NEW TESTAMENT COMMENTARY

New Testament Commentary

Exposition of Galatians,
Ephesians, Philippians,
Colossians, and Philemon

William Hendriksen

BakerBooks
A Division of Baker Book House Co
Grand Rapids, Michigan 49516

Originally published in separate volumes:

Galatians © 1968 by William Hendriksen

Ephesians © 1967 by William Hendriksen

Philippians © 1962 by William Hendriksen

Colossians and Philemon © 1964 by William Hendriksen

Galatians and Ephesians and Philippians, Colossians and Philemon combination volumes issued 1979
Double combination volume issued 1996

First printing, December 1995

Published by Baker Books
a division of Baker Book House Company

P.O. Box 6287, Grand Rapids, MI 49516-6287

Second Printing, July 2002

12 volume set, first available 2002

ISBN 0-8010-2606-7

Printed in the United States of America

ISBN 0-8010-2078-6

TABLE OF CONTENTS

LIST OF ABBREVIATIONS

The letters in book-abbreviations are followed by periods. Those in periodical-abbreviations omit the periods and are in italics. Thus one can see at a glance whether the abbreviation refers to a book or to a periodical.

A. *Book Abbreviations*

A.R.V.	American Standard Revised Version
A.V.	Authorized Version (King James)
Gram.N.T.	A. T. Robertson, *Grammar of the Greek New Testament in the Light of Historical Research*
Gram.N.T. (Bl.-Debr)	F. Blass and A. Debrunner, *A Greek Grammar of the New Testament and Other Early Christian Literature*
Grk.N.T. (A–B–M–W)	*The Greek New Testament,* edited by Kurt Aland, Matthew Black, Bruce M. Metzger, and Allen Wikgren, 1966 edition.
I.S.B.E.	*International Standard Bible Encyclopedia*
L.N.T. (Th.)	Thayer's *Greek-English Lexicon of the New Testament*
L.N.T. (A. and G.)	W. F. Arndt and F. W. Gingrich, *A Greek-English Lexicon of the New Testament and Other Early Christian Literature*
M.M.	*The Vocabulary of the Greek New Testament Illustrated from the Papyri and Other Non-Literary Sources,* by James Hope Moulton and George Milligan (edition Grand Rapids, 1952)
N.A.S.B. (N.T.)	New American Standard Bible (New Testament)
N.N.	*Novum Testamentum Graece,* edited by D. Eberhard Nestle, revised by Erwin Nestle and Kurt Aland, 25th edition, 1963
N.E.B.	New English Bible
N.T.C.	W. Hendriksen, *New Testament Commentary*
R.S.V.	Revised Standard Version
S.H.E.R.K.	*The New Schaff-Herzog Encyclopedia of Religious Knowledge*
Th.W.N.T.	*Theologisches Wörterbuch zum Neuen Testament* (edited by G. Kittel)
W.D.B.	*Westminster Dictionary of the Bible*

B. *Periodical Abbreviations*

ABR	*Australian Biblical Review*
BA	*Biblical Archaeologist*
BW	*Biblical World*
CTM	*Concordia Theological Monthly*
EQ	*Evangelical Quarterly*
ET	*Expository Times*
Exp	*The Expositor*
GTT	*Gereformeerd theologisch tijdschrift*
Int	*Interpretation*
JBL	*Journal of Biblical Literature*
TT	*Theologisch tijdschrift*

Please Note

In order to differentiate between the second person plural (see Gal. 6:1: "y o u who are spiritual") and the second person singular (same verse: "lest you also be tempted"), the letters in "y o u pl." are spaced; those in "you sing." are not.

Introduction

to

The Epistle to the Galatians

I. Why Is This Epistle Important?

"The epistle to the Galatians is my epistle. To it I am as it were in wed-lock. It is my Katherine." Thus spoke Luther, who considered Galatians the best of all the books in the Bible. It has been called "the battle-cry of the Reformation," "the great charter of religious freedom," "the Christian declaration of independence," etc.

It is important because *in any age* it answers the basic question asked by the human heart: "How can I find true happiness?" "How can I obtain peace, tranquility, freedom from fear?"

In his own strength and by his own wisdom man is totally unable to discover the answer. The slogan that has appeared in various forms, one of them being: "No Christ for a gift God gave us, Mankind alone must save us," fails completely. It fails in each of its manifestations, be it ritualism in obedience to the law of Moses—that was the snare in which the Galatians of Paul's day were becoming entangled (3:10; 5:2-4) —, rigorous asceticism, the affliction of the body, works of supererogation, the self-righteous deeds of "the moral man," strict obedience to "the laws of Nature," confidence in Science (these two here purposely spelled with a capital letter), or, lastly, the leaning either on oneself, as the captain of one's fate and the master of one's soul, or on this or that political Führer or false religious Messiah.

At times the attempt to satisfy man's deepest yearning takes an entirely different, even *opposite,* direction. *Legalism yields to license.* It is as if men were saying, "Since *obedience* to law—whether of Nature, of Moses, of the demagogue, or even of unenlightened conscience—has not brought the desired result, let us try *dis*obedience to law. Let us break their bonds asunder, And cast away their cords from us. Away with every restraint!" However, those who have sown the wind of (what *they* are pleased to call) "personal liberty"—in reality it is unbridled license!—with its emphasis on such things as sex and sadism, robbery and rioting (cf. 5:19-21), are reaping the whirlwind of intellectual impoverishment, moral decay, and spiritual bankruptcy. The solution, clearly, does not lie in this direction.

For all those who are willing to take God at his word Galatians shows the way to true freedom (5:1). That genuine liberty is neither legalism nor license. It is the freedom of "bondage to Christ." It consists in becoming a captive in his train, that is, surrendering oneself to God Triune as he has revealed himself in Jesus Christ unto salvation. It is discovered when one is willing to desist from every attempt to save oneself, and to accept Christ

3

Jesus as his Lord and Savior, glorying in his cross alone (6:14) and trusting in him as the fulfiller of the law (3:13). For all those who have by God's sovereign grace been led to do this the law ceases forevermore to be the means of attaining happiness now or the ticket to heaven when death arrives (2:16). Guided by Christ's Spirit, the redeemed, out of gratitude for the salvation which they have thus received as a gift, begin to adorn their lives with "the fruit of the Spirit: love, joy, peace, longsuffering, kindness, goodness, faithfulness, meekness, and self-control" (5:22, 23). Now fear has fled. Lust has vanished as a guiding principle (5:24). The prison-door has been opened. The air is exhilarating, invigorating. True freedom at last has been found. The sinner has been reconciled to his God. He is walking by the Spirit (5:16). Not only has he *found* the blessing, but he has also *become* a blessing, for it is through him that God blesses *the world*.

This last observation deserves emphasis. In Paul's day neither *legalism* nor *libertinism* (licentiousness) was winning any victories, real and lasting. It was exactly the gospel of *liberty in and through Christ* which was going forth conquering and to conquer. Had Paul surrendered to *legalism* Christianity would have become known as nothing more than a modified Judaism, which in no sense whatever could have conquered the world. The Gentiles would have rejected it. Had he compromised with *libertinism* after the example of those who had adopted the slogan, "Let us continue in sin that grace may abound" (cf. Rom. 6:1), the hearts of men chosen to eternal life would never have been satisfied. Sooner or later the falsity of "the new religion" would have been exposed. But because, by God's sovereign power, he succumbed to neither but proclaimed the riches of God's pardoning *and transforming* (!) grace, Christianity became—not just *a* but—*the* great world-religion, the religion destined to invade the hearts of all those whom God from eternity had chosen "out of *every* tribe and tongue and people and nation" (Rev. 5:9). *Legalism, libertinism,* or *true liberty,* that was the question then. It is the question also today.

II. To Whom Was It Addressed?

About the year 278 B.C. a large body of Gauls or Kelts, who had previously invaded and ravaged Greece, Macedonia, and Thrace, crossed over into Asia Minor. Their coming was not—at least not altogether—an unwarranted intrusion, for they arrived as a result of an invitation that had been extended to them by Nicomedes, king of Bithynia. So, here they were, with their wives and children, occupying the very heart-land of Asia Minor, a broad belt extending northward from the center (see accompanying sketch).

They belonged to three tribes: the Trochmi, Tectosages, and Tolisbogii, with whom are associated the cities, respectively, of Tavium, Ancyra, and

INTRODUCTION

Pessinus. All three of these tribes were *Galli,* that is, Gauls ("warriors"), also called *Galatae,* that is, Galatians ("nobles"). They rapidly gained the mastery over the native population of "Phrygians," of mixed ancestry, devotees of the ancient and impressive religion of Cybele. For a long time, due to constant raids into adjacent districts, the boundaries of the Gallic domain remained fluid, but the newcomers were finally forced by the Romans to live in peace with their neighbors and to remain within the limits of their own territory. In course of time, as happens often in such cases, the Gauls amalgamated with the earlier population, adopted their religion, but in most other respects remained the dominant strain.

Since the Gallic rulers were gifted with shrewdness they generally allied themselves with whoever happened to be "on top" in Rome. The latter reciprocated by allowing the former to be treated more as an ally than as a conquered nation. They were considered a "kingdom." During the reign of their last king, Amyntas IV, their realm was even extended southward. Upon the death of Amyntas (25 b.c.) the Romans fell heir to this already somewhat enlarged kingdom and converted it into the Roman "province of Galatia," which soon comprised, in addition to the *central and northern* territory, *to the south:* parts of Phrygia, Lycaonia, Pisidia, and Isauria (see the sketch).

It is understandable that the terms *Galatia* and *Galatians* could now be used in a twofold sense, as indicating either *a. Galatia proper* with its Gallic population, or *b. the larger Roman province,* inhabited not only by the Gauls as the dominant race in the central and north, but also by others farther south. When the term *Galatians* was used in the former sense, it naturally could not refer to those to whom the gospel had been proclaimed in the course of Paul's first missionary journey. The churches of Antioch (Pisidia), Iconium (Phrygia), Lystra and Derbe (cities of Lycaonia),[1] would then be excluded. On the other hand, when it was used in the latter sense it could very well refer to these early converts to the Christian faith about whom we read in Acts 13 and 14.

All of this leads to the question: "To whom was Galatians addressed: to the churches of Pessinus, Ancyra, Tavium and surroundings, or to those in Antioch (Pisidian), Iconium, Lystra, Derbe, and vincinity? Did the apostle use the term *Galatians* (3:1; cf. 1:2) in the racial (ethnic) or in the political sense? Was he thinking of people in the north or of those in the south?"[2]

---

[1] Ancient writers do not always link these cities with the districts as here indicated. There is much confusion, brought about to some extent by the individual author's point of departure, whether it be geographical or political. Moreover, boundaries shifted. See, however, Acts 13:14; 14:6.

[2] The great distance between the cities of the north and those of the south and also certain specific incidents mentioned in the letter (4:12-16) make it impossible to believe that he was addressing the churches of *both* North and South Galatia. Either the one or the other must be true.

5

For well-nigh two centuries there has been a sharp division of opinion with respect to this subject. Both camps of advocates have their great scholars as well as their lesser lights. For a representative defense of the North Galatian theory see J. B. Lightfoot, *The Epistle of St. Paul to the Galatians*, reprint,

WHO WERE THE GALATIANS?

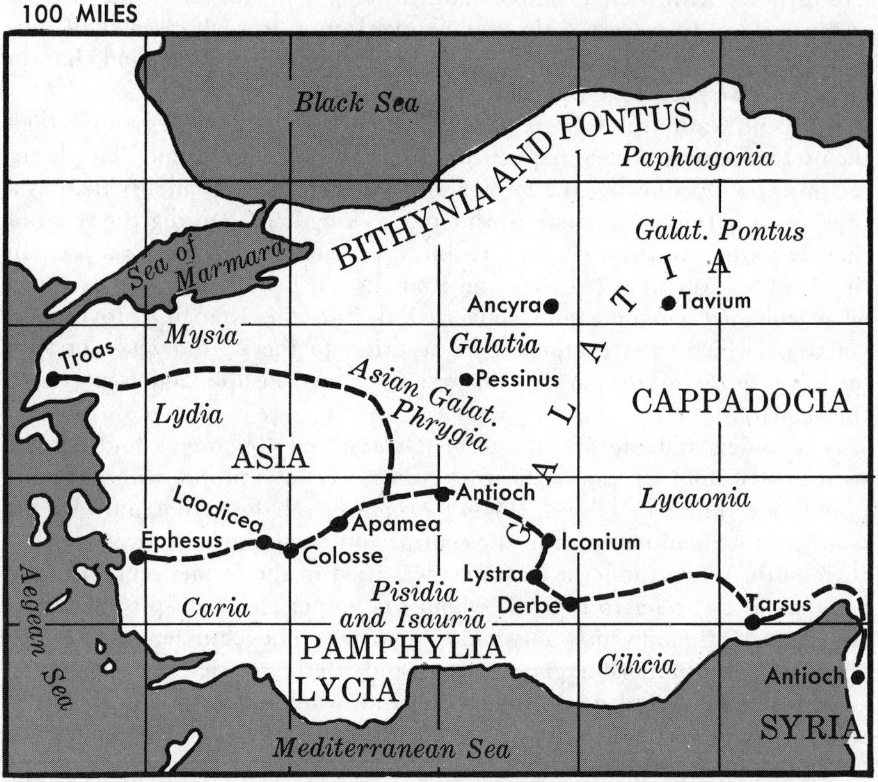

100 MILES

Black Sea

BITHYNIA AND PONTUS

Paphlagonia

Sea of Marmara

Galat. Pontus

Mysia

Ancyra●

Troas

Galatia

●Tavium

Lydia

Asian Galat. Phrygia

●Pessinus

CAPPADOCIA

ASIA

Antioch

Lycaonia

Laodicea

Apamea

Ephesus

Colosse

Iconium

Lystra

Caria

Pisidia and Isauria

Derbe

Tarsus

Aegean Sea

PAMPHYLIA

Cilicia

Antioch●

LYCIA

SYRIA

Mediterranean Sea

ASIA, GALATIA, etc.: Roman Provinces
Mysia, *Galatia*, etc.: Geographic Regions
— — — — — — — — — — : Beginning of second Miss. Journey: Antioch (Syria) to Troas; and of third: Antioch (Syria) to Ephesus

Grand Rapids, no date, pp. 1–35; for the South Galatian view see W. M. Ramsay, *The Church in the Roman Empire,* London, 1893, pp. 3–112; *St. Paul the Traveler and the Roman Citizen,* reprint, Grand Rapids, 1949, pp. 89–151; and *A Historical Commentary on St. Paul's Epistle to the Galatians,* reprint, Grand Rapids, 1965, pp. 1–234.[3]

---

[3] Among those favoring the North Galatian theory are also the following (for titles of their works see the Bibliography): Calvin, Coneybeare and Howson, Erdman,

INTRODUCTION

Excellent summaries of arguments and counter-arguments, logically arranged, can be found in several commentaries. In order to avoid duplication and, if possible, increase the interest in this subject, which is not wholly devoid of significance for the proper interpretation of certain Galatian passages, I shall follow a new approach, and present the matter in the form of a brief imaginary debate between a defender of the North Galatian theory and an advocate of the opposite view.

Resolved: That Galatians is addressed to the churches in North Galatia.

A. *Affirmative*

Mr. chairman, honorable judges, worthy opponent, and all other friends of biblical investigation:

In the days of the apostle Paul there existed in central and northern Asia Minor a people known as *Gauls* or *Galatians*. They were Gauls or Galatians by blood and descent. Even long before they had crossed over from Europe into Asia Minor they were known thus. The new kingdom which they established in Asia Minor was consequently a Gallic or Galatian kingdom. It is true that when this kingdom was converted into a Roman province, named Galatia, a few small districts were added, inhabited by people of a different nationality, who, in a remote or definitely secondary sense, were able, from that moment on, to call themselves Galatians. However, it cannot be denied that the primary meaning of this word *Galatians* is not "inhabitants of the province of Galatia," but *Gauls,* nothing else. When, therefore, a letter is addressed "To the Galatians," convincing proof to the contrary would be needed before it would be possible to interpret this address in any other way than in harmony with the long established connotation of the word.

Such convincing proof, however, is completely absent. Ask the ancient interpreters, the men who lived much nearer to the time when this letter was written, how *they* interpreted the term *Galatians* as used in Gal. 3:1, cf. 1:2. With one voice they will tell y o u that it refers to the Gauls of Galatia *proper,* and not to just anyone who, due to some political maneuvering, happened to be living within the Roman province of Galatia. Now this testimony of the ancients should be given its proper due. In all other disputes— for example, touching such matters as the origin of Infant Baptism or of the religious observance of the first day of the week—we are always asking,

Findlay, Greijdanus, Kerr, Moffatt, Schaff, and Schmoller. Kirsopp Lake's criticism of the South Galatian view (in *The Beginnings of Christianity,* Part I, London, 1933, pp. 224–240) "has tended to keep minds open on this issue," remarks Sherman E. Johnson, "Early Christianity in Asia Minor," *JBL,* 77 (March 1958), p. 9. For the defense of the South Galatian theory see (in addition to Ramsay's works) Berkhof, *New Testament Introduction,* p. 179 ff.; Bruce, *Commentary on Acts,* p. 300, Burton, Cole, Ellis, Emmet, Goodspeed, Jones, Rendall, Ridderbos, Ropes, Scott, Stamm, Tenney, Thiessen, Van Leeuwen, and Zahn.

"What does early tradition say about this?" Why should we ignore such unanimous tradition in *this* particular instance?

Besides, careful study of the contents of the epistle strengthens the proposition which I am defending. We note that those addressed are pictured as *fickle*. When the apostle arrived in their midst and preached to them the glorious gospel, they accepted it at once. Yes, they even welcomed him as they would have welcomed an angel or Jesus Christ himself, and had it been necessary, they would even have plucked out their very eyes and given them to Paul (Gal. 4:14, 15). Soon afterward, however, due to the arrival in their midst of some false teachers who slandered the apostle and belittled his preaching, they turn right around, so that they are now at the point of rejecting both Paul and his message (Gal 3:1-4). Now has not instability of character always been the outstanding trait of *Gauls,* yes, and even of their descendants to this present day? Do we not read in Caesar's *Gallic War* IV.5: "Caesar was informed of these events; and fearing the fickleness of the Gauls . . . decided that no confidence could be reposed in them"? These Galatians whom Paul addressed in his epistle were typical Gauls, therefore.

Moreover, when with Luke's account of the first missionary journey, during which the gospel was proclaimed to the people of Antioch (Pisidian), Iconium, Lystra, and Derbe, we compare the apostle's own account of his reception by the *Galatians* and his work among them (Gal. 4:13, 14), do we not see immediately that these two are completely different? This difference is not because one is true and the other false. Rather, it is because the two accounts deal with two entirely different subjects, two different missions. Thus, the apostle tells the Gauls or Galatians: "It was because of an infirmity of the flesh that I preached to y o u the gospel on that former occasion" (Gal. 4:13). Now compare this remark with Luke's review of Paul's work in Antioch, Iconium, Lystra, and Derbe (Acts 13 and 14). In that account is there even the least hint that it was because of infirmity that the apostle either *began* his work in these more southern cities or *continued* it for a longer period than he had at first intended? Of course not, for these are different people. They cannot be identified with Paul's *Galatians.*

Besides, when does Luke first mention the word *Galatia?* Not until he has reached the point in his story where Paul, on his *second* missionary journey, has left behind the more southern cities of Derbe, Lystra, etc., and is turning *northward* (Acts 16:6; cf. 18:23; 19:1). It is very clear, then, that when Paul's close friend and frequent companion, Luke, whom the apostle calls "the beloved physician," now finally speaks about *Galatia,* he cannot have been thinking of the cities of the south that had but recently been added[4]

---

[4] His opponent might have challenged this bit of information, as these people had been "Galatians" for at least 75 years. But in a debate you cannot delve into every minor point!

to the province of Galatia. His eyes are now turned toward the north. And if that was true with respect to Luke, why should it not hold for Paul? Why should we assume that the latter uses the terms *Galatia* and *Galatians* in any sense different than the ethnic?

There is one additional reason that makes it well-nigh impossible to identify the people of the more southern part of the Roman province of Galatia with the *Galatians* whom Paul addresses in his letter. It is clear from the entire contents of this epistle that those addressed were—either exclusively or at least almost exclusively—converts from the Gentile world (Gal. 4:8-11; 6:12). They were people who had never been circumcised (Gal. 5:2; 6:12), but were now in danger of accepting the rite of circumcision. They could not have been Jews, therefore, for the Jews were circumcised, and were even called "the circumcision." On the other hand, the churches established in the southern part of the Roman province of Galatia consisted of both Jews and Gentiles, perhaps in equal proportion. The Jews may even have predominated. In fact, in Antioch of Pisidia there were *"many* Jews" who turned to Christ (Acts 13:43). In Antioch and in Iconium there were found synagogues of Jews. Into these synagogues the apostle entered and preached. At Iconium "a great multitude both of Jews and of Greeks believed" (Acts 14:1). This decided difference between the constituency of the southern churches, described in the book of Acts, and the Gentile converts whom Paul addresses in his letter to the Galatians, proves that this letter cannot have been written to South and must have been intended for North Galatia.

B. *Negative*

Mr. president, noble referees, friendly adversary, and all those interested in scriptural research:

First of all I wish to remind y o u of the proposition which my worthy opponent was supposed to defend. It was this: "Resolved: That Galatians is addressed to the churches in North Galatia." Permit me to underscore the word *churches*. At what point in his argument did he ever give us a clear conception of these churches? All he told us was that at some point in the second missionary journey and also later Paul turned "to the north." He evidently wanted us to draw the conclusion that since Paul's letter was addressed to the Gauls, and since the more southern churches did not consist of Gauls, the apostle must have labored for a considerable time among the Gauls of the north, long enough to establish churches there. Am I being unfair when I state that his conclusion is drawn from a false premise? Fact is that when Paul says *Galatians* he does not necessarily mean *Gauls*. Rather, in distinction from Luke, he, Paul, in making mention of the churches under his care, and grouping them, uses the names of *Roman provinces* rather than those of races or nationalities. Thus, for example, in I Cor. 16:5 the apostle speaks of *Macedonia;* in the fifteenth verse of the same chapter he refers to

Achaia, and in the nineteenth verse to *Asia.* Now all of these were *Roman provinces.* Therefore, when in the opening of the chapter (I Cor. 16:1) he mentions "the churches of *Galatia,*" is it not logical to assume that here, too, as well as in the other three cases, he refers to it as *a Roman province?* And if in I Cor. 16:1 the meaning must be "the churches of the Roman province of Galatia," why should the identical phrase in Gal. 1:2 have a different meaning?[5] We see, therefore, that it is far better to say that the epistle of Paul which figures in this debate was addressed to "churches in the Roman province of Galatia" than to argue that this letter must have been intended for churches in *North* Galatia.

My opponent made much of the fact that it was in the old ethnic sense that the Church Fathers interpreted the terms *Galatia* and *Galatians.* He omitted to mention the reason for this patristic error. That reason was that in the days of these fathers the province of Galatia had again been restricted to virtually its old dimensions, so that for *them* "the territory inhabited by the Gauls" and "the province of Galatia" coincided. Hence, without further investigation they concluded that Paul, in addressing the churches of Galatia, was speaking to the people who had come from across the sea, the Gauls. But, as has been shown, this opinion of the fathers is not in harmony with Paul's use of political terms.

It somewhat amazes me that my beloved adversary, in the defense of his proposition, even resorts to the now seldom heard argument based on the *instability* of the Gauls. But is it ever fair and honest for us, who do not possess the gift of infallible inspiration, to characterize an entire nation as being fickle? Is instability a *national* characteristic? Is it not rather a weakness that pertains to unregenerate human nature in general? Let it be granted that the Galatians whom the apostle add.   in his letter were fickle in that they so quickly abandoned their initial enthusiasm with respect to Paul and the message he had brought. Of whom does this instability remind us? Does it not immediately recall the scene at Lystra, a city of Lycaonia in the *southern* part of the province of Galatia, whose inhabitants, after having first welcomed Paul and Barnabas, shouting, "The gods have come down to us," shortly afterward stoned the apostle almost to death? Truly, to be fickle one does not have to be a Gaul! Besides, strictly speaking, is it even correct to imply that at this late date, the first century A.D., the northern tribes were exclusively *Gauls?* Granted that the Gallic strain was dominant, is it not true that many tributaries had poured their water into the stream of their composite nationality?

---

[5] Moreover, I Cor. 16:1 speaks about the collection for the Judean saints, which had been recommended to "the churches of Galatia" (among others). According to Acts 20:4, among the delegates who carry this gift to Jerusalem were Gaius of Derbe and Timothy (of Lystra, Acts 16:1), both, therefore, of *South* Galatia. Not a single delegate from *North* Galatia is mentioned. Though there are ways to circumvent the force of this argument, it may, nevertheless, carry some weight.

INTRODUCTION

My opponent also appeals to the fact that the book of Acts does not speak of physical infirmity (cf. Gal. 4:13) as a reason why Paul either began or prolonged his mission in South Galatia. But, first of all, this difference between the two accounts can be removed by a different interpretation of Gal. 4:13, according to which it would not read *"because of"* but *"amid"* physical infirmity, which would fully harmonize with Acts 13:50; 14:5, 6, 19; cf. II Tim. 3:11. And secondly, even if we retain "because of," and assume a real difference between Gal. 4:13 and the account in Acts, let it be remembered that of those many afflictions which the apostle himself enumerates in II Cor. 11:23-33 Luke mentions only a few. Is it safe, then, to conclude that Paul never endured those which Luke does not record?

As to the Jew versus Gentile difference between Acts and Galatians, diligent study of Acts 13 and 14 leaves the impression that wherever there was a synagogue Paul entered it and proclaimed the gospel, reaching both Jews *and Gentiles,* proselytes (Acts 13:43; 14:1). Though Jews as well as Gentiles accepted the gospel, the former, on the whole, rejected it, causing the apostle to remark, "Since y o u thrust it from y o u, we turn to the Gentiles." Moreover, in some of the places visited, Jews were so few in numbers that there was not even a synagogue. This tallies with the situation as pictured in Paul's epistle. And as concerns the latter, the apostle assumes that those addressed have sufficient knowledge of the Old Testament to follow his reasoning, even including that of Gal. 4:21-31. Does not this fact rather point in the direction of the presence of at least some Jews among the addressed and of considerable Jewish influence even in these predominantly Gentile congregations?

I conclude by saying that my opponent has failed to show that *Galatians* is addressed to the churches of *North* Galatia. Of the founding and existence in Paul's day of such churches the book of Acts does not with certainty say anything at all, neither in 16:6 nor in 18:23; 19:1. And, on the other hand, of the establishment of churches in *South* Galatia it has given us a detailed account.

C. Rebuttal for the Affirmative

As to my opponent's contention that, in referring to groups of churches, Paul classifies them according to the Roman provinces in which they were located, and that, consequently, the term "the churches of Galatia" must refer to churches in the *province* of Galatia, that rule has its exceptions. Thus, it cannot be proved that the apostle is using political terminology when he speaks of Cilicia (Gal. 1:21), of Judea (Gal 1:22), and of Arabia (Gal. 4:25).

As for the rest, I must express my profound admiration for my opponent's cleverness. He can turn an argument from silence in either direction, to suit his purpose. It makes me think of what a child will at times say to his play-

11

mate to determine who will receive the biggest slice of the apple: "Let's flip a coin. Heads I win; tails you lose." When I called attention to the silence of the book of Acts with respect to any infirmity on Paul's part on his first missionary journey, during which he founded the churches of South Galatia, my opponent told us that such silence, if it were a fact, would mean nothing at all. Nevertheless, he was certain that when that same book of Acts fails to say in so many words that *churches* were established in North Galatia, this silence speaks volumes, and must mean that no churches were established there, churches to which Paul might have addressed his epistle. He maintains this in spite of the fact that Acts 18:23 states that the apostle went through this northern region "establishing *all* the disciples." Does not the word *all* indicate that there were *many?* Does not this imply that these many disciples must have organized themselves into churches? And does not the fact that on this third missionary journey Paul *established* or *strengthened* all these disciples indicate that these several churches must have been founded previously, a fact to which Acts 16:6 would seem to call our attention? Moreover, does not Acts 19:1 say that Paul, *having passed through the upper country,* came to Ephesus? What else can this "upper country" mean but North Galatia, with its cities of Tavium, Ancyra, and Pessinus? It is true that Luke does not tell us in so many words that churches were established in these cities, but neither does he tell us that a church was ever established in Colosse. Yet Paul wrote a letter to the Colossians. Luke does not even tell us anything about the founding of the church in Rome. Yet we know that a church was established there and that Paul wrote a letter to that church.

I conclude my summary, therefore, by stating once more that it is my firm belief that there were churches in North Galatia, . ˙ at it was to these genuinely *Galatian* churches that Paul addressed his letter.

D. *Rebuttal for the Negative*

It is clear, is it not, that my opponent has not succeeded to overthrow my contention that wherever in Paul's epistles we are in a position to determine with certainty the location and extent of any group of churches the apostle uses *political* terminology to describe it. He uses the names of Roman provinces.

As to these silences of the book of Acts, here my opponent fails to distinguish between expected and unexpected silences. When Luke presumably fails to mention Paul's infirmity, this *silence* is more or less *expected*. At least it cannot mean that there was no such infirmity, for by comparing Luke's account with Paul's own catalogue of sufferings (II Cor. 11:23-33) we learn that Luke is not in the habit of particularizing Paul's sufferings. Rather, he recounts Christ's work on earth, establishing a church here, a church there, and welding them into an organic unity. So when, while narrating a journey in which churches were being established, Luke omits any reference to the establishment of churches in a district covered on that journey or to Paul's preaching there, this would be an *unexpected silence,* unless nothing of importance happened in that district.

My opponent emphasized Acts 16:6; 18:23; 19:1, as if these three passages described Paul's work in the cities of *North* Galatia. Now in Acts 16:6-8 (second missionary journey), since God intended to send Paul to Europe via Troas, the route may well have touched the western edge of the more northerly part of the Roman province of Galatia. But this passage in Acts says nothing about establishing churches or even preaching there. As to Acts 18:23; 19:1 (third missionary journey), a look at the map suffices to show that the route from Antioch (in *Syria*) to Ephesus was probably not over Tavium, Ancyra, and Pessinus! The more southerly part of this same Roman province of Galatia is indicated.[6] And the words "establishing all the disciples" probably mean "in *South* Galatia." Cf. Acts 14:20-23; 16:1-5.

It is also significant that, as the last reference indicates, it was to the churches of *South* Galatia that the regulations of the Jerusalem Council were delivered, showing that it was exactly there that Judaism was a live issue, the very Judaism against which Paul contends in his letter. I believe, therefore, that Paul used the term *Galatians* in the political sense, as did also Peter (I Peter 1:1). It is hard to believe that the Judaistic errorists, with their sinister propaganda, would have bypassed *South* Galatia on their way to *North* Galatia. Moreover, Barnabas, mentioned three times in Galatians (2:1, 9, 13), had worked with Paul in *South* Galatia. And it was only with respect to the *South* Galatian churches, established on the *first* missionary journey, that Paul, at the time of the Jerusalem Council, could say, "(I did not yield to the infiltrators) in order that the truth of the gospel *might continue* with y o u" (Gal. 2:5).

I conclude, therefore, in stressing once again that the proposition according to which Paul's letter was meant for *North* Galatia is to be rejected.

Report of *one* of the judges (the author of this book. The readers are the other judges): I believe that both speakers have done justice to their assignment. Nevertheless, the speaker for the negative deserves a slight reprimand for having saved a few of his minor arguments to the very last, so that his opponent lacked any opportunity to answer him. Had the latter been given this opportunity, he would, no doubt, have somewhat diminished the force of these arguments. He would have shown, for example, that Barnabas is mentioned not only in Galatians but also elsewhere (I Cor. 9:6; Col. 4:10). Nevertheless, all things considered, I cast my ballot in favor of the negative and of the South Galatian theory. To believe that the South Galatian churches, so dear to Paul because of his blessed experiences among them

[6] See sketch; also N.T.C. on Colossians and Philemon, pp. 6–9.

(Acts 13:33, 44, 48; 14:1, 3, 20-23), and so vividly impinged upon his memory because of the persecutions which he had endured while laboring in their cities (Acts 13:50; 14:2, 5, 19; cf. II Tim. 3:11), would have played virtually no part in his correspondence and would have disappeared almost completely from sacred history, is difficult. And if the apostle did write to them, as I believe the speaker for the negative has proved, by what common name could he have addressed them better than by that of *Galatians?*

III. When, Where, and Why Was It Written?

A. *When and Where?*

On this subject there is a great diversity of opinion. Some accept as the *date* the close of the first missionary journey (about A.D. 50), and as the *place* of composition: Antioch. There are also those, at the other extreme, who assign this letter to the apostle's Roman imprisonment (A.D. 60 and afterward). While the former date once enjoyed great popularity and is still being favored by certain eminent scholars, the latter is now seldom met.[7] Various intermediate dates have gained large followings. Naturally, as a rule, the advocates of the *North* Galatian theory accept a rather late date because the apostle did not enter those parts until he was on his second missionary journey. As they see it, Paul revisited North Galatia during his third journey. And so, quite generally they hold that Galatians was written on the third missionary journey at Ephesus (Greijdanus), or, more precisely, at Ephesus a few weeks before I Corinthians (Warfield), or after I and II Corinthians but before Romans, and then either: a. on the journey from Macedonia to Achaia (Lightfoot) or b. at Corinth (Robertson). We who have adopted the South Galatian theory (see chapter II) arrive at an earlier date because during his three missionary journeys Paul labored in South Galatia earlier than in any other group of churches. Is it possible to be more specific? The following items may be of some help, though certainty cannot be attained:

1. Galatians was written *after the Jerusalem Council,* for it describes Paul's relation to the other leaders at that great meeting. The journey to Jerusalem mentioned in Gal. 2:1 must be identified with the one indicated in Acts 15:1-4. For proof see on Gal. 2:1.

2. It was written *after two previous visits to South Galatia,* the first of

---

[7] In addition to the various commentaries see the following articles all of which bear the identical title, "The Date of the Epistle to the Galatians": F. F. Bruce, *ET*, 51 (1939–1940), pp. 157, 158; Maurice Jones, *Exp*, 8th series, 6 (1913), pp. 192–208; D. B. Knox, *EQ*, 13 (1941), pp. 262–268; and B. B. Warfield, *JBL* (June and December, 1884), pp. 50–64.

which is indicated in Acts 13 and 14, the second in Acts 15:40-16:5. This is the most natural interpretation of Gal. 4:13 (see on that verse).

3. It was composed *not long after the conversion of the Galatians*—hence also: not long after Paul's two visits—, for Paul is amazed that the Galatians are "so quickly" moving away from God who had called them (see on 1:6).

4. It may well have been written, therefore, *on the second missionary journey, at Corinth, before the arrival of Timothy and Silas.*[8] This would explain the omission of greetings from these two men, both of whom occupied a special place in the hearts and memories of the South Galatian churches (Acts 15:40; 16:1-3). Contrast Gal. 1:1, 2, where these two names are omitted, with I Thess. 1:1; II Thess. 1:1, which mention both, the probable reason for the omission and the inclusion being that when Galatians was composed Timothy and Silas were still absent, but when the letters to the Thessalonians were written these two fellow-workers had arrived in Corinth and were again in Paul's company. This would fix the date of composition somewhere near the middle of the period A.D. 50-53 (second missionary journey), just previous to the writing of I Thessalonians.

Galatians, then, may well be the very first or oldest of all the letters of Paul that have been preserved. It has been objected that it is improbable that Paul, during his early Corinthian ministry, would dispatch in close succession letters as diverse in general theme as Galatians, on the one hand, and I and II Thessalonians, on the other. To the Galatians Paul writes: "A man is not justified by law-works but only through faith in Jesus Christ" (Gal. 2:16); while to the Thessalonians he writes: "For they [people everywhere] are reporting about us, what kind of entering in we had among y o u and how y o u turned to God from those idols (of y o u r s), to serve God, the living and real One, and to await his Son out of the heavens" (I Thess. 1:9, 10). The following, however, should be borne in mind:

1. The subject matter of Paul's epistles was determined not so much by the apostle's gradual mental development as by specific needs arising from concrete situations in the various churches. The Galatians needed to be reminded about the doctrine of salvation by grace through faith only. The Thessalonians needed encouragement in connection with their dramatic conversion and with respect to the return of Christ. *Each group receives what it needs!*

2. The Galatians and the Thessalonians lived in different continents, *amid different surroundings.*

3. The two differed also in their *degree of loyalty to the truth.*

4. Even so, the difference between the two situations is not nearly as radical as it is sometimes made to appear. For example, the doctrine of conver-

---

[8] In general this is also the position taken by Zahn, Berkhof, Hiebert, Lenski, Ridderbos, etc.

sion to the living God from dead idols was proclaimed among both (cf. Acts 14:15 with I Thess. 1:9). And as to the difference in content between the letters themselves: though it is true that the doctrine of the last things is stressed in Thessalonians far more than in Galatians, it is not absent from the latter (Gal. 5:21). Moreover, does *faith* working through *love* occupy a place of prominence in Galatians (Gal. 5:6)? It does also in I Thess. 1:3; 3:6; 5:8. Was Paul concerned lest he might have labored in vain among the Galatians (Gal. 3:4)? Before Silas and Timothy rejoined him he had entertained somewhat similar fears with respect to the Thessalonians (I Thess. 3:5). Cf. also Gal. 1:4; and 5:5 with I Thess. 1:10; and II Thess. 3:2; Gal. 5:3 with I Thess. 2:12; Gal. 5:13, 16, 19 with I Thess. 4:3; Gal. 5:21 with II Thess 2:5; Gal. 6:6 with I Thess. 5:12; and see footnote 129 on p. 175.

I can see no reason, therefore, to deny that the epistle to the Galatians was followed soon afterward by I Thessalonians, which, in quick succession, was followed by II Thessalonians, all three having been written from Corinth about the year A.D. 52.

B. *Why?*

Occasion and Purpose

In harmony with all that has been established, in this and in the preceding chapter, touching the identity of the Galatians, the time when, and the place from which Paul wrote his letter, the latter's historical background and purpose will appear from the following account:

In the church of Syrian Antioch there was great joy, for, after an eventful and perilous journey, Paul and Barnabas, who had been ordained for missionary work, and had been sent forth by the Holy Spirit and by a dedicated congregation committed to the grace of God, had returned in safety, with a wonderful story to tell (Acts 13:1-3; 14:25-27). "They rehearsed all things that God had done with them, and how he had opened a door of faith to the Gentiles," we read. The two then spent "not a little time" with the church at Antioch.

Now Antioch, "the queen of the east," was cosmopolitan in outlook. There was a colony of Jews here, to be sure (Acts 11:19), but the Christian community, which has been called "the cradle of Gentile Christianity and missionary endeavor," refused to be hemmed in within the narrow limits of Jewry. It was in Antioch that it had been most clearly discerned that the followers of Jesus were not just another Jewish sect but had a religion that was unique among all the religions of the empire. It was here that the disciples were first called "Christians." Hence, if anything were to occur that would tend to impede the worldwide progress of Christianity, the church of Antioch could be counted on to do something about it.

And something of this nature did indeed occur, for Antioch's joy because of the return of the missionaries and the tidings which they had brought, about multitudes of people, especially *Gentiles,* having embraced Christ and salvation in him, did not remain a secret. It spread far and wide. Jerusalem, too, heard about it. Also there, we may well believe, the church rejoiced. But this joy was not universal. In this Judean city among those who heard the news there were also some nominal converts from the sect of the Pharisees (Acts 15:5). In common with the disciples of the Lord, *all* Pharisees believed in the resurrection from the dead. In addition, the Pharisees mentioned here in Acts 15:5 may have been impressed by the strength of the evidence for *Christ's* resurrection, and by the indisputable grandeur of his miracles, and may for these reasons have joined the followers of the Nazarene. But at heart they had remained Jewish legalists. They were convinced that it took more.than simple faith in Jesus to be saved; and that strict observance of Jewish ceremonies, particularly circumcision, was also necessary.

So, when news of the conversion of the Gentiles *apart from the work of the law, and especially apart from the necessity of receiving circumcision,* reached the ears of these men, off to Antioch they went, with a protest in their hearts and an ultimatum on their lips. Arrived in the city, they hesitated not a moment to announce to the startled, mostly Gentile, congregation, "Unless y o u are circumcised according to the custom of Moses, y o u cannot be saved" (Acts 15:1). This stern pronouncement, whereby the majority of the congregation was relegated to the limbo of the lost, must have caused considerable consternation and alarm.

The church, however, decided to do something about it, encouraged no doubt by the growing and well-founded suspicion that these trouble-makers had not been authorized to deliver this scare-fomenting message (cf. Acts 15:24). And so it was agreed to refer this matter to a General Conference at Jerusalem, that is, to "the apostles and elders" (Acts 15:2) together with "the whole church at that place" (Acts 15:22). Paul, Barnabas, and certain other men were selected to go to Jerusalem in order to represent the church of Antioch (and, in a sense, every uncircumcised Gentile convert everywhere) with respect to this matter. As had been true when Paul was commissioned to go on his first missionary journey, so also now, the decision of the Antioch church and Paul's compliance with it were no merely human matters. God himself had a hand in it: the apostle went up to Jerusalem "by revelation" (Gal. 2:2).

In the company of men going to Jerusalem was also Titus, of heathen extraction both on his father's and on his mother's side, *a test case,* therefore, a manifest challenge to the Judaizers. The decision to place the entire matter, with reference to uncircumcised Titus and every Gentile convert, before the Jerusalem Council by no means implied that Paul was thereby abdicating his authority as an apostle or that the validity of his gospel ministry among the Gentiles was left in doubt úntil the mother church would come forth with an official answer to the question: "Must Gentiles be circumcised in order to be saved?" Paul, "an apostle not from men nor through man but through Jesus Christ and God the Father" (Gal. 1:1), knew that the divine approval rested on him and his work. But on a matter as important as this the church must not be divided, for this would hurt the great cause of evangelizing the Gentiles. The leaders, moreover, must speak clearly and unequivocally to the people, so that all may know what is the truth. Solutions must also be reached to problems which, though not basic, deal with temporary arrangements whereby in mixed churches Jews and Gentiles can dwell together in harmony (cf. Acts 15:29). For these various reasons and others, no doubt, the convocation of this General Council or Conference was entirely in order.

The Council, described in Acts 15, was, in all probability, preceded by *a private interview* of the leaders, to which Gal. 2:2-10 refers. Paul says, "I set before them the gospel which I am accustomed to preach among the Gentiles; but (I did this) privately, to 'those of repute,' to make sure that I was not running or had not run in vain" (Gal. 2:2). Complete agreement was evident on every point: Titus must not receive circumcision; the basic doctrine of salvation for Gentiles as well as for Jews by faith in Jesus Christ, apart from the works of the law, must be courageously upheld before the entire church; there must be a division (probably geographical) of labor, so that James, Cephas, and John will preach the gospel to the Jews, Paul and Barnabas to the Gentiles; the poor must be remembered. At the close of the interview the Jerusalem "pillars" give to Paul and to Barnabas "the right hand of fellowship."

At the meeting of the General Council the Judaists avail themselves of the opportunity to defend their position (Acts 15:5). However, when ample time has been allowed for this "questioning," *Peter* arises and in well-chosen words defends the perfect *parity* of Jew and Gentile: "God made no distinction between us and them." He points out that the way of salvation is exactly the same for both groups (15:7-11). After a respectful pause *Paul* and *Barnabas* take the floor and rehearse to the assembled multitude the *phenomenal blessings* which God had showered upon the Gentiles, "the signs and wonders" by means of which he had placed the seal of his approval on the work of his ambassadors (15:12). *James* then gives his *judgment.* Moved by the fact that what was happening in the Gentile world was a clear fulfilment of prophecy (Amos 9:11, 12), he states, "Wherefore my judgment is that we do not trouble those who from the Gentiles turn to God." Without in any way injuring the doctrine of justification by faith alone, apart from the works of the law, James, who is a very practical individual, suggests the adoption of certain regulations which, in this period of transition, would make it possible for Jewish and Gentile Christians to live together in peace and harmony (Acts 15:20, 21).

18

INTRODUCTION

The apostles and elders, together with "the whole church," reach a consensus, and decide to embody the decision in a written decree, a Charter of Freedom, as it were, which is to be brought to Antioch by Paul, Barnabas, and two other leaders (15:22-29). The arrival of these men and the message which they convey bring general rejoicing (15:31).

The decision of the Conference was made known in Antioch and Syria and Cilicia (15:23), and also in the cities of South Galatia (16:1-4). "So the churches were strengthened in faith, and increased in number daily" (16:5).

The Judaizers, however, are not about to give up the fight. They follow Paul at his heels in order to destroy the results of his labors. In Antioch they are partly to blame for Peter's reprehensible conduct (Gal. 2:11, 12). They traverse Galatia, insisting that the Gentiles be circumcised as a means unto salvation (Gal. 5:2, 3; 6:12). They do not deny that faith in Christ is necessary, but they loudly proclaim that circumcision and obedience to certain additional legal requirements are also necessary (4:9, 10). Yet, with amazing inconsistency, they do not insist on obedience to the whole law (5:3). In order to bolster their cause they cast suspicion on Paul. They attempt to discredit him, claiming that his apostleship is not from God but from men, and that his gospel is second-hand, therefore (Gal. 1:1; cf. I Cor. 9:1 ff.); that he is simply striving to win the favor of men (Gal. 1:10), and that when it suits him he himself preaches circumcision (Gal. 5:11).

Paul knew that these trouble-makers were Christians in name only. They were insincere and inconsistent, for while trying to force others to observe the law, they themselves failed to keep it (Gal. 6:13). Their aim was: a. to escape persecution from the side of the Jews, and b. out of personal ambition to glory in the flesh of their followers; that is, to be able to point with pride at those Gentiles who, due to *their* (the Judaizers') urging, had received circumcision (4:17; 6:13). "But far be it from me to glory except in the cross of our Lord Jesus Christ," says Paul (6:14).

Strange to say, *many* of the Galatians listen attentively to these usurpers. They are on the point of exchanging bread for a stone, a fish for a serpent. Big-hearted, solicitous Paul is filled with sadness when he hears that in Galatia the doctrine of Christian freedom is in danger. Guided by the Spirit and under the latter's direction, he decides to write a letter to these people who are so dear to his heart. Are they not among the first fruits of his labors as an *ordained* foreign missionary? To them the doctrine of sovereign grace in all its simplicity and glory must be set forth once again.

Yet, while glorying in the cross, the apostle knew that it was necessary to warn the Galatians against a perversion of this doctrine of grace, as if this new Christian liberty were tantamount to license. He emphasizes that if a person really walks by the Spirit, the Spirit of *freedom,* he will not fulfil the desire of the flesh but will instead bear fruit, even the fruit of the Spirit (Gal. 5:16-26).

19

Briefly, therefore, *the occasion* which prompted Paul to write this letter was the sinister and, to some extent, successful influence which Judaistic trouble-makers were exerting upon the churches of South Galatia. And *the purpose* was to counteract this dangerous error by re-emphasizing the glorious gospel of free grace in Christ Jesus: justification by faith alone, apart from the works of the law, and to urge those addressed to adorn their faith and prove its genuine character by means of a life in which the fruit of the Spirit would abound. Thus the cause of truth would be advanced, and sectionalism, caused in part by the sinister propaganda of the Judaizers, with which *many* agreed but others were undoubtedly not so ready to agree, would cease. By heeding Paul's—that is, the Holy Spirit's—admonitions the Galatian churches would be enabled to present a united testimony to the world.

IV. Who Wrote It?

Since the Pauline authorship of Galatians is almost universally acknowledged today, little need be said about it. In the middle of the nineteenth century under the influence of F. C. Baur, the Tübingen School, proceeding from the premise that only those writings can be ascribed to Paul in which he appears *prepared for combat,* denied the authenticity of all the letters passing under the apostle's name *except* Galatians, I and II Corinthians and Romans. Bruno Bauer, in his extreme radicalism, considered even these four epistles as products not of Paul but of the second century. In this rejection of the Pauline authorship of Galatians, etc. he was followed by the radical Dutch School: Loman, Pierson, Naber, and Van Manen. They held that the sharp clash between Pauline and Judaistic Christianity pictured in Gal. 2:11-21 (as interpreted by them), could not have developed as early as the days of the apostle Paul, and that the Christology of Galatians was far too lofty. All of this rests on purely subjective reasoning and is not worthy of further comment.

Eusebius, writing at the beginning of the fourth century, includes Galatians in the list of Paul's letters (*Eccl. History* III.iii. 4, 5). Origen, Tertullian, Clement of Alexander, and Irenaeus, in their respective writings, quote this epistle again and again. The Muratorian Fragment (about 180–200) places it second among Paul's epistles. The canon of the heretic Marcion is the first to mention the epistle by name (about the year 144), and places it first in the list of ten Pauline letters. It is found in the Old Syriac and in the Old Latin Versions. Polycarp (martyred 155) in his *Epistle to the Philippians* V.1 quotes Gal. 6:7, "God is not mocked." About the year 100 Clement of Rome writes, "Y o u kept his sufferings before y o u r eyes" (I Clement II.1), which reminds one of Gal. 3:1. And at about the same time Ignatius writes about a "ministry neither from himself nor through men, but in the love of God the Father and the Lord Jesus Christ" (*To the Philadelphians* III.1), in which there may be an allusion to Gal. 1:1. Barnabas, Hermas, Justin Martyr, *the Epistle to Diognetus* are among the other writings of very early date which contain passages which are viewed by many as allusions to Galatians.

But more important is the fact that as soon as this epistle was ascribed to anyone, it was ascribed to Paul. That has been the belief of the church throughout the centuries and is its conviction today. No argument of any merit has ever been presented to show that this view is in error. And the compromise theories, which are propounded every now and then up to the very present, according to which Galatians contains a Pauline core around which in post-apostolic times a pseudo-Pauline shell fastened itself, break down under the weight of their self-contradictions.

The author tells us that his name is Paul (1:1; 5:2). The letter is clearly a unit. It pictures a condition true to the times in which Paul lived (cf. Acts 15:1; I Cor. 7:19). It is, moreover, very personal, and reveals throughout "a man in Christ." Here is a mind so broad that it has room for both sovereign grace and human responsibility, a heart so loving that it administers stern rebuke just because it loves so deeply! The Paul of Gal. 1:15, 16; 2:20; 3:1; 4:19, 20 is clearly also the Paul of Rom. 9:2; I Cor. 9:22; 10:33; II Cor. 11:28; 12:15; Eph. 4:1; and Phil. 3:18, 19. It is Paul of Tarsus.

V. What Is Its Theme? Its Outline?

It has become clear that the apostle's chief concern was that the Galatians should not lose their hold on the only true gospel. It is significant how often the word *gospel,* either as a noun or as a component element of a verb, occurs in this small epistle: 1:6, 7, 8, 9, 11, 16, 23; 2:2, 5, 7, 14; 3:8; 4:13. The essence or content of this gospel is also affirmed and reaffirmed: "A man is not justified by law-works but only through faith in Jesus Christ" (2:16; cf. 2:21; 3:9, 11; 4:2-6; 5:2-6; 6:14-16).

Now *justification by faith apart from law-works* is also the theme of Romans. There is a close resemblance between the larger and the smaller epistle. Gen. 15:6: "Abraham believed God, and it was reckoned to him for righteousness" is quoted in both letters (Rom. 4:3; Gal. 3:6). Among other verbal resemblances are especially the following: Rom. 6:6-8 and Gal. 2:20; Rom. 8:14-17 and Gal. 4:5-7; Rom. 13:13, 14 and Gal. 5:16, 17. Nevertheless, there is a striking difference between the two. Romans sets forth calmly and majestically that for every sinner, whether he be a Jew or a Gentile, there is salavation full and free through faith in Christ, apart from law-works. Galatians, in a tone that is not nearly as calm and at times becomes fiery, defends this glorious gospel over against its detractors. Against the latter its denunciations are withering (1:8, 9; 5:12). With respect to those addressed, with whom there was a tendency to lend a listening ear to the impostors, the apostle's reprimands (1:6; 3:1-4) are as sharp as are the contrasts which characterize this epistle.[9]

The reason why Paul reprimands the Galatians so sharply and warns them so sternly is that he loves them with a love that is genuine, tender, and deep: "My dear children, for whom I am again suffering birth-pangs until Christ be formed in y o u, I could wish to be present with y o u now and to change my tone of voice, for I am perplexed about y o u" (4:19, 20).

The theme of Galatians, then, is:

The Gospel of Justification by Faith apart from
Law-works Defended against Its Detractors

Now in the first two chapters, by a selection of events from his life, the apostle defends himself against the charge, expressed or implied, that he had never received a divine commission and that his gospel was, accordingly, not to be trusted. This section is described at times as Paul's Self-defense. It is more than this, however. Calvin aptly expresses this by saying, "Let us remember, then, that in the person of Paul the truth of the gospel was assailed." The assailants attacked Paul in order thereby to destroy his gospel. They reasoned that if Paul's so-called apostleship was of merely human origin, then his gospel was also a merely human invention. Hence, at bottom it is *the gospel* with which we are dealing in Chapters 1 and 2 as well as in the rest of the epistle. Briefly, then, Galatians may be divided as follows:

ch. 1 and 2   I. This Gospel's Origination: it is not of human but of divine origin, hence, is independent.

ch. 3 and 4   II. Its Vindication: both Scripture—i.e., the Old Testament —and life (experience, past history) bear testimony to its truth.

ch. 5 and 6   III. Its Application: it produces true liberty. Let the Galatians stand firm, therefore, as does Paul, who glories in in the cross of Christ.

---

[9] only true gospel   versus   no gospel at all   (1:6-9)
 grace or promise   versus   law   (2:21; 3:18)
 faith   versus   law-works   (2:16; 3:2, 5, 10-14)
 flesh   versus   Spirit   (3:3; 5:16; 6:8)
 slave-woman   versus   free-woman   (4:21 ff.)
 Jerusalem of today   versus   Jerusalem that is above   (4:25, 26)
 freedom   versus   slavery   (5:1)
 to love   versus   to bite and devour (5:14, 15)
 circumcision   versus   new creation   (6:15)

INTRODUCTION

Extended Outline

ch. 1 and 2   I. *This Gospel's Origination: it is not of human but of divine origin (ch.1); hence, is independent (ch. 2).*

Chapter 1

A. Introduction which really introduces! Name of addressor, of the addressed; opening salutation.

B. I am amazed that y o u are so quickly moving to a different gospel. There is only one true gospel. Let him be accursed who preaches another. There! Is it the favor of men that I am now seeking to win or of God?

C. The gospel I preach is not a human invention. I received it through the revelation of Jesus Christ. Rescued by God's grace from intense Judaism, I did not immediately go to Jerusalem to seek men's advice, but went to Arabia, and again I returned to Damascus.

D. Not until three years later did I go up to Jerusalem to visit Cephas, for fifteen days. I saw none of the other apostles, only James. Then I went to Syria and Cilicia, but remained unknown by sight to the Christian churches of Judea. For the change wrought in me they glorified God.

Chapter 2

E. Then, on a visit to Jerusalem with Barnabas and Titus, its "pillars" in a private interview imparted nothing to me, but gave us the right hand of fellowship. Titus, a Greek, was not compelled to be circumcised. Thus, there was no yielding to infiltrators but continuation of blessing for y o u. A division of missionary labor was agreed on. The poor were to be remembered.

F. Far from receiving anything from Jerusalem's "pillars," at Antioch I even took Cephas to task for his reversion to legalism: separating himself from Gentile converts after first eating with them. A man is not justified by law-works but through faith in Jesus Christ. For I through law died to law, that I might live to God.

ch. 3 and 4   II. *Its Vindication: both Scripture—i.e., the Old Testament —and life (experience, past history) bear testimony to its truth.*

Chapter 3

A. O foolish Galatians! Was it by doing what the law demands that y o u received the Spirit or was it by believing the gospel message?

B. The law (Deut. 27:26) pronounces a curse upon the disobedient. Christ crucified, by bearing this curse (Deut. 21:23), redeemed us from it, so that we are saved through *faith* in him. Abraham, too, was justified by faith (Gen. 15:6), and blessed with him are all those who are of faith, according to God's promise (Gen. 12:3; 18:18; 22:18; Hab. 2:4).

C. This promise or covenant is superior to the law, for the latter reached us through mediation, the former came directly from God, and is still in force. The law, which came later, far from annulling the promise, serves it, by revealing our sinfulness and leading us to Christ. All who belong to Christ are Abraham's seed, heirs according to promise.

Chapter 4

D. We used to be in bondage to ordinances, regulations. God sent forth his Son to redeem those who were in bondage, that we might receive the adoption as sons. And because y o u are sons God sent forth the Spirit of his Son into our hearts, crying, "Abba! Father!" Do y o u then wish to exchange y o u r former bondage to heathenism for bondage to Judaism? I am afraid about y o u, lest somehow I have labored among y o u in vain.

E. Become as I am as I also became as y o u are. Where is now that blessedness which y o u experienced on that former occasion when y o u welcomed me so warmly? Those (perverters of the true gospel) who pay court to y o u do so selfishly. I could wish to be present with y o u now and to change my tone of voice, for I am perplexed about y o u.

F. History of the slave-woman (Hagar) and her son versus the free-woman (Sarah) and her son (Gen. 16:1-4; 21:8-12). Application: Cast out the slave-woman and her son. Not of a slave-woman are we children, but of the free-woman.

ch. 5 and 6   III. *Its Application: it produces true liberty. Let the Galatians stand firm, therefore, as does Paul, who glories in the cross of Christ.*

Chapter 5

A. For freedom Christ has set us free; continue to stand firm, therefore.

B. Do not try to combine both principles: *a.* justification by way of law and *b.* justification by grace through faith. If y o u let yourselves be circumcised, Christ will be of no advantage to y o u. If y o u cling to law, y o u have lost y o u r hold on grace. Practice faith working through love.

C. Y o u were running well; who was it that threw y o u off y o u r course? I am convinced that y o u will see the matter my way. If I am still preaching circumcision, why am I still being persecuted? Would that the disturbers might make eunuchs of themselves.

D. Remember that true liberty does not mean license. It means love. It does not welcome the works of the flesh but the fruit of the Spirit. It produces unity, not strife.

Chapter 6

E. Restore the fallen in a spirit of gentleness. Bear one another's burdens. Share all good things with y o u r instructor. Bear in mind that a man will reap what he sows. Let us do good to everybody, and especially to those who are of the household of the faith.

F. The Letter's End: Paul's "huge letters." Final warning against the disturbers and exposure of their motives: ease, honor. Concluding testimony: Far be it from me to glory except in the cross of our Lord Jesus Christ. Last plea: From now on let no one cause trouble for me, etc. Closing benediction.

Commentary

on

The Epistle to the Galatians

Chapter 1

Verses 1-5

Theme: *The Gospel of Justification by Faith apart from Law-works
Defended against Its Detractors*

I. *This Gospel's Origination: it is not of human but of divine origin*

A. Introduction which really introduces!

Name of addressor, of the addressed; opening salutation.

CHAPTER I

GALATIANS

1 1 Paul, an apostle—not from men nor through man but through Jesus Christ and God the Father, who raised him from the dead—2 and all the brothers who are with me, to the churches of Galatia; 3 grace to y o u and peace from God our Father and the Lord Jesus Christ; 4 who gave himself for our sins, that he might rescue us out of this present world dominated by evil; (having thus given himself) according to the will of our God and Father, 5 to whom (be) the glory forever and ever. Amen.

1:1-5

A. *Introduction*

The spiritual atmosphere is charged. It is sultry, sweltering. A storm is threatening. The sky is darkening. In the distance one can see flashes of lightning; one can hear faint muttering sounds. When each line of verses 1-5 is read in the light of the letter's occasion and purpose (see Introduction III B, pp. 16–19) the atmospheric turbulence is immediately detected. The apostle, though in perfect control of himself, for he is writing under the guidance of the Holy Spirit, is greatly agitated, deeply moved. His heart and mind are filled with a medley of emotions. For the perverters there is withering denunciation springing from holy indignation. For the addressed there is marked disapproval and an earnest desire to restore. For the One who has called him there is profound reverence and humble gratitude.

Now in these opening lines there is, to be sure, a measure of restraint. The most vivid flashes of lightning and the most deafening peals of thunder are reserved for later (1:6-9; 3:1, 10; 5:4, 12; 6:12, 13). Nevertheless, even now the storm is definitely approaching. This will be shown in connection with each element of this Introduction: *a.* the manner in which *the addressor* describes himself, *b.* the way in which he designates *the addressed,* and *c.* the qualifying clause by means of which he enlarges on his *opening salutation.*

1. Paul, an apostle. He is a *sent,* a *commissioned* one (cf. John 20:21), an *apostle* in the deepest, richest sense, fully clothed with the authority of the One who sent him. His apostleship is equal to that of the Twelve. Hence, we speak of "the Twelve and Paul." Elsewhere he even stresses the fact that the risen and exalted Savior had appeared to *him* just as truly as to Cephas (I Cor. 15:5, 8; cf. 9:1). The Savior had assigned to him a task so broad and universal that his entire life was henceforth to be occupied with it.

To the words "Paul, an apostle" the writer adds a very significant modifier, one which immediately points to the theme of the entire letter. Among uninspired men introductions do not always introduce. In fact, at times they may even confuse. But here is an Introduction which really introduces, for the words **not from men nor through man but through Jesus Christ and God the Father** can only mean: "My apostleship is genuine; hence, so is *the gospel* which I proclaim, no matter what the Judaizers who disturb y o u may say! I am a divinely appointed emissary." As was pointed out previously, Paul's opponents had infiltrated the South Galatian churches, and were casting slurs on his apostleship, in order to show that his gospel was not from God. They charged—or at least insinuated—that *Paul's apostolic office or commission was either not derived from God but merely from men,* from the church of Syrian Antioch perhaps, as if this church had acted without divine guidance and authorization (Acts 13:2); *or else,* though derived originally from God, *had been transmitted to him through this or that man* (Ananias or an apostle?), with the implication that in the process of transmission it had been substantially modified, adulterated.

Paul's answer is an unequivocal and double denial. Not only had he received his office *from* the historical Jesus, who is at the same time the Anointed One, but that very Jesus Christ *in person* had invested him with this high distinction. Hence, Paul is an apostle *through*—not only *from*— Jesus Christ. Moreover, since Jesus Christ, in turn, as Son is one in essence with the Father (John 1:1; 10:30), and as Mediator always performs his Father's will (John 4:34; 5:30, etc.), hence Paul's apostleship is *through*[10] Jesus Christ and God the Father.

The implication is clear: since Paul and his message are backed by divine authority, those who reject him and his gospel are rejectors of Christ, hence also of the Father who sent him and **who raised him from the dead.** The detractors *oppose* the very One whom the Father had *honored;* the very One upon whose work of redemption the Father, by the act of raising him from the dead, had placed the seal of his approval, thereby designating him as the complete and perfect Savior, whose work does not need to be, and cannot be, supplemented; the very One who from his exalted position in heaven had called Paul to be an apostle!

The divine source of Paul's mission, to which he here bears witness, is confirmed by the book of Acts, which shows that it was Christ *himself* who had appeared to Paul (9:1-5; 22:1-9). True, it was Ananias who encouraged Paul concerning his *commission* (Acts 22:15), but either *a.* Ananias con-

---

[10] *One* preposition διά governs both appellatives.

veyed that commission to Paul *so exactly* that the latter was able afterward to merge the words of Jesus and those of Ananias as if all had been spoken by Christ himself, or (better perhaps) *b. the commission itself* also had *first of all* been uttered directly by Christ, not by Ananias. When Acts 26:12-18 is interpreted either way, Gal. 1:1a remains true. See also on Gal. 1:16.

2. Paul adds, **and all the brothers who are with me.** Of these words there are three main interpretations: *a.* "all fellow-believers at the place from which I am writing this letter." Those who favor this view stress the fact that "brothers" is a very common term that is often used to indicate Christians in general (I Thess. 1:4; 2:1; I Cor. 5:11; 6:5-8; 8:12; etc.). Some also add that if it be true that this letter was written from Corinth in the early days of the work there, a *church* may not yet have been organized, though there were already some *believers* or *brothers.* Interpretation *b.* is: "all those mentioned under *a.* (above) plus all the members of the Galatian delegation that is with me." The adherents of this view point out that Paul must have received his information about the situation in the South Galatian churches from some reliable source (cf. I Cor. 1:11), perhaps from a delegation sent to him by the officials of these churches, who wanted him to know what was going on and who desired to benefit by his advice. Theory *c.:* "all my fellow-workers who are with me here." Those who favor this interpretation point to a similar phrase in Phil. 4:21, where it refers to the apostle's assistants in Rome, in distinction from "all the saints," namely, all of Rome's resident Christians, mentioned in the next verse. They are of the opinion, moreover, that a traveling missionary like Paul, one who stays in a place for a while and then moves on again, would hardly refer to the place's *residents* as "all the brothers who are *with me.*" A closer look as this argument, however, shows that it is not as strong as it may at first appear to be. The distinction drawn in Phil. 4:21, 22 between Paul's assistants and all of Rome's resident Christians is altogether natural in a city (Rome) where there was a numerically strong church that had been established long before the apostle's arrival. But in Corinth from which, probably on his second missionary journey, the apostle wrote Galatians (see our Introduction, pp. 14–16), and where the work had just begun and the number of believers may still have been rather small, the apostle could very well have referred to this small company as "all the brothers who are *with me.*" The word *all,* moreover, stresses unanimity of sentiment rather than numerical immensity. Even if there were only ten or twenty converts, as long as there was no disagreement among them the apostle would still be justified in writing in the name of "*all* the brothers who are with me." Also, as to the several fellow-workers who, according to theory *c.* were with Paul, I answer that if the time and place of the letter's composition was as has been surmised, their presence in any considerable quantity

31

would seem rather doubtful. On his second missionary journey only one assistant accompanied the apostle from the start: Silas; a little later also Timothy (Acts 15:40-16:3). Luke was with them for a little while, but soon left again (16:10-17). He was no longer present when Paul reached Corinth and did not rejoin him until the latter, returning from his third missionary journey, had reached Troas (20:5). As has been indicated previously, when Galatians was written even Silvanus and Timothy were probably not in Paul's company. All things considered, therefore, the true meaning of the words "and all the brothers who are with me" would seem to lie in the direction of theory *a.* or possibly *b.* rather than in that of theory *c.* Certainty on this point, is, however, unattainable.

What is often forgotten, however, is *the main lesson.* That lesson would seem to be this, that even though it is true that Paul alone—not Paul plus these brothers who are with him—authored this letter (note constant recurrence of first person sing.: Gal. 1:6, 10-17, etc.), nevertheless, before composing and sending it he thoroughly discussed *with all the brothers* the matter with which it was to deal. So unanimous was their agreement with Paul's proposed method of handling this difficult situation that the apostle writes in the name of all. Moral: when it becomes necessary to send someone a letter of sharp reproof, discuss the matter with others who also have the welfare of Zion at heart, if such can be done without violating any confidences or of coming into conflict with the principles established in Matt. 18. Were this rule always observed, what a difference it would make in the end-product! It is true that Paul was writing under the infallible guidance of the Holy Spirit. Even so, however, this work of inspiration makes use of means. It operates organically, not mechanically. Besides, Paul's loving heart, filled with intense yearning to reclaim the Galatians, makes use of every legitimate means to attain this end, one of these means being to impress upon the addressed that his own apprehensions concerning the course which they are now beginning to pursue is being shared by *all* the brothers who are *with*[11] him.

Those whom Paul addresses are designated as follows: **to the churches of Galatia.** Every commendatory modifier—for example, "beloved of God" (cf. Rom. 1:7), "sanctified in Christ Jesus" (cf. I Cor. 1:2), "saints and believers" (Eph. 1:1)—is lacking here. The apostle loves, but does not believe in flattery. The atmosphere remains tense.

Note: church*es* both here and in 1:22. Paul recognizes the autonomy of the local church. Nevertheless, he is also fully aware of the fact that all believers everywhere constitute *one* body of Christ, *one* church (1:13). He

---

[11] The flexibility or wide variety of connotations adhering to the preposition σύν makes it impossible for me to join those exegetes who are of the opinion that it must here mean *"supporting* (me)," in distinction from μετά, which would simply have meant "in (my) company." Is not the *support* already clearly implied?

keeps perfect balance, a lesson for all time! That these churches were in all probability located in the southern part of the Roman province of Galatia has been established (Introduction, Chapter II).

3. The opening salutation proper is as in Rom. 1:7; I Cor. 1:3; II Cor. 1:2; Eph. 1:2; and Phil. 1:2: **grace to y o u and peace from God our Father and the Lord Jesus Christ.** Although it is true that the apostle finds little to praise, much to deplore, in the churches of Galatia, this does not mean that he has given them up as being hopeless. Far from it. See on 5:10a; cf. 4:19, 20. Though he is "perplexed" about them, he still regards them as Christian communities, upon whom, accordingly, he is fully justified in pronouncing this salutation. *Grace,* as here used, is God's spontaneous, unmerited favor in action, his freely bestowed lovingkindness in operation, bestowing salvation upon guilt-laden sinners who turn to him for refuge. It is, as it were, the rainbow round about the very throne out of which proceed flashes of lightning, rumblings, and peals of thunder (Rev. 4:3, 5). We think of the Judge who not only remits the penalty but also cancels the guilt of the offender and even adopts him as his own son. Grace brings *peace.* The latter is both a *state,* that of reconciliation with God, and a *condition,* the inner conviction that consequently all is well. It is the great blessing which Christ by his atoning sacrifice bestowed upon the church (John 14:27), and it surpasses all understanding (Phil. 4:7). It is not the reflection of an unclouded sky in the tranquil waters of a picturesque lake, but rather the cleft of the rock in which the Lord hides his children when the storm is raging (think of the theme of Zephaniah's prophecy); or, to change the figure somewhat but with retention of the main thought, it is the hiding place under the wings, to which the hen gathers her brood, so that the little chicks are safe while the storm bursts loose in all its fury upon herself.

Now this grace and this peace have their origin in God *our* (precious word of appropriation and inclusion!) Father, and have been merited for believers by him who is the great Master-Owner-Conqueror ("Lord"), Savior ("Jesus"), and Office-Bearer ("Christ"), and who, because of his threefold anointing "is able to save to the uttermost them that draw near to God through him" (Heb. 7:25).[12]

For further details about certain aspects of Paul's opening salutations see N.T.C. on I and II Thessalonians, pp. 37–45; on Philippians, pp. 43–49; and on I and II Timothy and Titus, pp. 49–56; 339–344.

4. Everywhere else the opening salutation proper is very brief. Having read the words "from God our Father and the Lord Jesus Christ," the addition *here* of a modifier to the title of the second person of the Holy

---

[12] The *one* preposition *from* introduces the entire expression "God our Father and the Lord Jesus Christ," showing that these two Persons are placed on the level of complete equality.

Trinity comes as somewhat of a surprise. Clearly, in keeping with the occasion and purpose of the letter, there must be a reason why Paul *here* adds: **who gave himself for our sins, that he might rescue us out of this present world dominated by evil.** The reason is that the atmosphere continues to be loaded. The greatness and magnanimity of Christ's act of self-surrender is stressed in order to underscore the grievous nature of the sin of those who teach that this supreme sacrifice must be supplemented by law-works. Christ surrendered himself to sorrow and scorn, to the curse of eternal death during his entire sojourn on earth but especially at Gethsemane, Gabbatha, and Golgotha. He laid down his life for his sheep. No one took it from him, but he laid it down of his own accord, voluntarily (John 10:11, 17, 18). He did this motivated by love incomprehensible; hence, "for our sins," that is, to deliver us from the pollution, guilt, and punishment adhering to the many ways in which, by inner disposition, thought, word, and deed, we *miss the mark* of existing and living to the glory of God Triune.

Note: "He gave himself . . . that [meaning: that in so doing] he might rescue us." The word *rescue* is very descriptive. It presupposes that those to whom it applies are in great danger from which they are unable to extricate themselves. Thus Joseph *was rescued* out of all his afflictions (Acts 7:10), Israel out of Egypt's house of bondage (Acts 7:34), Peter out of Herod's hand (Acts 12:11), and thus also Paul would one day be delivered or rescued out of the hands of Jews and Gentiles (Acts 23:27; 26:17). The rescue described here in Gal. 1:4 is all the more glorious because: *a.* it concerns those who by nature are enemies of the Rescuer, and *b.* it was accomplished by means of the voluntary death (in this case *eternal* death) of the Rescuer. One is reminded of a swimmer who plunges into the fast moving current in order to rescue the child that has fallen into the stream and is about to be pitched over the cliff of the cataract to its death. In the act of seizing the youngster and hurling him to the side where loving arms reach out and catch him, he himself is swept over the precipice to his death. All comparisons fall short, however, since in the case of Christ the sacrifice was great beyond all comprehension, and the beneficiaries were thoroughly unworthy of such love!

Paul states that Christ gave himself that he might rescue us out of this present world dominated by evil.[13] For *world* Paul uses the term *aeon*. It denotes *the world in motion* in contrast with *cosmos* which, though used in a variety of senses, indicates *the world at rest*. The *aeon*, then, refers to the world viewed from the standpoint of time and change. This is especially true when the adjective *present* is added, as here. It is the world or transitory

---

[13] The position of the adjective πονηροῦ gives it special emphasis, which accounts for my translation "this present world dominated by evil" instead of simply "this present evil world."

era which is hastening to its close and in which, in spite of all its pleasures and treasures, there is nothing of *abiding* value. Over against *this present world or age* is *the coming world,* the glory-age, that will be ushered in at the consummation of all things (cf. Eph. 1:21; I Tim. 6:17; II Tim. 4:10; Titus 2:12).

The *rescue* from this present world dominated by evil, though not complete until the last trumpet has sounded, is progressive in character. It is being accomplished whenever a sinner is brought out of the darkness into the light and whenever a saint gains a victory in his struggle against sin.

It is not sufficient, however, to bow in adoration before *the Son,* as if he alone were deserving of thanksgiving and honor because of his marvelous, self-sacrificing, work of redemption. On the contrary, the Son gave himself for our sins, that he might rescue us, etc. (**having thus given himself**) **according to the will of our God and Father.**[14] The son gave himself; the Father—yes, *our* (see on 1:3) God and Father—"spared not his own Son, but delivered him up for us all" (Rom. 8:32). In fact, in the very act of the Son's self-sacrifice the Father's *will*—his decree as revealed *in time,* his *desire*—was being accomplished. Therefore the Father loved the Son! (John 10:17, 18; cf. 4:34; 6:38).—Let the trouble-makers bear in mind, therefore, that when they belittle the work of the Son, they make light of the Father also!

5. When the apostle contemplates the Father's marvelous love revealed in delivering up his own dear Son, the Only-begotten, for our salvation, his soul is lost in wonder, love, and praise, so that he exclaims: **to whom be**[15] **the glory**[16] **forever and ever. Amen.** When the wicked infiltrators *minimize* God's work of redemption, Paul will *magnify* it, calling upon all men to do this with him. So marvelous is this work that it is worthy of *never-ending* praise; hence, "to whom be the glory *forever and ever,"* literally: to the ages of the ages. With a solemn "Amen" he reaffirms his personal gratitude as again and again he ponders God's great undying love, the unfathomable depth of his grace and mercy in Jesus Christ.

---

[14] This modifier ("according to," etc.) belongs to verse 4 in its entirety, as brought out in the translation.
[15] Though the verb is missing, so that one could either insert ἐστιν, *is* (Rom. 1:25; I Peter 4:11) or εἴη *be* (Ps. 113:2; LXX:112:2), the resultant meaning would be about the same, for if his *is* the glory then glory should certainly *be* ascribed to him.
[16] On the concept *glory* see N.T.C. on Philippians, pp. 62, 63, footnote 43.

Chapter 1

Verses 6-10

Theme: *The Gospel of Justification by Faith apart from Law-works Defended against Its Detractors*

I. *This Gospel's Origination: it is not of human but of divine origin*

B. I am amazed that y o u are so quickly moving to a different gospel. There is only one true gospel. Let him be accursed who preaches another. There! Is it the favor of men that I am now seeking to win or of God?

6 I am amazed that y o u are so quickly moving away from him who called y o u (and turning) to a different gospel, 7 which (in reality) is not (even) another; but (the fact is that) certain individuals are throwing y o u into confusion and are trying to pervert the gospel of Christ. 8 But even though we ourselves or an angel from heaven were to preach to y o u any gospel other than the one which we preached to y o u, let him be accursed! 9 As we have said before, so now I say again, If anyone is preaching to y o u any gospel other than that which y o u have received, let him be accursed! 10 There! Is it the favor of men that I am now seeking to win or of God? Or is it men whom I am seeking to please? If I were still trying to please men, I would not be a servant of Christ.

1:6-10

B. *There is only one true gospel*

6, 7. We have reached the place in the letter where ordinarily, according to the custom of the day, words of thanksgiving would be found. It stands to reason that in Paul's epistles this expression of gratitude would be addressed to the one true God and not, as among the Gentiles, to this or that pagan divinity. For the apostle, then, it was generally a grateful acknowledgment of divine grace bestowed upon the addressed, whereby they had been enabled to make progress in knowledge, faith, love, etc. It was an expression of inner satisfaction and was frequently accompanied by a prayer that the advance already made might continue on and on (Rom. 1:8 ff.; I Cor. 1:4-9; Phil. 1:3-11; Col. 1:3 ff.; I Thess. 1:2 ff.; II Thess. 1:3 ff.). Sometimes the thanksgiving was in the form of a doxology (II Cor. 1:3 ff.; Eph. 1:3 ff.).

In Galatians, however, we are confronted with the very opposite. What we find *here* is not satisfaction but stupefaction: overwhelming amazement, painful perplexity. Says Paul: **I am amazed that y o u are so quickly moving away from him who called y o u (and turning) to a different gospel, which (in reality) is not (even) another.** Paul could be stern.[17] He was no flatterer. To be sure, he was very tactful. It was his custom to *commend* before he began to *condemn,* to use words of praise and encouragement before using words of criticism and warning. He does this even in I Corinthians, addressed to a church not lacking in failings both common and uncommon. But in Galatians *the very essence of the gospel* is at stake. Had this not been the case Paul would have been very tolerant, as Phil. 1:15-18 proves. But when the issue is momentous—God's glory and man's salvation—tolerance has its

---

[17] In the original the abruptness of this outburst is heightened by the absence of any introductory particle.

limits. In view of the occasion and purpose of Galatians, as previously explained, the unceremonious and uncompromising character of 1:6-10 is not surprising. Now this does not mean that in connection with those whom he addresses the apostle was unaware of anything whatever that he might be able to acknowledge with gratitude. In the present circumstances, however, such acknowledgment must bide its time (3:3; 4:12-15; 5:7).

But although 1:6-10 is in the nature of an outburst, nevertheless, *as far as the Galatians themselves are concerned* it is not an outburst of anger. There is consternation rather than indignation, amazement rather than resentment. Though Paul reproaches, he does not reject. Even now he is convinced that in the end everything will turn out favorably (5:10). The apostle is amazed or astonished to hear that the addressed are *in the process of changing their position.* The verb used can have either a favorable or an unfavorable sense; here obviously the latter. Moreover, the Galatians are transferring their loyalty *so quickly,* that is, so soon after their conversion (4:12-15; 5:7); hence also: so soon after the evangelistic labor that had been performed in their midst by Paul and his companions. And it is they themselves who are turning (themselves) away; they are not just being turned away.[18] Neither is it merely a theological position from which they are swerving. On the contrary, they are in the process of transferring their loyalty from the One who in his grace and mercy had called them—that is, from *God* (Rom. 4:17; 8:30; 9:11, 24; Gal. 1:15; Eph. 1:18; 4:1, 4; Phil. 3:14; I Thess. 2:12; 4:7; II Thess. 1:11; II Tim. 1:9)—to a different gospel. The *call* to which reference is made, is here, as everywhere in Paul, the internal or effectual calling: that act of the Holy Spirit whereby he savingly applies the gospel-invitation to the heart and life of certain definite individuals among all of those to whom, in the course of history, that invitation is extended. It is a call to salvation, full and free, via the avenue of sanctification. Speaking by and large, the apostle is convinced that the Galatians whom he here addresses had received *that* effectual call.

If it be argued that surely in the case of the Galatians the call cannot have been effectual since they were in the process of turning away from the God who had called them, the answer is that this position can be maintained only if it could be demonstrated that these people, after having first accepted the gospel by a true and living faith, afterward rejected it and died in that condition, not having given heed to Paul's admonition contained in this letter or to subsequent warnings. As has been pointed out, Paul himself is far more optimistic (5:10). It must ever be borne in mind that divine sovereignty does not abrogate human responsibility, and that

---

[18] It is true that the form of the verb can be interpreted either as a middle or as a passive, but passages like 3:1 ff.; 5:7 show that the apostle is definitely blaming the Galatians for lending a listening ear to the trouble-makers' false teaching.

God, accordingly, carries out his eternal purpose by so operating through his Spirit in the hearts of backsliders that they give heed to the earnest appeals that are made to them. Individuals who until their last breath persist in their disobedience prove that they had never embraced Christ with a true and living faith, even though they may have been church-members outwardly. The fact that the internal call results in salvation, in other words, that God's grace is irresistible, in the sense that it cannot be resisted effectively to the very end, is clear from such passages as John 4:14; 10:28; Rom. 8:28-39; 11:29; I Cor. 1:9; and Phil. 1:6. In the chain of means whereby this calling is made effectual, and this grace irresistible, earnest warnings and obedience to these warnings are important links. No one can ever afford to take his ultimate salvation for granted. Everyone must *strive* to enter in. "And as it has pleased God, by the preaching of the gospel to begin his work in us, so he preserves, continues, and perfects it by the hearing and reading of his Word, by meditation thereon, and by the exhortations, threatenings, and promises thereof, and by the use of the sacraments" (Canons of Dort, v. 14). Note *the threatenings and the warnings!*

In their present condition, then, the Galatians are turning to a *different* gospel, that is, to a gospel that differs radically from the one which they had received from Paul. The latter gospel was: "that a man is not justified by law-works but only through faith in Jesus Christ" (2:16; cf. Rom. 3:24; Eph. 2:8; Titus 3:4-7). That gospel the Galatians were abandoning in favor of a different gospel, one which proclaimed *faith plus law-works* as the way to salvation. It stands to reason that the substitute to which the addressed were turning was a gospel only in name, not in reality. It was really no gospel at all, exactly as Paul here declares: "a different gospel, which (in reality) is not (even) another." Much has been written about the combination *"different . . . not another."* [19] The translation which I favor and which, in one way or another, is also favored by A.R.V., N.E.B., N.A.S.B., (N.T.), Williams, Goodspeed, Weymouth, etc. (contrast A.V.), has been sharply criticized, even ridiculed at times! Some have arrived at the conclusion that Paul is saying that the Galatians are turning away to another gospel which in reality is not essentially different! But the context is clear and decisive: the gospel (?) to which the Galatians are in the process of turning is the perversion of the true gospel (verse 7); it is a gospel (?) different in quality from the one which Paul and his assistants had preached to the Galatians (verse 8), and which the latter had embraced (verse 9);

---

[19] On ἕτερος as compared with ἄλλος see, among many references that could be listed, M.M., p. 257. It should be obvious that the attempt at a consistent distinction between these two words, applicable in all cases, must fail, especially in Koine Greek. In the New Testament, for example, the two are sometimes used interchangeably (I Cor. 12:9, 10; II Cor. 11:4). For the rest, the rule "ἄλλος adds, while ἕτερος distinguishes" is often helpful.

it is a gospel (?) so bad that a curse is invoked upon him who *might*—and also upon him who actually *does*—proclaim it (respectively verses 8 and 9).

With disdain for such a perversion of the true gospel the apostle continues: **but (the fact is that) certain individuals are throwing y o u into confusion and are trying to pervert the gospel of Christ.** The reference is clearly to the extreme rightists, the Judean Judaizers (cf. Acts 15:1), who, though in a very general sense "coming from James" (Gal. 2:12), do not truly represent James at all (Acts 15:24). Very descriptively the apostle says that these "certain individuals"—they are not nearly as important as they assume themselves to be!—*are throwing y o u into confusion. Literally* this verb means *to shake, stir up, trouble, agitate,* as when Egypt's king is said to resemble a monster that *troubles the waters with its feet,* thereby contaminating the rivers (Ezek. 32:2). *Figuratively,* as here, it has reference to *upsetting* the mind and/or heart. Thus Herod was shaken, deeply disturbed, when he heard about the birth of a king of the Jews (Matt. 2:3); the disciples were troubled when they imagined that they were looking at a ghost (Matt. 14:26); and Zechariah when he saw an angel (Luke 1:12). Another unforgettable illustration of the meaning of the word is found in John 14:1, where Jesus, in the night of his betrayal, says to his disciples, who are gathered with him in the upper room, "Let not y o u r hearts any longer be troubled" (see N.T.C. on the Gospel according to John, Vol. II, pp. 262, 263).

The Galatians, then, were being thrown into confusion by men who were wishing and attempting *to turn upside down* the gospel which centers about Christ and glories in him, the Christ-gospel. Surely, a teaching according to which men are saved *through faith plus law-works* is a perversion of the true gospel which proclaims the glad tidings of salvation (by grace) *through faith alone.*

8. Paul continues: **But even though we ourselves or an angel from heaven were to preach to y o u any gospel other than the one which we preached to y o u, let him be accursed**; that is, "Even though we, God's human representatives (I, Paul, and my assistants[20]), or a good angel, one who descends out of heaven in the radiant blaze of his consummate holiness, should begin to preach to y o u any good news other than—hence, contrary to[21]—the gospel which we previously (on the first missionary journeys and on the first leg

---

[20] The fact that in the very next verse the author clearly distinguishes between "we" and "I," mentioning them in one breath, makes it quite clear that even in verse 8 his "we" is not a literary plural. On this subject see N.T.C. on I and II Thessalonians, p. 82, footnote 65.
[21] For this meaning of παρά see also Acts 18:13; Rom. 1:26; 4:18; 11:24; 16:17. The root idea of this preposition is *beside, alongside;* Cf. the English *parallel.* One can place things *side by side* for the sake of comparison. This easily shifts into that of *opposition;* for example, the worship of a false god *besides* the true God is carried on in opposition to—contrary to the will of—the true God.

of this second missionary journey) preached to y o u, let him (I myself in that case, any of my assistants, that angel) *be doomed.*[22] So far the *hypothetical* case. There follows *reality,*[23] *verse* 9. **As we have said before, so now I say again, If anyone is preaching to y o u any gospel other than that which y o u have received, let him be accursed.** The truth expressed in the first conditional sentence (verse 8) greatly strengthens that expressed in the second (verse 9). We have here the reasoning: if even, then all the more. In effect, Paul is saying, "If even we (I, or a fellow-worker) or a holy angel must be the object of God's righteous curse, were any of us ever to preach a gospel contrary to the one we humans previously preached to y o u, then *all the more* the divine wrath must be poured out upon those self-appointed nobodies who are now making themselves guilty of this crime." Here the storm is unleashed in all its fury. Paul's "Let him be anathema" is not a mere wish, but an effective invocation. The apostle, as Christ's fully authorized representative, is pronouncing the curse upon the Judaizers, who are committing the terrible crime of calling the true gospel *false,* and of substituting the false and ruinously dangerous gospel for the true and saving one.

But this word of severe condemnation for the trouble-makers is at the same time one of earnest remonstrance and warning for the Galatians, who were in the process of allowing themselves to be misled, and were actually moving away from the One who, in his love and mercy, had called them. That the addressed deserved this rebuke is clear *first of all* from the fact that they had been forewarned, and "forewarned is forearmed," that is, *if* one heeds the warning. When Paul says, "As we have said before," he probably means that immediately after the Jerusalem Council the apostle and Silas, fully realizing that the Judaizers were not at all satisfied with the decisions of this council and would do all in their power to render them ineffective, had plainly told the Galatians, "There is every possibility that soon after we, y o u r true shepherds, have left y o u, wolves will arrive and

---

22 According to H. L. Strack and P. Billerbeck, *Kommentar zum Neuen Testament aus Talmud und Midrasch,* Vol. III, p. 260, in the terminology of the Septuagint the word ἀνάθεμα indicates anything which by God or in God's name has been devoted to destruction and ruin. The rabbinical *"herem"* is a broader concept, inasmuch as it comprises *whatever* is devoted to God, not only that which is devoted to him for destruction. The same distinction is carried over into the New Testament, where the noun ἀνάθημα (Luke 21:5, according to the best reading) means that which has been devoted to God as a votive offering, naturally with no curse implications; while ἀνάθεμα (used here in Gal. 1:8, 9, and also in Acts 23:14; Rom. 9:3; I Cor. 12:3; 16:22) refers to that which is devoted to God without hope of being redeemed; hence, that which, or he who, is doomed to destruction, accursed. See also the entries ἀνάθεμα and ἀνάθημα in L.N.T. (Th.) and L.N.T. (A. and G.).
23 The first conditional sentence (verse 8) has ἐάν and the aorist middle subjunctive in the protasis, and is, accordingly, *future more vivid* or *third class.* The second (verse 9) has εἰ and the present middle indicative, and is *simple, first class.* It *assumes* that the condition is true to fact. In the present case we know that it is also *actually* true to fact. The apodosis, in both cases, uses the present imperative.

will try to destroy y o u, by substituting the false gospel of salvation by law-works for the true gospel of salvation by grace through faith. Be on y o u r guard against these destroyers." It is even possible that already on the first missionary journey similar warnings had been issued, but certainly on the second. Paul adds, "So now I say again,"[24] etc. He now says "I" and not "we" because he alone is the author of this epistle, he himself is *the apostle,* clothed with full authority, and his former associates are absent at this moment. Also later on in life Paul would continue to warn those entrusted to his care about impending dangers (Acts 20:29 ff.; cf. II Tim. 3:1-5; 4:1-5). In this, as in so many other respects, he was following the example of his Master (John 16:1, 4, 33). Since the Galatians had disregarded the earlier warning, they had earned the reprimand.

Secondly, they had merited this reproof because not only had the gospel been previously preached to them (verse 8), but they had also accepted it (verse 9). In this respect verse 9 says more than verse 8. By the power of the Holy Spirit the external message had been translated into an inward conviction. They should have guarded the deposit that had been entrusted to them.

The question might be asked, "But was not Paul too severe in his denunciation and in his rebuke? Is it not true that even now the Judaizers believed in Jesus Christ for salvation, the only difference between Paul and those who differed with him being that to this required faith the latter *added* strict obedience to certain Mosaic regulations?" The answer is that the "addition" was in the nature of a complete repudiation of the all-sufficiency of Christ's redemption. Read Gal. 5:2. A beverage may be very healthful and refreshing, but when a drop of poison is *added* to it, it becomes deadly. Christ, too, used severe language in condemning the hypocrites of his day (Matt. 23, especially verses 15 and 33). Pharisees and Judaizers had much in common, were in fact closely related (Acts 15:5; Luke 11:46; cf. Gal. 6:12, 13).

Moreover, Paul and the gospel were friends. To him that gospel was the good news of salvation which God addresses to a world lost in sin. He considered it indispensable for salvation (Rom. 10:14, 15), and was so enthused about it that affectionately he called it *"my* gospel" (Rom. 2:16; cf. Rom. 1:16; I Cor. 1:17; 9:16; II Cor. 4:4; Phil. 1:17; I Tim. 1:11). On the concept *gospel* and *preaching the gospel* see N.T.C. on Philippians, pp. 81–85.

Paul's sharp distinction between the true and the false gospel has a present day application. Illustrations:

---

[24] He cannot have meant, "I now repeat what I just said" (in verse 8), for there is too much difference in content between the two statements, as has been, and will be, indicated.

a. At a church service *hymns* are sung which set forth salvation by grace. The *sermon,* however, proclaims an entirely different "gospel" (?) .

b. The pastor calls on a family and enquires about the absent daughter. The parents exultantly inform him that she is about to marry "a very nice young man, a member of a church which our daughter, too, will soon join." Are these parents blissfully unaware of the fact that in that church the true gospel is not being proclaimed; or does this not matter?

c. At a "crusade" many people sign decision-cards. They begin to attend various churches, from some of which the "crusader's" gospel is banned!

10. Paul has used forceful language. That gives him an opportunity to answer a charge of the opponents. He writes: **There!**[25] **Is it the favor of men that I am now seeking to win or of God? Or is it men whom I am seeking to please?** Here one detects an echo of the opponents' accusations and insinuations, on this order: "Paul is trying to win human, rather than divine, favor. He tries to please everybody, so that everybody may follow him. Among his own people he preaches circumcision (Gal. 5:11; cf. Acts 16:3) , for he knows that they believe in it. But he withholds this rite from the Gentiles because they welcome exemption from it."

Paul answers: "Would a popularity-seeker hurl anathemas at people? Is it not clear that it is not men's but God's approval in which I am interested, and that I am seeking to please my Lord?" Continued: **If I were still trying to please men, I would not be a servant of Christ.**[26] Two misinterpretations:

a. "I *never* yield to human customs and traditions."

Total indifference on this score would not have been like Paul. It would bring Gal. 1:10 into conflict with I Cor. 9:22. Tactfulness is not a vice but a virtue when paired with honesty and truth. The apostle desired to be "all things to all men, in order in one way or another to save some." Hence, among the Jews he was willing, during this transition period, to observe certain traditions (Acts 16:3; 21:17-26; cf. 18:18) , as long as these were not considered *means unto salvation,* for on *that* issue he was adamant. When Judaizers tried to force circumcision upon Gentiles, declaring that otherwise salvation could not be obtained, the apostle invoked God's curse on these distorters. In Paul's religion there was room for flexibility, but ever *within* the limits prescribed by the gospel.

b. "If I were still, *as formerly,* trying to please men," etc.

This supposed reference to the apostle's unconverted state is out of line with the present context.

---

[25] By no means does γάρ always mean *for* or *because.* It can also be strongly confirmatory or exclamatory: Yes, indeed! Certainly! There! What! Why! (cf. Matt. 27:23; John 7:41; Acts 8:31; I Cor. 9:10; 11:22; Phil. 1:18) .

[26] This is a *contrary to fact* or *second class* conditional sentence: with εἰ and the imperfect indicative in the protasis; and the imperfect indicative with ἄν in the apodosis.

The true interpretation is this: "If, *in spite of* my claim that I am Christ's servant, I were *still,* or *nevertheless,* attempting to please men, my claim would be false." One who trims his sails to every breeze of opinion and bias, cannot be a *servant*[27] of Christ. Paul, on the contrary, is such a servant, for he joyfully acknowledges Jesus as his Redeemer, Owner, and Lord, and is fully surrendered to him. It was this very Christ who said, "No man can serve two masters" (Matt. 6:24). Paul realizes that for himself this life of complete loyalty means persecution (Gal. 5:1), but he glories in such affliction. Not Paul but his opponents are trying to avoid persecution (Gal. 6:12). *They* are the men-pleasers (Gal. 6:13), a type of conduct reprehensible even in slaves (Eph. 6:6; Col. 3:22). *Paul's* chief concern is God's glory.

---

[27] For the implications of the term *servant* see N.T.C. on Philippians, pp. 44, 109, 110.

Chapter 1

Verses 11-17

Theme: *The Gospel of Justification by Faith apart from Law-works*
Defended against Its Detractors

I. *This Gospel's Origination: it is not of human but of divine origin*

C. The gospel I preach is not a human invention. I received it through the revelation of Jesus Christ. Rescued by God's grace from intense Judaism, I did not immediately go to Jerusalem to seek men's advice, but went to Arabia, and again I returned to Damascus.

11 For I make known to y o u, brothers, with respect to the gospel that was preached by me, that it is not a human invention; 12 for as concerns myself, I did not receive it from men nor was I taught it; on the contrary (I received it) through the revelation of Jesus Christ. 13 For y o u have heard of my former manner of life when I practiced the Jewish religion, how beyond all bounds I was persecuting the church of God and was trying to destroy it; 14 and I advanced in the Jewish religion more than many of my contemporaries among my people, and was a more ardent enthusiast for the traditions of my fathers. 15 But when it pleased him, who separated me from my mother's womb and called me through his grace, 16 to reveal his Son in me, in order that I might preach his gospel among the Gentiles, I did not at once confer with flesh and blood, 17 nor did I go up to Jerusalem to those who were apostles before me, but I went away to Arabia; and again I returned to Damascus.

1:11-17

C. *This gospel originated in God, as shown by Paul's experiences before, during, and shortly after his conversion*

11. Paul continues to show that the gospel which he proclaims is the only one worthy of the name, being of divine origin. He writes, **For I make known to y o u, brothers, with respect to the gospel that was preached by me, that it is not a human invention.** In connection with the present context "for" must mean something like "In justification of the facts which I have stated, namely, that my gospel is of divine origin and is the only true gospel, so that anyone who distorts it is accursed, note the following corroborative facts selected from the story of my life."

In the verses which follow, the apostle is not trying to present a complete autobiography. He chooses from his career only those events which support his main contention with reference to the source of his calling as an apostle and of the message which he proclaims. Hence, when he omits an event mentioned elsewhere—for example, in Acts or in Paul's letters to the Corinthians—this must not be charged against him, as if he were purposely suppressing certain facts in order to win the argument against the Judaizers. On the contrary, he is deeply conscious of telling the truth (Gal. 1:20). The omitted incidents are left unmentioned for the simple reason that they have nothing to do with the point which Paul is trying to prove.

The beginning of the sentence is rather striking: "For I make known to y o u," as if they did not already know. But they must have known many of the facts which Paul is going to relate. However, they were acting as if they did not know them. Otherwise they would not be lending a listening ear to the distorters of the true and only gospel of salvation. And for this reason the apostle must remind them again of the truth with reference to himself and the gospel he proclaims. He does this in a very tactful and tender manner, calling them "brothers," for even now, in spite of their deviation, he regards them as members of the same spiritual family to which he, too, belongs, "the Father's Family" (Eph. 3:14). The subject to which he calls their attention is "the gospel that was preached by me," *preached;* hence, they have heard it and are responsible for what they have heard; *by me,* never mind what enemies have been proclaiming; *the gospel,* for, as stated previously, the apostle's defense of himself is in reality a defense of the one and only gospel. He makes known to them that this good news is "not a human invention." This rendering, adopted also by Phillips and by N.E.B.,[28] is well-founded. Literally Paul writes, "not in accordance with man." This might leave the impression that he is simply saying that his gospel is not "in human style." But though, to be sure, this is implied and is even basic, yet the next verse clearly shows that what Paul has in mind is that the gospel which the Galatians have heard from his lips differs not only in *character* and *content* from any human "gospel" (?), but also— and for that very reason—in *origin:* it is not the *result* of human ingenuity or devising.[29] Continued: **12. for as concerns myself, I did not receive it from men nor was I taught it,** probably meaning: "As far as I myself am concerned (note emphatic "I"), in no way whatever did it reach me from any human source. It was not transmitted to me by means of *tradition* from father to son (or from one generation to the next), nor by means of *instruction* from teacher to pupil."[30] Continued: **on the contrary (I received it) through the revelation of Jesus Christ.** Paul here declares that he had received the gospel by a direct revelation of Jesus Christ concerning himself, exactly as the other apostles had also received it (see also on Gal. 1:15, 16; cf. I Cor. 9:1; 15:8).

This introduces a problem. The question might be asked, "But were there not ever so many human agents that had taken part, at one time or another, in supplying Paul with the materials for his gospel? How then can he affirm, repeatedly and with great emphasis, that he had received his gospel from Christ, from him alone, and not at all from men?" Leaving out of consideration many speculative theories concerning contacts which Saul of Tarsus may have had with Jesus during the latter's sojourn on earth, when the future apostle was in Jerusalem, where as a young man he

---

[28] Similarly Williams "not a human message," and Beck "not a human idea."
[29] With the accusative κατά has this merging quality; see N.T.L. (A. and G.), p. 408: the meaning "in accordance with" merges with "the result of."
[30] Others, interpreting παρέλαβον differently, and emphasizing the role of oral tradition especially as employed in the rabbinical schools, believe that Paul meant, "I did not receive it by tradition from men, that is, I was not taught it."

was brought up as a pupil of Gamaliel (Acts 22:3), speculative theories for which it is hard to find solid support in II Cor. 5:16 or anywhere else, it remains true that even before his conversion Paul must have received a great deal of information about Jesus. If he had not known what believers were saying about Jesus, why would he have persecuted *them*—hence *him* (Acts 9:4)—so bitterly? The persecutor must have heard many a ringing testimony from the quivering lips of martyrs, uttered while, with *his* approval, they were being put in chains, dragged off to prison, and at times even put to death. He had been present when Stephen was being stoned, and had heard *his* testimony (Acts 7:58). It is safe to assume, therefore, that even before his conversion Paul must have been fairly well acquainted with many of the historical facts and happenings regarding Jesus. In his epistles he gives evidence of a vast amount of historical knowledge (Rom. 1:3; 9:5; I Cor. 1:23; 15:1 ff.; Phil. 2:5 ff.; I Tim. 3:16; and see also on Gal. 3:1), which he must have gathered little by little, much of it even before Christ had met *him,* Saul the persecutor, as he approached the ancient city of Damascus.

Moreover, these *historical facts* are important. Apart from these *events*—Christ's birth, suffering, death, resurrection, etc.—there is no basis for salvation. How is it, then, that Paul can say that he had received his gospel from Christ, and not from men? The answer is that no matter how detailed Paul's knowledge of these events may have been, their totality does not as yet constitute "the gospel." For, first of all, the persecutor rejected forthwith the fact of Christ's resurrection from the grave and that of his ascension to heaven. And secondly, as to the other facts and events of which he had been apprised, he failed to see them in their true significance. He was constantly giving the wrong answer to such questions as these: Was this Jesus merely born or had he come from heaven? Was his birth a mere happenstance, or had he been born with a purpose? Was he merely human, or divine and human in one person? Was he a dreadful danger to true religion, or a great blessing? Was he a tool of Satan, or the Son of God? Were his life and death a mere vapor that vanishes quickly, or were they of abiding and universal significance? When he died on the cross, was he merely a victim, or was he Victor?

It was when the light from heaven had suddenly descended upon him and had engulfed him, and when he had heard a voice saying to him, "Saul, Saul, why are you persecuting me? . . . I am Jesus whom you are persecuting," etc., it was *then* that *everything changed.* It was here, close to Damascus, that in principle the radical turnabout was accomplished, and Paul received his *gospel.* He now saw the Christ as the really risen and exalted One, full of majesty and power, but also . . . full of incomprehensible love, love so marvelous and condescending that it had sought and found this ruthless, mordacious foe in order to make of him an ardent and kind-hearted friend. He now saw Christ as Victor, full of mercy and grace, reaching out his loving arms to embrace both Jew and Gentile, yes *all* those who would place their (God-given) trust in him. The experience, therefore, on the way to Damascus shed a flood of light on all the information which had been reaching Paul. It changed vehement denial into rapturous conviction, vague outward awareness into marvelous insight.

13. Paul now briefly touches upon the three important facts of *a*. his life as a persecutor, *b*. his conversion, and *c*. his activity immediately and shortly after his conversion, in order to show with reference to each of these items that the gospel had not been given to him by any human agency but was a gift from heaven. He writes: **For y o u have heard of my former manner of life when I practiced the Jewish religion.** Yes, the Galatians have heard, probably both from Paul himself and from others, about the manner in which he had conducted himself when his life was still being regulated by the principles which governed the lives of the Jews, unconverted to Christ. Continued: **how beyond all bounds I was persecuting the church of God and was trying to destroy**[31] **it.** For his present purpose it was not necessary that Paul make mention of all the horrid details of this persecuting activity: that it concerned women as well as men, that the victims were bound with chains, imprisoned, urged to blaspheme, sometimes even put to death (see Acts 8:3; 9:1, 13, 14; 22:4, 5; 26:10, 11). What he does say here in Galatians speaks volumes, showing that the persecution of which Paul had been guilty was *a*. extremely violent ("beyond all bounds"), *b*. directed against God's peculiar treasure, the church (as Paul *now,* after his conversion, sees it), the body of those whom God had *called out* from among all the children of men, to be his very own; and *c*. most sinister in its purpose, namely, utterly to destroy this church. Note that the word "church" as here used is a universal concept (other than in 1:2, 22), and that as such it embraces both Gentiles and Jews, also both dispensations, as is made clear in this very epistle (3:7-9, 13, 14, 29; 4:27; cf. Gen. 22:18; Isa. 54:1-3; Amos 9:11 ff.; Matt. 21:33 ff.; Rom. 11:15-24; Eph. 2:14; I Peter 2:9; and Rev. 21:12, 14).

14. The activity of persecution has been described, though in general terms. And now the *drive* or *impetus* behind it is indicated. For Paul this incentive was supplied by the progress which he had made in Pharisaic Judaism, a religion of *works and bondage,* and by his recognition of the fact that this was the very opposite of the Christian religion of *grace and freedom.* He thoroughly understood that Judaism and Christianity were irreconcilable enemies. Moreover, lukewarmness was not in his blood. He

---

[31] The imperfect tenses make this summary very vivid; thus not "persecuted" but "was persecuting" and "was destroying" or "was trying to destroy." As to the second verb, this can be rendered either way: *a*. "was destroying," for Paul's efforts were partially successful; *b*. "was trying to destroy," for these efforts fell far short of their goal. God took care of that!

was not at all the kind of person who, in a mood of relative indifference, afflicts others because he has been ordered to do this. On the contrary, the man from Tarsus was *himself* bent on oppression and destruction, and he put his whole soul into it. He was a fully convinced persecutor, believing with all his heart that what he was setting out to do *must* be done (Acts 26:9). It is in this light that we should understand him when he now writes: **and I advanced in the Jewish religion more than many of my contemporaries among my people, and was a more ardent enthusiast for the traditions of my fathers.** Paul here pictures himself in his pre-conversion state as a dedicated enthusiast (cf. Phil. 3:6), filled with Pharisaic zeal. In fact, in the original the word "enthusiast" is literally "zealot." Elsewhere Paul describes himself as persecuting "this Way unto death" (Acts 22:4), and as being "exceedingly mad" against the saints (Acts 26:11). Luke writes that Saul of Tarsus "was breathing murderous threats against the disciples of the Lord" (Acts 9:1).

This is not surprising, for, as he tells us here in Gal. 1:14, he had been "chopping ahead" *in the Jewish religion,* "hewing out a path" as a pioneer who is cutting his way through a forest, destroying every obstacle in order to advance.

This Jewish religion (literally, "the Judaism") was not that of Old Testament revelation, whose lines—historical, typological, psychological, and prophetical—converge at Bethlehem, Calvary, Olivet.[32] No, the Jewish religion in which Paul had been pushing his way forward was that in which God's holy law was being buried under a load of human traditions, which Paul calls "the traditions of my fathers," the entire *"halakah"* or body of Jewish oral law which supplemented the written law. In such passages as Matt. 5:21 ff.; 15:3, 6; 23:2 ff., Jesus states his opinion about some of these oral traditions. According to one of them God's commandment, "You shall love your neighbor as yourself" (Lev. 19:18; cf. Exod. 23:4, 5; Prov. 25:21, 22) really meant, "You shall love your neighbor *and hate your enemy*" (Matt. 5:43); and according to another, the exhortation to honor father and mother (Exod. 20:12; Deut. 5:16) was similarly emasculated (Matt. 15:1-6). By means of obedience to the entire Mosaic law as interpreted by all these traditions, many of them trivial and at times even directly contrary to the very intention of the commandment as originally given, the Jews, including Paul before his conversion, tried *to work their way* into "the kingdom of heaven." And according to Paul's own testimony as here given, he had advanced in this Jewish religion more than many of his own age among his people. And as he made progress in the *Jewish* religion, he naturally also advanced in hatred against the *Christian* religion. In fact, he had been going ahead with such frightful fanaticism and terrorism that in this area,

---

[32] See W. Hendriksen, *Bible Survey,* p. 92 ff.

at least, he had already surpassed his own teacher, Gamaliel (Acts 5:33-39).

The apostle's purpose in reminding the Galatians of this sad episode in his life must be borne in mind in order to grasp what he is trying to convey. He is saying that no human persuasion would ever have been able to impart *the gospel* to such a confirmed and ferocious persecutor. His purpose is to show that his gospel is *from God,* not from men.

15, 16a. It is with this same purpose in mind that he now continues: **But when it pleased him,**[33] **who separated me from my mother's womb and called me through his grace, to reveal his Son in me, in order that I might preach his gospel among the Gentiles. . . .** Here Paul's conversion story is told "from the inside." To be sure, there was also the outward or physical side. Paul's conversion was not the product of mere subjective imagination. What he had seen was no hallucination. With his physical eyes he had really beheld the ascended Christ. With his physical ears he had actually heard his voice. But the outward and physical would never have sufficed. What Paul had seen and heard had to be applied to his heart. That story is told here. "But when it *pleased* him . . . to reveal his Son in me" can also be rendered, "But when in his *good pleasure* he . . . revealed his Son in me." Though, according to what is probably the best text, the name "God" is here not mentioned, the reference to him is clear. When God's name, attitude, or activity is clearly implied, he is not always mentioned by name. In fact, *not* mentioning his name but merely saying *"he who"* (or, as here, *"him who"*) places the emphasis on God's gracious deeds and attributes. Another striking instance of this type of omission is found in Phil. 1:6: "he who began a good work in y o u." (See N.T.C. on that passage.) The words "who separated me . . . and called me through his grace" form a combination in which both God's sovereign good pleasure and his marvelous love to one so undeserving are stressed. The expression "separated me from my mother's womb" refers to far more than the divine providential activity revealed in Paul's physical birth. It indicates that God did not, as it were, wait until Paul had first proved his worth before appointing him to an important function in his kingdom. No, from his very birth Paul had already been designed for his specific mission, that design being itself the expression of God's plan from eternity (Eph. 1:11). Hence, the verb *separated,* as here used, means nothing less than "set (me) aside," "consecrated" (me), "marked (me) off from the rest of mankind." Similarly, "called me through his grace" refers here not only to the effectual call to salvation through sanctification (see on verse 6), but also to the assignment unto

---

[33] Though the textual evidence for "God" is not too strong, it is clear that *God* is meant. In the original, with the verb εὐδοκέω and the cognate noun εὐδοκία, the name of God is not always expressed (Luke 2:14; Col. 1:19; Phil. 2:13). However, the reference to God is clear from the context; thus also in Eph. 1:5, 9; see 1:3.

plenary apostleship. There is a rather clear allusion here to Jer. 1:5: "Before I formed you in your mother's body I knew you; and before you came out of the womb I sanctified you; a prophet to the nations I ordained you." Cf. Luke 1:15. How wonderful this grace operated in the calling of Paul. It changed a man who was breathing *murderous threats* against Christ's church into one who breathed *doxologies* whenever he reflected on this marvelous redeeming love which had been shown to him, yes to *him so* undeserving! In fact, Paul's career as a relentless persecutor, and whatever intervened between his birth and his entrance upon his work as an effective missionary for Christ, made grace stand out all the more brilliantly!

The immediate. purpose of this separation and calling is here said to have been "to reveal his Son in me." To *reveal*, that is, "to remove the scales from the eyes of my heart, as the scales were removed from my physical eyes" (Acts 9:18). Moreover, Paul does not say "Jesus" or "Christ Jesus," but "his Son," for God wanted him to see that the Jesus whom in his disciples Paul had been persecuting, was indeed God's only Son, partaker of God's very essence, himself *God!* Yet, the words "to reveal his Son *in me*"[34] mean vastly more than "to my intellect." The phrase has reference to *illumining* grace ("to reveal") which is at the same time *transforming*. Cf. II Cor. 3:18. The more Paul sees that it was this very Son of God whom he had been persecuting but who, nevertheless, had taken pity on him, and in his infinite and tender love had sought him, had stopped him in his tracks, and had changed him into an enthusiastic ambassador of the mysteries of grace, so much the more he also loves and adores this Christ! And the more he adores him, so much the more his own mind, his inner disposition, is patterned after that of his Savior (cf. Phil. 2:5). It is thus that God's Son "was revealed" in Paul!

Now just as the *separation* and the *calling* had as its purpose "to reveal his Son in me," so, in turn, this revelation whereby, as just indicated, the image of Christ was engraved upon the very heart of Paul, had as *its* purpose: "in order that I might preach his gospel among the Gentiles"; literally, "in order that I might gospel him among the Gentiles." It should be obvious, therefore, that indirectly the "call" or "calling" was not just unto salvation but definitely also unto the office of "apostle to the Gentiles." In Paul's case these two cannot be separated. And in this connection one might well ask, "Is it ever possible to separate calling unto salvation from calling unto a task in God's kingdom?" Does not everyone who is called

---

34 The phrase ἐν ἐμοί has given rise to much discussion. It has been rendered "to me," "through me," "in connection with me," "in my case," and simply "in (or *within*) me." Though there are parallels for each of these uses, the inward look of the present epistle—cf. "Christ lives in me" (2:20); "until Christ be formed in y o u" (4:19) —has convinced me that "*in* or *within* me" is correct.

have a duty "to show forth the excellencies of the One who called him out of the darkness into his marvelous light"? (I Peter 2:9).

Throughout his apostolic career Paul remained very conscious of the fact that even though he had been called to be an apostle *to Jews and Gentiles* alike (Acts 9:15; 26:20, 23), yet he had been *especially* selected as God's ambassador to the latter (Acts 13:47; 15:12; 18:6; 22:21; 26:17; 28:28; Rom. 11:13; Gal. 2:2, 8; Eph. 3:1, 6, 8; I Tim. 2:7; II Tim. 1:11; 4:17). But was this purpose made clear to Paul *directly by Christ himself* or *indirectly through the mediation of Ananias or anyone else?* This question has already been touched upon in the discussion of verse 1, but requires a more detailed answer here. Now in connection with Paul's dramatic experience on the way to Damascus it must be admitted that either alternative makes sense. As long as Ananias was, as it were, "the mouth" of Christ, Paul's unshakable conviction that he had been called by Christ and had received his gospel from him, and not *"from* men," nor even *"through* man" in the sense that somehow it had lost its purity through this human intervention, was altogether justified. Nevertheless, if a choice must be made, I would favor the former alternative.[35] According to Acts 26:15-18, in answer to Paul's question, "Who art thou, Lord?" the Lord answers, "I am Jesus, whom you are persecuting. But arise and stand upon your feet because for this purpose have I appeared to you: to appoint you a minister and a witness not only to the things which you have seen but also to the things in connection with which I will appear to you; delivering you from the [Jewish] people and from the Gentiles, to whom I am sending you, to open their eyes so that they may turn from darkness to light and from the dominion of Satan to God, in order that they may receive forgiveness of sins and an inheritance among those who have been sanctified by faith in me." This account certainly leaves the impression that not only the words, "I am Jesus whom you are persecuting," reported in all three accounts (Acts 9:5; 22:8; 26:15), but also the call to apostleship among the Gentiles had come directly from the lips of Christ! And do not even the words of 22:15, where Ananias is saying to Paul, "You will be a witness for him to all men concerning the things which you have seen *and heard,"* imply that Paul had already heard *many things* from the lips of Christ? Is it not probable, therefore, that the accounts which we have in Acts 9 and 22 were never intended to reproduce *in full* the words which Jesus addressed to Paul?

To this should be added Paul's experience while he was praying in the temple at Jerusalem, "three years" after his conversion, and long before he wrote Galatians. While Paul had fallen into a trance it was the Savior

---

[35] This is also the view of S. Greijdanus, *Is Hand. 9 (met 22 en 26) in tegenspraak met Gal. 1 en 2?*, Kampen, 1935, p. 40.

who had said to him, "Depart, for I will send you far away to the Gentiles" (Acts 22:21).

It is clear, therefore, that not only in connection with Paul's experience before his conversion (Gal. 1:13, 14) but also in connection with his conversion itself the point has been established that the gospel which he received and the call to proclaim it originated not in man but in God.

16b, 17. This holds also with respect to the apostle's experience, immediately and shortly *after* his conversion, for he continues: **I did not at once confer with flesh and blood, nor did I go up to Jerusalem to those who were apostles before me, but I went to Arabia; and again I returned to Damascus.** Having been led by the hand to Damascus (Acts 9:8), Paul never gave anyone an opportunity to impose his subjective ideas upon him. To be sure, Ananias, at the direction of the Lord, had visited the former persecutor, had laid his hands upon him, had restored his sight, had baptized him, and had told him that he, Paul, would be a witness to all men (Acts 9:10-18; 22:12-16). But all of this had been done at Christ's own command. In fact, Ananias, having heard so many distressing reports with respect to Saul the persecutor, had been reluctant to carry out the order he received. His reluctance had to be overcome (Acts 9:13, 14).

Moreover, it is not at all strange that the Lord had told Ananias to speak to Paul about the latter's mission to "all men." After all, Paul's experience had been so sudden and had occasioned such a complete turn-about in his thinking, and such a radical reversal in his aiming, that a full discussion of its meaning under calmer circumstances was altogether natural and required. Kind-hearted Ananias was the right man for this task. But inasmuch as the message which the latter conveyed to Paul was not his own, Paul here in Galatians is fully justified in omitting any reference to this disciple of the Lord and his mission, since it did not in any way affect the point which he, Paul, is trying to establish, namely, that his gospel and his calling to proclaim it came from above, not from below.

Having spent a number of days in Damascus, Paul, instead of going to Jerusalem in order to receive from the other apostles—whom he fully acknowledges as such!—instruction in the contents of the gospel, at once decided *not* to go there. The words, "I did not at once confer with flesh and blood" do not mean "not at once but later," but rather "I immediately decided not to confer *with flesh and blood*"; that is, I decided not to consult mere man, man in all his weakness, over against God the Omnipotent (cf. Matt. 16:17; Heb. 2:14; and see N.T.C. on Eph. 6:12). So, Paul did not at that time go to Jerusalem. Literally he writes, "I did not at once *put myself upon* those who were apostles before me," seeking their advice or approval. He knew very well that, having seen the Lord and having already received the gospel and the call to proclaim it from *him,* he was on fully equal terms with the other apostles. So, instead of going to Jerusalem, he had gone *to*

Arabia! The fact that Luke does not make mention of this trip is not strange. Neither Luke nor Paul is trying to give us a complete biography of Paul. Paul's purpose has been stated more than once. And as to Luke, he is interested in setting forth the great works which Jesus, from his heavenly home, continued to do on earth in the establishment of his church (cf. Acts 1:1), mainly through the preaching of the Word. Since Paul, in all probability, did not carry out any preaching mission in sparsely settled "Arabia"—probably referring to the northern part of the large peninsula of Arabia, the part that extends almost to the very border of Damascus[36]—, it is not surprising that Luke omits mention of Paul's visit to that largely desert region. Surely, no one, not even the most confirmed Judaizer, would dare to claim that *in Arabia* Paul had received his gospel either *from* men or *through* man! And, on the other hand, the thought suggests itself that withdrawing to Arabia for rest, prayer, and meditation was exactly what Paul needed, so that his mind, violently shaken, would have time and opportunity to ponder the implications of the words which the Lord had spoken to him at the moment of his unforgettable experience. "And again I returned to Damascus," writes Paul. Note that he still does not go to Jerusalem to confer with the other apostles. Instead, having returned to Damascus, he begins to preach Christ in all his fulness. He does this not in this or that private dwelling (cf. Acts 18:7) or even in a school (cf. Acts 19:9), but *at once* in the synagogues (Acts 9:20). What courage! It reminds us of the "boldness" that characterized the other apostles when, shortly after Christ's resurrection, they addressed the people in the very courts of the temple (Acts 4:1). In both cases the reason for this lack of fear is to be sought in the conviction on the part of these men that they had seen *the risen Lord,* were proclaiming *his gospel,* and were discharging *the commission with which he himself had entrusted them.*

---

[36] See *Westminster Historical Atlas to the Bible,* Philadelphia, 1945, p. 87 and Plate XV.

Chapter 1

Verses 18-24

Theme: *The Gospel of Justification by Faith apart from Law-works Defended against Its Detractors*

I. *This Gospel's Origination: it is not of human but of divine origin*

D. Not until three years later did I go up to Jerusalem to visit Cephas, for fifteen days. I saw none of the other apostles, only James. Then I went to Syria and Cilicia, but remained unknown by sight to the Christian churches of Judea. For the change wrought in me they glorified God.

18 Then after three years I went up to Jerusalem to become acquainted with Cephas, and I remained with him fifteen days; 19 but none of the other apostles did I see, only James the Lord's brother. 20 Now take note: with respect to the things which I am writing to y o u, in the presence of God (I affirm) that I am not lying. 21 Then I came to the districts of Syria and Cilicia. 22 But I was still unknown by sight to the Christian churches of Judea. 23 They simply kept hearing, "He who formerly persecuted us is now preaching the gospel of the faith which he formerly was trying to destroy." 24 And they were glorifying God on my account.

1:18-24

D. *This gospel originated in God, as shown by Paul's experiences shortly after his conversion* (continued)

18. Then after three years I went up to Jerusalem to become acquainted with Cephas. Having spent some time in Arabia and in Damascus, Paul afterward went up to Jerusalem. This trip took place "after three years," this intervening period being figured from the main event mentioned in verses 15 and 16: Paul's dramatic conversion. What portion of this "three years" was spent in Arabia, what portion in Damascus, is not indicated. We do not even know whether these "three years" were three full years, or two full years and part of another year, or only one full year and fractions of two other years. The main point is this, that not immediately after his conversion but now at last, "after three years" Paul leaves Damascus for Jerusalem. It is evident that he does not go to Jerusalem in order to receive a mandate to preach the gospel, nor in order to discover the latter's contents. He has *already* received his commission and also the gospel, namely, from the Lord himself. Moreover, according to Acts 9:20 he has *already* been *effectively* preaching the gospel in the synagogues of Damascus. In fact, it was that very preaching of the gospel which stirred up the Jews, so that they took counsel to kill the preacher. Somehow—by means of slandering Paul, describing him as a dangerous person, and perhaps offering a bribe?—they persuaded the ethnarch of Damascus to assist them in their plot to kill Paul. The result: Paul's enemies guarded the city's gates, thinking that thus they would certainly get the apostle in their trap. However, Paul got wind of this scheme, and, by means of a large basket in which he was lowered to the ground from a window of a disciple's house built on the city-wall, he found safety and freedom (Acts 9:23-25; II Cor. 11:32, 33).

Southward he then wended his way, probably proceeding through the

59

darkness all by himself. But why did he turn his face toward the south, that is, toward Jerusalem? The answer, given here in Gal. 1:18, is that he wanted to *visit* or *become acquainted with*[37] Cephas (= Peter, John 1:42). He may have learned from traveling disciples that right at this moment Cephas was staying in Jerusalem.

Paul reached the place where Cephas was staying. He continues his report: **and I remained with him fifteen days.** Again, we cannot be certain whether the period was equal to our fifteen days or more nearly to our fourteen days (cf. the expression "three years" at the beginning of this verse, in connection with which we experience a similar difficulty). What was the purpose of this meeting, and what took place between these two men? One can only guess. It would seem probable that from Peter the escapee gained valuable information about the life of Jesus while still on earth, about the present state of the church in Jerusalem, and about plans for the future; while, in all likelihood Peter gained first hand knowledge concerning Paul's unforgettable experience as he drew near to Damascus, concerning the state of religion in that city and concerning the clever—and providential!—manner in which the plot of the Jews had been foiled. But whatever may have been the topics of discussion, one fact requires emphasis: the two men were meeting on a footing of perfect equality. Neither received his commission or his gospel from the other!

Paul's candid reporting of this visit with Cephas proves his honesty and historical objectivity. Had he been lacking in these qualities he would, no doubt, have left this incident unmentioned, for fear that the Judaizers would take advantage of it in support of their theory that Paul had received his gospel not from God but from men; particularly, in this case, from Peter. Paul, however, is not trying to hide anything that might be construed as being pertinent, one way or the other, to this basic point of contention (the gospel's origin). Besides, he must have been thoroughly convinced that, in the final analysis, the Judaizers in reality would derive little comfort from a visit so late in the day—that is, so long a time after the apostle's conversion—of such short duration, and for such a purpose ("to become acquainted"). Was it not altogether natural that Paul, an apostle of Jesus Christ, should wish to learn more about Peter, another apostle, commissioned by the same Lord, and should avail himself of the opportunity that presented itself?

19. Continued: **but none of the other apostles did I see.** The reason for this cannot have been that in Jerusalem Paul, out of fear, kept himself in hiding.

---

[37] The verb ἱστορέω (cf. the noun ἵστωρ, ἴστωρ) is from the stem ϝιδ; cf. εἴδω, οἶδα (*see, know*). From this same stem are derived the English *visit* (cf. *vision, wit*); A. S. *witan;* Dutch *weten,* and similar words in German, Danish, Swedish, etc. Hence, in Koine Greek the meaning of the verb under discussion is: *to visit with the purpose of getting to know, to become acquainted with.*

Lack of courage was not at all characteristic of this man (see Acts 14:19-21; 19:30; 20:24; 21:12-14; 27:21-26; I Cor. 4:9-13; II Cor. 11:22-33; Phil. 1:12-14; and I Thess. 2:2). For the "boldness" of the other apostles, displayed by them after Christ's resurrection, see Acts 4:29; 5:41. The real reason why Paul did not see the other apostles was probably the latters' absence from Jerusalem at this time. It is true that, according to Acts 8:1, immediately after Stephen's death the apostles had not joined in the flight of believers from that city. But do not Acts 11:30 and 12:1, 2 suggest that they, except Peter and James (the latter being John's brother whom Herod killed with the sword), did leave afterward? We are not told how long before the events reported in these two passages they had left. Besides, by this time there must have been many Christian communities scattered throughout the country that was inhabited by the Jews, communities in need of leadership. This guidance was provided, we may well assume, by the apostles. The point which Paul is making is that he did not deem it necessary to visit all these communities and meet all these apostles in order to be "approved" by them and receive instruction from them in the essence of the gospel. So he, already an apostle, had seen only Cephas, and this merely for the purpose of getting acquainted with him. None of the other apostles had he seen, **only** [or **except**] **James, the Lord's brother.** Does this mean that, after all, Paul had seen two apostles, namely, Peter, who, being one of the Twelve, was an apostle in the plenary sense of that term, and James, an apostle in a more general sense? Though from the point of view of grammar this possibility must be allowed, yet from the aspect of logic the alternative explanation would appear to be more reasonable, namely, "In addition to Cephas, the only apostle whom I saw in Jerusalem, I also saw one other person of special importance, James, the Lord's brother." This does not mean that Paul had seen no other *believers* in Jerusalem; only, that he saw no other individuals of special prominence in the kingdom, *Christian leaders.*[38]

Paul calls James "the Lord's brother." This distinguishes him from James, the brother of John (these two brothers being the sons of Zebedee), and from James, the son of Alphaeus (Matt. 10:2, 3). That James, the Lord's brother, was a man of prominence in the early church, particularly in Jerusalem, is clear from Acts 12:17; 15:13-29; 21:18; and Gal. 2:9, 12. In the days of Christ's earthly sojourn James and his brothers had remained unbelievers (John 7:5). But after the resurrected Christ had appeared to

---

[38] Accordingly, the charge that Gal. 1:19 and Acts 9:26-29 are in hopeless conflict is unfounded. Even Luke's statement that Paul was brought "to the apostles" is not necessarily in conflict with Paul's own declaration in the passage under discussion. The Praesidium of the Jerusalem church consisted originally of "the apostles," the Twelve. When, due to their absence, other men had to replace them—such as James, the Lord's brother, and certain "elders"—this governing body could very well continue to bear the name "the apostles." In Acts 14:14 Luke calls Barnabas an "apostle."

him (I Cor. 15:7), James and the other brothers of Jesus had become
believers (Acts 1:14). Of all of Christ's brothers James occupied a leading
role in the early history of the church. He was a person of special gifts
and wide sympathies. Objects of his tender affection were both the Jews
(Acts 15:21; 21:17 ff.) and the Gentiles (Acts 15:13-19). The endearing
phrase "our beloved Barnabas and Paul" may well have come from him
(Acts 15:25). He was a moderate, a man of peace, eager to weld Jew and
Gentile into a single Christian fellowship. He wisely accepted the position
that it was possible for believers of diverse origin and background to live
together harmoniously, even though in non-essentials the forms of religious
expression might not be exactly identical. In predominantly Jewish communities—for example, in Jerusalem—he favored, for the period of transition, the retention of the ancestral customs handed down from Moses, but
never as a substitute for (or supplement of) faith in Christ. He was
definitely opposed to burdening the Gentiles with the rite of circumcision
and other Jewish ordinances, but tactfully proposed that in mixed communities certain practices offensive to Jews be avoided (Acts 15:13-29).
Whether at times (cf. Acts 21:17-26), in pursuing his policy of conciliation
he may have bent backward too far in his attempt to satisfy, as far as possible, those from the Jews who, like himself, had turned to the Lord, is a
question that need not concern us here.

That James is here called "the Lord's brother" because he sprang from
the same womb as did Jesus, according to the latter's human nature, would
seem to follow naturally from such passages as Matt. 13:55, 56; Mark 6:3,
where the names of the other brothers are also mentioned, and the presence
of sisters is also indicated. The burden of proof rests entirely on those who
defend the idea that "brother," as used here, means *step-brother* (son of
Joseph by an earlier marriage) or *cousin*.[39]

For Paul, on his visit to Jerusalem, to have ignored a man of such
prominence as James, would have been unthinkable. However, the apostle's
testimony here in Gal. 1:19 is in line with his main contention, namely,
that he did not receive his gospel or his call to proclaim it from any man,
but from Christ. While Paul remained at the home of Cephas for a period
of two weeks, he only *saw*—in *this* connection meaning perhaps "briefly
contacted"—James. And there is not a hint of a clash between Paul and
James.

20. Since the apostle is well aware of the fact that his own representation
of the facts is going to be challenged by the enemies, he adds: **Now take
note: with respect to the things which I am writing to y o u, in the presence
of God (I affirm) that I am not lying.** Here *he solemnly affirms*, with an appeal
to God's own presence and omniscience, that what he says is true.

---

[39] On this see F. F. Bruce, *Commentary on the Book of Acts*, pp. 44, 45.

In reading Paul's epistles it is striking how often the apostle's awareness of the presence of God shines through his lines, as it were (Rom. 1:8, 9, 25; 6:17; 7:25; 8:35-39; 9:1, 5; 10:1; 11:33-36; 15:13, 32; 16:25-27; Eph. 1:3 ff.; 1:15 ff.; 3:14-21; and in all the other epistles). He was filled with a genuine and overpowering consciousness of living "in the very presence of God," the God whom he loved and, what is even more meaningful, who loved him. A good rule for each person to follow is, therefore, this one:

"When you think, when you speak, when you read, when you write,
When you sing, when you walk, when you seek for delight,—
To be kept from all wrong both at home and abroad,
Live always as under the eye of your God."

(First lines of a poem
of anonymous authorship)

21. Paul continues: **Then I came to the districts of Syria and Cilicia.** Luke states that it was because of another plot against Paul's life that the brothers in Jerusalem, having become aware of it, decided that he should leave the city. Paul agreed, for, as he himself reports, the Lord appeared to him and told him to depart quickly, adding the encouraging words, "I will send you far away to the Gentiles" (Acts 9:30; 22:17-21). So Paul was conducted on his way to Caesarea, and from there sent to his home-town, Tarsus, the chief city of Cilicia, from which, probably after a period of several years, Barnabas, overtaxed with evangelistic activity, brought him to Antioch in Syria to join in the work there.

Now this sequence of events raises the question, "If Paul first made his abode in Cilicia, afterward in Syria, why does he, in making his own report, reverse this order; in other words, why "Syria and Cilicia" instead of "Cilicia and Syria"? Some answers are: *a.* because Syria adjoins Palestine, so that, traveling by land, one would reach Syria before entering Cilicia; *b.* because in Cilicia the apostle remained inactive, but he worked in Syria; and *c.* because Cilicia, though a Roman province, was rather weak and under the jurisdiction of Syria. Whatever may be the truth as to this question, the main point which Paul is trying to stress must not be lost sight of. He is saying, as it were, "Then I left Jerusalem and went to places so remote that the possibility of contact with the Twelve, to receive the gospel from them or to be seriously influenced by them, was excluded."

22, 23. Continued: **But I was still unknown by sight to the Christian churches of Judea.** The apostle was fully justified in making this statement, for in former days his persecution activity, as far as it had been carried on in the southern part of Palestine, had been largely confined to Jerusalem; and as a convert and apostle he, having spent a fortnight with Cephas, had

63

not entered any of the surrounding territory.[40] Thus personally he was still unknown in these country churches, probably implying "and thus unknown also to the apostles who were serving them" (see on verse 19).

For various reasons the Christians in the outlying districts were used to making trips to Jerusalem. On these visits they would call on some of their fellow-believers. Also, those dwelling in Jerusalem would visit those outside the city. In both of these cases those of Jerusalem would joyfully and vividly impart to their friends and relatives the news about *the persecutor turned gospeler.* As a result **They,** that is, the members of the Christian churches of *Judea,* **simply kept hearing, "He who formerly persecuted us is now preaching the gospel of the faith[41] which he formerly was trying to destroy."** The underlying implication of this exuberant exclamation must not escape us. It is evident that the reporters, men and women of simple faith in Christ, approved of the gospel as preached by Paul! They recognized it as being the very same good news which they had accepted from the start, having heard it from the lips of Christ and his disciples. It was *that* gospel which at one time Paul had been trying to destroy. It was *that same gospel* which he was now preaching! What a crushing argument against the Judaizers, who were slandering the apostle for proclaiming the wrong kind of gospel, one that would not reach quite far enough to save people. What the church's "pillars" are reported to have done later on, namely, give expression to their conviction that the gospel as preached by Paul (and Barnabas, Gal. 2:6-10) was the true gospel, the Jerusalem saints were *shouting* even now, and their Judaean fellow-believers, who were constantly *hearing* it, were in glad accord with them. **24.** Paul concludes: **And they**—all of them together—**were glorifying[42] God on my account.** They were not *suspicious,* as those of Jerusalem had been at one time (Acts 9:26), nor *indifferent* (cf. Rev. 3:16), nor *unforgiving,* nor even *merely happy.* On the contrary, fully realizing that whatever comes from God must be returned to him in the form of praise and thanksgiving, and that this circle must never be broken, they declared the glorious character of God's marvelous attributes: power, sovereignty, wisdom, grace, mercy, etc., shown in saving a wretch, a relentless persecutor, and transforming him into a flame-tongued

---

[40] For use of the term "Judea" for the region round about Jerusalem, but excluding the latter, see also John 3:22. That here in Gal. 1:22 Jerusalem is indeed excluded follows naturally from verse 23, where the Jerusalem saints are introduced as referring to Paul's former activity as a persecutor in their midst. Certainly, if he had persecuted them, then *to them,* at least, he cannot have been unknown. It is impossible, however, to determine the exact boundaries of "Judea" as the term is employed here in verse 22. We do know, however, that from Jerusalem as a center the cause of the Lord had been spreading (Acts 8:4 ff.), so that the term "the churches of Judea in Christ" (thus literally) must not be taken in too narrow a sense.

[41] In this context the objective sense of the word *faith* surely predominates; that is, it is the *religion* or *doctrine* that is meant. See also on 6:10.

[42] On the cognate noun δόξα see N.T.C. on Philippians, pp. 62–64.

herald of the gospel! What depth of feeling must have overwhelmed Paul's soul as he wrote these last words: "They were glorifying God *on my account* (literally "in me") !"

Summary of Chapter 1

This chapter consists of four short paragraphs: verses 1-5; 6-10; 11-17; and 18-24. In the first of these subdivisions Paul's painful distress reveals itself in the manner in which he describes himself and the addressed, and in the qualifying clause by means of which he enlarges on his opening salutation. In that clause he clearly implies that to the sacrifice of Christ for sinners to purchase their salvation nothing can be added.

In the second paragraph Paul gives expression to his shocked amazement about those whom he addresses, because of their disloyalty to the God who had called them, and their readiness to accept a different gospel, which really was no gospel at all but a dangerous distortion. He pronounces God's curse upon anyone who might proclaim—or is actually proclaiming —a gospel other than the one which had been preached to the Galatians and had been accepted by them.

In this connection two facts must be borne in mind:

(1) Paul's anathemas have relevancy in every age. Anyone who teaches that God's grace and human endeavor are twin sources of salvation, that is, that *to a certain extent* men are able to lift themselves into heaven by the lobes of their ears, is here condemned. Implication: then would not this curse rest at least as heavily upon those who proclaim that salvation can be achieved apart *entirely* from divine help ("Mankind *alone* must save us") ?

(2) These anathemas are aimed at those who are leading the Galatians astray, not at the Galatians themselves. With the latter the apostle is sorely displeased. Nevertheless, in his love and patience he still regards them as *his* and *God's* children, grievously erring children though they be—a lesson for all pastors, parents, and leaders of men.

In verses 11-17 Paul proves that the charge of the opponents, namely, that he is not a true apostle and that his gospel had been imparted to him not by God but by men, and is accordingly a merely human invention, is false. He bolsters his argument by briefly setting forth certain relevant events from the story of his life. As to receiving the gospel from men, particularly from other apostles, he shows that *before his conversion* this would have been *psychologically impossible* for such a bitter persecutor; that *at the time of his conversion* it would have been *wholly unnecessary,* for Christ himself revealed the gospel to him by appearing to him and addressing him directly; and that *immediately after his conversion* it would, in addition, have been *geographically unthinkable,* for in Damascus and in Arabia, the places to which he wended his way, there were no apostles who could have imparted the gospel to him.

The same line of argumentation is continued in the closing paragraph. Paul shows that his first post-conversion visit to Jerusalem was of very short duration, had as its purpose "to become acquainted with Cephas (Peter)," *not* to receive the gospel from him, and was not followed by visits to the other apostles (though James, the brother of the Lord, was also briefly contacted). The writer had remained unknown to "the Christian churches of Judea," outside Jerusalem. Accordingly, when the wonderful news of his conversion began to spread, those who heard it did not begin to praise Peter or the rest of the apostles but "were glorifying *God*" on Paul's account, for it was from God—from Christ himself—that the former persecutor had received the glorious gospel of salvation full and free for Gentiles as well as for Jews.

Implication: since, then, this gospel is divine in origin and essence, no attempt must be made to distort it. It is the only good news whereby men are saved, enabled to be a blessing to their neighbors, and equipped to live to God's glory.

Chapter 2

Theme: *The Gospel of Justification by Faith apart from Law-works Defended against Its Detractors*

I. *This Gospel's Origination: it is not of human but of divine origin; hence, is independent*

E. Then, on a visit to Jerusalem with Barnabas and Titus, its "pillars" in a private interview imparted nothing to me, but gave us the right hand of fellowship. Titus, a Greek, was not compelled to be circumcised. Thus, there was no yielding to infiltrators but continuation of blessing for y o u. A division of missionary labor was agreed on. The poor were to be remembered.

CHAPTER II

GALATIANS

GALATIANS

2   1 Then, after an interval of fourteen years, I went up again to Jerusalem with Barnabas, also taking Titus with me. 2 I went up, moreover, as a result of a revelation, and I set before them the gospel which I am accustomed to preach among the Gentiles; but (I did this) privately to "those of repute," to make sure that I was not running or had not run in vain. 3 Yet even Titus who was with me, Greek though he is, was not compelled to be circumcised; 4 (in fact, the suggestion would never have arisen) but for the uninvited sham brothers, who had infiltrated our ranks to spy on our liberty which we have in Christ Jesus, and thus to reduce us to slavery; 5 to whom not even for a moment did we yield submission, in order that the truth of the gospel might continue with y o u. 6 Well, from those "who were reputed" to be something—whatever they once were makes no difference to me; God accepts no man's person—to me "those of repute" imparted nothing; 7 on the contrary, when they saw that I had been entrusted with the gospel to the uncircumcised just as Peter (with that) to the circumcised 8 —for he who was at work through Peter in apostolic mission activity for the circumcised was also at work in me for the Gentiles—, 9 and when they perceived the grace that was given to me, James and Cephas and John, "those who were reputed" to be pillars, gave to me and Barnabas the right hand of fellowship, that we should (go) to the Gentiles, and they to the circumcised. 10 Only, we were to continue to remember the poor, the very thing which I was also eager to do.

2:1-10

E. *The Validity of the gospel as proclaimed by Paul*
acknowledged by Jerusalem's "pillars";
the work divided; the poor to be remembered

In Chapter 1 the apostle has shown that he had received his gospel directly from Christ, not *from* men nor *through* this or that man. He now proceeds to show that, because of this very fact, *this gospel which he proclaims is independent of men's evaluation.* A God-given gospel does not need human validation. It can "stand on its own feet." And for this very reason, as soon as Jerusalem's "pillars" see that Paul and Barnabas had been thus divinely entrusted with the gospel, they extend to them the right hand of fellowship and agree to divide the work. James, Cephas, and John recognize *God's* hand when they see it!

1. The paragraph begins as follows: **Then, after an interval of fourteen years, I went up again to Jerusalem with Barnabas, also taking Titus with me.**

In 1:15, 16 Paul, in touching language, has spoken about his conversion. In verse 18 of that same chapter he has related how three years afterward he had gone to Jerusalem to become acquainted with Cephas. Leaving Jerusalem he had spent some time in Syria and Cilicia (verse 21). When he now continues by saying, "Then, after an interval of fourteen years, I went up again to Jerusalem," it is natural to interpret this statement as meaning that the trip to Jerusalem which he here introduces occurred fourteen years after that other visit to this city described in 1:18, *not* fourteen years after his conversion. If Paul's conversion occurred in A.D. 34, then the first trip to Jerusalem "after three years" took place *circa* A.D. 37. Nevertheless, as already indicated, it is impossible to be precise, since these "three years" may not have amounted to a full three years as we now count them. Thus, the real date may have been A.D. 36. Similarly, all we can safely affirm about the expression "after an interval of fourteen years" is that it probably means that the trip to Jerusalem described here in Gal. 2 took place *about* the year A.D. 50.[43]

Between the trip to Jerusalem indicated in Gal. 1:18 and the one here in 2:1 Paul had been in Tarsus, had labored with Barnabas in Antioch (Syria), about the time of the death of Herod Agrippa I (A.D. 44) had accompanied Barnabas on a relief mission to Jerusalem, had gone back to Antioch, and, together with Barnabas, had made his first missionary journey. It is from Antioch, to which they have again returned, that Paul and Barnabas now—after these fourteen years—make their trip to Jerusalem. They are sent to Jerusalem in order to assure *Gentile freedom over against the insistent demand of the Judaizers that the Gentiles be circumcised* (Acts 15:1, 2; Gal. 5:1). On this issue the minds of Paul and Barnabas are made up, but they are going to prove to the entire assembly, if such proof be required, that their own view and the course which they have been following is the only right one.

It is evident that, along with ever so many interpreters,[44] I accept the

---

[43] For a justification of this chronology which, with respect to several of its dates, cannot be more than *approximately* correct, see W. Hendriksen, *Bible Survey*, pp. 62–64, 70.

[44] For example, Berkhof, Erdman, Findlay, Greijdanus, Grosheide, Lightfoot, Rendall, Robertson. As I see it, the best and most detailed argument in favor of the view that the visit of Gal. 2 must be identified with that of Acts 15 is that of S. Greijdanus, *Is Hand. 9 (met 22 en 26) en 15 in tegenspraak met Gal. 1 en 2?*, Kampen, 1935. Ramsay, who did not commit himself to any fixed theory, states, "There is practically universal agreement among critics and commentators of every shade of opinion that the visit described as the third in Acts 15 is the one that Paul describes as the second in Gal. 2:1-10. Scholars who agree in regard to scarcely any other point of early Christian history are at one on this" (*St. Paul the Traveler and the Roman Citizen*, p. 154). I take exception to the phrase "as the second." P. Parker also links Acts 15 with Gal. 2, regrettably at the expense of Acts 9:26-30: "Once More, Acts and Galatians," *JBL*, 86 (June 1967), pp. 175–182.

identification of the Gal. 2 trip with that of Acts 15. My reasons are:

(1) The *big* question in both accounts amounts to this: "Is Christ sufficient unto salvation?" Phrased differently, this question may be expressed in these words, "Is it necessary to require of the Gentiles who have embraced Christ by a living faith that, for the sake of their salvation, they, in addition, observe the Mosaic ordinances?" Specifically, "Is it necessary that they be circumcised?" (cf. Acts 15:1-3, 10, with Gal. 2:3; 4:10; 5:2-4; 6:12, 13).

(2) Acts mentions the main speakers, namely, Peter, Barnabas, Paul, and James (15:7, 12, 13). These four are also mentioned in Galatians, as being, along with John, those who supply the leadership (2:7, 9).

(3) According to Acts, Barnabas and Paul relate before the whole assembly "what signs and wonders God had performed through them among the Gentiles" (15:12). And in Galatians Paul reports, "I set before them the gospel which I am accustomed to preach among the Gentiles." Also, "And he [God] was . . . at work in me for the Gentiles" (2:2a, 8).

(4) According to Acts "some of those who belonged to the party of the Pharisees" tell the assembly that for the Gentiles, too, circumcision is a necessity (15:5). The voices of these Judaizers are also heard in Galatians (2:4, 5).

(5) In Luke's account there is never any yielding to the expressed opinions and wishes of the Judaists or Judaizers (Acts 15:8-19). This is forcefully expressed in 15:10. The statement in Galatians is just as emphatic: "to whom [that is, *to the sham brothers*] not even for a moment did we yield submission" (2:5).

(6) From the start and throughout, according to Acts, there is perfect harmony among the leaders (15:8-29). This, according to the most reasonable interpretation, is also the case in Galatians: James and Cephas and John extend the right hand of fellowship to Paul and Barnabas (2:5, 9).

For the arguments which have, nevertheless, been advanced against this identification, see the footnote.[45]

---

[45] These arguments are as follows:

(1) If the visit of Gal. 2 must be identified with that of Acts 15, then very soon after this important Jerusalem Council, *in which Peter had taken a leading part,* he would have made himself guilty of conduct in direct conflict with its most important decision. This is inconceivable.

Answer. This objection is answered in some detail in the explanation of 2:11 ff.

(2) If it were true that Galatians was written soon after the Jerusalem Council, Paul would simply have referred the addressed to the decision of that Council.

Answer. Paul had *already* delivered to the Galatians the decrees of that assembly (Acts 16:4). The point is that *the Judaizers* had not been convinced, and, in turn, had succeeded to a certain extent in undermining the confidence of the Galatians in the wisdom of these decrees. Even today decisions of synods or general assemblies seldom convince those who, like the Judaizers, from the start have taken an opposite stand, or those who are influenced by them. Hence, in order to persuade the Galatians it was necessary for Paul to present arguments derived directly from

Scripture and—in close connection with this—from Christian experience. This he does in Galatians.

(3) Acts 15 deals with a *public* conference (verses 2 and 22); Galatians 2 with a *private* interview of the leaders (verse 2). Therefore, these two cannot refer to the same trip and the same meeting.

Answer. Galatians 2 leaves room for both. For the *public* conference see *especially* verse 2a (though some of the later verses may also refer to it). For the *private* interview see *especially* verse 2b. There is, accordingly, no conflict here.

(4) According to Galatians (2:2) Paul goes up to Jerusalem "as a result of a *revelation*"; but according to Acts the church of Antioch *delegates* Paul and Barnabas to go to Jerusalem.

Answer. This twofold description of whatever it was that induced Paul to go to Jerusalem raises no conflict at all. One possibility is that he was at first rather reluctant to accept the assignment given to him by the church of Antioch; fearing, perhaps, that by placing before the "apostles and elders" at Jerusalem the question with respect to the circumcision of the Gentiles, he might endanger his standing as an apostle, the independence of the gospel which he had been proclaiming, and thus also the cause—so dear to himself—of mission activity among the Gentiles. If he actually harbored that reluctance, it is understandable that a divine revelation was necessary to send him on his way. But even aside from this, the present merging of a human factor and a divine in bringing about Paul's departure from one city to go to another is not at all exceptional; see also Acts 13:1, 2; and compare Acts 9:30 with 22:17-21.

(5) According to Galatians (2:1) when Paul and Barnabas go to Jerusalem, Titus is also in their company. Acts 15, however, does not name Titus. In fact, in the entire book of Acts Titus is never even mentioned.

Answer. From other passages—besides Gal. 2:1, 3—we know that Titus became one of Paul's beloved companions (II Cor. 2:13; 7:6, 13, 14; 8:6, 16, 23; 12:18; II Tim. 4:10; and, of course, Titus 1:4). It is not strange, therefore, to learn from Galatians that, *on Paul's initiative*, Titus is taken along to Jerusalem. Moreover, though it is true that, for an unknown reason, Titus is not mentioned by name in Acts 15, neither is his presence excluded. In fact, room is provided for him when it is stated that not only Paul and Barnabas but also "some other persons" were appointed to go up to Jerusalem (15:2). Hence, here, too, Galatians and Acts are not necessarily in conflict.

(6) The regulations mentioned in Acts 15:20 are not found in Gal. 2.

Answer. These regulations do not touch the main issue on which Paul rivets the attention in Gal. 2. Besides, it is not even certain that Gal. 2 does not contain a veiled reference to these regulations (see on verse 6).

(7) According to the book of Acts Paul's Jerusalem visit mentioned in Chapter 15 was his *third* (after his conversion); the first being recorded in 9:26, and the second in 11:27-30; 12:25. But according to Paul's own account, the visit to which Gal. 2:1 makes reference was only his *second;* the first trip being mentioned in 1:18. Therefore, the visit described in Gal. 2 cannot be identified with that of Acts 15, but must have occurred earlier. Far more probable, therefore, is the identification of Paul's visit mentioned in Gal. 2 with that described in Acts 11:27-30; 12:25. In both cases this would be the *second* visit. The view according to which in Galatians Paul simply skips the Acts 11:27-30; 12:25 visit, so that the Gal. 2 visit must be identified with that recorded in Acts 15, is unsound. Reason: in Gal. 2 (as well as in Gal. 1) the apostle is trying to prove that on none of his post-conversion trips to Jerusalem could he have received his gospel from *men,* that is, from the leaders of the Jerusalem church. Had Paul failed to include even *one* visit, he would have exposed himself to the charge of misrepresenting the facts, for in that case his enemies would have been able to say, "You have been in Jerusalem more often than you are now admitting. Hence, you had abundant opportunity to receive your gospel *from men.*"

Answer. It is not true that Gal. 2:1 must be interpreted to mean that the trip

There are some[46] who prefer to identify the Gal. 2 visit with that of Acts 11:27-30; 12:25. Their reasons for doing this may be gathered from footnote 45; see especially item (7).

With due respect for the scholarliness of the eminent men who favor this theory and for the many valuable works which they, as well as those who disagree with them, have produced, I here state the reasons for my inability to concur with their opinion:

(1) *The two accounts differ in their main theme.* Galatians 2 deals with the question whether or not the Gentiles who turn to Christ must be circumcised; Acts 11, 12 describes a relief mission, and (in the section referred to) says nothing about circumcision.

(2) In Acts 11:27-30; 12:25 it is Barnabas who takes the lead (note "Barnabas and Saul" in 11:30 and 12:25). In Gal. 2 Barnabas has no such priority (see verses 2:1, 6, 8, 9).[47]

(3) If the visit recorded in Gal. 2:1-10 is that of Acts 11:27-30; 12:25, then the question whether or not the Gentiles should receive circumcision was officially settled long before the time of the Council of Jerusalem described in Acts 15. On that supposition would not the latter meeting have been superfluous?

(4) Acts 11:30 makes mention only of "elders" ("sending it to the elders"). No "apostles" are referred to, either as a group or individually. Also in this respect Gal. 2 (see verse 9) resembles Acts 15 (see verses 7, 12, 22) far more closely than it does Acts 11:27-30; 12:25.

(5) Chronologically the identification of the Gal. 2 visit with the relief mission described in Acts 11:27-30; 12:25, which occurred at about the time of the death of Herod Agrippa I—hence, about A.D. 44—, presents difficulties that are well-nigh insurmountable. It would mean that the apostle's first post-conversion visit to Jerusalem—fourteen years earlier— took place around A.D. 30 or 31, and the conversion itself "three years" earlier than that; that is, during Christ's earthly ministry. Only by a very unnatural explanation of Gal. 2:1 is it possible to avoid that conclusion. Perhaps Lenski's remark is not too strong, "The supposition that [in Gal. 2:1-10] Paul is speaking of the visit which he and Barnabas paid to Jerusalem to bring relief . . . (Acts 11:27-30; 12:25) is chronologically impossible" (*op. cit.,* p. 68).

---

here mentioned was Paul's *second* post-conversion visit to that city. The word *again* —in the clause, "I went up again to Jerusalem"—does not necessarily mean *for the second time*. Also, it is not true that in Gal. 2 the apostle is still trying to prove that he had received his gospel not from men but from God. On both of these points see the explanation of 2:1.

[46] For example, Bruce (in his *Commentary on the Book of the Acts,* pp. 244, 298– 301), Calvin, Duncan, Ellis, Emmet, Hoerber, Knox.

[47] Nor does he have this priority in Acts 15, which has both "Barnabas and Paul" (verses 12 and 25) and "Paul and Barnabas" (verses 2 and 22).

Now when Paul declares that after an interval of fourteen years he went up *again* to Jerusalem, this word *again* does not necessarily mean "for the second time."[48] It can just as well mean "once again," without indicating how many previous trips to Jerusalem there had been.[49] Moreover, it is not at all strange that here in *the second chapter* of Galatians Paul says not a word about the relief mission recorded in Acts 11:27-30; 12:25. The simple fact is that he is no longer talking *per se* about the source of his gospel but rather about the *implication* of the fact that he had obtained it directly from God; that implication being that this gospel is independent, does not need to stand, hat in hand, begging human approval for its existence and proper functioning.

It must be borne in mind that whatever happened in the year A.D. 44— whether it were a mission of relief or anything else—could have had no bearing whatever on the question how the gospel had *originally* been given to Paul, for by that time he had already been an apostle for some *ten years!* He had been preaching the gospel not only in Damascus and Jerusalem but also in (Tarsus? and) Antioch of Syria. It is exactly as Greijdanus says: "The question whether Paul in obtaining his gospel ministry had been dependent on the other apostles could have reference only to the early period of that ministry."[50] It is not even strictly necessary to argue that on this relief mission Paul and Barnabas had contacted only "elders" and not "apostles" in Jerusalem, for even if everyone of the apostles had been in the welcoming committee and if Paul had remained with them for an entire year, they could not have *given* him the gospel which he already *had,* and which he had been proclaiming for such a long period! This is the answer to objection (7), footnote 45.

Among the men who went up to Jerusalem three are definitely indicated here in Gal. 2:1: Paul, Barnabas, and Titus.

Paul was a man of boundless energy, steadfast determination, earnest devotion to his Lord, zeal for the work of winning souls, and resolute unwillingness that the great cause of the evangelization of the Gentiles be hindered in any way. He was not only an intellectual giant but also *deeply emotional* and *expertly tactful.* However, since this has been set forth in

---

[48] The word πάλιν is more indefinite than δεύτερον, as in John 3:4, where Nicodemus literally says, "He cannot *a second time* enter into his mother's womb and be born, can he?" or as in Rev. 19:3, "And *a second time* they cried, 'Hallelujah.'" Though the meaning of II Cor. 13:2 is a matter of sharp controversy, that difference of interpretation does not really affect the word δεύτερον, which also there means *second time.*

[49] If the trip of Gal. 2 was that of Acts 15, then, according to the latter's count, it was the third; just as the word πάλιν in John 18:27 refers not to the second but to the *third* denial, as the context indicates. See N.T.C. on the Gospel according to John, Vol. II, p. 389.

[50] *Is Handelingen 9 (met 22 en 26) en 15 in tegenspraak met Galaten 1 en 2?*, p. 66.

some detail in other commentaries of this series, it is not necessary to repeat it here. See N.T.C. on Philippians, p. 181; and on Colossians and Philemon, pp. 231, 232. Paul was truly "a man in Christ," and for all these reasons the proper person to be sent to Jerusalem for the purpose that has been indicated.

Most of these characteristics applied also to *Barnabas,* the Levite from the island of Cyprus. By means of the many biblical references to him—approximately thirty—we are given a rather complete picture. He was "a good man, and full of the Holy Spirit and of faith" (Acts 11:24). The very name, Barnabas, that is, "son of prophecy" (Acts 4:36), hence "of consolation" (A.V.) or "exhortation" (A.R.V.; N.E.B.) or "encouragement" (R.S.V.; Williams), had been appropriately substituted for the one that had been given to him at birth, namely, Joses or Joseph. He was a spiritually eloquent man. When he is first mentioned (Acts 4:36, 37) he has moved from Cyprus to Jerusalem, where he has bought some property. When he realizes that many of the saints in that city and surroundings are poor, to which condition not only a famine but also their conversion to faith in Jesus may well have contributed, he, being himself also a believer and filled with generosity, sells a field and lays the proceeds at the apostles' feet. That same spirit of generosity, now coupled with pleasing trustfulness, also manifested itself in a totally different way. It caused him to dispel the suspicions of the disciples when Saul of Tarsus, known as the most bitter persecutor of the church, suddenly entered the city of Jerusalem, and claimed that he had experienced a dramatic conversion. When nobody else believed this story, it was Barnabas who stood by the side of the convert, and secured his admission into the disciples' fellowship (Acts 9:26-28). To these traits of *eloquence, generosity,* and *trustfulness* should be added that of *mission-mindedness,* which is *broadmindedness* in the best sense of that term. He entertained no scruples about allowing Gentiles to enter the church on the basis of simple faith in Christ, "without the works of the law." Accordingly, when, in Antioch (Syria), due to the preaching of his own countrymen and others, a great number of Greeks "turned to the Lord," it was Barnabas who by the church of Jerusalem was sent to this new Christian community to give direction and leadership to it (Acts 11:19-22). Touchingly beautiful, in this connection, is the description of this warm-hearted missionary's reaction to the mighty work of the Lord that was taking place in Antioch: "When he came and saw the grace of God, he rejoiced; and he encouraged them all to remain faithful to the Lord with steadfast hearts" (Acts 11:23). What a picture of genuine, fatherly *sympathy!* Add also *wisdom,* a wisdom in one respect exceeding even that of Moses (see Exod. 18; Num. 11:17). While Moses overloaded himself with work and had to be advised to share responsibility with others, Barnabas, confronted with a similar situation, immediately went into action *of his own accord,* and secured the help of Paul, whom he sought and found in. Tarsus. Thus, the two men worked side by side for an entire year in this flourishing field (Acts 11:25, 26). And the Lord blessed their labors. Together also they are sent to Jerusalem with gifts for the needy (Acts 11:27-30; 12:25). And, having returned to Antioch, they are together ordained as missionaries and proceed on the trip that has become known as Paul's "First Missionary Journey" (Acts 13:1 ff.). At this point another virtue, of which Barnabas had so many, begins to stand out, namely, that of marked *humility;* for, though the man (Paul) who at the beginning was the *assistant* of Barnabas gradually becomes the *leader,* "the son of encouragement" (Barnabas) never shows the least resentment on that score. And to top it all, add unwearying *patience,* the willingness to give a deserter another chance. This characteristic was to manifest itself shortly after the Jerusalem Conference, to which Gal. 2 refers, but is mentioned here to fill out the picture. The deserter was John Mark, who, having started out with Paul and Barnabas on the first missionary journey, had left during its course and had returned to his home. Because of this act of disloyalty and cowardice Paul, after the close of the Conference, was going to turn down the suggestion of Barnabas that Mark be taken along on the second journey. Between the two leaders there was going to arise "a sharp contention" (Acts 15:36-41). But Barnabas was going to stand by John Mark, even though it would mean parting company with Paul. And his patience was gloriously rewarded, for this same Mark at a later time becomes "a comfort" to Paul (Col. 4:10b, 11), "very useful" to him for kingdom work (II Tim. 4:11), and the writer of the second Gospel!

The purpose of the description just given is not at all to exalt Barnabas above Paul, as if the former were the better of the two. As concerns Mark, did he not stand in need of *Paul's* stern discipline as well as of *Barnabas'* untiring patience . . . and, besides, of *Peter's* fatherly oversight? See N.T.C. on Colossians and Philemon, pp. 188, 189. Moreover, the fact that Barnabas, too, had his moments of weakness is clear from Gal. 2:13. And as to *leadership* qualities, *penetrating insight* into redemptive truth, and *consistency* in applying this truth to the conditions of everyday living, was there anyone in the days of the apostles who surpassed Paul? No one, not even Barnabas! The real purpose, therefore, of the descriptions of Paul and Barnabas was to show how eminently fit *both* of these big-hearted men were for accomplishing their task of making certain at Jerusalem that those who had already been gathered into Christ's fold from the Gentile world should not lose their freedom, that others, Gentile as well as Jew, should be added to the multitude of the saved, and that the glory of Christ as all-sufficient Savior should not be debilitated.

And then there was *Titus,* who was taken along on Paul's initiative, as verse 1 clearly implies: "also taking Titus with me." For a delineation of his character see N.T.C. on I and II Timothy and Titus, pp. 36, 37. From that description it will be evident that the apostle could not have taken along a better brother in the Lord, one who was more willing and eager to co-operate in every way, and who, being by race a Gentile of unmixed extraction, and thus *uncircumcised,* was *a test case,* a definite challenge to the Judaizers, as has already been explained. See p. 17.

2. Paul continues: **I went up, moreover, as a result of a revelation.** Whatever hesitancy there may have been on Paul's part when he and others were delegated by the Antiochian church to go to Jerusalem for the purpose already indicated, was removed by this divine revelation. See footnote 45, point (4). The Lord knew that the contemplated conference to be held in that city would prove to be of great value not only for Paul, Barnabas, Titus, etc., but also for James, Cephas, and John; and, in fact, for all the assembled brothers; yes, even for the entire church on earth both then and in the ages to follow. Continued: **and I set before them the gospel which I am accustomed to preach among the Gentiles.** For a commentary on this see Acts 15:4, 12. With enthusiasm and candor Paul and Barnabas related to the entire assembly the course which had been followed in proclaiming to the Gentiles the gospel of free grace, untrammeled by any ceremonial ordinances. They took special delight in rehearsing how astonishingly the Lord, by means of conversions, signs and wonders, had placed the stamp of his approval on this work.

In addition to the meeting which was attended by "the apostles and the elders and the whole church" (Acts 15:22), there had also been a private interview, a meeting of the *leaders:* Paul, Barnabas, James, Cephas, and John. Borrowing a term used with fondness by the Judaizers with respect to the last three of this list of five men, namely, the appellation "those of repute," Paul continues: **but (I did this) privately to "those of repute."** Exactly when this interview occurred, or whether these leaders met privately only once or more often, is of no great importance. It seems reasonable, however, to believe that upon arrival in Jerusalem the delegation from Antioch *first of all* went into conference with the local church leaders. Since the term "those of repute" occurs not only once but, in one form or another, no less than four times (2:2, 6a, 6b, 9), it is safe to assume that the apostle is here quoting the phraseology of the opponents. He is, however, not trying to belittle the men of prominence in the church at Jerusalem. He does not use the term "those of repute" to heap scorn upon them or to ridicule them. True, the language he uses here implies a degree of resentment, but the latter is not directed at James, Cephas, and John, but at the legalists who have made it a habit to exalt these three at the expense of Paul, a man altogether insignificant in their eyes, a merely second-hand apostle, not even worthy to be called "apostle." And be it always borne in mind that basic to their attack on Paul was their attack on *the gospel* which he proclaimed!

It is the worthiness and independence of this gospel that Paul is here defending.

Continued: **to make sure that I was not running or had not run in vain;** or, somewhat more literally, "lest by any means I should be running or had run in vain."[51] If, while Paul was preaching the gospel of justification by faith, *without the works of the law,* the other apostles, though in principle agreeing with him, would have been "soft" in their attitude toward those who seriously questioned the rightness of his convictions and of his preaching, the cause of mission work among the Gentiles would have been seriously undermined. The effectiveness of that which Paul had been doing in the past and was still doing would have been decisively weakened.

3-5. Any fears, however, which Paul may have entertained on this score were quickly dispelled. He writes: **Yet even Titus who was with me, Greek though he is, was not compelled to be circumcised; (in fact, the suggestion would never have arisen) but for the uninvited sham brothers.**[52] Even Titus! If

---

[51] It is probably correct to say that μή πως expresses negative purpose (cf. Robertson, *Word Pictures,* Vol. IV, p. 283). In such a construction τρέχω (probably subjunctive) followed by ἔδραμον (aorist indicative) is not unusual in Greek. See also N.T.C. on I and II Thessalonians, p. 85, footnote 68. The interpretation according to which Paul is here saying that he submitted to the Jerusalem pillars *the question* whether or not he were running or had run in vain seems unnatural and out of keeping with the apostle's strong convictions on this matter.

[52] The construction of διὰ δὲ τοὺς παρεισάκτους ψευδαδέλφους is difficult. It may well have been perfectly intelligible to the Galatians, Paul's contemporaries, who were better acquainted with the historical background and with the apostle's manner of speaking than we are today (see, however, II Peter 3:16). Ever so many translations have been proposed. A.V. has: "and that because of false brethren unawares brought in" (see also A.R.V. text). Interpreting δέ (which should be retained) adversatively, A.R.V., margin, has *"but* it was *because of"* (cf. R.S.V.). On either basis it is difficult to discover the connection of these words with the preceding clause. As I see it, Lenski's explanation on the basis of his translation—"even on account of the pseudo-brethren"—fails to do justice to what Paul says elsewhere about the reason for rejecting Gentile circumcision. See (2) below. The adversative rendering in R.S.V. yields no intelligible sense: Paul begins to say something but never finishes it: "But because of false brethren secretly brought in, who slipped in . . . that they might bring us into bondage—to them we did not yield submission," etc.

It is for this reason that the theory according to which certain words must be supplied is probably the best. Abbreviated expression is, after all, a characteristic of all living language. See N.T.C. on the Gospel according to John, Vol. I, p. 206. I, therefore, offer the rendering: "Yet even Titus . . . was not compelled to be circumcised; (in fact, the suggestion would never have arisen) but for the uninvited sham brothers." Another possibility would be: "Yet even Titus . . . was not compelled to be circumcised, (not even) on account of the uninvited sham brothers." If δέ is merely transitional and not to be translated, Beck's rendering has something to say in its favor: "But nobody forced him to be circumcised to please the false Christians." These last three possibilities are basically the same, since in each case the pseudo-Christians are considered to have been the only ones who demanded the circumcision of Titus, and also since in each case the demand was refused. As I see it, to be rejected are the following:

(1) Burton's suggestion that there were actually three parties in the situation: *a.* Paul and Barnabas, who favored receiving Gentiles as Christians without re-

a Christian of unalloyed Gentile extraction, though present here in the very heartland of the *Jews,* and in an assembly in which *Jewish* Christian leaders filled an influential role, was not compelled to be circumcised, then surely there could be no objection to waiving this requirement in the case of other non-Jewish converts who were living in a partly or wholly Gentile environment. From the very outset the leaders at Jerusalem agreed with the position of Paul and Barnabas anent the question of the circumcision of the Gentiles who accepted Christ. Was it not Peter who (in the plenary session of the assembly) uttered these emphatic words: "Now therefore why do y o u put God to the test by putting on the disciples a yoke which neither our fathers nor we have been able to bear?" (Acts 15:10). And did not James immediately endorse that position by adding that those who from among the Gentiles turn to God should not be troubled? (15:19). Not that everything went smoothly in the public gathering. It is implied both in Acts 15:5, 7 and in Gal. 2:4, 5 that the Judaizers voiced their opinions in no uncertain terms. But the point is: according to *both* accounts *the leaders* never wavered! The very suggestion that Titus be circumcised would never even have been broached had not the Judaizers

---

quiring them to be circumcised; *b.* the pseudo-brothers who insisted that such Gentiles be circumcised; and *c.* the "pillars," who urged Paul to yield to the wishes of the Judaizers, but finally agreed to Paul's point of view. His *translation* naturally harmonizes with that *explanation* (*op. cit.,* pp. 67, 77, 78). See also N.E.B. for similar view.

Objections. Nowhere else (either in Gal. 2 or in Acts 15) does Paul give any hint that the "pillars" urged the circumcision of Titus. Moreover, Gal. 2:5 indicates that it was to the false brothers that Paul had not yielded, showing that they were the ones who had done the urging, *they* and not the "pillars."

(2) Lenski's explanation that "what set everybody against circumcising Titus for any reason was the attitude of the 'pseudo-brethren.'" Again, "Even on account of these men . . . Titus was not compelled to be circumcised." (*op. cit.,* pp. 78, 79).

Objection. The non-circumcision of Titus is a matter of principle; hence, not dependent on the strength of the Judaizers' demand. See Gal. 2:15 ff.; 5:2, 3.

(3) Zahn's solution that οἷς οὐδέ at the beginning of verse 5 should be omitted, not being original, and that the true meaning is, accordingly, "For the sake of the false brothers we gave ground for a moment, namely, in consenting to go to Jerusalem" (*Der Brief des Paulus an die Galater,* 1922, p. 89 ff.).

Objections. The omission of οἷς οὐδέ has weak textual support. This method of connecting the thought of verse 5 with that of verses 1 and 2 is unnatural. Gal. 2:2 declares that Paul went up to Jerusalem not because of the false brothers but as a result of a revelation.

(4) The theory that οὐδέ at the beginning of verse 5 should be omitted, so that Titus, after all, was circumcised. Paul "yielded on the issue of the submission demanded." Cf. B. W. Bacon, "The Reading οἷς οὐδέ in Gal. 2:5," *J.B.L.,* Vol. 42 (1923), pp. 69–80; also N.E.B., footnote, "I yielded to their demand for the moment."

Objection. The textual support for the omission of οὐδέ is weak. The non-circumcision of Titus was a matter of principle with Paul, on which he certainly would not have yielded; especially in view of what he says in 2:15 ff.; 5:2, 3. (The omission of οἷς *only* would not change the sense of the passage. Nevertheless, there is no sufficient textual support for this omission.)

brought it up. They—they *alone*—were the ones who had started all the trouble. They, these uninvited guests, these intruders, *who had wormed their way into the assembly from the sidelines,*[53] were the ones, says Paul, **who had infiltrated our ranks to spy on our liberty which we have in Christ Jesus.** The interlopers mingled among the true believers with the purpose of *spying,* that is, discovering the strategic situation of those whom they opposed—their strong and their weak points—specifically, their *liberty,* that is, their freedom from the curse of the law, from the law as a way to salvation, and from the ceremonial observances which that law demands. This is the freedom which believers enjoy "in Christ," for had it not been for his atonement they would have been deprived of it (see on Gal. 3:13). Continued: **and thus to reduce us to slavery.** The word *slavery,* as used here, is none too strong, for the demands of the law constituted an unbearable yoke, as not only Peter put it (Acts 15:10) but Paul also (Gal. 5:1). The effort to comply with these demands amounted to a "bleeding to climb to God" in one's own strength, a tremendous effort to attain salvation by law-works, only to discover that this effort is hopeless, and that, like the fly in the spider's web, the more one struggles, the more he also imprisons himself.

With respect, then, to these pseudo-brothers, these infiltrators, the apostle continues: **to whom not even**[54] **for a moment**[55] **did we yield submission.** The meaning is clear and simple: not at any time during the Conference— whether in the private interview or at the public meeting; whether at the beginning, in the middle, or at the close—was there any yielding to the wishes of the enemies of the one and only true gospel. It was one and the same gospel, whether proclaimed by Paul or Barnabas; by Cephas, James, or John. It was not dependent on anything men might say about it. They were able neither to subtract from it nor to add to it. Neither did they wish to do so: **in order that the truth of the gospel**—that is, the gospel in all its purity—**might continue with y o u.** Those who oppose the South Galatian theory at times interpret this to mean, "that the truth of the gospel might continue with y o u, *believers (in general) from the Gentiles.*" It should be apparent, however, that in a letter written specifically to the Galatians, a missive with so much local color, the alternative explanation, namely, "that the truth of the gospel might continue *with y o u Galatians*" is more

---

[53] Greek παρεισάκτους. This harmonizes with παρεισῆλθον, which again stresses the idea of coming in from the side, "over the wall," as it were, and not "through the door." Cf. John 10:1, 2.
[54] On οἷς οὐδέ see footnote 52.
[55] Greek ὥρα (ν); literally "hour," but it is rather apparent that this is to be taken in a figurative sense, so that "not [or: not even] for an hour" (A.V., A.R.V.; cf. German *Stunde,* Dutch Statenvertaling *uur,* Spanish *hora*) is equivalent to English "not for a moment" (Beck, Berkeley, Goodspeed, N.E.B., R.S.V., Williams; cf. Dutch, new version, *ogenblik,* Swedish *ögenblick,* French *moment,* and Latin *momentum*).

natural. The Galatians had already been evangelized, namely, on Paul's first journey. Soon afterward the trouble had started: the Judaizers had tried to substitute their "gospel" (?) of *salvation by grace-plus-works* (with emphasis probably on the latter) for Paul's gospel of salvation *solely by grace through faith.* Which view was to prevail? The unyielding stand of Paul and Barnabas, supported from start to finish by Jerusalem's "pillars," had as its purpose that from now on the Judaizers would never be able to say to the Galatians, "Paul has deceived y o u. The really 'prominent leaders' of the mother church in Jerusalem agree with us, not with him." Thus, the inflexible stand taken at Jerusalem would contribute significantly to the perpetuation of the true gospel among the Galatians.

Here is a lesson for all time. Paul was by no means a stubborn, inflexible individual. On the contrary, he was ready to accommodate himself and his message to any situation, becoming a Jew to the Jews, a Gentile to the Gentiles (I Cor. 9:19-23). Striking instances of this are reported in Acts 16:3; 21:17-26. But he was not willing to put any obstacle in the way of the gospel of Christ (I Cor. 9:12). In fact, rightly viewed, it was his inflexibility with respect to doing everything in his power to promote the simple gospel of God's grace in all its immaculate purity that made him so flexible in all relatively minor matters.

6. Returning now to "those of repute" (for the meaning see on verse 2) Paul continues: **Well, from those "who were reputed" to be something— whatever they once were makes no difference to me; God accepts no man's person—to me "those of repute" imparted nothing.** The break in grammatical sequence ("anacoluthon") is clear: when Paul starts out by saying, "Well, from those 'who were reputed' to be something," we expect him to conclude the sentence by adding, "I received nothing." Instead of this he interrupts himself. The thoroughly unfair comparison which his opponents are constantly drawing between himself and "those of repute," as if he and his gospel were definitely inferior, causes him to insert a parenthetical comment with respect to these vaunted leaders, the Jerusalem "pillars," not out of disrespect for *them* but from disapproval of *the comparison.* He then returns to the subject, but instead of completing the sentence by means of a predicate, he comes up with another independent clause in which the words "those of repute" constitute the subject: "to me those of repute imparted nothing." *Essentially* this disruption of grammatical sequence makes very little difference in meaning. *If* there be any difference at all it may possibly be indicated thus: "Not only did *I,* on my part, not receive or accept any new doctrine or regulation from these men of prominence, but I wish to emphasize that *they,* on their part, did not try to impose any dictates upon me." The main point to be emphasized in this connection is, however, the fact that the anacoluthon, coupled with parenthesis, reveals strong emotion. It shows how deeply Paul was affected

by any attempt to downgrade his divine commission and/or his gospel. Hence, he stresses the fact that the Jerusalem leaders did not try in any way to propose any changes in the gospel (of salvation solely by grace through faith) which he had been proclaiming. Specifically, they did not advise Paul that he must tell the Gentiles that in addition to believing in Jesus Christ they must be circumcised. It is possible that the apostle also implies that these leaders did not urge him to impose upon *Gentile* believers any new rules of conduct. To help them to live in peace with *Jewish* believers, the Council of Jerusalem asked the converts from paganism to observe the rules mentioned in Acts 15:20, 28, 29: avoiding meats sacrificed to idols or from which the blood had not been properly drained, and avoiding marriage within the degrees of affinity or consanguinity offensive to Jews and contrary to the regulations laid down in Lev. 18. But Paul did not regard such rules as bothersome novelties, *impositions* either upon himself or upon Gentile believers. In fact, as is clearly indicated in Rom. 12:18; 14:1 ff.; I Cor. 8:1 ff.; 9:19 ff.; 10:14 ff.; 10:23 ff., Paul was in the habit of insisting that for the sake of peace and harmony, as also to promote the spread of the gospel, Christians should, of their own accord, deny themselves certain privileges. As remarked earlier, though entirely inflexible in matters of principle (see Gal. 1:6-9), in all other matters the apostle was ready to yield and conform to the habits and wishes of others. Naturally, he taught those whom the Lord had placed under his spiritual care to be similarly disposed.

As to the parenthesis, how could it make any difference to Paul, who had been divinely appointed and had received his gospel directly from Christ, exalted in heavenly glory, whether "those of repute" had been closely associated with Jesus during the latter's earthly ministry? Why were the Judaizers always emphasizing that earthly fellowship, as if, because of it, men like James, Cephas, John, etc., were intrinsically better than he and more to be trusted? "What (that is, *of what kind*) they once[56] were" makes no difference to Paul. God takes no account of a man's "face" or "person." An individual's *outward circumstances*—whether, for example, he has been closely associated with Jesus as a *disciple* (Cephas and John) or as his *brother* (James) ; whether he occupies a certain *position,* or has a *reputation*—matter nothing to God; hence, not to Paul either. Things of that nature can never determine the intrinsic value of the gospel as proclaimed by Paul. Cf. I Sam. 16:7; Matt. 22:16; Mark 12:14; Luke 20:21; II Cor. 12:5.

7-9. But though Paul is not impressed with the propaganda of the Judaizers, who are constantly playing off "those of repute" against him, he

---

[56] L.N.T. (A. and G.) , p. 579, ascribes no separate meaning to ποτέ here (cf. A.V., Williams, R.S.V.) ; as if it were not a temporal modifier but simply a generalizing suffix; cf. the Latin *qualescumque.* However, *this* enclitic use has no other example in the New Testament.

is very definitely impressed by the divine influence upon James, Cephas, and John, causing them to welcome the grace of God when they saw its manifestation in the apostle to the Gentiles. Having stated that the Jerusalem leaders had imparted nothing to him, the writer continues: **On the contrary, when they saw that I had been entrusted with the gospel to the uncircumcised just as Peter (with that) to the circumcised—for he who was at work through Peter in apostolic mission activity for the circumcised was also at work in me for the Gentiles—, and when they perceived the grace that was given to me, James and Cephas and John, "those who were reputed" to be pillars, gave to me and Barnabas the right hand of fellowship, that we should (go) to the Gentiles, and they to the circumcised.**

At Jerusalem "those of repute" (see on verse 2), having taken note of the soundness of the gospel as proclaimed by Paul, of the enthusiasm with which he spoke of it, of the manner in which the Lord had been placing his seal of approval upon its proclamation among the Gentiles, namely, by means of conversions, signs and wonders (cf. Acts 15:4, 12; I Cor. 9:2; II Cor. 12:12), heartily and enthusiastically endorsed both him and his co-laborer, Barnabas. Literally, Paul speaks about "the gospel *of the uncircumcision* just as Peter *of the circumcision.*" This is one and the same gospel (cf. Gal. 1:6-9), and the terms "the uncircumcision" and "the circumcision" use the abstract for the concrete (cf. Rom. 3:30; 4:9; Eph. 2:11; Col. 3:11). The distinction made is that between the gospel "to the Gentile world" and that "to the Jewish world."[57]

It is clear that equal honor is accorded to Paul and Peter. Since in this combination nothing is said about John, whereas we know, nevertheless, that Paul's designation "those of repute," a term borrowed from the Judaizers, included John, it would appear to be a fair conclusion that Peter represents The Twelve (cf. Matt. 16:15, 16; Acts 2:37), including John. Peter and John, in fact, were often found together (John 1:35-41; 13:23, 24; 18:15, 16; 20:1-10; 21:2, 7, 20-22; Acts 3:1-4, 11 ff.; 4:13 ff.; 8:14 ff.). That among the Twelve Peter was the recognized leader is shown by the fact that in every list of apostles his name is mentioned first of all (Matt. 10:2-4; Mark 3:16-19; Luke 6:14-16; Acts 1:13).

That the Lord had been *at work*—energetically operative—in connection with Peter, and this *especially* (though by no means exclusively) in connection with the latter's "apostolic mission activity"[58] for *the Jews,* is

---

57 The genitives, accordingly, are objective.
58 The word ἀποστολήν refers here not to the apostolic office as such (Acts 1:25; Rom. 1:5), but to its execution; hence, here: *apostolic mission activity.* Note absence of article, perhaps to prevent the idea from taking root that Peter had a monopoly on carrying out the apostolic mandate. The expression εἰς τὰ ἔθνη is probably an abbreviation of εἰς ἀποστολὴν τῶν ἐθνῶν, which is parallel to εἰς ἀποστολὴν τῆς περιτομῆς.

clear from many other passages besides Gal. 2:7, 8; namely, from Gal. 1:18 (by implication) ; Acts 1:15 ff.; 2:14 ff.; 2:37 ff.; 3:1 ff.; 4:8 ff.; 5:3 ff. (*notably* 5:15) ; 11:2 ff.; 12:1 ff.; 15:7 ff. That the same Lord who empowered Peter was also energizing Paul, but in his case *especially* (though by no means exclusively) in apostolic mission activity for the benefit of *the Gentiles,* was now being made clear at Jerusalem, where, both in the private interview and at the public gathering, Paul and Barnabas gave a run-down of the astonishing results that had been accomplished.

The result was that James and Cephas and John, the reputed "pillars," clearly recognized that a ministry carried on by Paul and Barnabas with such conscientious regard for the will and revelation of God, such unswerving and pious purpose, such boundless energy, such tender love for souls, and, last but not least, such marvelous results, must be the product of "the grace that was given" to the agents used by the Lord. They saw the amazing manifestation of God's undeserved, but energetically operating, favor.

Of the three Jerusalem leaders *James* is mentioned first. See on 1:19. As has been shown, he is definitely linked with Jerusalem, more so even than Peter and John. It is not surprising, therefore, that he is mentioned first. Though not properly an apostle (in the plenary sense) , his position as "the Lord's brother," his moderation, wisdom, and sympathetic nature, assured him a place of special prominence in this stronghold of Jewry, in which many people had already accepted Christ, and many more were to follow (Acts 2:41; 4:4; 21:20) . Peter, the leader of The Twelve, has just been described. See also on Gal. 2:11 ff. Probably because his influence and activity in Jerusalem are here emphasized, he is now called by his Aramaic name, *Cephas.* There follows *John,* Peter's frequent companion, as has been shown. Though for a while similarly linked with Judea, he probably left Jerusalem at the beginning of the Jewish War, and chose Ephesus as his headquarters. Banished to the island of Patmos, he was subsequently permitted to return to Ephesus. According to tradition he, "the disciple whom Jesus loved," survived all the other apostles.

By the Judaizers these three men were regarded as "pillars" (cf. I Tim. 3:15; Rev. 3:12) , that is, those who gave stability to the church, its genuine leaders, whom they loved to contrast with Paul at the latter's expense. Paul does not begrudge the three the honor that is bestowed upon them. The real thrust of his argument is to show that these "pillars," far from disagreeing with him, enthusiastically approve of him, and acknowledge the fact that his gospel and their gospel are one and the same, to which nothing can be added, and from which nothing must be subtracted.

The singularly striking manner in which they confirmed their enthusiastic endorsement of the two foreign missionaries, herein following the example, years earlier, of "the common people" of Judea who were believers (1:22-24) , is expressed in the words: "When they saw that I had been entrusted with the gospel to the uncircumcised . . . and when they perceived the grace that was given to me, they . . . gave to me and Barnabas the right hand of fellowship." Note that they themselves—James, Cephas, and John—took the initiative. This handshake, to be sure, was a sign of *mutual agreement and acknowledgment;* more than that, of *fellowship (koinonia)*, one of the richest terms in the entire New Testament. See the detailed treatment of this concept in N.T.C. on Philippians, pp. 51–54; 93–95. But it also served as *the confirmation of a solemn covenant*[59] into which these five men now entered, as they divided the work-load: "that we [Paul and Barnabas] should (go) to the Gentiles, and they [James, Cephas, and John] to the circumcised." This division of labor must be interpreted in general terms. It amounted to a ratification of what had already begun; for, as has been indicated, Paul and Barnabas were bestowing their special attention upon the Gentiles; James, Cephas, and John, upon the Jews. This did not prevent the two from *first of all* addressing the Jews, wherever there was a synagogue, nor the three from reaching out also to the non-Jews. Thus, Peter did not have to apologize for having worked among the Samaritans (Acts 8:14 ff.) and having preached to the Roman centurion Cornelius and his friends and relatives (Acts 10:1 ff.; 11:1 ff., *especially* 15:7!). Nevertheless, from now on and as long as circumstances would permit it, the Jews and the country they inhabited would be the chief responsibility of the three and of those whom they represented, while Paul and Barnabas were to proclaim the gospel "far away to the Gentiles" (cf. Acts 22:21).

In verses 7-9 the following lessons stand out:

(1) Under God Paul's gospel is independent; that is, it is able to maintain itself in relation to friends and foes. It vanquishes the arguments of its foes, and is enthusiastically endorsed by its friends, who recognize it as the gospel which they themselves charish.

(2) *One* gospel suffices for every age and every clime. Methods of presentation may have to vary, but essentially the gospel for the first century A.D. is the gospel for today. Those who maintain that it is "not relevant" for this day and age are committing a tragic error. Only then when the message of the love of God in Christ has penetrated heart and mind, resulting in a life of unselfish dedication to God and grateful observance of the principles

---

[59] The handclasp as a pledge of friendship and allegiance has long existed among many nations; for example, Parthians, Persians, Hebrews, Greeks. Cf. II Kings 10:15; I Chron. 29:24; Ezra 10:19; Lam. 5:6; Ezek. 17:18. The right hand was given to signify the conclusion of an agreement: "Now then let us give the right hand to these men, and make peace with them" (I Macc. 6:58); "Vespasian . . . sent two tribunes . . . having ordered them to give right hands to Josephus" (*Jewish War* III.viii.1); "I received (from him) and extended (to him) the right hand" (Xenophon, *Anabasis* I.vi.6); "I know that both of us have taken oaths and given right hands [pledges]" (*Anabasis* II.v.3).

of conduct he has laid down in his Word, will solutions be found for the problems that now vex the individual, the family, society, the church, the nation, and the world.

(3) The New Testament is not a hodgepodge of conflicting theologies— the theology of John, the theology of Paul, etc.—but a harmonious, beauti- fully variegated, unit. It is a remarkable fact that the five men, whose handclasp of ringing harmony is here described, produced, between them, no less than twenty-one of the twenty-seven New Testament books![60]

10. To the major agreement touching the essence of the gospel and the division of the field of labor, one stipulation was added: **Only, we were to continue to remember the poor,**[61] **the very thing which I was also eager to do.** The difficult situation of the Judean poor required that special measures be taken to help them. It would seem that this situation, though more severe at one time than at another, was rather constant (Acts 11:27-30; 12:25; II Cor. 8:14). A few years earlier Barnabas and Paul had been sent on a relief mission. Paul and Barnabas now agree that such aid should be continued. Paul says that he was *eager*—was taking pains, making every effort—to do this. In fact, so eager was he to engage in this work of mercy that his third missionary journey, the one that was to follow immediately the present (second) trip during which Galatians was written, had as one of its chief objects, in the words of the apostle himself, "to bring alms to my nation" (Acts 24:17). The words, "We were *to continue to remember*," probably do not only mean that the work already begun should be resumed and thus continued, but also that to help the poor should be and remain *the regular practice* of the church. I Cor. 16:1, 2 certainly points in that direction.

Work of this nature should be pushed with all vigor. This is demanded by the laws of God (Exod. 23:10, 11; 30:15; Lev. 19:10; Deut. 15:7-11), the exhortations of the prophets (Jer. 22:16; Dan. 4:27; Amos 2:6, 7), and the teaching of Jesus (Matt. 7:12; Luke 6:36, 38; cf. 21:1-4; John 13:29; Gal. 6:2). It also pertains to the expression of gratitude for benefits re-

---

[60] Paul, thirteen; John, five; Cephas (Peter), two; James, one. Tertullian's opinion that *Barnabas* was the author of Hebrews has recently been revived by the prominent Dutch New Testament scholar, Dr. H. Mulder, in his articles "De Eerste Lezers van de Brief aan de Hebreeën," *homiletica & biblica* (May, 1965), pp. 95–99, and in the same journal, "Barnabas en de Gemeente te Jeruzalem" (September, 1965), pp. 198–200. If that view should be correct, all five of the men who are joined in this handclasp would be represented in the list of authors of New Testament books. However, the statement of Origen is still a fact, namely, "But as to who actually wrote the epistle, God knows the truth of the matter."

[61] This ἵνα clause is probably co-ordinate with the one that immediately precedes it. Hence, the two ἵνα clauses could be rendered: ". . . *that* we should (go) to the Gentiles, and they to the circumcised" and " (adding only) *that* we should continue to remember the poor." The position of μόνον τῶν πτωχῶν before ἵνα emphasizes the idea that it was especially *the poor* who should be remembered.

ceived. Those to whom mercy has been shown should be merciful. Paul points to the fact that since the Gentiles have received so many *spiritual* blessings from the saints of Jerusalem, they should certainly be of service to them in matters *material* (Rom. 15:26, 27). *And the greatest text of all, in this connection, is surely II Cor. 8:9!* A rich reward awaits the generous (Matt. 25:31-40).

It is remarkable that Paul, the deep thinker, is at the same time the Christian benefactor, who believes wholeheartedly in "doing good to everybody, and especially to those who are of the household of the faith," as he says in this very letter (6:10). Such is Christianity. If it is genuine, it is concerned about the poor, their health and their housing, their spiritual but also their material welfare. It does all in its power to help the under-privileged, under-educated, undernourished, the migrants and those who belong to "minority" groups. Overwhelmed by the love of God in Christ, it is *eager* to do so! The five men who concluded this agreement must have been very happy, indeed, as they stood there, firmly clasping each other's right hand, brothers in a common cause. Accordingly, Paul and Barnabas entered into a solemn agreement with the others, promising that they would remind the Gentiles that they should help the poor; particularly, in the present instance, Jerusalem's saints. One of these five men was James, the Lord's brother, who, with respect to the rich and the poor, wrote the unforgettable words found in the second and fifth chapters of his epistle!

Chapter 2

Verses 11-21

Theme: *The Gospel of Justification by Faith apart from Law-works Defended against Its Detractors*

I. *This Gospel's Origination: it is not of human but of divine origin: hence, is independent*

F. Far from receiving anything from Jerusalem's "pillars," at Antioch I even took Cephas to task for his reversion to legalism: separating himself from Gentile converts after first eating with them. A man is not justified by law-works but through faith in Jesus Christ. For I through law died to law, that I might live to God.

11 Now when Cephas came to Antioch I opposed him to his face because he stood condemned. 12 For before certain individuals from James arrived he had been in the habit of eating his meals with the Gentiles. But when they came he began to draw back and to separate himself, being afraid of those who belonged to the circumcision party. 13 And the rest of the Jews joined him in playing the hypocrite, so that even Barnabas was carried along by their hypocrisy. 14 But when I saw that they were not pursuing a straight course in accordance with the truth of the gospel, I said to Cephas, in everybody's presence, "If you, though a Jew, can live like a Gentile and not like a Jew, how can you (now) force the Gentiles to live like Jews?"

15 "We ourselves, though by nature Jews and not 'Gentile sinners,' 16 yet, knowing that a man is not justified by law-works but only through faith in Jesus Christ, even we believed in Christ Jesus in order that we might be justified by faith in Christ, and not by law-works, because by law-works will no flesh be justified. 17 But if, in seeking to be justified in Christ, we ourselves also turn out to be sinners, is Christ then a sin-promotor? By no means! 18 For, if I start to rebuild the very things which I have torn down, it is then that I prove myself a transgressor. 19 For I through law died to law, that I might live to God. 20 I have been crucified with Christ; and it is no longer I who lives, but Christ who lives in me; and that (life) which I now live in flesh I live in faith, (the faith) which is in the Son of God, who loved me and gave himself up for me. 21 I do not set aside the grace of God; for if justification (were) through law, then Christ died in vain."

2:11-21

F. The gospel as proclaimed by Paul
maintained even over against Peter's deviation

Paul continues to prove "the essential independence both of his gospel and of his position."[62] That gospel which had been so enthusiastically endorsed by the "pillars," etc. at Jerusalem was able to assert itself, when necessary, even *over against* one of those very "men of repute." The theory according to which the rebuke here administered was addressed to some other *"Cephas,"* not to the apostle, is without a shred of evidence. The *Cephas* or *Peter* indicated here in 2:11 ff. must have been the one to whom Paul referred previously in this same letter (1:18; 2:7-9). And that person was one of Jerusalem's "pillars," none other than Peter the apostle, the leader of The Twelve.

---

[62] R. A. Cole, *The Epistle of Paul to the Galatians (The Tyndale New Testament Commentaries)*, p. 72. There is, accordingly, no sharp contrast between verses 1-10 and verses 11-21. Hence, (verse 11) can best be translated "now" or "and," not "but."

The episode in which Peter was involved may well have occurred during the interval between the Jerusalem Conference (Acts 15:1-29) and the beginning of the second missionary journey (15:40 ff.). We know from the book of Acts (15:22, 30-39) that it was then that Paul and Barnabas tarried for some time in Syrian Antioch. And here in Galatians the Paul-versus-Peter controversy immediately follows the conference (inclusive of private interview).

11. Paul writes: **Now when Cephas came to Antioch I opposed him to his face.** We are not told just why Cephas visited Antioch at this time. Various guesses have been made but none of them serves any useful purpose. The important fact is that Cephas committed an error of conduct so serious that Paul felt obliged to *oppose* or *resist*[63] him "to his face," that is, directly, openly, man to man. Peter's action was entirely inexcusable, to which Paul calls attention by adding: **because he stood condemned.** His own behavior condemned him. Why this was true will become clear from the discussion of verses 12-14.

These lines begin as follows: **12. For before certain individuals from James arrived he had been in the habit of eating his meals with the Gentiles. But when they came he began to draw back and to separate himself, being afraid of those who belonged to the circumcision party.**

The reference is, no doubt, to the fellowship meals or *agapae* ("love feasts") of the early Christians. The food which otherwise would have been consumed at home was brought to the meeting-place of the congregation. It would seem that originally the Lord's Supper took place at the conclusion of such a get-together. Whether such meetings were ordinary church services or congregational meetings is not always clear and, for the present purpose, does not matter. The abuses to which such social meals could lead are pointed out in I Cor. 11:17-34. In Corinth there was segregation according to wealth, the rich separating from the poor; in Antioch the segregation which threatened was of an ethnic character, the Jewish Christians separating from their Gentile brothers in the faith, as will become clear.

The question, "How can Jewish Christians eat with Gentile Christians?" was a very perplexing one in the apostolic age. It is true that, with a view especially to those who from the Gentiles turned to God (Acts 15:19), the Jerusalem Council had made an important decision, namely, "that y o u abstain from that which has been sacrificed to idols, and from blood, and

---

63 The verb ἀνθίστημι occurs in Matt. 5:39; Luke 21:15; Acts 6:10; 13:8; Rom. 9:19; 13:2; Eph. 6:13; II Tim. 3:8; 4:15; James 4:7; and I Peter 5:9. It does not necessarily mean *to resist an attack,* though at times it should be so interpreted (Matt. 5:39; Eph. 6:13). Whether or not it does depends upon the context. The present context may well point in that direction. If so, then Paul regards Peter's conduct as an attack upon the freedom proclaimed by the gospel. See also W. Hendriksen, *The Meaning of the Preposition ἀντί in the New Testament* (doctoral dissertation), pp. 48, 58; also N.T.C. on Eph. 6:13, footnote 172.

from anything that has been strangled . . ." (15:29) .[64] But even though this decision to a certain extent limits the area in which it was possible for Jews and Gentiles to enjoy meal-time fellowship, it did not by any means settle everything with reference to such eating and drinking.

First, there were the Old Testament rules concerning clean and unclean (Lev. 11). For centuries the Jews had observed such and similar divine ordinances. Josephus (*Antiquities* IV.vi.8) puts into the mouths of the Midianite women who came to entice the Israelites (cf. Num. 25 and 31) these words: "Y o u r kinds of food are peculiar to yourselves, and y o u r kinds of drinks are common to no others." Well-known is the Old Testament passage: "But Daniel resolved in his heart that he would not defile himself with the king's dainties, nor with the wine which he drank" (Dan. 1:8). From the apocryphal book Tobit (1:10-12) note the following: "And when I was carried away captive to Nineveh, all my brothers and those that were of my kindred ate the bread of the Gentiles, but I kept myself from eating because I remembered God with all my soul." There is also I Macc. 1:62: "And many in Israel were fully resolved and confirmed in themselves not to eat unclean things"; and the dramatic story of the mother and her seven sons who were martyred because they refused to eat "abominable swine's flesh" (II Macc. 7). In some of the cases listed above (for example, Dan. 1:8 ff.) the revulsion of the devout Jews aroused by the sight of heathen food may have been due to a combination of reasons; for example, some of the food set before them may have been *unclean* according to the regulations of Lev. 11, and most or all of it may have been previously consecrated to idols.

Secondly, there were the man-made restrictions and stipulations, handed down from generation to generation, by means of which the rabbis had sought to explain and expand the divinely imparted ordinances. These, in turn, were of various kinds. Some dealt with the purchase of meats from Gentile meat-markets; for example: "The Jews were permitted to get meat from a Gentile meat-market when the animal had not been slaughtered by a non-Israelite, when the meat had not been brought into contact with pagan religious ceremonies, and when the proprietor of the place where the meat was sold guaranteed that he did not handle inferior meat, the kind that had been prohibited for Jewish consumption."[65]

There was also the peculiar Pharisaic interpretation of the law of purity (Lev. 15). This may well furnish the true explanation of John 4:7-9 with reference to Christ's conversation with the Samaritan woman. Jesus said to her, "Give me a drink." Continued: "So the Samaritan woman said to him, 'How is it that you, a Jew, ask a drink of me, a Samaritan woman?'

---

[64] The question with respect to the value of the variant reading in the Western text belongs to commentaries on the book of Acts.
[65] Strack-Billerbeck, *op. cit.*, Vol. III, p. 420.

(For Jews do not use [vessels] together with Samaritans)." See N.T.C. on the Gospel according to John, Vol. I, pp. 160, 161.

Still another set of *halakoth* ("traditions of the elders") had to do with washing the hands before eating, a washing not for ordinary hygienic reasons but out of fear lest these hands had been contaminated by contact with a Gentile or with something that belonged to a Gentile (Matt. 15:1 ff.; Mark 7:1 ff.).

Finally, to mention only one more reason why it was so difficult for a devout Jew to eat with a Gentile, think of the many man-made rules which the rabbis had laid down regarding the consumption of food *on the sabbath!*

In view of all this, it is easy to see that for a Jew to eat in the company of a Gentile, whether on the sabbath or not, was considered by many to be positively wicked.

But had not Christ, by his death on the cross, fulfilled, and thereby abolished, the Old Testament "shadows"? And if even the divinely established rules had lost their validity, was not the same true—even more decisively—with respect to all the man-made regulations that had been embroidered upon these rules? True indeed, but this legitimate inference was not drawn by every believer in Christ. Many, especially in and around Jerusalem, held fast to their "traditions." Provided that no saving significance of any kind was ascribed to the continuation of such habits and that no offense was given, such persistence could be tolerated, particularly during what might be called the period of transition. However, in mixed communities problems immediately presented themselves. See I Cor. 8:1 ff.; 10:14 ff. Customs (Gentile versus Jewish) were bound to clash. The fact that the law of ordinances had been nailed to the cross was not always fully appreciated, and the further and closely related fact that "in Christ" the wall of separation between Jew and Gentile had been broken down, never to be rebuilt, was frequently ignored (as it is even today in certain circles!).

In *liberal* (I now use the word in its most favorable sense) Antioch the far-reaching *implication* of the Jerusalem Council had been fathomed. The logical deduction had been drawn, namely, that if the ceremonial ordinances regarding eating and drinking were not to be imposed upon the Gentiles, they should not be saddled upon the Jews either. Here it was understood that the unity of the church, consisting of Jew and Gentile, demanded, among other things, eating and drinking together in sweet fellowship, with restrictions reduced to the very minimum (those only that are described in Acts 15:20, 29). Were not *all* of the brothers "Christians," and was it not Antioch in which this beautiful new name had first been given to Christ's followers? (11:26). According to this principle of love and fellowship the members of the Antiochian church had now for some time been eating and drinking.

When Cephas arrived in Antioch he, too, had fallen in line with this new procedure and had continued in this manner for some time. But then something occurred which brought about an inexcusable and dangerous change in his behavior. Into the church-gathering walked "certain individuals from James."[66] In the light of such passages as Acts 15:1, 24 it is not necessary to conclude that these "investigators" actually represented the views of James or that they had been delegated by him. Far more natural would seem to be the explanation that they came from the church at Jerusalem, a church in which James occupied a position of special prominence. Although some cling to the theory that these "individuals from James" and "those who belonged to the circumcision party" are two different groups, the text does not demand this interpretation. In all probability the "individuals from James" belonged to the same group as the Judaizers to which reference is made in Acts 15:1. In the latter passage they demanded that the Gentiles, in order to be admitted to the church, be circumcised. Here we meet them once more in the same city of Antioch, and this time they insist (perhaps by their very presence and refusal to eat with Gentile believers) that Jews dine with Jews, Gentiles with Gentiles. And Cephas hesitates, then little by little begins to withdraw himself from the Gentiles, until at length he is completely separating himself and is no longer eating with the Gentiles.[67]

Peter, in so doing, was motivated by fear. Was he afraid that by means of continued eating with the Gentiles (believers in Christ, gathered from the Gentiles) he would antagonize the men from James to such an extent that the evil report which they would bring to their like-minded friends in Jerusalem would weaken his prestige in that city and might even cause him to be persecuted?

It is argued that the Peter who had spoken with such courage at the Council of Jerusalem would not have "turned around" so completely here at Antioch, certainly not so shortly afterward. This argument fails to give due consideration to two facts: a. Peter may not have been aware of the full implications of his action; for, after all, the decisions of that council *explicitly* dealt with Gentiles, not with Jews; b. inconsistency and momentary fear consituted the weak strain in Peter's character. Besides, though a believer's progress in sanctification is capable of being represented by a rising diagonal, so that the Peter of Acts 2:22-36; 4:19, 20; 5:12-16, 29 shows far more courage than the one of Matt. 27:69-75; Mark 14:66-72; Luke 22:54-62; and John 18:15-18, 25-27, nevertheless, this diagonal is not a straight line. It dips at times. And so it was here. Instability was again asserting itself,

---

[66] The word-order would seem to favor the construction of ἀπὸ Ἰακώβου with τινας rather than with ἐλθεῖν.

[67] The imperfects συνήσθιεν, ὑπέστελλεν, and ἀφώριζεν are very graphic.

as it had done so often before. Accordingly, far from saying that Cephas could not have changed so quickly from one kind of conduct to another, we should rather affirm that the description here given is exactly "in character" for that particular apostle. For proof see N.T.C. on the Gospel according to John, Vol. II, p. 232. The change from Peter's excellent emphasis on the unity of Jew and Gentile, when at the Council of Jerusalem he said, "And God made no distinction between us and them, cleansing their hearts by faith" (Acts 15:9) and his present encouragement of separation between these two groups, was certainly not any more drastic and sudden than that between his boast, "Even if I must die with thee, yet will I not deny thee" and his complete disavowal, "I do not even know the man."

13. Continued: **And the rest of the Jews joined him in playing the hypocrite.** Whether or not Peter had understood the full implications of the decisions of the Jerusalem Council, one thing at least is certain: he knew that in separating himself from the believing Gentiles he was acting contrary to his own inner convictions. He was hiding his real beliefs, just as an actor conceals his real face under a mask. He was playing the hypocrite. We know that this is true, for:

(1) During Christ's sojourn on earth Peter had been one of his closest disciples. He had heard the teaching of Jesus whereby he "made all meats clean" (Mark 7:19). He knew that this same Jesus had urged sinners, one and all, to come unto him and be saved by simple trust in him (Matt. 11:28-30). He knew, too, that the Master had welcomed non-Israelites (Matt. 8:11; 28:18-20; Mark 12:9; Luke 4:16-30; 17:11-19); and that in ever so many of his sayings he had emphasized the oneness in him of all believers throughout the whole wide earth (Matt. 13:31, 32; Luke 14:23; 19:10; John 3:16; 4:42; 10:16; 12:32; 17:19, 20).

(2) As if that were not sufficient, to Peter had been given—and this not once but three times!—the vision of the sheet. On the housetop at Joppa he had learned that it was wrong to regard as "unclean" that which God had cleansed (Acts 10:9-16).

(3) He had also understood the implication *of this vision* and had acted upon it. Boldly he had gone to Caesarea and had entered the house of the centurion Cornelius of the Italian band. It was to the group gathered at the home of this non-Jew that he had said, "Y o u yourselves know how unlawful it is for a Jew to associate with or to visit a person of another nation; yet to me God has shown that I should not call any man common or unclean" (Acts 10:28).

(4) Not only had he visited the uncircumcised but *he had even eaten* with them. And when those of the circumcision party had criticized him for such conduct, Peter had come forth with a lengthy defense (Acts 11:1-18). And, in the full assurance of the fact that he was following the only divinely approved course, he had in the beginning repeated at Antioch

what he had already done at Caesarea. In both cases he had taken his meals with the Gentiles.

(5) In fact, if it was right for Peter to eat with Gentile *enquirers* at Caesarea, it certainly must have been right for him to eat with Gentile *believers* in Antioch!

Accordingly, when Paul accuses Peter of insincerity or hypocrisy he is not using too strong a word. Peter's conduct was all the more reprehensible because he was a recognized leader. His example was prone to be followed by others. So it was also in the present case. When the courage of Cephas was oozing out, faint-heartedness also took possession of "the rest of the Jews" (that is, all the other Jewish Christians who were present). Even Barnabas, whom we would never have accused of narrow-mindedness (see on Gal. 2:1), who had co-operated heartily with Paul in the establishment of several churches in Gentile regions, and who must have enjoyed many a meal with the young converts from the heathen world, now meekly went along with Peter in the latter's insincere behavior: **so that even Barnabas was carried along by their hypocrisy.**

The courage and firmness of Paul's reaction to this inexcusable hypocrisy merit profound admiration: **14. But when I saw that they were not pursuing a straight course in accordance with the truth of the gospel, I said to Cephas, in everybody's presence, "If you, though a Jew, can live like a Gentile and not like a Jew, how can you (now) force the Gentiles to live like Jews?"**

Paul saw that Peter and all those who followed his example "were not straight-footing *toward,* or in *accordance with,* the truth of the gospel," thus literally. In the New Testament the verb *they are straight-footing*[68] occurs only here. The meaning is probably either that, as Paul saw it, these people were not advancing *toward,* i.e., *in the direction of,* the gospel-truth, or that they were not pursuing a straight course *in accordance with*[69] that truth. According to the latter view, to which I would give a slight preference, the two lines—of which one is the guideline and represents the gospel-truth, and the other represents the conduct of these segregationists—were not running parallel. On the contrary, they were pulling farther and farther apart. The straight course in accordance with gospel-truth is the gospel message presented in all its purity.

When Paul, after due consideration, understood that Cephas and his imitators were deviating from the straight course, he addressed himself directly to his fellow-apostle. This is generally far better than "talking behind a person's back." It stands to reason that Paul could not very well have waited for an opportunity to speak to Peter *privately,* for even though

---

[68] ὀρθοποδοῦσιν: *present* active indicative retained because of indirect discourse, where we would use the *imperfect.*
[69] The reason for the slight difference in interpretation is that πρός with the accusative can here mean either *toward* or *in accordance with.*

Peter was the leader, he was not the only sinner. The rest of the Jews were also guilty, including even Barnabas. It would have been impractical to visit each one separately. Besides, on this matter of *publicly* rebuking those who have erred *publicly,* worthy of serious consideration is John Calvin's comment on this verse, "This example instructs us that those who have sinned publicly must be publicly chastised, as far as the church is concerned. The purpose is that their sin may not, by remaining unpunished, form a dangerous example; and elsewhere (I Tim. 5:20) Paul lays down this rule expressly, to be observed in the case of elders, 'Those who do wrong you must rebuke in the presence of all, so that also the others may have fear,' because the position which they occupy renders their example more pernicious. It was particularly advantageous that the good cause in which all had an interest, should be openly defended in the presence of the people, that Paul might have the better opportunity of showing that he did not shrink from the broad light of day."

In everybody's presence, then, Paul said to Cephas, "If you, though a Jew, can live like a Gentile and not like a Jew, how can you (now) force the Gentiles to live like Jews?" Meaning: "If even you, Cephas, *though you are a Jew,* can allow yourself the freedom of ignoring the Jewish traditions with respect to eating and drinking, as you certainly did when you were eating your meals with the Gentiles, then how can you now impose these very traditions upon *Gentiles,* forcing them to live like Jews? It is undeniable that by separating yourself from the Gentiles at dinner time, you are saying to them, 'If y o u Gentiles wish to have fellowship with us—and such, of course, is desirable—y o u will have to adopt our customs; y o u will have to live like Jews.' "

As to verses 15-21 the question arises, "To whom were they addressed?" To Peter? To the entire multiude present at the love-feast? To the Galatians? The best answer is probably this, that even though Peter is never absent from Paul's mind, for it was this very Cephas who had led the others into serious error, yet the attention is gradually shifted away from one individual to the entire group present, which includes even Paul himself. The very change in the employment of pronouns would seem to point in that direction, for having used the singular pronoun *you* (συ) in verses 14, Paul now shifts to the plural "we ourselves" (verse 15). It should be added immediately, however, that inasmuch as the error which *the Galatians* were committing was similar to that of Peter and his followers, for both groups allowed themselves to be influenced by the Judaizers, the entire address (verses 14-21) was intended to be taken to heart also by those *to* whom, or *by* whom, this letter would be read.

15, 16. Clear and forceful are the words: **We ourselves, though by nature Jews and not "Gentile sinners," yet, knowing that a man is not justified by law-works but only through faith in Jesus Christ, even we believed in Christ Jesus**

in order that we might be justified by faith in Christ, and not by law-works, because by law-works will no flesh be justified.

If a Jew who, having turned to Christ, has learned that strict obedience to legal requirements, divine and human, will not bring even *him* into the kingdom, tries, nevertheless, to impose such legalism upon *Gentiles,* his effort to place this yoke upon them is inexcusable. Such would seem to be the connection between verses 15, 16 and that which immediately precedes.

The content of the present verses may be briefly paraphrased as follows: "Though we ourselves are by birth (race, descent) Jews, highly privileged people, and not coarse sinners of Gentile descent, yet, when we learned that our works done in obedience to law could never suffice to make us righteous in God's sight, and that this standing could be attained only by trusting in Jesus Christ, *even we,* who in self-esteem were always looking down upon the Gentiles, began to see that before God we were not any better than they. Hence, *even we* embraced Christ by a living faith, in order that by means of the exercise of this faith we might receive, as a free gift, the standing of being 'not guilty but righteous' in God's sight. It was *by faith* in Christ and *his* merits, and definitely not by law-works, that we received this blessing, for by works done in obedience to law no weak, earthly, perishable human being,[70] whose works never reach the goal of perfection, will ever be able to attain to the standing of righteousness before God."

The verb *to justify*—here in the passive voice; hence, *to be justified*—occurs here for the first time in Paul's epistles, and no less than three times in this one passage (verses 15, 16).[71] Since we are dealing here with one of the most important concepts in the writings of Paul, a closer study is called for.

"To Be Justified"

(1) *The Meaning Not Always the Same*

The exact connotation of the word will have to be determined in each case in accordance with the specific context. Thus it will become clear that its sense in I Tim. 3:16 differs from that in Rom. 3:24. Note also its difference in meaning in Rom. 2:13 as compared with Rom. 3:20. An appreciation of this fact is very important. It will greatly help in the solution of the problem *James versus Paul.* The latter again and again emphasizes the fact that a man is *not* justified by works, but the former states, "Y o u see that by works a man is justified and not only by faith" (James 2:24). If

---

[70] The Greek word is σάρξ, "flesh." The various meanings of this word in Paul's epistles are summarized in N.T.C. on Philippians, p. 77, footnote 55.

[71] δικαιοῦται (third per. sing. pres. indic. passive); δικαιωθῶμεν (first per. plur. aor. subj. passive); and διακιωθήσεται (third per. sing. fut. indic. passive).

James means that by works the genuine character of man's faith *is demonstrated,* Paul is in perfect agreement with him (cf. Eph. 2:10).

(2) *Justification Defined*

When used, as here in Gal. 2:15, 16, in the dominant forensic sense, *justification* may be defined as *that gracious act of God whereby, on the basis solely of Christ's accomplished mediatorial work, he declares the sinner just, and the latter accepts this benefit with a believing heart.* In defense of this definition see, besides Gal. 2:15, 16, the following: Gal. 3:8, 11, 24; 5:4; Rom. 3:20, 24, 26, 28, 30; 4:3, 5; 5:1, 9; 8:30; Titus 3:7. *Justification* stands over against *condemnation* (Rom. 8:1, 33).

(3) *Justification Compared to Sanctification*

Justification is a matter of *imputation* (reckoning, charging): the sinner's guilt is imputed to Christ; the latter's righteousness is imputed to the sinner (Gen. 15:6; Ps. 32:1, 2; Isa. 53:4-6; Jer. 23:6; Rom. 5:18, 19). Sanctification is a matter of *transformation* (II Cor. 3:17, 18). In justification the Father takes the lead (Rom. 8:33); in sanctification the Holy Spirit does (II Thess. 2:13). The first is a "once for all" verdict, the second a lifelong process. Nevertheless, although the two should never be identified, neither should they be separated. They are distinct but not separate. In justifying the sinner, God may be viewed as the Judge who presides over a law court. The prisoner is standing at the dock. The Judge acquits the prisoner, pronouncing him "not guilty but righteous." The former prisoner is now a free man. But the story does not end here. The Judge now turns to that free man and adopts him as his son, and even imparts his own Spirit to him (Rom. 8:15; Gal. 4:5, 6). Here justification and sanctification touch each other, as it were; for, out of gratitude, this justified person, through the enabling power of the Spirit, begins to fight against his sins and to abound in good works to the glory of his Judge-Father. Good works never justify anyone, but no truly justified person wants to be without them (Eph. 2:8-10).

(4) *The Basis of Justification*

As already implied in the definition (see point 2), justification, as a judicial act of God, rests not on human works (Rom. 3:20, 28; Gal. 3:11; 5:4), not even on faith as a work of man (Eph. 2:8), but solely on God's sovereign grace in Jesus Christ. It is *his* accomplished mediatorial work that furnishes the legal basis upon which man's justification becomes both possible and actual. Christ fully satisfied the demands of God's law: he both paid our debt and also rendered the obedience which we owed (Matt. 20:28; Rom. 3:24; II Cor. 5:21; Gal. 3:24; Eph. 1:7; Titus 3:7).

(5) *The Acquisition of Justification*

Man cannot earn it. He can only accept it as a gift. Faith is the hand that accepts this gift. Faith itself is also a gift. See N.T.C. on Eph. 2:8. This does not reduce man to sheer passivity. Is not a tree which *accepts*

water and minerals from the soil, light from the sun, etc., very active? So
it is also with faith. It is receptive but not passive. It is very active, indeed!
(John 3:16; Phil. 2:12, 13).

(6) *Justification an Imperative Need*

Neither poverty nor disease nor pain nor imprisonment is man's most
bitter woe. To remove any or all of these is not his most pressing need.
His unbearable curse is the fact that by nature he is a child of wrath (Eph.
2:3). He has no peace (Isa. 48:22) but only a terrifying expectation of
judgment (Heb. 10:27), so that he cannot even fully enjoy the natural
blessings which God bestows upon him. What he needs more than anything
else is to have his guilt removed. "How can man be just with God?" (Job
9:2; 25:4) is the question to which he must have an answer.

(7) *Justification and Man's Continuous Quest*

In his utterly lost condition, however, man fails to understand that by
his own efforts he will never be able to dispel his guilt complex and to
achieve peace. Over the years and the centuries man has employed various
means and methods in order to "justify himself" (Luke 10:29); such as,
a strenuous effort to live in accordance with law (human, natural, and/or
divine), rigorous asceticism, physical torture, sacrifices to appease the deity,
the invocation of angels and of saints, the purchase of letters of indulgence,
masses, humanitarianism, becoming a zealous member of a political movement (Fascism, Nazism, Communism), submitting to psychoanalysis, etc.

(8) *Man's Failure to Obtain Justification by His Own Efforts*

None of these attempts succeed. *Man,* dead in sins and trespasses, is
unable to atone for *man's* guilt or to bring an offering that will redeem
either himself or his brother (Ps. 49:7). Moreover, he is also totally unable
to perform even a single *perfect* deed. In God's sight no man living is
righteous (Ps. 143:2; cf. 130:3; Job 9:3; 25:4; 40:4; 42:5, 6; Rom. 3:9-20).

(9) *Justification by Faith as God's Free Gift* (see point 5 above) *by the
Gospel Offered to All, Regardless of Race, Social Position, Wealth, Degree
of Education, Sex, etc.*

All have sinned and have fallen short of the glory of God. The invitation
is that *all* should repent and accept the righteousness of Christ, including
forgiveness of sins (Ps. 130:3, 4; Isa. 1:18) and life eternal (Isa. 45:22; 50:8;
53:11; Ezek. 18:23; 33:11; John 3:16; Rom. 3:23, 24; 5:19; II Cor. 5:20, 21).

17a. Paul has just said, "We believed in Christ Jesus in order that we might
be justified by faith in Christ," etc. With a reflection, perhaps, on the
Judaizers, who claim that such faith in Christ will not quite reach far
enough and must be supplemented by law-works, the apostle continues:
**But if, in seeking to be justified in Christ, we ourselves also turn out to be
sinners, is Christ then a sin-promoter?** Of this difficult passage there are many
interpretations. Three of the most important are:

99

(1) "If, in seeking to be justified in Christ, *our sins are laid bare,* so that it becomes evident that not only the Gentiles but also we, Jews, are great sinners before God, is Christ then a sin-promoter?"

Objection. The expression "turn out to be sinners" (literally "are found to be sinners") is not the same as "must submit to having our sins laid bare." Besides, in such a connection, the question, "Is Christ then a sin-promoter?" does not make good sense, for how would the laying bare of sin, so that it is seen in its true character, make Christ a sin-promoter, an encourager (literally "a servant") or abettor of sin? By itself it is true that Christ, by his Spirit, lays bare or reveals the seriousness of sin. However, he does this in order to bring the sinner to repentance, and so to the joyful assurance of having been forgiven, and to gradual victory over sin. Christ, in all this, proves himself a Deliverer from—and not an Encourager of—sin.

(2) "If, in seeking to be justified in Christ, we Jews, law-*respecters,* turn out to be sinners just like the Gentiles, law-*rejecters,* then why should we not all live as if there were no law? Moreover, if this doctrine of justification is of Christ, must we then conclude that he encourages sin (lawlessness)?" Cf. Rom. 6:1, 15.

Objection. The introduction, at this point, of a kind of antinomian distortion of the doctrine of grace seems rather unnatural. Nothing in the preceding context has prepared us for it, and nothing in the succeeding context links with it. Contrast Gal. 5:13, where the danger of turning liberty into license is clearly stated and condemned.

(3) *"If the Judaizers are correct* in maintaining that we, in seeking to be justified solely in Christ, and thus neglecting law, turn out to be gross sinners just like the Gentiles, then would y o u say that Christ, who taught us this doctrine, is a sin-promoter?"

In favor of this interpretation note the following:

(a) *It obviously suits the preceding context.* In substance Paul is saying, "Peter and all of y o u who have followed his example, consider what y o u are doing! By y o u r action y o u are really saying that Christ was wrong when he taught y o u: that it is not what enters a man from without that defiles him but rather what proceeds out of his heart (Matt. 15:1-20) ; that all meats are clean (Mark 7:19) ; and that men are saved by simply coming to him and trusting in him (Matt. 11:25-30; John 3:16) . Is it really true, then, that Christ is a sin-promoter, that is, that he—by his teaching, example, death on the cross—makes y o u a greater sinner than y o u were already?"

(b) *It also establishes a smooth connection with the words which immediately follow,* for Paul continues:

17b, 18. By no means! A thousand times *NO* to the suggestion that Christ encourages sin, making y o u a greater transgressor than y o u were previously, *for* not by tearing down the ceremonial law and believing in salvation solely by grace, as y o u, Peter, etc., started out to do, do y o u show yourselves transgressors, but y o u very definitely prove yourselves transgressors by doing the very opposite, namely, rebuilding the very things which y o u have torn down. However, to spare their feelings, that is, to prevent those in his audience (*visible:* those actually present when the apostle was speaking—Peter, Barnabas, etc.—and *invisible:* the Galatians who would hear the letter as it was read to them) from thinking that they alone were capable of so great an error, Paul lovingly uses the first person instead of the third, as if to say, "The conclusion I am drawing holds for anyone who rebuilds what he had previously so wisely torn down. It holds in my own case, if I were to be guilty of it, as well as in y o u r s. Let each and every one of us then apply it to himself. Let him say, 'If *I* start to rebuild,' " etc. Accordingly, in close connection with the immediately preceding, as has now been shown, the apostle states: **For, if I start to rebuild the very things which I have torn down, it is then that I prove myself a transgressor.** I *prove* or *demonstrate* (cf. Rom. 3:5; II Cor. 7:11) myself a transgressor, because I know very well that what I am now doing—in rebuilding the doctrine of salvation by law-works—*a.* clashes with my deepest convictions based on past experience (see verse 19), and *b.* cancels the significance of Christ's death on the cross (see verses 20 and 21).[72]

19. Continued: **For I through law died to law.** If ever a man could have been saved by strict obedience to law, that man was Paul. He had tried O so hard! Elsewhere he reviews his life before his conversion in these words: "If anyone else imagines that he has reason for confidence in flesh, I (have) more: . . . *as to legal righteousness having become blameless*" (Phil. 3:4b-6). So strict had Paul been in his outward observance of the Old Testament law, as interpreted by the Jewish religious leaders, that in the pursuit of this legal rectitude he had become blameless, that is, in *human* judgment. His outward conduct, even during the days before he was converted to Christ, had been irreproachable. So it had seemed in the eyes of men, but not in the eyes of God! God's law, after all, demanded much more than the kind of behavior of which Paul's superiors approved. It demanded nothing less than *inward* (as well as outward) *perfection:* loving God with *all* the heart, soul, mind, and strength, and loving the neighbor as oneself. That standard Paul had been unable to meet. In fact, he had missed the target *by far.* In the meantime, moreover, the law had not relaxed its demands, nor its threats of punishment, nor its actual flagellations. It had not given Paul the peace with God which he so ardently desired. It had scourged him until, by the marvelous grace of God, he had found Christ (because Christ

---

[72] Others are of the opinion that Paul meant, ". . . then I prove that I *was* a transgressor previously" (e.g., Lenski, *op. cit.,* p. 113). But the more natural explanation would seem to be that Paul means: *"In the very act* of rebuilding the things which I have torn down, *I am, and show myself to be,* a transgressor." Besides, this explanation makes for a smoother connection with verse 19 ff.

had first sought and found him!) and peace in him. Thus, through the law he had died to the law. Through the law he had discovered what a great sinner he was, and how utterly incapable in himself of extricating himself from his position of despair and ruin (cf. Rom. 3:20; 7:7). Thus the law had been his custodian to conduct him to Christ (Gal. 3:24). And when by Christ he had been made alive, the law, viewed as being in and by itself a means unto salvation and as a cruel taskmaster who assigns tasks impossible of fulfillment and who lays down rules and regulations endless in their ramifications, had left him cold, dead like a corpse, without any response whatever. The response had been given *by Christ!* The satisfaction has been rendered *by him!*

Now in all this, God's wise purpose was being realized. What purpose? Answers Paul: **that I might live to God** (cf. Rom. 6:11; 14:7; II Cor. 5:15). And what is meant by living *to* or *for* God? Negatively, it means: no longer living for self. Positively it indicates: living as God wants me to live; hence, to his glory (I Cor. 10:31), according to his revealed will, his *law.*

It must never be overlooked that in the writings of the apostle the word *law*—as is true with respect to so many other great words—has more than one meaning. It is not my purpose at this point to present a detailed study of all the various meanings which this word has in Paul's epistles. That task would be more appropriate in a commentary on Romans. For the present the following must suffice. On the one hand Paul rejoices in the fact that he is not under law (Rom. 6:14, 15; cf. 7:6). He speaks of being delivered from the curse of the law (Gal. 3:13). He describes the law as "the hand-written document that was against us, which by means of its requirements testified against us" (Col. 2:14; cf. Eph. 2:15). And in the chapter now under study—see below—he even states, "If justification (were) through law, then Christ died in vain" (Gal. 2:21). Yet, on the other hand, he also tells us that he is "under law to Christ" (I Cor. 9:2), that he "delights in the law of God according to the inner man" (Rom. 7:22), that "the law is holy, and the commandment holy and righteous and good" (Rom. 7:12), and that love—the very love which is "the greatest of the three greatest" (I Cor. 13:13)—is the fulfilment of the law (Rom. 13:10; cf. Gal. 5:14; 6:2).

There is no warrant, therefore, to go to any extreme in denouncing the law. Whenever anything is said in disparagement of law, the concept *law* must be carefully described. The hue and cry of the present day, to the effect that as Christians "we have nothing whatever to do with the law" has no Scriptural justification at all. It is, in fact, a dangerous slogan, especially in an era of lawlessness!

Even in the passage now under consideration (Gal. 2:19) Paul does not think of *law* in an altogether negative sense or as something wholly useless. It was through a legal demand ("law")—the requirement that Paul be *perfect*—that Paul had died to the demand ("law"), and had been driven to Christ (cf. 3:24). That much good *law*, at least, had performed. Nevertheless, broadly speaking, it remains true that when Paul in Galatians places salvation *by law-works* over against salvation *by grace* (or "justification by faith"), he is using the term *law* in its definitely unfavorable sense. He is referring to the fact that man endeavors to save himself through his own efforts by means of strict adherence to the law of Moses, buried under a load of human regulations, many of them in direct conflict with the will of God (Matt. 5:43; Mark 7:9-13).

20, 21. Paul has shown that if he were to rebuild the very things—namely, salvation by law-works and everything connected with it—which he had torn down, he would prove himself a transgressor, because he would be doing something that would clash with his deepest convictions based on past experience (verses 18, 19). To this he now (in verses 20, 21) adds that such action would also destroy the meaning of Christ's death on the cross. In his own experience faith in Christ Crucified has thoroughly replaced confidence in whatever he might have been able to accomplish by means of law-works. That is the connection between verses 20, 21 and the immediately preceding context. Since the closing passage of the chapter has rightly endeared itself to believers of every age, I shall treat it in the manner in which similar most precious texts have been presented in this series of Commentaries, namely, in the form of a theme and a brief outline or summary:

The Riddle of Having Been Crucified with Christ

(1) The Riddle Propounded
Paul starts out by saying: **I have been crucified with Christ.** What a startling assertion! Here is the great apostle to the Gentiles at this love-feast of the Antiochian church. He is addressing an audience the bulk of which consisted of believers both of Gentile and Jewish origin. Peter and Barnabas are in this audience. Undoubtedly some of the men who had come from Jerusalem and who, though nominally confessing Jesus as their Savior, were always making trouble by stressing salvation by obedience to law far more than salvation by grace through faith, had also tarried in Antioch long enough to cause their presence at this particular meeting to be felt.

Now in this meeting-place that day there was a situation which at many a get-together would be considered improper, but which without any doubt is highly objectionable in a *church,* and most emphatically at a *love*-feast, a religious-social meeting characterized by all or most of the following elements: prayers, sacred songs, the reading and brief exposition of Scripture, eating and drinking together, and partaking of the Lord's Supper. That deplorable condition was this, that *the church-members were cliquing.* Segregation was being practiced, yes, right here in the church meeting:

103

Jews eating *exclusively* with Jews, leaving the Gentile believers no other choice than to eat with other Gentiles. This violation of the principle of the oneness of all believers "in Christ" occurred because undue respect was being accorded to the Judaizers. Peter, who previously had been freely eating with the Gentile believers, had allowed himself to be scared into withdrawing himself from them. He was now seen sitting or reclining in the company of Jews; Barnabas, ditto; and the same was true with respect to the rest of the Jews, as if *the cross of Christ* had been of no avail in taking down the barrier that had divided Jews and Gentiles!

It is under such circumstances that Paul arises and points to the significance which Christ Crucified had come to assume in his own life. Having first shown that "a man is not justified by law-works"—for example, by rigidly adhering to traditional regulations regarding eating and drinking—, but only through faith in Jesus Christ, the apostle closes his stirring address with the passage which starts out with these ringing words: "I have been crucified with Christ." Something marvelous had happened to Paul in the past, with abiding significance for the present and for all future time.[73]

But what can he mean by this? Must this saying be taken *literally*? Cases of survival after crucifixion have occurred, but certainly the present context, marked by use of words in an other-than-literal sense (for example, Paul also affirms that he is no longer alive!), cannot be interpreted literally. Are the words to be understood *emotionally*, perhaps (after the manner in which some explain Phil. 3:10)? Is it Paul's intention to convey the thought that with mind and heart he had been contemplating the story of Christ's great love for sinners, shown in his entire sojourn on earth but especially at Calvary, until he (Paul) had at last tearfully arrived at the point of identifying himself with the Great Sufferer, that is, of feeling, in some small degree, what *he* had felt and undergoing what *he* had experienced? But though such sharing in Christ's sufferings, when applied to the heart by the Holy Spirit, so that its boundaries are not overstepped, and its implications as to the sinner's guilt and his pardon are sanctified to the heart, can be very beneficial, this explanation would fail to do justice to the concrete situation that occasioned this famous testimony. Is it then to be explained *forensically*, that is, in terms of the law-court? Does Paul mean that he, too, along with all of God's children, had been declared "*Guilty* and exposed to the sentence of *eternal death*," but that at Calvary, due to Christ's redemptive suffering as our Substitute and Representative, this sentence had been changed into its very opposite, namely, "*Righteous* and an heir of *eternal life*"? Certainly, in such a case the apostle would have had the perfect right to say that he had been crucified along with Christ and also that with Christ he had arisen from the dead. Moreover, this forensic

---

[73] Paul uses the perfect tense: συνεσταύρωμαι.

explanation would bring the passage into line with many others (for example, Isa. 53:4-6, 8, 12; Matt. 20:28; Mark 10:45; John 1:29; Gal. 1:4; 3:13; Eph. 2:1, 3, 5, 6; Col. 2:12-14, 20; 3:1; I Tim. 3:6). But even though this meaning may well have been included, does it exhaust the contents of Paul's remarkable affirmation? Does it solve the riddle, and does it do justice to the present historical, as well as literary, context?

No doubt the best procedure is to let Paul be his own interpreter. Accordingly, we proceed to:

(2) *The Riddle Partly Clarified but Also Partly Intensified*

Paul continues: **and it is no longer I who lives, but Christ who lives in me.** This at least shows that when the apostle said, "I have been crucified with Christ" (literally, according to word order: "With Christ I have been crucified"), he meant that the process of crucifixion had been carried to its conclusion: he had been crucified, abidingly experiences the effects of this crucifixion, and, therefore, he is now no longer alive! But in what sense has he been crucified and is he no longer alive? The answer that suits the present context is this, that Paul is saying: *"As a self-righteous Pharisee, who based his hope for eternity on strict obedience to law, I, as a direct result of Christ's crucifixion, have been crucified and am no longer alive."* That, after all, was exactly the issue here at Antioch! "In order to be saved, is it necessary that, in addition to believing in Christ, we observe the old traditions; particularly, that we adhere to the laws concerning eating and drinking, and that we accordingly separate ourselves from the Gentiles?" That was the question. It is as if the apostle were saying, "I used to be of that persuasion myself. I was 'as to law a Pharisee, as to legal righteousness blameless' (Phil. 3:5, 6). But when, by God's marvelous grace, I was rescued from my sinful folly, then, 'such things as once were gains to me, these I counted loss for Christ.' And now I rejoice in no longer having 'a righteousness of my own, legal righteousness, but that which is through faith in Christ' (Phil. 3:9). Therefore 'it is Christ who now lives in me': it is from him that I receive all my strength. In him I trust completely. On his righteousness, imputed to me, I base my hope for eternity. 'On Christ, the solid Rock, I stand; All other ground is sinking sand.' "

For those in the audience who were used to interpreting everything literally (and there are such people, now as well as then!), the riddle may not as yet have been cleared up, however. They may have said to themselves, "But how can Paul say that he is no longer alive? If he were no longer alive, how could he be addressing us?" For them, accordingly, the riddle propounded by the man who was addressing them may have been intensified instead of solved. The apostle does not ignore them. He clears up this point also, for in the next line we see:

(3) *The Riddle Fully Explained*

Paul had not been trying to say that in no sense whatever was he still alive. He had not fallen into the error of those mystics who, on the basis of the present passage and of other passages, proclaim the doctrine of the merging of the believers' personality with that of Christ, in such a way that in reality only one personality can be said to exist, namely, that of Christ. The apostle fully clears up this point by stating: **and that (life) which I now live in flesh**[74] **I live in faith, (the faith) which is in the Son of God.** Paul has not been deprived of his life "in flesh," that is, earthly existence. It is still Paul, the individual, who thinks, exhorts, bears witness, rejoices. Nevertheless, the bond between himself and his Lord is a very close one, for it is the bond of faith. Humble trust in Christ is the channel through which Paul receives the strength he needs to meet every challenge (Phil. 4:13). By means of this unshakable confidence in his Redeemer he surrenders all to him and expects all from him. This faith, moreover, is very personal, and this both as to *subject* and *object*. First, as to *subject*. Note the constant use of the pronoun *I*. In verses 19-21 it is *twice* spelled out fully as a separate pronoun (first at the beginning of verse 19: "For *I—ego—*through law died to law," and then in verse 20, at the end of the clause which A.V. renders literally, "nevertheless I live; yet not *I—ego—*"). In addition "I" occurs no less than *seven* times as part of a verbal form. Finally, there are the *three* occurrences of this same pronoun in a case other than nominative, translated *me* in each instance (verse 20). That makes no less than *twelve* "I's" in all in just three verses! It shows that salvation is, indeed, a very personal affair: each individual must make his own decision, and each believer experiences his own fellowship with Christ, relying upon him with all the confidence of his own heart. Then also this faith is personal as to its *object:* Christ, not something pertaining to Christ but Christ *himself.* When Paul, who had been a bitter persecutor, reflects on the manner in which his Lord and Savior had taken pity on him, unworthy one, he, perhaps in order to emphasize the greatness of Christ's condescending love, reminds us of the fact that the One who so loved him was no less than "the Son of God," hence, himself God! ("the faith which is in the Son of God"). He adds: **who loved me and gave himself up for me.** Note: not just *gave,* but *gave up.* In that act of giving himself up to shame, condemnation, scourging, the crown of thorns, mockery, crucifixion and abandonment by his Father, death, and burial, the love of the Son of God for his people—"for me"—had become most gloriously manifest. How, then, would it ever be possible for Paul to minimize in any way the significance of the cross? This leads to the conclusion:

(4) *The Riddle Applied to the Present Concrete Situation*

Paul writes: **I do not set aside the grace of God.** Of this simple line, too, there are several explanations, some of them without any reference to the

---

[74] The Greek phrase is ἐν σαρκί. See footnote 70.

present context. The simplest interpretation is surely this one: "I do not set aside—declare invalid, nullify—the grace of God, which I surely would be doing if I were attempting by means of law-works—for example, strict obedience to regulations concerning eating and drinking—to secure my acceptance with God, my state of righteousness before him." In complete harmony with this thought the apostle adds: **for if justification (were) through law,**[75] **then Christ died in vain.** Paul is saying, therefore, to Peter, to Barnabas, to all those present that day at this love-feast in Antioch, to the Galatians, who have allowed themselves to be influenced by the Judaizers, and certainly also *to the modern man who imagines that by doing good and giving everyone his due he can be saved,* that a definite choice must be made, namely, between salvation by grace and salvation by law-works, by Christ or by self.

We are firmly convinced that Peter knew in his heart—and was glad—that his "beloved brother Paul" (II Peter 3:15) had rendered an incalculably valuable service to the cause of the unity of *all believers* in Christ, to the demands of Christian love, and to the doctrine of the all-sufficiency of Christ unto salvation. Barnabas and many of the others must have been similarly persuaded.

Summary of Chapter 2

This chapter consists of two paragraphs: verses 1-10; 11-21. The first describes what took place in Jerusalem fourteen years after the visit indicated in 1:18, 19. The apostle gives his version of The Jerusalem Conference (cf. Acts 15:1-29). The second paragraph concerns the Paul-versus-Peter affair in Syrian Antioch shortly afterward. In the first paragraph the foes are the Judaizers, Christians only in name, men who advocated faith plus law-obedience as the way to glory. One of their slogans was, "Unless y o u are circumcised according to the custom of Moses, y o u cannot be saved." Not being real Christians, they had no business at this synod. They were present as spies, bent on depriving true believers of their freedom in Christ. Now to this Conference the Antiochian church had delegated Paul and Barnabas, champions of Christian liberty. With them was Titus, a Christian of unmixed Gentile extraction, and thus uncircumcised, *a test case* therefore. Would the Judaizers succeed in persuading the assembly that Titus must be circumcised? If they do, then everywhere the position of Gentile Christians would be in jeopardy, Christianity would never become a worldwide religion, and the gospel of Christ's all-sufficiency for salvation

---

[75] In the original the verb is not expressed. Hence, some translate this protasis as belonging to the *first class* or *simple condition* group; others as *second class* or *contrary to fact*. In the end it makes no difference, as in each case the interpreters agree that Paul meant to convey the thought: *a.* that justification is not actually through law, and *b.* that Christ did not die in vain.

would vanish from the earth. But by God's decree that cannot happen! In a private consultation the truly Christian leaders—Paul and Barnabas, on the one hand; James, Cephas, and John, on the other—plan their strategy. Concerning God's work among the Gentiles Paul and Barnabas bear witness with such conviction, both before the Jerusalem leaders and before the full convention, that the opponents fail completely. The paragraph closes by picturing James, Cephas, and John in the act of extending the hand of friendship and brotherhood to Paul and Barnabas. The work-load is divided and help for the poor is provided.

Hardly was this battle won when a second had to be fought, as shown in verses 11-21. And in this struggle the foe was no one less than Cephas, the leader of The Twelve. Not that Peter was at heart an enemy of the gospel of grace, but here at Antioch he suffered a temporary lapse (cf. Matt. 16:23). When, at a public church-gathering he withdraws himself from the Gentiles, refusing any longer to eat with them, he is saying, in effect, "To be saved, more is needed than trust in Christ. Adherence to the ceremonial law is also necessary." He knows better, having been taught by Jesus and by the vision of the sheet. He is playing the hypocrite, having become alarmed by the arrival of a party of Judaizers. For a while things looked bad, for Peter's example was followed by others, including even Barnabas. Paul, however, rises to meet the challenge. We see him at the height of his fortitude. By inserting the substance of his remarks in this letter to the Galatians, he shows that his words are now also meant for these similarly erring brothers. In substance he says, "If you, Cephas, though a Jew, can live like a Gentile, as you proved when you ate with Gentiles, how can you now, by withdrawing from them, force them to live like Jews, so that they may be able to eat and have fellowship with us?" Then, turning to the entire audience, he stresses that not by law-works is anyone justified, but only by faith in Christ, and that if the Judaizers were right, Christ would be a promoter of sin. The real sinner, however, is the man who rebuilds the very structure—salvation by law-works—which he had previously pulled down. As to law Paul states, "For I through law died to law, that I might live to God." For a thematic treatment of verses 20, 21 see the explanation.

In the room silence prevails. The gospel of grace has triumphed once more. And may we not assume that not only Cephas but all true but momentarily erring believers who had followed his example were grateful to the Lord that they had been corrected by "our beloved brother Paul"?

Chapter 3

Verses 1-5

Theme: *The Gospel of Justification by Faith apart from Law-works Defended against Its Detractors*

II. *Its Vindication: both Scripture—i.e., the Old Testament—and life (experience, past history) bear testimony to its truth*

A. O foolish Galatians! Was it by doing what the law demands that y o u received the Spirit or was it by believing the gospel message?

CHAPTER III

GALATIANS

3 1 O foolish Galatians! Who has bewitched y o u, before whose very eyes Jesus was openly displayed as crucified? 2 This only would I learn from y o u: Was it by doing what (the) law demands that y o u received the Spirit, or was it by believing (the) gospel message?[76] 3 Are y o u so foolish? Having begun by the Spirit, now by fleshly means are y o u being made perfect? 4 Did y o u experience so many things in vain?—if (it be) really in vain. 5 He, accordingly, who supplies the Spirit to y o u and works miracles among y o u (does he bring this about) because y o u do what (the) law demands or because y o u believe (the) gospel message?[77]

3:1-5

A. *By what avenue did y o u receive the Spirit and its fruits?*

1. The apostle, having proved that the gospel as proclaimed by himself—that is, the good tidings of justification by faith apart from law-works—is of divine origin and is therefore able to maintain itself everywhere and at all times, now proceeds to show that both *Scripture* and *experience* bear testimony to its truth. He turns to *experience* first of all, that is, to that which the Galatians themselves had begun to experience when they, by sovereign grace, had accepted Jesus Christ as their Lord and Savior. He says: **O foolish Galatians! Who has bewitched y o u, before whose very eyes Jesus was openly displayed as crucified?** As is clear from a study of the word "foolish" or "senseless" in Luke 24:25; Rom. 1:14; I Tim. 6:9; and to a certain extent even in Titus 3:3, the original indicates an attitude of *heart* as well as a quality of *mind*. It refers not to bluntness but to a sinful neglect to use one's mental power to the best advantage. The Galatians, in lending a listening ear to the arguments of the legalists, must be considered not necessarily dull but thoughtless, not ignorant but senseless, not stupid but foolish. And is not everyone foolish who barters the truth of God for the lie of Satan, peace for unrest, assurance for doubt, joy for fear, and freedom for bondage?

---

[76] Alternate translation: "Was it as a result of law-works that y o u received the Spirit or was it as a result of faith-inspired listening?"
[77] Alternate translation: ". . . (does he bring this about) as a result of law-works or as a result of faith-inspired listening?"

Paul, deeply moved, asks, "Who has bewitched y o u?" Neither in Greek, however, nor in modern English does the word *bewitch* always have reference to literal witchcraft. In the interpretation of this passage much has been made of "the evil eye" (cf. Deut. 28:54, 56; Prov. 23:6; 28:22; Matt. 20:15; Mark 7:22). But Paul was probably not thinking about the sorcerer who had brought the Galatians under the baleful influence of his evil eye, but rather of the Judaizer who had cast a spell upon them *not* by means of his eyes but by means of his *words, his teaching;* specifically, by telling them that faith in Christ must be *supplemented* by Mosaic ritualism.[78] And the Galatians, by yielding to this influence, had failed to understand that a Christ *supplemented* is a Christ *supplanted.*

Moreover, such yielding was entirely inexcusable, since Jesus, as the source of salvation full and free to all who believe, had been *openly displayed, clearly and publicly proclaimed*[79] to the Galatians. With their very eyes, as it were, they had seen him. So clear and vivid had been the presentation of this Christ that they had formed a mental picture of him, dying for sinners and promising salvation to all who would accept him by true faith. When Paul says "before whose very eyes Jesus was openly displayed as crucified," he is thinking not so much of the historical details of the crucifixion as of the supreme value of Christ Crucified for a world lost in sin, and of the implication that obedience to law contributes nothing to this salvation.

2. Paul continues: **This only would I learn from y o u: Was it by doing what (the) law demands that y o u received the Spirit, or was it by believing (the) gospel message?** A somewhat different translation—not differing, however, in its basic idea—is also possible, namely, ". . . Was it as a result of law-works that y o u received the Spirit, or was it as a result of faith-inspired listening?"[80] The two renderings agree in this that according to

---

[78] See Delling, article βασκαίνω, Th.W.N.T., Vol. I, pp. 595, 596.
[79] The context makes clear that this rather than *written beforehand* (cf. Rom. 15:4; Eph. 3:3; Jude 4) is the sense of προεγράφη.
[80] The preference for either the one or the other translation hinges mainly on the answer which is given to the question, "What is the meaning of ἐξ ἀκοῆς πίστεως? The notion that πίστις is here used in the objective sense (body of doctrine, teaching) can be dismissed as being out of line with the context. It is also easy to agree on the meaning of ἐξ = *by, by way of, as a result of.* But the exact connotation, in the present instance, of ἀκοή-ῆς furnishes a real difficulty. Dismissing the meaning *ear, ears* (Mark 7:35; Luke 7:1; Acts 17:20; II Tim. 4:3), it is agreed that the word can refer to *a. hearing* or *listening (active* sense). It has this meaning in Rom. 10:17 and II Peter 2:8. The modifier πίστεως could then be interpreted as a qualitative genitive: "hearing characterized by faith, hearing with a believing heart," or as a subjective genitive: "hearing that comes of—or: is inspired by—faith." This interpretation of ἀκοῆς πίστεως as being, in either sense, the hearing or listening *of faith* yields a good sense in the passage now under discussion. There is then a contrast between *works performed in bondage to law* ("law-works"), on the one hand, and *listening inspired by (or: characterized by) faith,* on the other.

both *salvation by works* is placed over against *salvation by faith.* Paul's question is filled with significance and applies to every age. Let the tree be judged by the fruits it produces. It is as if Paul were asking, "My dear Galatians, does the course which y o u are now following make y o u more happy and contented than that which y o u previously selected? By what avenue were y o u first made conscious of having the Holy Spirit in y o u r hearts? Was it by the avenue of rigorous bondage to ceremonial ordinances or was it by the exercise of faith in Christ, so that y o u listened and listened and eagerly took to heart the marvelous message of the gospel?" In verse 5 the apostle is going to come back to this question and is going to expand it. See on that verse.

3. Continued: A̓re y o u so foolish? What their folly consisted of has already been explained (see on verse 1). Nevertheless, there is a further explication of the concept *Galatian Folly* in these words: **Having begun by the Spirit, now by fleshly means are y o u being made perfect?** [81]

In the original there is a double contrast, namely, *a.* between "having begun" and "being made perfect," and *b.* between "by the Spirit" and "by flesh" (in the sense of "by fleshly means"). This double contrast is made all the more effective by the chiastic (or letter X) arrangement of the words in the sentence:

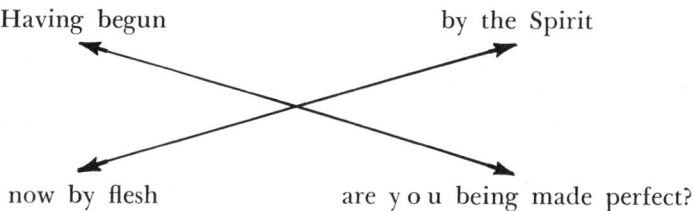

Having begun   by the Spirit

now by flesh   are y o u being made perfect?

However, ἀκοή also has a *passive* meaning: *b. that which is heard, report, preaching, message;* particularly now *the gospel message.* It has this meaning in Isa. 53:1 (LXX) and at least also in the New Testament quotations of that passage (John 12:38; Rom. 10:16). So rendered ἐξ ἀκοῆς πίστεως could then be translated: *by* (or: *as a result of*) *the gospel message which demanded faith* or . . . *which was the object of faith,* or even more simply but still correctly: *by believing the gospel message.* Here, too, the contrast between *doing* what the law demands, on the one hand, and *believing* the gospel message, on the other, is very clear. What especially interested the present author, in making a study of this verse, was that noted interpreters, *in each group* (*a.* and *b.*) claim that *their* rendering of ἀκοή-ῆς does better justice to the contrast which Paul has in mind than does the opposite rendering. As I see it, both do equal justice to this contrast, and at bottom, both interpretations and translations of the passage amount to about the same thing, for what is this *faith-inspired* (or *faith-derived*) *listening* if it be not a "listening with a believing heart to the gospel message"?

[81] The verb ἐπιτελεῖσθε is probably passive, not middle. Nowhere else in the New Testament does this verb occur in the middle voice. It is always either active (Rom. 15:28; II Cor. 7:1; 8:6, 11; Phil. 1:6; Heb. 8:5; 9:6) or passive (I Peter 5:9).

By placing *Spirit* and *flesh* so near to each other (as is done in the original and in my translation) the difference between the two receives the proper emphasis. The active presence of *the Spirit* spells the indwelling of Christ; hence, rebirth, the implantation of the seed of true faith, the sense of forgiveness and sonship, and the further gifts of illumination, liberty, joy, assurance of salvation, power against Satan, answered prayers, effective witness-bearing, etc. It produces gifts both outward and inward, as will be indicated (see on verse 5). On the other hand, *the flesh*[82] is the absence of Christ's indwelling. It indicates anything apart from Christ on which one bases his hope for salvation. The Galatians were beginning to renounce Christ as the all-sufficient Savior. Having begun in the Spirit they were now tending to place their confidence in fleshly means—such as trusting in the advice of the Judaizers, hence also in legal works, strict observance of ceremonies, circumcision, etc.—in order that by means such as these they might become perfected. What stupendous and disastrous folly! They remind one of the prodigal son who leaves the home of his father, with the security, peace, love, and understanding which that home offered, in order that he might roam about in a strange and hostile environment, where he would suffer hunger and want. Flesh spells doubt, fear, darkness, weakness, bondage, gloom, defeat, etc.

It is as if Paul were saying, "How hopeful was y o u r beginning, and how sad y o u r continuation! And just think of it: those false guides whom y o u are now beginning to follow have a name for this process of going downhill. They call it *becoming perfected!* What tragic irony!"

What the apostle writes applies not only to the Galatians of his own day. It applies equally to those who today are trusting in such things as ritual, the moral life, scientific achievement, intellectual attainment, physical charm, financial resources, political power, doctrinal liberalism, or even doctrinal purity. If one bases his hope for this life or the next upon anything apart from Christ he is placing confidence in *flesh*.

4. In close connection with the words "Having begun by the Spirit" (verse 3 and cf. also verses 1 and 2) Paul continues: **Did y o u experience so many things in vain?** A.V. reads, "Have ye suffered so many things in vain?" This wording (with *suffered* instead of *experienced*) is found also in many other translations, both ancient and modern, and is recommended by many interpreters. If it be correct, Paul would be introducing an entirely new thought at this point, one about which he has said nothing whatever in the preceding, which he drops immediately, and to which he never again alludes in the remainder of the letter! Now, it can hardly be questioned that the Galatians, along with all others who turn to Christ, had suffered. Cf. John 16:33; II Tim. 3:12. Even the book of Acts which dwells in some detail

---

[82] On σάρξ see N.T.C. on Philippians, p. 77, footnote 55, meaning g.

on Paul's sufferings in South Galatia (13:50; 14:2, 5, 19) and says but little about the afflictions which the Galatians themselves endured, nevertheless implies that many tribulations awaited them (14:22). It is also true that the word used in the original and translated *suffered* in A.V., etc., generally has that meaning. And, *taken in and by itself,* the question, "Have ye suffered so much in vain?" yields an intelligible sense, for the Galatians might well be asked whether "the game had been worth the candle," if they now were at the point of deserting the very faith which they had once confessed and for which they had suffered a measure of persecution.

Notwithstanding these arguments in support of the rendering *suffered,* there remain a few considerations which have moved many to part company with the A.V. at this point. First, it should be borne in mind that the verb used in the original is neutral. It really means no more than *to experience.* Whether the things which have been experienced were good or bad, favorable or unfavorable, is not indicated in the verb as such.[83] Then also the argument based upon the prevalent meaning of the word (namely, to suffer) in Paul's epistles (and elsewhere) loses much of its force as soon as it is discovered, after detailed examination of all the other Pauline passages in which it is found (I Cor. 12:26; II Cor. 1:6; Phil. 1:29; I Thess. 2:14; II Thess. 1:5; and II Tim. 1:12) that *in all these other cases* the context clearly demands, as translation, a form of the verb *to suffer,* but that the present context, on the contrary, points in the opposite direction. Both preceding and succeeding verses speak of past *favors:* the public proclamation of the Christ to the Galatians, the reception of the Spirit, and the occurrence of miracles in their midst. See also Gal. 4:14, 15. It is in *this* general context that Paul asks, "Did y o u experience so many things *in vain* (that is, *to no effect*)?"

The implied lesson, always applicable, is surely this, that the Lord wants everyone to profit spiritually by the experiences through which he has passed. He wants his people to use those experiences—in the present case *blessings,* but the lesson applies to *all* experiences—to good advantage. In the old dispensation Laban, though he refers to what he has learned from experience, made a selfish application (Gen. 30:27). The Galatians likewise were showing by their erring ways that theirs was not the proper response. On the other hand, David, reflecting on God's mercies, proves that these tokens of divine love had not been lost on him. He said, "Who am I, O Lord Jehovah, and what is my house, that thou hast brought me thus far?" (II Sam. 7:18). Cf. also Ps. 103; 116; 119:67; Luke 17:11-19; Acts 3:23-31; I Tim. 1:12-17; and Rev. 15:2-4. Paul adds: **if (it be) really in vain.** Some interpret this to mean, "If (it be) only in vain and not worse than

---

[83] Greek authors at times used an adverbial modifier—εὖ, κακῶς—to indicate whether the experience was good or bad.

in vain." I cannot agree with this—rather harsh (?)—interpretation. Gal. 5:10 definitely shows that Paul had not given up hope in connection with the Galatians. Even now he regarded them as being *his* "dear children" (Gal. 4:19), yes, as *God's* dear—but grievously erring—children. I agree with Calvin's remark on this verse: "But to mitigate the severity of this complaint, he [Paul] adds, 'if (it be) really in vain,' thus inspiring their minds with the expectation of something better, and rousing them to the exercise of repentance." Thus also Berkhof, Lightfoot, Luther, and most commentators. The opposite view is defended by Ridderbos (among others), *op. cit.*, pp. 115, 116.

5. As the word "accordingly" indicates, Paul now returns to the question which he had asked previously (see verse 2), changing the second person to the third, and the past tense to the present, for heightened effect: **He, accordingly, who supplies the Spirit to y o u and works miracles among y o u (does he bring this about) because y o u do what (the) law demands or because y o u believe (the) gospel message?** [84] Note the addition: "and works miracles among y o u." Instead of "among y o u" one can also translate "within y o u." This means that the *miracles, forces,* or *powers* of which the apostle makes mention can be viewed either as *outward charismata* (*special gifts*), such as healing, prophecy, tongues, interpretation of tongues (I Cor. 12:10; II Cor. 12:12), or as *inward moral and spiritual endowments,* such as faith, hope, and love. There would seem to be good reason to believe that Paul had both of these groups in mind, for when he himself enumerates the various blessings which the Holy Spirit had bestowed on another church, he proceeds, by a very easy transition, from the first group (in I Cor. 12) to the second (in I Cor. 13). Blessings of both kinds had been bestowed—yes, *liberally bestowed* [85]—upon the Galatians. But had they been imparted as a result of obedience to law or as a result of faith in the Lord Jesus Christ, as set forth in the gospel? And if the latter, as was most certainly true, then why are the Galatians turning away from *faith* to *works,* from *the Fountain* to *the broken cistern* that holds no water? "O foolish Galatians!" "O equally foolish modern man!"

---

[84] Or: "(does he bring this about) as a result of law-works or as a result of faith-inspired listening?" For a discussion of these different renderings see on verse 2.
[85] For the meaning of ἐπιχορηγέω see N.T.C. on Philippians, p. 74, footnote 50.

Chapter 3

Verses 6-14

Theme: *The Gospel of Justification by Faith apart from Law-works Defended against Its Detractors*

II. *Its Vindication: both Scripture—i.e., the Old Testament—and life (experience, past history) bear testimony to its truth*

B. The law (Deut. 27:26) pronounces a curse upon the disobedient. Christ Crucified, by bearing this curse (Deut. 21:23), redeemed us from it, so that we are saved through *faith* in him. Abraham, too, was justified by faith (Gen. 15:6), and blessed with him are all those who are of faith, according to God's promise (Gen. 12:3; 18:18; 22:18; Hab. 2:4).

6 (It is) even as (recorded): "Abraham believed God, and it was reckoned to him for righteousness." 7 Know then that those that are of faith, it is they who are sons of Abraham. 8 Now Scripture, foreseeing that it was by faith that God would justify the Gentiles, preached the gospel beforehand to Abraham, (saying): "In you all the nations shall be blessed." 9 Therefore, those that are of faith are blessed with Abraham, the man of faith.

10 For as many as rely on law-works are under a curse; for it is written, "Cursed (is) everyone who does not continue in all the things that are written in the book of the law, to do them." 11 Now it is evident that by law no one is justified before God, for "The righteous shall live by faith." 12 But the law does not belong to faith; on the contrary, "He who does them shall live by them." 13 Christ redeemed us from the curse of the law, having become a curse for us—for it is written, "Cursed is everyone who is hanging on a tree"—14 in order that the blessing of Abraham might come to the Gentiles in Jesus Christ, in order that we might receive the promised Spirit through faith.

3:6-14

B. *Faith: blessing . . . works: curse. The promise to Abraham*

For the idea that justification—hence, salvation in all its fulness—is obtained by way of faith and not by reliance on law-works Paul now appeals to Scripture, and first of all to the story of Abraham. In fact, the present section begins and ends with a reference to Abraham (verses 6-8, 14). We may well believe that throughout this entire paragraph (3:6-14), and, in a sense, throughout the entire chapter (cf. verses 15-18, 29), Abraham is never absent from the apostle's mind. Paul probably selected the scriptural references to Abraham in order to show *a.* that already at the very beginning of Israel's history it is clearly evident that God had chosen this one nation in order that in and through its great "seed" it might not only receive a blessing but also become a blessing to *the world;* and *b.* that equally from the very beginning the divinely appointed means of receiving this blessing, so as to be able to impart it to the nations, was *faith,* not works.

6. Accordingly, Paul writes: (**It is**) **even as** (**recorded**): "**Abraham believed God, and it was reckoned to him for righteousness.**" Probably an additional reason for devoting so much attention to Abraham was the fact that the opponents were constantly boasting about their descent from Abraham, as if this biological circumstance would give them a higher rating with God (Acts 15:5; Gal. 2:3; 5:2, 3; 6:12, 13, 15; cf. Matt. 3:9; Luke 3:8; John 8:33, 39, 40, 53), and as if the *righteousness* which Jehovah had "reckoned" to Abraham (Gen. 15:6) had been a *debt* which God owed him for his *work*

(cf. Rom. 4:4).[86] So Paul refers to this very passage from Genesis and shows that it teaches the exact opposite, and places the emphasis on *faith, not* on *work.* "Abraham believed God," that is, believed what God had spoken. Moreover, this faith, says Paul, in complete harmony with Gal. 3:1-5, was not a matter of merit on Abraham's part, but was by God graciously "reckoned" or "imputed" to him for righteousness. Also, if the opponents imagine that for their emphasis on the necessity of *circumcision* as a means unto salvation they can appeal to the story of Abraham (Gen. 17:23-27), let it then be emphasized that *the patriarch's justification preceded his circumcision* by many years (Gen. 15:6; 16:16; 17:24). Righteousness was reckoned to him not after but long before he had been circumcised (Rom. 4:9-12); so that, as a result of this prior justification, he became the father of *all* believers, the uncircumcised as well as the circumcised. That, in brief, is Paul's argumentation, according to Gal. 3:6-10 as illumined by Rom. 4:1-12.

Abraham's life is, in fact, an illustration of the manner in which men, in all ages, are saved. *Confidence* in God, come what may, and *resulting obedience* to God's revealed will, characterize Abraham's life. Of these two—confidence and obedience—the former is basic throughout. Abraham obeyed because he believed. He heeded God's command because, *first of all,* he trusted God. The *work* of obedience proved that the confidence was genuine.[87]

Abraham's faith is being constantly put to the test. By God's grace he triumphs again and again. When God appears to him in Ur of the Chaldeans (Acts 7:3; cf. Gen. 11:28-32) he is told to leave country and kindred. Fully trusting that God will make all things well, he obeys. When Jehovah appears the second time, in Haran of Mesopotamia (Gen. 12:1), the test is even more severe: Abraham[88] must leave his father's house. Again he trusts and obeys (Heb. 11:8). It is at this time that he receives the wonderful promise, "In you shall all the families of the earth be blessed." Here we notice that God's particularism—in selecting Abraham from among all of mankind—had a universalistic purpose: the salvation of men of every nation. At Shechem in the land of Canaan Jehovah appears again, this time with the promise, "To your *seed* I will give this *land*" (Gen. 12:6, 7). This promise constitutes another test of faith, for Sarai is barren (Gen. 11:30), and the Canaanite, who was not at all eager to yield his soil to a stranger, was then in the land. Again Abraham believes, and builds an

---

[86] For λογίζομαι, here ἐλογίσθη ("it was reckoned") see Heidland, Th.W.N.T., Vol. IV, especially pp. 293, 294.
[87] It is for this reason that James (2:20-24), with his stress on *works,* is able to make use of this same passage (Gen. 15:6) and to apply it to prove his point, doing so without coming into any real conflict with Paul.
[88] Until his name is changed he is called "Abram" (Gen. 17:5).

altar to Jehovah. After an unhappy incident in Egypt (Gen. 12:10-20), in which the weaker side of the man's character becomes manifest, Jehovah appears to him at Bethel. This occurred when Abraham had separated himself from Lot (Gen. 13:1-13). "God's friend" (James 2:23) is promised *a.* all the land which he sees, extending in every direction, and *b.* a seed as the dust of the earth (Gen. 13:14-18). But Abraham himself during his lifetime did not see the fulfilment of these promises. He lived *by faith* (Heb. 11:18-13). After his return from the slaughter of Chedorlaomer and his associates the word of Jehovah comes to Abraham in a vision, saying, "Fear not . . . I am your shield and your exceeding great reward." Offspring is promised to him as the stars in multitude. There follows the passage which Paul quotes here in Gal. 3:6 (cf. Rom. 4:3, 20, 22; James 2:23): "Abraham believed God, and it was reckoned to him for righteousness." Subsequently, to Abraham, aged ninety-nine, the promise is repeated (Gen. 17). With him, as prospective father of a numerous race, the covenant of grace is established (17:7). Even before the promised child's birth it is already given a name (17:19). A little later the very time of the birth is revealed to Abraham and his wife (18:10). Abraham, though overcome with wonder, continues to cling to God's promise. Isaac is born, Abraham being now a centenarian (21:1, 2, 5).

The most excruciating test of Abraham's faith occurs when God says to him, "Now take your son, your only son, whom you love, even Isaac, and go to the land of Moriah, and offer him there as a burnt offering upon one of the summits which I will indicate to you" (Gen. 22:2). Yet Abraham knows that Isaac is the very son who, in the line of descent, must some day produce "the seed" (as to his human nature), the very One in whom all the nations of the earth were to be blessed! How then can God command Abraham to offer up Isaac? By divine grace the father of all believers sustains even this fearfully bitter trial. He triumphs through faith in God, being deeply convinced that God was able even to raise up Isaac from the dead (Heb. 11:19). His faith is gloriously rewarded.

It is with this climax of Abraham's faith (Gen. 22) that James in his epistle links Gen. 15:6. He had every right to make this application, for whether Abraham professes his faith at the terebinths of Mamre, at the tamarisk of Beer-sheba, or on a high hill in Moriah, that marvelous confidence is still the same subtle chain that binds him to the Infinite, the same resting on the promises, the same looking forward to the city with the solid foundations, whose Architect and Builder is God. Paul, on the other hand, leaves Gen. 15:6 in its own historical context, as is clear from Rom. 4:3, 10. For Paul's reasoning, both in Galatians and in Romans, this actual historical context was very meaningful, since, as has been indicated, it showed that *even before his circumcision* Abraham's faith was already reckoned to him for righteousness. Hence, it also proved that circumcision was not nearly as important as the Judaizers were trying to make it appear!

Two questions demand an answer, however. The first one is this: "Is not forensic righteousness or justification a matter of the imputation of Christ's righteousness to the sinner? But if this be true, then how is it that here in Gal. 3:6 (cf. Rom. 4:3, 20, 22), as in Gen. 15:6, Abraham's *faith* is said to have been reckoned for righteousness, and this without any reference to Christ? Does not Christ figure in this account of imputation? Or must a reference to him be artificially superimposed upon the story or dragged into it?" The answer is: Scripture itself shows us the Christ in the story. He is there, for all to see who are willing to see. Even better: it is Christ himself who reveals himself with respect to this story. It was he who said to the hostile Jews of his day, "Abraham, y o u r father, was extremely happy that he was to see my day, *and he saw it and rejoiced*" (John 8:56). When the promise concerning a son was made to Abraham, the latter believed, therefore, that in the line of Isaac "the blessed seed" would at length arrive through whom God would bless all the nations. Thus, as is stated clearly in Heb. 11:13, Abraham (and others before and after him) "died in faith, not having received (the fulfilment of) the promises, but *having greeted them from afar.*" See N.T.C. on John 8:56, Vol. II, pp. 64–66.

It is not necessary, however, to establish to what extent Abraham had received clarity with respect to the coming Redeemer and the task assigned to him by the Father. It is far more important to take note of the fact that Paul himself, here in Gal. 3, links the promise that was given to Abraham with Christ and his redemptive work (verses 13, 14, 16, 22, 29). For Abraham also, therefore, the real basis of justification—pardon for sin, right standing before God, adoption as a son—was Christ's voluntary and vicarious sacrifice. For him, too, faith was the hand that laid hold on God's promise, however dimly apprehended. It is in that sense that Gen. 15:6 and Gal. 3:6 must be understood.

The second question, which also is being asked again and again is this: "Does Paul have any right, in his defense of faith over against law-works, to appeal to the faith of Abraham, which, after all, is mentioned in an entirely different setting?" A quick, true, and also at times the only possible, answer would be that it was the Holy Spirit who inspired both Moses and Paul, both Genesis and Galatians, and who therefore had the right to apply his own previous utterances to new situations. Having granted this, however, must it not be added that *basically* the two situations were very similar? When, step by step, we followed the life of Abraham up to Moriah, did it not become clear that (with few exceptions) he was constantly rejecting the flesh for the Spirit, the earthly in favor of the heavenly, the visible in the interest of the invisible? Did he not do exactly this when, purely at God's bidding, he left his home and kindred for regions unknown; again when he rejected the well-watered Plain of the Jordan, giving Lot first choice;

and once more when, in obedience to God, the God in whom he trusted, he even suppressed his strong and natural desire to keep alive his own dear and long-awaited son, in order that he might do God's bidding with respect to him? Is it not clear then that Abraham's chief desire was to lean for his salvation entirely on God and his will, and not on the arm of "flesh"? And was not the latter, namely, leaning on the arm of flesh, exactly what the Judaizers of Paul's day were doing when, prompted by fleshly considerations (Gal. 6:12), they continued to demand that the Gentiles supplement their faith in Jesus with fleshly trust in fleshly ordinances? Over against all those who placed their confidence in *flesh*—anything apart from Christ on which one relies—both Abraham and Paul manifested their *faith,* and were able to say, "We look not at the things that are seen but at the things that are not seen; for the things that are seen are temporal, but the things that are not seen are eternal" (II Cor. 4:18). Therefore the appeal to Gen. 15:6 is not only fully justified but even natural.

7. Paul continues: **Know[89] then that those that are of faith, it is they who are sons of Abraham.** To be "of faith" means to be characterized or controlled by faith, to have *trust in God* as one's guiding principle. When this can be truly affirmed of persons, then they are sons of Abraham; and if sons then also heirs, true partakers of the spiritual promise that was made to Abraham. Note the emphasis on the fact that they, *they alone* but also *all of them,* are the true sons of Abraham.

What Paul is writing was nothing new. Christ in his teaching had emphasized the same truth, namely, that not physical descent but spiritual likeness makes a person a true son of Abraham. Those are sons of Abraham who do the works of Abraham (Luke 19:9; John 8:39, 40; cf. Matt. 8:11, 12). And John the Baptist had taught similarly (Matt. 3:9; Luke 3:8). Just as it is true that to be a child of God one must be like God (Eph. 5:1; I John 2:29; 3:1, 8, 9), so also it cannot be denied that to be a son of Abraham one must be like Abraham, imitate his conduct, and thus become a partaker of his blessedness. Therefore, even though a man should be a Hebrew of Hebrews, he is not, in the spiritual sense, a son of Abraham unless he be a true believer. Conversely, if he be a true believer in the Lord Jesus Christ, he is a son of Abraham, whether he be a Gentile or a Jew by race.

8. Continued: **Now Scripture, foreseeing that it was by faith that God would justify the Gentiles, preached the gospel beforehand to Abraham, (saying): "In you all the nations shall be blessed."** In the words "Scripture foreseeing . . . preached the gospel beforehand" we have a very emphatic identification of

---

[89] Though construing γινώσκετε as a present indicative yields a good sense (for example, "You are able, therefore, to draw the conclusion"), the imperative is more immediately understandable: the Galatians were forgetting that in the sight of God racial distinctions had no value, that faith was all that really mattered. Hence, they are called back to their duty of realizing this truth.

God and his Word: what Scripture promises God promises, for he is the Speaker. Since the Holy Spirit is Scripture's Primary Author the conclusion is inevitable that God and his Word are most closely connected. The thing *foreseen,* because it had been thus ordained before the foundation of the world (Eph. 1:4, 11), was that it was "by faith"[90] and not "by works" that God would justify the Gentiles. If the Galatians would only understand this, they would not allow themselves to be misled by the Judaizers. "By faith" means "by trustfully receiving" God's gift out of his hand. It is thus, thus *only,* that the nations of the world were to receive pardon, right standing in the sight of God and his holy law, and adoption as sons; in a word: justification. This precious doctrine had been previously "gospeled" to Abraham. It had been proclaimed to him as good tidings of great joy for the entire world. This promise, though always valid, was to be realized *on an international scale* with the coming of Christ and of the dispensation which that coming would usher in. The content of the promise proclaimed to Abraham, recorded in words varying slightly but always essentially the same, was this: "In you all the nations shall be blessed" (Gen. 12:3; 18:18; 22:18). The blessing of which Paul is thinking is that of "justification by faith," as the context indicates; and this, in turn, was basic to all the blessings of salvation full and free. But inasmuch as the fulfilment of this promise, on a world-wide scale, was a matter of the future, it is readily understood that the phrase "in you" must be understood as Abraham himself also certainly understood it, namely, "in the Messiah," "the seed of the woman" (Gen. 3:15), Abraham's seed (see on verse 16).

9. A significant and logical conclusion is drawn. The assurances were: *a.* Those that are *of faith, they alone* but also *all of them* without exception, are sons of Abraham (verse 7); and *b.* "in Abraham," that is, "in his seed," shall *all the nations* be blessed, for it was foretold that it would be *by faith* that God would justify *the Gentiles* (verse 8). Conclusion: **Therefore, those that are of faith are blessed with Abraham, the man of faith.**[91] This conclusion

---

[90] The forward position of ἐκ πίστεως, indicating strong emphasis, is inexcusably lost in most translations.

[91] The English translation of such a simple phrase as τῷ πιστῷ Ἀβραάμ, with retention of the sound similarity which in the original characterizes the words οἱ ἐκ πίστεως, πιστῷ, is not easy. This is due to the fact that English has no suitable adjective that is built on the stem *faith.* To a modern reader A.V.'s "faithful Abraham" is somewhat confusing, since the word "faithful" in the sense of "full of faith" is today obsolete. Today a "faithful person" is simply one who is true to his word and shows loyalty, fidelity. It is only fair to state that several other languages, besides English, present the same difficulty. In German, however, the sentence runs very smoothly: *"Also werden nun, die des Glaubens sind, gesegnet mit dem gläubigen Abraham."* Dutch similarly: *"Zij, die uit het geloof zijn, worden dus gezegend tezamen met den gelovigen Abraham."* In English the best that can be done with τῷ πιστῷ Ἀβραάμ is to render it "Abraham, the man of faith" or, with R.S.V., "Abraham who had faith."

is warranted, for those who are "of faith" are the ones who exercise faith. As such they are the sons of Abraham; hence, they are blessed with him, the man of faith, who "in hope believed against hope, in order that he might become a father of many nations" (Rom. 4:18).

The passage (Gal. 3:6-9; cf. verses 14, 26-29) clearly teaches the important truth—by many so deplorably rejected—that the church of both dispensations, the old and the new, is *one*. All believers dwell in the same tent (Isa. 54:1-3). When the old dispensation ended it was not necessary to pitch a new tent; the old one was simply enlarged. All of God's children are represented by the same olive tree. The old tree did not have to be uprooted; new branches were grafted in among the old (Rom. 11:17). To each of the saints the same promise is given: "I will be your God." Note how this promise runs through both Testaments (Gen. 15:1, 2; 17:7, 8; Exod. 20:2; Deut. 5:6; Josh. 1:5; II Chron. 20:17; Jer. 15:20; 24:7; 30:22; 31:33; Ezek. 11:20; Zech. 8:8; 13:9; II Cor. 6:16; Heb. 8:10; Rev. 21:3, 7). All are saved by the same faith in the same Savior (Gen. 15:6; Isa. 53; Jer. 23:5, 6; Matt. 1:21; John 3:16; Acts 4:12; 10:43; 15:11; Rom. 3:24; 4:11). Apart from us those of the old dispensation do not reach perfection (Heb. 11:40). The names of all God's people are written in the same book of life. There are not two of those books: one for the old and one for the new dispensation; there is only one (Exod. 32:32, 33; Ps. 69:28; Dan. 12:1; Mal. 3:16, 17; Luke 10:20; Phil. 4:3; Rev. 3:5; 13:8; 17:8; 20:12, 15; 21:27; 22:19). All are foreknown, foreordained, called, justified (by faith), and glorified (Rom. 8:29, 30). All partake and will partake of the glories of Jerusalem the Golden, the city on whose gates are written the names of the twelve tribes of the children of Israel, and on whose foundation stones are engraved the twelve names of the twelve apostles of the Lamb (Rev. 12:12, 14). Cf. John 10:16; 17:11.

Once this is understood the Bible becomes a living book, for we begin to realize that when God says to Abraham, "Fear not . . . I am your shield and your exceeding great reward . . . your God," he is speaking also to us. This *central*[92] promise concerns all believers of both dispensations, for all those that are of faith are Abraham's children and heirs (Gal. 3:29). No clearer language could have been used than that which is found in Rom. 4:22-24. There Paul, having again made mention of the fact that Abraham's

---

[92] It is true, of course, that blessings of a more temporal character were also promised to Abraham—for example, "To thy seed will I give this land" (Gen. 12:7)—but it is the *central* promise, "I will be your God," with all that it implies as to salvation full and free in and through the promised Messiah, that is repeated throughout both the Old and the New Testament, as has been shown. To say that God's covenant with Abraham has no significance for us because in addition to its central promise it also comprised elements of a temporal and national character amounts to affirming that a river loses its identity when it decreases or increases in width or depth. Besides, the promised *land* typifies Canaan above. See on 3:16.

faith "was reckoned to him for righteousness," adds, "But not for his sake alone was it written that it was reckoned to him, but for our sake also."

10. Having shown that righteousness comes by way of faith, Paul now expresses this same truth negatively. What he states in verse 10 ff. may therefore be considered a corollary of the thought expressed in verses 6-9. Moreover, his attack against the false doctrine of the Judaizers, by which the Galatians were being influenced, thus increases in intensity and directness. It develops into a head-on collision: **For as many as rely on law-works are under a curse; for it is written: "Cursed (is) everyone who does not continue in all the things that are written in the book of the law, to do them."** This is a modified quotation from Deut. 27:26, which, according to the Hebrew reads: "Cursed (is) he who does not confirm the words of this law, to do them." In the Old Testament these words form the conclusion of the chapter that contains the curses that were to be pronounced from Mt. Ebal after the children of Israel would have passed over the Jordan. Now the curse which the law here pronounces is very real. Unless this be granted Gal. 3:13 will be meaningless. Nevertheless, it is a fact, often ignored, that in Deuteronomy not only the blessing which was to be shouted from Mt. Gerizim but also the curse occurs in a setting of love, the idea being that by means of proclamation of this blessing and curse Israel, tenderly addressed as "the people of Jehovah thy God," shall live a consecrated life to the glory of their merciful Deliverer. Paul's intentional departure from the Hebrew text when he writes, "the book of the law" may have been occasioned by his desire to emphasize the thought that the entire law, with all its precepts, considered as a unity, is meant. His reference to "everyone" and to "all the things" reminds one of the LXX rendering: "Cursed (is) every man who does not continue in all the words of this law, to do them." But these changes are not of an essential nature.

Now what was really the purpose of God's law? God gave his law in order that man, by nature a child of wrath, and thus lying under the curse (Gal. 3:13), as definitely declared in Deut. 27:26; John 3:36; Eph. 3:2, might be reminded not only of his unchanged obligation to live in perfect harmony with this law (Lev. 19:2), but also of his total inability to fulfil this obligation (Rom. 7:24).[93] Thus this law would serve as a custodian to conduct the sinner to Christ (Gal. 3:24; cf. Rom. 7:25), in order that, having been saved by grace, he might, in principle, live the life of gratitude. That life is one of freedom in harmony with God's law (Gal. 5:13, 14). However, the Judaizers were perverting this true purpose of the law. They were relying on law-works *as a means of salvation.* On that basis they would fail

---

[93] That total inability is brought to light even more sharply when the law is interpreted in its true, inner meaning. Thus Jesus showed that, in order to qualify as a murderer, being angry with one's brother would suffice, while similarly the lustful glance would suffice to make one an adulterer (Matt. 5:21-48).

forever, and Deut. 27:26, when interpreted in that framework, pronounced
God's heavy and unmitigated curse upon them; yes, *curse*,[94] not blessing.
The law condemns, works wrath (Rom. 4:15; 5:16, 18).

11. The fact that the opponents were diverting the law from its true
purpose and that this attempt was bound to result in tragic failure is
brought out clearly, as Paul continues: **Now it is evident that by law no one
is justified before God, for "The righteous shall live by faith."**[95] The law has no
power to subdue man's sinful tendencies. It cannot destroy the power of
sin within man (Rom. 8:3). How then can a sinner ever attain to the
ultimate blessing of being righteous in the sight of God? How can that
true, rich, full life in which man is at peace with his Maker, and abides in
sweet communion with him, ever be reached? The answer, which holds for
both dispensations, the old and the new, and for people of every race or
nationality, whether Gentile or Jew, is this: "The righteous shall live by
faith." It is the man who has placed his entire confidence in God, trusting
him implicitly, and accepting with gladness of heart the gracious provision
which that merciful Father has made for his salvation, it is he, he alone, who
shall live. This *living* consists in such things as: *a.* enjoying the peace of
God which passes all understanding (Phil. 4:7), in the knowledge that in
the sight of God's holy majesty the believer is *righteous* (Rom. 5:1; 8:15);
b. having fellowship with God "in Christ" (John 17:3); *c.* "rejoicing
greatly with joy unspeakable and full of glory" (I Peter 1:8); *d.* "being
transformed into the image of the Lord from glory to glory" (II Cor.
3:18); and *e.,* last but not least, striving to be a spiritual blessing to others
to the glory of God (I Thess. 3:8).

Now if the Judaizers had only paid more attention to the Word of God
and had accepted it, they would have known that not by trusting in his
own reasoning or in his own accomplishments but "by faith" the righteous
man attains to this bliss of "living." This had been clearly stated by
Habakkuk the prophet (Hab. 2:4). That man of God appeared upon the
scene of history during the reign of wicked Jehoiakim (608–597 B.C.). The
words "The righteous shall live by his faith" may even be considered the
theme of Habakkuk's prophecy. The divisions then would be: I. *Faith
tested:* the prophet's questions and Jehovah's answers (chapters 1 and 2),
and II. *Faith strengthened* by a vision shown in answer to the prophet's
prayer. What bothered Habakkuk was that it seemed as if wicked men were
getting away with their wickedness. Jehovah apparently tolerated such

---

94 In verse 10 (contrast beginning of verse 13) the word καταραν is used without
preceding article, no doubt to emphasize the quality of this curse, as if to say
"curse as opposed to blessing" (for the latter see verses 8, 9, 14).
95 The correct rendering is not "the righteous by faith" but "shall live by faith."
This is clear both from the preceding and the immediately following context; for
"live by faith" is contrasted with "justified by law" and with "live by (doing) them."

evils as the exploitation of the needy, strife, contention, violence, etc. So the prophet begins to ask questions. He addresses these questions to Jehovah. He complains, objects, and waits for an answer. Habakkuk's first question amounted to this, "Why does Jehovah allow the wicked in Judah to oppress the righteous?" Jehovah answers, "Evil-doers will be punished. The Chaldeans (Babylonians) are coming." But this answer does not quite satisfy the prophet. So he asks another one, which was tantamount to this: "Why does Jehovah allow the Chaldeans to punish the Jews, who, at least are more righteous than these foreigners?" The prophet stations himself upon his watch-tower and awaits an answer. The answer arrives: "The Chaldeans, too, will be punished. In fact *all sinners* will be punished . . . but the righteous shall live by his *faith*." It is his duty and privilege to trust, and to do this even then when he is not able to "figure out" the justice of Jehovah's doings. In this humble trust and quiet confidence he shall truly *live*.

But Jehovah does more than merely tell the prophet that he must exercise faith. He also strengthens that faith by means of a marvelous, progressive vision. Habakkuk sees the symbol of Jehovah's presence, descending from Mt. Paran. Having descended he stands firm and shakes the earth. The tent-hangings of Cushan and Midian are trembling and are being torn to shreds. One question worries the prophet: "Upon whom is Jehovah's wrath going to fall? Merely upon the realm of nature? Upon Judah perhaps?" Finally, the answer arrives: Jehovah destroys the Chaldeans and delivers his people.

So fearful and terrifying had been the appearance of Jehovah, so alarming the sound of the tempest, of crumbling mountains, etc., that the prophet is trembling in every part of his body. Nevertheless, having witnessed that Jehovah had descended for the defense of his own people, Habakkuk no longer questions the ways of God's providence. From now on he "waits quietly." He expresses his feelings in a beautiful Psalm of Trust: "For though the fig-tree shall not flourish. . . . Yet I will rejoice in Jehovah, I will joy in the God of my salvation."

In this case, too, as with the quotation from the story of Abraham (Gen. 15:6; cf. Gal. 3:6), I beg to differ from those who think that Paul's appeal to an Old Testament passage in his battle with the Judaizers is far-fetched. These interpreters seem to see little if any connection between "the faith versus law-works controversy" of Paul's day and the "faith versus Chaldean self-confidence contrast" described in Habakkuk's prophecy. It is an error, however, to restrict the latter contrast so narrowly. A rapid review of the contents of the Old Testament book has certainly shown that the quiet confidence which Jehovah so patiently teaches his servant is contrasted also—perhaps *especially*—with the prophet's own tendency to question the ways of God's providence. Fact is that the sinner is beset with enemies: the accusing voice of conscience, the doubting mind, etc. He must have peace. How will he obtain it? The Judaizers answer: "by trusting in his own works (circumcision, etc.)." Habakkuk, before he had fully learned the lesson which God was teaching him, gives evidence of answering: "by trusting in his own reason." That is why it was so difficult for him to harmonize the events that were happening in Judah with the existence of a holy God. That is why he had asked so many questions. But Habakkuk learned his lesson. When he sat down to write his prophecy he had learned it thoroughly, and gave an account of the experience through which he had passed. But whether a person trusts in his own *works* or in his own *reason,* in either case is he not trusting in "flesh"? As I see it, therefore, to clinch his argument Paul could not have chosen a better prophecy from which to quote than that of Habakkuk. The passage fits the situation exactly! In every age it remains true that "The righteous shall live by faith." "In quietness and confidence shall be y o u r strength" (Isa. 30:15).

12. Continued: **But the law does not belong to faith; on the contrary, "He who does them shall live by them."** In its own setting the included quotation from the book of Leviticus (18:5) is beautiful and comforting. It is introduced as follows: "Speak to the children of Israel and say to them, I am Jehovah y o u r God" (verse 2). This encouraging assurance is repeated in verse 4, and is followed by "Y o u must therefore keep my statutes and my ordinances; which, if a man do, he shall live by them: I am Jehovah" (verse 5). In summary this means: "As y o u r *sovereign* God I have a right to order y o u to keep my statutes, and as y o u r *faithful and loving God* I will help and strengthen y o u to observe these statutes out of gratitude." So interpreted, observing God's law is the believer's joy. Did not the Psalmist exclaim: "O how I love thy law! It is my meditation all the day"?

However, when one begins to *"rely* on law-works" (Gal. 3:10), as if such obedience to law amounts to a ticket of admission into the kingdom of heaven—and *that,* after all, is the context here in Galatians—he should bear in mind that, *so conceived, law* is the very opposite of *faith.* The two cannot be combined. Leaning on law means leaning on self. Exercising faith means leaning on Christ. As avenues by which men attempt to obtain salvation the two simply do not mix. They are thoroughly antagonistic. Paul himself supplies the best commentary: "But when the kindness of God our Savior and his love toward man appeared, he saved us, not by virtue of works which we ourselves had performed in a (state of) righteousness, but according to his mercy through the washing of regeneration and renewing by the Holy Spirit" (Titus 3:4, 5). Cf. John 1:17. Those who expect to be justified by observing all the statutes and ordinances of the law should remember that "He who does them shall live by them." They are even more foolish than those who imagine that they can quench their thirst by drinking salt water. Lev. 18:5 now becomes their accuser, but that is *their* fault!

13. The penitent sinner does not need to despair, however. To be sure, he is by nature under the curse of the law, as has been indicated. From this pitiable situation he is unable to deliver himself. But God has provided the remedy: **Christ redeemed us**—Gentiles as well as Jews (see verse 14)—**from the curse of the law, having become a curse for us.** Christ purchased us free from the curse of the law. He bought us back[96] from the sentence of condemnation which the law pronounced on us and from the punishment of eternal death which it exacted (Gen. 2:17; Deut. 30:15, 19; John 3:36; Rom. 5:12; 8:1; Eph. 2:3). He rescued us by the payment of a ransom (Exod. 21:30), the ransom price being his own precious blood (I Cor. 6:20; 7:23; Rev. 5:9; cf. I Peter 1:18, 19). He became a curse—that is, "an accursed one" —for us.

It is, indeed, difficult to conceive of the majestic Christ as being *accursed*. What! Jesus anathema? In the face of I Cor. 12:3 how would one dare to say that? This becomes all the more a problem when we consider that we generally—and rightly—associate the curse with *sin,* and Christ had no sin (Isa. 53:9; John 8:46; II Cor. 5:21; I Peter 2:22). The only solution is the one supplied by the beautiful words of Isa. 53:6: "Jehovah laid on him the iniquity of us all"; cf. also verses 10-12. Christ's curse-bearing, then, was vicarious: "Him who knew no sin he made to be sin for our sake, in order that in him we might become the righteousness of God" (II Cor. 5:21). This eminently scriptural truth of Christ's substitutionary atonement is being denied by ever so many people. It has been called "butchershop theology." Nevertheless, not only is it taught here in Gal. 3:13 in unmistakable language[97] but it is the doctrine of Scripture throughout (Exod. 12:13; Lev. 1:4; 16:20-22; 17:11; Ps. 40:6, 7; 49:7, 8; Isa. 53; Zech. 13:1; Matt. 20:28; 26:27, 28; Mark 10:45; Luke 22:14-23; John 1:29; 10:11, 14; Acts 20:28; Rom. 3:24, 25; 8:3, 4; I Cor. 6:20; 7:23; II Cor. 5:18-21; Gal. 1:4; 2:20; Eph. 1:7; 2:16; Col. 1:19-23; Heb. 9:22, 28; I Peter 1:18, 19; 2:24; 3:18; I John 1:7; 2:2; 4:10; Rev. 5:9; 7:14).

In support of the idea that Christ became a curse for us Paul appeals to Deut. 21:23: **for it is written, "Cursed is everyone who is hanging on a tree."** In its Old Testament context, however, that passage does not refer to death by crucifixion, which was not known among the Israelites as a mode of

---

[96] The verb is ἐξηγόρασεν. In the New Testament, besides its occurrence here and in 4:5, it is found only in Eph. 5:16 and Col. 4:5. But other verbs express the same or a very similar idea. See N.T.C. on Eph. 1:7 and on Col. 1:14.

[97] The idea of substitution, however, can hardly be derived solely from the preposition ὑπέρ. To say that in this passage ὑπέρ = ἀντί is precarious and wholly unnecessary. Entirely aside from the meaning of ὑπέρ the passage itself clearly teaches *a.* that we were under the law's curse; *b.* that we are now no longer under the curse; and *c.* that the reason for this changed situation is this: Christ took our curse upon himself. The logical conclusion, surely, is that Christ's curse-bearing was substitutionary.

capital punishment. It refers, instead, to the custom according to which after a wrong-doer had been executed, his dead body was nailed to a post or tree. But if, in the sight of God, the hanging of a *dead* body was a curse, how much more would not the slow, painful, and shameful death by crucifixion of a *living* person be a curse, especially when that dying one was experiencing anguish beyond the power of description! See Matt. 27:46.

14. The curse having thus been borne and lifted off our shoulders, the blessing can now flow forth: **in order that the blessing of Abraham might come to the Gentiles in Jesus Christ, in order that we might receive the promised Spirit through faith.** The two purpose clauses are co-ordinate. They cover the same ground, the second explaining the first. Among all the priceless gems sparkling in the crown of Abraham's blessing (the blessing he received) this surely was one of the most precious, namely, that through him—more precisely through his seed, the Messiah—a countless multitude of people was to be blessed. Through Christ and his Spirit (literally "the Spirit of promise," but this means "the promised Spirit," cf. Acts 1:4, 5; Eph. 1:13) the river of grace (cf. Ezek. 47:3-5; Ps. 46:4; Rev. 22:1, 2), full, flowing, freshening, fructifying, and free, would continue on and on, blessing first the Jews but subsequently men of every race, Gentiles as well as Jews. And to receive this blessing, namely, the realization of the promise, "I will be your God," all that is necessary is *faith,* confidence in Christ Crucified, for it is at Calvary that the fires of God's wrath have spent all their fury, and believers of every tribe and tongue and people and nation are therefore perfectly safe!

Chapter 3

Theme: *The Gospel of Justification by Faith apart from Law-works Defended against Its Detractors*

II. *Its Vindication: both Scripture—i.e., the Old Testament—and life (experience, past history) bear testimony to its truth*

C. This promise or convenant is superior to the law, for the latter reached us through mediation, the former came directly from God, and is still in force. The law, which came later, far from annulling the promise, serves it, by revealing our sinfulness and leading us to Christ. All who belong to Christ are Abraham's seed, heirs according to promise.

15 Brothers, I speak from a human standpoint: even a human testament, once ratified, no one sets aside or amplifies. 16 Now to Abraham were the promises spoken, and to his seed. He does not say, "And to the seeds," as (referring) to many, but as (referring) to one, "And to your seed," which is' Christ. 17 Now this is what I mean: a covenant that has been ratified by God, the law, which came into existence four hundred thirty years afterward, does not annul so as to make the promise ineffective. 18 For if the inheritance (is) due to law, it (is) no longer due to promise; but to Abraham it was through a promise that God graciously granted it.

19 Why then the law? By reason of the transgressions it was added, until the seed should come to whom the promise had been made, having been ordained through angels by the agency of an intermediary. 20 Now the intermediary does not represent (just) one party, but God is one.

21 (Is) the law then contrary to the promises of God? By no means. For if a law had been given that was able to impart life, then indeed righteousness would have come by law. 22 But Scripture has locked up the whole world under (the power of) sin, in order that as a result of faith in Jesus Christ the promise might be given to those who believe.

23 Now before this faith came, we were kept in custody under law, being locked up with a view to the faith that was to be revealed. 24 So the law became our custodian (to conduct us) to Christ, that by faith we might be justified. 25 But now that this faith has come we are no longer under a custodian.

26 For y o u are all sons of God, through faith, in Christ Jesus. 27 For as many of y o u as were baptized into (union with) Christ have put on Christ. 28 There can be neither Jew nor Greek; there can be neither slave nor freeman; there can be no male and female; for y o u are all one in Christ Jesus. 29 And if y o u belong to Christ, then y o u are Abraham's seed, heirs according to promise.

3:15-29

C. *The superiority of the promise over the law*

The promise is superior to the law because it was *earlier.* Moreover, being in the nature of a testament, already ratified and in force, this promise or covenant could not be set aside by the law which came so much later (verses 15-18). Besides, the promise came to Abraham *directly;* the law was given to Israel *indirectly,* by mediation (verses 19, 20). For both of these reasons the promise is superior to the law. The Galatians should remember this and repent of their error of listening to the Judaizers who exalt the law above the promise.

15. Paul writes: **Brothers, I speak from a human standpoint.** He is taking his illustration from human life so that the Galatians may understand all the better that those to whom they have been lending a listening ear are

133

false guides. Jesus also often made use of earthly stories (parables) to illustrate heavenly realities. Note that Paul calls the Galatians "brothers." This shows that when he exclaimed "O foolish Galatians" he was scolding them as a father or mother rebukes an erring son who is the object of tender love (cf. 4:19, 20). Continued: **even a human testament, once ratified, no one sets aside or amplifies.** It is a matter of common knowledge that among men a last will or testament, legally ratified, cannot be nullified. Nor can it be amplified: not a single codicil can be added to it. Then would not this be true all the more with respect to the covenant-promise which the immutable Jehovah made to Abraham and his seed? Was not this covenant in the nature of a testament?[98] Was it not re-affirmed to Isaac, Jacob, etc.? Did it not begin to go into effect immediately, namely, when "Abraham believed God, and it was reckoned to him for righteousness"? Surely, when God's will or testament has been thus decreed and ratified it cannot be set aside or changed. This logical deduction, already implied here in verse 15, is going to be clearly expressed in verse 17. However, the inviolability and immutability of God's promise will become all the more evident when it is understood first of all that, in the final analysis, it is a promise that concerns not physical Israel but Christ together with those who are "in him," for all the promises of God find their Yes in him (II Cor. 1:20; cf. Eph. 1:3). If this be understood it will be seen that the words which now follow are not really a parenthesis but part of the argument: **16. Now to Abraham were the promises spoken, and to his seed. He does not say, "And to the seeds," as (referring) to many, but as (referring) to one, "And to your seed," which is Christ.** Is this argument a bit of rabbinical casuistry, ingenious perhaps but unconvincing? Does not Paul know that even in Hebrew the word *seed* is a collective noun, so that no plural is needed to indicate more than one? See Gen. 15:5; 16:10; 22:17; 46:6; II Kings 11:1; II Chron. 20:7; Mal. 2:15; etc.[99] And as to the Greek word for *seed,* namely, *sperma,* does the apostle not realize that this word also is a collective noun (Matt. 22:24; Rom. 4:18; Acts 7:6; II Cor. 11:22), so that *spermata* (seeds) would have been unnecessary in any case? Shall we say then that in arguing against rabbinical adversaries Paul was using rabbinical methods that belonged to the exegesis of that happily bygone day and age? How can Paul say that the singular *seed* indicates one person, namely, Christ, when in Gal.

---

[98] The LXX translators used the word διαθήκη to render the Hebrew bᵉrîth. It appears thus nearly three hundred times. The New Testament also uses διαθήκη rather than συνθήκη, probably because the former stresses the one-sided character of God's disposition with respect to salvation for man and all that this implies. In Heb. 9:16, 17 and also here in Gal. 3:15 the context favors the rendering *testament.* Elsewhere the translation *covenant* is probably the best.

[99] Biblical Hebrew does not use the plural of *zera'* (see I Sam. 8:15) in referring to one's *descendants;* and even the Greek σπέρματα though occurring in classical literature, is elsewhere not plentiful (LXX Dan. 11:31; IV Macc. 18:1).

3:29 he himself uses that very word *in the singular* as a collective noun which refers to all believers? Besides, did he not realize that the seed promised to Abraham would be "as the stars in multitude" (Gen. 15:5; 22:17)?

As I see it, the answer is as follows:

(1) It is not true that the Hebrew word for *seed* always refers to more than one person. In Gen. 4:25 it refers to Seth, to him *alone;* in 21:13 to Ishmael; in I Sam. 1:11 to Samuel; in II Sam. 7:12 to Solomon as a type of Christ; so also in I Chron. 17:11. And obviously—see the context in each case—the Greek equivalent *sperma* has a singular reference not only here in Gal. 3:16 but also in 3:19; Acts 3:25; Rom. 9:7, 8; and Heb. 11:18.

(2) It should be readily admitted that Paul knew that both the Hebrew and the Greek word for *seed* (singular) often refer to more than one person. He knew that Abraham's seed would be as the stars in multitude. However, in keeping with the point which he is driving home, namely, that God promised salvation not to Abraham's physical descendants but to true believers, to them *all* (whether Jew or Gentile) and to them *alone,* he is saying that this great blessing is concentrated in *one* person, namely, Christ. It is in him, in him *alone,* that all these multitudes of believing Jews and Gentiles are blessed. It is in this sense that *seed* is singular, definitely not plural. It is true that the physical descendants of Abraham inherited the physical land of Canaan, according to God's promise (Gen. 12:7; 13:15; 15:18; 17:8; 24:7), but even Abraham already knew that there was more to this promise than appeared on the surface. The promised country on earth was the type of "the better country," the heavenly, reserved for believers in the Lord Jesus Christ, for them *all* and for them *alone,* as is beautifully stated in Heb. 11:8-16. Now the one and only heir of that "country" is Christ, for he is the Son by nature. It is by his grace that believers, as children by adoption, are joint-heirs with him (Rom. 8:17). And as for the basic promise, expressed from the beginning in spiritual terms, the promise according to which God assures Abraham that he will be his God and that in Abraham's seed all the nations of the earth will be blessed (17:7; 22:18), is it not very obvious that this promise also, in its fulfilment, was centered exclusively in *one* person, namely, Christ? The many are blessed in the One!

(3) In promising these rich spiritual blessings God had from the very beginning turned Abraham's attention away from the plural to the singular, from *seeds to seed:* "As for Ishmael, I have heard you . . . but I will establish my covenant with Isaac. . . . In Isaac shall your seed be called" (Gen. 17:20, 21; 21:12; cf. Rom. 9:7). Similarly, at a later time God made it very clear to Isaac and Rebekah that not in the line of Esau but in that of Jacob the promise would be continued (Gen. 25:23; cf. 27:27-29). Accordingly, Paul's distinction here in Gal. 3:16 between *seeds* and *seed* is based on the words which God himself addressed to the patriarchs.

(4) It appears to be clearly implied in such passages as John 8:56; Heb. 11:13, 17-19 that Abraham understood that Isaac would not himself be the Hope of mankind. He knew that Isaac's birth would pave the way for the coming of the real Messiah, the genuine *seed,* the *One* through whom God would bless all the nations. He was aware of the fact that the promised blessings would be concentrated in this one great person. At the time of Christ's birth even the highest court in Israel, the Sanhedrin, interpreted the prophecy of Micah 5:2 *personally,* that is, as referring to the birth of one definite person, Christ (Matt. 2:4-6). Is not the personal interpretation of Isa. 53—"Surely he has borne our griefs and carried our sorrows. . . . He was wounded for our transgressions, he was bruised for our iniquities," etc.—better by far than the exclusively *nationalistic?* Were not Isaiah and Micah contemporaries? And can we not go back beyond these two prophets, and their Messianic utterances, to II Sam. 7:12, 13? Does a reference to Solomon *exhaust* the meaning of the words, "I will establish the throne of his kingdom forever"? Does not also that promise refer to one exalted person, one greater by far than Solomon? Does not the same thing apply to Gen. 49:10? And does not this series of promises, everyone of which refers ultimately to one definite person, a person who had not yet arrived but was eagerly awaited, finally point back to Gen. 3:15, which concerns *the seed of the woman,* the very culmination of God's promise not only to Adam but also to Abraham?

The words which, according to Gen. 3:15, God addressed to the serpent —that is, to Satan—were as follows: "And I will put enmity between you and the woman, and between your seed and her seed; he shall bruise your head, and you shall bruise his heel." Is it not probable that Abraham knew this prophecy? It refers to the woman's *seed,* and here, too, the primary reference would appear to be to *one* person, though a further collective reference is not thereby ruled out. Dr. G. Ch. Aalders makes the following comment (my translation from the Dutch): "There is more here than merely this, that man will gain the victory over the serpent. . . . In that serpent a definite personality is being addressed. . . . And if the enemy whose discomfiture is here announced must be a definite personality, then would it even be possible that the One who conquers him could be other than also a definite personality? Even the contrast *head* and *heel* suggests that the struggle will finally be fought between two contestants. Also the Hebrew demonstrative pronoun [*that one* or *he*] strongly suggests that the conqueror is to be regarded as one person." Having pointed out that this protevangelium does not exclude the reference to a collective interpretation of the concepts "your seed" and "her seed," Aalders continues: "But in the end the figure of the Mediator stands in the foreground, and this so much so that in the words in which the final struggle is described there is definite mention of only one person, who is indicated by this seed of the woman.

The real struggle is won by no one else than by our Lord Jesus Christ"
(*Korte Verklaring, Genesis,* Vol. I, pp. 136–138).

As mentioned earlier, Abraham probably knew this prophecy. But more
important is the fact that the Holy Spirit, who inspired Galatians as well
as Genesis, knew what content he was pouring into Gen. 3:15; 13:15; 17:7,
8; 22:18; 24:7, as well as into Gal. 3:16. And is it not significant that in the
echo of Gen. 3:15 which we have in Rev. 12:1-6 the struggle is again *primarily* between the two personal antagonists: Christ and Satan? To be sure,
from this struggle "the woman" is not excluded (verses 6, 13); yet the
central figure, the One who really conquers, is *Christ.*

Accordingly, Paul's intention in writing, "He does not say, 'And to the
seeds,' as (referring) to many, but as (referring) to one, 'And to your seed,'
which is Christ," is to show *a.* that God's promise to Abraham, in its richest,
spiritual meaning, was to be fulfilled in connection with one—and not more
than one—definite person, Christ, the true seed; *b.* that all those—and only
those—who are "in him" are saved; *c.* that had the case been otherwise,
that is, had the promised blessings been dispersed indiscriminately among
an indefinite aggregate of individuals, such plurality would have been
definitely indicated; and *d.* that being thus concentrated unchangeably in
the one seed, Christ, nothing, not even the law, is able to nullify this promise, a truth to which the apostle gives further expression by continuing: **17.
Now this is what I mean: a covenant that has been ratified by God, the law,
which came into existence four hundred thirty years afterward, does not annul
so as to make the promise ineffective.** "Even a human testament, once ratified,
no one sets aside or amplifies" (verse 15); hence, this holds all the more
with respect to a *testament* or *covenant* (same word in the original) ordained and ratified by God. Between the giving of the promise and the
promulgation of the law at Sinai there had been an interval of "four hundred thirty" (Exod. 12:40) or, in round figures, "four hundred" years (Gen.
15:13; Acts 7:6). Surely a covenant that had been in effect for so long a
time, that partook of the nature of a testament, and had been established
by the unchangeable Jehovah, whose word never fails, could not be annulled
by the law!

With reference to these "four hundred thirty years" there is much difference of opinion. The question has been asked: Was there not an interval of
two hundred fifteen years between Abraham's call and Jacob's "descent"
into Egypt (Gen. 12:4; 21:5; 25:26; 47:9)? These two hundred fifteen years
plus the four hundred thirty years in Egypt (Exod. 12:40) add up to six
hundred forty-five years from Abraham's call to the exodus, and the same
number of years (plus a few months, Exod. 19:1) to the giving of the law
(Exod. 20). If the *repetition* of the promise of Gen. 12:1-3 in Abraham's
later years, with specific mention of *the seed* (Gen. 13:15; 15:5, 18; 21:12;
22:15 ff.; 24:7), be taken as the beginning of the interval between the

promise and the law, some years could be subtracted from the two hundred fifteen and from the total of six hundred forty-five, but even then the question would remain: How can Paul say that the law came into existence four hundred thirty years after the covenant-promise? Was not the intervening period considerably longer? Among the answers that have been suggested are the following:

(1) Paul errs, having been misled by the Greek Bible (LXX) which in Exod. 12:40 gives a total of four hundred thirty (or, according to another text, 435) years as the duration of the sojourn of the Israelites in Canaan *and* in Egypt (literally, "in Egypt-land and in Canaan-land").

(2) The period from the giving of the promise to Abraham, as recorded in Gen. 12, to the giving of the law at Sinai, actually covered only four hundred thirty years, as is clear from such passages as Gen. 15:16; Exod. 6:15-19 [Hebrew text: verses 16-20]; and Num. 26:57-59. Of this entire period two hundred fifteen years belong to the stay in Canaan, two hundred fifteen to the sojourn in Egypt.

I cannot accept either of these theories. The round figure "four hundred years," and the more exact figure "four hundred thirty years," for the sojourn *in Egypt* are too definitely established in Scripture as an indication of the time that the Israelites spent there to be so easily dismissed (Gen. 15:13; Acts 7:6; and Exod. 12:40 Hebrew text). Paul, thoroughly at home in the Old Testament, knew this. Besides, would not two hundred fifteen years have been too short a period for "three score and ten" people at the outset (Gen. 46:27) to grow into a nation so great that at the time of the exodus it had produced "about six hundred thousand men on foot (Exod. 12:37) besides the women and children? [100]

(3) We have here a case of "intentional understatement" made by Paul so that the Galatians may say: "Paul is certainly not exaggerating, for when the law finally came into existence the covenant had been in force much longer than four hundred thirty years, hence could certainly not be annulled."

As I see it, the best answer is the following:

(4) The covenant which God made with Abraham was repeated and confirmed in identical language in the promise addressed to Isaac and to Jacob. Compare, for example, Gen. 22:18 (to Abraham), 26:4 (to Isaac), and 28:14 (to Jacob), in each of which are found the words: "And in your

---

[100] As to the small number of "generations" mentioned or implied in Gen. 15:16; Exod. 6:15-19; and Num. 26:57-59, it is a well-known fact that the ancients counted generations differently than we do today: for one reason or another they would often skip certain ancestors in their count. In 15:16 one generation may represent one century. As to skipping generations, compare Matt. 1:8 with II Kings 8:25; 12:1, 2; 15:1. Therefore no solid argument as to the length of Israel's stay in Egypt can be based on such passages.

seed shall all the nations (in 28:14: "families") of the earth be blessed." "It may not be unreasonable to suppose that it was from such a time, at which the promise was confirmed (to Jacob) that Paul is measuring the interval which extends to the giving of the law at Sinai" (C. R. Erdman, *op. cit.,* p. 69). This, as I see it, best accounts for the figure "four hundred thirty years afterward."

The reasonable character of this explanation is evident from the fact that Scripture itself definitely points in this direction, for again and again it mentions Abraham, Isaac, and Jacob in one breath. Not only this, but in nearly every case when this occurs *it is in connection with the divine promise that the three patriarchs are grouped together as if they were one* (Gen. 28:13; 32:9; 48:16; 50:24; Exod. 3:16; 6:3; 32:13; Deut. 1:8; 9:5, 27; 29:13; 30:20; I Chron. 29:18; Matt. 22:32; Mark 12:26; Acts 3:13; 7:32).

18. It has been established, therefore, that justification, hence salvation in all its fulness, the entire "inheritance," is the result of God's promise, a covenant-promise that could not have been abrogated by Sinai's law, which did not enter into the picture until much later. Salvation, then, is not the result of law or law-observance. Neither is it possible to combine the two, as if *law* and *promise,* merit and grace, were twin sources of eternal bliss for God's children. Says Paul: **For if the inheritance (is) due to law, it (is) no longer due to promise; but to Abraham it was through a promise that God graciously granted it.** The Galatians will have to make up their minds once for all. They will have to choose between God's way and man's way of being saved. They must fully return to the position of faith in God and in his promise. In this connection there are especially four words that deserve emphasis, all of them underscoring the same idea, namely, that salvation is God's gift, not man's achievement:

(1) It is the result of God's *covenant,* and, as shown earlier, this covenant is of the nature of a *testament,* a sovereign *grant* (verses 15, 17). It is not a *contract* or *compact* reached after lengthy bargaining, bickering, and wrangling. It was God who established this covenant. It was he who stipulated the manner in which it would attain its purpose for man, namely, through faith. It is even God who grants this faith. He grants what he demands (Eph. 2:8).

(2) The main feature of this covenant is therefore God's *promise,* his solemn *assurance:* "I am (will be) your God," "In your seed I will bless you," "I will give you the land" (ultimately "the better land, Canaan above," as has been indicated).

(3) God's covenant with Abraham was therefore a "covenant *of grace.*" "To Abraham it was through a promise that God *graciously* granted it." Human merit has nothing to do with it. In fact, God's gift would be deprived of its gracious character if it were afterward made to depend on strict compliance with law.

(4) The promised salvation is an *inheritance*. Paul says, "If *the inheritance* (is) due to law, it (is) no longer due to promise." An inheritance is freely bestowed. It is a gift; hence, is not bought with money, nor earned by the sweat of human toil, nor won by conquest. Moreover, it is duly acquired (by right rooted in grace), and inalienable (cf. I Kings 21:3). As an inheritance it is future glory of which, however, the first instalment has even now become our possession (Eph. 1:13, 14).

Now it is certainly true that in the historical realization of the divine arrangement for man's salvation action proceeds from two parties: God and man. *God* makes the promise and points out the way in which it is to be fulfilled, namely, through faith (Gen. 15:1, 4, 5; 17:7; etc.). *Abraham* believes (Gen. 15:6; 17:1b, 9; etc.). God does not believe for him. When the Philippian jailer asked Paul and Silas, "Men, what must I do to be saved?" Paul did not answer, "Nothing at all, just wait until it pleases God to come and save you." What he did say was this, "Believe in the Lord Jesus, and you will be saved, you and your household" (Acts 16:30, 31). Nevertheless, this two-sidedness is completely subsidiary to the one-sided character of the covenant, as has already been indicated. If strict compliance with the demands of the law could have saved anyone, Paul certainly would have entered heaven by that gateway (Phil. 3:1-6). But the Lord had revealed to him the utter impossibility of success in this direction. No wandering sheep ever returns to the fold unless the Master finds him and brings him home.

19. This, however, raises a question: **Why then the law?** If the law given at Sinai was unable to impart righteousness, then what possible good could it do? Of what use was it? Perhaps the opponents had already asked that question. If not, they could be expected to ask it. Paul answers: **By reason of**[101] **the transgressions it was added**; that is, it was given to man in addition to the promise in order to bring about within his heart and mind an awakened sense of guilt. A vague awareness of the fact that all is not right with him will not drive him to the Savior. Only when he realizes that his sins are transgressions of the law of that God who is also his Judge and whose holiness cannot brook such *digressions,* such constant *stepping aside* from the appointed path, will he, when this knowledge is applied to his heart by the Holy Spirit, cry out for deliverance. "Where there is no law, there is no transgression," no stepping aside from the law (Rom. 4:15). "The law came in besides, that *the trespass*—the act of *falling away from* the proper course, as indicated by the law—might abound" (Rom. 5:20).

---

[101] Here χάριν probably means "by reason of," cf. Eph. 3:1; I John 3:12. The statement must be explained, as always, in the light of the context; see especially verse 24. This refutes the interpretation, favored by some, that Paul here views the law as a means of *checking* or *restraining* transgressions.

This—"that the trespass might abound"—has been interpreted to mean that the law actually makes a person a more determined wrong-doer than he ever was before. The more he is forbidden to steal, the more he will steal. Illustration: Boys pass an apple orchard a hundred times without attempting to pick one from the tree's overhanging branches. But let a sign be put up: "Those who steal apples will be prosecuted," and see if the pockets of these boys do not begin to bulge with apples!—Nevertheless, that is probably not the meaning here, but rather this: "Through the commandment sin becomes exceedingly sinful." It is *knowledge* of sin that comes through law (Rom. 3:20; 7:7, 13). The law acts as a magnifying glass. That device does not actually increase the number of dirty spots that defile a garment, but makes them stand out more clearly and reveals many more of them than one is able to see with the naked eye. "By reason of the transgressions," therefore, the law was added, so that when that law demands nothing less than perfect love for God and the neighbor, and the man sees clearly that there is very little of this love in his heart, he may by means of this realization be led to the Savior. This interpretation brings the present passage into harmony with another one taken from this very chapter (see on 3:24). It also blends with the words which immediately follow, namely, **until the seed should come to whom the promise had been made.** When by God's grace the sinner has learned to see himself in the light of the law as being damnable in himself, he yearns for Christ, the true seed, and for redemption in and through him. To this *seed* the blessing and the right and power to impart it had been promised. Therefore, while the law was given through Moses, grace and truth came through Jesus Christ (John 1:17), the One who entered the world in order to minister, and to give himself a ransom for many (Matt. 20:28; Mark 10:45). There was nothing wrong with the law. It had been given by God through Moses. But there was one thing which the law was unable to do: it was unable to pardon transgressors. It could point out but could not remove their sins. That mighty work in which God's justice and his love embrace each other was reserved for the Mediator.

With respect to the law Paul adds: **having been ordained through angels.** The law of Sinai was *ordained* or authoritatively decreed. By whom was it thus ordained? Though this is not stated here, it is clear from such passages as Rom. 7:22, 25; 8:7, that the law's Author was God himself. It was he who decreed it. "And God spoke all these words saying, I am Jehovah your God," etc. (Exod. 20:1 ff.).

Now a king's decree is issued, published, or promulgated *through* his servants. Moreover, these messengers do not always convey the king's order directly to the public at large. At times the sequence of communication is as follows: king, messenger, provincial governor, citizenry. Something of this nature must have happened also in connection with the giving of the law. We cannot be more precise. Where Scripture is silent, it is not proper for us to try to break this reserve. Did the holy angels communicate God's commands to Moses? Is that the meaning of Heb. 2:2: "the word spoken through angels"? Stephen also held that the angels were active in the giving of the law at Sinai (Acts 7:53). This belief may perhaps be traced back to Deut. 33:2, but the meaning of that passage, whether read according to the Hebrew text or according to the Septuagint, is not entirely clear. Farther than this we cannot go.[102] All kinds of speculations have been built up around the theme of angelic activity in connection with the giving of the law. It has been said, for example, that the angels had made the law their hobby, which they intended to defend against every encroachment. With the coming of Christ, so continues this theory, these angels became as it were, competitors of Christ, and tried to maintain the law over against the doctrine of salvation by grace. In the present passage, then, and in Gal. 4:3, 9, Paul is supposedly warning the Galatians against putting themselves in bondage again to these angels. However, the idea that Paul regarded the keeping of the law to be a bondage to angels is devoid of every shred of evidence. Paul never makes the angels responsible in any way for the idea of salvation through law-works. Here in Gal. 3:19 he clearly represents the angels as adding luster to the law. The point which the apostle is trying to drive home is of an entirely different nature, as will become clear in a moment. See also on 4:3, 9.

Whatever function the angels may have performed in connection with the giving of the law, the real intermediary between God and the people was Moses. The law was ordained through angels **by the agency**—literally, "in (the) hand"—**of an intermediary.** This would seem to be a clear echo of Deut. 5:5, where Moses says, "I stood between Jehovah and y o u at that time." The lesson, then, which Paul is teaching the Galatians is clearly this: the law given at Sinai, though ordained by God through his holy angels by the agency of Moses, and though, accordingly, holy, righteous, and good (Rom. 7:12; cf. 2:18; 8:7; 9:4), is inferior to the promise, for while *the law came indirectly from God to his people, the promise was made to Abraham (and thus to all believers) directly by God himself.* When a ruler—whether president, king, or queen—wishes to communicate a message to his people, there are all kinds of indirect avenues by means of which he is able to do this, but when the message is of supreme importance, he will unburden his very heart by addressing his people directly, today by means of radio or television. Thus also, the gospel of salvation by grace alone is so precious

---

[102] For example, to identify these angels with "the Angel" mentioned in Acts 7:38 or with "the Angel of Jehovah" of the Old Testament (Gen. 22:11; 48:16; etc.) is unwarranted. That God's holy angels are, in a sense, "ambassadors" is true, though also the passage in Josephus (*Antiquities* XV.v.iii) where this comparison is drawn, fails to shed light on the exact nature of the function of the angels at Sinai.

to the heart of the God to whom the impartation of this salvation meant nothing less than the agonizing death of his only Son, that he appeals to each of us directly and personally, saying, "My son—my daughter—give me your heart" (Prov. 23:26).

20. Moses, to be sure, was a great man. But God is greater by far. The Galatians must not permit the Judaizers to exalt Moses above God. Says Paul: **Now the intermediary does not represent (just) one party**—literally, "Now the intermediary is not of one"—**but God is one.** Instead of vexing the reader with the four hundred thirty different interpretations to which this passage has given rise, I shall immediately state the one which appears to me to be the most consistent with the context. It is this: Though a human intermediary may be ever so important, he is, after all, only a third party acting between two other parties. Moses served as a human link between God and the people. Such an intermediary lacks independent authority. God, however, is *One.* When he made his promise to Abraham—and through him to *all* believers, whether Jew or Gentile (Rom. 3:30!)—he did this on his own sovereign account, directly, personally. He was speaking from the heart to the heart.

21. Continued: **(Is) the law then contrary to the promises of God?** Paul has indicated that the inheritance was due to promise, not to law, and that law is, accordingly, inferior to promise. Must the conclusion then be drawn that the law is an enemy of the promise*s,* that is, of the oft-repeated, rich and varied promise of God? See on verse 16. Paul answers: **By no means** (literally, "Let it not be") or "That never," "Certainly not," "Perish the very thought." Continued: **For if a law had been given that was able to impart life, then indeed righteousness would have come by law.**[103] Only then when law and promise (works and grace) are both regarded as means whereby the sinner obtains salvation, can they be viewed as opponents. But as soon as it is understood that the two differ in their objectives—*the law* aiming to lead the sinner to Christ and his gracious promise; *the promise* "in Christ" aiming to save him—it becomes clear that they cannot be viewed as being in conflict with each other. By reason of human perversity the law is unable to deliver a man from the sentence of condemnation and to impart to him the blessing of justification (Rom. 8:2, 3). The law can never make a man spiritually alive, cannot regenerate him, or impart faith to him whereby he would be enabled to accept the righteousness of God in Christ. If a law had been given that could have done that, then, of course, righteousness would have come by law, but the law is not a vivifying power. It takes God's grace to function in that capacity. Phrasing it differently, it

---

[103] This is a *contrary to fact* or *second class conditional sentence,* relating to past time: εἰ with aor. indic. passive in the protasis, and ἄν with a past indicative in the apodosis. In such sentences ἦν may be regarded as aorist *in meaning.*

takes the promise of God, savingly applied to the heart by the Holy Spirit, to raise the dead to life (II Cor. 3:6, 17). As to the law, it is useful indeed. It accomplishes its very design by showing what it cannot accomplish! It causes the sinner to say, "Wretched man that I am! Who shall deliver me out of the body of this death?" Grace, already operative *in principle* when the question was asked, makes possible the answer, "I thank God through Jesus Christ our Lord" (Rom. 7:24, 25). Another way of expressing this truth is found in verse **22. But Scripture has locked up the whole world under (the power of) sin.** Did the law ever justify anyone? Did it ever set anyone free? "On the contrary," says Paul, "Scripture, in which the law plays such a prominent role, has locked up," that is, has shut in from every side without possibility of escape, "the whole world[104] under (the power of) sin." The words, "Scripture has locked up, etc." probably indicate that Scripture, that is, the Old Testament, has authoritatively declared that the whole world is under the power of sin; in other words, that sin is the jail-keeper who holds all men under the sentence of condemnation. These men are as truly chained as are prisoners with iron bands around their legs, bands that are fastened to chains that are cemented into the walls of their cells. Such spiritual convicts are unable to break their fetters. On the contrary, every sin which they commit draws tighter their bonds, until at last they are completely crushed (John 8:34; Rom. 6:23a; I John 5:19).

That this is indeed the picture that is drawn in the Old Testament is clear from such passages as the following: Deut. 27:26, already discussed (see on Gal. 3:10); Ps. 130:3, "If thou, Jehovah, shouldest mark iniquities, O Lord, who could stand?"; Ps. 143:2, "In thy sight no man living is righteous"; Isa. 1:5, 6, "The whole head is sick, and the whole heart is faint. From the sole of the foot even to the head there is no soundness in it, but bruises and sores and raw wounds"; and Jer. 17:9, "The heart is deceitful above all things, and it is exceedingly corrupt; who can know it?" Add to this Gen. 6:11, 12; 8:21; Job 40:4; Dan. 9:4 ff.; Zech. 3:3; as well as all those Old Testament passages that are quoted or alluded to by Paul in Rom. 3:9-18. And these are but a few. Many more could easily be added.

But, with the help of the Holy Spirit, the prisoners' very consciousness of their galling bondage and of their total inability to burst their chains, causes them to yearn for a divine Deliverer and to shout for joy when they hear his approaching footsteps. All this was in God's plan. Therefore Paul continues: **in order that as a result of faith in Jesus Christ the promise might be given to those who believe.** Who will want to be delivered unless he knows that there is something from which he needs to be delivered? But once men know this, and this knowledge has been sanctified to their hearts, they

---

[104] The neut. τὰ πάντα can refer to persons, and the present context favors the meaning "all mankind."

will hail the Rescuer, and place their trust in him, that is, in Jesus Christ, the Anointed Savior, the One whose very purpose *was* and *is* to save the lost (Matt. 1:21; 9:12, 13; Luke 19:10; I Tim. 1:15). This wonderful Redeemer does something for sinners that the law was not able to do. He sets the prisoners free, delivering them from the curse by taking it upon himself, and speaks peace to their hearts. In a word, he gives *the promise* to those who were perishing. The term "promise," as used here, must be interpreted in its fullest, richest sense, for the wretched ones not only receive a verbal promise, cheering tidings—"Be not afraid," "Only believe and all will be well"—but also the *fulfilment* of this promise; hence, justification by faith, salvation full and free, as a gift to all those who embrace Jesus Christ by means of simple trust apart from the works of the law.

23. Looking back from the vantage ground of faith in Jesus Christ, both Jew and Gentile had to admit that bondage to law had served the purpose of preparing them for this wonderful gospel of justification by faith alone, a thought which Paul expresses as follows: **Now before this[105] faith came, we were kept in custody under law, being locked up with a view to the faith that was to be revealed.** Note the slight transition from "locked up the whole world *under sin*" (verse 22) to "kept in custody *under law,* being locked up" (verse 23). The difference is not essential. If *sin* is the jail-keeper, then so is *the law,* for sin derives its power from the law (I Cor. 15:56). It is through the commandment that sin becomes exceedingly sinful (Rom. 7:13; see also 7:9 and 4:15).

When Paul says, "Before this faith came," he is not denying what he had before so emphatically affirmed, namely, that even during the old dispensation people were saved *by faith* (Gal. 3:6, 11, 17, 18). He is speaking now of faith in the incarnate Christ, the Deliverer already arrived.[106] Essentially there is no difference: the Object is still the same and the nature of the activity remains unchanged. The difference is this, that Abraham and all the other saints of the old dispensation looked *forward* to the coming Redeemer; Paul and his fellow-believers were able to look *back* to a Redeemer

---

[105] In connection with abstract nouns—faith, hope, love, etc.—the Greek (as also German, Dutch, and French) often uses the definite article where English would omit it. Thus the correct English rendering of the phrase "through the faith" of the original (verse 26) is "through faith." However, if the abstract quality has been mentioned in the immediately preceding context *and* the article's omission would lead to confusion, it is better to insert it—or the demonstrative "this" or "that"—in English. Hence, at the beginning of verse 23 I favor the rendering "this faith" (with Williams and N.E.B.), and toward the close of that verse "the faith" (with Williams), and again "this faith" in verse 25 (with Williams). On the use of the article in the original in such cases see Gram.N.T., especially pages 758 and 762.

[106] Some hold that "faith" must here be interpreted in the objective sense (religion, doctrine) as in 1:23. See also 6:10. However, the word obviously refers to the "faith in Jesus Christ" of the preceding verse, the subjective activity of believing in him.

who had already come into the flesh, had carried out his redemptive program on earth, and had returned to heaven, so that believers could now look *up* to him as the One who had been exalted to the Father's right hand, from which he was ruling the entire universe in the interest of the church.

Now *before* this faith in the Christ of history arrived, hence during the old dispensation, "we," says Paul, "were kept in custody" under law. God's *moral* law filled the hearts of the Jews with a sense of guilt and inadequacy. They were obliged to fulfil it, yet were unable to do so. Of course, even then there was a way of escape provided by the Lord himself, namely, trust in God's promise concerning the "seed," and thus salvation "without money and without price" (Gen. 3:15; 22:18; 49:10; II Sam. 7:13; Job 19:23-27; Ps. 40:6, 7; Isa. 1:18; 9:1, 2, 6; 40:1-5, 11; 53; 55:1, 6, 7; Jer. 23:6; Mic. 5:2; Zech. 13:1), but most of the Jews had failed to avail themselves of this glorious opportunity. They refused to grasp the hand that was extended to them, and instead began to look upon strict obedience to law as a means whereby they must try to obtain salvation *for* and *by* themselves. Not only the moral law must be kept, however, but also the *ceremonial*. The latter was interpreted and re-interpreted. It was "embellished" by the rabbis, augmented almost beyond recognition, until its observance had become an oppressive burden, a galling yoke, from which no mere man offered any way of escape. Because of their own stubbornness the law, in its most comprehensive sense, thus *held* the Jews *in strictest custody;* just as, for example, the governor under king Aretas *rigidly guarded* (same word in the original) the city of Damascus, in order, as he thought, to prevent any possibility that Paul might escape. The Jews, then, were *locked up*, shut in from every side (as in verse 22). But God's grand design was to be openly revealed, so that the stubbornness of men, for which they, they alone, were responsible, would lead to the open display of *his* mercy: "being locked up *with a view to* the faith that was to be revealed" in connection with the coming and work of the Redeemer and the outpouring of his Spirit.

As to the manner in which the strict custody of the law could be a means of leading a formerly self-righteous Pharisee to humble faith in Christ, note this autobiographical fragment, in which some years later Paul was going to describe himself as having been in his pre-conversion years "as to law a Pharisee, as to zeal persecuting the church, as to legal righteousness having become blameless." He was going to continue: "Nevertheless, such things as once were gains to me these have I counted loss for Christ. Yes, what is more, I certainly do count all things to be sheer loss because of the all-surpassing excellence of knowing Christ Jesus my Lord, for whom I suffered the loss of all things, and I am still counting them refuse, in order that I may gain Christ, and be found in him, not having a righteousness of my own, legal righteousness, but that (which is) through faith in Christ, the righteousness (which is) from God (and rests) on faith" (Phil. 3:5-9).

The question might be asked, "But in view of the fact that the Galatians, for the greater part, had been won for Christ from the *Gentile* world (Gal. 4:8-11), how can the given explanation, which depicts a change from legal righteousness to all-out surrender to Christ, suit the concrete situation with which the addressed confronted Paul? Are we not forgetting that the apostle was writing not to Jews but to those who were Gentiles by race and formerly also by religion?" The answer would be:

(1) It is clear that these Gentiles had of late been in very close contact with the Judaizers (1:6-9; 3:1, 2; 4:10, 17, 21-31; 6:13-15).

(2) Even before this, by means of the synagogue-service, which a considerable number of them had attended (Acts 13:16, 44, 45; 14:1), and also by means of daily contact with Jews, the Galatians had become acquainted with a somewhat adulterated version of the Jewish religion, a religion which, in its modified presentation, insisted on strict compliance with law *as the way to salvation*.

(3) Even apart from any contact with the Jews or with Judaizers, was not the attempt to reach life's fulfilment by purely human means (such as sacrifices to appease the gods, the infliction of self-torture) characteristic of paganism? In their "Do it yourself" philosophy of obtaining salvation, *all* Galatians, of whatever racial or religious origin, were basically equal. Therefore all needed this letter. And since this same sinful tendency, one that leads but to bankruptcy and despair, is a true description of every human heart as it is by nature, this epistle is ever up-to-date in the lesson which it teaches.

God's holy law daily confronts every man with a "must" which he is unable to fulfil and with the threat of punishment if he does not fulfil it. The clear revelation of God's love revealed in the birth, teaching, suffering, death, burial, resurrection, ascension, and coronation of Christ and in the outpouring of the Holy Spirit was necessary to bring about a mighty change on earth. Not that even then the bulk of the people accepted the proffered grace (John 1:5, 10, 11). But compared to the rivulet of grace during the old dispensation there was a mighty stream now. "The church in the wilderness" (Acts 7:38) was, without loss of identity as to essence, being replaced by the world-conquering church (Rev. 17:14; cf. 20:1-3; Luke 10:17, 18; John 12:31, 32). And the tension which had been generated by the discipline of the law had contributed its very significant share to the bringing about of this change. It had prepared the hearts of multitudes for the reception of Christ and his promise. Paul expresses this thought by means of a striking figure: **24. So the law became our custodian (to conduct us) to Christ, that by faith we might be justified.** In view of the explanation of verse 23 little need be added. The rendering "schoolmaster" (A.V.) is not a happy

147

one. It is true that the original calls the law "our pedagogue," but that word did not then have the meaning which it has now in our language.[107] It cannot be denied that in the execution of his duties the ancient "pedagogue" might also impart some elementary and useful instruction on various matters, but that was not his primary function. In the figure here used the "pedagogue" is the man—generally a slave—in whose custody the slave-owner's boys were placed, in order that this trusted servant might conduct them to and from school, and might, in fact, watch over their conduct throughout the day. He was, accordingly, an *escort* or *attendant,* and also at the same time a *disciplinarian.* The discipline which he exercised was often of a severe character, so that those placed under his guardianship would yearn for the day of freedom. And, as has been shown (see the explanation of verses 19, 22, and 23), that was exactly the function which the law had performed. It had been of a preparatory and disciplinary nature, readying the hearts of those under its tutelage[108] for the eager acceptance of the gospel of justification (for which concept see on 2:15, 16) by faith in Christ. Continued: **25. But now that this faith has come we are no longer under a custodian.** The time arrives when the boy is no longer a mere child. The grim discipline of his earlier days is not necessary any more. The rod can be laid aside, the custodian given a different assignment. Some parents seem to forget that little children grow up, and that there comes a time when from the discipline of *outward precepts* they can advance to the free expression of *inner principles.* Similarly the Judaizers, who were upsetting the Galatians, were forgetting that the tutelage of the law could not continue forever. They were ignoring the fact that when Christ himself had arrived, and trust in him had been established, those who had embraced him by this true and living faith had attained to majority and freedom.

26. This new-found freedom in Christ has nothing to do with race or former religion. Hence, Paul's "we" (verse 25) easily changes into "y o u" (verse 26), as he continues: **For y o u are all sons of God, through faith, in Christ Jesus.**[109] In proof, therefore, of the fact that the Galatians, too, are no

---

[107] In German one might say that the law is not here described as our *Schulmeister* but rather as our *Zuchtmeister;* or in Dutch: not as our *schoolmeester* but rather as our *tuchtmeester.*

[108] The rendering "the law became our *tutor,*" favored by many, is entirely proper, provided the figure be understood in the sense of *the guardian of a boy or girl below the age of puberty or majority,* and not in the sense which today many immediately attach to it, namely, that of *private instructor.*

[109] Thus the order of the words as in the original is maintained (as in A.R.V.); and at the same time, by the use of commas, room is provided for the probability that the phrase "in Christ Jesus" must here be regarded as a modifier of the entire statement. Another way of arriving at the same result would be to shift the phrase "in Christ Jesus" from the end of the sentence to the beginning: "For in Christ Jesus y o u are all sons of God through faith" (cf. R.S.V.). Although it is certainly possible to regard the phrase in question as modifying only the concept *faith* (cf.

longer under a custodian (verse 25) Paul emphasizes that they are no longer immature children but "in Christ Jesus" mature sons, yes, "sons of God," with all the rights and privileges implied in that term, and that this new state and condition has come about "through faith."

27. Let no one deny that in vital union with Christ *all* believers, Gentiles as well as Jews, are immediately sons of God, true Christians. Let no one deceive the Galatians into thinking that in order to become Christians they must first become Jews. Says Paul: **For as many of y o u as were baptized into (union with) Christ have put on Christ.** The "in Christ" relationship, therefore, expressed in verse 26 and here repeated in slightly altered form, is all that matters. And that holds for anyone, for the words "as many as" here in verse 27 are as wide in scope as is "all" (that is, "all believers") in verse 26. It should not be any matter of controversy that "being baptized into (union with) Christ" means more than being baptized with water, for surely not all those who were the objects of the outward administration of this sacrament have actually "put on Christ." The apostle is speaking, therefore, not about the merely outward administration of baptism, as if some magical healing power adhered to it, but about *the sign and seal in conjunction with that which is signified and sealed.* All those, then, who by means of their baptism have truly laid aside, in principle, their garment of sin, and have truly been decked with the robe of Christ's righteousness, having thus been buried with him and raised with him, have put on Christ (cf. Rom. 6:3 ff.; 13:14; Col. 2:12, 13). In Christ they have risen to newness of life. They have become united with him in the sense that he is the Life of their life, the Light of their light, the Strength of their strength. And this, let it be stressed once again, is true of *them all*, regardless of outward differences, for the apostle continues: **28. There can be[110] neither Jew nor Greek; there can be neither slave nor freeman; there can be no male and female; for y o u are all one in Christ Jesus.** In Paul's day fraticidal class-distinctions were the order of the day, just as they are still in many quarters. See N.T.C. on Colossians and Philemon, pp. 151–154, where this same

---

A.V.: "For we are all children of God by faith in Christ Jesus," note absence of commas), the alternative manner of construing the sentence (with ἐν Χριστῷ Ἰησοῦ regarded as a modifier of the whole) receives support from verse 27, in which not Christ as the object of faith but as the One with whom believers have become united is indicated. The *oneness* of Christ and his own is, moreover, not only a repeatedly recurring Pauline theme but also a central thought in the immediate context (verse 27).

110 Though οὐκ ἔνι = οὐκ ἔνεστιν is rendered variously, the translators agree that Christianity cannot tolerate any actions or decisions which because of race, social standing, or sex, would degrade certain individuals to the status of second-rate citizenship in the kingdom of heaven, or would even exclude them entirely from such citizenship. Thus, Moffatt and also Goodspeed translate: "There is no room for"; A.V. and R.S.V.: "There is neither"; N.E.B.: "There is no such thing as"; and Weymouth: "There cannot be."

subject is discussed in some detail in connection with Col. 3:11. For the present purpose it is necessary only to note that the Jews drew a sharp line of separation between themselves and the "swarms" or "hordes" ("*goyim*") of outsiders, heathen nations in contrast with Israel. Often such heathen were simply called "dogs." Even proselytes to the Jewish religion were never fully "accepted." After all, they were not "children of Abraham." It seems that the Judaizers of Paul's day had not broken away from this feeling of disdain for non-Jews. Gentiles, too, were often guilty of similar snobbery. They looked down upon the Jews as much as the latter looked down upon them. And as to their attitude toward slaves, it cannot have been far removed from that of Aristotle, who called a slave "an animated implement," a mere breathing tool. And as to the distinction between male and female, even such a man of culture as Josephus, if the passage in his work *Against Apion* (II.xxiv) be genuine, declared, "The woman, so says the law, is inferior in all things to man." What Paul is saying, then, is that all such distinctions—be they racial-religious ("neither Jew nor Greek"), social ("neither slave nor freeman"), or sexual ("no male and female") —must be thoroughly and forever abandoned, since in Christ all are equal.

This does not mean that common sense must now be cast overboard. Because of different historical backgrounds, different vocational interests, different skills, different degrees of educational advancement, and different geographic locations, it may be in the interest of all concerned that at times "birds of a feather flock together." The Bible recognizes this right. It was not wrong for Bezalel and Oholiab to work in conjunction with other artisans of similar ability in the construction of the tabernacle (Exod. 36:1, 2, 8). Neither was it wrong, as such, for Demetrius, "the silversmith," to meet with other men of his trade (Acts 19:25). Scripture clearly justifies distinctions of this nature. It teaches not only the unity but also the diversity of all believers and, in a sense, of all men (Acts 17:26; I Cor. 7:20; 12; 16:2; Eph. 4:7). Are there not some people today who, in their mania for unity and equality, have left common sense and genuinely scriptural teaching far behind? Is it not absurd, for example, in the interest of "integration" to force into the fourth grade children, of whatever race, who cannot do fourth grade work? Would it not be foolish for ministers, with little knowledge of electricity, to try to crash a Convention of Electrical Engineers? Or for *men* to barge into a meeting of the Sewing Circle?

On the other hand, it certainly remains true that in God's holy sight all men are, indeed, equal, for "all have sinned, and fall short of the glory of God" (Rom. 3:23; cf. 2:11; 3:9-18; 5:12, 18). Also, "the same Lord is Lord of all, and is rich to all that call on him" (Rom. 10:12). For a Jew to confess himself to be a Christian, and then to refuse to eat with Christians from the Gentiles, or to regard himself as being in any way superior to them in moral worth, is an abomination to the Lord. Similarly today the church cannot tolerate hurtful distinctions. All believers are in a sense one person, one body "in Christ" (I Cor. 10:17; 12:12; Col. 3:15), for he who is the Son of David is also the Son of man; he who is "the seed of Abraham" is also "the seed of the woman." From God's side the Holy Spirit, and from man's side Spirit-imparted faith, link believers with Christ, and thereby also with one another.

29. Paul concludes this beautiful chapter as follows: **And if**[111] **y o u belong to Christ, then y o u are Abraham's seed, heirs according to promise.** The close connection with verses 27, 28, as well as with verses 6-9 and 16-18, is immediately apparent. It is unnecessary, therefore, to repeat what has already been said in the discussion of these passages. Clearly, the apostle once again stresses the fact that "belonging to the seed of Abraham is not determined by physical descent but by faith" (Ribberbos, *op. cit.*, p. 150). "In Christ" the wall of separation between Jew and Gentile no longer exists. Therefore, the Judaizers have no right to demand of the Gentiles anything else than that which they demand of the Jews, namely, true and living faith in the Lord Jesus Christ. Throughout the whole vast earth the Lord recognizes *one,* and *only one,* nation as his own, namely, the nation of believers (I Peter 2:9). These are Abraham's seed. These, too, are the *heirs* (for this concept see on 3:18) according to the promise which centers in Christ.

Summary of Chapter 3

Having shown that the gospel which he, Paul, proclaims is of divine origin and therefore victoriously independent, the apostle now indicates that both Scripture and experience bear testimony to its truth. He begins (verses 1-5) with a lesson from *experience.* Now experience is very important. The way in which God has led men in the past must be constantly recalled and applied to new situations (cf. Ps. 78:1 ff.). This the Galatians had neglected to do. So in verse 1 Paul asks them, "O foolish Galatians! Who has bewitched y o u, before whose very eyes Jesus was openly displayed as crucified?" And in verse 2 he continues, "This only would I learn from y o u: Was it by doing what (the) law demands that y o u received the Spirit, or was it by believing (the) gospel message?" In verse 5 he repeats the question of verse 2 in somewhat expanded form. In verse 3 he asks, "Are y o u so foolish? Having begun by the Spirit, now by fleshly means are y o u being made perfect?" They had begun by yielding to the direction of the Spirit, but they were now continuing by placing their trust in fleshly means: observance of days, months, seasons, and years (4:10), believing in the necessity of circumcision (5:2, 3; 6:12-15); in short: adherence to

---

111 The εἰ δέ in this *simple* or *first class conditional sentence* does not suggest doubt, however. The meaning is that whoever is "of Christ" certainly also belongs to Abraham's seed. Throughout this epistle Paul regards the Galatians as Christians (3:15; 4:12, 19; 5:10), though grossly erring (3:1).

law as a means of obtaining salvation. And *this* was progress? Has all their past experience—the manner in which at their conversion they had been enriched with both special gifts and spiritual endowments—been in vain? Paul refuses to believe it, and by saying, "if (it be) really in vain," he "rouses them to the exercise of repentance" (John Calvin).

For the idea that justification—hence, salvation in all its fulness—is obtained by way of faith and not by reliance on law-works Paul now (verses 6-14) appeals to *Scripture*. He shows that from the very beginning of Israel's history—that is, already in the promise God gave to Abraham—the divinely appointed means of obtaining the blessing was faith, not works (Gen. 15:6). Hence, all those, and only those, who have faith as their guiding principle are the true sons of Abraham. Those, on the contrary, who rely on law-works are under a curse from which they cannot deliver themselves, for they cannot "continue in all the things that are written in the book of the law to do them" (Deut. 27:26). Therefore "by law no one is justified before God, for 'The righteous shall live by faith'" (Hab. 2:4). Leaning on law means depending on self. Exercising faith means resting on Christ. Considered as means of obtaining salvation these two do not mix. But penitent sinners do not need to despair, for Christ has redeemed them from the curse by taking it upon himself (Deut. 21:23), in order that thus "the blessing of Abraham might come to the Gentiles in Jesus Christ, in order that we might receive the promised Spirit through faith."

In the final paragraph (verses 15-29) Paul shows that this promise made to Abraham-Isaac-Jacob is superior to law, for two reasons: (1) Because the latter came much later, and was therefore unable to annul the earlier promise, just as even among men a last will or testament that has been legally confirmed and has gone into effect cannot be abrogated. Surely a promise that centered in Christ, the one and only seed, could not be withdrawn. Nevertheless, the law performed a useful function, namely, by serving as custodian to bring sinners to Christ, having aroused within them the sense of guilt and the yearning for salvation through him. (2) Because the law reached us through mediation (Moses), but the promise came *directly* from God, who, in establishing his covenant with Abraham, and thus with *all believers,* regardless of racial-religious, social, or sexual distinctions, did this on his own sovereign account, being filled with love. Nothing can ever remove God's love for all who belong to Christ. Nothing can deprive them of their inheritance, for "If y o u belong to Christ, then y o u are Abraham's seed, heirs according to promise."

Chapter 4

Verses 1-11

Theme: *The Gospel of Justification by Faith apart from Law-works
Defended against its Detractors*

II. *Its Vindication: both Scripture—i.e., the Old Testament—and life (experience, past history) bear testimony to its truth*

D. We used to be in bondage to ordinances, regulations. God sent forth
his Son to redeem those who were in bondage, that we might receive the
adoption as sons. And because y o u are sons God sent forth the Spirit of
his Son into our hearts, crying, "Abba! Father!" Do y o u then wish to
exchange y o u r former bondage to heathenism for bondage to Judaism?
I am afraid about y o u, lest somehow I have labored among y o u in vain.

CHAPTER IV

GALATIANS

4 1 What I mean is this, that as long as the heir is a child he differs in no respect from a slave though he is owner of all, 2 but is under guardians and stewards until the time fixed by the father. 3 So also we, when we were children, were enslaved by the rudiments of the world. 4 But when the fulness of the time came, God sent forth his Son, born of a woman, born under law, 5 in order that he might redeem them (who were) under law, that we might receive the adoption as sons. 6 And because y o u are sons, God sent forth the Spirit of his Son into our hearts, crying, "Abba! Father!" 7 So, no longer are you a slave but a son; and if a son then also an heir through God.

8 However, at that time, since y o u did not know God, y o u were slaves to those who by nature are no gods; 9 but now that y o u have come to know God, or rather to be known by God, how (is it) that y o u turn back again to the weak and beggarly rudiments by which all over again y o u wish to be enslaved? 10 Y o u observe days and months and seasons and years. 11 I am afraid about y o u, lest somehow I have labored among y o u in vain.

4:1-11

D. *Why exchange one bondage for another?*

Paul has shown that as many as rely on law-works are under a curse, that by law no one is justified before God, that no law was ever given that could impart life, and that the law served only in a preparatory way, namely, as a custodian to bring sinners to Christ. Here, so it might seem, the argument could have ended. Why is it that one entire chapter (ch. 4) is added to drive home the same central point: the sinners' inferiority "under law"? The answer is probably this, that the apostle loved his Galatians so very much (see verses 19 and 20) that he wished to leave no stone unturned in order to deliver them from their grievous error. Besides, what he now presents is by no means mere repetition. Though here, too, as in chapter 3, there is an appeal to past history and experience (verses 1-20), as well as to Scripture (verses 21-31), there is material difference. In chapter 3 the argument from experience centered about *the gifts* which at their conversion the Galatians had received, and the question was asked, "By what avenue did y o u receive them?" In chapter 4 it is rather *the joy or blessedness* that had accompanied the reception of these gifts that is recounted. Again, in chapter 3 the argument from Scripture centered about Abraham,

155

Habakkuk, and Moses. In chapter 4 the reference is to Abraham's wife Sarah and her son *versus* Abraham's concubine Hagar and her son.

In driving home his point Paul (in the present paragraph, verses 1-11, and the next, verses 12-20) appeals to both heart and mind: to feelings, desires, and considerations which could be counted on to affect profoundly the members of the Galatian churches. Accordingly he appeals to their desire for freedom, a yearning that dwells in every human breast (verses 1-11), their sense of honor, by reminding them of their past nobility in attitude and action (verses 12-14), their presupposed nostalgia for former bliss (verse 15), their presumed sense of fairness (verse 16), and their dread of being duped (verses 17, 18). Last but not least he mentions the birth-pangs endured at this very moment by his own tenderly loving heart (verses 19, 20).

The immediate connection with the preceding paragraph is found in the word *heir(s)*, which is found both in 3:29 and 4:1. Chapter 3 ended with the significant statement, filled with comfort for both Gentile and Jew, "And if y o u belong to Christ, then y o u are Abraham's seed, *heirs* according to promise." Hence, Paul continues: **1, 2. What I mean is this, that as long as the heir is a child he differs in no respect from a slave though he is owner of all, but is under guardians and stewards until the time fixed by the father.** When a young father dies[112] his minor child will have to wait for the inheritance until he is of age. Though this child is, accordingly, the legal heir and as such "lord," "master" or, as here, "owner" of everything, yet with respect to taking possession of, and exercising control over, the estate that has been left to him he is no better off than a slave. Until he attains to the age previously stipulated by the father, he is heir *de jure* (by right) but not as yet *de facto* (in fact). For the time being this child is under *guardians,* to whose care he has been personally entrusted, and under *stewards* (often slaves) to whom the oversight of his estate has been committed (cf. Luke 12:42; 16:1 ff.; Rom. 16:23). Continued: **3. So also we, when we were children, were enlsaved by the rudiments of the world.** Just as an immature child is governed by rules and regulations, so also before the dawning of the light of the gospel, *we* were in bondage to "the rudiments of the world." For a rather detailed study of this concept I refer the reader to N.T.C. on Colossians and Philemon, pp. 108–110, 130–137; especially to footnote 83 on pp. 135–137. The context in Gal. 3:3, 9 (see verse 10) and

---

112 Several commentators point out that in the illustration here used it is not necessary to assume that the father has died, since sons would at times take active possession of their inheritance or allotment before the death of the father had occurred (Luke 15:12; cf. Gen. 25:6). Nevertheless, normally a will or disposition to divide an inheritance does not go into effect until the testator has died (Heb. 9:17). We are safe, therefore, in making that assumption also in the present case. Besides, it is not the condition of the father but that of the son that is in the foreground in the present illustration.

in Col. 2:8, 20 (see verses 16, 18, 21-23), demands, as I see it, that we interpret these "worldly rudiments" as *elementary teachings regarding rules and regulations, by means of which, before Christ's coming, people, both Jews and Gentiles, each in their own way, attempted by their own efforts, and in accordance with the promptings of their own fleshly (unregenerate) nature, to achieve salvation.*[113]

There was nothing wrong with the law given at Sinai, but when the Jews and the proselytes to the Jewish religion began to look upon law-observance as the way whereby salvation could be achieved, and when, with this in mind, the Jewish religious leaders began to add their own multitudinous rules and regulations to those previously received, that law became their tyrant, to which they became enslaved. The same was true with respect to the prescriptions and ordinances by which the worshipers of pagan deities sought to achieve redemption. By all such means, whether Jewish or pagan, men were putting themselves in bondage. This interpretation is also in harmony with Paul's previous statement in 3:23 (see on that verse). With the coming of Christ and the full light of special revelation which he brought (John 1:17, 18) there was even less excuse than there had ever been for this servitude, this catering to false philosophy and empty deceit. To the Colossians Paul was going to say, "If with Christ y o u died to the rudiments of the world, why, as though y o u were (still) living in the world, do y o u submit to regulations, 'Do not handle, Do not taste, Do not touch'—referring to things that are meant for destruction by their consumption—according to the precepts and doctrines of men? Regulations of this kind, though to be sure having a reputation for wisdom because of their self-imposed ritual, humility, and unsparing treatment of the body, are of no value whatever, (serving only) to indulge the flesh" (Col. 2:20-23). Continued: **4. But when the fulness of the time came, God sent forth his Son. . . .** Christ's coming supplied the basis of freedom for man. He came, moreover, "in the fulness of the time"; that is, he arrived upon the scene of human history at the time previously fixed by the Father (cf. the illustration, verse 2).

This is about all we can say with certainty about the phrase "the fulness of the time." Other ideas, however, may have been included in the concept; for example, to mention but one, that of *ripeness of opportunity* for the scattering, far and wide, of the seeds of the gospel. In this connection think

---

[113] In my definition of these rudiments to which men were in bondage the two most important items are: *a.* "rules and regulations" (the law) and *b.* "fleshly nature." Essentially the same conclusion was reached independently by Dr. Andrew J. Bandstra, who on p. 71 (and elsewhere) of his doctoral dissertation states that the term *stoicheia* most probably refers to law and the flesh (for title of Bandstra's work see General Bibliography). Luther agrees, calling these "the two feeble beggars."

of: *a.* the spread of the *Greek* language throughout the civilized world, *b.* the presence of *Jewish* synagogues in many places, enabling Christian missionaries to reach both Jews and Gentiles (proselytes) simultaneously, and *c.* the help which these evangelists derived from the network of *Roman* roads and, to some extent, from the enforcement of *Roman* peace. But it is God alone who fully knows why, in his inscrutable decree, he had decided that *the long period of time* (*chronos*) in which all the preparatory events were to occur would run out at that specific moment. It was then that he "sent out from himself" his Son. We say that Jesus *was born* in Bethlehem, and that is correct. But in some respects his birth was not like that of any other child. Other children do not exist in any real sense before they are conceived in the womb. It is by means of conception and birth that they come into existence. But God's Son existed already from eternity with the Father (John 1:1; 8:58; 17:5; Rom. 8:3; II Cor. 8:9; Phil. 2:6; Col. 1:15; Heb. 1:3). He existed—and exists forevermore—*as to his deity.* Accordingly, the fact that he was now sent forth must mean that he now assumed the human nature (John 1:14), which was wondrously prepared in the womb of Mary by the Holy Spirit (Luke 1:35). Thus he now became, and would forever remain, the possessor of two natures, the divine and the human, united indissolubly in the one divine person. From the very beginning Christ's human (as well as his divine) nature was without sin and filled with positive holiness (Mark 1:24; Luke 1:35; John 4:34; 6:38; 8:29, 46; Acts 3:14; 22:14; II Cor. 5:21; Heb. 4:15; 7:26; I Peter 1:19; 2:21; 3:18; I John 2:1; 3:5). And so it will remain forever. Nevertheless, during the days of his humiliation it was oppressed by the effects of sin, for Paul continues: **born of a woman.**

Some have used this expression as a proof-text for the doctrine of the virgin birth, as if "born of a woman" meant "born without human paternity." Now it is certainly true that the Holy Spirit has seen to it that Paul expressed himself in a way which causes Gal. 4:4 to be in full harmony with the teaching elsewhere of the doctrine of the virgin birth. Nevertheless, direct evidence for the virgin birth—a most important truth, to be sure—is found not here in Gal. 4:4 but rather in Matt. 1:18-25 (cf. Isa. 7:14) and Luke 1:34, 35. The fact that Jesus was "born of a woman" does not *in and by itself* mean that he was virgin born. John the Baptist, too, was born of a woman, and so is everybody else, with the exception of Adam and Eve (Matt. 11:11).[114] J. G. Machen correctly observes: "This passage [Gal. 4:14] has

---

[114] In the defense of the theory that Gal. 4:4 is a proof-text for the virgin birth, some (Lenski, Orr, etc.) argue that the text should really be translated: ". . . his Son, *come to be* from a woman" (Lenski) or ". . . His Son, *become* of a woman" (James Orr, *The Virgin Birth of Christ,* New York, 1924, p. 119), instead of *"born* of a woman,"* since the aor. participle of the verb γίνομαι is used here, and not the aor. passive participle of the verb γεννάω, as in Gal. 4:29 (cf. forms of that same

sometimes been held to show that Paul did not believe in the virgin birth and sometimes also has been held to show that he did so. As a matter of fact both opinions are probably wrong; the passage does not enable us to draw any conclusion with respect to Paul's belief in the matter one way or the other" (*The Virgin Birth of Christ,* New York and London, 1930, p. 259).

Fact is that in order to save us Jesus Christ had to be in one person both divine and human, *divine* in order to give his sacrifice infinite value, to deliver us out of the realm of darkness, and to transplant us into the realm of everlasting light (Isa. 9:1, 2, 6; John 1:1-4; Col. 1:13, 14); and *human* because since it was man who sinned it is also man who must bear the penalty for sin and render his life to God in perfect obedience (Rom. 5:18; I Cor. 15:21; Heb. 2:14-17). It stands to reason that the Redeemer must be a *sinless* man, for one who is himself a sinner cannot satisfy either for himself or for others (Ps. 49:7, 8; Heb. 7:26, 27; I Peter 3:18). There is, accordingly, something special and something common about Christ's birth. That which is *special* is stressed in the words: "God sent forth his Son." That which is *common* is brought out in the phrase: "born of a woman," meaning: like any other human being, born to affliction, pain, trouble, etc. "Man that is born of a woman is of few days and full of trouble" (Job 14:1). Truly, Christ "was in every respect tempted as we are, yet without sin" (Heb. 4:15).

Continued: **born under law,** and this in the sense not only of being under *personal* obligation to keep that law, but also of being duty-bound (with a duty to which he voluntarily bound himself!) *vicariously* to bear the law's penalty and to satisfy its demand of perfect obedience.

The altruistic nature of Christ's coming is stressed in the purpose clause: **5. in order that he might redeem them (who were) under law.** Essentially we have here the same thought that was expressed previously in 3:13: "Christ redeemed us from the curse of the law, having become a curse for us." Even

---

verb in 4:23, 24). But, in speaking of Christ's conception and birth the sacred writers do not hesitate to use forms of the latter verb (Matt. 1:16; 2:1), not even in reproducing the message of Gabriel to Mary (Luke 1:35). In fact, Jesus himself, in speaking of his own birth, made use of this verb when he said to Pilate, "For this purpose *was I born,* and for this purpose I am come into the world, that I should bear witness to the truth" (John 18:37). Note, however, also a form of the verb γίνομαι—ultimately the two verbs can be traced to the same root—in the sense of *being born.* It is used in connection with the birth of Abraham (John 8:58, according to the best text), when Christ's Aramaic is rendered: "Before Abraham *was born* I am." As to *Paul's* usage in connection with Christ see also Rom. 1:3. In the Apocrypha this verb has reference to *being born* in such passages as Esd. 4:16; Tob. 8:6; Wisd. 7:3; etc. "To be born" or "to be begotten" is, accordingly, a recognized meaning of the verb γίνομαι. Hence, no argument in favor of the doctrine of the virgin birth can properly be derived from its use here in Gal. 4:4. See also L.N.T. (A. and G.), p. 157.

the verb—*redeem*—is the same. Hence, see the explanation of 3:13, and for the thought compare II Cor. 5:21. Yet, there is a difference, for here in Gal. 4:5 emphasis is placed on the fact that *we* (Gentiles, Jews; the addressed, the addressor, everybody destined to be redeemed) were "under law," and this not only in the sense of being subject to the moral law, which by nature we were unable to fulfil and whose curse we were unable to carry so as to get out from under it; but also (in the present context; see verses 3, 8-10; cf. Col. 2:8, 14, 20-23) in the sense that "we" regarded strict obedience to the ceremonial law and all its man-made additions to be necessary for salvation. Accordingly, the Father's object in commissioning his Son was that, in the most comprehensive sense, the latter might purchase those free that were under law; and not only that but also: **that we might receive the adoption as sons.** Cf. Rom. 8:15, 23; 9:4; Eph. 1:5. Plainly, then, the purpose of the Father in sending his Son, and of the Son in condescending to be born "of a woman, under law," was that we might not only be delivered from the greatest evil but might also be crowned with the choicest blessing. The best interpreter of Paul's statement in Gal. 4:4, 5 is Paul himself: "For y o u know the grace of our Lord Jesus Christ, that though he was rich, yet for y o u r sake he became poor, that y o u through his poverty might become rich" (II Cor. 8:9).

Rich, indeed, we become, for we are made members of "the Father's Family" (see N.T.C. on Eph. 3:14, 15). With respect to this *adoption* it is rather useless to look for human analogies, for it surpasses anything that takes place on earth. It bestows upon its recipients not only a new name, a new legal standing, and a new family-relationship, but also a new image, the image of Christ (Rom. 8:29). Earthly parents may love an adopted child ever so much. Nevertheless, they are, to a certain extent, unable to impart their *spirit* to that child; but when *God* adopts, he imparts to us the *Spirit* of his Son, as Paul indicates by continuing: **6. And because y o u are sons, God sent forth the Spirit of his Son into our hearts, crying, "Abba! Father!"** The redeemed are now sons, not minors but majors. They have reached maturity and with it freedom. It is remarkable that the apostle is saying this to *the Galatians!* He says, as it were, "Y o u, Galatians, weak, foolish, erring, must consider that y o u, yes even y o u, are sons of the heavenly Father, the Father of y o u r Lord Jesus Christ." In other words, he is not giving up hope with respect to them, even though he is baffled about their present behavior (4:11).

Now because they are sons, God, the Father, having adopted them as sons, has sent forth the Spirit into their hearts. They are sons; hence they receive the Holy Spirit. They receive the Spirit; hence they become conscious of their sonship (Rom. 8:15). All three persons of the Holy Trinity are indicated in this passage, and their harmonious co-operation as the one true God is beautifully set forth. Moreover, the third person is called "the

160

Spirit of his (God the Father's) Son." He is the Spirit of the Son because he proceeds from the Son (John 15:26), as well as from the Father, and because he glorifies the Son, causing men to ponder the Son's teaching, love unto death, heavenly intercession, and constant care (John 16:14).

"God *sent forth* his Son" (verse 4); "God *sent forth* the Spirit of his Son" (verse 6). The same word is used with reference to the sending of the Spirit as was previously used in connection with the sending of the Son. The two are equally real, and also equally important. In fact, the salvation that was *bought* for God's people by the Son will not avail except it be also *wrought* in their *hearts* by that Son's Spirit. The heart, moreover, controls the entire personality. It is the core and center of man's being, man's inmost self. It is the hub whence radiate all the spokes of his existence, the fulcrum of feeling and faith as well as the mainspring of words and actions (Rom. 10:10; cf. Matt. 12:34; 15:19; 22:37; John 14:1). "Out of it are the issues of life" (Prov. 4:23).

In dwelling on the great mysteries of salvation, matters in which he himself has become intensely and lastingly involved, Paul frequently changes from the second to the first person plural (Gal. 1:3, 4; 2:14, 15; Eph. 1:17, 19; 2:1, 5; 2:8, 10; 2:13, 14; 5:1, 2; 6:11, 12; Phil. 3:2, 3; 3:15, 16; Col. 1:11-13; 2:13; etc.). So also here: "And because y o u are sons, God sent forth the Spirit of his Son into *our* hearts." About such marvelous realities he is unable to write in an abstract, detached manner; hence not y o u . . . y o u r, but y o u . . . our. And why is his soul thus lost in wonder, love, and praise? The very contents of verses 4-6 clearly shows why. First, the Father had sent the Son, sent him from his very heart, as it were: "he *spared not* his *own* Son!" (Rom. 8:32), his *only* Son (John 3:16). He sent him into a world of sin and ruin, where for our sake and in our stead he was to suffer innumerable reproaches. And what did *we* (all those who were to be redeemed) do? *We* (that is, *our* sins) nailed him to the cross! This we did to him who came to dwell *with* us. Yet, instead of casting us away forever from his presence of love, the Father then sent the *Spirit* of his Son, in order that this Spirit (and in him also the Father and the Son) might draw even closer to us, dwelling not just *with* but *within* us, in our very hearts, and transforming these hearts from being hateful to being loving, from being rebellious to being obedient, from being distrustful to being faith-filled, and from being despondent to being exuberant with praise and adoration. Within these hearts the Spirit speaks peace, assurance. He bears witness with our spirit that we are God's very children, his adopted sons and heirs. Is it any wonder that such hearts begin to respond to the Father's love, so that love answers love, and a blessed interchange takes place? Is it not natural that the Spirit, dwelling within these hearts, impels them to address their Benefactor jubilantly, calling him "Father"? The text reads: crying, "Abba! Father!" In reality the outcry of joyful recognition, sweet response, appropriating love, overwhelming gratitude, and last but not least, filial trust, is ascribed to the Spirit. Nevertheless, this must be understood mediately, meaning that it is the Spirit "whereby we cry Abba! Father!" (Rom. 8:15). Similarly, in connection with the church's yearning for Christ's return we read, "And the Spirit and the bride say, Come" (Rev. 22:17). Here, too, the bride is moved by the Spirit. Spirit and bride always work together (Rom. 8:16).

It is a well-known fact that those who have acquired proficiency in more than one language will at times give preference to their native tongue as a vehicle for the expression of their deepest emotions. Being "a Hebrew of Hebrews" (Phil. 3:5), a Hebrew son of Hebrew parents, Paul must have been fond of the language spoken by the Jews as they returned from the lands of the captivity, namely Aramaic, akin to Hebrew (Acts 21:40). Aramaic, in fact, was a very important language in those days, being spoken not only by the Jews but by many others besides, even far outside the borders of Palestine. Jesus, too, spoke Aramaic, and it is altogether probable that in his frequent teaching about the Father, he had often used the term *Abba*. His disciples, therefore, relished the use of this word. Thus it passed into the vocabulary of the primitive church. Naturally, in writing to churches consisting for the greater part of people who were non-Jews, the word *Abba* had to be translated into the Greek *pátēr*, as Paul does here. Paul, then, is giving expression to his own inner devotion as well as to the deepest feelings of the early church when he tells us that now that freedom has arrived, through the redemption accomplished by Christ, and the way of access to the throne of God has been opened wider than ever, redeemed humanity, both Jew and Gentile, takes hold on God by crying, "Abba! Father!" By means of this expression of filial trust and *closeness* to the Father believers echoed the words of their Lord, spoken at a time when, in order to obtain this closeness of fellowship for us, he himself was being driven into isolation, was losing this very sense of nearness to his Father. It was in Gethsemane that Jesus, in deep anguish, said, "Abba," which by the evangelist Mark is similarly rendered into the Greek equivalent for "Father" (Mark 14:36).

7. At this point there is a change in the form of address which Paul uses. He has been addressing the Galatians as a group. He now turns to each one individually, saying: **So, no longer are you a slave but a son. . . .** Once a man has accepted Christ's sacrifice as the only ground of his salvation, and has drawn near with confidence to the throne of grace, addressing God as *"Abba! Father!,"* the shackles of bondage to law have been thrown off. No longer is man a slave. He not only *is* a son now (4:1, 2), but *knows* that he is. For him the way to the Father's heart is no longer blocked. Every valley has been raised, every mountain and hill made low, the crooked turns have been straightened, and all rough places have been made smooth. There are no longer any obstructions. Grace has removed them all. Continued: **and if a son then also an heir . . . ,** as was stated previously (3:29). For the comforting implications of heirship see on 3:18. The very word *heir* already implies that the son's salvation is not his own achievement but the gift of God's marvelous grace. But since this is hard for man's proud heart to admit, and since salvation by self-effort and not by grace was the very error against which Paul is here directing his attack, he adds: (according to the best reading) **through God.** Soli Deo Gloria! The sovereign, divine, nature of the work which made a man a son and an heir is stressed throughout Scripture (Deut. 7:7, 8; Isa. 48:11; Dan. 9:19; Hos. 14:4; John 15:16; Rom. 5:8; Eph. 1:4; I John 4:10, 19). This doctrine gives a person a sturdy foundation to stand on. It spells eternal security, without in any way violating personal responsibility.

> "The glory, Lord, from first to last,
> Is due to thee alone;
> Aught to ourselves we dare not take,
> Or rob thee of thy crown."
> —Augustus M. Toplady

8, 9. Assurance of full redemption through Christ, sonship, the blessed indwelling of the Spirit, freedom of access to the Father, heirship—are the Galatians now ready to sacrifice all these? Are they really going back to their former state of slavery, with this difference that they will be exchanging one type of bondage (to heathenism) for another (to Judaism)? It is evident that the apostle is here returning to the very occasion that had led him to write this letter. There is thunder in the sky, and the lightning flashes again, as it had done in 1:6-10 and 3:1 ff. Paul writes: **However, at that time, since y o u did not know**[115] **God, y o u were slaves to those who by nature are no gods.** Formerly the Galatians, then mostly pagans, had been without saving knowledge of God. It is not denied that by virtue of the manner in which God created man there is a certain kind of knowledge of God and of his law inherent in man's mind. Even the heathen show the work of the law written in their hearts (Rom. 2:14, 15). Nor is it denied that all men—including, therefore, non-Christians—derive from general revelation a certain amount of knowledge of God's attributes (Rom. 1:19, 20). That all of this knowledge is indeed important is plainly taught in the passages referred to. But *saving* knowledge is not found outside of Christ. Though the heathen have knowledge of God, they fail to render to God

---

[115] There is a cause and effect relationship between ignorance of God and slavery; hence, οὐκ εἰδότες is probably causal as well as temporal, with emphasis on the former.

the glory and the thanksgiving that is his due (Rom. 1:21). They do not *acknowledge* him but instead, in their perversity, serve the creature rather than the Creator, and for the glory of God they substitute "the likeness of an image of corruptible man and of birds and of four-footed beasts, and of creeping things," and make these the objects of their worship.[116] This foolish and wicked failure to acknowledge God results in slavery for those who are guilty of it, slavery to the products of their own wicked invention: gods which in reality are no gods at all, as is clear from their very nature, for they are but objects of wood, stone, etc. They have no breath, no power, no wisdom, and no concern for man. Instead of carrying man through his difficulties, they themselves must be carried (Isa. 46:1; contrast Isa. 63:9). Idolatry always spells slavery, not only the slavery of fear but also that of moral and spiritual degradation of every variety. Such, then, had been the former condition of most of those whom Paul here addresses.

A great change had occurred however, as Paul indicates by continuing: **but now that y o u have come to know God.** . . . In his marvelous grace it had pleased God to send Paul, Barnabas, etc. to preach the gospel to these wretched ones. And through the work of the Holy Spirit the Galatians had come to acknowledge the true God as he stands revealed in Christ. With respect to the dramatic and basic experience which these Galatians had undergone Paul is going to say more in verses 12-15. Here in verse 9 he adds one important point, however: **or rather to be known by God.** . . . This is an expression full of glorious significance. It means far more than that God would have a bare, factual knowledge with reference to them, or would simply be *acquainted* with them. In the case of the Galatians it indicates at least this, "that God had visited them in his mercy" (thus John Calvin). In view of what the apostle says in verse 6 ("Y o u are sons") is it not possible that also in the present passage the words are rich with such meaning as this: that they had been acknowledged as God's own; that, accordingly, God had set his love upon them and had chosen them to eternal life? This would certainly not have to apply to each and every one of them, but it could well apply to most of them, if we may assume that God blessed this letter to their hearts. We are reminded of such passages as: "I am the good shepherd, and I know my own" (John 10:14); "The Lord knows those who are his" (II Tim. 2:19). See also Gen. 18:19; Exod. 33:12, 17; Nah. 1:7; John 10:28; and Rom. 8:28, in all of which the statement that *God knows* or *has known* (or *foreknown*) a person is rich in meaning toward salvation. When Paul says, ". . . but now that y o u have come to know God *or rather* to be known by God" he is clearly stressing the fact

---

[116] John Murray gives an excellent explanation of the pertinent passages in Paul's Epistle to the Romans. See his book *The Epistle to the Romans*, Grand Rapids, Mich., 1959, Vol. I, especially pp. 34–42; 72–76.

that "We love him because he first loved us." Here, as at the close of verse 7 (see on that passage), there is, accordingly, a renewed emphasis on God's sovereignty in the effectuation of man's salvation. And that was exactly the lesson which the Galatians needed, and which, in a sense, we all need.

Right at this moment these Galatians were guilty of backsliding, so that Paul continues: (in view of these facts) **how (is it) that y o u turn back again to the weak and beggarly rudiments by which all over again y o u wish to be enslaved?** The apostle was shocked to learn that men who had been so enriched with the gospel of God's free and bounteous grace in Jesus Christ would now, under the influence of false teachers, be turning back again to those "rudiments of the world" (verse 3), which here, in verse 9, are described as being "weak and beggarly." What makes matters worse is that they are doing this by choice. Formerly they had been enslaved by the childish teachings of pagan priests and ritualists. They had been taught to obey all kinds of prescriptions regarding the discovery of the will of the gods by means of omens, the benefit of afflicting the body and of submission to fate. See on 5:1. There had been moral stipulations derived from nature, custom, and arbitrary will. Having been delivered from all this folly, do they now wish to become enslaved all over again, this time by Judaistic regulations? Paul calls these "rudiments" *weak and beggarly* because they have no power to help man in any way. Luther, commenting on this verse and applying the lesson to his own day, tells us that he had known monks who zealously labored to please God for salvation, but the more they labored the more impatient, miserable, uncertain, and fearful they became. And he adds, "People who prefer the law to the gospel are like Aesop's dog who let go of the meat to snatch at the shadow in the water. . . . The law is weak and poor, the sinner is weak and poor: two feeble beggars trying to help each other. They cannot do it. They only wear each other out. But through Christ a weak and poor sinner is revived and enriched unto eternal life."

The apostle then gives an illustration which sheds much light on what he meant when he spoke about turning back to the weak and beggarly rudiments: **10. Y o u observe days and months and seasons and years.** Since Paul in the entire preceding argument has made it abundantly clear that he is mainly attacking the false doctrine that law-works are the road to salvation (2:16, 19; 3:2, 5, 10-13, 17, 21; 4:5), and since by "law" he is referring specifically to that of Sinai, which came into existence four hundred and thirty years after the promise had been given to Abraham, Isaac, and Jacob, it follows that here in 4:10 he is not referring to days, months, etc., that pertained to this or that pagan system of religious worship, or even to some mixed ("syncretistic") cultus, but definitely to *the sabbath-days, days of the new moon, festival seasons* belonging to the Jewish cycle, and *either a. the sabbath and jubilee years, or b. the New Year* (Rosh

Hashana) on the first day of the month Tishri (September or October).[117] Paul is saying that strict observance of such days and festivals has nothing whatever to do with securing the divine favor. As a foundation upon which to build one's hope of being justified in the sight of God such a superstition is utterly futile, nothing but sinking sand! In fact, though deep down in his heart Paul certainly has not given up hope regarding the eternal welfare of the Galatians, as he indicates again and again (1:11; 3:4, 15; 4:6, 7, 9, 15, 16, 19; 5:10), he, as it were, shakes his head in utter disgust when he reflects on the fact that rigid, painstaking, adherence to the Mosaic law regarding sacred days, and to all kinds of man-made rules and regulations with respect to such celebrations, was actually beginning to be substituted for the simplicity of faith in Jesus Christ unto salvation full and free. Such folly staggers him. Have these Galatians learned nothing then? That seems to be the meaning of the words: **11. I am afraid about y o u, lest somehow I have labored among y o u in vain.** Note the word *somehow* or *perhaps*, strangely ignored in several translations,[118] yet of some importance, as it shows that the apostle has *not* definitely decided that all his efforts in the interest of the Galatians have been a waste of time. In fact, though admittedly this verse is one of Paul's gloomiest utterances in the entire epistle, so that, as some see it, the pendulum of his emotions, which is swinging between hope and fear, has here swung all the way to the latter, even here the door of hope has not been shut. Gal. 4:11 is not really in conflict with the somewhat similar 3:4. And the noble purpose of 4:11 as well as of 3:4 is "to rouse the minds of the Galatians to the exercise of repentance."

---

[117] The fact that the reference to *years* is not entirely clear is one of several reasons why the attempt that has been made to found upon it a theory with respect to the date when the epistle was written must be considered a failure.

[118] Greek πώς. Among those who do justice to this word in their translations are Beck, Berkeley Version, Goodspeed, Moffatt, N.A.S.B. (N.T.), Norlie, and Weymouth.

Chapter 4

Theme: *The Gospel of Justification by Faith apart from Law-works Defended against Its Detractors*

II. *Its Vindication: both Scripture—i.e., the Old Testament—and life (experience, past history) bear testimony to its truth*

E. Become as I am as I also became as y o u are. Where is now that blessedness which y o u experienced on that former occasion when y o u welcomed me so warmly? Those (perverters of the true gospel) who pay court to y o u do so selfishly. I could wish to be present with y o u now and to change my tone of voice, for I am perplexed about y o u.

12 Become as I (am), because I also became as y o u (are), brothers; (this) I beg of y o u. No wrong did y o u do me. 13 Y o u know, moreover, that it was because of an infirmity of the flesh that I preached to y o u the gospel on that former occasion; 14 and though my physical condition was a temptation to y o u, yet y o u did not despise or loathe me, but as an angel of God y o u welcomed me, as Christ Jesus. 15 Where, then, (is) y o u r (former) blessedness? For I testify to y o u that, had it been possible, y o u r very eyes y o u would have plucked out and given to me. 16 Have I then become y o u r enemy by telling y o u the truth? 17 These people are zealously courting y o u for no commendable purpose: on the contrary, they want to isolate y o u, in order that y o u may zealously court them. 18 Now (it is) commendable to be zealously courted in connection with a commendable cause (and this) always, and not only when I am present with y o u. 19 My dear children, for whom I am again suffering birth-pangs until Christ be formed in y o u, 20 I could wish to be present with y o u now and to change my tone of voice, for I am perplexed about y o u.

4:12-20

E. *Where is now y o u r blessedness?*

12. It is characteristic of Paul, the tactful shepherd of souls, the warm-hearted master-psychologist, that his rather sharp reproof (verses 8-11) is followed immediately by tender, urgent, intensely personal appeal. This paragraph is one of the most gripping in all of Paul's epistles. The apostle implores and agonizes, because he cannot endure the thought that those whom he addresses and who at one time had treated him with such sympathetic consideration and had accepted his gospel with such enthusiasm would now continue to wander farther and farther away from home. Hence, lovingly, as a parent speaking to children, for such in a sense they are (see verse 19), he writes: **Become as I (am), because I also became as y o u (are), brothers; (this) I beg of y o u.** In the light of such stirring passages as Gal. 2:16, 19, 20; Phil. 3:7 (cf. Titus 3:5) this must mean: "Cast aside all thought of being able, by means of law-works, to become righteous in the sight of God, for that is exactly what I by grace was taught to do. At one time, I, a proud Jew, imagined that I would be able to achieve my own righteousness before God. But I became as y o u Gentiles are, by nature condemnable in his sight, with nothing of self to appeal to."

Because Paul, by God's marvelous grace, has learned that this shedding of all self-righteousness is the only way to please and glorify God, he beseeches the Galatians to follow this course. They should return to the point from which they started out when they had accepted the gospel of salvation, full and free, on the basis solely of Christ's redemptive sacrifice. They should spurn once and for all the sinister teachings of the Judaizers. Let them, as his children, reveal their likeness to him. Let them return to that simple, childlike, faith which, in addressing the Savior, says, "Nothing in my hand I bring, Simply to thy cross I cling." Cf. 2:20; 6:14. That the plea is very earnest and touching appears from the affectionate word of address, "brothers" (1:11; 3:15; 4:28, 31; 5:11, 13; 6:1, 18), and from the emphatic appeal with which the sentence *ends*: " (This) I beg of y o u."[119] Continued: **No wrong did y o u do me.** At first glance this statement may surprise us because of its suddenness. Some have explained it as a response to an assertion made by the Galatians: "We have not wronged you in any way." But there is no basis for this theory. Nor is there any need for it. Paul's soul was in a state of intense agitation, brought about by grave concern about the present disloyalty of the Galatians, especially as contrasted with their past enthusiasm. Therefore, his abruptness is, after all, understandable. When he now says, "No wrong did y o u do me," he is reflecting on the manner in which he had been received by the Galatians when he had met them for the first time and worked among them, as is clear from verses 13-15. Continued: **13. Y o u know, moreover, that it was because of an infirmity of the flesh that I preached to y o u the gospel on that former occasion. . . .**[120] Paul had visited the Galatians twice, that is, on two separate missionary journeys: the first (see Acts 13 and 14) and the second (see Acts 15:40-16:5). He refers now to what had happened on the first of these two trips.

The apostle states that it was *because* of an infirmity of the flesh—an illness so severe that on the part of the Galatians it might have given rise to contempt and disgust (verse 14)—that he had preached the gospel to them on that former occasion. Some interpreters, however, do not look with favor on the rendering "because of." They prefer—or at least regard as worthy of very serious consideration—a translation such as "amid," or "while suffering from" or simply "in" bodily weakness.[121] Reference to this difference of opinion was made earlier. See p. 11. In favor of the idea that the infirmity of which Paul speaks was not *the cause* of the apostle's preaching but rather *the accompanying circumstance* it might be stated that not only Luke (see Acts 13:50; 14:5, 6, 19) makes some remarks about the physical

---

[119] This special emphasis is lost in most translations. It is retained, however, in N.E.B., and, in a way, also by Phillips.
[120] It is true that the Greek τὸ πρότερον at times simply means *formerly, before, previously* (John 6:62; 9:8; I Tim. 1:13). However, in the present instance Paul, by his very emphasis and rather lengthy expatiation on what had happened *on a definite earlier occasion,* shows that he is here using this expression in the sense of "on the former of two occasions."
[121] Thus respectively Cole (*op. cit.,* pp. 121, 122); Ridderbos (*op. cit.,* pp. 13, 30, 166); and Bruce (*The Letters of Paul, An Expanded Paraphrase,* p. 31).

afflictions which Paul, and to some extent also Barnabas, had to endure while working in Galatia, but so does also Paul himself, many years later. These experiences were never erased from the latter's memory. Even in his very last epistle that has been preserved the afflictions suffered on that journey march in rapid procession before his mind's eye, as he writes to Timothy: "You, however, followed my . . . persecutions, my sufferings, what kind of things happened to me at Antioch, at Iconium, (and) at Lystra, what kind of persecutions I underwent; yet from them all the Lord rescued me!" (II Tim. 3:10, 11). For this and other, more technical, reasons,[122] the *possibility* that this was actually what the apostle had in mind, and that what he wrote should be rendered, ". . . it was *amid bodily weakness* that I preached to y o u the gospel on that former occasion" must be granted. Nevertheless, it must also be admitted that the far more usual sense of the phrase found here is *because of an infirmity*. It is so understood by the vast majority of exegetes.[123] And on the basis of this interpretation of the phrase Ramsay's conclusion, that because of malaria with accompanying severe headaches Paul had been forced to leave the lowlands of Perga and vicinity for the considerably higher elevation of Antioch and the other cities of Galatia, has been accepted by many. It could be right. Yet, in reality we know nothing about the nature of the illness which, if the preferred rendering "because of an infirmity of the flesh" is accepted, caused the apostle to preach the gospel in Galatia and/or to continue his ministry there for a longer period than he had at first contemplated. The idea that verse 15 (cf. 6:11) points to an affliction of the eyes is not well grounded, since in that passage the apostle is no longer speaking about his physical infirmity. And so it is with the other guesses that have been made. Those who immerse themselves in such matters sometimes miss the real intention of the passage, as when a Bible study group, spending several evenings on the first few chapters of the book of Genesis, instead of taking to heart the marvelous spiritual lessons taught there, how God is there revealed in all his power, wisdom, and love, wholly concentrates its attention on the question: "How long were the days of the creation week?"

---

[122] The question may well be asked whether Koine Greek is so inflexible as never to allow διά to be used even with the accusative to indicate attendant circumstance, as it certainly does at times when it is used with the genitive. At any rate prominent Greek fathers (Chrysostom, Theodoret, and Theodore of Mopsuestia), well-versed in Greek, seem to interpret Gal. 4:13 with this sense of διά in mind.

[123] For example, by Burton (*op. cit.*, pp. 238, 239); Duncan (*op. cit.*, p. 139); Goodspeed (*Paul*, p. 42); Lenski (*op. cit.*, pp. 217, 218); Lightfoot (*op. cit.*, p. 174); and last but not least Ramsay (*St. Paul the Traveller and the Roman Citizen*, pp. 92ff.; Historical *Commentary on Galatians*, p. 424). Lightfoot states: "No instance has been produced, until a much later date, which would at all justify one explaining δι' ἀσθένειαν, as if it were δι' ἀσθενείας or ἐν ἀσθενείᾳ, as is frequently done."

By writing, "Y o u know that it was because of an infirmity," etc., the apostle causes the scenes and experiences of the not very distance past to flash vividly across the memory of the errant Galatians. Their thoughts are carried back to the events that had taken place at the time of the first meeting with the missionaries, and shortly afterward. The sentence continues: **14. and though my physical condition was a temptation to y o u, yet y o u did not despise or loathe me. . . .** This is a very compressed statement. Literally, according to what is probably the best reading, this clause reads: "And y o u r temptation in my flesh y o u neither despised nor loathed." Two ideas are here combined: *a.* "Y o u did not despise or loathe me because of my physical condition"; *b.* "Y o u did not yield to the temptation to do so." The resultant meaning is clear enough, just so also at this point we avoid wild conjectures. The first verb causes no difficulty: "Y o u did not regard (me) of no account, as good for nothing"; hence, "Y o u did not despise (me)." There follows, *if* the verb is to be taken literally: "or spit out (at me.)."[124] On the basis of that literal rendering some have said that Paul was surprised because the Galatians had not expectorated when they first met him, for that was their custom when they saw a person who was having an epileptic fit. The conclusion drawn from the use of this verb is, accordingly, that Paul was an epileptic. But since from very early times this verb was also used in a metaphorical sense—to loathe—, and since after "Y o u did not despise," this secondary meaning "or loathe" completes the pair of synonyms, the latter translation is certainly to be preferred. Besides, nowhere in Paul's epistles or in the book of Acts is there the slightest evidence to support the notion that Paul was an epileptic. Therefore, all we can really affirm is that when, during this first missionary journey, the Galatians saw Paul, they saw a man who was afflicted with a grievous physical illness. But even though such bodily infirmity was regarded by the Jews, and even more so by the Gentiles, as a token of God's displeasure (Job 4:7; John 9:2; Acts 28:4), so that the Galatians had been tempted to treat Paul with contemptuous scorn, they had done nothing of the kind. Continued: **but as an angel of God y o u welcomed me, as Christ Jesus.** So great had been their respect for Paul, so generous the welcome extended to him, as if his voice had been that of an angel of God, yes even that of Christ Jesus himself (cf. Acts 13:42, 44, 48; 14:1, 11-13, 21).

The Galatians had experienced a season of thrilling discovery, of joy unspeakable and full of glory. What had become of it? How completely different was their present condition. Says Paul: **15. Where,[125] then, (is) y o u r (former) blessedness,** the disposition of mind and heart in which,

---

[124] "At last, however, he [Odysseus] came up, and *spat forth* from his mouth the bitter brine that flowed in streams from his head" (Homer, *Odyssey* V. 322, 323).
[125] The textual evidence is decidedly in favor of the reading as here assumed.

because of our presence, y o u blessed or congratulated yourselves? Continued: **For I testify to y o u that, had it been possible, y o u r very eyes y o u would have plucked out and given to me.**[126] In the original the words "y o u r eyes" are, for the sake of emphasis, given a forward position: "y o u r eyes, having plucked (or: dug) out, y o u would have given to me." My translation preserves this special stress. What the apostle evidently means is this: "Y o u thought so highly of me at that time, and felt so happy in our presence, that, had it been possible, you would have given me the most precious member of y o u r body." Continued: **16. Have I then become y o u r enemy by telling y o u the truth?**[127] To what does Paul refer when he asks this question? In which way does he assume that he might have become their enemy? The opinions given may be classified as follows: *a*. by means of a previous letter which he had written to them but which was not preserved; *b*. by means of warnings against the Judaizers which he had issued on his *second* journey through Galatia (see Acts 15:40 ff.) ; *c*. by means of the strong language which he had used earlier in the very letter which he is now writing (1:6; 3:1 ff.; 4:11) . For the first of these suggestions I see no need whatever, nor probability. The second is very well possible. The Galatians may not have taken kindly to these warnings. The third impresses me as being the most natural, though *b* and *c* may well be combined. What Paul is telling the Galatians by means of this question is that he has proved himself their real friend, for the mark of such a friend is that he tells those whom he loves the truth even though it may hurt. Nathan, for example, proved that he was David's genuine supporter when, in the name of his Sender, he rebuked the king, saying, "You are the man!" (II Sam. 12:7) . Paul, then, is saying, "Y o u have heard what I have said. Now what is y o u r reaction? Have I become y o u r enemy by rendering this service to y o u, namely, telling y o u the truth?" Are the Galatians unable to tolerate the truth? Are they like a foolish woman who breaks her mirror because it reveals the wrinkles on her face? Do they not realize that were the apostle, in this important matter, concealing the truth, he would be committing a crime? Do they resemble those fickle church-members who are always demanding that their minister says nothing but "nice things" to them? Paul's own stand on this matter is that one should always practice integrity in all his dealings, and that he should do so in the spirit of love (Eph. 4:15) . Said Lincoln: "If it is decreed that I should go down because of this speech, then let me go down linked to the truth." This attitude gave him peace of

---

[126] I agree with Robertson (*Word Pictures*, Vol. IV, p. 305) that there is nothing unusual in the omission of ἄν in this *second class* or *contrary to fact* conditional sentence, but I disagree with his suggestion: "Did Paul not have at this time serious eye trouble?"
[127] For ἀληθεύω see N.T.C. on Eph. 4:15, footnote 118.

mind. And as to his influence? Though defeated in his bid for the Senate, he became President two years later.

It is but natural that Paul, who has just asked whether he had possibly become the enemy of the Galatians by telling them the truth, now states who are their *real* enemies. In what he is about to say he probes into and exposes the motives of the Judaizers, without mentioning them by name: **17. These people are zealously courting y o u for no commendable purpose: on the contrary, they want to isolate y o u, in order that y o u may zealously court them.** The Judaizers are trying to curry favor with the Galatians, ostensibly being deeply concerned about them. However, their purpose is not commendable, their motivation is not honorable. Literally Paul says "not properly," "not in the right way." Their real object is *to exclude* the Galatians, that is, to shut them out from all influences except their own; particularly, of course, *to isolate* them from any effect Paul and his associates might have upon them. But man cannot live in a vacuum. He is a social being. Once these opponents have succeeded in deluding the minds of the Galatians with an untrue image of Paul and of his message, the sadly deluded ones will then become wholly dependent upon these detractors of the only true gospel. Accordingly, the apostle states, "They want to isolate y o u, in order that y o u may zealously court them." *To zealously court someone* (active voice), to be deeply concerned about that person, and to bestow much attention upon him, need not be a bad thing. Good parents are deeply concerned about their children. The very idea that those so dear to them might succumb to the temptation of being led astray by evil companions, so that in that sense these parents might "lose" their children, fills them with dismay and incites them to earnest prayer and strenuous effort on their behalf. They are jealous for their children with God's own jealousy, as was, for example, Paul himself, with respect to the Corinthians (II Cor. 11:2: same verb in the original as here in Gal. 4:18). So also, says Paul, *to be zealously courted* (passive voice), diligently sought after, is not a bad thing in and by itself, no matter whom it concerns, provided, however, that it be "in something good," that is, "in connection with a commendable cause": **18. Now (it is) commendable to be zealously courted in connection with a commendable cause.** Then suddenly the apostle rivets the mind of the Galatians upon the fact that this rule applies also to himself. On that unforgettable "former occasion" had *he* not been the object of their whole-souled attention, intense interest, unmistakable favor, and genuine respect, and this in connection with the noblest of all causes, namely, the proclamation of the one and only true gospel? Would that this had endured and were true even today! Continued: **(and this) always, and not only when I am present with y o u.** That was the trouble. Their attachment to Paul had lost its warmth, to say the least. Their zeal for the truth had subsided. Their loyalty was in the process of being transferred from Paul to the proponents of dangerous error. Everything was fine, as long as Paul had been present with them. But once he was gone and the distorters of the true gospel had arrived, the alienation of affection had begun, to their own hurt!

This situation almost breaks Paul's heart. No wonder, for he knows so much better than they do what would be the result of such apostasy were it to run its full course. But this must not, this cannot be. So, in spite of the fact that their feelings toward him had cooled, he, still filled with the most tender love toward them, now addresses them in the language of warm, pastoral—and we may well add: parental—affection, as follows: **19, 20. My dear children,**[128] **for whom I am again suffering birth-pangs. . . .**

Paul compares himself to a mother who is giving birth to a child. Thus also in I Thess. 2:7[129] he says, employing a figure only slightly different: "But we were gentle in the midst of y o u, as when a nurse cherishes her own children," meaning: as when a mother-nurse warms, fondles, cherishes the children that are her very own because she gave them birth. Here in Gal. 4:19 note the word *again:* "for whom I am again suffering birth-pangs." Once before he had endured these labor pains for them, as Luke so vividly portrays in Acts 13 and 14. At that time he, as God's instrument, had brought these children to the point where they loved him and trusted him; even better: where they loved and trusted *Christ,* placing their hope for salvation in him alone. And now, having been displaced in their affections by others, Paul's birth-pangs have returned. He hopes with all the ardor of his soul that, for the sake of their own salvation, the Galatians will renew their former attachment to him. O that they might be his children once more, as children imitating him! O that they might become as he is (verse 12), trusting solely in Christ for their salvation! O that they would cast aside all reliance on self, on law-works, as he, by the grace of God, had learned to do!

The apostle is yearning for his children. He is afflicted. In his heartache also this element is included, "that the Galatians are making the maternal heart of Paul suffer all the birth-pains a second time, something which no offspring ever does in nature. . . . Unnaturally they are causing Paul to suffer all these pains over again, even in a more severe way" (Lenski, *op. cit.,* p. 227).

Though, according to the entire preceding context, it was especially the acceptance of legalism by the Galatians that made Paul suffer and yearn as he did, nevertheless the danger of libertinism (immorality) can hardly

---

[128] Whether with Grk.N.T. (A-B-M-W) on reads τεκνία μου (literally: "my little children," cf. John 13:33; I John 2:1, 12, 28; 3:7, 18; 4:4; 5:21) or with N.N. τέκνα μου ("O my children!"), cannot the rendering "My dear children" be considered proper in either case?

[129] This resemblance between Galatians and I Thessalonians can be added to those mentioned earlier. See p. 16.

have been absent from his mind, for in the very next chapter he earnestly warns the Galatians that they must not turn their freedom into an opportunity for the flesh (5:13, 16-24; cf. 6:7, 8). Hence, it is in that broad connection, reflecting on the situation in Galatia in its entirety, that he says: **until Christ be formed in y o u,** that is, until y o u r whole inner being[130] proclaims Christ's being and his ways, so that y o u will trust fully in y o u r Savior, will be like him in y o u r thoughts, wishes, and aspirations, and will reflect him in the common words y o u speak, in life's common looks and tones, in intercourse at hearth or board with y o u r beloved ones, in brief: in the entire gamut of y o u r existence and manifestation among men.[131] Continued: **I could wish to be present with y o u now and to change my tone of voice, for I am perplexed about y o u.** Though Paul was writing as a holy man of God who was being moved by the Holy Spirit (cf. II Peter 1:21; 3:15, 16), he, nevertheless, was conscious of the manner in which he was restricted by the limitations of time and space. Right now he wishes that he could be with those whom he addresses. However, with his hands full of work in Corinth (if that supposition be correct), he finds it impossible right now to rush off to distant Galatia. Ah, if he could only be with them, then, perhaps by hearing and seeing them and conversing with them, the change in them for which he so yearns might be brought about more speedily. Then possibly he might no longer have to rebuke them as he has done in this epistle, might not have to call them "foolish Galatians" any longer, but might be able to change his tone of voice. As of now, however, he is perplexed about them, at a loss to know why they have yielded to temptation. O that his dear children would return to the home from which they have wandered away! Yes, indeed, Paul is suffering birth-pangs . . . again!

The passage is one of the finest practical applications of I Cor. 13, written by Paul himself. Though the Galatians have failed Paul, his love toward them never fails, for love is longsuffering and kind, and even now hopes all things.

---

[130] The verb μορφωθῇ points to a desired change in inner essence. See N.T.C. on Philippians, pp. 102–105.
[131] The hymn "Fill Thou My Life" by Horatius Bonar provides an excellent commentary.

Chapter 4

Theme: *The Gospel of Justification by Faith apart from Law-works Defended against Its Detractors*

II. *Its Vindication: both Scripture—i.e., the Old Testament—and life (experience, past history) bear testimony to its truth*

F. History of the slave-woman (Hagar) and her son versus the free-woman (Sarah) and her son (Gen. 16:1-4; 21:8-12). Application: Cast out the slave-woman and her son. Not of a slave-woman are we children, but of the free-woman.

21 Tell me, y o u who desire to be under law, do y o u not hear the law? 22 For it is written that Abraham had two sons, one by the slave-woman and one by the free-woman. 23 But the son of the slave-woman was flesh-born; the son of the free-woman (was born) through promise. 24 Now things of this nature were spoken with another meaning in mind, for these two women represent two covenants: one from Mount Sinai, bearing children destined for slavery. She is Hagar. 25 Now Hagar represents Mount Sinai in Arabia, and corresponds to the Jerusalem of today, for she is in bondage with her children. 26 But the Jerusalem (that is) above is free, and she is our mother; 27 for it is written:

"Rejoice O barren one, you who do not bear;
Break forth and shout, you who have no birth-pangs;
For more are the children of the desolate than of her who has a husband."

28 Now y o u, brothers, like Isaac, are children of promise. 29 But as at that time he (who was) flesh-born persecuted the one (who was) Spirit-born, so (it is) also now. 30 But what does Scripture say? "Cast out the slave-woman and her son; for in no way shall the son of the slave-woman share in the inheritance with the son of the free-woman." 31 Wherefore, brothers, not of a slave-woman are we children, but of the free-woman.

4:21-31

F. *Instructive "Allegory"*

The proposition that those—those *alone, all* those—who by a true and living faith accept God's promise are the children of God, is defended once more, and now for the last time, with an appeal to Scripture. Rigid adherence to law, as if this were the way to be saved, is exposed as being in reality nothing but bondage, spiritual slavery. Faith, on the contrary, spells freedom. Accordingly, this section, too, is true to the theme of the entire epistle, namely, "The gospel of justification by faith apart from law-works defended against its detractors."

This time, however, the apostle makes use of a type of argumentation which he has not employed before. He avails himself of an allegory. It is not wrong to call it that, provided that the term *allegory* be interpreted in the most favorable sense (see on verse 24). Paul sets forth the spiritual meaning of a familiar story, that of two women that dwelt in Abraham's tents: *a.* his wife Sarah, and *b.* Sarah's personal slave Hagar, whom she gave to Abraham in order that she, Sarah, might obtain children by her. Hagar bore Ishmael. Several years later Sarah bore Isaac. Sarah and her son are now described as representing all those freedom-loving people who live by faith, as contrasted with Hagar and her son who are designated as representing those spiritually enslaved individuals who live by law. Cf. Gen. 16:1-4; 21:1-12.

Those who suppose that by using this kind of an argument Paul arrives at an interpretation that is fallacious, far-fetched, and fantastic, betraying the influence of his own early training in worthless rabbinical methods of exegesis, do him an injustice, and are themselves guilty of misinterpretation, for they misinterpret the apostle. What his allegory really amounts to is *an obvious lesson* plus a *self-invited comparison,* both of them derived from the ancient narrative in a manner so natural that in a mood of surprise Paul says: **21. Tell me, y o u who desire to be under law, do y o u not hear the law?** Those people—the Judaizers and also the Galatians themselves to the extent in which they allow themselves to be influenced by these legalists—are always talking about the indispensable necessity of keeping the Mosaic law (see on verse 10) ; nevertheless, they seem to forget that the law itself clearly contradicts their belief. In this second reference to *law* ("the law") Paul uses the term in a wider sense: Torah or Pentateuch. With a lively "Tell me," he calls his opponents to account. Continued: **22. For it is written that Abraham had two sons, one by the slave-woman and one by the free-woman.** As has been shown earlier (see on 3:6) , Paul's adversaries and their Jewish followers prided themselves in the fact that they were the descendants of Abraham, as if that biological relationship were of paramount significance for salvation, of such superior value that even the non-Jewish converts to Christianity should, by being circumcised, strive to resemble their Jewish co-religionists as closely as possible. Paul's argument, then, is this: Those who are always boasting about their descent from Abraham are forgetting that Abraham had not *one* son but *two* sons[132]: Ishmael by Hagar as well as Isaac by Sarah. Accordingly, if physical descent from Abraham is so all-important, then they who are Jews by birth are not any better off than are the Ishmaelites.

Nevertheless, so runs Paul's argument, there is, indeed, a marked difference between the son of Hagar, the slave-woman, and the son of Sarah, the free-woman, but that difference is not of a physical but of a spiritual nature. It represents the contrast between those who live by law and those who live by faith; in other words, between those who depend on that which they themselves are able to bring about and those who rely on the effectuation of God's gracious promise. The basic difference between Ishmael and Isaac, and between the two groups which they respectively represent, reveals itself in their contrasted birth (verses 23-28), their relation to each other (verse 29), and their lack of right, or right, to the inheritance (verse 30).

---

[132] The sons of Abraham's concubine Keturah are not within the range of vision here (Gen. 25:1 ff.; I Chron. 1:32, 33).

First, then, there is the contrast in birth: **23. But the son of the slave-woman was flesh-born; the son of the free-woman (was born) through promise.** Meaning: Ishmael was the product of his parents' natural power of procreation. He was born in accordance with that which Abraham and Hagar were able to accomplish in the ordinary course of nature (cf. John 1:13; Rom. 9:7-9). Accordingly, he represents all those who base their hope for eternity on what they themselves are able to effectuate, that is, on their own works.

There are those who think that this conclusion, already obvious, gains added strength when the full story, as related in Gen. 16:1-4, is taken into account. According to that passage Ishmael's birth was the result not only of a physical act but also of sinful deliberation. Abraham and Sarah, unwilling to bide God's time for the fulfilment of the promise, took matters into their own hands, so that, on the advice of Sarah, Abraham went in to Hagar, Sarah's Egyptian maid, with the result that she conceived and bore Abraham a son, Ishmael. However, the purpose of this scheme was not thereby realized, for Ishmael was not the child of promise. As these interpreters see it, therefore, when Paul here in Gal. 4:23 describes Ishmael as *flesh-born,* he attaches a double sense to this term, namely, "born according to carnal deliberation (Gen. 16:2), and by virtue of the physical capacity of both Abraham and Hagar, which had not yet died (Gen. 16:4)."[133] Thus, in the opinion of these exegetes, it becomes even more strikingly evident how the son of the slave-woman could represent all those who, instead of trusting in Christ for their salvation, labor slavishly to attain it by their own cunning, and are doomed to bitter disappointment. This double sense theory is attractive, but whether or not it be correct cannot be proved. Moreover, the theory is not necessary. Ishmael, as a son born in the usual, natural, way, is even so a true representative of all those who have experienced only the natural birth, not the birth from above. And on either theory he remains a slave, a fit symbol of all those who labor slavishly to enter into the kingdom.

Isaac, on the other hand, was born as a result of Abraham's faith in God's promise. It was as a reward for the exercise of this faith that God intervened miraculously, enabling Abraham, though he had become "as good as dead," to deposit seed, and making it possible for Sarah, heretofore barren, to conceive (Rom. 4:19; Heb. 11:11, 12). Isaac, then, was Spirit-born (verse 29), for it was the Holy Spirit who caused the promise to be realized. The conclusion, therefore, that Isaac is a symbol of all Spirit-born (now in the sense of *regenerated*) men is not far-fetched. It is all the more natural in view of the fact that he, in spite of his weaknesses, was going to manifest himself as a true believer, one who by faith rested in God's promise (Gen. 24:63; 26:18, 22-25; 28:1-4).

---

[133] Greijdanus, *Galaten* (Korte Verklaring), p. 126.

181

On the basis of the preceding it is not strange that Paul continues: **24. Now things of this nature were spoken with another meaning in mind, for these two women represent two covenants.** . . . Such historical events were designed to convey a meaning *other than*—in addition to—the strictly literal. God has given us such narratives not only to teach us what happened in the past, but also to enable us to apply the lessons of the past to our present situation (cf. Rom. 4:23, 24). Such things, then, are true as *history* and valuable as *graphic pedagogy*. It is in that sense that Paul is saying that things of this nature "are an allegory" (A.V.). The lesson here taught is derived as naturally from the narrative as an almond-kernel is picked out of an almond-shell. With this interpretation in mind we can understand that Paul was justified in saying, "Tell me, y o u who desire to be under law, do y o u not hear the law?" He meant, of course, that the lesson implied in the incident was so obvious that anyone who listened attentively to the narrative, when it was read, should have understood the deeper meaning immediately.

This shows that Gal. 4:24 provides no comfort whatever to "allegorizers" of the wild type; such, for example, as Rabbi Akiba, who was able to distil a mystical sense from the hooks and crooks of the Hebrew letters; Philo, who imagined that the cherubim placed at Eden's gates represented God's lovingkindness and his sovereignty; Origen, who on occasion "tortured Scripture in every possible manner, turning it away from the true sense" (Calvin); and the author of a certain very popular present day Bible which, though valuable in some respects, can hardly be considered a trustworthy guide when it pictures Asenath, the Egyptian wife of Joseph, as the type of the Christian church, called out from among the Gentiles to be the bride of Christ!

These two women, says Paul, *are* (that is, *represent*) two covenants, two distinct affirmations of God's one and only covenant of grace. See N.T.C. on Eph. 2:12. These two were: the covenant with Abraham (verse 18; cf. 3:8, 16-18) and the covenant of Sinai (Gal. 3:19, 24). Paul begins with the latter: **one from Mount Sinai, bearing children destined for slavery.** Though, as was shown earlier (see on 3:10, 25), God gave his law to Israel in a context of grace, that law was unable to save anyone. Besides, when it is, nevertheless, viewed as a force by means of which a person achieves deliverance and salvation, as the Jews and Judaizers actually viewed it, then it enslaves. It then not only leaves men in their bondage but more and more adds to their heavy burden. See on 2:4; 3:22, 23; 4:3, 7; 5:1; cf. Matt. 11:28, 29; Rom. 8:15. Paul adds: **She is Hagar,** for just as Hagar, being herself a slave, was able to bear only a slave-child, so also the law, as the Jews and Judaizers erroneously interpreted it, was able to bring forth none but drudges, whom it kept under its harsh dominion. Continued: **25. Now Hagar represents Mount Sinai in Arabia, and corresponds to the Jerusalem of today, for she is** in bondage with her children.[134] In the preceding verse Hagar and Mount Sinai have been linked. It was shown that, in the sense explained, both can produce nothing but slaves. Now the comparison is brought a step farther. What was implied right along is now clearly stated, namely, that *in line with* Hagar and Mount Sinai is also the Jerusalem of Paul's own day, earthly Jerusalem with her children (cf. Matt. 23:37): all of carnal Israel that had rejected Christ and his glorious gospel. It is hardly necessary to add that here Paul is thinking not only of the Jews who had openly repudiated Christ, but definitely also of those Jews who were Christians only in name, the Judaizers. Now here in verse 25 the emphasis is entirely on the third element in the comparison: Jerusalem and her children. These, too, as well as Hagar and Ishmael, are now said to be in bondage. They have enslaved themselves to Sinai's law, for they imagine that by strict obedience to this legal code—with emphasis on its ceremonial regulations, expanded by man-made additions—they can work their way into the kingdom of heaven. But they are wrong. Mount Sinai is in Arabia, and Arabia is a desert. It is not the land of promise; it is not "Zion" (Heb. 12:22; Rev. 14:1). When a person bases his hope for eternity on his own endeavors he is engaged in a sterile business!

The clause: ". . . and corresponds to the Jerusalem of today," calls attention to the fact that Hagar, Mount Sinai, and Jerusalem of today all stand in the same *row* or *line,* the same *"stich"* (line of poetry); hence, the same *category,* for they all spell *slavery,* the bondage that results from trusting in works of the flesh. Their opposites spell *freedom,* the blessing which those enjoy who trust fully in Christ, their Lord, who will never put them to shame:

> Hagar, Horeb, earthly Salem,
> Works of flesh will not avail them.
> Sarah, Zion, heavenly Salem,
> Christ, their Lord, will never fail them.

Continued: **26. But the Jerusalem (that is) above is free, and she is our mother.** Over against "the Jerusalem of today" we might have expected Paul to mention "the Jerusalem of the future." But he cannot very well do this, for the church, as the sum-total of all believers, here contrasted with carnal Israel, is being gathered even now, though her glorious consumma-

---

[134] The text here is somewhat obscure. There are many variants. Some of these are not very important. So, for example, whether one reads *Now* or *For* at the beginning of verse 25, the basic sense of the entire passage remains the same. The most debated question is whether or not the proper name *Hagar* belongs to the text. Though lengthy arguments have been presented for its omission, that rejection does not rest on solid textual evidence but is an unsubstantiated conjecture. On the basis of the information supplied by N.N.'s textual apparatus there would seem to be no good reason to accept any changes in the reading that is given in the text of both N.N. and Grk.N.T. (A.B.M.W.).

tion belongs, indeed, to the future. Not until Christ's return will she have been brought to completion, to shine forth in all her beauty, to the glory of God Triune.

Now when Paul speaks about "the Jerusalem (that is) above," he is thinking not only of the Church Triumphant but also of the many blessings which the exalted Christ lavishes upon this object of his love. And since from heaven these blessings also descend to the earth (cf. Eph. 1:3), creating and strongly influencing the church here below, producing conditions on earth which in some measure reflect those in heaven, it is clear that "the Jerusalem (that is) above" becomes in a sense the mother of all God's true children on earth, be they Gentiles or Jews. Essentially the same idea is found in the book of Revelation (3:12; 21:2, 10). In a vision John sees the holy city, new Jerusalem coming down out of heaven from God. That is happening now: whenever sinners are reborn—born "from above" (John 3:3, 6, 7)—; whenever, in principle, God's will is done on earth as in heaven (Matt. 6:10); and whenever, as a result of Christ's coming and work (Isa. 7:14; cf. 9:6), heaven's peace is reflected in the hearts and lives of God's children here below (Isa. 11:6-9; cf. Jer. 23:6; 31:31-34). But this is only an anticipatory fulfilment of the prophecies. Perfection belongs to the day of the great consummation.[135]

Heaven, then, is the church's mother, for it was heaven that gave birth to her children. Though many of them are still on earth, is not heaven their homeland (Phil. 3:20)? Are not their lives governed from heaven in accordance with heavenly standards? Are not their names inscribed in heaven's register? Is it not there that their rights are secured, and their interests promoted? Is it not to heaven that their thoughts and prayers ascend and their hopes aspire? Their Savior dwells there, living evermore to make intercession for them. Some of their friends are there even now, and they themselves, if they place their trust in the heavenly Highpriest, will be there shortly, to receive the inheritance of which they have an earnest even now. See John 14:1-4; Rom. 8:17; Col. 3:1-3; Heb. 4:14-16; 6:19, 20; 7:25; 12:22-24; I Peter 1:4, 5; Rev. 7:9-17.

"The Jerusalem (that is) above is free," says Paul. See John 8:36. She has been delivered from every form of bondage and enjoys perfect peace in the presence of her Lord. She is, moreover, *our* mother," the mother not only of the Jews who have gone to the deeps of God's promise but also of the Gentiles who have done the same thing; **27. for it is written:**

"Rejoice O barren one, you who do not bear;
Break forth and shout, you who have no birth-pangs;
For more are the children of the desolate than of her who has a husband."

---

[135] See my book *More Than Conquerors, An Interpretation of the Book of Revelation* (Grand Rapids, fifteenth edition, 1967), p. 237.

Isaiah, by prophetic vision, sees Zion bereft of her children, who have gone into Babylonian captivity. Jehovah, through his prophet, brings her a message of cheer. She, though now barren, will be fruitful; more so, in fact, than ever before (Isa. 54:1). The promise given to Sarah, who also was barren, will be fulfilled (Gen. 17:16). God's church will be extended among the Gentiles. Large multitudes will thus be added to the company of the saved. Zion, the Jerusalem (that is) above, will have an abundant posterity on earth. Hence, she will have to make her tent more spacious by lengthening its cords. At the same time she will have to see to it that the stakes are strengthened, that is, that the tent-pins are fixed into the ground more firmly, because the dwelling-place of the church as God sees it will never be broken up (Isa. 54:2, 3; Rev. 3:12; 7:9; cf. John 6:37, 39; 10:28).

Now all this is represented here as the work of the Lord, the result of the manifestation of his enduring lovingkindness (cf. Isa. 54:7, 8); not the product of human exertion but the realization of God's promise, the very promise that gave Isaac to Abraham and Sarah. This promise applies also to the Galatians if they accept it by means of a living faith: **28. Now y o u, brothers, like Isaac, are children of promise.** Here again we are pleased to take note of the affectionate manner in which Paul addresses those for whom the letter was intended. Again he calls them "brothers" (cf. 1:11; 3:15; 4:12, 28, 31; 5:11, 13; 6:1, 18). Are not all believers members of the same family, the Father's Family? See N.T.C. on Eph. 3:14, 15. They are brothers by grace, through the Spirit. Surely, if the Jerusalem (that is) above is their common mother (verse 26), then it follows that her children are brothers. Like Isaac, and by virtue of the promise realized in him but not in Ishmael, these Galatians who truly believe—whether they be Gentiles or Jews by birth makes no difference—are "children of promise." They are Abraham's legitimate sons, the true heirs. Let them understand, then, that what the Judaizers and their followers are doing is this: they are opposing the very work of God which he is gloriously effectuating whenever Gentiles, on equal terms with the Jews, are gathered into the church. See on 3:16-18, 29; 4:22.

The basic difference between Ishmael and Isaac, and between the two groups which they respectively represent, reveals itself not only in their birth (slave or free), but also in their relation to each other: **29. But as at that time he (who was) flesh-born persecuted the one (who was) Spirit-born, so (it is) also now.** The reference here is to Gen. 21:8, 9, which informs us that on the day when Isaac was weaned—which usually took place when the child was about three years of age—Abraham celebrated this event by means of a great feast. It was then that "Sarah saw the son of Hagar the Egyptian, whom she had borne to Abraham, mocking" (translation of the Hebrew text). Though the original lacks the words: (mocking) "her son Isaac," this object, added by the Septuagint and thus also by the Vulgate, etc., undoubtedly expresses what the writer had in mind, as the context

185

clearly indicates. Since Ishmael was fourteen years older than Isaac (cf. Gen. 16:16 with 21:5), he must have been a lad of about seventeen at the time when this incident occurred.

There are those, however, who interpret the Hebrew verb which describes Ishmael's conduct toward his brother as indicating nothing more serious than innocent play. Thus R.S.V. renders the Genesis passage: "playing with her son Isaac."[136] On the basis of this rendering it is at times further assumed that the guilty one was Sarah, not Ishmael. When Isaac's mother sees the older boy and her own little child having a good time together, she is stricken with jealousy, as she considers the future. She begins to worry about the possibility that the two might some day become joint-heirs of Abraham's wealth. That must not be. Hence, she demands Ishmael's ejection, so that her own son Isaac may be the sole heir. On the basis of this interpretation Paul's statement that Ishmael *persecuted* Isaac would, of course, be wrong. But the facts do not sustain this view of that which actually took place. Note the following:

(1) The Old Testament does not support this meaning for the verb that is here used to describe what Ishmael was doing. That verb does not generally refer to innocent fun. There was, for example, nothing innocent in the "jesting" with which Lot's prospective sons-in-law greeted the announcement of Sodom's imminent doom (Gen. 19:14). That jesting was coarse ridicule, mockery. Again, Potiphar's wife was not at all in the mood to accuse Joseph of having been "guilty" of a little innocent play. On the contrary, by implication she charged him with *insult,* to put it mildly (Gen. 39:14). The unrestrained hilarity of the Israelites around the golden calf was by no means innocent merrymaking (Exod. 32:6), neither was the "amusement" of the Philistines in connection with their prisoner Samson (Judg. 16:25). It is evident that in all these cases the word has an unfavorable sense, an acrid taste.[137]

(2) A look at the historical and psychological background also favors the rendering *mocking* rather than *playing with*. It should be borne in mind that the birth of Isaac and, even more, the fact that the little one had survived the earliest and most critical stage of his life, had brought about an important change in Ishmael's prospects as an heir of Abraham's vast estate. *Before* Isaac's arrival Ishmael must have regarded himself as the sole heir of unassailable assets. He must have felt all the more secure because of his father's ripe old age. And now suddenly the ground gives way from under his feet. Someone else has replaced him. Not only that, but

---

136 See also Strack-Billerbeck, *op. cit.,* Vol. III, pp. 575, 576.
137 In Gen. 26:8 the verb is used in a different sense: of a man *fondling* his wife. In all these cases in which the word occurs in the Old Testament the Hebrew uses a strengthened (Piël) form of the verb *çāhaq* (Gen. 19:14; 21:9; 26:8; 39:14; Exod. 32:6; and Judg. 16:25: the only instances of the Piël form).

at this particular *feast* everyone's interest is focused on this little brother, not on Ishmael. Seen in this light, it is not so strange that Ishmael, out of envy, *mocked* Isaac.

(3) Children often imitate their parents. Is it not possible, indeed rather natural, that the contempt with which Hagar had looked down upon Sarah was copied by Ishmael in his attitude toward Sarah's son? Cf. Gen. 16:4 and 21:9.

Paul, accordingly, was entirely correct in interpreting the Old Testament passage as he did. The one who was born in the natural way *had persecuted* the one who was born in a supernatural way, that is, born through special intervention of the Holy Spirit, who had enabled Abraham, though the latter had become "as good as dead," to deposit seed, and had quickened Sarah's womb. Cf. verse 23. So also today, says Paul, himself formerly a legalist and persecutor, the flesh-born Judaizers are persecuting those who are Spirit-born (now in the sense of *regenerated*). The wicked world, whether represented by legalists or by libertines, begrudges believers their joy in the Lord. To be persecuted is therefore the lot of the Christian (Matt. 5:11; John 15:20; 16:33; II Tim. 3:12; Rev. 12:13).

If there be any implied idea of relative "innocence" in this passage, it would be on the part of Isaac. If he complained at all, it is not mentioned. It was his mother who noticed that Ishmael was mocking. It is true that a child of three can do very little in the way of opposing a young man of seventeen. But it is characteristic of Isaac that also later on in life he bears persecution with admirable patience (Gen. 26:13-22), a virtue for which the Lord rewarded him (Gen. 26:23-25). He was not a vengeful person.

But though vengeance is wrong, evil must be resisted. Moreover, it was the duty of both Abraham and Sarah to protect the son of promise. Ishmael and Isaac cannot live side by side. Hence, Paul continues: **30. But what does Scripture say?** "**Cast out the slave-woman and her son; for in no way shall the son of the slave-woman share in the inheritance[138] with the son of the free-woman.**" The inheritance (see on 3:9, 18, 29) is not for mockers or persecutors. It is for believers, for them alone. This is the third item with respect to which the basic difference between Ishmael and Isaac reveals itself. For the others see on verses 23 and 29. *Law* (as interpreted by the Judaizers) *and grace cannot dwell in one camp.* Ishmael must be summarily ejected! Sarah demanded it (Gen. 21:10). What is more, God himself supported this demand (Gen. 21:12), giving Paul the right to imply that the order for Ishmael's expulsion was based on divine authority: "But what does *Scripture* say?"

31. With another, very affectionate, "brothers" (see on verse 28) the

---

[138] What we have here is a very strong negative, expressed by οὐ μή and the future indicative κληρονομήσει (the best reading).

apostle closes and summarizes the argument. He says: **Wherefore, brothers, not of a slave-woman are we children, but of the free-woman.** We—that is, Paul, the Galatians (as viewed by the judgment of love; cf. 4:6, 19; 5:10), all believers everywhere and throughout all time—are children not of *a* slave-woman—the definite article being omitted to emphasize her *slavish* quality—but of *the* free-woman, Sarah, as the true representative of "the Jerusalem (that is) above." We are the offspring of sovereign grace. Nevertheless, this in no way relieves us of responsibility, the very responsibility implied in the passage, namely, to guard the precious endowment which the Lord has bequeathed to us, and therefore to live by faith, in the joyful exercise of our freedom of access to the throne of grace. This freedom is at the same time a deliverance from the curse of the law. Let us then, so argues Paul, cling to this freedom, for Jerusalem (that is) above is a city of free men (Gal. 3:19-29; 4:26; 5:1).

Summary of Chapter 4

This chapter can be divided into three sections under the headings: Recapitulation (verses 1-11), Reminiscence (verses 12-20), and Reasoning by means of an Allegory (verses 21-31). In the first section Paul, in close connection with the preceding argument,[139] points out the folly of exchanging one type of slavery for another. Judaistic bondage is not any better than paganistic. God sent his Son to redeem men from every type of spiritual slavery. He changed slaves into sons. Moreover, he sent the Spirit into their hearts in order that those who were sons *in position* might also be sons in *disposition,* for *adoption* implies *transformation.* Deliverance means freedom of access, so that the ransomed one cries out, "Abba!" ("Father!").

In the next paragraph the apostle asks, "Where is now y o u r former blessedness?" His affectionate concern for the Galatians reveals itself as he recalls the warm welcome with which they had received him at the occasion of their first meeting. How blessed had been the experiences then enjoyed, how unforgettable the fellowship! What a contrast between then and now. One is reminded of the lines:

"Where is the blessedness I knew
When first I sought the Lord?
Where is the soul-refreshing view
Of Jesus and his Word?

---

[139] Cf. 4:1, 2 with 3:22, 25; 4:3, 8-10 with 3:23; 4:4 with 3:19; 4:5 with 3:13; 4:6 with 3:2, 3, 5, 14; 4:7 with 3:18, 29; and 4:11 with 3:4.

GALATIANS

"What peaceful hours I once enjoyed!
How sweet their memory still!
But they have left an aching void
The world can never fill."
                              William Cowper

In the case of the Galatians the former blessedness had been lost because Paul's earnest warnings had been left unheeded. The apostle exposes the motives of the enemies of the faith. They make much of the Galatians in order that the latter may make much of them. Now making much of someone is not wrong if it be in connection with a good cause. Thus, the fact that the Galatians had previously paid special attention to Paul, and, far from treating him with contemptuous scorn because of his bodily infirmity, had been willing, if necessary, to give him their most precious possession, was not wrong, because he proclaimed to them the gospel of salvation. Would that this interest in Paul and his gospel had continued! With sadness of heart Paul asks, "Have I then become y o u r enemy by telling y o u the truth?" Do the Galatians not realize that his warnings and criticisms were for their own good? The apostle concludes this section by saying, "My dear children, for whom I am again suffering birth-pangs until Christ be formed in y o u, I could wish to be present with y o u now and to change my tone of voice, for I am perplexed about y o u."

The chapter closes with a reminder—in the form of an allegory—that those who hear the law should take it to heart. When the Judaizers pride themselves in the fact that they are "sons of Abraham," and the Galatians are influenced by this boast, let it be remembered that Abraham had two sons: one by the slave-woman, the other by the free-woman. Slavish law-observance, as if this were the pathway to salvation, makes one similar to Ishmael, slave-son of a slave-woman (Hagar). On the contrary, the exercise of one's freedom in Christ, basing one's trust in him alone, makes one a true son of Abraham, similar to the free-born son Isaac, born to the free-woman, Sarah.

Chapter 5

Verse 1

Theme: *The Gospel of Justification by Faith apart from Law-works Defended against Its Detractors*

III. *Its Application: it produces true liberty. Let the Galatians stand firm, therefore, as does Paul, who glories in the cross of Christ*

A. For freedom Christ has set us free; continue to stand firm, therefore.

CHAPTER V

GALATIANS

5   1 For freedom Christ has set us free; continue to stand firm, therefore, and do not be loaded down again with a yoke of slavery.

5:1

A. *Maintain y o u r freedom!*

1. For freedom Christ has set us free.[140] There is every reason to agree with modern versions when they print Gal. 5:1 as a little paragraph all by itself, the first paragraph of a new chapter. That something new begins here is clearly evident from the contrast between the *argumentative* style of the earlier chapters, including the immediately preceding context, and the *hortatory* language that begins here in 5:1. Having been taught that in Christ we *are* free, we (here specifically the Galatians) are now encouraged to maintain that freedom (verse 1) and to interpret and apply it properly (verse 13 ff.). But this very statement also indicates the close connection between chapters 4 and 5. The truth stated and vigorously defended in the preceding chapters is applied to life in chapters 5 and 6.

That the idea of freedom is very much in the foreground is clear not only from verse 1 but also from verse 13 ff. The question arises: Just what does Paul mean when he speaks of freedom? It implies first of all *deliverance*. This deliverance is sometimes conceived of as rescue from the guilt and power of sin (Rom. 6:18); hence, from an accusing conscience (Heb. 10:22), from the wrath of God (Rom. 5:1; cf. Heb. 10:27), and the tyranny of

---

[140] Other translations of verse 1, such as, "Stand fast therefore in the liberty wherewith Christ hath made us free" (A.V.), though conveying the same meaning essentially, are not based upon the best text. Besides, in connection with the great central doctrines of salvation asyndetic expression is not uncharacteristic of Paul. Cf. Eph. 2:5b, "By grace y o u have been saved." Such omission of conjunctions produces emphasis. With respect to the question whether, with some, we should adopt the rendering, "For *this* freedom," or should favor the simple, "For freedom," my answer would be that it is probably best to allow either translation, since although the abstract quality *freedom* has not been mentioned in the immediately preceding context, it has nevertheless been implied in the words, "We are children of the free-woman." Translated either way, moreover, the close connection with the immediately preceding verses is clear. For the point of grammar see p. 145, footnote 105.

Satan (II Tim. 2:26; cf. Heb. 2:14). Nevertheless, although all of this is probably implied in Paul's use of the term here in Gal. 5:1, 13, the context indicates that he is thinking particularly of freedom from "the law," that is, deliverance from the curse which the law pronounces upon the sinner who had been striving—unsuccessfully, of course—to achieve his own righteousness (Gal. 3:13, 22-26; 4:1-7), but has now, by grace, turned to Christ and salvation in him. Cf. Phil. 3:4-9. For God's chosen one this freedom includes rescue from the results of the law's inability to make alive what is dead (Gal. 3:21). Implied is also freedom from fear, the fear that arises from *a.* the erroneous idea that both the moral and the ceremonial law must be strictly obeyed if one is to be saved, and *b.* the oppressing awareness of inability to meet this demand (Gal. 3:23; 4:21-31; Rom. 7:24-8:2).

Deliverance is, however, a negative concept, though the positive is clearly implied. *Freedom is more than deliverance. It is a positive endowment.* What the law could not do God has accomplished through Christ and the Spirit (Rom. 8:3, 4). Positively, then, freedom, as Paul sees it, is the state in which a person is walking and living in the Spirit (Gal. 5:25), so that he produces the fruit of the Spirit (5:22, 23), and with joy and gratitude does the will of God (5:14; Rom. 8:4), in principle fulfilling the law of Christ (Gal. 6:2), even "the law of liberty" (James 1:25). This liberty amounts to delighting in the law of God in one's inmost self (Rom. 7:22). The person who is truly free no longer acts from constraint but serves his God willingly, with cheerfulness of heart. Freedom of access to the Father is implied, of course, for the blessing of which Paul speaks is enjoyed by *sons* (Gal. 4:6; Rom. 8:15).

Such true freedom is therefore always a freedom *plus.* It is with freedom as with justification. See p. 98. When an accused man is declared not guilty, he is free. Likewise when a slave has been emancipated, he is free. But the judge or the emancipator does not, as a rule, adopt the acquitted individual as his son. But when the Son makes one free, he is free indeed (John 8:36). He then rejoices in the glorious liberty of sonship, with all that this implies as to "access," right to the inheritance, etc.

Paul emphasizes that it was Christ himself—not our own merits or our own deeds—that set us free. He did it by becoming a curse for us (Gal. 3:13); hence, by his blood (Heb. 10, 19, 22); and he did it and is constantly doing it through his Spirit (Gal. 3:2, 3, 14; 4:6, 29; cf. Rom. 8:4). Where the Spirit of the Lord is, there is liberty (II Cor. 3:17).

The thoroughly human Paul expresses himself in a manner which could almost be described as containing a bit of humor when he says, "For freedom Christ has set us free," as if to say, "Is it not ridiculous to imagine that Christ would have opened for us the gate of our prison—at such a cost!— merely to transfer us to another prison? Surely, he set us free in order that we might indeed be and remain free!" Continued: **continue to stand firm, therefore** (cf. II Thess. 2:15). Perseverance in the fight against re-enslavement is here prescribed. The Galatians had been running beautifully (5:7), but they had failed to carry on. They had, in fact, reversed their course. What Paul is saying, then, is that over against the opponents they should stand firm *and should so continue.* This standing firm is not that of a well-nigh unassailable fenced-in statue, but rather that of a tree firmly rooted in the midst of the raging storm. Even better, it is that of the soldier on the field of battle, not fleeing but offering stout resistance to the enemy and defeating him (Eph. 6:10-20). The very fact that it was no one less than Christ himself who had set the Galatians free, so that by standing firm, they are voluntarily continuing in the sphere of *his* activity, should encourage them; hence, "Continue to stand firm, *therefore.*" The crown of valor is victory (Matt. 10:22; Rev. 2:10).

Paul adds: **and do not be loaded down**[141] **again with a yoke of slavery.** Peter had spoken about an unbearable yoke (Acts 15:10). He was referring to the yoke of the law, including its many regulations, augmented subsequently by man-made "traditions." Under that yoke Israel had groaned. The Galatians, mostly of pagan origin (4:8), had been similarly subjected to rules and regulations pertaining to their former pagan religion. Ramsay speaks of "a highly elaborate system" of such burdensome stipulations, prevalent in Galatia. Hence, what the apostle is saying is that those who were delivered from this unbearable yoke of paganism should certainly not try to shoulder another similar yoke, that of Judaism. See also on 4:9. Having escaped from one ritualism are they now going to bow before another? Rather, let them flee for refuge to him whose yoke is easy and whose burden is light (Matt. 11:29, 30).

---

[141] The original uses a form of the verb ἐνέχω; literally, to *have or hold in.* Thus it is used in connection with Herodias who "had it in" for John the Baptist (had a grudge against him; Mark 6:19), and in connection with the scribes and Pharisees who were (violently) enraged against Jesus (Luke 11:53). In connection with a yoke, the best translation is probably "to be loaded down with" or "to be oppressed by."

Chapter 5

Theme: *The Gospel of Justification by Faith apart from Law-works Defended against Its Detractors*

III. *Its Application: it produces true liberty. Let the Galatians stand firm, therefore, as does Paul, who glories in the cross of Christ*

   B. Do not try to combine both principles: *a.* justification by way of law and *b.* justification by grace through faith. If y o u let yourselves be circumcised, Christ will be of no advantage to y o u. If y o u cling to law, y o u have lost y o u r hold on grace. Practice faith working through love.

2 Now I, Paul, say to y o u that if y o u let yourselves be circumcised
Christ will be of no advantage to y o u. 3 And I testify again to every man who lets
himself be circumcised, that he is under obligation to keep the whole law. 4 Y o u
are estranged from Christ, whoever (y o u are who) seek to be justified by way of
law; y o u have fallen away from grace. 5 For, as to ourselves, it is through the
Spirit, by faith, that we eagerly await the hoped-for righteousness. 6 For in Christ
Jesus neither circumcision nor uncircumcision is of any avail, but faith working
through love.

5:2-6

B. *Faith in Christ plus circumcision will not do*

It was a *gain* of incalculable value that Christ obtained for his people,
namely, freedom. Over against this stands the frightful *loss* that is incurred
by those who refuse to recognize him as their all-sufficient Savior. Therefore
the text continues: **2. Now I, Paul, say to y o u that if y o u let yourselves be
circumcised**[142] **Christ will be of no advantage to y o u.** From the stately style
it is evident that the writer is conscious of his authority as an apostle of
Jesus Christ. He has every right to speak thus, not only because he is, in
fact, a true apostle, invested with this office by Christ himself (1:1, 12), but
also because the matter at hand concerns the eternal weal or woe of those
addressed. For "I, Paul" see also II Cor. 10:1; Eph. 3:1; Col. 1:23; and I
Thess. 2:18. The substance of Paul's words is this, that a man's faith rests
on Christ either entirely or not at all. God's Anointed One must be recognized and worshiped as the one and only Savior. Since the Galatians were
already yielding to the Judaizers in the matter of observing "days and months
and seasons and years" (4:10), the danger was great that they would yield
also in the matter of circumcision, and that, as a result, their whole religion
would be reduced to ritualism with a slightly Christian tinge. It is for this
reason that the apostle uses such incisive language. If they accept circumcision, thinking that this is necessary for salvation, or at least for a full
measure of salvation, Christ will be of no advantage to them whatever.
A Christ supplemented is a Christ supplanted. Continued: **3. And I testify**

---

[142] It is important to note that this is a third class or future more vivid conditional
sentence, implying that, considered from the viewpoint of human responsibility,
the thing which Paul fears is possible, not that it necessarily has already occurred.
On circumcision see N.T.C. on Colossians and Philemon, pp. 114-116, including
footnote 85.

again to every man who lets himself be circumcised, that he is under obligation to keep the whole law. Continuing in the same solemn vein Paul *testifies*, so that the Galatians may act reverently, with a proper sense of respect for the will of God as revealed to them by his ambassador Paul. For *testify* see also Eph. 4:17 and I Thess. 2:12. The gravity of the expression is shown especially in the manner in which it is used in the speeches of Paul as reported by Luke in Acts 20:26 and 26:22. Paul testifies *to every man*. He is not only addressing the churches "en masse," or even the Galatian congregations one by one, but each *member* individually and personally. Let his warning be taken to heart by each and by all. Note the significant word *again* ("I testify again"). The sense, in connection with the preceding verse, is in all probability this, "Y o u must accept *the whole Christ* (Christ in all the fulness of his saving power and grace); *again,* if y o u refuse, then y o u will have to keep *the whole law.*" The one is implied in the other. If salvation is by law, why should one be obliged to keep just *one* ceremonial commandment, or even two or three, and not the rest? If the pathway to salvation is thought to lie in that direction one should travel it to the very end. He will discover, however, that the base from which he started was located in enemy territory—that his presupposition was a tragic error—and that the destination for which he is actually headed is "the curse" (3:10).

4. In this verse the same truth is reiterated: **Y o u are estranged**[143] **from Christ, whoever (y o u are who) seek to be justified**[144] **by way of law; y o u have fallen away from grace.** If the Galatians, whether all or some, should seek to be justified by way of law, and should persist to the end in this error, the cord that binds them to Christ would not be able to bear that strain. It would snap! They would then have fallen away from the domain of grace, would have lost their hold on grace. It would be with them like it is with withered flowers that fall to the ground and perish.

We should not try to diminish the force of these words, in the interest, perhaps, of this or that theological presupposition. It might seem as if what Paul is here saying is inconsistent with the doctrine of the preservation of the saints, a doctrine not only scriptural in general but also particularly dear to Paul. For evidence see N.T.C. on Philippians, pp. 54, 55. In reality, however, there is no conflict at all, as has been shown in connection with the explanation of Gal. 1:6, 7. Let it be borne in mind that Paul is speaking here from the standpoint of human responsibility.

5. In contrast with those who presumably might fall into the error against which the apostle issues his warning, Paul's own position, the

---

[143] Greek κατηργήθητε 2nd. person pl., aor. indic. passive of καταργέω. Cf. Rom. 7:2, 6.
[144] Greek δικαιοῦσθε 2nd. person pl. pres. indic. passive with conative force. See Gram. N.T., p. 880.

conviction of the Galatians who have remained loyal, and, in general, the firm persuasion of believers everywhere, is set forth in the following passage, in which the emphasis falls on the word which in the original heads the sentence, namely, "we" or, as we can also render it, "as to ourselves." Says Paul: **For, as to ourselves, it is through the Spirit, by faith, that we eagerly await the hoped for righteousness.** The conjunction γάρ can best be interpreted in its more usual sense as indicating the cause or reason for the thought that was expressed in the preceding verse. What Paul is saying then amounts to something along this line, "Those who yield to the Judaizers have fallen away from grace *because* they refuse to give due credit to the work of the Holy Spirit. On the contrary, as to ourselves, we recognize that Spirit as the source of all our striving and of our ultimate victory." That the word *pneuma,* which by itself can be rendered either *spirit* (6:1, 18) or *Spirit* (the Holy), must here be interpreted in the latter sense, as nearly always in Galatians, follows from all that Paul has been saying previously in this epistle and from all that he says elsewhere concerning the activity of the third person of the Trinity. Thus, the idea that it is through the Spirit that by faith we eagerly await the hoped-for righteousness is in line with the teaching that the law produces death (Rom. 7:10; 8:2), but the Spirit makes alive (Gal. 4:29; Rom. 8:3, 4, 10; cf. John 3:5); that the law creates fear and wretchedness (Rom. 8:15), but the Spirit brings about hope and assurance (Rom. 8:16; Eph. 1:13); that the law enslaves (Gal. 3:23; 4:24, 25), but the Spirit brings about freedom (Gal. 4:29-5:1). Considered from God's side, therefore, salvation is the gift of the Spirit (II Thess. 2:13; cf. Eph. 2:5, 8). Viewed from man's side it is received by faith, but even this faith, both in its initiation and at every step of the way, is Spirit-given. And if faith is God-given, why should not hope be also? And why should not the thing hoped for, in this case: the hoped-for righteousness,[145] be also assigned to the Holy Spirit, this all the more because the very presence of the Spirit in the hearts of believers is considered a pledge and first instalment of greater glories to come (Eph. 1:13, 14)?[146]

These greater glories to come are definitely in the mind of the writer, for he says that "through the Spirit, by faith we *eagerly await* (cf. Rom. 8:19, 23, 25; I Cor. 1:7) the hoped-for righteousness." To be sure, the verdict of acquittal has already been pronounced, so that even now the peace of God has smiled its way into our hearts (Rom. 5:1). But one day, namely, at Christ's glorious return, our righteousness will be declared *publicly.* Cf. Matt. 25:31-40; Luke 18:1-8; I Thess. 3:13; II Thess. 1:10. To

---

[145] Thus also in Col. 1:5 and Titus 2:13 "hope" refers to "the thing hoped for."
[146] For the reasons given I cannot accept the conclusion of Lenski (*op. cit.,* pp. 256, 257) who refuses to interpret Gal. 5:5 as containing a reference to the Holy Spirit. To be sure the Spirit may not be "a means that *we* use," but he may, nevertheless, very well be the Source of the exercise of our faith, hope, and love.

this day and to this blessing *we*, through the Spirit, by faith, eagerly look forward, not doubting that God will fulfil his promise.

6. This declaration concerning the eager forward look of Spirit-imparted faith is true, **For in Christ Jesus**[147] **neither circumcision nor uncircumcision is of any avail, but faith working through love.** As far as Christ Jesus is concerned —or, as one might say, in the sphere of Christian religion—*being circumcised* will be of no benefit toward salvation. But here as always Paul shows excellent balance by immediately adding, *nor being uncircumcised*. The circumcised person must not boast about the fact that his foreskin was removed, nor should the uncircumcised put on airs because he still has his. Cf. the similar statement in I Cor. 8:8 regarding food. What *is* important, however, is "faith working through love." Compare Rom. 14:17, "For the rule of God does not consist in eating and drinking but in righteousness and peace and joy in the Holy Spirit."

A controversy has long raged between Roman Catholic and Protestant interpreters with respect to the question whether Paul meant to say "faith wrought through love" or "faith working through love." According to the first view, generally favored by Rome, love precedes faith. Our works of love or "charity" give substance to faith. In this way the danger of ascribing too great a value to works and of making works basic in the effectuation of our salvation, is great indeed. This theory, therefore, contradicts the very thesis which the apostle is trying to establish in this epistle, namely, that justification is by faith, apart from works.[148] And as to which is first in order, whether *a.* love and the work it produces or *b.* faith, basically the priority should be given to faith. The works are fruits, not roots. Cf. Eph. 2:8-10; I Thess. 1:3; and see N.T.C. on I Tim. 1:5.

This having been said, it is well, nevertheless, to point out that just as in the natural sphere the young married woman who becomes the happy mother of a child, not only lavishes her love upon that child but is also herself reciprocally enriched, so also mother *faith,* having produced her child *love,* receives grace and glory from this child. Action begets reaction in this blessed circle of interrelationships.[149] The endowments with which

---

[147] On the title "Christ Jesus" in distinction from "Jesus Christ" see N.T.C. on I and II Timothy and Titus, p. 51, footnote 19.

[148] Moreover, also from the point of view of grammar this position is indefensible, for, in spite of articles that have been written in defense of the belief that ἐνεργουμένη, here used, is in the passive voice, the theory which regards it as a middle is far more natural and in keeping with Paul's usage elsewhere: "sinful passions are at work" (Rom. 7:5); "comfort—or patience—is at work" (II Cor. 1:6); so is also God's power (Eph. 3:20) and his word (I Thess. 2:13); and also "the mystery of lawlessness" (II Thess. 2:7). In each of these cases the verbal form is a middle, not a passive.

[149] I consider Lenski's discussion of this subject (*op. cit.*, pp. 259, 260) to be, on the whole, excellent. I have difficulty, however, with his statement, "Faith is ever complete in itself."

the Holy Spirit graces the believer overlap. None stands by itself. And is not this implied in Paul's very statement that faith works through love? It works, becomes effective, proves its genuine character, by means of love and loving deeds. Indeed, by works faith is made perfect (James 2:22). Paul and James are in complete agreement!

Whether or not those are right who say that the Judaizers must have accused Paul of minimizing love, and that in this passage the apostle is answering this charge, we do not know. One fact, however, stands out clearly: the faith which Paul proclaims is always far richer than mere understanding. It is fruitful (5:22, 23; cf. John 16:2, 5, 8), not barren. It is warm, not cold. The man who wrote Gal. 5:6 also wrote I Cor. 13:2.

Chapter 5

Theme: *The Gospel of Justification by Faith apart from Law-works
Defended against Its Detractors*

III. *Its Application: it produces true liberty. Let the Galatians stand firm,
therefore, as does Paul, who glories in the cross of Christ*

C. Y o u were running well; who was it that threw y o u off y o u r
course? I am convinced that y o u will see the matter my way. If I am still
preaching circumcision, why am I still being persecuted? Would that the
disturbers might make eunuchs of themselves!

7 Y o u were running well; who cut in on y o u so that y o u did not continue to obey the truth? 8 This persuasion (is) not (derived) from him who is
calling y o u. 9 A little leaven leavens the whole lump. 10 I on my part am persuaded in the Lord with respect to y o u, that y o u will not adopt a different view
(than mine). And the one who is throwing y o u into confusion will have to pay
the penalty, whoever he may be. 11 Now as for myself, brothers, if I am still
preaching circumcision, why am I still being persecuted? In that case the stumbling-
block of the cross has been removed. 12 Would that those who upset y o u might
make eunuchs of themselves!

5:7-12

C. *Y o u were running well. I am persuaded that y o u will repent*

7. Turning back once more (cf. 1:8, 9; 3:2, 3; 4:9, 12-15) to the time when
the Galatians had heard the gospel from the lips of Paul and had accepted
Christ as their Savior and Lord, the apostle says: **Y o u were running well.**
They had started out beautifully. Proof for this statement is found in 4:13,
14; cf. the account in Acts 13 and 14. The metaphor is taken from the foot-
race in the stadium. A similar figure underlies Gal. 2:2; Phil. 2:16; I Tim.
4:7, 8; Heb. 12:1, 2. If Paul was in Corinth when he wrote this letter, as
seems probable, he must have been hearing about such and other athletic
contests, and may even have been a spectator at one time or another. But
rivalry in games and sports was not confined to the city famous for its
Isthmian contests, but was prevalent in greater or lesser extent throughout
the world, then as well as now. The Galatians understood the metaphor.
Continued: **who cut in on y o u so that y o u did not continue to obey the truth?**
Paul is not asking for information. He is not necessarily referring to any
ringleader. In all probability he is simply saying to the Galatians, "Before
y o u continue to yield to the wishes of *any* person who belongs to this
group, would it not be wise to consider carefully what kind of a person it
was that threw y o u off y o u r course?" It is not the *identity* but the
character of the Judaizers which the apostle is bringing into the foreground.
This is in harmony with 6:12, 13. The Galatians, having been diverted
from their proper course, were now proceeding on a path that would lead
them to ruin, unless they returned to the base from which they had started
out. They had discontinued to obey the truth. By this "truth" is meant God's
special revelation as embodied in the gospel proclaimed by Paul and the
other apostles and fellow-workers. Cf. 2:5, 14. That *truth* is full of practical
implications. It concerns both doctrine and life. It not only tells men what
to believe but also how they should conduct themselves. It reveals to them

that God gave his Son as a complete and perfect Savior, and that, out of gratitude for the salvation that is freely given to all who embrace him by a living faith, the redeemed should spend their days showing forth God's praise in thought, word, and deed. Continued: **8. This persuasion**[150] **(is) not (derived) from him who is calling y o u.** For "calling" see on 1:6. The Galatians are being told that the persuasion that draws them away from the truth does not have its source in him who not only *called* them in the beginning but *is calling* them even now: "Day by day his sweet voice soundeth, Saying, 'Christian, follow me' " (Mrs. Cecil F. Alexander). They must realize that their present course of action means that they are saying "No" to no one less than God himself (cf. 1:15). And this is a mild way of declaring that they have begun to say "Yes" to Satan, who is using the Judaizers in the distortion of the only true gospel (cf. Matt. 13:25, 28).

9. The warning continues, this time in the form of a proverbial saying, found also in I Cor. 5:6: **A little leaven leavens the whole lump.** Seemingly insignificant causes can lead to momentous consequences, whether for good (as in Matt. 13:33) or for evil, as in the present case. Principles penetrate! When a person has forsaken the sound principle of salvation *by grace alone through faith* (the latter considered as God's gift; see N.T.C. on Eph. 2:8), and has taken his stand on a new "persuasion," namely, salvation *by grace plus works,* the attention is gradually shifted to works, until grace has disappeared completely, and so has Christ, on whom grace rests. Illustrations of the penetrating power of evil: *a.* In ancient Israel the deceptively *innocent* worship of Jehovah under the symbolism (and by means) of an image soon led to gross idolatry; *b.* it took only a "worm" to destroy Jonah's "gourd" (Jonah 4:7); *c.* cancer spreads (metastasizes), so that a malignant tumor, ever so small in its beginning, may in the end destroy the entire body (cf. II Tim. 2:17); *d.* a "little" (?) carelessness starts a forest-fire, with destruction of thousands of valuable lumber-producing trees, or sets fire to a hotel, killing several people; *e.* someone tosses a few roots of a "beautiful" flower into a stream; result: many of the rivers, canals, lakes, and bayous of beautiful Florida, etc., are choked with the water hyacinth, which menaces wildlife, causes floods, strangles navigation, costs a fortune in attempts at eradication, so far with no completely satisfactory remedy in sight; and *f.:*

"For want of a nail the shoe was lost; for want of a shoe the horse was lost; for want of a horse the rider was lost; for want of a rider the battle

---

[150] As is clear from the textual evidence presented in N.N., this is the best text. The words πείθεσθαι (verse 7), πεισμονή (verse 8), and πέποιθα (verse 10), present a sound-similarity that is difficult to reproduce in English. An attempt would be: "Who cut in on y o u so that y o u did not continue *to be persuaded by* (hence, to obey) the truth? This (new) *persuasion* of y o u r s is not derived from him who is calling y o u. . . . I on my part *am persuaded* in the Lord, . . ."

was lost; and for want of a battle the kingdom was lost. All this for want of a horseshoe nail" (Benjamin Franklin, according to one version).

10. But though again and again the apostle has expressed his deep concern with reference to the Galatians (1:6, 7; 3:1-5; 4:11-20; 5:1-4, 7), he now reiterates his conviction that the letter which he is writing will have the desired effect. For other traces of this confidence see 3:4b; 4:6, 7, and the frequent use of the endearing form of address: "brothers" (1:11; 3:15; 4:12, 28, 31; 5:11, 13; 6:1, 18). He writes: **I on my part am persuaded in the Lord with respect to y o u, that y o u will not adopt a different view (than mine).** His conviction or persuasion regarding the Galatians rests not on any innate goodness of theirs, but solely on *their* and *his* relation to Christ, *their* and also *his* Lord. It is that Lord who, having begun a good work in the Galatians, will carry it on toward completion. See N.T.C. on Phil. 1:6. Continued: **And the one who is throwing y o u into confusion will have to pay the penalty, whoever he may be.** For the meaning of the verb *to throw into confusion* see on 1:7. Here in 5:10, as in verse 7 above, some see a reference to a ringleader. Some venture even farther away from shore, embarking boldly upon the sea of speculation when they suggest that either the apostle Peter, or else James the brother of the Lord, was that ringleader. But as to Peter see II Peter 3:15; and as to James see Acts 15:19, 24-26. Fact is that in referring to the disturbers Paul again and again uses the plural (1:7; 4:17; 5:12; 6:12, 13). But he also does not hesitate to use the plural and the singular in one breath (1:7; cf. 1:9: "certain individuals . . . anyone"). Does that mean that from the *many* disturbers he suddenly turns to the *one* ringleader? That would be rather strange. So also here the very wording would seem to point in the opposite direction: "the one who is throwing y o u into confusion . . . whoever he may be." The probable meaning is: "There are several disturbers. Be on y o u r guard, therefore, so that if *one*—anyone at all—of these creators of confusion approaches, y o u resist him, bearing in mind that, whoever he may be, he will have to pay the penalty." Implication: "and y o u also will have to pay the penalty (literally: bear the judgment) if y o u become involved in his guilt."

That the apostle is referring to *God's* judgment upon the distorters of the truth is not open to doubt. Whether Paul was thinking of punishment *here and now,* or rather of retribution *in the hereafter,* is not indicated. He may well have been thinking of both.

11. It is but natural that in connection with the strong condemnation of the teachers of error Paul would be reminded of an accusation which, in all probability, these men had hurled against him; namely, that he himself was inconsistent in his presentation of the gospel; specifically, that in regard to circumcision, the very matter with respect to which he censured his opponents so unmercifully, he himself was not to be trusted. They charged him with duplicity. At one time, so they said, Paul would have nothing

whatever to do with this rite, and would denounce those who honored it. At another time he himself would preach it. Had he not circumcised Timothy? Viewed in the light of this accusation we understand what the apostle means when he continues: **Now as for myself, brothers, if I am still preaching circumcision, why am I still being persecuted?**[151] If there had *not* been a radical change in Paul's philosophy of life, so that he who at one time had been a self-righteous Pharisee and an ardent advocate of the Jewish traditions had even now *not* been truly converted, but was still clinging to his earlier beliefs, then why would he nevertheless be persecuted? In that case the Judaizers would have welcomed him as one of their own circle!

As to the circumcision of Timothy (Acts 16:3), it certainly was *one thing* to circumcise a person of mixed parentage, as was Timothy, in order to make him a more effective missionary among the Jews, and to do this without the least suggestion that in some way this circumcision would contribute toward his salvation; it was *an entirely different matter* to force circumcision upon the Gentiles, with the implication that unless they were circumcised they could not be saved! See Acts 15:1. In matters in which no principle was involved Paul was very accommodating, flexible, and conciliatory (cf. Acts 21:17-26), but when a deep principle was at stake—for example, Christ's all-sufficiency for salvation—he was unbending, and rightly so. Moreover, far from being inconsistent when, on the one hand, he circumcised Timothy, yet on the other hand strongly condemned the circumcision of the Galatians, he was most gloriously consistent, for in both instances he was promoting the spread of the one true gospel, subordinating everything else to this marvelous cause. If, therefore, the opponents, in charging Paul with inconsistency, were thinking of what he had done to Timothy, and were implying that by that very act he had been "preaching circumcision," they really had no case at all.—For a different interpretation of the passage see footnote.[152] See also on 2:5.

---

[151] This is a first class conditional sentence, with εἰ and the first per. pres. indic. active in the protasis; first per. pres. indic. passive in the apodosis. The sentence assumes the thought expressed in the protasis to be true, but in the present instance (as in Matt. 12:27) only *for the sake of the argument*, to show how absurd the conclusion would be if the assumption in the protasis were true.

[152] There are those who think that Paul's hypothetical clause bears no relation to his controversy with the Judaizers. In support of their theory they state that the Judaizers could hardly have called such an alleged inconsistency as the circumcision of Timothy "a *preaching* of circumcision." See Ridderbos, *op. cit.*, p. 266. I believe Lenski answers this objection when he points out that, as the Judaizers saw it, "Did Paul not thus preach circumcision by his own acts?" He refers to such acts as circumcising Timothy and refusing to object when Jewish Christians chose to circumcise their male children, as long as no legalistic and Judaistic ideas were connected with such circumcisions.

Certainly one also preaches by means of his actions and refusals to act! Besides, the explanation which I, along with many others—Berkhof, Burton, Lenski, Robert-

Paul continues: **In that case the stumbling-block of the cross has been removed.** For the Jews the death of the Messiah—even more so, the *accursed* death of the cross!—was a stumbling-block, a definite obstacle or hindrance to their acceptance of the Christian religion (I Cor. 1:23). They would say, "What, the Messiah crucified? Perish the thought!" What added to the offensiveness of this doctrine, as they saw it, was the claim that by means of this cross the old shadows had been fulfilled, the old ceremonial ordinances abrogated. Moreover, the burden of obedience to the law as a precondition of salvation had been lifted. And, to make things even worse *in their eyes*, by this cross the wall of separation between Jew and Gentile had been removed once for all, never to be rebuilt. Therefore, the all-sufficiency of Christ Crucified for salvation, completely obliterating the need of any additional props such as circumcision, was the stumbling-block for the Jews. But if the apostle were still preaching circumcision as a means of salvation, that offense would have been removed. Also, in that case Paul would no longer be persecuted by his kinsmen. Hence, the very fact that this persecution had not been discontinued was adequate proof that the charge of the opponents was false.

12. Paul closes this brief paragraph with a rather startling expression: **Would that those who upset y o u might make eunuchs of themselves!**[153]

In view of the fact that the basic meaning of the verb which Paul uses in expressing his wish is *to cut off*, there are those who think that the apostle voices his desire that the opponents may be "cut off" from the church ("I would that they were even cut off which trouble you," A.V.), or, better still, that they would *cut themselves off* (". . . would cut themselves off from you altogether," Phillips; cf. Ramsay, *Historical Commentary*, pp. 437–440). A more reasonable interpretation, however, one which (because it agrees with the use of the verb in such contexts in contemporary sources)[154] is supported by most commentators both ancient and modern, interprets the meaning to be this, that the apostle is saying, "As for these agitators, they had better go the whole way and make eunuchs of themselves!" (N.E.B). Paul reasons, as it were, as follows: Since circumcision has lost its religious value, it is nothing more than a concision (cf. Phil. 3:2), which differs only in degree but not essentially from the practices of pagan priests, practices well-known to the Galatians. But since the Judaizers who are upsetting the Galatians believe *a little* physical mutilation is of

son, etc.—accept, is also in harmony with the charge of *duplicity* which the Judaizers preferred against Paul (1:10).
[153] The text accepted by both N.N. and Grk.N.T. (A-B-M-W) has the third person pl. fut. indic. middle ἀποκόψονται. Some texts, including p46, favor the subjunctive -ψωνται, with very little difference in resultant meaning. The verb is used elsewhere in connection with the cutting off of a member of the body (Mark 9:43, 45; John 18:10, 26) or of the ropes by which a boat is held (Acts 27:32).
[154] See the entry ἀποκόπτω in L.N.T. (A. and G.), p. 92.

spiritual value, let them be consistent and cut away *more radically*. Let them go all the way, and castrate themselves, thus making eunuchs of themselves like the priests of Cybele in their wild "devotions."

The question arises whether Paul was justified in uttering this wish. A few points should be borne in mind in this connection:

(1) In the final analysis Paul, in expressing this wish, was responsible to God, not to us. It is God alone who is able to judge the ethical value of such an utterance.

(2) Did not even the sinless Jesus say, "Whoever causes one of these little ones who believe in me to stumble, it is better for him that a heavy millstone be hung around his neck, and that he be drowned in the depth of the sea"? (Matt. 18:6; cf. Mark 9:42; Luke 17:2) .

(3) The situation in which Paul found himself was similar: the Galatians, who were very dear to him (4:19) were being led astray. Also, the purity of the gospel was being undermined. Paul loved the Galatians and the true gospel deeply enough to be disturbed!

(4) Accordingly, instead of saying, "Shame on you, Paul, for wishing such a thing!" should we not rather say, "Shame *on ourselves,* that when in our own day and age the soundness of the gospel is being sacrificed upon the altar of ecumenism, and when ever so many people are being led astray by a so-called gospel that recognizes no contrast between saved and unsaved, but only "the brotherhood of all men" (as if, *in a redemptive sense,* all men were brothers) , our own cheeks have lost the ability to glow with righteous indignation!

(5) Nevertheless, in all our thoughts, wishes, and expressions, may the prayer of the Psalmist, uttered in connection with a somewhat similar revelation of indignation, be ours also:

> "Search me, O God, and know my heart;
> Try me, and know my thoughts;
> And see if there be any wicked way in me,
> And lead me in the way everlasting"
> (Psalm 139:23, 24) .

Such language reminds us of Paul's own sentiments (Eph. 4:31, 32; Col. 4:4, 6; Titus 3:2) .

Chapter 5

Verses 13-26

Theme: *The Gospel of Justification by Faith apart from Law-works Defended against Its Detractors*

III. *Its Application: it produces true liberty. Let the Galatians stand firm, therefore, as does Paul, who glories in the cross of Christ*

D. Remember that true liberty does not mean license. It means love. It does not welcome the works of the flesh but the fruit of the Spirit. It produces unity, not strife.

13 For y o u were called to freedom, brothers; only (do) not (turn) this freedom into an opportunity for the flesh, but through love be serving one another. 14 For the whole law is fulfilled in one word, namely, in this: "You must love your neighbor as yourself." 15 But if y o u bite and devour one another, watch out lest y o u be consumed by one another.

16 But I say, walk by the Spirit, and y o u will definitely not fulfil the desire of the flesh; 17 for the flesh sets its desire against the Spirit, and the Spirit against the flesh: for these are opposed to each other, so that these very things which y o u may wish to be doing, these y o u are not doing. 18 But if y o u are being led by the Spirit y o u are not under law. 19 Now obvious are the works of the flesh, which are: immorality, impurity, indecency, 20 idolatry, sorcery, quarrels, wrangling, jealousy, outbursts of anger, selfish ambitions, dissensions, party intrigues, 21 envyings, drinking bouts, revelries, and the like, of which I forewarn y o u, as I previously forewarned y o u, that those who indulge in such practices will not inherit the kingdom of God. 22 But the fruit of the Spirit is love, joy, peace, longsuffering, kindness, goodness, faithfulness, 23 meekness, self-control; against such there is no law. 24 And those who believe in Christ Jesus have crucified the flesh with its passions and desires.

25 If we live by the Spirit, by the Spirit let us also walk. 26 Let us not become boasters, challenging one another, envying one another.

5:13-26

D. *Freedom means love, not license*

Having previously dealt with the subject of freedom (2:4; 4:21-30; 5:1), Paul feels that further treatment is necessary, and this, it may well be surmised, particularly for two reasons: *a*. the charge of the Judaizers, that Paul's rejection of the law as a precondition of salvation would lead to lawlessness, and *b*. the presence of leftovers of pagan vices in the hearts and lives of the formerly chiefly pagan Galatians.

The Christian religion resembles a narrow bridge over a place where two polluted streams meet: one is called legalism, the other libertinism. The believer must not lose his balance, lest he tumble into the refined (?) faults of Judaism on the one side, or into the gross vices of paganism on the other. He must tread the safe and narrow path. Whether fashionable or coarse, both kinds of evils are products of "the flesh," that is, of sinful human nature. Since the apostle had devoted a large part of his epistle to the task of combating Judaistic self-righteousness, arrogance, exclusivism, etc., he now turns the attention of the Galatians, and of all who then or now read these warnings, to those sins which, though to a certain extent also present among the Jews (Rom. 2:1, 21-24), were *especially* conspicuous among the Gentiles. He fully realizes that even though the Galatians were now "brothers" in Christ, they were still plagued and beset by the sinster influences of contaminated heredity, long-existing habit, and dissolute environment. Generally speaking, sanctification does not complete its task in one day. So, this new section begins as follows: **13. For y o u were called to freedom, brothers; only (do) not (turn) this freedom into an opportunity for the flesh.** . . . For the meaning of *freedom* see on 5:1. The present passage is linked in thought especially with verse 8. When these two verses (8 and 13) are combined the meaning of *for* and of both passages becomes clearer: "This persuasion (is) not (derived) from him who is calling y o u. . . . For y o u were called to freedom, brothers; only (do) not (turn) this freedom into an opportunity for the flesh." When God applies the *outward* call, the gospel message, to the heart, thereby producing the *effectual* call, the person who experiences this basic change is introduced into the realm of freedom, the sphere of grateful and spontaneous living to the glory of his marvelous Benefactor, and is invited to roam about freely in this new country, delighting in its treasures and making full use of its opportunities. The Galatians must beware, nevertheless, that they do not accept a distorted interpretation of the concept *freedom,* as if it were an *opportunity,* that is, bridgehead, springboard, pretext, or incentive (cf. II Cor. 5:12; 11:12; I Tim. 5:14) for sinful human nature to assert itself.

Paul is not tilting at windmills when he issues this warning. Cf. Rom. 3:8; 6:1; Rasputin (cf. R. K. Massie, *Nicholas and Alexandra,* New York, 1967, p. 196). Turning liberty into license is an evil ingrained in sinful human nature. It is so easy to interpret *liberty* as "the right to sin," and to construe *freedom* as "the privilege to do whatever one's evil heart *wants to* do," instead of looking upon it as *the Spirit-imparted ability and desire to do what one should do.* Even today how often does it not happen that such baneful practices as attending places of *worldly* amusement, chain-smoking, "boozing," desecrating the sabbath, and reading smutty novels are defended with an appeal to "Christian liberty!" The apostle's own inspired interpretation of the meaning of true liberty is set forth both here in Galatians and in equally touching passages of his first epistle to the Corinthians: see especially 6:12; 8:9, 13; 9:12, 19, 22; 10:23, 24, 31; 11:1.

Surely no loftier description of the essence of true freedom has ever been offered than the one given in the words: **but through love be serving one another.** For the concept *love* see the explanation of verse 6, where Paul speaks about "faith working through love." Here in verse 13 note the paradox: "freedom . . . serving." A paradox, indeed, but not a self-contradiction, for such service is voluntary, from the heart. It is a service rendered in imitation of him who "took the form of a servant" (Phil. 2:7), and who, during the solemn night when he stepped upon the threshold of his most profound and indescribable agony, "rose from the supper, laid aside his garments, and having taken a towel, tied it around his waist, poured water into a basin, and began to wash the disciples' feet and to dry them with the towel" (John 13:4, 5). He was the thoroughly consecrated, wise and willing servant pictured by Isaiah (42:1-9; 49:1-9a; 50:4-11; and 52:13-53:12), the spontaneously acting servant who resolutely fulfilled his mission, so that with reference to him Jehovah said: "Behold, my servant, whom I uphold; my chosen, in whom my soul delights." It is such service that Paul has in mind when he says: ". . . through love be serving one another."[155] And what is meant by this *love* by means of which one brother voluntarily *serves* the other? Such ingredients as deep affection, self-sacrificing tenderness, genuine sympathy, readiness to render assistance, yearning to promote the brother's (and in a wider sense the neighbor's) welfare, spontaneous giving and forgiving: all these enter into it. But would it not be easier to count the glistening beads in the descending chains of rain than to catalogue all the elements that enter into that mysterious force which causes many hearts to beat as one?[156]

When Paul warns the Galatians not to turn freedom into an opportunity for the flesh but through love to be serving one another, he is placing *service* over against *selfishness*, the *positive* over against the *negative*. Paul does this frequently: see Rom. 12:21; 13:14; I Cor. 6:18-20; Eph. 4:28, 31, 32; 5:28, 29; 6:4; Col. 3:5-17; I Thess. 4:7, etc. Vice can only be conquered by virtue, which is the Spirit's *gift*, man's *responsibility*. Continued: **14. For the whole law is fulfilled in one word, namely, in this: "You must love your neighbor as yourself."** Paul quotes Lev. 19:18. One can also say that he is quoting the words of Jesus (Matt. 22:39, 40; Mark 12:31; Luke 10:27; cf. Matt. 7:12; 19:19; Rom. 13:8-10; and I Cor. 13). Love, then, is both the *summary* (interpretive epitome or condensation) and the *realization in practice* of the entire God-given moral law, viewed as a unit. True, in harmony with the immediately preceding context ("through love be serving *one another*"), the apostle here refers specifically to the second, not to the first, table of the law, but that first table is in the background, for the two are inseparable (I John 4:20, 21). Paul's teaching throughout is that though it would be a gross error to say that the sinner must love God and his neighbor *in order to be saved,* it is entirely true that the "saint," saved by grace, out of gratitude for (and by dint of) this salvation loves God and his neighbor.

---

[155] Accordingly, the rendering here given is to be preferred to that of Lenski: "by means of love slave for each other." On this point see also N.T.C. on Philippians, pp. 44, 109.
[156] The significance which Paul ascribes to *love* is evident from the fact that in his writings forms of the verb ἀγαπάω occur more than thirty times, and of the noun ἀγάπη more than seventy times. For the difference between ἀγαπάω and φιλέω see N.T.C. on the Gospel according to John, Vol. II, pp. 494–501.

Though love and the deeds which it produces must not be considered preconditions of salvation, they are, nevertheless, very important, namely, as fruits of the work of the Holy Spirit in man's heart. Once this is understood it becomes clear that Paul is entirely consistent when, on the one hand, he maintains that believers are not under law, yet, on the other hand, emphasizes that they are "under law to Christ" (I Cor. 9:21; and see on Gal. 6:2).

It has been maintained that the rule here quoted differs in no respect from that of the non-Christian moralist. The resemblance, however, is only superficial. The believer's *incentive* to obey this summarizing command is gratitude for the redemption accomplished by Christ; the *strength* to observe it is furnished by the Spirit of Christ (Gal. 5:1, 13, 25; cf. Eph. 3:16, 17; 4:20 ff.; 5:1 ff.); and it was also Christ who himself supplied the *example* of obedience (John 13:34).

When the question is asked, "But who is my neighbor?" (Luke 10:29), the answer is: anyone with whom, in God's providence, we come into contact; anyone whom we can assist in any way, even though he hates us and in that sense is our "enemy" (Matt. 5:43-48). Here, too, Christ himself has given us the supreme example (Luke 23:34; cf. I Peter 2:21-24). The parable of The Good Samaritan (Luke 10:25-37) proves, moreover, that, instead of asking, "But who is my neighbor?" each person should "prove himself a neighbor" to the one whom he is able to benefit in any way. Continued: **15. But if y o u bite and devour one another, watch out lest y o u be consumed by one another.** The attitude toward "one another" that is described and condemned in this passage is the very opposite of the one that was urged upon the addressed in verses 13 and 14. Here, in verse 15, people—church-members at that!—are pictured in the act of rushing at each other like wild beasts. By means of an ascending series of gruesome acts their violence and its threatening woeful result is pictured: they bite each other, "gulp each other down," and, if they persist, will in the end be totally consumed by one another. They obey the dictates of their old self, and resemble nature "raw in tooth and claw." Robertson reminds us of the story of "two snakes that grabbed each other by the tail and each swallowed the other." (*Word Pictures,* Vol. IV, p. 311). And Cole refers to "the two Kilkenny cats of Cromwellian times who fought so furiously that not a scrap of fur remained of either" (*The Epistle of Paul to the Galatians,* in *The Tyndale New Testament Commentaries,* p. 158). One might expect such acts of terror and violence from the enemies of God's people in their onslaught upon the righteous (Ps. 35:25; 79:2, 7; 80:13; 124:3), but surely those who style themselves "believers in the Lord Jesus Christ" and "members of the one holy universal church" cannot be accused of such behavior?

The question arises, therefore, "Just what does Paul have in mind? Is he merely warning the Galatians against certain sins which they might be considering, without in any way implying that such evils as 'biting' and 'devouring' already existed in their midst? Or, on the other hand, has he received information regarding actual conditions of dissension and strife, and is he now warning the churches as to what will be the inevitable result of the continuation of such discord and contention?" Some commentators favor the first,[157] some the second[158] alternative. I side with the latter. My reason is as follows. It is clear from the entire epistle—especially from 1:1-5:12—that a considerable segment of the membership here addressed was in the process of yielding to the wishes of the Judaizers. Also, it is equally obvious (see 5:19, 21) that there were others who leaned in the exactly opposite direction, and were abusing the doctrine of grace, as if it implied a license to sin. Paul surely must have had a reason to dwell in such detail on the vices enumerated in the verses that follow. And finally, does not the fact that he knew so much about the conditions that prevailed in these churches indicate that he must have had close friends there, who shared his views, were infected neither with legalism nor with libertinism, and were his informers? Does it not seem reasonable, therefore, to believe that, at least to some extent, there were "parties" or "factions" in these churches? Besides, as Ramsay points out, older rivalries, as between person and person, town and town, race and race, etc., may not have been *completely* and *immediately* eliminated with the coming of Christianity to these parts. Of course, it is not necessary or even reasonable to suppose that *all* the Galatians were engaged in internecine strife. If we accept the theory that at least *some* of the addressed were thus engaged, and that Paul writes as he does not only to prevent these quarrels from becoming more extensive and/or intensive, but also to put an end to them completely by urging the contending parties to adopt "the more excellent way" of love, have we not done justice to the meaning of his words? At any rate, the apostle shows "how distressing, how mad it is that we, who are members of the same body, should be leagued together, of our own accord, for mutual destruction" (Calvin).

---

[157] Thus Lenski, who states, "We thus decline to accept the conclusion that biting and devouring were actually in progress among the Galatians at this time" (*op. cit.,* p. 278). Rendall, *op. cit.,* p. 186; and Ridderbos, *op. cit.,* p. 202, express themselves more cautiously.

[158] This is the more general view. See, for example, the commentaries of Burton, Calvin, Duncan, Findlay, Greijdanus, and Ramsay. Duncan states, "Paul tactfully puts the case hypothetically, but we may be sure that he believes that these conditions actually exist."

Grammar does not help us to solve the puzzle. The condition here expressed is first class, assumed as true. The protasis has εἰ with two pres. indic. verbs. The apodosis has ἀναλωθῆτε, first aor. passive subjunctive of ἀναλίσκω in a negative final clause. Whether, in such a conditional sentence the condition *actually* corresponds with reality or whether it is a *mere* assumption, to show what would happen granted that the condition were real, must be established from the general context.

What, then, is the remedy for this evil? Paul mentions it in these words: **16. But I say, walk by the Spirit,**[159] **and y o u will definitely not fulfil the desire of the flesh.**[160] Let y o u r conduct be governed by the Spirit, that is, by God's gift imparted to y o u (3:2, 5). If y o u follow his directions and promptings y o u will not be dominated by y o u r human nature regarded as the seat and vehicle of sinful desire (as in 5:13), but instead will conquer it. It takes the tender leaves of early springtime to rid the oak tree of the remnants of last autumn's withered foliage. It is only the living that can expel the dead. It is only the good that can push out the bad. See also on verse 13 above.

Verse 16 clearly implies that there is a conflict between the Spirit and the flesh, therefore also between the believer's new, Spirit-indwelt, nature and his old, sinful, self. Hence, Paul continues: **17. for the flesh sets its desire against the Spirit, and the Spirit against the flesh: for these are opposed to each other. . . .** True, as long as one allows himself to be led by the Spirit he will definitely not fulfil the desire of the flesh, but how often does it not happen that the person in question does not allow the Spirit to be his Leader? And so, because the Spirit persists, a fierce conflict takes place inside the believer's heart. The antagonists are: the Spirit—hence also the Spirit-indwelt new nature—, on the one side; and on the other side: the flesh, that is, "the old man" of sin and corruption (same meaning as in verses 13 and 19 of this chapter, and as in 6:8; cf. Rom. 7:25; 8:4-9, 12, 13).

In connection with this contest, note the following:

(1) The *libertine* experiences no such struggle at all, for he follows his natural inclinations.

(2) The *legalist,* who is destined for grace and glory, having been reminded of his sinfulness by the law but for a while unwilling to accept grace, struggles and struggles but without achieving victory or experiencing the sense of certain, ultimate triumph. This condition lasts until grace finally breaks down all the barriers of opposition (Phil. 3:7 ff.).

(3) The *believer,* while still on earth, experiences an agonizing conflict in his own heart, but *in principle,* has already gained the victory, as the very

---

[159] Also here πνεῦμα refers to the Holy Spirit. Says Duncan, "Throughout this passage it is important to remember that Paul is writing to Christians, i.e., to men who have received the Spirit of God" (*op. cit.,* p. 166). I believe this to be the correct position, and over against Lenski's rendering and exegesis (*op. cit.,* pp. 278, 279) I would also refer to my interpretation of 5:5 above, including footnote 146 on p. 197. It seems to me that the only instances in Galatians of πνεῦμα in a sense other than Holy Spirit are 6:1: "a *spirit* of gentleness," and 6:18: "The grace of our Lord Jesus Christ (be) with y o u r *spirit,* brothers."
[160] For a word-study of ἐπιθυμία see N.T.C. on I and II Timothy and Titus, pp. 271, 272, footnote 147; and for σάρξ see N.T.C. on Philippians, p. 77, footnote 55; also pp. 152, 153 on Phil. 3:3.

presence of the Holy Spirit in his heart testifies. In full measure this victory
will be his portion in the hereafter; hence,

(4) For *the redeemed soul in glory* the battle is over. He wears the
victor's wreath.

As to (3), therefore, the very wording of the text—note: "sets its desire
against" and "are opposed to each other"—indicates the intensity of the life-
long tug of war. This shows that the Christian life means far more than
stepping forward to register one's decision at a great revival meeting, after
listening to a powerful, evangelical, and heart-warming message, and while
one is under the influence of the singing of old familiar hymns by a massive
choir. When, under such circumstances, the sudden change is genuine, it is
wonderful, but it must be borne in mind that as a rule a sinner is not
wholly saved all at once ("Presto!"). He does not leap into heaven in one
prodigious bound. On the contrary, he has to *work out* his own salvation
(Phil. 2:12). This takes time, struggle, intense effort and exertion. He is
his own most powerful enemy, as Paul proves by continuing: **so that these
very things which y o u may wish to be doing, these y o u are not doing.** What
a battle between the will and the deed! Paul, writing as a converted man
(Rom. 7:14-25) and recording his *present, "state of grace"* experiences (for
proof see Rom. 7:22, 25), complains bitterly about the fact that he practices
that in which his soul no longer takes delight; in fact, practices that which
his regenerated self *hates* (Rom. 7:15). He cries out, "Wretched man that
I am! Who will deliver me out of the body of this death?" (Rom. 7:24).
Nevertheless, he is also fully aware of the fact that in the struggle between
his own flesh and God's Spirit, the latter's victory—hence also Paul's—is
certain; in fact, *in principle* is a fact even now. Would there have been this
genuine, *God-centered* sorrow for sin, had not Paul been a truly converted
man? Of course not! This very conflict, therefore, is a charter of the apostle's
salvation. We are not surprised, therefore, that the exclamation "Wretched
man! . . . Who will deliver me?" is followed by "I thank God through Jesus
Christ our Lord. . . . There is therefore now no condemnation to them that
are in Christ Jesus" (Rom. 7:25; 8:1; cf. I Cor. 15:57). Similarly here in
Galatians the thought of victory through the Spirit is basic to the understanding of verse **18. But if y o u are being led by the Spirit y o u are not under
law.**[161] Being "under law" spells defeat, bondage, the curse, spiritual impotence, for the law cannot save (Gal. 3:11-13, 21-23, 25; 4:3, 24, 25; 5:1).
It takes the Spirit to set one free (4:29; 5:1, 5; II Cor. 3:17).

---

[161] This is a first class conditional sentence. Accordingly, the thought expressed
in the protasis is assumed to be a fact. Upon the presupposition that it is a fact the
thought expressed in the apodosis is the truth. Whether the protasis states an
actual fact, let each Galatian—and let each hearer or reader down the centuries—
decide for himself, after thorough examination in the light of the Word. Note present tense: "are being led."

215

Being Led by the Spirit

(1) *Whom It Concerns*

According to a rather popular view "spiritual leading" is the Spirit's gift to the select few, "the holiest men," the flower of the flock. It is imparted to them to protect them from physical harm, especially while traveling, to deliver them from dangerous situations, and sometimes even to insure them success in their business enterprises.

However, when, with Gal. 5:18 as our starting-point, we trace *back* the line of Paul's thinking, it becomes evident that this limitation of "spiritual leading" to a group of super-saints is completely foreign to his mind. Those who are being led by the Spirit (5:18) are the same as those who walk by the Spirit (5:16), and vice versa. Going back a little farther, we notice that these, in turn, are the ones who have been set free (5:1; 4:31, 26), who belong to Christ (3:29), and are "of faith" (3:9). All true believers, therefore, are being led by the Spirit.

Moreover, the powerful influence that is being exercised upon and within them by the Spirit is not of a sporadic character, being, as it were, injected into their lives now and then in moments of great need or danger. On the contrary, it is steady, constant, as even the tense here in Gal. 5:18 implies: they *are being led* by the Spirit. Even when they disobey the Spirit—and they certainly do, as has just been set forth (verses 13-17)—the Spirit does not leave them alone but works repentance within their hearts.

This representation is in keeping with the only other truly parallel passage in Paul's epistles, namely, Rom. 8:14: "For as many as are being led by the Spirit of God, these are sons of God." Here, too, being led by the Spirit is set forth as the indispensable characteristic of God's children. If a person is a child of God he is being led by the Spirit. If he is being led by the Spirit he is a child of God.

(2) *What It Is*

Before giving a positive answer to this question it may be well to point out what is *not* meant by being led by the Spirit. Naturally, it cannot refer to being governed by one's own sinful impulses and inclinations, nor to "being easily led" into waywardness by evil companions. Also definitely excluded here is the idea of those moral philosophers, ancient and modern, who hold that in every man there is a higher and a lower nature, and that each human being has within himself the power of causing the former to triumph over the latter. This idea is excluded even if for no other reason than this, that throughout, in Paul's teaching, the Holy Spirit is a distinct person, of one substance with the Father and the Son. He is not "our other or better self." See Rom. 8:26, 27; I Cor. 2:10; II Cor. 13:14. This also shows that, strictly speaking, being led by the Spirit cannot even be identified with the triumph of "the new man" (the regenerated nature) within us over "the old man" (our corrupt nature, not yet fully destroyed). That victory and that implied struggle are certainly very real; yet they are not *in and by themselves* what is meant by being led by the Spirit, but are rather *the result* of the Spirit's active indwelling. They are certainly *implied,* but are not basic.

What then does *the leading of the Spirit*—to change from the passive to the active voice, for the sake of the definition—actually mean? It means sanctification. *It is that constant, effective, and beneficent influence which the Holy Spirit exercises within the hearts of God's children whereby they are being directed and enabled more and more to crush the power of indwelling sin and to walk in the way of God's commandments, freely and cheerfully.*

By so defining it extremes are avoided. Thus, on the one hand, to be *led* by the Spirit means more than to be *guided* by him, though, to be sure, the Spirit is also our Guide (John 16:13; cf. Matt. 15:14; Luke 6:39; Acts 8:31; Rev. 7:17). But the very fact that, according to the passage now under consideration (Gal. 5:18), the enslaving power of the law has been broken for all those who are being *led* by the Spirit, indicates that this *leadership* which the Spirit provides implies more than "pointing out the right way." It reminds us not so much of the Indian guide who pointed out to the pioneer white explorers the pass through the Rockies, as of the blind man of Jericho who *was led* to Jesus (Luke 18:40; cf. Matt. 21:2; Luke 10:34; John 18:28; Acts 6:12; 9:2). Merely pointing out the way to him would not have helped him. When the Holy Spirit *leads* believers he becomes *the controlling influence* in their lives, bringing them at last to glory.

On the other hand, however, this representation also steers clear of the opposite extreme, that of denying human responsibility and activity. The blind man of Jericho was not *carried* or *borne* (II Peter 1:21) to Jesus, but did his own walking. Warfield has said very aptly: "It is his [the Holy Spirit's] part to keep us in the path and to bring us at length to the goal. But it is we who tread every step of the way; our limbs that grow weary with the labor; our hearts that faint, our courage that fails—our faith that revives our sinking strength, our hope that instills new courage into our souls—as we toil over the steep ascent" (*The Power of God unto Salvation,* p. 172). Being led by the Holy Spirit, to be fully effective, implies that one allows himself to be led. As to the interrelation of these two factors—the believers' self-activity and God's (the Holy Spirit's) leading—, Paul's own Spirit-inspired statement cannot be improved upon: "With fear and trembling continue to work out y o u r own salvation; for it is God who is working in y o u both to will and to work for his good pleasure" (Phil. 2:12, 13; and see N.T.C. on that passage).

217

(3) *Its Blessed Results*

a. Those who are being led by the Spirit breathe the exhilarating and invigorating air of moral and spiritual freedom. Being no longer under law's bondage, they obey God's precepts with gladness of heart (Gal. 5:1, 18).

b. They detest and vigorously oppose "the works of the flesh" (5:17, 19-21, 24).

c. They love the Word (whose very Author is the Spirit) and the Triune God revealed therein in all his marvelous attributes (Rom. 7:22; cf. Ps. 119; John 16:14).

d. "The fruit of the Spirit" abounds in their lives (Gal. 5:22, 23; 6:2, 8-10).

e. This enhances their freedom of access in approaching the throne of grace (Eph. 2:18; cf. Rom. 5:1, 2; Heb. 4:14-16).

f. It also goes hand in hand with the testimony of the Spirit in their hearts, assuring them that they are children of God (II Peter 1:5-11; cf. Rom. 8:16).

g. Finally, it (the fruit of the Spirit abounding in their lives) greatly strengthens their testimony to the world, all this to the glory of God Triune (Acts 1:8; cf. John 15:26, 27).

19-21. The various ways in which the desire of the flesh (verse 17) manifests itself are now set forth. With the majority of commentators I hold that the apostle mentions the particular vices in the list that follows because they needed to be mentioned. In other words, the Galatians had not as yet gained a complete victory over these evils, though here as always the degree of success must have varied with the individual.

The list which follows may be compared with similar ones in Paul's other epistles (Rom. 1:18-32; 13:13; I Cor. 5:9-11; 6:9, 10; II Cor. 12:20, 21; Eph. 4:19; 5:3-5; Col. 3:5-9; I Thess. 2:3; 4:3-7; I Tim. 1:9, 10; 6:4, 5; II Tim. 3:2-5; and Titus 3:3, 9, 10). Striking, for example, is the similarity (note, however, also the differences) between Gal. 5:19, 20 and II Cor. 12:20, 21. Whether there were factors other than identity of authorship (for example, already existing lists) that account for this and similar resemblances is difficult to ascertain. Paul writes: **Now obvious**—hence undeniable, self-evident as vices—**are the works of the flesh, which are: immorality, impurity, indecency, idolatry, sorcery,**[162] **quarrels, wrangling, jealousy, outbursts of anger, selfish ambitions, dissensions, party intrigues, envyings, drinking bouts, revelries, and the like. . . .**

There are fifteen items in the list. In content there is, of course, consider-

---

[162] Thus rendered, the first five, in addition to being true to the meaning of the Greek words, all end in "-y," and the originals of these five all end in -ια.

able overlapping: Thus, while each of the three vices *immorality*, *impurity*, and *indecency*, has a distinct meaning, yet the three have something in common, namely, departure from the will of God in the matter of sex. And so it is also with the other items in the list.

The first three vices, accordingly, are in the realm of *sex*. The next two pertain to *false gods*. There follow eight that have to do with *strife*. The last two indicate abuses in the sphere of *drink*. Or, dropping these mono-syllables, the fifteen items can be grouped as follows:

Immorality and kindred evils; hence, immorality, impurity, indecency

Idolatry and the sin associated with it; hence, idolatry, sorcery

Rivalry: quarrels, wrangling, jealousy, outbursts of anger, selfish ambi-tions, party intrigues, envyings

Inebriety: drinking bouts, revelries.

First on the list, then, is *immorality*, a term which in Paul's writings is used also in I Cor. 5:1; 6:13, 18; 7:2; II Cor. 12:21; Eph. 5:3; Col. 3:5; and I Thess. 4:3. It refers basically to unlawful sexual intercourse. It probably includes illicit, clandestine relationships of every description. Evil in the sexual realm was, and is today, a characteristic feature of life apart from Christ. In paganism it is often closely associated with idolatry. That even among those who had turned to Christ it was not unheard of is clear from I Cor. 5:1 ff. Closely associated with immorality, *impurity* (II Cor. 12:21; Eph. 4:19; 5:3; Col. 3:5; I Thess. 2:3; 4:7) is mentioned next. It is a very comprehensive concept, and includes not only uncleanness in deeds but also in words, thoughts, and desires of the heart. *Indecency* or *licentious-ness* ("lasciviousness," Rom. 13:13; II Cor. 12:21; Eph. 4:19) emphasizes the lack of self-control that characterizes the person who gives free play to the impulses of his sinful nature.

The next group begins with the mention of *idolatry*. As the other passages in which Paul uses the word indicate (I Cor. 10:14; Col. 3:5), it refers not only to the worship of images as such but also to any evil practice in con-nection with such worship; for example, to eating meats that had been offered to idols, when conscience forbids this, and, in fact, to the substitu-tion of anything at all for the adoration of the true God who has revealed himself in Jesus Christ. Thus, greed, too, is idolatry, for by means of it a person has substituted self for God. Closely associated with idolatry is *sorcery*. The Greek word is *pharmakeia;* cf. our "pharmacy." Though basi-cally *pharmakeia* is a term without moral implications, it is not difficult to understand how—particularly in an unscientific age—a "mixer of drugs" could be—or could be viewed as being—a "magician." "Pharmakeia," ac-cordingly, is used here in the sense of *sorcery*, by means of which mysterious powers were erroneously ascribed to certain articles, formulas, or incanta-tions (cf. Acts 8:9; 13:8; 19:13, 19). The sorcerer generally claimed to have access to this or that super-human power by means of which he plied his trade. The apostle uses the word "sorcery" or "magic" only in this one instance. See, however, also Rev. 9:21; 18:23; cf. Exod. 7:11, 22; 8:14; Isa. 47:9, 12; Rev. 21:8; 22:15. When faith in magic replaces trust in God it is exposed as a form of idolatry.

The third is the largest group and refers to *rivalry* of the baser sort. The reason why so much prominence is given to this category of sinful practices has been stated above (see on verse 15). The list begins with *quarrels.* Cf. Eph. 2:16 where the singular occurs in the sense of "hostility." Next is *wrangling*[163] (also rendered "variance," "strife," "contention," cf. Rom. 1:29; 13:13; II Cor. 12:20; Phil. 1:15; I Tim. 6:4; Titus 3:9), which, for example, occurs when people begin to choose sides, and each of the wranglers fairly worships his hero (I Cor. 1:11, 12; 3:3). Something of this nature may have occurred also in Galatia, as was suggested previously. *Jealousy*[164] is mentioned in connection with "strife" also in Rom. 13:13; I Cor. 3:3; II Cor. 12:20.[165] Psychologically the two—wrangling and jealousy—go together, for what started out as intense devotion to a leader, so that every other name is immediately dismissed amid much wrangling, degenerates into a jealous craving to retain the feeling of closeness to that leader, to "possess" him, as it were, and to enhance his prestige come what may. In such a context *outbursts of anger* or fiery flashes of rage, when a "rival's" name is mentioned, are natural. The men who are guilty of this vice pant with fury (Rom. 2:8; II Cor. 12:20; Eph. 4:31; Col. 3:8). Though the people who engage in such practices may never be willing to admit it, yet it is a fact that such and similar sins are often rooted in *selfish ambitions* (Rom. 2:8; II Cor. 12:20). That such ambitions at times invade even "the Christian ministry" is shown in Phil. 1:17; 2:3 (see N.T.C. on these passages). *Dissensions* (Rom. 16:17) result when men are actuated by selfish motives, each craving honor for himself. *Groups* working and scheming against each other (cf. I Cor. 11:19: "factions"), hence *party intrigues,* come into existence when one member *chooses* the side of this, and another the side of that leader.[166] The group of eight vices that can be summarized

---

[163] The textual evidence favors the singular.
[164] Here, too, the textual evidence supports the singular rather than the plural.
[165] The resultant meaning of ζῆλος in other Pauline passages is somewhat different. Thus, in Rom. 10:2; II Cor. 7:7, 11; 9:2; Phil. 3:6 *zeal* is the preferred translation. II Cor. 11:2 refers to a "godly" (or "divine") *jealousy.*
[166] The party that becomes guilty of error in doctrine or ethics advocates "heresy," which is the English form of the very word that is used in the original. But this was a later development of the meaning of the Greek word. Hence the rendering of "heresies" here in Gal. 5:20 (A.V.) is an error. Though at first the term simply indicated a "sect," as of the Pharisees (Acts 15:5; 26:5) or of the Sadducees (Acts 5:17), with no odium attached, passages such as Acts 24:5 ("a ringleader of the *sect* of the Nazarenes"); 24:14 ("according to the Way which they call a *sect*"); and 28:22 ("as to this *sect,* we know that everywhere it is being spoken against") show its gradual tendency toward the meaning "heretical sect."

under the caption *rivalry* closes with *envyings*[167] (Rom. 1:29; Phil. 1:15;
I Tim. 6:4; Titus 3:3). Paul has already mentioned "jealousy." Whenever
these two—jealousy and envy—are distinguishable, as here, the former can
be defined as the fear of losing what one has, while the latter is the displeasure aroused by seeing someone else have something. One of the most
soul-destroying vices is envy, an evil which, as the probable etymology of
the Greek word implies, causes one *to waste away*. Has not envy been
called that vice whose rage nothing can allay, "the eldest born of hell"? Is it
not "the rottenness of the bones" (Prov. 14:30)? Our English word *envy* is
from the Latin *in-video,* meaning "to look against," that is, to look with
ill-will at another person because of what he is or has. It was envy that
caused the murder of Abel, threw Joseph into a pit, caused Korah, Dathan,
and Abiram to rebel against Moses and Aaron, made Saul pursue David,
gave rise to the bitter words which "the elder brother" (in the Parable of
the Prodigal Son) addressed to his father, and crucified Christ. *Love* never
envies (I Cor. 13:4).

The fourth group denounces and warns against *inebriety,* that is drunkenness and the evils associated with it. The first member of this group is
drinking bouts (Rom. 13:13; cf. Luke 21:34). No doubt it refers to
repeated manifestations of intemperance. The entire list of vices closes
with *revelries* (Rom. 13:13; cf. I Peter 4:3). It should be distinctly noted
that Scripture considers alcoholism to be a *sin,* not *merely* a *disease*. It states
in words clear and simple that drunkards will not inherit the kingdom of
heaven (I Cor. 6:10). The last part of the verse which we are now considering speaks likewise. Though the *disease* aspect of this evil should, to be
sure, be given its due, the *responsibility* aspect must not be ignored. Minimizing personal accountability has been the destroyer of several civiliza-
tions. Is not our own civilization in danger of being destroyed by it? As to
the pagan revelries to which the apostle makes reference here, we see, as it
were, the disorderly night-time procession of fellows parading through the
streets, with their torches and songs honoring Bacchus. The boisterous
parade of half-drunks stops in front of the houses of friends, and the merrymaking is protracted until the small hours of the morning. To practices such
as these the Galatians, too, had been accustomed. When they turned to the
Lord it must have seemed difficult for some of them to break off, once and
for all, every association with this kind of a past.

The given list of vices is not meant to be exhaustive. It is representative,
as is indicated by the words, "and the like" or "and things like these."

Continued: **of which I forewarn y o u, as I previously forewarned y o u,**

---

[167] As the textual apparatus of N.N. clearly indicates, the addition (A.V.) of
"murders" (*φόνοι*) after "envyings" (*φθόνοι*) rests on an inferior text. Perhaps it
is due to Rom. 1:29.

that those who indulge in such practices will not inherit the kingdom of God. It is clear from these words that to the Galatians Paul, during his visits, must have imparted a considerable amount of instruction, and this not only theological but also moral, the two being very closely related. This gives the lie to the charge of his opponents that he taught, "Let us do evil, that good may come" (Rom. 3:8; cf. 6:1). It should also be observed that although according to Paul's argumentation it is not possible to gain entrance to the kingdom of God by means of what were deemed to be *good* practices (law-works), it is definitely possible to shut oneself out by *evil* practices. A person must bid farewell to *all* the works of darkness. Otherwise he proves that he is not as yet walking in the light (I Cor. 6:11; Eph. 4:20; 5:7-11). He must realize that even though he is *in* the world and has a mission to fulfil, he is not *of* the world, but is a sojourner or pilgrim on the earth (cf. Ps. 119:19).

Here, too, Paul has a message for every age, including the present, in which the complaint is often heard that the tenor of certain so-called *Christian* organizations is that of "paganism on the basis of the creed." The constitution of the organization demands loyalty to the creed on the part of every member, and declares that all the activities must be carried on in harmony with Scripture as interpreted by this confession, but the facts of life tell an altogether different story, if published reports by those "on the scene" are reliable. Those who confess Jesus Christ as their Savior and Lord must bear in mind that far more worldly people "read" *them* than read the Bible (II Cor. 3:2).

With a pastor's loving heart, therefore, Paul issues his warning that those who continue to indulge in their former evil habits will not *inherit* (see on 3:18) the kingdom of God: the new heaven and earth with all their glory.[168]

---

[168] In its broadest connotation "the kingdom of God" indicates *God's kingship, rule, or sovereignty recognized in the hearts and operative in the lives of his people, and effecting their complete salvation, their constitution as a church, and ultimately a redeemed universe.* However, in various passages now this, then that, aspect of the βασιλεία (τοῦ) θεοῦ is stressed. Thus, at times it is obedience *to the rule of God* upon which the emphasis falls: "Thy kingdom come, thy will be done" (Matt. 6:10; cf. Luke 17:21). Then again the main idea is *complete salvation,* i.e., all the spiritual blessings that result when God is recognized as King in heart and life: "It is easier . . . than for a rich man to enter the kingdom of God. And they said, 'Then who can be saved?'" (Mark 10:25, 26). A third meaning is *the community of men in whose hearts God is recognized as King.* Here the terms "kingdom of God" and "church" begin to approach each other in meaning: "And upon this rock will I build my church. . . . I will give to you the keys of the kingdom of heaven" (Matt. 16:18, 19). Finally, the term has reference to the final realization of God's saving power: *the new heaven and earth with all their glory:* "Inherit the kingdom prepared for y o u" (Matt. 25:34). These four meanings are not separate or unrelated. They all proceed from the central idea of the rule of God, his supremacy in the sphere of saving power.—For the theory according to which there is a sharp distinction between the kingdom of *God* and that of *Christ* see N.T.C. on Colossians and Philemon, p. 64, footnote 47.

The *works* of the flesh have been reviewed. Over against these is now placed the *fruit,* that is, the organic, spontaneous product, of the Spirit, for it is only by means of the Spirit that the flesh can be conquered. It is the good that expels the evil. By no means does this representation cancel human responsibility. On the contrary, it is by means of the operation of the Spirit in the hearts of God's children that the latter become very active. But such activity is no longer slavery. It is the free, voluntary, and grateful response of hearts and lives to God for favors received (Luke 6:44, 45). It is the natural expression of the new life, the life "in the Spirit." It should also be noted that the apostle is not now speaking about *extraordinary* and *temporary* manifestations of the Spirit's power in the lives of certain individuals, *special gifts (charismata),* such as speaking in tongues (see I Cor. 12), but rather about endowments bestowed upon all those who love the Lord. These endowments are here considered as a unit: "the fruit," that is, the harvest.

Paul writes: **22, 23. But the fruit of the Spirit is love, joy, peace, longsuffering, kindness, goodness, faithfulness, meekness, self-control. . . .** Perhaps the nine pleasing endowments can be divided into three groups, each group comprising three gifts. *If* this should be correct—it is by no means certain!—, the first group would refer to the most basic spiritual qualities: love, joy, peace. The next group would describe those virtues that reveal themselves in social relationships. We assume that it views believers in their various contacts with each other and with those who do not belong to their company: longsuffering, kindness, goodness. In the last group, though here especially there is room for a difference of opinion, the first item listed may well refer to the relation of believers to God and to his will as revealed in his Word: faithfulness or loyalty. The second probably pertains to their contact with men: meekness. The last, to each believer's relation to himself, that is, to his own desires and passions: self-control.

Mentioned at the very beginning of the first group is "the greatest of the three greatest," namely, *love* (I Cor. 13; Eph. 5:2; Col. 3:14). For this virtue see on 5:6 and 5:13 above. Not only Paul but also John assigns priority to this grace of self-giving (I John 3:14; 4:8, 19). And so does Peter (I Peter 4:8). In this they clearly followed the example that was given by Christ (John 13:1, 34; 17:26). Although, as these passages indicate, it is hardly legitimate *strictly to limit* this basic virtue to "love *for the brethren,*" yet, on the other hand, in the present context (over against quarrels, wrangling, jealousy, etc.," and see also verse 14) the reference may well be *especially* to this mutual affection. When love is present, *joy* cannot be far behind, for has not the author told us that love is the law's fulfilment, and does not the doing of God's law bring *delight* (Ps. 119:16, 24, 35, 47, 70, 174)? Moreover, the truth of this statement becomes even clearer when it is borne in mind that the ability to observe this divine ordinance of love is God's gift, being an element in that wonderful salvation which in *his* great love he has freely bestowed upon his children. Moreover, since all things work together for good to those that love God (Rom. 8:28), it is evident that believers can rejoice even amid the most distressing circumstances, as Paul himself proved again and again (Acts 27:35; II Cor. 6:10: "as sorrowful, yet always rejoicing"; 12:9; Phil. 1:12, 13; 4:11; II Tim. 4:6-8). Their gladness, moreover, is not that of the world, a mirth which is superficial and fails to satisfy the deepest needs of the soul, but is a "joy unspeakable and full of glory" (I Peter 1:8), and a foretaste of the radiant raptures that are still in store for Christ's followers. *Peace,* too, is a natural result of the exercise of love, for "Great *peace* have they that *love* thy law" (Ps. 119:165; cf. 29:11; 37:11; 85:8). This peace is the serenity of heart that is the portion of all those who, having been justified by faith (Rom. 5:1), yearn to be instruments in the hand of God in causing others to share in their tranquility. Hence, the peace-*possessor* becomes, in turn, a peace-*maker* (Matt. 5:9). Moreover, the one who is truly conscious of this great gift of peace which he has received from God as a result of Christ's bitter death on the cross, will, within the Christian fellowship, "make every effort to preserve the unity imparted by the Spirit by means of the bond (consisting in) peace" (Eph. 4:3).

The mention of peace is, as it were, a natural link between the first and the second group, for this virtue is often contrasted with strife among men, and this second group describes those virtues which believers reveal in their contacts with each other and with other men. The first of the Spirit's gifts mentioned in this second group is *longsuffering*. It characterizes the person who, in relation to those who annoy, oppose, or molest him, exercises patience. He refuses to yield to passion or to outbursts of anger. Longsuffering is not only a human but also a divine attribute, being ascribed to God (Rom. 2:4; 9:22) and to Christ (I Tim. 1:16) as well as to man (II Cor. 6:6; Eph. 4:2; Col. 3:12, 13; II Tim. 4:2). As a human attribute it is inspired by trust in the fulfilment of God's promises (II Tim. 4:2, 8; Heb. 6:12). Emphasis on this virtue was greatly needed by the Galatians, who, as has been shown, were probably being torn by strife and the party spirit. Besides, longsuffering is a mighty weapon over against the hostility of the world in its attitude toward the church. Hand in hand with this virtue goes *kindness*. It is mildness, benignity. The early Christians by means of it commended themselves to others (II Cor. 6:6). This endowment, as exercised by believers, is a faint reflection of the primordial kindness manifested by God (Rom. 2:4; cf. 11:22). We are, moreover, admonished to become like him in this respect (Matt. 5:43-48; Luke 6:27-38). The Gospels contain numerous illustrations of Christ's kindness shown to sinners. To mention but a few, see Mark 10:13-16; Luke 7:11-17; 36-50; 8:40-56; 13:10-17; 18:15-17; 23:34; John 8:1-11; 19:25-27. *Goodness,* which completes this group, is Spirit-created moral and spiritual excellence of every description.

Perhaps in the present connection, being mentioned after kindness, it could refer especially to generosity of heart and action.

Finally, the apostle mentions the three graces that conclude the entire summary. First is *faithfulness*. The word that is used in the original is often properly rendered *faith*. However, here occurring after "kindness" and "goodness," the rendering "faithfulness" would seem to strike a more consonant harmony. It means *loyalty, fidelity*. Since in this very letter Paul complains about the lack of loyalty toward himself which had become evident in the conduct of many of the Galatians (4:16), we can see that mentioning this virtue was definitely in order. However, in the final analysis it was not so much disloyalty to himself as to the gospel—hence, to God and his Word—that, to a considerable extent, had been lacking, as is evident from 1:6-9; 3:1; 5:7. Faithfulness *to God and to his will* is, accordingly, the virtue which, in all probability, Paul is here commending as a gift of the Spirit. This, however, does not exclude but includes loyalty toward men. In connection with the preceding context, which speaks of strife in its various manifestations (see verses 20, 21), it would seem to be proper *here* to interpret the next item, namely, *meekness*, as gentleness *toward one another and toward all men.* Cf. I Cor. 4:21. Also *this* virtue reminds one of Christ (Matt. 11:29; II Cor. 10:1). Meekness is the very opposite of vehemence, violence, and outbursts of anger. The final virtue which Paul mentions, and by implication commends, is *self-control,* a relation of the self *to the self.* The person who is blessed with this quality possesses "the power to keep himself in check," which is the meaning of the word that is used in the original. The previous mention of immorality, impurity, and indecency, among the *vices* (verse 19), shows that it was very appropriate to list self-control as an opposing *virtue.* Of course, the reference is to other things besides sex. Those who truly exercise this virtue compel *every* thought to surrender itself in obedience to Christ (II Cor. 10:5).

Continued: **against such there is no law.** Since Paul has just completed a list of virtues, which are *things,* not *people,* it is natural to interpret his words as meaning: "against such *things*—such *virtues*—there is no law." Grammar does not forbid this construction. It is also evident that, as was true with respect to the vices, so also this list of virtues is representative. By no means every item of Christian excellence is included in the list. Hence, Paul says, "against *such.*" By saying that there is no law against such things he is encouraging every believer to manifest these qualities, in order that, by so doing, the vices may be annihilated.

The *incentive* to exhibit these fine traits of character was furnished by Christ, for it is out of gratitude to him that believers adorn their conduct with them. The *example,* too, in connection with all of them, was given by him. And *the virtues themselves,* as well as the *strength* to exercise them, are imparted by his Spirit.

Though Paul has called the enumerated virtues "the fruit of the Spirit," he now shifts the emphasis from the Spirit to Christ. That he is able to do this so readily is due to the fact that when the Spirit occupies the heart, so does Christ (Eph. 3:16, 17). Christ and the Spirit cannot be separated. "In the Spirit" Christ himself inhabits the inner selves of believers (Rom. 8:9, 10). Was not the Spirit given by Christ (John 15:26; II Cor. 3:17)? The reason for the shift in emphasis is that the apostle is going to remind the Galatians of the fact that they *have crucified* the flesh. This, of course, immediately rivets the attention upon Christ and his cross. So Paul continues: **24. And those who believe in Christ Jesus have crucified the flesh with its passions and desires.** Christ Jesus had been openly displayed to them as the One who had been crucified for their sins (3:1). They had seen his amazing love, and along with it they had learned to recognize the horrible nature of their sins which had required such a death. And they themselves had accepted this crucified Savior as their own, had reposed their trust in him, and through union with him had made a definite break with "the flesh," their old, evil nature. By God's grace they had administered the death-blow to it. They, like Paul, had been crucified with Christ (see on 2:20). Let them therefore *be* what they *are*. Let them be *in practice* what they are *in principle,* for in principle they had crucified their old human nature, together with its sinful yearnings, whether these be viewed more passively as *passions* (probably the evil promptings working within their subconsciousness) or actively as *desires* (the wicked cravings which they consciously support and enliven).[169]

Because of the supreme importance of living a consistent Christian life, that is, of being in practice what one is already in principle, this thought is now rephrased as follows: **25. If we live by the Spirit, by the Spirit let us also walk.** This translation, favored also by A.R.V., is better than the one that is found in A.V., R.S.V., N.E.B., and others. It preserves the chiastic structure of the original. The phrases "by the Spirit," "by the Spirit" are in the center, and thus receive the strongest emphasis. Nevertheless, by means of placing the words "if we live" at the very beginning of the sentence, and the words "let us also walk" at the very close, the contrast between *living* and *walking,* as these terms are here employed, is brought out with full force. Meaning: "If the source of our life is *the Spirit, the Spirit* must also be allowed to direct our steps, so that we make progress, advancing step by step toward the goal of perfect consecration to the Lord." This walking by the Spirit is the only way to administer the finishing touch to that which has already been dealt a mortal blow. It is the only way to deal with "the flesh along with its passions and desires." We should destroy the power of the negative by means of The Invincible Positive, the Holy Spirit.

---

[169] See N.T.C. on I and II Timothy and Titus, pp. 271, 272, especially footnote 147.

Continued: **26. Let us not become boasters, challenging one another, envying one another.** In other words, "Let us neither brag about that which we have (or think we have), thereby calling forth equally pretentious swagger on the part of the person to whom we are speaking, nor grudge that other person what he has." Haughtiness and conceit, the "know-it-all" attitude, brutal aggressiveness, these ill become those who claim to be followers of him who was always showing the very opposite spirit (Isa. 42:2; Zech. 9:9; Matt. 11:29; 20:28; John 13:5; II Cor. 10:1; Phil. 2:8). God does not approve of windbags. If there had not been a special need for this warning Paul undoubtedly would not have issued it. Paul's main idea, accordingly, is this: Allow the fruit of the Spirit to expel the works of the flesh!

Galatians 5: Seed Thoughts
(one thought for each verse)

See Verse

1. Freedom is a precious gift. It is also an immense responsibility.
2. Christ is either our complete Savior or is not our Savior at all.
3. Whoever would be saved by works must render perfect obedience to the whole law. Nothing less will do!
4. Those who would be saved by their good works have lost their hold on grace. Nevertheless, it is grace alone that saves.
5. For the Christian it is true that "the best is yet to be."
6. Faith without love is not true faith.
7. "Excelsior" is the Christian's motto. He should allow no one to throw him off this course.
8. "Consider the source!" whenever anyone urges you to do that which is morally or spiritually questionable.
9. An evil intention, if unchecked, leads to a shameful deed. A shameful deed, if unrepented of, becomes a bad habit. A bad habit, if not discarded, will grow into a depraved character, which, in turn, leads to perdition.
10. Showing that you have confidence in a person, if you are at all able to do this with candor, is excellent psychology.
11. The devil does not persecute those whom he already has captured.
12. Are we becoming so selfish that our cheeks no longer glow with indignation when harm is being done to those whom, supposedly, we love?
13. *True liberty* is not the privilege to do whatever one's evil heart desires to do, but is the Spirit-imparted ability and desire to do what one should do.
14. The Christian's law is love.
15. Bitter (= biting) words harm the biter as well as the one bitten. They tend to destroy the fellowship.

16. "Overcome evil with good."
17. Satan has a "fifth column" in our hearts. But the Holy Spirit also resides there. Hence, the conflict!
18. A person enjoys true freedom when the Holy Spirit has taken the helm of the ship which bears him over the troubled sea of life.
19. What today is often called "sickness" is by Scripture called "obvious work of the flesh."
20. We should practice self-denial, not self-indulgence.
21. "Private" sins, such as jealousy and envy, are not any better than "public" sins, such as drinking bouts and revelries.
22. *Love* heads the list of virtues.
23. The true Christian is loyal to his God, gentle to his neighbor, and has himself under control, all this as the result of God's grace.
24. Be in practice what you are (have confessed to be) in principle!
25. You derive all your strength from the Spirit. Then let the Spirit lead you in every phase of your life and conduct.
26. Rude self-assertion is displeasing to the Lord.

Chapter 6

Theme: *The Gospel of Justification by Faith apart from Law-works Defended against Its Detractors*

III. *Its Application: it produces true liberty. Let the Galatians stand firm, therefore, as does Paul, who glories in the cross of Christ*

E. Restore the fallen in a spirit of gentleness. Bear one another's burdens. Share all good things with y o u r instructor. Bear in mind that a man will reap what he sows. Let us do good to everybody, and especially to those who are of the household of the faith.

CHAPTER VI

GALATIANS

6   1 Brothers, even if a man be overtaken in any trespass, y o u who are spiritual should restore such a person in a spirit of gentleness, constantly looking to yourself, lest also you be tempted. 2 Bear one another's burdens, and so fulfil the law of Christ. 3 For if anyone imagines that he amounts to something, while he amounts to nothing, he is deluding himself. 4 But let each one test his own work; then his reason to boast will be in himself alone, and not in (comparing himself with) someone else; 5 for each person will have to bear his own load.

6 Let him who receives instruction in the Word share all good things with his instructor. 7 Do not be deceived; God is not mocked; for whatever a man sows, that also will he reap; 8 for he who sows to his own flesh will from the flesh reap corruption, and he who sows to the Spirit will from the Spirit reap life everlasting. 9 And let us not grow weary in well-doing, for in due season we shall reap if we do not give up. 10 So then, as we have opportunity, let us do good to everybody, and especially to those who are of the household of the faith.

6:1-10

E. *Show this love to all*

Over against rudeness (5:26) the apostle places gentleness. He says: **1. Brothers, even if a man be overtaken in any trespass, y o u who are spiritual should restore such a person in a spirit of gentleness. . . .** Here, let us say, is a person who, without deliberately planning to perform a wicked deed or to embark upon a devious course, "is overtaken in a trespass."[170] Before he even realizes to the full extent the ethically reprehensible or injurious nature of the act he has already committed it. He "was overtaken." The

---

[170] For the verb προλαμβάνω see M.M., p. 542. Perhaps the various meanings of the word can be subsumed under the general heading: to take or undertake—or in the passive, to be taken—before (hand). Thus in Corinth each person grabbed his food *before* sharing it with the less-privileged (I Cor. 11:21). The woman whose deed is described in Mark 14:8 undertook to anoint Christ's body *before* the usual time. So here in Gal. 6:1 also, the person in question is ensnared by the tempter *before* he fully realizes what he is doing.

This also sheds some light on the meaning *here* of the word *trespass*. In general it indicates a deviation from the path of truth and righteousness. Such deviations may be of a gross or of a less serious nature. The milder sense—fault, error, mistake —would seem to attach to the word in the present instance (as perhaps also in Rom. 5:15, 17, 18). At least the serious nature of the offense is not here stressed. See R. C. Trench, *op. cit.*, par. lxvi.

question then arises, "How must such a case be handled?" The answer is
that those members of the churches who are more consistent in following
the promptings of the Spirit (5:16, 18, 25) should, *in the spirit of gentleness
or meekness* (cf. 5:23), restore the one who committed the trespass. This
word *restore* means *to mend,* to bring something or someone back to its
or his former position of wholeness or soundness. Thus, it is used with
respect to mending nets (Matt. 4:21; Mark 1:19), and perfecting human
character (II Cor. 13:11: "Be perfected"). Cf. Luke 6:40; I Thess. 3:10. The
main idea certainly is this: "Follow a positive, not a negative course with
respect to the trespasser. Do not hurt him but help him. Treat him as
y o u yourselves would wish to be treated if y o u were in his place."
Continued: **constantly looking to yourself**—note change from plural ("Y o u
who are spiritual, etc.") to singular—**lest also you be tempted.** Rudeness or
boastfulness ill befits the person who at any moment may himself also
be tempted. Instead of being self-righteous and arrogant let each one offer
the prayers suggested in such passages as Matt. 6:14; 26:41; Mark 14:38;
Luke 22:40. The man who thinks that he is standing erect should all the
more take heed to himself lest he fall (I Cor. 10:12, 13).

Note how Paul himself practices what he preaches. Was it not true that
many Galatians had erred, not mildly but grievously? Nevertheless, though
he did not spare them (1:6; 3:1 ff.; 4:11; 5:7), did he not treat them gently,
tenderly (4:12 ff., 19, 20)? For the endearing word of address "Brothers,"
with which this chapter opens, see on 6:18.

Entirely in line with the preceding verse is verse **2. Bear one another's
burdens, and so fulfil the law of Christ.** This does not merely mean "Tolerate
each other," or "Put up with each other." It means: "Jointly shoulder each
member's burdens." Everybody should put his shoulder under the burdens
under which this or that individual member is groaning, whatever these
burdens may be. They must be carried[171] jointly. Though the term "one
another's burdens" is very general, and applies to every type of oppressing
affliction that is capable of being shared by the brotherhood, it should be
borne in mind, nevertheless, that the point of departure for this exhortation
(see on 6:1) is the duty to extend help to the brother so that he may

---

[171] The verb βαστάζω occurs more than twenty-five times in the New Testament.
It is especially common in the Gospels and in Acts. It is used in connection with
carrying a water-jar (Mark 14:13; Luke 22:6), a coffin (Luke 7:14), stones (John
10:31), money (carrying it away, stealing it: John 12:6), a corpse (transferring it
from one place to another: John 20:15), a yoke (Acts 15:10), a man: Paul (Acts
21:35), and a woman (Rev. 17:7). Hence, here in Gal. 6:2 (and cf. Rom. 15:1) it
can best be taken in the figurative sense of "carrying" each other's burdens,
lightening each other's loads *of difficulty and grief.* For a slightly different metaphorical sense see Gal. 5:10 (bear one's judgment, pay the penalty). We should
not allow the exceptional sense which the word has in Rev. 2:2 (tolerate, put up
with) to determine the meaning here in Gal. 6:2, but should interpret it in accordance with its usual sense.

overcome his spiritual weaknesses.[172] Continued: **and so fulfil the law of Christ.** This law of Christ is the principle of love for one another laid down by Christ (John 13:34; see also on Gal. 5:14; cf. James 2:8). However, Christ not only promulgated this law; he also exemplified it. Note how tenderly he dealt with: the sinful woman (Luke 7:36-50), the pentitent thief (Luke 23:43), Simon Peter (Luke 22:61; cf. John 21:15-17), an invalid (John 5:14), and the woman taken in adultery (John 8:11). And note also the marvelously generous reception which, according to Christ's *Parable of the Prodigal Son* (commonly so described), is accorded to the returning penitent. Paul constantly holds before us the *example* of Christ (Rom. 15:3-8; II Cor. 8:9; Phil. 2:5-8), as well as Christ's *precept.*

What follows stands in very close connection with the thought of verses 1 and 2. The connection with verse 1 might be stated as follows: "Constantly look to yourself, lest you also be tempted . . . for if anyone imagines that he amounts to something. . . ." And with verse 2, thus: "Bear one another's burdens, for no one can stand by himself alone . . . for if anyone imagines that he amounts to something, . . ." Accordingly, the apostle writes: **3. For if anyone imagines that he amounts to something, while he amounts to nothing, he is deluding himself.** What makes us tender and generous, meek and humble, sympathetic and helpful, toward others is the realization that we ourselves amount to so little. This does not mean that anyone should lose courage, thinking, "I amount to nothing, and am completely unfit to perform any kingdom work." On the contrary, Paul says, "I can do all things through him that infuses strength into me" (4:13). Morbid self-contempt is unfair to the Giver of all good gifts. Paul would have none of this. He recognizes that when the Holy Spirit distributed his gifts he (Paul) had not been passed by. Accordingly, he calls himself a wise master-builder (I Cor. 3:10), and a steward of the mysteries of God (I Cor. 4:1; cf. 9:17). He ranks himself higher than ten thousand tutors (I Cor. 4:15). He knows that he is able to speak with tongues "more than y o u all" (I Cor. 14:18). He is convinced that as an apostle he has "labored more abundantly" than anyone else (I Cor. 15: 10). See also II Cor. 11:22-33; Gal. 1:1, 14; and Phil. 3:4-6. But he ascribes all of these gifts to the Giver (Rom. 12:3; Gal. 6:14), and never claims personal credit for any virtue or talent (Rom. 7:24, 25; I Cor. 4:7). Besides, it should be borne in mind that Paul does not say, "For if anyone imagines that he amounts to something he is deluding himself." He says, "For if anyone imagines that he amounts to something, *while he amounts to nothing,* he is deluding himself." Paul is attacking the spirit of overconfidence in oneself. It was this error that caused Peter to deny his Lord (Matt. 26:33, 35; Mark 14:29, 31; Luke 22:33; John 13:37), and that

---

[172] Excellent is the article written by H. P. Berlage, "De juiste verklaring van Gal. 6:2," *TT*, 25 (1891), pp. 47–61.

denied the blessing to the Pharisee (Luke 18:9-14), just as much earlier it had brought about the discomfiture of Goliath (I Sam. 17:42-44), of Benhadad (I Kings 20:1 ff.), of Edom (Obad. 1-4), and of Nebuchadnezzar (Dan. 4:30; cf. Isa. 14:12 ff.). See also Rev. 3:17; 18:7.

Instead, therefore, of looking down upon the rest of the members, each member should examine himself. Says Paul: **4. But let each one test**[173] **his own work; then his reason to boast will be in himself alone, and not in (comparing himself with) someone else.** "He who mirrors himself in the mirror of another person's conduct mirrors himself gently."[174] He should mirror himself in the mirror of God's law and of Christ's example. If, after doing this, there is still room for making any claims—as there may be, indeed![175]— then the possibilities of glorying will have arisen from himself, that is, from that which God has accomplished in his heart, not from comparing himself with someone else. The man who is constantly comparing himself with others is senseless (II Cor. 10:12). He that boasts, let him boast in the Lord (cf. 6:14; II Cor. 10:17; cf. I Cor. 9:16; 10:31).

The folly of trying to derive comfort for oneself by comparing oneself with someone else is obvious, **5. for each person will have to bear his own load.**[176] Responsibility cannot be transferred. Each man will be judged in accordance with his own deeds (Jer. 17:10; 32:19; Ezek. 18:20; Matt. 16:27; Rom. 2:6; Rev. 2:23; 20:13). Works do not save anyone. That truth has been emphasized over and over again in this epistle. Nevertheless, the "reward" will be measured out in harmony with each man's works. These works will show the degree in which each man has been true to his trust, the extent to which grace has been operative in his life. *Burdens* should be carried jointly, but

---

173 The verb δοκιμάζω has various meanings: *a. to put to the test, examine* (I Cor. 11:28; II Cor. 13:5); *b. to prove or verify by means of testing* (I Cor. 3:13; Eph. 5:10; I Peter 1:7); and *c. to approve* (I Cor. 16:3). Here the first meaning best suits the context.

174 Dutch: Die zich aan een ander spiegelt, spiegelt zich zacht.

175 For example, he can claim to be a sinner, saved by grace!

176 In such cases in which βάρος (verse 2) and φορτίον (verse 5) have reference to that which oppresses, is there a difference in meaning between the two words? As to βάρος, Matt. 20:12 refers to "the burden of the day and the scorching heat." There is also Acts 15:28: "to lay upon y o u no greater burden" (cf. 15:10; and see Rev. 2:24). As to φορτίον Matt. 23:4 mentions "heavy burdens," and Luke 11:46 says that these burdens are "grievous to be borne." Contrast Matt. 11:30. It would seem, therefore, that when these two words are used in the aforementioned sense (they also have other meanings which are not relevant to our present purpose) they are quite indistinguishable. This, however, does not mean that here in Gal. 6:5 the word φορτίον must be interpreted in a manner identical with that of βάρος in 6:2. It is the context in each case that must decide. And that context clearly shows that the resultant meaning in these two cases is not identical. And since this is true, and besides, the words used in the original are different, the decision to use two different terms in the translation, a decision reached by most of the more recent translators, was, I believe, a wise one. Contrast A.V. and A.R.V. (text), which have the word "burden" in both passages.

the *load of responsibility* differs for each individual, and in the Judgment Day the manner in which brother *A* has assumed his responsibility will not make things easier or harder for brother *B*. The latter, too, will have to carry his own load.

At first glance it might well seem as if there is no connection between verses 1-5, on the one hand, and what now follows in verse 6. This may, in fact, be the case. It is entirely possible that Paul, realizing that what he mainly wanted to say has been said, asks himself, "Are there any other matters on which I must briefly comment before dispatching the letter?" And it is possible that it then occurred to him—under the direction of the Spirit—that there was, indeed, one rather important matter, namely, that pertaining to providing materially for those in need, including those who had been entrusted with the oversight of the various flocks. Nevertheless, there may, after all, have been a closer connection between verses 1-5, on the one hand, and verse 6 ff., on the other. Ministers who are serving large congregations or have done so at one time or another, will probably sense the possibility of this connection at once. Paul has been speaking about restoring the erring brother. One should not immediately draw the conclusion that this weakling has deliberately cast aside the truth. He may have been caught in a trap. Before he knew it, he had allowed himself to be deceived. Or, theoretically he may have stood for the truth, but in defending it he completely lost his temper. In any event, as was pointed out previously, the party-spirit had left its mark upon these churches. Much work had to be done, and it had to be done firmly, yet lovingly, tactfully. And in this connection a disproportionate burden would rest on the leaders, particularly on those who gave instruction in the Word. We can well imagine that in these early days of the establishment of the church and of its growth in the midst of much opposition both from within and from without, it must have seemed almost impossible, at times, for a church-leader to earn his living and, in addition, to perform all of his spiritual functions. Could this possibly be the reason why the apostle now adds: **6. Let him who receives instruction**—literally, *the catechumen,* a word that is still being used in religious circles—**in the Word share all good things with his instructor,** that is, with *the catechist?* It is worthy of note that even at this very early date there was in existence something similar to today's official Christian ministry. Cf. I Cor. 12:28; Eph. 4:11. In a letter that was probably written very shortly afterward the apostle says, "Now we request y o u, brothers, to appreciate those who labor among y o u and are over y o u in the Lord and admonish y o u, and to esteem them very highly in love for their work" (I Thess. 5:12, 13). Paul was a great organizer (Acts 20:17; Phil. 1:1; Titus 1:5). Even during his first missionary journey he was already appointing "elders in every church" (Acts 14:23). That among the several duties of these elders there was also that of imparting instruction is understandable.

Just how long it took the church to divide the work of the elders between those who governed but did not specialize in imparting instruction, on the one hand, and those, on the other hand, who in addition to governing also specialized in catechizing, we do not know. It may not have taken very long. In any event the Galatians must bear in mind that there is such a thing as the principle of reciprocity (Rom. 15:27; I Cor. 9:4-14; II Cor. 8:7-9, 14; I Tim. 5:8). Hence, those who receive instruction in the Word should *share* (see also Rom. 15:26; II Cor. 9:13; and Heb. 13:16) all good things—including material things—with their instructor. Paul had laid the foundation. He asks nothing for himself. He does, however, definitely urge the Galatians to provide adequately for those who are building on the foundation that had been laid.[177]

With respect not only to what he has just said with reference to attending to the needs of the ministers but also to all the admonitions contained in this letter, the apostle summarizes as follows: **7. Do not be deceived; God is not mocked; for whatever a man sows, that also will he reap. . . .** This rule holds not only for church-members; it holds for everybody. God is not mocked. He does not permit anyone to make light of his gospel or of the exhortations that are implied in it. To sneer at him, thinking, "God is dead," will not go unnoticed. On the contrary, every person will be rewarded according to his works (see on verse 5). This also means, of course, that the manner in which anyone reacts toward the present letter, in which the doctrine of justification by faith apart from law-works is defended against its detractors (be they legalists or libertines), does not escape God's notice, and will definitely be taken into account. Continued: **8. for he who sows to his own flesh will from the flesh reap corruption, and he who sows to the Spirit will from the Spirit reap life everlasting.** *Sowing to the flesh* means to allow the old nature to have its way. So also, *sowing to the Spirit* means to allow the Holy Spirit to have his way. The one who does the latter is walking by the

---

[177] I have carefully read the completely different interpretation of this verse in Lenski's *op. cit.*, p. 299ff. Lenski regards the idea that the Galatians should be "generous with their money," and that "congregations should pay their pastors" to be "a cheap thought," one that would have been especially out of place "so close to the end of the entire epistle." But the apostle was a very practical man. He who wrote I Cor. 9:14 could certainly also urge the Galatians to support their pastors. And as to the place which this admonition occupies in the entire letter, namely, a place toward the close, also in Romans it is toward the close of the epistle that the obligation to reciprocate by means of giving of one's physical substance in return for spiritual goods, is tactfully imposed upon those addressed.

Moreover, in I Corinthians the marvelous chapter with reference to Christ's resurrection and ours (I Cor. 15), ending with the words of triumph: "Thanks be to God who gives us the victory through our Lord Jesus Christ, . . ." is followed, at the beginning of the very last chapter, by "Now concerning the collection"! All this is really not surprising, for Paul considers the putting into practice of Christian stewardship *a sacred ministry* (II Cor. 8:4; 9:1).

Spirit (5:16), and is being led by the Spirit (5:18). What happens to these contrasted representative individuals? Already in this life, but especially in and after the resurrection at the last day, he who has been sowing to please his flesh will from the harvest-field of the flesh reap destruction, decay. On the other hand, he who has been sowing to please the Spirit will from the harvest-field of the Spirit reap life everlasting.

The two terms "corruption" and "life everlasting" must be understood in a double sense: quantitative and qualitative. With respect to the former, the two are alike: both last on and on and on. "Corruption," for example, far from amounting to annihilation, indicates "everlasting destruction" (II Thess. 1:9). "Life everlasting" (occurring frequently in the Gospels, especially in the Gospel according to John—3:16, etc.—; further also in Acts 13:46, 48; Rom. 2:7; 5:21; 6:22, 23; I Tim. 1:16; 6:12; Titus 1:2; 3:7; frequently also in I John—3:15, etc.—; Jude 21) is equal in duration (Matt. 25:46). Qualitatively, and this with reference to both body and soul, the two—"corruption" and "life everlasting"—form a striking contrast. Those who have sown to the flesh will awaken unto shame and everlasting contempt (Dan. 12:2). Their worm will not die, neither will their fire be quenched (Mark 9:48). Their dwelling-place will be outside the banquet-hall (Matt. 8:11, 12; 22:13; 25:10-13). On the other hand, those who have sown to the Spirit will then shine as the brightness of the firmament and as the stars forever and ever (Dan. 12:3). They will bear the image of the heavenly (I Cor. 15:49), and physically will be conformed to the body of Christ's glory (Phil. 3:21). They will be like Christ, for they will see him even as he is (I John 3:2). For the qualitative content of the term "life everlasting" see also on Gal. 3:11; cf. N.T.C. on John 3:16.

9. The idea of *reaping* (verses 7 and 8) is continued in this verse, now with emphasis on the perseverance in well-doing that is required of believers if they are going to reap the blessings of life everlasting. There would also seem to be a connection between verse 9 and the matter mentioned in verse 6. Moreover, with respect to "well-doing" the connection between verses 9 and 10 is obvious. Says Paul: **And let us not grow weary in well-doing, for in due season we shall reap if we do not give up.** "Well-doing"—literally, doing that which is *beautiful*—is a very broad concept, as comprehensive as is "walking by the Spirit" and "being led by the Spirit." See also Rom. 7:21; II Cor. 13:7; and II Thess. 3:13. In each of these passages the meaning is general; that is, the term "well-doing" is not limited to "giving to the poor." This having been admitted, it should now also be affirmed that the idea of providing for *the needy* (in any sense) is certainly not excluded. Is not this work of charity and of giving spiritual guidance an essential ingredient of well-doing? In fact, it is entirely possible that in the present context Paul was thinking especially of "helping anyone who is in need," whether it be of things physical: food, clothing, shelter (see Gal. 2:10; II

Cor. 16:1) ; things spiritual: instruction, encouragement, advice, etc.; or both. The admonition contained in this verse may well be viewed as a commentary on verse 2: "Bear one another's burdens, and so fulfil the law of Christ."

When the apostle says, "Let us not *grow weary* (see especially Luke 18:1; II Thess. 3:13) in well-doing," he is pointing his finger at a well-known weakness of human nature (see 5:7). Well-doing requires *continued* effort, *constant* toil; but human nature, being fond of ease, lacks staying-power, is easily discouraged. This is especially true when results are not always apparent at once, when those who should help refuse to co-operate, and when no reward seems ever to be coming our way. It is entirely possible that it was especially this last thought—namely, the apparent delay with respect to the fulfilment of the promise regarding Christ's return to reward his servants—that troubled the Galatians. So the apostle reminds them of the fact that we shall reap "in due season," that is, "at the moment of time that is exactly right," not, however, as determined by us but as fixed in God's eternal plan. It is then that the reward of grace—not of merit!—will be conferred. We shall receive it *if we do not lose heart and give up* (cf. Heb. 12:3, 5). Continued: **10. So then, as we have**[178] **opportunity, let us do good to everybody.** . . . Here again the negative—"Do not grow weary," "Do not give up"—is followed by the positive, "Let us do good." Perseverance in good works as a product of grace is what Paul is constantly urging (3:3; 5:7, 18, 25; 6:2). God preserves his people by means of their perseverance. The power to persevere is from him; the responsibility is theirs. Accordingly, as long as—and since—we have opportunity, let us at each and every occasion that presents itself do good to everybody. The believer has been placed on this earth for a purpose. The best way to prepare for Christ's second coming is to use to the full every opportunity of rendering service. Moreover, this service should be rendered to everybody regardless of race, nationality, class, religion, sex, or anything else. As our Lord's active love overleaped boundaries (Luke 9:54, 55; 10:25-37; 17:11-19; John 4:42; I Tim. 4:10) , so should ours. This, however, does not mean that there is no sphere of special concern. This is altogether to be expected. Parents, for example, have a duty toward their neighbors. Nevertheless, their first obligation is toward their own children. So also here. Paul says: **and especially to those who are of the household of the faith.** In this respect, too, we should imitate our heavenly Father, "who is the Savior of all men, especially of those who believe." For explanation see N.T.C. on I Tim. 4:10. Note the term, full of comfort, "the

---

178 There is considerable textual support for both ἔχομεν and ἔχωμεν, as the textual apparatus in N.N. indicates. However, when ὡς is used with the subjunctive we also expect ἄν, which is absent here. Hence, with N.N. and Grk.N.T. (A-B-M-W) I accept ἔχομεν. In ὡς ("as") "while" and "since" are probably combined.

household of the faith." All believers constitute one family, "the Father's Family" (see N.T.C. on Eph. 3:14, 15). See also I Cor. 3:9; Eph. 2:19; I Tim. 3:15; and let us not forget Ps. 133. By the term "the household of the faith" is meant those who share the gospel. With respect to material aid, is it not altogether probable that it was exactly this "household of the faith" that was most direly in need of such assistance?

Chapter 6

Verses 11-18

Theme: *The Gospel of Justification by Faith apart from Law-works Defended against Its Detractors*

III. *Its Application: it produces true liberty. Let the Galatians stand firm, therefore, as does Paul, who glories in the cross of Christ*

F. The Letter's End: Paul's "huge letters." Final warning against the disturbers and exposure of their motives: ease, honor. Concluding testimony: Far be it from me to glory except in the cross of our Lord Jesus Christ. Last plea: From now on let no one cause trouble for me, etc. Closing benediction.

11 Look with what huge letters I am writing to y o u with my own hand. 12 It is those who desire to make a fine outward impression that are trying to compel y o u to be circumcised, their sole purpose being that they may not be persecuted for the cross of Christ. 13 For even those who favor circumcision are not law-observers themselves, but want y o u to be circumcised that they may glory in y o u r flesh. 14 As for myself, however, far be it for me to glory except in the cross of our Lord Jesus Christ, by which the world has been crucified to me, and I to the world. 15 For neither is circumcision anything, nor uncircumcision, but a new creation. 16 And as many as shall walk by this rule, peace (be) upon them and mercy, even upon the Israel of God.

17 From now on let no one cause trouble for me, for I, on my part, bear on my body the marks of Jesus.

18 The grace of our Lord Jesus Christ (be) with y o u r spirit, brothers. Amen.

6:11-18

F. *Conclusion*

Paul has arrived at the conclusion. This he introduces as follows: **11. Look with what huge letters I am writing**[179] **to y o u with my own hand.** Another translation is: "Ye see how large a letter I have written unto you with mine own hand" (A.V.) . The Greek allows either rendering. Galatians is, indeed, larger than any of eight other epistles that tradition ascribes to Paul. Only Romans, I Corinthians, II Corinthians, and Ephesians[180] are larger (the last one only slightly) . So, especially if, of all Paul's letters that have been preserved, Galatians was the very first one he wrote, as we have assumed, he could perhaps have written, "See (or "y o u see") what a big letter I wrote y o u." Nevertheless, today very few interpreters would adopt the translation found in A.V. The most valid reason for this rejection is probably this: whenever the apostle refers to a *letter,* in the sense of "a communication in writing," as distinguished from "a character of the alphabet," he always uses the word *epistle* (Rom. 16:22; I Cor. 5:9; II Cor. 7:8; Col. 4:16; I Thess. 5:27; etc.) . That word is not found here in Gal. 6:11.[181]

---

[179] Robertson (Gram.N.T., p. 846) calls ἔγραψα "a true epistolary aorist." He states that "it probably refers to the concluding verses 11-18." The reasons given by others who contend that this is not an epistolary aorist have not convinced me. If in essentially similar cases this would be an epistolary aorist, showing that the writer looks at what he writes as the recipient will look at it, why would it be different in this case?

[180] Hebrews, of anonymous authorship, is, of course, excluded from this list.

[181] Besides, if Paul had an epistle in mind the accusative of the word "letter" (6:11) would have been more natural.

Having then adopted the rendering, "Look with what huge letters I am writing to y o u with my own hand," the next question would be, "Does Paul say this with respect to the entire epistle or only in connection with the closing paragraph (verses 11-18)?" Although there are those who have expressed very positively that the apostle wrote the entire Galatians with his own hand, I cannot go along with this conclusion. It would mean a departure, at the very outset, from what was going to be Paul's usual course, namely, to write *the closing greeting* (and perhaps a few words in connection with it) with his own hand. Thus we read, *"The greeting* by the hand of me, Paul, which is a token of genuineness in every epistle; so I write" (II Thess. 3:17). Cf. I Cor. 16:21; Col. 4:18.[182] This also indicates *why* the closing words were written by the author himself. Besides, it may well be that—especially in the case of Galatians—there was still another reason, namely, to add emphasis to the concluding words. In reading verses 11-18 one seems to sense the author's special emphasis, as if he were saying, "Let me summarize the entire argument, and let me give y o u one final, emphatic fatherly warning."

This, therefore, may also account for the fact that these letters were huge, namely, for the sake of special emphasis. But there may have been other reasons for this. Here, however, we have already entered the realm of speculation; for example: *a.* Paul's eyesight was impaired; *b.* his writing hand was sore; *c.* he had never learned to write very well; etc.

The next five verses contain a final warning against the Judaizers. Paul once again exposes their motives and in no uncertain terms blasts their compromising doctrine. In the course of doing this he comes up with one of his marvelous sayings, a profession of his personal faith. The warning begins as follows: **12. It is those who desire to make a fine outward impression that are trying to compel y o u to be circumcised, their sole purpose being that they may not be persecuted for the cross of Christ.** Whatever the apostle has said earlier about these opponents (see especially 1:7-9; 2:4, 5, 12; 3:1, 10; 4:17; 5:2-5, 7, 11, 12) is here brought to a head. In a few crisp phrases he makes clear that these Judaizers are not at all interested in the welfare of the Galatians. On the contrary, they are concerned only about themselves: their own honor, their own ease (freedom from persecution). They desire to make a good outward impression; literally: "to present a pleasing front *in flesh,*" that is, *outwardly.* They are eager to cut a respectable figure when they come face to face with other Jews, those who have not even nominally accepted Christ. By making so much of circumcision—as if that were far more important than the cross of Christ—they are trying to work their way back into the good graces of their relatives and former friends. They know

---

[182] It was not unusual in those days for a writer to employ a secretary, and then to write the conclusion with his own hand. See A. Deissmann, *op. cit.,* pp. 171, 172.

very well that a Jew who departs from the Jewish traditions and accepts Christ wholeheartedly can expect nothing but bitter presecution: ostracism, threats, calumny, physical and mental torture, etc. (Matt. 10:17; John 11:57; Acts 4:27, 28; 5:33; 13:45, 50; 14:2, 19; 21:27-36; II Cor. 11:24; Col. 1:24; I Thess. 2:14-16; II Tim. 3:10-12; Rev. 2:9). They are trying to escape all this, therefore, by means of effecting a compromise; something like: "Salvation is achieved by means of faith in Jesus plus law-works, especially circumcision." Their hypocrisy and selfishness is evident: **13: For even those who favor circumcision**[183] **are not law-observers themselves, but want y o u to be circumcised that they may glory in y o u r flesh.** By all kinds of devious means and subterfuges these legalists tried to circumvent the law's real intention. The relation between the Judaizers and the Pharisees is clear from Acts 15:5. Jesus again and again characterized the Pharisees as being "hypocrites" (Matt. 23:13, 14, 15, 23, 25, 27, 29). He also called them "serpents and offspring of vipers" (Matt. 23:33), and declared that they made void the word of God by their tradition (Matt. 15:6). Relevant to the present context is also this saying of the Lord: "They tie together heavy loads, and lay them on men's shoulders; but they themselves are unwilling to raise a finger to lift them" (Matt. 23:4).

Paul therefore tells the Galatians: These hypocrites "want y o u to be circumcised that they may glory in y o u r[184] flesh," that is, that y o u r circumcised organ may provide them with a reason to boast. They would then be able to step up to their fellow-countrymen with an air of confidence, bragging, "Just think of it, we persuaded so many Galatians to become circumcised!"

Over against this type of "glorying" Paul now sets his own: **14. As for myself, however, far be it for me to glory except in the cross of our Lord Jesus Christ, by which the world has been crucified to me, and I to the world.**

The Cross: Paul's Only Reason for Glorying

(1) Why Paul Glories Only in the Cross
The cross is about the last thing which natural man would ever have selected as a reason for boasting. It was "to the Jews a stumbling-block, and to the Greeks foolishness" (I Cor. 1:23). The cross exposes man's desperate state, his utter bankruptcy that made such suffering necessary. Accordingly,

---

[183] The perfect: "those who have been circumcised," may have seemed more correct to a copyist than the present, which could be interpreted to mean, "those who have themselves circumcised." But the present can also be interpreted as indicating, "those who favor and advocate circumcision." The context points in the direction of the latter interpretation for it is clear that Paul is referring to the Judaizers.

[184] The original may imply a degree of emphasis, especially in the light of *a.* the emphatic "as for myself" at the beginning of verse 14, and *b.* verse 17 (see on that verse).

it reveals the folly of all human pride. It teaches man to say: "I never knew myself as a sinner, nor recognized Christ as my Savior,

> Until upon the cross I saw
> My God, who died to meet the law
> That I had broken; then I saw
> My sin, and then my Savior."

No one is ever able to see on that cross "the wonder of God's glorious love" unless he also sees "his own unworthiness," and "pours contempt on all his pride."

By God's marvelous grace Paul had come to view that cross as:

a. The Mirror, and this not only of his own unworthiness but also of God's resplendent attributes, that is, of such "excellencies" as God's righteousness which must receive its due (Rom. 8:3, 4); God's power and wisdom (I Cor. 1:24); and his love, mercy, and grace (II Cor. 5:19-21; Gal. 2:20); all of these in sublime harmony with each other (Ps. 85:10).

b. The Means of Redemption in its most comprehensive sense (Justification, Sanctification, Glorification). See such passages as Rom. 3:25, 26; 6:6; Gal. 3:13; Eph. 1:7; 2:16; Col. 1:20; 2:14. Cf. Heb. 9:22; Rev. 7:14.

c. The Magnet by means of which men of every tribe and nation, being drawn to Christ Crucified, are also drawn together as one body (Gal. 3:23-29; Eph. 2:16, 18; Col. 3:11. Cf. John 3:13, 14; 12:32).

d. The Model for men to imitate. The redemptive acts can never be imitated, but the spirit of self-sacrifice and love that is revealed in these acts should be reflected in the hearts and lives of God's children (Rom. 15:1, 2; II Cor. 8:9; Eph. 5:1, 2; Phil. 2:5-8). Cf. John 13:14, 34; I Peter 2:21-24.

Is it any wonder, then, that Paul glories only in the cross?

(2) *How Paul Glories in the Cross*

a. By surrendering himself to Christ Crucified as his own Lord and Savior (Gal. 2:20);

b. By praying that the power of the crucified and risen Savior may more and more assert itself in his own life (Phil. 3:7-16);

c. By proclaiming the crucified and risen Lord—notice full title "our Lord Jesus Christ"—wherever he is sent (Gal. 1:16), the love of Christ constraining him to do so (I Cor. 9:16; II Cor. 5:14); and

d. By courageously defending the gospel of Christ Crucified over against every attack upon it (as is shown by this very epistle to the Galatians, in its entirety).

(3) *What Effect Paul's Glorying in the Cross Has upon the Relation between Paul and the World*

a. By this cross, says Paul, "the world has been crucified to me." He does not say, "I crucified the world," but "the world has been crucified to me."

244

In other words, he bears testimony to the fact that the Holy Spirit, by means of the pure doctrine of the cross, had wrought a mighty work in his soul. The "world," that is, all those earthly pleasures and treasures, honors and values, that tend to draw the soul away from Christ, had lost their charm for Paul. *The world had become dead to Paul.* I am in complete agreement with Calvin when, in commenting on this expression, he states: "This exactly agrees with the language which Paul employs on another occasion," and then refers to Phil. 3:7, 8: "Nevertheless, such things as once were gains to me these have I counted loss for Christ. Yes, what is more, I certainly do count all things to be sheer loss because of the all-surpassing excellence of knowing Christ Jesus my Lord, for whom I suffered the loss of all these things, and I am still counting them refuse, in order that I may gain Christ" (my translation, not Calvin's).

b. Paul adds, "and I (have been crucified) to the world." Logic would seem to demand that, as far as possible, the two statements (*a.* and *b.*) be interpreted, in such a manner that the words "has—or: have—been crucified" have the same meaning in both cases. Hence, this second clause must mean that *Paul had become dead to the world,* an object of contempt to all those who place their confidence in earthly pleasures and treasures, honors and values, that tend to draw the soul away from Christ. Duncan expresses it very aptly: "Paul's ideals and outlook have now become so spiritual and unworldly that the world can ignore him, just as if he had ceased to be."

Paul continues: **15. For neither is circumcision anything, nor uncircumcision, but a new creation.** The conjunction *for* indicates the relation between this and the preceding verse. It shows that what Paul means is this: salvation by means of the cross of Christ is everything to me; worldly inventions, on the contrary, such as salvation through circumcision, mean nothing, "For (or: the reason being that) neither is circumcision anything. . . ." The present passage (6:15) comes very close to saying what Paul had said before, namely, "For in Christ Jesus neither circumcision nor uncircumcision is of any avail, but faith working through love" (5:6). See the explanation of that passage. Cf. I Cor. 7:19; II Cor. 5:17; Gal. 3:28; and Col. 3:10, 11. Being circumcised contributes nothing toward being saved, nor does *not* being circumcised; neither is it possible for either of these two states to assure us of salvation—or to make us effective witnesses for God. The one and only thing that really matters is "a new creation," that is, the new life, the life of regeneration, which the Holy Spirit brings about in a person's heart (John 3:3, 5; Rom. 2:29). That "creation" is "new," as contrasted with man's old, outworn nature. It is infinitely *better* than the old. It is *God's* work, and is therefore what really counts. It is the product of him who says, "Behold, I make all things new" (Rev. 21:5). It has come *fresh* from the heart of God Almighty, and is a firm pledge of even greater glories to follow, as a result of *his* transforming power, "For his handiwork are we, created in Christ Jesus for good works, which God prepared beforehand that we should walk in them" (Eph. 2:10).

Paul continues: **16. And as many as shall walk by this rule, peace (be) upon them and mercy, even upon the Israel of God.** According to the preceding context, this rule[185] is the one by which before God only this is of consequence, that a person places his complete trust in Christ Crucified, and that, therefore, he regulates his life by this principle. This will mean that his life will be one of gratitude and Christian service out of love for his wonderful Savior. Upon those—*all* those and *only* those—who are governed by this rule *peace and mercy* are pronounced. *Peace* is the serenity of heart that is the portion of all those who have been justified by faith (Rom. 5:1). In the midst of the storms of life they are safe because they have found shelter in the cleft of the rock. In the day of wrath, wasteness, and desolation God "hides" all those who take refuge in him (Zeph. 1:2 ff.; 2:3; 3:12). See on 1:3. Hence, peace is spiritual wholeness and prosperity. *Peace* and *mercy* are inseparable. Had not the *mercy* of God been shown to his people they would not have enjoyed *peace*. God's mercy is his love directed toward sinners viewed in their wretchedness and need. See N.T.C. on Philippians, p. 142, for a list of over one hundred Old and New Testament passages in which this divine attribute is described.

So far the interpretation runs smoothly. A difficulty arises because of the last phrase of this verse. That last phrase is: *"kai upon the Israel of God."* Now, varying with the specific context in which this conjunction *kai* occurs, it can be rendered: *and, and so, also, likewise, even, nevertheless, and yet, but,* etc. Sometimes it is best left untranslated. Now when this conjunction is rendered *and* (as in A.V., A.R.V., N.E.B.), it yields this result, that after having pronounced God's blessing upon all those who place their trust exclusively in Christ Crucified, the apostle pronounces an additional blessing upon "the Israel of God," which is then interpreted to mean "the Jews," or "all such Jews as would in the future be converted to Christ," etc.

Now this interpretation tends to make Paul contradict his whole line of reasoning in this epistle. Over against the Judaizers' perversion of the gospel

---

[185] Greek κανών was probably borrowed from the Hebrew word *qāneh*. According to etymologists our English word "cane" may be related to this. At any rate the Greek word has the basic meaning: *reed* or *measuring rod*. Thus, figuratively, it developed into the meaning *norm, standard*. Something similar has happened in connection with our English word "rule." The sense *norm, standard of measurement in ethical and spiritual matters,* clearly pertains to the word here in Gal. 6:16. In II Cor. 10:13-16 the meaning is slightly different: "sphere of action or influence," "boundary." The meaning "collection of divinely inspired, normative writings" was a later development. The word does not have that meaning in the New Testament.

he has emphasized the fact that "the blessing of Abraham" now rests upon all those, and only upon those, "who are of faith" (3:9) ; that all those, and only those, "who belong to Christ" are "heirs according to promise" (3:29) . These are the very people who "walk by the Spirit" (5:16) , and "are led by the Spirit" (5:18) . Moreover, to make his meaning very clear, the apostle has even called special attention to the fact that God bestows his blessings on all true believers, regardless of nationality, race, social position, or sex: "There can be neither Jew nor Greek; there can be neither slave nor free-man; there can be no male and female; for y o u are all one in Christ Jesus" (3:28) . By means of an allegory (4:21-31) he has re-emphasized this truth. And would he now, at the very close of the letter, undo all this by first of all pronouncing a blessing on "as many as" (or: "all") who walk by the rule of glorying in the cross, be they Jew or Gentile by birth, and then pronouncing a blessing upon those who do not (or: do not yet) walk by that rule? I refuse to accept that explanation. Appeals to the well-known "Eighteen petition prayer of the Jews," to the meaning of the word *Israel* in other New Testament passages, etc., cannot rescue this interpretation. As to the former, Gal. 6:16 must be interpreted in accordance with *its own specific context* and *in the light of the entire argument of this particular epistle*. And as to the latter, it is very clear that in his epistles the apostle employs the term *Israel* in more than one sense. In fact, in the small compass of a single verse (Rom. 9:6) he uses it in two different senses. Each passage in which that term occurs must therefore be explained in the light of its context.[186] Besides, Paul uses the term "the Israel of God" only in the present passage, nowhere else.

What, then, is the solution? In harmony with all of Paul's teaching in this epistle (and see also Eph. 2:14-22) , and also in harmony with the broad, all-inclusive statement at the beginning of the present passage, where the apostle pronounces God's blessing of peace and mercy upon "as many as" shall walk by this rule, an object from which nothing can be subtracted and to which nothing can be added, it is my firm belief that those many translators and interpreters are right who have decided that *kai,* as here used, must be rendered *even,* or (with equal effect) must be left untranslated. Hence, what the apostle says is this: "And as many as shall walk by this rule, peace (be) upon them and mercy, even upon the Israel of God." Cf. Ps. 125:5. Upon all of God's true Israel, Jew or Gentile, all who truly glory in the cross, the blessing is pronounced.[187]

---

[186] See also my little book *And So All Israel Shall Be Saved,* an interpretation of Rom. 11:26a. It was published in 1945 by Baker Book House, Grand Rapids, Mich., but is out of print at this writing.

[187] The rendering according to which *kai* is translated *even,* or is left untranslated, is also favored by the following: The Amplified New Testament, Berkeley Version, Calvin, Erdman, Lenski, Lightfoot, Phillips, Rendall, R.S.V., and Williams.

247.

17. Paul presents a final request: **From now on**[188] **let no one cause trouble for me, for I, on my part, bear on my body the marks of Jesus.** The apostle, loaded down with many responsibilities, asks that in the future he may not again be troubled by departures from the truth in the Galatian churches. He asks, in other words, that these churches may take his message to heart. Troublesome churches, and also troublesome individuals, at times forget that, while their own misbehavior is bad enough in itself, they also deprive others of the attention that could have been bestowed upon them. Cf. Luke 13:7. Besides, on the part of the person who must set them straight they often require energy that is exhausting. It is especially the latter thought which Paul has in mind when he reminds the Galatians that he bears on his body the marks of Jesus.

Evidently the apostle was referring to the scars (literally: *stigmata*)[189] that had been left on his body by the persecutions which he had endured while traveling through Galatia on his first missionary journey (Acts 13:50; 14:19; II Cor. 11:25; II Tim. 3:10, 11). At Lystra, for example, he had been almost stoned to death! Up to this point there is very little disagreement among commentators. However, when the question is asked, "In what sense were these scars the marks of Jesus?" the opinions vary widely. Some of them are as follows: They characterized Paul as *a.* a slave of Jesus, *b.* a prisoner of Jesus, *c.* a soldier of Jesus, *d.* in possession of an amulet or "Jesus-charm," as if the apostle were warning the Galatians: "Do be sensible, y o u cannot make any trouble for me, for I am protected by a charm" (a most unlikely explanation!). The best explanation, as far as I can see, is the one offered by Lenski (among others): "The scars on Paul's body belonged to Jesus, like the wounds he himself suffered, for Paul's scars were truly suffered because of Christ. Cf. II Cor. 1:5; 4:10; Col. 1:24" (*op. cit.*, p. 321). The wounds inflicted on Paul's body were evidence of the closeness of the fellowship between Jesus and Paul (Gal. 1:8-12, 15, 16; 2:19 ff.; 4:12-20).

It is just possible that Paul's emphatic "I, on my part"[190] forms a contrast with 6:13, where Paul tells the Galatians that the purpose of the Judaizers is "that they may glory in y o u r flesh." If that be so, then the apostle is, as it were, saying, "I, too, have *marks* or *scars,* namely those that link me with my Savior. Remember that, Galatians! And be reminded that when,

---

[188] Here τοῦ λοιποῦ probably means *in the future* (= τοῦ λοιποῦ χρόνου), in distinction from τὸ λοιπόν, as for the rest. At times the two are equivalent in meaning. and may both be rendered "finally." See N.T.C. on Eph. 6:10.

[189] These *stigmata* must not be identified in nature with the wounds in the hands, feet, and side of Francis of Assisi and many others after him. See the interesting account in E. M. Wilmot-Buxton, *St. Francis of Assisi*, New York, 1926, pp. 154-157. As some see it, such marks are connected with nervous or cataleptic hysteria. In any case, this subject has nothing to do with the explanation of Gal. 5:17.

[190] Note emphatic ἐγώ at the beginning of the last clause; also: "on *my body*."

because of departure from the faith, y o u trouble me, y o u are grieving my Savior, whose ambassador I am" (cf. Acts 9:4, 5; 22:7, 8; 26:14, 15) .

Verse **18.** contains the closing benediction: **The grace of our Lord Jesus Christ (be) with y o u r spirit, brothers. Amen.** It has been remarked that the brevity which characterizes this benediction reflects the tension under which the apostle wrote this letter. Accordingly, these few words have been compared with the rich and bountiful parting salutations found in Rom. 16:25-27; II Cor. 13:14; Eph. 6:23, 24; and Jude 24, 25. Nevertheless, further reflection indicates that Paul's final word, here in Gal. 6:18, is by no means wanting in beauty and meaning. Note the following:

a. It concentrates the attention of those to whom it is addressed on "the marvelous grace of our loving Lord." This is the grace (love to the undeserving) that had atoned for their sin, had brought about the operation of the Holy Spirit in their hearts, and their adoption as children and heirs. It is the grace that sustains them, equips them to be living witnesses, fills their hearts with peace that passes understanding and with joy unspeakable and full of glory, and brings them at last to their inheritance, incorruptible, undefiled, and never-fading. Is it not true that throughout the letter the emphasis is on the marvel of *God's grace* as contrasted with *human work?*

b. It mentions Jesus in all the fulness of his saving power, giving him his full title "our Lord Jesus Christ." The solemnity with which the apostle utters this full name deserves attention. As *Lord* he owns us, governs and protects us, and we belong to him and should do his bidding. As *Jesus* he, he *alone,* is our Savior (Matt. 1:21; Acts 4:12) . And as *Christ* he was appointed and (as to his human nature) gloriously qualified to be, in his capacity as our Mediator, "our chief Prophet, only Highpriest, and eternal King." See Acts 2:36.

c. It focuses the attention of the Galatians on the necessity of having this grace of the Lord Jesus Christ in their *inner personality,* viewed as contact-point between God and his children: " (be) with y o u r spirit." The Judaizers were fond of making a good *outward* impression. The Galatians are reminded of the fact that what they need is "grace that will strengthen and cleanse *within.*"

d. Finally, it does not take leave of these Galatians, many of whom were erring grievously, before it has once more, as so often before (1:11; 3:15; 4:12, 28, 31; 5:11, 13; 6:1) , addressed them with that term of endearment and close Christian fellowship: "brothers," members—by grace!—of the same family, "the Father's Family" (see N.T.C. on Eph. 3:14, 15) .

A church that was dear—in fact, very dear—to the heart of Paul was that at Philippi. Note how he was going to describe it in Phil. 4:1: "my brothers, beloved and longed for, my joy and crown . . . beloved." Surely Paul would put just as much love into the closing benediction addressed to that church as he now puts into the final blessing which he pronounces on the Galatians. Now compare the two:

Phil. 4:23	Gal. 6:18
"The grace of the Lord Jesus Christ (be) with y o u r spirit."	"The grace of our Lord Jesus Christ (be) with y o u r spirit, brothers. Amen.

Note: "brothers" in Gal. 6:18. The Philippians did not need to be reassured of this. They knew it (Phil. 1:12; 3:1, 13, 17; 4:1, 8). The Galatians must hear it once more; for the heart of Paul, that warm, throbbing heart, feels the need of once again embracing these erring "children" of his with his love!

The solemn word of affirmation and confirmation, "Amen," closes this epistle.

Galatians 6: Seed Thoughts
(one thought for each verse)

See Verse
1. Restore lovingly those who were caught in temptation's net.
2. Burdens must be shouldered jointly.
3. Be conceited and be cheated!
4. He who mirrors himself in the mirror of another person's conduct mirrors himself gently.
5. Responsibility's load cannot be transferred.
6. Provide well for God's servant, the minister.
7. Those who sow weeds must not expect to reap wheat.
8. "The wages of sin is death, but the free gift of God is life everlasting in Christ Jesus our Lord."
9. "Blessed are the merciful, for they will receive mercy."
10. Love overleaps—yet also recognizes—boundaries.
11. Do not soft-pedal the gospel.
12. Beware of compromising when principles are at stake.
13. Practice what y o u preach.
14. The cross of Christ: our only glory.
15. "On Christ, the solid Rock, I stand; All other ground is sinking sand."
16. This (No. 15) is the Rule of Gratitude for every Christian.
17. Do not trouble those who bear the marks of Jesus, but help them in every way.
18. The man who preaches "Salvation through Imitation" forgets that it even takes grace to imitate.

Paul's Epistle to the Galatians

Chapter 1

1 Paul, an apostle—not from men nor through man but through Jesus Christ and God the Father, who raised him from the dead—2 and all the brothers who are with me, to the churches of Galatia; 3 grace to y o u and peace from God our Father and the Lord Jesus Christ; 4 who gave himself for our sins, that he might rescue us out of this present world dominated by evil; (having thus given himself) according to the will of our God and Father, 5 to whom (be) the glory forever and ever. Amen.

6 I am amazed that y o u are so quickly moving away from him who called y o u (and turning) to a different gospel, 7 which (in reality) is not (even) another; but (the fact is that) certain individuals are throwing y o u into confusion and are trying to pervert the gospel of Christ. 8 But even though we ourselves or an angel from heaven were to preach to y o u any gospel other than the one which we preached to y o u, let him be accursed! 9 As we have said before, so now I say again, If anyone is preaching to y o u any gospel other than that which y o u have received, let him be accursed! 10 There! Is it the favor of men that I am now seeking to win or of God? Or is it men whom I am seeking to please? If I were still trying to please men, I would not be a servant of Christ.

11 For I make known to y o u, brothers, with respect to the gospel that was preached by me, that it is not a human invention; 12 for as concerns myself, I did not receive it from men nor was I taught it; on the contrary (I received it) through the revelation of Jesus Christ. 13 For y o u have heard of my former manner of life when I practiced the Jewish religion, how beyond all bounds I was persecuting the church of God and was trying to destroy it; 14 and I advanced in the Jewish religion more than many of my contemporaries among my people, and was a more ardent enthusiast for the traditions of my fathers. 15 But when it pleased him, who separated me from my mother's womb and called me through his grace, 16 to reveal his Son in me, in order that I might preach his gospel among the Gentiles, I did not at once confer with flesh and blood, 17 nor did I go up to Jerusalem to those who were apostles before me, but I went away to Arabia; and again I returned to Damascus.

18 Then after three years I went up to Jerusalem to become acquainted with Cephas, and I remained with him fifteen days; 19 but none of the other apostles did I see, only James the Lord's brother. 20 Now take note: with respect to the things which I am writing to y o u, in the presence of God (I affirm) that I am not lying. 21 Then I came to the districts of Syria and Cilicia. 22 But I was still unknown by sight to the Christian churches of Judea. 23 They simply kept hearing, "He who formerly persecuted us is now preaching the gospel of the faith which he formerly was trying to destroy." 24 And they were glorifying God on my account.

Chapter 2

1 Then, after an interval of fourteen years, I went up again to Jerusalem with Barnabas, also taking Titus with me. 2 I went up, moreover, as a result of a

revelation, and I set before them the gospel which I am accustomed to preach among the Gentiles; but (I did this) privately to "those of repute," to make sure that I was not running or had not run in vain. 3 Yet even Titus who was with me, Greek though he is, was not compelled to be circumcised; 4 (in fact, the suggestion would never have arisen) but for the uninvited sham brothers, who had infiltrated our ranks to spy on our liberty which we have in Christ Jesus, and thus to reduce us to slavery; 5 to whom not even for a moment did we yield submission, in order that the truth of the gospel might continue with y o u. 6 Well, from those "who were reputed" to be something—whatever they once were makes no difference to me; God accepts no man's person—to me "those of repute" imparted nothing; 7 on the contrary, when they saw that I had been entrusted with the gospel to the uncircumcised just as Peter (with that) to the circumcised 8—for he who was at work through Peter in apostolic mission activity for the circumcised was also at work in me for the Gentiles—, 9 and when they perceived the grace that was given to me, James and Cephas and John, "those who were reputed" to be pillars, gave to me and Barnabas the right hand of fellowship, that we should (go) to the Gentiles, and they to the circumcised. 10 Only, we were to continue to remember the poor, the very thing which I was also eager to do.

11 Now when Cephas came to Antioch I opposed him to his face because he stood condemned. 12 For before certain individuals from James arrived he had been in the habit of eating his meals with the Gentiles. But when they came he began to draw back and to separate himself, being afraid of those who belonged to the circumcision party. 13 And the rest of the Jews joined him in playing the hypocrite, so that even Barnabas was carried along by their hypocrisy. 14 But when I saw that they were not pursuing a straight course in accordance with the truth of the gospel, I said to Cephas, in everybody's presence, "If you, though a Jew, can live like a Gentile and not like a Jew, how can you (now) force the Gentiles to live like Jews?"

15 "We ourselves, though by nature Jews and not 'Gentile sinners,' 16 yet, knowing that a man is not justified by law-works but only through faith in Jesus Christ, even we believed in Christ Jesus in order that we might be justified by faith in Christ, and not by law-works, because by law-works will no flesh be justified. 17 But if, in seeking to be justified in Christ, we ourselves also turn out to be sinners, is Christ then a sin-promoter? By no means! 18 For, if I start to rebuild the very things which I have torn down, it is then that I prove myself a transgressor. 19 For I through law died to law, that I might live to God. 20 I have been crucified with Christ; and it is no longer I who lives, but Christ who lives in me; and that (life) which I now live in flesh I live in faith, (the faith) which is in the Son of God, who loved me and gave himself up for me. 21 I do not set aside the grace of God; for if justification (were) through law, then Christ died in vain."

Chapter 3

1 O foolish Galatians! Who has bewitched y o u, before whose very eyes Jesus was openly displayed as crucified? 2 This only would I learn from y o u: Was it by doing what (the) law demands that y o u received the Spirit, or was it by believing (the) gospel message? 3 Are y o u so foolish? Having begun by the Spirit, now by fleshly means are y,o u being made perfect? 4 Did y o u experience so many things in vain?—if (it be) really in vain. 5 He, accordingly, who supplies the Spirit to y o u and works miracles among y o u (does he bring this about) because y o u do what (the) law demands or because y o u believe (the) gospel message?

6 (It is) even as (recorded): "Abraham believed God, and it was reckoned to him for righteousness." 7 Know then that those that are of faith, it is they who are sons of Abraham. 8 Now Scripture, foreseeing that it was by faith that God would justify the Gentiles, preached the gospel beforehand to Abraham, (saying): "In you all the nations shall be blessed." 9 Therefore, those that are of faith are blessed with Abraham, the man of faith.

10 For as many as rely on law-works are under a curse; for it is written, "Cursed (is) everyone who does not continue in all the things that are written in the book of the law, to do them." 11 Now it is evident that by law no one is justified before God, for "The righteous shall live by faith." 12 But the law does not belong to faith; on the contrary, "He who does them shall live by them." 13 Christ redeemed us from the curse of the law, having become a curse for us—for it is written, "Cursed is everyone who is hanging on a tree"— 14 in order that the blessing of Abraham might come to the Gentiles in Jesus Christ, in order that we might receive the promised Spirit through faith.

15 Brothers, I speak from a human standpoint: even a human testament, once ratified, no one sets aside or amplifies. 16 Now to Abraham were the promises spoken, and to his seed. He does not say, "And to the seeds," as (referring) to many, but as (referring) to one, "And to your seed," which is Christ. 17 Now this is what I mean: a covenant that has been ratified by God, the law, which came into existence four hundred thirty years afterward, does not annul so as to make the promise ineffective. 18 For if the inheritance (is) due to law, it (is) no longer due to promise; but to Abraham it was through a promise that God graciously granted it.

19 Why then the law? By reason of the transgressions it was added, until the seed should come to whom the promise had been made, having been ordained through angels by the agency of an intermediary. 20 Now the intermediary does not represent (just) one party, but God is one.

21 (Is) the law then contrary to the promises of God? By no means. For if a law had been given that was able to impart life, then indeed righteousness would have come by law. 22 But Scripture has locked up the whole world under (the power of) sin, in order that as a result of faith in Jesus Christ the promise might be given to those who believe.

23 Now before this faith came, we were kept in custody under law, being locked up with a view to the faith that was to be revealed. 24 So the law became our custodian (to conduct us) to Christ, that by faith we might be justified. 25 But now that this faith has come we are no longer under a custodian.

26 For y o u are all sons of God, through faith, in Christ Jesus. 27 For as many of y o u as were baptized into (union with) Christ have put on Christ. 28 There can be neither Jew nor Greek; there can be neither slave nor freeman; there can be no male and female; for y o u are all one in Christ Jesus. 29 And if y o u belong to Christ, then y o u are Abraham's seed, heirs according to promise.

Chapter 4

1 What I mean is this, that as long as the heir is a child he differs in no respect from a slave though he is owner of all, 2 but is under guardians and stewards until the time fixed by the father. 3 So also we, when we were children, were enslaved by the rudiments of the world. 4 But when the fulness of the time came, God sent forth his Son, born of a woman, born under law, 5 in order that he might redeem them (who were) under law, that we might receive the adoption as sons. 6 And because y o u are sons, God sent forth the Spirit of his Son into our

hearts, crying, "Abba! Father!" 7 So, no longer are you a slave but a son; and if a son then also an heir through God.

8 However, at that time, since y o u did not know God, y o u were slaves to those who by nature are no gods; 9 but now that y o u have come to know God, or rather to be known by God, how (is it) that y o u turn back again to the weak and beggarly rudiments by which all over again y o u wish to be enslaved? 10 Y o u observe days and months and seasons and years. 11 I am afraid about y o u, lest somehow I have labored among y o u in vain.

12 Become as I (am), because I also became as y o u (are), brothers; (this) I beg of y o u. No wrong did y o u do me. 13 Y o u know, moreover, that it was because of an infirmity of the flesh that I preached to y o u the gospel on that former occasion; 14 and though my physical condition was a temptation to y o u, yet y o u did not despise or loathe me, but as an angel of God y o u welcomed me, as Christ Jesus. 15 Where, then, (is) y o u r (former) blessedness? For I testify to y o u that, had it been possible, y o u r very eyes y o u would have plucked out and given to me. 16 Have I then become y o u r enemy by telling y o u the truth? 17 These people are zealously courting y o u for no commendable purpose: on the contrary, they want to isolate y o u, in order that y o u may zealously court them. 18 Now (it is) commendable to be zealously courted in connection with a commendable cause (and this) always, and not only when I am present with y o u. 19 My dear children, for whom I am again suffering birth-pangs until Christ be formed in y o u, 20 I could wish to be present with y o u now and to change my tone of voice, for I am perplexed about y o u.

21 Tell me, y o u who desire to be under law, do y o u not hear the law? 22 For it is written that Abraham had two sons, one by the slave-woman and one by the free-woman. 23 But the son of the slave-woman was flesh-born; the son of the free-woman (was born) through promise. 24 Now things of this nature were spoken with another meaning in mind, for these two women represent two covenants: one from Mount Sinai, bearing children destined for slavery. She is Hagar. 25 Now Hagar represents Mount Sinai in Arabia, and corresponds to the Jerusalem of today, for she is in bondage with her children. 26 But the Jerusalem (that is) above is free, and she is our mother; 27 for it is written:

"Rejoice O barren one, you who do not bear;
Break forth and shout, you who have no birth-pangs;
For more are the children of the desolate than of her who has a husband."

28 Now y o u, brothers, like Isaac, are children of promise. 29 But as at that time he (who was) flesh-born persecuted the one (who was) Spirit-born, so (it is) also now. 30 But what does Scripture say? "Cast out the slave-woman and her son; for in no way shall the son of the slave-woman share in the inheritance with the son of the free-woman." 31 Wherefore, brothers, not of a slave-woman are we children, but of the free-woman.

Chapter 5

1 For freedom Christ has set us free; continue to stand firm, therefore, and do not be loaded down again with a yoke of slavery.

2 Now I, Paul, say to y o u that if y o u let yourselves be circumcised Christ will be of no advantage to y o u. 3 And I testify again to every man who lets himself be circumcised, that he is under obligation to keep the whole law. 4 Y o u are estranged from Christ, whoever (y o u are who) seek to be justified by way of law; y o u have fallen away from grace. 5 For, as to ourselves, it is through the Spirit, by faith, that we eagerly await the hoped-for righteousness. 6 For in Christ

Jesus neither circumcision nor uncircumcision is of any avail, but faith working through love.

7 Y o u were running well; who cut in on y o u that y o u did not continue to obey the truth? 8 This persuasion (is) not (derived) from him who is calling y o u. 9 A little leaven leavens the whole lump. 10 I on my part am persuaded in the Lord with respect to y o u, that y o u will not adopt a different view (than mine). And the one who is throwing y o u into confusion will have to pay the penalty, whoever he may be. 11 Now as for myself, brothers, if I am still preaching circumcision, why am I still being persecuted? In that case the stumbling-block of the cross has been removed. 12 Would that those who upset y o u might make eunuchs of themselves!

13 For y o u were called to freedom, brothers; only (do) not (turn) this freedom into an opportunity for the flesh, but through love be serving one another. 14 For the whole law is fulfilled in one word, namely, in this: "You must love your neighbor as yourself." 15 But if y o u bite and devour one another, watch out lest y o u be consumed by one another.

16 But I say, walk by the Spirit, and y o u will definitely not fulfil the desire of the flesh; 17 for the flesh sets its desire against the Spirit, and the Spirit against the flesh: for these are opposed to each other, so that these very things which y o u may wish to be doing, these y o u are not doing. 18 But if y o u are being led by the Spirit y o u are not under law. 19 Now obvious are the works of the flesh, which are: immorality, impurity, indecency, 20 idolatry, sorcery, quarrels, wranglings, jealousy, outbursts of anger, selfish ambitions, dissensions, party intrigues, 21 envyings, drinking bouts, revelries, and the like, of which I forewarn y o u, as I previously forewarned y o u, that those who indulge in such practices will not inherit the kingdom of God. 22 But the fruit of the Spirit is love, joy, peace, longsuffering, kindness, goodness, faithfulness, 23 meekness, self-control; against such there is no law. 24 And those who believe in Christ Jesus have crucified the flesh with its passions and desires.

25 If we live by the Spirit, by the Spirit let us also walk. 26 Let us not become boasters, challenging one another, envying one another.

Chapter 6

1 Brothers, even if a man be overtaken in any trespass, y o u who are spiritual should restore such a person in a spirit of gentleness; constantly looking to yourself, lest also you be tempted. 2 Bear one another's burdens, and so fulfil the law of Christ. 3 For if anyone imagines that he amounts to something, while he amounts to nothing, he is deluding himself. 4 But let each one test his own work; then his reason to boast will be in himself alone, and not in (comparing himself with) someone else; 5 for each person will have to bear his own load.

6 Let him who receives instruction in the Word share all good things with his instructor. 7 Do not be deceived; God is not mocked; for whatever a man sows, that also will he reap; 8 for he who sows to his own flesh will from the flesh reap corruption, and he who sows to the Spirit will from the Spirit reap life everlasting. 9 And let us not grow weary in well-doing, for in due season we shall reap if we do not give up. 10 So then, as we have opportunity, let us do good to everybody, and especially to those who are of the household of the faith.

11 Look with what huge letters I am writing to y o u with my own hand. 12 It is those who desire to make a fine outward impression that are trying to compel y o u to be circumcised, their sole purpose being that they may not be persecuted for the cross of Christ. 13 For even those who favor circumcision are

GALATIANS

not law-observers themselves, but want y o u to be circumcised that they may glory in y o u r flesh. 14 As for myself, however, far be it for me to glory except in the cross of our Lord Jesus Christ, by which the world has been crucified to me, and I to the world. 15 For neither is circumcision anything, nor uncircumcision, but a new creation. 16 And as many as shall walk by this rule, peace (be) upon them and mercy, even upon the Israel of God.

17 From now on let no one cause trouble for me, for I, on my part, bear on my body the marks of Jesus.

18 The grace of our Lord Jesus Christ (be) with y o u r spirit, brothers. Amen.

Bibliography

For other titles see List of Abbreviations at the beginning of this volume.

Aalders, G. Ch., *Het Boek Genesis* (*Korte Verklaring der Heilige Schrift met Nieuwe Vertaling*), 3 volumes, Kampen, 1949.

Ante-Nicene Fathers, ten volumes, reprint, Grand Rapids, Mich., 1950, for references to Clement of Alexandria, Irenaeus, Justin Martyr, Origen, Tertullian, etc.

Bacon, B. W., "The Reading οἷς οὐδέ in Gal. 2:5," *JBL*, 42 (1923), pp. 69–80.

Bandstra, Andrew J., *The Law and the Elements of the World, An Exegetical Study in Aspects of Paul's Teaching*, doctoral dissertation submitted to the Free University at Amsterdam, Kampen, 1964.

Barclay, W., *The Letters to the Galatians and Ephesians* (*The Daily Study Bible*), Philadelphia, 1958.

Barton, G. A., "The Exegesis of ἐνιαυτούς in Galatians 4:10 and Its Bearing on the Date of the Epistle," *JBL*, 33 (1914), pp. 118–126.

Bavinck, H., *Gereformeerde Dogmatiek*, Vol. 11, *Over God;* English translation by W. Hendriksen, *The Doctrine of God*, Grand Rapids, 1955.

Berkhof, L., *New Testament Introduction*, Grand Rapids, 1916.

Berkhof, L., *Brief aan de Galatiërs, Hoofdstuk 3.* Student notes on class-lectures on Gal. 3, given at Calvin Seminary, Grand Rapids, during the school year 1925-1926. Redactor: W. Hendriksen. Contents: a broad introduction to the epistle and detailed exegesis of the entire third chapter.

Berkhof, L., *Systematic Theology*, Grand Rapids, 1949.

Berkouwer, G. C., *Dogmatisch Studiën* (the series), Kampen, 1949, etc.

Berlage, H. P., "De juiste verklaring van Gal. 6:2," *TT*, 25 (1891), pp. 47–61.

Bible, Holy, In addition to references to Bible-versions other than English, there are references to the following English translations: A.V., A.R.V., R.S.V., N.E.B., N.A.S.B.(N.T.), Amplified New Testament, Beck, Berkeley, Goodspeed, Moffatt, Phillips, Weymouth, Williams. These are *references.* The *translation* which is found in N.T.C. and followed in the exegesis is the author's own.

Bruce, F. F., "The Date of the Epistle to the Galatians," *ET*, 51 (1939–1940), pp. 396–397.

Bruce, F. F., *Commentary on the Book of Acts* (*New International Commentary on the New Testament*), Grand Rapids, 1964.

Bruce, F. F., *The Letters of Paul, An Expanded Paraphrase*, Grand Rapids, 1965.

Bultmann, Rudolf, ΔΙΚΑΙΟΣΥΝΗ ΘΕΟΥ, *JBL* (March 1964), pp. 12–16.

Burton, Ernest DeWitt, "Those Trouble-Makers in Galatia," *BW*, 53 (1919), pp. 555–560.

Burton, Ernest DeWitt, *A Critical and Exegetical Commentary on the Epistle to the Galatians* (*The International Critical Commentary*), New York, 1920.

Calvin, John, *Commentarius in Epistolam Pauli Ad Galatas* (*Corpus Reformatorum*, Vol. LXXX), Brunsvigae, 1895; English Translation (*Calvin's Commentaries*), Grand Rapids, 1948.

Cole, A., *The Epistle of Paul to the Galatians* (*Tyndale Bible Commentaries*, edited by R. V. G. Taker), Grand Rapids, 1965.

GALATIANS

Conybeare, W. J. and Howson, J. S., *The Life and Epistles of St. Paul*, Grand Rapids, 1949.

Crownfield, F. R., "The Singular Problem of the Dual Galatians," *JBL*, 64 (1945), pp. 491–500.

De Boer, W. P., *The Imitation of Paul, An Exegetical Study*, doctoral dissertation, Kampen, 1962.

Deissmann, A., *Light from the Ancient East* (translated by L. R. M. Strachan), New York, 1927.

Duncan, George S., *The Epistle of Paul to the Galatians* (*Moffatt New Testament Commentary*).

Ellis, E. Earle, *Paul and his Recent Interpreters*, Grand Rapids, 1961.

Emmet, C. W., "Galatians, the Earliest of the Pauline Epistles," *Exp*, 7th series, 9 (1910), pp. 242–254.

Erdman, C. F., *The Epistle of Paul to the Galatians*, Philadelphia, 1930.

Findlay, G. G., *The Epistle to the Galatians* (*The Expositor's Bible*, Vol. V, pp. 811–925), Grand Rapids, 1943.

Goodspeed, E. J., *Paul*, Philadelphia and Toronto, 1947.

Greijdanus, S., *Is Hand. 9 (met 22 en 26) en 15 in tegenspraak met Gal. 1 en 2?*, Kampen, 1935.

Greijdanus, S., *Bizondere Canoniek*, two volumes, Kampen, 1949.

Greijdanus, S., *De Brief van den Apostel Paulus aan de Galaten* (*Korte Verklaring der Heilige Schrift met Nieuwe Vertaling*), Kampen, 1953.

Grosheide, F. W., *De Openbaring Gods in het Nieuwe Testament*, Kampen, 1953.

Grosheide, F. W., "De Synode der Apostelen," *GTT*, 11 (1910), pp. 1–16 [Gal. 2].

Hendriksen, W., *"And So All Israel Shall Be Saved," An Interpretation of Romans 11:26a*, Grand Rapids, 1945.

Hendriksen, W., *The Meaning of the Preposition ἀντί in the New Testament*, doctoral dissertation, Princeton, 1948.

Hendriksen, W., *Bible Survey*, Grand Rapids, 1961.

Hendriksen, W., *More Than Conquerors, An Interpretation of the Book of Revelation*, fifteenth printing, Grand Rapids, 1966.

Jackson, F. J. Foakes, and Lake, Kirsopp, eds., *The Beginnings of Christianity*, five volumes, especially Vol. IV and V, London, 1920–1933.

Johnson, Sherman E., "Early Christianity in Asia Minor," *JBL*, 77 (March 1958), pp. 1–17.

Johnson, Sherman E., "Laodicea and its Neighbors," *BA*, Vol. XIII (Feb. 1950), pp. 1–18.

Jones, Maurice, "The Date of the Epistle to the Galatians," *Exp*, 8th series, 6 (1913), pp. 193–208.

Kerr, John H., *An Introduction to the Study of the Books of the New Testament*, Chicago, New York, Toronto, 1892.

Knox, D. B., "The Date of the Epistle to the Galatians," *EQ*, 13 (1941), pp. 262–268.

Kouwenhoven, H. J., "Paulus' beroep op de litteekenen van den Heere Jezus in zijn lichaam," *GTT*, 13 (1912), pp. 105–115 [Gal. 6:17].

Lambert, J. C., "'Another Gospel that is not another'—Galatians 1:6, 7," *ET*, 12 (1900–1901), pp. 90–93.

Lenski, R. C. H., *Interpretation of St. Paul's Epistles to the Galatians, to the Ephesians, and to the Philippians*, Columbus, Ohio, 1937.

Lietzmann, Hans, *An die Galater* (*Handbuch zum Neuen Testament*), 2nd ed., Tübingen, 1923.

GALATIANS

Lightfoot, J. B., *The Epistle of St. Paul to the Galatians,* reprint, Grand Rapids, no date.

Loeb Classical Library, New York (various dates), for The Apostolic Fathers, Eusebius, Josephus, Philco, Pliny, Plutarch, Strabo, etc.

Luther, Martin, *In Epistolam S.Pauli ad Galatas commentarius.* The edition that was used by the author of N.T.C. contains the lectures that were *delivered* in 1531. They are found in *D. Martin Luthers Werke,* kritische gesamtausgabe, 40.Band, two volumes, Weimar, 1911–1914. Among the translations there is also Th. Graebner's *New Abridged* [English] *Translation,* Grand Rapids, no date.

Machen, J. G., *The Origin of Paul's Religion,* Grand Rapids, 1947.

Mackintosh, Robert, "The Tone of Galatians 2:1-10," *ET,* 21 (1909–1910), pp. 327–328.

Menzies, Allan, "The Epistle to the Galatians," *Exp,* 8th series, 7 (1914), pp. 137–147.

Moffatt, J., *An Introduction to the Literature of the New Testament (The International Theological Library),* 3rd ed., New York, 1918.

Moulton, J. H., "The Marks of Jesus," *ET,* 21 (1909–1910), pp. 283–284 [Gal. 6:17].

Mulder, H., "De Eerste Lezers van de Brief aan de Hebreeën," *homiletica & biblica* (May, 1965), pp. 95–99.

Mulder, H., "Barnabas en de Gemeente te Jeruzalem," *homiletica & biblica* (September, 1965), pp. 198–200.

Murray, J., *Christian Baptism,* Philadelphia, 1952.

Murray, J., *The Epistle to the Romans,* two volumes, Grand Rapids, respectively 1959 and 1965.

Parker, P., "Once More, Acts and Galatians," *JBL,* 86 (June 1967), pp. 175–182.

Parker, Thomas D., "A Comparison of Calvin and Luther on Galatians," *Int,* 17 (Jan. 1963), pp. 71–75.

Prins, J. J., "Nog iets over Gal. III:20 en, in verband daarmede, over vs. 13 en 16. Open brief aan Dr. A. H. Blom," *TT,* 12 (1878), pp. 410–420.

Ramsay, W. M., *Historical Geography of Asia Minor,* London, 1890.

Ramsay, W. M., *The Church in the Roman Empire,* London, 1893.

Ramsay, W. M., *Cities and Bishoprics of Phrygia,* two volumes, London, 1895–1897.

Ramsay, W. M., "A New Theory as to the Date of the Epistle to the Galatians," *ET,* 12 (1900–1901), pp. 157–160.

Ramsay, W. M., *The Letters to the Seven Churches of Asia,* London, 1904.

Ramsay, W. M., *The Cities of St. Paul,* reprint, Grand Rapids, 1949.

Ramsay, W. M., *The Bearing of Recent Discovery on the Trustworthiness of the New Testament,* reprint, Grand Rapids, 1953.

Ramsay, W. M., *St. Paul the Traveler and the Roman Citizen,* reprint, Grand Rapids, 1949.

Ramsay, W. M., *A Historical Commentary on St. Paul's Epistle to the Galatians,* reprint, Grand Rapids, 1965.

Rendall, F., *The Epistle to the Galatians (The Expositor's Greek Testament,* Vol. III, pp. 123–200), Grand Rapids, no date.

Ridderbos, H. N., *The Epistle of Paul to the Churches of Galatia (New International Commentary on the New Testament),* Grand Rapids, 1953.

Robertson, A. T., *Word Pictures in the New Testament,* New York and London, 1931, Vol. IV, on Galatians, pp. 272–319.

Robinson, D. W. B., "The Circumcision of Titus and Paul's 'Liberty,'" *AusBibRev,* 12 (1-4, '64), pp. 24–42.

GALATIANS

Ropes, J. H., *The Singular Problem of the Epistle to the Galatians,* Cambridge, 1929.

Schaff, P., *History of the Christian Church,* Vol. 1, New York, 1920.

Schlier, Heinrich, *Der Brief an die Galater (Meyer's Kommentar),* 10th ed., Göttingen, 1949.

Schmoller, Otto, *The Epistle of Paul to the Galatians (Lange's Commentary on the Holy Scriptures),* reprint, Grand Rapids, no date.

Scott, E. F., *The Literature of the New Testament,* New York, 1940.

Shedd, W. A., "The Date of the Epistle to the Galatians upon the South Galatian Theory," *ET,* 12 (1900–1901), p. 568.

Stamm, R. T., *The Epistle to the Galatians (Interpreter's Bible,* Vol. X), New York and Nashville, 1953.

Stewart, J. S., *A Man in Christ, the Vital Elements of St. Paul's Religion,* New York and London, no date.

Strack, H. L. and Billerbeck, P., *Kommentar zum Neuen Testament aus Talmud und Midrasch,* München, 1922–1928; especially volume III.

Tenney, M. C., *The New Testament, an Historical and Analytic Survey,* Grand Rapids, 1953.

Thiessen, H. C., *Introduction to the New Testament,* Grand Rapids, 1943.

Van Leeuwen, J. A. C., "Galaten (Brief aan de)," article in *Christelijke Encyclopaedie,* Kampen, 1925, Vol. II, pp. 218, 219.

Warfield, B. B., "The Date of the Epistle to the Galatians," *JBL* (June and December, 1884), pp. 50–64.

Warfield, B. B., *The Power of God Unto Salvation,* Grand Rapids, 1930.

Wood, H. G., "The Message of the Epistles; the Letter to the Galatians," *ET,* 44 (1932–1933), pp. 453–457.

Zahn, Th., *Einleitung in das neue Testament,* 1897–1900.

NEW TESTAMENT COMMENTARY

NEW TESTAMENT COMMENTARY

By

WILLIAM HENDRIKSEN

Exposition

of

Ephesians

TABLE OF CONTENTS

LIST OF ABBREVIATIONS

The letters in book-abbreviations are followed by periods. Those in periodical-abbreviations omit the periods and are in italics. Thus one can see at a glance whether the abbreviation refers to a book or to a periodical.

A. *Book Abbreviations*

A.R.V.	American Standard Revised Version
A.V.	Authorized Version (King James)
Gram.N.T.	A. T. Robertson, *Grammar of the Greek New Testament in the Light of Historical Research*
Gram.N.T. (Bl.-Debr.)	F. Blass and A. Debrunner, *A Greek Grammar of the New Testament and Other Early Christian Literature*
Grk.N.T. (A–B–M–W)	*The Greek New Testament,* edited by Kurt Aland, Matthew Black, Bruce M. Metzger, and Allen Wikgren, 1966 Edition
I.S.B.E.	*International Standard Bible Encyclopedia*
L.N.T. (Th.)	Thayer's *Greek-English Lexicon of the New Testament*
L.N.T. (A. and G.)	W. F. Arndt and F. W. Gingrich, *A Greek-English Lexicon of the New Testament and Other Early Christian Literature*
M.M.	*The Vocabulary of the Greek New Testament Illustrated from the Papyri and Other Non-Literary Sources,* by James Hope Moulton and George Milligan (edition Grand Rapids, 1952)
N.A.S.B. (N.T.)	New American Standard Bible (New Testament)
N.N.	*Novum Testamentum Graece,* edited by D. Eberhard Nestle, revised by Erwin Nestle and Kurt Aland, 25th edition, 1963
N.E.B.	New English Bible
N.T.C.	W. Hendriksen, *New Testament Commentary*
R.S.V.	Revised Standard Version
S.H.E.R.K.	*The New Schaff-Herzog Encyclopedia of Religious Knowledge*
Th.W.N.T.	*Theologisches Wörterbuch zum Neuen Testament* (edited by G. Kittel)
W.D.B.	*Westminster Dictionary of the Bible*
W.H.A.B.	*Westminster Historical Atlas to the Bible*

B. *Periodical Abbreviations*

EQ	*Evangelical Quarterly*
ET	*Expository Times*
Exp	*The Expositor*
Int	*Interpretation*
JBL	*Journal of Biblical Literature*
NTSt	*New Testament Studies*
RE	*Review and Expositor*
TSK	*Theologische Studien und Kritiken*
TT	*Theologisch Tijdschrift*
TTod	*Theology Today*

Please Note

In order to differentiate between the second person singular (see Eph. 6:2, 3) and the second person plural (see Eph. 2:1; 6:1), we have indicated the former as follows: "you," "your"; and the latter as follows: "y o u," "y o u r."

Introduction

to

The Epistle to the Ephesians

I. Timeliness

Loathsome wickedness marked the world of Paul's day (Eph. 2:2; cf. Rom. 1:18-32). Efforts to improve this condition were largely unsuccessful. Mankind was "without hope" (2:12). The same perversity coupled with pessimism obtains today. At the present time, too, efforts are being put forth to banish crime and to improve man's environment. Among the means to this end are the following: slum clearance, better housing, development of parks and playgrounds, a higher minimum wage scale, job retraining, rehabilitation of educational drop-outs, and psychiatric aid for those who find it hard "to adjust themselves." Some call for better laws. Others emphasize the need of more rigid law-enforcement or the establishment of rules that will no longer favor the criminal at the expense of society. The merit in all this must not be *under*-estimated. But neither should it be *over*-estimated. Government totalitarianism, the tendency to look upon the state to provide for every need "from the cradle to the grave," with consequent loss of the sense of individual responsibility and initiative, is one danger. Another is the misapprehension of man's *basic* need. That need is nothing less than the removal of the load of guilt by which he, being by nature a child of wrath (2:3), is oppressed. What he needs is something more than *job rehabilitation*. He needs *reconciliation to God*. Ephesians proclaims that for all true believers this great blessing has been provided by means of the vicarious, atoning death of God's own Son (2:13). The motivation for this supreme sacrifice was "his great love" (2:4).

Another fallacy that is implied in today's approach to the problem of relieving man's misery is the notion that human happiness can be brought about by means that operate *from without inward*. "Improve the environment and man's inner condition will be improved" seems to be the slogan. But man's inner condition is one that does not offer much hope for the success of this method. He is "dead through trespasses and sins." Apart from Christ he is living "in the lusts of his flesh and its reasonings" (2:1, 3). An act of God is necessary to save him. The removal of the *guilt* of his sin is not sufficient. *Sin itself*, the urge to do that which is contrary to God's holy law, must be removed. A mighty work must be accomplished within man's heart, so that as a result, man, having been basically renewed and being gradually transformed by the Holy Spirit, can now, in consequence, begin to react *from within outward* upon his environment, calling upon all of it to function *Pro Rege* ("for the King"). This regenerating and transforming work of the Holy Spirit, procured by the death of Christ (John 16:7), is beautifully de-

3

scribed in Eph. 3:14-19. Those who by nature are dead must be made alive (2:1).

Now all this does not in any way cancel human responsibility. On the contrary, it rather increases the sense of man's obligation to dedicate his life to his Benefactor. The believer, object of God's sovereign love, feels indebted to his Savior and Lord. He loves in return for love received (5:1, 2; cf. I John 4:19). Moreover, it stands to reason that, being drawn to God, the recipient of divine grace is in this very process also attracted to his brothers and sisters in the Lord. Thus Jew and Gentile, reconciled to God, are also reconciled to each other. The barrier between the two ethnic groups is removed by the same cross that made peace between the offended God and the offending sinner (2:11-22; cf. John 12:32; 15:12; I John 4:21); yes, by that very cross which to unconverted Jews was a stumblingblock and to unconverted Gentiles foolishness (I Cor. 1:23). Thus the divine mystery becomes disclosed to human view, and the church universal is born.

Since a new day has now dawned upon those who had surrendered themselves to Christ and to the influences of his Spirit, it follows that these children of light show in their new life the fruits of light: goodness and righteousness and truth (5:9). Spirit-born virtue drives out vice of every description, as is clearly indicated in the lengthy section, Eph. 4:17–5:21. Here then is the true solution to the "loathsome wickedness" which marked Paul's day as it does ours. It is God himself who "in Christ" has provided this way out of darkness and pessimism. It is the business of the church "to make all men see" that this is *the only solution*. The church must sing its mighty chorus of salvation by faith in Jesus Christ, in order thereby to drown out the thoroughly unrealistic paean of atheism. The latter also sings, to be sure, but its song has a hollow sound. It sings *the lie* in (the spirit of) *hatred*. The church sings "the truth in love" (4:15). Its daily life is, in fact, a walking in love, for it imitates the God of love (5:1). Thus, firmly united, it bids defiance to Satan and all his hosts, and for this purpose makes use of the weapons provided by God himself (6:10-20).

Never futile is the work of the church, for it is a product not of the mind of man but of the sovereign grace of God. The apostle, in exuberance of spirit, describes this church, dwelling in some detail on its eternal foundation, universal scope, lofty ideal, organic unity (amid diversity) and growth, glorious renewal, and effective armor. It is a church that exists for the purpose of serving as an agent for the salvation of men to the glory of God Triune, "principalities and authorities in the heavenly places" joining in the praise as they behold, in a kaleidoscope of changing colors, the wisdom of God reflected in his masterpiece, the church (3:10).

4

II. Comparison with Colossians

A. *Introduction*

With a view to answering those that deny the Pauline authorship of Ephesians and affirm that this epistle "is nothing but a verbose amplification of Colossians" it is necessary to compare the two. This comparison will also serve another purpose, for, once having established that Paul was indeed the author of both letters, we will have the right, in exegeting Ephesians, to allow parallel passages in Colossians to illumine the interpretation. By way of anticipation let it be affirmed even now that, as I see it, the traditional view which ascribes both epistles to the great apostle to the Gentiles is correct. Hence, the present chapter will become a handy tool for exegesis.

Observe, however, the following:

(1) Not all the parallels are equally striking, nor are they all of the same character. Though there are a goodly number of verbal resemblances, there are also many similarities in thought rather than in the actual words that are used.

(2) In a few instances the actual *word* resemblances are even closer in the original than in the translation. However, translations that have tried to eliminate this discrepancy (between Greek and English) in every instance by supplying a so-called "standard" (or "identical") English equivalent for each Greek word in whatever context the latter occurs, have not proved to be very satisfactory. Reasons: *a.* the same Greek word does not always have the same meaning, hence cannot always be faithfully rendered by the same English equivalent; *b.* idiomatic use in Greek does not always parallel idiomatic use in English.[1]

(3) As this is a Commentary on Ephesians — not on Colossians — it is proper that the basis for comparison be first of all the text of Ephesians, newly translated from the original. That text is accordingly to be found in the left main column, with comparable Colossian passages printed in the right column. It has not always been possible to place all the parallel passages *exactly* opposite each other. However, let the reader look not only directly opposite the Ephesian passage but also a little higher or lower in the column.

(4) It is impossible to present a list of parallels that will satisfy everyone. The question: "Is the resemblance in this or that passage in Colossians close enough to consider it a parallel to an Ephesian passage?" will not receive a unanimous answer. Some, for example, might wish to add, to the ones given below, such a "parallel" (?) as Eph. 4:10 = Col. 1:19; and even more remote parallels. I have chosen not to do so. But there is room here for difference of opinion.

---

[1] Moreover, for the Greek parallels one can use two Greek New Testaments, one for Ephesians, one for Colossians.

B. Comparison

In Ephesians Compare	Ephesians	Colossians
	Chapter 1	
	1 Paul, an apostle of Christ Jesus through the will of God, to the saints and believers who are in Ephesus in Christ Jesus; 2 grace to y o u and peace from God our Father and the Lord Jesus Christ.	1:1 Paul, an apostle of Christ Jesus through the will of God, and Timothy our brother, 2 to the saints and believing brothers in Christ at Colosse; grace to y o u and peace from God our Father.
2:6	3 Blessed (be) the God and Father of our Lord Jesus Christ, who has blessed us with every spiritual blessing in the heavenly places in Christ, 4 just as he	
5:27	elected us in him before the foundation of the world, that we should be holy and faultless before him, 5 having in love foreordained us to adoption as sons through Jesus Christ for himself, according to the good pleasure of his will, 6 to the praise of the glory of his grace, which he graciously bestowed on us in the	3:12 Put on, therefore, as God's elect, holy and beloved. . . . 1:22 . . . in order to present y o u holy, fault-less, and blameless before himself. . . . 1:13 the kingdom of the Son of his love.
1:18; 2:7; 3:8, 16	Beloved, 7 in whom we have our redemption through his blood, the forgiveness of our trespasses, according to the riches of his grace, 8 which he caused to over-	1:14 in whom we have our redemption, the forgiveness of our sins. 1:20 . . . having made peace through the blood of his cross. . . .

3:9 flow toward us in the form of all wisdom and insight, 9 in that he made known to us the mystery of his will, according to his good pleasure, the purpose which he cherished for himself in him,

10 to be put into effect in the fulness of the times, to bring all things together under one head in Christ, the things in the heavens and the things on the earth; in him

3:11 11 in whom we also have been made heirs, having been foreordained according to the purpose of him who accomplishes all things according to the counsel of his will, 12 to the end that we should be to the praise of his glory, we who beforehand had centered our hope in Christ;

1:9 . . . in all spiritual wisdom and understanding. . . .

1:26 the mystery hidden for ages and generations but now made manifest to his saints . . . .

2:2 . . . with a view to the clear knowledge of the mystery of God, namely Christ. . . .

4:3 . . . to speak forth the mystery concerning Christ. . . .

1:16 for in him were created all things in the heavens and on the earth, the visible and the invisible, whether thrones or dominions or principalities or authorities, all things through him and with a view to him have been created. . . .

1:19 For in him he [God] was pleased to have all the fulness dwell, 20 and through him to reconcile all things to himself, . . . through him, whether the things on the earth or the things in the heavens.

1:12 with joy giving thanks to the Father who qualified you for a share in the inheritance of the saints in the light. . . .

1:23 . . . and are not moved away from the hope that is derived from the gospel which you have heard. . . .

1:27 to whom God was pleased to make known what (is) the riches of the glory of this mystery among the Gentiles, which is Christ

In Ephesians Compare	Ephesians	Colossians
		in y o u, the hope of glory. . . . 1:5 . . . of which y o u have previously heard in the message of the truth, the gospel.
4:30	13 in whom y o u also (are included, having listened to the message of the truth, the gospel of y o u r salvation; and having also believed in him, y o u were sealed with the promised Holy Spirit, 14 who is the first instalment of our inheritance, for the redemption of (God's) own possession, to the praise of his glory.	
4:4	15 For this reason, because I have heard of the faith in the Lord Jesus that (exists) among y o u and of y o u r love for all the saints, 16 I do not cease to give thanks for y o u, while making mention of y o u in my prayers, 17 (asking) that the God of our Lord Jesus Christ, the Father of glory, may give y o u the Spirit of wisdom and revelation in the clear knowledge of him, 18 (having) the eyes of y o u r hearts illumined, so that y o u may know what is the hope for which he called	1:3 While praying for y o u we are always thanking God, the Father of our Lord Jesus Christ, 4 because we have heard of y o u r faith in Christ Jesus and of the love which y o u cherish for all the saints, 5 by reason of the hope laid up for y o u in the heavens, of which y o u have previously heard in the message of the truth, namely, the gospel. . . . 9 And for this reason, from the day we heard it we never stopped praying for y o u, asking that y o u may be filled with clear knowledge of his will (such clear knowl-

edge consisting) in all spiritual wisdom and understanding, 10 so as to live lives worthy of the Lord, to (his) complete delight, in every good work bearing fruit, and growing in the clear-knowledge of God. . . .

1:11 being invigorated with all vigor, in accordance with his glorious might, so as to exercise every kind of endurance and long-suffering; 12 with joy giving thanks to the Father who qualified y o u for a share in the inheritance of the saints in the light. . . .

1:29 for which I am laboring, striving by his energy working powerfully within me.

2:12 having been buried with him in y o u r baptism in which y o u were also raised with him through faith in the operative power of God who raised him from the dead.

3:1 If then y o u were raised with Christ, seek the things that are above, where Christ is seated at the right hand of God. . . .

1:16 for in him were created all things . . . whether thrones or dominions or principalities or authorities. . . .

3:15 . . . for which y o u were called in one body.

1:18 And he is the head of the body, the church; who is the beginning, the firstborn from the dead, that in all things he might

y o u, what the riches of the glory of his inheritance among the saints,

3:20

19 and what the surpassing greatness of his power (displayed) with respect to us who believe, as seen in that manifestation of his infinite might 20 which he exerted in Christ when he raised him from the dead and made him to sit at his right hand in the heavenly places,

3:10
6:12

21 far above every principality and authority and power and dominion and every name that is named, not only in this age but also in the coming one; 22 and he ranged everything in subjection under his feet, and him he gave as head over everything to the church,

In Ephesians Compare	Ephesians	Colossians
		have the pre-eminence, 19 for in him he [God] was pleased to have all the fulness dwell. . . .
		1:24 I am now rejoicing amid my sufferings for you and what is lacking in the afflictions of Christ I in his stead am supplying in my flesh, for his body, which is the church. . . .
		2:9 for in him all the fulness of the godhead dwells bodily, 10 and in him you have attained to fulness, namely, in him who is the head of every principality and authority. . . .
4:12; 5:30	23 since it is his body, the fulness of him who fills all in all.	2:13 And you, who were dead through your trespasses and the uncircumcision of your flesh, you he made alive together with him, having forgiven us all our trespasses. . . .
	Chapter 2	
1:21	1 And you, even though you were dead through your trespasses and sins, 2 in which you formerly walked in line with the course of this world, in line with the prince of the domain of the air, (the domain) of the spirit now at work in the sons of disobedience, 3 among whom we also once lived in the lusts of our flesh, fulfilling the desires of the flesh and its reasonings, and were by nature chil-	3:6 on account of which things the wrath

1:3

of God is coming; 7 in which things y o u also walked at one time, when y o u were living in them.

1:7

3:1 If then y o u were raised with Christ, seek the things that are above, where Christ is, seated at the right hand of God. . . .

1:10 . . . in every good work bearing fruit. . . .

2:11 . . . in whom also y o u were circumcised with a circumcision made without hands. 1:20 and through him to reconcile all things to himself, having made peace through the blood of his cross, through him, whether the things on the earth or the things in the heavens. 21 And y o u, who once were estranged and hostile in disposition, as shown by y o u r wicked works, 22 he in his body

---

dren of wrath even as the rest, 4 God, being rich in mercy, because of his great love with which he loved us, 5 even though we were dead through our trespasses made us alive together with Christ — by grace y o u have been saved — 6 and raised us up with him and made us sit with him in the heavenly places in Christ Jesus, 7 in order that in the ages to come he might show the surpassing riches of his grace (expressed) in kindness toward us in Christ Jesus. 8 For by grace y o u have been saved through faith; and this not of yourselves, (it is) the gift of God; 9 not of works, lest anyone should boast, 10 for his handiwork are we, created in Christ Jesus for good works, which God prepared beforehand that we should walk in them.

11 Therefore remember that formerly y o u, the Gentiles in flesh, who are called "uncircumcision" by that which is called "circumcision" — in flesh, handmade! — 12 that y o u were at that time separate from Christ, alienated from the commonwealth of Israel, and strangers to the covenants of the promise, having no hope and without God in the world. 13

2:19
4:17, 18
5:8

Colossians

of flesh through his death has now reconciled, in order to present y o u holy, faultless, and blameless before himself. . . .

3:15 And let the peace of Christ . . . rule in y o u r hearts.

2:14 having blotted out the handwritten document that was against us, which by means of its requirements testified against us, and he took it out of the way by nailing it to the cross. . . .

3:10 and have put on the new man, who is being renewed for full knowledge according to the image of him who created him. . . .

Ephesians

But now in Christ Jesus y o u who formerly were far away have been brought nearby through the blood of Christ. 14 For he himself is our peace, who made both one and has broken down the barrier formed by the dividing wall, the hostility, 15 by abolishing in his flesh the law of commandments with its requirements, in order that in himself he might create of the two one new man, (so) making peace,

16 and might reconcile both of them in one body to God through the cross, having slain the hostility by means of it; 17 and he came and proclaimed the good news: "Peace to y o u, those far away, and peace to those nearby"; 18 for through him we both have our access in one Spirit to the Father.

19 So then y o u are no longer strangers and aliens, but y o u are fellow-citizens with the saints and mem-

In Ephesians Compare

6:15
3:12

3:6

12

2:7 rooted and being built up in him and being established in the faith, just as you were taught, overflowing with thanksgiving.

2:19 and not keeping firm hold on the Head, from whom the entire body, supported and held together by joints and ligaments, grows with a growth (that is) from God.

1:23 . . . the gospel . . . of which I, Paul, became a minister.

1:24 I am now rejoicing amid my sufferings for you, and what is lacking in the afflictions of Christ I in his stead am supplying in my flesh, for his body, which is the church, 25 of which I became a minister, according to the stewardship of God given to me for your benefit, to give full scope to the word of God, 26 the mystery hidden for ages and generations but now made manifest to his saints; 27 to whom God was pleased to make known what (is) the riches of the glory of this mystery among the Gentiles, which is Christ in you, the hope of glory; 28 whom we proclaim, admonishing

bers of the household of God, 20 built upon the foundation of the apostles and prophets, Christ Jesus himself being the chief cornerstone, 21 in whom the entire building, harmoniously fitted together, is growing into a holy sanctuary in the Lord, 22 in which you also together with (all the others) are being built up for a dwelling-place of God in the Spirit.

Chapter 3

1 For this reason I, Paul, the prisoner of Christ Jesus for the sake of you Gentiles – 2 for surely you have heard of the stewardship of God's grace that was given to me for your benefit, 3 how that by revelation there was made known to me the mystery, as I wrote before in few words, 4 whereby, as you can read it you can perceive my insight into the mystery of Christ, 5 which in other generations was not made known to the sons of men as it has now been revealed by the Spirit to his holy apostles and prophets, 6 namely, that the Gentiles are fellow-sharers in the inheritance and fellow-members of the body and fellow-partakers

6:19-20

1:7-11
2:13, 18,
19

13

In
Ephesians
Compare

Ephesians

of the promise (realized) in Christ Jesus (as conveyed) through the gospel, 7 of which I was made a minister according to the gift of God's grace that was given to me according to the working of his power. 8 To me, the very least of all saints, was this grace given: to proclaim to the Gentiles the good tidings of the unfathomable riches of Christ, 9 and to enlighten all on what is the administration of the mystery which for ages has been hidden in God who created all things; 10 in order that now to the principalities and the authorities in the heavenly places might be made known through the church the iridescent wisdom of God, 11 according to the eternal purpose which he formed in Christ Jesus our Lord, 12 in whom we have the courage of confident access through faith in him. 13 Therefore I ask (y o u) not to lose heart over what I am suffering for y o u, which is y o u r glory —
14 For this reason I bend my knees to the Father, 15 from whom the whole

Colossians

every man and teaching every man in all wisdom in order that we may present every man perfect in Christ; 29 for which I am laboring, striving by his energy working powerfully within me.

2:2 . . . in order that their hearts may be strengthened, they themselves being welded together in love, and this with a view to all the riches of assured understanding, with a view to the clear knowledge of the mystery of God, namely, Christ. . . .

4:3 . . . to speak forth the mystery concerning Christ, on account of which I am in prison. . . .

1:24 I am now rejoicing amid my sufferings for y o u. . . .

1:16 for in him were created all things in the heavens and on the earth, the visible and the invisible, whether thrones or dominions or principalities or authorities, all things through him and with a view to him have been created.

1:27 the riches of the glory of this mystery
1:11 being invigorated with all vigor, in accordance with his glorious might. . . .

1:23 if, indeed, you continue in the faith, founded and firm. . . .
2:7 rooted and being built up in him and being established in the faith.

1:29 . . . striving by his energy working powerfully within me.
1:26 the mystery hidden for ages and generations.

1:10 so as to live lives worthy of the Lord. . . .
3:12 Put on, therefore, as God's elect, holy and beloved, a heart of compassion, kindness, lowliness, meekness, longsuffering, 13

family in heaven and on earth derives its name: the Father's Family, 16 (praying) that according to the riches of his glory he may grant you to be strengthened with power through his Spirit in the inner man, 17 that Christ may dwell in your hearts through faith; in order that you, being rooted and founded in love, 18 may be strong, together with all the saints, to grasp what is the breadth and length and height and depth, 19 and to know the love of Christ that surpasses knowledge; in order that you may be filled to all the fullness of God.

22 Now to him who is able to do infinitely more than all we ask or imagine, according to the power that is at work within us, 21 to him be the glory in the church and in Christ Jesus to all generations forever and ever; Amen.

Chapter 4

1 I, therefore, the prisoner in the Lord, entreat you to live lives worthy of the calling with which you were called, 2 with all lowliness and meekness, with longsuffering, enduring one another

4:32
5:1

15

Colossians

enduring one another and forgiving each other if anyone have a complaint against anyone. Just as the Lord has forgiven y o u, so do y o u also. 14 And above all these things (put on) love, which is the bond of perfection. 15 And let the peace of Christ, for which y o u were called in one body, rule in y o u r hearts, and be thankful.

In Ephesians Compare

Ephesians

in love, 3 making every effort to preserve the unity imparted by the Spirit by means of the bond (consisting in) peace. 4 (There is) one body and one Spirit, just as also y o u were called in one hope which y o u r calling brought y o u;

5 one Lord, one faith, one baptism; 6 one God and Father of all, who (is) over all and through all and in all. 7 But to each one of us this grace was given within the limits which Christ apportioned. 8 Therefore he says: When he ascended on high he led captive a host of captives, and he gave gifts to men. 9 – Now this expression, *he ascended*, what can it mean but that he had (previously) descended into the regions lower than the earth? 10 The one who descended is himself also the one who ascended higher than all the heavens in order that he might fill all things – 11 And it was he who gave some

1:24 . . . for his body, which is the church.
2:2 . . . with the view to the clear knowledge of the mystery of God.
2:9 for in him all the fulness of the godhead dwells bodily.

2:22 . . . according to the precepts and doctrines of men.

1:18 And he is the head of the body, the church. . . .
2:19 and not keeping firm hold on the head, from whom the entire body, supported and held together by joints and ligaments, grows with a growth (that is) from God.

1:21 And y o u, who once were estranged

1:23 (to be) apostles; and some, prophets; and some, evangelists; and some, pastors and teachers; 12 in order fully to equip the saints for the work of ministry, with a view to the building up of the body of Christ, 13 until we all attain to the unity of the faith and of the clear knowledge of the Son of God, to a full-grown man, to the measure of the stature of the fulness of Christ, 14 so that we may

6:11 no longer be children tossed to and fro by the waves and whirled around by every gust of doctrine, by the trickery of men, by (their) talent for deceitful scheming; 15 but adhering to the truth in love, may grow up in all things into him who is the head, even Christ, 16 from whom the entire body, harmoniously fitted together and held together by every supporting joint, according to the energy that corresponds to the capacity of each individual part, brings about bodily growth with a view to its own upbuilding in love.

17 This I say, therefore, and testify in the Lord, that y o u should no longer walk as the Gentiles also walk, in the futility of their mind, 18 being darkened

2:12 in their understanding, alienated from

In Ephesians Compare

Ephesians

the life of God because of the ignorance that is in them due to the hardness of their hearts, 19 because they have become callous and have abandoned themselves to licentiousness for the greedy practice of every type of impurity. 20 Y o u, however, did not so learn Christ, 21 for surely y o u heard of him and were taught in him, just as it is in Jesus that truth resides, 22 (having been taught) that with respect to y o u r former manner of life y o u must put off the old man, which is being corrupted through deceitful lusts, 23 and must be renewed in the spirit of y o u r minds, 24 and put on the new man, created after (the likeness of) God in true righteousness and holiness.

25 Therefore, laying aside falsehood, speak truth each (of y o u) with his neighbor, for we are members of one another. 26 Be angry but do not sin; let not the sun go down on that angry mood of y o u r s, 27 and do not give the devil a

Colossians

and hostile in disposition, as shown by y o u r wicked works. . . .

3:5 Put to death therefore y o u r members that (are upon the earth): immorality, impurity, passion, evil desire, and greed, which is idolatry.

3:8 But now y o u, too, lay them all aside: wrath, anger, malice, slander, shameful language from y o u r mouth. 9 No longer lie to one another, seeing that y o u have put off the old man with his practices, 10 and have put on the new man, who is being renewed for full knowledge according to the image of him who created him. . . .

18

4:6 Let y o u r speech always be gracious, seasoned with salt, so that y o u may know how to answer each individual.

3:12 Put on, therefore, as God's elect, holy and beloved, a heart of compassion, kindness, lowliness, meekness, longsuffering, 13 enduring one another, and forgiving each other if anyone have a complaint against anyone. Just as the Lord has forgiven y o u, so do y o u also.

3:14 And above all these things (put on) love which is the bond of perfection.

5:4

foothold. 28 Let him who steals steal no longer but rather let him labor, with his own hands accomplishing what is good, so that he may have something to share with the needy one. 29 Let no corrupt speech proceed from y o u r mouth, but (only) such (speech) as is good for edification, as fits the need, that it may impart grace to the listeners. 30 And do not grieve the Holy Spirit of God in whom y o u were sealed for the day of redemption. 31 Let all bitterness and anger and wrath and brawling and slander be put away from y o u, along with all malice. 32 And be kind to each other, tenderhearted, forgiving one another, just as God in Christ forgave y o u.

1:13

Chapter 5

1 Be therefore imitators of God, as beloved children, 2 and walk in love, just as Christ loved y o u and gave himself up for us, an offering and a sacrifice to God, for a fragrant odor.

4:2, 3

19

In Ephesians Compare	Ephesians	Colossians
	3 But immorality and impurity of any kind, or greed, let it not even be mentioned among you, as is fitting among saints, 4 also filthiness and silly talk or wittiness in telling coarse jokes, which things are improper, but rather the expression of thankfulness. 5 For of this you can be very sure, that no immoral or impure person or greedy individual — which is the same as an idolater — has any inheritance in the kingdom of	3:5 Put to death therefore your members that (are) upon the earth: immorality, impurity, passion, evil desire, and greed, which is idolatry. . . . 3:8 But now you, too, lay them all aside: wrath, anger, malice, slander, shameful language from your mouth.
2:2	Christ and of God. 6 Let no one deceive you with empty words; for it is because of these things that the wrath of God comes upon the sons of disobedience.	2:4 I say this in order that no one may mislead you by persuasive argument. 3:6 on account of which things the wrath of God is coming. . . .
2:11, 13	7 Therefore do not be their partners, 8 for you were formerly darkness, but now (you are) light in the Lord; as children of light ever walk 9 — for the fruit of light (consists) in all goodness and righteousness and truth — 10 verifying what is pleasing to the Lord. 11 And do not take any part in the unfruitful works of darkness but instead even expose them, 12	3:20 . . . for this is well-pleasing in the Lord.

20

4:5 Conduct yourselves wisely toward outsiders, making the most of the opportunity.

3:16 Let the word of Christ dwell among you richly; in all wisdom teaching and admonishing one another (and) by means of psalms, hymns, and spiritual songs singing to God in a thankful spirit, with all your heart. 17 And whatever you do in word or in deed (do) all in the name of the Lord Jesus, giving thanks to God the Father through him.

for the things done by them in secret it is a shame even to mention. 13 But when all these (wicked practices) are exposed by the light they are made visible; for everything that is made visible is light. 14 Therefore he says,

"Awake, sleeper,
And arise from the dead,
And Christ will shine on you."

15 Be most careful therefore how you walk, not as unwise but as wise, 16 making the most of the opportunity, because the days are evil. 17 Therefore do not be foolish but understand what (is) the will of the Lord. 18 And do not get drunk on wine, which is associated with unrestrained living, but be filled with the Spirit, 19 speaking to one another in psalms and hymns and spiritual songs, singing and making melody from your heart to the Lord; 20 giving thanks always for all things in the name of our Lord Jesus Christ to (our) God and Father, 21 subjecting yourselves to each other out of reverence for Christ.

5:10

In Ephesians Compare	Ephesians	Colossians
	22 Wives, (be subject) to your own husbands as to the Lord, 23 for the husband is head of the wife as also Christ is head of the church, he himself (being) the Savior of the body. 24 Then just as the church is subject to Christ so also wives (should be subject) to their husbands in everything.	3:18 Wives, be submissive to your husbands, as is fitting in the Lord. 1:18 And he is the head of the body, the church. . . .
5:33b		
5:28, 33a	25 Husbands, love your wives, just as also Christ loved the church and gave himself up for her; 26 that he might sanctify her, cleansing her by the washing of water in connection with the spoken word; 27 in order that he might present the church to himself brilliant in purity, having no spot or wrinkle or any such thing, but that she might be holy and faultless. 28 That is the way husbands also ought to love their own wives as their own bodies. He who loves his own wife loves himself; 29 for no one ever hated his own flesh; on the contrary, he nourishes it and cherishes it, just as also Christ (does) the church, 30 because we are members of his body. 31 "There-	3:19 Husbands, love your wives, and do not be harsh toward them.
1:4		1:22 . . . in order to present you holy, faultless, and blameless before himself. . . . 1:28 . . . in order that we may present every man perfect in Christ. . . . 3:19 Husbands, love your wives and do not be harsh toward them.
1:23		

22

3:19 Husbands, love your wives, and do not be harsh toward them. 3:18 Wives, be submissive to your husbands, as is fitting in the Lord.

3:20 Children, obey your parents in all things, for this is well-pleasing in the Lord.

3:21 Fathers, do not exasperate your children, in order that they may not lose heart. 22 Slaves, obey in all things those who according to the flesh are your masters, not with eye-service as men-pleasers but with singleness of heart, fearing the Lord. 23 Whatever you do, put your soul into the work, as for the Lord and not for men, 24 knowing that from the Lord you will receive the recompense, namely, the inheritance. (It is) the Lord Christ

---

fore shall a man leave his father and mother, and shall cleave to his wife; and the two shall become one flesh." 32 This mystery is great, but I am speaking with reference to Christ and the church. 33 Nevertheless, let each one of you also love his own wife as himself, and let the wife see to it that she respects her husband.

Chapter 6

1 Children, obey your parents in the Lord, for this is right. 2 "Honor your father and your mother", which is a commandment of foremost significance, with a promise attached: 3 "that it may be well with you" and that you may be on earth a long time. 4 And fathers, do not provoke your children to anger but rear them tenderly in the discipline and admonition of the Lord. 5 Slaves, be obedient to those who according to the flesh are your masters, with fear and trembling, in the sincerity of your heart, as to Christ, 6 not in the way of eye-service as men-pleasers, but as slaves of Christ, doing the will of God from the heart, 7 with ready mind rendering service

In Ephesians Compare	Ephesians	Colossians
	as to the Lord and not to men, 8 knowing that whatever good each one does this he will receive back from the Lord, whether (he be) slave or free. 9 And masters, do the same things for them, and stop threatening, knowing that (he who is) both their master and y o u r s is in the heavens, and there is no partiality with him.	(whom) y o u are serving. 25 For, the wrong-doer will receive (the consequences of) what he has wrongly done. And there is no partiality. 4:1 Masters, render to y o u r slaves that which is fair and square, knowing that y o u also have a Master in heaven.
4:14	10 Finally, find y o u r (source of) power in the Lord and in the strength of his might. 11 Put on the full armor of God in order that y o u may be able to stand firm against the crafty methods of the devil. 12 For not against flesh and blood is our wrestling but against the	1:11 being invigorated with all vigor, in accordance with his glorious might.
1:21; 2:2	principalities, against the authorities, against the world-rulers of this darkness, against the spiritual forces of evil in the heavenly places. 13 Therefore take up the full armor of God, in order that y o u may be able to stand y o u r ground in the day of evil, and having done everything, to stand firm. 14 Stand firm therefore,	1:16 . . . whether . . . principalities or authorities. . . .
6:11		

having fastened the belt of truth around y o u r waist and having put on the breastplate of righteousness, 15 and having shod y o u r feet with readiness derived from the gospel of peace, 16 and in addition to everything else, having taken up the shield of faith, by means of which y o u will be able to extinguish all the flaming missiles of the evil one; 17 and take the helmet of salvation, and the sword of the Spirit which is the spoken word of God, 18 by means of all prayer and supplication, praying at all times in the Spirit, and with a view to this, being on the alert in all perseverance and supplication, for all the saints; 19 and (praying) for me that when I open my mouth I may be given a message, so that I may make known courageously the mystery of the gospel, 20 for which I am an ambassador in a chain, that when I proclaim it I may speak with courage as I ought to speak.

21 But in order that y o u also may know my affairs how I am getting along, Tychicus, the beloved brother and faithful minister in the Lord, will make them all known to y o u, 22 whom I am sending

4:2 Persevere in prayer, keeping alert in it with thanksgiving; 3 at the same time praying also for us, that God may open to us a door for the message, to speak forth the mystery concerning Christ, on account of which I am in prison, 4 (praying) that I may make it clear, (and may speak) as I ought to speak.

4:7 All my affairs will Tychicus make known to y o u, the beloved brother and faithful minister and fellow-servant in the Lord, 8 whom I am sending to y o u for this very purpose, that y o u may know our

2:17

In
Ephesians
Compare

Ephesians	Colossians
to y o u for this very purpose, that y o u may know our circumstances and that he may strengthen y o u r hearts. 23 Peace (be) to the brothers, and love with faith, from God the Father and the Lord Jesus Christ. 24 Grace (be) with all those who love our Lord Jesus Christ with (a love) imperishable.	circumstances and that he may strengthen y o u r hearts.

26

INTRODUCTION

In order to be able to arrive at an objective conclusion regarding the relation between Ephesians and Colossians it is now also necessary to refer to the *Colossian* text as a basis for comparison. (For the actual *text*, as newly translated, see N.T.C. on Colossians and Philemon, pp. 202–205.)

In the following presentation the numbers in roman type (1 2 3 4, etc.) indicate those verses in the Colossian chapter that have parallels in Ephesians. Those in italics (*6 7 8 15*, etc.) refer to the verses that are without significant duplicate in the longer epistle. Those printed in boldface (**1:1 1:16 1:15 1:13, 18**, etc.) immediately under the corresponding Colossian references, indicate the Ephesian parallels.[2]

C. *Conclusions*

The above comparisons have made clear that there is, indeed, a substantial degree of resemblance between Colossians and Ephesians. To begin with *Colossians*, of its 95 verses about two-thirds are clearly or rather clearly paralleled in Ephesians, entirely or (more often) *in part*, either in thought conveyed or else both verbally and materially. This, however, by no means forces one to accept the conclusion that Ephesians is therefore the result of a skilful incorporation and amplification of phrases either remembered from Colossians or else copied from that shorter letter of Paul. Would a post-Pauline writer, whether he be thought of as writing from memory or from script, have rephrased the wording of Col. 1:12 into that of Eph. 1:11, that of Col. 1:13 into that of Eph. 1:6, that of Col. 2:11 into that of Eph. 2:11, that of Col. 2:4 into that of Eph. 5:6, and that of Col. 2:22 into that of Eph. 4:14, to list but a few parallels? Would not an imitator have adhered much more rigidly to the remembered or copied text? Surely, the remark of E. F. Scott is to the point: "When a writer borrows from himself he does what he likes with his own material. He cannot help revising and modifying in every sentence. It is only the unwarranted imitator who feels that he must stick

---

[2] If anyone compares the list here printed with that found in the work of C. L. Mitton, *The Epistle to the Ephesians*, pp. 316–318, he will discover that the two differ in some important details. Mitton, it must be remembered, denies the Pauline authorship of Ephesians. He sees a resemblance between Col. 1:8 and Eph. 3:5 and 6:18. However, the only item with respect to which all three passages are alike is the phrase "in the Spirit." This phrase, occurring both in those letters that are ascribed to Paul by almost everyone (Rom. 8:9; 9:1; 14:17; I Cor. 12:3), and in the Pastoral Epistles (I Tim. 3:16), is of little value in determining whether Paul himself or an imitator composed Ephesians. Further, it is hard to see any resemblance between Col. 1:17 and Eph. 5:1; between Col. 4:16 and Eph. 3:4, except for the fact that both refer to *reading*. And as to the closing benediction in Col. 4:18, though it is admitted that the words, "Grace (be) with y o u" resemble "Grace (be) with all those" of Eph. 6:24, yet when the two benedictions, in their entirety, are compared it is the contrast rather than the similarity that stands out. In certain other details also the list here given differs from that found in Mitton's work. It was made after careful examination of each individual passage.

Colossians

Chapter 1

1 1:1	**2** 1:1	**3** 1:16	**4** 1:15	**5** 1:13, 18
6	**7**	**8**	**9** 1:8, 15–17	**10** 1:17; 2:10; 4:1
11 1:19; 3:16; 6:10	**12** 1:11, 16	**13** 1:6	**14** 1:7	**15**
16 1:10, 21; 3:9, 10, 15; 6:12	**17**	**18** 1:22; 5:23	**19** 1:23	**20** 1:10; 2:13, 14, 16
21 2:12, 13, 16; 4:18	**22** 1:4; 2:13, 16; 5:27	**23** 3:1, 2, 6, 7, 17	**24** 1:22, 23; 3:1, 13	**25** 3:2, 7
26 3:3–5, 9, 10, 21	**27** 1:9, 18; 3:6, 9, 10	**28** 3:10; 5:27	**29** 3:7, 10, 20	

Chapter 2

1	**2** 1:9; 3:9, 10	**3**	**4** 5:6	**5**
6	**7** 2:20; 3:17	**8**	**9** 1:23; 4:13	**10** 1:21
11 2:11	**12** 1:20	**13** 2:1	**14** 2:15	**15**
16	**17**	**18**	**19** 2:21; 4:15, 16	**20**
21	**22** 4:14	**23**		

Chapter 3

1	2	3	4	5
1 1:20; 2:6	**2**	**3**	**4**	**5** 5:3, 5; 4:19
6 2:2, 3; 5:6	**7** 2:3	**8** 4:22, 29, 31; 5:4	**9** 4:22, 25	**10** 2:15; 4:24
11	**12** 1:4; 4:2, 32	**13** 4:2, 32	**14** 4:2, 3; 5:2	**15** 2:14; 4:1, 3, 4
16 5:19, 20	**17** 5:20	**18** 5:22, 24, 33	**19** 5:25, 28, 33	**20** 5:10; 6:1
21 6:4	**22** 6:5–7	**23** 6:5, 7	**24** 6:6, 8	**25** 6:8, 9

Chapter 4

1	2	3	4	5
1 6:9	**2** 6:18	**3** 1:9; 3:9; 6:19, 20	**4** 6:20	**5** 5:15, 16
6 4:29	**7** 6:21	**8** 6:22	*9*	*10*
11	*12*	*13*	*14*	*15*
16	*17*	*18*		

closely to his copy lest he may betray himself" (*The Epistles of Paul to the Colossians, to Philemon, and to the Ephesians,* p. 121) .

It is true that even so the lists given above, in which the four chapters of Colossians form the basis for comparison, show remarkable resemblance. Yet, this resemblance is by no means uniform. Similarities abound especially in chapters 1 and 3. It is but fair, however, to take note also of the *differ-ences.* In Colossians 2 and 4 (with exception of 4:7, 8; cf. the almost identical passage Eph. 6:21, 22) the *contrast* is as conspicuous as is the resemblance or even more so. We now clearly see that the theory according to which who-ever wrote Ephesians simply copied Colossians but added a paragraph here and a phrase there, is not in accord with the facts. There is definite *material* difference between the two letters. No *contradiction,* to be sure, but *differ-ence.* Alongside of everything that is similar there is a line of thought devel-oped in Colossians which does not reappear *with similar emphasis* in Ephe-sians. As especially the second chapter of Colossians indicates, with confirma-tion in the other chapters, the smaller epistle places great stress on Christ, the Pre-eminent One, the Only and All-Sufficient Savior. Its style, moreover, is *polemical.* It is a defense of the truth over against heresy. The theme of Ephesians is a different one, for which see this Introduction, Chapter V. And its style is *doxological.* The longer epistle is an outburst of humble praise and adoration.

Turning now to *Ephesians,* passages paralleled in Colossians are clear from the parallel columns on pp. 6–26 in which the basis of comparison is the text of the longer epistle, printed consecutively in the first column. It is, accordingly, not necessary at this point to give a table of references for Ephesians as we did for Colossians. Ephesians contains 155 verses, well over half of which are paralleled, or *partly* paralleled, in Colossians. Sometimes more than one Ephesian passage is paralleled by the same Colossian passage. Thus both Eph. 4:2-4 and 4:32–5:2 resemble Col. 3:12-15. And for both Eph. 5:22 and 5:33b see Col. 3:18; for both Eph. 5:25a and 5:33a see Col. 3:19; etc. (The converse is also true: for both Col. 1:11 and 1:29 see Eph. 1:19; for both Col. 1:22 and 1:28 see Eph. 5:27; etc.)

Also with respect to *Ephesians,* however, it is necessary to point out not only the passages which correspond with those in Colossians but also those which do not. Though the two epistles have been called twins, these twins are by no means identical.

Thus, taking as our starting point for comparison *the first chapter of Ephesians,* we note that the paragraph concerning the church's *eternal foun-dation in Christ* and the ascription of praise for every spiritual blessing to Father, Son, and Holy Spirit (vss. 3-6, 7-12, 13, 14) , has no parallel in Co-lossians. The references to the third person of the Holy Trinity (1:13, 17; and see also 2:18, 22; 5:16; 4:3, 4, 30; 5:9, 18; 6:17, 18) are not duplicated, as to frequency of occurrence, in the smaller epistle, which mentions the Holy

Spirit only once (Col. 1:8) .³ And the *many* references to "the church" in its most comprehensive sense, references beginning already in chapter 1 and continuing in later chapters (1:22; 3:10, 21; 5:23-25, 27, 29, 32) , distinguish Ephesians from Colossians.

When we turn to *the second chapter of Ephesians* we are again reminded that this letter is by no means a copy of Colossians. Though, to be sure, Colossians, as well as Ephesians, magnifies God's grace (1:6) , yet nowhere in that smaller epistle do we find anything that equals Eph. 2:7-10 in clearly stating and emphasizing the sovereign character of this grace and its relation to faith and to works. Moreover, the truth concerning *the universal scope* of the salvation which grace provides, so that through the blood of Christ men who were formerly bitter enemies are not only reconciled to *the Father* but also, because of that very fact, to each other (Eph. 2:11-18) , though *implied* also in Colossians, *is brought into the foreground* only in Ephesians.

There is little in Colossians that parallels the closing paragraphs of *the third chapter of Ephesians,* the section containing the stirring prayer (3:14-19) and the doxology (3:20, 21) . To be sure, the little there is suffices to show the reasonability of believing that he who wrote Col. 1:9b-14 (and Phil. 1:9-11) was also the author of Eph. 3:14-21 (cf. also Eph. 1:17-23) . Yet, *the lofty goal* described in the words, "in order that y o u . . . may be enabled, together with all the saints, to grasp what is the breadth and length and height and depth, and to know the love of Christ that surpasses knowledge, that y o u may be filled to all the fulness of God" (Eph. 3:17-19) is unique.

As the parallel columns also clearly indicate, there is much in *Ephesians 4:1-16* to which there is no parallel in Colossians. *The organic unity (amid diversity) and growth* of the church is described in a paragraph which is unlike anything in the twin epistle, though, to be sure, *the idea* itself is not altogether absent from the latter (cf. Col. 3:15) .

The *glorious renewal* on which *Eph. 4:17–6:9* dwells (note especially 4:23, 24; 5:14) and which becomes evident not only in the relation of believers to outsiders but also in the reciprocal attitudes of members of the same family (wives, husbands; children, fathers; slaves, masters) , though paralleled to a considerable extent in Colossians, is in Ephesians described as a work of the Holy Spirit (4:30) , by whom men are turned from "darkness" to "light" (5:6-14) . The *darkness to light* metaphor occurs in a touching paragraph which, again, has no real parallel in Colossians, though *the germinal idea* occurs there also (Col. 1:13) . And the striking thought that the relation between the believing husband and his wife is rooted in and patterned after that between Christ and his church (Eph. 5:23-32) stands by itself.

---

³ This reference is, however, disputed, though, as I see it, without good reason. See N.T.C. on Colossians and Philemon, pp. 53, 54.

In *Eph. 6:10-24* it is especially the section that describes the believers' *effective armor* (Eph. 6:10-20) that distinguishes the two epistles. Except for verses 18-20 Colossians has little that corresponds to it.

It has become clear that those paragraphs — some of them lengthy — and those many individual passages in which Ephesians differs from Colossians are too numerous and too significant to be considered mere amplifications. On the contrary, they form a pattern and give to Ephesians a distinct character. This will become even clearer in Chapter V of this Introduction, where the theme of Ephesians is discussed and the distribution of the material under this theme is considered.

III. Authorship

A. *Arguments Against Pauline Authorship Answered*

The epistle to the Ephesians has been called "the divinest composition of man," "the distilled essence of the Christian religion," "the most authoritative and most consummate compendium of the Christian faith," "full to the brim with thoughts and doctrines sublime and momentous," etc. It has made that impression upon professional scholars and laymen, upon believers throughout the history of the church and of every nationality. Accordingly, to deny the universal testimony of the early church, namely, that it was the apostle Paul, richly endowed by his Lord with talents of heart and mind, who wrote it, would seem to require what some call "courage," others "temerity." This is true all the more when to this denial is added the suggestion that the writer was a person far more obscure than the apostle. Nevertheless, such denials have been lashed out and such suggestions have been propounded.[4]

---

[4] It should not be necessary at this point to dwell on the denial by F. C. Baur (b. 1792, d. 1860) and his school. For men of that type the question whether an epistle is characterized by the anti-Judaistic line of argumentation seemed to settle everything. Thus, all of Paul's thinking was forced into one groove. The historical Paul, as Baur and his disciples saw him, was ever ready for combat. Hence, when, as is the case with Ephesians, a letter is conciliatory in tone, picturing the church universal, Jew and Gentile having become reconciled not only with God but also with each other through the cross, no further mark of its un-Pauline and post-Pauline origin was required. But if any were needed it would be (according to Baur c.s.) the evidence, in both Colossians and Ephesians, of gnostic trends, and in Eph. 4:9, of the doctrine of the descent into Hades. However, the fact that already in Paul's days *incipient* gnosticism had raised its head is today undisputed, and as to Eph. 4:9, see on that passage.

After Baur a vigorous attack upon the authenticity of Ephesians, resembling in some of its arguments that of more recent criticism, was made by S. Hoekstra of The Netherlands in his article "Vergelijking van de Brieven aan de Efeziërs en de Colossers, vooral uit het Oogpunt van Beider Leerstelligen Inhoud," *TT* (1868), pp. 562–599. Hoekstra viewed Ephesians as an attempt to rephrase the contents of Colossians in such a manner that Ephesians would resemble more closely the doc-

INTRODUCTION

The main arguments that have been urged against Pauline authorship are two which, at least to a certain extent, cancel each other out:

1. *The Resemblance Is Too Close*

   a. *Ephesians resembles Colossians*

The statement is made that this similarity is so very close that if Paul wrote Colossians he cannot have written Ephesians.

Answer: This argument has been fully answered in the preceding chapter. The traditional theory, according to which the same author at about the same time wrote letters to people living in the same Roman province, but elaborated on themes which, though closely related, are yet essentially different, fits all the data. Moreover, several Colossians-Ephesians parallels are found also in Paul's other epistles. In such cases, therefore, assuming that Colossians was written prior to Ephesians,[5] can it be said that whoever wrote

---

trine of the real Paul. As Hoekstra saw it, the author, whoever he was, was averse to all those theosophic theories about Christ which were found in Colossians, theories which severed Christianity from its historic foundation and from its abiding connection with the old dispensation.

Among those who more recently have rejected the Pauline authorship of this epistle are the British scholars James Moffatt, *Introduction to the Literature of the New Testament,* New York, 1918, who does not even classify Ephesians with Pauline literature; B. H. Streeter, who discusses "The Pauline Corpus" in his work *The Primitive Church,* New York, 1929; W. L. Knox, *St. Paul and the Church of the Gentiles,* Cambridge, 1939; and especially C. L. Mitton, *The Epistle to the Ephesians, Its Authorship, Origin and Purpose,* Oxford, 1951; see also, by the same author, *The Formation of the Pauline Corpus of Letters,* London, 1955; "Unsolved New Testament Problems: E. J. Goodspeed's Theory Regarding the Origin of Ephesians," *ET,* 59 (1947–1948), pp. 323–327; "E. J. Goodspeed's Theory Regarding the Origin of Ephesians," *ET,* 60 (1948–1949), pp. 320–321; "Important Hypotheses Reconsidered; VII. The Authorship of the Epistle to the Ephesians," *ET,* 67 (1955–1956), pp. 195–198. In America it was especially E. J. Goodspeed who attacked the Pauline authorship and suggested that Onesimus (the fugitive slave for whom Paul interceded in his letter to Philemon), in his later capacity as Bishop of the church at Ephesus, not only made a collection of the Pauline epistles but also himself wrote Ephesians as a covering letter or introductory commentary, *The Meaning of Ephesians,* Chicago, 1933; cf. also by the same author *New Chapters in New Testament Study,* New York, 1937, p. 32; and *The Key to Ephesians,* Chicago, 1956, xvi. F. W. Beare (Toronto, Canada) states his reasons for rejecting Pauline authorship in his commentary, *The Epistle to the Ephesians (Interpreter's Bible,* Vol. X, pp. 597–601).

Among the defenders of Pauline authorship the scholarly work of E. Percy, *Die Probleme der Kolosser-und Epheserbriefe,* Lund, 1946, deserves to be mentioned first of all. It is deplorable that C. L. Mitton, in a Preface to his aforementioned work: *The Epistle to the Ephesians, Its Authorship, Origin and Purpose,* had to admit that his book was already in the printer's hands before he had been able to gain access to Percy's dissertation. The traditional view, that Paul wrote Ephesians, is also defended by the following, to mention only a few: Abbott, Barclay, Barry, Bartlett, Bowman, Brown, Bruce, Findlay, Greijdanus, Grosheide, Hodge, Hort, Moule, Robinson, Scott and Westcott. For titles see General Bibliography at end of this volume.

[5] Whether Colossians preceded Ephesians or vice versa cannot be established with certainty. The usual — and it would seem logical — view is that Paul, having written Colossians which deals with a particular situation (the denial of Christ's all-

the Ephesian passages was necessarily using *only Colossians* as a basis for composition? May he perhaps also have had in mind Romans, I or II Corinthians, Galatians or some other Pauline epistle(s)? This leads to the next proposition:

b. *Ephesians resembles too closely Paul's other epistles*

The claim is made that words and phrases from the other Pauline epistles, for the moment leaving out not only Colossians but also the Pastorals, reappear far more frequently in Ephesians than in any genuine letter written by the great apostle. The conclusion is drawn that a capable imitator, having been a disciple of the renowned master, and being well acquainted with his genuine epistles and thus able to reproduce their words and phrases from memory, must have composed Ephesians.

Answer:

(1) There is wide divergence of opinion among scholars as to the actual extent of this resemblance. E. J. Goodspeed claims that out of 618 short phrases into which Ephesians may be divided as many as 550 have unmistakable parallels in Paul, in words or substance. On the other hand, A. S. Peake and T. K. Abbott see in Ephesians no or very little evidence of borrowing from any of Paul's epistles other than Colossians. C. L. Mitton, though convinced that the percentage as given by Goodspeed is an exaggeration, agrees with him in his general conclusion that the similarities are so numerous and of such a character that someone other than Paul must have written Ephesians. Nevertheless, detailed examination of the borrowings which Mitton considers the most striking has left many unconvinced. Would a disciple, reproducing from memory or even from the written page, Romans 3:24, "justified freely by his grace through the redemption that is in Christ Jesus," have reformulated this into "even though we were dead

---

sufficiency for salvation), afterward passed from the particular to the more general, from conditions existing in one particular church or in the churches of the Lycus Valley to God's plan of redemption with reference to the church universal. The fact that Ephesians is the longer epistle, enlarging on certain subjects that are merely touched upon in Colossians, can also be interpreted as pointing to that conclusion. Colossians 4:16b ("see to it that y o u also read the letter from Laodicea") is not a refutation of this theory. It does not indicate that Ephesians must have preceded Colossians. Even if the letter "from Laodicea" should refer to Ephesians, a supposition that cannot be proved (see N.T. on Colossians and Philemon, pp. 196, 197), this would still leave room for at least two possibilities neither of which would preclude the priority of Colossians: *a.* the apostle wrote (i.e., dictated) Colossians in its entirety, including 4:16, *having already planned to write Ephesians very soon afterward,* the two letters (plus the letter to Philemon) to be carried to their respective destinations by the same carrier, Tychicus, on the same trip (cf. Col. 4:7-9; Eph. 6:21, 22) ; or *b.* having written Colossians, with the exception of 4:16 (at least) and having afterward also composed Ephesians, Paul then revised the former by adding 4:16. For the very complicated theory of H. J. Holtzmann regarding the composition of the two letters see N.T.C. on Colossians and Philemon, p. 29. For defense of Colossian priority cf. E. P. Sanders, "Literary Dependence in Colossians," *JBL* (March 1966), p. 29.

through our trespasses (he) made us alive together with Christ — by grace y o u have been saved — " (Eph. 2:5) ? To be sure, there is agreement in doctrine here and the phrase "by grace" is used in both passages. But is it not more reasonable to ascribe the significant alteration in general phraseology to an original author who has thoroughly digested this central fact of redemption and is recasting his own thought? And the same holds also with respect to other parallels such as Rom. 8:28, cf. Eph. 1:11; I Cor. 3:6, cf. Eph. 2:21; Gal. 1:15, cf. Eph. 3:8; Philem. 13, cf. Eph. 6:20; etc. In all these cases there is, to be sure, a degree of similarity, but resemblance close enough to disprove Pauline authorship, not at all! In each case, if *the same author* wrote both corresponding passages, neither their resemblance nor their divergence is strange or in need of further explanation.

(2) Since the author of Ephesians has as his theme *The Church Glorious,* a church enriched by all the blessings of salvation which God, *solely by grace,* bestows upon both Jew and Gentile, "to the praise of his glory," it is not at all strange that at least as to content many passages in this prison epistle resemble those in the other letters where the same or a very similar theme is expressed. The theme *Salvation* ("Justification") *by Grace Alone* is also central in Romans and Galatians and is the basis for the exhortations in all the other epistles.

(3) Ephesians offers very little material of a polemical character, and there are *few* — according to some there are *no* — local references. This leaves more room for resemblances in positive teaching.

(4) Ephesians was written later than most of the other epistles. It contains, as it were, *a summary of doctrine.* Also for this reason in reading it one would expect to hear more echoes of the other epistles than one could expect to detect elsewhere.

Now in comparing Ephesians with Paul's other epistles there is not any good reason to omit the Pastorals (I and II Timothy and Titus), as if it is an established fact that these were not written by Paul. On the contrary, the attempt to disprove their Pauline authorship must be considered a failure. See N.T.C. on I and II Timothy and Titus, pp. 4–33; 377–381. The most reasonable explanation for the extent of the resemblances, often in substance or thought-content but at times even in exact phraseology, between Ephesians and the Pastorals, is that these four letters sprang from the same mind and heart. Note the following:

Ephesians	I and II Timothy and Titus
Doxologies break in suddenly	
"Now to him who is able to do infinitely more than all we ask or im-	"So to the King of the ages, the imperishable, invisible, only God (be)

35

Ephesians	I and II Timothy and Titus
agine . . . be the glory . . . forever and ever" (3:20). Cf. 1:3 ff.	honor and glory forever and ever!" (I Tim. 1:17). Cf. I Tim. 6:15, 16; II Tim. 4:18.

Believers are God's *elect*

". . . just as he elected us in him before the foundation of the world" (1:4).	"On account of this I endure all things for the sake of the elect" (II Tim. 2:10).

Man's chief purpose is God's glory

". . . to the praise of the glory of his grace" (1:6); ". . . to the praise of his glory" (1:12, 14).	"to him (*be* or *is*) the glory forever and ever. Amen" (II Tim. 4:18).

The gospel is "the *word* or *message* [logos] of the truth"

". . . the message of the truth, the gospel of y o u r salvation" (1:13).	". . . rightly handling the word of the truth" (II Tim. 2:15).

It was because of God's *love* that sinners were saved

". . . among whom we also once lived in the lusts of our flesh . . . God, being rich in mercy, because of his great love with which he loved us, even though we were dead through our trespasses, made us alive together with Christ" (2:3-6).	"For at one time we also were . . . enslaved to various passions and pleasures. . . . But when the kindness of God our Savior and his love toward man appeared he saved us" (Tit. 3:3-5).

It is grace — not works — that saved us

"For by grace y o u have been saved through faith; and this not of yourselves, (it is) the gift of God; not of works, lest any one should boast" (2:8, 9).	"(God) who saved us and called us with a holy calling, not according to our works but according to his own purpose and grace" (II Tim. 1:9). Cf. Tit. 3:5.

Nevertheless, good works are necessary, as the fruit (never the root!) of grace

"For his handiwork are we, created in Christ Jesus for good works, which God prepared beforehand that we should walk in them" (2:10).	". . . (our great God and Savior Christ Jesus) who gave himself for us in order . . . to purify for himself a people, his very own, with a zest for noble deeds" (Tit. 2:14). Cf. I Tim. 2:10; 6:18; II Tim. 3:17; Tit. 3:8.

Ephesians	**I and II Timothy and Titus**

Christ is the one and only Mediator

". . . for through him we both have our access in one Spirit to the Father" (2:18).	"For (there is but) *one* God, and (there is but) *one* Mediator between God and men, the man Christ Jesus" (I Tim. 2:5).

Paul considers himself unworthy

"To me, the very least of all saints, was this grace given" (3:8).	"Reliable (is) the saying, and worthy of full acceptance, that Christ Jesus came into the world sinners to save, foremost of whom am I" (I Tim. 1:15).

The mystery of salvation, once hidden, has now been disclosed

". . . the mystery which for ages has been hidden in God . . . in order that now . . . might be made known through the church the iridescent wisdom of God, according to the eternal purpose which he formed in Christ Jesus our Lord" (3:9-11).	". . . his own purpose and grace which was given to us in Christ Jesus before times everlasting but now has been manifested through the appearing of our Savior Christ Jesus" (II Tim. 1:9, 10).

The ascended Christ has instituted the offices for the perfecting of believers

"And it was he who gave some (to be) apostles . . . fully to equip the saints for the work of ministry, with a view to the building up of the body of Christ" (4:12).	". . . that the man of God may be equipped, for every good work thoroughly equipped" (II Tim. 3:17).

Wives should be submissive to their own husbands

"Wives (be subject) to y o u r own husbands as to the Lord" (5:22).	". . . so that they may train the young women to be . . . submissive to their own husbands" (Tit. 2:4, 5).

We are saved through a spiritual washing, that of regeneration, symbolized by baptism

". . . cleansing her by the washing of water . . ." (5:26).	". . . through a washing of regeneration" (Tit. 3:5).

The mystery which centers in Christ is great

"This mystery is great . . ." (5:32).

"And confessedly great is the mystery of (our) devotion" (I Tim. 3:16).

The grace and power of the Lord is the
believers' source of strength

"Finally, find y o u r (source of) power in the Lord and in the strength of his might" (6:10).

"You then, my child, be strengthened in the grace (that is) in Christ Jesus" (II Tim. 2:1).

When grace, love, and faith combine
true peace results

"Peace (be) to the brothers and love with faith, from God the Father and the Lord Jesus Christ. Grace (be) with all those who love our Lord Jesus Christ with (a love) imperishable" (6:23, 24).

"And it super-abounded (namely) the grace of our Lord, with faith and love in Christ Jesus" (I Tim. 1:14).

Now in all this the complete *harmony* with the leading ideas found in those epistles that are by nearly everyone ascribed to Paul, coupled, however, with rich *variety* of expression, points to identity of authorship and not to either of two suggestions, namely, *a.* that a disciple of Paul refurbished passages from Ephesians, thus producing material now found in the Pastorals, or *b.* that he who composed Ephesians borrowed from the Pastorals.

    c. *Ephesians resembles I Peter*

It must not be overlooked that some of the material found in Ephesians is similar to that contained in *non-Pauline New Testament literature.* There are, for example, significant resemblances between Ephesians and I Peter. Note the following:

	Ephesians	**I Peter**
"Blessed (be) the God and Father of our Lord Jesus Christ"	1:3	1:3
"before the foundation of the world"	1:4	1:20
"so that y o u may know what is the *hope* . . . what the *inheritance* . . . and what the . . . *power* . . . which he exerted in Christ when he raised him from the dead"	1:18-20	cf. 1:3-5

	Ephesians	I Peter
"he (God) raised him (Christ) from the dead, and made him to sit at his right hand . . . far above every principality and authority and power"	1:20, 21	cf. 3:21b, 22
"the sons of disobedience" . . . "children of wrath"	2:2, 3	cf. 1:14; 2:2
"Christ Jesus himself being the chief cornerstone"	2:20	cf. 2:4, 8
"in other generations not made known . . . that now might be made known . . . ."	3:5, 10	cf. 1:10-12
"lowliness . . . meekness . . . longsuffering . . . love," etc.	4:2, 3	cf. 3:8, 15; 5:5
"laying aside falsehood . . . bitterness and anger and wrath and brawling and slander, along with all malice"	4:25, 31	cf. 2:1
"tenderhearted"	4:32	3:8
table of household duties	5:22–6:9	cf. 2:18–3:7
"Put on the full armor of God in order that y o u may be able to stand firm against the crafty methods of the devil"	6:11	cf. 5:8, 9a

d. *Ephesians resembles Luke and Acts*

Similarly there are resemblances between Ephesians and the Lucan writings. In all three the divine love and grace, mercy and forgiveness are prominently displayed (Eph. 1:4, 6-8; 2:5-8; Luke 1:48; 4:18; 5:20; 7:47, 48; Acts 5:31; 11:23; 13:38, 43; 14:3, 26; 15:11, 40; 26:18). There is emphasis on prayer, often intercessory in content (Eph. 1:15, 16; 3:14; 6:18; Luke 1:9, 10, 13; 2:37; 3:21; 5:16; 6:12, 28; etc.; Acts 1:14; 2:42; 4:24-31; 10:4; 12:5; etc.). There is thanksgiving, praise, and song (Eph. 1:6, 12, 14, 16; 5:19, 20; Luke 1:46; 2:13, 14, 20, 29-32, 47; 3:8, 9; 5:67-79; 24:52, 53; Acts 2:47; 15:31; 16:25, 34). This is not surprising, for a world-embracing gospel is being proclaimed (Eph. 2:18; Luke 1:78, 79; 2:32; 13:29; Acts 2:17-21; 13:46, 47; 15:7-9; 22:21). It is the gospel of full and free salvation through the shedding of Christ's blood (Eph. 1:7; 2:13; Luke 22:20, 44; Acts 20:28). In the final analysis, therefore, every blessing proceeds from God, was included before the foundation of the world in his all-comprehensive decree, and flows forth from his sovereign "good pleasure" (Eph. 1:4, 5; Luke 2:14; 17:26-28).

Nothing either good or evil ever happens apart from his all-comprehensive, eternal decree (Eph. 1:11; Luke 22:22; Acts 2:23; 13:29). The blessings received on earth descend from heaven, from the ascended and exalted Mediator (Eph. 1:3, 20-22; 4:8-10; Luke 24:50, 51; Acts 1:6-11; 2:32-36; 7:55, 56). It is from that heavenly home that Jesus sent the Comforter, so that his own might be "filled with the Holy Spirit" (Eph. 5:18; Luke 1:15, 41, 53, 67; Acts 2:4, 33; 4:8, 31; etc.). In receiving these marvelous blessings men do not remain passive. On the contrary, by the power of the Holy Spirit, they, "with loins girded" (Eph. 6:14; Luke 12:35), and walking in the *light*, expose the works of *darkness* (Eph. 5:8-14; Luke 1:79; 11:33-36; 12:3; 16:8).

   e. *Ephesians resembles the Johannine writings*

The last mentioned contrast — *light* versus *darkness* — is found, however, not only in Ephesians and Luke but also in other sacred literature, notably in the writings of *John* (John 1:4-9; 3:19-21; 8:12; I John 1:5, 7; 2:8-10, etc.; cf. also Rev. 21:22-26). The claim has often been made that Ephesians emits a Johannine fragrance. Note, accordingly, not only the light-darkness contrast but also the very similar opposition between *life* and *death* (Eph. 2:1, 5; 4:18; John 1:4; 5:24; I John 3:14; Rev. 3:1). Another contrast — in this case not hostile but complementary — with respect to which Ephesians reminds one of John's terminology, is that between Christ's *descent* and his *ascent* (Eph. 4:9, 10; John 3:13; 6:38, 41, 50, 51, 58, 62; 16:28). Many blessings descend upon the church from the ascended Christ. Now it was in Christ that even "before the foundation of the world" (Eph. 1:4; John 17:24; cf. 17:5; Rev. 13:8; 17:8) believers were chosen. They were fore-ordained to adoption as *sons* (Eph. 1:5; John 1:12; I John 3:1). Moreover, all of them having been elected from eternity "in Christ," (Eph. 1:3, 4, 6, 7, etc.; John 15:5) who dwells in them (Eph. 3:17; John 14:20; cf. Rev. 1:13), form a unity and must do their utmost to promote spiritual unity (Eph. 4:1-16; John 15:12; 17:21-23). The purpose of Christ's active and energetic indwelling is that he may present the church to himself brilliant in purity, having no spot or wrinkle, thoroughly sanctified (Eph. 5:27; cf. 3:14-19; 4:17-24; John 15:2; 17:17-19), cleansed by the spoken word (Eph. 5:26; John 15:3). This church is the object of his love. Of very frequent occurrence both in Ephesians and in the Johannine literature is this word *love*, both as noun and as verb (*noun:* Eph. 1:4, 15; 2:4; 3:14-19; *verb:* 2:4; 5:2; *noun:* John 5:42; 13:35; 15:9; I John 2:5, 15; II John 3, 6; III John 6; Rev. 2:14, 19; *verb:* John 3:16; I John 2:10; II John 1, 5; III John 1, to list only a few references). And is it not true that, according to both Ephesians and John, Christ is "the Beloved" of the Father? (Eph. 1:6; John 3:35; 10:17; 15:9; 17:23, 24, 26). Because of his infinite and tender love and in his Spirit believers are "sealed" (Eph. 1:13; 4:30; John 6:27; Rev. 5:1-9; 6:1; 7:3-8). They receive the reassuring testimony of the Holy Spirit. *Within the limit* ("according to the measure," Eph. 4:7) in which, in any situation of life, believers have need of pardoning and sustaining grace, their Savior apportions it to them, for it is he who has received the Spirit *in unlimited degree* ("without measure," John 3:34). He has "known" his sheep from all eternity, and they aim "to *know* the *love* of Christ that surpasses knowledge" (Eph. 3:19). Note this combination of these two entities that match perfectly: *a.* experiential *knowledge* and *b. love* that is experienced. As has already been indicated, John's writings, too, refer to this *love* again and again. They also enlarge on this *knowledge* (John 8:32; 10:15; 17:3, 25; I John 2:3-5, 13, 14; 4:7, 8, 16; 5:2, 20; II John 1; Rev. 3:9).

    f. *Ephesians resembles Hebrews*

Both teach redemption through blood (Eph. 1:7; Heb. 9:12, 22); Christ's exaltation at God's right hand (Eph. 1:20; Heb. 1:3; 8:1; 10:12); and access to the Father through Christ (Eph. 2:18; 3:12; Heb. 4:16; 7:25). They also describe in similar terms those who are immature (Eph. 4:14; Heb. 5:13); warn against being whirled around or carried away by every gust of doctrine, that is, by strange and deviating teaching (Eph. 4:14; Heb. 13:9); recognize Christ's one and only offering of himself for the sin of his people (Eph. 5:2; Heb. 10:10); pronounce God's judgment upon every form of immorality (Eph. 5:5; Heb. 13:4); tell us that Christ offered himself for the church in order that he might sanctify it (Eph. 5:26; Heb. 10:10, 22; 13:12); and compare the word of God to a sword (Eph. 6:17; Heb. 4:12).

    g. *Ephesians resembles the Epistle of James*

The same figure of speech is used to describe the unstable person. He is said to be "driven" or "tossed to and fro" by the wind (Eph. 4:14; cf. James 1:6). Ephesians 5:8 calls believers "children of light." James 1:17 describes God as "the Father of lights." "Be angry but do not sin" (Eph. 4:26) reminds one of "Let every man be . . . slow to anger" (James 1:19). For other resemblances compare Eph. 4:2, 3 with James 3:17; 5:8; Eph. 4:29 with James 3:10; Eph. 4:31 with James 3:14; Eph. 5:19 with James 5:13; Eph. 6:18, 19 with James 5:16. To represent James as Paul's opponent with respect to the doctrine of good works is unfair. On the contrary, James championed the cause of Paul (Acts 15:13-29). To the very end he remained Paul's friend (Acts 21:18-25). Paul and James were not in conflict, but faced different issues. James valued genuine faith highly (1:3, 6; 2:1, 5, 22-24; 5:15). The "faith" which he condemns is that of dead orthodoxy and of demons (2:19). Paul would condemn that just as vehemently. And, on the other hand, Paul was a firm believer in the necessity of good works as a fruit of faith (Eph. 2:10; cf. Rom. 2:6-10; II Cor. 9:8; I Thess. 1:3; II Thess. 2:17; Tit. 3:8, 14).

As to any conclusion with respect to authorship that can be drawn from these resemblances between Ephesians and other New Testament writings see below, under heading 3.

41

2. The Difference Is Too Great

a. Different Words

It is claimed that the letter contains too many exceptional or new words; that is, either words found nowhere else in the New Testament (forty-two of them) , or else words which, though occurring elsewhere in the New Testament, are not found in any genuine epistle of Paul.

Answer:

(1) The same argument, if applied to Romans, Galatians, Philippians, or I and II Corinthians, would also exclude them from the list of Pauline letters. The number of new words in Ephesians is not disproportionately large.

(2) A different subject requires different words. In Ephesians, more than elsewhere, the apostle discusses "the unity of all believers in Christ." Hence, it is not surprising that here he uses such new words (those *in italics* which follow) as: *unity* (4:3, 13) , which resulted because Christ "made *both* one and has broken down the *barrier* formed by the *dividing wall*" (2:14) . In connection with this same stress on spiritual togetherness, this letter contains many sun-compounds, the prefix "sun-" meaning "together" or "fellow-." Paul uses the expressions: *harmoniously fitted together* (2:21) , *built together* (2:22) ; *fellow-citizens* (2:19) , *fellow-members of the body, fellow-partakers of the promise* (3:6) . The last two are preceded by *fellow-sharers in the inheritance* (co-heirs) , but this is not a new word, as it already occurs in Rom. 8:17.

Also, Paul stresses the fact that this entire united church should bid defiance to the forces of evil, and that in order to do so it should put on the spiritual armor which God provides (6:11 ff.) . In that striking little paragraph this battle and this panoply of faith are described with a fulness of detail found nowhere else in Paul's epistles. We therefore expect to find new words. When they occur they certainly cannot be used as an argument against Pauline authorship. The apostle speaks about *crafty methods of "the devil"* (*ho diábolos,* a word found, however, also in the Pastorals; see No. [4] below) . He reminds us of the fact that our *wrestling* is against . . . *world-rulers* of this darkness, against the spiritual forces of evil in *the heavenly places* (see No. [3] below) . He urges us *to fasten* the belt of truth *around* the waist, *to put on* (lit., "to bind beneath") shoes that symbolize the *readiness* derived from the gospel of peace, and to take up *the shield* of faith by means of which we shall be able to extinguish all the flaming *missiles* of the evil one. In all this, for the reason given, there is nothing that argues against Pauline authorship for Ephesians.

(3) It is not very convincing to say that Paul could write "God," but not *without God* (Eph. 2:12) ; "shameful" (I Cor. 11:6; 14:35) but not shamefulness or, as here, *filthiness* (Eph. 5:4) ; that he could use the verb "to

open" (I Cor. 16:9; II Cor. 6:11), but not the noun *opening* (Eph. 6:19); could call a man "wise" (I Cor. 1:26) but not *unwise* (Eph. 5:15); could write "to equip," to make complete (I Cor. 1:10), but not *equipment* (Eph. 4:12); "to persevere" (Col. 4:2), but not *perseverance* (Eph. 6:18); "holily" (I Thess. 2:10), but not *holiness* (Eph. 4:24); and "heavenly" (I Cor. 15:40 — twice; 48, 49), also "the heavenly beings" (Phil. 2:10, "of those in heaven"), but not *the heavenlies,* at least not five times (Eph. 1:3, 20; 2:6; 3:10; 6:12).

(4) The statement, made so often, that many words are found in Ephesians "but not in any genuine Pauline writing," generally proceeds from the tacit assumption that the Pastorals (sometimes also Colossians) are not "genuine Pauline writings." But, as has been indicated (N.T.C. on I and II Timothy and Titus, pp. 4–33; also footnote 193 on pp. 377–381), for this assumption there are no real grounds. It was Paul who wrote the Pastorals. Hence, from the list of exceptional words that have any value as an argument against Pauline authorship for Ephesians must also be subtracted those which this letter has in common with the Pastorals though they do not occur in any other Pauline epistle: *chain* (Eph. 6:20; II Tim. 1:16); *deceive* (Eph. 5:6; I Tim. 2:14); *dissolute behavior* or *unrestrained living* (Eph. 5:18; Tit. 1:6); *devil* (Eph. 4:27; 6:11; I Tim. 3:6, 7, 11; II Tim. 2:26; 3:3; Tit. 2:3; also used by Matthew, Luke, John, James, Peter, and the author of Hebrews, often interchangeably with *Satan*); *evangelist* (Eph. 4:11; II Tim. 4:5); *discipline* or *training* (Eph. 6:4; II Tim. 3:16) and the verb *to honor* (Eph. 6:2; I Tim. 5:3).

(5) As to the "exceptional" words that still remain after all of these others have been subtracted because they can have no value in supporting the proposition that Paul could not have written Ephesians, we may well ask whether Paul, an able writer, with originality and a fertile mind, should not be credited with a sufficient command of language to enable him to use synonymous words and phrases. At the beginning of his writing-career was the apostle handed a list of words with the requirement that, no matter what the circumstances might be, either of himself or of the readers, and no matter what might be the purpose of any epistle or the subject on which he would write, he must invariably use *these* words, and *only* these, and, in addition, must distribute them in equal proportion over all his letters, like the spots on a polka-dot dress? Vocabulary proves nothing at all against Pauline authorship of Ephesians! [6]

---

[6] The manner in which this argument, however, is still being used even in a relatively recent commentary, with many excellent features, leaves something to be desired. I refer to F. W. Beare's work on Ephesians in *The Interpreter's Bible*, Vol. 10, p. 598. After informing the reader that the number of new words is extraordinarily large in Ephesians, he *mentions* five of them. However, no less than *three* of

b. *Different Meanings*

It is also maintained that in Ephesians Pauline words are used in a new sense. Thus the word *plērōma,* fulness, in Col. 1:19; 2:9 indicates the fulness of deity dwelling in Christ, but in Eph. 1:23 it is used in a different connection. In Col. 1:26, 27 the term *mystery* indicates eschatological glory, but in Ephesians it refers to the acceptance of the Gentiles (1:9; 3:3 ff.) . So also in Col. 1:22 the word *sōma, body,* refers to the physical body of Jesus Christ offered as a sacrifice for sin, and in Col. 2:19 its English equivalent is cosmos or universe, but in Ephesians the body is the church. Finally, the word *oikonomia* (whence our "economy") , which in Colossians and elsewhere has reference to the special task or assignment which by God was entrusted to Paul, has the abstract meaning "God's wise planning or generalship" in Ephesians.

Answer: The word *fulness,* in Greek as well as in English, can be used in many different connections. See N.T.C. on Colossians and Philemon, footnote 56, pp. 79, 80. Its exact reference in Eph. 1:23 is disputed. Certainly no argument of value can be based on such a controversial passage. See also the explanation of Eph. 1:10, 23; 3:19; 4:13. As to the word *mystery,* it is clear from the context that even in Col. 1:26, 27, though the setting is eschatological, the reference is to "the glory of the mystery *among the Gentiles* . . . Christ *in y o u,* the hope of glory." As to the word *sōma, body,* is it fair to demand that it must have exactly the same reference in Ephesians as in Col. 1:22, when only in the latter case the author speaks of "his body *of flesh*"? It is not true that in Col. 2:19 the word *body* refers to the cosmos or universe. See N.T.C. on that passage. What is true is that (in Ephesians) the well-nigh consistent reference of this word to *the church,* with the human body in the background (1:22, 23; 2:16; 3:6; 4:4 ff.; 5:23, 30; exception 5:28) is also well represented in Colossians (1:18; 2:19; 3:15) . Hence, there is no real problem here. And finally, as to *oikonomia,* this word, wherever it occurs in the New Testament, is based upon the idea of *stewardship.* It has this meaning not only in Luke 16:2-4; I Cor. 9:17; Col. 1:25; and I Tim. 1:4 but also in Eph. 3:2. However, by a slight semantic shift the meaning "administration of one's stewardship" arises, and so, in general, *administration,* execution, effectuation, the carrying into effect of a plan or purpose (Eph. 1:10; 3:9) . One and the same author must certainly be allowed the privilege of using the same word both in its basic meaning and also, in a different context, in a somewhat modified sense. Is it not true that

---

these five are found in 6:11 ff., the paragraph on the Christian's spiritual armor, a new subject (at least as to detail) , with respect to which we *expect* new words (see No. [2] above). The remaining *two* words are not "new" at all: one is found also in Romans; the other in II Corinthians. Negative criticism will have to do better than this!

even in the same short sentence a word, used twice, can have two different connotations (see Luke 9:60; Rom. 9:6) ? It is clear, therefore, that the argument based on "different meanings" lacks validity.

Sometimes *an entire phrase* is used in Ephesians in a connection in which it is not found in Colossians or elsewhere in Paul. This, too, has been used as an argument against Pauline authorship. The most remarkable instance of this exception to the rule is held to be Eph. 5:20 as compared with Col. 3:17. The latter passage reads, "And whatever y o u do in word or in deed, (do) all in the name of the Lord Jesus, giving thanks to God the Father *through him";* but the former reads, "giving thanks . . . *in the name of our Lord Jesus Christ* to (our) God and Father." Mitton tells us that in the Ephesian passage the phrase "in the name of Jesus" is artificially associated with giving thanks. As he sees it this phrase is added "rather pointlessly." To him this wrenching of a phrase from its proper Colossian context speaks, more than perhaps any other item, against Pauline authorship. But should we not rather say that this type of reasoning speaks more than perhaps anything else against the convincing nature of Mitton's argumentation? What could be wrong with the idea that in Paul's mind the giving of thanks was associated with the name of Jesus? Does not the very passage in Colossians clearly state that *everything* — hence, also the giving of thanks — must be done "in the name of the Lord Jesus"? Is not the clause, "giving thanks to God the Father *through him,*" synonymous with giving thanks to God the Father *in the name of* the Son? If it be true that in Christ's name knees will bend (Phil. 2:20), commands are issued (II Thess. 3:6), and, in fact, all things must be done (Col. 3:17), is it then pointless to say that in his name thanksgiving must also be offered? Is it not rather true that since the Father blesses us through the Son, thanksgiving should also be brought to the Father through the Son, that is, "in his name"?

c. *A Different Style*

The style employed by the author of Ephesians is said to be too diffuse, deferential, and dulcifying to belong to the real Paul. First, it is said to be *diffuse*. It is a wordy epistle, and the words are widely spread. By means of almost interminable sentences the letter moves along slowly and majestically like a glacier that worms its way down the valley inch by inch. See 1:3-14; 1:15-23; 2:1-10; 2:14-18; 2:19-22; 3:1-12; 3:14-19; 4:11-16; and 6:13-20. Within these lengthy sentences there is often a descriptive verbosity that is completely uncharacteristic of the real Paul. Titles are written out in full, followed by modifying clauses; example, "Blessed (be) the God and Father of our Lord Jesus Christ, who has . . ." etc. Frequently, a noun is followed by its synonym, the latter being in the genitive or being preceded by a preposition: "the dividing wall of the barrier," probably meaning "the barrier formed by the dividing wall," to which, as if this were not enough, is added another synonym "the hostility" (2:14) ; "the law of commandments in ordinances," indicating "the law of commandments with its requirements" (2:15); and "the measure of (the) stature of the fulness of Christ" (4:13). See also 1:5, 11, 19. Now all this is in sharp contrast with the concise, abrupt, lively, impetuous style that characterizes the real Paul.

Answer: Much of Ephesians is in the nature of a prayer offered by a deeply grateful apostle who is witnessing the realization of his life's dream, namely, the coming into existence of a new and glorious spiritual entity, the *one* church of Jew and Gentile, the product of the marvelous grace of God. Now elevated language with its many synonyms is characteristic of adoration. See N.T.C. on Colossians and Philemon, p. 30. Also, by far the most of these lengthy sentences occur in the first of the two major divisions of the letter, that is, in the part that can be described as *Adoration* in contrast with Part II: *Exhortation.* It is not fair to contrast the style of this Adoration section of Ephesians with that of the Exhortation section of the other epistles, and then to say that, therefore, Paul cannot have written Ephesians. It is true that Ephesians contains more long and lofty sentences than is usual with Paul. There is, however, a reason for this. Nowhere else is there such an outpouring of the heart, such unrestrained praise, as there is in this letter. The author is moved to the very depths of his being by *a.* the contemplation of God's sovereign, eternal, redemptive love for sinners, *both Jew and Gentile, b.* the inner conviction that he, the author himself, is a recipient of this grace, and *c.* the reflection that he, Paul, yes even he himself, formerly a vehement persecutor of the church, had been predestined by God to play a very important role in the proclamation and realization of God's marvelous plan of the ages.

Yet, as already indicated, the described stylistic difference in this respect between Ephesians and the other epistles is one *in degree* only. Hence, it cannot be properly used as an argument against Pauline authorship. Lengthy sentences are also found in other epistles traditionally ascribed to Paul. Rom. 1:1-7 has 93 words in the original; 2:5-10 has 87; Phil. 3:8-11 has 78; and Col. 1:9-20 has no less than 218. And as to piling up closely connected synonyms, this feature, too, is by no means confined to Ephesians. On the contrary, such and similar pleonasms are found also in Rom. 11:33; Phil. 3:8; Col. 1:5, 11, 27; I Thess. 1:3, to mention only a few.

Secondly, the style of Ephesians has been described as *deferential.* It is maintained that an admirer of the great master is here speaking. Paul himself, according to this manner of argumentation, could never have written such a boastful clause as the following: "whereby, as y o u read it, y o u can perceive my insight into the mystery of Christ" (3:4). Surely, the man who wrote, "I am the least of the apostles, unfit to be called an apostle" (I Cor. 15:9), was far too humble to write Eph. 3:4 (or 3:4-9).

Answer: It is exactly characteristic of Paul to make enormous claims. He claims to have fully preached the gospel amid signs and wonders (Rom.

15:19) ; calls himself "a wise master-builder" (I Cor. 3:10), and a "steward of the mysteries of God" (I Cor. 4:1; cf. 9:17). He even dares to make comparisons between himself and others. He ranks himself higher than ten thousand tutors (I Cor. 4:15). He is able to speak with tongues "more than y o u all" (I Cor. 14:18). As an apostle he has "labored more abundantly" than any of the others (I Cor. 15:10). See also II Cor. 11:22-33; Gal. 1:1, 14; Phil. 3:4-6. Hence, the claim made by the author of Eph. 3:4 is in line with those made elsewhere in Paul's epistles and cannot be used as a valid argument against the traditional ascription of Ephesians to the great apostle to the Gentiles.

It should be noted, however, that Paul's claims are entirely valid, are made in order that, through confidence in his message, men may be benefited spiritually and may be won for Christ (I Cor. 9:19-21), and that the glory may be given not to the recipient of the enumerated distinctions but to God alone (I Cor. 9:16; 10:31; Gal. 6:14). The apostle never claims personal credit for any virtue or talent (Rom. 7:24, 25; I Cor. 4:7; Gal. 6:3). Here in Ephesians he is just as humble as he was in I Corinthians, perhaps even more so (cf. Eph. 3:8 with I Cor. 15:9). But that he, nevertheless, makes these great claims cannot be denied. In the light of all the evidence it is clear that also on this score there is no essential difference between Ephesians and the other Pauline epistles.

Finally, a *dulcifying* character has also been ascribed to the style of Ephesians. It has been said by those who deny the Pauline authorship of both Colossians and Ephesians that in addition to the desire to soften the extreme doctrinal utterances of the former, the author of the latter, whoever he may have been, tried to tone down the *exhortations* found in the shorter epistle. Hence, the demand that children obey their parents and that slaves obey their masters "in all things" (Col. 3:20, 22) is in Ephesians reproduced in the weakened form which omits the offensive modifier (6:1, 5).

Answer: It is not difficult to suggest possible reasons for the change, reasons that will in no way imply a rejection of Pauline authorship for both epistles. In the case of the exhortation addressed to the children, the author here in this longer epistle wishes to stress another aspect of the matter, namely, that such submission is proper and will be rewarded. And in connection with the admonition to the slaves we may well ask whether the command (6:5) does not already have a sufficient number of predicate modifiers (verses 5b, 6, 7, 8) to be able to dispense with an additional "in all things." Besides, was not the flight of Onesimus from his Colossian master a sufficient reason why exactly in *Colossians* the demand that slaves obey their masters had to be emphasized by the addition of the modifier? But there may have been other reasons. What, however, especially shuts the door against this type of argumentation against Pauline authorship for Ephesians is the fact that in connection with the requirement that wives obey their husbands it is exactly *Ephesians,* not Colossians, that adds, "in everything" (cf. Eph. 5:24 with Col. 3:18).

It has become clear, therefore, that there is nothing in the style of Ephesians that prevents it from being a genuine letter written by Paul.

d. *Different Doctrines*

(1) *The Doctrine of God*

Objection: According to Ephesians *God's eternal decree* is the source of salvation for his people (Eph. 1:4, 5, 11). Paul, however, glories in the cross (Gal. 6:14; cf. Rom. 3:24).

Answer: Ephesians, too, glories in the cross (2:16; cf. 1:7), and the other Pauline epistles also trace salvation to its source in God's sovereign, eternal plan (Rom. 8:29, 30; 11:2, 28, 36; Col. 3:12).

(2) *The Doctrine of Man*

Objection: Ephesians describes man's condition apart from grace in milder terms than does Paul in Colossians and elsewhere. Contrast the strong language of Col. 3:5-9 with the mere negatives of Eph. 2:12.

Answer: No language used to describe the sinner in his natural state could be stronger than that used in Eph. 2:1-3. Moreover, there is dynamite in those negatives of Eph. 2:12! See on that passage.

(3) *The Doctrine of Christ*

(a) Objection: Ephesians calls Christ "the head" of the church (1:21, 22; 4:15, 16; 5:23). According to Paul the head is merely one of the members of the body (I Cor. 12:21).

Answer: Different themes require different metaphors. The passage from I Corinthians describes the mutual obligations of church-members. Ephesians deals with the unity of all believers in Christ, their head. There is no contradiction here. Even in I Corinthians the fact that "the head of every man is Christ" is clearly taught (I Cor. 11:3). Colossians, too, recognizes Christ's headship in relation to his church (Col. 1:18; 2:19).

(b) Objection: According to Eph. 2:16 it is *Christ* who achieves reconciliation; according to Col. 1:20; 2:13, 14 it is *God* who does this. Similarly, Eph. 4:11 teaches that it is *Christ* who appoints apostles, prophets, evangelists, etc. This is contradicted by I Cor. 12:28 which indicates that it is *God* who exercises that function.

Answer: As is clear from II Cor. 5:18 and Eph. 4:32, it is ever *God in Christ* who is at work. Hence, deeds of this kind can be ascribed to either person. It is as the late Professor L. Berkhof remarks in his *Systematic Theology,* Grand Rapids, Mich., 1949, p. 89, "*Opera ad extra,* or those activities and effects by which the Trinity is manifested outwardly . . . are never works of one person exclusively, but always works of the Divine Being as a whole." Thus also according to John 14:16, 26 the "giving" or "sending" of the Holy Spirit is ascribed to *the Father,* but in 15:26 this "sending" is ascribed to *the Son.* There is no contradiction: it is "in the Son's name" that the Father sends the Spirit; it is "from the Father" that the Son sends him.

(c) Objection: In Ephesians *Christ's death* is no longer basic. All the attention is concentrated on *his exaltation* (1:20 ff.; 2:6; 4:8).

Answer: Although, due to the central theme of Ephesians, the emphasis has changed somewhat, Christ's death is basic, even for the author of Ephesians (1:7; 2:13; 2:16).

(d) Objection: According to Paul sinners are reconciled *to God* through the cross (II Cor. 5:20, 21; Col. 1:21, 22), but according to Ephesians the cross effects a reconciliation *between Jew and Gentile* (2:14-18; cf. 2:19-22; 3:5 ff.; 4:7-16).

Answer: There is no contradiction. By means of the cross Jew and Gentile are reconciled to God; *therefore also to each other.* That basically the reconciliation is "to God" is clearly taught in Eph. 2:16; cf. also verse 18. But, in harmony with the central theme of Ephesians — the unity of all believers in Christ; hence, the church universal — it is on the reconciliation between Jew and Gentile that the emphasis falls here.

(e) Objection: Ephesians emphasizes *Christ's ascension* (4:8 ff.). Paul has no ascension doctrine.

Answer: Christ's ascension is clearly implied in such passages as Rom. 8:34; Phil. 2:6-11; 3:20; I Thess. 1:10; 4:16; and I Tim. 3:16.

(f) Objection: Ephesians teaches Christ's descent into Hades (4:19), and is therefore clearly post-Pauline. The real Paul nowhere teaches this doctrine.

Answer: See the explanation of Eph. 4:8-10.

(4) *The Doctrine of Salvation*

(a) Objection: Ephesians teaches the doctrine of *salvation* — "for by grace y o u have been saved through faith"; Paul that of *justification* (Rom. 3:24; 5:1).

Answer: It is true that over against Jewish and Judaistic legalism the forensic aspect of the sinner's deliverance is stressed in some Pauline epistles, notably in Romans and Galatians, leading to the use of the terms "justification" and "no condemnation," while, in harmony with the theme of Ephesians — the *oneness* of all believers "in Christ" — here the mystical experience and fellowship with Christ receives somewhat more extensive treatment. However, this does not imply any contradiction. The essence of the doctrine of justification, the "not of works, but solely by grace" doctrine, is clearly expressed in Eph. 2:8, 9. See also on 4:24; 6:14. Paul never departed from this, and even subsequent to the writing of Ephesians gave eloquent expression to it (Titus 3:4-7). As to Paul's emphasis on being *saved*, and being used as God's agent in *saving* others, see Rom. 10:9, 13; 11:14; I Cor. 9:22; 15:2.

(b) Objection: The manner in which Ephesians treats *the law* is un-

Pauline. In Ephesians the law is viewed not as something of benefit to man but as an instrument of division between man and man (2:15). Paul, however, establishes a definite relation between the law and the process of salvation: he pictures the law as our guide ("tutor") who brings us to Christ (Gal. 3:24). According to him "the law is holy, and the commandment holy and righteous and good" (Rom. 7:12).

Answer: In Romans and Galatians Paul views the law from several different aspects. Viewed from one aspect it is good, as just indicated; from another it is inadequate (Rom. 8:3); and from still another it even pronounces a curse upon a person (Gal. 3:10, 13). Hence, here, too, there is no contradiction. It certainly was not necessary for the author of Ephesians to discuss *all* the various phases of the law. What he does say about it here is in harmony with what he says elsewhere.

(5) *The Doctrine of the Church*

(a) Objection: In Ephesians the term *church* always refers to the church universal (1:22; 3:10, 21; 5:23, 24, 25, 27, 29, 32). In the genuine Pauline epistles it does not (or: does not always) have this meaning.

Answer: Examples of the use of the word *church* without local reference are I Cor. 12:28; 15:9; Gal. 1:13; Phil. 3:6 (cf. Acts 20:28). In Col. 1:18, 24 the reference is to the church universal; in Col. 4:15, 16 a local congregation is indicated. Accordingly, the use of this term in Ephesians cannot be a good reason for denying Pauline authorship. Since in writing Ephesians it was not Paul's purpose to enlarge on any local conditions but rather to glorify God for the work of his grace in the church at large, the apostle naturally used the word here in this broad sense.

(b) Objection: The author's emphasis on the unity of the church shows that this epistle must have been written after Paul's death, at a time when various sects had arisen, and when it had become necessary to stress the need of a centralized ecclesiastical government.

Answer: The unity that is described and urged in Ephesians is of a spiritual character. Cf. John 17:21. It is not the organizational unity for which, in a later day, Ignatius pleaded.

(c) Objection: The extreme importance attached to "apostles and prophets" (2:20-22; 3:5), as if they were "holy" and "the foundation" of the church, befits a generation later than Paul. The apostle himself would never have written this. To him Jesus Christ is the only true foundation (I Cor. 3:11).

Answer: It is exactly because these men gave a true and enthusiastic testimony about Christ that, in a secondary sense, they could be called the foundation of the church. Not at all in themselves or because of any intrinsic merit were they entitled to this distinction, but as divinely appointed witnesses and ambassadors who were constantly pointing *away from themselves, to Christ.* This manner of speaking about Christ's plenipotentiaries originated with Christ himself (Matt. 16:18). John, the disciple whom Jesus loved, made use of the same symbolism in describing Jerusalem the Golden. He says, "And the wall of the city had twelve foundations, and on them twelve names of the twelve apostles of the Lamb" (Rev. 21:14). The fact that the author of Ephesians calls these men "holy" is no objection. They were, indeed, holy, that is, set apart and qualified by God for a unique office. All this does not plead *against* Paul as the author of Ephesians but rather *for* him. It is in strict harmony with all that he has to say about himself and about the other apostles and prophets. See the following passages: Rom. 1:1; I Cor. 3:10; 5:3, 4; 9:1; 12:28; II Cor. 10:13, 14; 12:12; Gal. 1:1, 11-17; 2:6-9.

(d) Objection: Paul could not have written Eph. 2:11. No true Jew could have viewed the sacrament of circumcision with such utter contempt.

Answer: Read what Paul says about this in Gal. 5:1-12; Phil. 3:2, 3.

(6) *The Doctrine of the Last Things*

Objection: Paul could not have written Ephesians, for in this epistle there is no suggestion of any second coming or of any event in connection with it.

Answer: The following Ephesian passages cannot be understood apart from an implied doctrine of the consummation: 1:14; 2:7; 4:13, 30; 5:5, 6, 27.

3. *Conclusion*

a. *as to the resemblance being too close*

(1) The striking *similarity* between Colossians and Ephesians is due *chiefly* to identity of authorship, time and place of writing, and general situation of those addressed. Identity of authorship also explains numerous *variations* in expressions and emphases. An imitator or forger would have adhered more closely to the original. Another reason for the *divergence* of the two letters is their different purpose, as has been explained.

(2) Since *the other letters* (that is, other than Colossians) that are traditionally ascribed to Paul were written under different circumstances with respect to both addressor and addressees (exception: Philemon), the resemblances between them and Ephesians are not quite as striking. Nevertheless, here too there are many clear parallels. And here also the same thought is frequently given a new turn. In addition to identity of authorship, hence also of doctrine, a second factor must be taken into consideration, namely, the rise, throughout the early Christian church, of common forms of expression, such forms as generally come into being whenever people become united by ties of deep convictions to which they feel impelled to bear unanimous testimony in the midst of a generally hostile environment. The increasing prevalence of such *forms* is also a factor in explaining the parallels existing between Ephesians, etc., and *the non-Pauline New Testament literature*. Among the forms there are *doxologies* of two types:

a. "Blessed be . . ." (Eph. 1:3; cf. Rom. 1:25; 9:5; II Cor. 1:3; 11:31; I Peter 1:3) and *b.* "Now to him be . . ." (Eph. 3:20, 21; cf. Rom. 11:36; Jude 24, 25); *hymns* or *hymn-fragments* (Eph. 5:14; cf. the nativity account in Luke; Col. 1:15-19; I Tim. 3:16; Book of Revelation); *tables of duties for the respective members of the family* (Eph. 5:22–6:9; cf. Col. 3:18–4:1; I Tim. 2:8-15; 6:1, 2; Titus 2:1-10; I Peter 2:12–3:7); *lists of virtues* (Eph. 4:1-3, 32; Col. 3:12-15; James 3:17; 5:8); and various others.[7] Some of these forms have an Old Testament origin. Hence, see also No. 5 below.

(3) The need of imparting uniform catechetical instruction to enquirers and recent converts would also promote unanimity in thought-expression.

(4) Similarity in form and content, whenever it occurs among New Testament writers, must also be traced further back, namely, to Christ, that is, to the Spirit-guided reflection on his person, work, and teaching. Thus, one can hardly fail to see the words recorded in Matthew 6:12 and the similar words *and action* in Luke 23:34 (forgiveness) reflected in Ephesians 4:32; I Peter 2:21-23; 3:8, 9; etc.; Christ's title, God's "beloved Son" (Matt. 3:17) echoed in Eph. 1:6; II Peter 1:17; the reference to this son's stoneship (Matt. 21:42) recurring in Eph. 2:20 and I Peter 2:4, 8; and the mention of his glorious exaltation to the Father's right hand (implied in Matt. 26:64) re-affirmed in Eph. 1:20; Acts 7:55; Heb. 1:3; 10:12; 12:2; I Peter 3:22; Rev. 12:5. Paul and the other New Testament authors were drawing water from the same Well, namely, Christ.

(5) The apostle and the other sacred writers were versed in the same Old Testament background. Thus, to take but two examples mentioned under No. (4) above, the idea of Christ's stoneship can be traced to Psalm 118:22; that of his exaltation to the Father's right hand, to Psalm 110:1.

(6) The combination of all these factors constitutes a far more satisfying explanation of the listed similarities than does the assumption that the traditional ascription of the authorship of Ephesians to Paul must be regarded as an error and that an imitator must have been at work.

b. as to the difference being too great

When this argument is applied to such matters as vocabulary and style, it has been shown in detail that whatever remains of it, after due allowance has been made for exaggeration, is accounted for by the overpowering emotion of gratitude which prompted Paul to write the letter and by the purpose he had in mind. As to alleged differences in doctrine, the following conclusion has been established: though it is certainly true that in Ephesians various doctrines receive not only greater emphasis but also broader amplification than elsewhere and new facets of well-known gems of truth are displayed, no doctrines found in other Pauline epistles find any contradiction here.

---

[7] See A. C. King, "Ephesians in the Light of Form Criticism," *ET* 63 (1951–1952), pp. 273–276.

B. *Arguments in Favor of Pauline Authorship Stated*

1. The writer calls himself "Paul, an apostle of Christ Jesus" (1:1); and "I, Paul, the prisoner of Christ Jesus for the sake of y o u Gentiles" (3:1; cf. 4:1). Just before he pronounces the final benediction he states, "But in order that y o u also may know my affairs, how I am getting along, Tychicus, the beloved brother and faithful minister in the Lord, will make them all known to y o u, whom I am sending to y o u for this very purpose, that y o u may know our circumstances and that he may strengthen y o u r hearts" (6:21, 22). Would a disciple of Paul, a collector of his letters whose mind was saturated with Pauline teaching, have dared to identify himself with Paul so brazenly? The burden of proof surely rests on those who say that the writer, though calling himself Paul and delegating someone to tell those for whom the letter was intended how he, Paul, was getting along, was not actually Paul but Onesimus, Tychicus, or someone else.

2. Ephesians has all the characteristics of such almost universally recognized Pauline epistles as Romans, I and II Corinthians, Galatians, and Philippians. It resembles Colossians in many ways, as has been shown. To prove this remarkable similarity between Ephesians and the other Pauline epistles one need only compare the list given below with that found in N.T.C. on Colossians and Philemon, pp. 33, 34. Limiting ourselves now to Ephesians note the following:

		Ephesians
a.	The author is deeply interested in those whom he addresses	1:16; 3:14-19; 5:15-21
b.	He loves to encourage and praise them	1:15; 2:1
c.	He traces every virtue of those whom he addresses to God, ascribing all the glory to him alone	1:3-5; 2:1
d.	He writes touchingly about the supremacy of love	5:1, 2, 25, 28, 33
e.	He is filled with gratitude to God who laid hold on him and made him, though unworthy, a minister of the gospel	3:6-9
f.	He lists virtues and vices	4:17–5:21
g.	He is never afraid to assert his authority	3:4; 4:17–6:22
h.	When conditions are at all favorable he thanks God for those addressed and at times assures them of his constant prayer for them	1:15 ff.; 3:14-19
i.	He warns earnestly against those who are seeking to lead others astray	4:14, 17-19; 5:3-7; 6:10 ff.
j.	He loves "the gospel"	1:13; 3:6; 6:15, 19

3. It is hard to believe that somewhere in the early church there existed a genius of a forger who blended the genuine writings of Paul into a com-

posite so excellent in style, logical in arrangement, and lofty in content that he must have been at least the apostle's peer in intellectual ability and spiritual insight, able even to provide the church with a further development of Pauline thoughts, and then leave no trace behind as to his identity.

4. The testimony of the early church is in harmony with the conclusion that has been established. Thus, Eusebius, having made a thorough study of the sources within his reach, states: "But clearly evident and plain are the fourteen (letters) of Paul; yet it is not right to ignore that some dispute the (letter) to the Hebrews" (*Ecclesiastical History* III.iii.4, 5). It is clear, therefore, that this great church-historian, writing at the beginning of the fourth century, was well aware of the fact that the entire orthodox church of his day and age recognized Ephesians as an authentic epistle of Paul.

From Eusebius we go back to Origen (fl. 210–250), who in his work *On Principles* (*De Principiis*) quotes several passages from Ephesians, assigning them to "the apostle" or to "Paul himself" (II.iii.5; II.xi.5; III.v.4). In his chief apology *Against Celsus* (*Contra Celsum*) he says (chapter 72), "The apostle Paul declares," and then quotes Eph. 2:3.

From Origen we go back still further, to his teacher, Clement of Alexandria (fl. 190–200). In his work *The Instructor* (*Paedagogus* I.5) he quotes Eph. 4:13-15, ascribing it to "the apostle" (according to the preceding context).

About the same time Tertullian (fl. 193–216) in his work *Against Marcion* (*Adv. Marcionem* V.17) declares, "We have it on the true tradition of the church that this epistle was sent to the Ephesians, not to the Laodiceans. Marcion, however, was very desirous of giving it the new title, as if he were extremely accurate in investigating such a point. But of what consequence are the titles, since in writing to a certain church the apostle did in fact write to all." Again (V.11), "I here skip the discussion concerning another epistle, which we hold to have been written to the Ephesians, but the heretics to the Laodiceans."

Earlier by a few years, but still for a long time a contemporary of Clement of Alexandria and of Tertullian, was Irenaeus, who in his work *Against Heresies* (*Adversus Haereses,* I.viii.5) states, "This also Paul declares in these words," and then quotes Eph. 5:13. Similarly (V.ii.3), ". . . even as the blessed Paul declares in his epistle to the Ephesians, 'We are members of his body and of his flesh and of his bones.' " Cf. Eph. 5:30. This testimony of Irenaeus, in which he clearly names Paul as the author of Ephesians, is very significant, for Irenaeus had traveled widely and was rather thoroughly acquainted with the entire church of his day and age, a period of early history in which the traditions of the apostles were still very much alive.

The Muratorian Fragment (about 180–200), a survey of New Testament books, definitely names Paul as the author of Ephesians.

But we can go back even further than the latter part of the second century A.D. Skipping disputed allusions to Ephesians in *The Shepherd of Hermas, The Teaching of the Apostles (Didache)*, the so-called *Epistle of Barnabas*, etc., because such controversial passages have but little if any decisive value, we come now to such authors who not only flourished at one time or another during the period 100–170, but also furnished clear evidence for the existence and recognition of this epistle in their day. At a time so close to that of the apostles it was not necessary to mention the very names of the latter. Quoting their *writings*, with implied assumption that these were well known and were considered authoritative by the church, is all that we can expect from these early witnesses. I do not deny that those who reject the Pauline authorship of Ephesians will, of course, even deny the relevancy of the passages about to be quoted. But in doing so they labor under difficulties that are but too evident. Note, then, the following:

Polycarp states, ". . . knowing that 'by grace y o u have been saved, not by works' " (*Letter to the Philippians* I.3, quoting from Eph. 2:8, 9). Again, "Only as it is said in these Scriptures, 'Be angry but do not sin,' and 'Let not the sun go down on that angry mood of y o u r s'" (XII.1, Latin, quoting Eph. 4:26). Anent this letter of Polycarp see also N.T.C. on Philippians, p. 16.

We come now to Ignatius and his letter *To the Ephesians*.[8] The clearest reference to Paul's Ephesians is found in the opening paragraph (I.1), ". . . being imitators of God." These words immediately remind one of Paul's exhortation, "Be therefore imitators of God" (Eph. 5:1). And when Ignatius compares believers to "stones of the sanctuary of the Father, made ready for the building of God our Father" (IX.1), is not the reference to Paul's statement in Eph. 2:20-22 rather obvious?

Clement of Rome (as representing the church of Rome) writes, "Through him the eyes of our hearts were opened" (*The First Epistle of Clement to the Corinthians* XXXVI.2). Is not this a near-quotation of Eph. 1:18: ". . . that the eyes of y o u r hearts may be illumined"? Compare also: "Or have we not one God and one Christ and one Spirit of grace poured out upon us, and one calling in Christ?" (XLVI.6) with this sentence from Paul, "There is . . . one Spirit, just as also y o u were called in one hope which y o u r calling brought y o u [lit. 'of y o u r calling'], one Lord . . . one God and Father of all" (Eph. 4:4-6).

According to Hippolytus, the Basilides, Ophites, and Valentinians used Paul's Ephesian letter. Now these three were among the earliest of the Gnostic sects. The Epistle to the Ephesians was, moreover, also included in Marcion's Canon (though, as has already been indicated, under a different

---

[8] However, I purposely skip the debate with reference to XII.2. It is not needed to prove the point.

title) , in the Old Latin, and in the Old Syriac. Finally, there is the possibility that Col. 4:16 refers to this letter. See N.T.C. on that passage.

It has been shown, therefore, that as soon as the church began to assign the New Testament writings to definite authors it "with one accord" named Paul as the author of Ephesians. There was no doubt or dissent. This definite ascription began about the latter part of the second century. But even earlier than this the existence of the letter and the high value which the church attached to it as inspired Scripture was everywhere recognized. There is no reason to depart from these traditional convictions.

IV. Destination and Purpose

A. *Destination*

1. *The Facts and the Problem Arising from Them*

A real difficulty confronts us because Eph. 1:1, which in A.V., etc., mentions those to whom the letter was addressed, does not read the same in all the Greek manuscripts. The opening words, "Paul, an apostle of Christ Jesus through the will of God, to the saints and believers in Christ Jesus who are," furnish no serious textual problem. The difficulty arises with the additional phrase "in Ephesus" ($\dot{\epsilon}\nu$ 'Εφέσῳ) . This phrase is not found in the oldest extant manuscripts: it is absent from p[46], dating from the second century, and from the unrevised *Sinaiticus* and *Vaticanus,* dating from the fourth.[9] As most scholars see it, a comment by Origen (early third century) implies that it was not in the text he used. A remark by Basil (about A.D. 370) has led to a similar conclusion with respect to the text on which he commented.

On the other hand, with one exception, from the middle of the second century *the title* above the letter has always been "To the Ephesians." The one exception was Marcion's copy in which the epistle bore the title "To the Laodiceans." It is commonly held, with good reason, that this departure from the rule was due to a misinterpretation of Col. 4:16. The manner in which Tertullian criticized Marcion for accepting (or originating?) this error has been noted (see III B 5 above) . Also, with near-unanimity later manuscripts have "in Ephesus" in *the text* of 1:1. The versions also with one accord support this reading.

The problem, accordingly, is this: How can we explain the absence of the phrase "in Ephesus" from the earliest extant manuscripts in the light of the otherwise well-nigh unanimous testimony in favor of its inclusion? And what light do these facts shed on the real destination of Ephesians?

---

[9] It was also left out by the corrector of 424, whose corrections were based on a very ancient manuscript, and by 1739.

2. *Various Proposed Solutions*

a. *The letter was not intended for any specific locality whether large or small but rather for believers everywhere and at any time.*

According to this view, whatever *the title* may say, the words "in Ephesus" were never meant by Paul to be inserted. There are two main forms of this theory. According to the first, Paul addressed his message to the saints "who *are*," that is, who alone have true *being*, since Christ, in whom they live, is the one who truly IS. Is not he the great I AM? (cf. Ex. 3:14; John 6:35, 48; 8:12; 10:7, 9, 11, 14; etc.; Rev. 1:8; 22:13). This interpretation was suggested by Origen. Basil also adopts it. According to the second, Paul is simply writing "to the saints who are also faithful in Christ Jesus." This, with omission of the words "in Ephesus," is found not only in the text of R.S.V. but favored also, with some variation in wording, by many others, both translators and expositors: Beare, Findlay, Goodspeed, Mackay, Williams, etc.

Evaluation: Elsewhere in Paul's epistles the words "who are" or (the church) "which is," when present in the original, are consistently followed by a place-designation (Rom. 1:7; I Cor. 1:2; II Cor. 1:1; Phil. 1:1). Accordingly, there is no valid reason to assume that the occurrence of the words "who are" in Ephesians was to be an exception to this rule. There is nothing in Paul's other epistles that lends support to the metaphysical explanation presented by Origen and Basil. And as to the similarly non-local rendering "the saints who are also faithful," this rendering, besides being likewise exposed to the objection just mentioned, can be given a reasonable sense only if it be not interpreted to mean that there were some saints who were faithful and other saints who were not.

Though for the reason stated (Pauline usage elsewhere) I cannot accept the theory endorsed by R.S.V., etc., I am, nevertheless, of the opinion that it contains a point of value that should not be passed by. What Tertullian already pointed out is true, namely, that "in writing to a certain church the apostle did in fact write to all" (see above III B 5). In Ephesians, as well as in all the other epistles, etc., the Spirit is addressing *all* the churches both then and now. In fact the ecumenical theme of Ephesians adds emphasis to this point! It is possible to stress too strongly the local reference. However, this does not mean that the question whether or not the words "in Ephesus" should be retained can be dismissed as of no value whatever.

b. *The letter, though sent to believers living in a definite and limited region, was not in any sense meant for Ephesus.*

This theory is defended, among others, by T. K. Abbott in his work *The Epistles to the Ephesians and to the Colossians* (*International Critical Commentary*), New York, 1916, p. viii; and by E. F. Scott in his brief exposition, *The Epistles of Paul to the Colossians, to Philemon and to the Ephesians* (*Moffatt New Testament Commentary*), New York, 1930, pp. 121, 122.

According to Abbott Ephesians was meant for the Gentile converts in Laodicea, Hierapolis, Colosse, etc. Scott writes, ". . . nothing is certain except
that the letter was not written to the Ephesians." Grounds: "in Ephesus" is
lacking in the best manuscripts; there are no intimate touches; the implication of 1:15; 3:2; 4:21, 22 altogether rules out Ephesus.

Answer: It is hardly conceivable that Paul, who had spent so much time
and energy in Ephesus, would write a letter to the churches of Proconsular
Asia, excluding Ephesus!

The next two theories should be considered together. They agree basically, for both proceed from the assumption that in one sense or another
the letter was sent to Ephesus. They differ in that c. interprets "in Ephesus"
regionally; d. locally.

    c. *The letter was addressed to the believers who resided in the prov-
ince of which Ephesus was the chief city. It was a circular letter intended
not only for the local church but also for the surrounding congregations in
Proconsular Asia.*

Today this is a widely accepted view.

    d. *The letter was sent to one specific, local church, namely, the one at
Ephesus, just as Philippians was sent to the church at Philippi, and I and
II Corinthians to the church at Corinth.*

For the defense of this view and the refutation of the circular-letter or
encyclical idea in any form see especially R. C. H. Lenski, *op. cit.*, pp. 329–
341.

Those who favor the circular letter theory, c., advance the following reasons for their view (these being the same as those under b. but with less
rigid application):

(1) The words "in Ephesus" are omitted in the best and most ancient
manuscripts. Hence, there is really no good reason to retain this place-
designation unless we interpret it as referring to the region of which Ephesus
was the metropolis.

(2) The words ". . . because *I have heard* of the faith in the Lord Jesus
that (exists) among y o u" (1:15) and ". . . *if so be that* y o u *have heard*
of the stewardship of God's grace that was given to me" (3:2; cf. 4:21, 22)
clearly imply that among the addressed there were those with whom Paul
was not acquainted and who had never stood in close personal relationship
to him. Had the letter been intended solely for believers living in the city
of Ephesus, with whom the apostle had established such very close ties (read
especially Acts 20:36-38), he could never have expressed himself in this
manner.

(3) In every epistle addressed by Paul to a congregation which he had
founded or with which he had become personally acquainted there is a reference to the fact that he was the spiritual father of the church and had

labored in its midst (I Cor. 1:14; 2:1; 3:5-10; 11:23; 15:1-11; II Cor. 3:3; Gal. 1:8; 4:13-20; Phil. 1:27-30; I Thess. 1:5; 2:1-5). No such reference occurs in Ephesians. On the contrary, the epistle is completely lacking in intimate touches, items of personal information, or allusions to the work which the apostle had performed in the city and church of Ephesus, as recorded in Acts 18:18-21; 19; 20:17-38. If Ephesians was never intended as a letter to one specific congregation but rather as a circular letter sent to *several* churches, including Ephesus, this is understandable.

(4) Sometimes — *but now seldom* — a fourth reason is added: The epistle contains no personal greetings; yet, if it had been intended exclusively for the congregation at Ephesus these would not have been lacking.

Those who believe that the epistle was addressed solely to the church at Ephesus and was not a circular letter answer as follows:

(1) In all ancient manuscripts (except Marcion's) the letter bears *the title: To the Ephesians.* All the ancient *versions* have "in Ephesus" in verse 1. How shall we explain that title and those versions if the letter was not originally intended for the congregation at Ephesus? As to the absence of "in Ephesus" from 1:1 of the most ancient manuscripts, is it not possible that someone tampered with the text? Nearly all the later Greek *manuscripts* contain the disputed phrase. How do those who reject its genuine character explain that?

(2) As to 1:15, 3:2, and 4:21, 22, this is a matter of interpretation. See Commentary on these passages.

(3) It is not certain that there is no connection between the record of Paul's work found in Acts and the contents of this epistle. On the contrary, of which letter can it be said more truly that it proclaims "the whole counsel of God" (cf. Eph. 1:3-14)? Now according to Acts 20:27 that is exactly the characterization of Paul's preaching at Ephesus. See also on Eph. 2:20-22. Absence of major local problems that troubled the congregation may explain why Paul does not in this letter refer to the manner in which he had been received when he founded the church. Moreover, as to intimate touches and news with respect to himself, this is explained in 6:21, 22: Tychicus was able to supply full information.

(4) II Corinthians, Galatians, I and II Thessalonians also lack greetings though written to churches founded by Paul. On the other hand, Romans, addressed to a church not founded by the apostle, contains a great many greetings.

Evaluation: It is clear that *not all the reasons advanced in favor of the circular letter theory are valid.* No. (4) particularly is weak, and has been dropped by many proponents of the encyclical idea. It is doubtful, though, whether the rebuttal to No. (3) is fully satisfying. The lack or rather inconsiderable amount of local color and of personal touches as well as the broad and exalted theme (the church universal) would seem to harmonize better with the encyclical theory than with the purely local. There is, moreover, another fact that would seem to lend even greater support to this circular letter view. It would have been almost impossible for Paul to address a letter to the believers in Ephesus and not also to include those in the surrounding churches. Ephesus was the heart and center of the Christian community, as is very clear from Acts 19:10, which implies that when Paul was laboring in this city people from all around came streaming to hear him. As a result, "all those who were living in Asia heard the word of the Lord, both Jews and Greeks." In the Book of Revelation, too, the very first of the circle of seven letters is addressed to the church at Ephesus (Rev. 2:1-7). Accordingly, I favor theory c. But on the basis of either view (c. or d.) the words "in Ephesus" can be safely retained in our translation of Eph. 1:1.

Now in elaborating on the circular letter theory a popular view (proposed by Beza and endorsed by Archbishop Ussher) is that originally a blank had been left after the words "who are," and that Tychicus or someone else had been asked to make several copies, one for this church, one for that, in order, in each separate case, to fill in this blank by *writing* into it the name of the church for which the particular copy was intended. Furthermore, according to this theory, in the end the phrase "in Ephesus" became standardized because the church in that city was the most important one.

Possible objections to this theory are the following: First, are we not thus assuming for Ephesians a method of letter-distribution which "savors more of modern than of ancient manner" (Abbott)? Secondly, how do we explain the fact that a totally different method of letter-circulation is clearly indicated in Col. 4:16? Thirdly, if this seriatim labeling of blank spaces is what actually took place, how is it that there is no trace of copies in which 1:1 has any other name than that of Ephesus?

We shall have to admit that we do not know how and why the change from omission of "in Ephesus" to its insertion (or vice versa) occurred. Lenski, proceeding from the idea that the words "in Ephesus" were in the text from the very beginning, conjectures that Marcion may have tampered with the text of his day. However, this is not the only and perhaps not even the most charitable manner of solving the problem. Another suggestion — *again, a mere possibility!* — would be that *in full harmony with the expressed wishes of the apostle* and with thorough candor toward all concerned, the following took place:

The original letter, the autograph, left a blank, let us assume, after the words "who are." When this letter was read to any congregation assembled for worship, this blank was filled in *orally*, in each case in a manner suitable to the place where it was read. After the letter had been thus read to the church at Ephesus, it began its circular journey, arriving next at Laodicea. Here, before it was sent forward on its way to the next church,

Colosse (Col. 4:16?), a copy was made, enabling the members of the Laodicean church and also the brothers and sisters across the river (in Hierapolis) to be reminded again and again of the beauty of the inspired contents. This copy was true in every way to the *written* original, even to the point of retaining the blank space. This state of the letter is reflected in *the oldest extant manuscripts.* Finally, each church having made a copy, the autograph, having completed its circuit of the various congregations for which it was originally intended, was returned to Ephesus to rest in the archives of that church. However, by previous direction from Paul, the words "in Ephesus" were now inserted, for by now believers everywhere would understand that this place-designation had reference to *Greater* Ephesus, that is, to *Ephesus proper and the surrounding churches.* Just how far out this circle extended we do not know. Moreover, though the letter was now resting in the Ephesian archives, it was not unproductive. From this great center copies went out whenever they were needed. These copies contained the phrase "in Ephesus," exactly as reflected in nearly all *the later manuscripts.*

I repeat: all this is merely one of many possibilities. What actually happened may have been something entirely different. Nevertheless, the suggested possibility is not burdened with the three objections, mentioned earlier, to which the theory of the immediate seriatim labeling of blank spaces is exposed. Neither does it heap even more odium on the name of Marcion. As to doing this, did not Tertullian take care of it in an astoundingly thorough manner? (*Against Marcion* I.1).

3. *Conclusion*

The destination of the letter was "Ephesus," in the sense explained: the churches of Ephesus and surroundings. Place and time of writing: Rome, somewhere near the middle of the period A.D. 61–63. See N.T.C. on Colossians and Philemon, p. 28; on Philippians, pp. 21–30.

B. *Purpose*

1. Paul wrote this letter in order to express his inner satisfaction with the Christ-centered faith of the addressed and their love for all the saints (1:15). The departure of Tychicus and Onesimus for Colosse (6:21, 22; cf. Col. 4:7-9) enabled the apostle to convey his warm greetings, etc., to the believers in Ephesus, through which city these emissaries would be passing. The same message must be communicated to the surrounding churches.

2. A closely related purpose was to picture God's glorious redemptive grace toward the church, bestowed upon it in order that it might be a blessing to the world and might stand united over against all the forces of evil and thus glorify its Redeemer.

In what Paul says about this glorious church he pushes every line of thought to its very limit. Thus he makes clear that neither good works nor even faith but the gracious plan of God "in Christ" from eternity, hence

61

Christ himself, is the church's true *foundation* (1:3 ff.). **Christ** controls nothing less than *the entire universe* in the interest of the **church** (1:20-22). *Both* Jew and Gentile are included in the *scope* of redemption (2:14, 18), in connection with which *all things* are brought under the headship of Christ, the things in the heavens and the things on the earth (1:10). The saving process does not stop when men are "converted." On the contrary, the believers' *goal* must be to attain to "the measure of the stature of the fulness of Christ" (4:13). In order to reach this goal *all* must manifest their *oneness* in Christ and must *grow up in all things* into him (4:1-16). Paul prays that believers may be enabled to know the love of Christ that surpasses knowledge, that they may be filled *to all the fulness* of God (3:19). The wisdom of God *in all its infinite variety* must be proclaimed by the church. Moreover, not only to the world must it be made known but also "to the principalities and the authorities in the heavenly places" (3:10). *Every* member of the household must make his *renewal* manifest (5:22–6:9). In the struggle against evil the church, acting as one body, must make effective use of *the entire panoply* provided by God (6:11 ff.).

It is not impossible that Paul's exuberant doxology at the beginning of this letter was due *in part* to the fact that he saw in the hearts and lives of the addressed, as reported to him, a partial but significant degree of progress in the realization of God's plan for his church. But this was not the only reason for joy and praise. See on 1:3.

3. It is possible that in writing this letter the apostle also intended to draw a contrast between the Roman empire, by which he was being held a prisoner, and the church. That this possibility cannot be entirely dismissed appears from another letter composed during this same imprisonment (Phil. 3:20). If so, then Rome's *glamor* may have suggested to him the church's *glory;* Rome's stern dictator who ruled over a vast yet limited domain, the church's gracious Lord, sovereign over all; its political consolidation by physical force, the church's organic unity in the bond of peace; its military might, the church's spiritual armor; and its foundation in time and "change and decay," the church's eternal foundation and endless duration.

V. Theme and Outline

If it be true that in Colossians Paul dwells on "Christ, the Pre-eminent One, the Only and All-Sufficient Savior," then in Ephesians he discusses its corollary, namely, "The Unity of All Believers *in Christ.*" For "All Believers" one can substitute "The Church Glorious." The ideas of "unity" and of the "in Christ" relationship can be given their proper place in the Outline. Careful study of Ephesians has led an ever-increasing number of exegetes to arrive at the conclusion that the concept of *the church* receives such emphasis in this epistle that the entire contents can be grouped around it without superimposing one's own subjective opinions upon the apostle's thinking.[10]

The term *church*, as here used, indicates the *body* (Eph. 1:22, 23; 4:4, 16; 5:23, 30), *building* (2:19-22), and *bride* (5:25-27, 32) of Christ; the totality of those, whether Jew or Gentile, who were saved through the blood of Christ and through him have their access in one Spirit to the Father (2:13, 18).

As in Romans and Colossians so also here in Ephesians there is a rather clear-cut division between *Exposition* and *Exhortation*, between the truth *stated* and the truth *applied;* chapters 1–3 belonging to the first, chapters 4–6 to the second part. The style, especially of the first division, is, however, so exalted that *Adoration* more precisely expresses what is offered here than *Exposition*. The soul of the apostle is filled with humble gratitude to God, the Author of the Church Glorious. He pours out his heart in sincere, spontaneous, lavish praise. *With Paul doctrine is doxology!* It is a matter not only of the mind but also of the heart, of Christian experience under the guidance of inspiration.

After the opening salutation (1:1, 2) the body of the letter begins, in the original, with the word *E u l o g ē t ó s* (Blessed!). The apostle *eulogizes* (bestows high praise upon) God for his marvelous blessings to the church. To aid the memory an *acronym* can be made of the first six letters of this opening word, read downward: E This yields the following

U

L

O

G

E

Brief Summary of Ephesians

Theme: *The Church Glorious*

I. *Adoration*
for its

ch. 1   *E* ternal Foundation "in Christ"

After the salutation (verses 1, 2) the doxology begins as follows:

"Blessed (be) the God and Father of our Lord Jesus

---

[10] See W. E. Ward, "One Body — the Church," *RE*, Vol. 60, No. 4 (Fall, 1963), pp. 398-413; F. W. Beare, *The Epistle to the Ephesians (Interpreter's Bible,* Vol. X), New York and Nashville, 1953, pp. 606, 607; and L. Berkhof, *New Testament Introduction*, Grand Rapids, 1916, p. 189. The latter points out that while Colossians discusses Christ, the head of the church, Ephesians is concerned more emphatically with the church, the body of Christ.

Christ, who has blessed us with every spiritual blessing in the heavenly places in Christ, just as he elected us in him before the foundation of the world, that we should be holy and faultless before him" (1:4, 5).

ch. 2   *U* niversal Scope (embracing both Jew and Gentile)
"For through him we both have our access in one Spirit to the Father" (2:18).

ch. 3   *L* ofty Goal
"in order that now to the principalities and the authorities in the heavenly places might be made known through the church the iridescent wisdom of God . . . (and) to know the love of Christ that surpasses knowledge; in order that y o u may be filled to all the fulness of God" (3:10, 19).

II. *Exhortation*
describing and urging:

ch. 4:1-16   *O* rganic Unity (amid Diversity) and Growth into Christ
"I, therefore, the prisoner in the Lord, entreat y o u to . . . make every effort to preserve the unity imparted by the Spirit by means of the bond (consisting in) peace . . . so that we . . . adhering to the truth in love may grow up in all things into him who is the head, even Christ" (4:1, 3, 14, 15).

ch. 4:17–6:9   *G* lorious Renewal
". . . with respect to y o u r former manner of life y o u must put off the old man . . . and must be renewed in the spirit of y o u r minds, and put on the new man" (4:22-24).

ch. 6:10-24   *E* ffective Armor
"Put on the full armor of God in order that y o u may be able to stand firm against the crafty methods of the devil" (6:11). Conclusion (verses 21-24).

Below is a more extended

Outline of Ephesians

Theme: *The Church Glorious*

I. *Adoration*
for its

ch. 1   *E* ternal Foundation "in Christ"
After the opening salutation (verses 1 and 2) Paul "blesses" God for the fact that this is a foundation:

1. resulting in "every spiritual blessing" for believers, unto the praise of the glory of God the Father and the Son and the Holy Spirit (1:3-14); and
2. leading to thanksgiving and prayer, that the eyes of those addressed may be illumined in order to see God's saving power, exhibited in the resurrection and coronation of Christ (1:15-23).

ch. 2   *U* niversal Scope (embracing both Jew and Gentile),
1. secured by the great redemptive blessings *for both* which center "in Christ" and parallel his resurrection and triumphant life (2:1-10);
2. shown by the reconciliation of Jew and Gentile through the cross (2:11-18);
3. and by the fact that the church of Jew and Gentile is growing into *one* building, a holy sanctuary in the Lord, of which Christ Jesus is himself the chief cornerstone (2:19-22).

ch. 3   *L* ofty Goal
1. *To make known* to the principalities and the powers in the heavenly places *God's iridescent wisdom,* reflected in the mystery revealed especially, though not exclusively, to Paul, namely, that the Gentiles are . . . fellow-members of the body of Christ (3:1-13); and
2. *To know the love of Christ that surpasses knowledge* so as to be filled to all the fulness of God (3:14-19). Doxology (3:20-21).

II. *Exhortation*
describing and
urging upon all:

ch. 4:1-16   *O* rganic Unity (amid Diversity) and Growth into Christ

urging

ch. 4:17–6:9   *G* lorious Renewal
1. *upon all* (4:17–5:21)
   a. "Put off the old man. Be renewed. Put on the new man."
   b. "Do not give the devil a foothold. Be imitators of God."
   c. "Y o u were formerly darkness, but now y o u are light in the Lord; as children of light ever walk."
   d. "Do not get drunk on wine, but be filled with the Spirit."

2. *upon special groups* (5:22–6:9)
   a. "Wives, be subject to y o u r own husbands. Husbands, love y o u r wives."
   b. "Children, obey y o u r parents. Fathers, rear them tenderly."
   c. "Slaves, obey y o u r masters. Masters, stop threatening."

urging all to put on
the Church's God-given

ch. 6:10-24   *E* ffective Armor. Conclusion
   1. "Put on the full armor of God" (6:10-20) ;
   2. Conclusion (6:21-24) .

Commentary

on

The Epistle to the Ephesians

Chapter 1

Verses 1-14

Theme: *The Church Glorious*

I. *Adoration*
for its

E ternal Foundation "in Christ"

After the opening salutation (verses 1 and 2) Paul "blesses" God for the fact that this is a foundation:

1. resulting in "every spiritual blessing" for believers, unto the praise of the glory of God the Father and the Son and the Holy Spirit (verses 3-14)

CHAPTER I

EPHESIANS

1 1 Paul, an apostle of Christ Jesus through the will of God, to the saints and believers who are in Ephesus in Christ Jesus; 2 grace to y o u and peace from God our Father and the Lord Jesus Christ.

3 Blessed (be) the God and Father of our Lord Jesus Christ, who has blessed us with every spiritual blessing in the heavenly places in Christ, 4 just as he elected us in him before the foundation of the world, that we should be holy and faultless before him, 5 having in love foreordained us to adoption as sons through Jesus Christ for himself, according to the good pleasure of his will, 6 to the praise of the glory of his grace, which he graciously bestowed on us in the Beloved, 7 in whom we have our redemption through his blood, the forgiveness of our trespasses, according to the riches of his grace, 8 which he caused to overflow toward us in the form of all wisdom and insight, 9 in that he made known to us the mystery of his will, according to his good pleasure, the purpose which he cherished for himself in him, 10 to be put into effect in the fulness of the times, to bring all things together under one head in Christ, the things in the heavens and the things on the earth; in him 11 in whom we also have been made heirs, having been foreordained according to the purpose of him who accomplishes all things according to the counsel of his will, 12 to the end that we should be to the praise of his glory, we who beforehand had centered our hope in Christ; 13 in whom y o u also (are included), having listened to the message of the truth, the gospel of y o u r salvation; and having also believed in him, y o u were sealed with the promised Holy Spirit, 14 who is the first instalment of our inheritance, for the redemption of (God's) own possession, to the praise of his glory.

1:1, 2

Opening Salutation

1. As is not unusual with Paul, the letter opens with a salutation and closes with a benediction. At the beginning God, as it were, walks into the church assembled for worship and breathes his blessing upon it. He remains throughout and at the close of the worship-service walks out again, not out *of* the church but out *with* the church. Yet, it is **Paul** himself who is speaking in this letter. And he is not playing back electrically recorded dictation. Ephesians is not a belt from a transcriber or a reel from a recorder. On the contrary, here is Paul in person, pouring out his heart in praise and thanksgiving. What he writes is in very fact the product of his own meditation and reflection. It is both a spontaneous utterance of *his* heart and a careful composition of *his* mind. The gold that pours forth from his heart has been

69

molded into definite and (one may even say) artistic shape by his mind. But this heart and this mind are so thoroughly Spirit-controlled that the *ideas* expressed and the very *words* by means of which they are conveyed are also (in a sense, were first of all) the ideas and the words of the Holy Spirit. Hence, the word of Paul is the Word of God. Ephesians, as well as the rest of Scripture, is God-breathed. Cf. II Peter 1:21; II Tim. 3:16; and on the latter passage see N.T.C. on I and II Timothy and Titus, pp. 301–304.

The author of this epistle was a man whose Hebrew name was Saul, and whose Latin name was Paul*us* (here, in the original, grecized to Paulo*s*). He is not just any private individual who happens to have something on his mind to which he wants to give expression. No, he is, and wants the Ephesians to know that he is, **an apostle of Christ Jesus,** and this not in the broader sense merely but in the fullest meaning that can properly be given to the word *apostle*. Has he not received his call to office directly from Christ? Were not the marks of plenary apostleship abundantly evident in his life and work? He belongs to Christ, and represents him, so that *Paul's* message is *Christ's* own message. When Paul salutes the Ephesians, "God the Father and the Lord Jesus Christ" are bestowing *their* blessing upon them.

Paul continues, **through the will of God.** The apostle has attained his high office neither through *aspiration* nor through *usurpation* nor yet through *nomination* by other men but by divine *preparation,* having been set apart and qualified by the activity of God's sovereign will.

Having thus in some detail set forth the name of the addressor, Paul now turns to the addressees. He is writing **to the saints and believers who are in Ephesus in Christ Jesus.** The saints are those who by the Lord have been *set apart* to glorify him, *the consecrated ones,* whose task it is to proclaim God's excellencies (I Peter 2:9). The phrase "the saints and believers" forms a unit. The same people who are called *saints* are also called *believers,* for saints who are true to their calling do, indeed, repose their trust in the one true God who has revealed himself in Christ.[11]

The phrase "in Ephesus" has been fully discussed in the *Introduction,* IV A. Destination. Paul writes to God's people in Ephesus and surroundings. Those addressed are "in Christ Jesus," that is, they are what they are by virtue of union with him.[12] This phrase may without exaggeration be

---

[11] That the expression is a unit is shown also by the fact that in the original the definite article is not repeated before the second word. This non-repetition also indicates that it is correct to translate the second as well as the first of the two words as a noun, not an adjective; hence, *believers,* not *faithful.* The *believers* here in Eph. 1:1 are comparable to the *believing brothers* in Col. 1:2.

[12] The rendering "to the saints and believers in Christ Jesus" (instead of "to the saints and believers who are in Ephesus in Christ Jesus") makes it appear as if Christ Jesus were here conceived as the object of the implied verb *believe.* But this would be contrary to the usual meaning of the phrase "in Christ Jesus," and would

called the most important one in all the Pauline epistles. In Ephesians it or its equivalent ("in him," "in whom," "in the Beloved") or near-equivalent ("in the Lord") occurs in 1:1, 3, 4, 6, 7, 9-13, 15, 20; 2:5-7, 10, 13, 21, 22; 3:6, 11, 12, 21; 4:1, 21, 32; 5:8; and 6:10, 21. It also occurs with greater or lesser frequency in Paul's other epistles (exception Titus). It was *by virtue of union with Christ* that the addressees were saints and believers, for in connection with him they receive "every spiritual blessing" (1:3); here particularly and basically *election* before the foundation of the world (1:4-6), *redemption* through blood (1:7-12), and *certification* ("sealing") as sons and therefore heirs (1:13, 14). It will be clear that this interpretation of the phrase fits the present context. Had it not been for their connection with Christ, a connection infinitely close, these people would not now be saints and believers. Moreover, their present life of faith has its center in him. For them "to live is Christ" (Phil. 1:21). They now love him because he has first loved them.

2. The salutation proper is as follows: **grace to y o u and peace from God our Father and the Lord Jesus Christ.** Thus, there is pronounced upon the Ephesian saints and believers *grace.* This word may at times indicate *kindness, as a quality or attribute of God or of the Lord Jesus Christ.* It may also describe *the state of salvation,* and thirdly, the *believer's gratitude* for the salvation received or for any gift of God. But in the present instance it refers undoubtedly to *God's spontaneous, unmerited favor in action, his freely bestowed lovingkindness in operation, bestowing salvation upon guilt-laden sinners. Grace* is the fountain. *Peace* belongs to the stream of spiritual blessings which issues from this fountain. This peace is the smile of God as it reflects itself in the hearts of the redeemed, the assurance of reconciliation through the blood of the cross, true spiritual wholeness and prosperity. It is the great blessing which Christ by his atoning sacrifice bestowed upon the church (John 14:27), and it surpasses all understanding (Phil. 4:7).

Now this grace and this peace have their origin in God the Father (James 1:17), and have been merited for the believer by him who is the great Master-Owner-Conqueror ("Lord"), Savior ("Jesus"), and Office-Bearer ("Christ") and who, because of his threefold anointing — namely, as Prophet, Priest, and King — "is able to save to the uttermost them that draw near to God through him" (Heb. 7:25).[13]

For further details about certain aspects of Paul's opening salutations see N.T.C. on I and II Thessalonians, pp. 37–45; on Philippians, pp. 43–49; and on I and II Timothy and Titus, pp. 49–56; 339–344.

---

also destroy the unity of the pair "saints and believers," as if the words "in Christ Jesus" modified the second word only.

[13] The *one* preposition *from* introduces the entire expression "God our Father and the Lord Jesus Christ," showing that these two Persons are placed on the level of complete equality.

1:3-14

Proceeding now to the body of the letter, Paul "blesses" God for the church's *Eternal Foundation* "in Christ," a foundation:

1. resulting *"in every spiritual blessing"* for *believers, to the praise of the glory of God the Father and the Son and the Holy Spirit.*

3. Blessed (be) the God and Father of our Lord Jesus Christ. Goodness, truth, and beauty are combined in this initial doxology, in which the apostle, in words that are *beautiful* both in the thoughts they convey and in their artistic arrangement, pours out his soul in *true* adoration for God's *goodness* in action. He ascribes to God the honor due him for spiritual blessings *past* (election), *present* (redemption), and *future* (certification as sons with a view to complete possession of the inheritance reserved for them). The apostle realizes that divine blessings bestowed upon God's people should be humbly, gratefully, and enthusiastically acknowledged in thought, word, and deed. That response is the only proper way in which these spiritual bounties can be "returned" to the Giver. The circle must be completed: what comes from God must go back to him! That is the meaning of saying, "Blessed (be). . . ."[14]

The sentence begun by "Blessed (be)" rolls on like a snowball tumbling down a hill, picking up volume as it descends. Its 202 words, and the many modifiers which they form, arranged like shingles on a roof or like steps on a stairway, are like prancing steeds pouring forward with impetuous speed. Says John Calvin, "The lofty terms in which he [Paul] extols the grace of God toward the Ephesians, are intended to rouse their hearts to gratitude, to set them all on flame, to fill them even to overflowing with this disposition." Paul's "heart aflame" is bent on setting other hearts aflame also, with sincere, humble, overflowing praise to "the God and Father of our Lord Jesus Christ." Cf. Rom. 15:6; II Cor. 1:3; 11:31. Since Jesus was and is not only God but also man, and since he himself addressed the first Person of the Trinity as "my God" (Matt. 27:46), it is evident that the full title "the *God* and Father of our Lord Jesus Christ" is justified. As to the term "Father," it is evident that if the title *"God* of our Lord Jesus Christ" places emphasis on Christ's *human* nature, that of *"Father* of our Lord Jesus Christ"

---

[14] On *blessedness* as applied to God see N.T.C. on I and II Timothy and Titus, pp. 71, 72 (including footnote 34). Although according to its form εὐλογητός is a verbal adjective properly meaning "worthy of praise," yet, according to later usage, there is nothing that prevents it from having the sense of a perfect participle. As to the copula, Lenski would leave it out entirely. He says, "Supply nothing, read the word as an exclamation." But even an exclamation of this type has an *implied* verb. Some favor the indicative ἐστίν (cf. Rom. 1:25 and LXX Ps. 118:12) and the rendering "Worthy of blessing is"; more usual is the translation "Blessed be" or "Praise be to," on the basis of the optative εἴη. Ultimately the difference is minimal, as even the expression "Worthy of blessing is" would imply, "Therefore, let him be blessed (or praised)."

calls attention to the Son's *divine* nature, for not *nativistic* but *trinitarian* sonship is referred to in this thoroughly trinitarian epistle, in which the Beloved, by whatever name he is called, is constantly placed on a par with, and mentioned in one breath with, the Father and the Spirit (2:18; 3:14-17; 4:4-6; 5:18-20). Christ is the Son of God by eternal generation. See also N.T.C. on the Gospel according to John, Vol. I, pp. 86–88. Now, calling the first person of the Holy Trinity "the Father of our Lord Jesus Christ" has a very practical purpose, as the apostle shows plainly in II Cor. 1:3. In his capacity as Father of our Lord Jesus Christ he is "the Father of mercies and God of all comfort." Via Christ every spiritual blessing flows down to us from the Father. And if Christ is "the Son of God's love" (Col. 1:13), then God must be the Father of love, the loving Father. Note also that beautiful word of appropriating faith, namely, *our:* "the Father of *our* Lord Jesus Christ." How close this draws Christ to the believers' hearts, and not only Christ but the Father also. Truly, Christ and the Father are *one!* On the title "Lord Jesus Christ" see verse 2 above.

Paul continues, **who has blessed us with every spiritual blessing in the heavenly places in Christ.** The Father blesses his children when he lavishes gifts upon them in his favor so that these bounties or these experiences, of whatever nature, work together for their good (Rom. 8:28). Together with the gift he imparts himself (Ps. 63:1; cf. Rom. 8:32). While it is *not* true that the Old Testament regards material goods as being of higher value than spiritual, for the contrary is clearly taught in such passages as Gen. 15:1; 17:7; Ps. 37:16; 73:25; Prov. 3:13, 14; 8:11, 17-19; 17:1; 19:1, 22; 28:6; Isa. 30:15; cf. Heb. 11:9, 10, it is true, nevertheless, that between the two Testaments there is a difference of degree in the fulness of detail with which earthly or physical blessings are described (Exod. 20:12; Deut. 28:1-8; Neh. 9:21-25). God is ever the wise Pedagogue who takes his children by the hand and knows that in the old dispensation, "when Israel is a child" it needs this circumstantial description of earthly values in order that by means of these as symbols (e.g., earthly Canaan is the symbol of the heavenly), it may rise to the appreciation of the spiritual (cf. I Cor. 15:46). The New Testament, while by no means deprecating earthly blessings (Matt. 6:11; I Tim. 4:3, 4), places all the emphasis on the spiritual (II Cor. 4:18), and it may well have been that in order to emphasize this difference between the old and the new dispensation it is here stated that the God and Father of our Lord Jesus Christ blessed us with every *spiritual* blessing. It is best to allow the context to indicate the nature and content of these blessings. Though, to be sure, the very word *every* clearly proves that it would be wrong to subtract even a single invisible bounty from the list of those "vast benefits divine which we in Christ possess," yet the context indicates that the apostle is thinking particularly of — or subsuming all these benefits under — those that are mentioned in the present paragraph, namely, *election* (and its accompaniment, foreordination to adoption), *redemption* (implying forgiveness and grace overflowing in the form of all wisdom and insight), and *certification* ("sealing") as sons and heirs.

The phrase "in the heavenly places" or simply "in the heavenlies" (used in a local sense also in 1:20; 2:6; 3:10, and probably also locally in 6:12) indicates that these spiritual blessings are heavenly in their origin, and that from heaven they descend to the saints and believers on earth (cf. 4:8; and see N.T.C. on Phil. 3:20 and on Col. 3:1).

For the meaning of "in Christ" see on verse 1 above. It or its equivalent occurs more than ten times in this short paragraph (1:3-14), clear evidence of the fact that the apostle regarded *Christ* as *the very foundation of the church,* that is, of all its benefits, of its complete salvation. It is in connection with Christ that the saints and believers at Ephesus (and everywhere else) have been blessed with every spiritual blessing: election, redemption, certification as children and heirs, and all the other benefits subsumed under these headings. Apart from him they not only *can do nothing* but *are nothing,* that is, amount to nothing spiritually.

4. Paul continues, just as he elected us in him before the foundation of the world.

Election

(1) *Its Author*

The Author is "the God and Father of our Lord Jesus Christ," as has been indicated (see on verse 3). This, of course, by no means cancels the fact that all the activities which affect extra-trinitarian relationships can be ascribed to Father, Son, and Holy Spirit. Nevertheless, it is the Father who, as here shown, takes the lead in the divine work of election.

(2) *Its Nature*

To elect means *to pick* or *choose out of* (for oneself). Although the passage itself does not indicate *in so many words* the mass of objects or individuals out of which the Father chose some, this larger group is, nevertheless, clearly indicated by the purpose clause, "in order that we should be holy and faultless before him." Accordingly, the larger mass of individuals out of which the Father chose some are here viewed as *unholy and vile.* This interpretation suits the context. It supplies one of the reasons (see Synthesis at end of chapter for more reasons) why the soul of the apostle is filled with such rapture that he says, "Blessed (be) the God and Father of our Lord Jesus Christ, who . . . elected *us.*" He means: us, thoroughly unworthy in his sight! He does not try to explain how it was possible for God to do this. He fully realizes that when men are confronted with this manifestation of amazing grace their only proper response is *adoration,* not *explanation.*

(3) *Its Object*

The object is "us," not everybody. This pronoun "us" must be explained in the light of its context. Paul is writing to "saints and believers" (verse 1). He says that the Father has blessed "us," that is, "all saints and believers" (here with special reference to those at Ephesus) including Paul (verse 3). Therefore, when the apostle now continues, "just as he elected *us*," this "us" cannot suddenly have reference to *all men whatever*, but must necessarily refer to all those who are (or who at one time or another in the history of the world are destined to become) "saints and believers"; that is, to all those who, having been set apart by the Lord for the purpose of glorifying him, embrace him by means of a living faith.

It is for this contextual reason (and for others also) that I cannot agree with the contention of Karl Barth that in connection with Christ *all men whatever* are elect, and that the basic distinction is not between elect and non-elect but rather between those who are aware of their election and those who are not.[15]

(4) *Its Foundation*

The foundation of the church, of its entire salvation from start to finish, hence surely also of its election, is Christ. Paul says, "He ("the God and Father of our Lord Jesus Christ") elected us *in him*." The connection between verses 3 and 4 hinges on this phrase. One could bring this out in the translation as follows, "God the Father blessed us with every spiritual blessing in the heavenly places *in Christ, just as in him* he elected us. . . ." In other words, *in time* the Father *blessed* us in Christ, just as *from all eternity* he *elected* us in him. Though some maintain that this "just as" denotes no more than *correspondence*, in the sense that there is perfect agreement between the blessings and the election, for both are "in Christ," it may well be asked whether this interpretation exhausts the meaning of the word used in the original.[16] Aside from a point of grammar (for which see the footnote), it is the teaching of Paul that election from eternity and the further steps

---

15 For the teaching of Karl Barth on this subject see his "Gottes Gnadenwahl," *Die Lehre Von Gott, Die Kirchliche Dogmatik,* II/2 (3e.Auflage, 1948). See also G. C. Berkouwer, *De Triomf der Genade in de Theologie van Karl Barth* (Kampen, 1954); C. Van Til, *The New Modernism: an appraisal of the theology of Barth and Brunner* (Philadelphia, 1946), and by the same author, *Has Karl Barth Become Orthodox?* (Philadelphia, 1954); F. H. Klooster, *The Significance of Barth's Theology: An Appraisal, With Special Reference to Election and Reconciliation* (Grand Rapids, 1961); and Edwin D. Roels, *God's Mission, The Epistle to the Ephesians in Mission Perspective*, doctoral dissertation presented to the Free University at Amsterdam (Franeker, 1962).

16 In similar case καθώς, at the beginning of a clause, is used as a conjunction and in a sense not merely of comparison or correspondence but of cause (4:32; also Rom. 1:28; I Cor. 1:6; 5:7; Phil. 1:7).

in the order of salvation are not to be considered as so many separate items but rather as links in a golden chain, as Rom. 8:29, 30 makes abundantly clear. Election, then, is the root of all subsequent blessings. It is as Jesus said in his highpriestly prayer, ". . . that to all whom thou hast given him he might give everlasting life" (John 17:2). See also John 6:37, 39, 44; 10:29. Hence, since election is from eternity, and since it is the foundation of all further blessings, and since it is "in him," Christ is not only the *Foundation* of the church but its *Eternal Foundation*.

The question must now be answered, "How is it to be understood that it was *in Christ* that saints and believers were chosen?" The answer that is often given is this, that it was determined in the counsel of God that *in time* these people would come to believe in Christ. Though, to be sure, that, too, is implied, it is not a sufficient answer and fails to do justice to all that is taught by Paul and other inspired writers with respect to this important point. The basic answer must be that from before the foundation of the world Christ was the Representative and Surety of all those who in time would be gathered into the fold. This was necessary, for election is not an abrogation of divine attributes. It has already been established that in the background of God's decree is the dismal fact that those chosen are viewed as being, at the very outset, totally unworthy, having involved themselves in ruin and perdition. Now sin must be punished. The demands of God's holy law must be satisfied. The God and Father of our Lord Jesus Christ does not, by means of election, cancel his righteousness or abolish the demands of his law. How then is it ever possible for God to bestow such a great, glorious, and basic blessing as election upon "children of wrath," and to do so without detriment to his very essence and the inviolability of his holy law? The answer is that this is possible because of the promise of the Son (in full co-operation with the Father and the Spirit), "Lo, I come; in the roll of the book it is written of me; I delight to do thy will, O my God; thy law is within my heart" (Ps. 40:7, 8. Cf. Heb. 10:5-7; Gal. 4:4, 5; Phil. 2:6-8). "In Christ," then, saints and believers, though initially and by nature thoroughly unworthy, are righteous in the very sight of God, for Christ had promised that *in their stead* he would satisfy all the requirements of the law, a promise which was also completely fulfilled (Gal. 3:13). This forensic righteousness is basic to all the other spiritual blessings. Therefore,

> "To thee, O Lord, alone is due
> All glory and renown;
> Aught to ourselves we dare not take,
> Or rob thee of thy crown.
> Thou wast thyself our Surety
> In God's redemption plan;

In thee his grace was given us,
Long ere the world began."
(Augustus M. Toplady,
1774; revised by Dewey Westra, 1931)

(5) *Its Time*

This election is said to have occurred "before the foundation of the world," that is, "from eternity." Moreover, since it occurred "in him," this is altogether reasonable, for he is the One who and whose "precious blood as of a lamb without blemish and without spot" were *foreknown even before the foundation of the world* (I Peter 1:19, 20).[17] The fixity of God's eternal plan with respect to his chosen ones was not a Pauline invention. It was the teaching of Jesus himself. It was he who referred to those whom he loved as *the given ones* (see John 6:39; 17:2, 9, 11, 24; cf. 6:44). The fact that from all eternity he had promised to make atonement for them may well have been an element that entered into the Father's love for him; cf. the words of the highpriestly prayer, "Father, I desire that they also, whom thou hast given me be with me where I am, in order that they may gaze on my glory, which thou hast given me, for thou lovedst me before the foundation of the world" (John 17:24). In such and similar passages (see also Matt. 13:35; Heb. 4:3) the universe is viewed as a building, and its creation as the laying of the foundation of this building.

The point that should be emphasized in this connection is the fact that if already before the foundation of the world those destined for everlasting life were elected, then all the glory for their salvation belongs to God, and to him alone. Hence, "Blessed (be) the God and Father of our Lord Jesus Christ!" See 2:5, 8-10.

(6) *Its Purpose*

The purpose of election is found in the words, **that we should be holy and faultless before him.** It is worthy of special note that Paul does not say, "The Father elected us *because* he foresaw that we were going to be holy," etc. He says, *"that* [or: *in order that*] we should be holy," etc. Election is not conditioned on man's foreseen merits or even on his foreseen faith. It is salvation's root, not its fruit! Nevertheless, it remains true that man's responsibility and self-activity are not diminished even in the least. When the divine decree unto salvation is historically realized in the life of

---

[17] If, with A.V. (and very similarly Berkeley Version and Lenski) Rev. 13:8 be rendered "the Lamb slain from the foundation of the world," the doctrine of election from eternity "in him" would receive additional support. And is it so certain that A.R.V., R.S.V., N.A.S.B. (N.T.), N.E.B., etc., are correct in linking the modifier ("from the foundation of the world") to the words "written in the book of life" (after the analogy of Rev. 17:8)? The word-order of Rev. 13:8, in the original, would seem to support A.V., etc., here.

any individual it does not operate by means of external compulsion. It motivates, enables, actuates. It *im*pels but does not *com*pel. The best description is probably that which is found in *Canons of Dort* III and IV. 11, 12:

"Moreover, when God accomplishes this, his good pleasure, in the elect, or works in them true conversion, he not only provides that the gospel should be outwardly preached to them, and powerfully illuminates their minds by the Holy Spirit, that they may rightly understand and discern what are the things of the Spirit of God, but he also, by the efficacy of the same regenerating Spirit, pervades the innermost recess of man, opens the closed, softens the hardened, and circumcises the uncircumcised heart, infuses new qualities into the will, and makes that will which had been dead alive, which was evil good, which had been unwilling willing, which had been refractory pliable, and actuates and strengthens it, that, as a good tree, it may be able to bring forth the fruit of good works. . . . Whereupon the will, being now renewed, is not only actuated and moved by God, but being actuated by God, itself also becomes active. Wherefore man himself, by virtue of that grace received, is rightly said to believe and repent." See Phil. 2:12, 13 and II Thess. 2:13.

From the stated purpose it is evident that election does not carry man half-way only; it carries him all the way. It does not merely bring him to conversion; it brings him to perfection. It purposes to make him *holy* — that is, cleansed from all sin and separated entirely to God and to his service — and faultless — that is, without any blemish whatever (Phil. 2:15), like a perfect sacrifice. Nothing less than this becomes the conscious goal of those in whose hearts God has begun to work out his plan of eternal election. It is their goal in this present life (Lev. 19:2), and it attains ultimate realization in the hereafter (Matt. 6:10; Rev. 21:27).

The absolute and undiminished perfection of the ethical goal is given added emphasis by the phrase "before him," that is, before God in Christ. Not what we are in the estimation of men but what we are in the sight of God is what counts most.

(7) Its Further Description

5. A further definition of election, showing the form it takes, is found in the words, **having in love** [18] **foreordained us to adoption as sons.** This fore-

---

[18] With N.N., F. W. Grosheide, *De Brief Van Paulus Aan De Efeziërs* (*Commentaar op het Nieuwe Testament*), Kampen, 1960, p. 18, R.S.V. (text), Berkeley Version, and many others, I construe ἐν ἀγάπῃ with verse 5, not with verse 4. In favor of linking it with verse 4 — with Grk. N.T. (A-B-M-W) — it is claimed:
  (1) that it is Paul's habit to place this phrase after the clause which it modifies (S. D. F. Salmond, *The Epistle to the Ephesians, The Expositor's Greek Testament,* Vol. 3, Grand Rapids, Mich., no date, p. 251); and
  (2) that the rhythm of the sentence requires this (R. C. H. Lenski, *op. cit.*, p. 359).

ordination is not to be regarded as a divine activity prior to election. It is the latter's synonym, a further elucidation of its purpose. The Father is described as having *pre-horizoned* or *pre-encircled* his chosen ones. In his boundless *love,* motivated by nothing outside of himself, he set them apart to be his own sons. "As the hills are round about Jerusalem, so Jehovah is round about his people" (Ps. 125:2). He destined them to be members of his own family (cf. Rom. 8:15; Gal. 4:5). It is rather useless to look for human analogies, for the adoption of which Paul speaks surpasses anything that takes place on earth. It bestows upon its recipients not only a new name, a new legal standing, and a new family-relationship, but also a new image, the image of Christ (Rom. 8:29). Earthly parents may love an adopted child ever so much. Nevertheless, they are, to a large extent, unable to impart their spirit to the child. They have no control over hereditary factors. When God adopts, he imparts his Spirit! This adoption is **through Jesus Christ for himself.** It is through the work of Christ that this adoption becomes a reality. By his atonement the new standing and also the transformation into the spirit of sonship were merited for the chosen ones. Thus, they become God's children who glorify him.

The modifier **according to the good pleasure of his will** not only fits the immediate context ("for himself"), but also harmonizes excellently with the words "having *in love* foreordained us." When the Father chose a people for himself, deciding to adopt them as his own children, he was motivated by love alone. Hence, what he did was a result not of sheer determination but of supreme delight. A person may be fully determined to submit to a very serious operation. Again, he may be just as fully determined to plant a beautiful rose garden. Both are matters of the *will.* However, the latter alone is a matter of *delight,* that is, of his will's *good pleasure.* Thus, God, who does not afflict from the heart (Lam. 3:33), delights in the salvation of sinners (Is. 5:4; Ezek. 18:23; 33:11; Hos. 11:8; Matt. 23:37; cf. Luke 2:14; Rom. 10:1).

However, as to (1) it may be replied that the passages referred to (Eph. 4:2, 15, 16; 5:2; Col. 2:2; I Thess. 5:13) prove that it is Paul's habit to place this phrase *close to the clause which it modifies;* and as to (2), why rhythm would require the linking of this phrase with the preceding clause is not made clear.

In favor of viewing the phrase as a modifier of προορίσας the following may be mentioned:

(1) There would seem to be no good reason to link the phrase with the far removed ἐξελέξατο instead of with the nearby προορίσας. With ἁγίους καὶ ἀμώμους it is unnatural.

(2) The idea that God *in his love* would foreordain his people to *sonship* — a son being the object of the love of his Father — makes excellent sense.

(3) The fact that in man's redemption God (or Christ) was motivated by love is in harmony with other passages in this very epistle (2:4; 3:19; 5:2, 25).

(4) It is Pauline doctrine throughout (Rom. 5:8; 8:28, 35, 37; II Cor. 5:14; 13:11; Gal. 2:20; II Thess. 2:16; Titus 3:4).

6. This election, which was further described as a foreordination to adoption as sons, is **to the praise of the glory of his [the Father's] grace.** That is its *ultimate* purpose. The *immediate* (or intermediate) design has already been designated, namely, "that we should be holy and faultless before him," and along the same line, that we should receive "adoption as sons." The final goal, to which everything else is contributory, is the adoring recognition ("praise") of the manifested excellence ("glory") of the favor to the undeserving ("grace") of him who was called "the God and Father of our Lord Jesus Christ." (The concept *glory* has been treated rather fully in N.T.C. on Philippians, p. 62 footnote 43. For the meaning of *grace* see also on 1:2; 2:5, 8.)

It is clear that it is especially that marvelous *grace* to which the emphasis now shifts. It was the rapturous contemplation of that freely bestowed love to those viewed as lost in sin and ruin which moved the soul of the apostle to cry out, "Blessed (be) the God and Father of our Lord Jesus Christ." That exclamation, moreover, was genuine. Heathen also at times ascribe praise and honor to their gods, but in their case the motivation is entirely different. They do it to appease them or to extract some favor from them. Actually, therefore, such praise ends in man, not in the god to whom honor is ascribed. It resembles Cain's offering, which the Lord could not accept. Here in Ephesians, however, at the close of each paragraph (see verses 6, 12, 14) there is genuine adoration, such adoration as was not only God's intention in saving man, but also the thanksgiving offering presented to God by his servant Paul, whose heart is in harmony with the purpose of his Maker-Redeemer.

It is but natural that the grace of "the God and Father of *our Lord Jesus Christ*" should center in the Beloved. Hence, Paul continues, **which** [19] **he graciously bestowed on us in the Beloved.** One might translate as follows: "with which he has generously blessed us." But the rendering, as given in bold type above, to some extent preserves the wordplay of the original.[20] When the Father imparts a favor he does so with gladness of heart, without stint. Moreover, his gift reaches the very heart of the recipient and transforms it. It is, of course, as explained earlier, in connection with the Son that the Father so generously bestows his grace on us (see on verses 3 and 4 above). That Son is here called "the Beloved." Cf. Col. 1:13, "the Son of his love." Since Christ by means of his death earned every spiritual blessing for us, and therefore wants us to have these goods, and since the Father loves the Son, it stands to reason that, for the sake of this Beloved One, the Father would gladly grant us whatever we need. To this must be added the

---

[19] ἧς is attracted to the case of its antecedent χάριτος.

[20] Even more literal, but not as euphonious in English, would be, "grace by which he graced us." Cf. Luke 1:21. Both the sense and the wordplay are beautifully preserved in the Dutch translation: "genade, waarmede hij ons begenadigd heeft."

fact that the Father himself gave his Son for this very purpose. Hence, "He that spared not his own Son, but delivered him up for us all, how shall he not also together with him *graciously give* us all things?" (Rom. 8:32).

It is said at times that Christ is the Father's Beloved because he always obeyed the Father. This is true and scriptural (John 8:29). However, it is necessary in this connection to point out that it was especially the *quality* of this obedience that evoked the Father's love. The Son, knowing what is pleasing to the Father and in harmony with his will, does not wait until the Father orders him to do this or that, but willingly *offers himself.* He *volunteers* to do the Father's will. He is not passive even in his death, but *lays down* his life. "For this reason the Father loves me because I lay down my life in order that I may take it again. No one has taken it away from me; on the contrary, I lay it down of my own accord" (John 10:17, 18; cf. Is. 53:10). It is this marvelous *delight,* on the part of the Son, in doing the Father's will and thereby saving his people even at the cost of his own death, yes, death by means of a cross (Phil. 2:8), that causes the Father, again and again, to exclaim, "This is my beloved Son." In substance the Father already made this exclamation "before the world began." Even then he bestowed his infinite love upon his Son (John 17:24), moved, no doubt, among other things, by the latter's glorious resolution, "Lo, I come" (Ps. 40:7; cf. Heb. 10:7). To be sure, this is a very human way of speaking about these realities, but how else can we speak about them? The Father's exclamation was repeated in connection with the Son's baptism (Matt. 3:17), when in a visible manner the Son took upon himself the sin of the world (John 1:29, 33); and once more in connection with the transfiguration (Matt. 17:5; II Peter 1:17, 18), when again, and most strikingly, the Son voluntarily chose the way of the cross.[21]

7. In the second paragraph the attention is shifted from heaven to earth, from the past to the present, and, in a sense, from the Father to the Son. I say "in a sense," for the change is by no means abrupt. The infinitely close connection between the Father and the Son in the work of redemption is fully maintained. It is *the Father* who caused *his* grace to overflow toward us (verse 8), made known to us the mystery of *his* will according to *his* good pleasure (verse 9), etc. Nevertheless, the emphasis has changed from the work of the Father to that of the Son. It is *the Beloved,* that is, *the Son,* in whom we have our redemption. It is *he* who shed *his* blood for us (verse 7). It is *he* also in whom the Father's purpose of grace was concentrated (verse 9), under whose headship all things are brought together (verse 10), in connection with whom we have been made heirs (verse 11), and in whom we centered our hope (verse 12). Accordingly, Paul continues: (the Beloved) **in whom we have our redemption.** *Redemption* here, as in Col. 1:14 (cf. also

---

[21] The subject of *election* has also been treated in N.T.C. on I and II Thessalonians, pp. 48–50.

Exod. 21:30; Matt. 20:28; Mark 10:45; Rom. 3:24; Heb. 9:12, 15), indicates *deliverance as a result of the payment of a ransom.*[22] There was no other way for sinners to be saved. God's justice must be satisfied. Anyone who doubts the necessary, objective, voluntary, expiatory, substitutionary, and efficacious character of the act of the Father's Beloved whereby he offered himself for his people should make a diligent study of the passages mentioned in N.T.C. on I and II Timothy and Titus, p. 376.

This redemption implies: *a. emancipation* from the curse, that is, from the guilt, punishment, and power of sin (John 8:34; Rom. 7:14; I Cor. 7:23; Gal. 3:13), and *b. restoration* to true liberty (John 8:36; Gal. 5:1). It was, moreover, a redemption **through his blood,** a redemption, therefore, which implied *substitution* of the life of One for the life of others. Thus, thus *only,* atonement could be made (Lev. 17:11; Heb. 9:22). Moreover, the blood through which alone redemption could be accomplished was *his* blood, that of the perfect Redeemer. The blood of animals was merely symbolical and typical (Ps. 40:6-8; Heb. 9:11-14; 10:1-14). Yet, when mention is made of redemption through his *blood,* this blood must never be dissociated from the voluntary sacrifice of the entire *life,* the *self* (Lev. 17:11; Isa. 53:10-12; Matt. 26:28; cf. 20:28; I Tim. 2:6). Expressions such as, "He gave his blood," "He gave his soul," and "He gave himself," are synonymous. They all indicate that the Redeemer was made (and made himself) an offering for sin (Isa. 53:10; II Cor. 5:21); that he suffered the eternal punishment due to sin; that he did this vicariously, and that he did all this for those who by nature were "children of wrath" (Eph. 2:3). What enhances the glory of this sacrifice even more is the fact that although the Beloved came into the world to do many things, for example, to still the boisterous waves, cast out demons, cleanse lepers, open the eyes of the blind, unstop the ears of the deaf, feed the hungry, heal the sick, and even raise the dead, yet the overarching purpose of his coming was to seek and to save the lost, to give himself a ransom for many (Isa. 53:12; Matt. 20:28; Mark 10:45; Luke 19:10; I Tim. 1:15). Truly, "Jesus from his throne on high came into this world *to die.*" No wonder that Paul cries out, "Blessed (be)," that Peter urges upon those committed to his charge the thankful response of a holy life, adding "knowing that y o u were redeemed not with corruptible things, with silver or gold . . . but with precious blood, as of a lamb without blemish and without spot, (even the blood) of Christ" (I Peter 1:15-19), that "angels desire to look into the sufferings of Christ and the glories that were to follow them" (I Peter 1:10-12), that, with their minds and hearts fixed on the infinite greatness of this sacrifice, the four living creatures and

---

[22] The more general connotation that adheres to the word in Luke 21:28; Rom. 8:23; I Cor. 1:30; Eph. 1:14; 4:30; Heb. 11:35, passages in which the idea of the payment of a ransom is dropped, and only that of deliverance, release, etc., is retained, does not change this fact.

the twenty-four elders in their new song are forever exclaiming, "Worthy art thou . . . for thou wast slain, and didst purchase with thy blood men of every tribe and tongue and people and nation" (Rev. 5:9), and that the ten thousand times ten thousand and thousands of thousands of angels join in with this grand jubilation by lifting up their voices in exuberant adoration, shouting, "Worthy is the Lamb who has been slain!" (Rev. 5:12).

Now the purpose of this redemption was "that we might from sin be free." It was with that objective in mind and heart that he "bled and died upon the tree." Hence, Paul says, "the Beloved, in whom we have our redemption through his blood," **the forgiveness of our trespasses.** These two — a. redemption by blood and b. forgiveness of trespasses — go together. Redemption would not be complete without procuring pardon. Even Israel in the old dispensation understood this. On the day of atonement the *blood* of one goat *was sprinkled* on the mercy-seat. The other goat, over whose head the people's *sins* had been confessed, *was sent away,* never to return. Now here in Eph. 1:7 this idea of *complete removal of sin* constitutes the very meaning of the word, used in the original, rendered *forgiveness* (or *remission*). Other passages that shed light on the meaning are Ps. 103:12 ("As far as the east is from the west, so far has he removed our transgressions from us"), Isa. 44:22 ("I have blotted out, as a thick cloud, your transgressions, and as a cloud your sins: return to me, for I have redeemed you"), Jer. 31:34 (". . . and their sin I will remember no more"), Mic. 7:19 ("Thou wilt cast all their sins into the depths of the sea"), and I John 1:9 ("If we confess our sins, he is faithful and righteous to forgive us our sins, and to cleanse us from all unrighteousness").

As to its derivation, the word rendered *trespass* means *a falling to the side of.* A trespass, then, is *a deviation from the path of truth and righteousness.*[23] Such deviations may be either of a gross or of a less serious nature. That in Ephesians no deviation is excluded, and that the totality of these deviations is regarded as a serious matter, one that is rooted in the very nature of man as corrupted by the fall, is clear from 2:1, "And y o u (he made alive) when y o u were *dead* through y o u r trespasses and sins" (cf. 2:3, 5). With reference to *forgiveness* see also N.T.C. on Colossians, pp. 118–120.

Now forgiveness takes place **according to the riches of his [the Father's] grace.** Forgiveness and grace are in complete harmony. The standard established by God's grace determines the measure of his forgiveness. For the meaning of *grace* see on 1:2 above; cf. also 1:6; 2:5, 7, 8. Note that the Father forgives not merely *of,* but *according to,* his riches, riches of grace. Illustration: Here are two very rich persons. When asked to contribute toward a good cause, both give *of* their riches. The first one, however, donates a

---

[23] See R. C. Trench, *Synonyms of the New Testament,* par. lxvi. He points out that although the milder meaning (fault, error, mistake) attaches to the word at times (see Rom. 5:15, 17, 18; Gal. 6:1), this is by no means always the case.

very paltry sum, far less than had been expected of him. He merely gives *of*
his riches, not *according to*. The second is lavish in his support of every
noble cause. He gives *according to* the amount of his wealth. God ever gives
and forgives *according to* his riches. And *he* is rich, indeed! His favor toward
the undeserving is infinite in character. 8. The apostle continues, **which** [24]
he caused to overflow [25] **toward us in the form of all wisdom and insight.**
In a similar passage (I Tim. 1:14) the apostle states, "And it *super-
abounded,* namely, the grace of our Lord, with faith and love in Christ
Jesus." Just as in that passage grace is said to have kindled *faith* and *love,*
so here grace floods the souls of believers with *wisdom* and *insight. Wisdom
is knowledge plus.* It is the ability to apply knowledge to the best advantage, enabling a person to use the most effective means for the attainment
of the highest goal. *Insight* (cf. Col. 1:9, *understanding*) is the result of
setting one's mind on God's redemptive revelation in Christ, the mystery
of his will, for Paul continues: 9. . . . **in that he made known to us the
mystery of his will.** God had made it known to Paul (3:3), who, in turn, rejoices in being able to proclaim it to others. In addition, grace sanctifies this
knowledge to the hearts of those destined to be saved. Paul says, "He made
it known to *us*" (cf. "toward us" in verse 8), that is, to myself and to those
whom I am addressing (see verse 1).

He caused his grace to overflow . . . in that *he made known* to us the
mystery of his will! He did not keep it to himself. The Father did not desire
that the saints and believers in Ephesus (and everywhere else) should be
like the people in the city of Samaria, described in II Kings 7:3-15, who
were unaware of their riches. The greatest story ever told, that of God's
grace in Christ, *must be made known.* In that respect, too, the true gospel
of salvation differs from "other gospels" invented by men. In the days of
Paul certain cults imposed on their devotees "tremendous oaths" *not* to reveal their secrets to the uninitiated. Even today there are societies which
demand that their members make similar solemn promises on pain of dire
punishment if they fail to keep them. It was the Father's will that the most
sublime secret be broadcast far and wide, and that it penetrate deeply into
the hearts of those who were his own. God's plan of salvation, moreover,
must be made known in order that it may be accepted by faith, for it is by
faith that men are saved.

Exactly what did Paul mean when he mentioned "the mystery"? Here in
Ephesians the answer is not given until we reach verse 10, and even then
it is merely *introduced.* Even so, however, we are told that the mystery of

---

[24] ἧς attracted to the case of its antecedent, as in verse 6 above.
[25] The verb περισσεύω is used in various senses: such as, to be left over (John 6:12),
surpass (Matt. 5:20; II Cor. 8:2), grow or abound (Phil. 1:9), have more than
enough (Phil. 4:18), excel (I Cor. 15:58). For the meaning *to cause to overflow,*
as here in Eph. 1:8, see also I Thess. 3:12.

which the apostle is thinking is that of God's *will*, that is, of the Father's *desire*. The mystery and the Father's *desire, good pleasure, cherished purpose,* go together. They cannot be separated, for the mystery is that *of* his eternal purpose. Its disclosure, too, was **according to his good pleasure. Cf.** verse 5 above, where *foreordination* is also ascribed to the Father's good pleasure. We learn from this that the Father, far from being less loving than the Son, *takes special delight* in planning whatever must be planned in order to bring about the salvation, full and free, of men who had plunged themselves into misery and ruin, and takes equal pleasure in telling them about this marvelous plan! Is it any wonder that Paul's heart was filled with adoration so that he exclaimed, "Blessed (be) the God and Father of our Lord Jesus Christ"?

The apostle further defines this *good pleasure* by adding: **the purpose which he cherished for himself in him.**[26] This "in him" must mean "in the Beloved," as the preceding context indicates. The Father "has blessed us with every spiritual blessing . . . *in Christ*" (1:3), "elected us *in him*" (verse 4), and "graciously bestowed his grace upon us *in the Beloved*" (verse 6). It is natural, therefore, that we should now be referred to the purpose which he cherished for himself "in him." In what sense this purpose of the Father was cherished *in* the Beloved has been explained above (see on verse 4).

10. The Father's good pleasure, his cherished purpose, the plan in which his soul delighted, a plan drawn up *in eternity,* was to be realized *in time.* Hence, Paul continues: **to be put into effect in the fulness of the times.** Literally, "for administration [or: for effectuation]," etc.[27] The expression "fulness of the times" (or: seasons) and the similar (though not exactly identical) one in Gal. 4:4 indicate *the moment* (Gal. 4:4) or *the period* (Eph. 1:10) when, as it were, the lower compartment of the hourglass of God's eternal decree had become filled, that is, when all the preceding times and seasons which the Father had set within his own authority had been completed (Acts 1:7; cf. 17:26). It is, in other words, "the appropriate time." As is evident from 1:20-23, in the present case the reference is to the entire New Testament era, particularly to the period which began with Christ's resurrection and coronation. It will not end until the Lord, upon his glori-

---

[26] Literally, the original reads: "(his good pleasure) which he purposed for himself in him." But since such a rendering is hardly idiomatic and fluent English, for we do not generally speak about "purposing a good pleasure," and since the shade of meaning in the word *good pleasure,* when its underlying idea is continued in the relative clause "which, etc.," shifts somewhat, so that it no longer refers exclusively to a divine disposition but also to the plan in which this disposition is expressed, I translated as I did. My rendering is somewhat similar to that proposed by R. F. Weymouth, *The New Testament in Modern Speech,* though I do not agree with his translation of this clause in its entirety. He offers: "the purpose which he has cherished in his own mind."

[27] The word οἰκονομία has been explained in Introduction, III A 2 b, p. 44.

85

ous return, will have pronounced and executed judgment (I Cor. 15:24, 25). It is well, in this connection, to stress what was said before, namely, that *mystery* and *purpose* go together: *the effectuation of the purpose is the revelation of the mystery,* for it was exactly the Father's purpose of love to reveal that which to men was a mystery. This effectuation and revelation was destined to take place, therefore, in the present Messianic age.

The purpose actualized in the fulness of the times, the mystery *then* revealed, is expressed in these words: **to bring all things together under one head in Christ,**[28] **the things in the heavens and the things on the earth.** What Paul is saying here receives amplification in verses 20-22. Therefore it is not necessary to enlarge upon it here. It is the identical doctrine expounded also in other letters that belong to this same imprisonment; see especially Col. 1:20 and Phil. 2:9-11, and the N.T.C. on these passages. As to the *mystery* which the apostle here introduces, but on which he later on expatiates in far greater detail (2:11-22, though in that paragraph the word *mystery* is not used; 3:1-13, note especially verse 4; 6:19), suffice it at this point to say that this mystery centers in Christ, and that one element in it is that which is expressed here, namely, that literally *everything*, things in heaven, things on earth, everything above us, around us, within us, below us, everything spiritual and everything material, has even now been brought under Christ's rule. This is, indeed, *a mystery*, for no one would ever have

---

[28] There is a great variety of opinion in connection with the rendering of ἀνακεφ-αλαιώσασθαι. On the one hand there are those who insist that since the cognate *noun* κεφάλαιον never means *head* but *sum* ("For a large sum of money I acquired this citizenship," Acts 22:28) or *summary, main point* ("Now the main point in what we are saying is this," Heb. 8:1) ; and since similarly, in its only other New Testament occurrence, the *verb* means *to sum up* ("For this, You must not commit adultery . . . and any other commandment, is summed up in this word, You must love your neighbor as yourself," Rom. 13:9), hence the only proper translation of the words of Paul here in Eph. 1:10 is *"to sum up* all things in Christ." Others, however, are of the opinion — I believe correctly — that this A.R.V. rendering is somewhat obscure, for just what does "summing up in Christ" really mean? Accordingly, they suggest various alternative renderings. A rather popular one centers about the concept of *bringing about unity* (cf. Col. 1:20). Hence, already A.V. translated, "that he might gather together in one all things in Christ." Similarly, R.S.V. offers, "to unite all things in him"; N.E.B., "that the universe might be brought into a unity in Christ"; and L.N.T. (A. and G.), "to bring everything together in Christ." This type of translation, provided that it be not interpreted to mean that in the end everybody will be saved, is undoubtedly on the right track. Is it possible, however, to be still more definite? Does the word used in 1:10 at all indicate what kind of bringing together Paul has in mind? A. T. Robertson (*Word Pictures in the New Testament*, Vol. IV, pp. 518, 519) points out that κεφάλαιον is derived from κεφαλή. Accordingly, he translates "to head up all things in Christ." F. F. Bruce (*The Letters of Paul, An Expanded Paraphrase*, pp. 267, 268) gives the sense of the passage in these words, "that all things in heaven and earth alike should find their one true head in Christ." As this is exactly what the apostle teaches in this very chapter (1:10-22; cf. also 4:10), it is difficult to believe that he can have meant anything else here in 1:10. This explains my rendering, "to bring all things together under one head in Christ."

guessed it, had it not been revealed. "Now we do not yet see all things subjected to him" (Heb. 2:8). It takes nothing less than *faith* — and not a very weak faith either — to "see Jesus crowned with glory and honor" (Heb. 2:9), actually ruling the entire universe from his heavenly abode. It is as Dr. Herman Bavinck has so aptly expressed it, "Round about us we observe so many facts which seem to be unreasonable, so much undeserved suffering, so many unaccountable calamities, such an uneven and inexplicable distribution of destiny, and such an enormous contrast between the extremes of joy and sorrow, that anyone reflecting on these things is forced to choose between viewing this universe as if it were governed by the blind will of an unbenign deity, as is done by pessimism, or, upon the basis of Scripture and by faith, to rest in the absolute and sovereign, yet — however incomprehensible — wise and holy will of him who will one day cause the full light of heaven to dawn upon these mysteries of life" (*The Doctrine of God,* my translation from the Dutch; Grand Rapids, Mich., second printing, 1955).

This bringing together of all things under one head in Christ, so that things are not allowed to drift by themselves but our Lord is fully in charge, is taught by many passages in Scripture. In heaven the exalted Mediator lives and reigns (Rev. 20:4), receiving the adoration of all the redeemed and of all the angelic hosts (Rev. 5). But the thoughts of this great Uniter are turned earthward also, so much so, in fact, that he not only *intercedes* for his people who are still engaged in struggle and turmoil (Rom. 8:34), but even *lives to make intercession* for them (Heb. 7:25), and is already preparing places for them (John 14:2). He imparts gifts to men (Eph. 4:8), performs acts of healing (Acts 3:6, 16), and through his Spirit dwells in the midst of "the seven light-bearers" (Rev. 1:13). This indwelling is very active and produces fruits of sanctification in the lives of believers (Eph. 3:17-19). At the same time Christ wages war victoriously against the dragon (Satan) and his allies (Rev. 17:14), and, in general, governs the entire universe in the interest of his church (Eph. 1:22).

That Christ's interest in this church is deep, indeed, is shown also in the statement which follows, namely, **in him 11. in whom we** — I, Paul, and y o u, the addressed — **also have been made heirs.** Note the word "also," meaning: *not only* did we, in vital union with Christ, receive such blessings as redemption, forgiveness of sin, and spiritual illumination (wisdom, insight), favors which have already been mentioned (verses 7-10 above), but, in addition to these initial favors, which, though they have *abiding* significance, focus the attention upon *the past* (deliverance from that terrible power by which we *were* bound, pardon of *past* sins, banishment of *former* darkness), the right to *future* glory was bestowed upon us. "We were made heirs," [29] says Paul. Heirs are those who, apart from any merit of theirs,

[29] The verb used in the original should be interpreted as a true passive, in harmony with such passives as "having been foreordained" (verse 11) and "were sealed"

87

were given the right to all the blessings of salvation in Jesus Christ, nevermore to lose them. The inheritance is given to them in two stages: certain blessings are bestowed upon them in the here and now, others in the hereafter (see on verses 13 and 14 below).

The objection might occur, "But will all the blessings of salvation — *future* as well as present — really be ours? Does God's plan for our lives also *secure* the future?" The apostle answers this by continuing: **having been foreordained according to the purpose of him who accomplishes all things according to the counsel of his will.**[30] Neither fate nor human merit determines our destiny. The benevolent purpose — that we should be holy and faultless (verse 4), sons of God (verse 5), destined to glorify him forever (verse 6, cf. verses 12 and 14) — is fixed, being part of a larger, universe-embracing plan. Not only did God *make* this plan that includes absolutely all things that ever take place in heaven, on earth, and in hell; past, present, *and even the future,* pertaining to both believers and unbelievers, to angels and devils, to physical as well as spiritual energies and units of existence both large and small; he also *wholly carries it out.* His providence in time is as comprehensive as is his decree from eternity. Literally Paul states that God *works (operates with his divine energy in)* all things. The same word occurs also in verses 19 and 20, which refer to the *working (energetic operation)* of the infinite might of the Father of glory, which he *wrought (energetically exerted)* in Christ when he raised him from the dead. Hence, nothing can upset the elect's future glory.

Moreover, although everything is included in God's universe-embracing

---

(verse 13). Moreover, the rendering "we were made a heritage" (A.R.V., and similarly, Barry, Berkeley Version, Greijdanus, Salmond, Van Leeuwen), though also passive, loses sight of the following facts:

a. the immediate context speaks of *"our* inheritance" (verse 14a). Though it is true that believers are regarded as God's own *possession* (verse 14b) yet *heirship* is not ascribed to God but to them.

b. In the New Testament *the inheritance* is ever said to be *ours* or *intended for us* (Acts 20:32; Gal. 3:18; Col. 3:24; Heb. 9:15; I Peter 1:4). Even Eph. 1:18 is no exception to this rule. See on that passage.

c. Eph. 1:5 informs us that the Father "in love foreordained us to adoption as sons." Now this very idea of being sons by adoption is elsewhere by Paul brought into immediate connection with the thought that *we* are therefore heirs (Rom. 8:15-16).

d. The parallel, Col. 1:12, also supports the idea that believers are the heirs: "with joy giving thanks to the Father who qualified y o u for a share in the inheritance of the saints in the light."

N.E.B. offers a translation which is essentially correct: "In Christ indeed we have been given our share in the heritage."

[30] It is not easy to distinguish between *will, counsel,* and *purpose.* Yet, Paul seems to have had a distinction in mind. Probably it is the best to regard God's *will* (θέλημα) as basic here. It is his sovereign volition. The βουλή would then be the *plan* or *counsel* that is viewed here as belonging to, springing forth from, his θέλημα. It would seem to indicate that God never acts arbitrarily, but with deliberation. Finally, God's πρόθεσις indicates the *purpose* of this plan, or, perhaps, *the plan itself* from the point of view of what it *aims* to accomplish; God's *design.*

plan and in its effectuation in the course of history, there is nothing in this thought that should scare any of the children of God. Quite the contrary, for the words clearly imply that the only true God, who in Christ loves his own with a love that passes all understanding, acts with divine deliberation and wisdom. All his designs are holy, and he delights to reward those who trust in him. Human responsibility and the self-activity of faith are never violated in any way. There is plenty of room for them in the decree and in its effectuation. Scripture is very clear on this (Luke 22:22; Acts 2:23; Phil. 2:12, 13; II Thess. 2:13).

Besides, God is not like the heathen deities who are moved by changing circumstances, by whim and caprice, so that one never knows how long their favor is going to last. He who in his love has foreordained his people to adoption as sons will never forsake them, but will finish that which he began in them (Phil. 1:6). He will carry out his plan to the very finish. Nothing will ever be able to frustrate his design. "Nor sin, nor death, nor hell can move his firm predestinating love."

12. If, then, God's decree from eternity is thus all-embracing, and if it is fully carried out in history, and if the destiny of his children was included in this plan, then Paul and the readers have no reason whatever for boasting in themselves. Whatever they *are* or *have* or *do* is from God. Hence, in language similar to that employed in verse 6 above, Paul concludes this section by saying: **to the end that we should be to the praise of his glory, we who beforehand had centered our hope in Christ.** *Before* the inheritance has been *fully* received — for only the first instalment has been received here and now (see verses 13, 14) — Paul and those addressed (see verse 1) have already centered their hope in Christ. That hope will not be crushed. "And the ransomed of Jehovah will return, and come with singing to Zion; and everlasting joy will be on their heads: they will obtain gladness and joy, and sorrow and sighing will flee away." (For contrasting interpretations of "we" in verse 12 and "y o u" in verse 13, see on verse 13.)

13. As the center of interest shifts once more, this time from the Son ("Christ," mentioned at the close of verse 12) to the Holy Spirit, here again instead of an abrupt change there is a gradual transition (cf. the beginning of verse 7, with its stair-step transition from the Father to the Son). Paul writes, **in whom y o u** [31] **also (are included), having listened to the message**

---

[31] On the basis of the words *"we, those having previously hoped in Christ"* (verse 12) as contrasted with *"y o u . . . having also believed in him"* (verse 13), many have endorsed the position that two ethnic groups are indicated here; namely, in verse 12 Jewish Christians; in verse 13 believers from the Gentiles.

Objections:

(1) This is a very unnatural interpretation, for in the preceding verses "we" and "us" always refer to Paul and all those addressed (see verses 11, 9, 8, 7, 6, 5, 4, 3). By far most of those addressed were believers from the Gentiles, not from the Jews. Why, then, the sudden change of meaning in verse 12?

of the truth, the gospel of y o u r salvation.[32] The Ephesians must not doubt their inclusion in Christ and all his benefits. They have heard, have listened attentively to, the message of the truth. Did not Luke report, "All those who lived in Asia heard the word of the Lord, both Jews and Greeks"? (Acts 19:10). Such *hearing* was necessary in order that by faith they might be saved. The answer to be given to those who say that men who can properly be considered objects (or potential objects) of missionary activity are able to be saved without hearing the gospel is, "And how will they believe in him whom they did not hear?" (Rom. 10:14; cf. Matt. 1:21; John 14:6; Acts 4:12). Of course, it makes a difference *how* men hear. Some hear and become gospel-hardened. As men may become deaf because of a constant pounding noise, so also hearers of the gospel may become completely immune to the preaching of the truth. ("And I heard him a bumming away like a buzzard clock over my head.") Moreover, to some the proclamation of the gospel is like a love-song sung beautifully and played well (Ezek. 33:32). They hear but do not take to heart (Mark 4:24; Luke 8:18). Christ told his audiences to take care *how* they heard. By means of unforgettable parables he emphasized this lesson (Matt. 7:24-27; 13:1-9, 18-23).

Christ, however, also stressed that men should give heed *what* they heard. The Ephesians had listened attentively to "the message of the truth." There were many errors abroad in those days, many false gospels (Col. 1:23; 2:4, 8; cf. Gal. 1:6-9). The Ephesians, by and large, had ignored or rejected them. They wanted to hear only the very best. It is called the message of *the truth* because it reveals man's true condition, proclaims and advocates the only true way of escape, and admonishes saved sinners to show true gratitude in

---

(2) The perfect participle προηλπικότας from προελπίζω, in the New Testament occurring only here, does not necessarily mean *having hoped before others did* or *having hoped before Christ arrived*. It may equally well mean *having hoped before having fully attained*. With "we had previously hoped" compare "y o u have previously heard" (Col. 1:5). In the latter passage, too, no contrast is implied between two groups of believers of different national origin.

(3) Finally, if such a contrast in origin must be maintained here in 1:12, 13, it would almost seem as if the apostle were writing, "We Jewish Christians, we alone, are destined for the praise of his glory," and "Y o u believers from the Gentiles, y o u alone, were sealed with the promised Spirit." The apostle obviously would never have taught this.

The only element of value I can see in the theory which I reject is this, that when Paul, who in verses 3-12 has been referring constantly to himself and the addressed as one group ("we," "us"), now in verse 13 (and see also 1:15-18; 2:1, 2, 8) begins to substitute the second person plural for the first person plural — meaning, however, *y o u as well as all believers* —, he is gradually preparing the hearers for the clear-cut distinction between Gentile Christians and Jewish Christians which begins at 2:11.

[32] This clear and positive statement, showing that the addressed had indeed heard the true gospel, sheds light on the proper explanation of 3:2; 4:21, passages which have often been enlisted in defense of the theory that this letter could not have been addressed to the Ephesians and/or that Paul could not have written it. See on these passages.

their whole lives. It is, accordingly, "the gospel of y o u r salvation," not in the sense that in and by itself it saves anyone, but thus that, when accepted by true faith in Christ, its good tidings of great joy become "the power of God for salvation" (Rom. 1:16). This true faith the Ephesians had shown, for Paul continues: **and having also believed in him. . . .** They had surrendered their lives to their Lord, had reposed their trust in him. The better they knew him, the more they had trusted him. The more they had trusted him, the better they had learned to know him. Hence, Paul says: **y o u were sealed with the promised Holy Spirit.** A seal — not stamped on but attached to an object in ancient times — was used *a. to guarantee* the *genuine character* of a document, etc. (Esther 3:12), or, figuratively, of a person (I Cor. 9:2); *b. to mark ownership* (Song of Sol. 8:6); and/or *c. to protect against tampering or harm* (Matt. 27:66; Rev. 5:1). The context (see verse 14) would seem to indicate that the first of these three ideas, that of authentication or certification, is basic in the present passage. The Spirit had testified within their hearts that they were children of God (Rom. 8:16; I John 3:24), and "if children, then heirs, heirs of God, and joint-heirs with Christ" (Rom. 8:17), people whom nothing can harm, and to whom "all things work together for good" (Rom. 8:28). It is immediately apparent that in such matters the three aforementioned purposes for which a seal is used combine: *authentication* implies *ownership* and *protection*. In this connection see also N.T.C. on I and II Timothy and Titus, pp. 266–270.

When the very practical question is asked, "How did the Ephesians — or how does anyone — get that seal, that inner assurance?" the answer is: not merely or mainly as the result of agonizing self-searching to see whether all the "marks" of having been elected are present, but rather by a *living* faith in the triune God, as revealed in Christ, a faith "working through love" (Gal. 5:6). That those addressed had indeed received it in no other way is a fact to which the apostle immediately calls attention (Eph. 1:15).

The Spirit who had given them this seal is here called by his full name, "the Holy Spirit," to indicate not only that he is holy in himself but also that he is the source of holiness for believers, a holiness which in the case of the addressed was expressed not only by their inner disposition but also by their loving words and deeds. Moreover, this third person of the Trinity is here called "the Holy Spirit *of promise,*" that is, *the promised Holy Spirit,* the One given in fulfilment of divine promises (John 14:16, 17; 15:26; 16:13; Acts 1:4). Does not the very fact that in his coming and work divine promises were gloriously fulfilled indicate that promises of future blessings for believers will also attain fruition? In that vein the apostle continues by writing, **14. who is the first instalment of our inheritance.** For "first instalment" Paul uses the word *arrabōn* (also spelled *arabōn*). In the papyri it often refers to earnest money in the purchase of an animal or even of a wife. In the LXX rendering of Gen. 38:17-20 the word occurs three times. It is of Semitic, probably Phoenician, origin. The Phoenicians were sea-faring traders who had not copyrighted their business-terminology. In the New Testament the word occurs also in II Cor. 1:22; 5:5, passages from which we learn that when God deposited the Spirit in the hearts of his children he obligated himself to bestow upon them subsequently the full remainder of all the blessings of salvation merited for them by the atoning sacrifice of Christ. The *first instalment* is, accordingly, a *pledge* or *guarantee* of glory to come, a glory arriving not only when soul and body part but also and especially in the great consummation of all things at Christ's return. The fruits which this indwelling and sanctifying Spirit bestows (Gal. 5:22, 23) — such as love, joy, peace, longsuffering, kindness, faithfulness, meekness, self-control, and their marvelous product: assurance of salvation (II Peter 1:5-11) — are "first-fruits" (Rom. 8:23). They are a foretaste of future, ineffable bliss.[33] The full *inheritance* — salvation viewed as God's gracious and abiding gift, not bought with money, nor earned by the sweat of human toil, nor won by conquest — will one day be the believers' portion, for them to possess and to enjoy, *to God's glory.*

Now the end or purpose of all things lies never in man but always in God: **for the redemption of (God's) own possession.**[34] At the moment when

---

[33] On ἀρραβών see also L.N.T. (A. and G.), p. 109; and Th.W.N.T., Vol. I, p. 474.
[34] Rather popular is the idea that the apostle has in mind not *God's* possession but *ours*. This is the view of T. K. Abbott, *op. cit.,* pp. 23, 24, who contends, "It is our inheritance that is in question; it is of it that the earnest is received. . . . Instead of this, the interpretation quoted supposes the figure entirely changed, so that, instead of receiving an inheritance, it is we that are the possession; a figure . . . involving a confusion of thought which we can hardly attribute to St. Paul." E. F. Scott, *op. cit.,* pp. 149, 150 reaches the same result. This type of reasoning is probably also basic to the rendering found in such translations as Berkeley, Moffatt, Goodspeed, and R.S.V. My objections are as follows:
(1) Is not the fact that it will become abundantly clear that we are *his* possession the very climax of *our* inheritance? A Christian young lady who is engaged to a young man of similar deeply rooted conviction, one who loves her with a love patterned after that of Christ for his church, looks forward with joyful anticipation to the moment when she will *belong to* her beloved.
(2) He who gives the engagement ring, in *pledge,* expects to receive the bride. It is God who gave the *arrabōn.* The word *arrabōn* and its cognates are used in modern Greek to indicate matters pertaining to a wedding engagement.
(3) The idea that God's people (in the Old Testament *Israel;* in the New Testament, *the church*) constitutes "his own possession," "a people, his very own," is repeated so often in Scripture that it may almost be said to belong to technical phraseology. For the linguistic aspect of the term see N.T.C. on I and II Timothy and Titus, p. 379, footnote 193. It occurs in one form or another in such passages as Exod. 19:5; 23:22; Deut. 7:6; 14:2; 26:18. Paul himself in Titus 2:14 states, " (our great God and Savior Jesus Christ) who gave himself for us in order to . . . purify for himself *a people, his very own,* with a zest for noble deeds." Peter states, "But y o u are . . . *a people for (God's) own possession,* in order that y o u may proclaim the excellencies of him who called y o u out of darkness into his marvelous light." Add also Isa. 43:20, 21; Ezek. 37:23; and Mal. 3:17. Surely Paul knew his Old Testament!

believers receive *their* full inheritance, which includes a glorious resurrection body (4:30), the redemption [35] of God's own possession takes place, that is, the full release to him of that which is his by virtue of the fact that he both made it and bought it. Fully released from all the effects of sin, his people will then be made manifest as being in very deed "his peculiar treasure." When the apostle also at the close of this third paragraph, which centers in the work of the Holy Spirit, adds **to the praise of his glory,** he is echoing what he had said in an earlier epistle: "Y o u are not y o u r own, for y o u were bought with a price; glorify God therefore in y o u r body" (I Cor. 6:19, 20). The fact that believers do not belong to themselves but to God (or: to Christ) is familiar Pauline doctrine: "Y o u belong to Christ" (I Cor. 3:23); "Whether we live, we live to the Lord, and whether we die, we die to the Lord; therefore, whether we live or whether we die, we are the Lord's" (Rom. 14:8). This, too, is the believers' only comfort both in life and in death. It is exactly as the Heidelberg Catechism expresses it:

"Question 1: What is your only comfort in life and death?

"Answer: That I, with body and soul, both in life and death, am not my own, but belong to my faithful Savior Jesus Christ; who with his precious blood has fully satisfied for all my sins, and delivered me from all the power of the devil; and so preserves me that without the will of my heavenly Father not a hair can fall from my head; yea, that all things must be subservient to my salvation, wherefore by his Holy Spirit he also assures me of eternal life, and makes me heartily willing and ready, to live unto him."

Moreover, the combination which we have here in Eph. 1:14, namely, "(God's) own possession . . . to the praise of his glory" reminds one immediately of Isa. 43:20, 21, "my people, my chosen, the people which I formed for myself, in order that they might proclaim my praise." Is it any wonder that when the apostle ponders the fact that he himself and also those addressed had been emancipated from the most dreadful evil and had been restored to the most unimaginable good, and this by the very God against whom they had rebelled, and at such a cost, and that God had even given to them the Holy Spirit as a pledge and foretaste of future climactic bliss when they would receive their full inheritance and would stand forth in dazzling splendor as God's very own, — in view of all this is it any wonder that he begins his magnificent doxology by saying, "Blessed (be)" and that he ends it with "to the praise of his glory"?

---

[35] For the two meanings of the word "redemption" see above, on verse 7, footnote 22; also N.T.C. on Colossians and Philemon, p. 64, footnote 48.

Chapter 1

Verses 15-23

Theme: *The Church Glorious*

I. *Adoration*
for its

E ternal Foundation "in Christ"
2. leading to thanksgiving and prayer, that the eyes of those addressed may be illumined in order to see God's saving power, exhibited in the resurrection and coronation of Christ (verses 15-23)

15 For this reason, because I have heard of the faith in the Lord Jesus that (exists) among y o u and of y o u r love for all the saints, 16 I do not cease to give thanks for y o u, while making mention of y o u in my prayers, 17 (asking) that the God of our Lord Jesus Christ, the Father of glory, may give y o u the Spirit of wisdom and revelation in the clear knowledge of him, 18 (having) the eyes of y o u r hearts illumined, so that y o u may know what is the hope for which he called y o u, what the riches of the glory of his inheritance among the saints, 19 and what the surpassing greatness of his power (displayed) with respect to us who believe, as seen in that manifestation of his infinite might 20 which he exerted in Christ when he raised him from the dead and made him to sit at his right hand in the heavenly places 21 far above every principality and authority and power and dominion and every name that is named, not only in this age but also in the coming one; 22 and he ranged everything in subjection under his feet, and him he gave as head over everything to the church, 23 since it is his body, the fulness of him who fills all in all.

1:15-23

2. Thanksgiving and Prayer

Christ as the eternal foundation of the church (cf. I Cor. 3:11), of its complete salvation, so that it was "in Christ" that believers received every spiritual blessing, is the theme not only of verses 3-14, as has been shown, but also of the rest of the chapter. This is evident from the fact that the apostle *begins* this single sentence of 169 words (in the original) by expressing gratitude because he has heard of the faith of those addressed "in the Lord Jesus." He *ends* it by describing the Christ as the One who *in the interest of the church* "fills all in all."

15. Paul's gratitude of heart was called forth by the blessings enumerated and described in verses 3-14 as well as by the report that had reached him, as he now relates: **For this reason, because I have heard of the faith in the Lord Jesus that (exists) among y o u. . . .** Traffic by sea was brisk in those days; visitors were allowed to see the famous prisoner in Rome; the bond of Christian fellowship was very strong. For all these reasons it is not surprising that although about four years had now elapsed since the apostle carried on his labors in Ephesus — labors from which the people of the surrounding territories also benefited (Acts 19:10, 26) — he had been kept well informed. Now not all of the information that had reached Paul was favorable. He knew that there were grave faults against which the Ephesians had to be warned, and he is going to do just that, but not immediately. Very tactfully he keeps these admonitions in reserve until the close of the letter is in sight (4:17–6:9). Paul was the kind of man who took pleasure in be-

stowing sincere praise upon those whom he loved, and in doing so at once. At the particular place in the letter where, had the apostle been a heathen, he would have thanked this or that deity for having kept the writer and/or the readers in good health, Paul expresses his humble gratitude to the only true God for having imparted to the addressed the quietness and confidence that is the portion of all those who lean on the everlasting arms of their Savior, *Jesus,* and revere him as their *Lord* who bought them and to whom they render joyful obedience. The rosebud of *faith,* moreover, had burst forth into the flower of *love,* for of this, too, Paul had received cheerful tidings: **and of y o u r love** [36] **for all the saints.** *Faith,* if it be genuine, and *love* go together, for the Magnet that draws sinners to himself draws them together also. Or, to change the figure, as the spokes of a wheel approach the hub they at the same time approach each other (see Gal. 5:6; I John 4:21). And because of this feeling of warm personal attachment to, and concern for, one another, present among the addressed, a disposition from which *all* of the saints benefited, Paul continues: **16. I do not cease to give thanks for y o u, while making mention of y o u in my prayers.** Honor to whom honor is due! It was God to whom gratitude was due for the marvelous changes which, by his grace, had been wrought in Ephesus and the region round about. Paul is shown here as a man who believed with all his heart in the necessity of thanksgiving, the latter being an essential element in every prayer that proceeded from his heart. As to prayer for others see also Rom. 1:9; Phil. 1:4; Col. 1:9; I Thess. 1:2; II Thess. 1:11; Philem. 4. All the more striking and beautiful is this expression of thanksgiving and prayer when it is seen in the light of the fact that it was uttered a. with great regularity ("I do not cease") and b. by a prisoner. The latter reminds one of Jonah's prayer "out of the fish's belly," a prayer which similarly included the note of thanksgiving (Jonah 2:1, 9). The content of the prayer is found in the words: **17. (asking) that the God of our Lord Jesus Christ, the Father of glory, may give y o u the Spirit of wisdom and revelation in the clear knowledge of him.** See verse 3 above for a similar manner in which the Object of prayer is indicated, and the explanation there given. Here in verse 17, however, we read "the Father of glory." Paul has just shown how magnificently the attributes of God shone forth in the works of election, foreordination, redemption, spiritual illumination, certification. It is understandable, therefore, that he speaks of "the Father *of glory,*" that is, "the glorious Father." See also Acts 7:2; I Cor. 2:8; and James 2:1. The apostle asks that the Spirit of wisdom and revelation be given to the Ephesians.

---

[36] Though p⁴⁶ Sinaiticus A B lack the word *love,* the alternative reading which includes *love* must be accepted. Otherwise the statement does not make sense. Though it is true that πίστις can mean both *faith* and *faithfulness,* it cannot have both meanings in any *single* occurrence. Hence, the rendering "faith in the Lord Jesus and faithfulness toward all the saints" must be rejected.

Most of the translations have "spirit" instead of "Spirit" (= the Holy Spirit). In favor of *Spirit*, however, are the following arguments:

(1) Paul writes ". . . of *revelation.*" We do not generally associate revelation with the purely human spirit or state of mind.

(2) As to ". . . of *wisdom,*" in Isa. 11:2 this is mentioned as the first of several gifts imparted by the Spirit of Jehovah.

(3) Such expressions as "Spirit of truth" (John 15:26) and "Spirit of adoption" (Rom. 8:15) also refer to the Holy Spirit.

(4) Ephesians abounds with references to the third Person of the Holy Trinity. Since the Comforter figured so prominently in this epistle, we may well believe that also in the present instance Paul has him in mind.

(5) It is rather characteristic of Paul that, having made mention of God the Father and of Christ the Son — and both have already been mentioned here in 1:16 — he then also refers to the Spirit. Cf. Rom. 8:15-17; II Cor. 13:14; Eph. 1:3-14; 3:14-17; 4:4-6; 5:18-21.[37]

(6) When the Father gives *enlightened eyes,* does he not do so through the Holy Spirit? See John 3:3, 5. Men cannot *see* the Kingdom of God, *to enter* it, except through the Spirit. Cf. Eph. 5:8; I John 1:7.

A question may occur, however, in this connection. It may be asked, "But how is it possible that Paul prayed that the Spirit of wisdom and revelation *be given* to those who already possessed that Spirit; in fact, according to verse 13, had been sealed by him?" One cannot escape this difficulty by reading "spirit" (state of mind) instead of Spirit (Holy Spirit). For even then the question would occur: "How can the apostle ask that a spirit of wisdom *in the clear knowledge of him* [that is, of God] *be given* to those who already knew him so well that they had reposed their trust in him?" (verse 13). However, this difficulty confronts us not only here in Ephesians, but throughout Paul's epistles. To give but two examples: contrast Col. 1:4 with 3:12; I Thess. 1:3; 2:13 with 5:15. If Paul could say the one how could he say the other also?

The answer is provided by Paul himself. It amounts to this: what is already present *must be strengthened.* The Holy Spirit is present, to be sure, but the apostle prays that the Ephesians "may be strengthened with power through his Spirit in the inner man" (3:16). The work begun in the heart must "be carried on toward completion" (Phil. 1:6). Love and all the other graces must "abound more and more" (Phil. 1:9; cf. I Thess. 3:12; 4:10). It is clear, therefore, that Paul's prayer here in Eph. 1:15-23, includ-

---

[37] Having recently made a contextual study and tabulation of every New Testament occurrence of πνεῦμα I have arrived at the conclusion that one should not rely too heavily on the rule, "When the article is used, the reference is to the Holy Spirit; when omitted, the reference is to an operation, influence, or gift of the Spirit." Each occurrence should be studied in the light of its own immediate context.

ing therefore also verse 17, is entirely consistent with what he had solemnly declared in verses 3-14. In fact, the connection between verses 15 and 16, on the one hand, and 17 ff., on the other, shows that it was exactly because so many spiritual gifts had been received that the apostle takes courage to ask for even more.

Paul, then, asks that the addressed may receive a continually growing supply of *wisdom* and *clear knowledge*. Combine the two, and note that he is asking that the Ephesians be given deeper penetration into the meaning of the gospel and a clearer insight into the will of God for their lives, enabling them at all times to use the best means for the attainment of the highest goal, namely, the glory of God Triune.

Now it was the Spirit who imparted wisdom, the Spirit also who revealed the truth. For these early Christians, who so recently had emerged from pagan fear, superstition, and immorality, who were able to communicate with Paul only by letter or through a messenger, and who were living in the midst of a heathen environment, wisdom and revelation were doubly needed, and this not only in order to gain a clearer insight into the way of salvation but also to know just what was the right course to follow in any given situation. What they needed above all was *clear knowledge* of God, including joyful *recognition* of God's way for their lives and a willingness to follow his direction. Now this was not merely a matter of the intellect. Far more than this was at stake. Hence the apostle continues his prayer as follows: **18. (having) the eyes of y o u r hearts illumined.**[38] In Scripture the heart is the fulcrum of feeling and faith as well as the mainspring of words and actions (Rom. 10:10; cf. Matt. 12:34; 15:19; 22:37; John 14:1). It is the core and center of man's being, man's inmost self. "Out of it are the issues of life" (Prov. 4:23). "Man looks on the outward appearance, but Jehovah looks on the heart" (I Sam. 16:7). Now apart from the work of the Holy Spirit the eye of the heart is blind (Isa. 9:2; John 9:39-41; I Cor. 2:14-16). Men thus blinded need two things: the gospel and spiritual apperception. The latter is what is meant by *eyes illumined* or *enlightened*. See also on 5:8 for the meaning of *light* versus *darkness*. In order to bring about this illumination the Spirit causes men to be reborn. He removes their mists of ignorance, clouds of lust, selfish and jealous dispositions, etc., and imparts to them sorrow for sin and faith working through love. The spiritual eye is enlightened when the heart is purified. "Blessed are the

---

[38] The construction of πεφωτισμένους τοὺς ὀφθαλμούς is not easy. One solution would be to infer that, because of the following infinitive, the dative (πεφωτισμένοις) is here replaced by the accusative (πεφωτισμένους). Another would be to regard the words in question as an accusative absolute. The simplest, and perhaps the best, would be the construction which looks upon these words as being governed by δώῃ, and accordingly as in apposition with the preceding πνεῦμα. This would yield the sense, ". . . that he may give y o u the Spirit of wisdom and revelation . . . (hence) eyes illumined."

pure in heart, for they shall see God" (Matt. 5:8). Paul continues: **so that
y o u may know what is the hope [39] for which he called y o u.** Paul knows
that the best way to drive away old sinful tendencies is no longer to concentrate on *them* but rather on the blessings of salvation. The Ephesians
had received *the effectual call.* The urgent invitation of the gospel (the
external call) had been applied to their hearts by the Holy Spirit, producing the *internal* call. In the latter sense *calling* is referred to everywhere in
the New Testament; cf. Rom. 11:29; I Cor. 1:26; 7:20; Eph. 4:1, 4 (in addition to the present 1:18); Phil. 3:14; II Tim. 1:9; Heb. 3:1; I Peter 2:9;
II Peter 1:10. Let those addressed then ponder how rich they are because
of *the hope* for which God had called them (literally, "the hope of his
calling"). This hope is firmly grounded in God's infallible promises. It is
the soul's anchor, moored to the very throne of God; hence, to the very
heart of Christ (Heb. 6:18-20). It is therefore a fervent yearning, confident
expectation, and patient waiting for the fulfilment of God's promises, a full
Christ-centered (cf. Col. 1:27) assurance that these promises will indeed be
realized. It is a living and sanctifying force (I Peter 1:3; I John 3:3). Paul
continues: (so that y o u may know) **what (is) the riches of the glory of his
inheritance among the saints.** "His" inheritance means the one given by
him, just like "his" calling was the call issued and made effective by him.
Paul is speaking about the glorious riches, the marvelous magnitude, of all
the blessings of salvation, particularly those still to be bestowed in the great
consummation of all things. See N.T.C. on Col. 1:12 ("the inheritance of
the saints in the light"). These blessings are called an *inheritance* because
they are the gift of God's grace, and once received will never be taken away
again ("I will not give you the inheritance of my fathers," I Kings 21:4).
See also above, on verse 14. The phrase "among the saints" (cf. Acts 20:32;
26:18) deserves special attention. When a believer's hope is what it should
be, he never looks forward to an inheritance *just for himself.* What will
make the inheritance so glorious is exactly the fact that he will enjoy it
together with "all who love his appearing" (II Tim. 4:8).

19. Paul continues by adding one more item to *the hope* and *the inheritance.* He says, "I pray that the eyes of y o u r hearts may be illumined, so
that y o u may know what is the hope . . . what the riches of the glory of
his inheritance among the saints," **and what the surpassing greatness of
his power (displayed) with respect to us who believe, as seen in that manifestation of his infinite might. . . .** This "surpassing greatness of his [God
the Father's] power" is needed as a link between the two other items which
were mentioned in the preceding verse, namely, *the hope* and the *inheritance.* The *power* (Greek *dúnamis,* cf. "dynamite") of God is necessary in
order that the *hope* may be realized, the *inheritance* obtained. The words

---

[39] Note the triad faith, love (verse 15) and hope (verse 18). See N.T.C. on Colossians and Philemon, pp. 47–50.

"with respect to us who believe" show that this power is exerted in the interest of believers, of no one else. They alone receive the inheritance. Paul is asking God to give the addressed enlightened eyes in order that they may know what is the surpassing greatness of God's power ". . . according to that working of the strength of his might," etc., thus literally. The three words which he employs to show how this *power* is used are: *enérgeia* (whence our "energy"), that is, *activity, working, manifestation; krátos: exercised strength;* and *ischús: might, great inherent strength.* Nevertheless, when such synonyms are piled up, as happens in this part of the sentence, it is a question whether we should distinguish them so sharply. F. W. Grosheide is probably correct when he says, "It is difficult to indicate an accurate distinction between the various words used for power. It is permissible to conclude that the apostle uses more than one term to indicate the fulness and the certainty of this power" (*op. cit.,* p. 30). In harmony with this view I suggest the translation "power . . . as seen in that manifestation of his infinite might," (continued) **20. which he exerted in Christ when he raised him from the dead and made him to sit at his right hand in the heavenly places.** The main thought expressed by these words when they are viewed in the light of what immediately precedes is this: the apostle prays that the Ephesians be given enlightened eyes so that they may see and discern that, in order to translate their steadfast hope into glorious realization so that they will receive their full inheritance, God has at his disposal *as great a power* as he exhibited when he raised his Son from the dead and set him at his own right hand. It is as if the apostle were saying, "Do not despair. Y o u can rely on God's infinite power. One day the inheritance held in store for y o u will be fully y o u r s."

But is it necessary to limit the meaning of Paul's words to *a comparison* between *a.* the power displayed in Christ's resurrection and coronation, and *b.* the power exercised in bringing believers to their ultimate victory? In the light of Rom. 6:8-11; I Cor. 15:20; Col. 3:1, may he not also have had in mind the fact that Christ's resurrection and session at the Father's right hand are *typical* of what happens to believers? They, too, will conquer death when they arise gloriously from their graves to live and reign with Christ forevermore. And even now Christ's resurrection is a type of their spiritual resurrection, their gradual victory over sin. There is, in fact, even a *causal* connection. Christ's resurrection, being proof-positive of the believers' justification, is a *pledge* of their eternal glory. His sitting at the Father's right hand, whence he has poured out his Spirit into their hearts, *guarantees* and *brings about* their ultimate bliss.

The tremendously important place which Christ's resurrection occupied in the thinking of the apostolic age is apparent not only from the present passage but also from the following: Matt. 28; Mark 16; Luke 24; John 20, 21; Acts 1:22; 2:32; 3:26; 10:40; 13:34; 17:31; 23:6; 26:8, 23; Rom. 4:25;

8:34; I Cor. 15; I Peter 1:3; etc. Similarly, the significance attached to Christ's coronation, so that as a reward for his mediatorial work he rules the entire universe in the interest of his church, is clear in the present epistle from 1:20-23; 4:8 ff., and elsewhere from Acts 2:33, 36; 5:31; 7:56; Rom. 8:34; Phil. 2:9; Col. 3:1; Heb. 2:8, 9; etc. See also Ps. 110:1. Two chapters of the Book of Revelation are devoted mainly to this theme (chapter 5, see verse 7; chapter 12, see verses 5 and 10). The living and ruling Christ was a living reality to the consciousness of the early church. For the phrase "in the heavenly places" see above, on verse 3.

21. The fact that the apostle was not thinking first of all of a particular point in space when he spoke of Christ's exaltation to the Father's right hand but rather of the extent or degree of this high position is clear from the words: **far above every principality and authority and power and dominion and every name that is named.** The enumeration of the mighty ones "far above" whom Christ was assigned his place of pre-eminence is almost the same as that in Col. 1:16. From that passage, in the light of Col. 2:10, as well as from the present Ephesian passage when compared with 3:10, it is clear that the reference is, or is primarily, to angels. Teachers of error, who at this very time were disturbing the churches of provincial Asia, particularly those of the Lycus Valley, grossly overestimated the position of the angels in relation to Christ and the work of salvation. The names of angels, the various categories into which they were to be classified, and the worship due to them, seem to have been some of the topics on which the heretics concentrated their attention. What Paul is saying, then, is this: the angels (whether good or bad) have no power apart from Christ. Call them by whatever name y o u wish, far above them all reigns Christ. (See on 4:10.) Moreover, his position of majesty will last forever, for he has been exalted above all these eminent ones and above every title that can be conferred **not only in this age,**[40] the present dispensation, **but also in the coming one,** the one that will be ushered in at the consummation of all things (cf. 2:7).[41]

---

[40] $al\acute{\omega}\nu$ has been defined as "the world in motion," as contrasted with $\kappa\acute{o}\sigma\mu os$, "the world at rest." However, the latter term is used in a great variety of senses; see N.T.C. on John, Vol. I, p. 79, footnote 26. The term $al\acute{\omega}\nu$ may be said to indicate the world viewed from the standpoint of time and change; hence, the *age*, whether present or future ("coming"), and its prevalent mood.

[41] At this point Lenski gets into a difficulty. Having interpreted "the coming" age as the one that Christ will usher in at his Parousia — a correct interpretation of the term as here used, I believe — and proceeding from the tacit assumption that at that moment time will cease to be, he must explain how the text can, nevertheless, speak about a *coming age*. His solution is as follows: "it is called 'the eon to come' only because we now wait for it in hope. Also we may note that human language is compelled to use terms indicating time when speaking of eternity [a fact which I do not call in question], although eternity is timelessness, the opposite of time, succession, progress, etc." On this point I differ. Nowhere does Scripture teach that the soul, either when it enters heaven or when it is reunited with the body at

22, 23. Accordingly, the God of our Lord Jesus Christ, the Father of glory manifested his infinite might when he raised Christ from the dead and made him to sit at his right hand **and he ranged everything in subjection under his feet.** In him, as *the Ideal Man* ("Son of Man" as well as "Son of God") Psalm 8 (of which verse 6 is here quoted; cf. LXX Ps. 8:7) attains its absolute fulfilment. See also I Cor. 15:27 and Heb. 2:8. The expression "everything" or "all things" must not be narrowed down to "all things in the church." Nor does it merely include such things as "sheep and oxen, the beasts of the field, the birds of the heavens, the fish of the sea, whatever passes through the paths of the seas" (Ps. 8:7, 8). Though, in a very limited manner, mankind, even after the fall, exercises a degree of dominion over these "lower" creatures, the sway that he thus wields is nothing compared to Christ's universal sovereignty, a dominion from which absolutely nothing that exists is excluded. Therefore *nothing* can prevent the realization of the believers' "hope." *Nothing* will be allowed to stand in the way of their acquisition and enjoyment, to the full, of that glorious "inheritance" of which they have a foretaste even here and now. Moreover, God's power does not lie dormant. In a manner that was clearly exhibited in Christ's exaltation it is being used for the government of the universe in the interest of the church. Hence, Paul continues: **and him** [42] **he gave as head over everything to the church, since** [43] **it is his body . . . ;** that is, since he is so intimately and indissolubly united with it and loves it with such profound, boundless, and steadfast love. It is the closeness of the bond, the unfathomable character of the love between Christ and his church that is stressed by this head-body symbolism, as is clearly indicated in 5:25-33. In this connection an important fact must not be ignored, namely, that throughout the letter Paul emphasizes God's (or Christ's) great love for his people, and the love they owe him and one another in return (1:5; 2:4; 3:19; 4:1, 2; 5:1, 2 ff.; 6:23, 24). There is not a single chapter in which this theme is not stressed. One who has not grasped this point does not understand Ephesians!

In the twin epistles, Colossians and Ephesians, the figure head-body appears for the first time in Paul's epistles, to indicate the relation between Christ and his church. It is true, of course, that here in Eph. 1:22, 23 Christ is not actually said to be the head of the church but rather "head over everything to the church . . . his body." But this manner of expressing it merely enhances the beauty of the symbolism. The meaning, then, is this:

Christ's return, acquires the divine attribute of timelessness. Also, "perfection" for believers does not necessarily rule out "progress." For my own views on this subject and also the views of others see my book *The Bible on the Life Hereafter*, pp. 70–78.

[42] Note forward position of αὐτόν for emphasis.

[43] The relative pronoun ἥτις has causal force. See Gram. N.T., p. 728.

since the church is Christ's body, with which he is organically united, he loves it so much that *in its interest* he exercises his infinite power in causing the entire universe with all that is in it to co-operate, whether willingly or unwillingly. Accordingly, the idea *Christ the Ruling Head over everything* (cf. Col. 2:10) does not cancel but rather strengthens and adorns the clearly implied doctrine *Christ the Ruling (and Organic) Head of the Church* (cf. Eph. 4:15; 5:23; Col. 1:18; 2:19). When, therefore, many commentators, dogmaticians, as well as the Heidelberg Catechism (Lord's Day XIX, edition with textual references, Q. and A. 50) appeal to Eph. 1:20-23, among other passages, in support of the position that Christ is head of the church, they are not committing an error. For further remarks on Christ's headship see above, on verse 10; also N.T.C. on Colossians, pp. 76–78, the latter particularly for the distinction between *ruling* and *organic* headship.

As a further description of the church as body of Christ, Paul adds: **the fulness** [44] **of him who fills all in all.**

The argument with respect to the exact meaning of *fulness* in this particular case covers many pages in scores of commentaries. With due respect for the reasoning of those who defend other theories, and whose pleas in corroboration of their views have been examined in detail,[45] I have, after

---

[44] The idea of G. G. Findlay and others that πλήρωμα modifies αὐτόν, and refers, therefore, to Christ rather than to the church, has found but little approval, the reason being that words used in apposition or as a modifier must be construed with a near, not with a remote, antecedent, unless a very good reason can be given for construing them differently.

[45] Some interpret πλήρωμα as "the full number of aeons as well as the uncreated monad from which they have proceeded" or, in general, as a term belonging to second century gnostic speculation. Nothing in the context favors this theory. Others, many of whom depend heavily on J. B. Lightfoot's contention (defended in his work, *Saint Paul's Epistle to the Colossians and to Philemon*, pp. 255–271) that "Substantives in *ma*, formed from the perfect passive, appear always to have a passive sense," favor the interpretation: (the church as body of Christ is) "that which is filled – or is being filled – by Christ." With variations as to detail this view is defended, among others, by Greijdanus, Percy ("die Gemeinde als von Christus erfüllt"), Robertson, Salmond, Scott. It is also favored by L.N.T. (A. and G.), p. 678, and by *The Amplified New Testament*. In support of this theory it can be said that the apostle stresses the fact that the church finds its fulness in Christ, in him alone (Col. 2:10), in whom God was pleased to have all the fulness dwell (Col. 1:19; cf. Eph. 4:10). Also, the combination of the noun πλήρωμα and the participle πληρουμένου then runs smoothly: the church is filled by him who fills all things. The theory is very attractive. It is weakened somewhat, however, by the contention of other interpreters that "In every other case in which πλήρωμα occurs it is used actively – *that which does fill*" (thus Hodge, *op. cit.*, pp. 89, 90; and for the titles of other sources showing that Lightfoot's position is indefensible see M.M., on πλήρωμα, p. 520). At any rate, contextual study of all the New Testament instances in which πλήρωμα is used shows that in interpreting Eph. 1:23 it is rather precarious to make use of Lightfoot's contention. See also N.T.C. on Colossians and Philemon, pp. 79, 80, footnote 56, for complete tabulation of the meaning of πλήρωμα in the New Testament. What is, perhaps, an even more cogent argument against the passive sense of the noun as here used is the fact that in that case the head-body metaphor which the apostle employs would seem to be hardly fitting. One can say that

lengthy study reached the conclusion that the following is the correct interpretation: *the church is Christ's complement*. In other words:

"This is the highest honor of the church, that, until he is united to us, the Son of God reckons himself in some measure imperfect. What consolation it is for us to learn that, not until we are in his presence, does he possess all his parts, or does he wish to be regarded as complete." (John Calvin in his comments on this passage. See Bibliography for title of work.) With variations as to detail, this view, namely, that the church is, indeed, represented here as *filling* or *completing* him who fills all in all, is also defended by Abbott, Barry, Bruce, Grosheide, Hodge, Lenski, Simpson, and many others.

This interpretation to which I, along with all of those just mentioned, cling does not any degree or manner detract from the absolute majesty or self-sufficiency of Christ. As to his divine essence Christ is in no sense whatever dependent on or capable of being completed by the church. But as *bridegroom* he is incomplete without the *bride;* as *vine* he cannot be thought of without *the branches;* as *shepherd* he is not seen without *his sheep;* and so also as *head* he finds his full expression in *his body,* the church.

There are also the following additional reasons that have induced me to regard this interpretation as being the correct one:

(1) The fact that the One who fills all in all does, nevertheless, have that which fills or completes him, is clearly taught by Christ himself and also by his disciple John (John 6:56; 15:4, 5; 17–21; I John 3:24) . "Abide in me, and I in y o u" shows that not only are the branches incomplete apart from the vine — which is the point that is stressed in John 15 — but, in a sense, the vine also finds fulfilment in the branches.

(2) In Col. 1:24 Paul speaks about himself as "supplying what is lacking

---

the church is filled by Christ, and conversely that, accordingly, Christ fills the church. But can one also say that the body is filled by the head, hence, that the head fills the body? Beare answers, "The head cannot be said 'to fill' the body." Is it not rather the body that fills, completes, expresses, carries out the directives of, the head?

Finally, there is an interpretation which would avoid placing any emphasis either on the active or on the passive sense of πλήρωμα. It interprets this noun as indicating simply "the full number or totality of those individual believers who are represented in the redemptive activity of the incarnate Christ." As I see it, this, too, is a plausible interpretation. The word πλήρωμα does at times seem to have the meaning *full number.* Rom. 11:12 and 11:25 ("total number of elect Jews," "total number of elect Gentiles") merit consideration here. And it is also true that, numerically speaking, the reference in Eph. 1:23 is, indeed, to none other than the full number of the elect. Why is it, then, that by far the most commentators insist that πλήρωμα, as used here in Eph. 1:23, must be interpreted either *passively,* "that which is — or is being — filled," or *actively,* "that which fills or completes," but not *quiescently,* "totality." Is it, perhaps, because it is felt by both classes of interpreters that the noun and the participle form a unit, and that if the latter implies *action,* whether received or exerted, the former must do the same?

in the afflictions of Christ." There is a sense in which the church, as it were, completes Christ's suffering. See N.T.C. on Col. 1:24. Those, therefore, who reject the idea that the church is the complement of the Christ, will experience great difficulty in interpreting Col. 1:24. Similarly, the church recapitulates Christ's death and resurrection (Rom. 6:4, 5; Col. 2:20; 3:1; II Tim. 2:11, 12).

(3) The head-body metaphor, when interpreted as meaning that the body fills or completes the head, resulting in an organic unity, so that the body carries out the will and purpose of the head, makes good sense. Christ uses the church in the realization of his plan in the government of the world and for the salvation of sinners.

(4) The idea stressed by Calvin, namely, that Christ refuses to regard himself as complete until he possesses all his parts, also harmonizes beautifully with the love-motif which, as I have shown, dominates this entire epistle.

(5) The description of the church as "the fulness of him who fills all in all" is, indeed, a "tremendous paradox" (to use Lenski's expression, *op. cit.*, p. 403). This, too, is exactly what we expect to find in Paul. Oxymora or seeming contradictions abound in his writings: "They are not all Israel that are of Israel" (Rom. 9:6). "In everything we commend ourselves . . . as deceivers, yet true; as unknown, yet well-known; as dying but behold we live; . . . as sorrowful, yet always rejoicing; as poor, yet making many rich; as having nothing, and yet possessing all things" (II Cor. 6:4-10). "When I am weak, then I am strong" (II Cor. 12:10). It is Paul who wants the Thessalonians to be ambitious about living calmly (I Thess. 4:11). And in this very epistle of Ephesians he speaks about *knowing* the love of God *that passes knowledge* (3:19)! The paradox of Eph. 1:23 fits nicely into this style category.

Commenting on the words "of him who fills all in all" Calvin continues as follows, "This is added to guard against the supposition that any real defect would exist in Christ if he were separated from us. His desire to be filled and, in some respects, to be made perfect in us, arises from no want or necessity; for all that is good in ourselves, or in any of the creatures, is the gift of his hand."

The words "who fills [46] all in all" mean that Christ fills *all* the universe *in all* respects; that is, the entire universe is not only dependent on him for the fulfilment of its every need but is also governed by him in the interest

---

[46] The participle is to be interpreted as a middle, not as a passive, which would result in a harsh construction. Whether or not this middle has retained something of its reciprocal or reflexive force — hence, "who fills the whole universe *for himself*" (or, according to others, "from himself as the center") — or simply has the sense of the active, would be difficult to establish, though the former alternative seems probable.

of the church, which, in turn, must serve the universe, and is replenished by his bounteous gifts. Thus he is constantly pervading all things with his love and power (cf. Jer. 23:24; I Kings 8:27; Ps. 139:7). I agree with the statement of Roels, "Paul most probably refers to the fact that the Christ, exalted over all, is now involved in the historical realization of the already accomplished reconciliation of the universe by directing all things to their determined, divinely appointed, end" (*op. cit.*, p. 248).

With such a Christ as *the Eternal Foundation* of its salvation the church has nothing to fear. Its *hope* will be realized, its *inheritance* fully enjoyed.

Summary of Chapter 1

The chapter consists of two main parts (after the opening salutation, verses 1-3). In the first of these (verses 4-14) Paul praises God Triune for the blessings of election by the Father, redemption through the Son, and certification in the Spirit. In the second (verses 15-23), having given utterance to his deep and humble thanksgiving, the apostle prays that the Ephesians may be enlightened so that they may behold: *a.* what is the *hope* for which they have been called; *b.* what the *inheritance* that awaits them; and *c.* what is the *power* of God to cause this hope to be realized and the inheritance to become their everlasting possession. Was not the proof of the operation of this power given when "the Father of glory" raised his Son from the dead and made him to sit at his right hand in the heavenly places?

In this chapter, more than in any other, the apostle underscores the fact that it is "in Christ" that every spiritual blessing descends upon God's people from "the heavenly places." Apart from him they are desperately poor. In intimate fellowship with him they are inexpressibly rich. Christ is, accordingly, in a very real sense the church's *Eternal Foundation*. Cf. I Cor. 3:11.

The question may be asked, "How is it that in this chapter and also in chapters 2 and 3 the apostle, a *prisoner,* gives expression to his profound gratitude in words of unrestrained adoration, beginning with 'Blessed (be) the God and Father of our Lord Jesus Christ!'?" The answer is that he had meditated on the following facts:

(1) The Father's *special delight* in planning the salvation of people who in themselves were entirely unworthy (1:5b; 2:3).

(2) The Father's *marvelous decision* to adopt these people as his very own, and to call them "the Father's Family" (1:5; 3:15).

(3) The Son's *solemn pledge,* made before the foundation of the world, whereby he became his people's Surety (1:4).

(4) The fact that "not until we are in his presence does he [the Son] wish to be regarded as complete" (Calvin's interpretation of the expression that the church is "the fulness of him who fills all in all" 1:23).

(5) The Spirit's willingness to dwell in the hearts of God's people, by his very presence assuring them of greater glory to come (1:13, 14).

(6) The Spirit's activity of enlightening the eyes, so that believers, thus illumined, may have a clear and definite knowledge of their *hope*, their *inheritance*, and of *the power of God* which transforms the hope into the actual possession of the inheritance (1:17-23).

(7) The revelation to Paul of the "mystery," namely, the establishment of the church gathered out of Jews and Gentiles and welded into *one* spiritual community with equality of membership for all regardless of race or nationality (1:15; 2:16; 3:6).

(8) The fact that this "united church" is being established before Paul's very eyes, the congregations of Ephesus and surroundings furnishing the proof (1:15).

(9) The fact that even he, Paul, once a bitter persecutor, had, in God's marvelous grace, been chosen to reveal the mystery to men and to see it go into effect (3:3-5).

(10) The reign of the resurrected and ascended Christ over the entire universe in the interest of the church, his body (1:22, 23).

Chapter 2

Verses 1–10

Theme: *The Church Glorious*

I. *Adoration*
for its

U niversal Scope (embracing both Jew and Gentile),
   1. secured by the great redemptive blessings *for both* which center "in Christ" and parallel his resurrection and triumphant life

CHAPTER II

EPHESIANS

2   1 And y o u, even though y o u were dead through y o u r trespasses and sins, 2 in which y o u formerly walked in line with the course of this world, in line with the prince of the domain of the air, (the domain) of the spirit now at work in the sons of disobedience, 3 among whom we also once lived in the lusts of our flesh, fulfilling the desires of the flesh and its reasonings, and were by nature children of wrath even as the rest, 4 God, being rich in mercy, because of his great love with which he loved us, 5 even though we were dead through our trespasses made us alive together with Christ — by grace y o u have been saved — 6 and raised us up with him and made us sit with him in the heavenly places in Christ Jesus, 7 in order that in the ages to come he might show the surpassing riches of his grace (expressed) in kindness toward us in Christ Jesus. 8 For by grace y o u have been saved through faith; and this not of yourselves, (it is) the gift of God; 9 not of works, lest anyone should boast, 10 for his handiwork are we, created in Christ Jesus for good works, which God prepared beforehand that we should walk in them.

2:1-10

1. Redemptive Blessings for Both Jew and Gentile

The record of the prayer and thanksgiving has ended. But the deep feeling continues, as is evident from such expressions as *"rich* mercy . . . *great love . . . surpassing* riches of grace." This, too, as well as in chapter 1, is the language of gratitude and adoration. Nevertheless a new subdivision begins here. There is no sudden break. In chapter 2, as in chapter 1, Christ, in whom the Holy Trinity is revealed, is regarded as the basis of blessing (2:6, 7, 9, 13, 21, 22). But the emphasis has shifted, as is shown by the fact that in this second chapter the phrase "in Christ" or its equivalent occurs with far less frequency. It is the *universal scope* or *extent* of the church on which chapter 2 concentrates our attention. The apostle begins to show that "in Christ" the palace of salvation has opened its gates to all, that is, to Gentiles as well as to Jews. When Jesus died on the cross the wall between these two formerly hostile groups came tumbling down, never to be re-erected (2:14). In him all are now *one,* that is, all those who have embraced him by a living faith.

The easy manner in which Paul shifts from "y o u" to "we" and back again, in verses 1-10 — with "y o u" in verses 1, 2, and 8; "we" in verses 3, 4, 6, 7, and 10; and a "we" that clearly includes a "y o u" in verse 5 — indicates that though a distinction is being drawn at times, it is upon what

109

all have in common that the emphasis falls. The blessings enumerated are shared by addressor and addressed, by Jew and Gentile alike, for all, being by nature dead through sins and trespasses, had to be made alive. Not until verse 11 is reached are we told how the two groups — Jew and Gentile — erstwhile bitter enemies, have become friends. The logic is simple and clear. The establishment of peace between God and man (verses 1-10), so that "children of wrath" stand revealed as objects of love, naturally precedes and brings about peace between man and man, in this case between Jew and Gentile (verse 11 ff.). The horizontal line is the proliferation of the vertical.

Not only does chapter 2 contain an echo of the main emphasis of chapter 1, namely, that Jesus Christ, as the revelation of God Triune, is the One "in whom" all blessings, past, present, and future, are bestowed upon believers, so that in that sense he is the church's *eternal foundation,* but it also foreshadows the ideas on which the apostle is going to dwell in greater detail in later chapters. Particularly, does it give a preview of 4:1-16: the church's *organic unity and growth.*

In the main, however, chapter 2, by implication, assails the spirit of sinful exclusivism, and stresses the fact that God's love is broader than the ocean, and embraces not only Jews but also Gentiles (cf. Rom. 1:14; Gal. 3:28; Col. 3:11; then also John 3:16; 10:16; Rev. 5:9; 7:9), welding them into an organic unity, and doing this by the strangest instrument imaginable, namely, a death upon a cross! The church's *universal scope* is the thought on which Paul's mind is centered here, and which he introduces as follows:

1. **And y o u, even though y o u were dead through y o u r trespasses and sins . . .** The word *y o u* is the object of the sentence, placed first for the sake of emphasis. It is as if the apostle were saying, "It was on *y o u,* so unworthy, that God took pity." Yet, in the original the subject of the sentence, namely, "God," and the predicate, "made alive," are not mentioned until verses 4 and 5. And even then Paul does not really say, "God made *y o u* alive," but "God made *us* alive." In dwelling on the great mysteries of salvation, matters with which the apostle is himself so vitally concerned, and the effects of which he has experienced so dramatically in his own life and is still experiencing, it was impossible for him to leave himself out of the picture. He is unable to write about such things in an abstract, detached manner. Hence, he is going to substitute "us" for "y o u." This "us" is, however, broad enough to include "y o u."

In many English translations, however, already in verse 1 subject and predicate are inserted, so that verse 1 reads, "And y o u did he make alive." Sometimes the words "did he make alive" (A.R.V.) or "hath he quickened" (A.V.) are printed in italics (A.R.V.; A.V.), to indicate their absence in the original; sometimes they are not (R.S.V.), which, as I see it, is worse.

Either way, their insertion in verse 1 beclouds Paul's purpose.[47] The apostle, I believe, was so completely overwhelmed by the sense of gratitude when he contrasted the former utter wretchedness of the addressed with their present riches in Christ that he purposely postponed the description of the latter until he had portrayed the former. No doubt he did this in order that the Ephesians, having been reminded at some length (verses 1-3) of the dreaded darkness of death in which they formerly walked, would rejoice all the more when at last (verse 4 ff.) they are told that all this is now past, since God, in his infinite mercy, love, and grace, had caused the light of life to dawn upon them (yes, upon "us"). The more men learn to see the dimensions of their utterly lost condition the more they will also, by God's grace, appreciate their marvelous deliverance.

Before their conversion, then, the addressed were "dead" in their trespasses (deviations from the straight and narrow path; see on 1:7) and sins (inclinations, thoughts, words, and deeds which "miss the mark" of glorifying God). Now the fact that these people are here described as having been *dead* does not mean that in their hearts and lives the process of moral and spiritual corruption had run its full course. Ursinus, in his explanation of the Heidelberg Catechism, John Calvin, and many, many others, have pointed out that even the unregenerate can perform *natural* good: eating, drinking, taking exercise, etc., and *civic* or *moral* good. Some worldly men have "uniformly conducted themselves in a most virtuous manner through the whole course of their lives." So wrote John Calvin, *Institutes of the Christian Religion* (translated by John Allen, Philadelphia, 1928), Vol. I, p. 263. To deny this would be to close our eyes to facts that confront us every day of our lives.[48] Also such a denial would amount to a rejection of the plain teaching of Scripture. King Joash "did what was right in the eyes of Jehovah all the days of Jehoiada the priest" (II Chron. 24:2). But note how his life ended (II Chron. 24:20-22). Jesus said, "If y o u do good to those who do good to y o u, what credit is that to y o u? For even sinners

---

[47] The Swedish Bible (Stockholm, 1946) inserts the words in verse 1. So do the Frisian (Amsterdam, 1946), the South African, though in italics (Kaapstad, 1938), etc. On the other hand, the Dutch (*Nieuwe Vertaling,* Amsterdam, 1951) and several others, including French and German versions, do not have this insertion. Some translators have taken Paul's one beautiful sentence (consisting at least of verses 1-7) and have chopped it up into so many brief statements, each followed by a period, that, whether in verse 1 they insert or omit these words, the resultant translation misses something of the flavor of the real Paul.

[48] The fact that *sinners* sometimes turn out better than expected, while *saints* often disappoint us, is discussed by A. Kuyper in his three-volume work *De Gemeene Gratie* (second edition, Kampen, no date); see especially Vol. II, p. 13 ff. Whatever one may think of Kuyper's solution, it is at least more scriptural and satisfying than that which is offered by Reinhold Niebuhr in his work *Man's Nature and His Communities: Essays on the Dynamics and Enigmas of Man's Personal and Social Existence* (New York, 1965). That author sees no real difference between saints and sinners!

do the same thing" (Luke 6:33). Truly at times "the barbarians" show us "no common kindness" (Acts 28:2; cf. Rom. 2:14). In an emergency the crowd that is willing to donate blood is frequently so numerous that at the proper time an announcement has to be issued, "No more blood needed." When a case of pitiable poverty makes the headlines, and is covered by an emotional write-up, accompanied by sensational pictures, men's feelings are stirred to such an extent that food, clothing, money, toys, etc., come pouring in to help those in distress. And by no means all the givers are believers!

However, though it would be foolish to deny that even apart from regenerating grace men "show some regard for virtue and for good outward behavior" (Canons of Dort, III and IV, article 4), such conduct does not even begin to compare with *spiritual* good. Only the Lord knows to what extent, in each man's life, the outwardly good deed springs from genuine sympathy because God's image in him was not completely lost, and in how far it resulted from the realization that absolute self-seeking is self-defeating, or from some other not exactly altruistic motive. In any event such a good deed does not spring from the root of gratitude for the salvation merited by Jesus Christ. It is not a work of faith, therefore. It is not done with a conscious purpose to please and glorify God and to obey his law. Now it is with respect to such *spiritual* good that men are by nature *dead*. It is a fact that even men with a reputation for virtue have been known to answer every gospel appeal with utter disdain. Their proud heart refuses to accept the urgent invitation to confess their sins and to accept Christ as their Savior and Lord. Natural man is not even able properly *to discern* God. The things of the Spirit are "foolishness" to him (I Cor. 2:14). He lacks the ability to bestir himself so as to give heed to that which God demands of him (Ezek. 37; John 3:3, 5). Only when God turns him is he able to turn from his wicked way (Jer. 31:18, 19). Besides all this, he is under the sentence of death, under the curse because of his sin in Adam (original sin) to which he has added his own trespasses and sins. 2. With respect to these trespasses and sins Paul continues: **in which** [49] **y o u formerly walked in line with the course of this world,** that is, in which environment y o u formerly moved about freely, feeling perfectly at home, conducting yourselves in complete harmony with "the spirit of the age that marks mankind alienated from the life of God," [50] **in line with the prince of the domain** [51]

---

[49] In view of the last antecedent the relative is feminine (αἷς). The reference is, however, to both trespasses and sins.

[50] αἰών see on 1:21, footnote 40.

[51] Just as βασιλεία can mean both *kingship* (or *rule*) and the realm in which it is exercised: *kingdom,* so also ἐξουσία can mean *authority, one who wields authority* (or at least *supposedly* does so, an angel for instance), or the *domain* or *realm* over which this authority extends. I believe that much of the difficulty with respect to the proper interpretation of this passage has arisen from failure to recognize this

of the air . . . Must this word "air" be taken more or less literally as indicating the region above the earth but below the heaven of the redeemed, or must it be interpreted in an ethical or figurative sense: "the moral atmosphere" or "prevailing mood" of the period in which one happens to live? Lenski's candor must be admired. He confesses that he does not know what to do with this term (*op.cit.*, pp. 408–410). He does, however, reject both the literal and the figurative meaning. Simpson accepts the figurative sense. In rejecting the literal meaning, calling it "a queer fancy," he adds, "else we should earnestly dissuade all Godfearing souls from setting foot in an aeroplane" (*op.cit.*, p. 48). At this point I allow myself the following observations:

(1) Why only "Godfearing souls"? If air-travel is so dangerous because of all those minions of evil, should not the wicked be warned also? Moreover, should not *the earth* be avoided also, or, in spite of Rev. 16:14, is its terrain "off limits" to the evil spirits? But if that be true why did Jesus call Satan "the prince of this world" (John 12:31; 14:30)?

(2) Is there even one other instance in Scripture where the word "air" is used in this figurative sense?

(3) As to Satan — for it is he who, in line with the references just mentioned, is "the prince of the domain of the air" — is he omnipresent like God? Are his servants, the demons, omnipresent? Is it wrong to ascribe *whereness* to them because they are spirits? Obviously the distinguished and scholarly author of the work on Ephesians in *New International Commentary* would not endorse such a view, for it would be in conflict with the demonology of the New Testament. According to Mark 5:13 "the unclean spirits came out (of the man) and entered into the swine." If, then, a *place* must be assigned to Satan's servants, so that, by means of them he can influence men, can that domain be restricted to *hell*, even in this present dispensation before Christ's return? But that opinion would clash with such passages as Matt. 8:29; 16:18; I Peter 5:8. Surely, neither Satan nor his agents are in the heaven of the redeemed (Jude 6). If, therefore, according to the consistent doctrine of Scripture, the evil spirits must be *somewhere*, but not in the heaven of the redeemed, and if in this present age they cannot be restricted to hell, is it so strange that Eph. 2:2 speaks about "the prince of the domain of the air"? Is it not rather natural that the prince of evil is able, as far as God in his overruling providence permits, to carry on his sinister work by sending his legions to our globe and its surrounding atmosphere?

(4) Does not also 6:12 ("the spiritual forces of evil in the heavenly

---

last meaning. Illustrations of its use in this sense are the following: in the Septuagint IV Km. 20:13 ("or in all his realm"); Psalm 113:2 ("Judah became his sanctuary; Israel his domain"). See further Luke 4:6, in the light of Matt. 4:8 ("all this domain"). Cf. Luke 23:7. And note Col. 1:13 ("the domain of darkness").

places") point in this same general direction? Surely, if the cherubim in Ezekiel's vision were able to be on earth one moment but "lifted up from the earth" into the sky the next moment (Ezek. 1:19; cf. 10:19; 11:22), it is not impossible that the demons too would have that power. Accordingly, whatever figurative overtones the word "air" may have — due to the fact that the air is the region of fog, cloudiness, darkness — *the literal meaning here is basic*. This passage, in conjunction with others (3:10, 15; 6:12), clearly teaches that God has tenanted the supermundane realm with innumerable hosts, and that in its lower region the minions of Satan are engaged in their destructive missions. Grosheide is right when in his comments on this passage he states that according to the New Testament "the atmosphere is inhabited by spirits, including evil spirits, who exert an evil influence on people" (*op.cit.*, p. 36).[52] Note this word "including." The *evil* spirits do not have it all to themselves by any means! And as far as they and their leader are concerned, the Christian's real comfort is found in such passages as 1:20-23; Col. 2:15; Rom. 16:20; Rev. 20:3, 10. Cf. Gen. 3:15; John 12:31, 32.

The Ephesians, then, had formerly conducted themselves "in line with the course of this world, in line with the prince of the domain of the air," to which Paul now adds: **(the domain) of the spirit now at work in the sons of disobedience.** That *spirit,* again, is Satan, who, by means of his agents, the demons, and probably even directly and personally (Zech. 3; I Peter 5:8), is busily engaged in the hearts and lives of those wicked people who by the use of a Semitic expression are here designated as "the sons of disobedience," that is, those who, as it were, spring from disobedience as the mother that gave them birth. Cf. II Thess. 2:3. This is the disobedience *of unbelief* (Heb. 4:6), and hence of rebellion against God and his commandments. Note the fact that this "prince" or "spirit" is said to be "at work," that is *energetically* engaged to make what is bad even worse. Satan never rests. Now it was in line with this spirit that the Ephesians had previously conducted themselves. 3. But not the Ephesians only. Paul is careful to add: **among whom we also once lived in the lusts of our flesh, fulfilling the desires of the flesh and its reasonings.** It is touching to read, "Among these sons of disobedience were also we," we Jews as well as y o u Gentiles.

---

[52] Salmond also adopts the literal meaning. Scott calls this idea "an out of date theory." Several commentators, however, are of the opinion that Paul is merely accommodating himself to current belief, and that the words he uses by no means necessarily imply that he himself held to this belief (thus Abbott, Robinson, and to a certain extent Van Leeuwen). Westcott emphasizes that the popular notion contained an element of truth, namely, "the unseen adversaries are within reach of us." Findlay interprets "air" figuratively. Hodge, having rejected the literal sense, wavers between the figurative sense "power of darkness" and the meaning "incorporeal power." No one today attaches any value to the grotesque and highly speculative notions of rabbinical literature regarding the abode, etc., of the demons.

Paul includes himself. Yet, this is the apostle who during this same imprisonment said concerning his own pre-Christian life, ". . . as to legal righteousness . . . blameless" (Phil. 3:6). The point is that both the Gentile, steeped in immorality, and the Jew, who imagines that he can save himself by obeying the law of Moses, are *living* (a synonym of *walking* in verse 2) "in the lusts of the flesh," for when the word *flesh* is used in such a context it refers to the corrupt human nature, or, more in general, to anything apart from Christ on which one bases his hope for happiness or salvation. "The moral man came to the judgment, But his self-righteous rags would not do." Cf. Rom. 7:18: ". . . in my flesh dwells no good thing." As to *desires,* in the present connection this can refer only to *unrighteous* cravings, such as belong to and are spawned by the flesh. For the Jew this undoubtedly included a yearning to enter the kingdom on the basis of his own supposedly meritorious law-works. For the Gentile the reference is to such matters as immorality, idolatry, drunkenness, and, in general, self-assertiveness in its several sinister manifestations.[53] The flesh or depraved human nature, accordingly, produces evil desires. These, in turn, in order to be realized, lead to reasonings, all kinds of hostile (cf. Col. 1:21), self-righteous, and/or immoral plans and cogitations, which finally result in wicked deeds. Cf. James 1:14, 15; 4:1. Illustrations of this process: the story of Cain and Abel (Gen. 4:1-8); of Amnon and Tamar (II Sam. 13:1-19); of Absalom in his rebellion against his father David (II Sam. 15 ff.); and of Ahab and Naboth (I Kings 21). However, though the indicated sequence of the elements in the progress of evil is as here summarized, life itself is too complex for such a simplification. There is constant interaction.[54] This is a matter that demands attention, for it shows how terrible is man's lost condition: the one sin breeds another which not only, in turn gives rise to still another but also "turns around," as it were, and reacts upon its begetter, adding to the latter's virility and effectiveness for evil! No wonder that Paul continues: **and were by nature children of wrath even as the rest.** This wrath is not to be compared to fire in straw, quickly blazing and quickly burnt out. On the contrary, it is *settled indignation,* the attitude of God toward men viewed as fallen in Adam (Rom. 5:12, 17-19) and refusing to accept the gospel of grace and salvation in Christ. It is with respect to them that it is written: "He who . . . disobeys the Son shall not see life, but the wrath of God remains on him" (John 3:36). "By nature" must mean "apart from regenerating grace." It refers to men as they are in their natural condition, as descendants of Adam; specifically, as included

[53] For a word-study of ἐπιθυμία see N.T.C. on I and II Timothy and Titus, pp. 271, 272, footnote 147; and for σάρξ see N.T.C. on Philippians, p. 77, footnote 55; also pp. 152, 153 on Phil. 3:3.
[54] Cf. the various sequences of the elements of Christian experience — such as knowledge, love, and obedience — in Scripture. See N.T.C. on the Gospel according to John, Vol. II, pp. 10, 11.

in him as their representative in the covenant of works. Such, then, says Paul, were we before the great change took place. It was true with respect to the addressed and true also with respect to the one who was addressing them. Moreover, in order that no one might conclude that among the children of men there were any at all to whom these words would not apply, Paul adds "even as the rest." Cf. Rom. 3:9-18. "Children of wrath" (another Semitism) means objects of God's settled indignation now and for all time to come (again John 3:36), unless God's marvelous grace intervenes to crush sinful pride and stubborn disobedience, the disobedience of unbelief.

"But is not God also merciful?" Yes, indeed, for though he hates the stubborn sinner because of his stubbornness, his inexcusable impenitence, yet he loves him as his creature. As such he loves all men. He loves *the world* (John 3:16). The amazing character of that love makes it understandable, at least to some extent, that God's wrath should rest on those who spurn it.

4, 5. And now the great change is vividly portrayed. Upon men so totally unworthy *such* mercy, love, and grace is bestowed: **God,**[55] **being rich in mercy, because of his great love with which he loved us, even though we were dead through our trespasses made us alive together with Christ — by grace y o u have been saved — .**

As far as the present paragraph is concerned the tragic account of man's forlorn condition is finished. But the main idea with which the apostle started out has not yet been expressed. The words "and y o u," as the *object* of the chapter's opening sentence, must not be left hanging in mid-air. *The Ephesians* cannot be left in their state of wrath and condition of misery. Both object and Ephesians must be "rescued." And it is high time that this be done. The great throbbing heart of this marvelous missionary, a heart so filled with compassion,[56] can wait no longer. Here then finally, after all these modifiers and in connection with the repetition in verse 5 of the words of verse 1 — "even though . . . dead through . . . trespasses" — comes the main clause: the subject and the main verb: "God (verse 4) . . . made alive" (verse 5). However, for the reason already given, the apostle chooses to take his stand alongside of the Ephesians. He is convinced that his own state (and, in fact, the state of all the Jews who in former days were

---

[55] Probably because spiritual darkness and light are here so strongly contrasted, and because of the particle δέ at the beginning of verse 4 (ὁ δὲ θεός), many feel that a new sentence begins here (A.V., R.S.V., N.E.B., etc.). However, the fact that in verse 5 the apostle (according to what appears to be the best reading) repeats the words of verse 1 in only slightly altered form, and now, in verses 4 and 5, adds the required subject and predicate, would seem to indicate that there was no serious "break" in the sentence structure. The anacoluthon which many see here is more apparent than real, and δέ in the present instance (as often) is best left untranslated. On this point I agree with Lenski (*op.cit.*, pp. 413, 414) over against many others.

[56] On this see N.T.C. on Philippians, p. 181.

trusting in their own righteousness for salvation) was basically no better than that of the Gentiles, and also that the new-found joy is the same for all. So instead of saying, "And y o u he made alive," he says, "And *us* he made alive." Now if this be a case of syntactical inconsistency it is one of the most glorious cases on record!

Paul ascribes the dramatic and marvelous change that has taken place, in his own life and in that of the others, to the *mercy, love,* and *grace* of God. *Love* is basic, that is, it is the most comprehensive of the three terms. Paul says, "God, being rich in mercy, because of his great love with which he loved us . . . made us alive," etc. This love of God is so great that it defies all definition. We can speak of it as his intense concern for, deep personal interest in, warm attachment to, and spontaneous tenderness toward his chosen ones, but all this is but to stammer. Those, and those only, who experience it are the ones who know what it is, though even they can never fully comprehend it (3:19). They know, however, that it is unique, spontaneous, strong, sovereign, everlasting, and infinite (Isa. 55:6, 7; 62:10-12; 63:9; Jer. 31:3, 31-34; Hos. 11:8; Mic. 7:18-20; John 3:16; I John 4:8, 16, 19). It is "the love that has been shed abroad in our hearts" (Rom. 5:5), "his own love toward us" (Rom. 5:8), the love from which no one and nothing "will be able to separate us" (Rom. 8:39).

Now when this love is directed toward sinners viewed in their wretchedness and need of commiseration and succor, it is called *mercy*. See N.T.C. on Philippians, p. 142 for a list of over 100 Old and New Testament passages in which this divine attribute is described, showing how "rich" this mercy is. It is as "rich" as God's love is "great." God's *grace* of which mention is made in the statement, "By grace y o u have been saved," is his love viewed as focused on the guilty and undeserving. Mercy *pities*. Grace *pardons*. But it does more than that. It *saves* all the way, delivering men from the greatest woe (everlasting damnation), and bestowing upon them the choicest blessing (everlasting life for soul and body). Being saved by grace is the opposite of being saved by merit, the merit that supposedly accrues from inherent goodness or from strenuous effort. Cf. 2:8, 9. The expression clearly indicates that the ground of our salvation lies not in us but in God. "We love him because he first loved us" (I John 4:19). This sovereign nature of divine love in its various aspects is illustrated in such beautiful passages as Deut. 7:7, 8; Isa. 48:11; Dan. 9:19; Hos. 14:4; John 15:16; Rom. 5:8; Eph. 1:4; I John 4:10.

It was because of the riches of his mercy, greatness of his love, and amazing character of his grace, that God "made us alive *together with Christ* even though we were dead through our trespasses." [57]

---

[57] With many expositors, but contrary to Lenski, *op.cit.*, p. 415, I adhere to N.N.'s punctuation which construes the words "even though we were dead through our trespasses" as a modifier of "God made us alive together with Christ." It seems to

"Together with Christ," for when the Father made his Son alive, by causing the latter's soul to return from Paradise in order to re-inhabit the body which it had left, he in this very act furnished proof that the substitutionary atonement had been accepted, and that, accordingly, the sentence of death which otherwise would have doomed believers had been lifted, their sins forgiven. And this justification, in turn, is basic to all the other blessings of salvation. **6.** This is true because vivification does not stand by itself, for the apostle continues: **and raised us up with him and made us sit with him in the heavenly places in Christ Jesus.** Christ's resurrection and exaltation to the Father's right hand in "the heavenly places" (here and in 1:3 the heaven of the redeemed is meant; contrast 6:12) not only foreshadows and guarantees our glorious bodily resurrection and all the consequent glory that will be our portion at the great consummation, but is also the basis of *present* blessings. Whatever happens to the Bridegroom has an immediate effect upon the Bride. This effect has reference not only to the church's *state* or legal standing before God's law, but also to its *condition,* the latter because from the place of his heavenly glory and majesty Christ sends forth the Spirit into the hearts of believers, so that they die to sin and are raised to newness of life. Therefore, both as to state and as to condition we can say that with Christ Jesus we ourselves were tried, condemned, crucified, buried (Rom. 6:4-8; 8:17; Col. 2:12; II Tim. 2:11), but also, made alive, raised, and set in heavenly places (Rom. 6:5; 8:17; Col. 2:13; 3:1-3; II Tim. 2:12; Rev. 20:4). To be sure, there is a time factor. Not at once do we receive this glory in full measure. But the right to receive it fully has been secured, and the new life has already begun. Even now our life "is hid with Christ in God." Our names are inscribed in heaven's register. Our interests are being promoted there. We are being governed by heavenly standards and motivated by heavenly impulses. The blessings of heaven constantly descend upon us. Heaven's grace fills our hearts. Its power enables us to be more than conquerors. And to heaven our thoughts aspire and our prayers ascend.

7. What now was the purpose which God had in mind when he bestowed on us this great salvation? Paul answers: **in order that in the ages to come he might show the surpassing riches of his grace (expressed) in kindness toward us in Christ Jesus.** Therefore, God's purpose in saving his people

---

me that this punctuation is justified by the consideration that Paul is here carrying toward completion the thought begun in verse 1. Lenski's objection, namely, that the apostle would certainly not mention the obvious fact that vivification concerns dead persons (*op.cit.,* p. 415) is not convincing. The point is: the addressed, as well as Paul, were dead *because of their own guilt.* This is clearly implied when they are called "children of wrath" and are pictured as in need of God's *grace.* Accordingly, when God makes them alive, in spite of the fact that they deserved nothing less than everlasting damnation, this is a marvelous deed, worthy to be mentioned.

reaches beyond man. His own glory is *his own* chief aim. It is for that reason that he displays his grace in all its matchless beauty and transforming power. To some this may seem somewhat cold or even "selfish." Yet, on re-reading the passage one will soon discover that God's overshadowing majesty and his condescending tenderness combine here, for the glory of his attributes is placed on exhibition as it reflects itself "in kindness toward us!" *We* are his sparkling jewels. Illustration: A Roman matron when asked, "Where are your jewels?" calls her two sons, and, pointing to them, says, "These are my jewels." So also, throughout eternity the redeemed will be exhibited as the monuments of "the marvelous grace of our loving Lord," who drew us from destruction's pit and raised us to heights of heavenly bliss, and did all this at such a cost to himself that he spared not his own Son, and in such a manner that not a single one of his attributes, not even his justice, was eclipsed.

In Christ Jesus this divine kindness [58] was displayed in various ways, mostly, of course, in the death on the cross. It was displayed also in such sayings as are recorded in Matt. 5:7; 9:13; 11:28-30; 12:7; 23:37; Mark 10:14; Luke 10:25-37, to mention only a few; and in such attitudes and actions, among many others, as are commemorated in Matt. 9:36; 14:14; 15:21-28; 20:34; Luke 7:11-17, 36-50; 8:40-42, 49-56; 23:34; John 19:27; 21:15-17.

Paul does not say "God's grace," nor even "the riches of his grace," but "the sur- (super) passing riches of his grace." This is characteristic Pauline language. Earlier he had written to the Romans, "Where sin abounded, grace *super*-overflowed" (Rom. 5:20). During the present imprisonment he was going to tell the Philippians about the peace of God which *"sur-* (super) passes all understanding" (Phil. 4:7). And, during his brief period of freedom between the first and second Roman imprisonments he would write to Timothy, "And it *super*-abounded (namely) the grace of our Lord, with faith and love in Christ Jesus" (I Tim. 1:14). See also II Cor. 7:4; I Thess. 3:10; 5:13; II Thess. 1:3. As Paul sees it, there is nothing narrow about this grace of God, nothing stingy. Its loving arms embrace both Gentile and Jew. It reaches even to "the chief of sinners" (Paul himself), and so "rich" is it that it enriches every heart and life which it touches, filling it with marvelous love, joy, peace, etc.

God will display the surpassing riches of his grace "in the ages to come." But what is meant by these ages? In the main, there are three opinions:

(1) *The ages that will precede Christ's Parousia.* The expression *ages to come* "must not be understood to refer to 'the future' world. Paul is speaking about the earthly dispensation which has not yet run its course" (Grosheide; cf. Barry). A possible objection to this view would be that in that case Paul would probably have spoken about "the fulness of the times" (as

---

[58] In the New Testament the word χρηστότης is used only by Paul (Rom. 2:4; 3:12; 11:22; Col. 3:12; Titus 3:4, etc.).

in 1:10) or about "this age" (as in 1:21). Though not even in his early epistles did he proceed from the assumption that the second coming was the very next item on God's program for the history of the world (see II Thess. 2:1-12), nevertheless, it was not his custom to posit continuing lengths of time that would intervene between his own day and Christ's return.

(2) *The ages that will follow Christ's Parousia.* With variations as to detail this view is held by Abbott, Greijdanus, Lenski, Salmond, Van Leeuwen, and many others. In its defense an appeal is made to 1:21: "the coming age." However, it is debatable whether this argument is valid, for in 1:21 a contrast is drawn between "this age" and "the coming one." That is not the case in 2:7. Also 1:21 has the singular *aeon;* 2:7, the plural *aeons.* And when, with one commentator, these post-Parousia ages, as they affect us, turn out to be "the timeless [?] aeons of eternity," while another — perhaps forgetting that in that glorious life there will be no more sin and misery? — in his comments on the grace that will then be expressed "in kindness toward us," interprets this to mean personal pity shown to those in need, one begins to wonder whether, after all, the restriction of "the ages to come" to the post-Parousia era is legitimate.

(3) *All future time.* In commenting on this passage John Calvin says, "It was the design of God to hallow in all ages the remembrance of so great a goodness." Scott expresses the same idea in these words, "The new life now begun will endure forever, so that the manifestation of God's grace will be always renewing itself. To bring out more forcibly this idea of goodness that will extend through all eternity Paul speaks not of the 'age' but *the ages* yet to come." And Hodge states, "It is better therefore to take it [the phrase "in the ages to come"] without limitation, for all future time."

Since nothing in the context limits the application of the phrase to any one period either before or after Christ's return, and since the apostle himself when he dwells more fully on the church's *lofty goal* (chapter 3) speaks about both the gathering in of the Gentiles in the present pre-Parousia age, and of the ultimate perfection of the church in the coming age, I regard explanation (3) as the best. The purpose, then, which God had in mind when he bestowed on us this great salvation described in verses 4-6, was that "in Christ Jesus" (see on 1:1, 3, 4) throughout this entire new dispensation and forever afterward he might place *us, Jew and Gentile alike,* on exhibition as monuments of the surpassing riches of his grace expressed in kindness of which we are and forever will be the recipients.

8. Reflecting on what he has just now said about grace, and repeating the parenthetical clause of verse 5b, the apostle says, **For by grace** [59] **y o u**

---

[59] The original has τῇ γὰρ χάριτι. Note the anaphoric use of the article. This is very common in Greek. See Gram. N.T., p. 762. Some translate: "this grace."

have been saved. . . . For explanation see on verse 5. He continues: **through faith; and this not of yourselves, (it is) the gift of God . . .**

Three explanations deserve consideration:

(1) *That offered by A. T. Robertson.* Commenting on this passage in his *Word Pictures in the New Testament,* Vol. IV, p. 525, he states, "Grace is God's part, faith ours." He adds that since in the original the demonstrative "this" (and *this* not of yourselves) is neuter and does not correspond with the gender of the word "faith," which is feminine, it does not refer to the latter "but to the act of being saved by grace conditioned on faith on our part." Even more clearly in *Gram. N.T.*, p. 704, he states categorically, "In Eph. 2:8 . . . there is no reference to διὰ πίστεως [*through faith*] in τοῦτο [*this*], but rather to the idea of salvation in the clause before."

Without any hesitancy I answer, Robertson, to whom the entire world of New Testament scholarship is heavily indebted, does not express himself felicitously in this instance. This is true first because in a context in which the apostle places such tremendous stress on the fact that from start to finish man owes his salvation to God, to him alone, it would have been very strange, indeed, for him to say, "Grace is God's part, faith ours." True though it be that both the responsibility of believing and also its activity are ours, for God does not believe for us, nevertheless, in the present context (verses 5-10) one rather expects emphasis on the fact that both in its initiation and in its continuation faith is entirely dependent on God, and so is our complete salvation. Also, Robertson, a grammarian famous in his field, knew that in the original the demonstrative (*this*), though neuter, by no means always corresponds in gender with its antecedent. That he knew this is shown by the fact that on the indicated page of his Grammar (p. 704) he points out that "in general" the demonstrative "agrees with its substantive in gender and number." When he says "in general," he must mean, *"not always* but most of the time." Hence, he should have considered more seriously the possibility that, in view of the context, the exception to the rule, an exception by no means rare, applies here. He should have made allowance for it.[60] Finally, he should have justified the departure from the rule that unless there is a compelling reason to do otherwise the antecedent should be looked for in the immediate vicinity of the pronoun or adjective that refers to it.

(2) *That presented, among others, by F. W. Grosheide.* As he sees it, the words "and this not of yourselves" mean *"and this being saved by grace through faith* is not of yourselves" but is the gift of God. Since, according to this theory — also endorsed, it would seem, by John Calvin in his Com-

---

[60] Though Lenski calls Robertson's statement ("Grace is God's part, faith ours") careless, his own explanation (*op.cit.*, p. 423), in which he likewise bases everything on the fact that τοῦτο is neuter but πίστις feminine, is *basically* the same as that of Robertson.

mentary — *faith is included in the gift,* none of the objections against theory (1) apply with respect to theory (2).

Does this mean then that (2) is entirely satisfactory? Not necessarily. This brings us to

(3) *That defended by A. Kuyper, Sr. in his book* Het Werk van den Heiligen Geest (Kampen, 1927), pp. 506–514.

Dr. Kuyper is, however, not this theory's sole defender, but his defence is, perhaps, the most detailed and vigorous. The theory amounts, in brief, to the following: Paul's words may be paraphrased thus, "I had the right to speak about 'the surpassing riches of his grace' *for* it is, indeed, by grace that y o u are saved, through faith; and lest y o u should now begin to say, 'But then we deserve credit, at least, for *believing,*' I will immediately add that *even this faith* (or: even this exercise of faith) is not of yourselves but is *God's gift.*"

With variations as to detail this explanation was the one favored by much of the patristic tradition. Supporting it were also Beza, Zanchius, Erasmus, Huigh de Groot (Hugo Grotius), Bengel, Michaelis, etc. It is shared, too, by Simpson (*op. cit.,* p. 55) and by Van Leeuwen and Greijdanus in their commentaries. H. C. G. Moule (*Ephesian Studies,* New York, 1900, pp. 77, 78) endorses it, with the qualification, "We must explain τοῦτο [*this*] to refer not to the feminine noun πίστις [*faith*] precisely, but to the fact of our exercising faith." Moreover, it is perhaps no exaggeration to say that the explanation offered is also shared by the average man who reads 2:8 in his A.V. or A.R.V. Salmond, after presenting several grounds in its favor, particularly also this that "the formula καὶ τοῦτο might rather favor it, as it often adds to the idea to which it is attached," finally shies away from it because "*salvation* is the main idea in the preceding statement," which fact, of course, the advocates of (3) would not deny but do, indeed, vigorously affirm, but which is not a valid argument against the idea that faith, as well as everything else in salvation, is God's gift. It is not a valid argument against (3), therefore.

I have become convinced that theory (3) is the most logical explanation of the passage in question. Probably the best argument in its favor is this one: If Paul meant to say, "For by grace y o u have been saved through faith, and this being saved is not of yourselves," he would have been guilty of needless repetition — for what else is *grace* but that which proceeds from God and not from ourselves? — a repetition rendered even more prolix when he now (supposedly) adds, "it, that is, salvation, is the gift of God," followed by a fourth and fifth repetition, namely, "not of works, for we are his handiwork." No wonder that Dr. A. Kuyper states, "If the text read, 'For by grace y o u have been saved, not of yourselves, it is the work of God,' it would make some sense. But first to say, 'By grace y o u have been saved,' and then, as if it were something new, to add, '*and* this having been

122

saved is not of yourselves,' this does not run smoothly but jerks and jolts
. . . . And while with that interpretation everything proceeds by fits and
starts and becomes lame and redundant, all is excellent and meaningful
when y o u follow the ancient interpreters of Jesus' church." [61] This, it would
seem to me also, is the refutation of theory (1) and, to a certain extent, of
theory (2).

Basically, however, theories (2) and (3) both stress the same truth,
namely, that the credit for the entire process of salvation must be given to
God, so that man is deprived of every reason for boasting, which is exactly
what Paul says in the words which now follow, namely, **9, 10. not of works,
lest anyone should boast.** This introduces us to the subject:

Works in relation to our salvation

(1) *Rejected*

As a basis for salvation, a ground upon which we can plead, works are
rejected. "Not the labors of my hands can fulfil thy law's demands." In this
connection it must be remembered that the apostle is not thinking exclusively or even mainly of works in fulfilment of the Mosaic law, by means
of which the Jew, unconverted to Christ, sought to justify himself. Surely,
also by such "works of the law" "no flesh will be justified in his sight"
(Rom. 3:20; cf. Gal. 2:16). But in view of the fact that Paul was addressing
an audience consisting mostly of Christians from the Gentile world it is
clear that he wishes to emphasize that God rejects every work of man, be he
Gentile, Jew, or believer in his moments of spiritual eclipse, *every work on
which any man bases his hope for salvation.* If, then, salvation is completely
from God, "who spared not his own Son but delivered him up for us all"
(Rom. 8:32), *every* ground of boasting in self is excluded (Rom. 3:27; 4:5;
I Cor. 1:31). When the Lord comes in his glory, those at his *left* hand will
do all the boasting (Matt. 25:44; cf. 7:22); those at his *right* hand will be
unable even to recall their good deeds (Matt. 25:37-39).

> Now all boasting is excluded,
> Unearned bliss is now my own.
> I, in God thus safely rooted,
> Boast in sovereign grace alone.
> Long before my mother bore me,
> E'en before God's mighty hand
> Out of naught made sea and land,

---

[61] As to grammar, from the works of Plato, Xenophon, and Demosthenes several instances of the use of τοῦτο to indicate a masculine or feminine antecedent are cited
by Kuyper. He also quotes the following from a Greek Grammar: "Very common
is the use of a neuter demonstrative pronoun to indicate an antecedent substantive
of masculine or of feminine gender when the idea conveyed by that substantive is
referred to in a general sense." The quotation is from the work of Kühnhert, *Aus-
führliche Grammatik der Griech. sprache* (Hanover, 1870), Vol. II, p. 54.

His electing love watched o'er me.
God is love, O angel-voice,
Tongues of men, make him your choice.[62]

(2) Confected

Paul continues: **for his handiwork are we, created in Christ Jesus for good works, which God prepared beforehand . . .** Fact is that though good works are non-meritorious, yet they are so important that God created us in order that we should perform them. We are his *handiwork:* that which he made, his product (cf. Ps. 100:3). To him we owe our entire spiritual as well as physical existence. Our very birth as believers is from God (John 3:3, 5). We are created "in Christ Jesus" (see on 1:1, 3, 4), for apart from him we are nothing and can accomplish nothing (John 15:5; cf. I Cor. 4:7). As "men in Christ," believers constitute a new creation, as the apostle had said previously (II Cor. 5:17): "Wherefore if any man is in Christ, there is a new creation: the old things are passed away; behold they are become new" (II Cor. 5:17). Believers were "made alive together with Christ" (see above on verse 5; and below on 4:24; also Gal. 6:15).

Now along with *creating us* God also *prepared good works.* He did this *first* by giving us *his Son,* our great Enabler, in whom good works find their most glorious expression (Luke 24:19; Acts 2:22). Not only does Christ enable us to perform good works but he is also our Example in good works (John 13:14, 15; I Peter 2:21). God did this *secondly* by giving us *faith in his Son.* Faith is God's gift (verse 8). Now in planting the seed of faith in our hearts, and causing it to sprout and with great care tending it, making it grow, etc., God also in that sense prepared for us good works, for good works are the fruit of faith. Living faith, moreover, implies a renewed mind, a grateful heart, and a surrendered will. Out of such ingredients, all of them God-given, God *confects* or *compounds* good works. Thus, summarizing, we can say that by giving us his Son and by imparting to us faith in that Son God prepared beforehand our good works. When Christ through his Spirit dwells in the hearts of believers, his gifts and graces are bestowed upon them, so that they, too, bear fruits, such as "love, joy, peace, long-suffering, kindness, goodness, faithfulness, meekness, and self-control" (Gal. 5:22, 23).

(3) Expected

Paul concludes this paragraph by adding: **that we should walk in them.** Though good works are a divine preparation, they are at the same time a human responsibility. These two must never be separated. If salvation can be illustrated by the figure of a flourishing tree, then good works are symbolized not by its roots nor even by its trunk but by its fruit. Jesus requires

---

[62] This is the product of my attempt to translate into English, with retention of meter, the first stanza of the beautiful Dutch hymn "Alle roem is uitgesloten."

of us fruit, more fruit, much fruit (John 15:2, 5, 8). He said, "I am the vine, y o u are the branches. He who abides in me, with me abiding in him, he it is that bears much fruit, for apart from me y o u can do nothing." *To bear much fruit* and *to walk in good works* is the same thing. When a certain occupation has the love of a man's heart, he is "walking" in it. Note: walk *in them*, no longer in "trespasses and sins" (verses 1, 2).

(4) *Perfected*

Combining (2) and (3) we see that by walking in good works we have entered into the sphere of God's own activity. Hence, we know that though our own efforts may often disappoint us, so that we are ashamed even of our *good* works, victory will arrive at last; not fully, to be sure, in the present life but in the next. Moral and spiritual perfection is our *goal* even here, but will be our *portion* in the life hereafter, for we are confident of this very thing that he who began a good work in us will carry it to completion (Phil. 1:6). Cf. Eph. 1:4; 3:19; 4:12, 13.

This doctrine of good works, when accepted by faith, deprives man of every reason for boasting in self but also takes away from him every ground for despair. It glorifies God.

Chapter 2

Verses 11–18

Theme: *The Church Glorious*

I. *Adoration*
for its

U niversal Scope (embracing both Jew and Gentile),
2. shown by the reconciliation of Jew and Gentile through the cross

11 Therefore remember that formerly y o u, the Gentiles in flesh, who are called "uncircumcision" by that which is called "circumcision" — in flesh, handmade! — 12 that y o u were at that time separate from Christ, alienated from the commonwealth of Israel, and strangers to the covenants of the promise, having no hope and without God in the world. 13 But now in Christ Jesus y o u who formerly were far away have been brought nearby through the blood of Christ. 14 For he himself is our peace, who made both one and has broken down the barrier formed by the dividing wall, the hostility, 15 by abolishing in his flesh the law of commandments with its requirements, in order that in himself he might create of the two one new man, (so) making peace, 16 and might reconcile both of them in one body to God through the cross, having slain the hostility by means of it; 17 and he came and proclaimed the good news: "Peace to y o u, those far away, and peace to those nearby"; 18 for through him we both have our access in one Spirit to the Father.

2:11-18

2. *The Reconciliation of Jew and Gentile*

When Paul wrote the present paragraph he was in high spirits. This is very clear from the fact that the prayer and the doxology found in chapter 3 are the natural climax to 2:11-18 and 2:19-22. In order to understand the present paragraph it should be borne in mind that the apostle knew by personal experience how difficult it was to weld Jew and Gentile into an organic unity, a unity of perfect equality. Jewish Christians had often been loath to admit Gentiles into the church except via Judaism. Immediately after Paul's return to Syrian Antioch from his first missionary journey "certain men came down from Judea and were teaching the brothers, 'Unless y o u are circumcised according to the custom of Moses, y o u cannot be saved'" (Acts 15:1). Even Peter, who, because of the vision he had received, should have known better (Acts 10, 11), refused for a while to eat with the Gentiles, and by his conduct merited Paul's stinging rebuke (Gal. 2:11-21). When Paul wrote Galatians the controversy over the question "How can salvation be obtained?," implying the further question "On what terms can the Gentiles be accepted into the church?," was at its height. The apostle reminded these "foolish Galatians" that those who desired to be justified by the law were severed from Christ (Gal. 5:4). The epistles to the Romans and to the Corinthians clearly indicate that when these were written the battle had not yet been completely won. In fact, until the end of Paul's life the fire which at one time had been raging furiously was never *completely* put out but showed intermittent flashes. That was true during

127

the present Roman imprisonment (see Col. 2:11-17; Phil. 3:2-11), during the brief period of freedom that followed it (I Tim. 1:6-11; Titus 3:5, 9), and even during the apostle's final incarceration (II Tim. 1:9, 10). But though this is true, yet *officially* the answer had been given long before the present letter was written. It had been furnished by the Synod of Jerusalem, before the apostle started on his second missionary journey. See Acts 15. The great principle that salvation in all its riches is freely given to all those — whether Jew or Gentile — who accept Christ through a living faith (this faith *also God-given*) had become the accepted doctrine of the church. Whatever remained of the struggle after the Jerusalem Synod had been held and Galatians had been written was "aftermath." The ferocious attack upon the truth had been repulsed. Yet all was not over. To the very end Paul defended the principle of freedom from the law in its saving and ceremonial aspects, the principle of salvation for "all men" without any distinction as to national or racial origin and without the requirement that anyone reach the church by means of a detour. (See I Tim. 2:3-7; Titus 2:11; II Tim. 4:1-8.)

Now it was especially in Ephesus and its surroundings that Jew and Gentile who had accepted Christ lived together in love and unity and constituted *one ecumenical church*. It was a flourishing church, from which, as from a center, many other congregations were founded (Acts 19:10; cf. Rev. 1:11; 2:1-7). This was one reason why Paul, though a prisoner, rejoiced greatly and glorified his God. Though even in Ephesus conditions were by no means perfect, yet, by and large, the apostle witnessed here the realization of his own ideal and, more important, of God's plan! Moreover, he bears testimony to the fact that Jew and Gentile, reconciled to God through faith in Christ, *are reconciled to each other also!* Hence, in the spirit of exultation he desires that the Ephesians, *mostly formerly Gentiles,* will rejoice with him in God's works. This goal can best be achieved by comparing their past wretchedness with their present reason for cheerfulness. **11, 12.** So Paul writes, **Therefore remember that formerly y o u, the Gentiles in flesh, who are called "uncircumcision" by that which is called "circumcision" — in flesh, handmade! — that y o u were at that time separate from Christ,**[63] **alienated from the commonwealth of Israel, and strangers to the covenants of the promise, having no hope and without God in the world.** "Therefore," that is, because y o u Ephesians, once dead, were made alive by grace through faith and for good works (verses 1-10), consider y o u r

---

[63] I do not agree with those expositors (including Lenski, *op.cit.*, p. 432, but see his translation, p. 429) who deny the predicative position of the phrase "separate from Christ." A harsh construction results, as was pointed out by Abbott (*op.cit.*, p. 57). Both the periphrastic nature of the predicate in verse 12 and the re-emphasis in verse 13 on the formerly "separate from Christ" idea, cause me to agree with most translators and exegetes in accepting *five* (not only four) predicate terms in verse 12: *separate from Christ, alienated, strangers, hopeless,* and *without God.*

present high estate in the light of y o u r former low position, that y o u may glorify God, y o u r Benefactor. As to y o u r past, y o u r case was in a sense even more hopeless than that of *the highly privileged* Jews, for y o u were Gentiles. Y o u carried the evidence of y o u r Gentile state in y o u r very flesh, for y o u were uncircumcised. Hence the Jews, unconverted to Christ, call y o u "uncircumcision" (that is, "the uncircumcised"). They do this even though they themselves, proud of being called "circumcision" (that is, "the circumcised"), possess only *the sign,* not *the thing signified.* They were circumcised only "in flesh," not in their hearts (Lev. 26:41; Deut. 10:16; 30:6; Jer. 4:4; Ezek. 44:7, ears (Jer. 6:10), and lips (Exod. 6:12, 30). It was all merely a matter of minor surgery, a manual operation, the cutting away of foreskin. It was outward, not inward. The real meaning or value of circumcision has been erased with Christ's death on the cross. Yet in this outward mark the Jews continue to glory, while they despise all others, including y o u Ephesians. Now at that time when y o u, as also now, were being held in such low esteem, y o u r misery was great, for y o u were *Christless, stateless, friendless, hopeless, and Godless.*

(1) *Christless: "separate from Christ"*

Paul cannot have meant that before their conversion Christ had paid no attention to them, for the apostle has clearly indicated that those whom he addresses had been included in the number of the elect from all eternity (1:3 ff.). He must mean that before their conversion this oneness "in Christ" had not been *experienced* by them in any sense whatever. They had been groping in the darkness, filth, and despair of sin. The light, holiness, and hopefulness of those who come to know Christ had not as yet become their portion. Hence, in that former state they had been unspeakably wretched. The Christians' greatest joy is the solemn assurance that no one and nothing can ever *separate* them from the love of Christ (Rom. 8:35). From this great joy the Ephesians had been *far removed.*

(2) *stateless: "alienated from the commonwealth of Israel"*

To be sure, they had not been stateless in every conceivable sense. But though included in the Roman province of Asia, they were excluded from the many blessings that pertained to the Jewish theocracy. They lacked citizenship among the chosen people. This was, indeed, a deplorable lack, for it was to Israel (for the meaning of the name see Gen. 32:28) that God of old had revealed himself in a special manner. To that people he had given his law, his special protection, his prophecies and promises. Read the following stirring passages: Deut. 32:10-14; 33:27-29; Ps. 147:20; Isa. 63:9; Ezek. 16:6-14; Amos 3:2. From all this the Ephesians had been excluded.

(3) *friendless: "strangers to the covenants of the promise"*

The essence of the covenant of grace, to which the present passage refers, is the experience of "the friendship of Jehovah" (Ps. 25:14). Now in their unconverted state the Ephesians had been strangers to this friendship. They

129

had been mere "foreigners" from whom the rights and privileges of citizens had been withheld. Ranking high among these withheld privileges were "the covenants of the promise." Paul speaks about *covenants,* plural. He has reference, no doubt, to *the many reaffirmations of the one and only covenant of grace.* He calls it the covenant "of promise," because its main element is, indeed, God's promise: "I will be your (or at times *y o u r*) God." That this promise was made to Abraham, reaffirmed to Isaac, to Jacob, and, in fact, to all God's people in both dispensations, so that, while in a sense there is only *one* covenant of grace, there were *many* reaffirmations (and in *that* sense many *covenants)*, is clear from such passages as the following: Gen. 17:7, 8; 26:1-5; 28:10-17; Exod. 20:2; Deut. 5:2, 3, 6; Jer. 24:7; 30:22; 31:33; Ezek. 11:20; Zech. 13:9; II Cor. 6:16; Gal. 3:8, 9, 29; Rev. 21:3. On the basis of all the passages that refer to it, this covenant can be defined as *that divinely established arrangement between the triune God and his people whereby God carries out his eternal decree of redemption by promising his friendship, hence full and free salvation, to his people, upon the basis of the vicarious atonement of Christ, the Mediator of the covenant, and they accept this salvation by faith.* Because of the greatness of God and the lowliness of man it stands to reason that such a covenant cannot be a fifty-fifty agreement but must be a one-sided disposition, a divine *grant, settlement, ordinance,* or *institution.* It is never a mere contract between two parties — God and man — each with equal rights. Though *in a sense* it is two-sided, because man must exercise faith, as has been indicated, yet even that faith is God's gift (see on verse 8 and cf. Jer. 31:33). In that respect this covenant partakes of the nature of a *testament.* In fact, the word used in the original, namely, *diathēkē,* has both meanings: *testament* and *covenant.* It means *testament* in Heb. 9:16, 17. See also Gal. 3:15. Elsewhere both in Hebrews and in the rest of the new Testament (as in the LXX) the translation *covenant* is probably the best. Now to this covenant, too, the Ephesians, in their lost condition, had been strangers. At that time God had never revealed himself to them as their special Friend. And the Jews, having robbed God's covenant of its real, spiritual meaning, and having substituted for it the hope of earthly glory, had not even been able to convey to the Ephesians the glory of God's promise. See Matt. 23:15.

(4) *hopeless: "having no hope"*

This follows very naturally, for the Christian's *hope* is based on the divine *promise.* Accordingly, since in the earlier period the covenant-promise had not been revealed to the Ephesians, as has just been indicated, hence they also lacked hope: solid, firmly-anchored assurance of salvation. Such hope is one of God's most precious gifts, and is mentioned alongside of faith and love (1:15, 18; cf. I Cor. 13:13). It is knowledge of God's promise plus confidence with respect to its fulfilment (cf. II Cor. 1:7). It is the proliferation of faith. It amounts to the conviction that all things will be well, even when all things seem to be wrong (Rom. 4:18). It never disappoints, because it, too, like faith and love, is a divine gift (Rom. 5:5).

In their state of unbelief the Ephesians had lacked this hope. Instead, they had been filled with fear and despair. The Greek and Roman world of Paul's day was, indeed, a *hopeless* world. For details on this see N.T.C. on I and II Thessalonians, pp. 110, 111.

(5) *Godless: "and without God in the world"*

Surely they had gods, but these were vain. The Ephesians were without the one true God. This cannot mean that they were "utterly abandoned by God," for we know that this is not true, for from eternity they had been included in God's decree of election. Moreover, for them, too, Christ had died (see 1:4 ff.). Besides, on the Ephesians, as well as on the people of Lystra, God had bestowed many blessings which they shared with all earth's inhabitants, though not with all in the same degree, namely, "rains and fruitful seasons, filling their hearts with food and gladness" (Acts 14:17). But they had been in truth "without God in the world" in the sense that they had been without the true knowledge of God, and therefore without holiness, righteousness, peace, and the joy *of salvation*. They had resembled mariners who without compass and guide were adrift in a rudderless ship during a starless night on a tempestuous sea, far away from the harbor. Nothing less than that is meant by the gloomy, awe-inspiring phrase "without God in the world." That world is the mass of fallen mankind, lost, sin-laden, and exposed to the judgment.

13. Out of the darkness and despair of heathendom the Ephesians had emerged *directly* into the radiance and rapture of Christianity. The great change is described in the following words: **But now in Christ Jesus y o u who formerly were far away have been brought nearby through the blood of Christ.** The words "but now" indicate a sharp contrast with "formerly" (verse 11) and "at that time" (verse 12). Formerly "far away," now "nearby." These expressions have an Old Testament background. In the old dispensation Jehovah, in a sense, had his dwelling in the temple. That temple was in Jerusalem. Israel, therefore, was "nearby." On the other hand, the Gentiles were "far away." [64] Not only was this true literally, but even more so in a spiritual sense: they generally lacked the true knowledge of God. All this, however, was going to change. Isaiah records, in words reflected here in Eph. 2:17: "I create the fruit of the lips: Peace, peace to him that is far off and to him that is near . . . and I will heal him" (Isa. 57:19). The fact that this type of phraseology was carried over into the New Testament is clear from Acts 2:39, "The promise is to y o u and y o u r children and to all that are *far away*." It should be evident that a person could be "nearby" and yet "far away." He could be "nearby" in a merely external

---

[64] In later days a *proselyte*, as the very name implies, was one who had come to be nearby.

sense, namely, because he was a sharer in the privileges of the Old Testament economy, or simply, a Jew. His heart, however, could still be "far away from God." Taken in the *external* sense, then, those who are "far away" are the Gentiles, those "nearby" are the Jews (as in verse 17). Through faith in Christ all those to whom the gospel is proclaimed have the opportunity *to draw near*. In the *spiritual* sense, however, those "nearby" are genuine *believers;* or as we today would say: Christians. The expression "nearby through the blood of Christ," here in 2:13, must mean *spiritually nearby*. Moreover, in order to do justice to the entire context, the idea "formerly far away but now nearby" must be explained in the light of verse 12 taken in its entirety. The meaning that results is this: formerly separate from Christ, now "in Christ Jesus" saved by grace through faith (verse 8); formerly alienated from the commonwealth of Israel, now "fellow-citizens with the saints and members of the household of God" (verse 19); formerly strangers to the covenants of the promise, now covenant members (Gal. 3:29); formerly without God, now at peace with him (verse 17) and in possession of the privilege of blessed access (verses 16-18).

With this explanation justice is done to the context, which shows that the terms "far away" and "nearby" must be construed both *perpendicularly* and *horizontally*. As to the first — the *God-man* relationship — the Ephesians in their former state had been so far removed from God that the intervening distance could be measured only by the greatness of the sacrifice required to bring them nearby. But by faith they had been brought close to God's heart. As to the second, the annihilation of the perpendicular distance had brought about the cessation of the horizontal also, for at the cross Jew and Gentile, both reconciled to God, had embraced each other. "Through the blood of Christ" (for explanation see on 1:7) *sin,* the great separator, had been vanquished. With reference to this horizontal reconciliation brought about by Christ crucified, the apostle continues: **14. For he himself is our peace, who made both one and has broken down the barrier formed by the dividing wall, the hostility.**[65] The forward position of the pronoun that

---

[65] With respect to the grammatical construction of verses 14 and 15 there is much difference of opinion among exegetes. Many connect τὴν ἔχθραν with the words that follow. This results in the rendering which is favored by A.V. and A.R.V., "having abolished in his flesh the enmity, *even* the law of commandments *contained in* ordinances." This makes good sense, for the law is, in a sense, an adversary, the accuser of transgressors (cf. Deut. 27:26; Gal. 3:10). Nevertheless, it is, perhaps, better to connect τὴν ἔχθραν with the immediately preceding λύσας, so that it would be in apposition with τὸ μεσότοχον. The participle καταργήσας has enough modifiers as it is. Hence, in harmony with N.N., I, too, would place a comma after τὴν ἔχθραν.

Essentially there is little difference between (a) the rendering favored by A.V. and A.R.V., and (b) that which R.S.V., I, and many others endorse. In both cases it remains true that when Jesus abolished in his flesh the law of commandments with its requirements, the barrier between Jew and Gentile ceased to be.

refers to Christ shows that the proper English translation is "he himself,"
or "he alone." He himself is our peace, that is, what everything else —
whether the law with its ordinances, human merit, law-works of whatever
kind, sacrifices, etc. — could not do, he, he alone in his own person, has done,
for he is the very embodiment of peace. In his capacity as the Prince of
Peace (Isa. 9:6) he, by means of his voluntary sacrifice, has brought about
peace (cf. John 14:27; 16:33; 20:19, 20) : reconciliation between God and
man, hence also between Gentiles and Jews. As to the latter groups, he has
made both [66] one, has welded them into one organic unit, namely, the
church. That the reference is here to the reconciliation between Gentiles
and Jews is clear from the fact that these are the two groups mentioned in
the immediate context (verses 11 and 12) .

Between the Gentiles and the Jews there had long been a formidable
obstacle, a hatred-barrier.[67] It is called a barrier "of" or "formed by" "the
dividing wall" or "fence," a figurative reference to the law considered as a
cause of separation and enmity between Jews and Gentiles. See on verse 15.
When Paul speaks about this *barrier* of hostility, there may be an allusion
to the barricade which in Jerusalem separated the court of the Gentiles from
the temple proper, and on which there was an inscription threatening death
to any non-Jew who tried to pass it:

"No foreigner may enter within the barricade which surrounds the sanctuary and enclosure. Anyone who is caught doing so will have himself to
blame for his ensuing death." [68]

But the allusion, if any, to that literal barricade is only by way of illustration. What the apostle was actually speaking of was something far more
serious and dreadful, namely, *inveterate hostility* between the two groups.
Humanly speaking, the wall of hatred and contempt that divided Jew and
Gentile had been strengthened by centuries of mutual disparagement and
mudslinging. A few more years and the pent-up hostility of generations
would burst into an open flame, and one of the most cruel and bitter wars
would be fought. It would result in the destruction of Jerusalem, A.D. 70.
To the Jews the Gentiles were "dogs." Many other vituperative expressions

---

[66] Though some suggest that the neuter here ($\tau\grave{a}$ $\dot{a}\mu\varphi\acute{o}\tau\epsilon\rho a$), contrasted with the
masculine ($o\acute{\iota}$ $\dot{a}\mu\varphi\acute{o}\tau\epsilon\rho o\iota$) in verses 16, 18, indicates an ellipsis, so that a word like
$\gamma\acute{\epsilon}\nu\eta$ should be applied, this is doubtful. Abbott (*op.cit.*, p. 60) may well be right
when he says, "It is simply an instance of the neuter being used of persons in a
general sense." Another instance of this same usage of the neuter is found in Heb.
7:7. Cf. also the use of the neuter $\tauo\tilde{\upsilon}\tauo$ in 2:8. See on that passage.
[67] The word $\mu\epsilon\sigma\acute{o}\tauo\chi o\nu$ is of rare occurrence. In the New Testament it is found only
here. Outside of the New Testament, too, it is found but seldom. See M.M., p. 400;
also L.N.T. (A. and G.), p. 509. Josephus, *Jewish Antiquities* VIII. 71, speaks about
a *middle wall*. Here in 2:14 the context favors the translation *barrier*.
[68] See J. H. Iliffe, "The ΘANATOΣ Inscription from Herod's Temple: Fragments
of a Second Copy," *Quarterly of Department of Antiquities in Palestine* VI (1938),
pp. 1 ff.

were used. Non-Jews were considered "unclean," people with whom one must have almost none but unavoidable dealings. By many prominent Jews and rabbis even *proselytes* were despised. Close association with Gentiles meant "defilement" (John 18:28). To be sure, the temple had its "court of the Gentiles," but even this space was at times filled with Jewish merchants and money-changers, with oxen, sheep, and doves, instead of being reserved for holy purposes. The result was that it failed to contribute its share in making the temple "a house of prayer" (Luke 19:46) *"for all peoples"* (Isa. 56:7). And, of course, the Gentiles treated the Jews similarly. By them the Jews were considered "enemies of the human race," a people "filled with a hostile disposition toward everybody." We can well imagine with what gesture of disdain and in what tone of contempt Pilate must have said, "I, surely, am not *a Jew,* am I?" (John 18:35). Across the centuries we can still hear the owners of the Philippian slave-girl denounce the Jewish trouble-makers (Paul and Silas!) in these words of contempt, "These men, *being Jews,* do exceedingly trouble our city" (Acts 16:20). Cf. Acts 18:2.

Yet, wonder of wonders, Christ Jesus, the Peace-maker, had broken down this barrier of hostility. *Believers* from the Jews and *believers* from the Gentiles were dwelling together in unity in the midst of a world of bitterness and turmoil. How had this been accomplished? Christ had broken down the barrier formed by the dividing wall, the hostility, **15. by abolishing** [69] **in his flesh the law of commandments with its requirements.** That law, in the sense here meant, was the dividing wall which had to be abolished if peace was to be established between Jew and Gentile. Now "in his flesh," that is, in his body nailed to the cross where he shed his blood (see verses 13 and 16; cf. Col. 1:20; 2:14; cf. Heb. 10:20), Christ abolished the law. Of course, this cannot mean that he did away with the law as a moral principle embedded in man's very conscience (Rom. 1:21; 2:14, 15), formalized in the decalogue (Exod. 20:1-17; Deut. 5:6-21), summarized in the rule of love for God and for one's neighbor (Matt. 22:34-40; Mark 12:28-34; Luke 10:25-28; Rom. 13:8-10; Gal. 5:14), and climaxed in "the new commandment" (John 13:34, 35). By God's grace and through the indwelling Spirit the believer, in principle, obeys this law out of gratitude for salvation received. He delights in it (Rom. 7:22). Also, since his obedience *in this life* is only in principle, never perfect, the believer rejoices in the fact that Christ, by means of his active and passive obedience, has fully satisfied the demands of this law and borne

---

[69] The verb καταργέω of which the aorist active participle occurs here is a favorite with Paul. It occurs frequently in Romans and in I Corinthians; also four times in II Corinthians and thrice in Galatians. In II Thess. 2:8 it indicates that the Lord Jesus *will utterly defeat* the lawless one; in II Tim. 2:8, that he *has utterly defeated* or *abolished* death. Another, rather common, meaning is *nullify, render useless or ineffective* (Rom. 3:3; 4:14; Gal. 3:17). In I Cor. 13:11 it means *set aside.* In the New Testament, outside of Paul, it is found only in Luke 13:7 and Heb. 2:14.

its curse. But while, according to many, the apostle here in verse 15, also refers to this satisfaction rendered by Christ, which opinion I believe to be correct, I agree with Grosheide (*op. cit.*, p. 45) that Paul was thinking *especially* of the ceremonial law. The very wording "the law of commandments with its requirements" points in that direction. So, and very clearly, does the parallel passage, Col. 2:14 (in the light of Col. 2:11, 16, 17). The reference then is especially to the many rules and regulations of the Mosaic Code, stipulations with respect to such matters as fasts, feasts, foods, offerings, circumcision, etc. The great error committed by the Jews was that they had shifted the emphasis from the moral to the ceremonial law, and as to the latter, had "made void the law of God by their tradition," having added ever so many rules and regulations of their own (cf. Matt. 15:3, 6). Since the return from the exile the Jewish religion had become formalistic to a very great extent. Obedience to traditional ordinances was stressed. Now it was this very emphasis on ceremonial stipulations, even those stipulations contained in the law of Moses, that formed the dividing wall between Jews and Gentiles. For example, the latter could see no reason why a man had to be circumcised in order to be saved. The passage (verse 15) teaches that Christ, by his suffering and death, put an end to the law of ceremonies, and caused its binding power to cease. These ceremonial regulations had served their purpose. During his entire life on earth, especially on Calvary, Christ fulfilled all these shadows **in order that in himself** [70] **he might create of the two one new man, (so) making peace.** Since Christ is both "the seed of the woman" and "the seed of Abraham" it is not surprising that in him Jew and Gentile meet so as to become "one new man," a new humanity (cf. 4:24; Col. 3:10, 11). In him the two were "created" (cf. verse 10) one! When the Christian was able to say to the Gentile, as well as to the Jew, "Believe in the Lord Jesus, and you will be saved, you and your household" (Acts 16:31), meaning, "Nothing less than this is required of you, but also *nothing more*," the dividing wall, which for so long a time had been a hostile barrier between Jew and Gentile, came crashing down. It was in that way that Christ by his atonement made peace, the very peace referred to in verse 14. In further explanation of the purpose of Christ's sacrifice whereby he abolished in himself the law of commandments in ordinances, the apostle adds, **16. and might reconcile both of them in one body to God through the cross, having slain the hostility by means of it.** What Paul describes in the present verse is not only the reconciliation between Jews and Gentiles but also that basic reconciliation, namely, between *a*. the two groups, *now viewed as one body, the church* (as in 1:22, 23; 3:6; 4:4 ff.; 5:23, 30), and *b*. God. In fact it is on that basic reconciliation that the emphasis falls in the first part of the verse. The meaning is that Christ's atoning death had

---

[70] Whether one reads αὐτῷ or ἑαυτῷ makes no essential difference, as, in either case, the sense is reflexive.

achieved its purpose: the proper relation between the Ephesians and their God had been established. By grace those estranged from God, having heard and accepted the gospel, had laid aside their wicked alienation from God and had entered into the fruits of Christ's perfect atonement. This miracle had been achieved "through the cross," that very cross which to the Jews was a stumblingblock and to the Gentiles folly (I Cor. 1:23). It was by means of Christ's death on the cross that the curse had been borne, and, having been borne, had been lifted off the hearts and lives of all believers (Gal. 3:13). The miracle of Calvary, however, was even more thrilling, for, *through the strange instrument of the cross*,[71] the Sufferer not only reconciled to God both Jews and Gentiles but also slew the deeply-rooted antipathy that had existed for so long a time between the two groups.

The basic lesson holds for all time. The reason why there is so much strife in this world, between individuals, families, social or political groups, whether small or large, is that the contending parties, through the fault of either or both, have not found each other at Calvary. Only then when sinners have been reconciled to God through the cross will they be truly reconciled to each other. This shows how very important it is to preach the gospel to all men, and *to beseech them* (!) on behalf of Christ to be reconciled with God (II Cor. 5:20). For a world torn by unrest and friction the gospel is the only answer.

17. The idea of *peace* between God and man, consequently also between man and man (Jew and Gentile), brought about by Christ's self-sacrifice (verses 14–16), is continued in the words: **and he came and proclaimed the good news: "Peace to y o u, those far away, and peace** [72] **to those nearby."** The *emphasis* here is on basic peace (between God and man), as verse 18 indicates. Not only did Christ by means of his substitutionary suffering merit this peace for his people, he also wanted them to know about it and to experience it in their hearts. This peace is the inner assurance that all is well because the curse of the law has been removed, the guilt transferred, the punishment borne, salvation procured. "He came" to proclaim this peace. This "coming" refers, in all probability, to all of Christ's work on earth, that which he himself in person performed during his earthly sojourn and that which he continued to accomplish by means of the apostles and others (John 14:12; Acts 1:1 ff.; 4:10, 30). That it was peace which he not only brought about but also proclaimed appears from the passages already referred to (see on verse 14). It is implied also in such beautiful texts as

---

[71] Contrary to Lenski, *op. cit.*, p. 444, but in agreement with most versions and commentators, I take αὐτῷ in verse 16 to refer to *its closest logical antecedent*, namely, τοῦ σταυροῦ. Col. 1:20, "having made peace through the blood of his cross" confirms this more common interpretation.
[72] The omission (see A.V.) of the second mention of *peace* is not supported by the best manuscripts.

Matt. 9:13; Luke 19:10; and I Tim. 1:15. Notice also the "wideness" of the mercy here revealed: he came to call *sinners, the lost*. Destined to be included in that category were not only Israelitish sheep but also "other sheep" (John 10:16). Christ, when lifted up from the earth, drew "all men," regardless of blood or race, to himself. Cf. Matt. 28:18-20; John 1:29; 3:16; 11:51. He, accordingly, *gospeled* [73] the gladsome message of that which the Triune God through him had done, urging *all* to receive it: both those *far away, the Gentiles* (see on verses 12, 13), and those *nearby, the Jews*, here called *nearby* because of the many privileges they had received, including the knowledge of the one true God.

18. Paul continues, as it were, We know that both Jew and Gentile have obtained this peace through Christ's suffering on the cross **for through him we both have our access in one Spirit to the Father.** It is through Christ, through him alone — that is, through the shedding of his *blood* (verse 13), the sacrifice of his *flesh* (verse 15), the curse borne by him on the *cross* (verse 16) — that access to the Father was made possible and real. There was and there is no other way. See 3:12; John 3:16-18; 10:9; 14:6; Acts 4:12; Rom. 5:1, 2 (note same sequence of *peace* and *access* there as here in Eph. 2:17, 18) ; 5:10; Heb. 4:14-16; Rev. 7:14. It was he who supplied the *objective* basis apart from which access would have been impossible. The word *access* occurs only here and in 3:12 and Rom. 5:12. It follows from 3:12 that it may be defined as *freedom of approach to the Father, in the confidence that we, Jew and Gentile, have found favor with him.* Subjectively speaking, it is "in" or "by means of" the Spirit that man has access to the Father. Though there are those who reject the common view that the reference is here to the Holy Spirit, the third person of the Holy Trinity, this departure from the usual interpretation is not well grounded. Here in 2:18, as well as so often in Ephesians (1:3-14; 1:17; 3:14-17; 4:4-6; 5:18-20), there is a clear confession of the doctrine of the Trinity. Besides, elsewhere, too, confident approach to the Father is associated with the indwelling and enabling power of the Holy Spirit (Luke 10:21, 22; Rom. 8:15, 16; Rev. 22:17).

However, to appreciate more fully how inestimably glorious is this privilege of *access* it should be seen in the light of concrete reality, that is, of actual cases in which it is superbly illustrated. In some of the instances about to be mentioned it is *one* quality that strikes us, in others it is *another*. Often it is a combination of two or more qualities. Among these pleasing attributes of access to the Father may be mentioned the following: reverence, earnestness, pertinacity ("importunity"), concern for the welfare of others and/or for the glory of God's name, ability to distinguish between what is needful and what is merely wishful, world-embracing sympathy, spontaneity or naturalness, pleasing simplicity of faith. Illustrations: Abra-

---

[73] For "proclaimed the good news" the original has εὐηγγελίσατο (cf. evangelize). See N.T.C. on Philippians, pp. 81–85.

2:18 **EPHESIANS**

ham's intercession for the cities of the plain (Gen. 18:23 ff.); Jacob's wrestling at the Jabbok (Gen. 32:26); Moses' entreaty for the people of Israel (Exod. 32:32); Hannah's prayer for a child (I Sam. 1:10, 11); Samuel's answer to Jehovah's call (I Sam. 3:10); his "cry" to God at Ebenezer (I Sam. 7:5-11); David's many confessions, pleas, expressions of thanksgiving and adoration (in the Psalms); Solomon's prayer at the dedication of the temple (II Chron. 6:12 ff.); the supplications of Jehoshaphat when beset by enemies (II Chron. 20:5 ff.), of Elijah on Carmel (I Kings 18:36 ff.), and of Hezekiah when he had received Sennacherib's defiant letter (II Kings 19:15 ff.); the prayerful "interjections" of Ezra (Ezra 9:5) and of Nehemiah (Neh. 5:19; 6:9, 14; 13:22, 29, 31); Daniel's confession (Dan. 9:3-19); the prayers of the publican (Luke 18:13), of the early church (Acts 4:24-31), of Stephen (Acts 7:59, 60), and of Paul (Eph. 1:15 ff.; 3:14-21; etc.); and the yearning of the bride for the coming of the Bridegroom (Rev. 22:17).

In a place all by itself, yet full of instruction for all his followers, is the manner in which Jesus, while on earth, approached his Father (Luke 10:21, 22; 23:34, 46; John 11:41, 42; 17). From these prayers not a single virtue of *access* is excluded.

It must be borne in mind, however, that, as defined above, *access* is more than prayer. It is first of all the condition of the soul that rests in the Lord, surrendering itself fully to him, trusting that he will, in answer to prayer, fulfil every need. Prayer, being the natural result of this state of heart and mind, is an essential element in access. And since Jew and Gentile, on equal terms, through the Son, have access in one Spirit to the Father, the world-embracing extent of Christ's church is once more emphasized. See Col. 3:11; cf. Gal. 3:28.

Chapter 2

Verses 19–22

Theme: *The Church Glorious*

I. *Adoration*
for its

U niversal Scope (embracing both Jew and Gentile).

3. shown by the fact that the church of Jew and Gentile is growing into *one* building, a holy sanctuary in the Lord, of which Christ Jesus is himself the chief cornerstone

19 So then y o u are no longer strangers and aliens, but y o u are fellow-citizens with the saints and members of the household of God, 20 built upon the foundation of the apostles and prophets, Christ Jesus himself being the chief cornerstone, 21 in whom the entire building, harmoniously fitted together, is growing into a holy sanctuary in the Lord, 22 in which y o u also together with (all the others) are being built up for a dwelling-place of God in the Spirit.

2:19-22

3. *A Sanctuary of Jew and Gentile*

Since, therefore, Christ has reconciled both Gentile and Jew to God through his suffering on the cross, and both have their access in one Spirit to the Father, hence all inequality between the two groups, as far as their *standing* in the sight of God is concerned, has ceased, a thought to which Paul gives expression in the words: **19. So then y o u are no longer strangers and aliens, but y o u are fellow-citizens with the saints and members of the household of God . . .** The Ephesians, believers from the Gentiles for the greater part, had been "strangers" (see verse 12), as it were citizens of another country, but no longer were they to be considered mere foreigners who happened to be visiting the people of another land. Nor were they even to be regarded as aliens or sojourners, mere Gibeonites who dwelt in the midst of Israel without having obtained full rights of citizens. Cf. Exod. 2:22; Acts 7:6. On the contrary, they are "fellow-citizens" (a word occurring only here in the New Testament) with the saints, that is, with all those who were separated from the world and consecrated to God as a people for his own possession. The church is not to be divided into first-class members (Jewish converts to Christianity) and second-class members (Gentile converts to Christianity). The *terms of admission* are the same for all: faith in the Lord Jesus Christ, a faith working through love. The *rank* or *standing* is also the same. Expressing this thought in language still more intimate, the apostle declares that these former Gentiles are now "members of the household" of God. The household or family is a more intimate unit than the state. "Brothers and sisters" (household-members) is a more endearing term than "fellow-citizens." **20.** The double sense of the Greek word *oikos* (household, house) makes it natural for the apostle, by an easy transition, to change his metaphor from family-life to architecture. Hence, he continues: **built upon the foundation of the apostles and prophets.**[74] The

---

[74] The fact that the article is not repeated before *prophets* does not mean that apostles and prophets indicate the same individuals. In fact, 3:5 and especially 4:11

141

sense in which the apostles and prophets were, indeed, though in a secondary sense, the foundation of the church,[75] has been indicated in the Introduction, p. 50. Not in the least does such a statement constitute any contradiction of I Cor. 3:11, where Paul teaches that *the real or primary foundation is, and can be none other than, Jesus Christ*. In fact, by calling Christ "the cornerstone," that is, that part of this foundation in which the latter achieves its super-excellence, luster is added to the metaphor. The joyful testimony made by the apostles and prophets *in confirmation of the very fact* that the *basic* or *primary* foundation is Christ makes it possible that, *in a secondary sense*, they, too, can be called the church's foundation. On the term *apostles* see 1:1; 4:11. The position that the term *prophets* as here used refers to the Old Testament bearers of that appellative, such as Moses, Elijah, Isaiah, Jeremiah, etc. (thus Lenski, *op. cit.*, pp. 450–453) , is open to serious objections; such as the following: (1) Apostles are mentioned first, then prophets; (2) the designation "foundation" of the house, a dwelling shared *equally* by Jew and Gentile, suits the New Testament prophets better than those of the old dispensation; (3) according to 4:8-11 the prophets there mentioned immediately after the apostles, just as here in 2:20, are "gifts" bestowed on the church by the *ascended* Christ; hence, prophets of the New Testament era; and (4) 3:5, where the same expression "apostles and prophets" occurs in a context from which the reference to the prophets of the old dispensation is definitely excluded, would seem to clinch the argument in favor of New Testament prophets. As to the office or function which these New Testament prophets performed, in distinction from the apostles, see on 4:11.

Paul continues: **Christ Jesus himself being the chief cornerstone.**[76] Other references to this stone, clearly showing that it symbolizes Christ, are Isa. 28:16; Ps. 118:22; Matt. 21:42; Acts 4:11. The cornerstone of a building,

---

show that this is not the case. True explanation of the non-repetition of the article: the apostles and prophets belong to the same large category, namely, that of teachers of the church.

[75] Among other interpretations the main ones are: (1) "the foundation of the apostles and prophets" means "Christ, the foundation on which the apostles and prophets have built." Objection: this introduces a confusion of metaphors, for here in 2:20 Christ is represented as the cornerstone, not the foundation. (2) It means "the foundation laid by the apostles and prophets," namely, Christ's teaching. Although both Matt. 16:18 and Rev. 21:14 point in the direction of the genitive of apposition (the apostles and prophets are themselves the foundation) , nevertheless, if it be understood that they are referred to as such not because of what they are in themselves but because of their office, representing Christ and his teachings to men, it will become evident that in the end meaning (2) , though probably not technically correct, does not miss the truth by much.

[76] With reference to this cornerstone see G. H. Whitaker, "The Chief Cornerstone," *Exp,* Eighth Series (1921) , pp. 470–472; also J. M. Moffatt, "Three Notes on Ephesians," *Exp,* Eighth Series (1918) , pp. 306–317.

in addition to being part of the foundation and therefore *supporting* the superstructure, finalizes its shape, for, being placed at the corner formed by the junction of two primary walls, it determines the lay of the walls and crosswalls throughout. All the other stones must adjust themselves to this cornerstone. So also, in addition to resting in Christ, the spiritual house is determined as to its character by him. It is he who settles the question as to what this house is to be in the sight of God, and as to what is its function in God's universe. It is Christ who gives the house its needed *direction*. Believers, as "living stones" (I Peter 2:5), must regulate their lives in accordance with the will of the cornerstone, Christ. **21.** The apostle adds: **in whom the entire building,**[77] **harmoniously fitted together, is growing into a holy sanctuary in the Lord.**

Another thought is added now to the one just expressed. We now learn that Christ, in addition to being the principle of the church's *stability* and *direction* is also the principle of its *growth*. It is in vital union with *him* that the entire building is "growing" or "rising." There is nothing static about this edifice. It is a living building consisting of living stones: believers. And since each living stone makes his own contribution to the growth and beauty of the building, the latter is described as "harmoniously fitted together." Compare 4:16. Thus the building becomes, ever increasingly, "a holy sanctuary in the Lord." It is *holy*, that is, cleansed and consecrated, because of the blood and Spirit of Christ.

Turning now from the general thought to the special application, Paul states: **22. in which y o u also together with (all the others) are being built up for a dwelling-place of God in the Spirit.** Very comforting is this assurance. The apostle says, as it were, The business of being built up concerns y o u, Ephesians, as well as all other believers; it has reference to y o u, who are for the most part Gentiles, as well as to the Jews. God's love is as wide as

---

[77] Although the best text omits the article, and Gram. N.T., p. 772, states that πᾶσα οἰκοδομή in Eph. 2:21 = "most probably 'every building,' " I, along with many others, believe that only one building is here indicated. Reason: verse 20 describes a *house* with a *foundation* and *cornerstone*, not several buildings. The unity of the church has been stressed right along. Nowhere in the context has the reader been prepared for the idea of several separate buildings or congregations. Besides, abstract nouns do not need the article to be definite, and "the entire building" may perhaps be viewed as "whatever is being (or *has been*) built." Again, it has been suggested that it is possible to regard the word in question as being in the nature of a proper name. Also in that case no article would be necessary. Cf. Matt. 2:3; Rom. 11:26. The renderings offered by A.V., R.S.V., and N.E.B. are to be preferred, therefore, to A.R.V.'s confusing "each several building."

As to the meaning of the word οἰκοδομή itself, in Matt. 24:1 and Mark 13:1 the literal meaning *building, edifice* is clear. In Eph. 4:12, 16, 29 *edification, building up* is indicated. This seems also to be the meaning in Rom. 14:19; 15:2; II Cor. 10:8; 12:19; 13:10, and in the several occurrences of the word in I Cor. 14. Subject of much controversy is the exact reference of the word in II Cor. 5:1.

the ocean. It is all-embracing. Moreover, y o u are being built up *together*, in the closest possible association with each other, through active fellowship. Thus, the church universal gradually rises. It will not be finished until the day of the consummation of all things. Then it will be *in perfection* what it is even now *in principle*, namely, "a dwelling-place of God *in* (that is, by virtue of the cleansing and transforming operation of) *the Spirit*."

That this house(hold) of God, rising building, holy sanctuary in the Lord, dwelling-place of God, is *a spiritual and not a physical entity* requires no proof. Paul is clearly speaking about the church glorious, gathered out of all the nations, until at last "the number of the elect is complete." The question arises, however, Is there any allusion here, however faint, to a physical temple, so that the image of the latter would serve as a kind of background? And if there be such an allusion is it possible that it might shed light on the meaning of the passage? In favor of the idea of an implied and indirect reference to a literal temple or to literal temples is the fact that when, during his second missionary journey, the apostle had made a tour of the city of Athens, observing closely its sacred places and objects, he had remarked, "The God who made the world and everything in it . . . does not live in sanctuaries made by (human) hands" (Acts 17:24). In the given context the meaning must have been: "he cannot be localized in (or restricted to) one of y o u r (heathen) temples." Yet the same words also applied to the temple at Jerusalem, as is shown by the use Stephen makes of them in Acts 7:46-50. It would seem to be established, therefore, that when the apostle concentrated his attention on God's dwelling-place, the contrast between the true and the false was not absent from his mind; and also that, being a Jew, the contrast between shadow and reality, type and antitype, was appreciated by him. He was "of the tribe of Benjamin, a Hebrew of Hebrews" (Phil. 3:5), and had received his early training in Jerusalem, at the feet of Gamaliel (Acts 22:3). After his conversion, the heavenly voice had spoken to him while he was praying in the temple (Acts 22:17, 18). Moreover, it was in this same temple at the close of his third missionary journey, that he had been mobbed and arrested (Acts 21). The result had been his incarceration, first at Caesarea, then at Rome for his first Roman imprisonment, during which Ephesians was written, as were also Colossians, Philemon, and Philippians. It would have been almost impossible, therefore, for Paul to have written Eph. 2:21, 22 without at least alluding to the Jerusalem temple. Most commentators who refer to this question at all — many skip it entirely — agree with this position. "He [Paul] thinks of the Sanctuary at Jerusalem, which was a type and symbol both of Christ (see John 2:18-22) and of his Church" (Lenski, *op. cit.*, p. 459). The same author definitely rejects the idea that in Paul's words there might also be an indirect reference to a pagan sanctuary. Others, however, stress the idea that "the famous image of the spiritual temple, in which perhaps we may trace some recollection of the magnificent temple of Artemis,[78] which all Asia and the world worshiped, belongs in Eph. 2:20-22, nowhere else." Though it is not possible to prove an allusion to the image which, according to popular belief, had fallen from heaven, there are, nevertheless, certain facts that would seem to favor it. Note the following: (1) It has already been pointed out that the words of Paul quoted in Acts 17:24 are applicable to *any* man-made temple, whether at Jerusalem or elsewhere. (2) The apostle was writing this letter to the people who lived in and around the very city which housed the temple of Artemis (by the Romans identified with Diana), one of the seven wonders of the ancient world. (3) During Paul's ministry at Ephesus his preaching had collided head-on with the cult of the goddess, a fact that had been thoroughly grasped by Demetrius and his fellow-craftsmen. Demetrius, in addressing his colleagues, had pointed out that because of Paul's preaching there was "danger that the temple of the great goddess Artemis would cease to command respect." This address had stirred up a riot so filled with excitement that for two hours the mob had shouted, "Great is Artemis of the Ephesians" (Acts 19:23-41). After the uproar ceased Paul had taken his departure, to continue on his missionary journey (the third), which, as was indicated, led to his arrest and imprisonment.

Now if we accept as probable the theory that in 2:20-22 the apostle is, by implication, contrasting the spiritual sanctuary with any and all others, whether the one at Jerusalem or the one at Ephesus,[79] exactly in what respect is there a contrast? What was the most important function of any earthly temple which the apostle may have had in mind when he wrote as he did? The answer must be that the literal temple — more definitely, the inner enclosure or *sanctuary* — "was not built for the comfort of the worshipers, but as a shrine to house the deity" (Moffatt). Thus, even though Solomon was well aware of the fact that "heaven and the heaven of heavens cannot contain God," nevertheless, he believed that Jehovah would reveal his glorious Presence in a special manner in the temple which had just been completed (II Chron. 6:1, 2, 41; 7:1; cf. Exod. 40:34 ff.). *The sanc-*

---

[78] Helpful is the full-color picture (No. 5) of "The Temple of Diana, Ephesus" in the View-Master reel "The Seven Ancient Wonders of the World." Also, the accompanying *Story Guide* with its description of this temple (Sawyer's, Inc., Portland, Oregon, 1962). On Ephesus and its famous temple see also Merrill M. Parvis, "Ephesus in the Early Christian Era," *The Biblical Archaeologist Reader*, 2 (edited by D. N. Freedman and E. F. Campbell, Jr.), New York, 1964, pp. 331–343. In the same volume also Floyd V. Filson, "Ephesus and the New Testament," pp. 343–352. See also: J. T. Wood, *Discoveries at Ephesus* (1877); D. J. Hogarth, *The Archaic Artemisia* (1908); and *Forschungen in Ephesos* (1906–37), published by the Österreiches Archaeologisches Institut of Vienna.

[79] "In order that he may dwell among men God requires the community of his people, which is henceforth to replace all the old temples made with hands" (Scott, *op. cit.*, p. 179).

tuary on Zion is God's dwelling-place (Ps. 132:1-5, 8, 13, 14; 135:21; etc.).
Similarly, the "cella" (inner shrine, sanctuary) of the temple at Ephesus
was by far the most important part of that marvelous building. It excelled
the rest of the temple in the value that was attached to it, the reason being
that *it contained the statue of the goddess. She dwelt there.* It is true, of
course, that between the dwelling-place of Jehovah at Jerusalem and that
of Artemis at Ephesus there was this vast contrast, namely, that it was, indeed, *the living God* who had made Zion his special abode, whereas, on the
contrary, it was a *mere statue,* perhaps a large meteorite, shaped into the
form of a human figure by a skillful artist, that was adored at Ephesus. But,
in contrast with both, what Paul is bringing out is this beautiful and comforting thought: *"Y o u yourselves, Ephesians, are now God's earthly sanctuary* (Isa. 57:15; 66:1, 2; I Cor. 3:16, 17; II Cor. 6:16; Rev. 21:3). *Y o u
are his dewlling-place, his home."* [80] "Dwelling-place, home" indicates per-
manence, beauty, close fellowship, protection, love. That dwelling-place
is very large. It is a home "where there cannot be Greek and Jew, circumcision and uncircumcision, barbarian, Scythian, slave, freeman" (Col. 3:11),
and where the "one new humanity" (Eph. 2:15) is at peace with its Maker-
Redeemer.

Summary of Chapter 2

The church's *Universal Scope,* its extent broader than any ocean, is described in this chapter. It embraces *both Jew and Gentile,* that is, *everybody*
who appropriates Christ by true faith. In verses 1–10 we are told that this
universality was secured by the great redemptive blessings *for both* which
center "in Christ," and which parallel his resurrection and triumphant life.

Paul shows that by nature *all* men are dead through trespasses and sins.
They are "children of wrath," and servants of "the prince of the domain of
the air." The great change, when it occurs, is due exclusively to the *rich
mercy* and *great love* of God, the *surpassing riches of his grace.* Salvation
in its entirety is from God, *even faith itself being "God's gift."* As to *good
works,* considered as a ground upon which to plead they are *rejected.* Yet
by God good works were "prepared" or *confected,* for he gave his Son and
imparted to his chosen ones faith in that Son, and good works are the fruit
of faith. Moreover, God prepared them in order that his people should
walk in them. In other words, these works are *expected* of them, as works
of gratitude. These good works, having been prepared by God, will by him
be *perfected,* for God always finishes what he has begun. Besides, Christ's
resurrection from the dead implies our resurrection from sin, for it is the
Spirit of the raised and ascended Christ who "raised us up with him." In

---

[80] Similarly, the church is "the Israel of God" (Gal. 6:16), the true "seed of Abraham" (Gal. 3:7, 16; cf. Rom. 4:16), "an elect race, a royal priesthood," etc.
(I Peter 2:9).

glory we shall be sinless. All this applies to all of God's children, both Jews and Gentiles.

The cross whereby Jew and Gentile were reconciled to God also brought about their mutual reconciliation (verses 11-18). This is an amazing fact, namely, that the very cross which to the Jews had been a stumblingblock and to the Gentiles foolishness was the means whereby the double reconciliation was secured. Paul shows how thankful *all* should be for this divine arrangement. The Jews should praise God because through the cross "the law of commandments with its requirements" had been abolished. But the Gentiles, too, had a reason for special thanksgiving. They should consider what great benefits Christ through his death on the cross had bestowed upon them. Formerly they had been separate from Christ; now they are "in him"; formerly alienated from the commonwealth of Israel, now, "fellow-citizens with the saints and members of the household of God"; formerly, strangers to the covenants of the promise, now covenant-members; formerly, hopeless, now filled with buoyant hope; formerly, without God, now at peace with him. To both Jews and Gentiles Jesus by his coming and work had proclaimed and was still proclaiming the good news: "Peace to y o u, those far away and peace to those nearby." Through him both have access in one Spirit to the Father.

Thus the church of Jew and Gentile is growing into one building, a holy sanctuary in the Lord, of which Christ Jesus is himself the chief cornerstone (verses 19-22). Of course, the real and primary foundation is, and can be none other than, Jesus Christ (I Cor. 3:11). But *in a secondary sense* the apostles and New Testament prophets can truly be called the church's foundation, namely, because they direct everyone's attention to Christ as the only true Savior. A parallel would be the fact that Jesus called himself "the light of the world" (John 8:12), but he also called his disciples "the light of the world" (Matt. 5:14). They derive their light from him. When the apostles are called the church's foundation, Christ is called that foundation's *cornerstone,* that is, the principle of the church's stability, direction, and growth. Day by day living stones are added to this building, the church. No earthly temple, whether Jewish or pagan, but the church alone is God's dwelling-place. Here he homes. That home is very large. It is peaceful, for Jew and Gentile being at peace with their Maker-Redeemer, are also at peace with each other.

Chapter 3

Verses 1–13

Theme: *The Church Glorious*

I. *Adoration*
for its

L ofty Goal

1. *To declare* to the principalities and the powers in the heavenly places *God's iridescent wisdom,* reflected in the mystery revealed especially, though not exclusively, to Paul, namely, that the Gentiles are fellow-members of the body of Christ

CHAPTER III

3 1 For this reason I, Paul, the prisoner of Christ Jesus for the sake of y o u Gentiles — 2 for surely y o u have heard of the stewardship of God's grace that was given to me for y o u r benefit, 3 how that by revelation there was made known to me the mystery, as I wrote before in few words, 4 whereby, as y o u read it, y o u can perceive my insight into the mystery of Christ, 5 which in other generations was not made known to the sons of men as it has now been revealed by the Spirit to his holy apostles and prophets, 6 namely, that the Gentiles are fellow-sharers in the inheritance and fellow-members of the body and fellow-partakers of the promise (realized) in Christ Jesus (as conveyed) through the gospel, 7 of which I was made a minister according to the gift of God's grace that was given to me according to the working of his power. 8 To me, the very least of all saints, was this grace given: to proclaim to the Gentiles the good tidings of the unfathomable riches of Christ, 9 and to enlighten all on what is the administration of the mystery which for ages has been hidden in God who created all things; 10 in order that now to the principalities and the authorities in the heavenly places might be made known through the church the iridescent wisdom of God, 11 according to the eternal purpose which he formed in Christ Jesus our Lord, 12 in whom we have the courage of confident access through faith in him. 13 Therefore I ask (y o u) not to lose heart over what I am suffering for y o u, which is y o u r glory —

3:1-13

1. *The Church Should Strive to Declare God's Marvelous Wisdom to the Principalities and the Powers in the Heavenly Places*

1. The very beginning of the present chapter, namely, the words **For this reason,** already indicate its close *material connection* with the preceding one. The meaning, accordingly, must be, Because blessings so great have been bestowed upon both Gentile and Jew — reconciliation with God and with one another, and the erection of *one* sanctuary consisting of Jew and Gentile — therefore, etc. In fact, in view of the equally close relation between chapters 1 and 2, and the recurrence in 3:4, 9 of the concept *mystery,* first mentioned in 1:9, it is very probable that the connection goes back even further and includes *all* that has gone before in this epistle.

The *mode* of humble gratitude and adoration also continues; see especially verses 8, 14-21. "Paul is about to resume his prayer on behalf of his readers. . . . This prayer forms the framework of the whole first half of the epistle. . . . His thought is pitched in a solemn key" (Scott, *op. cit.,*

149

p. 181). The first part of the epistle (chapters 1–3), which after the salutation began with one main type of doxology, namely, "Blessed (be)" (1:3 ff.), is going to end with the other main type, "Now to him . . . be the glory" (3:20, 21). That closing doxology is immediately preceded by one of the most glorious prayers to be found anywhere (3:14-19), a prayer which, in a sense, is already introduced in 3:1.

Nevertheless, there is *progress* in thought. Chapter 2 has shown what God has done. Chapter 3, therefore, is going to indicate what the church, mentioned distinctly in verse 10, now must do. It indicates the church's *Lofty Goal*. In the realization of this purpose Paul himself has played a prominent role, for to him, to him *especially* though not exclusively, the great mystery, to be published far and wide, has been disclosed.

So Paul continues, **I, Paul** (cf. II Cor. 10:1; Gal. 5:2; Col. 1:23; I Thess. 2:18; Philem. 19), **the prisoner of Christ Jesus** (cf. 4:1; Philem. 1, 9; II Tim. 1:8). In every reference to himself as a prisoner Paul stresses the fact that as such *he belongs to his Lord,* for it was while engaged in *his* service and thus for *his* sake that he was imprisoned. Moreover, all the details of the imprisonment as well as the outcome, whether it be the death-sentence or acquittal, are in the hands that were pierced for this prisoner, those very hands that now control the entire universe in the interest of the church (1:22). Paul's imprisonment is therefore a very honorable one. In fact, it strengthened his claim as an apostle of Jesus Christ. And since he is going to remind the church of its exalted task, its *Lofty Goal,* namely, to declare God's marvelous wisdom, it is entirely proper for him to make mention of his chains in authentication of his apostleship (cf. II Cor. 11:16-33). This is true all the more since enemies were constantly questioning his claims, as is clear from I and II Corinthians, Galatians, I and II Thessalonians, and from passages scattered here and there throughout his epistles. It is not improbable that these opponents viewed his very *imprisonment* as a sign of the falsity of his pretensions. So, instead of carefully avoiding this subject he starts right out by boldly calling attention to it. He emphasizes, however, that he is a prisoner in a righteous cause, so that his very confinement is a reason why they should listen all the more attentively to what he has to say. He regards it, in fact, as an honor, and this not only for himself but even *for them* (verse 13), for he is the prisoner of Christ Jesus **for the sake of y o u Gentiles —** It was because of the fact that he had been proclaiming the love of God for Gentile and Jew alike, without any racial or national distinction whatever, that he had been imprisoned (Acts 21:17 ff.; 22:21-24). The *Ephesians* especially knew about this, for surely they must have heard that at the close of his third missionary journey his association with Trophimus *the Ephesian* had led to the false charge which resulted in his capture and incarceration. Moreover, not only had his work *for the Gentiles* brought about his imprisonment but he had been specifically charged by his Lord to be an apostle *to Gentiles* as well as to Jews (Acts 9:15). In fact, to him, in distinction from the other apostles (Gal. 2:9), had been entrusted the glorious assignment of being above all else the apostle *to the Gentiles* (see verse 8; also: Acts 13:47; 22:21; 26:12 ff.; Rom. 11:13; 15:16; Gal. 2:8, 9; I Tim. 2:7; Titus 1:7).

It must be borne in mind, in this very connection, that big-hearted Paul wanted everybody to share his joy in the Lord. It was he who had said in a letter written previously, "I have become all things to all men, that in one way or another I may save some" (I Cor. 9:22). But in order to be saved men must accept the gospel-message which Paul had been commissioned to bring. And confidence in his credentials was necessary if his message was going to be accepted, his exhortations obeyed, his prayers appreciated. This also explains the digression (verses 2-13), in which he dwells at some length on the charge given to him by the Lord. Hence, having said, "For this reason I, Paul, the prisoner of Christ Jesus for the sake of y o u Gentiles," he does not at once add "bend my knees to the Father," but postpones this until verse 14 is reached. He never loses sight of this petition, however. It is definitely on his mind throughout the paragraph. But by inserting the words of verses 2-13 he adds strength to the prayer that he was about to utter and to the doxology which follows that prayer. **2.** Paul continues, accordingly: **for surely y o u have heard of the stewardship of God's grace that was given to me for y o u r benefit.** A strictly literal translation of what Paul actually writes is perhaps impossible in English. The nearest to it would be something like this: "If, indeed, y o u have heard." Cf. A.V., "If ye have heard"; A.R.V., "If so be that ye have heard." However, that type of rendering will hardly do, since it might suggest that Paul is questioning whether or not the Ephesians, by and large, have ever heard about the task committed to him by his Lord. There are those who, upon the basis of this kind of rendering, have argued that *Paul* could not have written Ephesians, and/or that this letter was never meant for *them*. They base their argument upon the fact that the book of Acts assigns a lengthy ministry to Paul at Ephesus, making it impossible for *him* to write to *the Ephesians*, "*If* y o u have heard of my stewardship," for Paul knew that *they* must have heard of his stewardship. However, such reasoning is not convincing. It proceeds from the assumption that the little word "if" — whether in Greek or in English — must indicate *uncertainty*. But that is incorrect. Two contrasted examples in the English language will make this clear: (1) "*If* our team wins, there will be a celebration." Here "if" expresses uncertainty, mere possibility. (2) "*If* you do not know the day of your death, you should be prepared now." Here "if" indicates an assumption that is taken for granted. This "if" could be translated "since." [81] But what ground have we for believing that in the

---

[81] Many commentators mention the fact that the expression εἰ γε, used here in Eph. 3:2, has the sense of "since" or "inasmuch as." They refer to II Cor. 5:3 as a paral-

present instance "if" means "*since* y o u heard" rather than "*maybe* y o u heard, *and maybe* y o u did *not* hear"? The answer is that this epistle, which from the beginning has been almost universally viewed as a writing of Paul "to the Ephesians" (in some sense), elsewhere clearly *states* (1:13; 2:17; 4:20) and throughout *implies* that the readers have heard the gospel. Would they then not have heard about *Paul's* part in it? Anent *Paul's* work in Ephesus Luke writes: "All those who lived in Asia *heard* the word of the Lord, both Jews and Greeks." With this cf. Eph. 3:2: ". . . y o u *have heard* of the stewardship of God's grace that was given to me for y o u r benefit." Therefore, such renderings as the following must be considered excellent: "Y o u have heard — have y o u not? — of the stewardship of God's grace" (Bruce's paraphrase) ; "If y o u have heard, as I presume y o u have" (Grosheide) ; ". . . assuming that y o u have heard" (R.S.V.) ; "Y o u must have heard" (Phillips) ; "Surely y o u have heard" (Moffat; N.E.B.). Of course, even on the basis of this translation and interpretation it must be granted that the "if" of the original may, perhaps, leave room for the possibility that a relatively small number of people living in the province of Asia, and addressed here, might never have heard about Paul and his commission, or that they might *claim* not to have heard. After all, the people to whom the epistle was addressed did not all live inside the city of Ephesus. The circle addressed was very wide! And some time had elapsed since Paul had labored in this region.

The apostle says that the addressed, by and large, must have heard about the *stewardship* of God's grace that had been granted to him. For a discussion of the word *stewardship* see Introduction, p. 44. The gospel of the *grace* (see on 1:2; 2:5, 8) of God in Christ had been assigned to Paul as a sacred trust (I Cor. 4:1, 2; 9:17; I Tim. 1:4; Titus 1:7). It had been given to him for the benefit of the Ephesians. Cf. Col. 1:25. In their case that was true in a special sense, for most of them had been won over from the Gentiles (3:1, 8), and, as has already been indicated, it was especially to the Gentiles that Paul had been sent. Paul continues, **3. how that by revelation there was made known to me the mystery.** Here begins a brief description of the stewardship of grace that had been entrusted to Paul. It had reference to "the mystery," that is, to something that would have remained unknown had it not been *revealed,* as Paul also indicates by writing "how that *by revelation* there was made known to me the mystery." Such revelation is generally in the form of a divine communication by means of voice or vi-

---

lel case. The probability of the correctness of this rendering does not depend exclusively on the particle γε, however. Even in the absence of this particle doubt is often excluded. Thus, the words, "*If* therefore there is any encouragement in Christ" (Phil. 2:1), do not mean that the apostle wonders whether there be such encouragement. On the contrary, the sense is, "If then there is any encouragement in Christ, *as there surely is.*" For similar illustrations of this second sense of "if" see I Cor. 11:6; 15:12, 32; II Cor. 3:7; Philem. 17; Heb. 2:2.

sion. Paul's stewardship with respect to the Gentiles had been made known to him by both of these forms of thought-transmission, as is clear *directly* from such passages as Acts 16:9; 22:21; 26:17, 18; and *indirectly* from Acts 9:15; Gal. 1:11-17; 2:8. Paul always insisted, over against the allegations of his critics, that the stewardship which he had received was not of human origin. As he had been one of the strictest of Pharisees it could not have occurred to him that God's grace would be extended to Gentiles as well as to Jews and on equal terms. And as far as Peter and other leaders of the church were concerned, Paul could not *originally* have received his commission as the apostle *to the Gentiles* from them, for the Book of Acts shows how difficult it had been for them to divest themselves of their Judaistic exclusivism. They only agreed *after* they had perceived the grace that had been given to Paul (Gal. 2:9). Peter, in fact, needed the vision of the sheet (Acts 10:9-16) and Paul's rebuke (Gal. 2:11 ff.) to get over his error.

In connection with the fact that the mystery had been made known to him *by revelation* Paul adds, **as I wrote before in few words.** Calvin prefers the translation "as I wrote a little before," that is, somewhat earlier. He inclines to the view, rather popular in his day, that the reference is to an earlier letter to the Ephesians, one that has not been preserved. But of such earlier epistles to the Ephesians there is no hint anywhere, and it would seem far more reasonable to interpret Paul's word as having reference to the brief account he had already given *in this same letter,* with respect to God's plan of salvation for both Gentiles and Jews, with special emphasis on the changed position of the former (2:11-22; cf. 1:9 ff.). Accordingly, the clause, "as I wrote before in few words" is tantamout to "as I briefly indicated above."

Continued, **4. whereby, as y o u read it, y o u can perceive my insight into the mystery of Christ.** When, in the various churches for which this epistle was intended, those of Ephesus and surroundings, this letter was read, particularly also 2:11-22, lectors and listeners would be able *to perceive* (cf. 3:20; I Tim. 1:7) Paul's insight into this Christ-mystery, that is, the mystery of which Christ is both the source and the substance. One can say that the mystery is, in a sense, Christ himself, that is *Christ in all his glorious riches actually dwelling through his Spirit in the hearts and lives of both Jews and Gentiles, united in one body, the church.* Cf. Col. 1:26, 27.[82] However,

---

[82] I prefer this interpretation to that which tries to distinguish sharply between "the mystery" in verse 3 and "the mystery of Christ" in verse 4, so that ὁ at the beginning of verse 5 would have to refer to the former, and 3b, 4 would have to be construed as a parenthesis (as in A.V.). More natural, it would seem to me, is the construction according to which ὁ refers to its nearest possible antecedent. Moreover, if the expression "this mystery . . . Christ" (Col. 1:27) can refer to the calling of the Gentiles (as it actually does according to the context), why should not the phrase "the mystery of Christ" (here in Eph. 1:4) describe the same theme?

here in Ephesians the actual *content* of the mystery is not given until verse 6 is reached.

We find no fault with Handel who said that when he began to compose the "Hallelujah Chorus" it seemed as if all heaven and earth were lying open to his gaze. Why then should we criticize Paul for saying, "Y o u can perceive my insight into the mystery of Christ"? The reason which prompted him to write this was altogether honorable, as was pointed out previously. See Introduction, p. 46, and also on verse 1 above. Besides, as did Handel in later days, Paul, too, gives the credit for his insight to God, not to himself (verses 3, 7, 8).

5, 6. In verse 5 Paul continues to speak about the mystery mentioned in verses 3 and 4, but still no description of its content is given. In verse 6, however, this description is finally supplied. Unless we know the content of the mystery it is impossible to interpret it, and to show in what sense it is true that it was concealed "in other generations." Therefore verses 5 and 6 should be considered together. The apostle writes: **which in other generations was not made known to the sons of men as it has now been revealed by the Spirit to his holy apostles and prophets, namely, that the Gentiles are fellow-sharers in the inheritance and fellow-members of the body and fellow-partakers of the promise (realized) in Christ Jesus (as conveyed) through the gospel.** It is a mystery which "in other generations," that is, at other times (cf. Acts 14:16: "in past times or ages"), was not made known to the sons of men (not even to *anybody*) *as* — meaning "as clearly as" — it has now *been revealed* or *unveiled* by the Spirit (the Holy Spirit, who imparts different gifts to different men, I Cor. 12:4-11) to his holy apostles and prophets (see on 1:1; 2:20; 4:11).[83] Cf. Rom. 16:25, 26; Col. 1:26, 27. This does not mean that before Pentecost no one, not even prophets, like Moses, Isaiah, etc., knew anything about the future blessing in which the Gentiles, too, would share. The Old Testament writers, in fact, did know about it and referred to it again and again (Gen. 12:3; 22:18; 26:4; 28:14; Ps. 72; 87; Isa. 11:10; 49:6; 54:1-3; 60:1-3; Hos. 1:10; Amos 9:11 ff.; Mal. 1:11, to mention only a few references). *But what these prophets did not make clear was that in connection with the coming of the Messiah and the outpouring of the Spirit the old theocracy would be completely abolished and in its place would arise a new organism in which the Gentiles and the Jews would be placed on a footing of perfect equality.* As has already been shown, even some of the leaders in the early church were slow to grant this point. Moreover, there is nothing which sheds so much light on the full meaning of a prophecy — a meaning not always *fully* grasped even by the Old Testament prophets (I Peter 1:10) — as does its fulfilment! The holy

---

[83] The connection of αὐτοῦ with *apostles,* and not with *prophets,* probably indicates "in the first place *to the apostles,* then also *to prophets* who followed them" (Grosheide, *op. cit.,* p. 52, footnote 8).

apostles and prophets of the *new* dispensation lived in the era of fulfilment. Illumined by the Spirit given to the church on the day of Pentecost, they were able to set forth with greater clarity than ever before the meaning of the prophecies and their application to the new order of events. Hence, for Gen. 12:3; 22:18 see Gal. 3:8; for Isa. 49:6 see Acts 13:47; for Isa. 54:1-3 see Gal. 4:27; for Amos 9:11 ff. see Acts 15:16-18; etc.

Paul makes it very clear that God's unveiled secret ("mystery") has to do not merely with an *alliance* of Jew and Gentile, or perhaps a friendly *agreement* to live together in peace, or even an outward *combination* or *partnership*, but, on the contrary, with a complete and permanent *fusion*, a perfect spiritual union of formerly clashing elements into *one* new organism, even a "new humanity" (2:15). In God's house there are no boarders; all are children. Note the climactic arrangement: the Gentiles are, in the first place, *fellow-sharers in the inheritance* (implied already in 1:14; cf. Gal. 3:29; 4:7). In the abstract it might, however, be possible for someone outside the inner family-circle (for example, a slave) to receive a share of an inheritance. So the next term makes the picture even clearer, namely, *fellow-members of the body;* [84] that is, the Gentiles are actually members of God's church (see 1:23; 2:16; 4:4, 16). As such they are equal in standing with all the other members. The blessed result and climax is that they are *fellow-partakers of the promise* (see on 2:11-13; cf. II Tim. 1:1). Full salvation is their portion, all this "in Christ Jesus," who merited it for them and apart from whom there can be no share in the inheritance or in the body or in the realization of the promise. And this marvelous union of the two who were formerly enemies but now in Christ have become *one* "elect race, royal priesthood, holy nation, people for God's own possession" (I Peter 2:9), was effected "through the gospel" preached, heard, and accepted by faith (Rom. 10:14, 15; I Cor. 4:15). On *the gospel,* its essence, power, author, emphasis, etc. see N.T.C. on Philippians, pp. 81–85.

7. Paul returns now to the very personal manner of speaking begun in verses 1-4. Perhaps the reason for this is that he has just made mention of *the gospel.* Paul and the gospel are friends. In Rom. 2:16 he speaks of "my gospel." It is a gospel in which he glories (Rom. 1:16, 17). In fact, he tells us that he was set apart in a special way to preach the gospel (Rom. 1:1). He just "cannot get over it" that God chose *him,* even himself, Paul, the great persecutor of the church, to proclaim the gospel of the grace of God in Christ. So, speaking about this glorious gospel and about his share in it, he writes: **of which I was made a minister.** That was the task that had been assigned to him, the cause which he had been called to serve **according to the gift of God's grace that was given to me.** Paul had not arrogated to himself the distinction of being a gospel-minister. He was no self-constituted

---

[84] Greek σύσσωμα, a word used only by Paul and Christian writers.

ambassador. The office with which he had been invested was a gift of God's grace, a fact which is stressed over and over in Paul's letters (Rom. 1:1; I Cor. 1:1, 17; 15:10; II Cor. 1:1; Gal. 1:1; etc.). The bountiful nature of this grace becomes all the more clear in the light of verse 8. But before coming to that the apostle adds: (God's grace that was given to me) **according to the working of his power.** How mightily that power of God had operated, and continued to operate, in the life and ministry of the apostle is clear from II Cor. 11:16-33; 12:9; cf. Phil. 4:13; and I Tim. 1:15, 16. For "the working of his power" see on 1:10. However, the thought which Paul emphasizes is rather this, that not he but his Lord deserves all the credit for whatever he, as gospel-minister, in proportion to the talents and opportunities given to him, may have accomplished. He continues: **8. To me, the very least of all saints,**[85] **was this grace given: to proclaim to the Gentiles the good tidings of the unfathomable riches of Christ.** That the man who wrote verse 4 — "whereby, as y o u read it, y o u can perceive my insight into the mystery of Christ" — was not a proud individual, appears very clearly here in verse 8. A similar note is struck in I Cor. 15:9, "For I am the least of the apostles, not fit to be called an apostle, because I persecuted the church of God"; and in I Tim. 1:15, "Reliable (is) the saying, and worthy of full acceptance, that Christ Jesus came into the world sinners to save, foremost of whom am I." Since in the present passage Paul does not give the reason for calling himself "the very least of all saints," it is impossible for any interpreter to supply this reason. The nearest we can come to a sensible conjecture would be to quote the apostle's own reference to his former life as a persecutor of the church. Note forward position of "to me," for emphasis. On "to the Gentiles" see 3:1, 2, 6. "Unfathomable riches" are riches that cannot be *tracked* or *traced,* the illimitable resources of the grace of God in Christ, ocean-depths that can never be plummeted, treasure-stores that are inexhaustible. See on 1:7 and on 3:17-19. Any one who wishes to learn how magnificently Paul fulfilled his God-given task, what excellent use he made of the "grace" (here "blessed but undeserved privilege") given to him should read such chapters and passages as the following: Rom. 5; 8; 12; 13:11-14; I Cor. 13; 15; II Cor. 4; 5; II Cor. 8 (see especially 8:9) ; 11; Gal. 5; 6; Phil. 2; 3; Col. 3:1-17; I Thess. 4; 5; etc.; also, of course, the account of Paul's life and preaching in the book of Acts.

9. To proclaim to the Gentiles the unfathomable riches of Christ was, however, only part of Paul's task. In two respects his mission was broader: *a.* it concerned not only the Gentiles but *all* men. Had not God described him as "a chosen vessel, to bear my name before the Gentiles and kings and the children of Israel"? (Acts 9:15) ; *b.* it had to do not only with the *proclamation* of the gospel but also with the *illumination* of men's eyes so that

---

[85] The word ἐλαχιστατέρῳ is a comparative formed on a superlative.

they might see how this gospel, accepted by faith, was operating in the hearts and lives of men. Not only must the mystery of the unfathomable riches of Christ be set forth. To be sure, that mystery is great and marvelous, and reveals salvation for both Jew and Gentile by grace through faith. But the attention must also be focused upon the manner in which in Paul's own day that mystery *was actually working out,* replacing fear by trust, gloom by gladness, hatred by love, and separation by fellowship. Speaking, then, about the *administration* or *effectuation* of the mystery, the apostle continues: **and to enlighten all on what is the administration of the mystery which for ages has been hidden in God who created all things.** In connection with the expression "to enlighten" see on 1:18 and 5:7-9. The original light is Christ himself. It is with reference to him that it was said, "The true light, which illumines every man, was coming into the world" (John 1:9). Jesus called himself "the light of the world" (John 8:12). In a secondary sense, Christ's followers, too, are "the light of the world" (Matt. 5:14). They are *light-bearers* (Rev. 1:20). The great missionary, Paul, was functioning in this capacity in a pre-eminent manner by bearing testimony, *even while in prison,* to "the light of the gospel of the glory of Christ" (II Cor. 4:4). As such he had become all things to *all men* that in one way or another he might save some. Hence, here in 1:9 he says, "to enlighten *all,*[86] (Jews and Gentiles alike) on what is the administration of the mystery." He describes the mystery as the one "which for ages has been hidden in God." Cf. Col. 1:26. From the beginning of time the mystery had been concealed. *Now,* however, it is being revealed both by the worldwide preaching of the gospel and by the crystallization of its precious truths in the life and conduct of the church universal. It is not clear why Paul adds: (God) "who created all things." If I may be permitted to add just one more guess to all those that have been made by others, I would say that the expression may, per-

---

[86] It is my conviction that πάντας should be retained. In the text of N.N. it is omitted. Grk. N.T. (A–B–M–W) retains it, though between brackets and with a D ("very high degree of doubt") rating. The external evidence is inconclusive. In such cases one must not slavishly follow the old rule "The more difficult reading must be adopted." That rule has long been in need of serious modification. Ernest C. Colwell in his article, "Biblical Criticism: Lower and Higher," *JBL* (March, 1948), p. 4, is correct when he states, "Today textual criticism turns for its final validation to the appraisal of individual readings, in a way that involves subjective judgment. The trend has been to emphasize fewer and fewer canons of criticism." One of the two canons which he mentions would apply especially in the present instance, I believe. It is this, "That reading is to be preferred which best suits the context." Surely, the words in the preceding context, namely, "to proclaim *to the Gentiles* the good tidings," etc., are followed very naturally by "and to enlighten all *(men)*." Note that the verb φωτίζω is followed by an object also in I Cor. 4:5 and in II Tim. 1:10. Cf. Rev. 21:23. However, in the present instance it really makes very little difference which reading one follows. It is as Abbott says *(op. cit.,* p. 87), "The general meaning is, indeed, pretty much the same with either reading, since the result of bringing oἰκ to light is that all men are enabled to see it."

haps, rivet the attention on God's sovereignty. He is the God who, by virtue of the very fact that he *created* all things, also proves himself to be the sovereign Disposer of their destinies. In other words, he does not owe it to any one to explain why for a long time the mystery was concealed from the Gentiles, and why it is now revealed to all, regardless of race or nationality.

The purpose which Paul has in mind in *proclaiming to the Gentiles the good tidings* of the unfathomable riches of Christ, *and in enlightening all men* on what is the administration of the mystery, is that by means of these two (to some extent overlapping) activities, the church, being formed and strengthened, might display God's marvelous wisdom even to the angelic world. He writes, 10. **in order that** [87] **now to the principalities and the authorities in the heavenly places might be made known through the church the iridescent wisdom of God.** The church, therefore, does not exist for itself. It exists for God, for his glory. When the angels in heaven behold the works and the wisdom of God displayed in the church, their knowledge of the God whom they adore is increased and they rejoice and glorify him. That the designation "principalities and authorities" refers to angels has been established. See on 1:21 and N.T.C. on Col 1:16 and 2:18. By no means all commentators who adopt this position are in agreement, however, with respect to the kind of angels indicated here (3:10). Some defend the position that the reference is to evil powers exclusively.[88] Robertson, in his *Word Pictures*, Vol. IV, p. 531, equates them with "gnostic aeons or what not." Greijdanus states that although the reference is, first of all, to the good angels, the fallen angels need not be excluded (*op. cit.*, p. 72). Now it is true, indeed, that the expression "principalities and authorities" is neutral just like "angels." Gabriel is an angel, but so is Satan. In each case it is the context that determines whether the designation refers to angels in general, as in 1:21, to evil angels, as in 6:12, or to good angels. Even the addition here in 3:10 of the words "in the heavenly places" is not decisive in determining whether good angels or demons are meant, as 6:12 proves. Nevertheless, I still see no reason for disagreeing with Calvin, Bavinck, Grosheide, Hodge, Lenski, and a host of other leading theologians and commentators, in believing that 3:10 refers to the good and not to the evil angels. My reasons are as follows:

---

[87] The purpose clause thus introduced must not be linked with the immediately preceding subordinate clause. According to that construction the sense would be, "God created all things in order that the principalities and the authorities might learn more about God's marvelous wisdom in the sphere of redemption." I agree with Hodge, *op. cit.*, when he states, "This connection of the clauses is unnatural, because the words 'who created all things' are entirely subordinate . . . and therefore not the proper point of connection for the main idea in the whole context."

[88] Thus, for example, Franz Mussner, in *Christus, Das All und die Kirche*, Trierer Theologische Studien, V, Trier, 1955, p. 21; E. F. Scott, *op. cit.*, p. 189.

(1) Here (3:10) there is no reference to any *conflict* between believers and spiritual hosts of wickedness. In 6:12 the matter is entirely different.

(2) Both language and thought-content are elevated. Calvin's comments may well be taken to heart. Says he, "Some prefer to refer these words to devils, but without due reflection . . . There can be no doubt about the fact that the apostle labors to place in the strongest light the mercy of God toward the Gentiles, and the high value of the gospel . . . Paul's meaning is, The church, composed of both Jews and Gentiles, is a mirror, in which the angels behold the astonishing wisdom of God displayed in a manner unknown to them before. They see a work which is new to them, and the reason whereof was hid in God."

(3) The fact that the church, as God's masterpiece in which his excellencies are mirrored forth, is an object of interest and scrutiny to the good angels is clear also from other passages (Luke 15:10; I Cor. 11:10; I Peter 1:12; Rev. 5:11 ff.). Eph. 3:10 harmonizes beautifully with all this.

Now what the principalities and powers see reflected in the church is "the iridescent wisdom" of God. The adjective that modifies *wisdom* means literally *multi-colored* or *much-variegated*. Unless the word used in the original has lost its full etymological significance, and should therefore simply be rendered *manifold* (as in A.V., A.R.V., R.S.V.) or *many-sided* (L.N.T. — A. and G.), which in the present highly elevated context is improbable, it calls attention to the *infinite diversity* and *sparkling beauty of* God's wisdom. For both of these characteristics one is reminded of the rainbow. Hence, *iridescent* or something on that order (like *"many-splendoured"* suggested by Bruce) would seem to be a reasonable English equivalent, unless one wishes to retain the literal rendering *multi-colored*. In every phase of redemption (as well as of creation) the brilliance of God's wisdom reveals itself. Since in chapters 2 and 3 of Ephesians (see especially 2:16; 3:6) the matter of the reconciliation of Jew and Gentile to God and to each other through the cross — which to the Jew was a stumblingblock and to the Gentiles foolishness (I Cor. 1:22-25) — is never absent from Paul's mind, it would seem that this is one of the manifestations of the divine "wisdom" which he mentions. Cf. Rom. 16:25-27, where *the revelation of the mystery* is ascribed to "the only *wise* God." *God's wisdom reconciles seeming irreconcilables.* So also the very word *wisdom* is again used in the text when elsewhere reference is made to the fact that the very rejection of carnal Israel results, by various links, in the salvation of all of God's people: "By their fall salvation is come to the Gentiles, to provoke them to jealousy . . . that by the mercy shown to y o u [Gentiles] they [Israel] may now obtain mercy. . . . O the depth of the riches and *wisdom* and knowledge of God. How unsearchable are his judgments; how untraceable his ways!" (Rom. 11:11, 31, 33). Accordingly, when in the past certain commentators, in interpreting the expression "iridescent wisdom," have fixed the attention upon various paradoxes such as the following, that God in Christ produces life by means of death, glory by means of shame (the "shame" of the cross), the blessing by means of the curse, power by means of weakness, etc., they were simply following where Scripture itself had led them.

The true dimensions of the term "iridescent wisdom" are, however, much broader than this. There is not a single work of God whether in creation or, as here, in redemption, where that richly variegated wisdom does not manifest itself. It is seen in the church as a whole when it strives earnestly to live to God's glory. It is seen also in every individual believer, drawn out of the darkness into God's marvelous light. We catch glimpses of it *now*, as we study Scripture or as we reflect on the divine providence in our own lives. By the sea of crystal, where at last all things become crystal-clear to us, we shall see it as we have never seen it before, and, filled with rapture, we shall say, "Great and marvelous are thy works, O Lord God Almighty. Righteous and true are thy ways, thou King of the ages" (Rev. 15:3). The words of the Psalmist with reference to God's works in the physical realm will then be applied, with emphasis greater than ever before, also to the *spiritual* realm, namely, "O Lord, how manifold are thy works, *in wisdom* thou hast made them all!" The more the church lives in harmony with its high calling, the more also will the angels be able to see in it God's marvelous wisdom. To make manifest in its life and character the "excellencies" of its Maker-Redeemer, so that the principalities and the authorities may, indeed, see this wisdom is, therefore, part of the church's *Lofty Goal.*

11. That God's iridescent wisdom might be made known through the church was **according to the eternal purpose which he formed in Christ Jesus our Lord.** Paul is speaking here about the plan which spans *the ages;* hence, his "eternal purpose," the same purpose which was mentioned also in 1:11. Cf. II Tim. 1:9. It governs the ages in all their continuity and contents. That this purpose centers "in Christ" has been made abundantly clear in chapter 1. Christ is, in fact, the church's *Eternal Foundation.* His very name, fully spelled out here in 3:11, namely, "Christ Jesus our Lord," is essentially the same as that mentioned in 1:2, 3, 17. See on 1:2, but note that the beautiful word of appropriating faith, namely, "our" is added only in 1:3, 17, and in the present passage. There are those who maintain that this very title points to Christ in his historical manifestation here on earth, and, accordingly, that the entire passage deals not with God's purpose in Christ from eternity but rather with the historical realization of that plan. Hence, they interpret the words "which he *formed* (or *made*) in Christ Jesus our Lord" to mean "which he has realized" in him (thus R.S.V.). But although the verb used allows that translation, it is hardly true that the church's *Lofty Goal* of making known God's iridescent wisdom has already been fully realized. Only in glory will it be fulfilled in perfection. And there

can be no objection to stating that even from eternity God's plan or purpose centered in him whom we now call "Christ Jesus our Lord." All things considered, therefore, it is best to interpret 3:11 as a very comforting passage, which assures believers that God's ultimate design for the church, namely, that it serve as a school in which the glorious angels may learn more and more about his marvelous wisdom, cannot fail to be realized, resting, as it does, not on the sinking sand of merely human striving but on the impregnable rock of the sovereign and eternal will of the Almighty, a will centered in the Anointed Savior, who is Lord of the entire Church Glorious, yes, *our* Lord. Continued, **12. in whom we have the courage of confident access through faith in him.** Literally, we would have to translate: "in whom we have *the courage and access in confidence.*" But if this be *hendiadys* we obtain the resultant meaning: *courage of confident access.* The three important words here are courage, access, and confidence. The word used for *courage*, namely, *parrēsia*, is very picturesque. It is derived from two Greek words, meaning *all* and *telling;* hence, telling all. The word occurs with great frequency in the New Testament, and in more than one resultant meaning. Light is shed upon its connotation here by such a passage as Phil. 1:20, "by my unfailing *courage* Christ will be magnified in my person," and by Heb. 4:16, "Let us therefore draw near with *courage* ("boldness," A.V., A.R.V.) to the throne of grace." The word *access* has already been explained. See on 2:18. It has been defined as *freedom of approach to the Father, in the confidence that we, Jew and Gentile, have found favor with him.* The third word, *confidence* (same meaning in II Cor. 1:15, but *ground of confidence* in Phil. 3:4), strengthens the idea already present in *access.*

Since, then, Christ Jesus is *ours* and we are *his,* bought with his blood, indwelt by his Spirit, we know that we have free and unrestricted access to the Father. Cf. 2:18. We can and should approach him without restraint, *telling* him *all* our troubles, asking him to help us in *all* our needs. We know that he will welcome us most heartily. Particularly, we should ask him to enable us so to live that the fruits of his grace may be exhibited in us, and the wisdom of God reflected in us, so that the angels may see us as the mirror of God's virtues. Such courage of confident access is possible only "through faith in him," namely, in "Christ Jesus our Lord," the very One "in whom" we were chosen from eternity. God's eternal purpose which cannot fail and the redemption accomplished by Christ Jesus our Lord make such fearless access possible.

13. The apostle concludes this parenthetical paragraph by writing: **Therefore I ask (y o u) not to lose heart over what I am suffering for y o u, which is y o u r glory —.** Meaning: because we have been endowed with this courage of confident access, we should rise above discouragement. Joy in the Lord should fill our hearts at all times, for no one can take from us the

blessings which are ours in Christ Jesus our Lord (see especially verses
6 and 12; cf. 1:3 ff.) . In the original we have here a case of abbreviated expression, of which the Bible, and literature in general as well as human
speech, is full. See N.T.C. on the Gospel according to John, Vol. I, p. 206.
Actually all we have in the Greek text is this: "Therefore I ask not *to lose
heart* (literally, *behave badly,* and so *become weary;* cf. II Cor. 4:1, 16; Gal.
6:9; II Thess. 3:13) in my afflictions for y o u," etc. In the abstract various
meanings are possible. The main ones are these:
  (1) Therefore I ask God that I may not lose heart
  (2) Therefore I ask God that y o u may not lose heart
  (3) Therefore I ask y o u that y o u may not lose heart
Since nothing in the context suggests God as the One to whom the request is presented, (1) and (2) can be ruled out. Also, another reason for
ruling out (1) is that in the situation in which the apostle, a prisoner in
Rome, finds himself, it was far more probable that those whom he addressed
would lose heart than that he himself would become discouraged. That this
is true appears quite clearly from another letter written, perhaps just a
little later, during this same imprisonment, namely, Philippians. The church
at Philippi seems to have been filled with anxious concern. It was for that
very reason that Paul was then going to write, "Now I want y o u to know,
brothers, that the things that have happened to me in reality turned out
to the advantage of the gospel" (Phil. 1:12) . We may well believe, therefore, that also here in Ephesus and surroundings not Paul but those whom
he addressed were in danger of losing heart. Accordingly, the third possibility, "Therefore I ask y o u that y o u may not lose heart," is the one
which I, along with many others, accept. It is as if the apostle were saying,
"What an honor it is for y o u that in the very eyes of God y o u are regarded as being worthy of so much suffering endured by me in y o u r behalf!" (see on verse 1) . How precious y o u must be to him! On the "glory"
of suffering for Christ's sake see N.T.C. on Philippians, pp. 90, 91.

Chapter 3

Verses 14–21

Theme: *The Church Glorious*

I *Adoration*
for its

L ofty Goal
  2. To know the love of Christ that surpasses knowledge so as to be filled to all the fulness of God

14 For this reason I bend my knees to the Father, 15 from whom the whole family in heaven and on earth derives its name: the Father's Family, 16 (praying) that according to the riches of his glory he may grant y o u to be strengthened with power through his Spirit in the inner man, 17 that Christ may dwell in y o u r hearts through faith; in order that y o u, being rooted and founded in love, 18 may be strong, together with all the saints, to grasp what is the breadth and length and height and depth, 19 and to know the love of Christ that surpasses knowledge; in order that y o u may be filled to all the fulness of God.

20 Now to him who is able to do infinitely more than all we ask or imagine, according to the power that is at work within us, 21 to him be the glory in the church and in Christ Jesus to all generations forever and ever; Amen.

3:14-21

2. The Church Should Strive to Know the Love of Christ That Surpasses Knowledge in Order to Be Filled to All the Fulness of God. Paul's Prayer That This Lofty Goal May Be Increasingly Realized. Doxology

In the preceding paragraph Paul has pointed out that the church of Jew and Gentile must live in harmony with its high calling, so that to the principalities and the authorities in the heavenly places it may display God's iridescent wisdom. How is this end going to be achieved? The answer is given in verses 14-19, which point to the strength-imparting Spirit and the indwelling Christ. These will enable believers to attain to an ever increasing, though necessarily never complete, realization of the second aspect of their *Lofty Goal,* namely, to learn to know the love of Christ in all its dimensions so as to be filled to all the fulness of God.

That the apostle is still writing about The Church Glorious is very clear. In fact, he supplies us with a double description of the concept *church,* calling it, first, "the whole family in heaven and on earth," and afterward, "y o u [Ephesian believers] together with all the saints." Similarly, the fact that here, too, as in verses 1-13, Paul is centering our attention on the church's *Lofty Goal,* the very word "goal" being used by several commentators,[89] appears from the wording: *"in order that* y o u may be enabled to grasp and to know; . . . *in order that* y o u may be filled." And surely no one can quarrel with the adjective *lofty* modifying the noun *goal,* for what could be a loftier purpose or ideal than to know the breadth and length and height and depth of the love of Christ, in order to be filled to all the fulness of God? Now inasmuch as in its own strength the church will never

---

[89] For example, by Lenski, *op. cit.,* p. 497; and by Simpson, *op. cit.,* p. 82.

be able even to make progress in trying to achieve this objective, the apostle makes this a matter of earnest intercession. He begins by writing, **14, 15. For this reason I bend my knees to the Father, from whom the whole family in heaven and on earth derives its name: the Father's Family.** It is clear that the apostle resumes the sentence begun in 3:1. The meaning of the opening words is therefore *here* as it was *there:* Because blessings so rich have been bestowed upon both Gentile and Jew — reconciliation with God and with one another, and the erection of *one* sanctuary consisting of Jew and Gentile — therefore I bend my knees to the Father. In the intervening verses 2-13 another element, however, has been added to this first reason. Paul has made clear that the Lord has highly favored him by imparting to him the privilege of proclaiming to the Gentiles the good tidings of the unfathomable riches of Christ, and by enabling him to illumine the minds and hearts of all men with respect to the fact that the marvelous mystery, now unveiled, is, on the part of many, being translated into actual day by day living, a fact of amazement and instruction even to angels. Surely, God's wonderful dealings with *him,* Paul, a man in himself so unworthy, have made him all the more confident in prayer. Blessings already received encourage him to ask for even greater ones. Summarizing, we can say, therefore, that what the apostle means when here in verse 14 he writes, "For this reason I bend my knees," is this: It is because God has dealt so kindly with y o u, Ephesians, and with me, Paul, that I have the courage of confident access to the Father in heaven.

The apostle speaks about *bending his knees.* Posture in prayer is never a matter of indifference. The slouching position of the body while one is supposed to be praying is an abomination to the Lord. On the other hand, it is also true that Scripture nowhere prescribes one, and only one, correct posture. Different positions of head, arms, hands, knees, and of the body as a whole, are indicated. All of these are permissible as long as they symbolize different aspects of the worshiper's reverent attitude, and as long as they truly interpret the sentiments of his heart. For a listing of various prayer postures to which Scripture makes reference see N.T.C. on I and II Timothy and Titus, pp. 103 and 104. As to kneeling, in addition to Eph. 3:14 see II Chron. 6:13; Ps. 95:6; Isa. 45:23; Dan. 6:10; Matt. 17:14; Mark 1:40; Luke 22:41; Acts 7:60; 9:40; 20:36; 21:5. This particular posture pictures humility, solemnity, and adoration. It is "to the Father" [90] that this moving supplication, a true pattern of intercessory prayer, is presented. It should be borne in mind, however, that the One addressed is our Father by virtue not only of creation (3:9) but also of redemption. In fact, it is upon this redemptive aspect that the emphasis clearly rests. He is the Father to whom both Jew and Gentile have access *through Christ,* through him alone, *in one*

---

[90] A.V.'s addition "of our Lord Jesus Christ," is not based upon the best textual evidence. It may have been interpolated from 1:3, 17.

Spirit (2:18). In this redemptive or soteriological sense he is definitely *not* the Father of all men.

Paul gives a further description of the Father in the words: (I bend my knees) "to the *patéra* (Father) from whom *every* or *all* or *the whole* (or *all the*) [91] *patriá* in heaven and on earth derives its name." The sound-similarity between *patềr* (here acc. *patéra*) and *patriá* is clearly an intentional play on words. It creates a problem in translation. The other question, as indicated in footnote 91, concerns the translation of the word *pâsa* which in the original precedes *patriá*, whether it should be rendered "every" or "all" or "the whole." The main translations that have been suggested are the following:

(1) *every family* (A.R.V., R.S.V., N.E.B.).

Objection: In a context in which the emphasis from start to finish is on *oneness*, how Jew and Gentile have become *one* organism (2:14-22; 3:6; 4:4-6), an emphasis so strong that the theme of the entire epistle is *The Church Glorious* or *The Unity of All Believers in Christ*, it is as dubious to speak of *every family* as it was in 2:21 to think of *each several building*. Those who, nevertheless, adopt this rendering become entangled in all kinds of questions such as: How many families does Paul have in mind? Do the Jews constitute one family, the Gentiles another? Do the angels form a family all by themselves or must we think of several angelic families: a family of "principalities" and another family of "authorities," etc.?

(2) *all fatherhood* (Phillips, Bruce). Simpson writes that *"Father of all fatherhoods"* is a rendering entitled to strong support (*op. cit.*, p. 79).

Evaluation: This translation has a certain appeal; first, because the play on words (paronomasia) of the original can thus be preserved in the translation, which then becomes, "I bend my knees to *the Father* from whom all *fatherhood* in heaven and on earth derives its name," or something similar; secondly, because it suggests a beautiful and comforting thought, in itself entirely true, namely, that, compared to the heavenly Father's *original* fatherhood, all other fatherhood anywhere in the universe is only *derived* and *secondary, a faint likeness*. If then human fathers love their children so intensely and care for them so generously, how marvelous must be the love and care of the heavenly Father! This thought, in turn, also provides an excellent basis for Paul's confidence that the request which he is about to make will be granted.

There are, nevertheless, two reasons that prevent me from adopting this translation: *a.* nothing in the context has prepared us for a discussion of

---

[91] The omission of the article before πᾶσα does not exclude the rendering "the whole" or "all the." This omission is not unusual with substantives that are viewed either as proper or as abstract nouns; probably the former in the present instance. Cf. footnote 77. Thus Robertson states that in Eph. 3:15 πᾶσα πατρία is "every family," though "all the family" is possible (Gram. N.T., p. 772).

167

the abstract concept of *fatherhood;* and *b.* the meaning *fatherhood* for *patriá* is foreign to Luke 2:4, "Joseph was of the house and *family* of David"; and to Acts 3:25, "In your seed will all the *families* of the earth be blessed." These are the only other New Testament passages in which the term *patriá* occurs. It is evident that even though it does not necessarily always refer to *family* in the most restricted sense of the term but can also indicate a wider group of persons united by descent from a common ancestor, it always has a concrete connotation. In the references given in M.M., p. 498, and in L.N.T. (A. and G.), p. 642, to contemporary Greek sources it also has the concrete sense.

(3) *the whole family* (A.V., footnote N.E.B.: "his whole family") .

Evaluation: I consider this rendering to be correct. It is entirely in harmony with the context. In fact, in words that differ but slightly, the apostle has just told us that all those who believe in Christ, whether they be Jews or Gentiles, now constitute one *household,* a synonym for one *family.* Not only that, but he has even mentioned *the Father's* relation to this household or family. His words were: "For through him we both have our access in one Spirit to *the Father.* So then y o u are no longer strangers and aliens, but y o u are . . . *members of the household of God"* (2:18, 19). In subsequent passages he has re-emphasized this same thought, though by the use of different metaphors (2:20-22; 3:6). He is going to stress it again in 4:1-6. It was, in fact, this very circumstance that filled his heart with great joy.

The only drawback which this translation has is its failure to reproduce the obviously intentional connection between *patḗr* (Father) and *patriá* (family), a sound-similarity almost impossible to reproduce in English while still retaining the meaning of the words in the original. Whether to give up the attempt, in which case A.V.'s rendering, or something similar, is still the best that has been offered: "the Father . . . of whom *the whole family* in heaven and earth is named," or else to look with favor upon my solution: "the Father, from whom the whole family in heaven and on earth derives its name: the Father's Family," I leave to anyone's preference. Perhaps someone can suggest a more excellent way.

What is Paul's purpose in attaching this modifier to the words "the Father"? I answer: He probably wishes to indicate that if it be true that the relation between believers and their heavenly Father is so very close that they constitute one family, whose very *name* — hence, existence, essence, character — as "the Father's Family" is derived from his name "Father," then this Father can be trusted to supply every need. See Matt. 7:11; Luke 11:13. This modifier, therefore, far from being inconsequential, furnishes an adequate introduction to the petition which Paul is about to present.

Another point must not be passed by, namely, that, according to this clause, "the family in heaven and on earth," "the Father's Family," is *one.* We speak about the Church Militant on earth and the Church Triumphant in heaven, but these are not two churches. They are *one* church, *one* family. It is in the interest of that *one* church that Christ governs the entire universe (1:22, 23). If even to us who are living in a day of travel by jet, short wave radio transmission, and the automatic relaying of electronic signals by means of synchronous satellites from and to any place on earth, distances seem to vanish, so that places on this planet once considered far apart are now viewed as close together, it should not be too difficult to understand that in the sight of the God who created all things the church of the redeemed in glory and the church of the redeemed on earth constitute *one* family. To be sure, there is nothing in Scripture that warrants the belief that there is *direct* contact between the dead and the living.[92] There *is*, however, indirect contact (Luke 15:7). Besides, the names of *all* believers, whether still on earth or already in heaven, are written in *one* book of life, and engraved on the breastplate of the *one* Highpriest. The Spirit, too, though in different measure, dwells in the hearts of all. All have *one* Father, of whom they are children by adoption (1:5; Rom. 8:15; Gal. 4:5). Christ, being the Son by nature, is not ashamed to recognize these adopted children as his brothers (Heb. 2:11). Every day the praise of the entire church, in heaven and on earth, is directed to *the same* Triune God.

The book of Revelation especially indicates how close are the ties that unite that part of the church which is in heaven with the part that is still on earth. In the early church this glorious truth was not a dead letter. Also in later times some have given beautiful expression to it. Thus, for example, the little girl, one of *seven* children, *two* of whom, however, had died, was certainly right when, according to Wordsworth's famous poem, she continued to maintain, "We are seven." The reader recalls, no doubt, the ending:

> "How many are y o u then?" said I,
> "If they two are in heaven?"
> Quick was the little maid's reply,
> "O master, we are seven."
>
> "But they are dead; those two are dead!
> Their spirits are in heaven!"
> 'Twas throwing words away; for still
> The little maid would have her will,
> And said, "Nay, we are seven!"

When we recite the "Apostles' Creed" and reach the line, " (I believe in) the communion of saints," we will have failed to pour full meaning into this part of our confession unless we understand that we are confessing that

---

[92] See the chapter devoted to this subject in my book *The Bible on the Life Hereafter,* pp. 62–65.

169

"we have come to mount Zion, and to the city of the living God, the heavenly Jerusalem, and to the innumerable hosts of angels [a different category of beings but vitally interested in our salvation], to the general assembly and church of the firstborn enrolled in heaven, to God the Judge of all, and to the spirits of just men made perfect" (Heb. 12:22, 23). We will have fallen short unless we cherish the memory of those who at one time were our leaders, reflect on the outcome of their life, and imitate their faith (Heb. 13:7). We will have missed the mark unless we bear in mind and are comforted by the fact that today too the ascended Christ is in the Spirit walking on earth in the midst of the lightbearers (Rev. 1:12, 13); and unless by faith we peer into heaven's opened door (Rev. 4:1), meditate upon the songs of its choirs (Rev. 4, 5, 12, 15, 19), and sense our oneness with all those who have come out of the great tribulation and, having washed their robes in the blood of the Lamb, are living and reigning with Christ in glory (Rev. 7:13-17; 20:4).

As to the intercessory prayer itself, it should be observed that it works its way toward a momentous climax. It is, as it were, a staircase consisting of three steps, a ladder with three rungs; steps or rungs, however, by means of which one is lifted to the very heights of heaven. The three parts of the prayer are readily visible, for the boundaries between them are marked out clearly by the words "in order that" in verses 17 and 19.[93]

16, 17a. Paul has introduced his moving trinitarian prayer by saying, "For this reason I bend my knees to the Father, from whom the whole family in heaven and on earth derives its name: the Father's Family," and he continues, **(praying) that according to the riches of his glory he may grant y o u to be strengthened with power through his Spirit in the inner man, that Christ may dwell in y o u r hearts through faith.** God is *glorious* in all his attributes, as has been indicated. See on 1:17. His power (1:19; 3:7) is infinite; his love (1:5; 2:4)` is great; his mercy (1:4) and his grace (1:2, 6; 2:7, 8) are rich; his wisdom (3:10) is iridescent; etc. Note particularly such expressions as "the surpassing riches of his grace (expressed) in kindness" (2:7) and compare "the unfathomable riches of Christ" (3:8). In the work of salvation it is never right to stress one attribute at the expense of another.[94] Hodge is right when he states, "It is not his power to the exclusion

---

[93] In the original this is represented by ἵνα in the *final* sense in these two verses. At the beginning of verse 16 ἵνα is clearly *non-final*.
[94] Is not Lenski guilty of this error when he states, "Omnipotence does not work in the spiritual domain, grace and grace alone does"? (*op.cit.*, p. 418; and cf. pp. 426, 475). On p. 500 this eminent commentator, whose works have been a blessing to many, blames Calvinism — as he does rather frequently — for what he considers an erroneous view. But if "omnipotence does not work in the spiritual domain," would Paul have been saved? Would even a single sinner have been saved? As to the "working of omnipotence in the spiritual domain" see the following New Testament passages (which could easily be supplemented by those from the Old Testament): Acts 1:8; 10:38; Rom. 1:16; 15:13, 19; I Cor. 1:18, 24; 2:4, 5; 4:20; 5:4;

of his mercy, nor his mercy to the exclusion of his power, but it is every-thing in God that renders him glorious, the proper object of adoration" (*op. cit.*, p. 181). Paul prays therefore that all of God's resplendent attributes may be richly applied to the spiritual progress of those whom he addresses. In particular, he asks that the One who, as 1:19 (cf. 3:7, 20; Col. 1:11) has shown, is himself the Source of power in all its various manifestations, may grant to the Ephesians that, in accordance with the measure of God's glory, they may be strengthened with power through his Spirit in the inner man. This "inner man" is not that which is rational in man as contrasted with man's lower appetites. Paul's terminology is not that of Plato or of the Stoics. On the contrary, the "inner man" is the opposite of the "outer" (or: outward) man. Cf. II Cor. 4:16. The former is hidden from the public gaze. The latter is open to the public. It is in the *hearts* of believers that the prin-ciple of a new life has been implanted by the Holy Spirit. See on 3:17. What the writer is praying for is therefore this, that within these hearts such a controlling influence may be exerted that they may be strengthened more and more with Spirit-imparted power. See on 1:19; cf. Acts 1:8. Another way of putting the same thought is this: "that Christ may dwell in y o u r hearts through faith." Wrong is the idea, rather popular among some commenta-tors, that *first,* for a while, the Spirit imparts strength to believers, *after which* there arrives a time when Christ establishes his abode in these now strengthened hearts. Christ and the Spirit cannot be thus separated. When believers have the Spirit within themselves they have Christ within them-selves, as is very clear from Rom. 8:9, 10. "In the Spirit" Christ himself in-habits the believers' inner selves. Cf. Gal. 2:20; 3:2. The heart is the main-spring of dispositions as well as of feelings and thoughts (Matt. 15:19; 22:37; Phil. 1:7; I Tim. 1:5). Out of it are the issues of life (Prov. 4:23). Christ's precious indwelling is "through faith," the latter being the hand that accepts God's gifts. Faith is full surrender to God in Christ, so that one expects everything from God and yields everything to him. It works through love (Gal. 5:6).

It is instructive to note that the long list of exhortations (4:1–6:17) by means of which the apostle is about to urge the Ephesians to work out their own salvation (Phil. 2:12) is wedged in between two references to prayer; the first one, here in 3:14-19, being Paul's own prayer; the second in 6:18 ff., being the exhortation unto prayer, in which connection Paul reminds the Ephesians that as he prays for them, they too should pray for him. It is as if the writer were saying: To be sure, believers should strive to reach their goal. They should exert themselves to the utmost. But they should remem-ber at all times that apart from the power of the Holy Spirit — or, stating

---

II Cor. 4:7; 6:7; 12:9; 13:4; Eph. 1:19; 3:16; 6:10; Col. 1:11; II Tim. 1:8; I Peter 1:5; Rev. 19:7; 21:22. Surely, when *the Almighty* reveals his *power,* he reveals his *almighty power, his omnipotence!*

it differently, apart from the indwelling of Christ — they are completely powerless. *"With fear and trembling work out y o u r own salvation; for it is God who is working within y o u both to will and to work for his good pleasure"* (Phil. 2:12, 13). And since so much — in a sense *everything* — depends on God, hence prayer for his strength-imparting power is all important.

The immediate purpose of the strengthening and the indwelling is stated in words which indicate, as it were, the second rung of this prayer-ladder: **17b-19a. in order that y o u, being rooted and founded in love,**[95] **may be strong, together with all the saints, to grasp what is the breadth and length and height and depth, and to know the love of Christ that surpasses knowledge.** Since faith works through love, and amounts to nothing without it (I Cor. 13:2), it is easy to see that if *by faith* Christ has established his abiding presence in the heart, believers will be firmly rooted and founded *in love,* a love for God in Christ, for the brothers and sisters in the Lord, for the neighbors, even for enemies. Moreover, this love, in turn, is necessary in order to comprehend Christ's love for those who love him. And in the measure in which the believers' vision of that love which proceeds from Christ expands, their love for him and their ability to grasp his love for them will also increase, etc. Thus the most powerful and blessed chain-reaction in the whole universe is established. It all *began* with God's love in Christ for the Ephesians (1:4, 5; I John 4:19). Like a continuing circle it will *never end.*

The words "rooted and founded" suggest a twofold metaphor: that of *a tree* and that of *a building.* To insure the stability of the tree roots are required, roots that will be in proportion to the spread of the branches. Similarly, as a guarantee for the solidity of a building a foundation is necessary, one that will adequately support the superstructure. Thus firmly rooted the tree, which represents all those who love the Lord, will flourish and bear the indicated fruit. Thus solidly founded the building will continue to grow into a holy sanctuary in the Lord, and will achieve its purpose.

That fruit and purpose is "to grasp what is the breadth and length and height and depth, and to know the love of Christ." Since such *grasping* or *appropriating*[96] and *knowing* can be practised only by those who are rooted and founded in *love,* it is clear that the reference is not to an activity that is purely mental. It is *experiential* knowledge, *heart*-knowledge, which Paul

---

[95] As I see it, the grammatical construction indicates that the phrase "rooted and founded" belongs to the purpose clause introduced by "in order that" at the beginning of verse 18 of the Greek text. The trajection of the particle ἵνα, or, if one prefers, the proleptic placing of the participles, is not unusual. As to the phrase "in love," neither here nor in 1:4, where it also occurs (see p. 78, footnote 18), is the *preceding* clause in need of any additional modifiers.

[96] M.M., p. 328, states that this is Paul's regular use of the verb in active and passive.

has in mind. And since the heart is the very core and center of life and influences all of life's inner activities and outward expressions, what is indicated is a grasping and a knowing with one's entire being, that is, with *all* the "faculties" of heart and mind. Mental appropriation is certainly *included*.

It should not be necessary to point out that when the apostle speaks of being *strong* (exercising great inherent strength; see on 1:19) *to grasp . . .* and *to know*, he does not have two objects in mind but one, namely, the love of Christ. So great is that love that no one will ever be able to appropriate and to know it all by himself alone; hence, "together with all the saints." The saints will tell each other about their discoveries and experiences with respect to it, in the spirit of Ps. 66:16, "Come and hear, all y o u that fear God, and I will declare what he has done for my soul." This activity of getting to know more and more about the love of Christ begins here on earth and will, of course, continue in the life hereafter. The fact that Paul in this very prayer is not forgetting about the church in *heaven* is clear from verse 14. The *Lofty Ideal* is to get to know *thoroughly* Christ's deep affection, self-sacrificing tenderness, passionate sympathy, and marvelous outgoingness. All of these are included in *love* but do not exhaust it. Paul prays that the addressed may appropriate and know this love in all its breadth and length and height and depth! Here, as I see it, the expositor should be on his guard. He should not pluck this expression apart, so that a separate meaning is ascribed to each of these dimensions. What is meant is simply this: Paul prays that the Ephesians (and all believers down through the centuries) may be so earnest and zealous in the pursuit of their objective that they will never get to the point where they will say, "We have arrived. *Now* we know all there is to know about the love of Christ." Just as Abraham was told to look toward heaven and number the stars, so that he might see that numbering them was impossible; and just as we today are being urged by means of a hymn to count our many blessings, and to name them one by one, so that their uncountable multitude may increase our gratitude and astonishment, so also the apostle prays that the addressed may concentrate so intensely and exhaustively on the immensity and glory of Christ's love that they will come to understand *that this love ever surpasses knowledge*. The *finite* heart and mind can never fully grasp or know *infinite* love. Even in the life hereafter God will never say to his redeemed, "Now I have told y o u all there is to be told about this love. I close the book, for the last page has been read." There will always be more and more and still more to tell. And that will be the blessedness of the heavenly life.

This introduces us to the climax. We now reach the top of the ladder: **19b. in order that y o u may be filled to all the fulness of God.** See also on 4:13. In other words, the knowledge just described is transforming in character: "But we all, with unveiled face beholding as in a mirror the glory

173

of the Lord, are transformed into the same image from glory to glory, even as from the Lord, the Spirit" (II Cor. 3:18). To contemplate the glory of Christ's love means to be increasingly transformed into that image. *In one sense* that process of transformation will cease at the moment of death. At the very moment when the soul of the believer enters heaven, a great change will take place, and he, who a moment before was still a sinner, a *saved* sinner, will be a sinner no more, but will behold God's face in righteousness. He will then be absolutely perfect, completely sinless, in every respect obedient to the Father's will (Matt. 6:10; Rev. 21:27). For "all the saints" it will cease, in the sense indicated, at Christ's return. *In another sense,* however, the transformation-process will not cease: growth in such things as knowledge, love, joy, etc., will continue throughout eternity. Such growth is not inconsistent with perfection. Even in the hereafter believers will still be creatures; hence, finite. Man never becomes God. God, however, ever remains infinite. Now when in glory, in a condition of total absence of sin and death, finite individuals are in continuous contact with the Infinite, is it even possible that the finite would not make progress in the matters that have been mentioned? When "the fulness of God" — all of those divine communicable attributes of which God is full: love, wisdom, knowledge, blessedness, etc. — is, as it were, poured into vessels of limited capacity, will not their capacity be increased? [97] To be sure, believers will never be filled *with* the fulness of God in the sense that they would become God. Even the communicable attributes, *in the measure in which they exist in God,* are incommunicable. But what Paul prays is that those addressed may be filled *to* all the fulness of God. Perfection, in other words, also in such matters as knowledge, love, blessedness must ever remain *the goal;* to become more and more like God, *the ultimate ideal.* What Paul is asking, therefore, with special reference, of course, to the church *still on earth,* though the answer to the prayer will *never* cease, is nothing strange, nothing new. It is a request similar to the exhortation of 5:1, "Be therefore imitators of God, as beloved children, and walk in love, *just as* Christ also loved y o u and gave himself up for us, an offering and a sacrifice to God, for a fragrant odor." And again, "It was he who gave some (to be) apostles . . . in order to fully equip the saints for the work of ministry . . . until we all attain to the unity of the faith and of the clear knowledge of the Son of God, to a full-grown man, to the measure of the stature of the fulness of Christ" (4:11-13). Cf. Col. 2:9, 10.

---

[97] On the entire subject of the possibility of progress in the life hereafter, may I once again call the readers' attention to my book *The Bible on the Life Hereafter,* pp. 70–78.

Doxology

20, 21. When the apostle surveyed God's marvelous mercies whereby, through the supreme sacrifice of his beloved Son, he brought those who were at one time children of wrath into his own family, and gave them "the courage of confident access," the privilege of contemplating in all its glorious dimensions the love of Christ, and the inspiring task of instructing the angels in the mysteries of God's kaleidoscopic wisdom, his soul, lost in wonder, love, and praise, uttered the following sublime doxology: **Now to him who is able to do infinitely more than all we ask or imagine, according to the power that is at work within us, to him be the glory in the church and in Christ Jesus to all generations forever and ever; Amen.** It is immediately clear that this doxology is not only a fitting conclusion to the prayer but also a very appropriate expression of gratitude and praise for all the blessings so generously poured out upon the church, as described in the entire preceding contents of this letter. Besides, it is Paul's way of making known his firm conviction that although in his prayer he has asked much, God is able to grant far more. On this point the apostle, who relished superlatives (see N.T.C. on I and II Timothy and Titus, p. 75), speaks very strongly. Literally he says, "Now to him — that is, to God Triune — who is able to do super-abundantly above all that we ask or imagine (or: think, conceive)," etc. In order to appreciate fully what is implied in these words it should be noted that Paul's reasoning has taken the following steps: *a.* God is able to do all we ask him to do; *b.* he is even able to do all that we dare not ask but merely imagine; *c.* he can do *more* than this; *d. far* more; *e. very far* more. Moreover, the apostle immediately adds that he is not dealing with abstractions. The omnipotence which God reveals in answering prayer is not a figment of the imagination but is *in line with* ("according to") that mighty operation of his power that is already at work "within us." It called us out of darkness and brought us into the light, changed children of wrath into dearly beloved sons and daughters, brought about reconciliation between God and man, and between Jew and Gentile. It is God's infinite might which he exerted when he raised Christ from the dead, and which is now operative in our own, parallel, spiritual resurrection.

Therefore to the One who does not need to over-exert himself in order to fulfil our desires but can do it with ease, "be *the glory* in the church and in Christ Jesus." In other words, may homage and adoration be rendered to God because of the splendor of his amazing attributes — power (1:19, 2:20), wisdom (3:10), mercy (2:4), love (2:4), grace (2:5-8); etc.— manifested in *the church,* which is the body, and in *Christ Jesus,* its exalted head. (On the concept *glory* see N.T.C. on Philippians, pp. 62, 63, footnote 43.)

The apostle's ardent desire is that this praise may endure "to all generations." The word *generation,* in addition to other meanings, has especially

175

two connotations that should be considered in the present connection: *a.* the sum-total of contemporaries (Matt. 17:17); and *b.* the duration of their life on earth; that is, the span of time intervening between the birth of the parents and that of their children. In the present case, as well as in verse 5 above, the latter or chronological sense is indicated, for the phrase "to all generations" is reinforced by "forever and ever." The latter expression means exactly what it says. It refers to *the flow of moments from past to present to future, continuing on and on without ever coming to an end.* Rather strangely it has been defined by some as indicating "the opposite of time," "time without progress," "timeless existence," etc. But as far as creatures and their activities are concerned, the Bible nowhere teaches such timeless existence. The popular notion, also found in some commentaries and in religious poetry, namely, that at death — or according to others, at the moment of Christ's return — believers will enter upon a timeless existence, finds no support in Scripture, not even in Rev. 10:6 when properly interpreted. If in the hereafter believers will acquire *one* divine "incommunicable" attribute, namely, *eternity,* why not the others also, for example "omnipresence"? For more on this see the work mentioned on p. 174, footnote 97.

The blessed activity of which believers have a foretaste even now but which in unalloyed and superabundant grandeur will be their portion in the intermediate state, and far more emphatically in the day of the great consummation, an activity with which the apostle is deeply concerned and for which he yearns in prayer, consists, therefore, in this, that forever and ever the members of the Father's Family ascribe praise and honor to their Maker-Redeemer, whose love, supported by the illimitable power which raised Christ from the dead, will lift their hearts to higher and higher plateaus of inexpressible delight and reverent gratitude. Arrived in glory, their minds unobscured by sin, advance from one pinnacle of spiritual discovery to the next, and then to the next, in an ever ascending series. Their wills, then fully delivered from all the enslaving shackles of willfulness, and invigorated with a constantly growing supply of power, find more and more avenues of rewarding expression. In brief, the salvation in store for God's children resembles the Healing Waters of Ezekiel's vision (Ezek. 47:1-5), which, though when one enters them they are ankle-deep, soon become knee-deep, then come up to the loins, and are finally impassable except by swimming. And because of this constant progress in bliss, the answering progress in praise to God also never ceases, for

> "When we've been there ten thousand years,
>   Bright shining as the sun,
>   We've no less days to sing God's praise
>   Than when we first begun."
>   (John Newton)

176

When the Holy Spirit inspired the prisoner Paul to write this overpowering doxology, Paul's heart was moved by that same Spirit to express hearty approval by means of the solemn "Amen."

Summary of Chapter 3

Paul now turns his attention to the church's *Lofty Goal*. This goal consists of two objects: a. to declare God's *wisdom* (1-13); and b. to learn more and more about Christ's *love* (14-21). Neither is possible without the other.

Paul arrives at the idea of God's wisdom by the contemplation of the "mystery" which had been revealed to him as to no other. The word *mystery* is used to indicate a truth which would have remained a secret had it not been divinely revealed. In the present instance and frequently when the word mystery is used, Paul is thinking of the fact that, according to God's eternal plan, in connection with the coming of the Messiah and the outpouring of the Spirit the old Jewish theocracy would be completely abolished and in its place would arise a new organism in which Gentiles and Jews would be placed on a footing of perfect equality. See Summary of Chapter 1, No. (7). Says Paul, "To me, the very least of all saints, was this grace given: to proclaim to the Gentiles the good tidings of the unfathomable riches of Christ and to enlighten all on what is the administration of the mystery which for ages has been hidden in God who created all things" (3:8, 9). When the apostle meditated on the fact that this mysterious organism of *a church gathered out of two formerly hostile groups, namely, Jews and Gentiles* was actually being established, and that the instrument which God was using to achieve it was nothing else than a totally unlikely one, namely, *the cross,* object of general derision and ridicule, he saw in this a manifestation of the wisdom of God, that is, of the latter's marvelous power to reconcile seeming irreconcilables, in order to carry out his gracious plan from eternity. By inspiration, he urges that this divine wisdom be made known by the church to all the good angels in heaven. Let the church of both Jews and Gentiles by their very striving to become more and more united for good be a mirror "in which the angels behold the astonishing wisdom of God displayed in a manner unknown to them before" (Calvin).

Not only God's *wisdom,* however, is displayed in the formation of the New Testament church, so is also his *love* in Christ. The apostle utters a prayer that is touching because of its depth of feeling, trinitarian character, and concentration on the love of Christ. He prays that through the indwelling of Christ's Spirit, believers, as it were pooling all their strength, may penetrate ever more deeply into the mysteries of Christ's transforming love, with the purpose of seeing that love in all its dimensions, and learning that it is so rich and marvelous that it can never be fully known.

True *idealism* which ever strives "to be filled to all the fulness of God" is at the same time the most *practical* thing on earth. The more believers, "rooted and founded in love" (otherwise they would not be qualified), make a devotional study of that love of Christ, the more also will they be filled with ardent desire to tell everyone about it. Thus sinners will be won for Christ and God Triune will be glorified. With the thought of the glory of God in his heart and openly expressed Paul closes this chapter.

Chapter 4:1-16

Theme: *The Church Glorious*

II. *Exhortation*
describing and urging upon all:

O rganic Unity (amid Diversity) and Growth into Christ

CHAPTER IV: 1-16

4 1 I, therefore, the prisoner in the Lord, entreat y o u to live lives worthy of the calling with which y o u were called, 2 with all lowliness and meekness, with longsuffering, enduring one another in love, 3 making every effort to preserve the unity imparted by the Spirit by means of the bond (consisting in) peace. 4 (There is) one body and one Spirit, just as also y o u were called in one hope which y o u r calling brought y o u; 5 one Lord, one faith, one baptism; 6 one God and Father of all, who (is) over all and through all and in all. 7 But to each one of us this grace was given within the limits which Christ apportioned. 8 Therefore he says: When he ascended on high he led captive a host of captives, and he gave gifts to men. 9 — Now this expression, *he ascended,* what can it mean but that he had (previously) descended into the regions lower than the earth? [98] 10 The one who descended is himself also the one who ascended higher than all the heavens in order that he might fill all things — 11 And it was he who gave some (to be) apostles; and some, prophets; and some, evangelists; and some, pastors and teachers; 12 in order fully to equip the saints for the work of ministry, with a view to the building up of the body of Christ, 13 until we all attain to the unity of the faith and of the clear knowledge of the Son of God, to a full-grown man, to the measure of the stature of the fulness of Christ, 14 so that we may no longer be children tossed to and fro by the waves and whirled around by every gust of doctrine, by the trickery of men, by (their) talent for deceitful scheming; 15 but adhering to the truth in love, may grow up in all things into him who is the head, even Christ, 16 from whom the entire body, harmoniously fitted together and held together by every supporting joint, according to the energy that corresponds to the capacity of each individual part, brings about bodily growth with a view to its own upbuilding in love.

4:1-16

It is clear as daylight and universally admitted that this section, especially in its opening verses, emphasizes unity. This unity, moreover, is not external and mechanical, but internal and organic. It is not superimposed, but, by virtue of the power of the indwelling Christ, proceeds from within the organism of the church. Those, therefore, who in their ecumenical zeal are anxious to erase all denominational boundaries and to create a mam-

---

[98] Or "into the lower regions [literally "parts"] of the earth?" Either translation is possible, with no essential difference in resultant meaning. In favor of "into the regions lower than the earth" is that it would balance "higher than all the heavens" in the next verse.

moth super-church can find no comfort here. On the other hand, neither can those who exaggerate differences and even stand in the way of inter-ecclesiastical co-operation when this can be accomplished without sacrificing any real principle.

The first six verses can be summarized as follows: the church *is* spiritually one; therefore, *let it be* spiritually one! This does not imply any contradiction, the meaning being that believers should "make every effort to preserve the unity imparted by the Spirit by means of the bond (consisting in) peace."

The unity is, however, not such that the individual believer becomes a mere "cog in the wheel." Personal initiative or individual expression, far from being crushed, is encouraged, as verses 7-12, 16, clearly indicate. Also, the oneness is not an end in itself. It is not a superficial desire for *togetherness* in the spirit of the familiar lines:

> "For your friends are my friends, and my friends are your
> friends; And the more we get together, the happier we'll be."

On the contrary, it is a unity with the purpose of being a blessing to one another, so that the church can be built up, and can thus be a blessing to the world. There is work to be done, as verse 12 clearly shows. And in order to accomplish the tasks assigned, believers should co-operate, each contributing his share to the inner growth of the church. This is all the more necessary because the opponents are very clever (verse 14). It is clear that in this section the idea of *growth* is just as prominent as is that of *unity*. If there be any difference in emphasis I would say the former is even more prominent, especially in verses 12-16. In verse 15 the apostle expresses the idea of growth in these words: ". . . that we, speaking truth in love, *may grow up* in all things into him who is the head, even Christ."

Everything considered, therefore, it would seem that the subtitle *Organic Unity (amid Diversity) and Growth into Christ* supplies the true key to the contents of this section.

1. The apostle begins, saying, **I, therefore, the prisoner in the Lord, entreat y o u to live lives worthy of the calling with which y o u were called.** Paul "the prisoner" (here "in the Lord"; cf. II Tim. 1:8; in Eph. 3:1 and in Philem. 1, 9 "of Christ Jesus," with no essential difference in meaning) has been faithful to his trust, as his very imprisonment, brought about by his loyalty, proves. He, therefore, is all the more justified in entreating the addressed to be likewise faithful, that is, "to live lives worthy of y o u r calling" (cf. Phil. 1:27; Col. 1:10; I Thess. 2:12; III John 6). Let them conduct themselves in harmony with the *responsibilities* which their new relationship to God had imposed upon them and with the *blessings* which this effectual *calling* (for which see on 1:18) had brought them. As to these *responsibilities,* the addressed had been foreordained to sonship (1:5). It is their re-

sponsibility, therefore, to behave in the manner in which adopted children of the heavenly Father could be expected to behave: believing his teachings, trusting his promises, and obeying his will. And as to the *blessings,* these were described in the preceding chapters: election, redemption, sealing, being made alive, being reconciled not only to God but also to those who had formerly been their enemies, having freedom of access to the throne of grace, etc. Surely, a life of gratitude, abounding in good works as its fruit, was in order! It is as if Paul were saying, "If y o u are believers, and wish to be known as such, live as believers." It reminds us of the manner in which Mordecai answered the accusations of those who found fault with him because he refused to obey the king's order to bow down to Haman. He simply answered, "I am a Jew" (implied in Esther 3:4). "Be what y o u are!" says Paul, as it were. He continues this thought by adding: **2, 3. with all lowliness and meekness, with longsuffering, enduring one another in love, making every effort to preserve the unity imparted by the Spirit by means of the bond (consisting in) peace.** The seven-fold description of the Christian life resembles very closely what is found in the twin-letter (see Col. 3:12-15).[99] To avoid repetition may I, accordingly, ask the reader to consult N.T.C. on Colossians and Philemon, pp. 155–160. What is about to be presented is *additional* material, not mere duplication. Though not intended as a complete list of qualities which believers should reveal in their lives, the Ephesian list furnishes a broad characterization of this new disposition and behavior. First mentioned is *lowliness* or *humility.* Having received blessings so great that their true value cannot be expressed in words, it is altogether proper that the recipients be filled with the very basic virtue of lowliness. Note the emphasis: *"all* lowliness and meekness." Humility has been called the first, second, and third essential of the Christian life. The mention of lowliness leads naturally to that of *meekness.* The meek individual is slow to insist on his rights. He realizes that in the sight of God he has no rights at all that are his by nature. All his rights were secured by grace. And although with reference to men he may at times have to insist on his rights (Acts 16:35-40), he does not rashly throw himself into the fray. He would rather "take" wrong than inflict it (I Cor. 6:7). With Abraham he prefers to let Lot have first choice (Gen. 13:7-18), with great reward . . . for Abraham! He exercises *longsuffering.* Emphasis on this virtue was greatly needed in the early church, when believers suffered misunderstanding, harshness, and cruelty from those who did not share their faith. For example, the lot of a Christian wife who was married to an unbeliever was by no means easy. Nevertheless, as long as her husband was willing to live with her in the marriage relationship, the wife must remain with him and try, by means of her God-fearing behavior, to win him for Christ. Thus,

---

[99] There compassion, kindness, forgiveness, and thankfulness are added to the list of seven characteristics mentioned here in Ephesians.

the grace of longsuffering would be beautifully illustrated in her life. See I Cor. 7:13 and I Peter 3:2. However, not only with respect to "outsiders" must this grace be exhibited, also with reference to fellow-believers. All have their faults and weaknesses. Let every one say to himself, therefore, "In view of the fact that God has been so longsuffering toward me, even though in *his* holy eyes my sins must stand out far more clearly than do my brother's blemishes in *my* eyes, I must surely be patient with my brother."

The mention of longsuffering is followed by that of *endurance* or *forbearance*. Literally the apostle says, combining two virtues, *"enduring* one another in *love."* The person who endures injury tries to pay no attention to it. He *holds himself up,* as the derivation of the word in the original implies, is not shaken up, but continues to keep himself erect and firm. We, too, at times use a somewhat similar expression when we say, "You should *put up* with his ill behavior." However, in saying this *we* do not always mean exactly what the apostle has in mind. We may simply be referring to suffering injury without *open* resentment, though we "boil" within! Paul, however, very aptly combines the forbearance of which he is speaking with the inner disposition of *love.* He everywhere emphasizes this virtue of outgoingness, true and tender affection toward the brother, the neighbor, and even the enemy, the noble endeavor to benefit him and never to harm him in any way. In addition to the Colossian verses to which reference was made earlier, see also Rom. 12:9-21; I Cor. 8:13; 9:22; 10:33; and Gal. 5:22, to select only a few references among the many that could be mentioned. The most complete and strikingly touching chapter on love toward all is I Cor. 13. To be appreciated it should be read, if possible, in the original, and if not possible, at least in several versions!

Now if, by the aid of the Holy Spirit and of prayer, a person truly endeavors so to conduct himself that his life will sparkle with these virtues, *unity,* to which Paul turns next, will be promoted. The spiritual oneness here indicated is an indispensable prerequisite for promoting the health and happiness of the church, for advancing the cause of missions, and for winning the victory over Satan and his allies. It does not come of its own accord but is the result of both effort and prayer; of *effort,* for the apostle says, "making every effort" ("giving diligence," "doing y o u r utmost," cf. II Tim. 2:15), and doing this *constantly* (note the present participle, continuative) ; and of *prayer,* for he refers to a unity "of the Spirit" (thus literally, but meaning: imparted by the Spirit) ; hence, the result of earnest prayer (Luke 11:13). It is a oneness of Jew and Gentile, as was emphasized by Paul (2:11-22; 3:6), of lofty purpose (3:10, 18, 19), and of true affection (4:2; 5:1, 2).

This unity is promoted by *peace.* Cf. I Cor. 14:33; II Cor. 13:11; Phil. 4:7; Col. 3:15; II Thess. 3:16; II Tim. 2:22. Here in Ephesians the apostle has already referred to it in 1:2; 2:14, 15, 17; and will refer to it again in

6:15, 23. When there is strife there is disunity. Peace, on the other hand, promotes the perpetuation of unity. Hence, it is, after all, not surprising that Paul writes, "making every effort to preserve the unity imparted by the Spirit by means of the bond ("of," that is, consisting in) peace." This *bond* or *tie that binds believers together* is *peace*, just as in Col. 3:14 it is *love*. This involves no contradiction, for it is exactly love that makes peace possible. Hence, both here in Eph. 4:2, 3 and in Col. 3:14, 15, love and peace are mentioned in close succession. Surely, if it be correct to say that the stability of the roof depends in a sense on the foundation that underlies the entire superstructure, then it is also correct to say that the roof's stability depends on the strength of the walls that immediately uphold it. And since especially in Ephesians the apostle dwells in such detail on the peace established between God and men, resulting in peace between Jews and Gentiles, it is entirely natural that he should *here* speak of *peace* as the bond. Take it in whatever sense one prefers, spiritual peace is ever the gift of love. Unity results.

The exhortation that the addressed may live in love and unity (verses 1-3) is followed by a description of this unity. In this description unity and all those characteristics associated with it are traced first to the Spirit, who had entered into the hearts of the believers; from there back to the Lord (Jesus Christ), whose vicarious sacrifice had made possible the gift of the Spirit; and, finally, to God the Father, who had given his Son and who, together with the Son, was also the Giver or Sender of the Spirit. In close association with the Spirit two other elements of Christian unity are mentioned, making three in all: "one body, one Spirit, one hope." So also, in connection with the Lord, two others, again resulting in a triad: "one Lord, one faith, one baptism." The Father is mentioned all by himself, for the six already named are traceable to him in the sense that whatever is associated with the Spirit and with the Son must, of necessity, also be associated with the Father, for it is he who is "over all and through all and in all." Accordingly, what we have here is a sevenfold description of a threefold unity, a statement of the character of Christian unity and of its trinitarian Source.[100]

4. The first triad is: (**There is**) **one body and one Spirit, just as also y o u were called in one hope which y o u r calling brought y o u.** The one body is, of course, the church consisting of Jews and Gentiles (2:14-22), the one family in heaven and on earth (3:15). Though in a sense, we are many, yet we are one body in Christ (Rom. 12:5). There is one loaf, one body (I Cor. 10:17). This body or church, moreover, is not an earth-born or

---

[100] I do not believe that there is any call for delving more deeply into the meaning of the number of the elements here mentioned. I find Lenski's numerical symbolism (*op. cit.*, pp. 510, 511) hardly convincing and, at any rate, unnecessary, since we are dealing here with the book of Ephesians, not with the book of Revelation.

man-made institution but a product of the Holy Spirit; hence, "one body and one Spirit." The urgent invitation of the gospel (the *external* call) has been applied to the hearts of the Ephesians by the Holy Spirit, producing the *internal* or *effectual* call. See on 1:18 and 4:1. Their call had brought them hope, a hope firmly grounded in God's promises which cannot fail. It was a hope of receiving the inheritance among the saints in the light (cf: 1:18 with Col. 1:12), as God's gracious reward for a life consecrated to him. The main reason, I believe, why the call had filled them with hope was that the very possession of the Spirit in their hearts was already the first instalment of their inheritance (1:14), and as such a pledge or guarantee of glory to come, a glory arriving not only when soul and body part but also and especially in the great consummation of all things at Christ's return. The fruits (Gal. 5:22, 23) which the indwelling and sanctifying Spirit was bestowing upon them were "firstfruits" (Rom. 8:23), a foretaste of future, ineffable bliss.

The Spirit, in the very process of imparting to the Ephesians the effectual call, also united them, so that they became one spiritual organism: "For by one Spirit we were also baptized into one body, whether we were Jews or Greeks, slaves or free, and we were all made to drink of one Spirit" (I Cor. 12:13; cf. 3:16; 6:19; Rom. 8:9, 11). Just as it is exactly because the human body is pervaded by the spirit that it is *one* and is able to function as a unit, every member in co-operation with all the others, so also it is precisely because the church, Christ's body, is indwelt and influenced throughout by the Holy Spirit that it is a single organism and operates as such.

5. Now the second triad: **one Lord, one faith, one baptism.** This Lord is "the Lord Jesus Christ." He is our Lord in the sense that since he bought us we are his. He owns us, loves us, cares for us, and protects us. We recognize his sovereignty, own him as our Deliverer and Ruler, trust, obey, love, and worship him (1:2, 3, 15, 17; 2:21; 3:11, 14; 4:1; etc.: cf. I Cor. 6:13-15, 20; 7:23; 12:3, 5; Phil. 2:11; I Peter 1:18, 19; Rev. 19:16). Whether Jew or Gentile, bond or free, male or female (Gal. 3:28; Col. 3:11), already in heaven or still on earth (Rom. 14:9), we all confess this *one* Lord as ours. We embrace him with *one* faith. What is meant by this one faith? Is it faith in the objective sense, *body of truth, creed* (Gal. 1:23; 6:10; Phil. 1:27 and frequently in the Pastoral Epistles), or is it faith in the subjective sense, *reliance on our Lord Jesus Christ and on his promises?* Among commentators there is great difference of opinion with respect to this question.[101] For

[101] Favoring the objective sense are Westcott and Lenski ("one truth"), though it is only fair to state that the latter does not entirely exclude the subjective meaning. He says, " 'One faith' includes our personal believing, but the stress is on the Christian faith as such, on what constitutes its substance." Simpson refuses to choose. Hodge and Greijdanus accept the theory that the term as here used combines subjective and objective faith. Abbott, Grosheide, Robertson, and Scott favor the subjective sense.

myself, the subjective sense seems to be the one indicated here. It is *one*
faith — not historical nor miraculous nor temporary but true and genuine
trust — by means of which we embrace the *one* Lord Jesus Christ. It is true
that the subjective and the objective cannot be separated: when a person
surrenders himself to Christ as his Lord he at the same time also accepts
the body of truth with reference to him. Yet this is not the same as saying
that the term *faith* is here used in a double sense. The fact that *faith* is
mentioned immediately after *Lord* and is immediately followed by *baptism*,
all in one very short sentence, would seem to indicate that the triad is a
closely knit unit (which was true also with respect to the first triad, mentioned in verse 4). Hence, I agree with Scott, *op. cit.*, p. 204, when he states,
"It is better to take the whole sentence as expressive of a single fundamental
fact: 'one Lord in whom we all believe and in whose name we have been
baptized.' "

With respect to the one baptism Grosheide states, "There is only one
baptism which is received by many (perhaps a number of persons simultaneously). All the members of the congregation are baptized in the same
manner, and we may well assume, after or in connection with the same
sermonic elucidation." By means of baptism the fellowship of believers with
their Lord was sealed (Gal. 3:27). "In baptism lies the evidence that all sorts
of people (cf. Gal. 3:28), without any discrimination, share in the grace
of Christ" (H. N. Ridderbos, *The Epistle of Paul to the Churches of Galatia*, a volume in *New International Commentary on the New Testament*,
Grand Rapids, Mich., 1953, p. 147).[102]

6. To show the unity within the Trinity as ultimate basis for the unity
of the church, the apostle, turning now to the Father, writes, **one God and
Father of all, who (is) over all and through all and in all.** The emphasis
here, as in 1:3, 17; 2:18; 3:14, 15, is on redemptive Fatherhood. The first
person of the divine Trinity is our Father in Jesus Christ. He is "the Father
from whom the whole family in heaven and on earth derives its name." To
be sure, as our Father he is also our Creator, for he created all things (3:9).
This fact makes his Fatherhood in the sphere of redemption stand out even
more beautifully. He recreated what he had created, so that we are his in
a double sense, and therefore all the more owe him our full devotion. But

---

[102] The question has been asked why Paul makes mention of only one sacrament,
namely, baptism. Why does he not also include the Lord's Supper? Lenski, having
enumerated several answers which he rejects, states categorically: "The correct
answer is that the *Una Sancta* includes also a host of babes and children, none of
whom are able to receive the Lord's Supper" (*op. cit.*, p. 514). However, the inclusion of the little ones — and they must be included — does not cancel the fact
that the Lord has instituted only *one* true Lord's Supper. Better, therefore, it would
seem to me, is Grosheide's observation: "I would remark that when a person does
not himself give the reason for omitting a subject it is difficult for anyone else to
state what that reason was" (*op. cit.*, p. 63, footnote 7).

that it is on his Fatherhood with reference to the family of believers that the emphasis here falls is clear not only from the fact that this is the prevailing sense in which the term *Father* is used in Ephesians but also from the immediate context. The first person of the Trinity is, accordingly, Father of all,[103] that is, of all those who belong to the family of the faith. Whether they are converts from the Jewish or from the Gentile world makes no difference, just so they are converts. As such he bears a threefold relationship to *all* his children: As Father he is *"over* all," for he exercises control over all. He is, however, also *"through* all," for he blesses us all through Christ our Mediator. And he is *"in* all," for he draws us close to his heart in the Spirit. Thus the three strands are gathered into one, and we perceive that the Spirit about whom verse 4 was centered, and the Lord (Jesus Christ) on whom verse 5 was concentrated, are not to be viewed as separate entities. We worship *one* God (Deut. 6:4), not three gods. Though it is true that Scripture ascribes election especially to the Father, redemption especially to the Son, and sanctification especially to the Spirit, yet in each of these departments all co-operate. The three never work at cross purposes. As has often been remarked, the Father thought our salvation, the Son bought it, the Spirit wrought it. Moreover, the unity amid diversity which pertains to the Trinity is the basis for the essential unity in the midst of the circumstantial variety which characterizes the church, and to which Paul now turns.

7. He writes, **But to each one of us this** [104] **grace was given within the limits which Christ apportioned** (literally, "according to the measure of the gift of Christ"). The apostle has dwelt in detail on the unity of the church. This was necessary, for only when the church recognizes its unity and strives more and more to preserve it, each member co-operating with all the others, will the gospel move mightily forward among the nations, will the church itself rejoice, will Satan tremble, and will the name of God be glorified. However, this *unity* makes allowance for *diversity* of gifts among the many members of the one body. In fact, this very diversity, far from destroying the unity, will, if properly used, promote it. The proper use of the gift, that is, the particular *endowment* (see on 3:2, 7) which in his grace God has bestowed on anyone, implies the following: *a.* that the recipient shall indeed recognize it as a gift, and not as the product of his own skill or ingenuity; *b.* that he view his gift as only one among many and as

---

[103] The entire context clearly indicates that the word πάντων is here not neuter. In the present connection the apostle has not been discussing God's relation to the universe or to nature.

[104] As Paul has previously referred to "the stewardship of God's grace" that had been given to him (3:2) and to "the gift of God's grace" (3:7), the article ἡ before χάρις in 4:7 is altogether natural. I see no reason, therefore, with B D*, etc., to omit it.

limited in extent, a measured gift; and *c.* that he be eager to use it not for his own glory but for the benefit of the entire body, and thus, to God's glory. The best commentary on this verse is what Paul himself writes in I Cor. 12, the entire chapter. In verses 4-6 he states, "Now there are diversities of gifts, but the same Spirit; and there are diversities of service, but the same Lord; and there are diversities of working, but it is the same God who works all in all." And significantly he adds, "But to each is given the manifestation of the Spirit for the common good" (verse 7). It seems that in the early church — as also today — there was a twofold danger: *a.* that those who had received very special endowments might overestimate their importance, give themselves the credit for them, and fail to use them for the benefit of the entire church; and *b.* that those who had not been so richly endowed might lose courage, thinking that they were of no benefit to the church. It was not only Paul who reacted against this real peril; in a slightly different sense so did James even earlier: "Let the brother of low degree glory in his high estate, and the rich in that he is made low" (1:9). The real comfort and glorious lesson for everyone must ever be: "I have received my gift, be it great or small, from Christ himself.[105] I must use it, therefore, as he requires. The Giver will not fail me when I use my gift for the benefit of all."

But is it really true that the Jesus who once walked the earth is now so highly exalted, so glorious, and so richly endowed with authority that he is able to bestow his gifts upon the church and upon its members in lavish quantity? In answer to this question the apostle writes about the ascended Christ and the gifts which he bestowed and is still bestowing. What follows in verses 8-16 is really a unit. However, since the reference to Christ's ascension and its implication is found especially in verses 8-10, this will be studied first of all. Paul writes **8-10. Therefore he says: When he ascended on high he led captive a host of captives, and he gave gifts to men.** — Now this expression, *he ascended,* what can it mean but that he had (previously) [106] descended into the regions [107] lower than the earth? The one who

[105] I see no good reason to regard τοῦ Χριστοῦ as an objective genitive (Lenski, *op. cit.,* p. 517: "the gift bestowed upon Christ"). Eph. 3:2, 7 as well as I Cor. 12:4-11 all point in the direction of regarding these special gifts as coming *from* Christ and *from* his Spirit. Eph. 4:8 points in the same direction: "he gave gifts to men."

[106] When Codex B and most of the later manuscripts and versions add πρῶτον (first, previously; see A.V.) after "he descended," they probably do this to clarify the text. Though the intention of this addition is to be appreciated, the proposed reading does not have quite sufficient textual support to be adopted. Nevertheless, as a clarification of the meaning of the text the word can be inserted in the translation *between parentheses,* as I have done.

[107] The omission of the word "parts" or "regions" in p46 D* G, etc., is of minor significance, as it affects the meaning very slightly, if at all; for in the present context, after "he descended into," the neuter pl. τὰ κατώτερα would still have to be translated "the lower regions (or *parts* or *lands* or something similar)."

189

descended is himself also the one who ascended higher than all the heavens in order that he might fill all things —.

The word "therefore" must here be interpreted to indicate something like "in accordance with this." By direction of the Holy Spirit Paul introduces a passage from the Psalms (Ps. 68:18; LXX 69:19) that has a bearing upon the present subject. He does not intend to quote literally but rather, as occurs so often in such cases, to elucidate a passage by showing how that which in the Psalter was said concerning *God* attained its fulfilment in *Christ*.[108] When we bear in mind the typical character of the old dispensation, the fact that "the Old is by the New explained," so that we do not have two Bibles but one Bible inspired by one original Author, the Holy Spirit, we will not be able to find fault with this method.

The expression "he says" means "God says." This appears rather clearly from the context in such passages as Rom. 9:25; Gal. 3:16, 17; and Heb. 1:5-7; and may be assumed also in such other passages as Rom. 15:10; I Cor. 6:16; II Cor. 6:2; etc.[109] There follows the application of Ps. 68:18 to Christ's ascension and the gifts he bestowed. In A.V. this passage reads as follows: "Thou hast ascended on high, thou hast led captivity captive; thou hast received gifts for men." In A.R.V. the first line is identical; the second reads "thou hast led away captives." This, however, is not a material change, for "captivity" can be interpreted as meaning "a host of captives" (see Judg. 5:12), just as, for example, "the circumcision" means "the circumcized" (Eph. 2:11). The third line is "thou hast received gifts among men." Paul appears to have had in mind the LXX version of the passage, with which, *with respect to the points which require comment,* our English versions agree substantially, though not in every little detail. However, in the apostle's *application* — for, as the passage from the Psalms reads *in Eph. 4:8* it is *applied* rather than literally *quoted* — the words undergo three changes. Two of them, however, are of such minor significance that they can be relegated to a footnote.[110] The one really important change is this, that the passage from which the apostle was borrowing stated that the One who ascended *received* gifts, but the apostle himself in referring to it here says that he *gave* gifts. According to the Old Testament passage God is repre-

---

[108] For other instances in which what is said of *God* in the Old Testament is referred to *Christ* in the New compare Exod. 13:21 with I Cor. 10:4; Isa. 6:1 with John 12:41; and Ps. 102:25-27 with Heb. 1:10-12.
[109] On this see B. B. Warfield, *The Inspiration and Authority of the Bible,* Philadelphia, 1948, pp. 299–348. His refutation of Abbott's contrary contention is interesting and, as I see it, convincing.
[110] Namely, the second person ("thou hast ascended") has been changed to the third ("he ascended"); and the finite verb has been changed into a participle ("having ascended"). As to "thou" or "he," except for the fact that what in the Old Testament applies to God is said here concerning Christ (on which I have already commented) there is no material change. And the change from the finite verb to the participle is merely stylistic.

sented, it would seem, as descending from heaven to wage war against his enemies. He ascends again as Victor, loaded with spoils. What gave Paul the right to apply this *receiving* of gifts to the activity of Christ whereby he *gives* gifts to his church? Ever so many explanations have been offered with which I shall not weary the reader. The one I accept is the following: *Under the guidance of the Holy Spirit the apostle had every right to make this application, for the Victor receives the spoils with a view to giving them away. The giving is implied in the receiving.* When Christ ascended he was not returning to heaven with empty hands. On the contrary, as a result of accomplished mediatorial work he returned *in triumph* to heaven, in the full possession of salvation for his people. These people were, so to speak, in his triumphant procession. They were captives in his train, chained, as it were, to his chariot. There was a vast host of captives. Among them was also Paul, destined, along with the others, to spread abroad the fragrance of the gospel. Thanks be to God! See II Cor. 2:14. Now Christ *received* in order *to give*. He *had earned* in order *to bestow*. He received these captives in order to give them to the kingdom, for kingdom-work. Reasons for adopting this interpretation:

1. The prevailing custom that the victor divides the spoil is recognized also in Scripture. Thus, when Abraham defeated Chedorlaomer and his allies he took booty with the intention of giving it away: to Lot, what he had lost; to Melchizedek, the tithe; to Aner, Eschcol and Mamre, their portion (Gen. 14). Did not David also receive the spoil in order to give it away? (I Sam. 30:26-31). Israel's enemies, too, were in the habit of dividing the spoil, first taking it and then distributing it (Judg. 5:30).

2. Isa. 53:12 says with reference to the coming Messiah, "He will divide the spoil with the strong."

3. According to Acts 2:33 Peter on the day of Pentecost distinctly reminded his audience that *"having received* of the Father the promise of the Holy Spirit, he [Christ] has *poured out* this which y o u see and hear."

4. The Aramaic Targum on the Psalter and also the Peshitta read, "Thou hast given gifts to men." At the root of this interpretation there must have been a very ancient oral tradition. Now the Targum explained the words of the Psalmist as having reference to Moses, *who received* the law on Sinai *in order to give* it to the people of Israel. All the same, the receiving implied the giving.

5. This explanation suits the present context in which the apostles, prophets, evangelists, etc., are described as *the gifts* of the ascended Christ to the church.

When Paul adds, "Now this expression, *he ascended,* what can it mean but that he had (previously) descended," the logic is not immediately clear. An ascent does not necessarily presuppose a previous descent. The fact, for example, that Elijah ascended to heaven does not mean that he

191

had previously come down from heaven. The solution lies in the fact that
Paul is not stating a general law but is speaking about Christ, and is saying
that *in his case* ascent implied (previous) descent. This is true, for, as we
have seen, Christ's ascension was glorious. He was welcomed back by his
Father into heaven (John 20:17; Acts 1:11), and at his entrance into glory
all heaven rejoiced (Rev. 12:5, 10). Now *this* ascension whereby he, as
Victor over Satan, sin, and death, re-entered heaven in the full merits of
his atoning sacrifice would never have been possible had he not first descended from the glories of heaven to earth's shame and suffering. This is
simply another way of saying that Christ's exaltation resulted from his
humiliation, a humiliation so deep and ineffable that the apostle characterizes it by saying that he "descended into the regions lower than the
earth." This expression of verse 9 is in direct contrast with "higher than
all the heavens" of verse 10. The two expressions can be understood only
when they are viewed in their relation to each other. And they should be so
considered for they concern the same person: "The one who descended is
himself also the one who ascended higher than all the heavens." Paul is the
best commentator of his own words. He furnishes this commentary in Phil.
2:5-11: "He emptied himself . . . and became obedient even to the extent
of death; yes, death by a cross. Therefore God raised him to the loftiest
heights," etc.[111]

---

[111] Since the interpretation here given of the expression "he descended into the
regions lower than the earth" fits the context and is in harmony with Paul's own
statement in Philippians, written during the same imprisonment, I comment on
other explanations as follows:

(1) The descent refers to Christ's burial or the entrance of his body into Joseph's
garden.

Objection: This does not go far enough. The burial is included, to be sure, but
only as part of Christ's deep humiliation.

(2) It indicates Christ's descent into the underworld — usually, but not always,
conceived of as having occurred during the interval between his death and resurrection — with the purpose variously represented as: *a.* releasing the souls of Old
Testament saints from the Limbus Patrum; *b.* proclaiming grace to the lost or to
some of them; *c.* taunting Satan with the announcement of his (Christ's) victory,
etc. In connection with *c.* it has been remarked that at Christ's arrival the devils
were so scared that some of them fell out of hell's window!

Objection: There is nothing in the context either of Ps. 68:18 or of the Ephesian passage to suggest such a descent. Nor is there any hint of it in Phil. 2 or,
for that matter, anywhere else in Paul's epistles. According to the Gospels the dying
Christ committed his soul to the Father. On the day of the resurrection it was restored to the body from which it had been taken. And as to I Peter 3:19 and 4:6,
these passages, too, which cannot now be considered, when contextually interpreted
do not teach anything of this nature. It is enough to say that they have reference
to preaching to those who, though now dead, were still living on earth when they
received God's warnings.

(3) It refers to a descent subsequent to the ascension but before the second
coming.

Objection: Leaving out of consideration the rhetorical or figurative use of the
verb καταβαίνω in Rom. 10:7, which cannot be used either in defense or refutation

For believers in every age it is certainly a comfort to know that he who ascended higher than all the heavens, an expression that must not be taken in a merely literal sense but in the sense of majesty and exaltation to the Father's right hand so that he reigns over the entire universe and over every creature (1:20-23), is still the same Jesus, filled with the same tender love and sympathetic concern which he showed when on Calvary's cross he descended to regions lower than the earth, that is, to the experience of the nethermost depths, the very agonies of hell (Matt. 27:46). Add to this the equally comforting truth that when he returns on clouds of glory he will still be "this same Jesus" (Acts 1:11), the *one* loving and ruling head of the *one* church. What an incentive to the spirit of *unity* among all the members of the church!

This Same Jesus

"This same Jesus!" Oh, how sweetly
Fall those words upon the ear,
Like a swell of far-off music
In a night-watch still and drear!

*　　*　　*

---

of the theory in question, it is safe to say that nowhere in the New Testament does the verb have this reference. In I Thess. 4:16 it is used in connection with the second coming. The other pertinent passages that speak of Christ's descent occur in the Gospel according to John (3:13; 6:33, 38; 6:41, 42, 50, 51, 58). All of them have reference to Christ's incarnation-descent, even though in John 3:13, as also here in Eph. 4:9, the ascent *is mentioned* before the descent. Note opposite order in Eph. 4:10. There is nothing in the context of Eph. 4:8-10 that points in the direction of a post-ascension descent. Ps. 68:18, which here in Ephesians is applied to Christ's ascension, is also best interpreted as indicating anthropomorphically *a descent* of Jehovah (cf. Hab. 3) *followed by ascent.* "In the Psalm it was Jehovah that ascended, but that was only after he had first descended to earth in behalf of his people from their proper habitation in heaven" (Salmond, *op. cit.,* p. 326).

(4) What we have here is a matter of simple apposition. The right translation is: "He descended into the lower parts, viz. the earth" (Hodge). Calvin favors this interpretation, and so do many other commentators.

Evaluation: This is a very attractive theory. The passages in John's Gospel, to which reference was made under (3), have been appealed to in its support. My hesitancy in accepting it is the objection which I share with many commentators, namely, that if Paul merely wanted to say that Jesus descended to earth he could have stated this in a far more simple manner than by inserting the reference to "the lower regions." Hence, the passages in John's Gospel are not necessarily completely parallel. However, in the final analysis the difference between the view of Calvin, Hodge, etc., and the one which I, along with many others, favor, becomes minimal when this descent to earth is interpreted in its most comprehensive sense, namely, as an *incarnation involving deep humiliation:* "Jesus from his throne on high *came into the world to die."* Thus Calvin comments as follows on Christ's *descent to the earth:* "And at what time did God descend lower than when Christ *emptied himself* (Phil. 2:7)? If ever there was a time when . . . God ascended gloriously, it was when Christ was raised *from our lowest condition on earth,* and received into heavenly glory." Here the two views, Calvin's and the one I favor, though based on two different renderings of the text, coincide completely!

He, the lonely Man of Sorrows,
  'Neath our sin-curse bending low,
By his faithless friends forsaken
  In the darkest hours of woe,—

* * *

"This same Jesus!" When the vision
  Of that last and awful day
Bursts upon the prostrate spirit,
  Like a midnight lightning ray;

* * *

Then, we lift our hearts adoring —
  "This same Jesus," loved and known;
Him, our own most gracious Savior,
  Seated on the great white throne.

* * *

(Frances Ridley Havergal)

Paul concludes this elaboration on Christ's humiliation and consequent exaltation by adding that his purpose was "that he might fill all things." This has been variously interpreted as meaning:

(1) that he might fulfill all predictions;

(2) that he might accomplish every task that had been assigned to him;

(3) that he might fill the universe with his omnipresence; and

(4) more in detail, that his human nature, including his body, might pass into the full enjoyment and exercise of the divine perfections, and thus become permanently omnipresent, omnipotent, etc.

I reject all these because, as I see it, they are foreign to the present context. This applies very clearly to (1) and (2) about which nothing is said in this context. As to (3), favored by Hodge and others, it is not clear how Christ, by means of his ascension, could become omnipresent. As to his deity he was already omnipresent. And as to his human nature, unless we accept the general proposition that by means of the ascension something peculiar to the divine nature is communicated to *the human nature* — which is *not* the Reformed position — it is hard to see how that human nature could now become omnipresent. And as to (4), the Lutheran position (see Lenski, *op. cit.*, pp. 524, 525), with reference to which, however, there is a difference of opinion among Lutheran theologians, here again the connection between the communication of divine attributes to the human nature, on the one hand, and the gift of apostles, prophets, etc., of which the context speaks, is not immediately clear. Besides, the ascension accounts as found in Luke 24:50-53 and Acts 1:6-11, while clearly describing the transition of Christ, as to his human nature, from one place to another, say nothing at all about any change in Christ's human nature so that it now entered into the full enjoyment and exercise of the divine perfections. Also, it is difficult to see how the human nature can continue its existence when it is fused with the divine.

A better interpretation, it would seem to me, is furnished by the immediate context, both preceding and following, namely, this, that as a result of Christ's descent into Calvary's hell where he made atonement for sin, and of his subsequent resurrection and ascension, which served as evidence that this atonement had been fully accepted, Christ, as the now exalted Mediator, *fills the entire universe with "blessings"* or, if one prefers, with "gifts," the very gifts which he had earned: salvation full and free and the services of those who proclaim it; such as apostles, prophets, evangelists, etc. Here also it is best to let Paul be his own interpreter. He has already called Christ the One "who fills all in all," which has been interpreted to mean, in part, that with a view to his universe-embracing program Christ replenishes the church with his bounteous gifts. See on 1:23. Cf. 1:3; John 1:16; I Cor. 12:5, 28-32. To some of these "gifts" of the ascended Christ Paul now turns his attention, as he continues: **11. And it was he who gave some (to be) apostles; and some, prophets; and some, evangelists; and some, pastors and teachers.** The ascended Savior gave what he had received: men who were to render service to the church in a special way. Before describing each of the groups mentioned in this passage, the following general observations are in order:

1. It is not Paul's intention to furnish us with a complete list of office-bearers, as a comparison with I Cor. 12:28 shows. In the latter passage there is a somewhat similar enumeration but no specific mention of evangelists. The combination "pastors and teachers" is also omitted, but other functionaries, not included in Eph. 4:11, are added. Though there is no scriptural warrant whatever for the tendency to get rid of the idea of "office" and "authority," [112] for these concepts are clearly implied in Matt. 16:18, 19; John 20:23; Acts 14:23; 20:28; II Cor. 5:3, 4; 10:8; I Tim. 1:18; 3:1, 5; 4:14; 5:17; II Tim. 4:1, 2; Titus 1:5-9; 3:10, nevertheless, "the emphasis in this passage [Eph. 4:11] does not lie on the apostles, prophets, etc. as officers, but as gifts of Christ to his church" (Roels, *op. cit.*, p. 185) .

---

[112] Thus A. Harnack, *The Constitution and Law of the Church*, New York, 1910. p. 5, quotes with approval the words of another: "The rise of ecclesiastical law and the constitution of the Church is an apostasy from the conditions intended by Jesus himself and originally realized." The position of these men — among whom may also be mentioned E. De Witt Burton, C. Von Weizsäcker, F. J. A. Hort, etc. — is that the apostles were not in any sense intended to be ecclesiastical officers but merely bearers of a message; that they were not vested with authority over life and doctrine but merely endowed with special spiritual gifts; or that, if they exercised any authority at all, it was not official but organic, spiritual, ethical. Scott's remark, "As yet there was no official ministry," *op. cit.*, p. 210; and Beare's "the ministry of function alone was known to Paul," *op. cit.*, p. 691, point in the same direction. See the refutation of this idea by O. Linton, *Das Problem der Urkirche in der Neuere Forschung*, Upsala, 1932, p. 71 ff.; and C. B. Bavinck, Art. "Apostel" in *Christelijke Encyclopaedia*, Vol. I, pp. 143–145.

2. The reason why in 4:11 ff. the apostle, whose heart went out to the lost (I Cor. 9:22) does not here stress the *numerical* growth of the church but rather its growth in love and other spiritual qualities, may well have been that the latter is the indispensable prerequisite of the former.

3. In order that the church may be strong it must not only have good leaders (verse 11) but also good, active followers (verse 12). Full salvation cannot be obtained until *all* of God's children obtain it together, a fact which Paul expresses beautifully in II Tim. 4:8, and which here in Ephesians he brings out by his constant use of the word *all* (1:15; 3:18, 19; 6:18).

4. Since here in 4:11 all who serve the church in a special way — not only "apostles, prophets, and evangelists," but also "pastors and teachers" — are designated as Christ's *gifts* to the church, they should be the objects of the love of the entire church. If, when they truly represent Christ, they are rejected, Christ is thereby rejected.

5. And, on the other hand, there is also here an implied admonition for the leaders themselves, namely, that these gifts were not given to them for their own sake but in the interest of Christ's body, the church.

A brief description of the "gifts" here enumerated is as follows:

a. Apostles, in the restricted sense of the term, are the Twelve and Paul. They are *the charter-witnesses of Christ's resurrection,* clothed with life-long and church-wide authority over life and doctrine, but introduced here, as already indicated, in order to stress *the service* they render. For a full statement of the characteristics of plenary apostleship see N.T.C. on I and II Timothy and Titus, pp. 50, 51.

b. Prophets, again in the restricted sense (for in a broader sense every believer is a prophet), are *the occasional organs of inspiration,* for example, Agabus (Acts 11:28; 21:10, 11). Together with the apostles they are described as being "the church's foundation." See also on 2:20 and 3:5; and see Acts 13:1; 15:32; and 21:9.

c. Evangelists, such as Philip (thus designated in Acts 21:8; his activity described in Acts 8:26-40) and Timothy (II Tim. 4:5), are *traveling missionaries,* of lower rank than apostles and prophets. Philip is mentioned first as one of the seven men chosen "to serve tables" (Acts 6:2). Timothy was one of Paul's assistants and representatives. For more about him and about the nature of his work see N.T.C. on I and II Timothy and Titus, pp. 33–39, 156–160, 312, 313. We know that Timothy had been ordained to office (I Tim. 4:14), as was true also with respect to Philip (Acts 6:6). For what office were these men ordained? In the case of Philip it is clear that he was ordained as "deacon," though the term deacon is not used in Acts 6. Must we then assume that when he was used by the Lord for the conversion of the Ethiopian eunuch he was "on his own," as it were, or serving in a different capacity? Similarly, must we take for granted that Timothy served in two separate offices: *a.* as apostolic vicar, and *b.* as evangelist? Is it not more consistent with scriptural data to infer from the account in Acts 6 that *only those* men were to be chosen as deacons who were "full of the Spirit and of wisdom," "full of faith," and that, accordingly, Philip was a *deacon-evangelist?* Are we doing full justice to the office of deacon if this is lost sight of? And does not the case of Timothy also indicate the flexibility of his office? If Timothy, as *evangelist* or *traveling missionary,* can serve the interests of the church best by being Paul's representative, why should he not function as such? Similarly today, instead of multiplying offices, would it not be better to put into practice the full implications of each office and to copy the flexibility of the early church, bearing in mind also that the special charismata of the early church are not ours today? The church of today is not able to produce an apostle like Paul, nor a prophet like Agabus. It is not in need of a Timothy to serve as apostolic delegate, nor of a Philip, addressed by an angel and "caught away" by the Spirit. In common with the early church, however, it does have ministers, elders, and deacons. It also has the Holy Spirit now as then. And it *now* has the complete Bible. Let *all* its offices then be utilized to the full as occasion demands, and in the spirit of true *service.*

d. Pastors and teachers are best considered *one* group.[113] Hodge remarks, "There is no evidence in Scripture that there was a set of men authorized to teach but not authorized to exhort. The thing is well nigh impossible" (*op. cit.,* p. 226). I fully agree. What we have here, accordingly, is a designation of *ministers of local congregations,* "teaching elders (or overseers)." By means of expounding the Word these men *shepherd* their flocks. Cf. Acts 20:17, 28; also John 21:15-17. They cannot do so properly without love for Christ.

12. The purpose of Christ's gifts to the church is now stated: **in order fully to equip the saints for the work of ministry, with a view to the building up of the body of Christ.** A.V. divides this verse into three separate phrases as follows: "For the perfecting of the saints, for the work of the ministry, for the edifying of the body of Christ." Along this line is also the rendering found in A.R.V. and the one in R.S.V. First, it should be pointed out that the original does not speak about "the work of *the* ministry" but about "the work of ministry," that is, of rendering specific services of various kinds. But even with this change the translation would still be a poor one, for it could easily leave the impression that the saints can be "perfected" without rendering service to each other and to the church. There

---

[113] The words τοὺς δε are not repeated before διδασκάλους. In itself this non-repetition might not be sufficient to prove that one group is meant, for see p. 141, footnote 74. However, in the present case we have a parallel in I Tim. 5:17b, where mention is made of men who, in addition to exercising supervision over the flock together with the other elders, also labor in the word and in teaching. These shepherds and teachers are *one* group.

197

should be no comma between the first and second phrases. A better solution, it would seem to me, is that favored by many of the older commentators and more recently by Salmond and by Lenski. These leave out both commas. The resultant idea is that Christ gave some men as apostles, others as prophets, etc., for the purpose of "perfecting" (cf. I Thess. 3:10; Heb. 13:21; I Peter 5:10) or *providing the necessary equipment* for all the saints for the work of ministering to each other so as to build up the body of Christ. I grant the possibility of the correctness of this construction. The meaning then would not differ very substantially from the third main rendering, the one to which I, along with many others, would still give the preference. According to this view of the matter the sentence *does not have two* commas (A.V., etc.) *nor no* commas (Salmond and Lenski) *but one* comma,[114] namely, after the word "ministry." This brings out more clearly that the *immediate* purpose of Christ's gifts is the ministry to be rendered by the entire flock; their *ultimate* purpose is the building up of the body of Christ, namely, the church (see on 1:22, 23).

The important lesson taught here is that not only apostles, prophets, evangelists, and those who are called "pastors and teachers," but the entire church should be engaged in spiritual labor. "The universal priesthood of believers" is stressed here. "Would that all Jehovah's people were prophets!" (Num. 11:29). Church attendance should mean more than "going to hear Rev. A." Unless, with a view to the service, there is adequate preparation, a desire for association, wholehearted *participation,* and the spirit of adoration, there is bound to be Sabbath-desecration. And during the week, too, every member should equip himself to be engaged in a definite "ministry," whether that be imparting comfort to the sick, teaching, neighborhood evangelization, tract distribution, or whatever be the task for which one is especially equipped. The meaning of 4:11, 12 is, moreover, that it is the task of the officers of the church to equip the church for these tasks. To all this it is important to add, however, that "the effectiveness of positive, conscious acts of Christian witness depends to a large extent upon the life of the person giving the witness in those moments not devoted to such witness" (Roels, *op. cit.,* p. 196).

The ideal in view with reference to the building up of the body of Christ is stated in verse **13. until we all attain to the unity of the faith and of the clear knowledge of the Son of God.** This brings us back again to the spiritual unity demanded in verse 3, and to the "one faith" to which reference was made in verse 5. It also reminds us of 3:19: "in order that y o u may be filled to all the fulness of God." When verse 13 is considered in the light of the preceding verses it becomes clear that what the apostle has in mind is

---

[114] The theory agrees with N.N.'s punctuation of the Greek text; also with that of Grk. N.T. (A–B–M–W).

this, that the entire church — consisting not only of apostles, prophets, evangelists, "pastors and teachers," but of all others besides — should be faithful to its calling of rendering service, with a view to the upbuilding of the body of Christ, so that true, spiritual unity and growth may be promoted. Note "we all." There is no room in Christ's church for drones, only for busy bees. To the Thessalonians the apostle had said, "For we hear that some among y o u are conducting themselves in a disorderly manner, not busy workers but busybodies" (II Thess. 3:11). Paul sharply rebuked that attitude. It is exactly *unity* that is promoted when all become busily engaged in the affairs of the church and when each member eagerly renders service for which the Lord has equipped him. Thus, it has happened repeatedly that young people began to be imbued with enthusiasm when they engaged in this or that church program. For example, the Board of Home Missions of a certain denomination launches a *S*(ummer) *W*(orkshop) *I*(n) *M*(issions) program. This program requires of the young people who are in it that at different places throughout the country for several weeks during the summer they not only receive special instruction in the aims and methods of missions but also make contact with those who have not been previously reached for Christ. They bring the message, teach, and organize various social and religious activities. They are not afraid to live for a while in a slum district in close and beneficial contact with the community. How the eyes of these young people sparkle upon their return, for they have a story to tell, and are far more aglow with interest in Christ and his church than ever before. Often the contacts made during the summer are continued by means of correspondence and return visits. Also, the Young People's societies and the congregations that have taken part in sponsoring the program, having become thus involved, receive an added blessing when the young witnesses bring their reports. Thus, unity has been promoted, a unity of faith in Christ and of knowledge — not just intellectual but heart-knowledge — of the Lord and Savior, who, because of his majesty and greatness, is here called "the Son of God" (cf. Rom. 1:4; Gal. 2:20; I Thess. 1:10). Thus all believers advance **to a fullgrown man.** The underlying figure is that of a strong, mature, well-built *male* (not just "human being"). In Col. 4:12 this maturity is described as follows: "fully assured in all the will of God." For a detailed tabulation of the meaning of the word *fullgrown* or *mature* see N.T.C. on Phil. 3:15, p. 176, footnote 156. Just as a physically robust man can be pictured as being filled with vibrant strength and without defect, so the spiritually mature individual, which is the ideal for all believers to attain, is without spiritual flaw, filled with goodness, that is, with every Christian virtue that results from faith in, and heart-knowledge of, the Son of God. Continued: **to the measure of the stature of the fulness of Christ.** One could also translate: "to an age-measure marked by the fulness of Christ" (cf. Lenski, *op. cit.,*

pp. 532, 536) .[115] It does not matter whether the underlying figure is fulness of *age* or fulness of *stature*, for in either case it is a "fulness of *Christ*"
that is meant (thus also Grosheide, *op. cit.*, p. 68, footnote 26). It is a fulness of him who completely fulfilled the earthly mission for which he had
been *anointed*, and who is willing to impart to those who believe in him
salvation full and free.

The question has been asked, Do believers during their present life on
earth attain to this "measure of the stature of the fulness of Christ"? According to some they do. Lenski, for example, mentions Paul as one who had
attained to it (*op. cit.*, p. 533). The passage itself, however, does not really
teach this. To be sure, it should be granted that not all remain "babes" in
Christ. A degree — in fact, a high degree — of maturity can be attained even
here and now. And the more wholeheartedly all the saints strive to promote it by rendering humble and wholehearted service to one another and
to the kingdom in general, the more also the ideal will be realized. Nevertheless, full, spiritual maturity, one that in the highest degree attains to
"the measure of the stature of the fulness of Christ," cannot be realized
this side of death. Paul himself would be one of the first to admit this. See
what he said concerning himself in Rom. 7:14: "I am carnal, sold under
sin"; and what he is going to say very shortly after Ephesians had been
delivered to its destination: "Brothers, I do not count myself yet to have
laid hold. But one thing (I do), forgetting what lies behind (me), and
eagerly straining forward to what lies ahead, I am pressing on toward the
goal, for the prize of the upward call of God in Christ Jesus" (Phil. 3:14,
15). For the rest, as to degree, time, and possibility of attainment, see on
3:19 where the same subject is discussed.

Marvelous growth in maturity, nevertheless, is certainly obtainable
through human effort springing forth from, and sustained from start to
finish by, the Holy Spirit. This is clear from the words which follow: **14,
15 . . . so that** [116] **we may no longer be children tossed to and fro by the
waves and whirled around by every gust of doctrine, by the trickery of men,
by (their) talent for deceitful scheming; but, adhering to the truth in
love, may grow up in all things into him who is the head, even Christ.**

---

[115] The word ἡλικία may refer either to *age* or to *height* or *stature*. Thus, Zacchaeus
was small in *stature* (Luke 19:3), Sarah was long past the *age* for conceiving (Heb.
11:11). The man born blind, healed by Christ, had reached the *age* of legal maturity (John 9:21, 23). No one can add a cubit to the length of his *life span* (Matt.
6:27; Luke 12:25). In such passages as Luke 2:52 ("Jesus increased in wisdom and
stature"; but according to others, "in wisdom and *age*") and Eph. 4:13 there is a
marked difference of opinion among commentators as to what is meant: *stature*
or *age*.

[116] The particle ἵνα clearly has a sub-final sense here. It cannot here mean "in order
that." The climax has been reached in verse 13. One does not attain to "the measure
of the stature of the fulness of Christ" (verse 13) *in order* not to be tossed, etc.,
and *in order* to grow (verses 14, 15).

The ideal of full Christian maturity is characterized in verse 14 from its negative aspect; in verse 15 positively. In striving to reach the goal and in advancing in that direction believers are goaded by the desire that they may no longer be like helpless children in a tempest-tossed boat which they cannot manage. Paul knew what it meant to be "driven to and fro" by the waves. While he was writing this, the trip which had brought him to his present Roman imprisonment must have been before him in all its vivid terror (Acts 27:14-44; note especially verse 27). But to be tossed to and fro and whirled around "by every gust of doctrine" is even worse than to experience the dangers of the sea. Just what did the apostle have in mind when he thus admonished the Ephesians? [117] Here we do well to bear in mind two facts: a. that most of the addressed were rather recent converts from heathenism; and b. that, although we must, therefore, conclude that his description was particularly fitting with respect to them, yet the apostle cannot have been thinking solely of these converts from the Gentile world, for he uses the first person plural, and says, "that *we* may no longer be children tossed to and fro," etc. The fact that heathen in their blindness and superstition are often swayed by the waves and winds of public opinion, believing whatever they have heard last, is vividly illustrated in Luke's account of the experience of Paul and Barnabas at Lystra. First the multitude held Paul to be Hermes, and Barnabas to be Zeus, and was ready to offer sacrifices in their honor. A little later these same people allowed themselves to be persuaded by wicked Jews, and stoned Paul nearly to death (Acts 14:8-20). But even followers of Jesus have much to learn in this respect. A typical example of unsteadfastness, before he became in very deed "a rock," was Simon Peter. In the Gospels he is pictured as a man who is constantly oscillating from one extreme to the other. Now he is seen walking courageously on the waters (Matt. 14:28); a little later he is crying, "Lord, save me" (Matt. 14:30). At one moment he makes a glorious confession (Matt. 16:16). Hardly have the echoes of that wonderful declaration faded, when he begins to rebuke the very Christ whom he has just confessed (Matt. 16:22). He promises to lay down his life for Jesus (John 13:37). A few hours later he is saying again and again, "I am not his disciple" (John 18:17, 25). After Christ's victorious resurrection he lags behind John to the tomb. Arrived, he enters the tomb before John does (John 20:4-6). At Antioch he first casts aside all ideas of racial segregation and eats with the Gentiles. Soon afterward he withdraws completely from the converts of the pagan world (Gal. 2:11, 12).

In addition to his bout with Peter, Paul had had other sad experiences with fluttering and fluctuating mankind. On his first missionary journey John Mark had deserted him (Acts 13:13; 15:38). The Galatians had de-

[117] This has been discussed in a most interesting fashion by J. M. Moffatt, "Three Notes on Ephesians," *Exp.*, Eighth Series, No. 87 (April, 1918), pp. 306–317.

serted the gospel (Gal. 1:6). And at this very time, while Paul was writing his "prison epistles," *some* of the members of the Colossian church must have been in real danger of lending a listening ear to false philosophers. The apostle knows that there is nothing so stabilizing as performing day by day loving service for Christ. No one learns truth faster than he who, with consecrated heart, teaches others. Let the Ephesians, therefore, withdraw their attention from "the trickery of men," and plunge into the work of the kingdom. That is the context here: all the saints, under the leadership of the apostles, prophets, evangelists, "pastors and teachers," united for the work of ministry.

The term "trickery," applied to those who in effect were attempting to lead believers astray, is *kubeia,* from *kúbos,* meaning *cube, die.* Paul is thinking, therefore, of *dice-playing* in which tricks were used in order to win. Hence, the word came to mean *trickery;* here "human trickery," "the talent literally, readiness to do anything for deceitful scheming." Constantly the thoughts and plans of these crafty fellows were directed toward (Greek πρός) "the method of deception." Cf. Col. 2:4, 8, 18, 23; then also Rom. 6:17, 18; II Cor. 2:17; 11:13; Gal. 2:4.

Now error is never overcome by mere negation. Over against the deceitfulness of the errorists the Ephesians should *adhere to the truth,* that is, *practice integrity.*[118] And what *ministry* (see verse 12) can be more noble than that which, while resolutely opposing deceit, setting *truthfulness* "of life and lip" over against it, does all this *in the spirit of love?* There are two great enemies of a successful ministry, whether carried on among believers or among unbelievers. One is departure from truth, compromise with the lie, whether in words or deeds. The other is chilling indifference with respect to the hearts and lives, the troubles and trials, of the people whom one is ostensibly trying to persuade. Paul has the real solution: *the*

---

[118] I agree with the statement of Simpson, "Whether the verb means to *speak* or to *act truly* is hard to decide" (*op. cit.,* p. 99). While some make a point of stressing that ἀληθεύω does not really mean "speaking the truth" but "adhering to the truth" or "living the truth," it remains a fact that the passages referred to in L.N.T. (A. and G.), p. 36, show that "speaking the truth" both here and in Gal. 4:16 is also possible. Thus in Josephus, *Jewish War* III. 322, we read, ". . . thinking that the man might be speaking the truth. . . ." and in his *Life* 132: "Even the inhabitants of Tarichaeae believed that the young men were speaking the truth." The possibility of the correctness of this rendering here in 4:15 must, therefore, be granted. The thought expressed in that case is not so foreign to the context to make it look impossible. On the other hand, there are two reasons why I, nevertheless, would give a slight edge to the rendering "adhering to the truth" or "practicing sincerity." In the first place, if in 4:15 the meaning be "speaking truth," the apostle would be repeating himself in 4:25, where the rendering "speaking truth" leaves no room for doubt. Secondly, the verb used in 4:15 "need not be restricted to truthfulness in speech" (Robinson, *op. cit.,* p. 185); especially not in the present instance where the context would rather seem to point in the direction of *being truthful* or *maintaining truthfulness* over against the deceitfulness of the men who practice trickery and perverse scheming.

truth must be practiced *in love* (3:18; 4:2; 5:1, 2), which was exactly what he was constantly doing (II Cor. 2:4; Gal. 4:16, 19; I Thess. 2:7-12); and telling others to do (I Tim. 4:11-13). In fact, *love* (for which see on 4:2) must mark *all* of life. By means of such behavior we will impart a blessing not only to others but to ourselves also, for we will "grow up in all things into him who is the head, even Christ." We must grow up into union with him. The same intimacy of conscious oneness with Christ is stressed in Rom. 6:5, where the idea is expressed that believers are "grown together" with him. Such statements do not in any way obliterate the infinite distinction between Christ and Christians. They do *not* indicate *identity but intimacy*. The distinction between believers and their Lord is clearly enunciated here, for the latter is called "the head," while the former are designated "the entire body." What is meant by growing up into Christ is interpreted by the apostle himself in Phil. 1:21, "For to me to live (is) Christ, and to die (is) gain." In other words:

> "So shall no part of day or night from sacredness be free,
> But all my life, in every step, be fellowship with thee."
> (Horatius Bonar)

16. Paul concludes this section by saying, **from whom the entire body, harmoniously fitted together and held together by every supporting joint, according to the energy that corresponds to the capacity of each individual part, brings about bodily growth with a view to its own upbuilding in love.** As *head* Christ causes his *body, the church, to live and to grow* (cf. Col. 2:19). He is its *Organic Head.* As head he also exercises authority over the church; in fact, over all things in the interest of the church (Eph. 1:20-23). He is its *Ruling Head.* It is doubtful whether either of these two ideas is ever completely absent when Christ is called head of the church, though sometimes one connotation and then again the other receives the greater emphasis, as the context indicates. And in such a passage as 5:23, 24 both ideas (*growth* and *guidance*) are brought to the fore. In the present passage (4:16) it is clearly the organic relationship that is stressed. The words reveal a marked resemblance to those found in Col. 2:19: ". . . the head, from whom the entire body, supported and held together by joints and ligaments, grows with a growth (that is) from God." The fact that the human body — which is the underlying figure — is, indeed, "harmoniously fitted together and held together by every supporting joint" is an astounding wonder. It is, however, common knowledge, not refuted by the most up-to-date science. The real message which the apostle is conveying both here in Ephesians and in the Colossian parallel is accordingly this, that to Christ the entire church owes its growth. Just as the human body, when properly supported and held together, experiences normal growth, so also the church, when each of its members supports and maintains loving contact with the others and above all with Christ, will, under the sustaining care of God (or *of Christ,* as here in Ephesians: "Christ, from whom"), proceed from grace to grace and from glory to glory (cf. I Cor. 12). There are, however, two main additions in the Ephesian passage, points not stressed in its Colossian parallel:

1. that the body is fitted together and held together . . . *according to the energy that corresponds to the capacity of each individual part.* Meaning: in the church, too, every spiritually alive member does his part, performing his ministry in accordance with his God-given ability. This is a fine repetition of the thought introduced in all the preceding verses of this section, particularly in verses 7, 12, 13.

2. dropping the underlying figure, that when all the individual "parts" (members) of the church co-operate, the entire church grows spiritually *with a view to its own upbuilding in love.* The love to which reference is made is the same as that mentioned in verse 2; see on that verse. With this marvelous word Paul ends this marvelous section.[119]

Seed Thoughts of Ephesians 4:1-16
(one thought for each verse)

See Verse

1. The best missionary method is the truly consecrated life.
2. The qualities which Christ demands of us are those which he himself exemplified.
3. Though peace is indeed a precious gift imparted by the Holy Spirit, it is at the same time the product of human effort.
4. The church is not a man-made institution but the product of the Holy Spirit whose call to repent and to follow Christ in service we should obey. Obedience to that call imparts hope.
5. The one Lord Jesus Christ in whom all Christians believe and in whose name they have all been baptized welds together into *one body* God's children, those still on earth and those already in heaven.
6. Anent the first person of the Holy Trinity, as Father he is *"over all,"* for he exercises control over all. He is, however, also *"through all,"* for he blesses us all through Christ our Mediator. And he is *"in all,"* for he draws us all close to his heart in the Spirit. Thus we perceive that we worship *one God,* not three gods. It is folly therefore to say, "God is dead but Jesus is still alive." The three are One.
7. A talent is a *gift,* and to no one has Christ imparted every gift. The fact that a person's ability in any direction is a *gift* should keep him hum-

---

[119] For problems in connection with this comparison of the relation between Christ and his followers, on the one hand, with the human body and its members, on the other, see N.T.C. on Col. 2:19, pp. 128, 129.

ble, for what has he that he has not received? It should also encourage him, for the way to the Giver and his inexhaustible gifts is known.

8. Not only Christ's suffering, death, burial, and resurrection were in our interest; so was also his ascension. He ascended not only to receive glory for himself but also to bestow gifts upon men.

9. The doctrine of Christ's descent into hell on Calvary should be retained. If our Savior did not suffer the torments of hell for us, is he then our Substitute?

10. *Did the descended* Jesus love us with a love so deep and intimate that nothing on earth can compare with it? The *ascended* Christ loves us no less!

11. An apostle was *a gift of Christ to the church*. This was true also with respect to the prophet; and also with respect to an evangelist. Today, too, the man to whom Christ has assigned the task of being "a pastor and teacher" should be so regarded. If, when he truly represents the will of his Sender, he is rejected, those who are guilty of this sin are rejecting the Master himself.

12. It is the duty of the pastor to impress upon everyone under his care the duty and privilege of *lay-ministry*. Only when every member does his part is the body of Christ being built up as it should be.

13. Not only *unity* but also *growth* is demanded of us. The Church's *Organic Unity and Growth* is the theme of this chapter. "Excelsior!" should be our motto. Reaching "the measure of the stature of the fulness of Christ," our aim.

14. The church should emphasize teaching right doctrine.

15. Over against the deceitfulness of the opponent the church should practice truthfulness; always, however, in a context of love.

16. Just as the human body when held together by every supporting joint grows strong, so also the church when it receives the active support of every member, each co-operating according to his ability, will be built up in love.

Chapter 4:17–6:9

Verses 4:17–5:21

Theme: *The Church Glorious*

II. *Exhortation
urging*

G lorious Renewal
1. upon all

CHAPTER IV:17–VI:9

EPHESIANS

17 This I say, therefore, and testify in the Lord, that y o u should no longer walk as the Gentiles also walk, in the futility of their mind, 18 being darkened in their understanding, alienated from the life of God because of the ignorance that is in them due to the hardness of their hearts, 19 because they have become callous and have abandoned themselves to licentiousness for the greedy practice of every type of impurity. 20 Y o u, however, did not so learn Christ, 21 for surely y o u heard of him and were taught in him, just as it is in Jesus that truth resides, 22 (having been taught) that with respect to y o u r former manner of life y o u must put off the old man, which is being corrupted through deceitful lusts, 23 and must be renewed in the spirit of y o u r minds, 24 and put on the new man, created after (the likeness of) God in true righteousness and holiness.

25 Therefore, laying aside falsehood, speak truth each (of y o u) with his neighbor, for we are members of one another. 26 Be angry but do not sin; let not the sun go down on that angry mood of y o u r s, 27 and do not give the devil a foothold. 28 Let him who steals steal no longer but rather let him labor, with his own hands accomplishing what is good, so that he may have something to share with the needy one. 29 Let no corrupt speech proceed from y o u r mouth, but (only) such (speech) as is good for edification, as fits the need, that it may impart grace to the listeners. 30 And do not grieve the Holy Spirit of God in whom y o u were sealed for the day of redemption. 31 Let all bitterness and anger and wrath and brawling and slander be put away from y o u, along with all malice. 32 And be kind to each other, tender-hearted, forgiving one another, just as God in Christ forgave y o u.

5 1 Be therefore imitators of God, as beloved children, 2 and walk in love, just as Christ loved y o u and gave himself up for us, an offering and a sacrifice to God, for a fragrant odor.

3 But immorality and impurity of any kind, or greed, let it not even be mentioned among y o u, as is fitting among saints, 4 also filthiness and silly talk or wittiness in telling coarse jokes, which things are improper, but rather the expression of thankfulness. 5 For of this y o u can be very sure, that no immoral or impure person or greedy individual — which is the same as an idolater — has any inheritance in the kingdom of Christ and of God. 6 Let no one deceive y o u with empty words; for it is because of these things that the wrath of God comes upon the sons of disobedience. 7 Therefore do not be their partners, 8 for y o u were formerly darkness, but now (y o u are) light in the Lord; as children of light ever walk 9 — for the fruit of light (consists) in all goodness and righteousness and truth — 10 verifying what is pleasing to the Lord. 11 And do not take any part in the unfruitful works of darkness but instead even expose them, 12 for the things done by them in secret it is a shame even to mention. 13 But when all these

(wicked practices) are exposed by the light they are made visible; for everything that is made visible is light. 14 Therefore he says,

"Awake, sleeper,
And arise from the dead,
And Christ will shine on you."

15 Be most careful therefore how y o u walk, not as unwise but as wise, 16 making the most of the opportunity, because the days are evil. 17 Therefore do not be foolish but understand what (is) the will of the Lord. 18 And do not get drunk on wine, which is associated with unrestrained living, but be filled with the Spirit, 19 speaking to one another in psalms and hymns and spiritual songs, singing and making melody from y o u r heart to the Lord; 20 giving thanks always for all things in the name of the Lord Jesus Christ to (our) God and Father, 21 subjecting yourselves to each other out of reverence for Christ.

4:17–5:21

The theme *renewal* is suggested by 4:23, where Paul tells the Ephesians, "Y o u must be renewed." This renewal, moreover, implies a complete, basic change, a *detachment* from the world which they had formerly served, and an *attachment* to Christ, their newly confessed Lord and Savior. In Paul's own words, it is a *putting* off of the old man and a *putting* on of the new man (4:22, 24). Now the idea of this *Spirit-born total transformation* governs the entire section: 4:17–6:9. Throughout what Paul is saying is, "Be done with the old and adopt the new." He is continually contrasting these two kinds of disposition and behavior. Thus he urges that falsehood be replaced by speaking the truth (4:25); sinful anger, by that which is not sinful (4:26); stealing, by sharing (4:28); corrupt speech, by edifying words (4:29); bitterness, anger, and wrath, by kindness, tenderness and love (4:31–5:2); filthiness and coarse wittiness, by the expression of thankfulness (5:3, 4), etc.

When the *general* admonitions (4:17–5:21) are ended and those *to special groups* (5:22–6:9) are issued, the idea of renewal continues. Husbands must love, not hate, their wives (5:28, 29). Fathers should not provoke their children to anger but should rear them tenderly in the discipline and admonition of the Lord (6:4). Slaves ought to render service not as to men but as to the Lord (6:5-8). Masters must stop threatening and must treat their slaves with consideration (6:9).

Although, to be sure, this renewal is a matter of strenuous, continuous, effort on the part of believers, a process of daily conversion, yet, as already stated, it is throughout a work of the Holy Spirit (4:30; 5:18), for it is only through the Spirit that men are able to put forth the needed effort and to succeed. Hence, it is a transformation or sanctification *full of glory*, nothing less than a change from dismal darkness to glorious light (5:7-14). Accordingly, I cannot find a better sub-title for this section than that of (the Church's) *Glorious Renewal*.

The section that covers the general admonitions has four parts, which may be divided as follows: 4:17-24; 4:25–5:2; 5:3-14; and 5:15-21.

a. 4:17-24

"Put off the old man. Be renewed. Put on the new man."

17. The paragraph begins as follows: **This I say, therefore, and testify in the Lord, that y o u should no longer walk as the Gentiles also walk.** This "therefore" connects the present paragraph with all that has gone before in 4:1-16. "Because of y o u r high calling, y o u r duty to render service with a view to the building up of Christ's body, no longer conduct yourselves as do the Gentiles." The apostle introduces this admonition with all the authority he is able to summon. He says, "I say and testify." As Bengel has pointed out: when the apostle *admonishes* he does it so that those addressed may act *freely;* when he *encourages,* so that they may act *gladly;* and when he *testifies,* so that they may act *reverently* (with a proper respect for the will of God) . Note also "in the Lord." He is speaking and testifying in the sphere of the Lord, with *his* authority, and in the interest of *his* cause. Cf. Acts 20:26; Gal. 5:3; I Thess. 2:12.

They must no longer behave as Gentiles,[120] for they no longer are Gentiles. When this statement is analyzed it becomes clear that two ideas are combined here: *a.* Lay aside y o u r former manner of life (cf. 2:1-3, 12; 4:14, 22) ; and *b.* do not imitate y o u r present evil environment. With reference to Gentile conduct Paul adds: **in the futility of their mind.** The rendering "vanity" instead of "futility" is not wrong, since the latter is one of the meanings of the former. Nevertheless, inasmuch as "vanity" also has another, very different and yet very common, meaning, namely, *excessive pride, conceit,* "futility" is to be preferred. The apostle emphasizes a very important point, namely, that all those endeavors which the Gentiles put forth in order to attain happiness end in disappointment. Their life is one long series of mocked expectations. It is a pursuing and not achieving, a blossoming and not bearing fruit. Cf. Rom. 8:20. All the rivers run into the sea, but the sea is never filled. The eye is never satisfied with seeing nor the ear with hearing. All this chasing after riches, honor, mirth, etc., is nothing but "a striving after wind" (Eccles. 1:7, 8; 3:9) . Their *mind* or *intellect* is fruitless. It produces naught that can satisfy. Continued: **18, 19. being darkened in their understanding, alienated from the life of God because of the ignorance that is in them due to the hardness of their hearts, because they have become callous and have abandoned themselves to licentiousness for the greedy practice of every type of impurity.** In order to see the entire picture of tragic hopelessness, these two verses should be viewed as a unit. It then becomes clear that the futility that characterizes the Gentile mind is a product of darkened understanding and estrangement from the God-given life,

---

[120] The reading upon which A.V. bases its rendering "not as other Gentiles," is weak.

these two, in turn, resulting from a type of ignorance that is by no means excusable but is due to willful hardening and surrender to unbridled license of every description. *Being darkened* is something that took place in the past but has continuing effect.[121] The "understanding" or power of discursive reasoning had been affected by sin. This understanding is treated here as if it were an eye that had become blind. This darkening, moreover, is far worse than *physical* blindness, for the man who is physically blind knows it and admits it, but the person who is spiritually and morally darkened is blind even to the fact that he is blind (John 9:40, 41). Not only is it true that people of this kind dwell in the darkness, but the darkness dwells in them. They have imbibed it, just as one day they will imbibe ("drink") God's wrath (Rev. 14:10). Contrast these blind eyes with the "enlightened" eyes of believers (2:18). They are, moreover, *alienated* or *estranged*,[122] and this not only from "the commonwealth of Israel" as was pointed out earlier (2:12) but also from "the life of God," that is, from God as the Source of eternal life. This darkening and alienation can be traced to their culpable ignorance, a condition they had brought upon themselves by hardening their hearts against the will of God. At one time, long, long ago their ancestors had had God's *special* revelation, but had rejected it. Many centuries had gone by. And now these distant descendants were suppressing even the light of God's general revelation in nature and conscience with terrible results. The picture, in all its lurid details, is drawn in Rom. 1:18-32; cf. 2:12 and 11:7. The very center of their being, their *hearts,* had become "callous" by their own deliberate action. For "callous" the A.V. and A.R.V. have "past feeling," which is also an excellent rendering, the root meaning of this perfect participle being "having arrived at a condition of freedom from pain," and thus, in general, "having become insensible" with reference here to the divine voice, to God's truth.

Some there are who *over-emphasize* feeling. Their religion never reaches any deeper than the emotions. Their picture is drawn in Matt. 13:5, 6, 20, 21. They are not firmly rooted. They lack conviction. The Gentiles whom Paul here describes as a warning example have followed the exactly opposite course, which, if anything, is even worse. By constantly saying "No" to God's voice in conscience and in the lessons which nature and history had provided, they had at last become hard as stone, dead to all responsiveness to that which is good and uplifting; not, however, dead to *all* feeling and *all* desire. Now there have been many people throughout the course of history who have taken pride in the stifling of *all* feeling. They were ashamed of shedding tears and even of revealing any but the most indifferent reaction

---

[121] That is the sense of the perfect periphrastic. It should not be necessary to remark that ὄντες in verse 18 and οἵτινες in verse 19, masculines, refer to τὰ ἔθνη neuter. This is not at all unusual and is a construction *ad sensum.*

[122] Another perfect participle, construed like *darkened.*

to *any* outside influence. Thus, for example, the Stoic's ideal was release from every emotion ("apatheia"). Again, according to a familiar story, the Spartan youth who had stolen a young fox and had hid it beneath his tunic, allowed the animal to tear out his vitals, without betraying himself by the movement of a muscle. In the camp of the Buddhists the best virtue is passion-lessness, and heaven ("Nirvana") has been defined as the cessation of all natural desires. And among the American Indians a captured Iroquois did his level best not to break down under torture, but instead to react to it with perfect equanimity. What we have here, in 4:18, 19, however, is some-thing far worse. The people of whom Paul was writing *did not try to squelch all feeling*. Far from it! They did not oppose *every* type of desire. On the contrary they suppressed only those feelings that are connected with good-ness. They were down on all desires that would have brought them into closer harmony with the will of God. By constantly arguing with con-science, stifling its warnings and muffling its bell, they had at last reached the point where conscience could no longer bother them. It was seared (I Tim. 4:2). They *did* have *feeling* and they *did* keep alive *desire,* namely, feeling and desire for evil indulgence. They had abandoned themselves to vice. They *gave themselves up* to it (thus literally, in the original). The result of such base surrender is always this, that, if persisted in, God *gives the sinner up* to suffer the full consequences of his sin, as Exod. 8:15, 32, cf. 9:12; Rom. 1:24, 26, 28 (where the same verb, "give up," is used as here in Eph. 4:19) clearly teach. See also Rev. 22:11. The vice to which they abandoned themselves is called *licentiousness* or "lasciviousness" (see also Rom. 13:13; II Cor. 12:21; Gal. 5:19). The literature of the day was deeply immoral. So corrupt had the Roman world become that somewhat later Origen states that when the people of his day committed adultery and whoredom they did not regard themselves as violating good manners. It has been remarked that it was not lava but lewdness that buried Hercu-laneum. And the frescoes found amid the ruins of nearby Pompeii show that this city was not any better.

The apostle says that the Gentiles of whom he speaks had abandoned themselves to licentiousness "for the greedy practice [literally: *practice in greed*] of every type of impurity." The greedy person is the one who over-reaches. He wishes "to have more than his due." He disregards the rights and feelings of all other people. He goes beyond what is proper and has no respect whatever for any laws of dignity or propriety. Cf. 5:3, 5; Col. 2:5; I Thess. 4:6. By means of his unbridled lust and wanton self-assertion he is digging his own grave. Note particularly: *every type* of impurity. For an enumeration of these types see 4:25-31; 5:3-11, 15, 18; cf. Rom. 1:26-32.

20. In principle, however, the people whom Paul addresses belong to a different category. This had been the case ever since Christ entered into their hearts and lives. Hence, Paul continues: **Y o u, however, did not so**

learn Christ. In the original the sentence begins with the word *y o u,* on which, accordingly, great emphasis is placed, as if to say, "Y o u did not learn Christ so as to continue to live as the Gentiles are doing." To learn Christ is more than to learn *about* Christ. Not only had the Ephesians received a body of teaching, namely, about Christ, and not only had they observed in the lives of those who brought it what this doctrine was able to achieve, but in addition, they themselves by an act of Spirit-wrought faith had welcomed this Christ into their hearts. Joyfully they had received the sacrament of holy baptism. And by constant and systematic attendance upon the means of grace, by prayer and answers to prayer, by daily living in accordance with the principles of the truth of the gospel, they had learned Christ, yes, Christ himself in very person.

Paul here presents the appropriation of Christ and of salvation in him as the result of a learning process, a learning with heart and mind. Believers, in other words, are not saved at one stroke. They do not become completely transformed all at once. They learn. There was the basic change wrought by the power of God. This was followed by a constant progress in sanctification, constant but not necessarily uniform. In one person it had been more clearly evident than in another. At one time the progress had been by leaps, but at another time at snail's pace. At times, in all likelihood, there had been reverses, retrogressions. The point which the apostle emphasizes, however, is that whatever had been their degree of advance in learning, they had definitely not learned Christ as an advocate of sin and selfishness, of lewdness and licentiousness. No longer were their minds futile, no longer was their understanding dark. Continued: **21. . . . for surely y o u heard of him and were taught in him.** Justification for this translation — "for surely," where A.V. and A.R.V. have "if so be" — was offered in the explanation of 3:2 where a similar "for surely" occurs. Many of the Ephesians had been taught by Paul himself during his lengthy ministry at Ephesus (Acts 19; 20:17-35). The apostle had been able to reach not only those who were actually living within the city of Ephesus but also people from the surrounding territory. Many had flocked to the city to attend feasts, for business, or for other purposes. Some, no doubt, had gone there for the very purpose of seeing and hearing Paul. But in addition there had been other multitudes, in surrounding cities and villages, who heard the gospel from the lips of those who had received it from Paul (Acts 20:17). It should be borne in mind constantly that this epistle is, in all probability, a letter addressed to a vast multitude of people, many of whom did not live in Ephesus. It was probably a circular letter. See Introduction, pp. 58-61. The addressed, then, had heard of Christ and had been taught not only *about* but "*in*" him; that is, the entire atmosphere had been Christian. Christ, speaking through his ambassadors, was the teacher. He was also the theme. Continued: **just as it is in Jesus that truth resides.** The truth with reference to man's fall into sin, his desperate condi-

tion by nature, the salvation procured by Christ, the necessity of faith working through love, principles of Christian conduct, etc.: all these doctrines
had Christ as their very center. In Christ's suffering and death by crucifixion
the addressed had been able to read how deeply fallen they were, necessitat-
ing the death of God's only-begotten Son, a death both painful and shameful. In his triumphant resurrection, ascension, and coronation they had
received proof positive that salvation had been achieved. In Christ's constant emphasis upon the fact that men must come to him and rely on him
completely, they had been given a lesson in the necessity of faith as appropriating organ of salvation. The Master's marvelous example in humility, self-sacrifice, love, etc. had been given for their instruction. Moreover,
had not Jesus himself said, "I am the way and the truth and the life"? (John
14:6). Was not he the very embodiment of the truth, the truth in person?
Were not "all the treasures of wisdom and knowledge" hidden in him, hidden in order to be revealed? (Col. 2:3). Was not he the active and living
truth, the truth that sets men free (John 8:32; 17:17), the very answer to
Pilate's question (John 18:38)?

Verse 21b was parenthetical in character. Continuing now with the main
idea expressed in verse 21a: "for surely y o u heard of him and were taught
in him," Paul writes: **22-24. (having been taught) that with respect to y o u r
former manner of life y o u [123] must put off the old man, which is being corrupted through deceitful lusts, and must be renewed in the spirit of y o u r
minds, and put on the new man, created after (the likeness of) God in true
righteousness and holiness.**

What the Ephesians had been taught "in Christ" was this, that nothing
less than a radical change in their mental outlook and manner of life was
necessary, a complete turnabout. Their former manner of life (2:2, 3;
4:17-19; 5:8, 14; cf. Col. 1:21; 2:13; 3:7) must cease. The directive which,
from the moment of their vital contact with Christ, was meant to control
their entire being in all its manifestations, and to confront them every day
and every hour, was curt and crisp: "Put off the old man," that is, "the old
nature, whatever y o u are apart from grace" (Col. 3:9; cf. Rom. 6:6), and
"Put on the new man," that is, "the new nature, whatever y o u have become, must be, and can become because of grace" (Col. 3:10; cf. Gal. 3:27).
It was *a summary formulation* [124] of a tremendously large order. In a sense,

---

[123] *Because of the parenthetical clause* ("just as it is in Jesus that truth resides,"
verse 21b) intervening between the main verb "y o u were taught" (verse 21a) and
the infinitives governed by it, namely, "to put off" (aorist middle, verse 22), "to
put on" (aorist middle, verse 24) and "to be (constantly) renewed" (present passive, verse 23), the subject of these infinitives "y o u" (ὑμᾶς) is written out.
[124] These aorists "to put off" and "to put on" do not indicate that the actions to
which they refer are done once for all, at this or that moment in the life of the
addressed. They simply *summarize*. They give *a snapshot view*. They do not indicate
anything at all with respect to whether putting off the old man and putting on the

they had already put off the old man and put on the new man, namely, when they had given their hearts to Christ, and had professed him openly at the time of their baptism. But *basic* conversion must be followed by *daily* conversion. Even though in principle the believer has become a new creature (or "creation") , he remains a sinner until he dies. The old nature, with which the Ephesians had been on such intimate terms for so many years, is not easy to shed. Getting rid of it is difficult and painful. It amounts, in fact, to a crucifixion (Rom. 6:6) . This is true all the more because it is always promising so much. It is being "continually corrupted" through lusts' illusions, those deceptive evil desires [125] with their mighty promises and minimal performances. This corrupting deceptiveness is present, moreover, wherever the old nature is represented, whether in the unbeliever or in the believer. Cain's murder of his brother, a deed which had appeared so attractive when planned, brought nothing but a curse. Absalom's prospective crown, so dazzling at first, resulted in his gruesome death. The vineyard, so luscious and so conveniently located that Ahab, in order to obtain this coveted prize, had not hesitated to sacrifice Naboth's life, brought ruin to the king's household and posterity. The thirty pieces of silver which had shimmered so brightly in Judas' scheming, once in his possession had burned his hands, tortured his soul, and sent the traitor himself scurrying on his way to hanging and to hell. And, not to omit one of God's chosen ones, David, in a moment of weakness, filled with passionate delight in the thought of pleasant days ahead with the object of his lustful yearning, was forced to listen to the words of the Lord which like thunder-bolts fell from the lips of the prophet: "You are the man. The sword will not depart from your house." Truly, the old nature flaunts a golden cup, but upon inspection it is found to contain nothing but filth and abomination (cf. Rev. 17:4) . Hence, the Ephesians had been warned most solemnly to put off the old man, to fight him with unrelenting and undiminished vigor in order to divest themselves completely of him.

But while "the old man" is wholly evil, "the new man" is wholly good. He is "created after (the likeness of) God." Cf. Col. 3:10. Other explanatory passages are Eph. 2:10; II Cor. 5:17; Gal. 6:15; and Titus 3:5. Day by day this new creation is advancing "in true righteousness and holiness." The Colossian parallel (3:10) adds "full knowledge." Grace restores what sin has ruinously impaired. God not only *imputes* but also *imparts* righteous-

---

new man takes place in a moment or covers a lifetime. The aorist in John 2:20 refers to an activity that had already lasted forty-six years! Here in Eph. 2:22-24 it is the nature of the indicated actions and the context in which the aorists occur — the fact that they are joined by means of the present durative infinitive referring to the continuing process of mental renewal — that establish the lifelong character of the *putting off* and *putting on*.

[125] With reference to the word ἐπιθυμία see N.T.C. on II Tim. 2:22, especially footnote 146, pp. 271, 272.

ness to the sinner whom he pleases to save. Thus, the believer begins to perform his duties toward his *fellow-men*. But *righteousness* never walks alone. It is always accompanied by *holiness*, so that the regenerated and converted person performs his duties with reference to *God* also. Cf. Luke 1:75; I Thess. 2:10; Titus 1:8. Moreover, the righteousness and holiness which God bestows are *true*,[126] not *deceptive*, as are the lusts spawned by the old nature. They bring life to its true, predestined fulfilment. They satisfy.

As to the figure underlying "putting off" and "putting on," it refers, of course, to what one does with a garment. Frequently such a robe indicates a person's nature or character: either good (Job 29:14; Ps. 132:9; Isa. 11:5; 61:10) or evil (Ps. 73:6; cf. Ps. 35:26; 109:29). How it clings to him! The figure is by no means confined to Scripture. It has become part of general literature. It also occurs in the prayers of God's children: "Disrobe us of ourselves and clothe us with thyself, O Lord."

Both the putting off of the old man and the putting on of the new man are necessary. Some people constantly stress the negative. Their religion is one of don't. Others turn their backs upon every don't, and take peculiar pride in overstressing the positive. Scripture avoids both of these extremes. Ephesians contains many a *do* and many a *don't*. Here in this life both are needed. They are inseparable and point to simultaneous activities. That is what Paul means when he states that the Ephesians had been taught to "put off" the old man and to "put on" the new man. A person can do very little with *one* scissorblade. Twin blades, operating in unison, compose the scissors that will work. He who says "Yes" to Christ is saying "No" to Satan. But though both are necessary, Paul's emphasis throughout is on the positive: "Overcome evil with good" (Rom. 12:21; cf. 13:14). So it is also here in Eph. 4:22-24, for we are taught that the only way in which one can progressively succeed in putting off the old man and putting on the new [127] man is by being renewed in the spirit of one's mind. This renewel is basically an act of God's Spirit powerfully influencing man's *spirit*, here, as also in I Cor. 4:21; Gal. 6:1; and I Peter 3:4, *mental attitude, state of mind, disposition,* with respect to God and spiritual realities.

---

[126] Literally "righteousness and holiness *of the truth*" (according to what is probably the best reading). So also in verse 22 "lusts of the deceit." In view of the presence of the article before *deceit* and before *truth* some deny the adjectival character of these modifiers. The meaning would then become "lusts springing from (the) deceit (or: deception)," and "righteousness and holiness springing from (the) truth." It is doubtful, however, whether there is good ground for this refinement. In any case it is clear that lusts, on the one hand, and righteousness and holiness, on the other, are here contrasted as to their character and value.
[127] In verse 23 note νέος-ον as a component element of the verb *renew*, while in verse 24 the adjective that modifies "man" is καινός-ον. In Col. 3:10, however, the roles are reversed. Accordingly, though it is true that basically νέος indicates *new* as to *time*, while καινός refers to *new* as to *quality*, it is obvious that the distinction cannot be pressed either here or in Colossians.

b. 4:25–5:2

"Do not give the devil a foothold. Be imitators of God."

25. The apostle now advances from the general to the particular: **Therefore, laying aside falsehood, speak truth each (of y o u) with his neighbor.** That there is a connection between this admonition and the preceding paragraph is clear from the repetition of the word "putting off" or "laying aside" (same verb in the original; cf. verses 22 and 25) and of the reference to "truth" (cf. verse 25 with verses 15, 20, 24). Based upon this evident connection one might interpret Paul's thinking at this point as follows: "In view of the fact that 'in Christ' y o u have been taught to put off the old man and to put on the new man, therefore, put off (or: lay aside) falsehood and speak truth."

One is, however, immediately confronted with a rather incisive difference of opinion among commentators with respect to the translation and meaning of these words. Perhaps the best way to bring out this difference would be to summarize the view of one representative of each of the two opposing theories. The first view is this: What Paul is saying is that since the Ephesians have once for all laid aside falsehood, namely, when they accepted the truth of the gospel, they should now speak truth each with his neighbor. The second is: "There is no need to render 'having put away,' which would seem to imply a separation in time between the two actions [that is, between laying aside falsehood and speaking truth]." [128] Grammatically both renderings — "having put away" and "putting away" (or: "laying aside") — are possible. In favor of the first view it can be argued that the Ephesians had experienced basic conversion. They had, therefore, already decisively repudiated the lie, namely, when they accepted the truth. The meaning of 4:25 could therefore be: "Be consistent. Let y o u r life adorn y o u r confession. Having put away falsehood, now practice the truth." This line of reasoning would also be entirely in harmony with Paul's logic as expressed, for example, in 4:1 ff. and elsewhere.

Nevertheless, although the possibility of the correctness of this theory must be granted, it would seem to me that the opposite view has the best of the argument. Why is it that so very many translators and interpreters have adopted it? *With minor variations* the rendering which I also favor, namely, "Therefore, laying aside falsehood, speak truth each (of y o u) with his neighbor" is that which one will find in A.V., A.R.V., R.S.V., and in substance also in the versions of those who use two imperatives: "Have done

---

[128] The first view is that of Lenski, argued with usual forcefulness, *op. cit.*, pp. 573, 574. He even states, "The participle is . . . aorist, hence not: 'putting away falsehood.'" But surely he must have been aware of the fact that there is also such a thing as *an aorist participle of simultaneous action!* The second view is that of Abbott, *op. cit.*, p. 139.

with falsehood; tell the truth to one another" (Bruce; and cf. Phillips, N.E.B., Williams, Beck, etc.). The reasons, no doubt, are as follows: *a.* it is felt that putting away falsehood and telling the truth are simply two sides of one and the same coin; and *b.* it is also rather apparent that the apostle, on the basis of his previous paragraph, is now beginning to list particular areas in which Christian conduct must reveal itself, one of them being the practice of truthfulness. To most interpreters these facts must have seemed so obvious that in their comments on this passage they do not even discuss the possibility of the opposite view.

Every missionary who has worked for a while with those still living in darkness can testify that not only thinking false thoughts but also definitely telling lies and spreading false rumors is characteristic of the heathen world. For those who had been converted rather recently it must not have been easy to break away from this evil habit. That could well be the reason why Paul, whether directly or indirectly, refers again and again to the necessity of putting a decisive end to the past manner of behavior in this respect, and of adopting an entirely new set of rules. Some, with an appeal to 4:15, 22, 25; 6:14, have even suggested that in and around Ephesus church-members behaved rather dishonestly (see Grosheide, *op. cit.*, p. 69). However that may have been, falsehood and dishonesty are typical of the Gentile way of life (Rom. 1:29) then as now.

The best way to kill the lie is by telling the truth. That is what Paul is actually saying, as by "Speak truth each (of y o u) with his neighbor" he is substantially quoting Zech. 8:16. Especially for those in the congregations addressed who were acquainted with the Old Testament, that is, for the Jewish Christians, the fact that this was a quotation from sacred literature must have added strength to the exhortation. In the opinion of Hodge the word "neighbor," though having the general sense of fellow-man of any creed or nation, here refers to fellow-Christian (*op. cit.*, p. 268); not as if it would be perfectly proper to lie to unbelievers, but because the context demands this interpretation. I believe Hodge is right, the context being: **for we are members of one another.** This recalls 2:13-22; 3:6, 14, 15; 4:1-6, 16, all of which stress the idea that though believers are many, they are also *one,* namely, one body with Christ as head. Lying is not only wrong because it makes light of the intrinsic excellence of the truth, but also because it causes trouble, friction, disunity and sadness in the church. The law of love certainly implies truthfulness.

26, 27. The next specific admonition has to do with such matters as anger and resentment: **Be angry but do not sin.** These words recall Ps. 4:4 (LXX: Ps. 4:5), which the apostle is here applying for his own use. The words should not be interpreted separately, as if the sense were, *a.* "Be sure to be angry once in a while"; and *b.* "do not sin." Much less is it true that all anger is here forbidden. Those who, by means of strange reasoning, favor this "interpretation" (?) do so with an appeal to verse 31, but see on that verse. The sense is simply, "Let not y o u r anger be mixed with sin." Anger as such need not be sinful. It is ascribed even to God (I Kings 11:9; II Kings 17:18; Ps. 7:11; 79:5; 80:4, 5; Heb. 12:29), and to Christ (Ps. 2:12; Mark 3:5; John 2:15-17). In fact, the age in which we are living could use a little more "righteous indignation" against sin of every type. Also, the more angry every believer is with his own sins, the better it will be. However, anger, especially with reference to the neighbor, easily degenerates into hatred and resentment. To love *the sinner* while one hates his *sin* requires a goodly supply of grace. The exclamation, "I cannot stand that fellow," is at times uttered even by one church member with reference to another. It is for that reason that the apostle immediately adds: **let not the sun go down on that angry mood** [129] **of y o u r s.** Having spoken about anger, the apostle now turns to that into which anger may easily degenerate, namely, the spirit of resentment, the angry mood, the sullen countenance that is indicative of hatred and of the unforgiving attitude. The day must not end thus. Before another dawns, nay rather, before the sun even sets — which to the Jew meant the end of one day and the beginning of another — genuine forgiveness must not only have filled the heart but must, if at all possible, have come to open expression so that the neighbor has benefited from its blessing. Phillips, though not really translating, does give the sense of the passage when he paraphrases it as follows: "Never go to bed angry." Continued: . . . **and do not give the devil** [130] **a foothold.** Literally, "And do not give a place to the devil." The devil will quickly seize the opportunity of changing our indignation, whether righteous or unrighteous, into a grievance, a grudge, a nursing of wrath, an unwillingness to forgive. Paul was very conscious of the reality, the power, and the deceitfulness of the devil, as 6:10 shows. What he means, therefore, is that *from the very start* the devil must be resisted (James 4:7). No *place* whatsoever must be given to him, no room to enter or even to stand. There must be no yielding to or compromise with him. He must not be given any opportunity to take advantage of our anger for his own sinister purpose.

28. From the warning against falsehood and the angry mood the apostle proceeds now to that against stealing. He writes: **Let him who steals steal no longer.** He does not say, "Let him that stole" (A.V.) but "Let him who steals." He is probably referring to people who before their conversion were used to enriching themselves by means of petty larceny, etc., and who were

---

[129] By means of this translation both the sense and the sound-similarity of the words used in the original for "anger" and "angry mood" are preserved.

[130] When *didbolos* is preceded by the article it is definitely *"the devil"* who is indicated. As an adjective it is rendered "slanderous (persons)," hence, "slanderers" (I Tim. 3:11; II Tim. 3:3; Titus 2:3). To avoid misunderstanding, therefore, the rendering "the devil" here in 4:27 is required.

now in danger of falling back into defalcations of various types. But must we then assume that there were thieves in the congregations here addressed? My answer is that at least the danger that some would slip back into this sin was very real. It must not be forgotten that some, perhaps many, of these early converts were slaves. Now lack of trustworthiness in matters material was characteristic of slaves, just as even today "servants" in heathen lands are not always honest, but will snitch things away from their employers when the latter happen not to be looking. According to Philem. 18 — a letter written during this same imprisonment and delivered at about the same time — Paul suspected Onesimus, the runaway slave, of having wronged his master in this respect. And after the release from the present (first Roman) imprisonment Paul was going to write to Titus: "Urge slaves to be submissive in every respect to their own masters . . . *not pilfering, but evincing the utmost trustworthiness*" (Titus 2:9, 10). Is it altogether improbable that even the "converted" slave might, in a moment of weakness, say to himself, "My master has left home. This is my opportunity to take something away from him. After all, he owes me much more, for by what right does he exact all this labor from me? Therefore, when I relieve him of some treasure, I am simply depriving him of that to which he has no right"? But we should not think exclusively of slaves. The sin against which Paul issues his warning was and is today, characteristic of heathenism.

What is Paul's solution? He wants the Ephesians to stop stealing and to practice honesty. But he wants more than that. He realizes that back of this sin of stealing lies a more basic fault, namely, *selfishness*. Hence, he strikes at the very root of the evil, for, by turning the attention of the thief, whether actual or potential, away from himself to the needs of other people, he strives to give him a new interest in life, a new joy. So he writes: **but rather let him labor, with his own hands accomplishing what is good, so that he may have something to share with the needy one.** The thief must stop stealing and begin to do some hard, honest *labor*. Paul uses this word *labor* or *toil* in connection with *manual* labor (I Cor. 4:12; II Tim. 2:6; cf. the noun in I Thess. 1:3; 2:9; II Thess. 3:8); and also in connection with *religious* work (Rom. 16:12 twice; I Cor. 15:10; Gal. 4:11; Phil. 2:16; I Thess. 5:12; I Tim. 4:10; 5:17). Here in 4:28 he has reference to manual labor, as the phrase "with his own hands" indicates. By using his hands in honest work, the worker will be accomplishing something that is good instead of doing that which is bad, contrary to God's law. As to working for a living, Paul himself had set an excellent example. Not only did he perform an amount of religious labor, of the highest quality, that is almost beyond belief, but in addition he at times even worked with his own hands in order to supply his own needs and those of others. He was able to say to the Thessalonians, "For y o u remember, brothers, our toil and hardship: by night and by day

219

(we were) working at a trade (or: "working for a living"), in order not to be a burden to any of y o u while we proclaimed to y o u the gospel of God" (I Thess. 2:9; cf. Acts 20:33, 34). For a detailed account of Paul's teaching with respect to *work* and receiving remuneration for it, see N.T.C. on I and II Thessalonians, pp. 65, 66, 201, 202.

Paul stresses the fact that the laborer should think not only of himself but also of his brother, especially of the one who is in need. The apostle himself was a man of tender and far-reaching sympathies (Gal. 6:10). He was "eager to help the poor" (Gal. 2:10). And he actually helped them! In fact, the very missionary tour which had resulted in his present imprisonment had been a benefit-journey in the interest of the Jerusalem poor. He had been gathering funds for the needy in that city. These needy ones were very dear to him, and by encouraging even those churches whose membership was drawn mostly from the Gentile world to extend a helping hand he was at the same time trying to do his part in welding the various churches into a fellowship of love and mutual helpfulness (Acts 24:17; Rom. 15:26; I Cor. 16:1-9; II Cor. 8; 9). In all this he was but following the example of his Lord and Savior, who while still on earth, spoke of the work of mercy again and again and whose pitying heart was deeply moved by the plight of the poor (Matt. 5:7; 19:21; 25:35, 36; Luke 4:18; 6:20; 14:13, 14; 16:19-31; John 13:29).

29. See also on 5:4. From a warning against the improper attitude toward material things Paul proceeds to an admonition against the improper use of the tongue, also in this case setting the positive over against the negative, in the spirit of Rom. 12:21, "Overcome evil with good." He writes: **Let no corrupt speech proceed from y o u r mouth.** Corrupt speech is that which is putrid, rotten; hence also corrupting, defiling, injurious (Matt. 15:18). We may well assume that for many years these rather recent converts to the Christian faith had been living in an impure environment, where foul conversation, at feasts and other social gatherings and parties, had been the stock in trade of everyone present. The change from this toxic environment to the pure and wholesome atmosphere of Christian fellowship must have been nothing short of revolutionary. Even believers who are well advanced in sanctification have at times complained about the fact that it was difficult for them to cleanse their minds entirely from the words and melody of this or that scurrilous drinking song. They hated it, fought against it, were sure at last that they had expelled it forever from their thoughts, and then suddenly there it was again, ready to plague and torture them by means of its reappearance. Thus also certain vile phrases or catch-words, sometimes even profanity, all too common in the pre-conversion period of life, have the habit in unguarded moments to barge right in and to befoul the atmosphere. Think of Simon Peter who, although a disciple of the Lord, "began to curse and to swear" when he thought that his life was in danger (Matt. 26:74).

Here, too, the only remedy, in addition to prayer, is to fill mind and heart with that which is pure and holy, in the spirit of Gal. 5:22 and Phil. 4:8, 9. Accordingly, Paul continues: . . . **but (only) such (speech) as is good for edification,** that is, for "building up the body of Christ" (4:12), **as fits the need** (literally, "edification of the necessity," meaning: edification required by a concrete or specific need), **that it may impart grace to the listeners,** that is, that it may spiritually benefit them. This recalls Col. 4:6, "Let y o u r speech always be gracious, seasoned with salt, so that y o u may know how to answer each individual." See also Col. 3:16.

We notice an interesting parallel between verses 25, 28, and 29. In each case the apostle urges the addressed *to be a blessing* for those with whom they have daily contact. Merely *refraining from* falsehood, stealing, and corrupt speech will never do. Christianity is not a mere "don't" religion, and believers must not be content to be mere zeros. Instead, they should copy the example of their Master, whose words were so filled with grace that the multitudes were amazed (Luke 4:22). "A word in due season, how good it is!" (Prov. 15:23).

30. When the apostle warns against ill behavior and urges Christian conduct upon all the addressed, he is never forgetting about all the "interested" parties. He has already mentioned the neighbor, the devil, the needy one, and the listeners (verses 25, 27, 28, and 29). It does not surprise us, therefore, that he now refers to one more interested party, *most interested indeed,* namely, the Holy Spirit. He writes: **And do not grieve the Holy Spirit of God in whom y o u were sealed for the day of redemption.** It is said at times that the church has failed to do full justice to the doctrine of the Holy Spirit; that it has neglected to bestow upon him the attention given to the Father and to the Son. There may be truth in this. As for Paul, however, he has no share in this blame. The term "the Holy Spirit" occurs about thirty times in his epistles, if we include such synonymous appellatives as "Spirit of God," "Spirit of Jesus Christ," etc. In addition I have counted at least seventy instances in which I, for one, would interpret the term *pneuma* (occurring without the adjective "holy") as referring to the third person of the Holy Trinity. On that subject, however, there is some difference of opinion among commentators. Be that as it may, the epistle to the Ephesians mentions the Holy Spirit again and again, using the very term (1:13; 4:30) or simply the designation: "the Spirit" (1:17; 2:18, 22; 3:5, 16; 4:3, 4; 5:18; 6:17, 18). In most of these cases there is general agreement that the reference is to the Paraclete.

The reason for this frequency of occurrence is obvious: Paul wishes to impress upon us that apart from God we cannot be saved; that is, that whatever good there is in us has its origin in the Holy Spirit. He both imparts life and sustains it. He causes it to develop and to reach its ultimate destination. It is he, therefore, who is the Author of every Christian virtue, every good fruit. Hence, whenever the believer pollutes his soul by any deceitful, vengeful, covetous, or filthy thought or suggestion, he is *grieving* the Holy Spirit. This is all the more true because it is the Spirit that dwells within the hearts of God's children, making them his temple, his sanctuary (2:22; I Cor. 3:16, 17; 6:19). By means of every evil imagination, cogitation, or motivation that indwelling and sanctifying Spirit is therefore, as it were, cut to the heart. Besides, not only does the Spirit *save* us but he also fills us with the joy, the assurance, of salvation; for, as was made clear earlier, and as is repeated in substance here in 4:30, it was "in" him ("in connection with," hence also "by means of," him) that we were *"sealed* for the day of redemption," that great day of the consummation of all things, when our deliverance from the effects of sin will be completed. It is the day of Christ's return, when our lowly body, refashioned so that it will have a form like Christ's glorious body, will rejoin our redeemed soul in order that in soul and body the entire victorious multitude may inhabit the new heaven and earth to glorify God forever and ever. The very meditation on the fulfilment of this hope should have a purifying effect on us (I John 3:2, 3). For further explanation see on 1:13, 14; cf. Luke 21:28; Rom. 8:23. Hence, reversion to pagan attitudes and practices is a sign of base ingratitude. How this must *grieve* the indwelling Spirit! We may call this a highly anthropomorphic expression, and so it is, both here and in Isa. 63:10 from which it is borrowed. It is, however, in a sense, a most comforting anthropomorphism, for it cannot fail to remind us of "the love of the Spirit" (Rom. 15:30), who "yearns for us even unto jealous envy" (James 4:5). That is also the context in Isaiah. Read Isa. 63:10 in connection with the verse which precedes it. To be sure, "grieving the Spirit" may not be as strong a term as "resisting" the Spirit (Acts 7:51); which, in turn, is not as trenchant as "quenching the Spirit" (I Thess. 5:19). Nevertheless, one step in the wrong direction easily leads to the next. Let the Ephesians, and all those down the centuries for whom the epistle was intended, take this to heart! Note also with what emphasis the Comforter's full name is spelled out: "the Holy Spirit of God," or, even more literally, "the Spirit, the Holy One, of God," with special emphasis on his holiness. The stress is both on his majesty and on his sanctifying power. He is "holy" and this not only as being spotlessly sinless in himself, but also as the very Source of holiness for all those in whose hearts he deigns to dwell!

31. Paul now returns once more to the sins of the tongue (cf. verses 25 and 29 above). Six specific items are mentioned, as he continues: **Let all bitterness and anger and wrath and brawling and slander be put away from y o u, along with all malice.** *Bitterness* is the disposition of the person with a tongue sharp as an arrow, keen as a razor. He resents his neighbor, and so he "needles" him, is ever ready to "fly off the handle" with a reply that bites or stings. *Anger* or *fury* (Latin: *furor*), is a strong feeling of an-

tagonism which is expressed in the tumultuous outburst, the hot retort. As here used, occurring in the evil company of words like *bitterness* and *brawling* (contrary to its use in verse 26) , it is potential murder (Matt. 5:21, 22) . *Wrath* (Latin: *ira*) is settled indignation, when the heart is like a roaring furnace. *Brawling* (cf. Acts 23:9) is the violent outburst of the person who has completely lost his temper and begins to yell at others. *Slander* or *reviling* is abusive speech, whether directed against God or against man.[131] This catalogue of the evil use of the tongue is summarized in the words "along with all malice." *Malice* is not merely "mischief" but, in general, the evil inclination of the mind, the perversity or baseness of disposition that even takes delight in inflicting hurt or injury on one's fellowmen. "Let all of these things be put away from y o u," says Paul by the inspiration of the Holy Spirit.

32. Now, in the final analysis, the putting away of the aforementioned evil dispositions, words, and actions can be accomplished only by the acquisition and development of the opposite virtues. Accordingly, turning once more to positive exhortations, the apostle states: **And be kind to each other, tender-hearted.** This may be compared with Col. 3:12, 13: "Put on, therefore, as God's elect, holy and beloved, a heart of compassion, kindness . . . , forgiving each other if anyone have a complaint against anyone. Just as the Lord has forgiven y o u, so do y o u also." *Kindness* is Spirit-imparted *goodness* of heart, the very opposite of the *malice* or *badness* mentioned in verse 31. The early Christians by means of kindness commended themselves to others (II Cor. 6:6) . God, too, is kind (Rom. 2:4; cf. 11:22) , and we are admonished to become like him in this respect (Luke 6:35) . When the kind person hears a piece of malicious gossip, he does not run to the telephone to let others in on the delectable tidbit. When someone's faults are pointed out to him, he tries, if he can at all do so in honesty, to offset these failings by pointing out the criticized individual's good qualities. Kindness marks the man who has taken to heart I Cor. 13:4. *Tenderheartedness* (cf. I Peter 3:8 and "the heart of compassion" of Col. 3:12) indicates a very deep feeling, "a yearning with the deeply-felt affection of Christ Jesus." [132] Paul adds: **forgiving one another, just as God in Christ forgave y o u.** Colossians says, "just as *the Lord*"; Ephesians, "just as *God in Christ*." There is no essential

---

[131] The Greek word used is *blasphemy.* But in Greek this word has a somewhat broader meaning than in English. While in our language it refers to abusive language with respect to God or things religious, that is, to *defiant irreverence,* in the original it refers to insults directed either against God or against men. In the present instance, as the context indicates, the latter is clearly meant: scornful and insolent language directed against a neighbor, slander, defamation, detraction.
[132] The tenderhearted person has *"good or strong bowels"* that is, those that are the seat of, or affected by, deep and powerful feelings of love and pity. That indicates the derivation of the word here used in the original. As to the problem in connection with this use of the term "bowels" see N.T.C. on Philippians, p. 58, footnote 39.

difference. Father, Son, and Holy Spirit are one. They co-operate in all of these activities that concern our salvation. To forgive "just as God in Christ" forgave means: just as freely, generously, wholeheartedly, spontaneously, and eagerly. For a justification of this interpretation see such passages as Matt. 18:21-27, 35 and Luke 23:34. Moreover, all the injuries that *we* have ever suffered because of the ill-will of our fellow-men can never be compared with the abuse *he,* the sinless One, endured: being spit upon, maligned, crowned with thorns, crucified. Yet he forgave! In doing this he left us *an example* (I Peter 2:21-25).

But he did more than this. He also left us a *motive* for exercising forgiveness. Having been forgiven so much, should not we forgive? See again Matt. 18:21-35. That example and that motive, however, relate to more than our duty *to forgive.* They touch the entire broad area of *love,* of which the exercise of forgiveness is only one manifestation, though a very important one. In *every* area of life love should manifest itself, the love patterned after, and motivated by, God's love in Christ. Hence, Paul continues: **5:1, 2.**[133] **Be therefore imitators of God, as beloved children.** Again and again Jesus and the apostles emphasized that believers should strive to be imitators of God. Now to people who are living in an age which proudly proclaims, *"We* have conquered space," and which drags God down to the level of a benign Santa Claus, it may not seem at all outrageous to strive to *imitate* God. But if, by the grace of the really living God, the words, "Be still and know that I am God!" have retained some meaning for us, this crisp command to imitate him may baffle us. We stand in awe before his majesty. How can we imitate him whom we cannot even fathom? With Zophar we are inclined to say, "Canst thou by searching find out God? Canst thou find out the Almighty to perfection? It is high as heaven; what canst thou do? Deeper than Sheol; what canst thou know?" (Job 11:7, 8). With Isaiah we see the Lord sitting upon a throne, high and lifted up, and we hear the voices of the flying seraphim, as they cover their faces and their

---

[133] Whether with Lenski, etc., we should begin an entirely new section here, to coincide with the chapter-division, on the basis of the circumstance that Paul's "therefore" often introduces something new (4:1, 17; 5:15; and so also 5:1), or should rather, with Bruce, Hodge, Scott, and many others, include 5:1, 2 with the preceding verses (so that, for example, 4:25—5:2 would form one paragraph), is largely a matter of choice. A good argument can be advanced for either position. The presence of "therefore" in 5:1 is not conclusive for the former of these two positions, for that word by no means always introduces a new paragraph (see 5:7). Also, why should it be necessary to accept a wide gap between 4:32 and 5:1, but an easy transition between 5:2 and 5:3? The new thought introduced in 5:1 is, after all, a logical conclusion and further development of that expressed in 4:32. Simpson remarks, "There is no real break here" (*op. cit.,* p. 114). But with respect to 5:3 Grosheide states, "With the mention of *immorality* the apostle arrives at an entirely new subject." One good way to treat 5:1, 2 may well be that followed by several exegetes, namely, to regard it as a sub-paragraph within the paragraph 4:25—5:2.

feet, and are crying continually, "Holy, holy, holy is Jehovah of hosts; the fulness of the earth is his glory." And we, too, answer, "Woe is me! for I am undone; because I am a man of unclean lips . . . for my eyes have seen the King, Jehovah of hosts" (Isa. 6:1-5). Rather than even faintly to imagine that we, creatures of the dust, would ever be able *to imitate God,* we feel like falling down upon our knees and saying, with Simon Peter, "Depart from me; for I am a sinful man, O Lord" (Luke 5:8). And we understand why John, when similarly overcome, said, "When I saw him, I fell at his feet as one dead" (Rev. 1:17).

It is only in that spirit of awe and humble reverence that we can properly study this glorious theme of "the imitation of God." It is only then that the Lord will lay his right hand upon us and say, "Fear not!" Obedience to the command to imitate him is, after all, possible. This is true for the following reasons: *a.* we are created as his image; *b.* his enabling Spirit dwells within us; and *c.* by his regenerating and transforming grace we have become his *children,* that is, *imitators.* To be sure, we cannot imitate God by creating a universe and caring for it day by day, or by devising a method of satisfying the demands of justice and of mercy in saving men from the pit into which they have cast themselves, or by raising the dead, or by creating a new heaven and earth. *But in our own finite way we can and must imitate him; that is, we must copy his love.*

It is amazing how often Jesus and the apostles emphasized that believers should strive to be imitators of *God* (Matt. 5:43-48; Luke 6:35; I John 4:10, 11), and of *Christ,* which essentially amounts to the same thing (John 13:34; 15:12; Rom. 15:2, 3, 7; II Cor. 8:7-9; Phil. 2:3-8; Eph. 5:25; Col. 3:13; I Peter 2:21-24; I John 3:16; a list of passages by no means complete). By adding that those addressed should do so as *children,* the idea is greatly strengthened, as if to say, "Are not children great imitators, and are not y o u God's children?" Moreover, the modifier "beloved" adds even more weight to this admonition, for, other things being equal, it is exactly *the child who is the object of love* that will be the most eager imitator of those who love him. Paul adds: **and walk in love,** that is, let love be the very tenor of y o u r life. Let it characterize all y o u r thoughts, words, and deeds. For *walking* see also 2:10; 4:1, 17; 5:8, 15. Continued: **just as Christ loved y o u.** Not just anything which men may wish to dignify with the name "love" should be the pattern for our thought and conduct, but very distinctly Christ's own purposeful, self-sacrificing love must be our example. And, to be even more specific, there is added: **and gave himself up for** [134] **us.** Here

---

[134] In connection with the preposition ὑπέρ two extremes must be avoided: *a.* to say that ὑπέρ = ἀντί. Though, on the basis of the occurrence of ὑπέρ in such passages as Gal. 2:20; 3:13 and in ancient letters in which one individual signs *for* another, this absolute identity of meaning has been maintained, it is extremely doubtful whether the two prepositions *as such* ever have *exactly* the same force. Moreover, we do not need Eph. 5:2 to prove the substitutionary atonement. Matt.

it must not escape our attention that when Paul urges the addressed to imitate *God* he, in one and the same breath, illustrates this love of *God* by directing our attention to that which *Christ* had done for us. This surely indicates not only that Father and Son are the same in essence but also that what the Father does he does in connection with the Son (4:32) and that neither loves us less than the other.

In his great love Christ *gave himself up,* surrendering himself willingly, to his enemies, and thus to his Father. This surrender is genuine. It was not forced upon him (John 10:11, 15). Among those for whom Christ had thus yielded himself as an offering for sin was also the great persecutor Paul. The thought of Christ's great love grips him to the extent that he changes the pronouns, so that y o u ("just as Christ loved y o u") now becomes *us* ("and gave himself up for us"). The apostle never writes in the abstract. Compare Gal. 2:20: "the Son of God who loved *me,* and gave himself up *for me."* See also Gal. 1:16. It is this spirit of giving oneself sacrificially and voluntarily which believers are urged to imitate.

The voluntary self-sacrifice of Christ during the entire period of his humiliation and especially on the cross is here called **an offering and a sacrifice** [135] to God. It was an *offering* for he willingly *brought* it (Isa. 53:10). It was a *sacrifice,* and as such could well remind one of the *fumes* rising from the altar when the burnt-offering was consumed whole, symbolizing *entire surrender to God.* But though the word used in the original does not always

---

20:28; Mark 10:45; John 1:29; Acts 20:28; I Cor. 6:20; Eph. 1:7; Heb. 9:28; I Peter 1:18, 19; 2:24 teach this clearly enough, especially when interpreted in the light of Exod. 12:13; Lev. 1:4; 16:20-22; 17:11; and Isa. 53. To be avoided also, however, is *b.* to deny that, in the light of all of Scripture, ὑπέρ, as here used, *implies* Christ's substitutionary death. The vicarious death of Christ is certainly *implied* here, for, according to the doctrine of Scripture throughout, in what other way could Christ have died *for* us — that is, *for our benefit, in our interest* — than by dying *in our stead?*

[135] The word προσφορά is very general in meaning. It might include peace, meal, and drink offerings such as were offered by (or *for*) those who wished to be released of a temporary Nazirite vow (Acts 21:26). It could also refer to alms or gifts to the poor, of whatever character (Acts 24:17), or even to the offering up of the Gentiles, now Christians, to God (Rom. 15:16). In Heb. 10:10, 14 it refers to Christ's offering of himself for sin, once for all.

The word θυσία, too, is very comprehensive in connotation. Its association with bloody sacrifices or with the altar upon which these are offered is common (Mark 12:33; Luke 2:24; Luke 13:1; Acts 7:42; I Cor. 10:18). Thus, it also suits Christ's bloody self-sacrifice upon the cross (Heb. 7:27; 10:12; cf. 10:27). But its use is not limited to bloody offerings or to anything that is consumed on the altar. Abel's offering was associated with blood; not that of Cain. Yet the same word θυσία refers to both of these offerings or sacrifices (Heb. 11:4). This is also the word used to describe the gift which Paul received from the Philippians by the hand of Epaphroditus (Phil. 4:18). In Phil. 2:17; Heb. 13:15, 16; and I Peter 2:5 the word is used in a definitely figurative sense. Christian life and conduct, springing from faith, the sacrifice of praise, goodness and generosity, all such things, when offered to God in the proper spirit of humility and gratitude, are *sacrifices.*

refer to sacrifices consumed on the altar but may also have a more general reference (for which see footnote 135), we learn from other passages of Scripture (e.g., Matt. 26:36-46; 27:45, 46; II Cor. 5:21; cf. Isa. 53) that as to his human nature Christ was indeed consumed by the wrath of God in the sense that "the weight of our sins and of the wrath of God pressed out of him the bloody sweat in the garden" and caused him to suffer "the deepest reproach and anguish of hell, in body and soul, on the tree of the cross, when he cried out with a loud voice: My God, my God, why hast thou forsaken me." Thus he had accomplished his task and had fulfilled the prophecies, with special reference now to Ps. 40:6 (LXX: Ps. 39:7, 8). In that passage the same two words, *offering* and *sacrifice,* are used, but now in reverse order, *sacrifice* and *offering,* in connection with the Messiah's offering of himself to God: *"Sacrifice and offering* thou hast no delight in . . . . Then said I, Lo, I am come; in the roll of the book it is written of me." By the author of the epistle to the Hebrews that passage is appropriately applied to Christ and his self-sacrifice (Heb. 10:5-7). In connection, then, with this offering and sacrifice to God, as an example and motive for us, Paul adds: **for a fragrant odor;** literally, "an odor of a sweet smell." Cf. Exod. 29:18; Ezek. 20:41; Phil. 4:18. The meaning is that this offering and sacrifice *was* — and *is* in our case, when we imitate the spirit in which Christ presented it — well-pleasing to God. Every deed done out of love and gratitude to God, whether it be Abel's (Gen. 4:4), or Noah's (Gen. 8:21), or that of the Israelites of old (Lev. 1:9, 13, 17) or that of new dispensation believers who dedicate themselves to God (II Cor. 2:15, 16), pleases God. Unique among them all is *Christ's* self-sacrifice. Yet, the latter's spirit must be reflected every day and every hour in the hearts and lives of his followers,[136] for a fragrant odor.

c. 5:3-14
"Y o u were formerly darkness, but now y o u are light
in the Lord; as children of light ever walk."

The Glorious Renewal of which Paul is speaking in this entire section (4:17–6:9) calls for self-sacrifice instead of self-indulgence. Since in the preceding verses great emphasis was placed on *self-sacrifice* in imitation of Christ, the attention is now shifted to its very opposite: *self-indulgence.* Stating it differently, the admonition to "walk in love" is followed here by the condemnation of love's perversion. Paul minces no words as he proceeds: **3. But immorality and impurity of any kind, or greed, let it not even be mentioned among y o u.** The list of vices which begins here may be compared with similar ones in Paul's other epistles (Rom. 1:18-32; I Cor. 5:9-11; 6:9, 10; Gal. 5:19-21; Col. 3:5-9; I Thess. 4:3-7; I Tim. 1:9, 10; II Tim. 3:2-5;

---

[136] On the imitation of Christ see also Willis P. De Boer, *The Imitation of Paul, An Exegetical Study,* doctoral dissertation submitted to the Free University of Amsterdam; Kampen, 1962.

and Titus 3:3). Christ, he alone, supplies the *example, motive,* and *power* to overcome them. Verse 3 centers around sexual perversion of every description. Though *immorality* (cf. Matt. 5:32; 15:19; 19:19; John 8:41; I Thess. 4:3) refers basically to unlawful sexual intercourse, it probably includes illicit, clandestine relationships of every description. Evil in the sexual realm was, and is today, a characteristic feature of paganism. It is often closely associated with idolatry. That even those who had turned to Christ had not thoroughly shaken off this sin is clear from I Cor. 5:1 ff. Is it also implied in the present epistle: 5:27? *Impurity* or *uncleanness,* not only in deeds but also in words, thoughts, intents of the heart, desires, and passions, is here condemned. The phrase "of any kind" covers a very large territory! For *greed* (cf. 4:19) the apostle uses a word which means *over-reaching.* Greed is *selfishness.* It characterizes the money-grubber. Nevertheless, in the present connection, because of its close association with *immorality* and *impurity,* it may well apply especially to ravenous self-assertion in matters of sex, at the expense of others: the going beyond what is proper and defrauding the brother (cf. I Thess. 4:6 where the related verb is used in a similar connection). "Let it not even be mentioned among y o u," says Paul, meaning: so far should y o u be removed from the sin of this type that the very suspicion of its existence among y o u should be banished once and for all. He cannot have meant that sex must never be discussed, and that warnings with respect to the evil of immorality and its attendant sins must never be heard, for he himself is at this very moment discussing it and issuing such a warning. With respect to the desirable absence of transgression in this area Paul adds: **as is fitting among saints.** Are not "saints" (cf. 1:1) those who have been set apart by God to be his very own? Have they not, by the power of the sanctifying Spirit, dedicated themselves completely to their Lord; hence also to a new walk of life?

4. Among the sins that should not even require mention are **also filthiness and silly talk or wittiness in telling coarse jokes.** *Filthiness* or *shamefulness* covers more than "shameful language" (Col. 3:8). It includes *any* thought, imagination, desire, word, or deed of which a believer who is sensitive to the demands of God's holy law and who views himself as living constantly in his presence would be ashamed. *Silly talk* is the kind of conversation one could expect to hear from the lips of a fool or of a drunkard. The next term is hard to translate. Judged on the basis of its derivation it is very innocent, for it means literally "that which turns easily." The closest to it as to etymological significance would be *versatility;* for this, too, has reference to turning easily. The versatile person is able to turn with ease from one subject to another, being at home in all of them. Similarly, the word which the apostle employs was often used in a favorable sense, to indicate the nimble-witted individual. However, it is also possible for certain speakers *to move very easily* into the mire of unbecoming expressions. They seem to have a garbage

can type of mind, and every serious topic of conversation reminds them of an off-color jest or anecdote. The word used in 5:4 has therefore come to mean *coarse jesting, wittiness in telling coarse jokes*. There need be nothing wrong with a joke. Good humor is what everybody needs. But the kind to which Paul refers should be thoroughly avoided. Regarding such practices the apostle adds: **which things are improper.** They are improper because they are *not worthy of the calling with which believers were called.* See on 4:1. What, then, is the remedy for the vices mentioned? The apostle answers this question by stating: **but rather the expression of thankfulness.** See further on 5:20. When mind and heart are centered on "all things bright and beautiful" which God grants to us and still has in store for us, the interest in squalid indecency will vanish. So the apostle places *thankfulness* over against *wittiness*. This translation not only gives the sense but preserves, to some extent, the wordplay of the original (*eucharistía* over against *eutrapelía*). *Clarion praise* should be substituted for the *clever* (but vulgar) *phrase*. Continued: **5. For of this y o u can be very sure, that no immoral or impure person or greedy individual — which is the same as an idolater — has any inheritance in the kingdom of Christ and of God.** The apostle wishes to emphasize this very important point, namely, that *immorality* and *salvation* are opposites. Hence, he says what literally could almost be translated, "For this y o u know, knowing." However, since in the original the finite verb and the participle which follows it are not forms of the same word, a better *literal* rendering would be, "For this y o u know, recognizing." Many translators and interpreters, though differing in their views of this expression, have, however, felt that the reason why the apostle makes use of these *two* words where ordinarily *one* would have sufficed is that he wished to lay special stress on what he is about to say. If we accept this position, the rendering would be: "For of this y o u can be very sure." [137] The fact of which the Ephesians can be very sure is this, that no one who practices the sins mentioned in verse 3 (and elaborated in verse 4) has any

---

[137] With Robertson, *Word Pictures*, Vol. IV, p. 542, I regard ἴστε to be not imperative but present indicative. His rendering is, "Y o u know recognizing by your own experience." Implied in this translation is the fact that basically the finite verb refers to a knowledge by intuition or by reflection, the participle to a knowledge by observation and/or experience. Hodge (*op. cit.*, p. 285) believed that the finite verb referred to what Paul had said in verse 3, the participle to what follows it in verse 5. Though this separation may appear somewhat unnatural, yet the very wording of verse 5 proves that Paul reverts to what he had said in verse 3. Still others refer to the familiar Hebrew idiom according to which two forms of the same word occurring in immediate sequence strengthen the idea that is being expressed: Thus, "dying thou shalt die" means "thou shalt surely die"; cf. "blessing I will bless" and "multiplying I will multiply." However, the idiom used here in 5:5 is not *exactly* the same, since the finite verb and the participle are forms of *different* verbs. As many translators see it, the combination of the two Greek forms so closely related in meaning could still convey an emphasis similar to that of the Hebrew idiom. If not, then Robertson's more literal rendering must be regarded as correct.

inheritance in the kingdom of Christ and of God. One of these sinful practices is greed. That calling a person "a greedy individual" is the same as calling him "an idolater" (cf. Col. 3:5) is clear even on the surface, for such a person is worshiping someone else than the true and living God. That someone else is *himself*. He has made of himself an idol and is therefore an idolater. To a Jew, like Paul and some of the Ephesians, there was no greater sin than that of idolatry (cf. I John 5:21).

Though conditions among those addressed cannot have been very bad morally or spiritually — for Paul praises the Ephesian believers in no uncertain terms (1:15) and has nothing to say by way of direct adverse criticism —, yet the impression is left that there was still considerable room for improvement. The danger of falling into the errors of licentious gnosticism was never far removed. This seems to have been especially the case in Asia Minor. A few years later, during his second Roman imprisonment, Paul was going to remind Timothy of this peril (II Tim. 3:1-9). Timothy was probably carrying on a ministry at Ephesus at that time. John, too, writing to people in this same region, would have to combat this nefarious error (I John 3:4-10; Rev. 2:6, 14, 15, 20). See also II Peter 2:12-19 and Jude 4, 8, 11, and 19.

With a pastor's loving heart, therefore, Paul issues his warning. No one who continues to practice the pagan vices, whether because he is following old habit and the course of least resistance or else because he has adopted a reasoned excuse (Rom. 6:1), has a share in the one and only kingdom, namely, that of Christ and of God. Cf. Rev. 21:27; 22:15. It is, of course, impossible to speak about the kingdom of Christ without speaking about the kingdom of God. In principle this kingdom is already present in the hearts and lives of God's children. One day it will be theirs in full measure (1:18; 3:6). See N.T.C. on Colossians and Philemon, pp. 63, 64, especially footnote 47. Continued: **6. Let no one deceive y o u with empty words.** Cf. Col. 2:4, 8; I Tim. 2:14; James 1:26. "Empty" words are those that are void of truth and filled with error. When heeded they will prove the sinner's downfall: **for it is because of these things that the wrath of God comes upon the sons of disobedience.** Cf. Col. 3:6. By means of what has been called "a prophetic present tense" (cf. John 4:21; 14:3) Paul stresses the fact that the coming of the wrath of God, to be visited upon those who live in the sins mentioned in verses 3-5 and who listen to empty words assuring them that all is well, is so certain that it is as if that wrath had already arrived, and *in principle* it actually has arrived. These sinister practices attract God's displeasure like a fully lit up enemy target attracts bombs. The wrath spoken of here, though in a sense already present, is also ever on the way, until on the day of the great consummation of all things it will be fully revealed (cf. John 3:36; Rom. 2:5-11; II Thess. 1:8-10; Rev. 14:9-12), for "sons of disobedience" are "children of wrath" (see on 2:2).

It should not escape our attention, however, that even this stern warning has repentance as its object, as the tender admonition which immediately follows in verses 7 and 8 clearly shows. See also verses 10, 14-17; and cf. Rev. 2:16, 21, 22; 3:19; 9:20, 21. As a father pleads with his children whom he dearly loves, so this prisoner of Christ Jesus, a hero of the faith who is facing the possibility of a death sentence and therefore weighs every word, continues: **7. Therefore do not be their partners,** "fellow-sharers" (cf. 3:6) in their sin, their guilt, and their everlasting punishment. Cf. II Cor. 6:4-18. Meaning: in the light of God's marvelous love and mercy in Christ, the upward call that was extended to y o u, y o u r own profession of faith, and the wrath of God coming upon the sons of disobedience, think on y o u r way, walk in paths of light and be done forever with the works of darkness. Continued: **8. for y o u were formerly darkness.** In earlier days (2:1-3, 11, 12; 4:14, 17) the Ephesians had been darkness. Cf. 4:18, "darkened in their understanding, alienated from the life of God," etc. Not only had they been *in* darkness as in an evil environment, but they themselves had been part of that realm. *The darkness had been in them,* namely, the darkness of lack of the true knowledge of God (II Cor. 4:4, 6), depravity (Acts 26:18), and despondency (Isa. 9:1, 2). Continued: **but now (y o u are) light in the Lord.** Now they belong to the realm of light, for they now have the true knowledge of God (Ps. 36:9), righteousness and holiness (Eph. 4:24), happiness (Ps. 97:11; Isa. 9:1-7). It is only "in the Lord," that is, in vital connection with him, that they are now light. Moreover, since now they are light, they have also become light-transmitters: from them light radiates forth to all those with whom they come into contact. Ever since Jesus, "the light of the world" (John 8:12), entered their hearts (II Cor. 4:6), they, too, in their own small way, had become "the light of the world" (Matt. 5:14). In their entire conduct they reflect Christ, as the moon reflects the sun. Hence, **as children of light ever walk.** Here is another and beautiful Semitism: they are now, by God's grace, the very offspring of him who is the light. No longer are they "children of wrath" (2:3) or "sons of disobedience" (2:2; 5:6), but "children of light." Then let them be consistent. Let them in their daily life *be and constantly remain* true to what in principle they have become. Let them walk and keep on walking as children of light; that is, let the true knowledge of God and of his will be their standard constantly; let righteousness and holiness characterize all their attitudes, words, and actions; and let the joy of salvation be the very tenor of their lives. On "walking" see also 2:10; 4:1, 17; 5:2, 15. That this is what they are and how they should walk is evident, as the apostle brings out in a parenthetical statement: **9. — for the fruit of light** [138] **(consists) in all goodness and righteousness and truth —.** How does

---

[138] The variant "fruit of the Spirit," though supported not only by many late and definitely inferior manuscripts but even by the valuable p[46], is probably an assimilation to Gal. 5:22.

one know whether or not he is walking as a child of light? The answer is that light bears fruit, and this fruit will supply the needed evidence (Matt. 5:16; 7:20). The *qualities* of heart and life from which good works proceed are to be considered light, fruit. Paul mentions *all goodness,* a very general term, the opposite of "all malice" (4:31). Such goodness is Spirit-created moral and spiritual excellence of every description. Another way of looking at this goodness is to call it *righteousness,* the joy in doing what is right in the eyes of God, walking the straight path and never deviating from it. And still another description is *truth:* integrity, reliability, over against the sham, falseness, and hypocrisy that characterized the old way of life in which the Ephesians had formerly walked (4:14, 25; 5:6).

Returning now to the main clause of verse 8b, "As children of light ever walk," Paul adds: **10. verifying what is pleasing to the Lord.** Meaning: by walking constantly as children of light, and thus producing the fruit of light, y o u will, by y o u r very attitudes and action, be *verifying or proving* [139] what is pleasing to the Lord. That is Paul's glorious answer to the question, "How can I know whether I am really a child of God, one with whom God is pleased?" The answer amounts to this: "Do not worry or speculate or philosophize or argue. Just go right ahead and do the will of God as he has revealed it. The proof or evidence for which y o u are looking will then be abundantly supplied to y o u. Y o u will have the verification in y o u r heart. The assurance or peace will be distilled into y o u r life as the dewdrops are distilled and impearled upon the leaves." This is Scripture's answer throughout (Rom. 8:16; 12:1, 2; II Cor. 5:9; Phil. 4:6, 7, 18; Col. 1:10; and II Peter 1:5-11). Since Jesus as the world's light, was ever walking in the light and doing the will of his Father (John 4:34; 5:30; 6:38), it is not at all surprising that more than once he was given the assurance that the Father *was pleased* with him (Matt. 3:17; 17:5; cf. 12:18). And, although in the present life we, his followers, should not expect to hear what he heard, namely, an audible voice from heaven, the Holy Spirit will nevertheless impart that assurance also to us when we walk in the light.

Another tender warning, the negative side of what in verses 8-10 was expressed in positive terms, follows, an admonition which recalls verse 7. Paul lovingly pleads: **11. And do not take any part in the unfruitful works of darkness.** By works of darkness are meant such things as immorality, impurity, greed, filthiness, silly talk, etc. (5:3, 4), and also those mentioned in 4:25-32; briefly, *any and all* works belonging to the realm of depravity and inspired by its prince. Such works are called *unfruitful.* They are sterile

---

[139] The verb δοκιμάζω has various meanings: *a. to put to the test, examine* (I Cor. 11:28; II Cor. 13:5); *b. to prove or verify* by means of testing (I Cor. 3:13; I Peter 1:7); and *c. to approve* (I Cor. 16:3). Here the second meaning best suits the context.

in the sense that they do not glorify God, do not win the neighbor for Christ, and do not bring inner peace or satisfaction. Note that Paul recognizes no twilight zone. Although according to Scripture there are degrees of sinfulness and also degrees of holiness, nevertheless, there is no region of the shades. A person is either a believer or an unbeliever. Works belong either to the light or to darkness. Those who have sworn allegiance to the Ruler of the realm of light *must take no part whatever* in the empty, futile, thoroughly disappointing, works of darkness.

Does this mean now that the Ephesians should withdraw themselves from the men of the world; that they should become hermits and move as far as possible away from wicked men? Not at all! Though they are not *of* the world, yet they are *in* the world and have a mission to fulfil. Says Paul: **but instead even expose** [140] **them**, that is, these unfruitful works of darkness. Those who belong to the realm of light cannot be neutral with respect to the work of darkness. Compromise, too, is definitely ruled out. For example, when God says, "Worship me alone," and another says, "Worship idols," it will not do to try to worship Jehovah under the symbolism of images which are on the way to becoming idols. The sin of Jeroboam was an abomination to Jehovah (I Kings 12:25-33). Sin must be *exposed*. One is not being "nice" to a wicked man by endeavoring to make him feel what a fine fellow he is. The cancerous tumor must be removed, not humored. It is not really an act of love to smooth things over as if the terrible evil committed by those still living in the realm of darkness is not so bad after all. With respect to this Paul continues: **12. for the things done by them in secret it is a shame even to mention.**

But if one feels ashamed even to mention the horrible deeds of those who live in darkness, how then can he expose these deeds? Lenski's answer is, "To state them in our reproof is shameful not for us who make the statement in reproof, but for those who engage in these works" (*op. cit.*, p. 609). This explanation, however, impresses me as being unnatural. I wonder whether any unbiased reader of Scripture would ever have drawn that conclusion. When the apostle tells the Ephesians *to expose* the works of darkness, does he not mean that *they* (and all others for whom the letter was intended throughout the course of history) should expose them? So when he now adds in one breath that it is a shame *even to mention* these secret practices, is not the obvious meaning: "*Y o u* should expose them, for they are so very wicked, that *for anyone* even to mention them is shameful"? But how were they able to expose them and yet not mention them? The answer which is clear from the entire context is that by means of a life of

---

[140] For a discussion of the verb ἐλέγχω and a tabulation of its seventeen New Testament occurrences see N.T.C. on the Gospel according to John, Vol. II, pp. 324, 325, footnote 200.

goodness and righteousness and truth (verse 9) they must reveal what a vast contrast there is between the works of those who walk in the light and the works of those who walk in darkness. There are sins so altogether repulsive that it is better by far never to mention them. Conditions in the pagan world of Asia Minor seem to have been particularly bad. Roland Allen, in his work, *Missionary Methods: St. Paul's or Ours?*, London, third edition, 1953, p. 49, remarks, "If the moral atmosphere of Greece was bad, in Asia Minor it was even worse." Continued: **13. But when all these (wicked practices) are exposed by the light** [141] **they are made visible.** Meaning: when, *by means of contrast with the conduct of believers as "children of light,"* the terrible deeds of wickedness that mark "the sons of disobedience" are thus exposed, these horrible practices are shown up for what they really are. That this is true is shown by the rule expressed in the following statement: **for everything that is made visible is light;** that is, *whatever,* whether attitudes, words, practices, etc., is made manifest by having been thus contrasted loses its hidden character, takes on the nature of light, and is seen for what it really is.

In verses 11-13 the emphasis has been on *deeds* rather than on the *doers.* It was the deeds that were exposed. However, it is readily understandable that when wicked men's evil deeds are thus laid bare, the doers are indirectly reproved. They are made to see how great their sins and miseries are; hence, how desperately they need a radical change of life. The transition to the next line is therefore very natural: **14. Therefore he says:**

> **"Awake, sleeper,**
> **And arise from the dead,**
> **And Christ will shine on you."**

There is no sound reason here to interpret "he says" in any other way than in 4:8; hence, "God says," for the apostle is obviously referring to these words as authoritative. What is their source? Among the many answers given the two most popular ones are: *a.* Isa. 60:1 (and perhaps certain somewhat similar passages, as Isa. 9:2; 26:19; 52:1) ; *b.* an early Christian hymn. As to the first, favored by Calvin, Findlay, Hodge, and others, today it seems to be in style to dismiss this at once with the remark that there is no, or only very slight, similarity between Eph. 5:14 and Isa. 60:1. For myself, the more I study Isa. 60:1 in the light of its own context the more I begin to see certain resemblances. It is perhaps instructive to place the two passages alongside of each other:

---

[141] As I see it the phrase ὑπὸ τοῦ φωτός modifies the immediately preceding ἐλεγχόμενα, just as in verse 12 the parallel phrase ὑπ' αὐτῶν should be construed with the similarly immediately preceding γινόμενα.

Isa. 60:1	Eph. 5:14
Arise, shine;	Awake, sleeper,
For your light has come,	And arise from the dead,
And the glory of Jehovah has risen	And Christ will shine on you.
upon you.	

1. In the context of the Isaiah passage the daughter of Zion is represented as forsaken, her land as desolate (Isa. 62:4). We read about captives and prisoners (Isa. 61:1). Also the Ephesian passage presupposes a condition of wretchedness, the sleep of death which *has* or *had* befallen the one addressed.

2. In both passages the one who is pictured as lying down in sleep or death is commanded to arise. Cf. Rom. 13:11; I Thess. 5:6.

3. In both the one addressed receives encouragement.

4. The substance of this encouragement is the same in both cases, namely, that light will be imparted to the one who heretofore has been in darkness.

5. In Isaiah the One who imparts this light is *Jehovah,* in a context which by Jesus himself was interpreted as referring to himself. Cf. Isa. 61:1, 2a with Luke 4:16-21. See also footnote 108. In Ephesians it is *Christ* who shines upon the formerly wretched one.

6. In Isaiah 40–66 deliverance from the *Babylonian* captivity through Jehovah's anointed Cyrus (see especially chapters 40–48) seems to be a symbol of deliverance from *spiritual* captivity through the gloriously anointed "Servant of Jehovah" (see especially chapters 49–57). Chapters 58–66, in which 60:1 occurs, speak of the glory of redeemed Zion. It is not impossible, therefore, that the early church of the new dispensation saw Christ in this passage (Isa. 60:1) as the One who causes the light of salvation to shine forth upon those who arise from their death-sleep of sin. If Jesus was able to interpret a passage from chapter 61 as referring to himself, as has just been indicated (see under 5.), why should it be impossible to explain or at least apply a passage from the immediately preceding chapter similarly?

It is my conviction, therefore, that the theory according to which, either directly or indirectly, the Ephesian passage has its root in Isa. 60:1 must not be readily dismissed as if it were entirely out of the question. There may not be sufficient reason to consider the connection between the two passages to have been definitely established, but there *certainly* is no ground whatever for rejecting even the possibility of this connection.

Even so, however, there could be an element of truth in theory *b.* It is conceivable that though Eph 5:14 is in the final analysis rooted in Isa. 60:1, the form in which the latter passage is here reproduced by Paul was that of lines from an early Christian hymn. The hymn, in other words, may have been based on the Isaiah passage. It is clear at any rate that when Paul was

235

writing what is now called the fifth chapter of Ephesians he had *hymns* in mind, for he mentions them only a few verses later, namely, in 5:19. Now if Eph. 5:14 was taken from a hymn, was it an Easter hymn, according to which the commemoration of Christ's physical resurrection reminded the one addressed to live a life in harmony with his *spiritual* resurrection, the two resurrections being related to each other as cause and effect? Or was it perhaps a song chanted in connection with the baptism of those who professed to have been awakened out of their sleep and to have been raised from the dead when they accepted Christ, and who were by means of this hymn urged to die more fully and constantly to "the old man" and increasingly day by day to put on "the new man"? We must confess that no one really knows for sure either the origin of these lines or the extent and manner of their use in the early church. What is certain, however, is the fact that they do not seem out of place in the present context. They apply to the man who is still living in paganism. When the wicked deeds of such a person have been exposed, the only way of escape must be clearly pointed out to him, so that he may wake up out of his sleep, may arise from the dead (cf. Luke 15:32) and Christ may shine on him.

In the light, however, of the entire preceding context (see especially verses 3-11) it is clear that the apostle has in mind not only the pagan but *also and especially* the convert. Paul's aim is to show that he who has renounced the wicked ways of the world should live a life consistent with his new standing. Therefore, instead of any longer taking part in the unfruitful works of darkness, he should emerge *completely* from his sleep and arise and withdraw *in every respect* from the wicked ways of the company of the spiritually dead. The blessed result will be that Christ will shine upon him. That would seem to be the meaning of the passage.

This, however, introduces another question. Do not these lines which the apostle is quoting with approval reverse the proper order of the elements in the process of becoming saved? Do they not seem to teach that it is man who turns to God before God turns to man? The sinner, so it would seem, is urged to wake up out of his spiritual sleep, and to arise from the dead (implying a resurrection from his death in sin), and only then will Christ shine upon him. The answer is: *a.* There is a long list of passages, both Old and New Testament, to which the same objection, if valid, would apply (for example, Deut. 4:29; 30:1-10; Ps. 50:14, 15; 55:16; Isa. 55:6, 7; Jer. 18:5-10; Matt. 11:28-30; Acts 16:31; Rev. 3:20). *b.* These passages stress human responsibility. *c.* None of them teaches that man is able, *in his own power,* to wake up or to arise from the dead. He can do this only by means of the grace of God and the power of the Holy Spirit. The very fact that he is called upon to arise *from the dead* implies this (see what was said about this in the interpretation of 2:1-9). In the process of becoming saved God always takes the lead. No one is able to become converted unless God first regenerates him. Also, after basic conversion has taken place there is never a moment in a person's life when he can do anything of spiritual value apart from his Lord. *d.* Christ, however, is not only the *Alpha* (beginning) of his salvation; he is also the *Omega* (the end); that is, he is not only salvation's *Originator;* he is also its *Rewarder.* Hence, when by divine grace and power the sinner puts off the old nature and puts on the new, when more and more he awakens and arises from the dead, the light from Christ shines upon him, illumining his entire life with tender, marvelous, mellow radiance, the radiance of the Savior's loving presence. It is thus that "the path of the righteous is as the dawning light that shines more and more unto the perfect day" (Prov. 4:18).

d. 5:15-21

"Do not get drunk on wine, but be filled with the Spirit."

Continuing his tender admonitions with respect to the church's Glorious Renewal Paul writes: **15. Be most careful therefore how y o u walk.**[142] Here again, in complete harmony with what has gone before, we are shown how very necessary it is for believers to show in every way and at all times that they have repudiated their old nature and have embraced the new and godly life. That is the only effective way of verifying one's own state of salvation, exposing the unfruitful works of darkness, calling the workers to repentance, and doing all this to the glory of God. Continued: **not as unwise but as wise.** Cf. 1:8, 17; Col. 1:9, 28; 3:16; 4:5. The unwise are those who, having no insight into things that pertain to God and salvation, are not aiming to reach the highest goal and therefore do not know and do not even care to know what are the best means to reach it. They regard as very important what is in reality of minor value or may even be harmful, and they do not appreciate what is indispensable. They conduct themselves accordingly. Those who are wise, on the other hand, have the proper insight and walk in harmony with it. They also make a judicious use of their time. In that trend Paul continues: **16. making the most of the opportunity.** They should not wait for opportunity to fall into their laps but should *buy it up,* not counting the cost. In the light of the entire context the opportunity referred to is that of showing by means of their life and conduct the power

[142] Should we read, "Look therefore *how carefully* y o u are walking"? Or rather, "Look therefore *carefully how* y o u walk"? In other words, is the correct reading πῶς ἀκριβῶς or is it ἀκριβῶς πῶς? A good case can be presented in defense of either. For myself I like Foulkes' reasoning in favor of the second reading. He writes, "This is a command that is essentially more likely to come from Paul's pen than that they should walk 'precisely' or 'strictly'. Paul could well use this word in its superlative form of his former life as a Pharisee (Acts 26:5), but to use it of the Christian life would have conveyed too much of a suggestion of renewed legalism" (*The Epistle of Paul to the Ephesians, An Introduction and Commentary,* Grand Rapids, Mich., 1963, p. 149). Either way, however, the emphasis is on the importance of Christian conduct.

and glory of the gospel, thus exposing evil, abounding in good works, obtaining assurance of salvation for themselves, strengthening the fellowship, winning the neighbor for Christ, and through it all glorifying God. The opportunity missed will never return. Let it therefore be used *to the full*. Read Mark 1:21-34 and see how much work Jesus was able to crowd into a single day, and what he did very early the next morning (Mark 1:35). Paul adds: **because the days are evil.** A single glance at the preceding context (see especially 4:14, 17-19, 25-31; 5:3-7, 10-12; cf. Rom. 1:18-32) will show how indescribably evil were the days when this letter was written. Similar admonitions are found in Rom. 13:11-14; I Cor. 7:29; II Cor. 6:14-18; Gal. 6:9, 10; and Col. 4:5. Continued: **17. Therefore do not be foolish but understand what (is) the will of the Lord.** The admonition of verse 15 — "not as unwise" — is repeated in slightly different language. The Ephesians must not be "without reflection or understanding." They must not show "want of sense," which amounts to saying that they must not be foolish. The connective "therefore" in the light of the preceding context may be interpreted as meaning: because the danger is so great, the wickedness so appalling, the opportunity so precious, and because constant watchfulness, earnest effort, and unwavering zeal are so necessary, do not be absurd. On the contrary, understand what is the will of the Lord, that is, of the Lord Jesus Christ. See 2:21; 4:1; 5:10. Do not depend on y o u r own acumen. Do not regard the advice of other people as the ultimate touchstone of the truth. Let the will of y o u r Lord as he has revealed it by means of his own word and example and by the mouth of his chosen messengers be y o u r standard and guide. See 5:10; cf. Rom. 12:2; I Peter 2:21.

One outstanding manifestation of "want of sense" is *drunkenness*. Its antidote, being "filled with the Spirit," indicates a far better avenue to true *understanding*. Hence, there is a double connection between verses 17 and 18. Paul writes: **18. And do not get drunk on wine, which is associated with unrestrained living, but be filled with the Spirit.** There are times when exhilaration of heart and mind is entirely proper. Scripture makes mention of shouting for joy (Ps. 5:11; 32:11; 35:27; etc.), fulness of joy (Ps. 16:11), good tidings of great joy (Luke 2:10), joy unspeakable and full of glory (I Peter 1:8). Exhilaration is wrong, however, when the method of inducing it is wrong. Thus it is improper to seek excitement from the excessive use of wine. It is the *abuse* of wine that is forbidden, not the *use* (I Tim. 5:23). That such abuse was a real danger in the early church, as it certainly is also today, appears from such restrictions as the following: "The overseer therefore must be above reproach . . . not (one who lingers) beside (his) wine" (I Tim. 3:3; cf. Titus 1:7); "Deacons similarly (must be) dignified, not . . . addicted to much wine" (I Tim. 3:8); and "Urge aged women similarly (to be) reverent in demeanor . . . not enslaved to much wine" (Titus 2:3).

Intoxication is not the effective remedy for the cares and worries of this life. The so-called "uplift" it provides is not real. It is the devil's poor substitute for the "joy unspeakable and full of glory" which God provides. Satan is ever substituting the bad for the good. Has he not been called "the ape of God"? Getting drunk on wine is "associated with unrestrained living" or "dissolute behavior," "recklessness" (Titus 1:6; I Peter 4:4). It marks the person who, if he so continues, *cannot be saved.*[143] But he need not so continue. The prodigal son of the unforgettable parable lived *recklessly* (an adverb cognate with the noun *recklessness* or *unrestrained living* occurring here in Eph. 5:18). *Extravagance* and *lack of self-control* were combined in his behavior, just as in all likelihood they are combined in the meaning of the word "unrestrained living" used in this passage from Paul's letter to the Ephesians. Nevertheless, there was salvation for him when he repented. Let anyone who may read this take courage (Isa. 1:18; Ezek. 33:11; I John 1:9).

The real remedy for sinful inebriation is pointed out by Paul. The Ephesians are urged to seek a higher, far better, source of exhilaration. Instead of *getting drunk* let them *be filled.* Instead of getting drunk on *wine* let them be filled with *the Spirit.* Note the double contrast. Although it is true that the apostle makes use of a word, namely, *pneúma,* which in the translation should at times be spelled *with,* at other times *without,* a capital letter (hence "Spirit" or "spirit"), it should be capitalized in this instance, as is often the case. Paul was undoubtedly thinking of the third person of the Holy Trinity, the Holy Spirit. Evidence in support of this view: *a.* the expression "filled with" or "full of" the *pneúma,* when the reference is to the Holy Spirit, is very common in Scripture (Luke 1:15, 41, 67; 4:1; Acts 2:4; 4:8, 31; 6:3; 7:55; 9:17; 13:9);[144] and *b.* the very contrast here in 5:18 between getting drunk on wine and being filled with the *pneúma* occurs also, though in a slightly different form, in Acts 2:4, 13, where the reference can only be to the Holy Spirit.[145]

---

[143] There are those who point out that etymologically ἀσωτία describes *the condition of the person who cannot be saved.* But here one would have to determine first of all what the word *saved* actually means in such a case. And even if this were determined, it would still remain true that, although derivations and word histories are instructive and do shed some light on meanings, *actual use of a word in a given context* is far more important. When, accordingly, I state that the person in question, if he so continues, *cannot be saved,* this conclusion is based not on etymology, nor on semantics, but on clear scriptural teaching (I Cor. 6:9, 10).

[144] The fact that here, in 5:18, by way of exception, we read ἐν πνεύματι does not invalidate this conclusion. The preposition ἐν covers a very wide area, especially in Koine Greek, in this case an area probably even broadened by the influence of Hebrew *be*, either directly, or indirectly via the LXX. Also, the suggestion that in the present case the unusual phrase was selected in order to convey the fact that the Holy Spirit is not only the agent *by* whom believers are filled but also the One *in* whom they are filled must not be lightly dismissed.

[145] This rather generally accepted view as to the reference here in 5:18 to the Holy Spirit must therefore be maintained over against Lenski who calls it "impossible" (*op. cit.,* p. 619).

By the ancients, moreover, an overdose of wine was often used not only to rid oneself of care and to gain a sense of mirth but also to induce communion with the gods and, by means of this communion, to receive ecstatic knowledge, not otherwise obtainable. Such foolishness, often associated with Dionysiac orgies, is by the apostle contrasted with the serene ecstasy and sweet fellowship with Christ which he himself was experiencing in the Spirit when he wrote this letter to the Ephesians (see on 1:3; 3:20). What he is saying therefore is this: getting drunk on wine leads to nothing better than debauchery, will not place y o u in possession of worthwhile pleasure, usable knowledge, and perfect contentment. It will not help y o u but hurt y o u. It leaves a bad taste and produces no end of woe (cf. Prov. 23:29-32). On the other hand, being filled with the Spirit will enrich y o u with the precious treasures of lasting joy, deep insight, and inner satisfaction. *It will sharpen y o u r faculties for the perception of the divine will.* Note the immediate context, verse 17. So, "do not get drunk on wine, but be filled with the Spirit." [146]

Being thus filled with the Spirit believers will not only be enlightened and joyful but will also give jubilant expression to their refreshing knowledge of the will of God. They will reveal their discoveries and their feelings of gratitude. Hence Paul continues: **19. speaking to one another in psalms and hymns and spiritual songs.** The term *psalms* in all probability has reference, at least mainly, to the Old Testament Psalter; *hymns,* mainly to New Testament songs of praise to God and to Christ (verse 14 above, in which Christ is praised as the Source of light, containing perhaps lines from one of these hymns); and finally, *spiritual songs,* mainly to sacred lyrics dwelling on themes other than direct praise to God or to Christ. There may, however, be some overlapping in the meaning of these three terms as used here by Paul.

The point to note is that by means of these psalms, hymns, and spiritual songs, Spirit-filled believers must *speak to each other.*[147] They are not merely *reciting* what they have committed to memory. "Daughter, do *you* know that *your* Redeemer lives?" said the director to the soloist. After an affirmative answer he continued, "Then sing it again, and this time *tell us* about it." She did, and there were tears of joy and thanksgiving in every eye. Continued: **singing and making melody from y o u r heart to the Lord.** The idea of some [148] that in the two parts of this one verse the apostle has reference to two kinds of singing: *a.* audible ("speaking") and *b.* inaudible ("in the stillness of the heart"), must be dismissed. If that had been his intention,

---

[146] On this passage see also J. M. Moffatt, "Three Notes on Ephesians," *Exp,* Eighth Series, No. 87 (April, 1918), pp. 306–317.

[147] The reflexive ἑαυτοῖς is here used as a reciprocal as was the case in 4:32; hence, not "for yourselves" (Lenski) nor "to yourselves" (A.V.), but "to one another." See N.T.C. on Colossians and Philemon, p. 161, footnote 137.

[148] See Salmond, *op. cit.,* p. 364.

he would have inserted the conjunction *and* or *and also* between the two parts. The two are clearly parallel. The second explains and completes the first: when believers get together they should not be having wild parties but should edify each other, speaking to one another in Christian song, and doing so *from the heart, to the* praise and honor of their blessed *Lord.* They should make music with the voice ("singing") or in any proper way whatever, whether with voice or instrument ("making melody"). Cf. Rom. 15:9; I Cor. 14:15; James 5:13. For further details of interpretation see N.T.C. on Colossians and Philemon, pp. 160–163 where a closely similar passage (Col. 3:16) is discussed more at length.

By means of psalms, hymns, and spiritual songs believers reveal their *gratitude* to God. On this theme Paul now enlarges as follows: **20. giving thanks always for all things in the name of our Lord Jesus Christ to (our) God and Father.** See what has been said about this passage earlier, on p. 45. In addition, the following:

Proper Thanksgiving

1. *What is it?*

Thanksgiving is grateful acknowledgment of benefits received. It presupposes that the person who engages in this activity recognizes three things: *a.* that the blessings which he enjoys *were bestowed upon himself,* so that in all honesty he cannot give *himself* the credit for them; *b. that he is totally unworthy* of them; and *c.* that they are *great and manifold.*

Paul has mentioned the giving of thanks once before in this chapter (5:4). He refers to it again and again in his epistles. So important does he regard it that he wants believers to be "overflowing with thanksgiving" (Col. 2:7). Gratitude is that which completes the circle whereby blessings that drop down into the hearts and lives of believers return to the Giver in the form of unending, loving, and spontaneous adoration. Properly pursued, such giving of thanks is a self-perpetuating attitude and activity, for it implies a review of blessings received. Naturally, such a review, the purposeful concentration of attention upon benefits, causes them to stand out more clearly, resulting in increased thanksgiving. The expression of gratitude is therefore a most blessed response to favors undeserved. While it lasts, worries tend to disappear, complaints vanish, courage to face the future is increased, virtuous resolutions are formed, peace is experienced, and God is glorified.

2. *When must it take place?*

The apostle says, "always." It is proper to give thanks *after* the blessing has been received, that is, when the situation that caused alarm has passed and quiet has been restored, as did the Israelites *after* their passage through the Red Sea (Exod. 15); as did the author of Ps. 116 *after* the Lord had heard his prayer; and as one day the glorious multitude will do on the

241

shores of the sea of crystal (Rev. 15). It is also proper to give thanks *in the very midst* of distress, as did Jonah when he was in "the fish's belly" (Jonah 2:1, 9). It is even proper to sing songs of praise and thanksgiving *before* the battle has commenced, as Jehoshaphat ordered (II Chron. 20:21). *Always* believers can and should give thanks because there is never a moment when they are not under the watchful eye of Jehovah whose very name indicates that his mercies are unchangeable and will never fail.

3. *For what must thanks be given?*

Paul answers, "for all things." Hence, gratitude must be felt and expressed for blessings physical and spiritual; "ordinary" and extraordinary; past, present, and future (the latter, because they are included in an infallible promise); and even for things withheld and for things received. It should be constantly borne in mind that the one who, under the guidance of the Spirit, issued this admonition was himself a prisoner while he so commanded. But *in spite of* his chain, nay rather *for* his chain, he thanked God (Phil. 1:12-14). He was able to "take pleasure in weaknesses, injuries, hardships, and frustrations" (II Cor. 12:10). Again and again during this imprisonment Paul thanks God and exhorts those whom he addresses to be thankful also (Eph. 1:16; 5:4, 20; Phil. 1:3, 12-21; Col. 1:3, 12; 2:4; 3:17; 4:2; Philem. 4). This may seem very strange. It is, however, entirely consistent with the rest of Paul's teachings, for it harmonizes beautifully with the assurance that "to them that love God *all things* work together for good" and that "in all these things we are more than conquerors through him that loved us" with a love from which we can never be separated (Rom. 8:28-39).

4. *How must thanks be given?*

The answer is "in the name of our Lord Jesus Christ," because it was he who earned all these blessings for us, so that we receive them all "together with him" (Rom. 8:32). It is also he who will purify our petitions and thanksgivings and, thus purified, will present them, together with his own intercession, before the countenance of the Father.

5. *To whom must it be offered?*

The answer is "to (our) God and Father." There are those who never give thanks at all. Like the rich fool in the parable that is recorded in Luke 12:16-21 they seem to give themselves the credit for everything they possess or have accomplished. There are others, however, who sense their obligations *to their neighbors*. They recognize *secondary causes,* but never the *First Cause* (Rom. 1:21). Since, however, the Ephesians knew that all their blessings were constantly coming from **God**, the God who in Christ Jesus is their Father, and since they also were aware of the fact that they constituted part of "the Father's Family" (see on 3:14, 15), so that every benefit which they had received, were now receiving, or would still receive, proceeded from his love, they must have been able to understand the reasonableness of the exhortation that to this God and Father of theirs they should ascribe constant thanksgiving and praise.

Having exhorted the Ephesians with respect to their duty to God, Paul very logically concludes this section by admonishing them in regard to their obligation toward each other. He does this in words which at the same time form an excellent transition to the thoughts with which he will be occupied in the next paragraph.[149]

Paul has been urging the Ephesians to express their thanksgiving to God by means of psalms, hymns, and spiritual songs. Now in order that this may be done successfully two things are necessary: *a.* that the thanksgiving and praise be addressed in the proper manner to the proper person, and *b.* that there be harmony among the singers. In a choir every singer must know his place so that his voice may blend with that of others. In an orchestra there must be no discord. Hence, Paul states: 21. **subjecting yourselves**[150] **to each other out of reverence for Christ.**[151] Again and again our Lord, while on earth, emphasized this very thought, namely, that each disciple should be willing to be the least (Matt. 18:1-4; 20:28) and to wash the other disciples' feet (John 13:1-17). Substantially the same thought is also expressed in Rom. 12:10: "in honor preferring one another" and in Phil. 2:3: "(doing) nothing from selfish ambition or from empty conceit, but in humble-mindedness each counting the other better than himself." Cf. I Peter 5:5. *Affection* for one another, *humility,* and a *willingness to co-operate* with other members of the body are the graces that are implied here in Eph. 5:21. The thought of the passage recalls what the apostle had said

---

[149] With A.R.V. and Lenski I include this verse in the present section, contrary to the paragraphing found in R.S.V., Hodge, etc. The reasons given by Lenski for so doing are mine also, namely, *a.* the sentence simply continues, with durative present participle similar to those that precede; *b.* the mention of mutual subjection here in verse 21 differs from subjection of wives to husbands, children to parents, and slaves to masters, discussed in the next section; and *c.* a new subject begins with verse 22: table of household duties.

It is necessary to add, however, that the relation between verse 21 and those that follow is close, since in both cases the matter of willingness to subject oneself is discussed. In fact verse 22 borrows its implied predicate from verse 21. Note how N.E.B., probably to indicate the transitional nature of verse 21, makes of it a little paragraph all by itself.

[150] The simplest construction would be to regard all these five present participles — speaking, singing, making melody, giving thanks, and subjecting (yourselves) — as governed by "be filled with the Spirit" (5:18). So construed, all of them have the force of present imperatives. When one is filled with the Spirit he will wish to engage in the activities indicated by the participles. A hostile attitude toward these activities, or an attempt at unconcern or so-called neutrality, shows that the individual to whom this would apply is not Spirit-indwelt.

[151] The better manuscripts read Χριστοῦ, not θεοῦ on which A.V. "in the fear of God" is based.

earlier in this same letter: "with all lowliness and meekness, with long-suffering, enduring one another in love, making every effort to preserve the unity imparted by the Spirit by means of the bond (consisting in) peace" (4:2, 3). Paul knew by experience what would happen in a church when this rule is disobeyed (I Cor. 1:11, 12; 3:1-9; 11:17-22; 14:26-33). He therefore stresses the fact that "out of reverence for Christ," that is, with a conscious regard for his clearly revealed will, every member of the body should be willing to recognize the rights, needs, and wishes of the others. Thus believers will be able to present a united front to the world, the blessing of true Christian fellowship will be promoted, and God in Christ will be glorified.

Chapter 4:17–6:9

Verses 5:22–6:9

Theme: *The Church Glorious*

II. *Exhortation*
urging

G lorious Renewal
  2. upon special groups

22 Wives, (be subject) to y o u r own husbands as to the Lord, 23 for the husband is head of the wife as also Christ is head of the church, he himself (being) the Savior of the body. 24 Then, just as the church is subject to Christ so also wives (should be subject) to their husbands in everything. 25 Husbands, love y o u r wives just as also Christ loved the church and gave himself up for her; 26 that he might sanctify her, cleansing her by the washing of water in connection with the spoken word; 27 in order that he might present the church to himself brilliant in purity, having no spot or wrinkle or any such thing, but that she might be holy and faultless. 28 That is the way husbands also ought to love their own wives as their own bodies. He who loves his own wife loves himself; 29 for no one ever hated his own flesh; on the contrary, he nourishes it and cherishes it, just as also Christ (does) the church, 30 because we are members of his body. 31 "Therefore shall a man leave his father and mother, and shall cleave to his wife; and the two shall become one flesh." 32 This mystery is great, but I am speaking with reference to Christ and the church. 33 Nevertheless, let each one of y o u also love his own wife as himself, and let the wife see to it that she respects her husband.

6 1 Children, obey y o u r parents in the Lord, for this is right. 2 "Honor your father and your mother," which is a commandment of foremost significance, with a promise attached: 3 "that it may be well with you" and that y o u may be on earth a long time. 4 and fathers, do not provoke y o u r children to anger but rear them tenderly in the discipline and admonition of the Lord. 5 Slaves, be obedient to those who according to the flesh are y o u r masters, with fear and trembling, in the sincerity of y o u r heart, as to Christ, 6 not in the way of eye-service as men-pleasers, but as slaves of Christ, doing the will of God from the heart, 7 with ready mind rendering service as to the Lord and not to men, 8 knowing that whatever good each one does this he will receive back from the Lord, whether (he be) slave or free. 9 And masters, do the same things for them, and stop threatening, knowing that (he who is) both their master and y o u r s is in the heavens, and there is no partiality with him.

5:22–6:9

As indicated previously (see p. 208) the theme Glorious Renewal is here continued but is now applied to special groups; as follows: wives and their husbands (5:22-33) ; children and their parents (6:1-4) ; and slaves and their masters (6:5-9) .

a. 5:22-33

"Wives, be subject to y o u r own husbands.
Husbands, love y o u r wives."

22. Wives, (be subject) [152] **to y o u r own husbands as to the Lord.** Some of the material found in 5:22–6:9 parallels Col. 3:18–4:1. Wherever it does,

---

[152] The verb is undoubtedly to be supplied from the preceding verse (cf. same verb in Col. 3:18) .

I refer the reader to N.T.C. on Colossians and Philemon, pp. 167–177, for *details* of exegesis. This will leave more room for expatiating in the present Commentary on those Ephesian passages that are not found in Colossians.

No institution on earth is more sacred than that of the family. None is more basic. As is the moral and religious atmosphere in the family, so will it be in the church, the nation, and society in general. Now in his kindness toward womanhood, the Lord, fully realizing that within the family much of the care of children will rest on the wife, has been pleased not to overburden her. Hence, he placed *ultimate* responsibility with respect to the household upon the shoulders of her husband, in keeping with the latter's creational endowment. So here, through his servant, the apostle Paul, the Lord assigns to the wife the duty of obeying her husband. This obedience must be a voluntary submission on her part, and that only to *her own* husband, not to *every man*. What will make this obedience easier, moreover, is that she is asked to render it "as to the Lord," that is, as part of her obedience to him, the very One who died for her. Continued: **23. for the husband is head of the wife.** A home without a head is an invitation to chaos. It spells derangement and disaster worse even than that which results when a nation is without a ruler or an army without a commander. For excellent reasons (see I Tim. 2:13, 14) it has pleased God to assign to the husband the task of being the head of the wife, hence also of the family. This headship, moreover, implies more than rulership, as is clear from the words which follow, namely, **as also Christ is head of the church, he himself (being) the Savior of the body.** This statement may come as a surprise to those who have been used to place undue stress on a husband's *authority* over his wife. To be sure, he has that authority and should exercise it, but never in a domineering manner. The comparison with Christ as head of the church (cf. 1:22; 4:15; Col. 1:18) reveals in what sense the husband is the wife's head. He is her head *as being vitally interested in her welfare.* He is her *protector. His pattern is Christ who, as head of the church, is its Savior!* What Paul is saying, therefore, amounts to this: the wife should voluntarily submit herself to her husband whom God has appointed as her head. She should recognize that, in his capacity as her head, her husband is so closely united to her and so deeply concerned about her welfare that his relation to her is patterned after the sacrificial interest of Christ in his church, which he purchased with his own blood! One is reminded of those many Old Testament passages in which Jehovah's love for his people is vividly portrayed. There is, for example, the story of Hosea's unfailing tenderness toward his wife Gomer. Though the latter was not true to him, went after other "lovers," and conceived "children of whoredom," nevertheless Hosea, instead of rejecting her, slips away to the haunt of shame, buys her back for fifteen pieces of silver and a homer and a half of barley, and mercifully restores her to her former position of honor (Hos. 1–3;

11:8; 14:4). For similar passages describing the Husband's (Jehovah's) marvelous reclaiming love see Isa. 54:1-8; 62:3-5; Jer. 3:6-18; 31:31-34. Let the wife, therefore, obey her husband who loves her so very, very much! And let her bear in mind that by being obedient to her husband she is being obedient to her Lord.

Not everyone accepts this interpretation of the passage. In addition to those who interpret the clause, "he himself (being) the Savior of the body" as a direct reference *not* to Christ but to *the husband* as being the defender of the wife (in which case the translation becomes *savior*, not *Savior*), an interpretation so completely out of line with the immediately preceding words that it deserves no further comment, there are also those who believe that the reference to Christ as the church's Savior is a kind of *aside,* or else expresses "a relation which Christ bears to the church which finds no analogy in that of the husband to the wife" (Hodge, *op. cit.,* p. 313). Just why the apostle would have inserted this clause if it had nothing to do with the subject is not explained. Calvin, on the other hand, in commenting on the words, "And he is the Savior [or "savior"] of the body," makes the following very apt remark, "The pronoun *he* is supposed by some to refer to *Christ;* and by others to *the husband.* It applies more naturally, in my opinion, to Christ, but still with a view to the present subject. In this point, as well as in others the resemblance ought to hold." Incidentally, I might call attention to the fact that in Calvin's own case the resemblance between *a.* Christ's love and care for his church and *b.* Calvin's love and care for Idelette certainly held. Contrary to the opinion of many who are ever picturing John Calvin as a stern, autocratic individual, here was a man who loved his wife very tenderly; while she, in turn loved and obeyed him with the same complete devotion.[153] Says P. Schaff, in commenting on Calvin's character, and in particular on the relation between Calvin and his wife, "Nothing can be more unjust than the charge that Calvin was cold and unsympathetic" (*History of the Christian Church,* New York, 1923, Vol. VII, p. 417).

Paul summarizes the contents of verses 22 and 23 as follows: 24. **Then,**[154]

---

[153] Read Edna Gerstner's *Idelette,* Grand Rapids, Mich., 1963. This is a biographical novel rich in authentic detail. Cf. L. Penning, *Life and Times of Calvin,* translated by B. S. Berrington, London, 1912, pp. 145–148.

[154] The interpretation of ἀλλά as if it is always adversative has led to many wrong interpretations, one of them being that the apostle meant to say, "*But* even though the relation of Christ to the church is unique, for he is the Savior of the body and as such cannot be imitated, *nevertheless* wives should be subject to their husbands," etc. What is forgotten is the fact that ἀλλά has other meanings besides *but, yet, nevertheless.* I agree with Grosheide when he states that in the present instance ἀλλά *summarizes* (*op. cit.,* p. 87). This view is also in line with L.N.T. (A. and G.), p. 38, which interprets the meaning of the particle as used here in 5:24 to be *now, then;* meaning No. 6. It is true that there is a sense in which the act whereby Christ saved the church cannot be imitated, as has been explained in detail in my comments on 5:1. There is, however, also a sense in which Christ's

just as the church is subject to Christ so also wives (should be subject) to their husbands in everything. The submission of the church to Christ is voluntary, wholehearted, sincere, enthusiastic. It is a submission prompted not only by a conviction, "This is right and proper because God demands it," but also by love in return for Christ's love (I John 4:19). Let the same be true with respect to the submission of wives to their husbands. Moreover, that obedience must not be partial, so that the wife obeys her husband when the latter's wishes happen to coincide with her own, but complete: "in everything." This little phrase must, however, not be interpreted as if it meant *"absolutely everything."* If the husband should demand her to do things contrary to the moral and spiritual principles established by God himself, submission would be wrong (Acts 5:29; cf. 4:19, 20). With this exception, however, her obedience should be complete.

The admonition addressed to *husbands* begins as follows: **25. Husbands, love y o u r wives, just as also Christ loved the church and gave himself up for her.** The love required must be deep-seated, thorough-going, intelligent and purposeful, a love in which the entire personality — not only the emotions but also the mind and the will — expresses itself.[155] The main characteristic of this love, however, is that it is spontaneous and self-sacrificing, for it is compared to the love of Christ whereby he *gave himself up* for the church. More excellent love than that is inconceivable (John 10:11-15; 15:13; I John 3:16). See also on 5:2.

When a believing husband loves his wife in this fashion obedience from the side of his believing wife will be easy. Illustration taken from life: "My husband loves me so thoroughly and is so good to me that I jump at the opportunity to obey him." That was putting it beautifully!

Christ loved the church and gave himself up for her, **26. that he might sanctify her,** separating her unto God and to his service, that *positively;* and *negatively:* **cleansing her,** that is, delivering her from sin's guilt and pollution (Heb. 9:22, 23; 10:29), this two-fold process (sanctifying and cleansing) of necessity occurring simultaneously and not finished until death.[156] Con-

---

sacrificial love can and should serve as an example. To be sure, *John* 3:16 is true, but so is *I John* 3:16! To deny this, as happens so frequently, even in the name of Calvinism, is a superimposition of doctrine on exegesis with which John Calvin himself would never have agreed, as is indicated by his own comments on this passage.
[155] I base this interpretation not so much on the use of ἀγαπάω instead of φιλέω here in 5:25, as on the manner in which the love that is required of husbands is here described, namely, as a love patterned after that of Christ for his church. As to the verb ἀγαπάω itself in comparison with φιλέω, Paul uses the latter only twice (I Cor. 16:22 and Titus 3:15). He uses ἀγαπάω more than thirty times. Evidently the verb ἀγαπάω, though in most cases (as here) retaining its full distinctive meaning, is beginning to push out the verb φιλέω, by absorbing some of its contents. A clear distinction is not always demonstrable. See N.T.C. on the Gospel according to John, Vol. II, pp. 494–500.
[156] The fact that the aorist active subjunctive ἀγιάσῃ is followed by the aorist active participle καθαρίσας does not necessarily mean that Christ by his death first cleansed

tinued: **by the washing of water.** As to the first noun, here, as in Titus 3:5, the only other occurrence of this word in the New Testament, the right translation is in all probability *washing*, rather than *laver* or *basin for washing*.[157] But while Titus 3:5 (on which see N.T.C. on I and II Timothy and Titus, pp. 391, 392) speaks of "a washing *of regeneration* and renewing by the Holy Spirit," the Ephesian passage mentions the washing *of water* in **connection with the spoken word.** Though the two passages are certainly closely related, they are not identical. This "washing of (or: "with") water" here in Eph. 2:26 can hardly have reference to anything else than to baptism. So much should be clear. However, does this mean that the rite *as such* purifies and sanctifies? If so I would have to retract everything I said a moment ago with reference to sanctifying and cleansing being two aspects of a lifelong process. The meaning then would simply be this: "Christ loved the church and gave himself up for her in order that he might *by means of the rite of baptism with water* sanctify and cleanse her." An outward rite would then impart an inward grace. An enormous significance would thus be assigned to baptism with water! That external rite would take care of just about everything. Having been baptized, little else would be needed. The death of Christ would have occurred in order to bring about that *one* and only necessary experience, so that thereby the person who undergoes it might be saved for all eternity. Not many would endorse such an extreme view. But let us guard ourselves also against moving too far in that general direction.[158]

---

his people and that he then subsequently sanctifies them. The aorist as such can refer to either antecedent or simultaneous action. In the present instance it is hard to construe this participle in the former sense. The fact that verb and participle are aorists, moreover, does not in any way indicate the amount of time involved, whether it be short or long. Although it is true that justification takes place once for all, while sanctification is a continuous process, the present passage does not in any way prove that the participle *cleansing* refers exclusively to *justification,* while the verb *sanctify* refers exclusively to *sanctification.* The distinction is probably simply between the *negative* and the *positive* aspects of the operation of the Holy Spirit in the hearts and lives of God's children.

[157] Simpson, who made a special study of this word, points out that ὁ λουτήρ, not τὸ λουτρόν, is the LXX vocable for the laver of Judaism, and that λουτρόν, both in Attic and Hellenistic Greek, as often signifies the act of washing as the vessel or the locality of ablution. See his work, *The Pastoral Epistles*, London, 1954, pp. 114 ff.

[158] It is interesting to read Lenski's very positively expressed views regarding this matter, *op. cit.*, pp. 632–635. He stresses the fact that Paul is referring to baptism with "actual water," "most definite water." He further emphasizes that this baptism with water is "a washing of regeneration in the Holy Spirit" (Titus 3:5), and that the phrase "in connection with the spoken word" unquestionably refers to *the baptismal formula* as spoken by the administrant. As to the statement by Robertson, namely, "Neither there [I Cor. 6:11] nor here [Eph. 5:26] does Paul mean that the cleansing or sanctification took place in the bath save in a symbolic fashion," he remarks, "The plainest Greek is not proof against dogmatic prejudice, — a warning to all exegetes." The warning in connection with the dogmatic prejudice should certainly be taken to heart by all of us. Was it taken fully to heart by Lenski?

It is not the rite of baptism with water that saves. It is "the washing of water *in connection with the spoken word*" that is used as means of sanctification and cleansing. And there is nothing in the context that would indicate that this "spoken word" is to be restricted to the baptismal formula. Let Paul be his own interpreter. In the very next chapter (6:17) he tells the Ephesians, "And take . . . the sword of the Spirit which is *the spoken word of God*." He surely cannot have meant that this sword of the Spirit which believers must wield is nothing else than the baptismal formula! It is, of course, *the gospel, the entire Word of God*. Compare Christ's petition, "*Sanctify them in the truth; thy word is truth*" (John 17:17). Hence, in connection with the present passage (5:26) the interpretation must be that when the meaning of baptism is explained to, understood by, and through the operation of the Holy Spirit applied to the minds and hearts of those who are baptized — and, of course, this takes place throughout life — the purpose of Christ's death is accomplished and believers are sanctified and cleansed. Baptism, to be sure, is important. It is a marvelous blessing. It is not only *a symbol* but also *a seal, a picture* and a definite *assurance* of the fact that God's gracious promise of salvation will certainly be realized in the life of the baptized individual who trusts in him. By means of this precious sacrament the gracious invitation to full surrender is made *very vivid* and *very personal*. But it has no saving efficacy apart from the word applied to the heart by the Spirit. Cf. John 3:5; Rom. 10:8; I Peter 1:25. It is exactly as Calvin, commenting on this passage, says: "If *the word* is taken away, the whole power of the sacraments is gone. What else are the sacraments but seals of the word? . . . By *the word* is here meant the promise, which explains the value and use of signs."

The *immediate* purpose of Christ's self-abasement (verse 25b) having been stated in verse 26, Paul now (in verse 27) indicates the *ultimate* purpose; or, expressing it differently, he shows to what end Christ sanctified and cleansed the church: **27. in order that he might present the church to himself brilliant in purity.** The church is even now *in essence* "Christ's bride." However, as such she has not yet been made manifest in all her beauty. The wedding is a matter of the future.

In order to understand the present passage it is necessary to review the marriage customs implied in Scripture. First, there was *the betrothal*. This was considered more binding than "engagement" with us. The terms of the marriage are accepted in the presence of witnesses and God's blessing is pronounced upon the union. From this day groom and bride are *legally* husband and wife (II Cor. 11:12). Next comes *the interval* between betrothal and the wedding-feast. The groom may have selected this period to pay the dowry to the father of the bride, that is, if this had not already been done (Gen. 34:12). Then there is *the preparation* and *procession* with a view to the wedding feast. The bride prepares and adorns herself. The groom also arrays himself in his best attire, and, accompanied by his friends, who sing and bear torches, proceeds to the home of the betrothed. *He receives the bride* and conveys her, with a returning procession, to the place where the wedding-feast will be held. Finally, the great event arrives: *the wedding-feast* itself, including *the wedding-banquet*. The festivities may last seven or even twice seven days (Matt. 22:1-14).

Now Scripture again and again compares the love-relationship between Jehovah and his people, or between Christ and his church, to a bridegroom and his bride (Ps. 45; Isa. 50:1; 54:1-8; 62:3-5; Jer. 2:32; 3:6-18; 31:31-34; Hos. 1-3; 11:8; 14:4; Matt. 9:15; John 3:29; II Cor. 11:2; Rev. 19:7; 21:2, 9). The church is betrothed to Christ. Christ has paid the dowry for her. He has bought the one who *is* essentially — *is to be* eschatologically — his bride:

> "From heaven he came and sought her
> To be his holy bride;
> With his own blood he bought her,
> And for her life he died."

> Samuel J. Stone, lines taken
> from the hymn, "The Church's
> One Foundation."

The "interval" of relative separation has arrived. It refers to this entire dispensation between Christ's ascension to heaven and his coming again. Now it is during this period that the bride must make herself ready. She will array herself in fine linen, glistening and pure. See Rev. 19:8 for metaphorical meaning. However, Paul looks at this preparation of the bride from the divine point of view. *It is the bridegroom himself, even Christ, who here in 5:27 is described as preparing the one who one day will be manifested as his bride, so that she will be "brilliant in purity."* The *presentation* here referred to must be viewed as definitely eschatological, that is, as referring to the great consummation when Jesus returns upon clouds of glory. Not only is it true that "the wife of the Lamb" *makes herself* ready (Rev. 19:7), and not only with a view to the future do God's duly appointed servants perform a function in this respect (II Cor. 11:2; Phil. 1:10; 2:16; Col. 1:28; I Thess. 2:19, 20; I John 2:28), but Christ himself readies her in order to present her to himself. The point stressed is, of course, that she, the church, can do nothing in her own power. She owes all her beauty to him, the bridegroom. It is for that very reason that when she is at last manifested in full view she is seen to be so brilliant in purity, that she answers the description as here given, namely, **having no spot or wrinkle or any such thing, but that she might be holy and faultless.** The word "spot" is in the New Testament confined to this passage and II Peter 2:13. In the latter passage the word used in the original has been rendered "spots" (A.V.,

253

A.R.V.) , and "blots" (R.S.V.) . It there refers to *persons.* M.M., p. 584, quotes a passage in which it is applied similarly and can be translated "dregs" ("the dregs of humanity from the city") . The word "wrinkle" is in the New Testament found only here in 5:27. It occurs neither in the Septuagint nor in the Apocrypha, but is otherwise not uncommon. It is useless to try to distinguish between the resultant reference or metaphorical sense of these two words. The combination of the two in the present passage simply *stresses* the fact that when in the day of days the victorious Lord of lords and King of kings presents the church to himself she will have *no moral or spiritual stain whatever.* The Bridegroom, *because of his great love for his bride* (note connection between verses 27 and 28) is going to present her *to himself* "holy and faultless" (see 1:4 for explanation) . To be sure, he performs this deed of *joyful public acknowledgment* with a view to himself, that *he* may therein rejoice and be glorified, for salvation never ends in man, always in God. Nevertheless, is not this marvelous welcome which the bride will receive also *her* supreme honor? Does it not indicate that she is and will forever remain the object of his everlasting delight? Cf. Zeph. 3:17. **28. That is the way husbands also ought to love their own wives as their own bodies;** not meaning: they should love their own wives just as they love their own bodies, but they should love their own wives, as being their own bodies. The husband is the head of the wife, as Christ is the head of the church. Hence, as the church is Christ's body, so the wife is in a sense the husband's body. Thus intimately are the two united. Therefore, husbands should love their wives. The thought of verse 25 is repeated here and strengthened. In the light of the immediately preceding context (verses 26 and 27) the thought now expressed is that not only should husbands love their wives with self-sacrificing love, a love patterned after that of Christ for his church, but also, in so doing, they should help their wives to make progress in sanctification. A large order, indeed! Husbands should love their wives for what they are and should also love them sufficiently to help them to become what they should be. **He who loves his own wife loves himself,** for, as already implied in the preceding statement, the wife is part of him, that is, has become intimately united with him. See on verse 31. Paul is already thinking of the words of Gen. 2:24 which he is going to quote a little later. Now if this fact, namely, that the wife is the husband's body, has been grasped, then the husband will indeed love his wife. **29. for no one ever hated his own flesh,** that is, his own body; **on the contrary, he nourishes it,** supplies it with food, etc., **and cherishes it.** For *nourishing* see also on 6:4; for *cherishing,* I Thess. 2:7. Each of these words in its own right, and even more, in combination with the other, indicates the attention that is paid to the body. Paul is, however, not thinking only of supplying the body with barely enough food, clothing and shelter to enable it to eke out a mere existence; he refers instead to the bounteous, elaborate, unremitting, and sympathetic care we bestow on our bodies. Continued: **just as also Christ (does) the church, 30. because we are members of his body.**[159] There is never a moment that Christ does not tenderly watch over his body, the church. We are under his constant surveillance. His eyes are constantly upon us, from the beginning of the year even to the end of the year (cf. Deut. 11:12). Therefore we cast all our anxiety upon him, convinced that we are his personal concern (I Peter 5:7), the objects of his *very special* providence.

It is striking that the apostle, who has been referring to Christ as the head and to the church as his body (see especially verses 23 and 29) and who, by clear implication, has described him as the bridegroom and the church as the bride (verse 27), now suddenly refers to *the individual members* of that body, and even more strikingly, though not at all contrary to his custom, *includes himself:* "*we* are members of his body" (cf. Rom. 12:5). The reason must be that Paul, *the prisoner* — this must never be lost sight of — is deeply touched by this marvelous fact that his own life, too, is dear to the heart of him who is enthroned in heavenly majesty; and, adds Paul, as it were, so are the lives of *all* believers. Paul loved them all and was never able to think of himself alone (II Tim. 4:8). It soothes the apostle to reflect on the truth that "Christ leaves us not when the storm is high, and we have comfort for he is nigh." Therefore, also, thus is his argument, we as members of his body, urged on by his example and enabled by his Spirit, should do to others as Christ does to us. And since Christ as our head, so assiduously cares for us, members of his body, let husbands take this to heart and let them strive to emulate Christ in the loving attention which they focus upon *their* bodies, that is, upon their wives. This, moreover, is in harmony with the divine command [160] recorded in Gen. 2:24, an ordinance that has been in the background of Paul's thinking all the while and which he now finally quotes, almost exactly [161] according to the Septuagint (Greek) translation of

---

[159] Although Hodge, Simpson and others favor the retention of the words "of his flesh and of his bones" (A.V.), the latter claiming that they have "strong MSS. support," and the former that "they are required by the context," I cannot join their company. The external evidence for their retention does not impress me as being nearly as strong as is that for their omission, and since in the present paragraph the oneness of Christ and his church has been stressed over and over, I do not see that anything is lost when they are left out.

[160] As G. Ch. Aalders has pointed out in his commentary *Het Boek Genesis* (a volume in *Korte Verklaring der Heilige Schrift*), Kampen, 1949, Vol. I, p. 127, this is indeed a divine command or ordinance. If those were right who are of the opinion that the Genesis passage (whether ascribed to Adam or to Moses) merely indicates what usually happens, or prophetically, what will generally happen, namely, that a man will leave his father and his mother, etc., the Lord would not have appealed to it as to an ordinance of God (Matt. 19:5, 6).

[161] The phrase ἀντὶ τούτο, with which the passage opens here in Eph. 5:31 and which has been interpreted variously, should really present no difficulty. It represents the Hebrew 'al-kēn = "therefore." The Septuagint has ἕνεκεν τούτου: *on account*

the Hebrew passage: **31. "Therefore shall a man leave his father and his mother and shall cleave to his wife."** The word "therefore" does not connect with anything here in 5:31. It belongs to the Genesis context. Adam rejoiced when he received Eve from the hand of Jehovah God. He gave expression to his joy and to his faith by saying, "This, indeed, is bone of my bones and flesh of my flesh! She shall be called *Ishshah* (Woman), because she was taken out of *Ish* (Man)" (Gen. 2:23). There follows: "Therefore shall a man leave his father and his mother," etc. The reasoning in Genesis is accordingly on this order: since, by virtue of creation, the bond between husband and wife is stronger than any other human relationship, surpassing even that between parents and children, therefore it is ordained that a man shall leave his father and his mother and shall cleave to his wife. God mercifully bases his *marriage ordinance* upon man's own natural inclination, the strong bent or desire with which the Almighty himself endowed him. Quotation continued: **"and the two shall become one flesh."** Whatever else this may mean as to oneness in mind, heart, purpose, etc., basically, as the very words (*cleave, flesh*) in their combination imply, the reference is to sexual union. Cf. I Cor. 6:16. In a very real sense, therefore, the two are no longer two but one. When we consider the fact that this intimate conjugal act is here placed in a context of love so deep, so self-sacrificing, so tender and pure that it (this love) is patterned after that of Christ for his church, it will be clear that no more noble description of the relation of a husband to his wife has ever been presented or is even possible. Incidentally, we are also shown here that consistent Christian living touches every phase of life, not excluding sex. The chain of our conduct as believers is as strong as is its weakest link. Note also, that according to this passage *the two* — not the three, four, five, or six — become *one* flesh. Cf. Matt. 19:5, 6. All adultery and promiscuity, by whatever fancy name it may be called, is here condemned. Cf. Matt. 5:32; Rom. 7:1-3.

Paul adds: **32. This mystery is great, but I am speaking with reference to Christ and the church.** In a footnote I list various explanations of this passage which I cannot accept.[162] Unless the context is kept in view a cor-

---

of this, but the meaning is the same. See my doctoral dissertation *The Meaning of the Preposition ἀντί in the New Testament,* 1948, p. 93.

[162] The following are just a few of the many that have been offered. The mystery is: God's purpose to unite all things in Christ, the oneness of believers with Christ, the fact that two can become one, the mysterious attraction of male for female and vice versa, the *sacrament* of marriage. The Roman Catholic view is in line with the rendering found in the Vulgate: *sacramentum hoc magnum est.* Calvin comments: "They have no ground for such an assertion [that marriage is a sacrament], unless it be that they have been deceived by the doubtful signification of a Latin word, or rather, by their ignorance of the Greek language. If the simple fact had been observed that *Mystery* is the word used by Paul, a mistake would never have occurred. We see the hammer and anvil by which they fabricate this sacrament. . . . This blunder arose from the greatest ignorance." And it is true, indeed, that if in

rect interpretation will be impossible. Paul has just now spoken about the marriage ordinance, in accordance with which *two* people become so intimately united that in a sense they become *one*. "*This mystery* is great," he says. He must, therefore, be referring to marriage. However, he makes very clear that he is not thinking of marriage *in and by itself*. He definitely mentions once more the link between it and the Christ-church relationship. Accordingly, I can find no better answer to the question, "What is meant here by *the mystery*, that is, by *the secret that would have remained hidden had it not been revealed?*" than the one given by Robertson in his *Word Pictures*, Vol. IV, p. 547: "Clearly Paul means to say that the comparison of marriage to the union of Christ and the church is the mystery." The union of Christ with the church, so that, from the sweep of eternal delight in the presence of his Father, God's only begotten Son plunged himself into the *dreadful darkness and awful anguish of Calvary* in order to save his *rebellious people*, gathered from among all the nations, and even to dwell in their hearts through his Spirit and at last to present *them* — even these utterly undeserving ones — to himself as his own bride, with whom he becomes united in such intimate fellowship that no earthly metaphor can ever do justice to it, *this* even in and by itself is a mystery. Cf. 3:4-6; Col. 1:26, 27. But the fact that this marvelous love, this blissful Christ-church relationship, is actually reflected here on earth in the union of a husband and his wife, so that by the strength of the former bond (Christ-church), the latter (husband-wife) is now able to function most gloriously, bringing supreme happiness to the marriage-partners, blessing to mankind, and glory to God *that,* indeed, is the Mystery Supreme!

This idea of marriage should never be lost sight of by those who have been united in Christian matrimony. Every day the husband should ask himself, "Does my love for my wife reveal the marks of Christ's love for his church?" That high ideal must never be relinquished. A step toward its realization is mentioned in the words: **33. Nevertheless, let each one of y o u also love his own wife as himself.** Note: "his own" wife, not someone else; "each one," there is no room for exceptions; "as himself," no less; "constantly" (implied in the present, durative imperative), not off and on. And as far as the wife is concerned: **and let the wife see to it that she respects her husband** (see on verse 22). The rendering "respects" is probably the best one. In our English language "fear" (A.R.V.) is somewhat ambiguous. Though it may not be a *wrong* translation, for the verb *fear* can be employed in the sense of reverencing (A.V. "reverence"), nevertheless since, because of popular usage this word so easily conjures up visions of awe, dread, and fright, and since "There is no fear in love; but perfect love

---

order to be a *sacrament* a custom must have been instituted by Christ and if it must be "a visible sign of invisible grace" (Augustine), then marriage cannot properly be called a sacrament.

casts out fear" (I John 4:18), it is probably better to use the word "respects" (R.S.V.). Let, therefore, the wife see to it that she "pays her husband all respect" (N.E.B.).

b. 6:1-4

"Children, obey y o u r parents.
Fathers, rear them tenderly."

6:1. Children, obey y o u r parents. Compare the following passages: Exod. 20:12; 21:15-17; Lev. 20:9; Deut. 5:16; 21:8; Prov. 1:8; 6:20; 30:17; Mal. 1:6; Matt. 15:4-6; 19:19; Mark 7:10-13; 10:19; 18:20; Col. 3:20. The apostle assumes that among those who will be listening when this letter is read to the various congregations the children will not be lacking. They are included in God's covenant (Gen. 17:7; Acts 2:38, 39), and Jesus loves them (Mark 10:13-16). Were Paul to be present with us today he would be shocked at the spectacle of children attending the Sunday School and then going home just before the regular worship service. He has a word addressed directly and specifically to the children. The implication is clear that also today sermons should be such that even the children can understand and enjoy them, at least to some extent, varying with age, etc., and at times the pastor should direct his attention *especially to* them.

What the apostle tells the children is that they should obey their parents. This obedience, moreover, should flow not only from the feeling of love, gratitude, and esteem for their parents, though these motivations are very important, but also and especially from reverence for the Lord Jesus Christ. Paul says that it should be an obedience **in the Lord,** and he adds, **for this obedience is right.** The proper attitude of the child in obeying his parents must therefore be this: I must obey my parents because the Lord bids me to do so. What he says is *right* for the simple reason that *he* says it! It is he who determines what is right and what is wrong. Hence, when I obey my parents I am obeying and pleasing *my Lord*. When I disobey them I am disobeying and displeasing *him*. It is true that, in so ordering, God — or, if one prefers, Christ — shows his wisdom and love. Under God, these children owe their very existence to their parents. The parents, moreover, are older, have had more experience, know more, and as a rule are wiser. Also, when conditions are normal, until the time of marriage no one *loves* these children more intensely than do their parents. And even after the parent-child relationship has been replaced by the (in a sense) even closer bond of husband-wife, the parents, if still alive, continue to love their children no less than before.

Paul's emphasis on the fact that such obedience is right is strengthened by a reference to an express divine command: **2, 3.** "Honor your father and your mother," which is a commandment of foremost significance, with a promise attached: "that it may be well with you" and that you may be on

earth a long time. The apostle shows what an excellent pedagogue he is, for just as even today *the ten commandments* are among those portions of Scripture which children learn by heart in their early youth, so — and probably even more so — was this true in Israel. And may we not also believe that even the children in formerly *Gentile* families were soon taught the decalogue, so that their sense of guilt and instant need of the Savior might be sharpened and their gratitude to God for salvation received might find adequate expression in consecrated conduct? [163]

The quotation is from Exod. 20:12 and Deut. 5:16, the first part of it literally according to the Septuagint. *To honor* father and mother means more than *to obey* them, especially if this obedience is interpreted in a merely outward sense. It is the inner attitude of the child toward his parents that comes to the fore in the requirement that he *honor* them. All selfish obedience or reluctant obedience or obedience under terror is immediately ruled out. To honor implies to love, to regard highly, to show the spirit of respect and consideration. This honor is to be shown to *both* of the parents, for as far as the child is concerned they are equal in authority. What follows, namely, "which is the first commandment with promise" (A.V., A.R.V., and very similarly also R.S.V., N.E.B., Phillips, Moffatt, Weymouth, Berkeley) has led to much difficulty, in view of the fact that an earlier commandment, regarded by some as the first and by others as the second, also has a promise attached to it: "showing lovingkindness to thousands of them that love me and keep my commandments" (Exod. 20:6). Surely that promise *precedes* the one that accompanies the commandment to honor father and mother. How then can Paul say that the latter is *the first* commandment with a promise? Some proposed solutions:

1. Paul means: the first commandment of the second table of the law. Objection: The division into tables is not always the same. Besides, the Jews generally regarded the commandment to honor father and mother as belonging to the first table.

2. It was the first commandment that spoke to the heart of the child, the first one which had special meaning for him. Objection: The text does not read: "the first commandment *for the child*" but ". . . *with a promise.*"

3. It was actually the first commandment with a promise, for the earlier

---

[163] In the teaching of Jesus there is constant reference to the ten commandments either as a group or singly (Matt. 5:27-32; 15:4-6; 19:18, 19; 22:37-40; Mark 10:19; 12:28-31; Luke 18:20; and perhaps John 4:24). Paul, too, refers to one or more of them not only here in Eph. 6:2, 3, but also in Rom. 7:7-12; 13:8-10; Gal. 5:14, but never as a means to be saved. *The Didache,* which has been ascribed to the period A.D. 120–180, opens with a summary of the law and in its second chapter mentions several of its commandments. See also the so-called *Letter of Barnabas,* chapters 15 and 19. It seems that not only did the Jews diligently teach the commandments to their children and to Gentile proselytes but that these commandments also figured prominently in *Christian* instruction, although, of course, the *purpose* of this teaching differed widely in the two camps.

promise (Exod. 20:6) is of a general nature. It is a promise to all who love God and keep his commandments. Objection: Though the general nature of that earlier promise must be granted, it remains true that it was attached to *the second* (or *first,* whichever way one prefers to count) commandment, so that the commandment that children honor their parents was not *the first* with an attached promise.

4. It was *the most important commandment* of the entire decalogue, *the first,* therefore, *in rank,* though not in order of enumeration. Evaluation: I believe this comes close to the truth, though it is still erroneous. Is not *the first* commandment, "Thou shalt have no other gods before me," at least as important as is *the fifth* (or *fourth*)?

There is, however, another solution which I personally accept as the right one. We arrive at it by bearing in mind two things: *a.* that the word generally translated *first* may indicate *rank* as well as numerical sequence. Thus, when a scribe asked Jesus, "Which commandment is *the first* of all?" he did not mean, "Which commandment *is mentioned first?*" but *"Which is first in importance?"* And *b.* the original does not read *"the* first commandment"; it reads, *"a* commandment first," that is, "commandment of foremost significance," not necessarily *the* most important of all.

In what sense is it true that this commandment is *one of extraordinary significance,* being so important, in fact, that in Lev. 19:1 ff. the list of commandments under the general heading, "Y o u shall be holy, for I Jehovah y o u r God am holy" opens with this one? The answer is found in the promise that is attached to it, namely, "that it may be well with you and that you may be on earth a long time." Notice the slight change in the wording from what is found in Exod. 20:12 and Deut. 5:16. Paul, by divine inspiration, lifts the promise out of its old, theocratic form. He speaks not of living long "in the land which God has given you" but of *being on the earth a long time.* The promise "that it may be well with you" (Deut. 5:16) is, however, retained. When the objection is raised that in spite of this promise many disobedient children prosper and become very old, while many obedient children die early, the answer is that the principle here expressed is, nevertheless, entirely valid. To be sure, obedience or disobedience to parents is not the only factor that determines a person's span of life, but it is an important factor. Disobedience to godly parents indicates an undisciplined life. It leads to vice and dissipation. This, in turn, *all other things being equal,* shortens life. For example, when a devout father warns his son against the evil of chain-smoking, addiction to alcohol, sins pertaining to sex, etc., and the son disregards his advice, he is following a course that does not as a rule lead to long life on the earth. In addition it should be borne in mind that though a disobedient child may live on and on and become a centenarian, as long as he continues in his wickedness *it will not be well with him.* He will have no peace! Living, as we do, in an age in which such matters as self-discipline and respect for authority are frowned upon, it is well to take to heart what is taught here in 6:2, 3. Undisciplined children spell ruin for the nation, the church, and society! The promise of God to reward obedience still holds.

Not only to wives, children, and slaves are these admonitions directed, however. Also to husbands, parents, and masters. *Glorious Renewal* must be experienced by all. So Paul, having addressed the children, turns now to the parents, and in particular to the fathers, though with application also to the mothers. **4. And fathers, do not provoke y o u r children to anger.** Note the fairness of these admonitions. The duty of wives is not stressed at the expense of that of husbands, nor that of slaves to the neglect of that of masters. So also here: the admonition addressed to fathers follows hard upon that directed to children. Although it is true that the word "fathers" at times includes "mothers" (Heb. 11:23), just as "brothers" may include "sisters," and that the directive here given certainly *applies also* to mothers, nevertheless it would hardly be correct in the present passage to substitute the word "parents" for "fathers." The fact that in verse 1 Paul employs the more usual word for *parents* seems to indicate that here in verse 4 *fathers* means just that. The reasons why the apostle addresses himself *especially* to them could well be *a.* because upon them as heads of their respective families the chief responsibility for the education of the children rests; and *b.* perhaps also because they, in certain instances even more than the mothers, are in need of the admonition here conveyed.

The parallel passage (Col. 3:21) has: "Fathers, do not exasperate y o u r children," meaning: "Do not embitter them or stir them up." There is very little essential difference between that and "Do not provoke y o u r children to anger." The cognate noun is "angry mood" (4:26). Some ways in which parents may become guilty of this error in bringing up their children:

1. *By over-protection.* The fathers — and mothers too — are so fearful that harm may befall their darlings that they fence them in from every direction: "Do not do this and do not do that. Do not go here and do not go there," until this process of pampering arrives at a point where we can almost imagine them to advise their offspring, "Do not venture into the water until you have learned to swim." Yet swim they must! To be sure, children should be warned against great dangers. On the other hand, a modicum of risk-taking is necessary for their physical, moral, and spiritual development. If the little bird remains in the safety of its nest it will never learn to fly. Besides, the over-protective attitude has the tendency of depriving the children of confidence and of instilling in them the angry mood, especially when they compare themselves with other children who are not receiving this special treatment.

2. *By favoritism.* Isaac favored Esau above Jacob. Rebekah preferred Jacob (Gen. 25:28). The sad results of such partiality are well known.

3. *By discouragement.* Example taken from life: "Dad, I am going to study hard and become a doctor," or perhaps a lawyer, teacher, mechanic, minister, or whatever it was the boy had in mind. Dad's answer: "You might as well forget about that. That will never happen anyway."

4. *By failure to make allowance for the fact that the child is growing up, has a right to have ideas of his own, and need not be an exact copy of his father to be a success.*

5. *By neglect.* In the quarrel between David and his son Absalom was the fault *entirely* on Absalom's side? Was not David also partly to blame because he neglected his son? (II Sam. 14:13, 28).

6. *By bitter words and outright physical cruelty.* Here is a father who loves to throw his weight around and to make use of his superior strength. Scolding his children and inflicting severe physical punishment has become a habit with him. Court records are filled with cases of unbelievable cruelty to boys and girls, including babes.

Paul places the positive over against the negative by continuing: **but rear them tenderly.** Fathers — mothers too — must provide their children with food, not only physical but also mental and spiritual. They must *nourish* them (see on 5:29), *rear them tenderly.*[164] "Let them be fondly cherished" (Calvin). However, this does not exclude *firmness:* **in the discipline and admonition of the Lord.** In Heb. 12:11 this word "discipline" refers to "chastening," which, though at the time when it is administered may not be pleasant, is appreciated afterward and produces excellent fruit. Cf. I Cor. 11:32; II Cor. 6:9; II Tim. 2:25. In II Tim. 3:16 this "discipline" is the *"training* in righteousness." "Discipline," accordingly, may be described as training by means of rules and regulations, rewards, and when necessary, punishments. It refers primarily to *what is done to the child.*

The meaning of the word rendered "admonition" appears from I Cor. 10:11, "These things were written for our *admonition,"* and from Titus 3:10, "After the first and second *warning* (or: admonition) have nothing to do with a factious person." "Admonition" is therefore prevailingly training by means of the spoken word, whether that word be teaching, warning, or encouragement. It refers primarily to *what is said to the child.* "Admonition" would seem to be somewhat milder than "discipline." Nevertheless, it must be earnest, not just a feeble observation such as, "No, my sons; it is not a good report that I hear" (I Sam. 2:24). In fact, it is distinctly reported that Eli "did not admonish them [his sons]" (I Sam. 3:13).[165]

All of this discipline and admonition must be "of the Lord." That should

---

[164] Since ἐκτρέφετε is used here as the antonym of *provoke to anger,* full justice should be done to its prefix; hence, *love* must replace *anger.* The children should be reared *tenderly.*
[165] See Trench, *Synonyms of the New Testament,* paragraph xxxii, an excellent treatment of the two terms παιδεία and νουθεσία.

be its *quality*. It should amount to *Christian* training, therefore, and this in its most comprehensive sense, certainly including giving the child a noble *example* of Christian life and conduct. The entire atmosphere in which the training is given must be such that the Lord can place the stamp of his approval upon it.

It is improper, in this connection, to overlook the fact that according to this passage (and cf. Deut. 6:7) not the state or society in general or even the church is *primarily* responsible for the training of the youth, though all of them have a vital interest in it and also a measure of responsibility with respect to it. But *under God* the child *belongs* first of all and most of all to the parents. It is they who should see to it that as far as they can help it those agencies that exert the most potent influence upon the child's rearing are definitely Christian. *The very heart* of Christian nurture is this: to bring *the heart* of the child to *the heart* of his Savior.[166]

c. 6:5-9

"Slaves, obey y o u r masters. Masters, stop threatening."

A rather detailed account of *Scripture on Slavery* will be found in N.T.C. on Colossians and Philemon, pp. 233–237. **5. Slaves, be obedient to those who according to the flesh are y o u r masters.** Paul does not advocate the immediate, outright emancipation of the slaves. He took the social structure as he found it and endeavored by peaceful means to change it into its opposite. His rule amounted to this: Let the slave wholeheartedly obey his master, and let the master be kind to his slave. Thus the ill-will, dishonesty, and laziness of the slave would be replaced by willing service, integrity, and industry; the cruelty and brutality of the master, by considerateness and love. Slavery would be abolished *from within*, and a gloriously transformed society would replace the old. "Be obedient" is the same command used with reference to *children* in verse 1. There is comfort in the words "masters *according to the flesh*," for it implies: "Y o u have another Master, who watches over y o u, is just and merciful to y o u in all his dealings, and to whom both y o u and y o u r earthly masters are responsible." Continued: **with fear and trembling.** Cf. II Cor. 7:15. Must they be filled with this spirit because they are slaves? No, "fear and trembling" befits anyone to whom the Lord has assigned a task (Phil. 2:12), Paul himself not excluded (I Cor. 2:3). It does not mean that slaves must approve of tyrannical methods or that they must melt with fear before their masters. It does mean, however, that they should be filled with conscientious solicitude when they recognize the real nature of their assignment, namely, so to conduct themselves toward their masters that the latter whether they be believers or not, will be able

---

[166] For a discussion of the subject *Principles and Methods of Education in Israel: Background for the Understanding of II Tim. 3:15* see N.T.C. on I and II Timothy and Titus, pp. 296–301. A brief bibliography is included in footnote 160 on p. 299.

to see what the Christian faith accomplishes within the hearts of all who practice it, not excluding slaves. This implies, of course, that slaves will recognize their own inadequacy and ask the Lord to help them to realize this high purpose. Continued: **in the sincerity of y o u r heart;** or "with single-ness of heart." That is, with an undivided mind, with integrity and upright-ness (cf. I Chron. 29:17). This obedience should be rendered **as to Christ,** that is, fully realizing that they are actually rendering it to their heavenly Master, the Lord Jesus Christ. Hence, **6. not in the way of eye-service as men-pleasers, but as slaves of Christ, doing the will of God from the heart.** They must not obey simply to catch the eye of their masters for selfish pur-poses. They should not seek to please men with the ulterior motive of seek-ing profit for themselves. The apostle means, therefore: "Fill y o u r service with the energy and the enthusiasm with which y o u would fill it were it done for Christ, *for it really is being done for Christ.* It is to him that y o u belong. Take then that service of y o u r s and lift it to a higher plain. Do the will of God from the heart, with all enthusiasm. And remember that y o u have nothing to be ashamed of. Y o u r Lord himself was also a servant, even *the Servant of Jehovah.* It was he who girded himself with a towel and washed the feet of his disciples (John 13:1-20). It was also he who said, 'For the Son of man also came not to be ministered to (or: to be served) but to minister (or: to serve), and to give his life a ransom for many' (Mark 10:45). And it was he who 'emptied himself, as he took on the form of a servant . . . humbled himself and became obedient even to the extent of death, yes, death by a cross' (Phil. 2:7, 8)." Continued: **7. with ready mind rendering service as to the Lord and not to men.** In spirit people really cease to be slaves as soon as they begin to work for the Lord and are no longer working *primarily* for men. Beyond their master they see their Master. Illustration: when the man who was conveying a load of bricks on his wheel-barrow was asked what he was doing, his answer was, "I am building a cathedral for the Lord." With that thought in mind he was putting his whole soul into his job. Paul ends his admonition to slaves by writing: **8. knowing that whatever good each one does this he will receive back from the Lord, whether (he be) slave or free.** With God there is no partiality (Lev. 19:15; Mal. 2:9; Acts 10:34; Col. 3:25; James 2:1). This is brought out very forcefully, for literally the apostle says, "knowing that *each one* [note forward position of "each one" for emphasis] whatever he does (that is) good, this he will receive back from the Lord, whether slave, whether free." It is the intrinsic good that was done that will matter in the day of judgment. And that intrinsic good is not determined by the social position of the doer, whether he was a master or a slave. Matt. 25:31-46 brings this out beautifully. *It is the nature of the deed that determines the reward.* And in that "nature" *the motivation* is, of course, included. Not only *what* one has said or has done is important but also, and especially, why he said or did it. Did his deeds prove that he really meant what he said? (Matt. 7:21-23).

Only the good is mentioned here. Both good and bad are spoken of in Eccles. 12:14; Col. 3:25; and II Cor. 5:10. Reason for the difference? We simply do not know. There may be truth in the answer of those who say that *only good* was mentioned here for the greater encouragement of the Ephesians. It is certain, at any rate, that no good deed is ever done in vain. "There's but one life [on this earth]; 'tWill soon be past. Only what's done for Christ will last." That God Triune, or that the Lord Jesus Christ in his capacity as Judge, will reward the services that were rendered in love and obedience to him, is clear from many a Scripture passage: Gen. 15:1; Ruth 2:12; Ps. 19:11; 58:11; Isa. 40:10, 11; 62:11; Jer. 31:16; Matt. 5:12; 6:4; 25 (the entire chapter); Luke 6:35; 12:37, 38; I Peter 1:17; II John 8; and Rev. 2:7, 10, 11, 17, 23, 26-28; 3:4, 5, 9-12, 20, 21; 22:12. This reward is entirely of grace, not of merit. Just as by reason of sin all *men* stand condemned before God (Rom. 3:22, 23), so also by reason of grace all *believers,* whether slave or free, receive a reward for the good they have done.

Among those to whom this letter was addressed there were probably not many "slave-owners." Cf. I Cor. 1:26-28. Yet, there were some. In fact, the same messenger who delivered this letter to its destination also delivered another letter, one addressed to a "slaveowner," namely, Philemon. This was on the same trip when the Colossians, too, received their epistle. To the masters, therefore, a word must also be addressed, but as these were relatively few in number, and as even that part of the admonition that had been addressed to the slaves was full of implied significance also for their masters, the exhortation directed specifically to the latter could be brief: **9. And masters, do the same things for them.** Co-operation must be a two-way street. It must be shown by both groups: masters and slaves. So, in effect Paul is saying to the masters: "Promote the welfare of y o u r slaves as y o u expect them to promote y o u r s. Show the same interest in them and in their affairs as y o u hope they will show in y o u and y o u r affairs." Continued: **and stop threatening.** In other words, "Let y o u r approach be positive, not negative." Hence, not, "Unless you do this, I will do that to you," but rather, "Because you are a good and faithful servant, I will give you a generous reward." Before threatening, the slave stood helpless. He had no means of defending himself, not even, generally speaking, before the law. But as a believer he did have a real Defender. Hence, the apostle directs the attention of the masters to this fact, saying: **knowing that (he who is) both their master and y o u r s is in the heavens, and there is no partiality with him.** See James 5. Because of all that has already been said on this subject of impartiality (see on verse 8), no further comment is necessary.

Summary of Chapter 4:17–6:9

This section consists of two main divisions. In the first (4:17–5:21) the admonitions are addressed to the entire church; in the second (5:22–6:9), to the different members of the family: wives, husbands; children, fathers; slaves, masters. The general theme is (The Church's) *Glorious Renewal*. This renewal or transformation has the following characteristics:

(1) As already indicated, it has reference to the church in general, but also to the individual member.

(2) It is both negative ("Put off the old man") and positive ("Put on the new man"). For the first see 4:17, 22, 25a; etc.; for the second, 4:23, 24, 25b, 28b, 32; 5:1, 2; etc. *It stresses the positive* in the sense that evil must be overcome with good (5:18-21).

(3) It opposes self-indulgence (5:3-7, 18a) and encourages self-sacrifice (5:2, 25).

(4) Its Author is the Holy Spirit (4:30; 5:18) but it fully recognizes the role of human responsibility (in all the admonitions).

(5) It relates to *the past* (break with it, 4:17, 22), *the present* (be what y o u are, 5:8), and *the future* (the inheritance *or* the experience of God's wrath, what will it be? 5:5, 6).

(6) It combats specific sins: immorality, greed, falsehood, wrath, dishonesty, corrupt speech, slander, malice, drunkenness, etc. (4:25-31; 5:18; etc.) but also the underlying evil nature (4:17, 22). Similarly, it recommends specific virtues: truthfulness, industry, generosity, gracious speech, kindness, tenderheartedness, the forgiving disposition, love, thankfulness, righteousness (4:25b, 28b, 29b, 32; 5:2, 4b, 9) but also the basic godly nature (4:23, 24).

(7) It is fair to all and believes in the principle of reciprocity in human (and especially in family) relationships (5:22–6:9).

(8) It derives its example, motive, and strength from Christ (4:32; 5:2, 23, 24).

(9) It banishes the darkness and welcomes the light (5:7-14).

(10) It is gladdening, for it causes the one who experiences it to break forth into cheerful thanksgiving, into the singing of psalms, hymns, and spiritual songs, and into making melody from the heart to the Lord.

Chapter 6:10–24

Theme: *The Church Glorious*
II. *Exhortation*
urging all to put on
the Church's God-given

E ffective Armor. Conclusion.

CHAPTER VI:10-24

10 Finally, find y o u r (source of) power in the Lord and in the strength of his might. 11 Put on the full armor of God in order that y o u may be able to stand firm against the crafty methods of the devil. 12 For not against flesh and blood is our wrestling but against the principalities, against the authorities, against the world-rulers of this darkness, against the spiritual forces of evil in the heavenly places. 13 Therefore take up the full armor of God in order that y o u may be able to stand y o u r ground in the day of evil, and having done everything, to stand firm. 14 Stand firm therefore, having fastened the belt of truth around y o u r waist, and having put on the breastplate of righteousness, 15 and having shod y o u r feet with readiness derived from the gospel of peace, 16 and in addition to everything else, having taken up the shield of faith, by means of which y o u will be able to extinguish all the flaming missiles of the evil one; 17 and take the helmet of salvation, and the sword of the Spirit which is the spoken word of God, 18 by means of all prayer and supplication, praying at all times in the Spirit, and with a view to this, being on the alert in all perseverance and supplication, for all the saints; 19 and (praying) for me, that when I open my mouth I may be given a message, so that I may make known courageously the mystery of the gospel, 20 for which I am an ambassador in a chain, that when I proclaim it I may speak with courage as I ought to speak.

21 But in order that y o u also may know my affairs, how I am getting along, Tychicus the beloved brother and faithful minister in the Lord, will make them all known to y o u, 22 whom I am sending to y o u for this very purpose, that y o u may know our circumstances and that he may strengthen y o u r hearts. 23 Peace (be) to the brothers, and love with faith, from God the Father and the Lord Jesus Christ. 24 Grace (be) with all those who love our Lord Jesus Christ with (a love) imperishable.

6:10-20

1. *"Put on the full armor of God"*

The church's

E ternal Foundation

U niversal Scope

L ofty Goal

O rganic Unity and Growth, and

G lorious Renewal

having now been set forth, there remains the exhortation that believers arm themselves with the church's God-given

E ffective Armor. This is followed by the Conclusion to the entire letter: a warm recommendation of the letter's bearer and an equally warm and unique benediction.

In all the preceding sections Paul has described salvation as being, on the one hand, the product of God's sovereign grace, on the other hand the promised reward of human effort, the latter being made possible from start to finish by the former. These two elements — divine grace and human responsibility — are again most beautifully combined in this closing section. *Man* must equip himself with a full suit of arms, that is, it is he who must *put it on.* It is also *he, he alone,* who must *use* this entire panoply. Nevertheless, the weapons are called "the full armor *of God.*" It is *God* who has forged them. It is *God* who gives them. Not for one single moment is man able to employ them effectively except by *the power of God.*

But what is it that makes the taking up of this formidable armor absolutely necessary, so essential that salvation is impossible without it? The answer is that the church has an enemy hell-bent on its destruction. So Paul begins this remarkable concluding exhortation with respect to the church's Effective Armor by saying: **10. Finally,**[167] **find y o u r (source of) power** [168] **in the Lord and in the strength of his might.** It is the exercise or manifestation of the might of the Lord that is the source of power for believers.[169] Apart from Christ Christians can accomplish nothing at all (John 15:1-5). They are like branches severed from the vine. On the other hand, in close fellowship with their Lord they can do whatever they need to do: "I can do all things in him who infuses strength into me" (Phil. 4:13; cf. II Cor. 12:9, 10; I Tim. 1:12). The reason is that the might of the Lord is infinite. By his strength God not only created the heavens and the earth, caused the mountains to tremble, the rocks to melt, Jordan to be driven back, the cedars of Lebanon to be broken in pieces, and the forests to be stripped bare, but specifically, as already emphasized in the *Ephesian* context, by his strength he caused *a. the Savior to arise from the dead (1:20)* and *b. his chosen ones to be made alive from their death in trespasses and sins (2:1).* It is, therefore, as if Paul were saying: "When I urge y o u to find y o u r source of power in the Lord and in the strength of his might, I am not making an unreasonable request, for y o u yourselves know that his omnipotence has been revealed *by these two marvelous deeds.* Hence, we are not

---

[167] In view of the present context there is only a minimal difference in meaning between τοῦ λοιποῦ ("in respect of the rest") and τὸ λοιπόν ("as for the rest"). Either reading may here be rendered "finally." Thus also N.T.L. (A. and G.), p. 481; Lenski, *op. cit.,* p. 657; and Robertson, *Word Pictures,* Vol. 4, p. 549. Contrast Simpson, *op. cit.,* p. 142.

[168] The question whether this present imperative should be construed as middle or as passive (cf. Acts 9:22; Rom. 4:20; II Tim. 2:1) is academic since the former "strengthen yourselves" or the latter "be strengthened" coalesce because of the modifier "in the Lord."

[169] For the meaning of the nouns δύναμις (implied in the verb ἐνδυναμοῦσθε), κράτος, and ἰσχύς see on 1:19.

dealing with abstractions but with *the power of God demonstrated in human history.* Y o u are aware, therefore, of the fact that when y o u ask him to strengthen y o u, he will certainly hear y o u, for he is able to do infinitely more than all we ask or imagine" (3:20).

Paul continues: **11. Put on the full armor of God in order that y o u may be able to stand firm against the crafty methods of the devil.** The question might be asked, "In view of the fact that by means of the two marvelous deeds mentioned above it has become clear that the power of God in Christ is *infinitely superior* to that of Satan and his allies, need we be so concerned about the onslaught of the prince of evil?" The answer is: "Assurance of this superiority, however, does not diminish the seriousness of any given conflict on any 'evil day' nor give certain assurance of victory in any particular battle" (Roels, *op. cit.*, p. 216). I find myself in complete agreement with the words quoted, and wish only to add that, looked at from the angle of man's responsibility, it is even possible to say that not only this or that particular battle but the entire war will be lost unless we exert ourselves. It is true that the counsel of God from eternity will never fail, but it is just as true that in that plan of God from eternity it was decided that victory will be given to those who overcome (Rev. 2:7, 11, 17, etc.). Overcomers are conquerors, and in order to conquer one must fight!

Moreover, the war must be waged *strenuously,* for the foe is none other than *ho diábolos,* that is, the devil (Matt. 4:1, 5, 8, 11; John 8:44; I Peter 5:8; Jude 9; Rev. 2:10; 12:9; 20:2). It is clear that the apostle believed in the existence of a personal prince of evil. Paul was writing to people most of whom before their rather recent conversion to the Christian faith had been in great fear of evil spirits, as is true also today among pagans. It is almost impossible to appreciate how widespread, haunting, and overwhelming is this dread of demons which one encounters throughout heathendom. How did Paul counteract this fear? Did he say what many are saying today, namely, "The world of evil spirits is one huge untruth, a mere figment of the imagination"? He did not. Instead, without accepting paganism's demonology or animism, he, nevertheless, emphasizes the great and sinister influence of Satan. So do the other inspired writers. What they all say in describing the power of the devil can be summarized somewhat as follows: Having been cast out of heaven, he is filled with fury and envy. His malevolence is directed against God and his people. His purpose is, therefore, to dethrone his great Enemy, and to cast all God's people — in fact, *all* people — into hell. He walks about as a roaring lion seeking whom he may devour. He has a powerful, well-organized army (as will be shown in a moment), and has established an outpost within the very hearts of those whom he aims to destroy.

Also, his *methods,* says Paul, are *crafty* (see on 4:14). They are the schemes *of the deceiver.* Of this fact believers are not ignorant (II Cor. 2:11).

271

Now this expression "crafty methods" will be no more than a hollow sound unless we give scriptural content to it. Some of these clever ruses and vicious stratagems are the following: mixing error with just enough truth to make it appear plausible (Gen. 3:4, 5, 22), quoting (really misquoting!) Scripture (Matt. 4:6), masquerading as an angel of light (II Cor. 11:14) and causing his "ministers" to do likewise so that they "fashion themselves as apostles of Christ" (II Cor. 11:13), aping God (II Thess. 2:1-4, 9), strengthening people in their belief that he does not even exist (Acts 20:22), entering places where he is not expected to enter (Matt. 24:15; II Thess. 2:4), and above everything else promising people that good can be attained through wrongdoing (Luke 4:6, 7).

In view of all this, therefore, it is clear why, in the name of his Sender, the apostle issues the mobilization order: "Put on the full armor of God." Leave nothing out. Y o u will need every weapon. Do not try to advance against the devil and his host with·equipage from y o u r own arsenal. Rather, say with David, "I cannot go with these, for I have not proved them" (I Sam. 17:39). Such weapons as trusting in human merits, in one's own erudition or mental acumen, in seclusion from the world, in the invocation of saints and of angels, in the theory that sin, sickness, and Satan do not exist, etc. will not avail in "the evil day." Therefore, "put on the full armor *of God,* forged by him and furnished by him. Put it on, equip yourselves with it so that y o u may be able *to stand,* not *to stand idle* but in the battle *to stand firm, to hold y o u r ground* against the devil's crafty methods." Continued:

12. For not against flesh and blood is our wrestling but against the principalities, against the authorities, against the world-rulers of this darkness, against the spiritual forces of evil in the heavenly places. The reason for the urgent character of the admonition is that we are not fighting against "flesh and blood," [170] that is, against mere, frail men (Gal. 1:16), with all their physical and mental infirmities (respectively I Cor. 15:50 and Matt. 16:17). On the contrary it is against an innumerable supermundane host of evil spirits: the devil himself and all the demons under his control, that we are waging warfare. These fallen angels are here characterized as "principalities" and "authorities" (on which see 1:21 and N.T.C. on Col. 1:6); as "the world-rulers of this darkness," that is, as those who — under the permissive providence of God — are in tyrannical control of the world of ignorance, sin, and sadness; and as "the spiritual forces of evil *in the heavenly places,*" that is, in the supermundane realm. The term, "heavenly places," although *everywhere,* including here, referring to what may be called in a very broad sense "the celestial sphere" cannot have *precisely the same* meaning here as elsewhere. While in the remaining Ephesian passages it

---

[170] Literally here and in Heb. 2:14 "blood and flesh," but it is futile to search for any important difference in meaning between this word order and the reverse in Matt. 16:17; I Cor. 15:50; and Gal. 1:16.

indicates the heaven whence blessings descend (1:3), where Christ sits enthroned at the Father's right hand (1:20), where the redeemed are seated with Christ (2:6), and where the good angels have their abode (3:10), it must *here* (6:12) refer to the region above the earth but below the heaven of the redeemed; in other words, it must here indicate what in 2:2 is called "the domain of the air." Inasmuch as the reference is to "the world-rulers of this darkness" with whom believers must *contend*, this alteration in the application of the term should not cause any difficulty. See further on 2:2.

When the apostle implies that with "the full armor of God," including such weapons as *shield* and *sword* (verses 16, 17), we must "wrestle" against the innumerable spiritual host, he must not be accused of inconsistency, as if he started out with the idea of believers opposing the foe on the field of battle, and then quickly changed the scenery from that of the battle-field to that of the gymnasium. The true explanation is probably far more simple: the apostle means that *the battle* is such a violent hand-to-hand encounter that *in that respect* it amounts to *wrestling*. If this is a mixed metaphor it is not inconsistent.

Now it is because of this very intense and personal nature of the warfare against the devil and all his minions that Paul repeats and also develops the thought already expressed in verse 11, by saying: **13. Therefore take up the full armor of God.** The language used here is very incisive. The command is curt and crisp, as if to say, "Do not allow the enemy to find y o u defenseless. Take up y o u r armor. Do so at once, without any hesitancy or waste of time. And remember: take up the *full* panoply!" [171] The purpose is: **in order that y o u may be able to stand y o u r ground in the day of evil,** that is, in the day of severe trial, the critical moments in y o u r lives when the devil and his sinister underlings will assault y o u most vehemently (cf. Ps. 41:2; 49:5). And inasmuch as one never knows when these crises will occur, the clear implication is: be ready *always*.

We must be careful, however, not to infer from this that Christians are pictured here as sitting back, as it were, waiting in the shelter of their fortress for Satan's attack. The context (see on verses 17 and 19) does not allow this rather common interpretation. The "standing" of which Paul speaks (verses 11, 14) is not that of a brick wall that is waiting passively, as it were, for the assault of the battering ram. The soldiers referred to here are drawn up in battle array and rushing into the fight. They are both defending themselves and attacking. Only when they make full use of God's armor will they be able to "stand their ground," that is, to withstand the foe, stand up against [172] him, repulse his onrush and even gain ground, for the sentence

---

[171] The urgency of the command appears from the five aorists that are used in this one sentence.
[172] ἀντιστῆναι from ἀνθίστημι, an ἀντί-compound, occurring also in the following passages: Matt. 5:39; Luke 21:15; Acts 6:10; 13:8; Rom. 9:19; 13:2; Gal. 2; 11;

continues: **and having done everything, to stand firm.** The assumption is that they *will have accomplished thoroughly* — will have carried through to the end, as implied in the original — marvelous things. Resisting the devil, standing up against him, has this comforting result that, at least for the moment, the devil will flee (James 4:7; cf. Matt. 10:22).

To give even more substance to the character and the necessity of this battle against the devil and his hosts, this intense and vehement struggle, see what it meant in the life and labors of Paul himself. For him it had been, and/or was even now, a fight against Satan-inspired Jewish and pagan vice and violence; against Judaism among the Galatians and others; against fanaticism among the Thessalonians; against contention, fornication, and litigation among the Corinthians; against incipient Gnosticism among the Ephesians and far more among the Colossians; against fightings without and fears within; and last but not least, against the law of sin and death operating within his own heart.

It may be regarded as a trite saying, but it is true nevertheless, that the best defense is an offense. All of Paul's missionary journeys may be regarded as manifestations of offensive warfare. Paul was invading the territory which heretofore had been the devil's own, for "the whole world lieth in the evil one" (I John 5:19). The reason he had made these incursions into the hostile territory, and was going to make even more, was that the devil had something that was earnestly desired by the apostle, namely, the souls of men. Paul wanted them in order to present them to God. He yearned with all his heart to be used as God's agent in bringing about the rescue of men from the realm of darkness and their transfer into the kingdom of light. Whenever he refers to this subject he uses language that is expressive of deep feeling (Rom. 1:13; 10:1; I Cor. 9:22; 10:33; etc.). Paul loved ardently!

We see, therefore, that in order properly to interpret what the apostle meant by this battle it must be borne in mind that the church and Satan are on a collision course. They are rushing at each other. They clash!

With all this by way of introduction, showing why believers must by all means be fully equipped for battle against the forces of evil, their suit of armor is now described. In order to do this the apostle makes use of six metaphors derived from the armor of the Roman hoplite, the heavily armed Roman legionary going forth to battle. To be sure, there is also a seventh weapon, the climax of them all. However, that seventh one stands in a place all by itself. It is not indicated by any figure or metaphor. To do jus-

---

II Tim. 3:8; 4:15; James 4:7; and I Peter 5:9. While in all of these passages it means *to resist*, in some it implies *to resist successfully* (Luke 21:15; Acts 6:10; Rom. 9:19). In the present instance (Eph. 6:13) the successful character of the resistance is brought out especially in the words: "and having done everything, to stand firm." See also footnote 161.

tice to the six one should see the entire picture all at once. Hence, verses 14-17 are printed together here:

14-17. Stand firm therefore,

a. having fastened the belt of truth around y o u r waist,

b. and having put on the breastplate of righteousness,

c. and having shod y o u r feet with readiness derived from the gospel of peace,

d. and in addition to everything else, having taken up the shield of faith, by means of which y o u will be able to extinguish all the flaming missiles of the evil one;

e. and take the helmet of salvation,

f. and the sword of the Spirit which is the spoken word of God.

When the question is asked, "What was the source of this imagery?" the answer is anything but unanimous. Some are of the opinion that *the Roman guard* to which Paul was attached by means of a "chain" or handcuff (verse 20) naturally suggested the various pieces of the panoply of which mention is made here. But it is hard to believe that a guard inside a prison would be holding the huge shield of which mention is made in verse 16. *The lightly armed fighter*, equipped with bow and arrows, will not do either as a basis for the symbolism we find here. As to *the Roman warrior*, the Greek historian Polybius describes him as having a shield, sword, two javelins, a helmet, greaves, and heart-guard or something more elaborate to replace it. It is evident at once that Paul mentions neither greaves nor javelins. On the other hand, he does mention the girdle or belt and, by implication, the shoes. Perhaps the best answer to the question as to source would seem to lie in this general direction: the apostle is thinking of the heavily armed Roman soldier, but in the use of his metaphors is being constantly influenced by such Old Testament passages as Isa. 11:5; 49:2; 59:17; etc., passages which he does not slavishly copy but modifies for his own purpose. Also, it must be borne in mind that much earlier than this Paul had already made use of somewhat similar language: "But since we belong to the day, let us be sober, putting on a breastplate of faith and love, and for a helmet (the) hope of salvation" (I Thess. 5:8). Cf. I Cor. 9:7; II Cor. 6:7. Later he was going to write II Tim. 2:3, 4. After all, the imagery found here in Eph. 6:14-17 would naturally suggest itself to a battle-scarred veteran like Paul.

When we study the various pieces of the panoply there is one item that must not be left unmentioned, namely, the (by and large) natural order in which the various pieces are mentioned: the soldier would first of all fasten his *belt*, next put on his *breastplate*, then his *sandals*. Also, having taken his shield with his left hand and now holding it, he could not very well follow up this action immediately by taking his sword with his right hand, not sheathing it but *holding* it in readiness for immediate use, for in that case he would have no hand left with which to take the helmet. Hence, the order is *shield, helmet, sword*. This, to be sure, was not the only possible sequence, and may not even have been the actual order in which a soldier would equip himself. The order: helmet, sword, and shield suggests itself. But possibly in order to work his way toward a climax Paul mentions first those weapons which in physical warfare are considered defensive, and saves the sword, as the most emphatically and obviously offensive weapon, to the very last.

Now before setting out to do battle with as formidable a foe as the devil and all his host, one may well ask the question: *"Do I really want to fight him at all? Am I sincere about this spiritual warfare?"* Hence, Paul says, "Stand firm, therefore, having fastened the belt of truth around y o u r waist." The girdle or belt, in physical warfare, was fastened or buckled around the short tunic worn by the soldier. Thus his limbs were braced up for action. Both breastplate and sword (the latter when not in use) were subsequently attached to this cincture. The belt, therefore, was very important. It was basic. So also in spiritual warfare *truthfulness* — which Paul has been stressing right along over against the *deceitfulness* that characterizes the man of the world (4:15, 25; 5:6, 9) — is the basic quality needed by the warrior. By this truthfulness is meant *sincerity of mind and heart,* removal of all guile and hypocrisy. There must be "truth in the inward parts" (Ps. 51:6).[173] "Whosoever is fearful and trembling, let him return home" (Judg. 7:3). And more than two-thirds of the army went home! In the battle against Satan and his armies there is no room for Demas! Sincerity is a mighty weapon, and this not only defensively. All other things being equal, the sincere person is far more likely to be a blessing to all those with whom he comes in contact than is the hypocrite.

The second question is: *"Am I living the kind of life that enables me to engage in this conflict?"* Have I put on "the breastplate of righteousness"? Cf. Isa. 59:17. In the underlying figure the breastplate has been described as the armor that covered the body from neck to thighs. It consisted of two parts, one covering the front, the other the back (cf. I Sam. 17:5, 38; I Kings 22:34; II Chron. 26:14; Neh. 4:16). Spiritually the breastplate is *the devout and holy life, moral rectitude* (Rom. 6:13; 14:17). It will be recalled that in I Thess. 5:8 Paul speaks of "the breastplate of faith and love." In both of the previous Ephesian instances the word "righteousness" was employed in an ethical sense (4:24; 5:9). And in II Cor. 6:7 Paul mentions "the armor of righteousness on the right hand and on the left," that is, such armor as enables one to meet attack from any quarter. This occurs in a context in which purity, kindness, etc. are also mentioned. In addition it should be borne in mind that the apostle in this very epistle has been plac-

---

[173] Along this line the figure is interpreted by Calvin, Erdman, Greijdanus, Salmond, Scott, and others.

ing great stress on the necessity of living lives worthy of the calling with which believers were called (4:1). Apart from such a life the would-be Christian has *no defense* against Satan's accusations. He has no assurance of salvation. And he also lacks the power to attack, for the testimony of the lips will be ineffective, the neighbor will not be won for Christ, and the evil one will not be vanquished. On the other hand, when *righteousness* in conduct is present, what a mighty weapon for defense and offense it becomes! [174]

"Am I prepared to fight?" is the next question. In other words, Have I shod my feet with "readiness derived from the gospel of peace"? The meaning of this expression has been much debated. Nevertheless, the following facts must be admitted: *a.* In order to promote facility of motion over all kinds of roads Roman soldiers were in the habit of putting on "shoes thickly studded with sharp nails" (Josephus, *Jewish Wars* VI. i. 8). Thus, one important reason for Julius Caesar's success as a general was the fact that his men wore military shoes that made it possible for them to cover long distances in such short periods that again and again the enemies were caught off guard, having deceived themselves into thinking that they still had plenty of time to prepare an adequate defense. In the victories won by Alexander the Great this same factor had played an important role. Accordingly, proper footwear spells readiness. *b.* A person who experiences within his own heart the peace of God that passes all understanding, the very peace which the gospel proclaims, has been delivered of a great burden. The conviction of being reconciled with God through the blood of Christ gives him the courage and the zeal to fight the good fight. If *the gospel,* accepted by faith, had not given him this peace, how could he be prepared to engage in this battle? *c.* The fact that this *readiness* is actually *derived from the gospel whose message or content is peace* is clear from such passages as 2:15, 17; cf. Rom. 5:1. The expression "having shod y o u r feet with readiness derived from the gospel of peace" makes good sense, therefore. Here again the believer has a twofold weapon, defensive and offensive.

"Am I able to defend myself against Satan's attack?" Prominent among the weapons of defense were *the shield* for the protection of the body (especially the heart, lungs, and other vital organs) and *the helmet* for the protection of the head. As to the shield, the one to which reference is made here measured four feet in length by two and one half feet in breadth and was oblong in shape and covered with leather. It was a kind of "door" for protection against enemy-missiles dipped in pitch or similar material and

---

[174] This explanation is favored by Calvin, Erdman, Salmond, Westcott, etc. Lenski, on the other hand, rejects it, and interprets the figure as having reference to imputed righteousness, *op. cit.,* p. 667. It is true, of course, that imputed and imparted righteousness can never be separated. They can, however, be distinguished. For the reasons given the reference here in 6:14 is to *imparted* righteousness.

set on fire before being discharged. When these darts collided with the shields their points were blunted, their flames extinguished. Similarly the exercise of genuine God-given faith enables one "to extinguish all the flaming missiles of the evil one." In the devil's quiver there are all kinds of fiery bolts. Paul mentions "tribulation, anguish, persecution, famine," etc. Some of these missiles enkindle doubt, others lust, greed, vanity, envy, etc. Only by looking away from self to God Triune, placing one's trust in him for life, death, and eternity, relying on his word of revelation and promise, is it possible to repel this shower of flaming arrows. Things looked thoroughly hopeless to Jairus when his servants arrived with the announcement, "Your daughter is dead, do not bother the Teacher any more." But Jesus answered, "Fear not, only believe" (Luke 8:49, 50). But faith is more than a weapon of defense. It is also "the victory that overcomes the world" (I John 5:4).[175] Surely, this shield must be taken up "in addition to everything else."

"And take the helmet of salvation," says Paul, borrowing this metaphor from Isa. 59:17. However, Paul applies the figure differently, for in Isaiah it is Jehovah who wears this helmet, but here in Ephesians believers are called upon to receive it. In I Thess. 5:8 the apostle had identified the helmet with "the hope of salvation," here with salvation itself. The difference is perhaps not as important as it may seem, since salvation is both a present possession and an inheritance not yet fully acquired in this life; hence, the object of firmly anchored hope.

"Take it," says Paul. The verb might also be translated: *accept* (it). Just as a helmet is *accepted* by the soldier out of the hand of the officer in charge of supply and distribution, so salvation and all that pertains to it, including even the faith whereby we accept it (2:8), is God's free gift. The helmet of iron and brass (I Sam. 17:5, 38; II Chron. 26:14; cf. I Macc. 6:35) afforded a measure of protection for the head, as did the breastplate for the heart, etc. In the Herodian period Greek and Roman helmets both of leather and brass were used extensively. It is easy to see that for the Christian salvation is indeed a weapon of *defense*. Were it not for the fact that in the midst of hardship and persecution the assurance of salvation both present and future dwells in his heart he might easily give up the fight. It is exactly this precious treasure that fortifies him with strength to continue the fight, for *as to himself* he knows that what God has begun in him will be carried on to completion (Ps. 138:8; Phil. 1:6). *As to the neighbor* whom the helmeted believer is trying to rescue from the power of darkness, God's word will never return to him void but will accomplish that which he pleases (Isa. 55:11). Hence, the Christian soldier continues the fight, with "blessed as-

---

[175] While by far the most commentators view this shield as a symbol of faith in action, which, as I see it, is the correct explanation, Lenski places the emphasis on "the objective content of faith" (*op. cit.*, p. 671).

surance" clearly evident in his looks and entire demeanor and with a testimony upon his lips. It is clear therefore that also the helmet as Paul here interprets it (= salvation) is not only a piece of *defensive* armor. Do not the *songs* of salvation, considered as an essential part of salvation, constitute a mighty weapon in the believers' *offensive* as well as defensive armor?

The final question is, *"Have I learned the art of offensive warfare?"* We have been studying those weapons that are generally included under the heading *defensive armor*. We have seen, however, that though in physical warfare this description may be entirely adequate, in spiritual combat it hardly reaches far enough. Even *truthfulness* or *integrity* — the belt — is not exclusively defensive. *It captivates! Righteousness* — the breastplate — not only serves as a protection; it also wins the neighbor for Christ, that God may be glorified (Matt. 5:16). The *peace* that provides *readiness* for the spiritual battle — the *shoes* — furnishes both time and energy for invading the enemy's domain and robbing him of the spoils he has taken. *Faith* — the shield — overcomes the world, recapturing the lost. And *salvation* — the helmet — sings its way into the enemy's prison-camp, setting the prisoners free. But although all this is undoubtedly true, nevertheless, *the most conspicuously offensive weapon,* offensive both in physical and spiritual combat, is certainly the sword. Says Paul: " (and take) the sword of the Spirit which [176] is the word of God."

The underlying figure is that of *the short sword,* the one carried and wielded by the heavily armed Roman soldier.[177] With it he not only defended himself, but sallied forth into the ranks of the enemy and won victories. As has already been indicated (see on 5:26), *this sword is the gospel* (cf. I Peter 1:25), *God's utterance;* if you wish, *the Bible, the entire Word of God.* First it was spoken by him, and now his servants proclaim it to others. *As long as what they proclaim is really in harmony with God's special revelation as it was subsequently deposited in written or printed form in what we now call the Bible it remains the very sword here referred to.* Even the least deviation from the word as originally given is, of course, the word of man, not of God. Errors in transcription or translation, in doctrine or in ethics, no matter how enthusiastically these may be defended from the pulpit, are no part of "the spoken (or: uttered) word." It is this word that "stands forever" (Isa. 40:8), and cannot be defeated. The hammers that would destroy it will be broken. The anvil remains.

This spoken word is called "the sword *of the Spirit*" because it is given by the Spirit (II Tim. 3:16; II Peter 1:21) and perhaps also because by the Spirit it is applied to the heart. Soldiers for Christ handle the word, heed

---

[176] The neuter ὅ may be due to the influence of ῥῆμα, which is stressed.
[177] This μάχαιρα is distinguished from the ῥομφαία (Luke 2:35; Rev. 1:16; 2:12, 16; 6:8; 19:15, 21). The latter is the heavy great-sword that proceeded out of Christ's mouth as John saw him in a vision on Patmos.

it, hide it in their hearts, and hold it forth among the nations. The sword, thus wielded, is "living and active, sharper than any two-edged sword, piercing even to the dividing of soul and spirit, of joints and marrow, and quick to discern the thoughts and intentions of the heart" (Heb. 4:12).[178] By using this powerful sword Paul and his associates had won amazing victories. And any victory that is being won today either at home or abroad is the result of the wielding of this sword. *God is not dead!* He lives and speaks in and through his message.

It is by means of it that man's state of guilt before God is revealed, his sinful condition exposed. Through it, too, when applied to the heart by the Spirit, man is led to the Savior from sin, and to thanksgiving and praise. Through it doubts are dispelled, fears driven away, assurance of salvation given, and Satan put to flight. When Jesus was tempted he answered every word of the devil by an appeal to the written Word of God!

The Four "All's"[179] of Prayer

The *word of God directed to men* (verse 17) is very powerful indeed, especially when it is in close association with *the word of men directed to God* (verses 18-20), not as if God and men were equal partners but because the word of men directed to God is Spirit-given, Spirit-guided ("in the Spirit"). Paul writes:

18. by means of all prayer and supplication,
    praying at all times in the Spirit,
    and with a view to this, being on the alert in all perseverance and supplication,
    for all the saints.

In his own power the soldier can do nothing against so great a foe. Hence, as he takes and puts on each piece of his armor and as he makes use of it in the battle he must pray for God's blessing.

1. *The Variety of Prayer: "all* prayer and supplication"

The apostle makes a special point of it that the soldier's communion with his General — the believer's fellowship with his God — should not be of just one kind. Some people are always asking for things. Their entire prayer-life consists of that. But *prayer* — the first word is very general — should include not only cries for help but also confession of sin, profession of faith, adoration, thanksgiving, intercession. Moreover, prayer-life should be definite, not just "O Lord, bless all that awaits thy blessing," which is a big order, but "supplication" or "petition" for the fulfilment of definite

---

[178] In this passage the *"word"* is λόγος, not ρῆμα, but the central thought is the same for either, for the two terms are coextensive.
[179] The word πᾶς ("all") is used four times in verse 18: πάσης, παντί, πάσῃ, and πάντων, four different forms.

needs, a request for specific benefits. This means that the man who prays should become acquainted with concrete situations all over, at least not limited to his own contracted horizon, situations in connection with which help is needed. He should set aside, perhaps, *today* to stress this need, *tomorrow* to remember another.

2. *The "when" and the "where" of Prayer:* "at *all* times . . . in the Spirit."

Prayer in time of "great calamity" or "catastrophe" has long been in vogue. For many people, however, "Thanksgiving Day" comes just once a year. It is the day set aside by the national government. The apostle admonishes the addressed to take hold on God "at every occasion." "In *all* thy ways acknowledge him" (Prov. 3:6).

As to the "where" of prayer, it is not to be confined either to "Jerusalem" or to "this mountain" but should always be "in (the sphere of) the Spirit," that is, "with his help" and "in harmony with his will" as revealed in the Word which he inspired.

3. *The Manner of Prayer:* "being on the alert in *all* perseverance and supplication." Cf. Col. 4:2.

Those who are not "alert" but listless and indifferent to what is going on in their homes, in the streets of their city, in their state or province, in their country, in their church, in their denomination, or in the world at large will have a very restricted prayer-life. Those who do not know the will of God because they devote so little time to the study of the Word will fail to harvest the fruits of prayer. Those who do not know the promises cannot be expected to "go to the deeps of God's promise" in their devotions. They will not partake of a deep and satisfying communion with God. Consequently, they will perhaps pray now and then only. There will be no "perseverance" and little "supplication" (petition for definite benefits).

4. *The Indirect Objects of Prayer:* "for *all* the saints"

Christ during his sojourn on earth evaluated intercessory prayer ("prayer for others") very highly, as is shown by many incidents (Matt. 9:18-26; 15:21-28; 17:14-21; etc.). So did Paul. The heart of our Great Intercessor who not only intercedes for us but actually *lives in order to do so* (Heb. 7:25) is deeply touched by such petitions! Thus the fellowship of saints is kept alive and real.

In this fellowship of prayer the Jewish convert must not forget the Gentile convert, the old must not ignore the young, the free must not neglect those in bondage, nor vice versa. It must be prayer "for *all* the saints." With God there is no partiality.

Up to this point the apostle has said very little about his own physical circumstances. He is not a complainer. He has made brief mention of the fact that he was writing as a prisoner (3:1; 4:1), and has also urged the

Ephesians "not to lose heart" over what he was suffering for them (3:13).
But that was all; and even in the given passages he was thinking not of himself so much as of the welfare of those addressed.

Now at last he for one brief moment centers the attention on himself, his
own needs, and asks that when prayer is made "for all the saints," he, too,
may be remembered in a special way. Notice, however, how nobly he expresses himself: **19. and (praying) for me, that when I open my mouth I
may be given a message, so that I may make known courageously the
mystery of the gospel.** Cf. Col. 4:2, 3. Even the requested prayer for himself
is in reality to be a petition for the progress of the gospel! Paul knew that
the Lord had chosen him to be a prominent leader. As such, a heavy load of
responsibility rested on his shoulders! Yet, he was aware of his own weakness,
of the fact that he stood in need of divine strength and guidance every
moment. So, as he had done on other occasions (Rom. 15:30; I Thess. 5:25;
II Thess. 3:1, 22) and was doing now also in another letter (Col. 4:3), he
asks that those whom he addresses will remember him in their prayers. He
does not ask, however, that they may pray for his release from prison. What
he does ask is that they may invoke God's blessing upon him as an effective
witness for Christ. "Ask God to give me two things," he says, as it were:
a. "a message when I open my mouth" (Matt. 10:19), and *b. "courage* at all
times to deliver that message in a worthy manner" (cf. Acts 4:13). In his
zeal for the salvation of sinners to the glory of God the apostle considered
even his present difficult circumstances to be an opportunity to tell everyone
— the constantly changing guards, the visitors, the Roman tribunal in case he
should (or should *again*) be summoned to appear before it — "the mystery
of the gospel" (= "the mystery concerning Christ," Col. 4:3), the blessed
truth which would have remained a secret had not God revealed it, namely,
that in Christ there is salvation full and free for *everyone* who embraces him
by faith, even for both Jew and Gentile on a basis of perfect equality. Cf.
3:3, 4, 9; Rom. 16:25; Col. 1:26, 27; 2:2; 4:3; I Tim. 3:9, 16. Continued:
20. for which I am an ambassador in a chain. The fact that when Paul arrived in Rome he, by a chain at the wrist, was fastened to a Roman guard is
implied in Acts 28:20. Though his first Roman imprisonment, during which
Colossians, Philemon, Ephesians, and Philippians were written, seems never
to have been as harsh and severe as his second was going to be, he was a
"prisoner," nevertheless. (For the first imprisonment compare 3:1; 4:1; with
Acts 28:16, 30. For the second imprisonment see II Tim. 1:12; 2:3, 10; 4:6-8,
14-16).

His imprisonment, however, is not a shame. It is an honor; for whatever
men may think, the truth of the matter is that he is, and is conscious of being, *an ambassador* [180] *in a chain*. What a paradox! Is not an *ambassador*

---

[180] The verb used is πρεσβεύω, meaning: "I am a πρεσβευτής, an ambassador." This
word πρεσβευτής must not be confused with πρεσβύτης, old man (Philem. 9).

supposed to be *free?* But here is an official representative of him who is King of kings and Lord of lords, and *this* ambassador is chained! May he never forget whom he represents. Therefore, whenever he proclaims the glorious *mystery of the gospel* may he do so in a manner befitting his high office. "Pray," says he, that when I proclaim it I may speak with courage as I ought to speak; virtually repeating, for the sake of emphasis, what he has said in the preceding verse.

On this high level Paul ends the main part of his epistle. He has been setting forth "the benefits divine which we in Christ possess." As an ambassador equipped with this message he is writing, both *defending and attacking,* both *reacting against* anyone who might wish to oppose his Sender's gospel *and* at the same time *taking the initiative* and with his message invading the enemy's territory. Does not this passage (6:19, 20) shed light on the manner in which the immediately preceding "whole armor of God" should be interpreted, that is, as indicating *a panoply that is both defensive and offensive?* It is as if we can hear the apostle making his appeal and saying:

"On Christ's behalf, therefore, we are ambassadors, seeing that God is entreating through us. We implore (y o u) on behalf of Christ, be reconciled to God! Him who knew no sin he made (to be) sin on our behalf that we might become God's righteousness in him."

6:21-24

2. *Conclusion*

The item of information contained in verses 21 and 22, including a warm recommendation of Tychicus, the bearer of these letters (Colossians, Philemon, Ephesians), is almost identical with Col. 4:7, 8. The slight differences can be seen by comparing the parallel passages in Ephesians and Colossians on p. 25. If Colossians (right column) was written before Ephesians (left column), as I have assumed, then the word "also" (in "that y o u *also* may know my affairs") here in Eph. 6:21 can be explained as meaning: "y o u as well as the Colossians." The entire passage in Ephesians is as follows: **21, 22. But in order that y o u also may know my affairs, how I am getting along, Tychicus, the beloved brother and faithful minister in the Lord, will make them all known to y o u, whom I am sending to y o u for this very purpose, that y o u may know our circumstances and that he may strengthen y o u r hearts.**

Tychicus [181] was one of Paul's intimate friends and highly valued envoys. He hailed from the province of Asia, and had accompanied the apostle when

---

[181] For the meaning of the name see N.T.C. on Philippians, pp. 138, 139, footnote 116, where the explanation of many other personal names is also given. For more on Tychicus, e.g., his relation to Paul after the latter's first Roman imprisonment, see N.T.C. on Titus 3:12 and on II Tim. 4:12.

at the close of the third missionary journey the latter was returning from Greece through Macedonia and then across into Asia Minor and so to Jerusalem on a charitable mission (Acts 20:4); that is, on that trip Tychicus had traveled in advance of Paul from Macedonia to Troas, and had been waiting for the apostle in that city. And now, some four years later, having spent some time with Paul in Rome during the latter's first Roman imprisonment, Tychicus had been commissioned by the apostle to carry these letters to their destination, as is clear from the present passage, from its parallel in Colossians, and from a comparison of Col. 4:9 with Philem. 1, 8-22. It stands to reason that Tychicus, having just now spent some time with Paul and being a "beloved brother" — a member of the Father's Family, along with all believers — and "faithful minister in the Lord" — Christ's special servant, loyal to his Master in every respect — , would be the right person, as he traveled from church to church, to supply all the necessary information about Paul and his companions and fellow-Christians in Rome. Besides, paper was not as plentiful and cheap as it is today, the circumstances under which Paul had to dictate his letters were not altogether favorable, and certain things are better *said* than *written*, especially in a letter intended for a wide circle of readers (which was true also of Colossians, as Col. 4:16 indicates, though probably in a more limited way). The oral message which Tychicus will bring will be not only *informative*, however, but also *consolatory*. Hence, Paul writes: "that y o u may know our circumstances and that he may strengthen y o u r hearts," the latter, no doubt, by stilling their fears (see on 3:13; cf. Phil. 1:12-14) and by supplying the "atmosphere" of consolation and spiritual strengthening based on the promises of God. The most substantial consolation of all would be the very letter of Paul which Tychicus would deliver.

The closing benediction follows: **23. Peace (be) to the brothers, and love with faith, from God the Father and the Lord Jesus Christ.** Peace, love, and faith are among the themes most often referred to in this epistle. For *peace* see 1:2; 2:14, 15, 17; 4:3; and 6:15; for *love* among the brothers or within the community (including the love of a husband for his wife) see 1:15; 4:2, 15, 16; 5:25, 28, 33; in a more general sense: 3:17; 5:2a; for the love of God in Christ for believers: 1:4; 2:4; 3:19; 5:2b; and for *faith* see 1:15; 2:8; 3:12, 17; 4:5, 13; 6:16. These were the very qualities that needed to be emphasized in that day and age. Is not the same true also today?

The *peace* of which the apostle is thinking is harmony among brothers. Nevertheless, it cannot exist unless through faith in Christ and his atoning sacrifice it has been established first of all in the heart of individual believers. It is impossible to separate these two. *Love*, too, though here again emphatically that among brothers, cannot be separated from the love toward God in Christ; both of these resulting from the love of God in Christ for those who are his own. *Faith* means trusting in God Triune who has revealed himself to the church in Jesus Christ. It is the gift of God (2:8). Verse 24 adds *grace*.

There are those who lay special stress on what they believe to be "the reverse order" in which these items are here mentioned. As they see it, in this enumeration the effect precedes the cause, the "proper" order being: first *grace*, because it is that divine attribute to which man owes everything; next *faith*, because it is the fruit of grace; and finally *peace and love*, as twin children of faith. I have no objection whatever against this representation as long as it makes allowance for an important qualification. To be sure, God's grace is basic. None of the others can ever begin to approach it as the cause or producer of every virtuous quality or activity in man. Yet, the relationship between the items here mentioned is richer and more bountiful by far than the simple sequence: grace → faith $\Big\langle$ peace & love indicates. Each quality, as soon as it is present, reacts upon the others and enriches them. The more a person exercises his faith in the Lord Jesus Christ, the more also the work of divine grace will blossom forth in his life; and so also with the others. Love has been described as faith's fruit, but it also enriches faith; etc. All these qualities, attitudes, and activities proceed from "God the Father," who is their Source, and "the Lord Jesus Christ" (see on 1:17) who by the shedding of his blood merited them as gifts for his children. The perfect equality of Father and Son is again clearly evident: *one* preposition ("from") precedes both. Continued: **24. Grace (be) with all those who love our Lord Jesus Christ with (a love) imperishable.** It has been pointed out that in verse 23 the love to which reference is made is "emphatically that among brothers." Here in verse 24 it is the love for *the Lord Jesus Christ* that is stressed. Grace was the root of this love. The enrichment of grace is the fruit of the love that has the Savior as its object. Once this love for Christ is present in the heart it can never vanish for it is a divine endowment. Literally, the apostle says, "Grace" — that is, *the* very grace to which he has referred so often (see especially 2:5-8) — "(be) with all those loving our Lord Jesus Christ *in imperishability*." For *imperishability* or *incorruptibility* see also Rom. 2:7; I Cor. 15:42, 50, 53, 54; II Tim. 1:10. It is, however, not in conflict with good grammar to construe this last phrase as an adverb; hence, "imperishably." As to what it modifies it surely seems more natural that it would belong to the nearby *loving* than to anything more remote. In harmony with many interpreters, therefore, and also with most translators, I, therefore, translate as follows: "those loving imperishably," which is the same as saying, "Grace (be) with all those who love our Lord Jesus Christ with a love which, once present, can never perish."

Seed Thoughts of Ephesians 6:10-24

(one thought for each verse)

See Verse

10. The exhortation to find one's source of power in the Lord is reasonable, for the Lord has demonstrated his power again and again both in nature and in grace and is still doing this.

11. The omission of a single piece of armor is dangerous, for the devil will soon discover a person's Achilles' heel.

12. Denial of the existence and activity of a personal devil and his well-organized hosts is becoming more foolish every day.

13. In order to stand your ground in the day of evil or crisis, stand your ground *today!*

14. A sincere resolve to fight Satan in the strength of the Lord, coupled with right conduct, points the way to victory. Make full use therefore of the God-given *effective Armor.*

15. It is the guilt-eased heart that makes the feet nimble.

16. Against Sinai's lightnings, hell's rage, and the atheist's ridicule the firm grip of faith in God and his promise always wins.

17. Assurance of salvation is contagious: almost everyone likes to listen to the martial music of an army marching on to victory. The word of God is mightier than any two-edged sword.

18. If prayer-life is weak, is it because you have not done justice to the four "all's" mentioned in this verse?

19. There is great power in intercessory prayer.

20. Some take special pride in speaking "bluntly." It is far better to ask for grace to speak "courageously."

21. Believers take a keen interest in each other's welfare.

22. Giving out information may be perfectly proper, particularly when the purpose is to strengthen the hearts of the listeners.

23. The peace that passes all understanding, the love that is the greatest of the three greatest, and the faith that overcomes the world, these three precious treasures *are given away* to anyone who sincerely requests them of God the Father and the Lord Jesus Christ.

24. The gifts of God's grace are imperishable.

General Bibliography

For other titles see List of Abbreviations at the beginning of this volume.

Aalders, G. Ch., *Het Boek Genesis (Korte Verklaring der Heilige Schrift)*, Kampen, 1949, Vol. I.

Abbott, T. K., *The Epistles to the Ephesians and to the Colossians (International Critical Commentary)*, New York, 1916.

Allan, J. A., *The Epistle to the Ephesians (Torch Bible Commentaries)*, London, 1959.

Allen, R., *Missionary Methods: St. Paul's or Ours?*, London, 1953.

Ante-Nicene Fathers, ten volumes, reprint, Grand Rapids, 1950, for references to Clement of Alexandria, Irenaeus, Justin Martyr, Origen, Tertullian, etc.

Barclay, W., *The Letters to the Galatians and Ephesians (The Daily Study Bible)*, Philadelphia, 1958.

Barnes, A., *Notes on the New Testament, Ephesians, Philippians and Colossians*, reprint Grand Rapids, 1949.

Barnette, H., "One Way of Life: Personal and Social," *RE*, Vol. 60, No. 4 (Fall 1963), pp. 414–429.

Barry, A., *The Epistles to the Ephesians, Philippians, and Colossians (C. J. Ellicott's New Testament Commentary for English Readers)*, New York, 1896.

Barth, K., "Gottes Gnadenwahl," *Die Lehre Von Gott, Die Kirchliche Dogmatik*, II/2, 3e. Auflage, Zürich, 1948.

Barth, M., "Conversion and Conversation," *Int*, Vol. 17, No. 1 (Jan. 1963), pp. 3–24.

Bartlett, W., "The Saints at Ephesus," *Exp, Eighth Series*, No. 107 (Nov. 1919), pp. 327–341.

Bavinck, C. B., Art. "Apostel" in *Christelijke Encyclopaedia*, Vol. I, pp. 143–145.

Bavinck, H., *Gereformeerde Dogmatiek*, Vol. II, *Over God;* English translation, *The Doctrine of God*, translated by W. Hendriksen, Grand Rapids, 1955.

Beare, F. W., *The Epistle to the Ephesians (Interpreter's Bible, Vol. X)*, New York and Nashville, 1953.

Benoit, P., *La Sainte Bible traduite en français sous la direction de l'École Biblique de Jerusalem*, 1949.

Berkhof, L., *New Testament Introduction*, Grand Rapids, 1916.

Berkhof, L., *Systematic Theology*, Grand Rapids, 1949.

Berkouwer, G. C., *De Triomf der Genade in de Theologie van Karl Barth*, Kampen, 1954.

Bible, Holy, In addition to references to Bible-versions other than English, there are references to the following English translations: A.V., A.R.V., R.S.V., N.E.B., N.A.S.B. (N.T.), Amplified New Testament, Beck, Berkeley, Goodspeed, Moffatt, Phillips, Weymouth, Williams. These are *references*. The *translation* which is found in N.T.C. and followed in the exegesis is the author's own.

Bowman, J. W., "The Epistle to the Ephesians," *Int*, Vol. 8 (April 1954), pp. 188–205.

Braune, K., *The Epistle of Paul to the Ephesians (Lange's Commentary on the Holy Scriptures)*, republished, Grand Rapids, no date.

Brown, R., "Ephesians among the Letters of Paul," *RE*, LX, No. 4 (Fall 1963), pp. 372–379.

Bruce, F. F., *The Epistle to the Ephesians, A Verse-by-Verse Exposition*, London, 1961.

EPHESIANS

Bruce, F. F., *The Letters of Paul, An Expanded Paraphrase,* Grand Rapids, 1965.

Cable, J. H., *The Fulness of God,* Chicago, 1945.

Calvin, John, *Institutes of the Christian Religion* (translated by John Allen, Philadelphia, 1928), Vol. I.

Calvin, John, *Commentarius In Epistolam Pauli Ad Ephesios (Corpus Reformatorum,* Vol. LXXX), Brunsvigae, 1895; English Translation *(Calvin's Commentaries)* Grand Rapids, 1948.

Chafer, L. S., *The Ephesian Letter,* New York, 1935.

Colwell, E. C., "Biblical Criticism: Lower and Higher," *JBL* (March 1948), p. 4.

Conybeare, W. J., and Howson, J. S., *The Life and Epistles of St. Paul,* Grand Rapids, 1949.

Coutts, J., "Ephesians I.3-14 and I Peter I.3-12," *NTSt,* Vol. 3, No. 2 (Jan. 1957), pp. 115–127.

Dale, R. W., *The Epistle to the Ephesians,* 1961.

Dalmer, J., "Bemerkungen zu I Kor. 10.3-4 und Eph. 4.8-10," *TSK,* 63 (1890), pp. 569–592.

De Boer, W. P., *The Imitation of Paul, An Exegetical Study,* doctoral dissertation, Kampen, 1962.

Deissmann, A., *Light from the Ancient East* (translated by L. R. M. Strachan), New York, 1927.

Dibelius, M., *An die Kolosser, Epheser, an Philemon* (Lietzmann's *Handbuch zum Neuen Testament),* 3rd edition, revised by H. Greeven, Tübingen, 1953.

Erdman, C. F., *The Epistle of Paul to the Ephesians,* Philadelphia, 1931.

Filson, F. V., "Ephesus and the New Testament," *The Biblical Archaeologist Reader,* 2 (edited by D. N. Freedman and E. F. Campbell, Jr.), New York, 1964, pp. 343–352.

Findlay, G. G., *The Epistle to the Ephesians,* New York, 1931. This is also included in *The Expositor's Bible,* Vol. VI, pp. 1–108.

Foulkes, F., *The Epistle of Paul to the Ephesians (The Tyndale New Testament Commentaries),* Grand Rapids, 1963.

Gerstner, E., *Idelette,* Grand Rapids, 1963.

Gerstner, J. H., *The Epistle to the Ephesians (Shield Bible Study Series),* Grand Rapids, 1958.

Goodspeed, E. J., *New Solutions to New Testament Problems,* Chicago, 1927.

Goodspeed, E. J., *The Meaning of Ephesians,* Chicago, 1933.

Goodspeed, E. J., *New Chapters in New Testament Study,* New York, 1937.

Goodspeed, E. J., *The Key to Ephesians,* Chicago, 1956.

Greijdanus, S., *Bizondere Canoniek,* Kampen, 1949, two volumes.

Grosheide, F. W., *De Brief Van Paulus Aan De Efeziërs (Commentaar op het Nieuwe Testament),* Kampen, 1960.

Harnack, A., *The Constitution and Law of the Church,* New York, 1910.

Hendriksen, W., *The Meaning of the Preposition ἀντί in the New Testament,* doctoral dissertation, Princeton, 1948.

Hendriksen, W., *Bible Survey,* Grand Rapids, 1961.

Hendriksen, W., *More Than Conquerors, An Interpretation of the Book of Revelation,* Grand Rapids, 1963.

Hendriksen, W., *The Bible on the Life Hereafter,* Grand Rapids, 1963.

Hodge, C., *A Commentary on the Epistle to the Ephesians,* Grand Rapids, 1954.

Hoekstra, S., "Vergelijking van de Brieven aan de Efeziërs en de Colossers, vooral uit het Oogpunt van Beider Leerstelligen Inhoud," *TT* (1868), pp. 562–599.

Hogarth, D. J., *The Archaic Artemisia,* 1908.

EPHESIANS

Holtzmann, H. J., *Kritik der Epheser und Kolosserbriefe*, 1872.

Hort, F. J. A., *Prologomena to St. Paul's Epistles to the Romans and the Ephesians*, London, 1895.

Iliffe, J. F., "The ΘΑΝΑΤΟΣ Inscription from Herod's Temple: Fragments of a Second Copy," *Quarterly of Department of Antiquities in Palestine* VI (1938), pp. 1 ff.

King, A. C., "Ephesians in the Light of Form Criticism," *ET*, 63 (1951–1952), pp. 273–276.

Klooster, F. H., *The Significance of Barth's Theology: An Appraisal with Special Reference to Election and Reconciliation*, Grand Rapids, 1961.

Knox, W. L., *St. Paul and the Church of the Gentiles*, Cambridge, 1939.

Kuyper, A., Sr., *De Gemeene Gratie*, three volumes, Kampen, no date.

Kuyper, A., Sr., *Het Werk van den Heiligen Geest*, Kampen, 1927.

Lenski, R. C. H., *Interpretation of St. Paul's Epistles to the Galatians, to the Ephesians, and to the Philippians*, Columbus, Ohio, 1937.

Lightfoot, J. B., *Saint Paul's Epistle to the Colossians and to Philemon*, reprint of 1879 edition, Grand Rapids.

Lightfoot, J. B., *Notes on the Epistles of St. Paul*, London, 1895. This volume contains notes on the Greek text of Eph. 1:1-14.

Linton, O., *Das Problem der Urkirche in der Neuere Forschung*, Upsala, 1932.

Lock, W., *St. Paul's Epistle to the Ephesians* (*Westminster Commentaries*), London, 1929.

Loeb Classical Library, New York (various dates), for Eusebius, Herodotus, Josephus, Philo, Plato, Pliny, Plutarch, Strabo, Xenophon, etc.

Mackay, J. A., *God's Order, The Ephesian Letter and This Present Time*, New York, 1957.

Mackay, J. R., "Paul's Great Doxology," *EQ*, Vol. 2 (1930), pp. 150–161.

McNicol, J., "The Spiritual Blessings of the Epistle to the Ephesians," *EQ*, Vol. 9 (1937), pp. 64–73.

Metzger, B. M., "Paul's Vision of the Church; A Study of the Ephesian Letter," *TTod*, 6 (1949–1950), pp. 49–63.

Mitton, C. L., "Unsolved New Testament Problems: E. J. Goodspeed's Theory Regarding the Origin of Ephesians," *ET* 59 (1947–1948), pp. 323–327; and *ET* 60 (1948–1949), pp. 320–321.

Mitton, C. L., *The Epistle to the Ephesians; Its Authorship, Origin, and Purpose*, Oxford, 1951.

Mitton, C. L., *The Formation of the Pauline Corpus of Letters*, London, 1955.

Mitton, C. L., "Important Hypotheses Reconsidered: VII. The Authorship of the Epistle to the Ephesians," *ET*, 67 (1955–1956), pp. 195–198.

Moffatt, J., *Introduction to the Literature of the New Testament*, New York, 1918.

Moffatt, J., "Three Notes on Ephesians," *Exp*, Eighth Series, No. 87 (April 1918), pp. 306–317.

Moule, H. C. G., *Ephesian Studies*, New York, 1900.

Murray, J., *Christian Baptism*, Philadelphia, 1952.

Mussner, F., *Christus, Das All und die Kirche*, Trierer Theologische Studien, V, Trier, 1955.

Niebuhr, R., *Man's Nature and His Communities: Essays on the Dynamics and Enigmas of Man's Personal and Social Existence*, New York, 1965.

Ockenga, H. J., *Faithful in Christ Jesus, Preaching in Ephesians*, New York, 1948.

Parvis, M. M., "Ephesus in the Early Christian Era," *The Biblical Archaeologist*

EPHESIANS

Reader, 2 (edited by D. N. Freedman and E. F. Campbell, Jr.), New York, 1964, pp. 331–343.

Paulus, H. E. G., *Philologisch-kritischer Kommentar über das Neue Testament,* Lübeck, 1800.

Peake, A. S., *Critical Introduction to the New Testament,* 1909.

Penning, L., *Life and Times of Calvin,* translated by B. S. Berrington, London, 1912.

Percy, E., *Die Probleme der Kolosser- und Epheserbriefe,* Lund, 1946.

Piper, O. A., "Praise of God and Thanksgiving," *Int,* Vol. 8, No. 1 (Jan. 1954), pp. 3–20.

Ramsay, W. M., *The Letters to the Seven Churches of Asia,* 1904.

Ridderbos, H. N., *The Epistle of Paul to the Churches of Galatia (New International Commentary on the New Testament),* Grand Rapids, 1953.

Robertson, A. T., *Word Pictures in the New Testament,* New York and London, 1931, Vol. IV, on Ephesians, pp. 514–552.

Robinson, J. A., "The Church as the Fulfilment of the Christ: a Note on Ephesians 1:23," *Exp.,* 5th series, 57 (1898), pp. 241–259.

Robinson, J. A., *St. Paul's Epistle to the Ephesians,* London, 1907.

Roels, E. D., *God's Mission, The Epistle to the Ephesians in Mission Perspective,* doctoral dissertation, Franeker, 1962.

Salmond, S. D. F., *The Epistle to the Ephesians (The Expositor's Greek Testament,* Vol. Three), Grand Rapids, no date.

Sanders, E. P., "Literary Dependence in Colossians," *JBL* (March 1966), pp. 28–45.

Schaff, P., *History of the Christian Church,* New York, 1923, Vol. VII.

Schille, "Liturgisches Gut im Epheserbrief," doctoral dissertation, Göttingen, 1952.

Scott, E. F., *The Epistles of Paul to the Colossians, to Philemon, and to the Ephesians (Moffatt Commentary),* New York, 1930.

Simpson, E. K., *The Pastoral Epistles,* London, 1954.

Simpson, E. K., *Commentary on the Epistle to the Ephesians (New International Commentary on the New Testament),* Grand Rapids, 1957.

Smalley, S. S., "The Eschatology of Ephesians," *EQ,* Vol. 28, No. 3 (July–September, 1956), pp. 152–157.

Stewart, J. S., *A Man in Christ, The Vital Elements of St. Paul's Religion,* New York and London, no date.

Streeter, B. H., *The Primitive Church,* New York, 1929.

Summers, R., "One Message — Redemption," *RE,* Vol. 60 (Fall 1963), pp. 380–398.

Talbot, L. T., *Lectures on Ephesians,* Wheaton, Ill., 1937.

Thiessen, H. C., *Introduction to the New Testament,* Grand Rapids, 1943.

Trench, R. C., *Synonyms of the New Testament,* edition Grand Rapids, 1948.

Van Leeuwen, J. A. C., *Paulus' Zendbrieven aan Efeze, Colosse, Filemon, en Thessalonika (Kommentaar op het Nieuwe Testament),* Amsterdam, 1926.

Van Til, C., *The New Modernism: an appraisal of the theology of Barth and Brunner,* Philadelphia, 1946.

Van Til, C., *Has Karl Barth Become Orthodox?,* Philadelphia, 1954.

Ward, W. E., "One Body — the Church," *RE,* Vol. 60, No. 4 (Fall 1963), pp. 398–413.

Warfield, B. B., *The Inspiration and Authority of the Bible,* Philadelphia, 1948.

Westcott, B. F., *Saint Paul's Epistle to the Ephesians,* London, 1906.

Whitaker, G. H., "The Chief Cornerstone," *Exp,* 8th series (1921), pp. 470–472.

Wood, J. T., *Discoveries at Ephesus,* 1877.

Wright, G. E., *Biblical Archaeology,* London and Philadelphia, 1957.

Zahn, Th., *Einleitung in das Neue Testament,* 1897–1900.

NEW TESTAMENT COMMENTARY

NEW TESTAMENT
COMMENTARY

By

WILLIAM HENDRIKSEN

Exposition
of
Philippians

TABLE OF CONTENTS

LIST OF ABBREVIATIONS

The letters in book-abbreviations are followed by periods. Those in periodical-abbreviations omit the periods and are in italics. Thus one can see at a glance whether the abbreviation refers to a book or to a periodical.

A. *Book Abbreviations*

A.R.V.	American Standard Revised Version
A.V.	Authorized Version (King James)
Gram.N.T.	A. T. Robertson, *Grammar of the Greek New Testament in the Light of Historical Research*
H.B.A.	Hurlbut, *Bible Atlas* (most recent edition)
I.S.B.E.	*International Standard Bible Encyclopedia*
L.N.T. (Th.)	Thayer's *Greek-English Lexicon of the New Testament*
L.N.T. (A. and G.)	W. F. Arndt and F. W. Gingrich, *A Greek-English Lexicon of the New Testament and Other Early Christian Literature*
M.M.	*The Vocabulary of the Greek New Testament Illustrated from the Papyri and Other Non-Literary Sources,* by James Hope Moulton and George Milligan (edition Grand Rapids, 1952)
N.N.	*Novum Testamentum Graece,* edited by D. Eberhard Nestle and D. Erwin Nestle (most recent edition)
N.T.C.	W. Hendriksen, *New Testament Commentary*
R.S.V.	Revised Standard Version
Th.W.N.T.	*Theologisches Wörterbuch zum Neuen Testament* (edited by G. Kittel)
W.D.B.	*Westminster Dictionary of the Bible*
W.H.A.B.	*Westminster Historical Atlas to the Bible*

B. *Periodical Abbreviations*

AThR	*Anglican Theological Review*
Bib Sac	*Bibliotheca Sacra*
Coll Mech	*Collectanea Mechliniensia*
ExT	*Expository Times*
JBL	*Journal of Biblical Literature*
JThS	*Journal of Theological Studies*
NTS	*New Testament Studies*

Please Note

In order to differentiate between the second person singular (see Phil. 4:3) and the second person plural (see Phil. 1:3), we have indicated the former as follows: "you"; and the latter as follows: "y o u."

Introduction
to
The Epistle to the Philippians

I. Reasons for Studying Philippians

The search for "tranquility" is on, and in a big way! In order to attain peace of mind Americans are swallowing tons of tranquilizers. In addition to the *drugs* there are the tranquilizing *books.* These have become best-sellers overnight, single editions running into the hundreds of thousands. Those who read them are urged to wind themselves like clocks, and to begin the day by saying to themselves:

"What a wonderful morning this is! And what an exceptionally fine wife (or husband) I have! And what lovely children! What a wholesome and delicious breakfast awaits me! And what a congenial boss I have at my job!"

But such "peacefulizers" may do more harm than good. They provoke the following objections:

First, whenever the soothing thought fails to comport with reality, the ease of mind which results will fail to be of an enduring character.

Secondly, the most stubborn fact of all is *sin.* No amount of mental push-ups or "positive thinking" can brush it aside.

Thirdly, the only peace that is worthy of the name is peace with God. This cannot be self-manufactured.

Fourthly, those *trusting in* tranquilizers, whether books or pills, could be proceeding from the false assumption that spiritual unrest or soul-struggle is an evil in itself. But it is often far better to *face* reality than to try to *escape* it. Evasion leads to spiritual torpor. Confronting the facts about oneself is the only course which can lead to "the peace of God that surpasses all understanding."

Now if one wishes to know how this *real* peace or tranquility of heart and mind can be obtained, he should turn to that epistle which contains the very expression which was just quoted (Phil. 4:7). This little gem of four sparkling chapters pictures a man who has actually found it. He has unearthed life's most cherished treasure. He is "the happiest man in the world." Listen to him, as he says in this epistle:

"Rejoice in the Lord always; again I will say, Rejoice."

"I have learned in whatever circumstances I am to be content. I know what it means to live in straitened circumstances, and I also know what it means to have plenty. In any and all circumstances I have learned the secret, both to be filled and to be hungry, both to have plenty and to be in want. I can do all things in him who infuses strength into me . . . I am amply supplied."

3

And this man who had learned life's greatest secret was a prisoner in Rome, facing possible death by execution!

So, the reasons for studying the epistle to the Philippians are the following:

1. It reveals *the secret* of true happiness. How this happiness can be obtained is clearly disclosed in this letter.

2. It reveals *the man* who had learned the secret. Philippians is one of the most personal of all of Paul's epistles. It shares this characteristic with II Corinthians, I Thessalonians, and Philemon. Nowhere are we brought closer to the real Paul, pouring out his heart to those whom he deeply loves.

3. It reveals *the Christ* who taught him the secret. Christ as our Pattern and Enabler is portrayed here in the greatness of his condescending love (Phil. 2:5-11; 4:13).

II. The City of Philippi

Without a knowledge of the history and geography of Philippi it is impossible to derive the most benefit from a study of Philippians.

A man of restless energy, determination, and organizing talent was Philip II, the father of Alexander the Great. When he seized the throne in 359 B. C., the "Macedonia" over which he began to reign was about the size of the state of Vermont or of Maryland. Consult a map of Northern Greece. (It was a small segment of that vast region which originally was called *Thrace*.) To the East it did not even touch the Strimon River. To the South it left the three-fingered Chalcidice Peninsula outside its boundary. To the West it hardly touched what is now Albania. And to the North it pushed up for a distance of perhaps nowhere more than forty miles into what is now Jugoslavia.[1] Philip set about at once to "modernize" his army. He gave it longer spears, charging cavalry, better organization, etc. With this new tool he began to extend his domain.

Armies and expeditions, however, are expensive. So Philip annexed the gold-region[2] in the neighborhood of a place which because of its numerous springs was called Krenides, meaning "The Little Fountains." He enlarged this town, naming it after himself, "Philippi." With such eagerness did he work the gold-mines that he secured from them more than one thousand talents a year, using some of the revenue to maintain his army and some to enlarge his kingdom by means of bribes. He is reported to have made the statement, "No fortress is impregnable to whose walls an ass laden

---

[1] See the map on p. 313 of H. G. Wells, *The Outline of History*, Garden City, New York, Star-edition, 1930; cf. this with the map "Lands of the Bible Today" in the December, 1956 issue of *The National Geographic Magazine*.
[2] Cf. Strabo VII, 34.

4

INTRODUCTION

with gold can be driven." And so, "This gold of Krenides spread itself over Greece, preceding the phalanx like an advance guard and opening more gates than the battering rams and catapults" (Heuzey). And the territorial expansion begun by Philip was continued on an even larger scale by his son, Alexander.

Inestimable consequences flowed from this conquest. It has been truly said that if Philip and Alexander had not gone East, Paul and the gospel which he proclaimed could not have come to the West. For, these conquerors brought about the *one* world of Hellenistic speech that made possible the spread of the gospel to many regions.

The city founded by Philip was situated fully ten miles inland from the Gulf of Neapolis (now Kolpos Kavallas), northwest of the island of Thasos in the Aegean Sea. By Paul it must have been regarded as a city in the North, for while the place of his birth, Tarsus, was situated 37° N. lat. (like Springfield, Missouri), and Jerusalem where he received his training 32° N. lat. (like Montgomery, Alabama), Philippi was located 41° N. lat. (like the city of New York). To reach Philippi from the sea a person would have to enter a port which, in common with many other places, bore the name Neapolis (cf. "Naples"), that is, "new city." Probably because this was the place where Paul landed, bringing the gospel of Christ, it was subsequently called Christopolis. It still exists under the name of Kavalla, and is today the heart of the Greek tobacco industry.[3]

Proceeding from Kavalla a person crosses the Pangaeus Range through a narrow depression. A stretch of the old Roman highway, the Via Egnatia, connects the port with the ruins of Philippi. From the crest of the hill between the thriving port and these ruins one has a marvelous view. Looking *back,* one beholds the Aegean Sea with its islands: Thasos to the southeast and Samothrace much farther away, to the east. One can even discern to the south the towering summit of Athos. Looking *ahead* one sees the plain of Drama, skirted by mountains and watered by the Gangites. This plain can be lovely. It can also be a terrible marsh. The contrast depends on the season of the year when one happens to view it. On a hill which dominates this plain lay Philippi. An air-view reveals the ruins of two churches and the remains of the Roman forum.[4]

---

[3] See the article "Jerusalem to Rome in the Path of St. Paul," in *The National Geographic Magazine,* December 1956, p. 747; also the photograph on p. 179 of *Everyday Life in Ancient Times,* 1953, published by the National Geographic Society, Washington, D.C.; and the air-views in connection with the text of Acts 16 and of Philippians 1 on pp. 18 and G11 of *The Good News, The New Testament with over 500 Illustrations and Maps,* published by The American Bible Society.

[4] Cf. W. J. Conybeare and J. S. Howson, *The Life and Epistles of St. Paul,* reprint 1949, Grand Rapids, pp. 219-226; Herodotus vi. 46, 47; vii. 113; Strabo VII. 34, 35; 41-43; W. Keller, *The Bible As History,* New York, 1957, p. 384; E. G. Kraeling, *Rand McNally Bible Atlas,* New York, 1956, pp. 438–440; and G. Ernest Wright, *Biblical Archaeology,* London, 1957, pp. 255-257.

Two centuries after the founding of Philippi Rome conquered Macedonia, and divided it into four political districts. To the famous Roman general Aemilius Paulus belongs the credit for the decisive victory at Pydna (near Mt. Olympus) on the western shore of the gulf of Salonica (168 B. C.).[5] By this time, however, the gold mines having become nearly exhausted, the city of Philippi had been reduced to "a small settlement" (Strabo VII. 41). In the year 146 B. C., Macedonia became one of the six provinces governed by Rome.

The subsequent enlargement of the city resulted from the important event which occurred here in 42 B. C. It was then that the historic battle of Philippi took place between Brutus and Cassius, defenders of the Roman republic, on one side, and Antony and Octavian, avengers of Caesar's death, on the other. After two engagements Antony and Octavian were victorious, Brutus and Cassius were dead.[6]

Soon afterward Philippi was made a Roman *colony* and was called *Colonia Julia Philippensis.* Antony settled some of his disbanded veterans there. There followed (31 B. C.) the naval battle of Actium, an ancient Grecian promontory in Epirus off the Ionian Sea (see N.T.C. on Titus 3:12). It was here that Octavian won the victory over Antony, who had become hopelessly infatuated with the woman who was his undoing, namely, Cleopatra, the romantic Egyptian queen who previously had been the mistress of Julius Caesar. Realizing the hopelessness of their cause both Antony and Cleopatra committed suicide.[7]

Octavian had now become sole head of the Roman Empire. His new name was *Caesar Augustus:* in 29 B. C. he was declared *Imperator;* in 27 *Augustus.* When he dispossessed the partisans of Antony of their estates in Italy, these people were now given the privilege of joining earlier Latin-speaking settlers in Philippi. The name of this city now became

COLONIA JULIA AUGUSTA VICTRIX PHILIPPENSIUM

Philippi, then, was a Roman *colony.* As such it was a Rome in miniature, a reproduction on a small scale of the imperial city. Its inhabitants were predominantly Romans, though the natives lived alongside of them and gradually coalesced with them. The Roman citizens naturally took great pride in being Romans. Moreover, they enjoyed all the rights of Roman citizens everywhere, such as freedom from scourging, from arrest except in

---

[5] Plutarch's *Aemilius Paulus* is unforgettable; especially the manner in which he contrasts the Roman general with the Macedonian king, Perseus.
[6] Cf. Plutarch, *Brutus* XXXVI–LIII and (same author) *Caesar* LV–LXIX (Shakespeare's *Julius Caesar* is based on Plutarch); also F. B. Marsh, *A History of the Roman World From 146 to 30 B. C.,* London, second edition 1953, pp. 281-284.
[7] Cf. Plutarch, *Antony;* see especially XXV–LXXXVII; Shakespeare, *Antony and Cleopatra* (based on Plutarch); Dryden, *All For Love* (a reworking of Shakespeare); G. B. Shaw, *Caesar and Cleopatra* (dealing with Cleopatra's earlier years); F. B. Marsh, *op. cit.,* pp. 295-311.

extreme cases, and the right to appeal to the emperor. Their names remained upon the rolls of the Roman tribes. Their language was Latin. They loved to dress according to Roman style. The coins of Philippi bore Latin inscriptions. Each veteran received from the emperor a grant of land. Upon the entire community, moreover, the *Jus Italicum* was conferred, so that the inhabitants of this city enjoyed not only economic privileges, such as exemption from tribute and the right to acquire, hold, and transfer property, but also political advantages, such as freedom from interference by the provincial governor, and the right and responsibility to regulate their own civic affairs.

In control of the government of the city was a pair of officials who were fond of calling themselves *praetores duumviri,* that is, *the two civic commanders,* freely translated στρατηγοί in Greek. And as in Rome, these *civic commanders* or *magistrates* had their fasces-carrying *lictores,* that is, *policemen* or *constables* (ῥαβδοῦχοι).

In creating here and there such *colonies* Rome knew what it was doing. The advantages were mutual: not only did *the colonists* receive many privileges, as has been shown, but also *Rome* profited by this arrangement, for thus its frontiers were being safeguarded against the enemy and its veterans were being rewarded.

We are now in a better position to understand (a) Luke's account in Acts 16 with reference to the establishment of the church in Philippi, and (b) Paul's epistle to the Philippians. As to the former, see the next section: The Church at Philippi. As to the latter, note the following:

(1) Paul, writing from a prison in Rome, mentions the progress of the gospel among the members of *the praetorian guard* (1:13). He refers to this guard because he knows that his readers, many of whom belonged no doubt to the families of veterans, would have a lively interest in it. In no other epistle does the apostle mention this guard.

(2) He says, "Only continue to exercise y o u r citizenship in a manner worthy of the gospel of Christ" (1:27).[8] In the light of the facts which have been enumerated it is probable that the earthly (Roman) citizenship of which the Philippians were proud is *the underlying idea* of the heavenly citizenship to which the apostle refers. Spiritual realities, however, always transcend earthly symbols. Thus, though many citizens of Philippi probably felt perfectly at home in their city, so that they would not have exchanged Philippi for Rome to take up residence there, believers, on the contrary, can never feel at home here on earth. They realize that their homeland, the country to which they as citizens belong, is in heaven, and that they are sojourners and pilgrims here below (Phil. 3:20).

---

[8] Cf. W. J. Conybeare and J. S. Howson, *op. cit.,* pp. 223-226; Raymond R. Brewer, "The Meaning of POLITEUESTHE in Philippians 1:27," *JBL* LXXIII, Part II (June, 1954), pp. 76-83.

(3) He speaks about the grievous suffering which the readers have to endure and the bitter conflict in which they are engaged (1:27-30). Philippi, being Roman to the core, had its imperial cult. It can be assumed that the non-Christian community — especially the *Augustales* who deified the emperor — exerted heavy pressure upon the Christians to join in this emperor-worship. Resistance to this pressure resulted in reproach and persecution. This, no doubt, was *part of* their suffering. It was not the *whole* of it. See comments on the passage.

(4) Here in a Roman colony, more than almost anywhere else, there was a tendency to flatter Nero with divine titles and honors. Hence, it is in such an epistle as this that the glory of Christ, his full deity, is set forth (2:5-10), in order that the readers may remain unswervingly loyal to *him* as to their *only* God and Savior.

(5) Greetings from members of *Caesar's household* (4:22) are mentioned *in this letter only.* See on 4:22.

III. The Church at Philippi

In the course of his second missionary journey (A. D. 50/51-53/54) Paul, accompanied by Silas and Timothy, reached Troas, located to the south of what is considered the site of ancient Troy. Although Troas is today a deserted ruin, in the time of the apostle it was one of Asia's chief ports. Here the vision of "the man of Macedonia" summoned the missionaries to Europe. Here also they were joined by Luke (Acts 16:9, 10). The ship on which they sailed must have passed the Aegean outlet of the Hellespont, for it made a straight course to the island of Samothrace, where Demetrius had set up the world-famous statue of Victory. On the next day the party reached Neapolis, Philippi's port. Here the boat-trip ended. It had been a speedy one, having taken only *two* days. The winds must have been favorable; contrast the trip in the opposite direction — Neapolis to Troas — toward the close of the third missionary journey, which was going to take *five* days (Acts 20:6). From Neapolis the missionaries proceeded at once on foot to Philippi. In obedience to the direction of the Spirit Paul performed most of his labors in important centers; such as Pisidian Antioch, Philippi, Corinth, Ephesus, Rome. It has long been held that this was a policy which he followed in the firm belief that from the more strategic centers the gospel-message would fan outward,[9] as it actually did. At any rate, Philippi was an important center. Luke says, "and from there to Philippi, since it is

---

[9] In *Paul and the Salvation of Mankind,* Richmond, Va., 1959, J. Mund rejects this idea.

INTRODUCTION

a leading city of the district of Macedonia, a colony" (Acts 16:12). In addition to *political*, Philippi also had *geographical* and *commercial* significance. From Philippi on the Egnatian Way the traffic moved via Dyrrachium, Brundisium and the Appian Way, to Rome (and vice versa).

This city of Philippi was so unlike any which the travelers had visited thus far that they had to spend a few days here to get their bearings. Then came their first Sabbath in Europe. At the western exit of the city a great colonial arch-way spanned the Via Egnatia, which about a mile farther crossed the swift and narrow Gangites River that empties into the Strymon. Somewhere along the bank of the Gangites the men found "a place of prayer." The word used in the original occurs at times as a synonym for "synagogue." Here, however, there seems not to have been a synagogue: no *men* were present; there was no formal worship, and no reading of law and prophets. There were probably few Jews in Philippi. Is it possible that also in showing a hostile spirit toward the Jews this *Roman colony* had followed the mother-city? These were the days of Emperor Claudius (A. D. 41-54) who, though at first friendly to the Jews, had subsequently ordered them to leave Rome (A. D. 50 or shortly afterward). At any rate, Paul and his companions spoke to *the women* that were gatherered at this place of prayer for their Jewish religious devotions.

In the little group assembled here was a woman named Lydia. Her home-town was Thyatira (now Akhisar, Turkey), on the way from Pergamum to Sardis (Rev. 2:12, 18; 3:1), in the province of Lydia, in what today is called Western Asia Minor. Though a born pagan, she had become acquainted — in her native town? — with the religion of the Jews and had accepted it as her own, having become a proselyte of the gate. Hers surely was a far superior way of worshipping God than any pagan cult with it foolish idolatry and gross immorality. Yet, somehow it had failed to give her complete satisfaction, the peace which her soul craved.

She was a business-woman, and may have been a widow who was continuing the pursuit of her late husband. We may think of her as an importer. She was a seller of purple. That should cause no surprise, for the place of her birth was located in the heart of the region of the purple-garment industry. Such garments were expensive, for the purple dye was derived from the shellfish in the waters of Thyatira, and the throat of each shellfish produced only *one* drop of the dye! (A cheaper grade was obtained by simply crushing the shellfish.) Now since Philippi was a Roman colony it was naturally an excellent market for purple garments. Romans loved the royal color! With it they trimmed togas and tunics. They wove it into their rugs and tapestries. Philippians were eager to copy Rome and its customs. To handle such an expensive product Lydia must have been a woman of means. The account in Acts supports this conclusion, for it implies that she

9

had a spacious mansion in Philippi, perhaps a typical Roman town-house of the better class, one that had ample room to accommodate several guests.[10]

As has often been remarked, Lydia had come from Asia with her earthly treasures, and was about to discover spiritual treasures in Europe. Though she probably had to walk a considerable distance to get to the place of prayer on the river-bank outside the city, and though she did not expect, perhaps, that the scheduled meeting would be of any great significance, *she went!* And here she met the missionaries, who spoke with great conviction, proving that the Old Testament prophecies, with which she was acquainted, had been fulfilled in Jesus Christ. The chief speaker was Paul. Whether Lydia was converted at that first meeting or subsequently is not clear from the text and is unimportant. The main fact is that by means of the preaching of Paul this woman, whose heart the Lord had opened, was led to accept Christ. So was her "household" subsequently. Then she and all the members of her family were baptized.

At once Lydia gave evidence of the genuine character of the great change in her life. Her eager generosity reminds one of Mary of Bethany (see N.T.C. on John 12:1-8). With rare tact she extended an invitation which the missionaries could not refuse, for rejecting it would have amounted to an insult. She said, "If y o u have judged me to be faithful to the Lord, come into my house and stay." Her wish, so urgently expressed, prevailed (Acts 16:15).

It is clear from Acts 16:40 that Lydia was by no means the only convert in Philippi. Moreover, men as well as women were translated from the kingdom of darkness into that of light. But while matters were proceeding favorably something occurred which at the time must have been considered an unpleasant interruption. One day, as the missionaries were going to the place of prayer, a female fortune-teller met them. She was a slave owned by masters who were making money out of her gift. Her lot was indeed a sorry one. She had "a spirit, a Python" (thus literally, Acts 16:16).

In Greek mythology the word *Python* refers, first of all, to a serpent or dragon that dwelt in the region of Pytho at the foot of Parnassus in Phocis, north of the Gulf of Corinth. It was believed that this dragon used to guard the oracle of Delphi with its oracular sanctuary. He was, however, slain by the god Apollo, as Ovid describes most interestingly.[11]

---

[10] Cf. N.T.C. on John, Vol. II, p. 392. For the general plan of a Roman house of the well-to-do see T. G. Tucker, *Life in the Roman World of Nero and St. Paul*, New York, 1922, ch. 9; also *Everyday Life in Ancient Times*, pp. 322, 323.

[11] "Accordingly, when the earth, mud-covered by reason of the recent deluge, became heated up by the hot and genial rays of the sun, she brought forth innumerable species of life; in part she restored the ancient shapes; and in part she created new monsters.

"She, indeed, would have wished not to do so, but she then also bore *you*, enormous Python, you hitherto unknown snake. You were a terror to the new population, so vast a space of mountainside did you occupy.

INTRODUCTION

By an easy transition this word Python began to be applied to divination or fortune-telling in general, so that "a spirit, a Python" indicated "a spirit of divination."

Plutarch, Greek essayist and biographer (about A. D. 46-120), tells us that in his day ventriloquists were called Pythons. But though it is possible that the slave-girl referred to in Acts 16:16 was a ventriloquist, this cannot be proved. The meaning here seems to be simply that she had "a spirit of divination." [12] She was a demon-possessed girl who was regarded by the superstitious people of this region as being able to predict future events. And they were willing to pay for her predictions.

Now one day as she was going *into* or *toward* the city, she *met* the missionaries who were on their way to the prayer-meeting *outside* the city's gates. But having met them she first walked past them and then turned around and followed them. She began to cry out, "These men are servants of the Most High God who proclaim to y o u a way (or "the way") of salvation." [13]

It is understandable that Paul did not cherish the idea of being advertised by a demon-possessed girl (cf. Luke 8:28, 29), as if there were some connection between the kingdom of light and that of darkness, between the servants of the Most High God and . . . Beelzebub! So at last, after the girl had behaved in this fashion for several days, the apostle, worn out through and through by the unwelcome notoriety he was receiving, suddenly turned around and said to the spirit, "I order you in the name of Jesus Christ to get out of her." And it came out that very hour.

But now the real trouble started. The masters of the slave-girl, men who had been making money out of her, became very bitter, and having grabbed Paul and Silas (as the most important of the four?) dragged them to the Agora, the public square or forum. Brought before the *praetors,* the two bringers of good tidings were denounced as *Jewish* trouble-makers. How shrewd this charge and also how inconsistent! The *accusers* were proud of being *Romans, not Jews!* But they forgot that they were never more like wicked Jews than they were right now! Note the similarity:

"This monster the god of the glittering bow destroyed with arms never before used except against does and wild she-goats, well-nigh emptying his quiver, crushing him with countless darts till his poisonous blood flowed from black wounds.

"And in order that the fame of his deed might not perish through lapse of time he instituted sacred games whose contests throngs beheld. These were called Pythian from the name of the serpent he had overthrown" (Metamorphoses I. 434-447. See also T. Bulfinch, *The Age of Fable,* New York, edition 1942, pp. 21, 159, 297.

[12] Cf. M.M., p. 559.

[13] Was she hinting that there were several ways of salvation, and that what Paul and his companions proclaimed was only *one* way out of many? Note that the original lacks the definite article, and *can* therefore be translated *a* way, instead of *the* way. But over against this stands the fact that in Greek the article is not always necessary to make a word definite.

11

The charge of the Jewish leaders against Jesus:	*The charge of these Romans against Jesus' messengers: Paul and Silas:*
"We found this man perverting our nation, and forbidding (us) to give tribute to Caesar, and saying that he himself is Christ, a king" (Luke 23:2). *It was a lie and a piece of hypocrisy.* The *real* reason for their agitation is stated in Matt. 27:18: *"Out of envy* they had delivered him up."	"These men, being Jews are exceedingly disturbing our city, and are advocating customs which it is not lawful for us to accept or to practise, since we are Romans." *This, too, was a lie and a piece of hypocrisy.* The real reason for their agitation is stated in Acts 16:19: "Her masters saw that the hope of their gain was gone."

The charge was of an inflammatory character, for Roman colonists were very jealous of their rights and customs as Romans. Besides (as was stated earlier), had not the emperor Claudius recently ordered all Jews from Rome? And now here were these two Jewish vagrants making trouble in Miniature-Rome! Roused by the infuriated, wailing rabble, the praetors caused the two men to be stripped and beaten with rods. Such a flogging was exceedingly painful. Moreover, among the Romans there was no fixed number of lashings, no rule limiting them to "forty stripes less one." To make matters even worse, when the lictors had inflicted many blows, Paul and Silas were thrown into prison, and the jailer was charged to guard them securely. That individual, having received the order, threw them into the inner dungeon, a musty hole, where their feet were locked wide apart in gruesome stocks. Were their wrists also manacled in irons, attached to chains which were bolted into the walls, as was the case with other prisoners? Truly horrible was their condition. Yet this, too, was providential, for it meant that deliverance from such profound agony, from such seemingly unbreakable bonds, would stand out all the more clearly as an act of God and not of man!

As happens so often, "man's extremity was God's opportunity." At midnight Paul and Silas were praying and singing hymns to God. Were any of the following among these hymns: Psalm 2, 16, 20, 23, 27, 42, 43, 46, 68, 69, 71, 130? Such singing surely required a very special measure of God's grace. And then suddenly there was a great earthquake, so that the foundations of the prison were shaken. At one stroke all the prison-doors were opened, the bolts in the tottering walls loosened, and the locks in the stocks sprung. Naturally the jailer, asleep in the house which adjoined the prison, woke up, and came rushing out to the prison-court. It being night he could not see much. Yet, through the semi-darkness he discerned that the prison-doors were open! Filled with terror, he quickly concluded that this could mean one thing only, namely, that the prisoners had escaped. This, he was sure, meant *shameful* death for him (cf. Acts 12:19). Rather than suffer such a disgrace, he would take his own life. Was not this in effect what Cassius and Brutus had done in this very vicinity? Had not Antony and Cleopatra also committed suicide? Was not Seneca constantly defending suicide as a right and privilege? Though the jailer may not have been acquainted with the opinions of the philosophers, it is at least certain that, being a pagan, he cannot have evaluated life as highly as did the Jew (King Saul, Ahithophel, Zimri, and Judas Iscariot were *exceptions*) and especially the Christian. So, in despair he quickly drew his sword and would have killed himself had not Paul, having by this time perhaps stationed himself before the main entrance where he saw what was about to happen, called out loudly, "Do not harm yourself, for we are all here." The astonished jailer then called for lights. Trembling with fear the man fell down before Paul and Silas, brought them outside to the prison-court, and asked, "Sirs, what must I do to be saved?" What did he mean? Merely this, "How can I escape from my present predicament, and hold on to my job?" In the light of the entire situation and also of the answer which he received it is hard to believe that this was all he meant. The following items must not be overlooked:

a. The demon-possessed girl had been telling the people, "These men are servants of the Most High God who proclaim to y o u a way (or "the way") of salvation." It is very well possible that the jailer had heard about this.

b. It is also not improbable that the man had been for some time worried about the condition of his soul.

c. He must have noticed that the behavior of Paul and Silas under the terrible lashings which they received and subsequently in the dungeon was entirely different from anything he had ever seen or heard.

d. It is wholly probable that he knew that at Paul's word the slave-girl had experienced a remarkable change. News, especially of this character, travels fast. And did he perhaps see a connection between these men and the occurrence of the earthquake? Had he become convinced, therefore, that the slave-girl might not have been entirely wrong, that there was indeed a close relation between these two men and divinity, and that they would be in a position to answer the deepest question of his soul?

All these considerations lead me to conclude that the explanation which the man in the pew generally ascribes to the jailer's question is probably the right one. And on this basis the answer which he received was very fitting: "Believe on the Lord Jesus, and you will be saved, you and your household." Of course, this advice needed amplification. So Paul and Silas, having entered the jailer's house, spoke the word of the Lord to the jailer and to all that were there. Moreover, those who heard the message accepted it. And their faith revealed its genuine character in loving deeds. Having taken the missionaries back to the courtyard, where there must have been a cistern or tank with water, or perhaps a spring, the jailer now tenderly washed their wounds. Then immediately he himself was baptized and all those of his household. In the house once more, the jailer set the table for the missionaries. General rejoicing followed.

At break of day the praetors sent the lictors, saying to the jailer, "Release those men." What may have been the motivation of the praetors' change of mind? Can it be that Codex Bezae is correct when it suggests that the authorities had seen a connection between the earthquake and the missionaries, and that in their fear they had arrived at the conclusion: Paul and Silas are actually what they claim to be? Or had thorough investigation convinced the praetors that the strangers had been falsely accused? Whatever may have been the reason for the sudden turnabout, one fact is definitely stated, namely, that, informed by the jailer that he had been officially instructed to release the prisoners, the latter, who meanwhile had re-entered their dungeon, refused to heed the command: "Now therefore come out and go in peace." Instead of leaving the prison, Paul said, "They have beaten us publicly, without trial, men that are Romans, and have thrown us into prison, and do they now throw us out secretly? No indeed! But let them come themselves and lead us out!"

Gross injustice had been done, and Roman law had been violated on more than one count: Roman citizens had been scourged, publicly disgraced, and imprisoned; all this without a trial! Moreover, justice had been trampled by its would-be defenders! The honor of the missionaries, the rights of every Christian in Philippi, the cause of the gospel, and even the good reputation of Roman jurisprudence demanded that the men who had been "shamefully treated" (cf. II Thess. 2:2) be officially vindicated. Hence, Paul acted with sound judgment when he insisted on an honorable discharge for himself and his companion. In fact, that was *the least* he could have demanded!

When the lictors reported to their superiors the true state of affairs regarding these prisoners, particularly that they were *Romans,* the praetors were frightened. They realized that not only their position but their very life was in danger because of the crimes which they had committed. Hence, they readily complied with Paul's request. It must have been quite a scene: purple-robed praetors descending into the dungeon and then "eating crow," offering humble apologies as they politely led Paul and Silas to liberty! And when they had brought them out, they begged them to leave the city. The colonists of Philippi must not get to know that the two strangers who had come into town and had been so deeply humiliated were *Roman citizens!* Surely, these colonists would not have spared the praetors. So, the sooner the strangers leave the city the better!

The latter, in turn, were willing enough to comply with the urgent request. The work in Philippi had met with a considerable measure of success. Lydia and the jailer were by no means the only converts. This appears from the fact that when the missionaries have departed from the prison and have re-entered Lydia's hospitable mansion, they find a number of "brothers" there. To this assembled congregation, the first church in Europe, they speak words of encouragement. Then Paul and Silas wend their way to Thessalonica. Timothy accompanies them or follows a little later. For the present Luke remains in Philippi.

Glancing back at this account of the establishment of the church at Philippi we see that among those who undoubtedly continued for some time to exert a wholesome influence upon it there were especially two that were alike in their unselfish devotion to the cause of Christ and in their bigheartedness, namely, Lydia and Luke. In Lydia's home believers were always more than welcome. And as to Luke, in his Gospel he reveals not only the love of God in Christ but also his own personality. Hence, as we read it we are not surprised to see how mercy is bestowed upon the penitent prodigal, how the sick are healed, the weary strengthened, women (especially widows) and children honored. Moreover, if to these two (Lydia and Luke) a third must be added, the converted jailer certainly deserves consideration (in view of Acts 16:33, 34).

Now the church of Philippi seems to have drawn its character from that of its leading members. Accordingly we are not surprised to learn that when on this second missionary journey Paul was proclaiming the gospel in the next place after Philippi, namely, Thessalonica, he was cheered once and again by a gift from the church of Lydia and Luke (Phil. 4:16). The same thing happened a little later, making possible the work in Athens and Corinth (Phil. 4:15; and see also II Cor. 11:9). Paul's second visit to Philippi and vicinity occurred during his third missionary journey, outward bound. Writing to the Corinthians he praises the eager generosity of the churches of Macedonia (among them, of course, Philippi), in contributing toward the relief of the Jerusalem saints (II Cor. 8:1-5). The third visit to Philippi occurred on this same third missionary journey, but now homeward bound. Paul had planned to set sail directly from Corinth to Syria, when a plot was discovered which caused him to change his plans. So he reversed his course and proceeded toward Jerusalem by way of Macedonia. At this time, however, his contact with the church of Philippi seems to have been very brief. One event of some significance is clearly implied, however: at Philippi Luke rejoined him (Acts 20:5, note "us"). (Some add that Paul attended a Passover at Philippi, but that is not necessarily implied in Acts 20:6.)

For the purpose of understanding the epistle to the Philippians the next contact, though it was not a visit of Paul to the church, is the most important of all. This contact, so characteristic of the church at Philippi, occurred during the apostle's first imprisonment in Rome. See the next section: Paul's Purpose in Writing Philippians.

During this imprisonment Paul wrote that he hoped to send Timothy to visit the church, and he added, "But I trust in the Lord that I myself shall also come soon" (Phil. 2:19, 24). It is certainly within the realm of probability that the apostle actually carried out this plan, and that upon his release he journeyed from Rome by way of Crete and Asia Minor to Philippi. The latter may have been his headquarters when he wrote the epistles known to us as I Timothy and Titus (see N.T.C. on The Pastoral Epistles, pp. 39-42). As far as we know this was Paul's last visit to the church at Philippi.

Fully a half century afterward Polycarp wrote his *Letter to the Philippians*.[14] The occasion was as follows: Ignatius, on his way to Rome and martyrdom, had passed through Philippi. The Philippians had written to Polycarp concerning Ignatius and had expressed a desire that the former make a collection of the latter's letters. Perhaps they had also asked for advice concerning a matter of discipline. Polycarp now answers them, praising them for having followed the pattern of true love and having shown sympathy to those who were bound in chains. He tells them that he rejoices about the fact that the firm root of their faith, famous in times past, is still flourishing and bearing fruit for Christ. He remarks about the incomparable wisdom of the glorious and blessed Paul who had been among them, and he reminds them of the fact that Paul had boasted about them to all the churches. He warns them, however, against avarice. In this connection he states that he feels deeply grieved for Valens and his wife (called by Lightfoot "the Ananias and Sapphira of the Philippian community"), and offers advice with respect to the treatment which such offenders should receive. This writing of Polycarp is at the same time a covering letter, for in the same package Polycarp includes the letters of Ignatius for which the Philippians had asked.

All in all it appears, therefore, that two generations after Paul's death the church at Philippi was still standing firm. The information which has come down to us concerning the state of the church in the immediately succeeding centuries is too scanty to furnish a basis for generalization. A not too encouraging glimpse into the situation that obtained there about the fifth

---

[14] Perhaps there were two letters. The one-letter theory does not fully explain the final sentence in Chapter 13, which seems to imply that when it was written Ignatius was still alive (or at least that Polycarp had not yet been informed about Ignatius' death), while according to Chapters 1-12 (see especially Chapter 9) Ignatius is considered dead. Hence, there are those who think that what the manuscripts have handed down as a single letter of Polycarp to the Philippians is in reality two letters, and that the earlier of these two letters comprises Chapters 13 and 14 of the traditional text. See P. N. Harrison, *Polycarp's Two Letters to the Philippians*, London, 1936.

century is afforded by the inscription in marble which was attached to the city gate on the Egnatian Way (toward Neapolis). This inscription contains the wholly spurious correspondence which king Abgar V is alleged to have had with Jesus! By the Philippians of that later day the inscription was regarded as a charm against enemies and catastrophies! But the charm was wholly ineffective. During the Middle Ages the city was repeatedly attacked by hostile forces and ravaged by earthquakes and fires. The last inhabitants finally left the swampy place.

There are, however, a few records of bishops of Philippi whose names are appended to the decisions of various councils (held in the years 344, 431, 451). We also know that in the year 1212 Philippi must still have been a town of some importance, for in that year Pope Innocent III made it a see. Its last archbishop died in the year 1721. However, it would seem that the see outlived the city itself.

An arched enclosure built by the Romans is held by many to have been the prison where Paul and Silas sang their songs and the jailer was converted. This belief receives some support from the fact that in a day when presumably the memory of these things had not yet faded away the enclosure was covered with a chapel. In the vicinity of Philippi evidences — such as grotto-shrines and chiseled reliefs — of several different pagan religions have been found. One shrine was devoted to the Egyptian gods Isis and Serapis.

From 1914–1938 a French archaeological expedition excavated this region. It found what remained of paved streets and squares, the forum, temples, public buildings, and pillared arcades. However, many of the discoveries concern the post-apostolic history of the city. Except for a few inscriptions — for example, a monument which a presbyter set up in honor of his parents and his wife — and the remains of Byzantine churches, especially the huge piers of the Derekler basilica, there remains today little evidence of the Christianity which once flourished here to such an extent that Paul called this church "my joy and crown." But the apostle's letter to the Philippians makes up for the loss.[15]

IV. Paul's Purpose in Writing Philippians

One day, while Paul was in prison, he received a welcome visitor. His name was Epaphroditus. He was a leader in the church at Philippi. He had been sent to Paul as a delegate from that church. He carried with him a

---

[15] For archaeological sources see General Bibliography at the end of this book; also I.S.B.E., art. "Philippi" (note "Literature" at the close of the article); and article "Archaeology, Christian" (and Bibliography at the end of that article) in *The New Schaff-Herzog Encyclopaedia*, Volume I of *The Twentieth Century* augmentation.

generous gift from the Philippians. If he took the land-route, his journey was comparable to that from New York to Chicago. In both cases it would be a journey of a little more than eight hundred miles of actual travel, from east to west, and from 41 N. lat. (for Philippi and for New York) to 42 N. lat. (for Rome and for Chicago). However, due to the radical difference in modes of travel, ancient versus modern, it took Philippi's messenger much longer than it would take us to travel the comparable distance. He was probably on the way about a month.[16] Moreover, the journey by land from Philippi to Rome would have taken even longer had it not been for those good Roman roads, the products of excellent highway engineering. They were usually about fourteen feet wide, of sturdy construction (large blocks of carefully fitted hard stone laid on concrete which capped a well-prepared base), well maintained, relatively safe, pointing straight ahead in spite of obstacles, and marked by milestones.[17] From Philippi to Dyrrachium on the Adriatic one would take the Egnatian Way; then, after crossing the Adriatic to Brundisium (this crossing would take about a day), one would continue on the Appian Way to Rome. It is possible, however, that Epaphroditus made his journey by the sea-route, either through the Gulf of Corinth or around the promontory of Malea. Under favorable circumstances one could save some time by doing this.

The background of the epistle may now be summarized as follows:

(1) Between the delegate's arrival in Rome and the writing of Philippians there had been a time-interval of at least two months, probably more. (See the next section: The Time and the Place of Writing.) The gift which Epaphroditus had brought was deeply appreciated by Paul. It was, indeed, a meaningful *Remembrance,* and in a sense the messenger who had brought it was also himself a gift from the church which he represented, for the intention probably was that he should be the apostle's constant attendant and assistant. Grateful *written* acknowledgment was surely in order.

(2) Epaphroditus must also have brought a *Report* about conditions that prevailed in the Christian community which he had left. Moreover, it is entirely possible that, in the weeks which followed, others had added to this report. It must be borne in mind that, due to Philippi's strategic location on the Egnatian Way and also because of blood-relationships and political ties between the inhabitants of the two cities, travel between Philippi and Rome was heavy and constant. It is at any rate clearly evident that, although by now several weeks had elapsed since Epaphroditus had arrived in Rome,

[16] For proof see J. B. Lightfoot, *Saint Paul's Epistle to the Philippians,* reprint, Grand Rapids, Mich., 1953, p. 38, footnote 1.
[17] See the pictures and description in W.H.A.B., p. 77; *Everyday Life in Ancient Times,* pp. 304, 305; G. E. Wright, *Biblical Archaeology,* Philadelphia, 1957, p. 265; T. G. Tucker, *Life in the Roman World of Nero and St. Paul,* New York, 1922, pp. 16-29; and L. H. Grollenberg, *Atlas of the Bible* (tr. of *Atlas Van De Bijbel*), New York (Thomas Nelson and Sons), 1956, p. 134.

the apostle's knowledge about conditions in the church at Philippi continued to be rather up-to-date (Phil. 1:5; 1:27-29). He had heard that although the Philippians were certainly adorning their confession with a life to God's honor, were willing even to suffer in behalf of Christ, were ever ready to do more than their share in contributing toward the need of others, were, in fact, setting a wonderful example for others to follow, nevertheless their church was *not entirely* free from personal friction (Syntyche and Euodia, for example, were not of the same mind, Phil. 4:2) and from *every* danger of giving heed to "those dogs," "those evil workers," namely, "the *concision*" (Judaistic teachers). See Phil. 3:1-3. There were those, moreover, "whose god is the belly, and whose glory is in their shame, who set their mind on earthly things" (Phil. 3:19).

(3) Epaphroditus (and others too, perhaps) had also told Paul, we may well assume, that the church at Philippi was deeply concerned about the apostle, and that it wanted to know more about his present condition. Did Paul think that he would soon be set at liberty? What was his own spiritual reaction to the bonds which he had to endure? If he regained his liberty, would he favor them with an early visit? Questions such as these amounted to a *Request* for detailed information about Paul. See Phil. 1:12-26; 4:18, 19.

(4) Finally, Epaphroditus, having been exposed to considerable danger, having suffered and recovered from grave illness, and having become deeply concerned about the effect of all this upon the church which had delegated him, was anxious to wend his way homeward to Philippi. This expressed desire met with the apostle's full approval, so that the latter not only *allowed* him to go back but actually *sent* him back (Phil. 2:25). But surely those by whom he had been delegated (the church at Philippi, especially its officers) had never intended that he would return to them so soon. What kind of *Reception* would be accorded him upon his return? Would it be critical or friendly?

In view of this background — and linked with it point by point — *the purpose* of Paul's letter can now be stated. *The immediate occasion* for dispatching a letter at this time was undoubtedly the return of Epaphroditus to Philippi. In all probability he carried with him the apostle's letter and delivered it to the church.[18] *Paul's purpose,* then, was as follows:

(1) To give *written* expression to his *Gratitude.*

In all probability, when the apostle received the gift he had acknowledged it as soon as possible, either by mouth of those who presumably had accompanied Epaphroditus on his journey to Rome and had immediately returned or through others who a few days or weeks later had traveled from Rome to Philippi. But, some time having now elapsed, the apostle also wishes to

---

[18] For a different view see one of the two suggestions offered by S. Greydanus, *Bizondere Canoniek,* Kampen, 1949, Vol. II, p. 159.

express his appreciation in *writing*. (It is possible that Paul's letter was delayed by the illness of Epaphroditus.) That the Epistle to the Philippians is indeed the first *written* acknowledgment seems to be clearly implied in Phil. 4:10, 18. However, not only does Paul thank the Philippians for their gift; he also thanks God for the Philippians! See Phil. 4:10-20; then 1:3-11.

(2) To provide the spiritual *Guidance* which the congregation needed.

Let the Philippians continue to exercise their citizenship in a manner that is worthy of the gospel of Christ (Phil. 1:27-30). Let them remain united in mind and purpose (Phil. 2:2). Let the attitude of Christ who humbled himself and became obedient unto death, even death on a cross, be descriptive also *of them* (Phil. 2:1-11). In the midst of a crooked and perverse generation let them be light-bearers, holding forth the word of life (Phil. 2:14-16). Let them beware of *the Judaizers* (Phil. 3:1-3). Let them not think that spiritually they have already "arrived." On the contrary, imitating Paul, let them "press on toward the goal" (Phil. 3:4-16). Their homeland being in heaven, let them beware of *sensualists,* the enemies of the cross, whose god is the belly (Phil. 3:17-21). Let them, in brief, strive after *courage* (Phil. 1:27, 28), *oneness* (Phil. 2:2; 4:2, 3), *lowliness* (2:3), *helpfulness* (2:4), *obedience* (2:12), *perfection* (3:12-16), *holiness* (3:17, 20), *steadfastness* (4:1), *joy and trust in the Lord* (4:1-7). In reaching out toward this ideal let them fix their attention on "whatever things are true, honorable, just, pure," etc. Then the God of peace will be with them (Phil. 4:8, 9).

(3) To fill the minds and hearts of the Philippians with the spirit of *Gladness*.

Do the Philippians request information about Paul? "Do not be unduly disturbed about me," he says, as it were: "The things that have happened to me have fallen out to the advantage of the gospel (Phil. 1:12-17). . . . In every way, whether in pretense or in truth, Christ is being proclaimed, and in this *I rejoice. Yes, and I shall continue to rejoice,* for I know that . . . this will turn out to my salvation . . . Now as always Christ will be magnified in my person, whether by life or by death . . . For the rest, my brothers, *rejoice in the Lord . . . Rejoice* in the Lord always. Again I will say *Rejoice . . .* Now *I rejoice* in the Lord greatly." From beginning to end the letter is bathed in this sunshine of joy. We can understand Bengel when he said: *Summa epistolae: Gaudeo, gaudete* (The sum of the epistle is: I rejoice; y o u must rejoice), even though we would not put it quite that strongly. Not less than sixteen times do the words *joy, rejoice* occur in this letter: Phil. 1:4; 1:18 (twice); 1:25; 2:2; 2:17 (twice); 2:18 (twice); 2:28; 2:29; 3:1; 4:1; 4:4 (twice); and 4:10. Yet, it is hardly correct to say that joy is *the summary or theme* of the letter.

Now the joy of which Paul makes repeated mention is the joy unspeakable and full of glory. It is the *great* joy which, far from being dependent upon outward circumstances, wells up from the heart of this prisoner who faces possible death and is chained night and day to a soldier, with few friends to comfort him and several enemies who are ever ready to raise up affliction to him in his bonds (Phil. 2:20, 21; 1:15-17). The apostle writes this letter in order that the readers, by fully sharing in this joy, may make full his own joy. Paul's case is in process before the imperial court. There had been a trial (Phil. 1:7), and the final verdict cannot be long delayed. Is he going to be set free? Deep down in his heart he believes that this is exactly what is going to happen. Yet, he does not exclude the opposite possibility. But, come what may, he is ready. See Phil. 1:22-26. As soon as the verdict has been made known, he will send Timothy to Philippi with the news. He adds, "But I trust in the Lord that I myself shall also soon come" (Phil. 2:19-24).

(4) To prevail upon the Philippians' Spirit-wrought *Goodness* of heart to extend to Epaphroditus a most cordial "Welcome Home."

A wonderful person, this Epaphroditus! The apostle calls him "my brother and fellow-worker and fellow-soldier," as well as "y o u r messenger and minister to my need." In the course of his labors for Christ the King he had suffered much. He had, in fact, risked his life, and had experienced days of illness so grievous that he had lain at death's very door. But God had shown mercy to this hero and had healed him. Meanwhile Epaphroditus had been informed that the members of the home-church, having heard about his illness, were worried about him. Epaphroditus naturally wants to remove that anxiety and so does Paul. Hence, the apostle decides to send him back to Philippi, and in his letter he states the purpose, namely, "Accordingly, I am sending him back the more eagerly in order that when y o u see him again y o u may rejoice and I may be less sorrowful. So extend to him a most joyful welcome in the Lord, and hold such men in honor" (Phil. 2:28-29). Thus the apostle provides a hearty reception for Epaphroditus, upon his probably unexpectedly early return.

V. The Place and the Time of Writing

Philippians belongs to a group of four letters — Colossians, Philemon, Ephesians, and Philippians — that are commonly designated the Prison Epistles. Here for the first time Paul writes as *a prisoner* (Col. 4:3, 18; Philem. 10, 13, 22, 23; Eph. 3:1; 4:1; 6:20; Phil. 1:7, 13; 2:17).[19] In reading

---

[19] It is true that at a later time also II Timothy was written from prison, but that epistle is in an altogether different category. Like I Timothy and Titus it was written to one of the apostles' official representatives, comparable, but only *to a certain extent*, to "pastors." Hence, these three form a group. See N.T.C. on The Pastoral Epistles.

these letters one notices how deeply the writer is affected by his imprisonment. Nevertheless, he does not lose heart. Is he not the prisoner *of Christ Jesus?* The greatness of Christ Jesus is described in Colossians, Ephesians, and Philippians. Tychicus seems to be the bearer of the letter to the Colossians and the one to Philemon. The fugitive slave Onesimus accompanies him and must be returned to his master in Colossae; not as a slave, however, but as a brother. See Col. 4:7-9; Philem. 10-12, 16. It is not at all surprising that Tychicus also has a letter for the church at Ephesus (Eph. 6:21, 22), located near Colossae. It is clear, therefore, that Colossians, Philemon, and Ephesians belong together. They are in all likelihood delivered to their respective addresses by the same person, Tychicus. And though Philippians seems to have been brought to its destination by someone else, namely, Epaphroditus (Phil. 2:25-29; 4:18), and therefore, in a way stands outside the group of three, nevertheless, all four have this in common, as already noted, that they are Prison Epistles, which by most interpreters are regarded as having been written during the same imprisonment.

Now the question arises: Where was this prison? According to the book of Acts Paul was in prison in Philippi (Acts 16:23-40), in Jerusalem (Acts 21:33–23:30), in Caesarea (Acts 23:35–26:32), and in Rome (Acts 28:16–31). However, Philippi and Jerusalem can be ruled out at once, for the apostle did not have the time to write from these prisons. (Besides, as far as Philippians is concerned, the prison in Philippi would be ruled out anyway: one does not write to the Philippians from Philippi!) There remain Caesarea and Rome, to which (because of what Paul writes in I Cor. 15:32; II Cor. 1:8-11; 6:5; and II Cor. 11:23) some would add Ephesus.

As a result we now have four theories with respect to the place from which these letters may have been written: (a) the traditional position, according to which they were written from Rome; (b) the view that they were composed in Caesarea; (c) the theory which supports Ephesus as the place of their origin; and (d) the "mixed" hypothesis, according to which a distinction is made of one kind or another; for example, Colossians, Philemon, and Ephesians were written from Caesarea, but Philippians was written from Rome (or, according to others, from Ephesus); or the three were written from Ephesus, Philippians from Rome.[20]

---

[20] For the various views consult J. Schmid, *Zeit und Ort der Paulinischen Gefangenschaftsbriefe,* 1931. For the view that all were written from Rome see J. B. Lightfoot, *St. Paul's Epistle to the Philippians,* reprint Grand Rapids, Mich., 1953, p. 30; R. C. H. Lenski, *Interpretation of Galatians, Ephesians, Philippians,* Columbus, Ohio, pp. 325-329, 699, 700; M. R. Vincent, *The Epistles to the Philippians and to Philemon* (in I.C.C.), New York, 1906, pp. xxii-xxv and 160-162; S. Greydanus, *Bizondere Canoniek,* Kampen, 1949, Vol. II, pp. 127-140. The influence of the Caesarean and of the Ephesian theories is gradually beginning to "wear off," and in most recent works the traditional Rome-view, which was the view either expressed or assumed by all the earlier exegetes, is beginning to be endorsed more strongly

INTRODUCTION

In harmony with most interpreters, ancient and modern, I accept the Rome-view for all four Prison Epistles. It is true that the distance between Rome and Philippi was greater than, for example, that between Ephesus and Philippi. But since there was an excellent and much-traveled "highway" between Rome and Philippi, this matter of greater distance has very little value as an argument against the view that the apostle was at Rome when he wrote the four Prison Epistles. In fact, it is so weak that it can be disregarded.

The following points may be adduced in refutation of the Caesarean and Ephesian hypotheses and in favor of the Rome-view. Instead of enumerating them in haphazard fashion, I have tried to arrange them in such a manner that the grouping is both *logical* and *memorizable*. It will be seen that the first three points concern *the general situation* pertaining to Paul's imprisonment: he was *under guard;* which, as we know from the book of Acts, was true *in Rome;* he was experiencing *a lengthy imprisonment;* and he was in a city where there was *a multitude of preachers.* The fourth point has to do with *the contents* of the Prison Epistles. Points five and six pertain to *the verdict* which Paul was awaiting: he more or less expected it to be *favorable;* he knew that it would be *decisive.* Points seven, eight, and nine fix the attention on: a faithful church, few faithful friends, and the ever-faithful Christ.

So far, *Philippians* has been the starting-point for much of the argumentation, though wherever possible the other three Prison Epistles have also furnished material for arriving at a conclusion. Points ten and eleven, however, are derived not from Philippians but from *Colossians, Philemon, and Ephesians.* Point twelve is a tradition-summary touching all four letters. We now consider these twelve points.

---

than ever. As far as Philippians is concerned, the Rome-theory has never been eclipsed. In *The Interpreter's Bible* E. F. Scott favors Rome for Philippians, and F. W. Beare likewise favors Rome for Colossians; but John Knox seems to incline toward Ephesus for Philemon. F. W. Grosheide supports the traditional Rome-view (*Openbaring Gods In Het Nieuwe Testament*, Kampen, 1953, pp. 204, 208).

The Caesarean theory was proposed by H. E. G. Paulus, *Philologisch-kritischer Kommentar über das Neue Testament* (Lübeck, 1800-1804). It has had many defendants since his day. (See especially E. Lohmeyer, *Die Briefe an die Philipper, an die Kolosser und an Philemon*, Göttingen, 1930; Meyer's *Kommentar.*) Among others who favor this view are J. Macpherson, F. Spitta, and O. Holtzmann.

The Ephesian theory was advanced by H. Lisco (*Vincula Sanctorum*, Berlin, 1900). However, three years earlier A. Deissmann, while lecturing at the Theological Seminary at Herborn, had already introduced it with application to Colossians, Philemon, and Ephesians (see *Light From the Ancient East*, tr. from the German by L. R. M. Strachan, New York, 1927, pp. 237, 238, in which book he endorses this theory for all four Prison Epistles). What is, perhaps, the best defense of the Ephesian theory is found in G. S. Duncan's book, *St. Paul's Ephesian Ministry*, New York, 1930. Cf. D. Rowlingson's article "Paul's Ephesian Imprisonment, An Evaluation of the Evidence," *AThR*, XXXII (1950), pp. 1-7. Among others the following favor this theory: Bowen, Appel, and Michaelis.

(1) *"Throughout the whole praetorian guard," and "Caesar's household."*
It has been argued that the expression "throughout the whole praetorian guard" (Phil. 1:13) should be rendered "in the whole praetorium," and that since a praetorium is simply a government house or provincial governor's residence (see N.T.C. on John 18:28) it may have been located at Caesarea (cf. Acts 23:35), or even at Ephesus; but not at Rome.

However, in the present instance the phrase is immediately followed by "and to all the rest," and refers, therefore, to *people,* not to a building. According to the most natural interpretation it indicates the imperial guard, nine thousand in number, which was instituted by Augustus.[21] It is exactly at Rome that the apostle would be constantly guarded by a soldier from this guard and because it rotated, the reason why this remarkable man was imprisoned would gradually become known "throughout the whole praetorian guard and to all the rest."

In the same category is the expression, "All the saints greet y o u, especially those of Caesar's household" (Phil. 4:22). Here again *the most natural interpretation* would refer the expression to that large number of slaves and freemen who served in the emperor's palace at Rome. They were household servants, cooks, gardeners, porters, doorkeepers, etc. See also on Phil. 4:22.

(2) *Established Facts versus Questionable Inferences. A Lengthy Imprisonment as a New Way of Life.*
In order to prove the Ephesian theory an appeal is made to four passages in Paul's Corinthian correspondence: I Cor. 15:32 ("If after the manner of men I fought with beasts *at Ephesus*"), II Cor. 1:8-11 (". . . the affliction which befell us *in Asia* . . ."), II Cor. 6:5 ("in imprisonments"), and II Cor. 11:23 ("in far more imprisonments"). The argument is as follows: since these passages antedate both the Caesarean and Roman imprisonments, they show that Paul must have been in prison during his stay at Ephesus, while he was on his third missionary journey.

However, when examined carefully, in the light of their contexts, these passages do not compel one to accept that conclusion. As to I Cor. 15:32, this can hardly be taken literally. It is not easy to believe that Paul, *the Roman citizen,* would have been *literally* cast before beasts at Ephesus. As to II Cor. 1:8-11, the "affliction in Asia" was not necessarily an imprisonment. As the context clearly indicates, it was of a kind that is still continuing, now that the apostle has reached Macedonia. The other two passages *may,* but do not necessarily, refer to an imprisonment *in Ephesus.* But even if they refer to an Ephesian imprisonment, it is very doubtful whether the latter would be of the nature implied in the Prison Epistles. These letters imply a lengthy period of imprisonment, imprisonment as *a new way of life*

---

[21] See J. B. Lightfoot, *op. cit.,* pp. 99-104; M.M., pp. 532, 533.

and not as a brief experience. Paul's ministry of less than three years at Ephesus, a ministry filled with kingdom-activity (see Acts 19:8, 10), leaves no room for such a protracted incarceration. Moreover, in his detailed account of Paul's activity in Ephesus Luke has not a word to say about it.

On the other hand, from the book of Acts (Chapter 28; cf. 23:11) *we know* that Paul was a prisoner in Rome. It is *possible* that when he wrote Philippians he had been transferred from his "rented house" (Acts 28:30) to the soldiers' barracks or that in some other way he had been placed under stricter custody (*custodia militaris instead of custodia libera*). But it is hard to prove this. One thing, however, is clear: *in general,* the conditions of Paul's imprisonment as described in Acts were the same as those which are implied in the Prison Epistles: for example, soldiers guarded Paul (cf. Acts 28:16 with Phil. 1:13, 14); he enjoyed freedom to receive visitors (cf. Acts 28:30 with Phil. 4:18); and he had the opportunity to bear testimony concerning his faith (cf. Acts 28:31 with Phil. 1:12-18; Col. 4:2-4; Eph. 6:18-20). As to this last item, it would seem that *at Caesarea* the apostle's opportunities to reach others with the gospel were far more limited (see Acts 23:35 and 24:27).

Hence, the view that Paul wrote these four epistles while he was a prisoner in Rome rests on *the established facts* with reference to his Roman imprisonment, while other theories are based on *questionable inferences.*

(3) *The Multitude of Preachers.*

From Phil. 1:14-18 it appears that in the city of his imprisonment there were *many* heralds of the gospel. Some were motivated by envy and rivalry, others by love. This multitude of preachers suits the large city of Rome far better than the far smaller Caesarea. (Cf. also Col. 4:2-4; Eph. 6:18-20.)

(4) *Arguments Based on Contents.*

It is urged that in material contents Philippians approaches the earlier epistles (especially Romans and Galatians; but see also I and II Corinthians; e.g., II Cor. 11), and that for this reason it cannot belong to the period A. D. 61-63 when Paul was imprisoned in Rome, but must be earlier, dating back to Ephesus and in general to the third missionary journey (A. D. 53/54-57/58). Reference is made, for example, to the scathing denunciation of what the apostle contemptuously calls *the concision* and to the immediately following emphatic affirmation of the doctrine of justification by faith alone (Phil. 3:2-16). This is then compared with similar emotion-filled utterances on the same subject in Romans (2:25-29; 9:30-33; 10:3); and Galatians (3:1-14; 4:12-20; 5:1-12; 6:12-16).

But even if it be granted that the subject-matter here in Phil. 3:2-16 is the same as that in Galatians (which is true except that Paul *rebukes* the Galatians, but *warns* the Philippians), similarity in subject-matter by no means proves identity in the place from which one is writing. *The apostle wrote as the concrete situation in any given case demanded!* And the warmth with which he was able to write on the theme of salvation not by law-works but solely by grace through faith never left him. We find touches of it even in the Pastoral Epistles (see I Tim. 1:12-17 and Titus 3:4-7). Moreover, if a change in subject-matter indicates a change in the author's whereabouts, then, considered by and large, the Prison Epistles (so largely Christological) and the Earlier Epistles (largely Soteriological) must come from *different* places!

Some, favoring the Caesarean theory, link the denunciation of the *concision* (Phil. 3:2-16) with the hostility which *the Jews* showed to Paul during the latter's Caesarean imprisonment (Acts 24:1; 25:7). But Phil. 3 is clearly not directed against Christ-hating Jews but against Judaizers, so-called "converted" (nominally Christian) Jews who were still clinging to the Mosaic ritual. See on Phil. 3:2-16.

It is exactly the contents of the Prison Epistles that point away from Ephesus and Caesarea. For, if written from Ephesus, during the third missionary journey, when Paul had on his mind *the collection* for the needy saints at Jerusalem, they would in all probability have contained references to this subject. Moreover, had Paul been in Ephesus, Epaphroditus, his friend and prison-attendant, could have made a quick visit to Philippi. All this discussion about "sending (back)" Epaphroditus (Phil. 2:25-30) would not have been necessary.

And if these epistles had been written from Caesarea, they would most likely have contained a kind word about Philip the evangelist who lived there and who a moment before had so generously entertained the apostle (Acts 21:8). In none of the Prison Epistles is anything said about this man or about his four remarkable daughters. The entire situation is clearly different. Paul is now in Rome, not in Ephesus or Caesarea.

(5) *Expectation of a Favorable Verdict.*

There are passages in these Prison Epistles which show that Paul *hopes* and, to a certain extent, *expects* to be acquitted (Phil. 1:25; 2:24). Upon his release he plans to go to Colossae and asks that a guest-room be kept ready for him there (Philem. 22). Now his plan *had been* to visit Spain (Rom. 15:28). The question is asked, accordingly, "If it were true that Paul was writing from Rome, with plans to proceed farther West, to Spain, would he have asked that a guest-room be kept ready for him at a place located not at all on the way from Rome to Spain but in the very opposite direction?"

The answer is that the plan to visit Spain had been announced when the apostle was still a free man, writing Romans from Corinth on his third missionary journey. At that time he intended to go to Rome and then to Spain. From there he probably planned to return to the churches in Asia Minor, Macedonia, etc. But God willed differently. Paul did indeed go to Rome after his third missionary journey, but as a prisoner! In all, his Caesarean and Roman imprisonments probably lasted about five years (cf. Acts 24:27; 25:1; Chap. 27; 28:30). It is altogether natural that when now at last he expects to be released, he announces a revision in his plan: he will first see the familiar faces in the East — moreover, in Asia Minor a dangerous heresy is threatening! — , and then visit strangers in the far West. In all probability the apostle carried out this revised plan.

Besides, the very expectation of *a favorable verdict* fits *Rome* far better than, for example, Caesarea. For Paul to be released while at Caesarea would have meant either bribing Felix (Acts 24:26) or consenting to the wish of Festus, namely, to be tried by the Jews at Jerusalem (Acts 25:9). Paul will have nothing to do with either suggestion. When the second one is made, he immediately appeals to Caesar in Rome (Acts 25:10). — On the other hand the closing chapters of Acts point toward *release from Roman imprisonment*. See N.T.C. on Pastoral Epistles, pp. 25-27; 39-40.

(6) *The Decisive Character of the Verdict.*

Though Paul rather expected to be released, he did not exclude from his mind the thought that he might, after all, be sentenced to death. One thing he knew for sure: *the verdict, whatever it was, would be decisive:* it would mean either life or death, with no possibility of further appeal (Phil. 1:20-23; 2:17, 23). Hence, he must have been *at Rome* when he wrote these letters, for at Ephesus or at Caesarea he, as a Roman citizen, would have been able to appeal to Caesar. In neither of these two places would the verdict have been decisive.

(7) *A Faithful Church Established Long Ago.*

In Phil. 4:15 Paul gratefully recalls what the Philippians had done for him "in the early days [literally, "in the beginning"] of the gospel." And they had remained faithful *ever since*. This sounds as if those early days were "long ago." But when the apostle was in Ephesus on his third missionary journey, the church at Philippi, established on the second missionary journey, was only a few years old. The solution: Philippians was written from Rome, as were the other Prison Epistles.

(8) *Few Faithful Friends, Timothy a Notable Exception.*

Often Timothy is enlisted in the cause of the Ephesian theory. The argument runs as follows: We know that Timothy was with Paul *in Ephesus,* but there is no source that informs us that he was with the apostle in Rome, though he *may* have been. We also know definitely that Paul sent Timothy *from Ephesus* (I Cor. 4:17; 16:10) to Macedonia, in which Philippi was located (Acts 19:22). And this exactly harmonizes with Paul's intention as expressed in Phil. 2:19-23. Hence, Paul must have been *at Ephesus* when he wrote Philippians. See, for example, J. H. Michael, *The Epistle of Paul to the Philippians* (in The Moffatt New Testament Commentary), New York, 1929, pp. xvi, xvii.

This argument impresses me as being rather superficial. There is nothing to prove that I Cor. 4:17 (cf. 16:10) and Phil. 2:19-23 refer to *the same errand*. The context, in fact, argues strongly against this identification. For in Phil. 2:21 the apostle states, that, with the exception of Timothy, all those who are with him "look after their own affairs, not those of Jesus Christ." But surely this expression even when interpreted in a qualified sense (see on 2:21) would not have suited Ephesus where the apostle had very many warm friends (cf. Acts 20:36-38), among them Priscilla and Aquila, his helpers in Christ Jesus who were ever ready to sacrifice their very lives for him (Rom. 16:3, 4; cf. Acts 18:18, 19, 26).

An expression such as this (Phil. 2:21) suits the last days of the first Roman imprisonment. It does not suit any other place or time, least of all Ephesus and the third missionary journey

Moreover, as to Timothy's having been (or *not* having been) with Paul in Rome, *we know* from the book of Acts that both Timothy and Aristarchus accompanied Paul to Jerusalem where Paul was arrested (Acts 20:4-6); also, that Aristarchus was with the apostle aboard the ship, when the apostle departed from Caesarea to go to Rome (Acts 27:2). (For the idea of Lightfoot, namely, that Aristarchus disembarked at Myra, there is no evidence whatever.) It must certainly be considered very probable that ever-faithful Timothy, if he was not actually with Paul on that ship, followed his master soon afterward. Any other course would have been unlike Timothy. See N.T.C. on the Pastoral Epistles, pp. 33-36.

(9) *The Faithful Christ, Not the Roman Emperor, Is God.*

As has been pointed out in Section II (The City of Philippi), the Roman citizen Paul and the inhabitants of the Roman colony of Philippi had much in common. In *Rome* emperor-worship reached its climax. Of course, it was also found elsewhere, in fact throughout the Roman empire, but elsewhere particularly in *the Roman colonies,* such as Philippi. If Paul is writing from *a prison in Rome* it is even easier to understand his words to the effect that writer and readers are "engaged in *the same* conflict" (Phil. 1:30, note especially the context, Phil. 1:27) than if he is writing from any other place. If he is writing from Rome his reason for placing added stress on the fact that the faithful Christ, and he alone, is God, becomes doubly clear (Col. 1:15; 2:9; Phil. 2:6).

(10) *The Flight of Onesimus*

The purpose of one of the Prison Epistles was to secure a kind reception for the fugitive slave Onesimus upon his return to his master, Philemon, who lived in Colossae. See the epistle addressed to the latter (cf. Col. 4:9). The slave had found his way to the city of Paul's imprisonment, had been brought into contact with the apostle, through whose instrumentality he had been converted. It is argued, accordingly, that it is easier to imagine that from Colossae Onesimus had fled to Ephesus, only about a hundred miles away, or even to Caesarea, about five hundred miles, than *all the way* to Rome, about a thousand miles of actual travel.

Now this reasoning may be correct when it pertains to a certain class of fugitives in any age. In the case of others, however, it is faulty. Understandably they love *distance,* and they love to boast about it ("I took my flight and ran away, *All the way* to Canaday!"). They also long to hide behind *the curtain of anonymity* which the large city with its teeming multitudes provides. Rome has been called "a haven for runaways"!

(11) *The Return of Onesimus.*

In this same connection some say that had the three epistles — Colossians, Philemon, and Ephesians — been written from Rome, Onesimus, who was returning to his master in the company of Tychicus, would have reached Ephesus before reaching Colossae, and, therefore, would have been commended to the Ephesian as well as to the Colossian church. They argue that the omission of his name from Ephesians (contrast Col. 4:9) indicates that Tychicus, traveling from Paul's prison in *Caesarea,* had already left Onesimus at Philemon's home in Colossae. Alone he traveled on to Ephesus.

But this argument, too, is very unrealistic. To have commended the fugitive slave to the church at Ephesus, so that this church would have been urged to accept him with open arms even before his own master at Colossae had had the opportunity to act in the case would have been a breach of etiquette, to say the least.

(12) *The Voice of Tradition.*

According to the tradition of the early church it was from Rome that Paul wrote the four Prison Epistles. Not until about the year 1800 did the Caesarea theory arise, and not until 1900 the Ephesus theory. In the absence of any cogent reasons to depart from the traditional position it is certainly wise to cling to it.

As has been indicated, in all probability Colossians, Philemon, and Ephesians were despatched at the same time and were carried to their respective destinations by the same messenger, namely, Tychicus. The only remaining question, then, is this: Did these three letters precede or did they follow Philippians? Some defend the latter position [22] but on grounds that have failed to impress most commentators. Lightfoot, arguing for the priority of Philippians, says that in this letter we have "the spent wave" of the Judaistic controversy which was brought so prominently to the fore in earlier epistles, especially in Romans (cf. Phil. 3:3 with Rom. 2:28; Phil. 3:9 with Rom. 9:30-33; 10:3), while in Colossians and Ephesians we are beginning to deal with incipent Gnosticism which subject is continued in the Pastorals. But about four years must have elapsed between Romans and Philippians, while, on the other hand, the time-interval between Philippians and the other

---

[22] J. B. Lightfoot, *op. cit.,* pp. 30–46. Thus also Bleek, Sanday, Hort, and Beet.

Prison Epistles cannot have been much more than a year (perhaps less; cf. Philem. 22 with Phil. 2:23, 24). It is hard to believe that in this very brief interval there can have been any great change either in the character of the heresy by which the church, as a whole, was threatened, or in the system of thought which (as some assume) was gradually being developed in the apostle's mind. Whatever difference in emphasis there be between Philippians, on the one hand, and Colossians, Philemon, and Ephesians, on the other, is mainly due to difference in situations and needs of the respective readers.

Although the question which letter was first or last cannot be answered with certainty, yet, if any choice must be made, placing *Philippians last,* as is done by most interpreters, seems to have by far the better of the argument. Among the many reasons that have been advanced for this position the following are, perhaps, the most convincing:

(1) Luke and Aristarchus, who accompanied Paul on his perilous journey to Rome (Acts 27:2), and were still with him when he wrote Colossians (4:10, 14) and Philemon (23), are no longer with him when he writes Philippians.

(2) Between Paul's arrival in Rome and the despatch of Philippians much time has elapsed. See Phil. 2:25-30; 4:10, 18. The distance between Philippi and Rome had probably been covered no less than four times:

a. Someone travels from Rome to Philippi with the news of Paul's arrival and imprisonment in Rome.

b. The Philippians collect a gift for Paul and send it to him by the hand of Epaphroditus.

c. Epaphroditus becomes gravely ill, and someone conveys this information to the Philippians.

d. Someone from Philippi reaches Rome and tells Epaphroditus (who in the meantime has fully recovered) about the deep concern of the Philippians for his health and safety.[23]

(3) The reaction of the praetorian guard and that of two categories of gospel-heralds to the presence and preaching of Paul (Phil. 1:12-18) indicates that when Philippians was written the apostle had been in Rome for some time.

(4) The apostle is expecting a verdict *any moment* (Phil. 2:23, 24; cf. 1:7). Yet, though there surely is a difference between Philemon 22 and Phil. 2:23, 24, inasmuch as in the former passage the apostle expresses *the hope* that release from imprisonment *will take place,* whereas in the latter he expresses

---

[23] Lightfoot's attempt to reduce these four journeys to two (*op. cit.,* pp. 35–37) has left most exegetes (myself included) unconvinced. But a criticism of this point belongs to a Commentary on the Book of Acts (27:2).

the confidence that such a release *is about to take place,* the implied differ-
ence in the time of writing was probably rather brief. If we place all four
Prison Epistles in the period A. D. 61–63,[24] with Colossians, Philemon, and
Ephesians followed shortly afterward (and toward the close of the first
Roman imprisonment) by Philippians, we are probably about as near to
the truth as we can get.

VI. Authorship and Unity

The question, "Who wrote Philippians?" is readily answered. It was the
apostle Paul. Timothy, to be sure, was associated with him, so that we read,
"Paul and Timothy, servants of Christ Jesus, to all the saints in Christ Jesus
who are in Philippi," but from the fact that Paul is throughout writing in
the first person singular it is clear that it is Paul with whom the main responsibility rests. Not Timothy but Paul was the author.

It was Ferdinand Christian Baur who, conducting a siege against the
fortresses of traditional Christian doctrine, assailed the Pauline authorship
of all the letters passing under the apostle's name, except Galatians, I and II
Corinthians, and Romans. See his *Paulus,* Stuttgart, 1845. His arguments
against Philippians were in the main as follows:

(1) The mention of "overseers and deacons" (Phil. 1:1) points to a post-
Pauline stage of church government.

Answer: A study of Acts 6:1-6; 11:30; 14:23; 30:27, 28; and I Thess. 5:12,
13 indicates that these offices existed long before Philippians was written.
See on Phil. 1:1.

(2) The epistle shows no originality. It is full of imitations of Paul's
genuine epistles.

Answer: If Paul wrote Philippians as well as Romans, etc., similar expressions would be entirely natural.

(3) The epistle shows traces of Gnosticism, especially in 2:5-8, where the
writer was thinking of the last of the aeons, namely, Sophia, who, attempting
to comprehend the Absolute, falls from *fulness* into *emptiness.*

Answer: This weird interpretation contradicts the context. See on Phil.
2:5-8; also II Cor. 8:9.

(4) The epistle is a post-Paulinic attempt to reconcile the Jewish-Christian
and Gentile-Christian parties, typified respectively by Euodia and Syntyche
(Phil. 4:2).

Answers: The context (see especially Phil. 4:3) clearly indicates that these

---

[24] For a discussion of this date and of the entire Pauline chronology see my *Bible
Survey,* pp. 62-64, 70.

names belong to women in the church at Philippi, and that neither of them had ever been the leader of any party that opposed Paul. On the contrary both had been "laboring *with* Paul" in the gospel. Baur's interpretation must be considered a very fanciful application of his Hegelian principle, a notion hardly worthy of consideration.

At first Baur's arguments were accepted by several of his Tübingen school disciples. But soon some began to disagree. Among those who regarded most of Baur's arguments as irrelevant or worse it was especially Karl Christian Johann Holstein who, nevertheless, revived the attack against the genuineness of the letter. He accepted in modified form *one* of the arguments of Baur that has not yet been mentioned, namely, that the doctrine of justification which Philippians sets forth is not that of Paul. He added other arguments. His reasoning, then, was as follows:

(1) Paul's doctrine of forensic, imputed righteousness is here in Philippians replaced by that of infused righteousness (see Phil. 3:9-11).

Answer: The author of Philippians clearly speaks of imputed righteousness in Phil. 3:9: "not having a righteousness of my own, which (is) of the law, but that (which is) through faith in Christ, the righteousness (which is) from God (and rests) on faith" (cf. Rom. 3:21-24; even Titus 3:4-8 is no different). It is true, of course, that by means of an infinitive of purpose the passage in Philippians links this imputed righteousness with subjective righteousness: "that I may know him," etc. (Phil. 3:10, 11).

(2) According to Paul the pre-incarnate Christ was *a heavenly man* (I Cor. 15:47-49), but according to Philippians (2:6: "existing in the form of God") this pre-incarnate Christ belongs to an order of beings *higher than heavenly humanity*.

Answer: The Corinthian passage refers not to the preincarnate but to the risen and ascended Christ, as is evident from the context (see I Cor. 15:49).

(3) The same people who are denounced by Paul (Gal. 1:6, 7) are more than tolerated by the author of Philippians (1:15-18). While Paul says that they are accursed individuals who *pervert* the gospel of Christ, Philippians says that they are *proclaiming* the Christ, a fact in which he rejoices though they preach Christ from envy and rivalry.

Answer: These are not the same persons. Those to whom Phil. 1:15-18 refers are not preaching a different doctrine. They are proclaiming the true Christ, but their motives are not pure. As to the people who are condemned in Gal. 1:6, 7, these are probably referred to in Phil. 3:2, where the denunciation is similarly sharp.

(4) The real Paul is no boaster. He says, "When I would do good, evil is present" (Rom. 7:21). But the author of Philippians says that he was *blameless* when measured by the standard of the law (Phil. 3:6).

Answer: There is no contradiction. A person can be blameless, indeed, with respect to the law considered as an external commandment, but he may still be very guilty with respect to the law viewed in its deeply spiritual meaning.

It will have become evident that the arguments against the Pauline authorship of Philippians are very superficial. They have been called frivolous. Scholarship in general, throughout the centuries, has always considered this letter to be a genuine product of the mind and pen of Paul. Weizsäcker was right when he said that the reasons for attributing the epistle to Paul are "overwhelming." And so was McGiffert when he declared: "It is simply inconceivable that anyone else would or could have produced in his name a letter in which the personal element so largely predominates and the character of the man and the apostle is revealed with so great vividness and fidelity" (*The Apostolic Age*, p. 393).

Not only does the letter claim to have been written by Paul, and not only do the conditions reflected in it harmonize, on the whole, with those described in Acts 28, as has already been indicated, but the character of Paul, as revealed in his other letters, is also clearly expressed in Philippians. Here, too, we find a person who is deeply interested in those whom he addresses (cf. Phil. 1:3-11, 25, 26; 2:25-30 with Rom. 1:8, 9; I Thess. 1:2 ff.; II Thess. 1:3, 11, 12); is anxious to see them (cf. Phil. 2:24 with Rom. 1:11; I Thess. 2:17, 18); and loves to encourage and praise them (cf. Phil. 4:15-17 with II Cor. 8:7; I Thess. 1:3, 6-10). Nevertheless, here, as well as in the other epistles, his praise never ends in man but always in God (cf. Phil. 1:6 with Rom. 8:28-30; Gal. 5:22-25; I Thess. 1:4, 5; II Thess. 2:13). Here, too, as elsewhere, he likes to review his past relations with the church (cf. Phil. 2:12; 4:15, 16 with I Cor. 2:1-5; 3:1, 2; I Thess. 2:1-12). He shows great tact in admonishing (cf. Phil. 4:2, 3 with II Cor. 8:7; I Thess. 4:9, 10; Philem. 8-22). Nevertheless, he is never afraid to assert his authority (cf. Phil. 2:12-18; 4:1-9 with I Cor. 16:1; I Thess. 5:27). He is a very humble man who is filled to overflowing with gratitude for the mercies which God showed to one so unworthy (cf. Phil. 3:4-14 with I Cor. 15:9; II Cor. 11:16-12:10; Eph. 3:8).

The testimony of the early church is in harmony with the conclusion which has been derived from the epistle itself.

Thus Eusebius, having made a thorough investigation of the oral and written judgment of the church, writes: "But clearly evident and plain are the fourteen (letters) of Paul; yet it is not right to ignore that some dispute the (letter) to the Hebrews" (*Ecclesiastical History* III.iii). Obviously Eusebius, writing at the beginning of the fourth century, knew that the entire orthodox church accepted Philippians as being among "the true, genuine, and recognized" epistles of Paul (*op cit.*, III.xxv).

From Eusebius we go back to Origen (fl. 210-250). His works are full of quotations from Philippians; for example, "For we do not hesitate to affirm that the goodness of Christ appears in a greater and more divine light because . . . he humbled himself, and became obedient to death, even death on a cross, than if he had judged existence in a manner equal to God something to keep in his grasp, and had shrunk from becoming a servant for the salvation of the world" (*Commentary on John* I.xxxvii), clearly a reference to Phil. 2:6-8. He considered Paul to be the author of Philippians (same book I.xvii, a comment on Phil. 1:23).

Hippolytus, said to have been a bishop of Portus near Rome, was martyred somewhere about A. D. 235–239. He was a disciple of Irenaeus, who was a disciple of Polycarp, who was a disciple of the apostle John. Hippolytus quotes from Philippians again and again. Among the passages from this epistle which he uses frequently is the very one of which Origen was also fond, namely, Philippians 2:6-8. And he ascribes Philippians to "the blessed Paul" (*Fragment from Commentaries,* on Gen. 49:21-26).

From Origen we can go back to his teacher, Clement of Alexandria (fl. 190–200), and from Hippolytus we can go back to his teacher, Irenaeus. But before doing so, it is necessary to point out that also Tertullian who in his famous work against Marcion (begun A. D. 207) combats the notion that such expressions as "form of a servant" and "fashion as a man" prove that Christ did not truly become man, thereby definitely indicates that he was well acquainted with Philippians (*Against Marcion* V.xx). Moreover, references to that epistle abound in his various writings. He considers Paul the author (see, for example, *Antidote to the Scorpion's Sting,* Chapter XIII).

This brings us then to Clement of Alexandria and to Irenaeus. So frequently does the former refer to Philippians, which he regards to be the work of "the apostle," that in his *Stromata* or *Miscellanies* he quotes more than once from each of its four chapters.

What Irenaeus says about the authorship of Philippians must be considered of great significance, and this because of his many travels and intimate acquaintance with almost the entire church of his day. His voice in a matter as important as this may be considered the voice of the church. Now in his work *Against Heresies* (written about A. D. 182-188) he refers to passages from every chapter of Philippians. Particularly instructive is his explanation of the phrase "obedient unto death" (V.xvi.3, on Phil. 2:8), and the one with reference to Christ's subsequent exaltation (I.x.1, on Phil. 2:10, 11). Without the least hesitation he ascribes Philippians to Paul (III.xii.9) that is, to "the one who received the apostolate to the Gentiles" (IV.xxiv.2).

The Muratorian Fragment, an incomplete list of New Testament books, written in poor Latin and deriving its name from Cardinal L. A. Muratori (1672–1750) who discovered it in the Ambrosian Library at Milan, may be assigned to the period 180-200. It contains the following: "Now the epistles of Paul, what they are, whence or for what reason they were sent, they themselves make clear to him who will understand. First of all he wrote at length to the Corinthians to prohibit the schism of heresy, then to the Galatians against circumcision, and to the Romans on the order of the Scriptures, intimating also that Christ is the chief matter in them — each of which it is necessary for us to discuss, seeing that the blessed apostle Paul himself, following the example of his predecessor John, writes to no more than seven churches by name in the following order: to the Corinthians (first), to the Ephesians (second), to the Philippians (third), to the Colossians (fourth), to the Galatians (fifth), to the Thessalonians (sixth), to the Romans (seventh)." Philippians is also included in Marcion's Canon and in the Old Latin and Old Syriac Versions.

How gloriously did the Christians of Lyons and Vienna, many of whom were subjected to indescribable torture for the sake of their faith and to the cruelest forms of death, make use of Phil. 2:5-8! They became imitators of their Lord's humility and refused even to be called "martyrs." See their unforgettable *Letter to the Brothers in Asia and Phrygia*. This letter was written A. D. 177, and is found in Eusebius, *op. cit.*, V.i, ii.

But it is possible to go back even farther. Polycarp's beautiful Letter (or *Letters*) to the Philippians has (or *have*) already been described (see Section III, The Church At Philippi). Those who accept the two letter theory give the dates as A. D. 135 and 115. He definitely states that the blessed and glorious Paul had written to the Philippians. In his day, therefore, that fact was well-known.

Ignatius, on his journey to Rome, where he was going to be killed by beasts in the amphitheatre (about A. D. 108), wrote several letters. He clearly shows that he is well acquainted with Philippians. It is true that a few of the references are rather vague, but surely when he describes people who are "enemies of the cross of Christ . . . whose god is the belly" (*To the Magnesians* IX; *To the Trallians* XI), he is quoting Phil. 3:18, 19.

Finally, Clement of Rome, writing to the Corinthians probably about the last decade of the first century, uses a few expressions which remind one immediately of Paul's letter to the Philippians. This resemblance is seen especially when both are read in the original or in a translation that adheres closely to the original:

Philippians	*I Clement*
"Only continue to exercise y o u r citizenship in a manner worthy of the gospel of Christ" (1:27).	"(This will be so) if we are not exercising our citizenship in a manner worthy of him" (i.e., worthy of Christ, XXI).
"in (the) beginning of the gospel" (4:15).	"in (the) beginning of the gospel" (XLVII).

The conclusion of the entire matter is this: All the evidence, external and internal, points to Philippians as a genuine, authentic epistle, recognized as such already in the earliest written sources that have been preserved, and, whenever ascribed to anyone, always ascribed to *Paul*.

Closely connected with the authorship of Philippians is its unity. It is well at the very outset to define the exact question that is of importance in this connection. That question is *not*, "Did Paul write more than one letter to the Philippians?" The possibility that he did can be readily granted. Did he not also write a letter to the Corinthians which has not come down to us? See the reference to it in I Cor. 5:9. There are scholars who believe that the proposition, "Paul wrote more than one letter to the Philippians," can be defended on the basis of Polycarp's statement, "For neither am I, nor is any other like me, able to follow the wisdom of the blessed and glorious Paul, who . . . when he was absent wrote *epistolas* to y o u" (*To the Philippians* III.2). Others, for various reasons, dispute this conclusion. The real question, however, is *this*, "Does the existing, canonical letter of Paul to the Philippians consist of more than one letter?" Among those who deny the unity of Philippians are the following: Beare, Goodspeed, Hausrath, Lake, McNeile, Rahtjen, J. Weiss. Their reasons (with individual variations) are as follows:

(1) The *tone* of the letter suddenly changes from that of tender address to that of harshness, as the apostle begins to use terms like *dogs, evil workers, the concision.* Cf., 3:1 with 3:2 ff.

(2) The *content* also changes. There is a sudden attack on Judaizers, out of keeping with the contents of the rest of the letter. This is followed by a warning against sensualists. Clearly, the section 3:2-4:1 is an interpolation, which must have belonged to another letter. Then there is also the note of thanks for the gift that had been brought to the apostle by Epaphroditus (4:10-20). This, too, stands by itself, must be viewed as a separate letter. Perhaps this was written first of all.

This shows that what we actually have here is three letters (complete or incomplete) : *a.* 4:10-20; *b.* 1:1-3:1; 4:2-9, 21-23; and *c.* 3:2-4:1. (It must be added immediately, however, that the critics are by no means united on the extent of each of the letters that supposedly entered into the combination which we now call Philippians.)

(3) The word *finally* (3:1) also indicates that the letter is about to end at this point, but in the canonical epistle it introduces two entire chapters, and stands nowhere near the end of the letter.

Reasons for rejecting this view and maintaining the unity of Paul's Epistle to the Philippians:

(1) The change of tone (if it is correct to call it that) can be easily explained. See my comments on 3:1, 2.

(2) It is not true that the section 3:2-4:1 comes as a complete surprise. Paul has already spoken about *the adversaries* (1:28) and about *a crooked and perverse generation* (2:14). Besides, the change from one subject to another when writing to friends is altogether natural. Must we assume, for example, that when Paul in a thrilling manner climaxes his glorious paragraph on the Resurrection and the Second Coming with the exclamation, "O death, where is thy victory," etc., and adds a very fitting and moving admonition, "Wherefore, my beloved brothers, be steadfast," etc. (I Cor. 15), and then suddenly changes to "Now concerning the collection" (I Cor. 16:1), he must have made use of two letters to convey these sentiments?

The unity of Philippians stands out very strikingly. The same ideas recur again and again; such as: the note of rejoicing, the oscillation between expectation of acquittal and leaving room for the possibility of being sentenced to death, eschatological references, the evil of disharmony. The thank-y o u note (4:10-20) also has been anticipated (see 1:5-7; 2:25).

(3) It is not true that the words used in the original and translated "Finally" necessarily indicate that the letter will end almost immediately. See my comments on 3:1, footnote 124.

(4) Philippians appears, as a letter of Paul, in all the Canons of Scripture during the second century. In them all the reference is to *one* letter, never to two or three letters. No valid evidence has been presented to upset that well-established tradition. A fine and very recent article confirming the unity of the epistle is that by B. S. Mackay, "Further Thoughts on Philippians," *NTS*, Vol. 7, Number 2, (Jan. 1961) pp. 161-170.

VII. General Contents

Attempts have been made repeatedly to construct a formal outline for Philippians, a central theme with its subdivisions. Several themes have been tried; for example, *Christ-mindedness* (suggested by Phil. 2:5), *Paul's Joy in Christ,* etc. But such themes either lack distinctiveness (is not Christ-mindedness in action in all the epistles?) or comprehensiveness (though joy is certainly a very prominent characteristic of this letter, it is not an all-inclusive theme: faith, hope, and love are also in evidence). What we have here is a genuine letter from Paul to his beloved church at Philippi. The writer passes from one subject to another just as we do today in writing to friends. (The difference is that Paul's letter is inspired; ours are not.) What holds these subjects together is not this or that central theme but the Spirit of God, mirrored forth, by means of a multitude of spiritual graces and virtues, in the heart of the apostle, proclaiming throughout that between God, the apostle, and the believers at Philippi there exists a blessed bond of glorious *fellowship*.[25]

And what a marvelous heart, what a rich and many-sided personality, was that of Paul! We see the apostle first of all as *a joyful servant of Christ Jesus:* "Paul and Timothy, servants of Christ Jesus. . . . I thank my God every time I remember y o u, always in every supplication of mine in behalf of y o u all making my supplication with joy . . ." (Phil. 1:1, 3).

Presently we see him as *an optimistic prisoner* (prisoner *of the Lord,* that is!) : "Now I want y o u to know, brothers, that the things that have happened to me have in reality turned out to the advantage of the gospel . . . and most of the brothers have been heartened in the Lord through my bonds" (Phil. 1:12, 14).

Again we see him as *a humble cross-bearer:* ". . . in humblemindedness each counting the other better than himself. In y o u r inner being continue to set y o u r mind on *this,* namely, on that which (was) also in Christ Jesus, who . . . humbled himself. . . . In fact, even if I am to be poured out as a libation upon the sacrificial offering of y o u r faith, I rejoice, and I rejoice with y o u all" (Phil. 2:3, 5, 7, 17).

Anon we see him as *a thoughtful administrator:* "But I hope in the Lord Jesus to send Timothy to y o u soon so that I also may be heartened by knowing y o u r affairs. For I have no one likeminded who will be genuinely interested in y o u r welfare. . . . But I consider it necessary to send (back) to y o u Epaphroditus, my brother and fellow-worker and fellow-soldier, and y o u r messenger and minister to my need" (Phil. 2:19, 25).

Then we see him as *an indefatigable idealist* (and in *that* sense, *perfectionist*) : "Not that I have already gotten hold or have already been made perfect, but I am pressing on (to see) if I can also take hold of that . . . for which I was laid hold on . . . forgetting what lies behind (me) and eagerly straining forward to what lies ahead, I am pressing on toward the goal for the prize of the upward call of God in Christ Jesus" (Phil. 3:12-14).

Next we see him as *a tactful pastor:* "I entreat Euodia and I entreat Syntyche to be of the same mind in the Lord. . . . Lend these women a hand, for they strove side by side with me in the gospel" (Phil. 4:2, 3).

And finally we see him as *a grateful recipient:* Nevertheless, y o u did nobly in sharing my affliction. . . . I am amply supplied, having received from Epaphroditus the gifts (that came) from y o u, a fragrant odor, a sacrifice acceptable, well-pleasing to God" (Phil. 4:14, 18).

Two further items must be stressed, in this connection. First, that the various facets of Paul's rich personality, the multiple categories in which he functions, *overlap.* Not a single one of them can be separated from any of

[25] In his excellent book, *Philippians, The Gospel at Work*, M. C. Tenney has a fine chapter on "The Fellowship of the Gospel," pp. 35-50. And see also my comments on Phil. 1:5.

the others. The same man who writes as a joyful servant of Christ Jesus is also writing as an optimistic prisoner, humble crossbearer, etc. Hence, in the following arrangement of the contents the name by which Paul is characterized in any given section is a matter *not of rigid classification but merely of emphasis.*

Secondly, throughout our attention is riveted not alone on Paul himself, but *on him in relation to his dearly beloved Philippians.* Remember the *fellowship!*

Thus understood, the contents of this genuine letter may be summarized as follows:

The Apostle Paul Pours Out His Heart to the Philippians, Whom He Prizes Highly and Loves Profoundly.

Chapter I

Verses 1-11

The Joyful Servant of Christ Jesus,

by means of
   salutation,
   thanksgiving,
   and prayer,
revealing his warm affection for the Philippians with whom he is united in a blessed fellowship.

Verses 12-30

The Optimistic Prisoner,

rejoicing in his imprisonment for the advantage of the gospel, and in the fact that Christ will be magnified in his person whether by life or by death; and exhorting the Philippians to remain steadfast, united, and unafraid.

Chapter II

Verses 1-18

The Humble Cross-bearer,

by an appeal to a fourfold incentive exhorting the Philippians to live the life of oneness, lowliness, and helpfulness, after the example of Christ Jesus, and to shine as lights in the midst of a wicked world, thereby filling the hearts of Paul and of themselves with joy.

Verses 19-30

The Thoughtful Administrator,

promising to send Timothy to the Philippians as soon as his (Paul's) own case has been decided,
and even now sending Epaphroditus back to them.

Chapter III

(the entire chapter)

The Indefatigable Idealist,

warning against evil workers (the *concision*) who by placing confidence in flesh seek to establish *their own* righteousness and perfection; as contrasted with God's true servants (the *circum*cision) ;

for example, with Paul, who could boast of many prerogatives, but has rejected them all, and relies completely on the righteousness of Christ, in whom he is pressing on to perfection;

exhorting the Philippians to imitate him, to honor the friends and beware of "the enemies of the cross," sensualists, who set their minds on things of earth, while believers know that *their* homeland is in heaven.

Chapter IV

Verses 1-9

The Tactful Pastor,

in general, exhorting the brothers at Philippi to remain firm; and in particular, entreating Euodia and Syntyche to be of the same mind, and Syzygus to help these gospel-women;

urging the Philippians to rejoice in the Lord, to be big-hearted to all, and instead of worrying to bring everything to God in prayer that brings peace; finally, admonishing the addressees to meditate only on praiseworthy things, practising these in imitation of Paul and with promise of rich reward.

Verses 10-23

The Grateful Recipient,

rejoicing in the generosity of the Philippians, and testifying that he has learned the secret of contentment and of readiness for every task;

resuming and completing his expression of appreciation for the generosity which the Philippians have shown both in the more recent and in the more distant past;

confessing his faith in God who will supply every need, and ascribing glory to him; and

concluding his letter with words of greeting and benediction.

Commentary

on

The Epistle to the Philippians

Summary of Chapter 1

Verses 1-11

Paul, the Joyful Servant of Christ Jesus

by means of salutation, thanksgiving and prayer, revealing his warm affection for the Philippians with whom he is united in a blessed fellowship.

1:1, 2 The Salutation.
1:3-11 The Thanksgiving and Prayer.

CHAPTER I

1   1 Paul and Timothy, servants of Christ Jesus, to all the saints in Christ
      Jesus who are in Philippi, together with overseers and deacons; 2 grace to
y o u and peace from God our Father and the Lord Jesus Christ.

1:1, 2

I. *The Salutation*

1. In structure the letters which we find in the New Testament differ from
those written today.   Our letters *end* with the name of the sender.   In Paul's
day that name was mentioned first.   Then came the name of the person(s)
addressed and the rest of the opening salutation.   There followed, generally
in the order given: the thanksgiving and/or prayer (often both), the body
of the letter, and finally the concluding items; such as greetings, word of
farewell or even a benediction.   It should be emphasized that this was the
letter-plan as it existed in the polite society of Paul's day.   The apostle
simply took it as it was and poured a definitely Christian content into the
customary form.[26]   A glance at Philippians shows that Paul is following the
then-prevailing letter-plan.

The sender's name is **Paul,** with whom *Timothy* is associated.

In a world held together politically by Rome and culturally by Greece it
was natural that the writer should use his Greek-Roman name *Paul* instead
of his Jewish name *Saul*.   (For details on the meaning and use of these
names see N.T.C. on I and II Thessalonians, p. 38.)   It is also natural that
he writes his own name first, for it was he himself who was the author of
the letter, as is evident from the fact that in its entire contents, with the
exception of the salutation, he uses the first person singular ("I" and "my"
instead of "we" and "our"), while he refers to Timothy in the third person
("his," "him").   Examples:

"*I* thank *my* God in all *my* remembrance of y o u. . . . God is *my* witness

---

[26] See examples in A. Deissmann, *Light From the Ancient East* (translated from the
German by L. R. M. Strachan), New York, fourth edition, 1922, p. 179 ff.; and in
C. M. Cobern, *The New Archaeological Discoveries and Their Bearing upon the
New Testament,* New York and London, seventh edition, 1924, pp. 582-590; and
see also Acts 15:23-29; 23:25-30.

how *I* am yearning for y o u. . . . *I* hope in the Lord to send Timothy to y o u. . . . Y o u know *his* proved worth. . . . *Him,* then, *I* hope to send at once."

To the mention of his own name Paul adds **and Timothy,** as he also does in two other epistles written during the same imprisonment: Col. 1:1; Philem. 1:1; and as he had done in three earlier letters: II Cor. 1:1; I Thess. 1:1; II Thess. 1:1. The reasons for the addition of Timothy's name here in Philippians were probably the following: Timothy, though *not* co-author, was in full agreement with the message of the letter. Moreover, he was deeply interested in the Philippians, for he had been associated with Paul in bringing the gospel to them (Acts 16:11-40; I Thess. 2:2) ; had in all probability revisited them on more than one occasion (Acts 19:21, 22; 20:3-6; Phil. 2:22) ; and was destined soon to be˙ sent to them again (Phil. 2:19-23). Moreover, Timothy was in Paul's vicinity when this letter was dictated, in a position to visit him. He may even have been the actual *writer* (not *author*) of the letter, Paul's secretary. That Paul dictated his letters appears clearly from Rom. 16:22; and may be inferred from I Cor. 16:21-24; Gal. 6:11; Col. 4:18; and II Thess. 3:17 (on which see N.T.C. on I and II Thessalonians, pp. 208, 209). (For details with respect to the life and character of Timothy see N.T.C. on The Pastoral Epistles, pp. 33-36.)

Paul calls himself and Timothy **servants.** James (1:1), Peter (II Peter 1:1), and Jude (verse 1) introduce themselves similarly. The Greek word is *doulos* (δοῦλος) singular, *douloi* (δοῦλοι) plural. Some prefer the translation *slaves.* It is true that *something* can be said in favor of that rendering. In a sense even deeper than that which pertains to ordinary slaves and their earthly masters, Paul and Timothy had been *bought* with a price and were therefore *owned* by their Master (I Cor. 3:23; 7:22) on whom they were *completely dependent* and to whom they owed *undivided allegiance.* If by thus defining the concept *doulos* as used here in Phil. 1:1 its meaning were exhausted, and if our word *slaves* conveyed nothing of a sinister nature, the translation *slaves* might be unobjectionable. But such is definitely not the case. As Paul uses the term, a *doulos,* in the spiritual sense, is one who *ministers* to his Lord with gladness of heart, in newness of spirit, and in the enjoyment of perfect freedom (Rom. 6:18, 22; 7:6), receiving from him a glorious reward (Col. 3:24). Love and good will toward God and man fill the heart of this *doulos* (Gal. 5:13; Eph. 6:7). But with the English word *slave* we immediately associate the ideas of involuntary service, forced subjection, and (frequently) harsh treatment. Hence, in the light of Paul's own use of this noun and of the cognate verb, it is clear that the rendering *slaves* in passages such as Phil. 1:1 is not the best, and that the translation *servants* (as in A.V., and as in the text of A.R.V. and of R.S.V.), though not fully adequate, is the better of the two. It must be borne in mind, however, that these servants serve their Lord all the more heartily because they know that they have been redeemed by his blood from the bondage of sin, and accordingly belong to him, who is the Disposer of their destinies, the Director of their lives.[27]

By adding **of Christ Jesus** Paul accomplishes two things: (1) He directs the attention to *his Lord* and away from himself and from Timothy. Not Paul and Timothy are all-important; Christ Jesus is. In the deepest sense Philippians is *Christ's* letter to the church. Let the Philippians remember that. (2) He focuses the light upon *his heavenly Master rather than upon Rome* which considered itself to be the master of the earth. It is not surprising that Paul, being a prisoner who by dint of circumstances was being constantly reminded of the servile attitude of Roman soldiers, and writing to people living in a Roman colony many of whose citizens worshiped the Roman emperor, was comforted by the fact that the Anointed One, the Savior, and not the emperor, was his real Master. (For a detailed treatment of the names *Jesus* and *Christ* see N.T.C. on I and II Thessalonians, pp. 41, 42; and for the order in which the words occur here — *Christ Jesus* instead of *Jesus Christ* — see N.T.C. on The Pastoral Epistles, p. 51, footnote 19.)

Now in the opening salutation of every one of his letters, with the exception of Philippians, I and II Thessalonians, and Philemon, Paul calls himself *apostle*. In fact, even in Rom. 1:1 and Titus 1:1, where as in Phil. 1:1 he refers to himself as *servant*, he still immediately adds *apostle*. Why then does he omit the designation *apostle* here in Phil. 1:1? The probable reason is that the Philippians were Paul's "beloved and longed for," his "joy and crown" (Phil. 4:1), with whom he knew himself to be on the most pleasing and intimate terms of Christian fellowship and among whom his authority stood unassailed. It is possibly for this same reason that in writing to this church founded by himself Paul does not deem it at all necessary to indicate any distinction between himself and Timothy. Humbly he writes, "Paul and Timothy, servants of Christ Jesus." Compare with this II Cor. 1:1 and Col. 1:1 (apostle . . . brother), and Philemon, verse 1 (prisoner . . . brother). The thoroughly sympathetic and understanding Philippians did not have to be told that Paul was the apostle and that Timothy was his delegate. Besides, in Christ, the two, though differing in age, authority, and experience, were equal in the sense that both were saved by the same grace and were engaged in the same exalted task.

Paul addresses his letter **to,** and pronounces his salutation upon **all the saints in Christ Jesus who are in Philippi.** He is not merely interested in

---

[27] In the Old Testament the prophets as a group (Amos 3:7 and other passages) are called *douloi*, that is, *servants*, and the name *doulos*, translated *servant*, is also applied to individual men of God, such as Joshua (Judg. 2:8), David (Ps. 35:27 = LXX 34:27), Solomon (I Kings 8:28), and the author of Psalm 116 (Ps. 116:16 = LXX 115:7). And see the great Servant passages in Isaiah (42:1-9; 49:1-9a; 50:4-11; and 52:13-53:12).

certain prominent individuals, "the pillars of the church," for instance. Moreover, he hates cliques or unnecessary dissensions (cf. Phil. 4:2 and see also I Cor. 1:12, 13; 3:4; 11:21). He prays for *all* (Phil. 1:4), loves *all* (1:7), yearns for *all* (1:8), hopes to continue with them *all* (1:25), and greets *all* (4:21).

In writing or in preaching, the character of the message will be affected by the writer's or preacher's opinion of the addressed. It will make a difference whether he views them as *sinless ones in their own right* or, on the other hand, as nothing else than *gross sinners,* mere pagans, whether baptized or unbaptized. Paul avoids both extremes. He views the addressed as they exist not in themselves but in Christ. As such they are **the saints.** A *saint* is someone who by the Lord has been *set apart* to glorify him. It is in that sense that the addressed are called *holy.* Thus also during the old dispensation there were certain places, objects, and people that had been *set apart* or *consecrated* unto the service of God; for example, the holy place of the house of Jehovah (I Kings 8:10), the most holy place (Exod. 26:33), the tithe of the land (Lev. 27:30), the place of the bush (Exod. 3:5), holy water (Num. 5:17), the ark and the Levites (II Chron. 35:3), the priests (Lev. 21:6, 7) and the Israelites, in distinction from other nations (Exod. 19:6; Lev. 20:26; Deut. 7:6; Dan. 7:22; and cf. Num. 23:9; Amos 3:2). It is this latter idea which in the New Testament is applied to Christians generally. They are the Israel of the new dispensation, *set apart* to proclaim God's excellencies (I Peter 2:9). A saint, then, is a person to whom the Lord has shown great favor and upon whom, accordingly, there rests a great responsibility. He who is a *saint* (II Cor. 1:1) must remember that he has been *called to be a saint* (Rom. 1:7; I Cor. 1:2). Ideally, saints are, indeed, *believers* (Eph. 1:1; Col. 1:1).

But even redeemed sinners are never saints *in their own right.* Hence, Paul addresses the members of the church at Philippi as saints **in Christ Jesus,** that is, *by virtue of union with him.* Of this phrase ("in Christ," "in him," etc.) the apostle is very fond. So was also our Lord ("in me") as reported by the disciple whom he loved (see John 15:1-7). Paul uses the phrase repeatedly throughout his epistles. The union indicated is not "an actual physical union," as some have thought. Neither is it true that in Paul's writings there are two contradictory "ways of salvation," the one forensic or legal (Jesus paid for my sins, delivering me from guilt and condemnation), and the other experimental, mystical, or practical (I live in him, having died with him and having risen with him). On the contrary, the forensic and the experiential are two essential elements in the one great work of salvation. Christ's death *for* the believer must never be separated from the faith exercised *by* the believer. There is, moreover, a link between these two, namely, the regenerating and sanctifying work of the Holy Spirit *within* the believer. That Spirit applies to the believer's heart the merits of Christ's death, and, having planted in that heart the principle of faith, qualifies him to embrace his Lord by means of a living faith. Thus *for* and *within* and *by* form one golden chain, and the person who slights any one of these three links is wrong in theory and in practice. Paul, in some of the very passages in which the expression *in Christ (Jesus)* is used, combines the two ideas (what Christ did *for* the believer and what is now done *by* the latter) and also shows that the Bond of union between the two is *the Holy Spirit* working *within* the heart.

Examples:

FORENSIC	PRACTICAL
"There is therefore now *no condemnation* to them that are *in Christ* Jesus	*who walk* not after the flesh but after *the Spirit*" (Rom. 8:1, 4).
"And *he died for* all	that they who live should no longer *live* for themselves . . . wherefore if any man is *in Christ* he is *a new creature*" (II Cor. 5:17).

See also the explanation of another famous *in him* passage, which beautifully combines the related ideas, namely, Phil. 3:9, 10; and cf. I Cor. 6:19, 20; Titus 2:14.

Paul addresses his letter in general and his opening salutation in particular to all the saints in Christ Jesus that are in Philippi **together with** (that is, in association with) **overseers and deacons.** Against the traditional view according to which it was Paul who wrote Philippians the objection has been advanced that during the apostle's life there were as yet no "overseers and deacons." The sources, however, do not sustain the objection. Note the following:

As to *overseers* (Acts 20:28; Titus 1:7) or *elders,* that is, *presbyters* (Acts 20:17; Titus 1:5), these are mentioned again and again from early apostolic times on. The Lucan and Pauline references are as follows:

Acts 11:27-30

About A. D. 44, during a famine, a relief commission, consisting of Barnabas and Saul, is sent to Judea with a gift for the needy believers in that province. This gift is delivered to *the elders.* It is no surprise to find *elders* in this Jewish-Christian community. Surely, the much-debated view that this Christian eldership was a divinely sanctioned outgrowth of the eldership in ancient Israel (Josh. 24:31) and even more directly of the eldership in the contemporary non-Christian Jewish community right here in Jerusalem and surroundings is hard to refute. After all, the people who started the Judean churches were *Jews,* and the church is the true *Israel.*[28]

Acts 14:23

Sometime between A. D. 44 and 50, on his first missionary journey, Paul appointed *elders* in every church.

I Thess. 5:12, 13

About the year 52, on his second missionary journey, the very journey on which the church at Philippi was founded, the apostle writes to the Thessalonians, "Now we request y o u, brothers, to appreciate those who labor among y o u and are over y o u in the Lord and admonish y o u, and to esteem them very highly in love because of their work." See N.T.C. on that passage. That *overseers* or *elders* were included in this reference would seem probable.

Acts 20:17-38

In the year A. D. 57 or 58, Paul, on his third missionary journey, comes to Miletus on the coast of Asia Minor, and sends for the *overseers* (verse 28) or *elders* (verse 17) of the Ephesian region, and bids them farewell in a touching address.

I Tim. 3:1-7; Titus 1:5-9

A little later than Philippians, but not much later than A. D. 63, Paul after his release from the first Roman imprisonment, writing from Macedonia, enumerates the requirements for the office of *overseer* (I Tim. 3:1; Titus 1:7) or *elder* (Titus 1:5), and states that the *elders* who rule well should be counted worthy of double honor (I Tim. 5:17). See N.T.C. on The Pastoral Epistles; pp. 117-129; 179, 180; 344-349.

Though there are those who dispute it, yet a comparison between verses 17 and 28 of Acts 20, and between verses 5 and 7 of Titus 1, would seem to indicate that *elder* and *overseer* indicate the same person. The man who with respect to age and dignity is called *elder* is called *overseer* or *superintendent* with respect to the nature of his task.

As to *deacons,* about the year A. D. 33, when Greek-speaking Christians from among the Jews complained that their widows were being neglected in the daily distributions, seven men were chosen to attend to this matter and, no doubt, to matters of similar nature. The term *deacon* is not used in Acts 6:1-6, but that makes no material difference: the purpose for which these men were chosen is clearly indicated. The requirements for the office of *deacon* (the very term is used now) are found in I Tim. 3:8-12. (Other

---

[28] From the well-nigh endless literature on this subject I wish to select only two articles of very recent date and excellent contents. Both occur in *The Twentieth Century Encyclopedia of Religious Knowledge* (An Extention of *The New Schaff-Herzog Encyclopedia*), Grand Rapids, Mich., 1955. They are F. C. Grant, "Organization of the Early Church," pp. 823, 824; and D. J. Theron, "Presbyter, Presbyterate," p. 905.

supposed New Testament references to the office of deacon are debatable. See N.T.C. on The Pastoral Epistles; pp. 129-134.)

Now into this frame of references the mention of *overseers* and *deacons* here in Philippians (written probably A. D. 62/63) fits very well. It is definitely not an anachronism.

Another question is: Just why did Paul make special mention of these overseers and deacons in *this* (and in no other) opening salutation? Some answer: because these leaders had taken the initiative in gathering the gifts sent to Paul by the Philippians both now and on previous occasions. The apostle wishes to express his appreciation to them. Others are of the opinion that the particular reference to these leaders was in the nature of a hint to them that they must see to it that the instructions contained in the letter are carried out. And still others stress the idea that Paul by making special mention of these men thereby furnishes a needed endorsement of their authority (in view of the *dogs* and the *enemies of the cross of Christ* who were threatening the church, and who might lead some astray, Phil. 3:2, 18). Any or all of these explanations may be correct. And there may also have been an entirely different reason. We do not know.

2. The rest of the salutation — one might also say *the salutation proper* — is as follows: **grace to y o u and peace from God our Father and the Lord Jesus Christ.** Thus, there is pronounced upon all the saints in Christ Jesus that are in Philippi, together with overseers and deacons, *grace,* that is, God's spontaneous, unmerited favor in action, his sovereign, freely bestowed loving-kindness in operation, and its result, *peace,* that is, the conviction of reconciliation through the blood of the cross, true spiritual wholeness and prosperity, these two blessings (grace and peace) coming from God our Father and the Lord Jesus Christ.

This salutation is exactly as in Rom. 1:7; I Cor. 1:3; II Cor. 1:2; Gal. 1:3; Eph. 1:2; Philemon 1-3; and substantially also as in II Thess. 1:1. For further details of explanation and for a discussion of the question whether this salutation is an exclamation, a declaration, or perhaps merely an expression of a pious wish, see N.T.C. on I and II Thessalonians, pp. 40-45, 153, 154.

---

3 I thank my God in all my remembrance of y o u, 4 always in every supplication of mine in behalf of y o u all making my supplication with joy, 5 (thankful) for y o u r fellowship in the gospel from the first day until the present, 6 being confident of this very thing that he who began a good work in y o u will carry it on toward completion until the day of Christ Jesus; 7 just as it is right for me to be thus minded in behalf of y o u all, because I am holding y o u in my heart, y o u all being partakers with me of grace (as evidenced) both in my bonds and in the defense and confirmation of the gospel. 8 For God is my witness how I am yearning

for y o u all with the deeply-felt affection of Christ Jesus. 9 And this is my prayer that y o u r love may abound more and more with full knowledge and keen discernment, 10 so that y o u may approve the things that are excellent and may be pure and blameless with a view to the day of Christ, 11 filled with the fruits of righteousness that come through Jesus Christ to the glory and praise of God.

1:3-11

II. *The Thanksgiving and Prayer*

1:3-8

A. *The Thanksgiving*

3. In the letters that present themselves as coming from Paul (and, we firmly believe, actually did come from him) the salutation is in all except two cases (Galatians and Titus) followed by hearty words of thanksgiving. This praise is addressed not to the gods or to any particular deity (as was customary in Paul's day among pagans) but to that glorious Being whom Paul here (and in Rom. 1:8; Philem. 4) calls *my God.* His words are **I thank my God.**[29] The apostle is jubilant. He reflects on the wonderful way in which he has been led and on the evidences which the church at Philippi has given of its love for the gospel and for himself. Hence, he says, I thank *my God.* Cf. Ps. 42:11; 63:1. He continues **in all my remembrance of y o u.**[30] The many individual reflections on the work of grace in the lives of the Philippians are grouped together in the phrase *all my remembrance* (literally "all *the* remembrance," but in the light of the immediate context the article surely has possessive force).

4. Now thanksgiving, by causing a person to reflect on *blessings,* increases his *joy.* Hence, there now follows the parenthesis, which indicates a circumstance accompanying the thanksgiving: **always in every supplication of mine in behalf of y o u all making my supplication with joy.** (For *prayer* and its synonyms see N.T.C. on The Pastoral Epistles pp. 91, 92). A *supplica-*

---

[29] Not, "I, however, thank God," based on a reading preferred by Ewald, Zahn, Moffatt, and others. No more here than in comparable passages (Col. 1:3; I Thess. 1:2) is Paul trying to draw a contrast between (a) himself and Timothy, or (b) himself and the Philippians. As to the latter, the view that he wishes to say, "I for my part do not feel as meanly as y o u do about this last gift y o u sent me," rests upon a fanciful reconstruction of the historical background.

[30] Not "in all y o u r remembrance of me." Here as well as elsewhere μνεία is followed by the objective genitive (see Rom. 1:9; Philem. 4). Besides, the parallelism is evident: "my remembrance of y o u" underlies "in every petition of mine in behalf of y o u." In both cases it is *Paul's* activity that is indicated: *Paul* remembers, *Paul* makes petition.

50

tion is a petition for the fulfilment of a definite need that is keenly felt. Even in Philippi there were definite spiritual needs. There were imperfections (Phil. 1:9-11; 2:2, 4, 14, 15; 4:2) and dangers (Phil. 3:2, 18, 19). So Paul again and again (always . . . in every supplication) beseeches the Lord that these needs may be supplied. In these supplications Paul omitted no one (in behalf of y o u all). The main point, however, is this: since there was much room for thanksgiving, Paul is ever making his supplication *with joy,* for prayer with thanksgiving is joyful prayer.

5. The *immediate* reason for the thanksgiving is given in verse 5, the *ultimate* reason in verse 6. These two must not be separated. What Paul is saying is in substance this, "Y o u r *perseverance* in sympathetic participation in the work of the gospel (verse 5) has convinced me that y o u are the objects of divine *preservation* (verse 6). For all this I thank my God (verse 3), making my supplication with joy (verse 4)." We find exactly the same reasoning in I Thess. 1:2-5, where the believers' day-by-day Christian living is regarded as the unquestionable evidence of their election from eternity. And for all that Paul gives thanks to God (see N.T.C. on I and II Thessalonians, pp. 45-51).

Returning then to the immediate reason for thanksgiving we read: **thankful** (supplied from verse 3) **for y o u r fellowship in the gospel.**

The Fellowship of all Believers in Christ [31]

(1) It is a fellowship *of grace.* It is not a natural or Platonic fellowship, nor is it man-made, that is, called into being or organized by men, like a club or society. It is not even *merited* by men. It is sovereignly effected by Jesus Christ (I Cor. 1:9), and is the gift of the Spirit (II Cor. 13:13; Phil. 2:1) sent from the Father. Apart from Christ and his Spirit this fellowship is entirely impossible. Ideally speaking, the fellowship between Christ and his people even precedes *time,* for they were chosen in him *from eternity* (Eph. 1:4).

In time, Jesus Christ is, as it were, the Magnet, for it is he who *draws* to himself those given to him by the Father (John 12:32; 17:2, 9, 11, 24). He draws them through his Word and Spirit. This Spirit applies to them the merits of the Savior's death. Jesus, by means of his crucifixion, resurrection, ascension, and coronation, attracts to himself (that is, to abiding faith in himself) all of God's elect, from every age, clime, and nation. Moreover, in the person of their Surety, Jesus Christ, they themselves were tried, condemned, and crucified. They also were made alive and raised with him. With him they live in heavenly places. Their life is hid with Christ in God. This truth, accordingly, concerns both their state and their condition. Their santification as well as their justification is mediated through Christ

---

[31] Because of its length this footnote has been placed at the end of the chapter, page 93.

51

alone. *It is all of grace.* And it is a very close fellowship. In fact, so closely connected with him are believers that while they are on earth they even complete what is lacking in his suffering (see on Col. 1:24).

(2) It is, consequently, a fellowship *of faith.* Just as *Christ* draws sinners to himself through his redemptive acts, revealed to them by the Word and applied by *the Spirit,* so *they* approach and embrace Christ through a living, Spirit-given, *faith.* There is accordingly a faith-participation in Christ's sufferings, body, and blood (Phil. 3:10; I Cor. 10:16; II Cor. 1:7; and cf. Philem. 6), as well as in his resurrection and glory (Phil. 3:10; Col. 3:1). Faith commemorates Christ's death, rejoices in his presence, and awaits his revelation in glory.

(3) It is a fellowship *in prayer and thanksgiving.* Faith comes to expression in these devotions. Believers pray both individually and unitedly. Through their prayers they glorify *God.* Also they remember *one another* in prayer and thanksgiving (Phil. 1:3, 5, 9-11). Hence,

(4) It is a fellowship *of believers with one another; a fellowship in love for one another.* The same Magnet who attracts sinners *to himself,* also, in the very act of doing so, draws them into a close relationship with *each other.* Thus, the believer enshrines his fellow-believers in his heart and yearns for them (Phil. 1:7, 8; 2:2; 4:2; cf. John 13:34).

(5) It is therefore a fellowship *in helping each other; hence also, a fellowship in contributing to each other's needs.* Believers make their fellowship of love felt by remembering the poor among their number, no matter who they are, to what race they belong, or where they are living (Rom. 15:26; II Cor. 8:4). They, moreover, also make it a practice to support the missionaries in their needs. This was true especially with respect to the *Philippian* believers. These had even "entered into a partnership" with Paul in an account of expenditures and receipts (Phil. 4:15, which also belongs under 6).

(6) It is, accordingly, a fellowship *in promoting the work of the gospel.* It is an active co-operation in gospel-activity (Phil. 1:5; cf. I Cor. 9:23). Those who in this joint-participation are brothers give each other the right hand of fellowship with a view to hearty co-operation in kingdom-work (Gal. 2:9).

(7) It is a fellowship in *separation.* This sounds paradoxical but is true. The **koinonia** is a fellowship over against the world. Attachment to Christ always means detachment from the world, that is, from worldly thoughts, purposes, words, ways, etc. For what fellowship could there possibly be between light and darkness? (II Cor. 6:14; cf. James 4:4; I John 2:15).

(8) Finally, it is a fellowship in *warfare.* Believers struggle side by side against a common foe (Phil. 1:27-30; 2:25).

It is with all this in mind that the expression "I thank God for y o u r fellowship in the gospel" must be considered. It will then be clear that it indicates not only that the Philippians had "received the gospel by faith" (John Calvin), but much more. This acceptance by faith is implied, of course. But the emphasis is on *hearty co-operation in the work of the gospel* (cf. I Cor. 9:23), a *sympathetic participation* which had been shown **from the first day until the present** (for "the present" see also Rom. 8:22). As soon as the Lord had opened Lydia's *heart* for the gospel, that wonderful woman had opened her *home* for the gospel-workers (Acts 16:14, 15), and she had *kept* it open; in fact, she had opened it ever wider, so that what had been "headquarters" for the missionaries became "church" (place of assembly) for all the early converts at Philippi (Acts 16:40). How tenderly also the jailer had washed the missionaries' stripes and placed food before them (Acts 16:19-34). Is it not logical to believe that the man continued to reveal this same spirit? Moreover, when on his second missionary tour Paul had reached the very next place after Philippi, namely, Thessalonica, the Philippians had once and again sent gifts to him to further the work of the gospel (Phil. 4:16). When, on that same journey, the apostle had gotten to be in want at Corinth, he had not found it necessary to burden the Corinthians, for his needs had once more been supplied by "the brothers who came from Macedonia" (II Cor. 11:9). And thus, whenever the opportunity had presented itself — sometimes it had not presented itself (Phil. 4:10) — this noble band of Christians had proved the truth of the proverb, "A friend in need is a friend indeed!" The recent heroic mission of Epaphroditus, who had risked his very life in the interest of the good cause, was, as it were, the climax of this glorious manifestation of "fellowship in the gospel from the first day until the present" (Phil. 2:25; 4:13, 18).

There are several facts which cause this active co-operation to stand out all the more remarkably:

(1) It was a fellowship *for the furtherance of* (note εἰς) *the gospel,* not only in the interest of a good friend, Paul. In fact, in the hearts of the Philippians there was room for others besides Paul. Thus, for example, they (and also other believers in Macedonia) had given a magnificient example of Christian charity in supplying the needs of the poor saints at Jerusalem (II Cor. 8:1-5).

(2) It was *exceptional.* No other church had manifested such a high degree of fellowship (Phil. 4:15).

(3) It was *spontaneous.* Whenever there was need and opportunity to supply it, the Macedonians (surely including the Philippians) had given of their own free will and joyfully (II Cor. 8:2, 3).

(4) It included a giving *according to* their means, yes, *and at times even beyond their means* (II Cor. 8:3).

(5) It was *not a matter of fleeting impulse but of lasting principle.* The very phrase (here in Phil. 1:5) "from the first day until the present" stresses *perseverance* in spite of all obstacles. The prayers, the sympathies, the tes-

timonies, the willingness to make a pecuniary contribution, all these had
never ceased. The Philippians had not lost their first love (contrast Rev.
2:4) during this entire decade.

6. Paul thanks God for this, for it was God who had grafted his own
image in the hearts of the Philippians. Hence, to the *immediate* reason for
the thanksgiving the apostle now adds the *ultimate* reason: **being confident
of this very thing that** [32] **he who began a good work in y o u will carry it
on toward completion.** Note how closely the apostle links *human perseverance* ("y o u r fellowship in the gospel from the first day until the present")
with *divine preservation* ("*he who* began a good work in y o u will carry it
on toward completion"). Any doctrine of salvation which does not do full
justice to both of these elements is unscriptural. See Phil. 2:12, 13; II Thess.
2:13. Although it is true that God brings his work to completion, it is
equally true that when God has once begun his work in men, the latter by
no means remain merely passive instruments!

"*He who* began a good work in y o u," is God, as is evident from the context, "I thank *my God* . . . being confident that *he who* began a good work
in y o u, etc." When God's name, attitude, or activity is clearly implied, he
is not always mentioned by name. In fact by *not* mentioning his name but
merely saying *he who* there is often in such instances a greater opportunity
to stress his disposition or his activity: "*He who* does *this* will also certainly
do *that*." Thus William Cullen Bryant says beautifully (in his poem "To
A Waterfowl") :

> "*He who,* from zone to zone,
> Guides through the boundless sky thy certain flight,
> In the long way that I must tread alone,
> Will lead my steps aright." [33]

The good work which God had begun within the hearts and lives of the
Philippians was that of *grace,* whereby they had been transformed. This
work, indeed, was good in origin, quality, purpose, and result. The result
had been their own willing and working for God's good pleasure (Phil.

---

[32] The connective ὅτι is, of course, anticipatory: "confident of this very thing,
namely, that he, etc." The main clause (verse 3) , "I thank my God in all my remembrance of y o u," has as its object, "for y o u r fellowship in the gospel from
the first day until the present" (verse 5). That is the *immediate* reason for the
thanksgiving. The adverbial modifiers of accompanying circumstance (modifying
"I thank my God") are a. "always making my supplication with joy" (verse 4) and
b. "being confident of this very thing, etc." (verse 6). However, verse 6 expresses
more than this: also the *ultimate* reason for the thanksgiving.
[33] Other instances where God's name does not occur in the very phrase or clause
but the divine being or one of his attributes is mentioned in the immediate context or is clearly implied are Luke 2:14b (men of good pleasure = of *God's* good
pleasure) ; Rom. 8:11; Gal. 1:6; 2:8; 3:5; 5:8; I Thess. 5:24.

2:12, 13); specifically, their own hearty co-operation in whatever pertained to the advancement of the gospel.

Now Paul is confident that God will not permit his good work of transforming and qualifying grace to remain unfinished. The expression "will carry it onward toward completion" implies "and will present it complete."

Accordingly, out of the darkness and the distress of a prison in Rome a message of cheer reaches each Philippian believer, enabling him to say:

> "The work thou hast in me begun
> Shall by thy grace be *fully* done."

God, accordingly, is not like men. Men conduct *experiments,* but God carries out *a plan.* God never does anything by halves. Men often do.

This teaching of divine *preservation* for a life of service (hence, with implied human *perseverance*) is in harmony with that of the entire Bible, which tells us about:

a faithfulness that will never be removed (Ps. 89:33; 138:8),

a life that will never end (John 3:16),

a spring of water that will never cease to bubble up within the one who drinks of it (John 4:14),

a gift that will never be lost (John 6:37, 39),

a hand out of which the Good Shepherd's sheep will never be snatched (John 10:28),

a chain that will never be broken (Rom. 8:29, 30),

a love from which we shall never be separated (Rom. 8:39),

a calling that will never be revoked (Rom. 11:29),

a foundation that will never be destroyed (II Tim. 2:19),

and an inheritance that will never fade out (I Peter 1:4, 5).

It should be stressed, however, that according to the present context (and all of Scripture) this preservation is not for a purely selfish purpose but is *for service.* God's work of grace qualifies men *for work.*

Now God will carry his good work on toward completion **until,** and will actually have it all completed on, **the day of Christ Jesus.** This day is also called:

the day of Christ (Phil. 1:10; 2:16),

the day of our Lord Jesus (Christ) (I Cor. 1:8; cf. II Cor. 1:14),

the day of the Lord (I Thess. 5:2; II Thess. 2:2; cf. I Cor. 5:5),

the day (I Thess. 5:4),

that day (II Thess. 1:10),

the parousia (of the Lord, of our Lord Jesus, etc.) (I Thess. 2:19; 3:13; 4:15; 5:23; II Thess. 2:1, 8; cf. I Cor. 15:23; etc.). See also N.T.C. on I and II Thessalonians, pp. 76, 122-124, 141, 146-150, 161, 167, 168.

It is called the day *of Christ Jesus* because on that day *he* will be manifested in glory, will be met by his bride (the church), will judge, and will thus be publicly vindicated.

Not until that day has arrived will *that* work of God be completed which qualified the addressees for hearty co-operation in spreading the gospel and which ends in the completed fellowship. Moreover, it takes *all* God's ransomed children to make *one* ransomed child complete. A brick may have the appearance of a finished product, but it will still look rather forlorn until it is given its proper place in row and tier, and all the rows and tiers are in, and the beautiful temple is finished. So also God's children, like so many living stones, will form a finished temple when Jesus returns, not until then. Believers are like the dawning light that shines brighter and brighter unto the coming of the perfect day, for it is then that he who began a good work in them will have completed it.

7. The confidence (see verse 6) which Paul has with respect to the Philippians is well-founded, as he shows by adding: **just as it is right for me to be thus minded in behalf of y o u all, because I am holding y o u in my heart.**[34] Paul's *attitude* toward the Philippians (not just his *opinion* about them) has been made clear in the beginning of this long sentence: he thanks God for them, makes supplication for them with joy, being thankful for their fellowship in the gospel, etc. For this *disposition* on his part the apostle does not claim any special credit. He says, "It is *right* (morally obligatory) for me to be thus *minded* (or *disposed*) " (cf. Phil. 2:5; 3:15, 19; 4:2; also Rom. 8:5; 11:20; I Cor. 13:11; Gal. 5:10). Ill-will toward the Philippians, a refusal to thank God for them, while in his inmost being he is convinced of their loyalty to God's cause, would have been highly improper. The apostle is holding them in his *heart*, and the heart is the mainspring of dispositions as well as of feelings and thoughts (see Matt. 15:19; 22:37; I Tim. 1:5). Out of it are the issues of life (Prov. 4:23). And the fact, in turn, that the apostle is cherishing the Philippians in his heart finds its ready explanation in the situation upon which the emphasis really falls, namely, **y o u all being partakers with me of grace.** These Philippians have given proof that they belong to *the fellowship* (see on Phil. 1:5). Accordingly, Paul calls them "my fellow-partakers of the grace" (thus literally), that is, of that operation of God's grace which enables one to work in the interest of the gospel, to suffer for it, and to assist those who proclaim and defend it. (On the word *grace* see N.T.C. on I and II Thessalonians, p. 42). Paul continues: **(as evidenced) both in my bonds and in the defense and confirmation of the gospel.**[35]

---

[34] "*I* am minded," and "*I* am yearning"; hence also (in parallelism with "*I* am yearning") "*I* am holding y o u in my heart"; not: "Y o u are holding me in y o u r heart." Note also the word-order in the original.

[35] The word-order is as follows: ". . . because I am holding y o u in my heart both in my bonds and in the defense and confirmation of the gospel my fellow-partakers of the grace y o u all being." This raises the question. Does Paul mean that he is holding the Philippians in his heart both in his bonds and in the defense and con-

The Philippians had given evidence of their participation with Paul in the grace of God. They had proved it in his *bonds*, that is, his *imprisonment* (see on this word N.T.C. on The Pastoral Epistles, p. 251) and they had also proved it in something which, as it stood in the closest possible association with this imprisonment, is mentioned immediately afterward, namely, *the defense and confirmation of the gospel*.[36] It is evident from this clause that when these words were written Paul had already appeared before the Roman authorities. He had given an account *of himself as a herald of the gospel*.[37] He had *defended* the gospel by removing doubts and suspicions, and had *confirmed* it by setting forth its meaning positively. Naturally the two activities (defense and confirmation) overlapped. And the Philippians had shown that they were deeply concerned in all this. They had prayed for Paul. They had sympathized with him in his experiences — Were not their own experiences similar? Were not they engaged in the same conflict? See on Phil. 1:29, 30. — And they had even sent their personal representative to him with a gift and in order to assist him in every possible manner. (Phil. 2:25; 4:10-14, 18). Epaphroditus had delivered the gift and had begun his work in Rome. The fact that subsequently for a certain space of time he had not been able to assist Paul was nobody's fault. The reason for that was that this worthy ambassador, probably while busily engaged as Paul's attendant and assistant, had become a very sick man, on the verge of death! (Phil. 2:27).

8. Paul has just written: I am holding y o u in my heart (verse 7). He now shows that this is no exaggeration: **For God is my witness how I am yearning for y o u all with the deeply-felt affection of Christ Jesus.** Because it is important that the Philippians shall know how ardently he loves them, that they may be confirmed in the truths which he conveys and may take to heart his admonitions, the apostle appeals to the God who cannot lie and who judges the hearts of men (I Sam. 15:29; Jer. 11:20; John 14:6; 15:29; Rom. 2:23; II Tim. 2:13; Titus 1:2; Heb. 6:18).[38] That is the mean-

---

firmation of the gospel; or does he mean that all these Philippian saints are his fellow-partakers of God's grace, and that this participation is evidenced both in the apostle's bonds and in the defense and confirmation of the gospel? Obviously the latter. See verse 5. *Y o u all being* (πάντας ὑμᾶς ὄντας) is in apposition with *y o u* (ὑμᾶς). Hence, the clause means: I am holding y o u in my heart, y o u all being my fellow-partakers of grace (as evidenced) both in my bonds, etc.
[36] Some commentators seem to dissociate these two (a. bonds and b. defense and confirmation of the gospel), and regard b. as referring to Paul's preaching in general over the course of the years. But the fact that the apostle mentions b. immediately after a. is significant and shows that in the present instance the two should not be thus separated.
[37] See on Phil. 1:27 for a word-study of the concept *gospel*.
[38] As Calvin says aptly: *neque enim parum hoc valet ad fidem doctrinae faciendam cum persuasus est populus a doctore se amari*: "for it tends in no small degree to

ing of the words, "For God is my witness." Cf. Rom. 1:9; II Cor. 1:23; I Thess. 2:5, 10. The fact with reference to which Paul calls upon God to be witness is that the apostle yearns deeply for all these Philippians. He is tenderly attached to them and longs to see them again (cf. Phil. 4:1; Rom. 1:11; I Thess. 3:6; II Tim. 1:4). In fact, he yearns for them all "with the deeply-felt affection (or: "in the tender mercies") of Christ Jesus." Meaning: Paul's love is patterned after (cf. Phil. 2:5) and energized by Christ's indwelling love (Gal. 2:20).[39]

---

secure faith in the doctrine when the people are persuaded that they are loved by the teacher" (*Commentarius In Epistolam Pauli Ad Philippenses,* Corpus Reformatorum, vol. LXXX, Brunsvigae, 1895, on this passage).

[39] The word "deeply-felt affection" or "tender mercies" has given rise to much discussion. The original has σπλάγχνα (ἐν σπλάγχνοις) A.V. renders "bowels"; A.R.V., "tender mercies"; R.S.V. "affection." The primary, literal meaning is *inward parts, intestines, entrails.* See Acts 1:18, "He (Judas) burst open in the middle and all his *entrails* gushed out." It is when Scripture links the affections (love, mercy, pity) with the σπλάγχνα that objections arise. We are told that on this point the Bible is untrustworthy. Paul, being a child of his own day, is simply perpetuating a crude notion of the ancients.

However, over against this attack on Scripture and on Paul stand the following facts:

(1) Experience has proved again and again that emotions (sorrow, joy, pity, love, hatred, anger, etc.) do, indeed, affect the internal organs. A person, let us say, attends a joyous banquet. The feasting is suddenly interrupted by a message of sadness. Moved by grief and sympathy the banqueters — particularly those most directly concerned — lose their appetite.

(2) Science confirms this fact, and has shed some light on the function which the autonomic nervous system performs with respect to it.

(3) We are dealing here with figurative language. Paul has just as much right to use the term σπλάγχνα *figuratively* as we have to make a similar use of the term *heart.* The word σπλάγχνα which literally means *entrails* — and often especially the nobler entrails: heart, liver, lungs — , by way of metonymy, begins to indicate the spiritual center of the emotions, what we today call *the heart,* and even the emotion of *tender love* itself.

In our translation of the term σλπάγχνα we must remember that metaphorical terminology differs in various languages. With this in mind, I suggest the following rendering of the word in the New Testament passages in which it occurs:

(1) The literal rendering *entrails* (Acts 1:18, already quoted).

(2) Figurative usage:

  a. The heart:

    Luke 1:78: "merciful heart."

    II Cor. 6:12: "in y o u r own hearts."

    II Cor. 7:15: "his heart goes out to y o u."

    Col. 3:12: "compassionate heart."

    Philem. 7: "the hearts of the saints have been refreshed by you."

    Philem. 12: "my very heart."

    Philem. 20: "refresh my heart."

    I John 3:17: ". . . and closes his heart against him."

  b. Deeply-felt affection, tender mercies:

    Phil. 1:8: "the deeply-felt affection (or: the tender mercies) of Christ Jesus."

    Phil. 2:1: "deeply-felt affection (or: tender mercies) and compassion."

    Cf. L.N.T. (A. and G.) entry σπλάγχνον

1:9-11

B. *The Prayer*

9. Having thus reaffirmed his great love for the Philippians, Paul is able to proceed as he does; for, though the words which immediately follow imply that perfection had not yet been attained among those to whom this epistle would be read, the very tactful introduction (verses 3-8) has removed every legitimate reason for taking offense.

Verses 9-11 contain the substance of the prayer to which reference was made in verses 3 and 4. This should be compared with Paul's recorded prayers found in the other epistles of this first Roman imprisonment: Eph. 1:17-23; 3:14-21; Col. 1:9-14. Combining them we noticed that the apostle prays that those addressed may abound in wisdom, knowledge, power, endurance, longsuffering, joy, gratitude, and love. Also, we observe that Jesus Christ is regarded as the One through whom these graces are bestowed upon the believer; and that the glory of God is recognized as the ultimate purpose. Truly, one cannot afford to ignore Paul's lessons in prayer-life.

Accordingly, in the present section we have:

(1) *Its Burden:* **And this is my prayer that y o u r love may abound more and more.** The word *love* (ἀγάπη) crowds the pages of Paul's epistles. For its use in Philippians see, besides our present passage, 1:16; 2:1; 2:2. He views this love as being entirely dependent upon and caused by God's love which it strives to imitate (Eph. 4:32-5:2; 5:25-33). Though it is true that when the apostle speaks about the love which believers should exercise, he generally does so in a context which makes *men* the object of that love (Rom. 13:10; 14:15; I Cor. 4:21; II Cor. 2:4, 8; Gal. 5:13; Eph. 1:15; 4:2; etc.), yet no one who has made an earnest study of the closeness of *the fellowship,* which involves both God and men (see on 1:5), can long cling to the idea that for Paul *God* would be removed from the range of this object. (See Rom. 8:28; I Cor. 2:9; 8:3; Eph. 6:24; II Tim. 4:8.) And particularly when, as in the present passage and its context, there is nothing which in any way restricts this object, such rigid limitation seems unjustifiable. The love of which Paul speaks is, accordingly, intelligent and purposeful delight in the triune God, the spontaneous and grateful outgoing of the entire personality to him who has revealed himself in Jesus Christ, and consequently, the deep and steadfast yearning for the progress of his kingdom and for the true prosperity of all his redeemed. This yearning becomes manifest in one's attitude (humility, tenderness, the forgiving spirit even toward "enemies"), in words (of encouragement, truthfulness, and mildness) and in deeds (of self-denial, loyalty, and kindness). The best description of love is found in I Cor. 13.

Now Paul does not pray that the Philippians may *begin* to exercise this love, but that the ocean of their love may rise to its full height, overflowing its entire *perimeter;* in fact, that it may thus abound *more and more.* It is characteristic of Paul that he is never satisfied with anything short of perfection (see Phil. 2:11, 12; 3:13; 4:17; then also I Cor. 15:58; II Cor. 4:15; I Thess. 3:12; 4:1, 9, 10; II Thess. 1:3; Eph. 3:14-19; 4:12, 13; Col. 1:9, 10; 3:12-17; and cf. N.T.C. on The Pastoral Epistles, p. 75).

However, *fully developed* love never travels alone. It is accompanied by all the other virtues. It functions in beautiful co-operation **with full knowledge and keen discernment.** Though knowledge apart from love leaves its possessor a spiritual zero (I Cor. 13:2), and though "knowledge puffs up but love builds up" (I Cor. 8:1), love also needs knowledge, particularly *real, full, advanced spiritual knowledge* (ἐπίγνωσις) in the sense in which the word is used in Rom. 10:2; and cf. also the related verb used similarly in I Cor. 13:12). With the blessing of God such penetrating insight into God's wonderful, redemptive revelation will produce gratitude in an ever-increasing measure, which, in turn, will increase the supply and enhance the quality of love to God and to the brotherhood.

The apostle prays that as a further ingredient of their love the Philippians may have *keen discernment,* the taste and feeling for that which in any concrete situation is spiritually beautiful, *the aesthetic sense* in the sphere of Christian duty and doctrine (αἴσθησις is the Greek word, occurring only here in the New Testament). Love, in other words, should be *judicious.* This keen discernment or perception, born of experience, is the ability of mind and heart to separate not only the good from the bad, but also the important from the unimportant, in each case choosing the former and rejecting the latter. This is, indeed, necessary. A person who possesses love but lacks *discernment* may reveal a great deal of eagerness and enthusiasm. He may donate to all kinds of causes. His motives may be worthy and his intentions honorable, yet he may be doing more harm than good. Also, such an individual may at times be misled doctrinally. There must have been a good reason why Paul here stressed the necessity of abounding in love "with full knowledge and keen discernment" (see Phil. 3:1-3; 3:17-19).

(2) **10.** *Its Purpose:* **so that y o u may approve the things that are excellent.** That naturally follows from what has just been said. Certain commentators here prefer the rendering "so that y o u may distinguish the things that differ." In the abstract this translation is possible. Besides, the difference between the two is not great, for the ability to distinguish between the good and the bad would be for the purpose of electing the former and rejecting the latter. Nevertheless, the rendering found (with slight variations) in A.V., A.R.V. (text), and R.S.V. is to be preferred. It best suits the context: the man who not only has the ability to distinguish but also actually chooses

the things that really matter, in preference to those that are either bad or of little importance, does this with a view to being "pure and blameless," etc. Besides, Paul is his own best interpreter. Phil. 1:10 finds its best commentary in Phil. 4:8, 9 (see on that passage).⁴⁰ The prayer, accordingly continues, **and may be pure and blameless.** Underlying the first adjective is probably the image of precious metal from which the dross has been removed; hence, *unmixed, without alloy;* and so, in the moral sense, *pure.*⁴¹ Underlying the second is that of arriving at one's destination *not stumbled against,* i.e., *uninjured* by any obstacles in the road; hence, morally uninjured, and so, *not worthy of blame, blameless* (the word is used in that passive sense also in Acts 24:16; for the active sense see I Cor. 10:32). The prayer, then, is that the Philippians, their faculties having been trained to prefer the good to the evil, and the essential to the trivial (cf. Heb. 5:14), may be pure and blameless **with a view to the day of Christ.** For the expression "the day of Christ" see on verse 6. Their whole life must be a preparation for that great day, for it is then that the true character of every man's life will be revealed (I Cor. 3:10-15), and everyone will be judged according to his work (Dan. 7:10; Mal. 3:16; Matt. 25:31-46; Luke 12:3; I Cor. 4:5; Rev. 20:12).

11. It is not enough, however, to pray that with a view to the day of Christ's return no flaw and no blame may be found in the Philippians. The implication of this negative petition must now also be stated positively. Hence, the prayer continues: so that y o u may be . . . **filled with the fruits of righteousness.**⁴² Paul prays that in the hearts and lives of the Philip-

---

⁴⁰ As to the verb δοκιμάζω here −ειν, this does not settle the issue either way. It may mean *to put to the test, examine* (I Cor. 11:28; II Cor. 13:5); *to prove by means of testing* (cf. I Cor. 3:13 and I Peter 1:7); or *to approve* (I Cor. 16:3). As to the *diaphora*, these are opposed to the *adiaphora* (the things that do not matter). Hence, the *diaphora* would seem to be the things that really matter, the important or excellent things. Although basically the verb διαφέρω, used intransitively, means *to differ,* yet the sense *to be of* (*more*) *value, to be superior or excellent* finds abundant illustration not only in the New Testament (Rom. 2:18; see the context there; Matt. 6:26; 10:31; 12:12; Luke 12:7, 24) but also elsewhere (see the entry διαφέρω in L.N.T., A. and G.). The context and the parallel passage (Phil. 4:8, 9) must decide the issue. And these favor the rendering "approve the things that are excellent."

⁴¹ The actual *usage* of the word favors this explanation. The etymology is not of much help, because of its uncertainty.

⁴² Literally *fruit,* where (after "filled with") we could also say *fruits.* Moreover, according to the best reading, the word *fruit* is here in the accusative, καρπόν, the accusative of the remote object (cf. also Col. 1:9; II Thess. 1:11); elsewhere the apostle uses πληρόω with the dative (Rom. 1:29; II Cor. 7:4) or with the genitive (Rom. 15:13, 14). This simply shows that there is no fixed rule with respect to the case which follows this verb. The tendency, moreover, was toward the accusative.

pians there may be a rich spiritual harvest, consisting of a multitude of the fairest fruits of heaven; such as, love, joy, peace, longsuffering, kindness, goodness, faithfulness, gentleness, self-control (Gal. 5:22, 23), and the works which result from these dispositions. One of these works, a very important one, is soul-winning (Prov. 11:30). As is shown by the passage just mentioned (and see also Amos 6:12, cf. James 3:18), the expression "fruits of righteousness" is taken from the Old Testament. These are fruits that are produced by the right relation between God and believers. No mere man is ever able to produce them by his own unaided efforts. They are fruits **that come through Jesus Christ,** for apart from him the disciple can do nothing (John 15:5). It is Christ who by means of his sacrifice secured for the believer a new state and consequently also a new condition, so that by virtue of that new relationship the believer by the power of the Holy Spirit is now able to produce fruit, more fruit, much fruit (John 15:2, 5; cf. Matt. 7:17, 18). In fact, believers are "his workmanship, created in Christ Jesus for good works, which God prepared beforehand that we should walk in them" (Eph. 2:10).

Paul concludes his prayer by beseeching God that the ultimate purpose of all that is mentioned in the entire sentence, beginning with verse 9, may be **to the glory** [43] **and praise of God.** The circle must be completed. Fruits

---

[43] Paul uses the word δόξα, *glory,* more than seventy-five times in his epistles. Since it is a word with many different, though related, meanings, a closer study is profitable. The noun is related to the verb δοκέω; hence, has the primary meaning *opinion* (IV Macc. 5:18). It is but a small step to the meaning *good opinion* concerning someone; hence, *praise, honor, homage.*

The Hebrew *kābhōdh,* which is the most common word for *glory* in the Old Testament, has the primary meaning *weight, heaviness, burden* (Is. 22:24); hence, *substance, wealth, dignity.* It is used to describe Jacob's *substance,* his flocks and herds (Gen. 31:1). At times the element of brightness, radiance, splendor is added to that of substance. Thus, the word is used to indicate *the brilliant physical manifestation of Jehovah's presence* (Exod. 16:7; Is. 6:1-5).

In a study of the meaning of δόξα in Paul's epistles both the Greek derivation and use and the Hebrew background must be borne in mind. Accordingly, the different senses in which the word is used by Paul may be summarized as follows:

(1) *praise, honor bestowed upon creatures, or belonging to them* (their *reputation*). Here the antonym is *dishonor* (II Cor. 6:8) or *shame* (Phil. 3:19). The synonym of δόξα, so used, is τιμή (Rom. 2:7; 2:10).

(2) *adoration or homage rendered to God.* Thus the word is used here in Phil. 1:11, as is shown by its synonym *praise.* See also Rom. 3:7; 3:23; 4:20; 11:36; I Cor. 10:31, etc.

(3) *the thing which reflects honor or credit on someone, or the person whose virtues redound to the glory of another* (I Cor. 11:7; 11:15; II Cor. 8:23; I Thess. 2:20).

(4) *external splendor, brightness, brilliance, or radiance* (of the heavenly bodies, I Cor. 15:40, 41).

(5) *the bright cloud by which God made himself manifest, the Shekinah* (Rom. 9:4).

(6) *the manifested excellence, absolute perfection, royal majesty or sublimity of*

descending from heaven must waft their fragrance back to heaven again. The chief end of man is "to glorify God and enjoy him forever" (cf. Matt. 5:16; John 15:8; 17:4). Call this Calvinism if you wish; every man who loves the Word, be he a Baptist, Methodist, Lutheran, Calvinist, or whatever he may be, subscribes to it from the bottom of his heart. It was a thought embedded very securely and deeply in the heart and thoughtlife of Paul (I Cor. 10:31; Eph. 1:6, 12, 14). God must be magnified. His virtues must be extolled. The majesty of the redeeming love and power of him who when his people rejoice rejoices over them with singing (Zeph. 3:17) must be acknowledged gratefully, in spontaneous anthems of praise and adoration.

Synthesis of 1:1-11

This section consists of three parts: salutation, thanksgiving, and prayer. Thanksgiving and prayer are, however, so closely connected that they may be considered together.

In the salutation Paul associates Timothy with himself, so that the letter must be regarded as coming from both, though Paul alone is the author. Paul calls himself and Timothy servants of Christ Jesus, for they recognize Christ Jesus as their sovereign Lord, whom they serve willingly and with gladness of heart. The salutation — of grace and peace — is officially pronounced upon all the spiritually consecrated people in Philippi, viewed as gathered for worship. For a reason unknown to us Paul adds, "together with overseers and deacons." Happy the church with overseers and deacons whom a man like Paul can trust.

Paul thanks God because whenever he thinks of and prays for the Philippians, joy wells up in his heart. Truly, he is writing as Christ's *joyful servant,* yes joyful even though he writes from a Roman prison. The Philippians have always shown that the work of God's grace, proof of their eternal security and preservation, is functioning in their hearts and lives. They have shown and are showing, by their very deeds, that they understand the implications of the blessed *fellowship* of all those who are in Christ. Hence, though from a distance, they co-operate with Paul in his defense. In response to this splendid sharing, he yearns for them all with the deeply-felt affection of Christ Jesus.

God (Rom. 1:23; II Cor. 4:6), *or of Christ* (II Cor. 3:18; 4:4), *particularly also at his second coming* (Titus 2:13; II Thess. 1:9).

(7) *God's majestic power* (Rom. 6:4).

(8) *the light that surrounds those who are, or have just been, in contact with God* (II Cor. 3:7).

(9) *the state and/or place of blessedness into which believers will enter* (Rom. 8:18) *and Christ has already entered* (I Tim. 3:16).

(10) in general, *the pre-eminently excellent or illustrious condition of something or of someone, manifested excellence, either now or in the future* (I Cor. 15:43; II Cor. 3:10; Eph. 1:6; 1:14; 1:18; Phil. 3:21; 4:19).

63

He prays that their love may increase not only, but may also become fully rounded so as to include the graces of deep insight into the way of salvation and keen discretion in every concrete situation of life, that sense of true values which always chooses whatever is best. Thus may they all be filled with the fruits of righteousness to the glory and praise of God.

Summary of Chapter 1

Verses 12-30
Paul, the Optimistic Prisoner

rejoicing in his imprisonment for the advantage of the gospel, and in the fact that Christ will be magnified in his (Paul's) person whether by life or by death; and exhorting the Philippians to remain steadfast, united, and unafraid.

1:12-18a The Imprisonment for the advantage of the gospel.

1:18b-26 Christ magnified in Paul's person whether by life or by death.

1:27-30 Exhortation to steadfastness, unity, and fearlessness.

12 Now I want y o u to know, brothers, that the things that have happened to me have in reality turned out to the advantage of the gospel; 13 so that it has become clear throughout the whole praetorian guard and to all the rest that my bonds are for Christ, 14 and most of the brothers have been heartened in the Lord through my bonds and are showing far more courage in telling the message of God without being afraid.

15 Some, to be sure, are heralding Christ from envy and rivalry, but others from good will. 16 The latter do it out of love, knowing that I am appointed for the defense of the gospel; 17 the former proclaim Christ out of selfish ambition, not sincerely, thinking to raise up affliction (for me) in my bonds. 18 What then? Only that in every way, whether in pretense or in truth, Christ is being proclaimed, and in this I rejoice.

1:12-18a

I. The Imprisonment for the Advantage of the Gospel

12. Being the Joyful Servant of Christ Jesus, Paul is also the Optimistic Prisoner. The Christ whom he so willingly serves will take care of him; in fact, is doing so already, and not of *him* alone, but what is far more important, of *the gospel* also. For the concept *gospel* see on 1:27.

In all probability this optimism was not wholly shared by those whom Paul addresses. The church at Philippi was on tenterhooks. "What is going to happen to Paul; will he be condemned or will he be acquitted?" That was the question which everyone was anxiously asking. "Too bad for him . . . and for the cause of the gospel, this imprisonment!" That was what many people were thinking.

Now on both of these points Paul was of a different mind. With him the primary question was not, "What is going to happen to me?" It was, "How is the gospel-cause affected by whatever happens to me?" And his answer was not, "It is being retarded." It was, "It is actually being advanced by my imprisonment." Accordingly, Paul writes first about "the gospel," "the message of God," "the Christ" (verses 12-18), and then about his own hope of release (verses 19-26). And even in that second paragraph he writes not so much about himself as about "Christ magnified" in his (Paul's) person and work.

The opening clause, **Now I want y o u to know, brothers,** is substantially the same in meaning as the slightly differently worded one in I Cor. 11:3 and Col. 2:1. Similar is also the expression, "I (or *we*) do not wish y o u to be in ignorance" (Rom. 1:13; I Cor. 10:1; 12:1; II Cor. 10:1; 12:1; II Cor.

1:18; I Thess. 4:13) ; and cf. "I (or *we*) make known to y o u" (I Cor. 15:1; II Cor. 8:1; Gal. 1:11) . Introductions of this character serve to call attention to the fact that something of considerable interest or importance is going to follow. The word *brothers* (also in 1:14; 3:1, 13, 17; 4:1, 8, 21) is one of endearment, and indicates that the apostle regards these Philippians as being, along with himself, children of the same heavenly Father, by virtue of the merits of Christ and the work of the Spirit, and accordingly as being included in the glorious fellowship (see on verse 5 above) .

Paul continues, **that the things that have happened to me have in reality turned out to the advantage of the gospel.** The apostle's recent experiences (literally, "the things concerning me" or "my affairs"; cf. Eph. 6:21; Col. 4:7) have had the same effect on the gospel-message as the work of sturdy engineers has on the progress of an army. These men are sent ahead in order to remove obstructions and clear the roads for the rest of the army. Now in the path of the gospel, too, there had been formidable obstructions. On the part of those who had heard vague rumors but were unacquainted with the real essence of the gospel, there had been mistrust and hostility. And on the part of many a church-member there had been fear and cowardice. Paul's experiences and reactions — his bonds, trial, constant witness for Christ, conduct in the midst of affliction — had served the purpose of tending to remove these obstacles. Thus, road-blocks set up by Satan to hinder and stop the progress of the gospel (see N.T.C. on I Thess. 2:18; cf. I Cor. 9:12) had become stepping-stones to better understanding and deeper appreciation of God's redemptive truth and to rising courage in defending it. Paul had been bound, but the word of God could not be bound (see II Tim. 2:9; cf. Isa. 40:8; 55:11) . When the apostle went to Rome as a prisoner, it was in reality *the gospel* that went to Rome.

Thus it has ever been. Joseph, cast into a pit and sold into slavery, by and by magnifies God and praises his providence (Gen. 37:23, 24; 50:20) . Israel, pursued by Pharaoh's army, a moment later is heard singing a song of triumph (Exod. 14 and 15) . Job, deprived of his children, earthly goods, and health, arrives at a deeper insight into the mysteries of God's wisdom than ever before (Job 1 and 2; then 19:25-27 and 42:5, 6) . Jehoshaphat, threatened by the Ammonites and Moabites, offers a soul-stirring prayer in the midst of his distress. There follow praise, victory, and thanksgiving (II Chron. 20) . Jeremiah, cast into a muddy cistern and suffering other afflictions, coins the famous phrase immortalized in Scripture and song, "Great is thy faithfulness" (Jer. 38:6; Lam. 3:23; cf. verses 2 and 7) . Our Lord Jesus Christ, crucified, by means of his very cross gains the victory over sin, death, Satan, causing every true believer to exclaim, "Far be it from me to glory save in the cross of our Lord Jesus Christ" (Matt. 27:5; Acts 4:27, 28; Gal. 6:14; cf. Heb. 12:2) . Peter and John, imprisoned, become bolder than ever in proclaiming Christ to be the only Savior (Acts 4) . The early church, scattered abroad, improves that very opportunity to go about preaching the word (Acts 8).

The manner in which this wonderful progress has been achieved is now described. First, Paul's experiences have affected the outside-world, notably, the praetorian guard (verse 13). Secondly, they have exerted their wholesome influence upon insiders, the "brothers" (verse 14).

13. Beginning with the first group, Paul states, **so that it has become clear throughout the whole praetorian guard and to all the rest that my bonds are for Christ.** On the expression *the praetorian guard* see *Introduction,* II, V. Paul was under constant guard (cf. Acts 28:16, 20). The guards relieved each other. In this way ever so many of them came into contact with this apostle to the Gentiles. They took note of his patience, gentleness, courage, and unswerving loyalty to inner conviction. They were deeply impressed. Yes, even these hardened soldiers, these rude legionaries, who presumably would be the very last to be affected in any way by the gospel, were deeply moved by what they saw and heard and felt in the presence of Paul. They listened to him as he talked to friends who came to visit him, or to his secretary to whom he dictated his letters, or to his judges, or to God in prayer, or even to themselves. It is not difficult to imagine that at first they listened with a measure of disdain or hardly listened at all. But after a while they became interested, and then . . . enthusiastic. And what they learned they began to spread. "We are guarding a very remarkable prisoner," they would say, "and we are firmly convinced that his imprisonment is not for any crime he has committed but solely *for his connection with the Christ* whom he proclaims." And so the news spread, from guard to guard, to the families of the guards, to Caesar's household (see on Phil. 4:22), and thus to "all the rest," the inhabitants of Rome, in general. Paul's *case* and, even better, Christ's *cause,* became "the talk of the town." That meant *progress* for the gospel, for *the real issue* was being clarified.

14. And now the effect upon "the brothers": **and most of the brothers have been heartened in the Lord** [44] **through my bonds and are showing far more courage in telling the message of God without being afraid.**

---

[44] What does "in the Lord" modify? Must we read, "brethren in the Lord" (A.V.)? This is possible, but it would be the only instance in the New Testament in which the noun *brothers* is so modified. However, we do have "brothers in Christ" in Col. 1:2. Hence, "brothers in the Lord" cannot be entirely dismissed. Or is it "bonds in the Lord"? But the order of the words in the original pleads against this meaning. Besides, the interpretation, "trusting in my bonds in the Lord" makes little sense. Probably the best is "heartened in the Lord through my bonds." That is entirely in harmony with the context here: Paul's bonds have become manifest as being for the sake of Christ, and so by means of these bonds and the testimony of the man in bonds most of the brothers have been heartened in the Lord. And see also Phil. 2:24 and 3:3, 4 (in the original).

Who were these *brothers?* Clearly, the believers in Rome. Here, years ago, a congregation had been established to which the apostle had addressed his famous Epistle to the Romans. That congregation consisted largely of converts from the Gentile world. However, when Paul, as prisoner, arrived in Rome, he immediately proclaimed the gospel to the *Jews,* with the result that "some believed . . . some disbelieved" (Acts 28:24). The Jews who believed founded *their own* churches in Rome. Nevertheless, we may be sure that between the members of the first group, the believers from the Gentiles, and the second, those from the Jews, there existed a bond of Christian fellowship, so that when Paul here speaks of the *brothers* he has reference to members of both groups, that is, to those among them who had not left Rome.[45] Similarly we read in Acts 28:30 that during his two years of imprisonment in Rome Paul welcomed *all* who came to him, proclaiming the kingdom of God and teaching about the Lord Jesus Christ openly and without hindrance (Acts 28:30, 31).

Now what had been the brothers' attitude to Paul and his message? And what had been the attitude of their leaders? As soon as they knew that Paul was on trial had they offered help? Had they remained steadfast in spreading the tidings of salvation, the good news? Here in verse 14 it seems to be implied that at first they had not shown a very commendable degree of courage. *Some* courage here and there, yes, but not very much. Instead, they seem to have been "frightened by the adversaries" (verse 28), definitely in need of the warning that each man should look out not only for his own interests but also for the interests of others (2:4). All had been looking after their own affairs (cf. 2:21). At his defense no one had been at Paul's side but all had deserted him.

But things were changing now. Let it be borne in mind that when this letter was written, the author speaks as a man who is awaiting not *a trial* but *a verdict.* The trial had reached its crisis; the case was about to be terminated (Phil. 2:19, 23, 24). Everyone had had a chance to observe Paul's steadfastness and courage while "under fire." The Lord had sustained him most wonderfully (Phil. 4:13), and this not only during his trial but even earlier, on his way to Rome as a prisoner (Acts 23:11; 27:23). So now at last, as a result of having seen what the grace of God is able to accomplish in the heart of his "bound" apostle, *most* of the brothers (not just "many," A.V.) have taken courage, the courage which is "in the Lord," imparted and kept alive by him. Not only was there official proclamation of "the message of God," that is, the gospel, but this message had even become the theme for discussion without restraint, the topic for ordinary conversation or *talk,* and this now *far more* than ever before. Yet this was the case not among *all* but only among *most* of the brothers. The fact that even

[45] See also my *Bible Survey,* pp. 206, 207; 210-212; 353-357; 427.

now conditions were not exactly ideal even among the preachers at Rome is clear from that which follows, which, however, also shows Paul's magnificent optimism:

15. Some, to be sure, are heralding Christ from envy and rivalry, but others from good will.

It stands to reason (and should never have been denied) that when Paul now begins to speak about those who "are heralding Christ from envy and rivalry . . . out of selfish ambition, not sincerely, *thinking to raise up afflic-tion (for me) in my bonds*" he is no longer referring to those people for whom he has nothing but praise because they have been *"heartened in the Lord through my bonds* and are showing far more courage in telling the message of God without being afraid."* The apostle approaches the subject from a different angle now. He has already indicated two favorable results of his imprisonment experiences: a. *the issue has been clarified for the out-siders* (praetorian guard, etc.), so that these now realize that Paul's bonds are *for Christ;* b. *most of the believers in the great metropolis have shaken off their former fears,* and are now at last telling the message of God cou-rageously. He now accentuates a third reason for his optimism (a reason in reality already implied in a. and b.), namely, c. *Christ is being proclaimed!* Now with this thought uppermost in his mind he is saying that this herald-ing of the Christ is, sad to say, not always actuated by the proper motives.

The men of whom Paul is thinking are *all heralding* Christ (see verses 15, 17, 18).[46] They are exercising their ambassadorship, and are publicly and authoritatively proclaiming him as the one only name under heaven that is given among men by which we must be saved. (On this verb *to herald* or *to preach* and its synonyms see N.T.C. on The Pastoral Epistles, pp. 309, 310.) As far as one is able to gather from the text, none of the heralds is a preacher of false doctrine. None of them, for example, is giving undue prominence to the observance of the law as a means of salvation. None of those referred to here in Phil. 1:15-18 is "preaching a different gospel" (Gal. 1:6; cf. 5:1-6) or "another Jesus" (II Cor. 11:4). None of them is "a dog" or "an evil worker" (Phil. 3:2). But while all are proclaiming the true gospel, not all are actuated by pure motives. *That* is the point! It is with respect to this point that Paul is here dividing the preachers at Rome into two groups.

The first group consists of those who are heralding Christ from *envy* and *rivalry.* (For this combination see also I Tim. 6:4. For a word-study of *envy* see N.T.C. on The Pastoral Epistles, p. 388). It should be borne in

---

[46] The contention of S. Greydanus, that the verb κηρύσσουσιν belongs only with "others from good will," because those who are filled with envy and rivalry cannot really be said to herald Christ, must be considered an error. Words have a history and cannot be so strictly circumscribed or delimited. Besides, if τινὲς . . . διὰ φθόνον καὶ ἔριν does not have κηρύσσουσιν as its predicate, what is its predicate? It would be a subject without a predicate.

mind that there was a church in Rome long before Paul arrived there. It can scarcely be doubted, therefore, that certain preachers in Rome had attained a degree of prominence among the brothers. With the arrival of Paul and especially with the spreading of his fame throughout the city (see verses 13 and 14) is it easy to understand that these leaders were beginning to lose some of their former prestige. *Their* names were no longer mentioned so often. Hence, they became envious of Paul. Their motives in preaching Christ were not pure or unmixed.

16. *The second group* consisted of those who were motivated by *good will* (used here of *human* good will; in Phil. 2:13; Luke 2:14; 10:21; Eph. 1:5, 9 of *divine* good pleasure). That the essence of this *good will* was love for Paul and for the gospel which he proclaimed is evident from the words which immediately follow: **The latter do it out of love, knowing that I am appointed for the defense of the gospel.**[47] These men do not begrudge Paul the authority which he exercised by divine appointment, nor the great gifts he had received from God and the honor which was bestowed upon him by many people. They heralded Christ out of *love* (see on verse 9), a love for Christ, hence also for his gospel and for the man whom they knew to have been *set, destined, or appointed* (see for this verb I Thess. 3:3; cf. Luke 2:34) for *the defense* (see on verse 7) of *the gospel.*

17. The former proclaim Christ out of selfish ambition. Like many a hired servant discards idealism and has his mind set chiefly on the wages which he will receive, so also these envious preachers are actuated by selfish motives (cf. Phil. 2:21). They crave honor and prestige, at least they have permitted this motive to crowd the nobler incentives into a corner. Hence, Paul continues: these men proclaim Christ **not sincerely,** that is, not from unmixed motives, not purely, **thinking to raise up**[48] affliction (for me) in

---

[47] The A.V., on the basis of the Textus Receptus, reverses the order found in the A.R.V. and R.S.V. (so that A.V. verse 16 is A.R.V. and R.S.V. verse 17; and A.V. verse 17 is A.R.V. and R.S.V. verse 16). This change was probably made in order that the sequence in verses 16 and 17 might be the same as that in verse 15. But the *chiastic* arrangements, so that the third clause parallels the second, and the fourth parallels the first, is based on the best texts (see textual apparatus in N.N.).

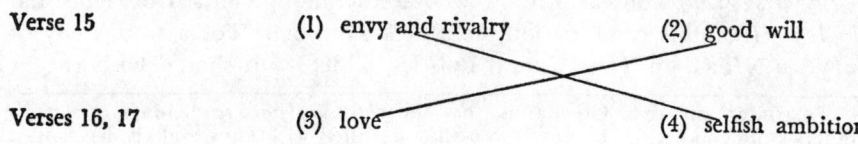

Verse 15	(1) envy and rivalry	(2) good will
Verses 16, 17	(3) love	(4) selfish ambition

For another illustration of chiastic parallelism in Paul see N.T.C. on The Pastoral Epistles, pp. 138, 139; cf. Prov. 13:24; 23:15, 16.

[48] This verb, rather than "to add to" is supported by the best texts.

my bonds. They would just as soon aggravate Paul's affliction, as long as their own selfish interests are served.

18a. What then? or "What really matters?" **Only that**[49] **in every way, whether in pretense or in truth, Christ is being proclaimed, and in this I rejoice.** Paul's self-forgetfulness excites affectionate admiration. We love him all the more for having written this beautiful passage. Sensitive soul though he was, he does not begin to pity himself because certain jealous preachers were trying to win applause at his expense. What really matters to him is not what they are doing to *him* but what they are doing for *the gospel.* But is it possible, then, that such selfish individuals can render service to the gospel in any way? Yes, for it must be borne in mind that those who hear them do not know what Paul knows. The listeners hear only the *good* preaching. They do not see the *bad* motive. What matters then is that *in every way,* that is, whether *in pretense* — as by those who know how to cover up their selfish ambition — or *in truth* — as by those whose sole aim is actually the glorification of their Lord and Savior — Christ is proclaimed. In *this,* says Paul, *I rejoice* (see also 1:25; 2:2, 17, 18, 28, 29; 3:1; 4:1, 4, 10). It would seem that the apostle's joy is so great that it crowds out every other consideration.

18b Yes, and I shall continue to rejoice. 19 For I know that through y o u r supplication and the help supplied by the Spirit of Jesus Christ this will turn out for my salvation, 20 in accordance with my eager expectation and hope that in not a single respect I shall ever be put to shame, but that now as always by my unfailing courage Christ will be magnified in my person, whether by life or by death. 21 For to me to live (is) Christ, and to die (is) gain. 22 Now if (what awaits me is) to live in the flesh, this for me means fruit resulting from work; yet which I shall choose I cannot tell. 23 So I am hard pressed between the two, having the desire to depart and be with Christ, for that is very far better; 24 but to remain in the flesh is more necessary for y o u r sake. 25 And being convinced of this, I know that I shall remain, yes remain with y o u all, for y o u r progress and joy in the faith, 26 in order that in connection with me, because of my being with y o u again, y o u r exultation in Christ may abound.

1:18b-26

II. *Christ Magnified in Paul's Person whether by Life or by Death*

18b, 19. Paul is the Optimistic Prisoner not only because he realizes that his imprisonment is for the advantage of the gospel (1:12-18), but also be-

---

[49] B has ὅτι; D,E,K, and L have πλήν without ὅτι. But πλήν ὅτι, Aleph, A,F,G,P, though rather unusual not only fits the context very well but is also used by Paul as reported by Luke in Acts 20:23.

cause he is deeply convinced that in his person Christ will be magnified, and that this happy result will be attained whether he, the apostle, is set free (as he rather expects) or is put to death (1:19-26).

At first glance it might seem as if from the lofty height of glorying in the fact that Christ is being proclaimed — verse 18 — Paul now descends to the somewhat lower plane of rejoicing in his own salvation — verse 19. However, by reading not only verse 19 but also verse 20 it will be seen that for Paul *salvation* consisted in this — to quote his own words — "that . . . Christ be magnified in my body, whether by life or by death." Christ's glory and Paul's salvation cannot be separated.

Yet there is progress in thought. The apostle advances from the consideration of his joy in the present (verse 18) to the consideration of his joy in the future. He writes: **Yes, and I shall continue to rejoice.** He states as the reason for his continued rejoicing: **For I know that through y o u r supplication and the help supplied by** [50] **the Spirit of Jesus Christ this will turn out for my salvation.** This present imprisonment with all its attending woe will result in Paul's truest welfare, his highest good, namely, Christ magnified more than ever in Paul's person. Note that this glorious result will be brought about by means of *two factors* which because of their great difference in magnitude — the one human, the other divine — we would probably hesitate to place next to one another: *y o u r supplication* . . . and . . . *the help supplied by the Spirit of Jesus Christ!* Yet, they certainly belong together: the very same Spirit which sustained Jesus Christ, the Mediator, in *his* trials, will cause all things to work together for good in the case of Paul also, and this in answer to the prayer of fellow-believers. The apostle sets much store by the intercession (here *supplication,* that is, fervent petition or request for the fulfillment of a definite need; cf. Phil. 1:4; 4:6; see N.T.C. on I Tim. 2:1) of his friends (cf. Rom. 15:30, 32; II Cor. 1:11; Col. 4:2; I Thess. 5:25; II Thess. 3:1). Note that *Paul* makes supplication for the Philippians (1:4), and that he knows that *they* are doing the same thing for him (1:19). The *fellowship* is operating (see on verse 5).

20. The "knowledge" of which Paul speaks is in complete harmony with an underlying conviction born of experience. Hence, the apostle continues:

---

[50] The verb χορηγέω means basically *to lead a chorus* i.e., to furnish a chorus at one's own expense, *supplying* whatever is necessary to fit out the chorus. Hence, it comes to mean simply *to supply or furnish,* with the added idea *abundantly* (II Cor. 9:10; I Peter 4:11). Similarly, the compound verb ἐπιχορηγέω means *to furnish or provide* (II Peter 1:5); *to give or grant* to someone (II Cor. 9:10; Gal. 3:5; passive II Peter 1:11). Without acc. the verb becomes *to support* (Col. 2:19). Hence, also the noun as used here in Phil. 1:19 means *support* or *help.* In Eph. 4:16 the reference is to a ligament that serves as support. The idea that this support is *generous* may well be implied in Phil. 1:19. See L.N.T. (A. and G.) pp. 892, 305; also M.M., pp. 251.

in accordance with my eager expectation and hope that in not a single re-spect I shall ever be put to shame, but that now as always by my unfailing courage Christ will be magnified in my person. The apostle is not bragging. Quite the opposite is true. He ascribes nothing to self but everything to the power of the Spirit of Jesus working within him. It is his *eager expectation* (see Rom. 8:19; yearning, looking forward to something with head erect) *and well-founded hope* that this Spirit will never put him to shame. He will never permit Paul to seek an easy way out of his imprisonment; for example, by denying his Lord. On the contrary, he will equip the apostle with *un-failing courage;* literally, *complete outspokenness,* a courage which reveals itself in a frank and unhesitant proclamation of the good tidings of salva-tion to all who are willing to listen, and which has as its source confidence in God and in his promises, the confidence of one who knows that at all times he can approach his God without fear (cf. Eph. 3:12).[51]

Thus Christ will be magnified in Paul's *person;* literally *body,* but here *body* indicates *the entire personality* (cf. also Rom. 12:1; Eph. 5:28),[52] as is evident from the addition of the words **whether by life or by death.** If Paul is acquitted and released, he will continue his apostolic labors. If he is condemned to death, he will go to his Lord with unwavering faith and with a song in his heart. Either way it will become evident what the Lord through his grace can accomplish in the heart of his child. Thus Christ will be magnified.

21. There is no sharp division between verses 20 and 21. They should stand together. Paul says that he knows that in his person Christ will be magnified, **For to me to live (is) Christ, and to die (is) gain.** Were this not true, Christ would not be magnified in him.[53]

What Paul means by saying, "For to me to live is Christ," may be learned from the familiar lines of the well-known hymn by Will L. Thompson:

> "Jesus is all the world to me,
> My life, my joy, my all;
> He is my strength from day to day,
> Without him I would fall.

---

[51] See D. Smolders, "L'audace de L'apôtre selon saint Paul. Le thème de la par-rêsia (suite et fin)," *Coll Mech* 43 (Feb., 1958), 117-133.
[52] L.N.T. (A. and G.), p. 807.
[53] It is clear that both here and also in verse 22 we are dealing with abbreviated language: "is" has to be inserted (cf. N.T.C. on John, Vol. I, p. 206). There should also be no doubt about the fact that the expression "to live" and "to die" belong to the same physical sphere: "to live" means "to live in the flesh," and "to die" means "to depart" from this earthly scene (see verses 22 and 23).

> When I am sad to him I go,
> No other one can cheer me so;
> When I am sad he makes me glad,
> He's my friend."

And the stanzas which follow.

When the apostle says so emphatically "to me" placing this word at the very beginning of the sentence, he is giving a personal testimony and is at the same time drawing a contrast between himself and those to whom he has just been referring and who, no doubt, are still very much in his mind; namely, preachers "who proclaim Christ out of selfish ambition." *Paul*, then, in contrast with them, is not *self*-centered but *Christ*-centered. He is concerned with the honor and glory of his wonderful Redeemer.

To determine even more exactly just what the apostle has in mind when he says, "to live (is) Christ," parallel Pauline passages must be consulted. It means: to derive one's strength from Christ (Phil. 4:13), to have the mind, the humble disposition of Christ (Phil. 2:5-11), to know Christ with the knowledge of Christian experience (Phil. 3:8), to be covered by Christ's righteousness (Phil. 3:9), to rejoice in Christ (Phil. 3:1; 4:4), to live for Christ, that is, for his glory (II Cor. 5:15), to rest one's faith on Christ and to love him in return for his love (Gal. 2:20).

"And to die (is) gain." Dying physically means gain *for Paul*. It will mean that he will actually be *with* Christ (see verse 23), "at home with the Lord" (II Cor. 5:8). But gain for Paul can never be dissociated from gain for the cause of Christ, for the one objective in which Paul rejoices most is that in *his* person Christ may be magnified. Death will be a distinct gain because it will be the gateway to clearer knowledge, more wholehearted service, more exuberant joy, more rapturous adoration, all of these brought to a focus in Christ. Surely, if even now Christ is magnified in Paul's person, he will be thus magnified even more on the other side of death. Cf. I Cor. 13:12. Death is gain because it brings more of Christ to Paul, and more of Paul to Christ.

22. From the words "whether by life or by death" and "For to me to live (is) Christ, and to die (is) gain," it follows that the apostle was weighing the two possibilities, and was asking himself, "Now if the choice between these two were mine, which would I choose?" This thought, which in verses 20 and 21 is in the background, comes to the fore now, as Paul continues **Now if (what awaits me is) to live in the flesh, this for me (means) fruit resulting from work.** The words placed in parentheses show that here again we are dealing with abbreviated expression, but the sense is clear enough.[54]

---

[54] Both A.V. and R.S.V. are better here than the text of A.R.V., which reads as follows, "But if to live in the flesh, — if this shall bring fruit from my work, then what

If Paul is acquitted, so that his life *here on earth* is prolonged,[55] this will mean *fruit:* souls won for eternity through his further ministry, the edification of believers, the establishment of churches, etc. The prospect is wonderful. Paul knows that, should he be acquitted and released, he will again avail himself of every opportunity to proclaim the gospel far and wide. What is more, *he knows that this work will not be in vain.* In the realm of the Spirit there is *always* fruit of labor. When one abounds in the work of the Lord, his labor is never futile (I Cor. 15:58). To be sure, not every seed germinates, nor does every plant bear fruit (Matt. 13:1-9). Many people there are who experience "so many things" *in vain* (Gal. 3:4). But it is equally true that by no means all the seeds that are scattered are wasted. He who goes forth weeping, bearing the seed for sowing, will come home with shouts of joy, bringing his sheaves with him (Psalm 126:6). The word that proceeds from the mouth of Jehovah never returns to him empty (Is. 55:11). Hence, blessed are those who sow beside all waters (Isa. 32:20, cf. also 32:17). And let no one think that if the seed does not *at once* appear above the ground and if the plant does not rush to maturity like Jonah's gourd, the work of sowing has been in vain. Rather, *at God's own time* the seeds scattered broadcast will ripen into a blessed harvest (Eccles. 11:1; cf. Mark 4:26-29). And in this fruit-bearing Christ will be glorified, *the Christ who was Paul's very life.*

And since for Paul to live was Christ, hence for him to die was gain (vs. 21). In fact it was better by far, by *very* far (vs. 23). Hence, it is not surprising that the apostle continues **Yet which I shall choose I cannot tell.**[56]

I shall choose I know not." In addition to several other objections to this reconstruction there is the basic one that it would imply that the apostle doubted whether a prolonged ministry on earth would mean fruitful labor. However, as is clear from verse 24, he entertained no doubts with reference to this.

[55] The expression "to live in the flesh" means to go on living *in this world.* In Paul's epistles the word σάρξ (flesh) has the following meanings:

a. the chief substance of the body, whether of men or of animals (I Cor. 15:39) ;
b. the body itself, in distinction from the spirit, mind, heart (Col. 2:5) ;
c. earthly existence (Gal. 2:20; Phil. 1:22, 24);
d. a human being, viewed as a weak, earthly, perishable creature (I Cor. 1:29; Gal. 2:16). This usage depends heavily on the Hebrew. Cf. Isa. 40:6, "All flesh is grass," etc.
e. physical descent or relationship (Rom. 9:8) ;
f. the human nature, without any disparagement (Rom. 9:5) ;
g. human worth and attainment, with emphasis on hereditary, ceremonial, legal, and moral advantages; the self apart from regenerating grace; anything apart from Christ on which one bases his hope for salvation (Phil. 3:3).
h. the human nature regarded as the seat and vehicle of sinful desire (Rom. 7:25; 8:4-9, 12, 13; Gal. 5:16, 17, 19; 6:8).

[56] A.V. has "What I shall choose I wot not." Similarly A.R.V. "What I shall choose I know not." This rendering is possible. That γνωρίζω can have the meaning *to know* is clear. See N.T.L. (A. and G.), p. 162. However, in all other New Testament occurrences this verb probably has the meaning *to cause to know, to make*

23, 24. The apostle loves Christ, and loves to be with him to glorify him forever, free from sin and from suffering. But he also loves the Philippians and knows that they have definite spiritual needs, and that a further ministry among them will be very fruitful and to the glory of the Redeemer. The choice is a difficult one, which is expressed even more clearly in the words: **So I am hard pressed between the two, having the desire to depart and be with Christ, for that is very far better; but to remain in the flesh is more necessary for yo u r sake.** Torn between conflicting considerations Paul is being pressed from both sides:

On the one side there is the desire,[57] the strong yearning, *to strike* (literally, to loosen) *the tent* of his earthly, temporary existence; the desire "to break camp," or "to loosen the cables of a ship," hence, *to depart.* See II Tim. 4:6. Note the words: to depart *and be with Christ.* The apostle knows that when his soul departs from this earthly life, it is immediately *with Christ.* It does not "go out of existence" until the day of the resurrection, nor does it "go to sleep" (cf. Ps. 16:11; 17:15; Matt. 8:11; Luke 16:25; John 17:24; I Cor. 13:12, 13; II Cor. 5:8; Heb. 12:23; Rev. 6:10; 20:4). It at once enjoys blessed fellowship with the Savior. That is "very far better" [58] than to remain in the flesh. Just why is this far more appealing, subjectively considered? Consult such passages as Rom. 8:18; II Cor. 5:8; II Tim. 4:7, 8; and Phil 3:14 for the answer. Note the contrast between

Remaining here ********	and	*Departing to be with Christ* ********
Here:		There:
a. A temporary residence, a mere tent-dwelling		A permanent abode
b. Suffering mixed with joy		Joy unmixed with suffering
c. Suffering for a little while		Joy forever
d. Being absent from the Lord		Being at home with the Lord
e. The fight		The feast
f. The realm of sin		The realm of complete deliverance from sin, positive holiness.

On the other side there is the need of the Philippians. The apostle places this objective need over against his own subjective desire. He is convinced

---

known (hence, *to tell*). This is definitely true of all other occurrences in the Prison Epistles (Eph. 1:9; 3:3, 5, 10; 6:19, 21; Phil. 4:6; Col. 1:27; 4:7, 9). The causative rendering makes excellent sense also in the present passage, though the possibility of the other meaning must be admitted.
[57] legitimate desire; see N.T.C. on The Pastoral Epistles, pp. 271-274, especially footnote 147.
[58] This rendering of the A.R.V. is more exact than that of either the A.V. or the R.S.V., for it preserves the flavor of the *triple* comparative used in the original: "much more the better."

that his continued life on earth, enabling him to bestow further pastoral care upon the believers at Philippi, must be given serious consideration. The church had existed for not much longer than a decade. Only yesterday some of its members had emerged from the idolatry and immorality of heathendom. Though it was a wonderful church in many ways, it had its weaknesses and it was confronted with real dangers (see Phil. 3:1-3; 3:19; 4:2). Accordingly, big-hearted Paul is ready for the present, if that be God's plan, to forego the entrancing glories of heaven in order that his span of life on earth may be lengthened in the interest, among others, of the Philippians. The *need* of the church weighs heavier with him than the *desire* of his own soul.

25, 26. He therefore continues, **And being convinced of this, I know that I shall remain, yes remain with y o u all.** Because the apostle is convinced of *this,* namely, of that which he has just written: that the lengthening of his life's span would mean fruit resulting from work, and that such work was needed by the church at Philippi, he regards it as altogether probable that he will remain on earth a while longer. "It is my definite opinion," says he, as it were, that "I shall even remain by the side of *y o u all.*" This *y o u all* probably includes more than the church at Philippi.

The purpose of this expected release and prolonged ministry is expressed in *the phrase* **for y o u r progress and joy in the faith,** and in *the clause* that stands in apposition with it (see verse 27).

Again and again in Philippians and also in Paul's other epistles the idea of spiritual *progress* is stressed. Such progress means growth in love (Phil. 1:9), in knowledge (1:9), in fruitfulness (1:11), and in obedience (2:12). Why is it important that believers progress? Because *not to progress* means *to regress.* Standing still spiritually is impossible. And *regression produces depression* (dejection). But *progress means happiness,* the joy unspeakable and full of glory. Hence, Paul very neatly unites these two concepts and writes that he expects to remain with his friends on earth for their *progress and joy* in the faith. There follows the elucidation: **in order that in connection with me, because of my being with y o u again, y o u r exultation in Christ may abound.** The apostle's release — should it please God to grant this, as Paul rather expects — would result in more than merely sentimental rejoicing. Not only would the Philippians exclaim, "Paul, we are very happy to have you with us once more." They would also thank their Anointed Savior. In connection with God's mercies bestowed upon Paul they would make their boast in the Lord, praising *him,* and this particularly for bringing their dear friend to them *again.* Note that word *again.* It implies that the apostle had been in Philippi before (on the second missionary journey, Acts 16:11-40; the third, outward bound, II Cor. 8:1-5; and the third, homeward bound, Acts 20:5).

All the historical evidence points to the fact that Paul's expectation was fulfilled, and that, having been released, he actually visited the Philippians once more. For proof see N.T.C. on The Pastoral Epistles, pp. 23-27, 39, 40.

---

27 Only continue to exercise y o u r citizenship in a manner worthy of the gospel of Christ, that whether I come and see y o u or am absent, I may hear of y o u that y o u are standing firm in one spirit, with one soul striving side by side for the faith of the gospel, 28 and not frightened in anything by the adversaries, which is for them a clear sign of destruction, but of y o u r salvation, and this from God. 29 For to y o u it has been granted in behalf of Christ not only to believe in him but also to suffer in his behalf, 30 being engaged in the same conflict which y o u saw me having and now hear me having.

1:27-30

III. *Exhortation to Steadfastness, Unity, and Fearlessness*

27, 28. It is in keeping with his character as Optimistic Prisoner that Paul now exhorts the Philippians to remain steadfast, united, and unafraid, and to regard it a privilege to be counted worthy to suffer for Christ. He writes, **Only continue to exercise y o u r citizenship in a manner worthy of the gospel of Christ.** Paul says, "Only," that is, "whatever happens to *me* personally, whether I come and see y o u or am absent," *in any event* be sure to conduct yourselves as believers. With respect to the words, "Continue to exercise y o u r citizenship," commentators differ rather sharply. According to some the meaning is, Continue to discharge y o u r obligations as citizens and residents of Philippi faithfully. According to others the idea that there is even so much as an allusion here to Roman citizenship is far-fetched.[59] But why should it be necessary to accept either of these rather extreme positions? In opposition to the first opinion the question may be asked, Does not Phil. 3:20 ("For *our* homeland is in heaven") clearly indicates that the apostle is referring to *heavenly* citizenship? And in answer to the second view, the question is pertinent, Does not that very passage and also the position of the Philippians as Roman citizens make it altogether probable that this Roman citizenship is *the underlying idea?* Paul is drawing a parallel, making a comparison. It is as if the apostle were saying, "Y o u are Roman citizens and proud of it (and so am I, Acts 16:21, 37). But constantly bear in mind that what matters *most* is the fact that y o u are citizens of *the kingdom of heaven.* Continue, therefore, to exercise *that* citizenship in a manner worthy of the gospel of Christ." The verb has reference, accordingly, to Christian conduct, a manner of life that befits a citizen-soldier who be-

---

[59] For the first idea see Raymond R. Brewer, "The Meaning Of POLITEUESTHE In Philippians 1:27," *JBL* 73 (June, 1954), 76-83. For the second, R.C.H. Lenski, *op. cit.,* p. 756.

longs to the kingdom and army of Jesus Christ.[60] Naturally, good citizens of the realm of Christ will also be good citizens of the Roman realm.

To exercise their citizenship "in a manner worthy of the gospel of Christ" means to conduct it in harmony with the responsibilities which that gospel imposes and with the blessings which it brings. The word *gospel* occurs twice in this verse, and not less than six times in this one chapter. This is therefore the proper place to answer the question:

What Is the Gospel?

It is the God-spell, the *spell* or *story* that tells us what God has done to save sinners. Hence, it is *evangel* or *message of good tidings*. It is *the glad news of salvation which God addresses to a world lost in sin*.[61] Not what *we* must do but what *God* (in Christ) has done for us is the most prominent part of that news. This is clear from the manner in which the noun *evangel* and the related verb *to proclaim an evangel, to bring good news* are used in the Old Testament. See LXX on Psalm 40:9; 96:2; Isa. 40:9; 52:7 in relation to Chapter 53; 61:1; and Nahum 1:15.

Isa. 61:1

"The Spirit of the Lord Jehovah is upon me,
because Jehovah has anointed me,
to bring good tidings to the afflicted.
He has sent me to bind up the broken-hearted,
to proclaim liberty to the captives,
and the opening (of the prison) to those who are bound;
to proclaim the year of Jehovah's favor;
and the day of vengeance of our God;
to comfort all who mourn;
to grant to those who mourn in Zion —
to give them a garland instead of ashes,
the oil of gladness instead of mourning,
the garment of praise instead of the spirit of heaviness;
that they may be called oaks of righteousness,
the planting of Jehovah, that he may be glorified."

---

[60] Thus interpreted, the meaning of the verb πολιτεύομαι approaches, but is not entirely identical with, that of περιπατέω (Phil. 3:17, 18 and frequent in Paul). This emphasis on conduct is also found in the only remaining New Testament instance of the verb πολιτεύομαι (Acts 23:1). For its use both in and outside of the New Testament see also L.N.T. (A. and G.), p. 693.

[61] In Paul the emphasis falls at times on *the contents* of God's message, namely, *salvation;* at other times on *the proclamation* of this message. These two meanings may occur side by side: Rom. 1:1, 2; I Cor. 9:14. In the sense of Gospel (with a capital "G") "a *book* containing the story of Christ's life and teaching" the word is not used in Scripture. See G. Friedrich's article on this concept in Th.W.N.T., Vol. II, pp. 705-735.

In his sermon at Nazareth Jesus referred these words to himself, quoting the first part of the passage (Luke 4:18; cf. Isa. 61:1, 2b).

Isaiah 52:7 in relation to Chapter 53; cf. Nahum 1:15:
"How beautiful upon the mountains (are) the feet of him *who brings good tidings,* who publishes peace, *who brings good tidings of good,* who publishes salvation" (thus Isaiah, and cf. Nahum).

In Romans 10:15 Paul refers to these words. According to the contexts in Nahum and Isaiah freedom from the foreign yoke or return to the native soil was good tidings for Israel of old. But even during the old dispensation the good news had reference to blessings far beyond the national and physical horizon. One has no right to exclude from the glad tidings of Isaiah 52 the precious contents of Chapter 53; e.g.,

> "Surely, he has borne our griefs
>   and carried our sorrows;
> yet we esteemed him stricken,
>   smitten by God, and afflicted.
> But he was wounded for our transgressions,
>   he was bruised for our iniquities;
> the chastisement of our peace was upon him;
>   and by his stripes we are healed."

Between the evangel of the old dispensation and that of the new there is a very close connection. Thus, for example, apart from Isaiah 53 the New Testament cannot be understood:

When John the Baptist proclaimed his gospel, pointing to Jesus as the Lamb of God who takes away the sin of the world, was he not thinking of Isaiah 53? (I John 1:29; cf. Isa. 53:7, 10).

When Matthew referred to Christ's humble origin and the lowly conditions of his birth, was there not a clear reference to Isaiah 53? (Matt. 2:23; cf. Isa. 11:1; 53:2).

When this same Matthew-passage and also many other New Testament references showed that Christ was despised, was not this in fulfilment of Isaiah 53? (Matt. 2:23; Luke 18:31-33; 23:35, 36; John 1:46; I Peter 2:4; cf. Isa. 53:3).

When John, the apostle and evangelist, summarized Israel's reaction to Christ's earthly ministry, did he not do it in words taken from Isaiah 53? (John 12:36-38; cf. Isa. 53:1).

When Jesus healed the sick, gave himself a ransom "for many," and "was reckoned with the transgressors," did he not fulfill Isaiah 53? (Matt. 8:16, 17; cf. Isa. 53:4; Matt. 20:28; Mark 10:45; cf. Isa. 53:11, 12; Luke 22:37; cf. Isa. 53:12).

When Matthew stated, "And there came a rich man and asked for the body of Jesus," was he not thinking of Isaiah 53? (Matt. 27:57; cf. Isa. 53:9).

When Jesus stressed that he regarded not only his suffering and death but also his entrance into glory (resurrection, etc.) as fulfilment of prophecy, was he not thinking of a series of Old Testament passages which included Isaiah 53? (Luke 24:25, 26; cf. Isa. 53:10-12).

When Philip *the evangelist* told the Ethiopian eunuch the evangel or good news of Jesus, was not his text taken from Isaiah 53? (Acts 8:32, 33; cf. Isa. 53:7, 8).

When Peter described Christ's sinlessness and vicarious suffering for his wandering sheep, did he not do so in the very terms of Isaiah 53? (I Peter 2:22-25; cf. Isa. 53:4, 5, 6, 9, 12).

When the author of Hebrews dwelt on Christ's self-sacrifice for many, was not his source Isaiah 53? (Heb. 9:28; cf. Isa. 53:12).

When to John on Patmos the Lamb revealed himself in visions, was it not *the slaughtered Lamb* of Isaiah 53? (Rev. 5:6, 12; 13:8; 14:5; cf. Isa. 53:7).

And so also when Paul proclaimed what he delighted to call "my gospel," did he not base it on God's glorious redemptive revelation found in principle even in the Old Testament, and did he not include Isaiah 53 among his sources? (Rom. 4:25; I Cor. 15:3; cf. Isa. 53:5; Rom. 10:16; cf. Isa. 52:7; 53:1). *Note that not a single verse of Isa. 53 is ignored in the New Testament!*

The *evangel of the new dispensation is that of the old dispensation, gloriously amplified.* The gospel of the Coming Redeemer is transformed into the gospel of the Redeemer who came, who is coming again, and who imparts salvation, full and free, *to every believer on a basis of perfect equality.*[62]

The following elements are included in the concept *gospel* as set forth by Paul:

(1) *Its Power*

Romans 1:16 states: "For I am not ashamed of *the gospel:* for it is *the power* ($\delta \acute{v}v\alpha\mu\iota s$, cf. our *dynamite*) *of God unto salvation* to every one who believes, to the Jew first and also to the Greek."

The person who accepts the gospel by a true and living faith is saved, delivered, reconciled, redeemed, justified, etc. See Rom 3:23, 24; 7:24, 25; 8:1; I Cor. 15:1, 2; II Cor. 5:18-21; I Tim. 1:15. Dynamite, by being *destructive,* can be very *constructive.* So is the gospel when it takes hold of a person.

---

[62] In Paul the noun *gospel* ($\epsilon\dot{v}\alpha\gamma\gamma\dot{\epsilon}\lambda\iota\sigma\nu$) occurs about 60 times; the verb ($\epsilon\dot{v}\alpha\gamma\gamma\epsilon\lambda\dot{\iota}\zeta\omega$) in the original, nontheological sense, *to bring or announce good news,* once (I Thess. 3:6), and in the theological sense, *to proclaim the divine message of salvation,* twenty times. In addition there is the noun *evangelist* ($\epsilon\dot{v}\alpha\gamma\gamma\epsilon\lambda\iota\sigma\tau\dot{\eta}s$). which Paul uses twice (Eph. 4:11; II Tim. 4:5); and the verb *to proclaim good news in advance* ($\pi\rho\sigma\epsilon\nu\alpha\gamma\gamma\epsilon\lambda\dot{\iota}\zeta\sigma\mu\alpha\iota$) which he uses once (Gal. 3:8).

(2) *Its Author*

The Author, both of salvation itself and of the gospel which promises salvation, is *God in Christ:*

"the gospel of God" (I Thess. 2:9).

"the gospel of Christ" (I Thess. 3:2).

Paul stresses the fact that his gospel is not man-made. The apostle has received it by revelation from God (Gal. 1:11, 12; 2:16). Man by nature is totally unable to devise a gospel or to save himself. He is dead through trespasses and sins, a child of wrath. His works have no merit unto salvation (Eph. 2:1, 5, 9). God, and he alone, can save him. From start to finish it is *God* who saves, never man.

(3) *Its Emphasis*

Accordingly, the gospel places all the emphasis on sovereign, unmerited *grace.* Paul calls it:

"the gospel of the grace of God" (Acts 20:24). Other Pauline passages in which this doctrine of the gospel of grace is set forth most beautifully are such as Rom. 3:23, 24; Eph. 2:6-10; and Titus 3:4-7.

(4) *Its Message*

What, then, is *the message* or *the news* which this gospel brings? What has *grace* done to effectuate salvation? This message centers in *Christ:*

"Now I make known to y o u, brothers, *the gospel* . . . that Christ died for our sins according to the scriptures; and that he was buried; and that he was raised on the third day according to the scriptures," etc. (I Cor. 15:1-11). See also Gal. 2:20: "Christ lives in me . . . loves me, and gave himself up for me." Hence also, "I have been crucified with Christ, have been raised with him, sit in heavenly places with him."

(5) *Its Implication*

The implication is clearly this, that the sinner should accept this gospel, that he should appropriate this salvation, *repenting* (II Cor. 7:10; II Tim. 2:25), and embracing Christ by living *faith:*

"For I am not ashamed of *the gospel:* for it is the power of God unto salvation to *every one who believes;* to the Jew first and also to the Greek. For in it the righteousness of God is revealed *from faith to faith;* as it is written, the just shall live *by faith*" (Rom. 1:16, 17). See also Gal. 3:11; Eph. 2:8; Phil. 2:12, 13. It is, therefore, definitely the "whosoever-*believes*" gospel.

(6) *Its Ambassadors*

Some have been set apart in a special way by God to proclaim this gospel. Thus, for example, Paul had been

"separated unto the gospel of God" (Rom. 1:1). The apostle was so deeply convinced of this and so thoroughly enthused about his solemn obligation that he cried out, "Woe to me if I preach not the gospel!" (I Cor. 9:16). In a broader sense all believers are ambassadors of the gospel of God's marvelous grace.

(7) *Its Appeal*

Since, then, apart from the gospel there is no salvation and no life that is truly to the glory of God, an earnest, emphatic, ringing appeal is addressed to men, urging them to be reconciled with God:

"We are ambassadors therefore for Christ, God as it were making his appeal through us. We beseech y o u for Christ's sake, be reconciled to God" (II Cor. 5:20).[63] This clearly is more than a mere *implication* (see 5 above). What is *implied* is also *urged*.

Are the Philippians living in harmony with this gospel? And are they doing this regardless of whether they are being watched by Paul? Hence, the apostle says, Only continue to exercise y o u r citizenship in a manner worthy of the gospel of Christ, **that whether I come and see y o u or am absent, I may hear of y o u that,** etc. It is certainly in harmony with Paul's compressed emotional style that we interpret these words as meaning, ". . . that whether I come and see y o u, or am absent and hear about y o u, I may learn that," etc.[64]

What the apostle hopes to learn with respect to the Philippians he expresses as follows: **that y o u are standing firm in one spirit, with one soul striving side by side for the faith of the gospel, and not frightened in anything by the adversaries.** We see here not only

What Paul Expects Of The Philippians
but also
What God Expects Of His Children

(1) *Their attitude toward God and his gospel must be one of Tenacity*

They must *stand fast* in the Lord, rooted in him, trusting him, loving him, hoping in him, clinging to the traditions, the authoritative teachings which they have received, the *faith* (body of redemptive truth) [65] that pertains to and is revealed in *the gospel.* For this idea of *standing firm* see also Rom. 14:4; Gal. 5:1; I Thess. 3:8; II Thess. 2:15; and especially the beautiful passage, I Cor. 16:13, 14. There must be no compromise with error. That Paul has in mind loyalty *to the Lord* is clear from the context (and see 4:1), and that this firmness must be exercised *over against the opponents or adversaries* and *in the midst of persecution* appears clearly from verses 28-30. Divine *preservation* does not cancel but implies human *perseverance.*

(2) *Their attitude toward each other must be one of Harmony*

---

[63] For the *contents* of the gospel-message see also N.T.C. on the Gospel according to John, Vol. I, pp. 139-142; for the concept *salvation* see N.T.C. on The Pastoral Epistles, pp. 76-82; and on *heralding* or *preaching* this gospel see N.T.C. on The Pastoral Epistles, pp. 309, 310.

[64] On the general subject of Abbreviated Style in the New Testament see N.T.C. on John, Volume I, p. 206.

[65] Used in this sense also elsewhere in Paul's epistles (Gal. 1:23; 6:10, and frequently in the Pastoral Epistles). See the discussion in N.T.C. on The Pastoral Epistles, pp. 11 and 12.

Note: "in one *spirit,* with one *soul* striving side by side." [66]

Paul's central thought here reminds one of a song popular in The Netherlands (I refer to *Eén in Geest en Streven*), which may be rendered as follows:

> One in our endeavor,
> One in song forever,
> One in word and deed,
> One in adoration,
> One in thank-oblation,
> One in praise: our creed.
> One glorious aim,
> Our goal the same
> One in strength and one in striving,
> Help from God deriving.
>
> Lift now hearts and voices
> While our soul rejoices
> In our God above.
> Render adoration,
> Grateful exultation
> for his changeless love.
> Bless, bless the Lord,
> To him accord
> Praise in song, in all our striving
> Help from God deriving.

This matter of Christian unity, active harmony, was much on Paul's mind as he wrote Philippians (see also Phil. 2:2, 3; 4:1). Conditions in the Philippian church were not entirely ideal in this respect. Are they *ever* ideal *anywhere?* For other passages in which the apostle stresses the desirability of believers acknowledging their oneness in Christ, living together in peace, and working together in harmony, see Rom. 12:5; 12:12; I Cor. 1:10; 10:17; II Cor. 13:11; Gal. 3:28; Eph. 2:11-22; 4:3, 4; 4:13. Note also what was said above on the subject of Christian "fellowship" (Phil. 1:5). The danger of mutual discord is pointed out in I Cor. 11:17-22; Gal. 5:15. Paul and Peter were in full agreement also on this point (see I Peter 3:8-12). The unity here envisioned is one of *striving or struggling side by side, like*

---

[66] Although it is true that when the word *spirit* ($\pi\nu\epsilon\tilde{\upsilon}\mu\alpha$) is used, the reference is often to man's power of grasping divine things, the thinking and reasoning mind, and that when the word *soul* ($\psi\upsilon\chi\acute{\eta}$) occurs, this same invisible substance is viewed as the seat of sensations, affections, desires, feeling and will, it is probably best to view the sequence "in one spirit, with one soul" as meaning "united in heart and soul," "with common purpose and ardor." (See also N.T.C. on I Thess. 5:23, pp. 146-150.)

gladiators, against a common foe. In Phil. 4:3 the apostle also speaks about those who struggled side by side with him. This struggle, moreover, is not only *against* a foe, but *for* the gospel-truth. Some people are always struggling *against*, never *for*. Paul is interested not only in fending off attacks, but also and mainly in spreading God's glorious redemptive truth which centers in Jesus Christ and salvation in him.

(3) *Their attitude toward the foe must be one of Intrepidity*

They must not be frightened, like a timid horse shying in view of an unexpected object.[67] Over against the adversaries the Philippians must show undaunted courage, never even for a moment becoming frightened as did Peter when he denied his Lord.

But who are these *adversaries?* Several commentaries simply skip this question. Some (for example, R. Johnstone, *Lectures on the Epistle of Paul to the Philippians,* p. 125; R. C. H. Lenski, *op. cit.,* p. 759) are positive that the opponents cannot have been Jews, but must have been pagans. The arguments for this view are as follows: Is it not true that the Jews in the Roman colony of Philippi were so few in number that Paul did not even find a synagogue there? Besides, does not the apostle state in verse 30 that the Philippians are engaged in *the same conflict* which they had seen Paul having and now hear him having? Surely, Paul suffered *Roman* imprisonment both at Philippi and now again at Rome!

In spite of these arguments others continue to adhere to the view that it is not at all necessary to exclude either Jew or Gentile, either legalist or sensualist, from the category of the adversaries which Paul has in mind. I believe that this is the right solution. We should permit Paul to explain his own terms. In other words, when in Chapter 3 he warns against *dogs, evil workers, the concision;* also against *the enemies of the cross of Christ, whose end is destruction, whose god is their belly, and whose glory is in their shame, who set their mind on earthly things,* then, unless the immediate context forbids, we must be willing to accept such descriptive terms as giving meaning and content to the term *the adversaries* here in 1:28. This all the more because in Chapter 3 the apostle states that *he is there repeating his previous warnings* (3:1). This is the proper procedure, unless we have solid evidence that Chapter 3 belongs to another letter. Such evidence is lacking.

It is a well-known fact that among *the Gentiles,* not only in Rome but also certainly in its *colonies,* etc., the early Christians were suspected of being atheists (because they worshipped no *visible gods*), haters of mankind, etc. In the pursuit of their daily vocations and in their social intercourse the followers of Jesus, who condemned all idol-worship and emperor-worship, were

---

[67] This does not necessarily mean, however, that Paul was thinking of a chariot-race. The word is applied not only to animals but also to people. Thus Polycrates says in Eusebius, *Ecclesiastical History* V. xxiv. 7 "I am not *frightened* at what is threatened us." For other sources see the entry πτύρω in L.N.T. (A. and G.).

subjected to all manner of hardships, and this was happening long before Christianity had been declared an illegal religion. Besides, the Gentile world of that day was steeped in immorality. The Church was still young. Many of its members had been drawn from these Gentile circles. There were tares among the wheat. It is therefore altogether probable that some would-be converts who had come out of an immoral environment distorted their new faith by making Christian liberty an excuse for license (cf. Rom. 3:8; 6:1; Jude 1). Whether some of these voluptuaries had actually become *members* of the Philippian church is an open question. At any rate, they constituted a real threat. They were *adversaries*.

But what about *the Jews?* Is it really true that when Paul wrote about *the adversaries* he was altogether leaving them out of consideration? Is it not natural to assume that he included at least those Jews who had nominally accepted Jesus, but refused to see in him the *complete Savior?* In Chapter 3 he warns the church against Jewish, that is *Judaistic,* errorists ("the concision"). He does this in language that is clear and cutting (3:2). Is it psychologically probable that in this short epistle the opponents who are condemned in such scathing terms in Chapter 3 would be totally absent from the mind of the writer when in Chapter 1 he makes mention of the *adversaries?* Besides, the readily explainable fewness of the Jews in Philippi in the year when this church was founded (about 51/52) does not prove that a full decade later (62/63), when this letter to the Philippians was written, the Jews (Judaizers) could not have been *present or passing through in sufficient numbers* to have become a menace. Cf. Acts 15:1. If Thessalonica was troubled by Jews A. D. 51/52, why could not nearby Philippi be troubled by Judaizers A. D. 62/63? [68]

---

[68] The fortunes of the Jews under various political rulers were constantly changing. Under Augustus 27 B. C. – A. D. 14) and Tiberius (14-37) the Jews enjoyed a measure of tolerance. At the beginning of the reign of Caligula (37-41) they were even somewhat optimistic. Did they not have a good friend at court? But when that emperor, driven by insane ambition, demanded divine honor, a real clash was in the making, and would have occurred had not his death intervened. Under Claudius (41-54) their fortunes varied. Their tumultuous action in Rome led to *the order* for their expulsion from that city (Acts 18:2, probably about the year 49/50). Shortly after this, Paul came to *the Roman colony* of Philippi and not surprisingly found few Jews there. But does this prove that also afterward the Jewish population in Rome and its colonies remained at a minimum? According to the testimony of Cassius Dio it is by no means true that all the Jews were even actually driven out of Rome. At any rate, when Paul arrives in Rome for his first Roman imprisonment the Jews are living there in goodly numbers (Acts 28:17-28). Would it have been so strange if some Jews, including *nominal* Christians, had entered or re-entered Philippi, with the purpose of stopping a few days to make propaganda for their views, or of establishing a temporary or even a more or less permanent residence there? This at any rate would seem to be a more obvious explanation of Phil. 3.2 than that of those who, having based too much on Acts 16:13, regard Phil. 3:2 as nothing but *prophecy!* When Paul wrote Philippians (A. D. 62/63) the reigning emperor was Nero (54-68). He was at first rather reason-

Moreover, whether the struggle is against Jew or Gentile, legalist or sensualist, it is "the same conflict" in any case. See on verse 30. Let not the Philippian church be frightened by these enemies of the gospel.

Now of this calm endurance and undaunted courage in the face of formidable adversaries the apostle says **which with respect to them is a clear sign of destruction, but of y o u r salvation.**[69] Paul is ever cognizant of the higher hand that rules the affairs of men (see N.T.C. on I Thess. 1:3, 4). The failure of the adversaries to intimidate believers, and the latter's fearlessness, is *proof* that God is carrying out his program. The word which I have rendered *clear sign* occurs also in Rom. 3:25, 26; II Cor. 8:24 (its only other New Testament occurrences), and in each case has the meaning of *proof*, here in Phil. 1:28 with the added touch of *prophecy*. The point is not that the adversaries themselves see this, though perhaps they may have a dim awareness of it, but that for God's children this intrepidity on their own part is solid evidence of the doom which threatens their enemies unless they repent, and of their own salvation, now in principle and by and by in perfection. For the concept *salvation* see N.T.C. on I Tim. 1:15. *Destruction* or *perdition* is in every way the opposite of *salvation*. The reason why this undaunted courage is proof of salvation and of invincibility is that it is not man-made. Hence, Paul adds **and this**[70] **from God.** If intrepidity

---

able and tolerant. And *even after* the celebrated quinquennium or first five years (54-58), Poppaea Sabina, who proved to be Nero's evil star, a very ambitious and scheming woman who was regarded by the Jews as a proselyte to their religion, exerted enough influence upon the emperor to protect the Jews. The Jewish faith was regarded as a *religio licita* (religion to be tolerated). The blame for the devastating conflagration of Rome during the night of the 18th to the 19th of July 64 was by Nero placed not on the Jews but on the Christians. *Christianity* became a *religio illicita* (a religion not to be tolerated). Poppaea died (as a result of a cruel kick inflicted by Nero in a fit of rage?) in the year 65. But even before her death, Nero's character had shown evidences of deterioration. Led by evil counsellors he had become very extravagant. The great fire added to the expenses of the empire. As a result, the taxation of conquered peoples, including the Jews, became more and more unbearable. Related to this was the maladministration of Gessius Florus in Judea, and the consequent Jewish insurrection which resulted in the fall of Jerusalem (66-70).

If this brief summary of historical detail is borne in mind, it will be understood why the scarcity of Jews in Philippi shortly after the edict of Claudius cannot be used to prove the theory that when Paul wrote Philippians a full decade later and spoke about *the adversaries* he could not have been thinking about Jews (who had nominally accepted Christ; hence, Judaizers) as well as Gentiles. Besides, Phil. 3:2 remains an insuperable barrier to this view.

[69] The reading upon which the A.V. is based — "to them of perdition . . . to you of salvation" instead of "of y o u r salvation" is clearly a change for the sake of balancing the clauses, smoothness of style.

[70] To what exactly does τοῦτο refer? There has been much controversy on this point. According to many the antecedant is ἔνδειξις. The sense, as some of these interpreters see it, is something like this: in order to know what will happen to them, believers do not need to wait, like stricken gladiators, for a sign — say, the flick of a thumb or the wave of a handkerchief — from the fickle crowd. They get

were merely a homemade article, a state of mind into which a person enters without divine assistance, it would prove nothing as to *salvation*. But if, without in any way cancelling human responsibility, such fearlessness can and must be considered a gift of God, the product of his Spirit working in the heart, then certainly the conclusion follows that he who began a good work will carry it on toward completion (see the context, Phil. 1:6). This is entirely in the spirit of Ps. 27:1-3; 56:11; Rom. 8:31-39.

29, 30. What follows in these verses is elaboration of what has already been said. The proposition "Fearlessness is a gift of God, hence proof of salvation," is true "For," or "Seeing that," etc. Says Paul, **For to y o u it has been granted in behalf of Christ not only to believe in him but also to suffer in his behalf.** It has been *granted* to y o u, says Paul; that is, as *a privilege*, a gift of God's *grace*. The double blessing is this: in behalf of Christ not only to believe in him but also to suffer in his behalf.

First, *to believe in him,* that is, to rest on Christ, surrendering oneself to his loving heart, depending on his accomplished mediatorial work. The form of the expression as used in the original shows that here genuine, personal trust in the Anointed One is meant. (See also N.T.C. on John, Vol. I, pp. 76, 77, 141, footnote 83; Vol. II, p. 51.) Whether or not one regards Eph. 2:8 as proof for the proposition that such faith is God's gift, the conclusion is at any rate inescapable that here in Phil. 1:29 faith — not only its inception but also its continued activity — is so regarded. It is at one and the same time God's gift and man's responsibility.

Secondly, *to suffer in his behalf*. The emphasis falls on this in the present connection. There are *adversaries* who cause believers to suffer. Now suffering is not a privilege *in itself*. One should not court suffering. But suffering *in behalf of Christ,* in the interest of him and his gospel is different. Such suffering is indeed a blessing, a gracious privilege (Acts 5:41), because:

a. It brings Christ nearer to the soul of the Christian. In his suffering for Christ's sake the believer begins to understand the One who suffered redemp-

---

their *sign* directly from God. Others, however, hesitate to accept the view which regards ἔνδειξις as antecedant. With some this hesitancy seems to be connected with the idea that the neuter demonstrative pronoun τοῦτο cannot very well refer to a feminine noun. That theory, however, is grammatically debatable. Better, it would seem to me, is the argument that Paul does not elsewhere use the word ἔνδειξις in any sense other than *proof, positive evidence,* a sense which, with the added touch of *prophecy,* also fits very well in the present context. The strongest argument for the position that τοῦτο refers here not so much to a single word as to the entire idea of the believers' standing firm is supplied by the context, both preceding and following. Note: "standing firm in one spirit . . . not frightened in anything by the adversaries . . . and this from God. *For* to y o u it has been granted (or 'graciously, freely granted') in behalf of Christ not only to believe in him but also to suffer in his behalf." This firmness, this willingness to suffer for Christ and his cause, is God's gracious gift to the church.

tively for him and receives the sweetness of his enduring fellowship. It is "without the gate" that God's child, reproached by the enemy, meets his Lord (Heb. 13:13). See also such other wonderful passages as Job 42:5, 6; Psalm 119:67; II Cor. 4:10; Gal. 6:17; Heb. 12:6.

b. Accordingly, it brings assurance of salvation, the conviction that the Spirit of glory and the Spirit of God rests upon the sufferer (I Peter 4:14; cf. John 15:19-21).

c. It will be rewarded in the hereafter (Rom. 8:18; II Cor. 4:17; II Tim. 2:12; 4:7, 8; I Peter 4:13).

d. It is often a means of winning unbelievers for Christ and of encouraging fellow-believers (that thought is stressed in the very context; see Phil. 1:12-14).

e. By means of all these avenues it leads to the frustration of Satan (book of Job) and the glorification of God (Acts 9:16).

In a most amiable manner Paul now comforts the Philippians by telling them that they are standing on common ground with him. This is a tactful little touch which we often find in Paul's letters. It is beautiful because it is genuine. See I Thess. 1:6; 3:3; II Tim. 1:8; 3:10-15; 4:5-8; Titus 1:4, to mention only a few instances. Cf. N.T.C. on I and II Thessalonians, pp. 28, 29. Says Paul, with reference to the believing and suffering Philippians: **being engaged in the same conflict which y o u saw me having and now hear me having** (literally, "the same conflict having which y o u saw in me and now hear in me").

In Philippi Paul had been "advertised" by a demon-possessed girl, had been slandered, mobbed, stripped, flogged, thrown into a dungeon, his feet locked in gruesome stocks. The devil was behind all this. Influenced by Satan the masters of the slave-girl, the infuriated rabble, and many others had joined in inflicting upon him this "shameful treatment" (Acts 16:16-24; I Thess. 2:2; see also Introduction III). The Philippians had *seen* this conflict between the kingdom of light and that of darkness. And now, through this very letter (see, for example, Phil. 1:12-17; 4:14), and through Epaphroditus (Phil. 2:25-30), they *are hearing* about Paul's bonds and about those people who, encouraged by Satan, were raising up affliction for him in his bonds. For Paul it was like being engaged in a gladiatorial *contest* or *conflict*, a life or death *fight* or *struggle*.[71] It implied prodigious exertion of energy against that very powerful foe, namely, Satan. And the Philippians, vexed in a variety of ways by idol-and-emperor-worshippers, legalistic Judaists, paganistic sensualists, quarelling church-members, all of these the result of Satanic influence, were engaged in *the same conflict*. The conflict is *the same* because at bottom the arch-enemy is the same! Even more definitely, as Paul himself in this very context stresses by saying it *twice*, the conflict

---

[71] Paul's epistles contain numerous references to athletic and gladiatorial contests. See N.T.C. on The Pastoral Epistles, pp. 150, 151, 203, 314, 315.

is the same because it is "in behalf of Christ," in the interest of his cause and kingdom. If then the suffering which this conflict brings upon them is God's gracious gift, the victory is sure, both for Paul and for them. Thus, by divine inspiration, speaks The Optimistic Prisoner.

Synthesis of 1:12-30

In the first subdivision of this section Paul points out that, far from what others may be saying, he himself regards his imprisonment as having turned out for the advantage of the gospel. He speaks, therefore, as *optimistic prisoner*. Road-blocks set up by Satan have become stepping-stones for the progress of the message of salvation. Paul's bonds have had a good effect, *first* on the members of *the praetorian guard,* who have begun to see that this noted prisoner is not a criminal at all but is suffering as a proponent of a very worthy cause, namely, that of Christ and his gospel. From the mouths of the guards Rome's population in general has heard about this and has begun to take an interest in the gospel. *Secondly, believers in Rome,* too, though fearful at first, have of late received courage, so that they are telling the message of God without being afraid.

This does not mean, however, that all is wonderful. *Rome's heralds of salvation,* preachers of the gospel, can be divided into two classes. Some are filled with envy and would just as soon add to Paul's suffering, if only they can harvest popular acclaim. Others, however, proclaim the gospel from good will, being motivated by love both for God and for Paul. The thing that really matters, though, is this, that in every way Christ is being proclaimed. In this Paul rejoices.

In the second subdivision the optimistic prisoner expresses his deep conviction that whatever happens to him, whether it be life or death, acquittal or condemnation, Christ will be magnified in his (Paul's) person. Though he desires to be with Christ, regarding this as being very far better, yet he is willing to place the need of the Philippians above his own immediate enjoyment of eternal bliss.

In the final subdivision Paul urges upon the addressees the spirit of:

a. *tenacity.* Paul's absence or presence should make no difference. They should *stand firm,* and continue to exercise their heavenly citizenship in a manner worthy of the gospel of Christ.

b. *unity:* "with *one* soul striving side by side for the faith of the gospel."

c. *intrepidity.* Whether the enemies be emperor-worshipers, Judaizers, sensualists, or whoever they may be, let the God-given fearlessness of the Philippians be a double sign, namely, of the destruction of their enemies and of their own salvation. Let them meditate on the fact that suffering in behalf of Christ is a privilege, and that Paul himself shares with them in this suffering, as they know very well.

PHILIPPIANS

31 The following sources have been consulted:
Campbell, J. Y., "*Koinonia* and its Cognates in the New Testament," *JBL* 51 (1932) 352-380.
Cranfield, C. E. B., art. "Fellowship, Communion," in *A Theological Word Book of the Bible* (A. Richardson, editor), New York, 1952.
Endenburg, P. J. T., *Koinonia bij de Grieken in den klassieken tijd*, 1937.
Ford, H. W., art. "The New Testament Conception of Fellowship," Shane Quarterly 6 (1945), 188-215.
Groenewald, E. P., *Koinonia (gemeenskap) bij Paulus*, doctoral dissertation, Amsterdam, 1932.
Hauck, D. F., entry κοινός and cognates, Th.W.N.T., Vol. III, pp. 789–810.
Jourdan, G. V., "*Koinonia* in I Cor. 10:16," *JBL* 67 (1938), 111-124.
L.N.T. (Th.) entries κοινός and cognates.
L.N.T. (A. and G.) entries κοινός and cognates.
Liddell and Scott, *Greek-English Lexicon*, Oxford, 1940, entries κοινός and cognates.
M. M., entries κοινός and cognates.
National Herald English-Greek, Greek-English Dictionary, entries κοινός and cognates.
Tenney, M. C., *Philippians, the Gospel at Work*, Grand Rapids, 956, pp. 35-50.

The concept *koinonia — fellowship* or *communion* — merits more than passing notice. Examples of usage:
Plato uses the phrase: "the dissolution of a *koinonia*" (*business-partnership, Republic*, 343 D).
He also writes, "Where there is no *koinonia (communion)*, there can be no friendship" (*Gorgias*, 507 E).
The word *koinonia* lives on in modern Greek in various meanings; such as *society, communication*, and (holy) *communion*.
Throughout it has also been used to indicate *the marriage-bond*.
Does the term also indicate fellowhip between God (or the gods) and men?
In ancient Greece, since in so many respects the gods resembled men, a certain amount of contact between the two was considered possible. In fact, the Age of Fable records many instances of such contact.
Even when in the more enlightened circles mythology was shorn of its cruder elements, the idea of fellowship between the gods and men persisted. For example, Plato wrote "Wise men tell us, Callicles, that *heaven and earth and gods and men* are held together by *koinonia* (fellowship) and friendship . . . and that is the reason, my friend, why they call the whole of this world *order* (kosmos) . . ." (*Gorgias*, 508 A).
Plato evidently had no eye for the fact that sin has brought about *separation* between God and man. Apart from special revelation and from saving faith that philosopher was not able to appreciate the truth with respect to the sovereign majesty and holiness of God, on the one hand, and the enormity of sin, on the other. Fellowship between the divine and the human seemed altogether normal and natural to the Greek, for the simple reason that his mind, darkened by sin, was unable to discover the truth.
Accordingly, between the teachings of Plato and those of the Old Testament there is a sharp contrast. The Old Testament stresses *the distance* between God and man. Jehovah is the Holy One. He is separate from all that is sinful, and exalted above all that is weak. He is seated above all people and even above all the gods, which are but vanities. He is unsearchable in his judgments and "terrible" in his mighty acts (Ps. 47:2; 65:5; 66:3, 5; 68:35; 99:3; Is. 61:1-5; 45:15; 55:8, 9; etc.). In fact, the transcendence of God is stressed to such an extent that although the Hebrews did have words indicative of fellowship (from the root ḥ b r; e.g., Prov. 28:24; Is. 1:23), these words were never used to indicate the relation between God and

93

man (Ps. 94:20 is a very doubtful exception). Moreover, the LXX never employs the word *koinonia* to describe any communion between the two.

Nevertheless, the *existence* as such, of the fellowship, even during the old dispensation, must be granted. Though after the entrance of sin with its devastating effect upon the human race, such communion was no longer *natural*, it was present *as a special gift of God to his children*. Thus, Enoch walks with God (Gen. 5:22). Jehovah knows Moses face to face (Deut. 34:10). Jehovah is his people's Shepherd (Ps. 23). He dwells in the hearts of those who are of a contrite and humble spirit (Is. 57:15). He loves, pities, and redeems his own, and even hides them in his own pavillion (Ps. 103:13, 14; Is. 63:9; Ps. 27:5). But *the word koinonia* is not used to indicate this divinely bestowed favor.

As we turn to the New Testament we observe that it was *the incarnation of the Son,* so that God came to dwell *with* men, and *the outpouring of the Holy Spirit,* so that God came to dwell *in* men, that gave the word *koinonia* its full scope. It was Jesus who spoke of himself as the Vine and of his followers as the Branches, adding, "Abide in me, and I (will abide) in y o u." See N.T.C. on John, Vol. II, pp. 293-304 (on John 15:1-11). The disciple whom Jesus loved (John) was glad to record this marvelous truth. It was also he who used the word *koinonia* no less than four times in the first chapter of his first epistle (twice in verse 3, once each in verses 6 and 7).

Nevertheless, it was not John but Paul who, under the guidance of the Spirit, brought this concept to its fullest development. He uses the word *koinonia* no less than thirteen times (Rom. 15:26; I Cor. 1:9; 10:16, twice, II Cor. 6:14; 8:4; 9:13; 13:14; Gal. 2:9; Phil. 1:5; 2:1; 3:10; and Philem. 6). The only remaining passages of the New Testament (i.e., outside of John and Paul) in which the word appears are Acts 2:42 and Heb. 13:16.

In reality the stress which *Paul* places on this concept is even more striking than has been indicated in the comparative statistics already given. In summary,

(a) He uses *koinonia* more than twice as often as all the other New Testament authors combined.

(b) He employs *koinonos,* in the sense of *participant, sharer* (I Cor. 10:18; II Cor. 1:7) or *partner* (I Cor. 10:20; II Cor. 8:23; Philem. 17). This word occurs in Paul's letters alone as often as in all the rest of the New Testament together (Matt. 23:30; Luke 5:10; Heb. 10:23; I Peter 5:1; II Peter 1:4).

(c) Paul also has *sun-koinonos,* co-sharer, using this word three out of the four times that it occurs in the New Testament (Rom. 11:17; I Cor. 9:23; Phil. 1:7; only other instance of its use: Rev. 1:9).

(d) The main verb is *koinoneo,* occurring in Paul's epistles five out of a total of eight times: have a share in (Rom. 15:27; I Tim. 5:22); give a share to (Rom. 12:13; Gal. 6:6); enter into partnership with (Phil. 4:15). The only other occurrences are in Heb. 2:14; I Peter 4:13; and II John 11.

(e) The related compound is *sun-koinoneo,* used by Paul two out of three times: to share with someone in something (Phil. 4:14); to share in something (Eph. 5:11) non-Pauline occurrence: Rev. 18:4.

(f) Finally, there is *koinonikos,* ready to share. Paul is the only New Testament writer who used this word (I Tim. 6:18).

Even this falls short of being a full summary of the meaning which Paul poured into the idea of the fellowship, as a study of the derivation of the word *koinonia* will now show. It comes from *koinos,* which (not only means but) is by etymologists related to our English word *common. Koinonia,* then, is basically a *community-relationship. It is a sharing together; a having a share, giving a share, fellowship:* 1. *Anteilhaben,* 2. *Anteilgeben,* 3. *Gemeinschaft* (thus, D. F. Hauck, Th.W.N.T., Vol. III, p. 798). Experts in word-derivation connect *koinos* with *xyn* or *syn* (ξύν, σύν), related to the Latin *cum,* English *syn-, con-,* meaning *with, together with, joined (joint-, fellow-).* Thus in English we have:

*sym*pathy (a feeling *with* another, *fellow*-feeling), *sym*phony, *syn*agogue, *syn*chronism, etc.

*con*currence (an occurring *together*), *con*nect, *com*mon, *com*munity, etc.

Accordingly, in order to obtain a comprehensive view of Paul's use of the word *koinonia* one should take note of the numerous *syn*-compounds (words which in the original begin with the prefix *syn*-), which occur in his letters.

First we have the basic idea: *Believers have fellowship "with" Christ.* They suffer *with* Christ, have been crucified *with* him, died *with* him, were buried *with* him (Rom. 8:17; 6:6; 6:8; cf. II Tim. 2:11; Rom. 6:4; Col. 2:12). But they also are made alive *with* Christ, are raised *with* him, are joint-heirs *with* him, glorified *with* him, enthroned *with* him, and reign *with* him (Col. 2:13; Col. 3:1; Rom. 8:17; II Tim. 2:12. and cf. Rev. 20:4).

Then, there is the implied idea: *Believers have fellowship "with" each other.* They are *joint*-partakers (Phil. 1:7, *joint*-imitators (3:17): *joint*-souled (2:2); *jointly* striving (1:27; 4:11) *jointly* rejoicing (2:17, 18); *joint*- (or *fellow*-) workers (2:25; 34:3). See also the following: *jointly* comforted (Rom. 1:12); *jointly* refreshed (15:32); *joint*- (*fellow*-) prisoners (16:7); *fellow*-citizens (Eph. 2:19); *jointly* framed (2:21); *jointly* built (2:21); *fellow*-heirs, *fellow*-members, and *fellow*-sharers (3:6). Paul can hardly conceive of *Christians* holding themselves aloof from other *Christians!*

Finally, all of this beautifully harmonizes with:

a. the Pauline use of the phrase "in Christ" (or "in him," etc.). *Unitedly* believers are *in* Christ, and he is *in* them.

b. the Pauline metaphor of the body, its head, and its members (Rom. 12:3-8; I Cor. 12:12-31; Eph. 4:16).

c. the Pauline metaphor of the temple with its chief cornerstone and its many stones (Eph. 2:19-22; cf. I Peter 2:4-7).

d. the Pauline teaching (received from the Lord) concerning the Lord's Supper, in which the fellowship of believers with Christ, and with one another, is beautifully set forth (see especially I Cor. 10:17).

Summary of Chapter 2

Paul, the Humble Cross-bearer

by an appeal to a fourfold incentive exhorting the Philippians to live the life of *oneness, lowliness,* and *helpfulness,*
after the example of Christ Jesus,
and to shine as lights in the midst of a wicked world, thereby filling the hearts of Paul and of themselves with joy.

2:1-4   The Stirring Appeal with fourfold incentive and threefold directive.

2:5-11   The Example of Christ.

2:12-18 Shining lights producing mutual joy.

CHAPTER II

2   1 If therefore (there is) any encouragement in Christ, if any persuasive appeal springing from love, if any fellowship of the Spirit, if any tender mercy and compassion, 2 make full (the measure of) my joy by being of the same mind, having the same love, with souls united setting y o u r minds on unity; 3 (doing) nothing from selfish ambition or from empty conceit, but in humble-mindedness each counting the other better than himself, 4 each looking not (only) to his own interests but also to the interests of others.

2:1-4

A new section begins here, in which Paul reveals himself as ready to be poured out as a libation upon the sacrificial offering of the faith of the Philippians (see verse 17). Accordingly, he appears here as *the Humble Cross-bearer,* and his very humility is shown in this, that he focusses attention not *on* himself but *away from* himself, *on Christ,* the unique Cross-bearer (verses 5-11).

But though this is indeed a new section, it is closely connected with that which precedes. In the closing paragraph of Chapter 1 the apostle had expressed the ardent wish that he might learn that the Philippians "are standing firm in one spirit, with one soul striving side by side for the faith of the gospel" (verse 27). In the present section (2:1-11) he re-emphasizes the necessity of *oneness* among the brothers, a quality that is possible only then when there is true *lowliness* of mind and *helpfulness* of disposition.

Verses 1-4 are in the nature of a stirring appeal. The intensity of this appeal or plea would seem to indicate that there was among the Philippians, at least among some of them, a measure of personal strife, perhaps for ecclesiastical honor or preferment.

I. *The Humble Cross-bearer's Stirring Appeal*

A. *Its Fourfold Incentive*

1. If then (there is) any encouragement in Christ, if any persuasive appeal springing from love, if any fellowship of the Spirit, if any tender mercy and compassion. . . .

To be sure, the church of Philippi was characterized by many excellent qualities. Paul calls its members, "my brothers, beloved and longed for, my joy and crown" (Phil. 4:1). Warmly he praises them for their fellowship in the gospel and for their generosity (Phil. 1:5; 4:10, 14-18). But, as is often the case, the "domestic affairs" of the church were not entirely as ideal as were the "foreign affairs." There was some trouble on the Home Front. Did some of the members see too much of each other? Were they getting on each other's nerves? Were some beginning to exaggerate the weaknesses and to minimize the virtues of other church-members? At any rate, not only Abraham (Gen. 13:7, 8) and James (James 3:16) were acquainted with the disastrous results of disunion, but so was also Paul (Rom. 13:13; I Cor. 3:3; Gal. 5:20; I Tim. 6:4). Brothers *attacking* or even just *belittling* each other make a sorry spectacle before the world. Their inner spiritual growth is retarded and their witness to the world is weakened.

This evil often results from inconsistency. On the one hand men will give glowing accounts of the blessings which they have received since they became Christians and of their spiritual experiences. On the other hand, among *some* of them the fruits of gratitude for all these favors are not particularly impressive *in one area;* namely, *at home.* Accordingly, the main thrust of what the apostle is saying is this: If then y o u receive any *help* or *encouragement* or *comfort* [72] from y o u r vital union with Christ, and if *the love* of Christ toward y o u does at all provide y o u with an incentive for action; if, moreover, y o u are at all rejoicing in *the marvelous Spirit-fellowship,*[73] and if y o u have any [74] experience of *the tender mercy and compassion* [75] of Christ, then prove y o u r gratitude for all this by loving

---

[72] The word is παράκλησις. For this meaning see also II Cor. 1:4-7; 7:4, 13; Philem. 7; II Thess. 2:16. Cf. N.T.C. on I and II Thessalonians, p. 62, and 189; and on John, Vol. II, p. 276

[73] This genitive transcends both objective and subjective; one might call it adjectival. That it is a fellowship *with* the Holy Spirit, an actual participation in that Spirit and in all his benefits cannot be doubted (cf. I Cor. 10:16; I John 1:3). But Paul also here regards it as the *gift* of the Spirit, just as he here considers the *persuasive appeal* as springing from love, and just as in II Cor. 13:13 he views *grace* as being the gift of the Lord Jesus Christ, *love* the gift of the Father, and *fellowship* the gift of the Holy Spirit. For a discussion of the fellowship see above under Phil. 1:5.

[74] The majority of the oldest manuscripts has τις. Is this an error of an early transcriber (for τινα or else for τι, the τι changed to τις by accidental repetition of the first letter of the following word)? See J. B. Lightfoot, *op. cit.,* p. 108; A. T. Robertson, *Word Pictures,* Vol. IV, p. 443. No better explanation has as yet been advanced. Lenski's defense of the reading τις, by interpreting the passage as if the meaning were, "If any such fellowship, let it be tender mercies and compassions," and so also in the preceding line, "if any fellowship, let it be of spirit," does not satisfy. Paul does not thus separate *fellowship* and *spirit.* The expression κοινωνία πνεύματος is a unit as is κοινωνία τοῦ ἁγίου πνεύματος in II Cor. 13:13.

[75] Literally "tender mercie*s* (deeply felt affections) and compassion*s.* For the literal meaning of σπλάγχνα and the argument resulting from it see on Phil. 1:8.

y o u r brothers and sisters *at home!* (that is what the threefold directive amounts to, as will become clear). All true Christian activity begins at home, as the Gadarene demoniac discovered (Mark 5:18-20).

Note: Paul says "If," not as if he doubts whether the condition is really true, but simply to emphasize that when the condition is present, the conclusion should also be present. One might translate, "If then (there is) any encouragement in Christ, as there surely is, if any persuasive appeal springing from love, as there surely is, . . . make full (the measure of) my joy."

B. *Its Threefold Directive*

2-4. The conclusion is a very natural one: "If then to any extent y o u have all these experiences and share in these benefits, then . . ." and here follows the threefold directive. Not really three directives, but a *threefold* directive: essentially the command is *one*, yet *three* graces, very closely related, can be distinguished. The three are:

Verse 2: *oneness*
Verse 3: *lowliness* (of mind or disposition)
Verse 4: *helpfulness*

Paul says, **make full (the measure of) my joy.** The manner in which he thus prefaces the threefold directive is touching. There was joy in the heart of the apostle (Phil. 1:4; 4:10). The Philippians, because of their many virtues, had been a source of this joy. But its measure was not yet full. A higher degree of oneness, lowliness, and helpfulness on the Home Front can supply what is still lacking in Paul's cup of joy. While none of the Philippians would have been able to claim perfection in these virtues, in the case of some the lack was rather noticeable (see on 4:2). This is Paul's deep concern. Not speedy release from prison but the spiritual progress of the Philippians — of *all* of them — is his chief desire. This shows how big-hearted he is.

(1) *Oneness*

Paul continues . . . **by being of the same mind, having the same love, with souls united setting y o u r minds on unity.**[76] Read what has been said with respect to the general theme of oneness or harmony (see on Phil. 1:27, 28). *The mind or inner disposition* is basic. This fundamental attitude will reveal itself by having *the same love* (for God in Christ, hence for fellow-members, with emphasis on the latter in the present connection), and by setting their minds on *the one*, that is, on *oneness* or *unity*.

Note that according to the context the oneness for which Paul pleads is of a distinctly spiritual nature. It is a oneness in disposition, love, and aim

---

[76] The harmonious connection between the elements of this lengthy apodosis would seem to demand that no comma be inserted after σύμψυχοι. The construction then is as follows: modifying *be of the same mind* are the four participles *having, minding* ("setting y o u r mind on"), *counting*, and *looking*.

(see also N.T.C. on John 17:21). It is the oneness set forth so strikingly in Ps. 133.

(2) Lowliness

Oneness cannot be achieved without lowliness, that is humility. Hence, Paul continues: **(doing)** [77] **nothing from selfish ambition or from empty conceit.** If everyone is constantly thinking of himself alone, how can unity ever be brought about? The Philippians must not be actuated by unholy rivalry, by selfish motives, craving honor and prestige for themselves, like certain preachers in Rome (see on Phil. 1:17, where the identical word — selfish ambition — is used). Selfish ambition and empty conceit (cf. Gal. 5:26) go together, for "the emptier the head the louder the boast." As often so here also Paul balances a negative with a positive formulation of the same idea. Thus, the thought advances to: **but in humble-mindedness each counting the other better than himself.** The word used in the original and here rendered *humble-mindedness* or *lowliness* (of disposition) was by non-Christians used in an evil sense (cowardliness, meanness; see Josephus, *Jewish War* IV.494; *Epictetus* III.24.56). When grace changes the heart, submission out of fear changes to submission out of love, and true *humility* is born. By Paul this virtue is associated with those of tenderheartedness, kindness, forbearance, longsuffering, meekness (Acts 20:19; Eph. 4:2; Col. 3:12). It is the happy condition which arises when in a church each member counts the other to be better than himself. Thus the members, filled with tender affection, will be outdoing one another in showing honor (Rom. 12:10).

But is not this rule impracticable? How can a man who knows that he is industrious regard the rather lazy fellow-member as being better than himself? The answer will probably be somewhat along this line:

a. The rule does not mean that one must consider *every* fellow-member to be *in every respect* wiser, abler, and nobler than he is himself.

b. As a general principle the rule certainly should control our lives, for while to a certain extent (never *completely,* see Psalm 139:23, 24; Jer. 17:9) a Christian is able to scrutinize *his own* motives (I Cor. 11:28, 31), and knows that they are not always good or unmixed, which knowledge leads him at times to utter the prayer, "O Lord, forgive my *good deeds!*" he has no right to regard *as evil* the motives of his brothers and sisters in the Lord. Unless a consistently wicked pattern is clearly evident in the life of one who has with his mouth confessed the Lord, that individual's outwardly good deeds must be ascribed to *good* and never to *evil* motives. On this basis it clearly follows that a truly humble child of God, who has learned to know *himself* sufficiently so that at times he utters the cry of the publican (Luke

---

[77] Or *minding,* that is, *contemplating,* if φρονοῦντες instead of ποιοῦντες is to be supplied here, from the immediately preceding clause.

18:13), or of Paul (Rom. 7:24), will regard *others* to be indeed better than himself. And not only *better* but *in certain respects abler,* for the Lord has distributed his gifts (I Cor. 12). There is generally something, of value to the kingdom, which the brother or sister can do better than y o u or I.

It is easy to see that when this spirit of *genuine* mutual regard and appreciation is fostered, unity will result. True Christianity is still the best answer to the question, "How can I win friends and influence people?" And the ecumenicity which it proclaims is the only kind that is really worthwhile.

It is probably not too bold an assertion to say that Paul himself had grown in this grace of humble-mindedness. He who during his third missionary journey called himself "the least of the apostles" (I Cor. 15:9), styled himself "the very least of all saints" during his first Roman imprisonment (Eph. 3:8), and a little later, during the period that intervened between his first and second Roman imprisonments, climaxed these humble self-descriptions by designating himself "chief of sinners" (I Tim. 1:15).

It took a humble cross-bearer to urge humble-mindedness. Is not Paul's humility also one of the reasons why even in the midst of his imprisonment, facing a verdict, he was filled with joy? The man who has learned to view himself as a great sinner before God appreciates God's saving grace, and thanks God even in the midst of his tears.

(3) Helpfulness

The apostle concludes this paragraph by adding **Each looking not (only) to his own interests but also to the interests of others.**

This follows from the immediately preceding. If one regards the brother very highly, he will wish to look to his interests in order to help him in every possible way. The apostle surely implies that a believer should look to his own interests. But he should obey the command, "You must love your neighbor as yourself" (Matt. 19:19), a commandment which receives added stress when the neighbor is a brother in Christ (John 13:34; Gal. 6:10). The more one realizes how fervently Christ loved the brother, and went all out to save him, the more he will wish to advance that brother's interests. Thus, too, true unity will be promoted, and before the world the glorious fellowship will begin to stand out in all its beauty, as a mighty testimony.[78]

---

5 In y o u r inner being continue to set y o u r mind on *this,* which (is) also in Christ Jesus, 6 who, though existing in the form of God, did not count his existence-in-a-manner-equal-to-God something to cling to, 7 but emptied himself, as he took on the form of a servant, and became like human beings. 8 So, recognized in fashion as a human being, he humbled himself and became obedient even to the extent of death; yes, death by a cross.

---

[78] See the poem "Living For Others," by Charles E. Orr, in *Treasures of Poetry,* published by the Gospel Trumpet Co., Anderson, Indiana, 1913, p. 221.

9 Therefore God raised him to the loftiest heights and bestowed on him the name that is above every name, 10 that in the name of Jesus every knee should bend, of those in heaven, and of those on earth, and of those under the earth, 11 and that every tongue should confess to the glory of God the Father that Jesus Christ is Lord.

2:5-11

By means of *a fourfold incentive* Paul has urged the Philippians to be obedient to *the threefold directive,* namely, that they should manifest to one another the spirit of oneness, lowliness, and helpfulness (Phil. 2:1-4). In order to underscore this exhortation and to indicate the source of the strength needed to live up to it, he now points to *the example of Christ, who with a view to saving others renounced himself, and thus attained to glory.*

John Calvin has given an excellent summary of the present paragraph and has indicated its proper divisions into two parts or "members," (a. verses 5-8; b. verses 9-11) and the reason for both and for each. Says he: "The humility to which he had exhorted them in words, he now commends to them by the example of Christ. There are, however, two members, in the first of which he invites us to imitate Christ because this is the rule of life; in the second he allures us to it because this is the road by which we attain true glory." [79]

II. *The Example of Christ*
Who with a View to Saving Others Renounced Himself

2:5-8

A. *Invitation to Imitate Christ because this is the rule of life*

5. Says Paul, **In y o u r inner being continue to set y o u r mind on** *this,* **which (is) also in Christ Jesus.**[80] The apostle desires that the Philippians keep on cherishing the disposition described in verses 1-4, a disposition that also characterizes Christ Jesus. This admonition is in line with many similar

---

[79] *Humilitatem, ad quam hortatus verbis fuerat, nunc commendat Christi exemplo. Sunt autem duo membra: quorum in priore invitat nos ad Christi imitationem, quia sit vitae regula: secundo allicit, quia sit haec via, qua ad veram gloriam pervenitur* (*Commentarius in Epistolam Pauli Ad Philippenses,* Corpus Reformatorum, vol. LXXX, Brinsvigae, 1895, p. 23).

[80] K. S. Wuest adopts a similar rendering: "This be constantly setting your mind upon in your inner being, that which is also in Christ Jesus," "When Jesus Emptied Himself," an article in *Bib Sac,* Vol. 115, No. 458 (April, 1958) pp. 153-158. The reading without γάρ and with φρονεῖτε instead of φρονείσθω has the best support. The rendering, "Have the same thoughts among yourselves as you have in your communion with Christ Jesus," injects into the text an idea that is foreign to it, is not in harmony with the context, and misconstrues ἐν ὑμῖν.

rules that urge us to follow the example of him who is the Anointed Savior. To be sure, there is an area in which Christ cannot be our example. We cannot copy his redemptive acts. We cannot suffer and die *vicariously*. It was he, he alone, who was able to satisfy the divine justice and bring his people to glory. But with the help of God we can and should copy *the spirit* that was basic to these acts. The attitude of self-renunciation with a view to helping others should be present and should grow in the life of each disciple. And *that* obviously is the point here (see verses 1-4). *Oneness, lowliness,* and *helpfulness* were manifested by our Savior (John 10:30; Matt. 11:29; 20:28). These should characterize his disciples also. In *that* sense there is truth in those simple lines:

> "Oh, dearly, dearly has he loved,
> And we must love him too;
> And trust in his redeeming blood,
> *And try his works to do.*"

Other passages which bring out the idea that Jesus is our Example are such as the following: Matt. 11:29; John 13:12-17; 13:34; 21:19; I Cor. 11:1; I Thess. 1:6, I Peter 2:21-23; I John 2:6. It is exactly because Jesus is our Lord that he can be our Example. If he is not our Example, faith is barren, orthodoxy dead.

6, 7a. Accordingly, the apostle continues: **who, though** [81] **existing** [82] **in the form of God.** . . . But what is meant by existing in God's *form?* In the paragraph under study two words — *morphe* ($\mu o \rho \phi \dot{\eta}$), that is, *form*, and *schema* ($\sigma \chi \tilde{\eta} \mu a$), that is, *fashion* — occur in close connection: "existing in the *form* of God . . . recognized in *fashion* as a human being.[83] Now

---

[81] The preceding context has prepared us for the idea of *sacrifice;* hence, the rendering *"though* existing" (taking the participle as *concessive*) is correct here as in II Cor. 8:9 (*"though* being rich").

[82] The present participle $\dot{\upsilon} \pi \dot{a} \rho \chi \omega \nu$ stands in sharp contrast with all the aorists which follow it, and therefore points in the direction of continuance of being: Christ Jesus was and is eternally existing "in the form of God."

[83] In the New Testament the first word *morphe* is found only here in Phil. 2:6, 7 and in Mark 16:12. The second one *schema* is found only here in Phil. 2:8 and in I Cor. 7:31. Both of these words are, however, also component elements in other words. Consult the original: (1) for *morphe* as a word-element: a. Rom. 2:20; II Tim. 3:5; b. Matt. 17:2; Mark 9:2; Rom. 12:2; II Cor. 3:18; c. Phil. 3:10; d. Rom. 8:29; Phil. 3:21; (2) for *schema* as a word-element: a. I Cor. 12:23; b. I Cor. 7:36 13:5; c. Rom. 1:27; Rev. 16:15; d. Mark 15:43; Acts 13:50; 17:12; I Cor. 7:35; 12:24; e. I Cor. 12:23; f. Rom. 3:13; I Cor. 14:40; I Thess. 4:12; g. I Cor. 4:6; II Cor. 11:13, 14, 15; Phil. 3:21; and h. Rom. 12:2; I Peter 1:14.

Do these two words — *morphe* and *schema* — have the same meaning? At times, throughout Greek literature, as any good lexicon will indicate, both can have the meaning *outward appearance, form, shape.* In certain contexts they can be just about interchangeable. But at other times there is a clear difference in meaning. The context in each separate instance must decide.

this very transition from *form* to *fashion* would seem to point to a difference in meaning.[84] Besides, from several New Testament passages in which one or the other or both of these words occur, generally as component elements in verbs, it is evident that *in these given contexts morphe or form refers to the inner, essential, and abiding nature of a person or thing, while schema or fashion points to his or its external, accidental, and fleeting bearing or appearance.*[85]

---

[84] Cf. the change from ἀγαπάω to φιλέω in John 21:15-17 see N.T.C. on John Vol. II, pp. 494-500.

[85]

MORPHE, FORM	SCHEMA, FASHION
Rom. 8:29	I Cor. 7:31
"whom he foreknew he foreordained to be *conformed* to *the image* of his Son." An *inner change* takes place. A person's *nature* is renewed.	"the *fashion* of this world passes away." Though the universe is not destroyed as to its inner essence, the *scheme* or *outward aspect* of things is rapidly changing.
	"Change and decay in all around I see, O thou that changest not abide with me."
II Cor. 3:18	II Cor. 11:14
"we are . . . *transformed* into the same *image* from glory to glory." Again, an abiding change takes place, a change that affects *the inner nature.*	"Satan *fashions* himself into an angel of light." He cannot change his inner self, but can and does assume *the garb* of a good angel. He *masquerades!*
Gal. 4:19	I Peter 1:14
"My little children, for whom I am again suffering birth-pangs, until Christ be *formed* in y o u." Paul is not satisfied with mere beginnings. He wants to see the completed *image* of Christ in *the inner life and character* of the Galatians. — Similar is the following example:	"Be sober . . . not *fashioning* yourselves according to y o u r former lusts." Those addressed must show that their *scheme of life* — words, habits, actions, manner of dress, etc. — is not suggestive of the passions that were formerly in control of them. *Outward bearing and conduct* must be in harmony with the new life.

Phil. 3:10
"that I may gain Christ. . . . becoming *conformed* unto his death."

Rom. 12:2
"Stop being *fashioned* after the pattern of this (evil) age, but be constantly *transformed* by the renewal of y o u r mind." Here we have both words (each occurring in a compound verb): *fashion* and *form*. Stop adopting the external customs of the world round about y o u. There must be a *gradually progressing and abiding inner change*, a *metamorphosis.*

What Paul is saying then, here in Phil. 2:6, is that *Christ Jesus had always been (and always continues to be) God by nature, the express image of the Deity. The specific character of the Godhead as this is expressed in all the divine attributes was and is his eternally.* Cf. Col. 1:15, 17 (also John 1:1; 8:58; 17:24).

This thought is in harmony with what the apostle teaches elsewhere: II Cor. 4:4; Col. 1:15; 2:9 (and cf. Heb. 1:3).

A closely related question, namely, "Is Paul speaking here in Phil. 2:5-8 about the pre-incarnate or about the incarnate Christ?" is not difficult to answer. The two must not be separated. The One who in his pre-incarnate state exists in a manner equal to God is the same divine Person who in his incarnate state becomes obedient even to the extent of death, yes, death by a cross. Naturally, in order to show the greatness of our Lord's sacrifice, the apostle's *starting-point* is the Christ in his pre-incarnate state. Then follows of necessity Christ in his incarnate state. This strongly reminds one of II Cor. 8:9, "Though he was rich, yet for y o u r sake he became poor." One might compare this transition to what is found in the Gospel of John, Chapter 1:

"In the beginning was the Word, and the Word was face to face with God, and the Word was God. He himself was in the beginning face to face with God . . . And the Word became flesh, and dwelt among us as in a tent, and we beheld his glory."

Thus, though existing in the form of God, he **did not count his existence-in-a-manner-equal-to-God** [86] **something to cling to** [87] **but emptied himself.**

He did not regard it as *something that must not slip from his grasp.* On

---

Similarly, we immediately recognize the fact that *basically and in certain contexts* there is a difference between:

forma	and	*habitus* (Latin)
Gestalt	and	*Gebärdung* (German)
gestalte	and	*gedaante* (Dutch)
And so also between		
form	and	*fashion* or *figure* (English)

The fact that *in certain contexts* the word *form* is the more basic one is clear also from the following two examples:

A de*form*ed individual is generally in a worse condition than a dis*figur*ed person.

The *form* or *inner nature* of an apple tree remains the same throughout the year: short and stocky trunk, scaly bark, gnarled branches, rounded head. But the *fashion* of the tree changes with the seasons. As the year progresses we see the tree budding, blossoming, bearing fruit, picked clean, and finally entirely bereft of both leaf and fruit.

[86] The word ἴσα is adverbial, meaning "in a manner of equality."

[87] Because of its length this footnote has been placed at the end of the chapter, page 129.

the contrary, *he* . . . and here follow the two words that have given rise to much discussion and dispute: *emptied himself.*[88]

The question is: of what did Christ Jesus empty himself? Surely *not* of his existence "in the form of God." He never ceased to be the Possessor of the divine nature. "He could not do without his deity in his state of

---

[88] Tyndale's rendering "he made him silfe of no reputacion" was taken over by Cranmer, the Geneva Version, and the A.V. Cf. also The New English Bible "he made himself nothing." Similarly, the Dutch (*Statenvertaling*) has, "*hij heeft zichzelven vernietigd.*" In favor of that translation it is usually argued that in all the other instances in which the apostle employs the verb κενόω a metaphorical sense must be given to it (see Rom. 4:14; I Cor. 1:17; 9:15; and II Cor. 9:3). Dr. B. B. Warfield even goes so far as to call the alternative rendering ("emptied himself") a mistranslation (*Christology and Criticism*, p. 375).

But is this argument against the translation "emptied himself" really valid? Is it not possible to retain the translation "emptied himself" and still give a metaphorical — at least a non-strictly-literal — meaning to the verb? R.S.V. renders I Cor. 1:17 as follows, ". . . let the cross of Christ *be emptied* of its power." And cf. the use of this verb in I Cor. 9:15. At any rate the meaning that must be given to the verb in these other instances of its New Testament use hardly proves the position that here in Phil. 2 it cannot mean *he emptied.*

It is significant that the rendering *he emptied himself* has always had defenders; for example,

Latin: *sed ipse sese inanivit*
French: *il s'est aneanti lui-même*
English (Rheims translation of 1582) : he exinanited himself.

This rendering "is nearer the Greek and in every way more satisfactory than that of the A.V." (J. H. Michael). It is accepted by: The Amplified New Testament, W. G. Ballentine (*The Riverside New Testament*), R. C. H. Lenski, J. Moffatt, A. T. Robertson, G. Verkuyl (*The Berkeley Version*), K. S. Wuest, R. Young (*Literal Translation of the Holy Bible*), as well as by A.S.V. and R.S.V. Similarly, the new Dutch translation has, "*maar Zichzelf ontledigd heeft*"; the South African, "*maar het Homself ontledig*"; and the Swedish, "*utan utblottade sig själv.*"

A strong argument in favor of this rendering is the fact that it expresses precisely the idea that one expects after "he did not count his existence-in-a-manner-equal-to-God something to cling to." If a person refuses to cling to something, he empties or divests himself of it. Note: *of it.* Most commentators agree that when one empties himself, he empties himself *of something.*

Some excellent exegetes, whose doctrinal position and emphasis I share, reject the secondary object, "of it." In line with their preference for a translation other than "he *emptied* himself," they stress the fact that "of it" is not actually in the text. However, the difference between the two groups of interpreters becomes very minor when both accept the following propositions:

(1) Christ Jesus gave *himself*, nothing less.
(2) He did not in any sense whatever divest himself *of his deity.*
(3) The meaning of the clause "he emptied himself" or "he made himself of no reputation" (whichever is preferred) is set forth in greater detail in the words which follow it, namely, "as he took on the form of a servant . . . humbled himself and became obedient even to the extent of death; yes, death by a cross."

Many translators, though not actually using the verb *emptied*, express the same idea by their translation: "stripped himself of his glory" (R. F. Weymouth), "stripped himself of all privilege" (J. B. Phillips), or "laid it aside" (E. J. Goodspeed, M. R. Vincent, C. B. Williams).

humiliation. . . . Even in the midst of his death he had to be the mighty God, in order by his death to conquer death" (R. C. H. Lenski).[89]

The text reads as follows:

"Christ Jesus . . . though existing in the form of God, did not count his existence-in-a-manner-equal-to-God something to cling to, but emptied himself."

The natural inference is that *Christ emptied himself of his existence-in-a-manner-equal-to-God.*[90]

On the basis of Scripture we can particularize as follows:

(1) *He gave up his favorable relation to the divine law.*

While he was still in heaven no burden of guilt rested upon him. But at his incarnation he took this burden upon himself and began to carry it away (John 1:29). And so he, the spotlessly righteous One, who never committed any sin at all, "was made to be sin in our behalf, that we might become the righteousness of God in him" (II Cor. 5:21). This is basic to all the rest.

---

[89] The Kenotists who teach otherwise are clearly wrong. These defenders of the Kenosis-theory in any of its many forms teach that in one way or another Christ at the incarnation divested himself *of his deity,* whether absolutely or relatively. Christ's human nature is just "shrunken deity." Of the vast literature of this subject I select only the following titles:

Karl Barth on Phil. 2:5-8 in his *Erklärung des Philipperbriefes;* also the pertinent pages in his *Kirchliche Dogmatik* IV (for example, IV:1, pp. 138 f, 146, 147; Engl. transl. pp. 126 f, 133, 134; IV:2, pp. 37, 38; Engl. transl. pp. 35, 36) ; and C. Van Til, "Karl Barth on Chalcedon," W. Th. J. XXII (May 1960), pp. 147-166.

C. A. Beckwith, article "Kenosis" in *The New Schaff-Herzog Encyclopedia of Religious Knowledge,* Vol. VI, pp. 315-319

L. Berkhof, *The History of Christian Doctrine,* pp. 124-126

A. B. Bruce, *The Humiliation of Christ,* pp. 134-192

E. D. La Touche, *The Person of Christ in Modern Thought,* pp. 351-366

H. R. Mackintosh, *The Doctrine of the Person of Jesus Christ,* pp. 223-284

J. J. Müller, *Die kenosisleer in die christologie sedert die Reformatie,* doctoral disseration, Amsterdam, 1931

W. Sanday, *Christologies Ancient and Modern* (advocates the rather strange theory that the divinity of Christ was located in the subliminal consciousness)

B. B. Warfield, *Christology and Criticism,* pp. 371-389

[90] This is the position of L. Berkhof: ". . . the verb *ekenosen* [he emptied] does not refer to *morphe theou* [form of God] but to *einai isa theo[i]*, that is, his being on an equality with God" (*Systematic Theology,* p. 328).

That is also the view of A. T. Robertson (*Word Pictures in the New Testament,* Vol. IV, p. 444) : "Of what did Christ empty himself? Not of his divine nature. That was impossible. He continued to be the Son of God. . . . Undoubtedly Christ gave up his environment of glory."

Of Greijdanus (*De Brief van den Apostel Paulus aan de Philippenzen,* in Korte Verklaring, p. 50) : "He laid aside his majesty and glory (John 17:5) but remained God."

And of H. Ridderbos (*Commentaar op het Nieuwe Testament, Romeinen,* p. 25) : "He divested himself of his divine power and majesty by becoming like human beings."

(2) *He gave up his riches*

". . . because for y o u r sake he became poor, though being rich, in order that y o u through his poverty might become rich" (II Cor. 8:9).

He gave up everything, even *himself,* his very *life* (Matt. 20:28; Mark 10:45; John 10:11). So poor was he that he was constantly *borrowing:* a place for his birth (and what a place!), a house to sleep in, a boat to preach from, an animal to ride on, a room in which to institute the Lord's Supper, and finally a tomb to be buried in. Moreover, he took upon himself a debt, a *very heavy* debt. His debt, voluntarily assumed, was the heaviest that was ever incurred by anyone (Isa. 53:6). One so deeply in debt is surely *poor!*

(3) *He gave up his heavenly glory*

Very keenly did he feel this. That is why, in the night before his crucifixion, out of the very depths of his great heart he uttered the prayer: "And now Father, glorify thou me in thine own presence with the glory which I had with thee before the world existed" (John 17:4).

From the infinite sweep of eternal delight in the very presence of his Father he willingly descended into this realm of misery, in order to pitch his tent for a while among sinful men. He, before whom the seraphim covered their faces (Isa. 6:1-3; John 12:41), the Object of most solemn adoration, voluntarily descended to the realm where he was "despised and rejected of men, a man of sorrows and acquainted with grief" (Isa. 53:3).

(4) *He gave up his independent exercise of authority*

In fact, he became a servant, *the* servant, and "even though he was a Son, learned obedience by what he suffered" (Heb. 5:8). He said: "I do not seek my own will, but the will of him who sent me" (John 5:30; cf. 5:19; 14:24).

Impatiently we voice an objection, namely, "But if Christ Jesus actually *gave up* his favorable relation to the divine law, riches, glory, and independent exercise of authority, *how could he still be God?"*

The answer must be that he, who was and is and ever remains the Son of God, laid aside all these things *not* with reference to his *divine* nature but with reference to his *human* nature, which he voluntarily took upon himself and in which he suffered all these indignities.

In his Commentary on this passage Calvin reasons as follows: It was *the Son of God himself* who emptied himself, though he did it *only with reference to his human nature.* This great Reformer uses the illustration: "Man is mortal." Here the word "Man" refers to *man himself,* man in his entirety, yet man's mortality is ascribed *to the body only,* not to the soul.

Further than this we cannot go. We stand before an adorable mystery, a mystery of power, wisdom, *and love!*

7b. It has become clear by this time that the clause, "He emptied himself" derives its meaning not only from the words which immediately precede it (namely, "he did not count his existence-in-a-manner-equal-to-God something to cling to") but also from those that follow, namely, **as he took on the form of a servant.** In fact, this clause, "he emptied himself," "includes all the details of humiliation which follow, and is defined by these" (Vincent). In the likeness of a human being taking on the form of a servant, so that he was recognized in looks and manners as a human being, humbling himself and thus becoming obedient to the extent of death; yes, death by a cross — *all this* is included in "he emptied himself." When he laid aside his existence-in-a-manner-equal-to-God, he in that very act took upon himself its very opposite (that is, *as to his human nature*).

The type of reasoning which we have here in verses 6-8 is not at all similar to that which goes on in the mind of a child who is building with blocks, each block being a unit in itself, separate from all the rest. On the contrary, it is *telescopic* reasoning: the various sections of the telescope, present from the start, are gradually drawn out or extended so that we see them.

Hence, he emptied himself *by taking* the form of a servant. "He emptied himself by taking something to himself" (Müller). Moreover, when he became a servant, he was not play-acting. On the contrary, *in his inner nature* (the *human* nature, of course) he became a servant, for we read, "He took on *the form* of a servant." (Read what was said previously with respect to the meaning of the word *form* in distinction from *fashion*.) This is great news. It is, in fact, astounding. He, the sovereign Master of all, becomes servant of all. And yet, he remains Master. The text cannot mean that "he *exchanged* the form of God for the form of a servant," as is so often asserted.[91] He took the form of servant while he retained the form of God! It is exactly that which makes our salvation possible and achieves it.

It was, moreover, the form of *a servant* — and *not* that of a *slave* — which he took upon himself. From the very beginning of his incarnation he was the thoroughly consecrated, wise and willing servant pictured by Isaiah (42:1-9; 49:1-9a; 50:4-11; and 52:13-53:12), the spontaneously acting servant who resolutely fulfills his mission, so that with reference to him Jehovah said: "Behold, my servant, whom I uphold; my chosen, in whom my soul delights."

The passage under study has as its starting-point the very beginning of this servant-career, the point where Christ *took* the form of a servant. But it implies, of course, that he remained servant to the very end of that career. Of his earthly mission it has been truly said, "The only person in the world who had the right to assert his rights waived them" (Wuest). It was Christ Jesus who said, "I am in the midst of y o u as one that serves" (Luke 22:27). In the very act of being servant to men (Matt. 20:28; Mark 10:45), he was accomplishing his mission as servant of Jehovah. We see

---

[91] Even H. Bavinck commits that error (*Gereformeerde Dogmatiek,* Vol. III, third edition, p. 456).

him, Jesus, the Lord of glory . . . with a towel around his waist, pouring water into a basin, washing the feet of his disciples, and then saying to them:

"Do y o u know what I have done to y o u? Y o u call me Teacher and Lord, and y o u say (this) correctly, for (that is what) I am. If therefore, I, y o u r Lord and Teacher, have washed y o u r feet, y o u also ought to wash each other's feet, for I have given y o u an example, in order that just as I did to y o u, so also y o u should do" (John 13:12-15).

And that is exactly Paul's point. He is saying to the Philippians and to us, "Follow the example of y o u r Lord" (see verse 5).

Never did any servant serve with more unswerving loyalty, unwavering devotion, and unquestioning obedience than did this one.[92]

Paul continues, **and became like human beings** (or more literally, "in the likeness of human beings having become"). When Christ took the form of a servant, he, who from all eternity had the divine nature and who continues to have it unto all eternity, took upon himself the human nature. Accordingly, the divine Person of the Christ now has two natures, the divine and the human (John 1:1, 14; Gal. 4:4; I Tim. 3:16). But he assumed that human nature not in the condition in which Adam had it before the fall, nor in the condition in which Christ himself now has it in heaven, nor in the condition in which he will reveal it on the day of his glorious return, but in its *fallen* and therefore *weakened* condition, burdened with *the results* of sin (Isa. 53:2).

Surely, that human nature was *real,* and in so far just like that of other human beings (Heb. 2:17). But though it was real, it differed in two respects from that of other men:

(1) His, and only his, human nature from its very conception was joined in personal union with the divine nature (John 1:1, 14); and

(2) Though it was burdened with *the results* of sin (hence, subject to death), it was not sinful in itself. Therefore this passage *"in the likeness* of human beings having become," and the similar one, "God sending his own Son *in the likeness* of sinful flesh" (Rom. 8:3) must be read in the light of Heb. 4:15, "One who was in all points tempted as we are, *yet without sin.*" There was likeness, similarity. There was no absolute, unqualified identity.

8. Paul continues, **So, recognized in fashion as a human being.**

When Jesus had come into the flesh, how did men regard him? What did they find him to be? The answer is: in their estimation he was a human being, just like themselves in ever so many respects:

---

[92] See further what has been said with reference to the meaning of δοῦλος in Phil. 1:1. Dr. John A. Mackay wrote an excellent article on this subject in The Princeton Seminary Bulletin (Jan., 1958). The title is "The Form of a Servant." He states, "The servant image is the most significant symbol in the Bible and in the Christian religion. . . . It denotes a complete absence of external compulsion. It means voluntariness, spontaneity, a certain inner joy and even exultancy."

Had they come into this world through the natural process of birth? So had he (Luke 2:7). (The mystery of the *virgin*-birth they did not fathom.)

Had they been wrapped in swaddling clothes (cf. Ezek. 16:4)? So had he (Luke 2:7).

Had they grown up? So had he (Luke 1:80).

Did they have brothers and sisters? So did he (Matt. 13:56).

Had they learned a trade? So had he (Mark 6:3).

Were they at times hungry, thirsty, weary, asleep? So was he (Matt. 4:2; John 4:6, 7; Mark 4:38).

Were they ever grieved or angry? So was he (Mark 3:5).

Did they weep at times? So did he (John 11:35).

Did they rejoice, for example, at weddings? He too attended a wedding (John 2:1, 2).

Were they destined to die? So was he, though in *his* case that death was physical, eternal, voluntary, and vicarious (John 10:11), and *this* they did not understand.

In his entire *fashion,* therefore, he was recognized as a human being. He had the looks and outward bearing of men. His way of dress, customs and manners resembled those of his contemporaries.

To a considerable extent *they were right* in so regarding him. Accordingly, it is open to doubt whether the following very familiar lines really tell the truth:

"The cattle are lowing, the Baby awakes,
  But little Lord Jesus, *no crying he makes.*"

Should it not be assumed that a normal baby cries at times, but that in the case of Jesus this crying, too, like everything else, was "without sin"?

Better are the words composed by Susanne C. Umlauf, of which I shall quote only two stanzas:

"Hast thou been hungry, child of mine?
  I, too, have needed bread;
For forty days I tasted naught
  Till by thy angels fed.
Hast thou been thirsty? On the cross
  I suffered thirst for thee;
I've promised to supply thy need,
  My child, come unto me.

"When thou art sad and tears fall fast
  My heart goes out to thee,
For I wept o'er Jerusalem —
  The place so dear to me:

And when I came to Lazarus' tomb
I wept — my heart was sore;
I'll comfort thee when thou dost weep,
Till sorrows all are o'er."

But though they were right in recognizing his humanity, *they were wrong* in two respects: they rejected a. his *sinless* humanity and b. his *deity*. And so, though his entire life, particularly also his mighty words and acts, implied the command, "Veiled in flesh the godhead see!" yet, by and large, they disavowed his claims and hated him all the more because of them (John 1:11, 5:18, 12:37). They heaped scorn upon him, so that "he was despised and rejected of men" (Isa. 53:3).

The amazing fact is, however, that "when he was reviled, he reviled not again" (I Peter 2:23), but **he humbled himself.** (For the meaning of the concept *humblemindedness* see on verse 3.) From the very beginning of his incarnation he bowed himself under the yoke. Implied in this act of humbling himself is: **and became obedient,** namely, to God the Father, as verse 9 clearly indicates (note, "Therefore *God,*" etc.). Moreover, his obedience knew no bounds: **even to the extent of death.** In that death he, functioning both as Priest and Guilt-offering, gave himself as an expiatory sacrifice for sin (Isa. 53:10). Hence, this death was not just an ordinary death. Says Paul, **yes death by a cross.**

Such a death was very *painful.*

It has been well said that the person who was crucified "died a thousand deaths."

It was also very *shameful.*

Compelling the condemned person to carry his own cross, expelling him from the city to a place "outside the gate," and there executing him by means of a death which, as we learn from Cicero, was considered the death of a slave (*Actio in Verrem.* i. 5, 66; *Oratio pro P. Quinto* viii. 4), was surely shameful. See John 19:31; I Cor. 1:23. "Let the very name of the cross be far removed not only from the body of a Roman citizen, but even from his thoughts, his eyes, his ears" (Cicero, *Pro Rabirio* 5). Hence, being a Roman, Paul, even should he after all be sentenced to die, would in all probability not have to die such a shameful death! Did he think of that when, with reference to his Master's death, he wrote, "yes, death by a cross"?

It was *accursed.*

"He that is hanged is accursed of God" (Deut. 21:23). And if this was true even with respect to a dead body, how much more with reference to a living person! Christ Jesus humbled himself, becoming obedient to a death whereby he vicariously bore the curse of God (Gal. 3:13). See also N.T.C. on John, Vol. II, pp. 425-427.

Thus, while he was hanging on that cross, from *below* Satan and all his hosts assailed him; from *round about* men heaped scorn upon him; from *above* God dropped upon him the pallor of darkness, symbol of the curse; and from *within* there arose the bitter cry, "My God, my God, why hast thou forsaken me?" Into this hell, the hell of Calvary, Christ descended.

The underlying thought of verses 5-8 is this: Surely, if *Christ Jesus* humbled himself so very deeply, y o u Philippians should be constantly willing to humble yourselves in y o u r own small way.   Surely, if *he* became obedient to the extent of death, yes death by a cross, y o u should become increasingly obedient to the divine directions, and should accordingly strive more and more to achieve in y o u r lives the spirit of y o u r Master, that is, the spirit of oneness, lowliness, and helpfulness, which is pleasing to God.

Note the chiastic (that is, the crisscross) parallelism:

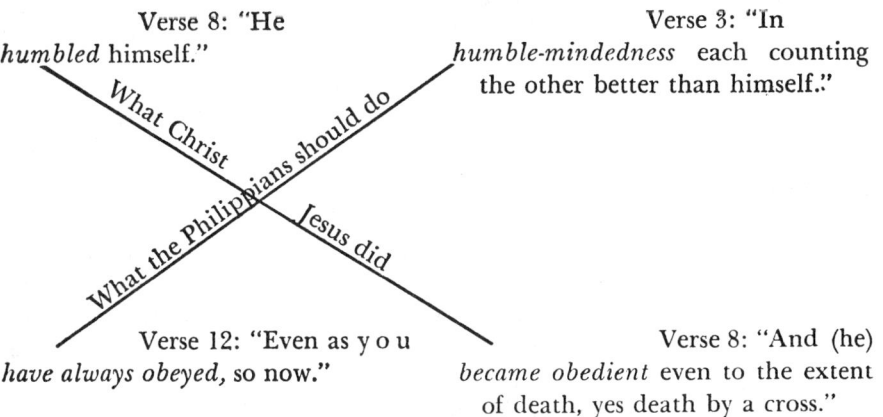

Verse 8: "He *humbled* himself."

Verse 3: "In *humble-mindedness* each counting the other better than himself."

Verse 12: "Even as y o u *have always obeyed,* so now."

Verse 8: "And (he) *became obedient* even to the extent of death, yes death by a cross."

B. *Invitation to Imitate Christ*
because this is the road by which we attain to glory

9. The glorious reward which Christ Jesus received is described as follows: **Therefore God raised him to the loftiest heights.**   He who humbled himself was exalted.   The same rule which he had himself laid down for others was now applied in his own case.   For this rule see Matt. 23:12; Luke 14:11; 18:14; and cf. Luke 1:52; James 4:10; and I Peter 5:6.   It was "because of the suffering of death" that his reward was given to him (Heb. 2:9; cf. Heb. 1:3; 12:2).   Yet, there is a difference between *his* exaltation and *ours.*   To be sure, he, too, was *exalted.*   The very same verb which applies to his followers (II Cor. 11:7) is used at times with respect to him (John 3:14b; 8:28; 12:32, 34; Acts 2:33; 5:31).   But in the present passage a verb is used which in the New Testament occurs only in this *one* instance and is here applied only to *him,* namely, the verb *"super*-exalted."   God the Father elevated the Son *in a transcendently glorious manner.*   He raised him *to the loftiest*

113

heights.[93] Do believers go to heaven? See Psalm 73:24, 25; John 17:24; II
Cor. 5:8; Heb. 12:18-24. The Mediator "passed through the heavens" (Heb.
4:14), "was lifted high above the heavens" (Heb. 7:26), and even "ascended
far above all the heavens" (Eph. 4:10). His super-exaltation means that
he received the place of honor and majesty and is accordingly "seated at the
right hand of God's throne" (Mark 16:19; Acts 2:33; 5:31, Rom. 8:34; Heb.
1:3, 12:2), "far above all rule and authority and power and dominion and
every name that is named not only in this age but also in that which is to
come" (Eph. 1:20-22). *Resurrection, ascension, coronation* ("session" at
God's right hand), all these are implied and included in the statement,
"God raised him to the loftiest heights" (verse 9). Moreover, before the
sentence is finished the final step in Christ's exaltation is also described
(verses 10 and 11), the *consummation* of his glory when on the day of his
coming every knee shall bend before him and every tongue shall proclaim
his lordship.

All this happened (and with respect to the last step *will happen*) in fulfilment of prophecy: Gen. 3:15; II Sam. 7:13; Psalm 2:7-9; 8; 47:5; 68:17-19;
72; 110:1; 118:22, 23; Isa. 9:6, 7; 53:10-12; Micah 5:2; Zech. 9:9, 10; cf. Luke
24:26; Rev. 1:7.

The exaltation is the reversal of the humiliation. He who stood condemned in relation to the divine law (because of the sin of the world which
rested on him) has exchanged this penal for the righteous relation to the
law. He who was poor has become rich. He who was rejected has been
accepted (Rev. 12:5, 10). He who learned obedience has entered upon the
actual administration of the power and authority committed to him.

As *king,* having by his death, resurrection, and ascension achieved and displayed his triumph over his enemies, he now holds in his hands the reins
of the universe, and rules all things in the interest of his church (Eph. 1:22,
23). As *prophet* he through his Spirit leads his own in all the truth. And
as *priest* (High-priest according to the order of Melchizedek) he, on the
basis of his accomplished atonement, *not only intercedes but actually lives
forever to make intercession* for those who draw near to God through him
(Heb. 7:25).

Though it was *the person* of the Mediator upon whom these honors were
conferred, it was of course *the human nature* in which the exaltation itself
took place, since the divine nature is not capable of either humiliation or
exaltation. But these two natures, though ever distinct, are never separate.
The human nature is so very closely linked with the divine that though it
never becomes divine, it shares in the glory of the divine. Therefore Christ's
assumption of glory is in a sense also *resumption* of glory. There is no real
conflict between Phil. 2:9 and John 17:5.

---

[93] Super-combinations are typically Pauline. See N.T.C. on The Pastoral Epistles,
p. 75.

Paul continues: **and bestowed on him the name that is above every name.** God the Father *bestowed* on him (literally, he *graciously,* that is *whole-heartedly,* granted to him) *the* name (thus according to the best reading, not merely *a* name). The apostle does not as yet fully tell us what that name is. He does say, however, that it is the name which excels that of every creature in the entire universe.

10. The purpose of the exaltation is: **in order that in the name of Jesus,** that is, *not* in the name *"Jesus"* but in the full name with which Jesus is now rewarded and which he now bears — a name which trembles on Paul's lips but which even now he does not yet fully mention but reserves as a climax — **every knee should bend, of those**[94] **in heaven, and of those on earth, and of those under the earth.** *At his return in glory* Jesus will be worshiped by "the whole body of created intelligent beings in all the departments of the universe" (M. R. Vincent). Angels and redeemed human beings will do this joyfully; the damned will do it ruefully, remorsefully (*not* penitently), see Rev. 6:12-17. But so great will be his glory that all will feel impelled to *render homage* to him (cf. Isa. 45: 23; Rom. 14:11; I Cor. 15:24; Eph. 1:20-22; Heb. 2:8; Rev. 5:13).

Note the three classes of created intelligent beings:

(1) those in heaven: the cherubim and seraphim, yes *all the* ten thousand times ten thousand *good angels,* including archangels; also, of course, *all redeemed human beings who have departed from this earthly life* (Eph. 1:21; 3:10; I Peter 3:22; Rev. 4:8-11; 5:8-12).

(2) those on earth: *all human beings on earth* (I Cor. 15:40).

(3) those under the earth: *all the damned in hell,* both *human beings* and the *evil angels* or *demons* (for if the adjective *heavenly* refers, among others, to the *good* angels, then its antonym, which literally means *under-earthly,* a word occurring only here in the New Testament, in all probability includes the *evil* angels).[95]

---

[94] In the abstract the three adjectives here used, in their genitive form, can be translated either as neuter or as masculine. A.V. and A.R.V., and also several commentators, prefer the neuter. And it is entirely true that the work of Christ is of value for the entire creation, both animate and inanimate (Isa. 11:6-9; Rom. 8:18-22; II Peter 3:7, 11-13; Rev. 21:1-5). However, we generally associate such actions as *knees bending* and *tongues confessing* with *persons,* not with things. So, unless it can be proved that the context here in Philippians 2:9-11 is very highly poetical (cf. Job 38:7; Ps. 65:13; 98:8; 148:3, 4, 7-10; Isa. 55:12, etc.), the view which refers these designations to *persons* deserves the preference.

[95] *Use of the term* καταχθόνιος-οι *in Greek mythology.*

Zeus (by the Romans identified with Jupiter) becomes the supreme deity and rules the heavens; Poseidon (Rom. Neptune), the ocean; Hades or Pluto (Rom. Dis), the realm of the dead; and the goddess Demeter (Rom. Ceres) the fruitful earth, agriculture.

Daughter of Demeter is Persephone (Rom. Proserpine). Hades abducts Persephone and makes her his wife. Demeter implores Zeus to restore her daughter to her. It is agreed that each year Persephone shall spend part of the time with her

11. Finally Paul arrives at the climax for which he has been preparing. Now at last he actually completes the mention of the name which is above every name: **and that every tongue should confess** [96] **to the glory of God the Father that *Jesus Christ* is *Lord*.** [97] Cf. Isa. 45:23; Rom. 14:11. Not only will all *make obeisance* but in doing so they will also *openly acknowledge and proclaim* the sovereign lordship of Jesus. They will *confess* that JESUS CHRIST (is) LORD, ΚΥΡΙΟΣ ΙΗΣΟΥΣ ΧΡΙΣΤΟΣ.

The solemnity with which the apostle utters this full name, deserves special attention. To him and to others in the early church *this* fact was one of tremendous significance, namely, that the humble "servant" Jesus had even now been crowned with glory and honor and as the great Conqueror is even now celebrating his triumph and actively ruling all things in the interest of his people. *This was the paramount confession of the very early church,* which longed for the day when the marvelous fact would be acknowledged by all. It must have imparted sweet comfort to Paul, the prisoner awaiting a verdict! It must have strengthened the Philippians in all their struggles and afflictions. *Not the earthly emperor but Jesus Christ is the real Ruler!* In order to appreciate somewhat the intense feeling and enthusiasm of the apostles when they thought of *Jesus Christ* as LORD (ΚΥΡΙΟΣ) one should note such passages as the following:

---

husband Hades, and the rest with her mother Demeter. (Here clearly is a symbol of Nature dying and reviving.) Hades and Persephone are therefore, respectively, the god and goddess of the underworld, and in Greek religion are to be counted among *the subterraneans* or καταχθόνιοι.

Use of this term in the New Testament.

In Paul's solitary use of the term the subterraneans are the damned, for according to the context the region "under the earth" is the symbol of that which is opposed to heaven. There are commentators who (with M. R. Vincent) argue that the term in question does not include the infernal spirits or demons, since according to Eph. 2:2; 6:12 demons are not regarded by Paul as being in Hades.

Over against this, note the following:

(1) The context shows that the apostle has in mind the whole body of created intelligences. From this category the demons cannot be excluded.

(2) The reference is to the judgment day. Surely *then* the demons will be assigned to hell, to dwell there forever.

(3) Even now these demons are *hellish ones.* They belong to hell, are hellish in character, and are elsewhere represented as streaming forth upon their sinister missions out of the gates of Hades (Matt. 16:18). The place of "everlasting fire," "is prepared for the devil and his angels" (Matt. 25:41). What Paul says in Eph. 2:2; 6:12 is not in conflict with all this.

[96] Though it is true that the future indicative ἐξομολογήσεται, supported by A,C,-D,F,G, etc., may have been changed to the aorist subjunctive ἐξομολογήσηται, supported by p[46], Aleph and B, in order to conform it to κάμψῃ, yet this is merely a possibility. One expects the aorist subjunctive. Besides, since in subordinate clauses these two forms (future indicative and aorist subjunctive) frequently interchange, there is no essential difference in meaning. See also Gram. N.T., pp. 188, 872.

[97] For alternate translation see footnote 99.

Peter:

"Let all the house of Israel therefore know assuredly that God has made him both Lord and Christ, this Jesus whom y o u crucified" (Acts 2:36).

Paul:

"If you confess with your lips that Jesus is Lord and believe in your heart that God raised him from the dead, you will be saved" (Rom. 10:9).

"No one can say, 'Jesus is Lord' except in the Holy Spirit" (I Cor. 12:3).
"Maranatha" (meaning, "Our Lord, come!")   (I Cor. 16:22).

John:

"These will war against the Lamb, and the Lamb will conquer them, for he is Lord of lords and King of kings" (Rev. 17:14).

"And on his robe and on his thigh he has a name inscribed, KING OF KINGS AND LORD OF LORDS" (Rev. 19:16).

This *name* meant very, very much to Paul and to sincere believers everywhere, because a name, as then understood, was not as with us merely a convenient means of distinguishing one individual from another. On the contrary, in biblical usage the name is intimately associated with the person who bears it and is frequently that person himself as he reveals himself. It expresses that person's character, reputation, dignity, work, power, or his peculiar position in the divine economy. Hence, often the name keeps pace with the person. Abram becomes Abraham. Sarai develops into Sarah. Jacob changes to Israel. Solomon receives the name Jedidiah. Simon is called Cephas, that is, Peter. See Gen. 17:5, 15; 32:28; II Sam. 12:25; John 1:42. Sometimes the old name is not wholly dropped. Sometimes it is.

Now this applies also to the glorious name *Jesus Christ . . . Lord.* It is not just a word or title, a kind of signal for knees to start bowing and for tongues to start shouting. It is not *at* (the mere mention of) the name but *in* the name that great things begin to happen. Phil. 2:9-11 means, accordingly, that by virtue of the power and majesty of Jesus Christ and the recognition of him as Lord every knee will bend and every tongue will proclaim him.[98]

Though *now* the proclamation of Christ's name, the open avowal of his sovereign majesty, is muffled on earth, but echoed forth in heaven, *one day* all creation shall bow to our Lord, as stated beautifully in the words of the Dutch Hymn (translated by Rev. W. Kuipers):

---

[98] That the name is often equivalent to the person himself as he stands revealed is seen in such contexts as: Ps. 8; Matt. 10:22; 24:9; 28:19; Mark 13:13; Luke 21:17; Acts 4:30; 9:15; 10:43; I Cor. 1:10; I John 2:12; 3:23.

117

"One day all creation shall bow to our Lord;
E'en now, 'mong the angels his name is adored.
May we at his coming, with glorified throng,
Stand singing his praises in heaven's great song:
'Jesus, Jesus, Savior adored,
Of all men and angels forever *the Lord.*' "

Great, indeed, was the reward which Jesus received. But every reward must be to the glory of God, the Father (representing the Trinity). The glory of God is ever the goal, the final purpose, of all things. Hence, Paul, who accordingly loves doxologies and near-doxologies, and who breaks into them again and again (Rom. 9:5; 11:36; 16:27; Eph. 1:3 ff.; 3:20; Phil. 4:20; I Tim. 1:17; 3:16; 6:15, 16; II Tim. 4:18; Titus 2:13, 14), also climaxes the present sentence with the words "to the glory of God the Father." [99] By means of the universal proclamation of Jesus' lordship the glory of God the Father, who raised him to the loftiest heights and gave him the most excellent name, will naturally be enhanced.[100] Cf. John 13:31, 32; 14:13; 17:1. Between the Father and the Son there exists a most intimate love-relationship. When the Son is glorified, the Father is glorified also, and vice versa; and when the Son is rejected the Father is rejected also, and vice versa. (In this connection see N.T.C. on John, Vol. II, p. 372, the diagram.)

Let the Philippians then continue to set their mind on Christ. Let them copy his example. Let them do this because this is the rule of life and because both for Christ and for his followers it is the road to that true glory by which God himself is glorified.

---

12 So then, my beloved, even as y o u have always obeyed, so, not as in my presence only but now much more in my absence, with fear and trembling continue to work out y o u r own salvation; 13 for it is God who is working in y o u both to will and to work for his good pleasure.

---

[99] Of course, these words modify the verb "should confess." Hence, in order to avoid ambiguity I translated as follows, "and that every tongue should confess to the glory of God the Father that Jesus Christ is Lord" (so also the Berkeley Version). A.V., A.R.V., and R.S.V. also avoid ambiguity, *if* due note is taken of the comma after the word *Lord.* Since this glorious lordship of the Anointed Savior is the burden, the main message, of the statement, so filled with thought and emotion, it is probably not incorrect to bring out this emphasis in English by slightly changing the word-order of the original and placing the word *Lord* at the very end. Nevertheless, in order to show that the final purpose of the praise rendered by every creature is God's glory, the word-order of the original may be retained and conveyed in some such manner as the following: "and that every tongue should confess that Jesus Christ is Lord (this confession redounding) to the glory of God the Father" (or, with Goodspeed, "and thus glorify God the Father").

[100] On the concept *glory* see the detailed study in connection with Phil. 1:11, including the footnote there. On *Lord* see N.T.C. on John, Vol. I, p. 103; Vol. II, pp. 234, 235; and N.T.C. on I and II Thessalonians, pp. 40, 41.

14 Practise doing all things without mutterings and argumentations, 15 that y o u may become blameless and guileless, children of God without blemish in the midst of a crooked and perverse generation, among whom y o u are shining as stars in the universe, 16 holding forth the word of life, (which will be) for me something to be proud of with a view to the day of Christ, (as indicating) that I did not run in vain or labor in vain. 17 In fact, even if I am to be poured out as a libation upon the sacrificial offering of y o u r faith, I rejoice, and I rejoice with y o u all; 18 and in the same manner do y o u also rejoice, and rejoice with me.

2:12-18

III. *Shining Lights Producing Mutual Joy*

2:12, 13

A. *Work Out Y o u r Own Salvation*

(1) *The Exhortation*

12. So then, my beloved. This establishes the connection between verses 12-18 and verses 1-11, especially 5-11. In fact, the connection goes back even farther, for there is a close parallel between 2:12 and 1:27 (as will be shown). Very tenderly Paul addresses the Philippians as "my beloved." He means, "Y o u whom Christ loves and I also love, with a love that is deepseated, thorough-going, intelligent, and purposeful."

By saying "So then" or "Therefore," the apostle means:

a. Since Christ Jesus by means of his unrestricted, voluntary obedience gave y o u an example (verse 5-8) ; and

b. since the reward which he received shows that there are great things in store for those who follow this example (verses 9-11) ; and finally,

c. since this highly exalted divine and human Mediator imparts strength from heaven to all who trust in him and yearn so to live as he would have them live (implied in verses 9-11) , *therefore,* etc.

The apostle continues his tactful procedure as follows: **even as y o u have always obeyed.** By and large the members of the Philippian church have always *hearkened* to the demands of *God* as expressed in *the gospel* (cf. Rom. 10:16; II Thess. 1:8), to *Christian teaching and admonition* (Rom. 6:17; II Thess. 3:14). Yet, there was danger. There was a tendency to lean too heavily on Paul, that is, on his physical presence with the church at Philippi. These people were overcome with an emotion bordering on nostalgia when they revived in their memory the events that had transpired when Paul had been personally present with them, enabling them to listen to his very voice, and to go directly to him with their problems. Similarly, at present they can hardly wait until, in God's good pleasure, Paul will be with them again. —Now, in such an attitude there is much that is beautiful and to be appreciated. Yet, it is *not altogether* healthy. The Philippians must learn to

119

lean *completely* on God, not just mostly on God and partly on Paul's physical presence with them. That Paul was keenly aware of this weakness is clear from the fact that he has hinted it once before. Note the aforementioned parallel between 1:27 and 2:12:

1:27	2:12
"Only continue to exercise y o u r citizenship in a manner worthy of the gospel of Christ, that *whether I come and see y o u or am absent,* I may hear of y o u that y o u are standing firm in one spirit," etc.	"So then, my beloved, even as y o u have always obeyed, so, **not as in my presence only but now much more in my absence, with fear and trembling continue to work out** y o u r **own salvation.**[101]

The obedience of the Philippians must not be motivated by,[102] and last only as long as, Paul's presence among them. On the contrary, his very absence must impress upon them the fact that *now more than ever* they must take the initiative. *Now especially* they must exert themselves, for *now they are on their own;* not, to be sure, as far as *God* is concerned, but as far as *Paul* is concerned. They must now work out "their own salvation," that is, they must work it out *apart from the assistance of Paul.* Yes, they must *work it out,* that is, carry it to its conclusion, thoroughly digest it, and apply it to day-by-day living. They must strive to produce in their lives all the fruits of the Spirit (the entire long list enumerated in Gal. 5:22, 23!). They must aim at nothing less than spiritual and moral perfection.

In such a context we do not go amiss when we say that *the tense* of the verb indicates that Paul has in mind *continuous, sustained, strenuous effort:* "Continue to work out." Believers are not saved at one stroke. Their salvation is *a process* (Luke 13:23; Acts 2:47; II Cor. 2:15). It is a process in which they themselves, far from remaining passive or dormant, take a very active part. It is a pursuit, a following after, a pressing on, a contest, fight, race (see on Phil. 3:12; also Rom. 14:19; I Cor. 9:24-27; I Tim. 6:12).

Putting forth such a constant and sustained effort is not easy. It is a battle

---

[101] This very comparison clearly shows that the words "not as in my presence only but now much more in my absence" modify "with fear and trembling continue to work out y o u r own salvation," and not "even as y o u have always obeyed." Besides, the negative μή (instead of οὐ, οὐχ) is more natural with limitations of the imperative than with the indicative. Cf. John 13:9; James 1:22. It also stands to reason that Paul, facing a verdict and possible death, would be deeply concerned about the question: How will Christian character and conduct develop among the Philippians if I remain absent? Are there perhaps *even now* certain individuals in that congregation who are taking sinful advantage of my absence? Cf. Phil. 4:2, 3. — Hence, from every point of view — exegetical, grammatical, and psychological — the construction of the sentence which, along with most commentators, I favor must be regarded as the best. This is my answer to R. C. H. Lenski, *op. cit.,* p. 803.

[102] Note: "not *as* in my presence." The retention of the rather difficult "as" probably represents the best reading. As in Rom. 9:32; II Cor. 2:17; and Philemon 14 ὡς indicates inward motivation.

on three fronts, a warfare against the tremendously strong and wily combination of the world, the flesh, and the devil. It will mean making full use of every God-appointed means to defeat the evil and bring out the good within them ("within them" because God placed it there!) .

It is one thing to shout, "Do all to the glory of God," but it is quite a different thing to carry this out in practice.

It is one thing to pray "as we have forgiven our debtors," but it is not so easy *really* to forgive.

It is one thing to display a beautiful plaque saying,

CHRIST IS THE HEAD OF THIS HOME

but it is something else again actually to recognize him as Head by submitting every important question to him in prayer and by obeying his every command.

It is one thing to assert very piously, "God's sovereignty is the ultimate principle for faith and practice," but it is far more difficult to submit trustfully to this sovereign will when a dear one is growing gradually weaker and finally dies. Thus one could continue. In fact, so very difficult is the task that is here laid upon the Philippians, that, left to their own resources, they can no more fulfil it than the invalid described in John 5 could get up and walk. Yet Jesus told the latter, "Get up, pick up your mat, and walk." And in substance he tells the Philippians that they must consider *working out their own salvation* to be their life's task. Note: their *salvation,* here with emphasis on that aspect of salvation which is called *sanctification.* (For the rest, see N.T.C. on I Tim. 1:15 for the meaning of the term *Salvation* as used by Paul.)

Because this task is so vital it must be performed "with fear and trembling." This phrase, because of its importance, even precedes the verb which it modifies. We read, "With fear and trembling continue to work out y o u r own salvation."

"With fear and trembling" (cf. I Cor. 2:3;
II Cor. 7:15; Eph. 6:5) . Meaning:

NOT in the spirit of:	BUT in the spirit of:
half-heartedness, the divided mind (1 Kings 18:21)	wholeheartedness, singleness of purpose (Ps. 119:10, 34)
disrespect and disdain (Acts 17:18)	reverence and awe, *being afraid* to offend God in any way (Gen. 39:9; Heb. 12:28)
trust in self (Matt. 26:33)	trust in God (II Chron. 20:12)
self-righteousness (Luke 18:11)	humility (Luke 18:13) .

(2) *The Incentive for heeding it*

13. Such fear and trembling does not spell despair. Quite the contrary. Encouragingly Paul says, as it were, Y o u, Philippians, *must* continue to work out y o u r own salvation, and y o u *can* do it, **for it is God who is working in y o u.** Were it not for the fact that God is working *in* y o u, you Philippians would not be able to work *out* y o u r own salvation. Illustrations:

The toaster cannot produce toast unless it is "connected," so that its nichrome wire is heated by the electricity from the electric power house. The electric iron is useless unless the plug of the iron has been pushed into the wall outlet. There will be no light in the room at night unless electricity flows through the tungsten wire within the light-bulb, each end of this wire being in contact with wires coming from the source of electric energy. The garden-rose cannot gladden human hearts with its beauty and fragrance unless it derives its strength from the sun. Best of all, "As the branch cannot bear fruit of itself unless it abides in the vine, so neither can y o u unless y o u abide in me" (John 15:4).

So here also. Only then can and do the Philippians work out their own salvation when they remain in living contact with their God. It is exactly because God began a good work in them — are they not the "beloved" ones? — and because he who began that good work will also carry it toward completion (Phil. 1:6), that the Philippians, as "co-workers with God" (cf. I Cor. 3:9), can carry this salvation to its conclusion. Not only at the beginning but at every point in the process salvation is from God (John 1:12; 15:5b; I Cor. 15:10; Eph. 2:8; Phil. 1:6, 28, 29; 3:9, 12; especially 4:13). "We are God's workmanship," his creation, his "poem." He has made us what we are. By means of his Spirit working in the hearts of his people (Phil. 1:19), applying to these hearts the means of grace and all the experiences of life, God is the great and constant, the effective Worker, the Energizer,[103] operating in the lives of the Philippians, bringing about in them **both to will and to work.** Note: not only *to work* but even *to will,* that is, to resolve and desire:

> " 'Tis not that I did choose thee,
> For, Lord, that could not be;

---

[103] Paul employs the present participle of the verb ἐνεργέω. He uses this verb with respect to:
a. God (I Cor. 12:6, 11; Gal. 2:8, twice; 3:5; Eph. 1:11, 20; Phil. 2:13, first of two instances; Col. 1:29; cf. also Eph. 3:20 and I Thess. 2:13.
b. the spirit of Satan (Eph. 2:2; cf. II Thess. 2:7).
c. sinful passions (Rom. 7:5).
e. death and life (II Cor. 4:12)
d. comfort (II Cor. 1:6)
f. faith (Gal. 5:6)
g. believers (Phil. 2:13, second of two instances).
The word indicates the effective exercise of power.

> This heart would still refuse thee,
> Hadst thou not chosen me.
> Thou from the sin that stained me
> Hast cleansed and set me free;
> Of old thou didst ordain me,
> That I should live for thee."
>
> (Josiah Conder)

The impotent man whose story is related in John 5 was unable to walk. Yet, at the word of Jesus he gets up, picks up his mat, and starts walking. That which he cannot do in his own strength, he can, must, and does do *in the strength of the Lord.*

As to *willing* and *working*, the facts are exactly as stated in *The Canons of Dort* III and IV, articles 11 and 12: "He infuses new qualities into the will, which though heretofore dead he quickens; from being evil, disobedient, and refractory, he renders it good, obedient, and pliable; actuates and strengthens it, that like a good tree, it may bring forth the fruits of good actions. . . . Whereupon the will thus renewed, is not only actuated and influenced by God, but in consequence of this influence becomes itself active." [104] Nowhere is the manner in which God operates within the heart of his child, enabling him to will and to work, more beautifully described than in Eph. 3:14-19.

It is comforting that the apostle adds **for his good pleasure.** It is *for the sake of* and *with a view to the execution of* God's good pleasure that God, as the infinite Source of spiritual and moral energy for believers, causes them to work out their own salvation. *"Causes* them," yet without in any way destroying their own responsibility and self-activity. Note, moreover, the word *good pleasure.* Says Dr. H. Bavinck *(The Doctrine of God,* English translation, p. 390), "Grace and salvation are the objects of God's delight; but God does not delight in sin, neither has he pleasure in punishment." This statement is in harmony with Scripture (Lam. 3:33; Ezek. 18:23; 33:11; Hos. 11:8; Eph. 1:5, 7, 9).

2:14-18

B. *Thus Y o u Will Be Shining Lights Producing Mutual Joy*

14-16. Paul has been speaking about the necessity of obedience (verse 12) in the great task of working out salvation. But obedience may be of two kinds: grudging or voluntary. "On the outside I may be sitting down, but

---

[104] How Lenski can speak in this connection of Calvinistic error is not clear to me *(op. cit.,* p. 806). Calvinism, like Paul, maintains both divine sovereignty and human responsibility. Man is neither "a self-starting and self-perpetuating organism" nor "a mechanized automaton."

on the inside I am still standing up," said the boy who after repeated admonitions to sit down and finally "obeyed," fearing that otherwise he might be punished. Such grudging obedience is in reality no obedience at all. Example: rendering hospitality while you pity yourself (cf. I Peter 4:9). True religion is never *merely* external compliance. Hence, Paul continues, **Practise doing all things without mutterings and argumentations.** In the original "all things" heads the command; hence really, "All things practise doing without mutterings and argumentations." All the dictates of God's will must be obeyed cheerfully; in such a manner that *the will* of man does not rebel against them by means of discontented, undertone *grumblings,* nor *his mind* by means of perpetual ingenious disputations. Cf. Exod. 4:1-13; 16:7-9, 12; Eccles. 7:29; Num. 17:5, 10; John 6:41-43, 52; I Cor. 10:10. Paul continues . . . **that y o u may become blameless and guileless,** "blameless" in the judgment of others, and "guileless" (literally "unmixed," or "unadulterated," that is, without any admixture of evil) in y o u r own inner hearts and lives. Further, **children of God without blemish.** Note, "that y o u *may become* children of God." But were they not *even now* children of God? The answer should probably be sought in this direction: One becomes *a child* ($\tau\acute{\epsilon}\kappa\nu o\nu$) *of God by regeneration,* for a child of God is one who is *begotten* of God. But this is not the end. *Regeneration* is followed by *sanctification.*[105] Those who by virtue of regeneration (and partial sanctification) *are* children of God must endeavor *to become children of God without fault or blame.* And this **in the midst of a crooked and perverse generation.** The description of the worldly contemporaries and neighbors of the Philippians is borrowed from The Song of Moses (LXX Deut. 32:5). Close parallels are found in Matt. 12:39 ("evil and adulterous generation"); 17:17 ("faithless and perverse generation"); and Acts 2:40 ("crooked generation"). People who are crooked are "morally warped." They cannot be trusted. They have arrived at this terrible condition by having turned and twisted themselves in different directions, but always away from the straight path pointed out by the law of God. They are spiritually perverted or distorted. **Among whom,** continues Paul, y o u, by y o u r sanctified, blameless and guileless character, **are shining as stars in the universe.**[106] As the stars

---

[105] There are other explanations. Some deny that Paul is here using $\tau\acute{\epsilon}\kappa\nu o\nu$, pl. $-\alpha$, in the Johannine sense. But the context, which stresses the process of sanctification, surely reminds one of John 1:12. See N.T.C. on that verse. "A child of God" should strive *to become* (hence also "to become manifest as") "a child of God without blemish."

Some commentators, failing to see how children of God can, in any progressive sense, still *become* children of God, re-arrange the clause so that it would read "that y o u, being children of God, may become blameless and guileless," etc. But this change is neither necessary nor justifiable.

[106] Whether $\varphi a\acute{\iota}\nu\epsilon\sigma\theta\epsilon$ is taken as (present, middle) *indicative* or as *imperative* makes little difference as long as the main clause "Practise doing all things without mutterings and misgivings" is imperative. *Indicative* here impresses me as the more

dispel physical darkness so believers banish spiritual and moral darkness. As the former illumine the firmament, so the latter enlighten the hearts and lives of men. Moreover,

> "The spacious firmament on high,
> With all the blue ethereal sky,
> And spangled heavens, a shining frame,
> Their great Original proclaim."
> (Addison — *Ode*.
> *The Spacious Firmament on High*)

Similarly also believers, by *being* "the light of the world" (Matt. 5:14, 16; cf. Eph. 5:8; I Thess. 5:5), *are constantly proclaiming* their Maker and Redeemer to a world lost in sin. They perform this glorious missionary-task by **holding forth** [107] **the word of life,** the gospel of salvation, not only

---

natural of the two, especially because the verb occurs in a dependent clause removed so far from the main clause. With Lex. N.T. (A. and G.) I agree that even in the middle voice φαίνεσθε with respect to light and its sources can mean *"are shining"* and need not be translated "are seen." Cf. Isa. 60:2. The transition from *to be seen* to *to shine* is a very natural semantic shift when the verb is used in connection with stars, etc. For φωστήρ, *luminary,* in the sense of *star* see same lexicon. The word κόσμος is used in various senses. See N.T.C. on John, Vol. I, p. 79, footnote 26. Here the meaning *universe* would seem to be the most fitting. Hence, there is much to be said for the rendering, "y o u are shining as stars in the universe" (or perhaps even "in the firmament," see for this possibility The New English Bible, footnote on Phil. 2:15; and H. G. Liddell and R. Scott, *Greek-English Lexicon,* entry κόσμος). Daniel 12:3 is a close thought-parallel.

[107] Lenski, among others, definitely rejects this rendering of ἐπέχοντες. Along with many others, before and after him, he favors *holding* or *holding fast.* Among versions and commentaries the two interpretations are about equally divided. Favoring the rendering *holding* or *holding fast* or something similar (for example, *being attached to*) are Moffatt, R.S.V., Berkeley Version, Dutch (Nieuwe Vertaling), Luther, Bengal, Michael, Kennedy (*Expositor's Greek Testament*), and Robertson, to mention only a few of a much longer list. Favoring the translation *holding forth* or *holding out* (to them) are A.V., A.R.V., (The New English Bible has "proffer"), Weymouth, Goodspeed, Wuest, Amplified New Testament, Dutch (Statenvertaling); Eadie, Alford, Vincent (*International Critical Commentary*), Scott (*The Interpreter's Bible*), Greijdanus, Müller, and many others. (Still others favor "being in the place of," "possessing," etc.) The most detailed and, as I see it, the most satisfactory discussion on this subject is found in Greijdanus (*Kommentaar op het Nieuwe Testament, Philippensen,* on Phil. 2:16). He favors *holding forth. Both renderings make good sense.* Here in Phil. 2:16, however, the rendering "holding forth" or "holding out (to them)" or "proffering" (offering for acceptance) would seem to be best suited to the context. As for the missionary idea, this is already present in the words, "among whom y o u are shining as stars in the universe." Surely, lives that are shining in the darkness of this world of sin and unbelief are exhibiting to men the power of the gospel in sanctified living. Cf. Matt. 5:16. They do it by *holding out* to them the word of life, just like, according to Homer, who uses the identical verb, red wine was *held out* or *offered* to a person (*The Odyssey* XVI, 442-444). When Lenski states that,

as *preached* but also as *practised*. See John 6:68; Acts 5:20; Eph. 2:1; I John 1:1. Light and life go together. "In him was life. And the life was the light of men." See N.T.C. on John 1:4. It is the life and light of salvation.

Says Paul, Such spiritual shining among men, such holding forth the word of life, is that **(which will be) for me something to be proud of with a view to (the) day of Christ.** If the Philippians so conduct themselves in word and deed, then on the glorious day of Christ's Return (see on Phil. 1:10) the apostle, far from being ashamed, will be able to point with pride to the Philippians, to their life and to their testimony. For him this will be *a reason for exultation* (see on Phil. 1:26). Says Paul, I can then be proud of y o u r accomplishment **(as indicating)** that — looking back from the glorious day to the days of my ministry on earth — **I did not run in vain or labor in vain.** "Not *for empty glory*" did I exert myself so strenuously. Not *for nothing* did I run or labor. Here *running* is a metaphor taken from the foot-race in the stadium. Paul frequently employs such figures. See N.T.C. on the Pastoral Epistles, I Tim. 4:7, 8 and II Tim. 4:7, 8. *Laboring* indicates exerting oneself in exhausting toil. Paul, looking back, would be able to point to fruit upon his heavy missionary toil for Christ. Cf. Phil. 4:1; then also I Cor. 3:12, 13; 4:3-5; II Cor. 1:4; and I Thess. 2:19, 20.

17, 18. Accordingly, if the Philippians will continue to work out their own salvation, shining as stars, holding forth the word of life, then there will be every reason for joy. And this remains true even though sooner or later Paul himself should fall a victim to his labors for Christ. Says Paul, **In fact, even if I am to be poured out** [108] **as a libation upon the sacrificial offering of**

so interpreted, "it would be the only instance of this meaning in the New Testament," the answer is as follows:

(1) The meaning *holding*, which he adopts, would indeed be the only instance of this meaning in the New Testament. The only other New Testament passages in which this verb occurs are: Luke 14:7 ("holding out the mind to," "focusing the attention upon," "marking"), Acts 3:5 ("held out his mind to," "focused his attention on," "gave heed to"); I Tim. 4:16 ("hold out your mind to," "focus your attention on," "look to") and Acts 19:22 ("he held out in Asia — remained in Asia — for a while").

(2) If Paul intended to say, "holding," "holding on to," or "holding fast" the word of life, would he not have made use of the verb κατέχω, just as he does elsewhere? Cf. I Cor. 11:2; 15:2; II Cor. 6:10; and I Thess. 5:21?

[108] The present σπένδομαι must be understood as a vivid reference to the future. Paul is probably thinking of his present imprisonment as "the beginning of the end" for himself, whether that end be climaxed at the close of the present imprisonment or a few years later.

I agree with H. A. A. Kennedy (*The Expositor's Greek Testament*), who in commenting on this passage states, "Here again unnecessary difficulties have been raised over the question whether Paul or the Philippians are to be regarded as offering the sacrifice. There is no evidence that the apostle wishes to strain the metaphor to the breaking point." The *passive* here as well as in II Tim. 4:6 is natural, the supposition being that the apostle's life is being — or is to be — poured out like a drink-offering.

y o u r faith, I rejoice. The pouring out of Paul's blood is a reason for joy to him as long as it can be considered *a drink-offering* [109] which crowns *the sacrificial offering* [110] brought by the Philippians. By this *sacrificial offering* which the Philippians must bring — and have already begun to bring (see Phil. 1:29) — is to be understood their Christian life and conduct, springing from faith. It is *their faith in action in the midst of persecution and trial.* If that offering is fully presented by the Philippians, then the apostle can truly rejoice, even in the face of death. He can be happy because it will have become evident that God has been willing to use him to bring the Philippians to their goal of the fully surrendered life. That surely would be an honor for Paul personally. He adds, **and I rejoice with y o u all.** He rejoices with them, because they will thus be fully experiencing the joys of redemption in Christ. **And in the same manner do y o u also rejoice** in the blessings of redemption, **and rejoice with me,** that is, in my having obtained the martyr's crown as a result of my labor for y o u and for others like y o u.

So speaks *Paul, the humble cross-bearer,* humble even to the point of rejoicing at the thought that "some day he would be the lesser part of the sacrifice poured out upon the major part, the Philippians' Christian testimony and service to God" (K. S. Wuest, *Philippians in the Greek New Testament,* p. 78).

Synthesis of 2:1-18

There is here a stirring appeal with a *fourfold incentive* to Christian living. Has not Christ given them his:

(1) encouragement

(2) love

(3) closeness (Spirit-fellowship)

(4) tender compassion?

Then let them exercise toward one another:

(1) oneness

(2) lowliness (humility)

(3) helpfulness.

That is the *threefold directive.*

In Christ this spirit has been beautifully exemplified. Let them therefore constantly turn their attention to him. If Christ Jesus humbled himself so deeply, Philippians should surely be willing to humble themselves in their own small way. If he became obedient to the extent of death by a cross, they in their own small way should be obedient to his directives. If he was rewarded, so will they be rewarded.

---

[109] Whether the underlying figure is the *Jewish* libation, poured out *beside* the altar, or the *pagan* libation, poured out *over* the sacrifice, makes no difference.

[110] ἐπὶ τῇ θυσίᾳ καὶ λειτουργίᾳ to be understood as *hendiadys.*

PHILIPPIANS

From all eternity Christ existed and continues to exist in the form of God. He is God. His deity cannot be diminished or shrunken in any way whatever. Yet, he emptied himself, not of his deity of course, for that were impossible, but of his existence-*in-a-manner*-equal-to-God. By taking on the form of a servant and becoming like human beings, he, in that human nature, became poor that we through his poverty might become rich.

As a reward for this humiliation, and following hard upon it, God the Father raised the Mediator to the loftiest heights, seating him at his right hand in the highest heaven, and bestowing on him the name that is above every name, in order that at his glorious Return all intelligent creatures — angels, men, demons may confess to the glory of God the Father that JESUS CHRIST is LORD.

A few propositions can be safely laid down:

(1) According to the clear teaching of this passage — note "Christ Jesus *existing* in the form of God" — Christ's divine nature is immutable. Note how in this passage *the present durative* stands in sharp contrast with *the aorists* which follow it. Any theory which ascribes to the divine nature mutability and the ability to become temporal and spatial finds no support here. Christ's divine nature will be what it has been from all eternity: fully divine.

(2) Exaltation clearly *follows* humiliation. It was because Christ became obedient even to the extent of death, yes death by a cross, that God raised him to the loftiest heights. The view which teaches that these two states coincided, so that Christ was exalted in his humiliation and humiliated in his exaltation, throws overboard the plain meaning of words, and cannot be regarded as being in accordance with sound principles of exegesis.

(3) Christ's two natures, though united in his one person, are and ever remain clearly distinct. He who exists eternally as God took upon himself the human nature, and now has both. The rejection of the two-nature doctrine is in direct contradiction to the plain teaching of Phil. 2:5-11. Exegesis should never surrender to mere fancy, wild speculation. But even the most careful exegesis will be insufficient if it ignores the real reason why the apostle was led by the Holy Spirit to write this paragraph, namely, that we should pattern ourselves after the spirit of Christ who for our sake was willing to humble himself so deeply!

True, if one so conducts himself, persecution from the side of the kingdom of darkness is in store for him. Paul, accordingly, presents himself as *humble cross-bearer,* willing to be poured out as a libation upon the sacrificial offering of the faith of the Philippians. He urges the addressees: with fear and trembling to continue to work out their own salvation, this all the more in the absence of their leader (Paul). Let their incentive be that there is One who is working within them both to will and to work for his good pleasure. And let them do it from the heart, without complaining. Thus, as stars in the universe they, too, will shine in the midst of a crooked and

128

PHILIPPIANS

perverse generation, holding forth the word of life, that is, fulfiling their mission-task, so that Paul can rejoice in them, and this both now and on the day of Christ's Return. "And in the same manner," concludes Paul, "do y o u also rejoice, and rejoice with me."

---

[87] The word ἁρπαγμός, acc. –ον, has given rise to several questions: Should it be taken in the active sense — an act of robbery or usurpation — or in the passive sense — *a prize* to be held on to, a treasure to be clutched? Is it *an action* or is it *a thing?* Several Latin fathers, notably also Augustine, favor the former. Most of the early Greek writers prefer the latter, that is, they interpret the passage to mean that Christ Jesus did *not* regard his existence in a manner equal to God as a prize to be retained at all hazards.

The active sense — robbery —is favored by the A.V. But this meaning is in conflict with *the words that precede* (see Phil. 2:1-4). The apostle has just exhorted the Philippians to be humble and not always to be insisting on their own rights but to be thoughtful of others. Surely, in such a context the idea that Christ *asserted* his rights — "thought it not robbery to be equal with God" — does not fit. Also, the rendering does not do justice to *the words that follow*. The conjunction *but* suggests a direct contrast. This demand is satisfied only when the clause "he emptied himself" is preceded by something like "he did not cling to," or as the text actually reads, "He did not count his existence-in-a-manner-equal-to-God something to cling to." Certainly when a word can have either an active or a passive meaning it is the specific context that decides the issue.

But is not ἁρπαγμός after all an active concept because of its suffix –μος which is an active-ending, in contrast with –μα, which is a result-ending? The answer is: this rule allows for many exceptions. Note the following:

ἐπισιτισμός	(in Luke 9:12) means	food.
θερισμός	(in Luke 10:2) means	harvest or crop.
ἱματισμός	(in John 19:24) means	vestment.
ὑπογραμμός	(in I Peter 2:21) means	writing-copy, hence example.
φραγμός	(in Luke 14:23) means	hedge or fence.
χρηματισμός	(in Rom. 11:4) means	oracle.
ψαλμός	(in I Cor. 14:26) means	psalm.

And as to ἁρπαγμός Eusebius in his Commentary on Luke (vi) uses this very word, and *in the passive sense,* as meaning *prize.*

This, however, brings up another matter. Such a *prize* can be either *res rapta*, that is, *something which one already has in his possession, ostensibly displays, and retains in his grasp,* or (as in the case of Peter's death on a cross) *res rapienda*, that is, *something which one does not yet have in his possession, a prize to be eagerly sought.* But here, too, it is the context in each given case that is decisive. The idea that also here in Phil. 2:6 the futuristic sense (*res rapienda*) should be ascribed to the word ἁρπαγμός is defended by H. A. A. Kennedy (*The Expositor's Greek New Testament,* Vol. III, pp. 436, 437); J. H. Michael (*The Moffat New Testament Commentary: Philippians,* pp. 88-89); A. M. Hunter (*Paul and his Predecessors,* pp. 45-51); J. Ross (*J Th S,* July, 1909); W. Warren (*J Th S,* April, 1911); and more recently by J. M. Furness (*J Th S,* Dec., 1957); and D. R. Griffiths, "Harpagmos and heauton ekenōsen in Philippians 2:6, 7" (*Ex T* 69, No. 8, 1958). With variations as to detail this view may be summarized as follows: Jesus might have used his miraculous powers in such a way as to compel men to worship him as God. He might have reached out for this honor in order to *grab* it. Is not that what, in substance, "*the first Adam*" did (see Gen. 3:4, 5 and cf. Phil. 3:6)? And was not that the very thing which in the desert of temptation and in fact throughout our Lord's earthly sojourn Satan tempted "*the second Adam*" to do? But Jesus said

129

"No." Instead of using *force* he showed *obedience*. And on account of his great renunciation and obedience God now highly exalted him and bestowed upon him, as a reward, the name that is above every name (Phil. 2:9-11).

The theory is very interesting, but will not do, and this for the following reasons: (1) To imply that the One who is here described as "existing in the form of God" lacked "existence in a manner equal to God," so that he looked forward to it as a reward is indefensible. Surely, as a starting-point, one must proceed from the idea that he who is the possessor of the divine nature also had the divine glory and authority.

(2) The clearly parallel-passage, II Cor. 8:9, teaches that *Christ gave up the glory which he already had!*

(3) The context, as has been shown, requires the idea that the Philippians must be willing *to sacrifice* certain things in the interests of others.

Summary of Chapter 2

Verses 19-30

Paul, the Thoughtful Administrator

promising to send Timothy to the Philippians as soon as his (Paul's) own case has been decided,
and even now sending Epaphroditus back to them.

2:19-24 The contemplated mission of Timothy.
2:25-30 The authorized return of Epaphroditus.

19 But I hope in the Lord Jesus to send Timothy to y o u soon, so that I also may be heartened by knowing y o u r affairs. 20 For I have no one likeminded who will be genuinely interested in y o u r welfare. 21 For they all look after their own affairs, not those of Jesus Christ. 22 But y o u know his proved worth, how as a child (serves) with (his) father, so he served with me in the gospel. 23 Him, then, I hope to send at once, that is, as soon as I can see (how) my affairs (will turn out). 24 But I trust in the Lord that I myself shall also come soon.

2:19-24

I. *The Contemplated Mission of Timothy*

19. Paul, the joyful servant of Jesus Christ, the optimistic prisoner, the humble cross-bearer, is also the thoughtful administrator. Even from his prison in Rome he manages in a masterly fashion the spiritual terrain entrusted to his care, so that we marvel at his practical wisdom, gracious consideration of the needs and feelings of others, and delightful unselfishness. Are the Philippians anxious to receive a report about the verdict that is about to be pronounced regarding Paul? As soon as this decision is known, a messenger will be rushed to Philippi with the news. See verse 23. However, the apostle wants the Philippians to know that he is as concerned about them as they are about him. In fact, it is of importance to note that the *first* reason which he mentions for dispatching someone to Philippi is that he, Paul, may be brought up to date in his information concerning *them*. He writes, **But** — though it is possible that my blood will be poured out presently (implied in verses 17 and 18), yet — **I hope in the Lord Jesus to send Timothy to y o u soon.** Although in this letter Paul never entirely dismisses from his mind the possibility of an unfavorable verdict (Phil. 1:20-23; 2:17, 18, 23), yet his expectation of an imminent acquittal and release predominates (Phil. 1:25, 26; 2:19; 2:24; cf. Philem. 22). He is full of hope. This hope is, of course, "in the Lord Jesus" (Phil. 1:8, 14; 2:24; 3:1). It is cherished in complete and humble subjection to him who alone is *Lord*, sovereign Ruler of all, the One with whom the apostle is living in intimate fellowship.

Now for this important mission of imparting information to the Philippians and (as here) obtaining news from them the apostle has selected no one less than Timothy. See on Phil. 1:1. And since hopefully this is to be a mission of good news and encouragement, Timothy will be sent not only *to* them but *for* them, *in their interest.*

Paul continues . . . so that I also may be heartened by knowing y o u r affairs. Just as the apostle expects that the Philippians will be heartened by news from him, so he *also* expects to be refreshed in his soul when he receives Timothy's report with reference to them.

Paul does not indicate the place where he, if released, hopes to meet Timothy again when the latter, having performed his task at Philippi, will make his report. Perhaps at Ephesus? See N.T.C. on The Pastoral Epistles, pp. 39, 40.

20, 21. A description of Timothy's unique fitness for his task follows: **For I have no one likeminded who will be genuinely interested in y o u r welfare.** For detailed description of Timothy's life and character see N.T.C. on The Pastoral Epistles, pp. 33-36.

As far as temperament, disposition, and inclination were concerned, and this especially with a view to the present assignment, there was no one who could compare with Timothy.[111] There was no one with a heart like his. His was a fine, sympathetic, amiable spirit. It is as if Paul were saying, "Y o u, Philippians, must not be disappointed if upon my release I cannot *in person* immediately come to see y o u. As soon as ever possible (see verse 23) I will dispatch Timothy. No one is better qualified and more favorably disposed. Already as a child he was an eager student of the sacred writings, a teachable and obedient son (II Tim. 3:15). As he grew up he was highly recommended by those who knew him best (Acts 16:2). Upon his conversion to the Christian faith he became my beloved and faithful child in the Lord (I Cor. 4:17), and a little later my special deputy and fellow-worker (Rom. 16:21), always ready to go wherever I sent him or to be left behind wherever I told him to remain (Rom. 16:21). To top it all, he is *God's* minister in the gospel of Christ (I Thess. 3:2). And do not forget either that from the very founding of y o u r church he has known y o u, and y o u have known him, for not only was he present when y o u r church was established (Acts 16:11-40; I Thess. 2:2) but subsequently he has also visited y o u upon more than one occasion (Acts 19:21, 22; 20:3-6; II Cor. 1:1). He therefore is a *natural.* Yes, y o u can surely bank on it that he will be genuinely interested in y o u r welfare (literally, *in the things concerning y o u*)."

But is it not true that upon his release Paul would like nothing better than to keep Timothy in his own immediate company? Was not Timothy the man whom Paul could least afford to spare? True, but in his mind and heart the apostle has already decided on this personal sacrifice. And this

---

[111] As is indicated by the relative clause ("who will be genuinely interested in y o u r welfare") which refers to Timothy, the word "likeminded" means "in comparison with Timothy," not "in comparison with myself (Paul)."

willingness always to subordinate his own immediate interests to those of the kingdom (see I Cor. 10:33) also explains, at least in part, why the apostle can use such strong language with respect to those who are of an opposite disposition. Surely, the names of others had occurred to him when he had decided that upon the publication of the verdict concerning himself some-one must convey the news to Philippi. But a moment of reflection — or per-haps *their* excuses when approached on this subject — had convinced him that *they* were not qualified. Says Paul, **For they all look after their own affairs, not those of Jesus Christ.** Attempts have been made to tone down the sharpness of this judgment. This is hardly warranted. The words are simple and direct, whether read in the original or in translation. With many interpreters I believe, however, that they do not apply to absolutely every gospel-worker who was at this time in any way whatever associated with the apostle, but rather to those only who might be available at this particular juncture, and who might for a moment be regarded as qualified for a mission to Philippi.

The following facts must be borne in mind:

(1) Paul was not thinking of men like Luke and Aristarchus. These, though having been with him in Rome (Col. 4:10, 14; Philem. 24), were now no longer with him. Paul in writing Philippians cannot even send their greetings. The apostle is in the habit of sending his envoys to various sta-tions, wherever they are needed. Thus later also, during his *second and far more severe* Roman imprisonment, he was not selfishly going to try to keep around him as many friends as possible, but was going to send Tychicus to Ephesus and also "Crescens to Galatia and Titus to Dalmatia" (II Tim. 4:10-12). Accordingly, here in Phil. 2:21, apostolic deputies absent on various missions must be subtracted from the number of those whom Paul judges so severely.

(2) The statement "For they all look after their own affairs, not those of Jesus Christ," is, nevertheless, indicative of the keen disappointment which the apostle suffered. Now Phil. 1:15, 17 has already shown that not every gospel-worker in Rome was inspired by the highest motives. And this was not the only disappointment Paul was going to experience in his missionary labors in the great metropolis. For example, Demas, whose name is still mentioned in earlier epistles that belong to this imprisonment (Col. 4:10; Philem. 24), but who is no longer mentioned in Philippians (perhaps because he too was absent on some legitimate mission?), *is going to* prove a bitter disappointment (II Tim. 4:10). And then there is II Tim. 4:16, "At *my first defense* no one was at my side but all deserted me." See N.T.C. on The Pastoral Epistles, pp. 325-330. If this "first defense" is connected with the first imprisonment, as may well be the case, then in II Tim. 4:16 we would have a statement similar to that in the Philippian passage now under consideration. The very people from whom Paul had expected help during

his trial had disappointed him. And so also, the very people whose names had momentarily occurred to Paul when the decision was made to send someone to Philippi, either had offered excuses or upon further reflection were simply dismissed from the apostle's mind as spiritually unqualified because of their previous failures, inability to endure the trial of fire, and lack of *genuine* interest. In the light of such passages as Phil. 1:15, 17; II Tim. 4:10, 16, *we are no longer surprised* to read Phil. 2:21. Paul here graciously withholds the names of those who because of their evident selfishness were unfit for a mission to Philippi.

22. How altogether different was Timothy! Hence, Paul continues in the spirit of verse 20, **But y o u know his proved worth.** Timothy is no novice. To be sure, he is still young, perhaps in his middle thirties. See N.T.C. on I Tim. 4:12. But he is not inexperienced. "The crucible of affliction" was known to him. Yes, the life of this young Christian had been subjected to the searching eyes of God and had stood the test.[112] He had been "approved." Timothy's reliability was by now a well-established fact. "Y o u know," says Paul, **how as a child (serves) with (his) father, so he served with me**[113] **in the gospel.** For the details, showing how the Philippians had become aware of this, see above on verse 20. Timothy's association with Paul was like that of a child with his father, father and son being intensely interested in the same cause. Willingly, enthusiastically, the younger man had subjected himself, in filial attachment, to his spiritual father, for the latter's aim was also his own. Timothy's service was a thoroughly dedicated, spontaneous, loving ministry in the interest of and for the promotion of *the gospel.* See on 1:27. In order that God's truth might be established in the hearts of men — including the Philippians — Timothy had been doing all in his power to lighten Paul's heavy load.[114]

23, 24. After this brief aside on Timothy's virtues the apostle resumes the thought of verse 19, the *sending* of Timothy: **Him, then, I hope to send at once, that is, as soon as I can see (how) my affairs (will turn out). But I trust in the Lord that I myself also shall come soon.** Once the verdict has been pronounced, the Philippians, far from being left in the dark, will be informed by no one less than beloved Timothy, who will carry the news to

---

[112] For the meaning of δοκιμή see on Phil. 1:10; also N.T.C. on I Thess. 2:4; and W. Grundmann, art. and related words, in G. Kittell, Th.W.N.T., II, pp. 258-264.
[113] This is better than *he slaved with me.* See on Phil. 1:1; 2:7.
[114] The idea of some that Paul started to write, "Timothy served me," but changed this to, "Timothy served with me," when it occurred to him that both men were after all servants of Jesus Christ, is probably not the most natural way to account for the structure of the sentence. If allowance is made for "compressed style," so characteristic of New Testament writers, especially of Paul, the sentence as it stands is sufficiently clear.

them without any delay. Will that verdict be condemnation or acquittal? Paul does not know for sure but is rather confident that it will be the latter. In any event his trust in the Lord remains unshaken. The best commentary on this underlying pendulation of thought with emphasis on hope of release and especially on complete trust in the Lord is found in Paul's own words recorded in 1:19-26 and 2:17, 18 (see comments on these verses). Was the apostle released? And did he soon follow Timothy to Philippi? The answer must be that this was actually what happened. See N.T.C. on The Pastoral Epistles, pp. 23-27 for detailed argument.

---

25 But I consider it necessary to send (back) to y o u Epaphroditus, my brother and fellow-worker and fellow-soldier, and y o u r messenger and minister to my need, 26 for he has been longing for y o u all, and he has been distressed because y o u heard that he was sick. 27 And sick he was indeed, on the verge of death. But God had mercy on him, and not only on him but also on me, that I might not have sorrow upon sorrow. 28 Accordingly, I am sending him (back) the more eagerly in order that when y o u see him again y o u may rejoice and I may be less sorrowful. 29 So, extend to him a most joyful welcome in the Lord, and hold such men in honor, 30 because for the work of Christ he came to the brink of death, risking his life that he might supply what was lacking in y o u r service to me.

2:25-30

II. The Authorized Return of Epaphroditus

25. Paul, the thoughtful administrator, now turns from Timothy to Epaphroditus. See Introduction, IV. Briefly the facts concerning him were the following:

---

(1) He was *a spiritual leader* in the church at Philippi.

(2) He had been commissioned by that church to bring a bounty to Paul, the prisoner, and to be his constant assistant and attendant.

(3) While engaged in this service he had become dangerously ill.

(4) His friends in Philippi had heard about this illness and had become alarmed, in turn. He learns about their anxiety.

(5) God graciously restores Epaphroditus.

(6) He yearns to return to the church which had delegated him, in order to allay its fears with respect to his health.

(7) Paul, in complete accord, sends him back to Philippi, bespeaks a cordial "Welcome home!" for him, and in all probability makes him the bearer of this letter.

Now *the fact* of Epaphroditus' authorized return, together with a brief *description* of the man, is found in verse 25; *the reasons for his return* are stated in verses 26-28; and *the manner in which he should be received* is indicated in verses 29, 30.

Says Paul: **But I consider** [115] **it necessary to send (back) to y o u Epaphroditus, my brother and fellow-worker and fellow-soldier, and y o u r messenger and minister to my need.** Epaphroditus! His name [116] means *lovely,*

---

[115] Instead of "I consider" in verse 25 and "I am sending" in verse 28 the original has "I considered" and "I sent." The latter are epistolary aorists written from the point of view of the readers. When Paul's letter is received by them the considering and the sending will belong to the past. Hence, in Greek a past tense is used, where our language, viewing the situation from the point of view of the writer, would use the present.

[116] The name, a rather common one, is related to that of the goddess of love and beauty, Aphrodite. Since in this predominantly heathen community the church was of fairly recent origin the conjecture that Epaphroditus descended from a Greek family *devoted to Aphrodite* may well be correct. The following facts must, however, be borne in mind:

A. (1) As a result of Alexander's conquest with its spread of Hellenistic culture names of Greek-pagan origin had become popular all over the wide-stretching empire.

(2) Jews, too, had adopted the habit of giving their children Greek names, and even Christians did not hesitate to copy and retain these names; just as today Christian parents often do not hesitate to name their children Dennis, Dion, Diana, Isadora, Minerva. They also retain the pagan names of the days of the week.

(3) In such names as Timothy (I Tim. 1:2, honoring God), Theophilus (Luke 1:3, Acts 1:1, loved of God) and Theudas (Acts 5:36, contraction of Theodorus, gift of God) the deity referred to is not definitely indicated. Hence, these lend themselves to Christian interpretation. This holds too for several others, including in a sense even Epaphroditus. See B 2.

B. Names derived from heathen deities abound on the pages of the New Testament. For our present purpose it is necessary to note only the following items of ancient mythology:

Many or all the Olympic deities are reflected in Olympas (Rom. 16:15). Offspring of Cronos and Rhea were the Olympic deities Demeter and Zeus.

Demeter (see also footnote 95), goddess of agriculture, of the fruitful earth, protectress of the social order and marriage (by the Romans identified with Ceres; cf. our "cereals"), finds her echo in Demetrius (Acts 19:24). Zeus (Acts 14:12), chief of the gods, ruler of the heavens (by the Romans identified with Jupiter) returns to us in the name Zenas (Titus 3:13, abbreviation of Zenodorus, given by Zeus), and in Diotrephes (III John 9, nourished by Zeus).

Zeus had several wives and children:

(1) *Offspring of Zeus and Leto:* Apollo and Artemis.

Apollo was considered the god of the sun; later, of healing, music, poetry, prophecy, youthful male beauty. Hence, we have Apollos (Acts 18:24, abbreviation of Apollonius) and Apelles (Rom. 16:10).

The twin-sister of Apollos was Artemis, the goddess of the moon; later, of youth, health, freedom, the dance, the dewy meadows and green forests, especially of the chase, "the virgin-huntress" (by the Romans identified with Diana); whence Artemas (Titus 3:12). Another name for Artemis was Phoebe, the bright and radiant moon-goddess; hence Phoebe (Rom. 16:1).

(2) *Offspring of Zeus and Dione* (but according to others sprung from the seafoam, ἀφρός): Aphrodite (by the Romans identified with Venus).

Epaphroditus and its abbreviation Epaphras are derived from Aphrodite (hence, *devoted to Aphrodite,* the goddess of love; and so *lovely*). Yet though the two

and a lovely person he was! Paul describes him first in his relation to himself, then in his relation to the church at Philippi. With respect to Paul he is *my brother, fellow-worker, and fellow-soldier.* The words are evidently arranged in an ascending scale. In common with every believer Epaphroditus is Paul's *brother,* united with him *in faith.* He is a member of the same spiritual family, with God in Christ as Father. Paul is fond of this word *brother,* for it is a term of affection (cf. 4:1). It is no surprise, therefore, that in the present letter, written to his dearly-beloved Philippians, the famous prisoner uses it more often than in any other prison-epistle (1:12, 14; 2:25; 3:1, 13, 17; 4:1, 8, 21). But Epaphroditus is even more than Paul's *brother.* He is united with him not only in faith but also *in work,* the work of the gospel; hence, *fellow-worker,* a title given elsewhere to such kingdom-laborers as Apollos, Aquila and Priscilla, Aristarchus, Clement, Mark, Onesimus, Philemon, Timothy, Titus, Tychicus, etc. Finally, Epaphroditus is united with Paul not only in faith and in work but also *in battle.* He is a *fellow-soldier,* a *companion in arms.* A *worker* must needs be a *warrior,* for in the work of the gospel one encounters many foes: Judaistic teachers, Greek and Roman mockers, emperor-worshippers, sensualists, the world rulers of this darkness, etc. Accordingly, on the part of every worker there must be prodigious exertion of energy against the foe, and unquestioning obedience to the Captain, in the full assurance of ultimate victory (cf. Philem. 2; II Tim. 2:3, 4; 4:7, 8). How Epaphroditus had fulfilled his commission as a worker and a soldier is explained in verse 30.

In relation to the church of Philippi Epaphroditus is called y o u r *messenger and minister to my need.* The word *messenger* is literally *apostle,* but this term is here used in its widest sense,[117] indicating someone who has been delegated by the church to carry out an assignment, *an official representative through whom the church itself speaks and acts.* In the present case the assignment was not only to bring to Paul the gift of the

---

names are the same, the Epaphroditus of Philippians is not the Epaphras of Colossians, for the respective contexts (cf. Phil. 2:25 with Col. 1:7) show that these two belong to different cities.

(3) *Offspring of Zeus and Maia:* Hermes (Acts 14:12).
He was the herald and messenger of the gods, the god of roads, commerce, invention (by the Romans identified with Mercury); whence Hermas (Rom. 16:14; abbreviation of several names, including Hermodorus, that is, given by Hermes) and Hermogenes (II Tim. 1:15, born of Hermes).
C. Even the lesser deities and supernatural beings are reflected in Biblical personal names. Thus Hymen, the god of marriage, returns to us in Hymenaeus (II Tim. 2:17); Nereus, a lower sea-deity, father of the Nereids or sea-nymphs, in Nereus (Rom. 16:11); and with less certainty Tyche (by the Romans identified with Fortuna), the goddess of fortune, chance, luck, in Tychicus (Acts 20:4), Syntyche (Phil. 4:2), and Eutychus (Acts 20:4, 9). Some find the sea-nymphs in Nymphas (Col. 4:15), but because of a textual-critical problem this is very uncertain.
[117] For the various meanings of the word *apostle* see N.T.C. on The Pastoral Epistles, pp. 49-51.

Philippian church but also to serve Paul in whichever way that service might be *needed* (note: minister *to my need;* cf. Phil. 4:16; Acts 20:34; Rom. 12:13) ; for example, as his personal attendant and as his missionary-assistant. Hence, Epaphroditus had been sent both to *bring* a gift and to *be* a gift from the Philippians to Paul. The very word used in the original for *minister,* namely *leitourgos,* indicates that the task of Epaphroditus was viewed as one in which he — and the church of Philippi through him — rendered *official* and *sacred* service, and this not only to Paul but to the cause of the gospel; hence, to God himself. The sending of Epaphroditus, with all that it implied, was a religious act, a true offering or sacrifice! Proof: see Phil. 2:17 (*"sacrificial offering* of y o u r faith") and 2:30, which use the cognate noun *leitourgia;* and also 4:18, which calls the gift which this messenger brought *"a sacrifice,* acceptable, well-pleasing to God." Cf. also Rom. 15:16 and II Cor. 9:12.[118]

Epaphroditus had done whatever he was able to do. He had done it in the right spirit. Let no one criticize this worthy servant when he now returns to his church at Philippi. Let no one say, "How shameful for you to have acted contrary to the charge which we gave you, and to have deserted Paul at the very time when that honored prisoner, who is awaiting a life-or-death verdict needs you most." Says Paul, as it were, "Bear in mind, Philippians, that Epaphroditus is returning to y o u because I myself consider it necessary to send him back to y o u."

26-28. The reasons for the authorized return are now stated. These reasons are three and are closely intertwined. They concern *him* (Epaphroditus), *y o u* (Philippians), and *myself* (Paul) :

(1) In order that the ardent wish of *Epaphroditus* may be satisfied (verses 26 and 27) ;

(2) In order that y o u may rejoice (verse 28a) ; and

(3) In order that *I* (Paul) may be less sorrowful (verse 28b) .

Beginning with (1) Paul says, **for he has been longing for y o u all, and he has been distressed because y o u heard that he was sick.** This implies that word of the illness of Epaphroditus had reached Philippi, and that the report of Philippi's resulting alarm had been brought back to Rome. The result for Epaphroditus was twofold:

First of all, he is worried over their worry! Severe distress of mind and

---

[118] As the Greek *leitourgos,* motivated by love for his city and its gods, financed a great drama or fitted out a warship, so the Philippians, impelled by a love for the one true God in Jesus Christ, had sponsored this truly great undertaking, namely, the gathering of a substantial gift for Paul and the sending to Paul of this wonderful bounty and of its even more wonderful bearer. See also N.T.C. on The Pastoral Epistles, p. 225, footnote 113.

heart, profound agony, overwhelms his soul. The word used in the original to express this disturbance (a word of uncertain derivation) is the one that is used in connection with the unspeakable anguish which Jesus experienced in Gethsemane (Matt. 26:37; Mark 14:33).

Secondly, his love for the church that had sent him becomes so overpowering that he yearns to see again the familiar faces of those whose sympathy is so real, and whose anxiety must be removed.

Now this anxiety of the Philippian church cannot be removed by stating that the report concerning the sickness of their beloved leader was unfounded or had been exaggerated. On the contrary; Paul continues: **And sick he was indeed, on the verge of death.**

The question is asked, "But why had not Paul, by means of a miracle or by means of prayer, prevented this illness, or at least quickly healed Epaphroditus, even long before his illness had taken such a grave turn?" The answer must be: first, that even in that charismatic era the apostles could not perform miracles whenever they felt so inclined. *Their* will was subject to *God's* will. And as to prayer, even though this is indeed a mighty means of healing and often leads to recovery, it is no cure-all. It does not operate mechanically like pressing a button. It, too, is ever subject to God's will, which is wiser than man's desiring. And in this all-wise providence of God it has been determined that believers too at times become ill, sometimes gravely ill (Elisha, II Kings 13:14; Hezekiah, II Kings 20:1; Lazarus, John 11:1; Dorcas, Acts 9:37; Paul, Gal. 4:13; Timothy, I Tim. 5:23; Trophimus, II Tim. 4:20; and so also Epaphroditus, Phil. 2:25-27). Yes, they get sick and they even die! The passage, "With his stripes we are healed," does not mean that believers have been exempted from the infirmities of the flesh, from grave illness or from death. But when believers are stricken, theirs is the comfort of such passages as Psalm 23; 27; 42; John 14:1-3; Rom. 8:35-39; Phil. 4:4-7; II Tim. 4:6-8; Heb. 4:16; 12:6, to mention only a few among many references.

Another question is, "What was the nature of Epaphroditus' illness?" Many guesses have been made, but all that is really known is that it was in connection with the work of the Lord and more specifically in connection with his loving attendance upon and assistance to Paul that Epaphroditus had become sick (see verse 30). Was the illness a result of over-exertion? Had he been trying to do too much? Had this wonderful fellow-believer, worker, soldier, after a very difficult and exhausting journey exerted himself to the utmost in the work of attending to Paul's every need, caring for believers in Rome, preaching to everyone willing to listen to the glorious gospel of the Crucified One, and doing all this amid great difficulty and personal danger, in a city whose multitudes paid homage not to Christ but to the emperor? At any rate, he had lost every bit of strength, and at last had been brought to death's very door, so close to it that he could, as it were,

141

touch it. For a while his life, humanly speaking, had been hanging by a thread. But then — in answer, to be sure, to the prayers of many — the experience of the author of Ps. 116 had become his also. Epaphroditus had been graciously restored to health. This surely is implied in the words which now follow: **But God had mercy on him.** God *compassionated, pitied* Epaphroditus! [119] He had mercy on him, **and,** continues Paul, **not only on him but on me also that I might not have sorrow upon sorrow,** that is, sorrow that would have resulted from the death of Epaphroditus added to sorrow because of his grave illness.

God *pitied* both Epaphroditus and Paul! It is comforting to know that the heart of God is filled with *mercy,* that is, with *lovingkindness and active pity.* In Christ he is "touched with the feeling of our infirmities."

> "Mindful of our human frailty
> Is the God in whom we trust;
> He whose years are everlasting,
> He remembers we are dust.

> "Changeless is Jehovah's mercy
> Unto those who fear his name,
> From eternity abiding
> To eternity the same."

The following are some of the beautiful passages in which this comforting doctrine is set forth or illustrated:[120]

Gen. 39:21; Exod. 3:7; 20:6; Deut. 30:3; 33:27; II Sam. 7:15; 24:14; II Chron. 36:15; Neh. 1:5; Ps. 5:7; 23; 34:6; 36:5, 7; 81:10; 86:5; 89:28-34; 103:14-17; 108:4; 116:1-9; 136; Is. 1:18; 40; 42:3; 53:4-6; 54:7; 55:1-7; 63:7-9; Jer. 12:15; 31:34; Lam. 3:22, 32, 33; Ezek. 33:11; Hos. 11:4, 8; Joel 2:13; Jonah 4:11; Mic. 7:18-20; Nah. 1:7; Zeph. 3:17; Zech. 9:9; Matt. 5:7; 9:13, 27-31, 36; 11:28, 29; 12:7; 14:14; 15:21-28; 17:14-18; 18:27, 33; 20:29-34; 23:23, 37; Mark 1:41; 5:19; 6:34; 10:14, 46-52; Luke 1:46-80; 7:13; 8:54, 55; 10:25-37; 12:32; 14:23; 15:7, 20-24; 16:24; 17:11-19; 18:35-43; 23:34, 43; John 3:16, 17; 10:11-16; 11:5, 35; 14:1-3; 17; 19:25-27; 21:15-17; Acts 2:46, 47; Rom. 5:8-10; 8:26-39; 9:15-18, 23; 11:30-32; I Cor. 7:25, II Cor. 4:1; 6:17, 18; Gal. 2:20; 6:16; Eph. 2:1-10; 3:14-19; Col. 3:12-17; I Thess. 4:17, 18; I Tim. 1:2, 13-16; II Tim. 1:2, 16, 18; 4:8, Titus 2:11; 3:5; Heb. 2:17; 4:14-16; 7:25;

---

[119] The original has, "God *mercied* him," but this does not sound well in English. German: *Gott hat sich über ihn erbarmet;* Swedish: *Gud förbarmade sig över honom;* Dutch: *God heeft zich over hem ontfermd.*
[120] Here in Phil. 2:27 the original has ἠλέησεν; cf. the noun ἔλεος: mercy. See the word-study of this concept in N.T.C. on The Pastoral Epistles, pp. 54-56, including footnote 23 on p. 55 there.

James 2:13; 3:17; 4:5; I Peter 1:3, 18, 19; 2:10; I John 1:9; 3:1-3; II John 3; Jude 2, 21; Rev. 7:9-17; 21:1-7.

This divine tenderness of heart that expresses itself in helpful deeds is beautifully reflected in Paul. To satisfy his faithful helper's ardent yearning and to relieve his deep distress he orders him to return to Philippi. Epaphroditus, now fully recovered, longs to be reunited with the church that had sent him. In all probability he wanted to present himself in person so that all could see that he had regained his health. No doubt he also wished to express his personal thanks to them for the prayers that had been offered and for the interest shown. And we may well believe that above all he was eager to help the Philippians in their continuing difficulties and afflictions (Phil. 1:29, 30; 3:2, 17–19; 4:2). Yet, on the other hand, he fully understood the charge he had received, loved Paul dearly, and would certainly not have left him had not the thoughtful administrator ordered him to do so.

The second reason for sending Epaphroditus back to Philippi is stated as follows: **Accordingly, I am sending him (back) the more eagerly in order that when y o u see him again y o u may rejoice.** Paul is sending his friend home again in order that the membership of the Philippian church, on seeing him again fully recovered, may leap for joy. This affords a glimpse into the inner soul of the great apostle. Easing the mind of his dearly beloved Philippians and imparting to them gladness of heart meant more to him than any personal service he might be able to derive from Epaphroditus.[121]

But although Paul's appreciation of his friend and of the services which he rendered in Rome was genuine, *he himself* is able to rejoice when he reflects on the usefulness of Epaphroditus to the Philippians. Accordingly, the third reason for bidding the valiant helper to return to his own church is stated as follows: **and I may be less sorrowful.** The joy of the Philippians upon the return of Epaphroditus will make Paul's own burden lighter. The great apostle proves himself to be a true imitator of God (cf. Eph. 5:1, 2) , who rejoices in the joy of his beloved ones, in fact rejoices over them *with singing* (Zeph. 3:17) .

29, 30. The manner in which Epaphroditus should be received by the church of Philippi is stated in these words: **So, extend to him a most joyful welcome in the Lord,** or more literally, "So, receive him in the Lord with all joy." This faithful minister must be received with deep gratitude to the Lord. Certainly, no welcome could be too cordial. And he deserves more than a welcome. Hence, **and hold such men in honor.** Note: *such men,* Epaphroditus and others like him (cf. I Tim. 5:17) . When Paul wrote this,

---

[121] Sending Epaphroditus back to Philippi was a real sacrifice for Paul. The idea of some, that Epaphroditus had become a burden on the apostle's hands, and that for this reason he wanted to get rid of him, is completely contrary to the entire context.

he could not foresee that at a later date men would twist these words as if a person who in any way had become a martyr for Christ must always be given the privilege of casting the deciding vote in important ecclesiastical matters. The apostle, however, was saying no more than this, namely, that due respect must be shown to those who have proved themselves willing, if necessary, to surrender their lives for Christ. This implies, of course, that weight must be attached to their judgments and opinions, but not *undue* weight. The teaching of the Word must remain the final criterion, and the advice of the entire church must be carefully considered. Returning now to Epaphroditus personally — though as an eminent example of the entire class of loyal, valiant, and self-effacing ministers — Paul states the reason why honor should be accorded to this attendant and assistant, namely, **because for the work of Christ** (see on verse 25) **he came to the brink of death.** Epaphroditus had been in mortal danger, **risking**[122] **his life,** as a gambler will take risks for possible gain.

By saying that for the cause of Christ Epaphroditus had exposed himself to the peril of losing his life, Paul probably had reference to more than the violent illness which seized his loyal friend, bringing him to death's very door. Likely the phrase also points to the danger involved in the delegate's very presence in Rome in the capacity of the constant and intimate attendant and assistant of a prisoner who might be on his way to execution. Peter, in a somewhat analogous situation, denied his Lord! Yes, Epaphroditus risked his life, says Paul, **that he might supply what was lacking in y o u r service to me.** This must not be viewed as a reprimand, as if Paul were in any way dissatisfied with the *sacred, sacrificial service* (see on Phil. 2:17; 2:25; 4:18) which the Philippians had rendered. What he meant was probably this: "Y o u r favors shown to me are deeply appreciated. If there were anything lacking in y o u r kindness toward me, y o u have certainly made up for it by sending me Epaphroditus."[123]

The example of Epaphroditus, who was willing to risk his very life for Christ, was copied by others. Accordingly, in the early church there were societies of men and women who called themselves *the parabolani,* that is, *the riskers or gamblers.* They ministered to the sick and imprisoned, and they saw to it that, if at all possible, martyrs and sometimes even enemies

---

[122] παραβολευσάμενος, aorist participle of παραβολεύομαι. The variant παραβουλευσάμενος must be regarded as a scribal substitute for the less familiar original. Deissmann (*Light from the Ancient East,* p. 88) cites an example of παραβολευσάμενος from an inscription at Olbia on the Black Sea, probably of the second century A.D.
[123] Similarly, at a previous occasion Stephanus, Fortunatus, and Achaicus had made up for the *lack* or *deficiency* of the Corinthians. They had done what, because of distance, the Corinthians had not been able to do personally (I Cor. 16:17). That the Philippians had fallen short in their duty toward Paul Phil. 2:30 does not imply any more than Col. 1:24 ("filling up whatever is lacking in the sufferings of Christ") implies that Christ in his own person had not suffered enough.

would receive an honorable burial. Thus in the city of Carthage during the great pestilence of A. D. 252 Cyprian, the bishop, showed remarkable courage. In self-sacrificing fidelity to his flock, and love even for his enemies, he took upon himself the care of the sick, and bade his congregation nurse them and bury the dead. What a contrast with the practice of the heathen who were throwing the corpses out of the plague-stricken city and were running away in terror!

Synthesis of 2:19-30

Paul appears in this section as *thoughtful administrator,* who even from his prison in Rome, under God, in a wise, considerate, and unselfish manner directs the affairs of his extended spiritual domain. In the first subdivision of the present section he says that as soon as he knows how his affairs will turn out he will send Timothy to the Philippians, and this not only with news concerning himself (Paul) but "that I also may be heartened by knowing y o u r affairs." He warmly recommends Timothy, whose unselfish devotion to the cause of Christ contrasts sharply with the attitude of all such other persons who might be considered for this mission. The apostle adds, "But I trust in the Lord that I myself shall also come soon."

In the second paragraph Paul informs the Philippians that he is sending (back) to them the man who was probably the bearer of the letter, namely, Epaphroditus. The latter had been sent to Rome as a gift and with a gift from the church of Philippi. While busily engaged in gospel-work and as Paul's personal attendant he had become grievously ill, having been brought to death's very door, but by God's marvelous mercy he had been completely restored. In returning him to Philippi Paul had a threefold purpose:

(1) To satisfy the wish of Epaphroditus, who desires to go back to the brothers at Philippi in order to remove their alarm.

(2) To gladden the hearts of the Philippians who will rejoice when they see Epaphroditus fully restored.

(3) To rejoice in the joy of the Philippians.

The apostle, who could surely have made good use of the continued services of Epaphroditus in Rome, gladly makes this sacrifice, and, to offset possible criticism on the part of some, emphasizes that this faithful servant of Christ must be given a hearty welcome and that he and others like him should receive the honor which they so richly deserve.

Summary of Chapter 3

Paul, the Indefatigable Idealist

warning against evil workers (the *con*cision) who by placing confidence in flesh seek to establish *their own* righteousness and perfection; as contrasted with God's true servants (the *circum*cision) ; *for example,* with Paul, who could boast of many external prerogatives, but has rejected them all and relies completely on the righteousness of Christ, in whom he is pressing on to perfection; *exhorting* the Philippians to imitate him, to honor the friends and beware of "the enemies of the cross," sensualists, who set their minds on things of earth, while believers know that *their* home-land is in heaven.

3:1-3   Warning against Judaizers.
3:4-16   Paul's Example as an Argument against the Judaizers.
       3:4-6   I, Paul, the Jew, had the following advantages (these are enumerated) .
       3:7-8a   I repudiated these advantages as basis of my righteousness before God.
       3:8b-11 I now rely on another righteousness.
       3:12-16 In Christ I press on to perfection (Paul, the runner) .
3:17-21 Warning against Sensualists. The Home-land in Heaven.

CHAPTER III

3 1 For the rest, my brothers, rejoice in the Lord. To write the same things to y o u is no trouble to me, and for y o u it is a safeguard. 2 Beware of those dogs, beware of those evil-workers, beware of the *conci*sion. 3 For, it is we who are the *circum*cision, we who worship by the Spirit of God, and glory in Christ Jesus, and put no confidence in flesh.

3:1-3

I. *Warning against Judaizers*

1. Paul, the joyful servant of Jesus Christ, the optimistic prisoner, the humble cross-bearer, the thoughtful administrator, is also the indefatigable idealist, and in that sense, perfectionist. He seeks perfection *in Christ*, in whom his soul rejoices. His creed is, "Nothing in myself I bring, only to thy cross I cling." Redemption in Christ is all-sufficient. When the apostle hears that the church of Philippi is being harassed by false teachers who deny this all-sufficiency and trust in ceremonial rites to supplement divine grace, he is deeply disturbed, and writes: **For the rest,**[124] **my brothers,** — members of the same spiritual family (see on 1:12 and on 2:25 — **rejoice.** This is by no means the first time Paul has touched on the exalted theme of joy (see also 1:4; 2:17, 18; 2:28, 29), but this time he specifically adds **in the Lord,** that is, only in union with him, and then solely in the person and work of the Lord Jesus Christ, not in anything that man might wish to contribute. This naturally leads the apostle to refer once more to a theme on which he has dwelt repeatedly; namely, that believers should acknowledge their oneness in Christ, and should not permit this unity to be undermined by enemies. It is entirely natural that before returning to this subject he

---

[124] The words "for the rest" or "finally" are very appropriate when a letter is gradually drawing to a close (Phil. 4:8; also II Cor. 13:11; I Thess. 4:1; II Thess. 3:1). It is not true, however, that this expression proves that Paul was about to end the letter at this very point, for (τὸ) λοιπόν may also simply introduce a new paragraph in which the apostle proceeds to a subject different from the one he has just now been discussing, a subject which he regards as very important and which he now wishes to stress. Besides, if "for the rest" when there are still forty-four more verses in Philippians disproves the unity of Philippians, would not the same expression followed by forty-six more verses (I Thess. 4:1) disprove the unity of I Thessalonians?

147

states: **To write the same things to y o u is no trouble to me, and for y o u it is a safeguard.**

It is *the duty of militant unity in a world of unbelief and hostility* that Paul has set before the church of Philippi previously; first, no doubt, orally, while he was present among them, later in writing. In this selfsame letter to the Philippians he had already written:

"Only continue to exercise y o u r citizenship in a manner worthy of the gospel of Christ, that whether I come and see y o u or am absent, I may hear of y o u that y o u are standing firm in one spirit, with one soul striving side by side for the faith of the gospel and not frightened in anything by the adversaries . . . make full my joy by being of the same mind, having the same love, with souls united setting y o u r minds on unity, doing nothing from selfish ambition or from empty conceit, but in humble-mindedness each counting the other better than himself; each looking not only to his own interests but also to the interests of others. . . . that y o u may become blameless and guileless, children of God without blemish in the midst of a crooked and perverse generation, among whom y o u are shining as stars in the universe, holding forth the word of life . . ." (1:27, 28; 2:2-4; 2:14-16).

Thus he had clearly warned against "the adversaries" and had just as clearly summoned the members of the church *unitedly* to be on their guard against these enemies and to combat them with the only effective weapon, namely, "the word of life." But in view of the fact that these opponents are very shrewd, numerous, and determined, and that he, Paul, is filled with love for the Philippians, he writes that to *him* it is "no trouble," no irksome task, to repeat previous warnings, and that for *them* this is a precaution for their spiritual safety.[125]

---

[125] Other explanations of "to write the same things to y o u" are:

(1) F. W. Beare and others see here an abrupt break in the course of the letter, a complete lack of connection between this chapter and the remainder of the letter. Answer: the unity of the letter has already been defended. See Introduction, VI.

(2) John Calvin represents those who think that the apostle means, "To repeat the same things to you which, while present, I told you." Answer: in view of such passages as Phil. 3:18; II Thess. 2:5, a reference to previous *oral* teaching may indeed be included in the meaning. *Written* admonitions, and these in this very letter, urging believers to take a courageous, united stand against the adversaries, are clear, as has been shown.

(3) H. Alford, etc., regard the expression as referring to the immediately preceding exhortation to rejoice in the Lord. Answer: the words, "for y o u it is safe" (or "a safeguard") are an indication of *danger*, which hardly suits the exhortation to rejoice.

(4) J. B. Lightfoot implies that the expression "to write the same things" is an allusion to admonitions against dissension. He points out that several of these warnings are found in this very letter. Answer: see under the next point (5).

(5) R. C. H. Lenski regards 3:1b to refer to the warning found in Phil. 1:27-30 to stand firm against opponents. Answer: On the whole I agree with Lightfoot and Lenski, and have combined the two views. Paul, as I see it, refers to his previous

And so the "adversaries" of 1:27, 28 appear once more here in Chapter 3, but now explicitly; first *the Judaists* (3:2); then *the sensualists* (3:18, 19).

2. With respect to the Judaists or Judaizers Paul writes, **Beware of those dogs, beware of those evil-workers, beware of the concision.** Note the threefold re-iteration, Beware . . . beware . . . beware! This can be very effective; for example,

"Holy, holy, holy is Jehovah of hosts" (Isa. 6:3);
"The temple of Jehovah, the temple of Jehovah, the temple of Jehovah, is this" (Jer. 7:4);
"Alleluiah! Alleluiah! Alleluiah! Amen" (in the refrain of *Hark! Ten Thousand Harps and Voices*);
"Goodnight! Goodnight! Goodnight!" *(in The Christian's Goodnight)*;

all the more effective when, as in "Beware . . . beware . . . beware!" they occur in the form of terse commands or exhortations; compare:

"O land, land, land, hear the word of Jehovah" (Jer. 22:29); or
"Break, break, break" (Tennyson, giving expression, in a beautiful little poem, to the burdensome sense of loss on the death of a beloved one).

Here in Philippians also, the three words are, as it were, blows of the gavel, signaling for attention, in order that the church of Philippi by giving heed may be safeguarded against spiritual and moral loss.

It is clear that the apostle had become profoundly disturbed by continued news from Philippi. It was a wonderful congregation, to be sure (4:1), but danger was threatening. It is entirely possible that just now fresh tidings of a renewed onslaught against the very essence of the gospel of salvation through Christ alone had reached him. At any rate, Paul uses vigorous language to guard against the evil. He speaks of dogs, evil-workers, the concision.

It has been said that his language undergoes a sudden change here; that unexpectedly it turns from tenderly loving address to sharp rebuke and denunciation; and that for this reason the present section must belong to another letter. With this judgment I cannot agree. To be sure, there is here something bordering on fiery vehemence. But an incisive caution against a dangerous foe is not necessarily a sign of lovelessness. On the contrary, the warmer a father's affection for his son, the deeper will be his distress when that son's life is being persistently threatened by shrewd

---

exhortations that believers take a *united* stand against *the adversaries.* I believe, however, that Lenski has somewhat weakened his case by writing that here in Chapter 3 the apostle has in mind another set of opponents than before. As he sees it, 1:28 refers exclusively to *pagan* opponents; 3:1b, 2, to the *Judaizers.* But in that case would Paul have said, To write *the same things* to y o u?

enemies, and the more earnest will be his warnings. So it is also in the present instance. What Paul writes here in verse 2 is in complete harmony with the tender appellation in verse 1, where he addresses the members of the Philippian church as "my brothers."

Now when Paul describes the opponents as those dogs, those evil-workers, the concision, he has in mind *one* kind of enemy, not three different types. This is clear from the context, which in the present paragraph concerns itself with *one* foe only: the concision over against the circumcision (see 3a). Besides, also in 3b a threefold description is given of *one* type of people, namely, God's true worshipers.

But when Paul speaks about the enemy, whom precisely does he have in mind? That he is thinking of Jews is clear from the use of the term "the concision" and from the entire argument in verses 2-6. But is he thinking of those Jews who persisted in their sullen rejection of the Christ? Or of those Jews who had indeed confessed Jesus but insisted that in order to attain salvation — at least *complete* salvation — it was necessary for all, Gentile as well as Jew, to keep the law of Moses, with special emphasis on circumcision? To save space, I shall from this point on call the first group *Jews,* the second, *Judaizers.* As I see it, it was the latter group he had in mind. The words here used form a striking parallel to Paul's denunciation of Judaizing teachers in Galatians (1:6-9; 3:1; 5:1-12, note especially verse 12 there; 6:12-15) and II Corinthians (11:13, cf. "deceitful workers" there with "evil workers" here). To be sure, the *Jews* had followed Paul on his missionary journeys, in order to contradict his message (Acts 13:50; 14:2, 19; 17:5, 13; 18:12; etc.), but so to some extent had the *Judaizers* (Acts 15:1). The theory that this latter opposition ceased completely after the council of Jerusalem (Acts 15:6-29) cannot be substantiated. Rather the opposite. Else why would it have been necessary for Paul to write Galatians? And is it not true that even the Pastoral Epistles (later than Philippians) combat a heresy consisting of the error of the Judaizers mixed with ingredients of other sinister falsehoods? (See N.T.C. on the Pastoral Epistles.)

When Paul reflects on the fact that the Judaizers are attacking the doctrine of salvation by grace alone and are striving to substitute for it a mixture of divine favor and human merit, with emphasis on the latter, he flings at them the derisive epithet which the Jews were always applying to the Gentiles. *Dogs* he calls them. He is thinking not of pets but of pariahs, large, savage, and ugly. One could see them almost everywhere, prowling about the garbage and the rubbish thrown into the streets. In comparing the Judaizers with these loathsome scavengers Paul has in mind *all,* or more likely *some,* of the following items; certainly item (1).

Are these dogs (1) unclean and filthy (Prov. 26:11; cf. II Peter 2:22; Matt. 7:6; Rev. 22:15)? So are also the Judaizers as to their motives. Do these (2) howl and snarl (Ps. 59:6)? So do also those, uttering loud and angry words against the true doctrine. Are these (3) greedy and shameless (Isa. 56:11)? So are also those, for they would devour the church. Are the former (4) contemptible (II Sam. 9:8; 16:9; II Kings 8:13)? So are also the latter. Other characteristics common to both dogs and Judaizers might be added; such as, (5) insolent, (6) cunning, and (7) roaming. The metaphor was apt.

Workers Paul also calls these men. Yes, church-workers are they. Right inside the church they themselves, as church-members, recognized as such somewhere, are carrying on their work. Missionaries are they, propagandizers! Was there not — and is there not always — a crying need for workers? Cf. Matt. 9:37, 38. But note the modifier: *evil* workers. These men are *wicked* laborers, *malicious* toilers. Cf. "deceitful workers" (II Cor. 11:13) and "workers of iniquity" (Luke 13:27). By no means are they "workers of righteousness." Instead of *helping* the good cause, they actually *harm* it. They draw the attention away from Christ and his accomplished redemption, and fix it upon an outworn ritual, and upon human worth and attainment in insisting upon its perpetuation and application. Here is Satan's demolition crew. It is working very hard to demolish God's beautiful palace of grace and peace.

The scorching parody continues as Paul adds: The *con*cision, that is, the mutilation-party, a name here scornfully given to those who insisted on the cutting away of the foreskin of *the body* only, not also of *the heart*. The apostle contrasts *con*cision with *circum*cision.[126]

What he means when he thus castigates the Judaizers with their emphasis on the outward rite of circumcision, as if the mere rite apart from the inner consecration of the heart were of any value, is set forth by himself in these words: "For he is not a Jew who is one outwardly; neither is that circumcision which is outward in flesh; but he is a Jew who is one inwardly; whose circumcision is that of the heart, in spirit, not in (the) letter; whose praise is not of men but of God" (Rom. 2:28, 29). For circumcision of *heart* cf. Lev. 26:41; Deut. 10:16; 30:6; Jer. 4:4; Ezek. 44:7; of *ear*, Jer. 6:10; and of *lips*, Exod. 6:12, 30. This is *Christian* circumcision (Col. 2:11, 12). On the other hand, the circumcision *merely* of the body, especially when this is performed and insisted upon by those who profess to believe in Jesus as Savior, is worse than useless. It is actually *mutilation*, cutting away, spiritual destruction, for if anyone receives this kind of circumcision, Christ

---

[126] He is fond of this kind of pun; cf., for example, "not busy workers but busybodies" (see N.T.C. on II Thessalonians 3:11). This style-characteristic is found in many languages. Often the real punch of such paronomasia (the use of words similar in sound but different in meaning) is lost in translation. But from the Latin compare the charge of pope against antipope, that the latter was "not consecrated but execrated (accursed)," and from the German note Luther's letter addressed to the pope, calling him, "Your hellishness" instead of "Your holiness."

will profit him not at all (Gal. 5:2; cf. 1:6-8). He will be farther removed
from Christ than he ever was before!

3. Beware of such leaders, says Paul, **for it is** not they but **we who are the
circumcision.** We Christians out of Jews and Gentiles (Rom. 9:24) are the
truly circumcized ones. The Jew is no better than the Gentile (Rom. 3:9).
"There is no distinction; for all have sinned and fall short of the glory of
God; being justified freely by his grace through the redemption that is in
Christ Jesus" (Rom. 3:24). This Jew-Gentile church, the church in which
neither circumcision nor uncircumcision amounts to anything, is the Israel
of God (Gal. 6:16). All those who belong to this church have Abraham as
their father (Gal. 3:9, 29). The middle wall of partition, separating Jew
and Gentile, has been completely broken down, never to be rebuilt. Through
Christ both have their access in one Spirit unto the Father (Eph. 2:14, 18).
Language could not be clearer. The notion that God even today recognizes two favored groups — on the one hand the church and on the other
the Jews — is thoroughly unscriptural. What Paul teaches here is, moreover, entirely in harmony with what is taught elsewhere. Jesus said, "I also
have other sheep that do not belong to this fold. Them also I must lead,
and they will listen to my voice, and become one flock, one shepherd" (John
10:16). And Peter applies to the church of the New Testament period the
very terms which in the old dispensation pertain to the people of Israel.
He writes, "But y o u are an elect race, a royal priesthood, a holy nation,
a people for (God's) own possession" (I Peter 2:9).
A threefold description is now given of the truly circumcized. Yet,
although in this description there are three grammatically parallel elements,
items two and three describe essentially the same mark, first positively, then
negatively. Hence, there are just two distinctive marks. The first one is:
we who worship by the Spirit of God.[127] Their *religious worship* [128] is
Spirit-guided. It proceeds from personalities renewed and energized by the
Holy Spirit. Hence, it is wholly from the heart, and is not hampered by
physical considerations. It does not ask, "Is the flesh of the worshipers
circumcized or not circumcized?" "Is the place of worship a beautiful
cathedral or a simple home?" "Must we worship on Mt. Gerizim or in
Jerusalem?" (John 4:19-24).
The second distinctive mark is expressed positively as follows: **and glory in
Christ Jesus.** Paul is fond of this word *glorying, boasting,* or *exulting.* He
uses it about 35 times (see also on Phil. 1:26), mostly in I and II Corinthians.
In all the rest of the New Testament it occurs only twice (James 1:19; 4:16).

---

[127] The textual evidence for this reading is stronger than that on which are based
the renderings "which worship God in the spirit" (A.V.) and "who worship God
in spirit" (R.S.V.).
[128] See R. C. Trench, *Synonyms of the New Testament* xxxv.

The apostle loves the beautiful Jeremiah passage (Jer. 9:23, 24), and in abbreviated form quotes it both in I Cor. 1:31 and in II Cor. 10:17. Those whose hearts — hence also lips and ears — have been circumcized make their boast in the Lord, in him alone. Such boasters rely entirely on Christ Jesus, the Anointed Savior; on his *person* and *work*. They glory in his *cross*, that is, in his atonement, as the only basis for their salvation. His presence is their consolation. His power provides them with energy to endure persecution and to raise and carry forward into battle the banner of the cross. On his unfailing, sovereign grace they rest for time and for eternity. Let the apostle be his own interpreter: "For I determined not to know anything among y o u but Jesus Christ, and him crucified" (I Cor. 2:2). "But far be it for me to glory, except in the cross of our Lord Jesus Christ, through which the world was crucified to me, and I to the world" (Gal. 6:14).

> "My hope is built on nothing less
> Than Jesus' blood and righteousness;
> I dare not trust the sweetest frame,
> But wholly lean on Jesus' name.
> On Christ, the solid Rock, I stand;
> All other ground is sinking sand."
>
> (Edward Mote)

Negatively, this is expressed as follows: **and put no confidence in flesh.** It stands to reason that if a person is constantly making his boast in Christ Jesus, he will put no confidence in flesh, for what is flesh? In broad terms, *flesh is anything apart from Christ on which one bases his hope for salvation.* In the present context it refers to merely human advantages and attainments, ceremonial, hereditary, legal, and moral in character (note Paul's own explanation in verses 4-6). It is the merely carnal self, viewed as a ground of eternal security.[129] It was on this self that the Judaizers relied. They boasted in mere *flesh.* In fact the term fitted them not only in the broader sense, as explained, but even in a more restricted sense, for they insisted on the circumcision of the literal, physical flesh.

Now the *truly* circumcized place confidence not in flesh but in Christ alone.

Paul had been saying, "For it is we who are the circumcision, we who worship by the Spirit of God, and glory in Christ Jesus, and put no confidence in flesh." Turning now from *we* to *I* he continues:

---

4 though I myself have reason for confidence even in flesh. If anyone else imagines that he has reason for confidence in flesh, I (have) more: 5 circumcized on the eighth day, of the people of Israel, of the tribe of Benjamin, a Hebrew

---

[129] For the various meanings of the term *flesh* as used by Paul see on Phil. 1:22, footnote 55. Here in Phil. 3:3 meaning g. applies.

of Hebrews, as to law a Pharisee, 6 as to zeal persecuting the church, as to legal righteousness having become blameless. 7 Nevertheless, such things as once were gains to me these have I counted loss for Christ. 8 Yes, what is more, I certainly do count all things to be sheer loss because of the all-surpassing excellence of knowing Christ Jesus my Lord, for whom I suffered the loss of all these things, and I am still counting them refuse, in order that I may gain Christ, 9 and be found in him, not having a righteousness of my own, legal righteousness, but that (which is) through faith in Christ, the righteousness (which is) from God (and rests) on faith; 10 that I may know him, and the power of his resurrection, and (the) fellowship of his sufferings, becoming increasingly conformed to his death, 11 if only I may attain to the resurrection from the dead.

　　12 Not that I have already gotten hold or have already been made perfect, but I am pressing on (to see) if I can also take hold of that for which I was laid hold on by Christ Jesus. 13 Brothers, I do not count myself yet to have laid hold, but one thing (I do) , forgetting what lies behind (me) and eagerly straining forward to what lies ahead, 14 I am pressing on toward the goal for the prize of the upward call of God in Christ Jesus. 15 Accordingly, let us, as many as are mature, continue to set our mind on this, and if on some minor point y o u are differently minded, that, too God will make plain to y o u. 16 Only, let our conduct be consistent with the level we have attained.

3:4-16

II *Paul's Example as an Argument against the Judaizers*
　A. *I, Paul, the Jew, Had the Following "Advantages"*
　　(1) *I, not They* (at least not in the same degree)
　　(2) *What My Parents Gave Me*
　　　a. Circumcision
　　　　"circumcized on the eighth day"
　　　b, c, d. Noble Birth
　　　　　"of the people of Israel"
　　　　　"of the tribe of Benjamin"
　　　　　"a Hebrew of Hebrews"
　　(3) *What I, Through My Own Efforts Attained*
　　　e. Recognition as a Pharisee
　　　　"as to law a Pharisee"
　　　f. Zeal
　　　　"as to zeal persecuting the church"
　　　g. Legal Rectitude
　　　　"as to legal righteousness having become blameless"

3:4-6

A. *I, Paul, the Jew, Had the Following "Advantages"*
(1) *I, not They* (at least not in the same degree)

4. By means of a telling argument, taken from his own experience, the apostle now presents himself as being, by God's grace, an example (Phil. 3:17) of God's true servants, as contrasted with those who were putting confidence in flesh. He writes, **though I myself have reason for confidence** [130] **even in flesh.** He emphasizes "I myself" (even more than the Judaizers). He cannot very well say, "*We* ourselves," for though the trusting in Christ alone is true of *all* God's genuine servants, yet the particular experience which the apostle is about to relate (in verses 4-7) pertained to himself alone, not literally to all Christians or to all the members of the church at Philippi, in Rome, or anywhere else. When he now writes that he himself *has reason for confidence even in flesh,* he does not mean that, after all, he does regard ceremonial and hereditary advantages and personal attainments to have *saving* value. On the contrary, he means that *if* this were actually the case, then he himself, even more than the Judaizers, would be entitled to such a ground of trust. This is in line with his own explanation, namely, **If anyone else** — he has the Judaizer in mind, of course — **imagines that he has reason for confidence in flesh, I (have) more.** The question might be asked, "But if Paul does not attach any merit for eternity to these Jewish distinctions, why then does he give us this list of special privileges which he, as a Jew, had enjoyed?" Two reasons immediately present themselves. He does this:

a. To answer the possible charge, "Paul is decrying privileges to which he himself cannot lay claim. He minimizes them because he never had them and cannot get them. The grapes are sour." This possible charge is answered in verses 5 and 6.

b. To refute the argument of the Judaizers that there is saving value in these distinctions. The apostle is going to show, from his own experience, that what he had considered gain turned out to be loss. This he does in verses 7-11.

As to a., the apostle shows that if the Judaizers present their list of special advantages, and Paul places his own list next to theirs, he, adopting for the sake of argument their "foolish" line of reasoning, emerges as a winner in this competition. On that basis the apostle has a right to speak, being in every sense an authentic Jew.

It is in that sense that the apostle now presents his credentials. In particulars the list here is on the whole substantially different from that in II Cor. 11:22-33. Yet *the argument* is the same, namely, "If there must be

---

[130] πεποίθησις , acc. −ν, not used here in the sense of subjective confidence (as in II Cor. 1:15; Eph. 3:12) but as the context clearly shows, *ground of confidence.* Similarly, in the next line, πεποιθέναι, second perfect active infinitive from πείθω, means (imagines) *to have reason for confidence.* Compare the use of ἐλπίς and χαρά in I Thess. 2:19. The use of words like confidence, hope, joy, for the ground of the feeling is found in many languages.

boasting, I, too, can indulge in it" (II Cor. 11:21). And so we come to Paul's list here in Phil. 3:5, 6, with its seven items.

(2) *What My Parents Gave Me*

5, 6. circumcized on the eighth day. The reason why the apostle mentions circumcision before giving any details with respect to his ancestry is probably that it was this very rite for which the Judaizers contended most of all. "With respect to circumcision I am an eighth-day-er," [131] writes Paul. This was in strict accordance with the law (Gen. 17:12; Lev. 12:3). Isaac was circumcized when he was eight days old (Gen. 21:4); [132] so was Jesus (Luke 2:21). But the same thing could probably not be said for every Judaizer. In all likelihood *some* of these were proselytes from the Gentile world, and as a result had been circumcized not on the eighth day but as adults. In this respect, therefore, Paul excelled them, that is, *if* circumcision according to law was an advantage.

of the people of Israel. His parents did not belong to a mixed stock, like so many people who were living in Palestine at that time, nor had they been grafted into Israel. He was a direct descendant not only of Abraham (the Ishmaelites were also Abraham's offspring), nor only of Abraham and Isaac (the Edomites could claim as much), but of Abraham, Isaac, *and Jacob.* It was to Jacob, after his wrestling with God, that God himself had given the new and significant name *Israel* (Gen. 32:28). Of this very *Israel* Paul was a descendant. He belonged therefore to the chosen people, the people of the covenant, the specially privileged people (Exod. 19:5, 6; Num. 23:9; Ps. 147:19, 20; Amos 3:2; Rom. 3:1, 2; 9:4, 5). Were the Judaizers able truthfully to claim such purity of descent for every one of their party?

of the tribe of Benjamin. Why does Paul mention this? According to several commentators, for reasons such as the following: the Benjamites were Israel's élite, its highest aristocracy. Did not the tribe always have the place of honor in Israel's line of battle? (Judg. 5:14; Hos. 5:8) This tribe, moreover, produced "seven hundred picked men lefthanded; every one could sling stones at a hairbreadth, and not miss" (Judg. 20:16); also "mighty men of valor, archers" (I Chron. 8:40). These interpreters add that Israel's first king was a Benjamite (I Sam. 9:1, 2). According to J. B. Lightfoot, in Acts 13:21 it is "with marked emphasis" that Paul himself refers to King Saul.

---

[131] Cf. for the Greek idiom "for he is a fourth-day-er" (or "fourth-day man"), that is, "for he (Lazarus) has been dead four days" (John 11:39). In such cases the ordinal is used with persons.
[132] Ishmael and the Ishmaelites at the age of thirteen (cf. Gen. 17:25).

Had not the apostle received his Hebrew name from this very king? [133] It is also said that the tribe of Benjamin was unique among all the tribes of Israel in always remaining loyal to the Davidic dynasty. A very noble, a most illustrious tribe, this tribe of Benjamin!

I fear, however, that this oft displayed picture is somewhat off balance, that this representation suffers from lack of careful exegesis. Is it correct to say that Judg. 5:14 and Hos. 5:8, in their respective contexts, prove that this tribe always held the place of honor in Israel's line of battle? It is doubtful, to say the least, whether Paul, in referring with pride to his descent from Benjamin, was thinking of Ehud and the other "southpaws" (Judg. 3:15; 20:16); or of the archers, for that matter. As to Israel's first king, he was hardly a person of whom a deeply religious Jew could be particularly proud (see I Sam. 15:10, 11, 23; 28:15-19). [134] I believe that Lightfoot is wrong in his interpretation of Acts 13:21, and that Lenski is right when he states that no motive of pride actuated Paul in making mention of King Saul. And finally, as to this tribe's unswerving loyalty to David, fact is that after Saul's death Benjamin yielded rather reluctantly to David (read II Sam. 2 and 3). And at the disruption of the kingdom it was indeed the *one* tribe of *Judah* but by no means the entire tribe of Benjamin that followed the house of David (see I Kings 11:32; 12:20).

Not only is the lavish praise bestowed on Benjamin somewhat out of line with history and exegesis, but other well-established and recorded facts with reference to this tribe are being conveniently ignored. Left unmentioned, for example, is the fact that it was precisely in this very tribe of Benjamin that a great atrocity had been committed, described in some detail (Judg. 19:22-26). When the other tribes demanded punishment for the wrongdoers, this was refused, with, as result, dire retribution for the guilty tribe (Judg. 20:35). Then there was the rape at Shiloh! (Judg. 21:20, 21). Surely, there must be a more honorable solution to the wife-shortage problem than the horrible expedient adopted by the tribe of Benjamin, upon the advice — let this be added in the interest of complete objectivity — of the other tribes. Finally, there was Shimei, who cursed and threw stones at God's anointed, David. This profane fellow, too, was a Benjamite (II Sam. 16:5-14). He repented, at least outwardly (II Sam. 19:16-20). Subsequently, however, he failed to keep his oath to Jehovah, and was slain (I Kings 2:36-46).

Since then it is a fact that the tribe of Benjamin presents such a mixture of light and shadow, virtue and vice, with the latter frequently predominating, why did Paul, in his pre-Christian state to which he here refers (and in a

[133] For a discussion of the apostle's names see N.T.C. on I and II Thessalonians, pp. 38, 39.
[134] David, in II Sam. 1:23, is being very magnanimous.

sense even later, Rom. 11:1), take such pride in being a Benjamite? The probable answer is as follows: *Israel,* as a theocratic people, was the recipient of God's special promises. Hence, the more convincingly Paul would be able to prove the proposition, "I am, indeed, an Israelite," the more inescapable would be the conclusion, "Therefore I am a specially privileged person." Now of all the tribes none was more Israelitish than Benjamin.

Whether or not the circumstance that Benjamin was the only son of Israel who was born in the land of promise (Gen. 35:16-20) has any particular bearing here would be hard to establish. But the following facts surely are significant. First, in common with Joseph but in distinction from the other patriarchs, Benjamin was not only a son of Israel but also of Israel's most beloved wife, Rachel (Gen. 35:17, 18). And secondly, of these two favored sons (Joseph and Benjamin) it was Benjamin alone (be it only *part* of his tribe) who, together with Judah, after the disruption formed *Israel Reconstituted* (I Kings 12:21); after the return from the captivity, *Israel Restored* (Ezra 4:1); [135] and who in connection with the plot of Haman, was God's chief agent in bringing forth *Israel Delivered* (see Book of Esther). Moreover, in thinking of the tribe of Benjamin it would be unfair to mention Shimei and then to leave out that other Benjamite, Mordecai. It was he who encouraged Esther to perform a great deed of faith and courage, and who gave us that marvelous saying, "For if you keep altogether silent at such a time as this, then relief and deliverance will rise for the Jews from another quarter, but you and your father's house will perish. And who knows whether you have not come to the kingdom for such a time as this?" (Esther 4:14).

The conclusion then is this: *if* indeed there were saving value, merit for eternity, in the special distinction of being an Israelite, then Paul was entitled to it, for, *being a Benjamite,* he surely was a most authentic Israelite. Could the Judaizers make an equally strong case for themselves? Yes, Paul was "of the tribe of Benjamin," and therefore:

a Hebrew of Hebrews. Paul was, indeed, a Hebrew, that is, an Israelite.[136] He was in fact "a Hebrew of Hebrews," that is, "purest of the pure." The

---

[135] Not all of those who returned belonged to Judah and Benjamin, but these two tribes formed the nucleus. See my *Bible Survey,* pp. 119, 120.

[136] Paul himself uses the terms *Hebrews, Israelites,* and *seed of Abraham* synonymously (II Cor. 11:22). The Old Testament uses the term *Hebrew* in a broader and in a more restricted sense. Long before Israel (Jacob) was born, there were Hebrews; e.g., Abraham (Gen. 14:13; cf. 40:15; 43:32). According to some, Abraham was a Hebrew because he was a descendant of Eber (Gen. 10:21, 24, 25). Others are of the opinion that the noun *Hebrew* is related to a verb meaning *to cross over.* On that theory the Hebrews are the people from across the Euphrates (cf. Josh. 24:2). In a more restricted sense the Hebrews are the descendants of Israel (Exod. 1:15; 2:6, 11, 13; 3:18; 21:2; Deut. 15:12; I Sam. 4:6, 9).

idiom stresses *at least* [137] the purity of his lineage: Hebrew son of Hebrew parents; hence, *definitely* a Hebrew, a Hebrew if there ever was one! In this way he emphasizes what was already implied in the preceding. He is proving this *one* point.

(3) *What I, Through My Own Efforts, Attained*

as to law a Pharisee. With reference to the law of Moses Paul had chosen to become a Pharisee. Was he not a son of Pharisees (Acts 23:6)? [138] And here he reflects how in his pre-Christian period he prided himself in this fact, namely, in his position and honor as a Pharisee. He had advanced in the religion of the Jews beyond many of his own age among his countrymen and had been exceedingly zealous for the traditions of his ancestors (Gal. 1:14). "After the strictest sect of our religion I lived, a Pharisee," he himself declared (Acts 26:5).

But how could a Jew ever take pride in being a Pharisee? Did not Jesus describe the Pharisees in language which plainly states or else implies that they were snobs and peacocks (Matt. 6:2, 16; 23:5-7), hair-splitters and fools (Matt. 23:16-22), serpents and the offspring of vipers (Matt. 23:33), cheats and hypocrites (Matt. 23:3, 13, 15, 23, 25, 27, 29)? Did they not make one think of green-eyed monsters (cf. Matt. 27:18)?

All this is true, but not all Pharisees were equally bad. Pharisaism, moreover, in its origin was not nearly as bad as it became later on. This religious party originated during the inter-testamentary period as a reaction to the excesses of those careless and indifferent Jews who had imbibed the Hellenistic spirit in its unsavory aspects. So the Pharisees or Separatists had withdrawn themselves from these worldly persons. They abstained also from politics and placed great stress on religious purity. They accepted the entire Torah, the doctrines of the immortality of the soul, the resurrection of the body, and the existence of angels. They were neither chauvinists like the Zealots, nor radicals like the Sadducees, nor politicians like the Herodians. Their high regard for the law of God deserves admiration. It explains Paul's pre-Christian pride expressed in the words "as to law a

---

[137] Many are of the opinion that the phrase "a Hebrew of Hebrews" *also* calls attention to the fact that the apostle was a Jew not only by race but also by language and customs. They think that the distinction (see Acts. 6:1) between Hellenists (Greek-speaking Jews) and Hebrews (Aramaic-speaking Jews) applies here. Paul, then, is not a Hellenist but a Hebrew as were his parents. He spoke Aramaic fluently (Acts 21:40; 22:2), was trained by a Hebrew teacher in Jerusalem (Acts 22:3), often quotes from the Hebrew Old Testament, etc. The possibility that the apostle had this additional idea in mind when he called himself "a Hebrew of the Hebrews" must be granted. Yet, with the early Greek commentators I believe that the explanation I have given is probably all that is required in the present context. See also H. A. A. Kennedy, *The Epistle to the Philippians,* in The Expositor's Greek Testament, vol. III, p. 451.
[138] Or, according to another reading, *of a Pharisee.*

Pharisee." They made their great mistake when they began to attach high value to the entire system of legalistic interpretations which the scribes superimposed upon the law, burying the law itself under the load of their traditions (cf. Mark 7:13), and when they began to think that by means of their own strict adherence to the law, so interpreted, they could bring about the coming of the Messiah and secure for themselves entrance into the kingdom of heaven. Of course, the attempt to achieve all this was far too great a strain on human nature. Hence, it is no wonder that many of them became hypocrites, some worse than others; also self-righteous, looking down with disdain upon the mere riffraff, "this rabble that does not know the law" (see N.T.C. on John 7:49). Now Paul must have been one of the better Pharisees (cf. Acts 26:9), but deluded nevertheless.

as to zeal persecuting the church. Paul had been one of the most bitter haters of the early Christians. In his zeal for the law, as misinterpreted by the scribes and Pharisees (Matt. 23:23), he had breathed threatening and slaughter against the disciples of the Lord, that is, the "Church" in its ecumenical sense, carrying out his program of molestation "even to foreign cities," "putting in chains and committing to prisons both men and women" (Acts 9:1, 2; 22:1-5; 26:9-15; I Cor. 15:9). If persecuting zeal could ever have opened the gates of heaven, Paul would have walked right in! Here, too, his "advantage" over the Judaizers was great. *They* merely proselyted. *He* had been a persecutor even "unto the death."

as to legal righteousness having become blameless. So strict had Paul been in his outward observance of the Old Testament law, as interpreted by the Jewish religious leaders, that in the pursuit of this legal rectitude he had become *blameless* (cf. Phil. 2:15), that is, in *human* judgment. His outward conduct had been irreproachable. Could the Judaists claim the same with respect to themselves? Or was Matt. 23:3, 4 also applicable, to some extent, to *them?*

3:7, 8a

B. *I Repudiated These Advantages As Basis of My Righteousness before God*

7, 8a. In the two preceding verses Paul has enumerated his superior advantages as a genuine Israelite, of noble birth, orthodox in his belief, and scrupulous in his conduct. By means of these advantages the apostle, in his pre-conversion period, had been "bleeding to climb to God." But had it not been a case of

"Gaining a foothold bit by bit
Then slipping back and losing it"?

Worse even, for never at all had there been any *real* progress, no matter how hard he, Paul the Pharisee, had labored to establish his own righteousness. But on the way to Damascus to persecute Christians the great event occurred which changed his entire life. Christ, as it were, came down the stairs to him (read the gripping account in Acts 9:1-31; 22:1-21; 26:1-23). In a moment Paul saw himself as he really was, a deluded, self-righteous, damnable sinner. Then and there he embraced the One whom until now he had been persecuting with might and main. He became "a new creature." In mind and heart he experienced a complete turn-about, a sudden and dramatic reversal of all values. The cause which with every means at his disposal and with all the zeal of heart and will he had been trying to wipe out now became very dear to him. And also, those things which to *Paul, the Pharisee,* had seemed very precious *became* at this moment — and ever after *remained* — useless to *Paul, the sinner, saved by grace;* and not merely *useless* but definitely *harmful.* Writes Paul, **Nevertheless, such things as once were gains to me these have I counted loss.** Not that any of these things which he enumerated in verses 5 and 6, and other things like them, were bad in themselves. Quite the contrary. To receive the sign of the covenant is not bad in itself. It is, in fact, a blessing. And was it not a blessing to belong to that people to which the oracles of God had been entrusted? Orthodoxy, too, is in itself a good thing. So is zeal, and so certainly also is irreproachable conduct. Paul himself elsewhere informs us that he considers such things as these to be blessings (Rom. 3:1, 2; 9:1-5; cf. 11:1). They are blessings because they can be of inestimable value if properly used, namely, as a preparation for the reception of the gospel. But when these same privileges begin to be viewed as a basis for self-satisfaction and self-glorification, when they are regarded as a ticket to heaven, they are changed into their opposites. All these separate *gains* become *one huge loss.* This is Paul's deliberate, considered judgment. He considered the gains, and counted [139] them loss. And in that judgment he persisted, as is implied in the tense of the Greek verb. On his balance-sheet those things which once were included, one by one, in the column of *assets* have now been transferred to the column of *liabilities,* and have been entered as *one gigantic liability.* Note that the plusses have not become a zero (0), but have become even less than zero, that is, one colossal MINUS (−). "For what will it profit a man if he gains the whole world and forfeits his life?" (Matt. 16:26; cf. Mark 8:36).

---

[139] Compare "I have counted" (perfect tense) here with "he did not count" (aorist) in 2:6. The verb indicates arriving at a sure judgment based on careful weighing of facts. Cf. Phil. 2:3. The similarity between 3:7 and 2:6 is striking. Christ *"did not count* his existence-in-a-manner-equal-to-God something to cling to, but *emptied* himself." This *counting* and this *emptying* is reflected in Paul, who, by *having counted* things that were gain to him to be loss for Christ, *emptied* himself of "all things" (Phil. 3:8) that he might gain Christ.

The word *loss* which Paul uses here in verses 7 and 8, and nowhere else in his epistles, occurs in only one other New Testament chapter, Acts 27 (verses 10 and 21), in the story of The Voyage Dangerous. And it is exactly that same chapter which also indicates how *gain* may become *loss*. The cargo on that ship bound for Italy represented potential *gain* for the merchants, for the owner of the ship, and for hungry people. Yet, had not this wheat been thrown into the sea (Acts 27:38), *loss,* not only of the ship but even of all those on board, might well have been the result. Thus also, the advantage of being born in a Christian home and having received a wonderful Christian home-training, becomes a disadvantage when it is viewed as a basis upon which to build one's hope for eternity. The same holds with respect to money, the charming look, a college education, physical strength, etc. All such helps may become hindrances. The stepping-stones will be turned into stumbling blocks, if wrongly used.

When the question is asked, "Why was it that, in Paul's considered judgment, these gains had become a loss?" the answer is **for Christ,** that is, for the sake of Christ; for, had Paul been unwilling to renounce his former estimate of these privileges and achievements, they would have deprived him of Christ, the one real gain (see verse 8).

Paul continues, in a sentence that is almost untranslatable,[140] **Yes, what is more, I certainly do count all things to be sheer loss because of the all-surpassing excellence of knowing Christ Jesus my Lord.**

In verse 8 Paul strengthens his previous statement, and this in two ways. First, he underscores what was implied in the preceding, namely, that what he counted loss at the moment of his conversion he is still counting to be loss. It is as if he were saying, "On this subject no Judaizer will ever be able to change my mind." Secondly, he now affirms that he considers not only the things mentioned in verses 5 and 6 to be a liability, a detriment, but also all other things that could stand in the way of fully accepting Christ and his righteousness. We may think of such matters as making too much of earthly possessions, delight in intimate fellowship with former anti-

---

[140] The sentence begins with the piling up of particles: ἀλλὰ μενοῦν γε καί. As in every language, when the heart is deeply stirred and when thoughts crowd the mind, the utterance becomes compressed, and words are left out. See N.T.C. on John 5:31 with respect to Abbreviated Style. A word for word, literal, rendering, so that the English sentence would start as follows, *"But, indeed, therefore, at least, even,"* would make little sense. By inserting a word here and there, an attempt could be made to get into our sentence everything that is in the original; somewhat as follows, *"But, indeed* (that is not all), *therefore* (I affirm) *at least even* (this, that) I do count all things to be loss because of the all-surpassing excellence of knowing Christ Jesus my Lord." Not only would this be rather clumsy but perhaps even unwarranted: it is a question whether, for example γε is translatable at all. It could be equivalent (in English) to a tone of voice rather than an actual word. The manner in which I have rendered the sentence is, accordingly, not literal but, I trust, natural.

Christian friends, anticipation centered on even more brilliant prospects as a Pharisee, etc. All such matters and many more are nothing but sheer loss, and this *because of* — hence also *in comparison with* — the all-surpass-ingness,[141] that is, the all-surpassing excellence or value, of "knowing Christ Jesus [142] . . . Lord." On the way to Damascus Paul had learned to know Jesus. Although there had been ample preparation for this knowledge — such as, Paul's acquaintance with the Old Testament, the testimonies he had heard from the lips of the martyrs, their behavior under fire —, when it broke in upon the soul, the experience was sudden and dramatic. Prophecy and testimony began to take on meaning now. It was an unforgettable experience, that meeting with the exalted Christ, while, a moment before, the apostle had still been breathing threatening and slaughter against Christ's Church, hence against this very Christ himself! Yes, he now *saw and heard* the actual Jesus, about whom he had been told so much. And he saw and heard him now as *Christ Jesus . . . Lord,* the name above every name (see on 2:9-11). And at the same time he here and now began to understand something of the condescending pity and tenderness of Christ's great and merciful heart, a love poured out upon *him,* even upon *Paul, the bitter persecutor!*

All this had occurred about thirty years ago. And during the period that intervened between the "Great Experience" and the writing of the present epistle to the Philippians, the joy of knowing, with a knowledge of both mind and heart (see on verse 10), *Christ Jesus . . . Lord* had been growing con-stantly, so that it outshone everything in beauty and desirability. Hence, Paul inserts a little word which makes "that beautiful name, that wonder-ful name, that matchless name" of Jesus even more adorable. He says "Christ Jesus *my* Lord." What this appropriating *my* implies is better explained by Paul himself. Read Phil. 1:21; 4:13; Rom. 7:24, 25; II Cor. 12:8-10; Gal. 1:15, 16; 2:20; 6:14; Eph. 5:1, 2; Col. 3:1-4:6; I Tim. 1:5, 16; II Tim. 1:12; 4:7, 8. According to these passages Christ Jesus is much more than Paul's Example and Friend. He is his Life, Lover, Strength, Boast, Rock, Re-warder, and especially as here, his Anointed Savior and Sovereign.

As before the rising sun the stars fade out, and as in the presence of the pearl of great price all other gems lose their luster, so fellowship with "Christ Jesus my Lord" eclipses all else. And it is Christ himself of whom

---

141 τὸ ὑπερέχον, the neuter of the present participle of ὑπερέχω (see also Phil. 2:3; 4:7; Rom. 13:1; I Peter 2:13). For other substantivized neuters in Paul see Rom. 2:4; 8:3; 9:22; I Cor. 1:25. The word *super-ness,* that is, *all-surpassing greatness* is one of a list of super-combinations used by the apostle. See N.T.C. on the Pastoral Epistles, p. 75. In Phil. 4:7 we have another.
142 Literally, "of the knowledge of Christ Jesus," etc. As is clear from verse 10, "that I may know him," the apostle is thinking of Christ Jesus not as the subject but as the object; hence, to avoid ambiguity, the translation "knowing Christ Jesus" com-mends itself.

Paul is thinking, not this or that matter about Christ. Paul is in complete agreement with the poet who said, (not *"What"* but) *"Whom* have I in heaven but thee? And there is none on earth that I desire besides thee" (Ps. 73:25). The apostle continues, **for whom I suffered the loss of all these things.**[143] It was for the sake of his Lord and Savior that Paul had lost whatever was at one time very dear to him: pride of tradition, of ancestry, of orthodoxy, of outward conformity with the law, and of whatever else there had been on which he had formerly depended as gateways to the heavenly city. Moreover his attitude of having willingly suffered this loss has not changed at all. So he continues, **and I am still counting them refuse.** What the Judaizers prize so very highly, the apostle considers to be nothing but *refuse,* something that is fit only to be thrown to the *dogs.*[144] The apostle is very consistent. Had he not, just a moment ago (see 3:2), called these dangerous enemies *dogs?* Paul, then, considers all these inherited privileges and human attainments, *considered as merits,* to be something that must be discarded as worthless leavings, abominable trash.

3:8b-11

C. *I Now Rely on Another Righteousness*
(1) It is Christ's
(2) It is not merited by works performed by man, law-works
(3) It is appropriated by faith
(4) It comes from God
(5) It results in a striving after spiritual perfection

(1) *It is Christ's*

8b, 9a. "I am still counting them refuse," says Paul, **in order that I may gain Christ and be found in him.**[145] Paul wishes to make Christ more and

---

[143] τὰ πάντα in the summarizing sense, as in II Cor. 4:15; Col. 3:8; hence, "all these things."

[144] This, in fact, may be the very derivation of the word σκύβαλον, pl. –a. By some it is said to be derived from τὸ τοῖς κυσὶ βαλλόμενον (what is thrown to the dogs). Others, however, connect it with σκώρ, dung. Though M.M. gives the preference to the meaning *dung* here in Phil. 3:8, which may be correct, the connotation *refuse* is well attested. Cf. Ecclesiasticus 27:4, "When a sieve is shaken the refuse remains"; Josephus, *Jewish War* V. 571, "they ate the refuse therefrom;" and Philo, *The Sacrifice of Abel and Cain* 109, "The chaff and husk and other refuse are scattered."

[145] The simplest and most natural construction here would seem to be that which makes κερδήσω καὶ εὑρεθῶ dependent on the nearest preceding verb, the second ἡγοῦμαι of verse 8, present middle indicative. The words κερδήσω καὶ εὑρεθῶ then state the purpose or motive of this continued act of counting all these things to be mere refuse, that purpose or motive being "that I may gain Christ and be found in Him." Now gaining Christ is indeed a life-long activity. More and more fully does

more fully his own. As long as one keeps clinging, even in the slightest degree, to his own righteousness, he cannot fully enjoy Christ's. The two simply do not go together. The one must be fully given up before the other can be fully appropriated. It is Paul's great aim that in the observation of all his fellow-believers he may be *found* to be completely *in him*, that is, in union with Christ. For the meaning of "in Christ" see also on Phil. 1:1. Here in Phil. 3 this "in him" relationship is described as to its forensic side in verse 9, and as to its practical side in verse 10. The "in him" relationship means that Christ's righteousness is imputed to the sinner, so that it is reckoned as his own. This implies redemption from the claims of Satan (Rom. 8:31, 33), reconciliation with God (II Cor. 5:18-21), forgiveness of sins (Eph. 1:7), hence, the state of being in conformity with the law of God (Rom. 8:1-4).

Now when Paul states that he is counting everything to be refuse in order that he may gain Christ and may be found in him, this sacrifice with the purpose of capturing the one, real prize must not be interpreted in a selfish, mercenary sense. It must, of course, be interpreted in the light of such passages as Rom. 11:36 and I Cor. 10:31. It is the glory of God that Paul has in mind, not just his own selfish benefit. To be sure, he is not forgetting himself. His is, in fact, seeking to promote his own welfare, which is altogether right and proper. But this ideal is never separated from the highest possible objective. The two go together. Hence, Paul is not like a man who sells an article in order to make a huge profit for himself, to be used entirely on himself. He is not like a fisherman using bait in order to catch a big fish, to be proudly displayed. Nor even like a chess-player who "sacrifices" Knight and Queen in order to checkmate his opponent's King, for the simple pleasure of winning the game. No, the apostle is more like a sea-captain who in time of war, *for patriotic reasons* jettisons his cargo, thereby lightening his ship so that it will have the speed needed to overtake and capture the enemy's vessel that contains a far more precious treasure. Even better, he is like a young man, heir to a going concern, who cheerfully gives up this inheritance in order that he may prepare himself for the ideal of his life: that of *rendering service to the Lord* in the work of the ministry, whether at home or abroad. Cf. Mark 10:21.

(2) *It is not merited by works performed by man, law-works*

Christ become united with the believer, and the believer with Christ. The fact that the *aorist* subjunctive is used to indicate this purpose or motive does not in any way cancel the duration of the process. *The aorist simply states the fact*, without indicating the time-element, whether long or short. It is simply "the flashlight picture." Also, since the aorist is properly indefinite as to time, and the subjunctive "is future in relation to the speaker," the interpretation which, along with many others, I give of this passage does not contradict grammar. See Gram. N.T., pp. 848, 849, 1380. Hence, I cannot accept Lenski's reasoning on p. 846 ff. of his Commentary.

9b. Says Paul, **not having a righteousness of my own, legal righteousness** (or: *a righteousness proceeding from law*). The apostle's meaning is: not in any sense can the righteousness that counts before God be regarded as based on my own accomplishments in conformity with the Old Testament law. *Sin earns wages* (Rom. 6:23). This return is *paid* to those who *deserve* it. But *God's righteousness is given to the undeserving.* God justifies the ungodly. Christ died for the ungodly (Rom. 4:5; 5:6; Titus 3:5).

(3) *It is appropriated by faith*
Not righteousness proceeding from law, says Paul, **but that (which is) through faith in Christ.** Faith is the appropriating agent, the hand extended to receive God's free gift. Since the only righteousness that has any value before God is Christ's righteousness *imputed* to the sinner as God's free gift to the undeserving, it stands to reason that the only possible way to obtain this righteousness is to *accept* it (one *accepts,* one does not *earn,* a gift!) by simple faith, that is, by appropriating confidence in the Giver; hence also in his word. God's Anointed is himself the object of this childlike trust (Rom. 1:16, 17; 3:21, 22; Gal. 2:20; 3:22; cf. Hab. 2:4; John 3:16).

(4) *It comes from God*
The faith-appropriation is repeated for the sake of emphasis, but first one more element is added: the divine origin of this righteousness. Hence, **the righteousness (which is) from God (and rests) on faith.** This righteousness is provided by God and avails before God (Rom. 3:24, 25; 8:3; II Cor. 5:19). Its possession and enjoyment rests on, is conditioned on, faith, faith possessed and exercised by man, to be sure (John 3:16), and for which man is fully responsible, but given, nurtured, and rewarded by God (Eph. 2:8).

(5) *It results in a striving after spiritual perfection*
10. Paul continues, **that I may know him.** Here he resumes the thought of verse 8 ("the all-surpassing excellence of knowing Christ Jesus, my Lord"), but also links his words to the immediately preceding idea of *the righteousness (which is) from God (and rests) on faith.* The progress of thought here is altogether natural. The experience of every person who has been brought out of the darkness into God's marvelous light, and has felt in his heart the glory of Christ's pardoning love is that he will sing:

"More about Jesus would I know,
More of his grace to others show;
More of his saving fulness see,
More of his love who died for me.

"More, more about Jesus,
More, more about Jesus,

166

More of his saving fulness see,
More of his love who died for me."
(E. E. Hewitt)

Thus the *faith-appropriation* of "the righteousness (which is) from God" and *contemplation* upon this fact implies, calls forth, the ardent yearning, that I may get to know Christ better and better.[146] And, considering the matter from God's side, we can say that when God justifies his child he also sends forth his sanctifying Spirit into the heart. Hence, from the divine side the link between righteousness *imputed* and righteousness *imparted* is the Holy Spirit; from the human side — ever dependent upon the divine — the link is the gratitude of faith.

Now "that I may know him" refers to a knowledge not only of the *mind* but also of the *heart*. (See also a similar use of *know* in John 17:3; Gal. 4:9; I John 2:18, 29; 4:8.) Though the first should never be excluded, the emphasis here is on the second. See N.T.C. on John 7:17, 18, for details on the inter-relation of the various elements of Christian experience. The apostle, being *an indefatigable idealist,* and in that sense *perfectionist,* wants to gain as full an understanding of Christ's person and love as possible. He is not satisfied with anything short of perfection. When he expresses his yearning *to know* Christ, he has in mind not only or even mainly the learning of certain facts about Christ but also and especially the sharing of certain experiences with him, as is clearly indicated by the rest of verse 10 and by verse 11. He wishes to become entirely "wrapped up" in Christ, so that Jesus will be "all the world" to him.[147] One gains such *experiential knowledge* by wide-awake attendance at public worship and proper use of the

---

[146] The articular second aorist infinitive τοῦ γνῶναι may, therefore, be called an *explanatory* infinitive, or also an infinitive of *contemplated result* or *purpose.* It sets forth what is the result and purpose of embracing the righteousness of Christ, by a living faith, what is *implied* in this act. My interpretation here differs but slightly from that which would connect the infinitive with the entire thought of verses 8b and 9. Least satisfactory, as I see it, is the explanation of those who leapfrog the second ἡγοῦμαι of verse 8, and, ignoring what lies in between, connect τοῦ γνῶναι with ἐζημιώθην, so that the thought would be "I suffered the loss of all things . . . that I might get to know Christ." My objection is this: Paul clearly is here no longer speaking about his experience on the way to Damascus but of his *present* yearning to get to know Christ better and better right along, in order to reach spiritual perfection in him, as is clear not only from the immediately preceding context but also from verses 11-14.

[147] The word used in the original for *that I may know* is a form of γινώσκω. See N.T.C. on John 1:10, 11, 31; 3:11; 8:28, 55; 16:30; 21:17, for distinction between γινώσκω and οἶδα.

Besides, the concept *knowledge* as referred to by Paul in verses 8 and 10 was probably also influenced by the use of the related word in the Old Testament where *to know* Jehovah means *to revere* him, *to be consecrated* to him (Prov. 1:7; Isa. 11:2; Hab. 2:14). It is a distinctly *personal, intimate, practical, religious* knowledge that Paul has in mind.

sacraments (Heb. 10:25; cf. Matt. 18:20, 28:19; Luke 22:14-20; I Cor. 11:17-24) ; by showing kindness to all, practising the forgiving spirit, above all love; by learning to be thankful; by studying the Word of Christ both devotionally and exegetically so that it dwells in the heart; by singing psalms, hymns, and spiritual songs to the glory of God, and continuing steadfastly in prayer; and thus by redeeming the time as *a witness of Christ to all men* (Col. 3:12-17; 4:2-6).

To show what this knowledge of Christ implies Paul continues: **and the power of his resurrection.** He longs for an ever-increasing supply of the power that proceeds from the risen and exalted Savior. That resurrected Savior, *by dint of his very resurrection,* assures Paul, through the Spirit, *of justification* (Rom. 4:25; 8:1, 16; I Cor. 15:17) ; for when the Father raised the Son he thereby proved that he had accepted the ransom paid by Christ (Matt. 20:28; Acts 20:28; I Peter 1:18) as full satisfaction for Paul's sin.

It was that same resurrected Christ who sent his Spirit into Paul's heart for the purpose of *sanctification.* Christ's life in heaven is ever the cause of Paul's new life (John 14:19). Paul desires a growing supply of this cleansing power, this *dynamite* that destroys sin and makes room for *personal holiness and for effective witness-bearing!*

Finally, this resurrected Christ also seals Paul's *glorification* and this with respect not only to the soul but also to the body, and not only for one person separately but for Paul together with all the saints. (Rom. 8:11; I Cor. 15; Phil. 3:21; II Tim. 4:8).

Now when the life of the risen Christ has entered into the heart of the believer and makes itself more and more manifest in his entire conduct, the inevitable result will be a sharing in Christ's *sufferings.* Hence, the apostle continues, **and (the) fellowship of his sufferings.** Paul yearns to participate more and more fully in the reproaches and afflictions of his Lord and Savior. He wants to "fill up whatever is lacking in the sufferings of Christ for his body, the Church" (Col. 1:24). Not as if Christ's atonement were incomplete (Heb. 10:14). But though the atonement left nothing to be desired, suffering *for the sake of Christ and his cause* (Rom. 8:17; II Cor. 11:24-28; 12:10) continues. Such suffering is a privilege (for detailed proof see on Phil. 1:29). It implies beatings, stonings, hunger, thirst, cold, nakedness, etc., endured in the work or being *a witness for Christ to all men* (Acts 9:15, 16; 22:15). It includes also the experience of the hatefulness and hurt of one's own sins, the sins that caused the Savior to suffer such indescribable agonies (Rom. 7:9-25). Hence, the desire to participate in the sufferings of Christ is part of the intense longing and striving for complete holiness, as is clear also from the words which follow immediately: **becoming increasingly conformed to his death.** This, as the apostle himself explains in a closely parallel passage (Rom. 6:4-11), means to become *dead to sin.* It implies death to selfishness; hence, eagerness to be a blessing to others, as was Christ in his death. Thus a person becomes *conformed* to Christ's death.

Union with Christ implies that all of Christ's redemptive experiences are duplicated unredemptively in the believer. The Christian, accordingly, suffered with Christ (Rom. 8:17), was crucified with him (Rom. 6:6), died with him (Rom. 6:8; II Tim. 2:11), was buried with him (Rom. 6:4; Col. 2:12), made alive with him (Col. 2:13), raised with him (Col. 2:12; 3:1), made joint-heirs with him (Rom. 8:17), is glorified with him (Rom. 8:17), enthroned with him (Col. 3:1; Rev. 20:4), and reigns with him (II Tim. 2:12; Rev. 20:4).

11. However, one should be careful to avoid the conclusion that these experiences are all *literally* reflected in the life and death of believers. Failure to note this important point has given rise to errors in exegesis both here and in connection with verse 11. Thus, when the apostle yearns to become increasingly conformed to Christ's death, this has been interpreted to mean that he longed for death by crucifixion or at least for death as a martyr. But why not allow the apostle himself to clarify the meaning? When with a believing heart the Christian appropriates the saving value of Christ's death, he dies to sin, for the guilt of his sin is removed, and its power over him is gradually reduced and at death completely annihilated by the work of the Holy Spirit. Rejecting sin and selfishness he throws himself into the work of being a means in God's hand to open men's eyes, that they may turn from darkness to light, and from the power of Satan to God (Rom. 6:4-11; Acts 26:18). It is in that sense that the believer experiences fellowship with Christ's sufferings and becomes conformed to his death.[148]

Similarly, when it is stated that the believer was crucified with Christ or was buried with him or raised with him, these expressions cannot be taken *literally* to mean that Christ's followers suffered physical death by crucifixion, that their bodies were interred, or that they have already been physically raised. The immediate context and parallel passages must be permitted to explain the meaning. And this also holds with respect to the next statement, in which Paul expresses his intense longing thus: **if only I may attain to the resurrection from the dead.** What is meant by this *out-resurrection out of the dead* (thus literally)? In the light both of the preceding and following contexts, these words give expression to Paul's intense longing and striving

---

[148] Entering into the fellowship of Christ's suffering and becoming conformed to his death by dying unto sin and selfishness and thus becoming, like Christ in his death, a blessing to others, is beautifully illustrated by M. C. Tenney in his book *Philippians, The Gospel At Work*, Grand Rapids, Michigan, 1956, pp. 77, 78. Not for a moment does the apostle forget his great missionary task, his exalted calling, as is evident not only from verses 12-14 of the present chapter, but also from Phil. 1:12-14, 18; 2:15, 16.

*to be raised completely above sin and selfishness, so that he can be a most
effective agent for the salvation of men to the glory of God.* Cf. Rom. 6:4,
5, 11; 7:24; I Cor. 9:22-24. *This is his aim even now.* However, absolute,
spiritual perfection for the entire person will not be fully attained until
Christ's brilliant Return, when in both soul and body Paul will glorify God
in Christ forevermore, and will delight in all the blessings of fellowship
with him and with all the saints in the new heaven and earth. This will be
the gracious reward, the prize, given to all who aim for perfection even now.
Such is the apostle's teaching not only here but everywhere (see verses 12-14,
20, 21 of the present chapter; also I Cor. 15:50-58; I Thess. 3:11-13; 5:23;
II Tim. 1:12; 4:7, 8; Titus 2:13, 14.[149]

When Paul, with reference to this *out-resurrection out of the dead* writes,
"If only I may attain," he is not expressing distrust in the power or love of
God nor doubt as to his own salvation. Paul often rejoices in assurance of
salvation (Rom. 6:5, 8; 7:25; 8:16, 17, 35-39. In this assurance he was
strengthened as the years went by (I Tim. 1:15-17; II Tim. 1:12; 4:7, 8).
But he wrote it in the spirit of *deep humility* and commendable distrust *in
self.* The words also imply *earnest striving.* They show us Paul, the Idealist,
who applies to himself the rule that he imposes on others (Phil. 2:12, 13).

It is in this same humble spirit that in verses 12-14 Paul enlarges on the
theme, "In Christ I press on to perfection."

3:12-16

D. *In Christ I Press on to Perfection*
Paul, the Runner
His
(1) *Frame of Mind*
(2) *Exertion*
(3) *Goal*
(4) *Reward*

(1) *Frame of Mind*
12. Paul's intense yearning and striving for spiritual perfection is expressed
now under the symbolism of the familiar foot-race.[150] In order to grasp the
apostle's meaning the underlying figure must be borne in mind at every
point. Picture then the ancient Greek stadium with its course for foot-races
and tiers of seats for the spectators. At Athens the length of the course was
one-eighth of an old Roman mile; hence, about 607 feet in our measurement.
The one at Ephesus was somewhat longer. The purpose of the race was to

---

[149] Because of its length this footnote has been placed at the end of the chapter,
page 185.
[150] See N.T.C. on I Tim. 4:7, 8; II Tim. 4:7, 8. Cf. I Cor. 9:24; Phil. 2:16; Heb.
12:1. Other references that come in for consideration in this connection are:
Acts 13:25; 20:24; Rom. 9:16; Gal. 2:2; 5:7; II Thess. 3:1.

reach the goal opposite the entrance, or to run up and back, and this once or even twice. Near the entrance the contestants, stripped for the race, have been assigned their places on a stone threshold. In fact, several of the old stadia show what is left of rows of stone blocks at either end of the track. These blocks contain grooves to give the sprinter's feet a firm hold for a quick take-off. Here the contestants stand, body bent forward, one hand lightly touching the threshold, awaiting the signal: the letting down of a cord that has been stretched in front of them. At the signal they leap forward.

When the question is asked, "Will this contestant succeed?" the answer is, "Much will depend on his frame of mind." If he tells himself, "I'm a sure winner, no matter what I do," he will probably undergo the experience of the hare, in the fable, *The Hare and the Tortoise.* While the tortoise was plodding steadily on, the hare took a nap, and on awakening discovered, too late, that his opponent had already reached the goal!

The same holds in the spiritual race. Here, too, much depends on the frame of mind. Paul completely rejects the idea that even now the race is as good as won. Says he, **Not that** [151] **I have already gotten hold or have already been made perfect.** Paul was a firm believer in the doctrine of election "before the foundation of the world" (Eph. 1:4), and accordingly also, as has been pointed out, in the possibility of assurance of salvation. But not in election apart from human responsibility, in salvation apart from human effort, or in assurance without constant recourse to the promises. Even though he had already sacrificed everything in his service for the Lord, he is certain of one thing, namely, that he has not yet completely gotten hold of the spiritual and moral resurrection that lifts one out from among those who are dead in sin; in other words, he is sure that he has not yet been made *perfect.* In principle, yes! But in full measure, no! Far from it! The struggle against sin, fear, and doubt is not yet over. The fact, moreover, that believers do not attain this perfection in the present life is the teaching of Scripture throughout (Ps. 51:1-5; Matt. 6:12; 23:75; Luke 18:13; Rom. 7:14-24; James 3:2; I John 1:8). Paul continues, placing the positive over against the negative, as he often does, **but I am pressing on (to see) if I can also lay hold on that for which** [152] **I was laid hold on by Christ Jesus.** Paul is *pursuing* with the purpose of *overtaking and laying hold on.*[153] Has

---

[151] Rejecting a possible misunderstanding; cf. Phil. 4:11, 17: II Cor. 3:5; 7:9; II Thess. 3:9.

[152] ἐφ' ᾧ either "on that for which" (cf. Luke 5:25) or "for this reason that" (or simply "because"). The difference is minor. In either case the apostle is saying that had not Christ Jesus laid hold on him, he would never be able to lay hold on Christ Jesus, that is, on perfection in him.

[153] For the idea of *pressing on* or *pursuing, keeping up the chase, eagerly seeking or running after* see N.T.C. on I Tim. 6:11; II Tim. 2:22; cf. I Cor. 14:1. For the combination *pursue — overtake* (or *firmly lay hold on, capture*) see Exod. 15:9 (LXX); Rom. 9:30. Interesting in the present connection (pursuing *one* definite

he not been laid hold on by Christ Jesus? When Paul was on his way to Damascus had not the exalted Lord and Savior commissioned him to a definite task? See Acts 9:1-19, especially verse 15; also 22:15, 21; 26:15-18. Encouraged and enabled by this very fact, namely, that it was Christ Jesus who *has laid a firm hold* on him, so as to *possess* him completely, the apostle is now pressing on in hot pursuit of the objective assigned to him. Cf. Phil. 2:12, 13; 4:13; II Thess. 2:13. He continues,

13. Brothers, I do not count myself yet to have laid hold. This is no superfluous repetition of a confession of imperfection. On the contrary, something is added now. The very word that introduces the sentence — namely, *brothers,* a word of endearment and also in this case of deep concern (see on 1:12) — shows that the apostle is deeply moved. Far more clearly than before, he is now intimating that the church at Philippi is being vexed by people who imagine that *they* have laid hold on perfection. These errorists probably based this claim on the fact that, as they saw it, they had not only accepted Jesus as their Savior but were also scrupulous in their adherence to Judaistic rites (see above, on verses 1-3). The apostle summarily rejects their claims by saying, as it were, "Such has not been *my* experience. Legal rectitude, slavery to outworn ordinances, hindered me instead of helping me. Moreover, as a believer in Christ alone, I for one am still far removed from the goal of spiritual perfection. Whatever any one else may claim, *I* have not yet laid hold on it."

This, however, does not mean that Paul is indolent or despairing. On the contrary, he refuses to acquiesce in sin. As a runner in the race he stresses his *exertion*.

(2) Exertion

Paul writes, **But one thing (I do).** The runner in the race practises *persistent concentration* on one, and only one, objective, namely, to press on toward the goal for the prize. He permits nothing to divert him from his course. His aim is definite, well-defined.

So it is also with Paul. On reading his epistles one is amazed by this unity of purpose which characterizes the apostle's entire life after conversion. Paul aimed at gaining Christ and perfection in him, a perfection not only of uninterruptible assurance but also of loving consecration: "Teach me to love thee as thy angels love, *one holy passion* filling all my frame."

> "Lord Jesus, I long to be perfectly whole;
> I want thee forever to live in my soul,
> Break down every idol, cast out every foe,

---

object and not permitting oneself to be sidetracked or distracted) is Ecclesiasticus 11:10, "My son, do not busy yourself with many matters. If you *pursue,* you will not *overtake.*" Cf. also Herodotus IX. 58, "They (the enemies) must be *pursued* until they are *overtaken.*" On the verb see also N.T.C. on John 1:5.

Now wash me, and I shall be whiter than snow.
Whiter than snow, yes, whiter than snow;
Now wash me, and I shall be whiter than snow."

(J. Nicholson)

Such concentration is absolutely necessary. In everyday life distractions are often disastrous. Excitement about an impending trip to Asia distracts a motorist. The result: a serious accident. Similarly, in the spiritual realm worldly cares, the false glamor of wealth, and all kinds of evil desires enter in to choke the word of the gospel (Mark 4:19). Over-emphasis on sports, clothes, physical charm, etc., prevents the runner from reaching the spiritual goal. Real, undivided concentration is a matter of ceaseless effort on man's part. It is at the same time the product of the operation of grace in the heart. It is the answer to the prayer, "*Unite* my heart to fear thy name" (Ps. 86:11).

Such concentration presents its requirements. The first is *mental oblitera-tion* of that part of the course which the runner has already covered. Paul says, **forgetting what lies behind (me).** The runner does not look back. He knows that if he does, he will lose his speed, his direction, and finally the race itself. Looking back while running ahead is always very dangerous.

So it is also spiritually. Here too looking back is forbidden. Remember Lot's wife (Luke 17:32). Now when Paul says that he forgets what lies behind, he refers to a type of forgetting which is no mere, passive *oblivion.* It is active *obliteration,* so that when any thought of merits, piled up in the past, would occur to Paul, he immediately banished it from his mind. This is not Nirvana. It is not the state resulting from drinking the waters of Lethe. It is a constant, deliberate *discarding* of any thought of *past attain-ments.*[154]

The second indispensable requisite of effective concentration is *unwaver-ing progression.* Hence, Paul continues, **and eagerly straining forward to what lies ahead.** The verb used in the original is very graphic. It pictures the runner straining every nerve and muscle as he keeps on running with all his might toward the goal, his hand stretched out as if to grasp it.

No less necessary is unwavering progression in the spiritual sphere. But if it be true that Paul on this side of the grave never reaches ethical-spiritual perfection — the perfection of *condition,* that is, holy living, and of constant,

---

[154] ἐπιλανθανόμενος, present participle, durative. Just what is Paul forgetting or discarding: his pre-Christian experiences or his previous progress as a Christian? If a choice must be made, the context (see especially verses 7 and 8) would seem to favor the former; logic, consistent application of the figure of the Christian race, the latter. But is it necessary to make a choice? Is it not possible that Paul is sim-ply stating that, in his race for perfection, he refuses to become absorbed in past at-tainments of whatever kind; in other words, that in order to win the race one should, with eyes fixed on the goal, advance steadily toward it?

never-interrupted, full assurance of his *state* —, then why strive so eagerly for it? Is not the apostle foolish when he strives with such constancy and ardor to reach a goal which he knows he cannot fully attain in this life? The answer is twofold:

a. Although a person cannot actually reach this objective here and now, he can, indeed, make progress toward it. This matter of ethical-spiritual perfection is by no means an all-or-nothing proposition. As Paul himself teaches everywhere, there is such a thing as *making progress* in sanctification. The line of progress may indeed be zig-zag, but this does not rule out the possibility of real progress. In fact, such advancement, such gradual development when the seed of true religion has been implanted in the heart, must be considered normal (Mark 4:28; Phil. 1:6, 9, 26; 4:17; then Eph. 4:12, 13; Col. 1:9-11; I Thess. 3:12; 4:1, 10; II Thess. 1:3; I Tim. 4:15; II Tim. 2:1).

b. Such spiritual perfection in Christ, considered as God's gracious *gift,* is actually *granted* only to those who *strive* for it! The *prize* is given to those who *press on* toward the *goal* (verse 14; cf. II Tim. 4:7, 8).

Concentration, obliteration, progression, accordingly, are the key-words of that spiritual *exertion* which results in *perfection.* It is by these means that one presses on toward the goal.

(3) *Goal*
14. So Paul continues, **I am pressing on toward the goal.** By derivation, the word translated *goal* is that on which one fixes his eyes. Throughout the race the sight of that pillar at the end of the track encouraged the contestant to redouble his exertions. He was ever running goal-ward, that is, *in accordance with* [155] the line from his eyes to the goal.

In the spiritual race that goal is Christ, that is, ethical-spiritual perfection in him (see Phil. 3:8, 12). With all his heart the apostle desired to be completely raised above sin. He sought eagerly to promote the glory of God by every tool at his disposal, particularly by being a witness to all men (Acts 22:15, 21; 26:16-18), that he might by all means save some (I Cor. 9:22).

(4) *Reward*
Never does the runner forget the prize (I Cor. 9:24, 25; II Tim. 4:8; Heb. 12:2). Hence, Paul continues, **for the prize of the upward call of God in Christ Jesus.** At the end of the race the successful runner was summoned from the floor of the stadium to the judge's seat to receive the prize. This prize was a wreath of leaves. At Athens after the time of Solon the Olympic victor also received the sum of 500 *drachmai.* Moreover, he was allowed to eat at public expense, and was given a front-row seat at the theater.

Probably some of these facts were in the background of Paul's thinking when he stated that he was pressing on toward the goal for the prize of the

[155] Note κατὰ σκοπὸν διώκω.

174

upward call of God in Christ Jesus. However, *underlying figure* and *spiritual meaning* do not completely correspond here — do they ever? —, for though *the prize* in both cases is awarded at the end of the race, the *upward call* of which the apostle is here speaking was issued already at his *conversion,* hence not only at the *end* of the race. Here as elsewhere in Paul there is *the effective gospel call.* It is the *heavenward* call, the *holy* calling, a calling to holiness of life. Thus God is summoning Paul upward continually. See N.T.C. on II Thess. 1:11, p. 162, footnote 162 there; also N.T.C. on II Tim. 1:9. Nevertheless, *the prize* which corresponds to this call, and is given to those in whom this call has performed its work, is awarded when the race is over and has been won. Then Paul, too, together with all the saints, is called upward to meet the Lord in the air and to remain forever with him in the new heaven and earth (I Thess. 4:17). It is only *in Christ Jesus* that this upward call, this holy calling, is possible. Without him it could neither have been given nor obeyed. Apart from his atoning sacrifice the glorious prize to which the call leads the way could never be awarded.

Is there a real difference between *goal* and *prize?* In a sense they are the same. Both indicate *Christ, perfection in him.* Nevertheless, *goal* and *prize* represent different aspects of the same perfection; as follows,

a. When this perfection is called *goal,* it is viewed as the object of human striving. When it is called *prize* it is viewed as the gift of God's sovereign grace. God imparts everlasting life to those who accept Christ by living faith (John 3:16). He imparts perfection to those who strive to attain it. Though it is true that this believing and this striving are from start to finish completely dependent on God's grace, nevertheless it is *we* who must embrace Christ and salvation in him. It is *we* who must strive to enter in. God does not do this believing and striving for us!

b. The *goal* rivets the attention on the race that *is being run* or *was run;* the *prize* upon the glory that *will begin* in the new heaven and earth. Thus, bringing sinners to Christ, and doing this with *perfect* devotion, pertains to the *goal. Perfect* fellowship with these saved ones on and after the day of the great consummation pertains to the *prize.* Hence, it is correct to distinguish between goal and prize, as Paul also does both here and, by implication, in II Tim. 4:7, 8.

With this glorious prize in mind — namely, the blessings of everlasting life; such as *perfect* wisdom, joy, holiness, peace, fellowship, all enjoyed *to the glory of God,* in a marvelously restored universe, and in the company of Christ and of all the saints — Paul is pressing on toward the goal.

15, 16. Now, in the earthly race the prize is perishable; in the heavenly, imperishable (I Cor. 9:25). In the former only *one* could win (I Cor. 9:24); in the latter *all* who love Christ's appearing win (II Tim. 4:8). They win the prize by being minded as is Paul, and by conduct in harmony with this disposition. Hence, Paul continues, **Accordingly, let us, as many as are mature, continue to set our mind on this.** Do we, the Philippians along with ourselves, desire the prize? Then let us — note tactful use of *us* here! — set our mind on the objective as just described; that is, fully realizing that we are still far from the goal of ultimate moral-spiritual perfection, let us earnestly and continually endeavor to reach this goal. Are we not *mature?* [156] Let us then leave behind any childish notions of reaching perfection by means of rigid law-observance, and let it be our disposition *in Christ* to seek ever higher ground:

> "I'm pressing on the upward way,
> New heights I'm gaining every day;
> Still praying as I onward bound,
> Lord, plant my feet on higher ground.
> Lord, lift me up and let me stand,
> By faith, on heaven's table-land,
> A higher plane than I have found;
> Lord, plant my feet on higher ground."
>
> (J. Oatman)

But while this rule is excellent and necessary, its exact application to all phases of life is not always immediately clear. Hence, Paul continues, **and if on some minor point y o u are differently minded, that, too, God will**

---

[156] Of all the explanations offered to explain τέλειος, pl. –οι, as here used, the one which regards it as meaning *mature, full-grown,* here with respect to knowledge of the way of salvation, would seem to be the best. The frequency with which the apostle uses the term in that sense is striking. Probable meanings as used by Paul:

Rom. 12:2:	*perfect* (will of God)
I Cor. 2:6:	*the mature, the full-grown,* as contrasted with *babes* (I Cor. 3:1)
I Cor. 13:10:	*the total, wholeness,* as contrasted with that which is "in part" (I Cor. 13:9)
I Cor. 14:20:	*mature, grown up, of full age:* "in malice babes, in mind grown-up"
Eph. 4:13:	*full-grown* man, *mature* manhood
Col. 1:28:	*perfect* or *mature*
Col. 4:12:	*mature, ripe, complete*

(Cf. also Heb. 5:14, "Solid food is for *full-grown* men.")
Meanings a. "full-grown" and b. "spiritually perfect" (without any defect and filled with positive goodness) sometimes coincide: the full-grown man is the one who has reached "the measure of the stature of the fullness of Christ." Cf. also Col. 4:12.
The question whether the use of τέλειοι here in verse 15 in connection with the same word implied in the verbal form used in verse 12 presents a play on words cannot be answered definitely. Lenski denies it. Many others are of the opposite opinion to which I also lean. If a play on words — rather frequent in Paul — is intended, then the full meaning is probably as follows: Judaizers may regard themselves as being τέλειοι (perfect), but it is *we* who are the real τέλειοι (mature individuals), for the τέλειοι are exactly the ones who in full awareness of their own imperfection reach for the goal.

make plain to y o u. If the Philippians will adhere to the rule as laid down, then if with respect to this or that minor point of application their views should be defective, God, through his Spirit, will unveil to their hearts and minds the truth also regarding such a matter. Cf. Ps. 25:14; Matt. 7:7; Luke 19:26; John 7:17; 16:13. Emphasizing this same thought, the apostle continues, **Only, let our conduct be consistent with the level we have attained.** Or, more literally, "Only, to what we have attained, with the same let us keep in line." The rule [157] has been established. The principle — namely, "We are still far from perfect, but in Christ we should strive to become perfect" — has been enunciated and exemplified. Let our lives be regulated by the consistent application of this principle. It must never be surrendered.[158]

True religion, then, is a matter not of precept upon precept but of basic principles. These are few but very important. If by the light of God's special revelation these principles are consistently applied, then all the rest will follow. God will not refuse to give further light to him who walks by the light already given.

---

17 Brothers, join in being imitators of me, and watch closely those who are walking according to the example that we have set y o u. 18 For many are pursuing a walk of life, of whom I told y o u often and now tell y o u even weeping (that they are) the enemies of the cross of Christ; 19 whose end is destruction, whose god is their belly, and whose glory is in their shame, who set their mind on earthly things. 20 For our homeland is in heaven, from which we also are eagerly awaiting, as Savior, the Lord Jesus Christ, 21 who will refashion our lowly body so that it will have a form like his own glorious body, (and who will do this) by the exertion of that power which enables him to subject even all things to himself.

3:17-21

III. *Warning against Sensualists. The Homeland in Heaven*

A new paragraph begins here. Warnings continue, but now against a foe described in terms that differ from those used in verse 2 above. Not about dogs, evil workers, the concision does Paul speak now but about men whom he considers as "the enemies of the cross of Christ, whose end is destruction, whose god is their belly, whose glory is in their shame, who set their mind on earthly things." It is well before entering upon a detailed exegesis to answer the question, "Who are these dangerous errorists?"

---

[157] The better text does not have "by that same rule." Nevertheless, that is the idea; cf. Gal. 6:16.
[158] Note use of present active infinitive στοιχεῖν with imperative connotation, here as also in Rom. 12:15.

In harmony with very many interpreters [159] I am firmly convinced that they are *sensualists, men who catered to the flesh, gluttonous, grossly immoral people,* all this though they pretended to be Christians. Reasons for accepting this view:

(1) This would seem to be the most natural explanation of the term "whose god is their belly." It is the interpretation that immediately occurs to the mind.[160] Only the most compelling reason should be permitted to cause one to surrender it. No such reason has been given.

(2) This view is strengthened by some of the other descriptive phrases that occur here; especially, "whose glory is in their shame, who set their mind on earthly things."

(3) This explanation is also in harmony with Pauline language elsewhere. In Romans the apostle warns against those who said, "Let us do evil that good may come" (Rom. 3:8), and "Let us continue in sin that grace may abound" (Rom. 6:1). It can hardly be doubted that these were the very individuals who in Rom. 16:18 are described as "serving not our Lord Christ but *their belly*," language very similar to that found here in Phil. 3:19.

(4) The transition from a warning against *legalists* (Phil. 3:2) to one against *libertines* (verses 17-21) is, after all, rather natural. We find it also in Galatians (cf. Gal. 5:1 with 5:13). Sinful human nature is prone to jump from one extreme into another. Hardly has it become clear to a person that he should not be "entangled again in the yoke of (Judaistic) bondage" when he begins to use his new-found freedom as "an opportunity for the flesh."

(5) In a parallel passage Peter warns against similar loose individuals, men who forget that the believers' homeland is in heaven, and that, acccordingly, the followers of Jesus are sojourners and pilgrims here below (cf. Phil. 3:19, 20 with I Peter 2:11). Peter clearly implies that these seducers indulge in "fleshly lusts which war against the soul." There is, therefore, every reason to interpret the passage in Philippians similarly.

Other views as to the identity of the errorists against whom Paul warns here are discussed in a footnote.[161]

---

[159] Alford, Barclay, Barnes, Braune (in Lange's "Commentary on the Holy Scriptures"), Beare, Ellicott, Erdman, Johnstone, Kennedy (in "The Expositor's Greek Testament"), Laurin, Lightfoot, Meyer, Michael (in "The Moffatt New Testament Commentary"), Rainy (in "The Expositor's Bible"), The Amplified New Testament.

[160] Similar language is used by Eupolis, 5th century B.C. Athenian comic poet; by Athenaeus who wrote *Banquet of the Learned;* by Euripedes (*Cyclops* 335); and by Xenophon (*Mem.* I.vi.8: note how he uses "slavery to the belly" in close connection with "incontinence").

[161] Such views are as follows:

(1) The people against whom Paul issues his warning here in Phil. 3:17-21 are *the heathen* (B. Weiss, A. Rilliet).

Objection: Would Paul have written, "of whom I told y o u often and now tell y o u even in tears"; in other words, would he have been so deeply disturbed if he had heard a report that *heathen* were guilty of the sin here described? The

17. Deeply moved by what he is about to write, Paul addresses the Philippians with the endearing word **Brothers** (see on 1:12; cf. 1:14; 3:1, 13; 4:1, 8, 21). He continues, **join in being imitators of me.** Should not brothers show that they belong to the same spiritual family, and are, therefore, really *brothers?* Should not their attitude of heart, speech, and conduct remind one of the same model? "Let me be that model," says Paul, as it were, and this in self-renunciation over against self-complacency; in humble, Christ-centered trust instead of arrogant self-esteem; in idealism versus indolence (Phil. 3:7-14); and thus also in spirituality as contrasted with sensuality, that is, in heavenly-mindedness as opposed to worldly-mindedness (verses 18-21).

But is selection of himself as an example consistent with Christian humility? Answer:

(1) Before pointing to himself as an example, the apostle had reminded the Philippians of *Christ* as the chief example (Phil. 2:5-8). Accordingly, they knew that what Paul meant was simply this, "Be imitators of me, as I also am of Christ" (I Cor. 11:1).

(2) The apostle was not placing himself on a pedestal, as if he were perfect, but, quite the contrary, was urging his friends *to strive after perfection,* in the full realization that they were still far removed from the ideal, as was he himself.

(3) Surrounded by immorality on the part both of pagans and of nominal Christians (see verses 18 and 19), these Philippians needed a concrete example of Christian devotion, a picture-lesson. The apostle had every right to point to himself as such an example.

---

apostle certainly knew that! Is it not far more likely that immorality practised by those who professed to be Christians caused him to weep so profusely?

(2) The persons against whom the warning is issued may have been *either* Judaistic legalists *or* Epicurean libertines (Martin, Robertson, Vincent).

Objection: I admire caution in exegesis. However, in the present instance I believe we can be certain, as I have tried to prove.

(3) The Judaizers are meant, just as in verse 2 (Barth, Greijdanus, Lenski, Müller in "The New International Commentary").

Objection: When it is said that the Judaizers made the belly their god *by demanding only kosher food,* and that their glory was in their shame because they gloried *in their circumcized flesh,* that is, *in their private parts,* proof should have been given to show that such interpretations are in line with New Testament usage. The proposition that strictness in the observance of dietary regulations would be tantamount to making a god of one's belly, so that, for example, Paul himself before his conversion was guilty of this sin, is in need of proof. And as to the word αἰσχύνη (shame), nowhere else in the New Testament does this word as such refer concretely and specifically to a person's private parts (Luke 14:9 *disgrace;* II Cor. 4:2, associated with *craftiness;* Heb. 12:2, *disgrace, ignominy;* Jude 13, *shameful deeds* cast up like seafoam; Rev. 3:18, *shameful nakedness*).

But does not the description "the enemies of the cross of Christ" fit the Judaizers? It certainly does, but it is an equally correct characterization of the sensualists!

Surely, far stronger arguments will have to be submitted before the majority of commentators can become convinced that when Paul warned against men whose god was their belly he was referring to Judaizers with their rigorous food laws!

179

(4) The justifiable character of his exhortation becomes even more clearly evident when it is seen in the light of what immediately follows, showing that when Paul urged the Philippians to imitate him, he was not thinking of himself *alone* but of *himself in company with others,* such as Timothy (Phil. 2:19-24) and Epaphroditus (2:25-30). Note the pronoun *we* instead of *I* in the continuation: **and watch closely those who are walking according to the example that we have set y o u.** Instead of fixing y o u r attention upon individuals who have confused Christian liberty with license, focus it upon those who are safe guides of Christian conduct. Let them be y o u r *example* (see N.T.C. on I Thess. 1:7).

18, 19. The apostle supports his urgent appeal by continuing, deeply moved, **For many are pursuing a walk of life, of whom I told y o u often and now tell y o u even weeping (that they are) the enemies of the cross of Christ.** The wicked life of these persons who wished to be regarded as Christians belied the confession of their lips. They deceived themselves, exerted a most sinister influence upon those who listened to them, kept unbelievers from becoming truly converted, and dishonored God. They may have been traveling "missionaries." They were *numerous* — note the word *many* —, from which, however, it does not follow that they constituted a considerable proportion of the membership of the *Philippian church.* If that had been the case, the apostle could not have praised this church in such glowing terms (see Phil. 4:1). Nevertheless, they were a real menace. Paul, while present among the Philippians, had often warned against this class of deceivers. He considers them not just enemies but *the* (note the definite article here) enemies of the cross of Christ. If *the friends* of the cross are those who show in their lives that they have caught the spirit of the cross, namely, that of *self-denial* (Matt. 20:28; Luke 9:23; Rom. 15:3; Phil. 2:5-8), then surely *the enemies* of the cross are those who manifest the very opposite attitude, namely, that of *self-indulgence. The friends* of the cross do not love the world. In fact, the world is crucified to them, and they to the world, and this because they glory in the cross (Gal. 6:14; cf. 5:24). *The enemies* of the cross love the world and the things that are in the world (I John 2:15). They set their minds on earthly things (Phil. 3:19).

Because of his great love for the Philippians the apostle actually *weeps* when he reflects on the fact that these enemies of the cross are trying to seduce the members of the first church established in Europe. He weeps as did Mary of Bethany because of her brother's death (John 11:31, 33; see N.T.C. on John 11:35), and as did Mary Magdalene on the morning of Christ's resurrection (John 20:11). One of the secrets of Paul's success as a missionary was his genuine, personal interest in those whom the Lord had committed to his spiritual care. Because his love for them was so real and tender, his heart was stirred to its very depths when danger threatened them.

Besides, the apostle was not only a man of penetrating insight and rugged determination but also of profound, surging emotion.

Paul's Deeply Emotional Nature

Various phases of the apostle's intensely emotional personality are exhibited in the book of Acts and in the epistles. Here was a truly *great* soul! What he did he did with all his might, never in a merely detached manner. Having formerly persecuted the followers of Jesus, after his conversion Sorrow, hearty and profound, walked with him (I Cor. 15:9; I Tim. 1:15). That to such a bitter persecutor Christ had revealed himself as a loving Savior baffled him. He just could not get over it (Eph. 3:8; I Tim. 1:16). It caused his heart to overflow with lasting, humble gratitude! For this and for other reasons his epistles are full of magnificent doxologies (Rom. 9:5; 11:36; 16:27; Eph. 1:3; 3:20; Phil. 4:20; I Tim. 1:17; 6:15; II Tim. 4:18) which are the spontaneous utterances of the man who wrote, "For the love of Christ constrains us" (II Cor. 5:14). Having been "laid hold on" by Christ, the apostle in turn was eager to burn himself out for the salvation of others (I Cor. 9:22; 10:33; II Cor. 12:15). His heart ached intensely because so many of his own people (Israelites) were not saved (Rom. 9:1-3; 10:1). Anxiety for all his churches pressed upon him daily (II Cor. 11:28). How fervent and touching were his prayers for them (Eph. 3:14-19; I Thess. 3:9-13). How he loved them, so that he could write, "We were gentle in the midst of y o u as a nurse cherishes her own children. So, being affectionately desirious of y o u, we gladly shared with y o u not only the gospel of God but also our own souls . . . For now we really live if y o u stand fast in the Lord" (I Thess. 2:7, 8; 3:8). How earnest were his pleadings (II Cor. 5:20; Gal. 4:19, 20; Eph. 4:1), and how tactful! Though for their own good he was able to rebuke the wayward very sharply (Gal. 1:6-9; 3:1-4), even this was a manifestation of the love of his great, throbbing heart. Is it any wonder that, when occasion demanded it, out of the eyes of a man with such an ebullient spirit and loving heart there welled forth fountains of tears (Acts 20:19, 31), so that not only here in Phil. 3:18 but also in II Cor. 2:4 these are mentioned? And is it at all surprising that, on the other hand, on one occasion the tears of his friends, because of his imminent departure and the afflictions in store for him, well-nigh broke his heart (Acts 21:13)? Truly Paul's *weeping* when he writes about the enemies of the cross of Christ is as glorious as is the *joy, joy, joy* that sings its way through this marvelous epistle!

Speaking about these enemies of the cross of Christ Paul continues, **whose end is destruction.** This is their appointed destiny, for God has ordained that "their end shall be according to their works" (II Cor. 11:15). This end is the *fruit* of their wicked lives (Rom. 6:21). It is the *wages* earned by their sin (Rom. 6:23). *Destruction,* however, is by no means the same as *annihilation.* It does not mean that they will cease to exist. On the contrary, it means *everlasting punishment* (Matt. 25:46), for this destruction is an *everlasting* destruction (II Thess. 1:9).[162] This destruction *begins* even in the present life, but is climaxed after death. Paul continues, **whose god is their belly** (cf. Rom. 16:18). Instead of striving to keep their physical appetites under control (Rom. 8:13; I Cor. 9:27), realizing that our bodies are the Holy Spirit's temple, in which God should be glorified (I Cor. 6:19, 20), these people surrendered themselves to gluttony and licentiousness. They worshipped their sensual nature. In this they were prompted, no doubt, by causes such as the following: immoral background (cf. I Peter 1:18), wicked pagan surroundings, licentious incipient gnosticism (see N.T.C. on I Tim. 4:3), perversion of the doctrine of grace (Rom. 3:8; 6:1), and, last but not least, evil lusts within the heart (James 1:14). The apostle further characterizes them as those **whose glory is in their shame:** Their pride was in that of which they should have been ashamed. Not only did they carry out their wicked designs, but they even boasted about them. They were the persons **who set their minds on earthly things.** Being carnal, "after the flesh," they pondered the things of the flesh (Rom. 8:5). Now the mind of the flesh is *"enmity* against God" (Rom. 8:7), and these people were *"the enemies* of the cross of Christ." In a parallel passage the apostle shows us what these *earthly things* were on which these people set their minds, namely, immorality, indecency, lust, evil desire, greed, evil temper, furious rage, malice, cursing, filthy talk (Col. 3:2, 5, 8).

20, 21. Such conduct would certainly be ill-fitting for *the citizens of the kingdom of heaven,* Paul implies, as he continues, **For**[163] **our**[164] **homeland is in heaven.** Do citizens of Philippi think of Rome as their native land to which they belong, in whose tribal records they are enrolled, whose dress they wear, whose language they speak, by whose laws they are governed, whose protection they enjoy, and whose emperor they worship as their Savior? In a sense far more sublime and real these *Christians* dwelling in Philippi must realize that *their homeland* or *commonwealth*[165] has its fixed location in heaven. It was heaven that gave them birth, for they are born from above. Their names are inscribed on heaven's register. Their lives are being governed from heaven and in accordance with heavenly standards. Their rights are secured in heaven. Their interests are being promoted there. To heaven their thoughts and prayers ascend and their hopes aspire.

[162] See W. Hendriksen, *The Bible on the Life Hereafter,* pp. 195-199.
[163] The idea for which the conjunction γάρ states the reason must often be inferred from the context. So also in this instance. See L.N.T. (A. and G.) entry γάρ, under 1, e., p. 151.
[164] Note position of ἡμῶν at the very beginning of the sentence.
[165] On the term πολίτευμα, *Gemeinwesen* or *Heimat* (*commonwealth* or *homeland*), see Hermann Strathmann's article in Th.W.N.T., Vol. 6, p. 535.

Many of their friends, members of the fellowship, are there even now, and they themselves, the citizens of the heavenly kingdom who are still on earth, will follow shortly. Yes, in heaven their inheritance awaits them. Their heavenly mansions are being prepared. See such passages as John 3:3; 14:1-4; Rom. 8:17; Eph. 2:6; Col. 3:1-3; Heb. 4:14-16; 6:19, 20; 7:25; 12:22-24; I Peter 1:4, 5; Rev. 7:9-17. Yes, Jerusalem that is above is their mother (Gal. 4:26). They are fellow-citizens with the saints and of the household of God (Eph. 2:19). On this earth they are strangers, sojourners, and pilgrims (Heb. 11:13; I Peter 2:11). "They desire a better country, that is, a heavenly one. Therefore God is not ashamed to be called their God, for he has prepared for them a city" (Heb. 11:16). Above all, in heaven dwells their *Head*, and they are *the Body;* so infinitely close is their relation to heaven! And this Head is, indeed, Savior. In fact, he is the only, the real Savior, who is coming again to deliver them from all their enemies and to draw them as closely as possible to his own bosom. Hence, Paul continues, **from which** [166] **we also are eagerly awaiting as Savior, the Lord Jesus Christ.**

The hope of Christ's Return has sanctifying power: "every one who has this hope set on him purifies himself even as he is pure" (I John 3:3). If a person makes a god of his belly and sets his mind on earthly things, how can he ever expect to be welcomed by the spotlessly holy and infinitely glorious Christ at his brilliant advent? This surely is the reason — at least one of the chief reasons — why the coming of Christ is here mentioned.

Believers *are eagerly awaiting* [167] their Lord. Theirs is not the attitude of the men of Laodicea, that of lukewarmness (Rev. 3:14-22); nor the attitude of some people in Thessalonica, that of nervousness (II Thess. 2:1, 2); but rather the attitude of the Smyrniots, that of faithfulness. The latter, while looking forward to the crown of life, remained faithful unto death (Rev. 2: 8-11). The citizens of the kingdom of heaven, looking *away from* all sinful pleasures, *eagerly* yearn *to welcome* their Savior, the Lord Jesus Christ. They await his manifestation in glory (I Cor. 1:7; Col. 3:4). It is a waiting *in faith* (Gal. 5:5), with *patient endurance* (Rom. 8:25), and *unto salvation* (Heb. 9:28). In a sense, the entire creation is eagerly looking forward for this great event, when from its present corruption and futility it shall be delivered, being transferred into the sphere of the glorious liberty of the children of God (Rom. 8:21).

Note that believers are yearning for *the Lord Jesus Christ* (see on Phil. 2:10) in his capacity as *Savior.* Even as Judge he will still be *their* Savior. The word Savior is also applied to Christ in Eph. 5:23; II Tim. 1:10; Titus

---

[166] The flexible character of Greek grammar certainly makes it possible for ἐξ οὗ to refer adverbially to οὐρανοῖς, plural. The latter noun, though plural in form, must frequently be regarded as singular in connotation.
[167] See Walter Grundmann's article on δέχομαι and cognates in Th.W.N.T., Vol. II, p. 49 ff., especially p. 55.

1:4; 2:13; 3:6. In fact, in Titus 2:13 Jesus is called "our great God and Savior." Not this or that heathen deity nor the Roman emperor but the Lord Jesus Christ is the real Savior whom believers are eagerly expecting. As their Savior he will deliver them from the final results of sin, will completely vindicate them and their cause, and will bestow upon them the glorious inheritance of the saints in the light, in a marvelously rejuvenated universe.

Though the glories of the intermediate state, that is, the happiness that will be the believer's portion during the interval between death and bodily resurrection, are not absent from the mind of the apostle (see Phil. 1:21, 23), nevertheless, he does not fall into the error into which we are so prone to become ensnared, namely, that of emphasizing the intermediate state at the expense of the Lord's advent! Will not the latter glory — in which *all* the saints of *all* the ages will take part, and in which Christ will be vindicated before *all* the world — be even greater than the former?

Paul continues, **who will refashion our lowly body so that it will have a form like his own glorious body.** By many Greek pagans the body was viewed as a prison from which at death the soul will be delivered. The body was intrinsically "vile." To Paul, however, that body was a temple, even the sanctuary of the Holy Spirit (I Cor. 6:19). To be sure, right now, as a result of the entrance of sin, it is "the body of our *humiliation*" (cf. cognate verb in Phil. 2:8, "he *humbled* himself"). As such it is exposed to sin's curse in the form of weakness, suffering, sickness, ugliness, futility, death, but at his coming the Savior — who is a *complete* Savior — will refashion it in such a manner that this new outward *fashion* or *appearance* will truly reflect the new and lasting inner *form*,[168] for it will have a *form* like the glorious body of the ascended Lord. We shall be "conformed to the image of his (the Father's) Son" (Rom. 8:29). We shall "bear the image of the heavenly" (I Cor. 15:49). "When he will be manifested, we shall be like him, for we shall see him even as he is" (I John 3:2). The nature of this great change is detailed in I Cor. 15:42-44, 50-58.

The question occurs, however, "But how will this be possible?" What about those martyrs who were devoured by lions? What about those who were burned alive? Yes, what about millions of others, particles of whose dead and decaying bodies, through various stages of disintegration, finally enter into other living bodies? An answer that would be completely "satisfying" to the mind of man — the mind darkened by sin! — is not available. One outstanding fact remains, however. That fact is the almightly power of One who could not be held even by death. Hence, the apostle concludes this exalted paragraph by saying **(and who will do this) by the exertion —** or **exercise — of that power which enables him to subject even all things to himself.** Marvelous is the *energy* of Christ's *dynamite*, that is, of his

---

[168] As to distinction between *fashion* and *form* see on Phil. 2:5-8.

power. This *energy* is *his power in action,* the exercise of his power. Surely, if that *energy* enables him to do the greater, how would it not enable him to do the lesser? If he can subject *even all things,* the totality of all the powers of the universe, unto himself (cf. Ps. 8:6; I Cor. 15:27; Heb. 2:5-8), will he not be able to refashion our lowly body so that it will have a form like his own glorious body?

Thus, Paul, the Indefatigable Idealist, ends this great chapter. He has reached the highest rung of the ladder. From *conversion,* with its repudiation of all human merits (verse 7), *justification* and *sanctification,* with the goal of *perfection* always in view (the main parts of verses 8-19), he has reached the great *Consummation,* when soul *and body,* the entire person, together with all the saints, will glorify God in Christ in the new heaven and earth, forever and forever. All this, through God's sovereign grace and power, and to his everlasting glory!

---

149 On the meaning of this passage interpreters differ widely:

(1) Some simply skip it, either saying nothing at all about the meaning of the verse or else merely affirming that it speaks about the resurrection of believers, not of unbelievers. That point can, of course, be readily granted. The context deals with Paul the believer, not with unbelievers. Also it has been pointed out by many that in Scripture the resurrection *out of* the dead always pertains either to Christ or to believers (Luke 20:35; Acts 4:2; I Peter 1:3). This, however, does not touch the real question. That question is not, "Does the resurrection for which Paul yearns pertain to believers or to unbelievers?" It is this, *"What kind of* believer-resurrection does the apostle have in mind here, physical, spiritual, or both perhaps?" It must be borne in mind that though there are other New Testament passages in which the phrase *resurrection out of the dead* occurs, the present is the only passage which speaks of an *out-resurrection out of the dead.*

(2) Among those who answer the real question there are some who feel assured that it is *the physical resurrection,* the resurrection of the body, that is meant. Some of these interpreters are convinced that the idea of a spiritual resurrection, particularly such a resurrection while still in the body, "lacks all support."

(3) Others sense a real difficulty with the explanation given under (2); for, so interpreted, the thought does not seem to proceed smoothly. The apostle then would be saying (verses 11 and 12), "If only I may attain to the resurrection of the body; not that I have already gotten hold of it (as if anyone could doubt that!) *or have already been made perfect."* But this last clause seems to imply that, after all, in verse 11 he was thinking *not* or *not chiefly* of physical resurrection but of *perfection.*

In order to avoid that break in the chain of reasoning, the following solutions have been proposed:

a. The verb "gotten hold" (verse 12) has no object at all, either expressed *or implied.*

Objection: It is difficult to conceive of *getting hold* of nothing at all. A person gets hold of *something;* he *arrives* somewhere!

b. Though the phrase (verse 11) *the out-resurrection out of the dead* refers to the believers' physical resurrection, yet the verb *gotten hold* (verse 12) does not refer as its object to that physical resurrection but to "the knowledge of Christ Jesus my Lord, and all that it implies" (see verses 8 and 10).

Objection: Why go back that far when "attain to" and "gotten hold (of)" seem to be parallel, and thus *the out-resurrection out of the dead* would seem to be the more natural and *immediate* object? It is granted, of course, that *the out-resurrec-*

tion out of the dead and "the knowledge of Christ Jesus my Lord, and all that it implies" coincide. Loosely the object includes *all* the fine things of verses 10 and 11.

(4) S. Greijdanus, conscious of the break in the chain of reasoning when solution (2) is adopted, believes that the expression *out-resurrection out of the dead* means "full, complete resurrection," and implies *both* physical resurrection at Christ's return and resurrection from sin now. Similarly Scott (in *The Interpreter's Bible*) argues that the compound word *out-resurrection* denotes not only inward resurrection in this life but also the final outward rising from the dead.

Objection: While the reference to a spiritual resurrection is indeed demanded by the context, the question may be asked, "Why must this compound noun refer to the compound idea of *present spiritual plus future physical resurrection?*" Does this not make the concept too cumbersome?

(5) F. W. Beare makes this *out-resurrection out of the dead* refer to "the final attainment of blessedness at the Parousia." It refers, therefore, in a sense to *spiritual perfection*. And *The Amplified New Testament* proposes the view that the phrase in question indicates "the spiritual and moral resurrection that lifts one out from among the dead even while in the body."

In favor of the *spiritual-perfection* interpretation the following arguments could be advanced:

a. It suits the *preceding* context. If *becoming conformed to Christ's death* has reference to the work of sanctification, why not also *the out-resurrection out of the dead?*

b. It suits the *following* context. The chain of thought then is, "If only I may attain to the spiritual and moral resurrection that lifts me out from among the dead. Not that I have already gotten hold of this condition of being raised completely above sin or have already been made perfect, but I am pressing on," etc.

c. It harmonizes with the idea that Paul regards this resurrection as the object of earnest yearning *and striving!*

d. It also tallies with the fact that Paul often refers to *resurrection* or its synonyms in a *spiritual* sense (Rom. 6:4-11; II Cor. 4:10, 11; Gal. 2:19, 20). It is particularly striking that whenever *in the Prison Epistles* the term *raised* or any of its synonyms is used in connection with believers, and without specific mention of either body or soul, the context shows that the reference is to the *spiritual* resurrection (see Eph. 2:5, 6; Col. 2:12, 13; Col. 3:1). If this is true everywhere else in these epistles, then why not also in this other passage from a Prison Epistle, namely, Phil. 3:11?

This spiritual resurrection, the condition of being "perfectly whole," while earnestly desired and pursued in this life, does not reach its *complete* (body and soul, together with all the saints) consummation until the end of the age.

PHILIPPIANS

Synthesis of Chapter 3

For this see the Summary at the beginning of the chapter.

Seed-thoughts of Chapter 3

(1) Christian joy can be cultivated (verse 1).

(2) Even Paul repeated himself, *when necessary* (verse 1).

(3) *Meekness* does not mean *weakness*. The maxim "See no evil" is in need of explanation and perhaps qualification (verse 2).

(4) No *demerit* is so great and harmful as *self-merit* (verse 3).

(5) The Christian has not truly *arrived* until he arrives in glory: "If only I may attain" is the language of the truly saved man. The believer is the enemy of the *status quo* (verses 4-14).

(6) Though justification is a once-for-all affair, the believer desires an ever richer assurance of having obtained this great blessing. Absolute perfection also in this respect is not reached in the here and now. He who spoke the words of Ps. 27:1 also spoke those of I Sam. 27:1. He who praised God by those of I Kings 18:36, 37, also uttered the lamentation found in I Kings 19:4, 10. And then there is the need of sanctification in all other respects (verses 8b-14).

(7) Every Christian is a true perfectionist or idealist (verses 8b-14).

(8) "We love him because he first loved us." We take hold on him because he first took hold of us (verse 12).

(9) Divine preservation implies human perseverance (verses 12-14).

(10) Not only mulling over past failures but also gloating over past "successes" is an enemy of spiritual progress (verse 13).

(11) Those who major on minors, forgetting the real goal of the Christian life, are immature (verse 15).

(12) Be consistent (verse 16).

(13) The sensualist is not a Christian (verses 17-19).

(14) Not the intermediate state but the state of final glory in the new heaven and earth, together with all the saints, at Christ's Return, should be most strongly emphasized in preaching and in meditation (verses 20, 21).

Summary of Chapter 4

Paul, the Tactful Pastor

in general, exhorting the brothers at Philippi to remain firm; and in particular, entreating Euodia and Syntyche to be of the same mind, and Syzygus to help these gospel-women;

urging the Philippians to rejoice in the Lord, to be big-hearted to all, and instead of worrying to bring everything to God in prayer that brings peace; finally, admonishing the addressees to meditate only on praiseworthy things, practising these in imitation of Paul and with promise of rich reward.

4:1-3 Exhortations: to all, Remain firm; to two women, Live in harmony; to Syzygus, Help these women.

4:4-7 The secret of true blessedness: Rejoice, Be big-hearted, Instead of worrying pray.

4:8, 9 Summary of Christian Duty: proper meditation, proper action.

CHAPTER IV

4 1 So then, my brothers, beloved and longed for, my joy and crown, so stand fast in the Lord, beloved.
2 I entreat Eudia and I entreat Syntyche to be of the same mind in the Lord. 3 Yes, I request you also, Syzygus (Yoke-fellow), in deed as well as in name,[169] lend these women a hand, for they strove side by side with me in the gospel, along with Clement and the rest of my fellow-workers, whose names (are) in the book of life.

4:1-3

I. *Various Exhortations: General and Specific*

1. Here we are face to face with *Paul, the tactful pastor.* The opening words of the chapter, **So then,** clearly indicate that there is the closest connection with what precedes. That connection may be stated as follows: Because the believers' homeland is in heaven and not on earth, and because a glorious inheritance awaits them at Christ's Return, when even their bodies will be made to resemble Christ's body both outwardly and inwardly, let nothing sway them from their firm foundation. Let them always remain steadfast and sure, so that these glories may be theirs indeed.

Very touching is the manner in which the tactful pastor addresses his charges. Note: **my brothers** — just as in 3:1 —, **beloved,** with a love that is deep-seated, self-sacrificing, thorough, intelligent, and purposeful, a love in which the entire personality takes part,[170] **and longed for,** "with the deeply-felt affection of Christ Jesus" (see on Phil. 1:7, 8), **my joy and crown.** The Philippians are the joy of the apostle's heart because the fruits of the Holy Spirit are clearly evident in their lives. Hence, he praises them again and again, and thanks God for them (Phil. 1:3-7, 29, 30; 2:12, 17; 4:10, 14-20). For the same reason they are also his *crown,* his *adorning-wreath* or *festive garland.* This is true, in a sense, even now but will become even more clearly evident at the coming of the Lord, when it will become manifest to all that these are the fruits of Paul's missionary labors, showing that he did not run in vain or labor in vain (Phil. 2:16). The passage should

---

169 Or simply, *genuine Syzygus* (Yoke-fellow).
170 For the meaning of the cognate verb ἀγαπάω see detailed discussion in N.T.C. on the Gospel of John, Vol. II, pp. 494-500, footnote 306.

be compared with similar language in I Thess. 2:19, 20. It is evident from these words that this was, indeed, a fine congregation, and that the heart of the prisoner went out to them. He pours out his affection upon them, without any attempt to hold back. His exhortation to them all is: **So stand fast in the Lord, beloved.** In view of their high calling, the blessings they have already received, and the inheritance that awaits them (Phil. 1:6; 3:20, 21), let them remain ever firm and steadfast, over against hostile pagans, merely nominal Christians such as legalists and libertines, and the promptings of their own sinful hearts. Let them do so by the continued exercise of their faith in the Lord Jesus Christ.

2. After such an endearing introduction addressed to each and to all, the needed admonition intended for two individuals cannot seem harsh: **I entreat Euodia** — the name means *prosperous journey* — **and I entreat Syntyche** —meaning *fortunate* [171] — **to be of the same mind in the Lord.** Here once again as so often before (Phil. 1:27, 28; 2:2-4; 2:14-16; 3:1) the apostle stresses the idea of militant *unity* in a world of unbelief and hostility. This time, however, the admonition is given a *particular* application.

With respect to Euodia and Syntyche the following facts only can be safely affirmed:

(1) They were, at this writing, and had been for some time, members of the church at Philippi.

(2) When the church was founded and/or at a later visit of Paul to Philippi, they had been the apostle's fellow-workers, and as such had co-operated harmoniously and enthusiastically with each other and with Paul and his companions (verse 3).

(3) An important disagreement, related to kingdom-work, had arisen between them, which called forth this apostolic admonition.

(4) They are still the object of Paul's high regard and deep-rooted, Christian love. They are Christians!

Views which are highly speculative and fanciful are the following:

(1) One of them was Lydia (Acts 16:14, 15).

(2) The two names represent the Jewish and the Gentile section of the church at Philippi (F. C. Baur and the Tübingen School).

(3) The two are the Philippian jailer and his wife. Objection: "these *women,*" verse 3.

Paul tenderly *pleads with* — as it were, *calls to his side* — *each* of these women, begging each to return to a harmonious disposition so as to work together as a team. Note the tactful repetition of the verb. The apostle does not say "I entreat Euodia and Syntyche," but, as if to emphasize his tender solicitude and high regard *for each,* he says, "I entreat Euodia and

---

[171] See on Phil. 2:25, footnote 116 under C.

I entreat Syntyche." A wonderful hint for pastors here! Let Euodia and let Syntyche reflect on the fact that their Lord has been — and still is — very gracious to them, and that their present open disharmony does not further his cause. The result of this pious reflection will be that "in the Lord" — praying together and leaning hard on him — they will again become of the same mind.

3. Paul now enlists the aid of another member of the church at Philippi, namely, Syzygus, in order that he may help these women to compose their difference: **Yes, I request you also, Syzygus (Yoke-fellow) in deed as well as in name, lend these women a hand.** Literally, the original has here, "Yes, I request you also, genuine Syzygus." In all probability, however, the apostle is making use here of a play on a name, for Syzygus means Yoke-fellow, a person who pulls well in a harness for two, and Paul is saying that Syzygus was true to his name. A similar pun occurs in Philem. 11: "Onesimus (Useful) who once was *useless* to you but now is *useful* to you and to me." It is safe to infer that Syzygus, about whom we have no further information, was one of Paul's comrades or associates in the work of the gospel. When this letter was written he was a prominent member of the church at Philippi, a man of influence who was highly esteemed by his people. Like the apostle himself, he must have been a man of extraordinary tact. Otherwise Paul would not have requested him to lend a hand in restoring harmony between two women.[172]

Speaking of these women Paul continues, **For they[173] strove side by side with me in the gospel.** These women deserve to be assisted. They were, after all, *noble* women. Well does the apostle remember the time when they *contended at his side* (for the verb, see on Phil. 1:27) against a common foe and in the gospel-cause. Eagerly they had worked together, and this not only with Paul but also, says the apostle, **along with Clement,** not otherwise known,[174] **and the rest of my fellow-workers, whose names (are) in the book**

---

[172] The reading as proper name is preferable. Other views as to the identity of this individual:
(1) "true yoke-fellow," not a proper name, merely descriptive. Objections: a. This is out of line with the other proper names here mentioned: Euodia, Syntyche, Clement. b. Nowhere else does Paul call his fellow-workers by the name *yoke-fellows*.
(2) Lydia. Objection: the adjective γνήσιε is vocative, sing., *masc.*
(3) Paul's wife. Objection: same as above, as well as other objections.
(4) Timothy. Objection: he was one of the senders of the letter (see on Phil. 1:1).
(5) Epaphroditus. Objection: he was in all probability the man who carried and delivered the letter. For the apostle to address him in the body of this letter would have been very unnatural.
(6) Other guesses, equally unnatural, or in some cases even more so: Silas, Luke, Christ!
[173] αἵτινες: inasmuch as they, etc.
[174] That he is to be identified with Clement of Rome is mere fancy.

of life. Why are not these other fellow-workers mentioned by name? Were there too many to mention? Is the apostle unable at this moment to recall all their names? Or is he implying that some had already died and their names had been forgotten? At any rate their names were known to God! They are in *the book of life.* "When earthly citizens die, their names are erased from the records; the names of the spiritual conquerors will never be blotted out; their glorious life will endure. Christ himself will publicly acknowledge them as his very own! He will do this before the Father and before his angels. Cf. Matt. 10:32; Luke 12:8, 9." [175] With respect to this *book of life* see also Exod. 32:32; Ps. 69:28; Dan. 12:1; Mal. 3:16, 17; Luke 10:20; Rev. 3:5; 13:8; 17:8; 20:12, 15; 21:27; 22:19.

---

4 Rejoice in the Lord always; again I will say, Rejoice. 5 Let y o u r big-heartedness be known to everybody. The Lord (is) at hand. 6 In nothing be anxious, but in everything by prayer and supplication with thanksgiving let y o u r petitions be made known before God. 7 And the peace of God that surpasses all understanding will keep guard over y o u r hearts and y o u r thoughts in Christ Jesus.

4:4-7

II. *The Secret of True Blessedness*

4:4-6

A. *What to Do to Obtain It*

(1) Let joy reign *within*

4. Once again, as so often before, the apostle stresses the duty of rejoicing. He says, **Rejoice in the Lord always; again I will say, Rejoice.** The exhortation is repeated, probably because on the surface it seems so unreasonable to rejoice *in obedience to a command,* and perhaps even more unreasonable to rejoice *always,* under all circumstances no matter how trying. Can one truly rejoice when the memory of past sins vexes the soul, when dear ones are suffering, when one is being persecuted, facing possible death? But there is Paul, who does, indeed, remember his past sins (Phil. 3:6; cf. Gal. 1:13; I Cor. 15:9), whose friends are really suffering (Phil. 1:29, 30), who is even now a prisoner facing possible death; yet, who rejoices and tells others to do likewise! It is evident from this that circumstances alone do not determine the condition of heart and mind. A Christian can be joyful *within* when *without* all is dark and dreary. He rejoices *in the Lord,* that

---

[175] Quoted from my book *More Than Conquerors,* p. 92.

is, because of his oneness with Christ, the fruit of whose Spirit is *joy* (Gal. 5:22). This is reasonable, for in and through Christ all things — also those that seem most unfavorable — work together for good (Rom. 8:28).

It was not unreasonable for Paul *to exhort* the Philippians to rejoice, for the disposition of joy can be and should be cultivated. This can be done, as the apostle indicates in the context (see verse 8), by meditating on the proper subjects, that is, by taking account of the things that should stand out in our consciousness. For Paul such reasons for joy, the joy unspeakable and full of glory, were the following: that he was a saved individual whose purpose was in his entire person to magnify Christ (1:19, 20); that this Savior, in whose cross, crown, and coming again he glories (2:5-11; 3:20, 21; 4:5), was able and willing to supply his every need (4:11-13, 19, 20); that others, too, were being saved (1:6; 2:17, 18), the apostle himself being used by God for this glorious purpose; that he had many friends and helpers in the gospel-cause, who together formed a glorious *fellowship* in the Lord (1:5; 2:19-30; 4:1, 10); that God was causing all things, even bonds, to work together for good (1:12-18; cf. Rom. 8:28), so that even death is gain when life is Christ (1:21, 23); and that at all times he has freedom of access to the throne of grace (4:6). Let the Philippians meditate on these things and rejoice, yes rejoice *always*.

5a. (2) Let big-heartedness be shown *all around*.

A Christian should cultivate an outgoing personality. The secret of his happiness is not confined within the walls of his own meditation and reflection. He cannot be truly happy without striving to be a blessing to others. Hence, Paul continues, **Let y o u r big-heartedness be known to everybody.** For *big-heartedness* one may substitute any of the following: forbearance, yieldedness, geniality, kindliness, gentleness, sweet reasonableness, considerateness, charitableness, mildness, magnanimity, generosity. All of these qualities are combined in the adjective-noun that is used in the original. Taken together they show the real meaning. When each of these would-be-English-equivalents is taken by itself alone, it becomes clear that there is not a single word in the English language that fully expresses the meaning of the original.[176]

The lesson which Paul teaches is that true blessedness cannot be obtained by the person who rigorously insists on whatever he regards as his just due. The Christian is the man who reasons that it is far better to *suffer* wrong than to *inflict* wrong (I Cor. 6:7). Sweet reasonableness is an essential ingredient of true happiness. Now such big-heartedness, such forbearance, the patient willingness to yield wherever yielding is possible without violating any real principle, must be shown *to all*, not only to fellow-believers.

---

[176] For the adjective ἐπιεικής see I Tim. 3:3; Titus 3:2; James 3:17; I Peter 2:18; for the noun ἐπιείκεια see Acts 24:4; II Cor. 10:1.

This Christian magnanimity probably stands in very close connection with the comfort which the Christian derives from the coming of the Lord, which coming has already been mentioned (Phil. 3:20, 21) and is about to be mentioned once more (4:5b, "the Lord is at hand"). The idea seems to be: since Christ's coming is near, when all the promises made to God's people will become realities, believers, in spite of being persecuted, can certainly afford to be mild and charitable in their relation to others.[177]

5b, 6. (3) Let there be no worry but prayerful trusting in God *above*.

Joy *within,* big-heartedness *all around,* and now prayerful trusting in God *above.* Says Paul, **The Lord (is) at hand.** In view of the immediate context (3:20, 21) the meaning is probably not, "The Lord is always nearby or present," (cf. Ps. 145:18) but rather, "The Lord is coming very soon." This, of course, is strictly true with respect to every believer. If the Lord arrives from heaven before the believer dies, then no one surely will be able to doubt that this coming was, indeed, *at hand.* But if the death of the believer occurs before the day of Christ's coming, then two facts remain true both for the believer's own consciousness and according to the clear teaching of Scripture: a. The believer's life-span here on earth was very, very brief. In fact, it amounted to a mere breath (Ps. 39:5; 90:10; 103:15, 16); and b. the interval between the entrance of his soul into heaven and the Lord's second coming was but "a little season" (Rev. 6:11), for in heaven he was geared to a different kind of time-scale.[178] Hence, take it either way, Paul had every right to say, "The Lord (is) at hand." Whatever happens in history is a preparation for this coming, which, as has been shown, will in either case be *soon.* This does not mean that the apostle excludes the possibility that *by earthly reckoning* there could still be an interval of many years before the Lord's arrival. He is not setting any dates (see I Thess. 5:1-3; II Thess. 2:1-3). In view of the fact that no one knows the day and the hour when Jesus will return (Matt. 24:36), it behooves every one to be ready, working, watching at all times (Matt. 25:1-13). At the coming of the Lord all wrongs will be righted, and the believer will stand in the presence of his Lord, fully vindicated. Hence, let him not make too much of disappointments, or unduly trouble himself about the future. So Paul continues, **In nothing be anxious** or "stop being anxious about anything." (See also N.T.C. on John 14:1-4.) There is such a thing as *kindly concern,* that is, *genuine interest* in the welfare of others. The verb (used in Phil. 4:6, and here rendered "be anxious") can elsewhere have a favorable meaning, as it does, in fact, in this very epistle (2:20): Timothy *was genuinely interested* in the welfare of the Philippians. Often, however, it indicates

---

[177] Thus also H. Preisker, article ἐπιείκεια, ἐπιεικής, Th.W.N.T., Vol. II, pp. 585-587.
[178] See my book *The Bible and the Life Hereafter,* Chapter 14, "Is There Time in Heaven?" pp. 70-74.

to be unduly concerned about, to be filled with anxiety, to worry. Such worry may be about food or drink or clothes or one's life-span or the future or words to be spoken in self-defense or even about "many things" (Matt. 6:25-28, 34; 10:19; Luke 10:41; 12:11). The cure for worry is prayer. Hence, the apostle continues, **but in everything by prayer and supplication with thanksgiving let y o u r petitions be made known before God.**

The cure for worry is not *inaction.* If one wishes to plant a garden, build a house, make a sermon, or do anything else, he cannot attain his objective by prayer *alone.* There must be careful planning. There must be *reflection* leading to *action.* Paul is not forgetting this. In fact, the *reflection* is stressed in verse 8, the *action* in verse 9. On the other hand, however, it is also true that reflection and action without prayer would be futile. In fact so very important is prayer to the Christian that it is mentioned first of all (verse 6b).

Neither is the cure for worry *apathy.* God never tells us to suppress every desire. On the contrary, he says, "Open your mouth wide, and I will fill it" (Ps. 81:10). Proper desires should be cultivated, not killed.

The proper antidote for anxiety is *the outpouring of the heart to God.* Here questions occur:

a. *In connection with what situations or circumstances should this take place?*

Answer: "in everything." Note the sharp contrast: *"In nothing* be anxious but *in everything* . . . let y o u r petitions be made known before God." Because of the specific context here, *the emphasis* is, nevertheless, on all such circumstances which might otherwise cause one to worry: "Cast all y o u r anxiety upon him, because he cares for y o u" (I Peter 5:7). The outpouring of the heart to God should, of course, not be *restricted* to this.

> "Sweet hour of prayer, sweet hour of prayer,
> That calls me from a world of care,
> And bids me at My Father's throne.
> Make all my wants and wishes known!"
> (W. W. Walford)

b. *In what frame of mind should this be done?*

Answer: *with reverence and true devotion.* That is implied in the words, "by prayer." *Prayer* is any form of reverent address directed to God.

c. *What is the nature of this activity?*

Answer: *it amounts to supplication.* Note: "and supplication." By this is meant the humble cry for the fulfilment of needs that are keenly felt.[179]

---

[179] προσευχή is the more general term; δέησις the more particular. The two words occur together also in Eph. 6:18; I Tim. 2:1; 5:5. The former is always addressed to God; the latter to either God or man. See R. C. Trench, *Synonyms of the New Testament,* paragraph li. Also N.T.C. on I Tim. 2:1.

d. *What is the condition of acceptance?*

Answer: that this be done "with thanksgiving." This implies humility, submission to God's will, knowing that this will is always best. There must be grateful acknowledgement for: a. past favors, b. present blessings, and c. firmly-grounded assurances for the future. Paul begins nearly every one of his epistles with an outpouring of thanksgiving to God. Throughout his writings he again and again insists on the necessity of giving thanks (Rom. 1:21; 14:6; II Cor. 1:11; 4:15; 9:11, 12; Eph. 5:20; Col. 3:15; etc.). Prayer without thanksgiving is like a bird without wings: such a prayer cannot rise to heaven, can find no acceptance with God.

e. *What are the contents?*

Answer: not vague generalities. The prayer, "Lord, bless all that awaiteth thy blessing" may be proper at times but can be overdone. It is easy to resort to it when one has nothing definite to ask. Paul says, "Let y o u r *petitions* be made known before God." There must be *definite, specific requests* (I John 5:15). That is also clear from the example given us in what is commonly called "The Lord's Prayer" (Matt. 6:9-13). Note also the preposition *before,* in "before God." One enters into the very presence of God, realizing that nothing is too great for his power to accomplish nor too small for his love to be concerned about. Is he not our Father who in Christ loves us with an infinite love?

4:7

B. *The Result*

7. Now if joy in the Lord reigns *within* the heart, if magnanimity is shown *all around* to everybody with whom one comes into contact, and if there be constant prayer to God *above,* the result will be *peace.* Paul begins the next sentence by saying, **And the peace of God that surpasses all understanding.** This sweet peace originates in God who himself possesses it in his own being. He is glad to impart it to his children. It is, therefore, "the gift of God's love." He not only gives it; he also maintains it at every step. Hence, it has every right to be called "the peace *of* God." It is founded on grace. It is merited for believers by Christ (see John 14:27; 16:33; 20:19, 21, 26). Paul speaks of this peace in every one of his letters, often at the opening and at the close, sometimes also in the body of the epistle. In Philippians Paul mentions it, as almost always, immediately after *grace* (in I and II Timothy *mercy* is interposed between *grace* and *peace*). See on Phil. 1:2. Peace is the smile of God reflected in the soul of the believer. It is the heart's calm after Calvary's storm. It is the firm conviction that he who spared not his own Son will surely also, along with him, freely give us all things (Rom. 8:32). "Thou wilt keep him in perfect peace, whose mind is stayed on thee, because he trusts in thee" (Isa. 26:3). In the present context it is the God-given reward resulting from *joyful* reflection on God's bounties, *magnanimity* toward the neighbor, and trustful *prayer* to God.

This peace *passes all understanding*. With respect to this modifier an interpretation favored by many is this: "God's gift of peace will do far more for us than will any clever planning or calculating on our part. In that sense *peace* surpasses our *understanding*." Objections, which I share with many, are the following:

(1) This interpretation takes the word *understanding* in a too limited sense.

(2) The parallel, Eph. 3:19, is clear. In that passage the love of Christ is said to surpass knowledge in the sense that, try as they may, believers will never succeed in measuring it in all its breadth, length, height, and depth (Eph. 3:18). Surely, if the passage about Christ's love means that this love is *unfathomable*, why should not the passage about God's *peace* have the same meaning?

By nature man is as totally unable to comprehend this wonderful peace as is a blind man to appreciate a glorious sunset (I. Cor. 2:14). And even the believer will never be able fully to grasp the beauty of this Christ-centered gift that surpasses in value all other gifts of God to man. One reason why it is justly esteemed to be very, very precious is that it **will keep guard over y o u r hearts and y o u r thoughts in Christ Jesus**. The Philippians were used to the sight of Roman sentinels standing guard. Thus also, only far more so, God's peace will mount guard at the door of heart and thought. It will prevent carking care from corroding the heart, which is the main-spring of life (Prov. 4:23), the root of thinking (Rom. 1:21), willing (I Cor. 7:37), and feeling (Phil. 1:7; see on that passage). It will also prevent un-worthy reasonings from entering thought-life. Thus, if any one should tell the believer that God does not exist and that everlasting life is a mere dream, he would get nowhere, for at that very moment the child of God would be experiencing within himself the realities which the infidel is trying to reason out of existence. The man of trust and prayer has entered that impregnable citadel from which no one can dislodge him; and the name of that fortress is *Christ Jesus* (note: "in Christ Jesus").

---

8 For the rest, brothers, whatever things are true, whatever things (are) honorable, whatever things (are) just, whatever things (are) pure, whatever things (are) lovely, whatever things (are) of good report; if (there be) any virtue and if (there be) any praise, be thinking about these things. 9 The things which y o u not only learned and received but also heard and saw in me, these things put into constant practice; and the God of peace will be with y o u.

197

4:8, 9

III. *Summary of Christian Duty*

A. *Proper Meditation*

8. For the rest — see on 3:1 — **brothers** — see on 1:12 — **whatever things are true.** Many are of the opinion that the apostle is here copying a paragraph from a pagan book on morality or from this or that Manual of Discipline circulated by an Essenic sect. Objections:

(1) The definitely Christian character of this exhortation is clear from the reference to *the peace of God* which precedes it and *the God of peace* which follows it.

(2) It is also clear from the fact that the apostle states that *these things* have been heard and seen *in himself.* Surely, the Philippians had seen *Christian* virtues displayed in Paul!

(3) Wherever possible, words used by Paul in any passage should be interpreted in the light of their true parallels in Scripture, especially in Paul's own letters.

Note the six occurrences of *whatever,* followed by two instances of *any.* Believers should exhibit not just this or that trait of Christian character but "all the graces in choral order and festal array" (Johnstone).

The apostle tells the Philippians to meditate on whatever things are *true.* Truth stands over against falsehood (Eph. 4:25). It has its norm in God (Rom. 3:4), goes hand in hand with goodness, righteousness, and holiness (Eph. 4:24; 5:9) and is climaxed in gospel-truth (Eph. 1:13; 4:21; Col. 1:5, 6). Truth belongs to the armor of the Christian soldier (Eph. 6:14).

Paul adds, **whatever things (are) honorable.** In his speech and in his entire behavior believers should be dignified, serious. Proper *motives, manners,* and *morals* are very important. In an environment then as now characterized by *frivolity* whatever things are honorable surely merit *earnest consideration.* See also I Tim. 2:2; 3:4; Titus 2:2, 7; 3:8.

So also **whatever things (are) just.** Having received from God *righteousness* both of imputation and impartation, believers should think righteous thoughts. They should, in their mind, gratefully meditate on God's righteous acts (Rev. 15:3), appreciate righteousness in others, and should plan righteous words and deeds. Masters, for example, should take account of what is fair and square in dealing with their servants. They should realize that they, too, have an Employer in heaven (Col. 4:1). In all his planning, let the Christian ask himself, "Is this in harmony with God's will and law?"

Next, **whatever things (are) pure.** The Philippians, because of their background and surroundings (both *pagan,* cf. Eph. 5:8, and *antinomian,* cf. Phil. 3:18, 19) were being constantly tempted by that which was *unchaste.* Let them therefore fill their minds with whatever is pure and holy. See also II Cor. 11:2; I Tim. 5:22; Titus 2:5. Cf. James 3:17; I John 3:3. *Let them overcome evil with good* (Rom. 12:21). A wonderful direction also for the present day!

Whatever things (are) lovely follows immediately. The word *lovely*, though occurring only in this one instance in the New Testament, is rather common in epitaphs. That which is *lovely, amiable, pleasing*, breathes love and evokes love. Let believers meditate and take into account all such things.

Whatever things (are) of good report (only occurrence of this adjective in New Testament, but see cognate noun in II Cor. 6:8) closes this list of six whatever's. These things are *well-sounding, appealing*. Even upon non-Christians they may make a good impression. The main consideration is, however, that in their inner essence they are actually worthy of creating that impression.

Paul summarizes: **If (there be) any virtue and if (there be) any praise, be thinking about these things.** Nothing that is really worthwhile for believers to ponder and take into consideration is omitted from this summarizing phrase. Anything at all that is a matter of moral and spiritual excellence, so that it is the proper object of praise, is the right pasture for the Christian mind to graze in. *Nothing* that is of a contrary nature is the right food for his thought. It is hardly necessary to repeat that the *virtue* of which the apostle speaks is the fruit which grows on the tree of *salvation*. The trunk of this tree is *faith*, and its roots are imbedded in the soil of God's sovereign, saving *grace* (Eph. 2:8-10; II Peter 1:5). To be sure, the believer is not at all blind to the fact that "there remain in man, since the fall, the glimmerings of natural light, whereby he retains some knowledge of God, of natural things, and of the difference between good and evil, and shows some regard for virtue and for good outward behavior" (Canons of Dort III and IV, article 4). In a sense even sinners *do good* (Luke 6:33), and even publicans *love* (Matt. 5:46). To deny this, in the interest of this or that theological presupposition, would be to fly in the face of the clear teaching of Scripture and the facts of everyday observation and experience. But surely when Paul told the Philippians to be constantly thinking about anything that is virtuous and worthy of praise, he, great idealist that he was, could not have been satisfied with anything that was less than goodness in the highest, spiritual sense (that which proceeds from faith, is done according to God's law, and to his glory).

This follows also from the continuation:

B. *Proper Action*

9. The things which y o u not only learned and received but also heard and saw in me these things put into constant practice. It becomes very clear now that the *thinking* or *meditation* of which the apostle spoke in the preceding passage was not of an abstractly theoretical character. It was thinking *with a purpose,* and that purpose lies in the sphere of *action.* This is also the teaching of The Sermon on the Mount and of Christ's parables (Matt. 7:24; 13:23; Luke 8:15). True believers *hear.* They meditate until they *understand.* Then they *act* upon it, putting it into *constant practice,* thereby showing that their house was built upon a rock.

The *learning and receiving* of which the apostle speaks here in verse 9 represents one idea; the *hearing and seeing* the other. Paul and others had taught the Philippians the matters summarized in verse 8, and they had accepted them. But the apostle had also exemplified these virtues in his own daily conduct. The Philippians had heard about this from various sources and by the mouth of ever so many messengers. Even by means of the present letter they are hearing about it, and Epaphroditus will surely fill in the details. Moreover, both on his first visit and on subsequent stopovers they have seen these graces displayed in Paul. Hence, the apostle had a right to say, "Brothers, join in being imitators of me" (Phil. 3:17).

The result of such constant Christian practice is stated in the words, **And the God of peace will be with y o u.** The expression *the God of peace* here in verse 9 complements and brings to a climax the phrase *the peace of God* of verse 7. Not only will the Philippians who obey these instructions receive God's most wonderful gift; they will also have as their constant Helper and Friend the Giver himself!

Synthesis of 4:1-9

Exhortations (general and specific) to remain firm and live in unity, an *answer* to the question how true blessedness can be obtained, and a *summary* of Christian duty: these thoughts fill the present section.

In a world of unbelief and hostility believers should continue to take a definite stand for their convictions. Theirs should be the attitude of militant unity. Very tactfully and lovingly Paul admonishes two women of the congregation to settle their dispute and live in harmony. While he administers a veiled rebuke, he yet praises them for their earnest and co-operative effort in days gone by. In fact, he even honors them by mentioning them in one breath with other then-famous gospel-workers. He appoints Syzygus — Yoke-fellow is his name and a true Yoke-fellow he is! — to lend them a hand in arriving at the ideal of true, Christian unity.

He points out that the secret of true blessedness consists in permitting spiritual joy to reign *within,* showing magnanimity *all around,* and trustfully bringing every need to the attention of God *above.* Such taking hold on God must be *reverent* (it must be true *praying*), *humble* (*supplicating*), *thankful* (no prayer is complete without *thanksgiving*), and *definite* (making definite *petitions* or *requests*). Result: God's peace incomprehensible in its grandeur, will stand guard at the door of the believers' hearts and thoughts, preventing the entrance of fears and doubts.

The summary of Christian duty may be expressed in this one thought that in all their thinking with a view to future deeds believers should strive to overcome evil with good; that is, that which is true, honorable, just, pure, lovely, and of good report must crowd out whatever is base. Let virtue conquer vice! Reward: not only the peace of God but the God of peace will be with them.

Summary of Chapter 4

Verses 10-23

Paul, the Grateful Recipient

rejoicing in the generosity of the Philippians, and testifying that he has learned the secret of contentment and of readiness for every task;

resuming and completing his expression of appreciation for the generosity which the Philippians have shown both in the more recent and in the more distant past;

confessing his faith in God who will supply every need, and ascribing glory to him; and

concluding his letter with words of greeting and benediction.

4:10-13   Thank-y o u note begun; testimony: the secret learned.

4:14-18   Thank y o u note resumed and completed.

4:19, 20 Assurance of God's loving care, Doxology.

4:21-23   Conclusion.

10 Now I rejoice in the Lord greatly that now at length y o u caused y o u r concern for my welfare to bloom afresh; a matter with reference to which y o u were indeed concerned, but y o u lacked opportunity. 11 Not that I mention (this) because of want; for I have learned in whatever circumstances I am to be content. 12 I know what it means to live in straitened circumstances, and I also know what it means to have plenty; in any and all circumstances I have learned the secret, both to be filled and to be hungry, both to have plenty and to be in want. 13 I can do all things through him who infuses strength into me.

4:10-13

I. *Thank-y o u Note Begun. Testimony: the Secret Learned*

10. One of Paul's purposes in writing Philippians was to give written expression to his gratitude for the gift received (see Introduction, IV). Says C. R. Erdman in his Exposition on Philippians, p. 131, "This message of thanks is a rare blending of affection, of dignity, of delicacy, with a certain under undertone of gentle pleasantry. It is an embodiment of ideal Christian courtesy." [180] It begins as follows, **Now I rejoice** [181] **in the Lord greatly that now at length** [182] **y o u caused y o u r concern for my welfare to bloom afresh.** [183] To be sure, there had been this concern, this interest, all along, just as throughout the winter-season the tree that seems to be dead is actually alive. But just as in spring-time the tree puts forth fresh shoots, thereby *proving* that it is alive, so also the Philippians' interest in Paul had at last found a way *to express and demonstrate* itself concretely. "In the Lord," that is, motivated by the highest possible considerations as being in the closest union with his Lord, Paul not only rejoices but, in consideration of

[180] The question as to Paul's attitude toward accepting remuneration or gifts for gospel-work has been discussed under ten points in N.T.C. on I and II Thessalonians, pp. 66, 67.
[181] Thus to be rendered if ἐχάρην is an *epistolary* aorist. Something can be said, however, in favor of the rendering, "I rejoiced," simple *historical* aorist, going back to the moment when Paul, after a terrible voyage (see Acts 27), had arrived in Rome, and then, at some later time, was heartened by the visit of Epaphroditus bringing not only the gift itself but, bound up with it, also the assurance that his dear friends in Philippi had by no means forgotten him, and, on the whole, were standing firm in their faith. It is, however, impossible to say definitely whether this aorist is a direct reference to the past or is epistolary, and this point is surely of very minor interest, as in either case the apostle must have *rejoiced greatly* whenever he thought of the Philippians and their gift.
[182] ἤδη ποτὲ as in Rom. 1:10. Not "because of late" (Berkeley Version).
[183] This, it would seem to me, makes better sense than to interpret ἀνεθάλετε intransitively, "Y o u revived with respect to y o u r concern for me." Transitive meaning also in LXX; e.g., Ezek. 17:24.

the *implications* of this gift, even rejoices *greatly*. The apostle guards against misinterpretation by continuing, **a matter with reference to which** [184] **y o u were indeed concerned, but y o u lacked opportunity.** The "matter" of which Paul speaks was, of course, that pertaining to his *welfare*. As soon as the news of Paul's imprisonment had become known in Philippi the desire had sprung up "to do something" to help him. But at first no favorable opportunity had presented itself. It may have been that no messenger had been immediately available, or that for some reason or other it had been impossible to collect the gift from the various members. These are only two out of many possibilities. At any rate, for a while opportunity to send the gift had been lacking. As soon as this situation changed, the Philippians had acted with characteristic enthusiasm and devotion.

11. Paul had been exuberant in his praise. He had said, "I rejoice *greatly*." Here, too, misinterpretation was possible. The question might be asked, "Is not this a weakness in Paul, to go into such raptures over merely *earthly goods,* as if he were a child who had just received a new toy? Or were his remarks to be taken as an expression of dire want, a kind of complaint with the implication, Please send me another gift soon?" To prevent any inferences of this nature the apostle continues, **Not that** [185] **I mention (this) because of want; for I have learned in whatever circumstances I am to be content.** Meaning: "The satisfaction of a material need must not be construed as being either the real reason for or the measure of my joy. On the contrary, regardless of outward circumstances, I would still be satisfied. My conversion-experience, and also my subsequent trials for the sake of Christ and his gospel, have taught me a lesson. The path which I traveled led me ever closer to Christ, to his love, and to his power, yes to Christ and *contentment* in him. That very contentment is riches to me."

12. It is to be noted that this *contentment* or soul-sufficiency (see on I Tim. 6:6) is derived not from any resources which the soul has *in itself*. Paul is no vain boaster who exclaims, "I am the Captain of my soul." He is no Stoic who, *trusting in his own resources,* and supposedly unmoved by either joy or grief, endeavors with all his might to submit without complaining to unavoidable necessity. The apostle is no statue. He is a man of flesh and blood. He knows both joys and sorrows, yet is content. But his contentment has its cause in One other than himself. The real Source or Fountain of Paul's soul-sufficiency is mentioned in verse 13. And that Fountain never runs dry, no matter what may be *the circumstances*. With reference to the latter Paul continues, **I know what it means to live in straitened circumstances, and I also know what it means to have plenty. In any and all**

---

[184] Of the various ways in which ἐφ' ᾧ can be rendered this yields the best sense.
[185] See on 3:12.

circumstances I have learned the secret, both to be filled and to be hungry, both to have plenty and to be in want.

Paul *has learned the secret* (a verb used only here in the New Testament and related to *mystery*).[186] He has been thoroughly *initiated* into it by the experiences of life applied to the heart by the Holy Spirit. To those who fear him God reveals this mystery (Ps. 25:14). Those who reject Christ cannot understand how it is possible for a Christian to remain calm in adversity, humble in prosperity.

The words in the present passage which require some elucidation are the following:

to live in straitened circumstances

Again and again Paul had been "brought low," same verb as used with reference to Christ in Phil. 2:8, the Christ who *humbled* himself. That the apostle indeed knew what it meant to be reduced to such straitened circumstances is clear from the following passages: Acts 14:19; 16:22-25; 17:13; 18:12; 20:3; Chapters 21-27; II Cor. 4:11; 6:4, 5; 11:27, 33. He knew what was meant by hunger, thirst, fasting, cold, nakedness, physical suffering, mental torture, persecution, etc.

to be hungry

Hunger and thirst are often mentioned together (Rom. 12:20; I Cor. 4:11; II Cor. 11:27; and cf. for spiritual yearning, Matt. 5:6). In glory there will be neither hunger nor thirst (Rev. 7:16), and this because of Christ's submission to these afflictions for his own children (Luke 4:2).

to be in want

The apostle had often *fallen behind*. He had suffered from *lack* of such comforts as many other people would have considered necessities. He had *come short*. Yet, none of these things had deprived him of his contentment.

Over against the expressions indicating poverty and affliction are those referring to riches and glory:

to have plenty

Before his conversion Paul has been a prominent Pharisee. The future looked bright and promising. Paul had had plenty, and this in more ways than one. Yet, he had lacked the greatest boon of all: Christ-centered peace of soul. But even after his conversion there had been moments of refreshment when even physically he had experienced what it meant, in a sense, to have plenty (Acts 16:15, 40; 16:33, 34; 20:11; 28:2; Phil. 4:15, 16, 18), and now no longer apart from but in connection with peace of soul. Now, to carry oneself properly in the midst of plenty is no easy matter (Prov. 30:8;

---

[186] On the verb μυέω see Bornkamm, Th.W.N.T., Vol. 4, p. 834. It is not necessary to suppose that the word was "borrowed from the mystery-cults." Nor is it at all certain that Paul's frequent use of the cognate noun *mystery* has been taken over from these cults. To Paul a mystery is a truth which, had it not been for special divine revelation, would not have been known.

Mark 10:23-25). As the adage has it, "In order to carry a full cup one must have a steady hand." Paul, however, by the grace of the Holy Spirit had been schooled to abundance as well as to want.

to be filled

This word, though used at first with respect to the feeding and fattening of animals (of which meaning there is an echo in the clause: "all the birds *gorged themselves* with their flesh," Rev. 19:21), and applied to men chiefly by the Comic poets, was gradually losing its depreciatory sense and is here simply used as a synonym for *to have plenty.*

13. Paul, then, is saying that *in every particular circumstance as well as in all circumstances generally* he has learned the secret of contentment. The cause that accounts for this soul-sufficiency, that is, the Person who taught and is constantly teaching him this secret, is indicated in the words, **I can do all things in him** [187] **who infuses strength into me.** Surely, a wonderful testimony! Whatever needs to be done Paul can do, for he is *in Christ* (Phil. 3:9), being by the indwelling presence of Christ's Spirit and by Spirit-wrought faith in vital union and intimate fellowship with his Lord and Savior. Christ's grace is sufficient for him and his power rests on him (II Cor. 12:9). This wonderful Helper is standing by him (II Tim. 4:17) as the great Enabler (I Tim. 1:12). The Lord is for Paul the Fountain of Wisdom, encouragement, and energy, actually infusing strength into him for every need. It is for that reason that the apostle is even able to say, "Wherefore I take pleasure in infirmities, in insults, in distresses, in persecutions and frustrations, for when I am weak, then I am strong" (II Cor. 12:10).

---

14 Nevertheless, y o u did nobly in sharing my affliction. 15 Moreover, y o u Philippians yourselves also know that in the early days of the gospel, when I departed from Macedonia, not even a single church entered into partnership with me in an account of expenditures and receipts except y o u only; 16 for even when I was in Thessalonica y o u once and again sent me something to alleviate my need. 17 Not that I seek the gift, but I seek the fruit which increases to y o u r credit. 18 But I have received payment in full and am enjoying abundance. I am amply supplied, having received from Epaphroditus the gifts (that came) from y o u, a fragrant odor, a sacrifice acceptable, well-pleasing to God.

4:14-18

II. *Thank-y o u Note Resumed and Completed*

The Thank-y o u note is now resumed (from verse 10) and completed. The apostle indicates the relation of the gift to:

---

[187] The reading Χριστῷ at the end of the sentence is wanting in the best manuscripts. It was probably added for the sake of clarity, influenced by such passages as II Cor. 12:9, 10; I Tim. 1:12; II Tim. 4:17.

(1) *himself the recipient:* it relieved his need and brought joy to his heart (verses 10, 14-16, 18a).

(2) *the givers:* it enriched them (verse 17).

(3) *God:* it was well-pleasing to him (verse 18b).

14. Paul is careful not to leave the impression that the gift had been superfluous and that he did not appreciate it. On the contrary, he indicates that he was definitely pleased with it. Hence, he says, **Nevertheless, y o u did nobly in sharing my affliction.** It was, says Paul as it were, *a noble, a beautiful deed,* like that of Mary of Bethany (Mark 14:6). Had the Philippians not been true sympathizers, so that they felt Paul's affliction as if it were their very own, they would not have performed their generous deed. The gift indicated that they had made common cause with Paul's affliction, were true sharers in it. Truly, the *fellowship* (see on Phil. 1:5) was operating beautifully!

15, 16. Paul continues, **Moreover, y o u Philippians yourselves also know that in the early days of the gospel, when I departed from Macedonia, not even a single church entered into partnership with me in an account of expenditures and receipts but y o u only.** Paul gratefully acknowledges the fact that the present gift was the continuation of a series of gifts. He mentions something well-known to both the Philippians and himself, namely, that when the Philippian church was *in its infancy,* having just been established — this was at least a decade ago — then already, in those early days of gospel-proclamation in their region, they, and *they alone,* had entered into partnership with himself in (and here follows a business-term) *an account of expenditures and receipts,* that is, an account in which the Philippians were the givers, Paul the receiver. Defining the occasion more exactly as to time, the apostle says that this generosity had been shown in connection with his departure from Macedonia (in which Philippi and nearby Thessalonica were located), a rather sudden departure, as Acts 17:14 indicates. The friends in Philippi had heard about Paul's troubles in Thessalonica and had immediately rushed to his aid in a material way, enabling him to continue his work elsewhere (in Achaia: Athens and Corinth; cf. II Cor. 11:8, 9). Nor was this all, **for even when I was in Thessalonica y o u once and again sent me something to alleviate my need.** This help which had been given during Paul's work in Thessalonica naturally even preceded his departure from Macedonia. So young a church, that of Philippi, yet so prompt and spontaneous in extending help! Truly the stamp of Luke's and Lydia's commendable generosity was upon this congregation! See Introduction, III.

17. Paul's fear of being misunderstood when he speaks about receiving gifts appears again and again, no doubt because his enemies were constantly misconstruing his motives (II Cor. 11:7; 12:14; I Thess. 2:3, 5, 8). If he accepted a gift or if his enemies suspected that he did, they were ready to charge him with selfishness, greed; if he did not, they accused him of making a show of his humility. Yet, in the final analysis it was not the gift but the giver that was the object of Paul's concern. Hence, he says, **Not that I seek the gift, but I seek the fruit which increases to y o u r account.** Note again the business-term *account*. The gift was really *an investment* entered *as a credit* on *the account* of the Philippians, an investment which is increasingly paying them rich dividends. These *dividends* or *fruits* in the lives of his friends are the object of Paul's concern. In this letter he has already mentioned fruits (Phil. 1:11), and he does so also elsewhere (Rom. 1:13; 7:4; Gal. 5:22, 23; Eph. 5:9; Col. 1:6). Right giving always enriches the giver. "The liberal soul will be made fat" (Prov. 11:25). "He who pities the poor lends to the Lord" (Prov. 19:17). "Blessed are the merciful, for they will obtain mercy" (Matt. 5:7). "God loves a cheerful giver" (II Cor. 9:7). And cf. also Luke 21:1-4. Among the fruits that are harvested by such givers may be mentioned the following: a good conscience, assurance of salvation, enriched fellowship with other believers, a broadened outlook into the needs and interests of the church universal, increased joy and love (both of these imparted and received), a higher degree of glory in heaven, Judgment Day praise.

18. In all probability commercial phraseology is continued in the words, **But I have received payment in full and am enjoying abundance.** According to the evidence supplied by papyri and ostraca the term *apecho* (ἀπέχω) here used has the meaning "I have received." The technical sense is, "This is my receipt." A. Deissmann (*Light From the Ancient East*, fourth edition, pp. 111, 112, 331) also informs us that in receipts *apecho* is frequently (as also here in Phil. 4:18) combined with *panta* (πάντα), meaning *everything* that was owed, *full payment*. In a more or less humorous manner, therefore, the apostle is here saying, "I have received full payment, and even more" (or "and am affluent," thus Erdman). He continues, **I am amply supplied, having received from Epaphroditus the gifts (that came) from y o u.** Just what was included in those gifts we are not told. Possibilities: money to cover expenses, reading material, clothes (cf. II Tim. 4:13 for the last two items for which Paul asks at a later occasion). On Epaphroditus see Phil. 2:25-30. The finest thing that can be said about these gifts is this: they are described as a **fragrant odor, a sacrifice acceptable, well-pleasing to God.** Higher praise even Paul could not have bestowed upon the givers. The gifts are "an odor of a sweet smell," "an offering presented to God, welcome and very pleasing to him." They are comparable to the thank-offering of Abel (Gen. 4:4), of Noah (Gen. 8:21), of the Israelites when in the proper frame of mind they brought whole-burnt-offerings (Lev.

1:9, 13, 17), and of believers generally in dedicating their lives to God (II Cor. 2:15, 16), as did also Christ, but he in a unique manner (Eph. 5:2). Whether or not an offering is really acceptable and well-pleasing to God (cf. Rom. 12:1) depends on the motive of the one who brings it (Gen. 4:1-15; Heb. 11:4).

> "Not what we give but what we share,
> For the gift without the giver is bare."
>
>   (Lowell)

The apostle credits the givers with the proper spirit, that is, the attitude of faith, love, and gratitude. He acknowledges that their deed was not merely an act of sympathy shown to a friend in need but a genuine offering presented to God to promote his cause, and thus to Paul as God's representative! That made the deed so grand and beautiful!

---

19 And my God will gloriously supply every need of y o u r s according to his riches in Christ Jesus. 20 Now to our God and Father (be) the glory forever and ever. Amen.

4:19, 20

III. *Assurance of God's Loving Care. Doxology*

A. *Assurance of God's Loving Care*

19. Approaching the end of his epistle Paul now assures the addressees that God will supply their every need: **And my God will gloriously supply every need of y o u r s according to his riches in Christ Jesus.** Had not God's care rested in a marvelous manner upon the apostle himself, during this very imprisonment? Note Paul's later testimony regarding this care: "But the Lord stood by my side and gave me strength in order that through me the message might be fully heralded, and all the Gentiles might hear it. And I was rescued out of (the) mouth of (the) lion" (II Tim. 4:17). So also this same compassion would bless the Philippians. Touching is the expression *"my* God." See on Phil. 1:3. It was the God who meant so very, very much to Paul. This God will not fulfill *every wish* but will supply *every need!* He will do this "in glory," which in the sense of *gloriously* must in all probability be construed as modifying the verb *supply;* hence, "God will gloriously supply." Paul is not primarily thinking of what God will do for believers when they have entered the glory of heaven, but what he will do for them in this earthly realm of needs, as they present these needs to him. These he will fulfill not merely *out of* his riches (as a millionaire might do when he donates a trifling sum to a good cause, subtracting the amount from his vast possessions) but *according to* his riches, so that the gift is actually *in proportion to* God's infinite resources! Of course, this loving care, this glorious help in need, is based on the merits of Christ Jesus. "How vast the benefits divine which we *in Christ* possess" (cf. Rom. 8:32). It is only because believers are in vital union with him that they receive all these bounties.

The assurance of this manifestation of God's *very special providence* [188] does not mean that the Philippians would now be justified in becoming lazy, disregarding or even rejecting every means and avenue of caring for themselves. "God's word does not advocate fanaticism, nor does it say that one should throw his pocketbook into the nearest river and then announce that he is going to live by faith" (Tenney). To be sure, God was taking care of Paul, but one of the ways in which he was providing for him was the gift from Philippi which Paul here acknowledges.

Among the many passages in which this tender and loving care of God for his children in the *here* and *now* is described, passages which have given comfort to God's people in many generations, are also the following: Gen. 28:15; 50:20; Exod. 33:14; Deut. 2:7; 32:7-14; 33:27; Josh. 1:9; I Sam. 7:12; I Kings 17:6, 16; II Chron. 20:17; Ps. 18:35; 23; 31:19; 91; 121; Isa. 25:4, 32:2; 40:11; 41:10; 43:1, 2; 46:3, 4; Joel 2:21-27; Mal. 3:10; Matt. 6:32; 14:20; 23:37; Luke 6:38; 12:7; 22:35; John 10:27, 28; 17:11; Rom. 8:28, 31-39; II Tim. 1:12; 4:18; I Peter 5:7.

4:20

B. *Doxology*

20. For Paul doctrine is never a dry matter. Whenever it occupies his mind it also fills his heart with praise. Hence, reflecting on this marvelous care which God bestows on his children he exclaims, **Now to our God and Father (be) the glory forever and ever. Amen.** Note *"our* God and Father," through Christ, of course. To this God who in his Son is the Father *of all believers* Paul ascribes *adoration*. See on Phil. 1:11 for detailed word-study of the concept *glory*. The ardent yearning of the apostle's heart is that all God's redeemed children will do their utmost to give *never-ending* praises unto their God, praises "for the ages of the ages," that is, *forever and ever*. The solemn Amen, a word of affirmation or confirmation, underscores the fact that the doxology is not merely a matter of the lips or of the "pen" but is the spontaneous utterance of the heart redeemed by grace. Paul's epistles

---

[188] I am here using the familiar terminology favored by those theologians who distinguish between God's *general providence* over all his creatures, including even plants and animals; his *special* providence over all his rational creatures, including all men, both believers and unbelievers; and his *very special providence* of which believers are the objects. See L. Berkhof, *Systematic Theology*, p. 168.

abound in doxologies. For this see above, on Phil. 3:18, 19, under the heading *Paul's Deeply Emotional Nature.*

---

21 Greet every saint in Christ Jesus. The brothers (who are) with me greet y o u. 22 All the saints greet y o u, especially those of Caesar's household. 23 The grace of the Lord Jesus Christ (be) with y o u r spirit.

4:21-23

IV. *Conclusion*

4:21, 22

A. *Words of Greeting*

21. It is entirely possible that Paul wrote these last three verses with his own hand (see N.T.C. on II Thess. 3:17). To every member of the church of Philippi who by virtue of union with Christ Jesus has been set apart to a life of consecration to the Lord the apostle sends his greeting as a token of brotherly love: **Greet every saint in Christ Jesus.** He adds, **The brothers (who are) with me greet y o u.** Paul's fellow-workers in Rome, having heard that Paul is sending a letter to the Philippians, have asked that their greetings, too, be extended. Some see here a discrepancy or inconsistency. They point to the fact that elsewhere in this same epistle the apostle has spoken disparagingly about this group of colleagues (see on 1:15a, 17; 2:21). So, how can he now convey their kind regards? The following, however, should be noted:

(1) One of the fellow-workers was Timothy. Paul has had nothing but good to say about him (Phil. 1:1; 2:20, 22).

(2) There were also others, with reference to whom Paul had already said that they were "heralding Christ from good will . . . out of love, knowing that I am appointed for the defense of the gospel" (1:15b, 16a).

(3) The so-called contradiction results from a too absolutistic interpretation of Phil. 2:21 (see on that passage).

(4) And if even some of the envious colleagues (who nevertheless, preached soundly!) had joined in asking Paul to convey their greetings, would this have been refused?

22. Paul continues, **All the saints greet y o u.** The circle of greeters widens now so that it includes all believers in Rome. They all tender their regards and good wishes, for

"In Christ there is no East or West,
In him no South or North;

211

But one great fellowship of Love
Throughout the whole, wide earth."
(John Oxenham)

Paul believed very strongly in ecumenicity of the highest type, ecumenicity indeed, but without sacrifice of the truth. Did he not during this same imprisonment devote an epistle to the theme, *The Unity of All Believers in Christ* (Ephesians)? Had he not been the active promoter of a collection for the needy saints in Jerusalem (read II Cor., Chapters 8 and 9)? Was he not the author of I Cor. 12 and 13? How he loved to send to the saints of *Philippi* the greetings from all the saints in *Rome* (cf. John 17:20, 21). Truly, this was not just a merely formal, polite, customary way of ending a letter. These greetings were "from the heart to the heart." The fellowship was functioning (see on Phil. 1:5). Paul adds, **especially those of Caesar's household.**[189] This expression does not as such refer to the emperor's blood-relatives. It refers rather to all persons in the emperor's service, whether slaves or freedmen. Such people who had been given employment in the domestic and administrative establishment of the emperor were found not only in Italy but even in the provinces. Nevertheless, it is rather questionable reasoning to base on this circumstance the conclusion that, therefore, the epistle to the Philippians may have originated outside of Rome, say in Ephesus or Caesarea. No matter how far and wide Caesar's household extended, its heart and center was in Rome and consisted of *servants in and about the emperor's palace*. Besides, Phil. 4:22 does not stand alone. There is, for example, also the reference to "the whole praetorian guard" (Phil. 1:13). Taken together and in connection with similar additional evidence which has been discussed in the Introduction everything points to Rome.

Why did *especially* these members of Caesar's household send their greetings? We simply do not know. The following are among the guesses that have been made. It is impossible to establish which (if any) of these reasons, or which combination of them, furnishes the true answer to the question.

(1) Philippi was a colony; hence, had many servants employed by the government. Because of the work they performed these were acquainted with similar government employees in Rome.

(2) These members of Caesar's household were earlier converts to Christianity. They had become believers before Paul arrived in Rome (see the long list of names in Romans 16); hence, there had been more time for them to establish contact with believers elsewhere, particularly also in Philippi.

(3) It is a known fact that a considerable percentage of those who be-

---

[189] On this see the following: J. B. Lightfoot's *Commentary on St. Paul's Epistle to the Philippians*, pp. 171-178; entry οἰκία in L.N.T. (A. and G.); and the article on this word in Th.W.N.T., Vol. 5, p. 136.

longed to Caesar's household in Rome had come from regions east of Rome. Hence, those — or at least some of those — who were sending these special greetings may have come from Macedonia, and therefore wished to be remembered to their friends and relatives.

Far more important is the fact that Christianity had entered even the circles of these palace-servants. Their position in the midst of a definitely pagan environment in which by many the emperor was worshiped as if he were a god, did not keep them from remaining true to their only Lord and Savior, from spreading the good news to others, and from strengthening the church in Philippi by means of their greetings. Eternity will tell what great blessings must have resulted from lives dedicated to Christ amid such worldly surroundings!

4:23

B. Benediction

23. The best textual evidence supports the reading which can be rendered, **The grace of the Lord Jesus Christ (be) with y o u r spirit.**[190] One is reminded immediately of Gal. 6:18 and Philem. 25; but see also I Cor. 16:23; I Thess. 5:28; II Thess. 3:18; and II Tim. 4:22. Picture the situation when this letter, having been delivered by Epaphroditus to the overseers and deacons at Philippi (see on Phil. 1:1), is at their order, read to the Philippian congregation, assembled for worship. Upon them all, thus gathered with God's Spirit in their midst, Paul the apostle, as God's official representative, pronounces God's grace, that is, God's unmerited favor in the Anointed Lord and Savior, based on his merits, conveyed by his Spirit. If this pronouncement is accepted with a believing heart, then from this basic blessing of grace all others flow forth, filling the very spirit, the inner personality viewed as contact-point between God and his child, with the peace of God that surpasses all understanding!

Synthesis of 4:10-23

For this see the Summary at the beginning of this section.

Seed-thoughts of 4:10-23

(1) The Christian is neither too proud nor too thoughtless to say, "Thank you" (verse 10).

(2) Deeds of kindness resemble a tree putting forth fresh shoots (verse 10).

(3) It is easy to find *excuses* to cover *real* neglect on our own part; it re-

---

[190] p46, Aleph A, the Koine, D most witnesses, Vulgate, and important Syriac translations add Amen, which is wanting in B, G and some other MSS.

213

quires grace to search out *reasons* for *seeming* neglect on the part of others (verse 10).

(4) One is not *born* with contentment; it must be *learned* (verse 11).

(5) Contentment is a jewel which no amount of gold or silver can buy and which does not depend on outward circumstances (verses 11, 12).

(6) The Author of true contentment is the indwelling, strength-imparting Christ (verse 13).

(7) Sharing your goods with a person in need is good and necessary. Sharing his affliction is even better. The first should be done in the spirit of the second (verse 14).

(8) Kindnesses which others have shown us in the past should be remembered and recalled (verses 15 and 16).

(9) *The fruit* is even more important than *the gift* (verse 17).

(10) The giver enriches two people: the recipient and himself (verse 17).

(11) True gifts are fragrant offerings (verse 18).

(12) When God gives us anything he does so *according to* (and not merely *out of*) his riches (verse 19).

(13) The climax of Christian speech, whether spoken or written, is the doxology. In fact, the Christian breathes doxologies (verse 20).

(14) If among the early Christians there were those who belonged to *Nero's* "household," today's government-employees in far more favorable circumstances will have great difficulty when they try to find an excuse for failing to bear witness for Christ (verse 22).

(15) In the final analysis our entire salvation from start to finish depends on God's sovereign favor in Jesus Christ (verse 23).

SELECT BIBLIOGRAPHY

An attempt has been made to make this list *as small as possible.*

Calvin, John, *Commentarius In Epistolam Pauli Ad Philippenses* (*Corpus Reformatorum*, vol. LXXX), Brunsvigae, 1895; English translation (in *Calvin's Commentaries*), Grand Rapids, 1948.
Lightfoot, J. B., *St. Paul's Epistle to the Philippians*, reprint Grand Rapids, 1953.
Vincent, M. R., *The Epistles to the Philippians and to Philemon* (in *The International Critical Commentary*), New York, 1906.

GENERAL BIBLIOGRAPHY

Barclay, W., *The Letters to the Philippians, Colossians, and Thessalonians* (in *The Daily Study Bible Series*), second edition, Philadelphia, 1959.

Barnes, A., *Notes on the New Testament, Ephesians, Philippians and Colossians*, reprint Grand Rapids, 1949.

Barth, K., *Erklärung des Philipperbriefes*, Zürich, 1927.

Beare, F. W., *The Epistle to the Philippians* (in *Harper's New Testament Commentaries*), New York, 1958.

Braune, K., *The Epistle of Paul to the Philippians* (in *Lange's Commentary on the Holy Scriptures*), Vol. VII, reprint, Grand Rapids.

Brewer, R. R., "The Meaning of POLITEUESTHE in Philippians 1:27," *JBL* 73, Part II (June, 1954), 76-83.

Bullfinch, T., *The Age of Fable*, New York, 1942.

Calvin, John, *Commentarius In Epistolam Pauli Ad Philippenses* (*Corpus Reformatorum*, vol. LXXX), Brunsvigae, 1895; English translation (in *Calvin's Commentaries*), Grand Rapids, 1948.

Campbell, J. Y., "Koinonia and its Cognates in the New Testament," *JBL* 51 (1932), 352-380.

Cobern, C. M., *The New Archaeological Discoveries and Their Bearing upon the New Testament*, seventh edition, New York and London, 1924.

Collart, P., *Philippes, ville de Macédoine depuis ses origines jusqu'à la fin de l'époque romaine*, Paris, 1937.

Conybeare, W. J., and Howson, J. S., *The Life and Epistles of St. Paul*, reprint Grand Rapids, 1949.

Cranfield, C. E. B., "Fellowship, Communion" (in *A Theological Word Book of the Bible*, A. Richardson, editor), New York, 1952.

Deissmann, A., *Light From the Ancient East* (translated by L. R. M. Strachan), New York, 1927.

Dibelius, M., *An die Thessalonicher I–II. An die Philipper* (in H. Lietzmann's *Handbuch zum Neuen Testament*), third edition revised, Tübingen, 1937.

Duncan, G. S., *St. Paul's Ephesian Ministry*, New York, 1930.

Endenburg, P. J. T., *Koinonia bij de Grieken in den klassieken tijd*, 1937.

Erdman, C. R., *The Epistle of Paul to the Philippians*, Philadelphia, 1932.

Ewald, P., *Der Brief des Paulus an die Philipper* (in T. Zahn's *Kommentar zum Neuen Testament*, XI.), Leipzig and Erlangen, 1923.

Ford, H. W., "The New Testament Conception of Fellowship," *Shane Quarterly* 6 (1945) 188-215.

Greijdanus, S., *Bizondere Canoniek*, Kampen, 1949, two volumes.

Greijdanus, S., *De Brief van den Apostel Paulus aan de Gemeente te Philippi* (in *Kommentaar op het Nieuwe Testament*, Vol. IX, part 2), Amsterdam, 1937.

Greijdanus, S., *De Brief van den Apostel Paulus aan de Philippenzen* (in *Korte Verklaring der Heilige Schrift*), Kampen, 1949.

Griffiths, D. R., " Harpagmos and heauton ekenōsen in Phil. 2:6, 7," *Ex.T* 69, No. 8 (1958), 237-239.

PHILIPPIANS

Groenewald, E. P., *Koinonia (gemeenskap) bij Paulus*, doctoral dissertation, Amsterdam, 1932.

Grollenberg, L. H., *Atlas of the Bible*, London and Edinburgh, 1956.

Grosheide, F. W., *De Openbaring Gods in het Nieuwe Testament*, Kampen, 1953.

Harrison, P. N., *Polycarp's Two Letters to the Philippians*, London, 1936.

Hendriksen, W., *Bible Survey*, Grand Rapids, Mich., sixth printing, 1961.

Hendriksen, W., *More Than Conquerors, An Interpretation of the Book of Revelation*, Grand Rapids, eleventh edition, 1961.

Hendriksen, W., *The Bible on the Life Hereafter*, Grand Rapids, 1959.

Heuzey, L., and Daumet, H., *Mission archeologique de la Macedoine*, Paris, 1876.

Jourdon, G. V., "Koinonia in I Cor. 10:16," *JBL* 67 (1938), 111-124.

Keller, W., *The Bible As History*, New York, 1957.

Kennedy, H. A. A., *The Epistle to the Philippians* (in *The Expositor's Greek Testament*, Vol. III), Grand Rapids.

Kraeling, E. G., *Rand McNally Bible Atlas*, New York, 1956.

Laurin, L. R., *Where Life Advances*, Wheaton, Ill., 1954.

Lenski, R. C. H., *The Interpretation of St. Paul's Epistles to the Galatians, to the Ephesians, and to the Philippians*, Columbus, Ohio, 1937.

Lightfoot, J. B., *St. Paul's Epistle to the Philippians*, reprint Grand Rapids, 1953.

Loeb Classical Library, New York (various dates), for The Apostolic Fathers, Josephus, Eusebius, Homer, Herodotus, Plutarch, Strabo, etc.

Lohmeyer, E., *Die Briefe an die Philipper, an die Kolosser und an Philemon* (in Meyer's Kommentar), Göttingen, 1930.

Marsh, F. B., *A History of the Roman World from 146-30 B. C.*, second edition, London, 1953.

Martin, R. P., *The Epistle of Paul to the Philippians* (in *The Tyndale New Testament Commentaries*), Grand Rapids, 1959.

Michael, J. H., *The Epistle of Paul to the Philippians* (in *The Moffat New Testament Commentary*), New York, 1929.

Müller, J. J., *The Epistles of Paul to the Philippians and to Philemon* (in *The New International Commentary on the New Testament*), Grand Rapids, 1955.

Mund, J., *Paul and the Salvation of Mankind*, Richmond, Va., 1959.

National Geographic Magazine, "Lands of the Bible Today" (Dec. 1956); in the same issue, "Jerusalem to Rome in the Path of St. Paul." Also published by National Geographic: *Everyday Life in Ancient Times*, 1953.

Paulus, H. E. G., *Philologisch-kritischer Kommentar über das Neue Testament*, Lübeck, 1800.

Robertson, A. T., *Word Pictures in the New Testament*, New York and London, 1931, Vol. IV.

Rowlingson, D., "Paul's Ephesian Imprisonment, An Evaluation of the Evidence," *Anglican Theological Review* XXXII (1950), 1-7.

Schaff-Herzog Encyclopaedia of Religious Knowledge, The New, thirteen volumes, edition Grand Rapids, 1950. The articles which have been consulted are not listed separately in this Bibliography.

Schmid, J., *Zeit und Ort der Paulinischen Gefangenschafts-briefe*, 1931.

Scott, E. F., *The Epistle to the Philippians* (in *The Interpreter's Bible*, Vol. XI), New York and Nashville.

Shakespeare, W., *Julius Caesar;* also *Antony and Cleopatra*.

Shaw, G. B., *Caesar and Cleopatra*.

Smolders, D., "L'audace de L'apôtre selon saint Paul. Le thème de la parrêsia," *Coll Mech* 43 (Feb. 1958), 117-133.

PHILIPPIANS

Tenney, M. C., *Philippians: The Gospel at Work,* Grand Rapids, 1956.

The Good News, The New Testament with over 500 illustrations and maps, published by the American Bible Society, New York, 1955.

Tucker, T. G., *Life in the Roman World of Nero and St. Paul,* New York, 1922.

Van Til, C., "Karl Barth on Chalcedon," *W.Th.J.* (May, 1960), 147-166.

Vincent, M. R., *The Epistles to the Philippians and to Philemon* (in *The International Critical Commentary*), New York, 1906.

Warfield, B. B., *Christology and Criticism,* New York, 1929.

Wells, H. G., *The Outline of History,* Star-edition, Garden City, New York, 1930.

Wright, E., *Biblical Archaeology,* London, 1957.

Wuest K. S., *Philippians in the Greek New Testament,* Grand Rapids, 1942.

Wuest, K. S., *Philippians Through the Revelation, An Expanded Translation,* Grand Rapids, 1959.

NEW TESTAMENT COMMENTARY

NEW TESTAMENT COMMENTARY

By
WILLIAM HENDRIKSEN

Exposition
of
Colossians and Philemon

TABLE OF CONTENTS

LIST OF ABBREVIATIONS

The letters in book-abbreviations are followed by periods. Those in periodical-abbreviations omit the periods and are in italics. Thus one can see at a glance whether the abbreviation refers to a book or to a periodical.

A. *Book Abbreviations*

A.R.V.	American Standard Revised Version
A.V.	Authorized Version (King James)
Gram.N.T.	A. T. Robertson, *Grammar of the Greek New Testament in the Light of Historical Research*
Gram.N.T.Bl.-Debr.	F. Blass and A. Debrunner, *A Greek Grammar of the New Testament and Other Early Christian Literature*
I.S.B.E.	*International Standard Bible Encyclopedia*
L.N.T. (Th.)	Thayer's *Greek-English Lexicon of the New Testament*
L.N.T. (A. and G.)	W. F. Arndt and F. W. Gingrich, *A Greek-English Lexicon of the New Testament and Other Early Christian Literature*
M.M.	*The Vocabulary of the Greek New Testament Illustrated from the Papyri and Other Non-Literary Sources,* by James Hope Moulton and George Milligan (edition Grand Rapids 1952)
N.N.	*Novum Testamentum Graece,* edited by D. Eberhard Nestle and D. Erwin Nestle (most recent edition)
N.E.B.	New English Bible
N.T.C.	W. Hendriksen, *New Testament Commentary*
R.S.V.	Revised Standard Version
S.H.E.R.K.	*The New Schaff-Herzog Encyclopedia of Religious Knowledge*
Th.W.N.T.	*Theologisches Wörterbuch zum Neuen Testament* (edited by G. Kittel)
W.D.B.	*Westminster Dictionary of the Bible*
W.H.A.B.	*Westminster Historical Atlas to the Bible*

B. *Periodical Abbreviations*

ATR	*Anglican Theological Review*
BA	*Biblical Archaeologist*

BibZ	*Biblische Zeitschrift*
ET	*Expository Times*
Exp	*The Expositor*
GTT	*Gereformeerd theologisch tijdschrift*
HTR	*Harvard Theological Review*
Int	*Interpretation*
JBL	*Journal of Biblical Literature*
JTS	*Journal of Theological Studies*
TSK	*Theologische Studien und Kritiken*
TZ	*Theologische Zeitschrift*
WTJ	*Westminster Theological Journal*

Please Note

In order to differentiate between the second person singular (see Philem. 4) and the second person plural (see Col. 1:2), we have indicated the former as follows: "you"; and the latter as follows: "y o u."

Introduction

to

Colossians and Philemon

I. Why Should We Study Colossians and Philemon?

The basic reason for the study of any Bible-book is given in II Tim. 3:16, 17. In addition we may well ask, Why should we, *especially today*, study these letters?

1. First of all because we are living in *the space-age*.

We hear and read about space-programs, galaxies, lunar probes, men-in-orbit. To a certain extent we can even see orbital flights on the television-screen. We discuss the prospects of inter-stellar flight. So, we as Christians naturally ask, "How is our Lord and Savior, Jesus Christ, related to this vast universe of space and of star-systems? Or does he, perhaps, stand outside of it?" For the great comfort of all believers this basic question is answered in Colossians (see especially on 1:16, 17, 20).

2. Again, this is the age of *ecumenicity*.

Today in religious circles *interdenominational Christian fellowship* — also called *ecumenicity* — is making headway. As many see it, this interdenominational fellowship must become organic union. They dream about a super-church. Will this be a body without a head? And if there is to be a head, will it be an earthly head? Today this question is very real, for not only Protestantism but also Roman Catholicism is looking forward toward ultimate ecclesiastical union. Even while this book is being written Protestant leaders are meeting in an ecumenical council at the invitation of the pope. Has he not loudly proclaimed that "the separated brothers" should be gathered, that they should return to the fold and recognize the supreme authority of . . . Rome? But must the Church have an earthly head at all? Who, after all, is the Head of the Church, both organic and ruling? Yes, and not of the Church alone but of all things? Colossians answers *this* question too (see on 1:18, 19, 24; 2:10, 19). May its teaching never be rejected or compromised in any way.

Now in the ecumenical movement there are men who are earnestly desirous of promoting the type of spiritual oneness of which Christ would approve; in fact, which he has commanded (see N.T.C. on John 17:21). Accordingly, it is their intention that members of various denominations and backgrounds shall sit down together and discuss their differences, in order, *without any sacrifice of essentials,* to resolve them if possible, to merge denominations wherever that can be done with spiritual benefit to all concerned, and in any event to investigate possible avenues of co-operation for philanthropic and cultural enterprises. All this is to be encouraged. Ecu-

3

menicity in that sense is not something to be avoided but to be welcomed.

There are others, however, who seem to have surrendered — if they ever had it! — the idea of *the finality of the Christian religion* and of *the all-sufficiency of Christ*. Their purpose seems to be to establish a *world-church*, that is, not only to merge the Protestant, Roman Catholic, and Russian Orthodox groups, but even to wed Christianity and the non-Christian religions. They seem to feel that Christ, to be sure, has something, in fact, has *much* to offer, but *not everything*. Rama, Vishnu, Zoroaster, Buddha, Confucius, Moses, and Mohammed have made their contributions too. It has been reported that Gandhi accepted all great religions as his. The extremists in the present ecumenical movement seem to be imitating Gandhi.

Now this virtual denial of the all-sufficiency of Christ was the very heresy — though presented in a different form — which Paul faced when he wrote Colossians. Is the Christian religion final or is it not? Is Christ all-sufficient or do we need other Saviors to supplement him? Colossians answers that question. The entire epistle is really an answer, but see especially 1:18; 2:9, 10.

3. The present era calls for basic reflection on *Christ's deity*.

The very emphasis on ecumenicity confronts the Church with the necessity of re-examining its basic beliefs regarding the Christ. If Christ is really God in the same sense in which the Father (and the Spirit) is God, then must the Unitarian, the Jew, and the Mohammedan be excluded from the ecumenical movement, or is there a possibility of compromise here? Reflection upon similar basic questions with respect to Christ — such questions as, "Are there three *persons* in the one, divine essence?" — is also forced upon us by the influence of the theology of Karl Barth. We see, therefore, that this space-age, this age of ecumenicity, is also *the age which forces upon us re-examination of our historical and confessional beliefs regarding the relation of Christ to the Father and to the Trinity*. And on this point, too, Colossians speaks with great clarity (see on 1:15a; 2:9).

4. This is the age of *pragmatism*.

It must be granted that by no means every one is interested in meditation and reflection upon deep theological truths. Today's slogan is: "Ideas must be tested by their practical value." Not, "Is it true?" but "Does it work?" is what people generally want to know. Colossians points out that these two questions cannot be separated. To be sure, Christianity is a life, but it is *a life based upon a belief*, a mighty energizing doctrine. He who is the Object of our faith is also the Source of our life. a. What this *faith* amounts to, and b. how this Christian *life* is lived, is here set forth with such surpassing beauty and grandeur that the remark of A. Deissmann was to the point, "When I open the chapel door of the epistle to the Colossians it is as if Johann Sebastian [Bach] himself sat at the organ." For a. see especially Col. 1; for b. especially 3:5-17.

4

INTRODUCTION

5. The age in which we are living is also marked by a re-emphasis on the great truth of *the equality of all men in relation to their Maker*.

There are many who agree that all men are equally helpless by nature, all equally in need of salvation, all equally duty-bound to live a life to God's glory; and that consequently no man has a right to oppress his fellow-man. Now if this be true then what should be the relation between race and race, husband and wife, parents and children, master and slave, employer and employee? And if the relationships be strained, how can the tension be removed? There is much disagreement on this score. Here, too, Colossians comes to the rescue. The teaching of Col. 3:18–4:1 cannot be neglected without harm.

It is, however, especially in Philemon that we have a practical illustration — an example in actual life, for all to see — of the manner in which such a problem is to be solved. The lesson there taught is of immense practical significance for the age in which we are living. As a bonus this little epistle also grants us a fascinating insight into the soul of Paul, *the man, the warmhearted, practical Christian*.

6. Finally, as the signs of the return of our Lord are beginning to multiply there is today *a renewed interest in the doctrine of the last things*.

With longing eyes believers are looking forward to "the inheritance of the saints in the light" (Col. 1:12). On this point too Colossians has much to offer. It is Paul's aim "to present every man perfect in Christ" (1:22, 28). To his fellow-Christians in Colosse he holds out the hope — a hope steadfast and sure — that "when Christ is manifested they, too, will be manifested with him in glory" (3:4). This *must* be true, for is not their life even now "hid with Christ in God"? That living Lord is "Christ in y o u, the hope of glory."

Viewed from every angle, therefore, this gem of an epistle is abreast of and even in advance of present-day discussion and reflection. It is timely. It is this because it presents the Christ who is the same yesterday, today, and forever, and who is:

    a. the Architect and Sustainer of the universe;

    b. the Head of all things, and especially the organic and ruling Head of his own Body, the Church, its all-sufficient, one and only Savior;

    c. the image of the invisible God, the embodiment of all the divine fulness;

    d. the Source of the Christian's life and peace and joy;

    e. the Rewarder of those who strive to be a blessing to others, regardless of social position; and

    f. as present within us, our "Hope of glory."

II. The City of Colosse

A. *Geography*

Essential to an understanding of Paul's Epistle to the Colossians is an acquaintance with the general features of the territory in which Colosse was located. The letter makes mention of three cities: Hierapolis (4:13), Laodicea (2:1; 4:13-16), and Colossae or Colosse (1:2). Though originally these were Phrygian cities, in Paul's day they had become part of the Roman province of "Asia." Their ancient site is included in today's Turkey in Asia (Minor). A few simple sketches, proceeding from the familiar to the less familiar and purposely omitting all unnecessary detail, may be helpful. Everyone is acquainted, of course, with the shape of western Asia Minor. Hierapolis, Laodicea, and Colosse are shown in this first sketch, in relation to the entire region and particularly to Ephesus which was Paul's center of missionary activity for this part of the third missionary journey during which the *three* churches, and probably also others, must have been established (Acts 19:10; Rev. 1:11). Distances are easy to see at a glance, since the side of each square represents 100 miles. Accordingly, Ephesus was located approximately 100 miles west of the three cities.

MAP 1

**Western Asia Minor
with Ephesus
and the Three Cities**

About 900 air-miles WNW of the three cities was Rome. By actual travel it was well over 1000 miles away from the triad, the exact distance varying according to the route taken. Far to the East, by slightly south, of the three cities was Paul's birthplace, Tarsus, to the SE of which lay Antioch in Syria, from which Paul started out on his third missionary journey. Also with re-

INTRODUCTION

spect to the places to the east of the three cities it must be borne in mind
that the actual *travel* distances were usually considerably greater than the
direct or flying distances indicated on the map. In those days there was
nothing like our Pennsylvania Turnpike with its seven tunnels. Lesser obstacles, too, had to be skirted. If one wished to travel by land from Antioch
in Syria to Tarsus, he had to go around the Cilician Gulf, as indicated by
the dotted line.

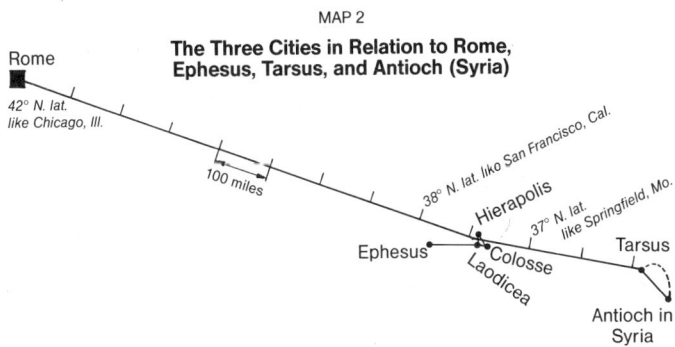

MAP 2

**The Three Cities in Relation to Rome,
Ephesus, Tarsus, and Antioch (Syria)**

The three cities were situated in the Lycos (or -us) Valley. The Lycus
River, also known as "The Little Maeander," branches off from the Maeander, shown on present-day maps as the Menderes River. The valley of the
Lycus is in the form of a right triangle, with the mountains of Mossyna as
its *hypotenuse,* the Salbakus and Cadmus ranges as *base,* and the Maeander
Valley as *altitude.* Hierapolis and Laodicea were located one on one side and
the other on the opposite side of the river. A distance of about six miles
separated them. Colosse straddled the river, and was situated eleven or
twelve miles farther east and slightly to the south. The acropolis of the city
was on the south bank; the tombs and buildings on the north. Colosse therefore occupied a narrow glen of the upper Lycus. It was beautifully and
strategically located, with the Cadmus Range rising very steeply to the
south, and the Mossyna Range to the north. The Eastern Highway passed
through Colosse, for roads naturally follow valleys.

Note that in Map 3, which follows, the side of each square represents 10
miles.

The question arises, "When Paul traveled from Antioch in Syria to
Ephesus in the Roman province of Asia, what road did he take?" Did he or
did he not touch Colosse? Bible atlases offer a variety of possibilities:

1. L. H. Grollenberg, *Atlas of the Bible,* map inside back cover, seems
to have adopted the Northern Galatia view, and makes the apostle travel to
the far north. Even when Paul at last wends his way toward Ephesus, he is
too far north to come into contact with Colosse. Discussion of this theory

7

MAP 3

Sketch of the Lycus Valley

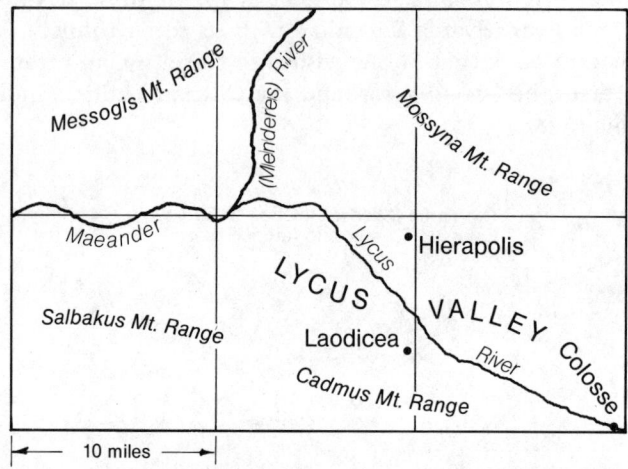

Messogis Mt. Range

(Menderes) River

Mossyna Mt. Range

Maeander

Lycus

•Hierapolis

LYCUS

VALLEY

Salbakus Mt. Range

Laodicea •

River

Colosse

Cadmus Mt. Range

|← 10 miles →|

does not belong to the present Commentary. Those who are interested in the reasons why I reject this Northern Galatia theory can find them stated in my book *Bible Survey*, pp. 334-336.

2. Others — such as J. L. Hurlbut, *A Bible Atlas*, p. 121; G. E. Wright and F. V. Filson, *The Westminster Historical Atlas to the Bible*, Plate XV — send Paul across the hills from Pisidian Antioch to Ephesus, an unusual and difficult way of travel. This road, too, avoids Colosse, being too far north.

3. The most natural route for Paul to have taken is the one indicated among others by Emil G. Kraeling, *Rand McNally Bible Atlas*, Map 20. It is the road from Antioch in Syria, over Tarsus, Derbe, Lystra, Iconium, Antioch in Pisidia, Apamea, Colosse, Laodicea, and thus, following for a while the Maeander Valley, to Ephesus. This road passes right through Colosse. It is the route illustrated on the next sketch. The idea of the sketch is *not* to suggest that this has now been established — Paul *may* have taken the route indicated under Number 2 above — but that room should certainly be left for this possibility since it was the more natural way of travel.

When the question is asked, "Why do most maps scrupulously avoid Colosse in routing Paul's third journey?" the answer could well be that this is the result, in part, of the influence of that great scholar, to whom the entire world of biblical scholarship is deeply indebted, namely, Sir William Mitchell Ramsay (see especially his *Historical Geography of Asia Minor;* and his *Cities and Bishoprics of Phrygia*) . Now Ramsay himself admits that "the ordinary and frequented route for trade between Antioch and the west coast passed through Apamea and Colosse." Why then does he not follow this lead? Here is his own statement, "But it would appear from the Epistle

MAP 4

**First Part of Paul's
Third Missionary Journey**

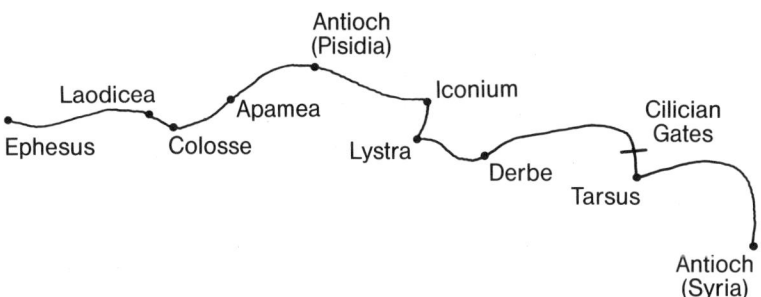

to the Colossians (2:1) that the Christians at Colosse and Laodicea had not seen his [Paul's] face." But does it actually follow from the indicated reference (Col. 2:1) that Paul *never passed through* Colosse? Is not this a case of basing too much on too little? Is it not possible that Paul passed through *the place* though he never personally founded *the church?* More careful, therefore, it would seem to me, is the statement of L. Berkhof, "Though Paul may have gone into the Lycus Valley, he certainly did not find nor found the Colossian church there since he himself says in Col. 2:1 that the Colossians had not seen his face in the flesh." [1] And as to the mountain-road on which many commentators and geographers send Paul, Sherman E. Johnson states, "But this is an unnatural and unlikely route." [2] The *present* highway and railroad are where we would expect them to be: in the valleys of the Menderes and Lycus rivers (see "Lands of the Bible Today," published by the National Geographic Society, December, 1956). Contrary to what happened on the *second* journey, when Paul's itinerary was changed by divine direction (Acts 16:6-8), on the *third* journey the trip from Antioch in Syria to Ephesus was carried out according to his own previous plan, as Acts 18:21 indicates (cf. that verse with 19:1), the divine approval resting upon it. It may be safely assumed, therefore, that he may have taken the easier and more usual route.[3]

---

[1] L. Berkhof, *New Testament Introduction,* p. 214.

[2] "Laodicea and its Neighbors," *BA,* Vol. XIII, No. 1 (Feb. 1950), pp. 1-18. The quotation is from p. 4.

[3] Lightfoot's observation that Paul "would not be deterred by any rough or unfrequented paths" can be answered by the counter-remark that one does not ordinarily choose such paths unless there be a special reason to do so. And as to other routes that have been suggested, such as require considerable detours, why would Paul take them when his purpose, namely, to confirm the churches already established, and continue on his way to Ephesus according to promise, did not require this?

B. *History*

The valley of the Lycus was plagued by many an earthquake.[4] Asia Minor is included in a belt of volcanic activity. Now earthquakes and volcanic activity spell disaster; think, for example of what the earthquake *circa* A. D. 60 did to Laodicea and Hierapolis! Nevertheless, volcanic ground is also fertile ground. It is excellent for grass and vegetation. Hence, on the rich meadows of the Lycus Valley grazed great flocks of sheep, bringing riches to the manufacturers of garments. This was all the more true because the waters of this valley were impregnated with chalky deposits. Now although these chalk-formations rendered parts of *the soil* barren, *the chalky waters* were just right for the purpose of dyeing cloth. This was an additional reason why the garment-industry flourished here. The trade of the dyer was practiced in all the three cities. It is not surprising, therefore, that the cities in this valley prospered, though in course of time their fortunes varied widely, as will be indicated.

1. *Colosse*

No one knows when Colosse (or Colossae) was founded. All we do know is that already in the days of Xerxes, king of Persia (485-465 B. C.), it was a thriving community. This Xerxes was the "Ahasuerus" of the book of Esther, who deposed Queen Vashti because she refused to yield to his unreasonable demand. He was the despot who commanded the waters of the Hellespont to be scourged with 300 lashes and the workmen to be beheaded because, due to a violent storm, the first attempt to bridge the narrow channel ended in failure. Having conquered Egypt, this terrible dictator had made extensive preparations for the invasion of Greece.

Now it was while he and his army were on their way toward the Hellespont that, seeking to avoid more difficult terrain, they passed through Colosse and the Lycus Valley. The Greek historian Herodotus, who in his *History* has given us a vivid — though not always thoroughly trustworthy — account of this ill-fated expedition, in this connection describes Colosse of the year 480 B. C. as "a great city of Phrygia" (VII.30) .

Xerxes was followed by Artaxerxes I (465-425 B. C.) , who allowed Ezra to

---

Here, too, I must beg to differ with Lightfoot when he states, "On the second occasion, St. Paul's primary object is to visit the Galatian churches which he had planted on the former journey (Acts 18:23) , and it is not till after he has fulfilled this intention that he goes to Ephesus." On the contrary, Ephesus, too, was clearly in the plan from the beginning, as has been indicated. See J. B. Lightfoot, *Saint Paul's Epistles to the Colossians and to Philemon,* pp. 24-28.

[4] Strabo (*Geography* XII.viii.16) describes it as *seismic, subject to earthquakes.* J. B. Lightfoot on pp. 38-40 of his book, *Saint Paul's Epistles to the Colossians and to Philemon,* gives documentary evidence for the many earthquakes which visited Laodicea and the surrounding region in the years preceding and subsequent to the birth of Christ.

lead a number of Jews back to Jerusalem and sanctioned the building of the walls under the direction of Nehemiah. Shortly afterward Darius II began to reign over the tottering empire (423-404 B. C.). Now "Darius [II] and Parysatis had two sons born to them: the elder Artaxerxes and the younger Cyrus" (Xenophon, *Anabasis* I.i.1). Darius II, then, was succeeded by his oldest son Artaxerxes II (404-358). But the latter's younger brother, Cyrus, because of his conviction that he himself should have been the heir to the throne and also by reason of a personal grievance against Artaxerxes, in all secrecy planned a revolt, gathering allies from various regions and under various pretexts. A contingent of roundly "10,000" Greeks attached itself to Cyrus. However, at Cunaxa, near the gates of Babylon, Cyrus, the very able and handsome pretender, was killed (Xenophon, *op. cit.*, I.viii.24-29). In connection with this campaign Xenophon, a bright young Athenian, gained for himself lasting fame, and this in two areas: a. as leader of the retreat of the "10,000," proving his rapidly acquired and amazing military skill, and b. as a master of narrative, in his *Anabasis* giving to posterity a brilliant account of the march.

Now it was very shortly after the beginning of this expedition, while marching south-eastward from Sardis, that the army reached Colosse and remained there seven days. It is in this context that Xenophon calls the Colosse of the year 401 B. C. "a city inhabited and prosperous and great" (I.ii.6). And Colosse was great indeed, and this not only in relative size and population, but also in strategic importance. Was it not situated on a highway that linked East and West Asia? Was it not the key to the entrance of the Lycus Valley and at the same time to the road eastward toward Apamea and the Cilician gates? But in course of time in this same valley other cities were founded, so that Colosse received competitors, as will now be set forth.

2. *Laodicea*

The march of the "ten thousand" had demonstrated the weakness of Persia's vast but unwieldy and antiquated army. Accordingly, Alexander the Great (336-323 B. C.) saw and grasped his opportunity. In the symbolic language of Daniel 8, very suddenly the he-goat (Greco-Macedonia under Alexander) comes from the west, storming across the earth and charging the two-horned ram (the Medo-Persian Empire), throwing it to the ground and trampling upon it. Even the wrath of man was praising God: Alexander brought not only Greek dominion but also the Greek language to the regions which he conquered, with the result — unforeseen by Alexander but included in God's plan — that at a later time this language could be used as a very effective vehicle for the spread of the gospel. God's ways are wonderful.

Sometime after Alexander's death his empire was divided into four parts (Dan. 8:8). Lysimachus received Thrace; Cassander, Macedonia; Ptolemy Soter, Egypt; and Seleucus, Syria and a vast region to the east of it. After some time Antiochus II (Theos) ruled over Syria (261-247 B. C.); Ptolemy II Philadelphus (283-246 B. C.) — builder of cities, patron of art and literature — over Egypt. These two kings entered into an agreement whereby Syria's king was to divorce his wife and marry the Egyptian king's daughter Berenice. The execution of the unholy plan brought nothing but trouble (Dan. 11:6). Now the name of this scheming, crafty, vindictive divorced wife was *Laodice*. It was for this woman that the new city of *Laodicea,* which replaced a smaller town, was named.

Though Laodicea did not prosper immediately, once the Roman province of Asia was founded (190 B. C.) the city began to flourish as a mighty center of industry. Soon Laodicea became famous for the fine, black wool of its sheep. Besides, due to a change in the road-system, it became a very important highway-junction, a place where the Eastern Highway met four other roads. The combination of these favorable factors meant trade, commerce, banking operations, riches (cf. Rev. 3:14-22) and political prestige; also the latter, for by the Romans Laodicea was made the capital of a political district embracing twenty-five towns.

3. Hierapolis

In a volcanic region there are generally many chasms out of which arise vapors and springs. These springs, supposedly, have healing power. They are by many considered of value in the treatment of such conditions as rheumatism, gout, dyspepsia, etc. Hence, resorts are often established in the vicinity of such springs. For present-day examples think of such European resorts as those at Aachen, Baden-Baden, Bath, Spa; or of similar places in the United States: Hot Springs, Las Vegas Springs, White Sulphur Springs. And so Hierapolis, too, became a famous spa, a city "full of self-made baths." By the thousands people would gather here to drink the healing waters and to bathe in them. The "flowing rills" of the city became its "jewels."

Besides, Hierapolis had its Charonion or Plutonium, which was a hole reaching far down into the earth whence issued a vapor reportedly so dreadful that it even poisoned the birds that flew over it. Naturally these springs and this deep cave were by the superstitious people of that age connected with and dedicated to divinities that were worshiped here. Hence, Hierapolis had a multitude of temples. In this connection it is often said that the original meaning of the name Hierapolis is *holy city.* This possibility must be granted. It is also possible, however, that the name was derived from the mythical Amazon queen Hiera.

4. The Further History of Colosse in Relation to Laodicea and Hierapolis

In view of the facts as related it is not surprising that in the long run Colosse was not able to keep abreast of its younger and more lavishly endowed competitors. In fact even the earthquake which did such damage to Laodicea and Hierapolis *circa* A. D. 60 could not reverse the trend. The prosperous citizens of Laodicea immediately rebuilt their city, and that without accepting aid from the government. Hierapolis, too, was restored, though not immediately. But long before A. D. 60 Colosse had already lost the race. If one was looking for health, pleasure, or relaxation, he would go to Hierapolis; if he was interested in trade or politics, he would direct his steps to Laodicea. But as for Colosse, the Greek historian and geographer Strabo, writing about two generations before Paul wrote Colossians, calls the Colosse of his day "a small town" (*Geography* XII.viii.13).

Today the ruins of Laodicea are still rather extensive. However, when nearby Denizli was built, some of these ruins were used as a quarry, and more recently many of the remaining stones were used in the construction of a railroad. But here is still that little hill tenderly embraced by two small tributaries of the Lycus River. On this hill Laodicea once stood. Here may be seen the ruins of the two theaters, one still rather well preserved; also what is left of the gymnasium, aqueduct, a large necropolis, and stones from the Eastern gate.

Hierapolis is more conspicuous. It stood on a lofty terrace. Over the precipitous cliffs which support this terrace glistening cataracts of pure white stone, the chalky deposits of the streams, come tumbling down into the plain below. In the autumn these frozen falls, glistening in the sunlight and visible from a distance, afford a beautiful sight. The ruins of Hierapolis are extensive. On the lofty plateau the city-walls can still be traced; also the pillars of the ancient gymnasium, the remains of what may well have been the statuary hall, ruins of arches, of a temple, churches, and baths. Especially remarkable are the ruins of two theaters, the smaller one from the Hellenistic age and the larger one from the Roman period. The latter stands at the east edge of the city, on the hill-side. As seen even today it can be described as one of the most perfect theaters of Asia Minor.

Now compare with all this what is left of Colosse. Though it is true that in the year 1835, when the archaeologist W. J. Hamilton visited the site, a few foundations of buildings, some pillars, fragments of cornices, and a necropolis with stones of a peculiar shape could still be seen, there was nothing to compare with the extensive and well-marked ruins of the other two cities. And today much of what was still there in 1835 has disappeared, having been used for building operations in Honaz and elsewhere.

It is a wonderful thought that to a church located in a town which in Paul's day was already so insignificant, a church which in all probability was small in membership, the very important Epistle to the Colossians was sent. What may seem small in the eyes of man is frequently great and important in the eyes of God.

Let us now consider the people to whom this Epistle was addressed.

C. *People*

Colosse, situated farther to the east than Laodicea and Hierapolis, was the most Phrygian of the three. It was populated by natives of Phrygia, pagans who worshiped various deities, as will be pointed out later. Nevertheless, a rather considerable number of Jews mingled with this heathen population, for Antiochus the Great (223-187 B. C.) had transported two thousand families from Mesopotamia and Babylon to Lydia and Phrygia.[5] These Jews prospered in the Lycus Valley and attracted others of their countrymen. The traffic in dyed wools and other business prospects acted like a magnet. Inscriptions in Phrygia have furnished ever so many indications of Jewish settlers there.[6] Thus, by the year 62 B. C., in the single district of which Laodicea was the capital there lived at least eleven thousand Jewish freemen. The entire Jewish population (including women and children) was, of course, far larger than that.[7] We know from the second chapter of the book of Acts that Jews from Phrygia were among those present at the feast of Pentecost described there.

It would be an error to infer from the preceding that the Jews who had emigrated to the Lycus Valley, and their descendants, were interested in this region only because it offered good prospects for business. To some of them the baths of Hierapolis were even more of an attraction than the commerce of Laodicea and (for a while) of Colosse. Listen, for example, to the complaint of the Talmudist: "The wines and the baths of Phrygia have separated the ten tribes from Israel." [8]

Now since, as has been shown, Colosse was a typically pagan city, with a strong intermingling of Jews, we cannot be surprised if we discover that the danger to the church that was planted here stemmed from two sources, namely, pagan and Jewish and even from a mixture of these two.

The Lycus Valley belonged to the Roman Empire from 133 B. C. During the seventh and eighth centuries A. D. it was overrun by the Saracens. About this time too the city became deserted. An earthquake was probably a contributing factor. The population moved to Chonas (the later *Honaz*), a little to the south, near the foot of Mt. Cadmus. In the twelfth century the city of Colosse disappears completely.[9]

---

[5] Josephus, *Ant.* XII.iii.4.
[6] See William M. Ramsay, *Cities and Bishoprics of Phrygia*, the chapter on "The Jews in Phrygia."
[7] For the evidence see Lightfoot, *op. cit.*, pp. 20, 21.
[8] *Talm. Babl.* Sabbath 147 b.
[9] For studies with respect to the Geography and Archaeology of Colosse and its surroundings see General Bibliography at the end of this volume.

III. The Church at Colosse

A. *Its Founding*

Was Paul ever in Colosse? According to some he never set foot there.[10] According to others not only did he spend some time there but he himself in person founded the church.[11] Now it has already been shown that Paul may have passed through Colosse on his third missionary journey, traveling from Antioch in Syria to Ephesus in Asia Minor. But the book of Acts (18:23; 19:1) gives no hint that the apostle founded any churches on this trip. So far as it traversed the country where no churches had as yet been established, the journey must have been to a large extent uninterrupted, for "there is no allusion to preaching in new places, but only to the confirming of old converts" (Ramsay). And it cannot be proved that during his stay at Ephesus Paul visited Colosse *with a view to founding or meeting with a church there.* Moreover, according to what is probably the best interpretation of Col. 2:2, at the time when Paul wrote his letter to the Colossians the membership as of then had not seen his face. Though this may have been intended as a general statement, allowing for exceptions, it was the truth.

Within this framework of established facts there is room for various possibilities, none of which should be entirely excluded. But however it may have been, it is certain that among the many who came to hear the apostle when he labored in his headquarters at Ephesus there were people from the Lycus Valley (Acts 19:8-10). It must have been during this period (A. D. 54-56) that also the church at Colosse was established.

Now in this church Paul had many notable friends:

1. *Epaphras. This man,* probably of heathen extraction,[12] having been converted through the instrumentality of Paul, *was in all probability the actual founder of the churches of the Lycus Valley* (Col. 1:7). He was a Colossian (Col. 4:12), a servant of Christ Jesus (again Col. 4:12), Paul's fellow-prisoner in Christ Jesus (Philem, 23; for explanation see on Col. 4:10a), and a hard worker in the three neighboring congregations of the Lycus Valley (Col. 4:13). He was vigilant in prayer and loyal to the point of being willing to suffer whatever hardships were in store for him as Christ's ambassador.

---

[10] Herman Ridderbos, *De Brief van Paulus aan de Kolossenzen (Commentaar op het Nieuwe Testament)*, p. 104. H. C. Thiessen, *Introduction to the New Testament*, p. 231.
[11] F. Wiggers, "Das Verhältniss des Apostels Paulus zu der christlichen Gemeinde in Kolossä," *TSK* (1838), pp. 165-188.
[12] For the meaning of his name and for any possible connection with the Epaphroditus who is mentioned in the letter to the Philippians see N.T.C. on Philippians, pp. 138, 139, footnote 116.

2. *Philemon, Apphia, and Archippus.* Since these three are mentioned in one breath (Philem. 1, 2) as the addressees of Paul's smallest extant letter, and since we are told that the church (evidently the one at Colosse; cf. Col. 4:9 with Philem. 10, 16; Col. 4:12 with Philem. 23; and Col. 4:17 with Philem. 2) was wont to meet at Philemon's home, the conclusion is warranted that Philemon, Apphia, and Archippus were closely connected. They may even have belonged to the same family: Philemon the husband and father, Apphia the wife and mother, Archippus the son.

3. *Onesimus* (in later years). He was Philemon's slave. Around his escape, conversion, and return centers Paul's letter to Philemon. See Section IV B; also Commentary on Philemon in this volume.

These, then, were some of Paul's friends and helpers in the congregation at Colosse which was established during his ministry at Ephesus. After this ministry had been completed Paul left for Troas. Then, having crossed the Aegean Sea, he came to Macedonia, and from there went to Corinth. From there he reversed his course and proceeded back toward Jerusalem by way of Macedonia. Tychicus, a Christian from the province of Asia, was one of those who traveled on in advance of Paul from Macedonia to Troas, and was waiting for the apostle in that city (Acts 20:4). His name will come up again at the close of section B.

When Paul arrived in Jerusalem, at the close of his third missionary journey, he was falsely accused and apprehended. Soon his imprisonment began. It lasted about five years, and was endured first at Caesarea and then at Rome. Now it was during this imprisonment in the empire's capital that Epaphras, the minister of the Colossian church, made a trip to Rome, traveling anywhere between 1000 and 1300 miles (the distance depending upon the route he took) to reach that city. On the whole the report which he brought was favorable (Col. 1:3-8), yet not entirely. Paul was made painfully aware of the fact that the church faced a twofold danger.

B. *Its Perils*

In order to understand the nature of the dangers that faced this church it is well to bear in mind that it consisted either entirely or well-nigh entirely of converts from the Gentile world (Col. 1:21, 22, 27; 2:11-13; 3:5-7). Paganism of almost every then-known variety thrived in this region. Such deities as the Phrygian Cybele Sabazius, Men, Isis and Serapis, Helios and Selene, Demeter and Artemis, were worshiped here. Accordingly, the basic evil with which the young church was confronted was

1. *The Danger of Relapse into Paganism with its Gross Immorality*

A careful reading of Col. 3:5-11 proves that this peril was basic. The members of the Colossian church were, at least for the most part, rather recent converts from the darkness and coarse sensuality of heathendom. As such

16

INTRODUCTION

the danger of relapse into their former multiform licentiousness was very real, and this for the following reasons:

There was first of all the cable of their evil past. A habit is like a cable. A person weaves a thread every day until it becomes well-nigh impossible to break the cable.

Secondly, there was the current of a wicked environment. It is hard to row against such a current, and to oppose the opinion and the will of the majority.

Thirdly, there was also the undertow of passion in hearts not wholly consecrated. Though the Colossians had accepted Christ, they had not become "perfect" overnight.

And finally, there was the lure of Satan, seeking by means of ever so many clever devices, to snatch the sheep out of the hand of the Shepherd (cf. John 10:28).

In view of all this we can understand Paul's repeated admonition that the Colossians must continue in their newly acquired faith, must not be moved from the gospel which rather recently they had accepted, must not return to their evil works, must "put to death" such things as immorality, impurity, passion, evil desire, greed, wrath, anger, malice, slander, shameful language, and the telling of untruths (Col. 1:21-23; 2:6; 3:5-11).

2. *The Danger of Accepting the Colossian Heresy*

Now what does the so-called "Colossian Heresy" have to do with all this? Clearly it was exactly the purpose of the teachers of error to show the Colossians how they would be able to triumph over the sins just mentioned, that is, over "the indulgence of the flesh." It was as if they were saying, Are y o u putting up a tremendous but losing battle against the temptations of y o u r evil nature? We can help y o u. Faith in Christ, though fine as far as it goes, is not sufficient, for Christ is not a *complete* Savior."

There is a distinct possibility that in this connection they made use of the word *fulness* (see below, footnote 56), as if to say, "Christ will not give y o u *fulness* of knowledge, holiness, power, joy, etc. Therefore, in order to attain such *fulness,* in addition to believing in Christ y o u must follow our rules and regulations. If y o u do this, y o u will conquer and will attain to maturity, to ultimate happiness and salvation." [13]

That this was actually the connection is clear from the fact that Paul, having summarized "the philosophy of empty deceit" of these peddlers of lies with their persuasive arguments about rules and regulations and their boasting about visions they had seen, concludes his criticism by saying, "*Regulations of this kind* have indeed a show of wisdom . . . (but) *are of no value,*

---

[13] C. F. D. Moule has shown that "the Colossian rules were meant to combat indulgence" (*The Epistles to the Colossians and to Philemon,* in *The Cambridge Greek Testament Commentary,* p. 110). The entire context points in this direction.

serving only to indulge the flesh" (Col. 2:23). In other words, they will *hurt* y o u rather than help y o u. He then proceeds to indicate a far better way — in fact, the *only* way — in which the battle against the flesh can be won (chapters 3 and 4), the way epitomized so strikingly by himself in Rom. 12:21b: "Overcome evil with good," and in Rom. 13:14 (the passage that meant so much to a great leader of the early Church, namely, Augustine), "Put on the Lord Jesus, and make no provision for the flesh."

"The Colossian Heresy" was accordingly a second danger added to the first, and to a certain extent an outgrowth of it. It may be characterized as follows:

a. *False Philosophy* (Col. 2:8) which, though claiming to have discovered secrets and to have seen visions (2:18), denied the all-sufficiency and pre-eminence of Christ. Paul states that the reason why he sets forth the greatness of Christ is that there are those who deny it and are trying to delude others into denying it also (2:2b-4; 2:8, 9; 2:16, 17). The sovereign majesty and complete adequacy of Christ as the perfect Savior and Lord is stressed in such passages as 1:13-20; 1:27, 28; 2:2-4; 2:8-10; 2:16, 17; 2:19; 3:1-4. This is basic to all that follows.

b. *Judaistic Ceremonialism* (Col. 2:11, 16, 17; 3:11), which attached special significance to the rite of physical circumcision, to food-regulations, and to observance of such special days as pertained to the economy of the old dispensation. All such things, says Paul, are but "shadows." They have lost their significance now that *the object casting the shadow,* namely Christ, has himself arrived (Col. 2:17).

c. *Angel-worship* (Col. 1:16; 2:15; 2:18), which also would detract from the uniqueness of Christ, as if he were insufficient for complete salvation.

d. *Asceticism* (Col. 2:20-23), which in its unsparing treatment of the body went beyond Judaism. The apostle exposes its utter futility and points to Christ as the real answer to the problems of doctrine and life that vex the Colossians (2:20-23, contrast 3:1-4).

Questions arise to which the letter does not supply the answer; for example, What is the larger context of this Colossian Heresy? How did this false philosophy originate? Was it an offspring of incipient gnosticism of the ascetic type? Could it be an outgrowth, perhaps, of the theories of the Essenes, in this case covered with a varnish of Christian belief? Was it an intermixture of incipient gnosticism, Essenism (itself already infected with gnostic error), and Christianity? Do the recently discovered Dead Sea Scrolls shed any further light on it?

Here we must tread very carefully. We are perhaps safe in stating that the Colossian Heresy was a syncretism, that is, a weird mixture of Jewish and pagan elements. Gnosticism, with its stress on "knowledge," seems to have had something to do with it, for it is evident from the epistle that the false teachers placed undue emphasis on such things as "knowledge," "wisdom," "philosophy," "mystery" and "mystic insight." Yet, the evidence for this is usually indirect, that is, it is often not directly stated but to be inferred from Paul's insistence that the *real* knowledge, wisdom, mystery, etc., is to be found in Christ, in him alone (1:26, 27; 2:2; 4:3). Once in a while, though, the errorists are clearly exposed from this particular point of view (2:4, 8a, 18, 23). It is also known that gnostics exalted the spirit, and viewed matter as the seat of evil. To some of them this meant that the body should be neglected, that its natural cravings should be suppressed, if one were ever to reach the goal of *fulness*. There are those, accordingly, who see a reflection of this fallacy in Paul's rather stern rebuke, "Why . . . do y o u submit to regulations, 'Do not handle, Do not taste, Do not touch' " (2:20, 21). They also see the gnostic doctrine of *emanations* reflected and refuted in the apostle's warning against angel-worship (2:18).

A word of caution may, however, well be in order, for (1) we do not as yet have a reasonably *complete* description of gnosticism in the *first* century A. D., (2) neither was it Paul's intention to present *a full account* of the heresy which he is combating. When, therefore, certain authors, taking their cue from the expression "rudiments of the world" (2:8), which they translate "elemental spirits of the universe," present a more or less complete and detailed reconstruction of the heresy, we may well hesitate to accept this. It is all very interesting to picture these "astral spirits" or "planetary lords" as being also guardians of the Mosaic law. It is fascinating to describe them as entering into combat with Christ who, however, "despoils" them (2:15); to present them further as having instituted sacred days by means of the very planets over which they exercise control, and as laying down elaborate rules of abstinence so that by means of obedience to these rules the spirit of man may become disinfected with earthliness and may begin to ascend through various "spheres" to God. But have we any right to form all these conjectures, and to fill the gaps which Paul has left wide open?

There is another objection: Granted that in the Colossian Heresy it is proper to detect some influence exerted by incipient gnosticism of whatever origin — and to grant this seems altogether reasonable —, it still remains true that, all in all, the falsehood which Paul scores so severely had a definitely Jewish background. It insisted on the rite of circumcision (2:11-13) and on the strict observance of the law of Moses with its stipulations regarding foods and feasts (2:14, 16). That this is really what Paul has in mind is clear from the fact that he views the law as fulfilled in Christ (2:16, 17).

It is true that the heresy, while Judaistic, went beyond the Judaism which Paul exposes in Galatians. This is clear especially from its rigorous asceticism, that is, its insistence on obedience to rules which were nothing but "precepts and doctrines *of men*" (2:20-23). Are we dealing here with an extreme form of Pharisaism, or with the doctrines of the Essenes, perhaps?

With respect to the Essenes see Josephus, *The Life* (autobiography) 7-12;

Jewish War II.119-161; Pliny the Elder, *Natural History* V.73; Philo, *Fragment of the Apology for the Jews* XI.1-17; Lightfoot, *op. cit.,* pp. 82-94, 355-419.

Josephus, who at one time himself belonged to this sect, has many fine things to say about it. He calls its members "masters of their temper, champions of fidelity, ministers of peace," etc. His description also shows, however, that the very errors which marked the Colossian Heresy were found among them. They were infected with a strain of incipient gnosticism for, as he tells us, "It is their fixed belief that the body is corruptible and its constituent matter impermanent, but that the soul is immortal and imperishable." They looked upon the soul as "having become entangled in the prison-house of the body." As to Judaistic Ceremonialism and Asceticism, he relates that "after God they hold most in awe the name of their lawgiver [Moses], any blasphemer of whom is punished with death." Also, "They are stricter than all the Jews in abstaining from work on the sabbath day." He refers to "their invariable sobriety and the limitation of their allotted portions of meat and drink." He implies that they were divided into two groups: *celibate* and *marrying.* As to the first group: "Marriage they disdain. . . . They do not on principle condemn wedlock . . . but they wish to protect themselves against women's wantonness," etc. As to the second group, "They give their wives a three-year probation." Further, "Riches they despise." As to attitude toward angels, "They carefully preserve the names of the angels."

Must we conclude from this that the false teachers who vexed the Colossians with their sinister doctrines were Essenes who had nominally turned to Christ, but had retained many of their former beliefs? It is held by some that this is impossible because no Essenes lived in Asia Minor. However, Josephus also states, "They occupy no one city, but settle in large numbers in every town." Pliny the Elder fixes their headquarters "on the west side of the Dead Sea." Philo adds, "They live in many cities of Judea and in many villages and are grouped in great societies of many members." That author also seems to make the Essenic view of marriage a springboard for his own rather uncomplimentary estimate of women, "No Essene takes a wife, because a wife is a selfish creature, excessively jealous, and adept at beguiling the morals of her husband and seducing him by her continued impostures," etc. It is clear at any rate that Essenic influence can easily have reached as far as Colosse. It has been shown earlier that many Jews lived in that particular region.

Now inasmuch as the Qumran sect, which gave us the Dead Sea Scrolls, shows many of these same characteristics, and had its headquarters in the same locality, it is today the conviction of many that the Qumran sect is to be identified with the Essenes. Its *Manual of Discipline* is probably our best source of information with respect to them. In reading it one cannot help wondering whether perhaps Paul's warning, "If with Christ y o u died to the rudiments of the world, why, as though y o u were (still) living in the world, do y o u submit to regulations, Do not handle, Do not taste, Do not touch" was his answer to the Manual's repeated admonitions in the form of, "He shall not touch," and "He shall not taste."

Here we must carefully distinguish between the actual *teaching* of the New Testament, on the one hand, and *the current ideas and beliefs* which it reflects and against which it reacts on the other. As to *teaching*, the New Testament is, of course, entirely distinctive, in the sense that "Jesus Christ spake unlike any other man, for the simple reason that he was unlike any other man," as E. J. Young has stated in a fine article, "The Teacher of Righteousness and Jesus Christ," *WTJ*, Vol. XVIII, No. 2 (May, 1956), p. 145. But as to the *errors* which it combats, there is no principial reason why these could not include the asceticism of the Essenes. This does not mean, however, that we are certain that the apostle Paul in writing Colossians was combating a party of Essenes who claimed to have been converted to Christ. We know too little about conditions that prevailed in Asia Minor during the first century A. D. to draw such a risky conclusion. I agree with the statement of Millar Burrows, "What the Dead Sea Scrolls actually demonstrate has been well summed up by Albright: they show that the writers of the New Testament 'drew from a common reservoir of terminology and ideas which were well known to the Essenes and' — this I would emphasize — 'presumably familiar also to other Jewish sects of the period' " (*More Light on the Dead Sea Scrolls*, p. 132). We can, however, state that the available sources do give us such a picture of the state of syncretistic religion in the days of Paul that the error which he combats in Colossians no longer seems so strange. See also on Col. 2:8, 18, 21; 3:18; footnote 76; and N.T.C. on I Tim. 4:3. The chief point to remember is that the errorists, by riveting so much attention on *man-made* remedies for relapse into paganism, were in reality denying the all-sufficiency of Christ for salvation.

Now, in order to combat this doubleheaded danger — the peril of relapse into paganism with its gross sensuality, and that of accepting the wrong solution — Paul wrote his letter to the Colossians. A more detailed statement as to the purpose of this epistle is found in the next Section (IV).

The one who delivered the letter to its destination was Tychicus, mentioned earlier. He was accompanied by Onesimus, the converted slave who was to be returned to his master Philemon (Col. 4:7-9). They also carried with them for delivery the letter to Philemon regarding Onesimus (Philem. 10-17) and the letter that has been transmitted to us as "The Epistle of Paul to the Ephesians" (Eph. 6:21, 22); but see also on Col. 4:16.

C. *Its Later History*

Paul was released from his first Roman imprisonment, the imprisonment during which he wrote Colossians, Philemon, Ephesians, and Philippians. For proof of this release see N.T.C. on I and II Timothy and Titus, pp. 23-27. Having regained his freedom he probably journeyed to Ephesus and from there to Colosse, just as he had intended (Philem. 22). What happened during his visit with the Colossians has not been revealed. He must have returned to Ephesus soon afterward. With respect to his further travels, all of them conjectural as to their sequence, see N.T.C. on I and II Timothy and Titus, pp. 39 and 40.

As to the congregation at Colosse, its further history is obscure. It would seem that the gradual decay of the church went hand in hand with that of the city. For a while the church had a bishop of its own. However, when the population moved to Honaz, the episcopal see followed the population, until at length, with the coming of the Turkish conquest, "the golden candlestick was removed forever from the Eternal Presence" (J. B. Lightfoot, *op. cit.*, p. 72).

IV. Paul's Purpose in Writing Colossians and Philemon

A. *Colossians*

One day, during his first Roman imprisonment, Paul received a visit from the "minister" of the Colossians, Epaphras (already discussed). The latter informed the apostle about the condition of the church. To a large extent the report was favorable: faith, love, and hope were in evidence. The gospel was bearing fruit increasingly (Col. 1:1-6; 2:5). Yet, there was always the danger of slipping back into the former grossly sinful habits. Moreover, right at this moment false teachers were trying to delude the church by offering a solution which was no solution at all but would make matters worse ("the Colossian Heresy" already described). A letter must therefore be written so that the church may not depart from the pure teaching of its faithful pastor.

In accordance with this background the purpose of this letter was as follows:

1. To warn the Colossians against relapse into their former state with all its soul-destroying vices (Col. 1:21, 23; 3:5-11) and against the "solution" urged upon them by those who refuse to recognize Jesus Christ as the complete and all-sufficient Savior (chapter 2).

2. To direct their attention to "the Son of God's love," so that they may trust, love, and worship him as the very image of the invisible God, the first-born of all creation, the Head of the Church, the One who is in all things

pre-eminent and in whom — in whom *alone* — believers attain their fulness
(1:13-18; 2:8, 9).

3. To this very end to enhance among them the prestige of their faithful
minister, Epaphras (1:7; 4:12, 13), who, though now with Paul in Rome,
joins others in sending greetings, is ever wrestling for them in prayer, and is
filled with the deepest concern for them.

In view of the fact that Tychicus was the bearer of the letter to the Colossians and also of the one to Philemon, a member of the Colossian church
and owner of the slave Onesimus who was being returned to his master, to
the three points already mentioned a fourth must now be added, namely,

4. To emphasize among the Colossians the virtue of forgiveness and kindness. Not too strong is the statement of John Knox, "The whole of Colossians is more or less overshadowed by Paul's concern about Onesimus"
(*Philemon among the Letters of Paul*, p. 35). This may well account, at
least in part, for the fact that the apostle writes somewhat at length about
the importance of showing *tenderness of heart* (3:12-14) and also for the
fact that he devotes much space to the relation between slaves and masters
(3:22-4:1, 5 verses, 4 of them lengthy), while he says far less about the relation between wives and husbands and about that between children and
fathers (3:18-21, *together* only 4 short verses; in contrast with Eph. 5:22-6:4,
16 verses!).

B. *Philemon*

1. A Theory That Departs from the Traditional

Point 4 of the preceding section shows the close relation between Colossians and Philemon. Accordingly, when Herman Baker, the publisher of this
New Testament Commentary, suggested that Colossians and Philemon be
treated in *one* volume his advice was excellent. These two letters, the one
written to a church and the other primarily to a family in that church,
should not be separated. Much credit for having stressed this truth is due to
the labors of such exegetes as Edgar J. Goodspeed and John Knox.

This, however, does not mean that we can agree wholeheartedly with the
position which these men have taken with respect to the Purpose of Philemon. Having carefully studied their writings and the books and articles of
those who either agree or disagree with them,[14] it has become our convic-

---

[14] See the following: E. J. Goodspeed, *New Solutions to New Testament Problems;
The Meaning of Ephesians; The Key to Ephesians;* J. Knox, *Philemon among the
Letters of Paul;* criticized by C. F. D. Moule in his valuable work, *The Epistles of
Paul the Apostle to the Colossians and to Philemon,* see especially pp. 14-21, which
criticism J. Knox tries to answer in the Revised (1959) edition of his aforemen-
tioned book. From Knox is also *The Epistle to Philemon* (Introduction and Exege-
sis, in *The Interpreter's Bible,* Vol. XI). Further: P. N. Harrison, "Onesimus and
Philemon," *ATR,* XXXII (1950), pp. 286-294. C. L. Mitton, *The Epistle to the
Ephesians; The Formation of the Pauline Corpus of Letters;* Heinrich Greeven,
"Prüfung der Thesen von J. Knox zum Philemonbrief," *TZ,* 79 (1954), pp. 373-

tion that while we owe them a debt of gratitude for the light which they have shed on the closeness of the relationship between Colossians and Philemon, we cannot accept their reconstruction of history. What is at best merely probable is at times presented as if it were well-nigh certain, what is merely possible as if it were probable, and what is very questionable as if it were at least possible. Since there are minor differences between Knox and Goodspeed the presentation given below is (unless otherwise stated) substantially that of Knox.

Briefly, then, according to his view the primary purpose of Paul's letter to Philemon is *not* that Onesimus shall be forgiven his offense of having run away from his master and having probably defrauded him besides, but rather *that this slave shall be set free and returned to Paul for the service of the gospel.*

As Knox reconstructs the events pertaining to Onesimus they become a very fascinating story, a kind of romance appropriate for dramatization:

a. Here, then, is this slave who though bearing the name *Profitable* (Onesimus) was not profitable to his superior. He lived with his owner in Colosse, but the latter's name was *not* Philemon but Archippus (*Philemon among the Letters of Paul,* p. 58). This Archippus was a befriender and member of the Colossian church. Church-members would gather in his house for worship. Philemon, though also mentioned in the opening verses of the small epistle, lived elsewhere; see point d.

b. Onesimus, not being in favor with his master, may have run away, though this is not expressed in so many words. And he may have visited Paul in the place of the latter's imprisonment, though also this is not specifically stated. Paul, at any rate, was in prison, perhaps in Ephesus (p. 33), not very far from Colosse.

c. Through the ministry of Paul the slave becomes a Christian. The once useless one becomes very useful. In fact so helpful does he become that the apostle would have liked to have kept him with him, and this not for personal reasons but for evangelistic work. However, after due consideration Paul decides to return the slave to his owner Archippus in order that the latter may of his own free will emancipate him and return him to Paul for kingdom work (p. 29).

d. However, will Archippus really consent to release his slave? If Onesimus has actually defrauded his master, will he not receive severe punishment? Paul finds a solution. In the company of faithful Tychicus the slave will be sent to his owner. In the hand of Tychicus there will also be a letter from Paul in the interest of the slave. It is to Archippus that the body of

378. Earlier: E. R. Goodenough, "Paul and Onesimus," *HTR,* 22 (1929), pp. 181-183; and Albert E. Barnett, *The New Testament: Its Making and Meaning,* pp. 79-92; 184-185.

the letter is addressed (p. 62). Now, in order to add weight to his request the apostle puts forth efforts to get others to support his appeal. Was not Laodicea located very close to Colosse? And did not the churches of the Lycus Valley look for leadership to a man — namely, Philemon — who had his headquarters in Laodicea (p. 70)? Let Philemon read the letter, therefore, and let him attach his support to Paul's request. Then let this letter, thus endorsed, be read to the church at Colosse. Having reached Colosse via Laodicea it can now be properly designated as "the letter from Laodicea." In his epistle to the Colossians (4:16) the apostle requests that this small letter which concerns Onesimus be read to the Colossians. Says Knox, "In my opinion there is a probability approaching certainty that this letter [the one "from Laodicea"] was our Philemon" (p. 45).

e. In Col. 4:17 Paul states, "And say to Archippus, See that you fulfil the ministry that you have received." *This "ministry" is the charge to release Onesimus and to send him back to Paul for gospel-activity.* The letter which we call Philemon is therefore "a letter to an individual, the reading of which, it was desired, should be *overheard* by a group to which the individual belonged and which was able to exercise some control over his conduct" (p. 60).

The plan works. In the company of Tychicus the slave travels to Laodicea. There Philemon endorses Paul's request. Slave and letter finally reach Colosse. The church supports Paul's Christian demands upon one of its members (p. 53). Thus Onesimus goes back to Paul.

f. And now the most interesting turn of all. Paul uses Onesimus as he had planned. And lo and behold, the one-time slave at a later time becomes nothing less than *bishop of the church at Ephesus!* Ignatius, bishop of the church of Syrian Antioch, on his way to Rome and martyrdom, stops at Smyrna in Asia Minor. He writes a letter to the Ephesians, in which he expresses his gratitude for the visit of Onesimus and others. In that letter Ignatius says, "Since then in the name of God I received your entire congregation in the person of Onesimus, a man of inexpressible love and your bishop, I beseech you in Jesus Christ to love him and all those who are like him. For blessed is he who granted you to be worthy to receive such a bishop" (Ephesians, I.1; cf. VIII.2).

The climax of this exegetical embroidery is the suggestion that after Paul's death Bishop Onesimus, the ex-slave who was so deeply indebted to the apostle, made a collection of the Pauline epistles; that is, the publication of the corpus of Paul's letters was done under his oversight (p. 107). Goodspeed leans to the conclusion that Philemon himself wrote Ephesians as a covering letter (*The Key to Ephesians*, xvi). Knox seems to endorse this position (p. 96). But the discussion of this theory belongs not here but in a Commentary on Ephesians.

2. Criticism

In what follows, paragraphs a, b, etc., respectively answer paragraphs a, b, etc., above.

a. The most natural interpretation of Philemon 1, 2 is that which views Philemon, Apphia, and Archippus as belonging to one and the same household, together with the slave Onesimus. They lived in Colosse (Col. 4:9). The owner of the slave, moreover, was *not* Archippus but Philemon, the one addressed first and throughout.

b. In all probability Paul was in Rome, not in Ephesus, when he wrote Colossians and Philemon. See V in *this* Commentary. Also, N.T.C. on Philippians, pp. 21-30.

c. In verse 14 the apostle is not asking that Onesimus be returned to him. The very next verse (verse 15b) seems rather to imply that Onesimus will remain in the company of Philemon ("that you should have him forever") who will, however, no longer regard him as a slave but as a brother beloved (verse 16). Moreover, Paul, who has his mind set on leaving the place of his imprisonment and who is already asking that at his destination a lodging be prepared for him (Philem. 22), would hardly be requesting that Onesimus be returned to him.

d. Col. 4:16, though admittedly difficult, seems to refer to an *exchange of letters addressed to churches* (see further on that verse).

e. It is surely more natural to interpret the words, "Attend to the ministry which you have received in the Lord" (Col. 4:17) as referring to the duty of Archippus to carry out a spiritual mission than as referring to his obligation to free a slave, be it even for evangelistic work. See comments on this verse.

f. If about a half century later Ignatius in his letter to the Ephesians had been actually referring to the ex-slave on behalf of whom Paul had made his marvelous plea, a *clear* reference to this previous letter by the great apostle would have been natural; just as, for example, Polycarp, writing to the Philippians, *clearly* reminds them of Paul's earlier letter. The fact that Ignatius had read Paul's Philemon and supplies the evidence of this in his *Ephesians,* does not in any way prove that Bishop Onesimus was the ex-slave.

Thus, it has been shown that Knox's theory, though valuable in showing the close connection between Colossians and Philemon, as a historical reconstruction lacks proof. No damage has been done to the traditional view.

3. Real Purpose of Paul's Letter to Philemon

The real background, then, is as follows:

Philemon was one of the pillars of the church at Colosse. He loved the Lord and the brethren, and had given concrete evidence of this fact again and again (Philem. 7). He was Paul's spiritual son, for, whether directly or indirectly (see on Philem. 19) God has used Paul to change him. His new life had affected not only himself but also his household. It is considered probable that Apphia was his wife, and Archippus their son. Friends who had accepted the Lord regularly gathered for worship at their home (Philem. 2). In the absence of Epaphras, Archippus would probably have charge of the service (Col. 4:17). He may have been a young man who, like Timothy, was in need of encouragement (cf. I Tim. 4:12).

Now, Onesimus was one of the slaves of Philemon's household. This slave ran away, journeying all the way to Rome. In Rome he came into contact with Paul. Just as the Lord had formerly blessed the work of the great missionary to the heart of the master so he now blessed it to the heart of the slave. So dear did the latter become to the apostle that Paul calls him "my child, whom I have begotten in my bonds" (verse 10), "my very heart" (verse 12), "a brother beloved especially to me but how much more to you, both in the flesh and in the Lord" (verse 16), "the faithful and beloved brother" (Col. 4:9). Gladly would Paul have kept Onesimus at his side as an assistant, for his character had finally caught up with his name. In this connection read Philemon 11, and notice the play on a synonym of the name of this slave:

"Onesimus who formerly to you was useless, but now both to you and to me is useful." Cf. also verse 20 in the original.

But Paul does not deem it right to keep Onesimus in Rome. He decides to send him back to his master with the very carefully and politely worded request that the latter accept him as one who is no longer merely a slave but a brother beloved. If he in any way has defrauded his master, Paul is ready to assume full responsibility for the payment of the debt. With insurpassable tact the great apostle adds:

"not to mention to you that you owe me your very self besides," verse 19.

Paul does not command, though, as he himself states, he has a *right* to do so; he rather *appeals* to the heart of Philemon (verse 9). He is fully confident that the latter will do "even better than" what is asked of him (verse 21). The apostle entertains hopes of being released from his present imprisonment and trusts that Philemon will "prepare a guest room" for him (verse 22).

It is hardly necessary to add that although this fully inspired epistle does not in so many words condemn the institution of slavery it strikes at its very spirit and transforms the slave into a brother beloved.

Accordingly, Paul's purpose in writing Philemon may be summarized as follows:

1. To secure forgiveness for Onesimus.
2. To strike at the very heart of slavery by tactfully requesting that, in accordance with the rule of Christ, love be shown to all, including slaves.

3. To provide for himself a place of lodging after his release from imprisonment.

V. The Place and the Time of Writing
Colossians and Philemon

Colossians and Philemon, as well as Ephesians and Philippians, are Prison Epistles. The place of origin and in general the date of *one* determines the date of *all four*. See detailed discussion in N.T.C. on Philippians, pp. 21-30.

Colossians, Philemon, and Ephesians are carried to their destination by Tychicus and Onesimus, all on one trip (cf. Col. 4:7-9, Philem. 10-12; and Eph. 6:21, 22).

As to Paul's circumstances, he is a prisoner (Col. 1:24; 4:3, 10, 18; Philem. 1, 9, 23). In addition to Onesimus other names are mentioned both in Colossians and Philemon. These are Paul's companions: Luke, Aristarchus, Mark, Epaphras, and Demas (Col. 4:10-14; Philem. 23, 24); also Timothy, mentioned together with Paul in the *opening* verse of both letters. Jesus Justus is also with Paul (Col. 4:11), but is not mentioned in Philemon. Paul is enjoying a measure of freedom to preach the gospel (Col. 4:3, 4). He hopes to be released (Philem. 22).

In all this there is nothing that contradicts the traditional view of the Roman origin of these letters. The measure of freedom which Paul enjoys harmonizes with the report of his circumstances in Rome (Acts 28:30, 31), but not with that of his imprisonment in Caesarea (Acts 24-26). Luke's presence is unaccountable if these letters were sent from a prison in Ephesus, for Luke has given us a rather detailed narrative of Paul's ministry in that city (Acts 19) but says nothing about any imprisonment there, and, in fact was not with Paul at that time. But Luke did definitely go with Paul to Rome (Acts 27:1; 28:16). And so did Aristarchus (Acts 27:2). Furthermore, if Rome is the place of Paul's imprisonment when Colossians and Philemon were written, then, in view of I Peter 5:13, Mark's presence is readily understandable, for Mark seems to have been in this "Babylon" shortly afterward.

And as to time, everything points to a date during the period A. D. 61-63, perhaps somewhere in or near the middle of this period, at least *before* the writing of Philippians.[15]

---

[15] See N.T.C. on Philippians, pp. 29 and 30; and for a discussion of the entire Pauline chronology see W. Hendriksen, *Bible Survey*, pp. 62-64, 70.

VI. The Authorship of Colossians and Philemon [16]

A. *Colossians*

In the main three arguments have been urged against the Pauline authorship of Colossians. It has been shown by many commentators that all three are rather readily answered when the facts are examined. The "objections," [17] then are as follows:

(1) *Language and Style show that Paul cannot have been the author.*

a. *Words Used and Words Omitted*

Colossians contains thirty-four words not found elsewhere in the New Testament and several additional words that occur nowhere else in Paul's epistles. On the other hand, such familiar Pauline words as *righteousness* ($\delta\iota\kappa\alpha\iota\sigma\sigma\nu\eta$), *salvation* ($\sigma\omega\tau\eta\rho\iota\alpha$), *revelation* ($\dot{\alpha}\pi\sigma\kappa\dot{\alpha}\lambda\upsilon\psi\iota\varsigma$), and *to abrogate* ($\kappa\alpha\tau\alpha\rho\gamma\epsilon\hat{\iota}\nu$) are not found in Colossians.

Answer: The percentage of such exceptional words found in Colossians but not elsewhere is comparable to that in other epistles, for example Romans (in a section of similar length) and Philippians. *A different subject requires different words.* Hence many of these words are found in Colossians 1 and 2, where the author combats a unique heresy; see especially 2:16-23.[18] This also accounts for the fact that other words, used in other epistles, in the discussion of other themes, are not found *here*. Why should they be? Percy is entirely correct when he states, "It can be safely affirmed, therefore, that from the aspect of lexicography no serious argument against the genuine character of this epistle can be advanced" (*op. cit.,* p. 18).

---

[16] See the detailed discussion in Ernst Percy's important work, *Die Probleme der Kolosser-und Epheserbriefe,* 1946.

[17] E. Th. Mayerhoff began the attack. See his work, *Der Brief an die Colosser mit vornehmlicher Berücksichtigung der drei Pastoralbriefe kritisch geprüft.* He regarded Colossians as an imitation of Ephesians which he viewed as written by Paul. F. C. Baur and his followers, the Later Tübingen School, denied the authenticity of all the letters passing under the apostle's name, except Galatians, 1 and II Corinthians, and most of Romans. But Baur's denial is vitiated by the Hegelian bias upon which it rests. For Baur the question whether or not an epistle is characterized by the anti-Judaistic line of argumentation seems to settle everything. Thus all of Paul's thinking is forced into one groove. This is manifestly unfair. H. J. Holtzmann in his work *Kritik der Epheser-und Kolosserbriefe,* views the letter which has come down to us as Colossians as being in reality an original shorter authentic Colossians plus interpolations from Ephesians which was composed by a Paulinist who in the process of writing it made use of the original and genuine Colossians. A. S. Peake is certainly correct when he states, "The complexity of the hypothesis tells fatally against it" (*Critical Introduction to the New Testament,* p. 52). Another and more recent author who finds a genuine nucleus in our Colossians is Charles Masson, *L'Épitre de Saint Paul aux Colossiens* (in *Commentaire du Nouveau Testament X,* 1950, pp. 83 ff).

[18] And some of these words are probably borrowed from the technical terminology of the false teachers.

b. *Stylistic Characteristics*

Colossians contains well-nigh endless sentence-chains. Thus, chapter 1 has only five sentences in the original, and one of these, verses 9-20, is a sentence of 218 words.

Also, this letter heaps up synonyms: pray and ask (1:9), endurance and longsuffering (1:11), holy, faultless, and blameless (1:22), founded and firm (or "grounded and stedfast," 1:23), ages and generations (1:26), rooted, built up, and established (2:7).

Again, it is rich in appositional clauses, such as, "the Father . . . who rescued us . . . and transferred us into the kingdom of the Son of his love, in whom we have our redemption (1:12-14), . . . who is the image of the invisible God," etc. (1:15-20).

And finally, certain particles that are of frequent occurrence in Paul's genuine epistles ($\gamma\acute{\alpha}\rho$, $o\tilde{v}v$, $\delta\iota\acute{o}\tau\iota$, $\H{\alpha}\rho\alpha$, $\delta\iota\acute{o}$) are rarely used here or do not even occur at all in Colossians.

Answer: It should be freely admitted that some of these stylistic characteristics are found in Colossians in a somewhat greater degree than elsewhere in Paul's epistles. Yet, the difference is by no means striking, as the following will indicate:

Lengthy sentences are also found in other Pauline epistles. Thus, Rom. 1:1-7 has 93 words in the original; 2:5-10 has 87. Phil. 3:8-11 has 78.

Synonyms abound in Romans; see 1:18, 21, 25, 29, etc. Also in other epistles; for example, in Philippians: full knowledge and keen discretion (Phil. 1:9), pure and blameless (1:10), glory and praise (1:11), envy and rivalry (1:15), eager expectation and hope (1:20), and so one could easily continue.

Appositional clauses, particularly those descriptive of the deity, are often of a liturgical nature. They are frequently found in ancient hymns in praise of Jehovah, God, Christ, in brief confessions of faith, and in doxologies. Paul has many of them. So have the prophets. And they abound in the liturgies of the synagogue even to the present day. When believers — either individually or collectively — are filled with gratitude to God, they will give humble and enthusiastic expression to this feeling of thankfulness and adoration by describing in clause upon clause God's greatness, faithfulness, wisdom, and love. Does not Romans begin with such an outburst of joyful testimony (1:3-5)? Add the following as a few of the clearest examples: II Cor. 1:3, 4; I Tim. 3:16; and then going back to the Old Testament: Isa. 44:24-28; Ps. 103:2-5; 104:2-5; 136. Besides, Col. 1:15-20, with its appositional clauses, may be a hymn which Paul quotes. See on that passage.

And finally, as to these particles, the argument based upon them has very little if any value: $\H{\alpha}\rho\alpha$ does not occur at all in Philippians; $\delta\iota\acute{o}$ only once in Galatians; $\delta\iota\acute{o}\tau\iota$ only once in the entire lengthy first epistle of Paul to the

Corinthians, not at all in II Corinthians; hence only once in the entire twenty-nine chapters of Paul's Corinthian correspondence that has come down to us! Hence, not much of an argument for rejecting Colossians as a genuine epistle of Paul can be based on the fact that in the 4 chapters of that letter διότι is not found. And the relative infrequency of οὖν in Colossians as contrasted with its frequency in Romans and in I Corinthians is easy to explain. It arises from the fact that in these epistles of earlier date the apostle is arguing with those whom he addresses, whereas in Colossians he is warning against a heresy.

One of the most recent to deny the Pauline authorship of Colossians — and of all the epistles which tradition ascribes to Paul, with the exception of Galatians, Romans, I and II Corinthians — is Andrew Morton. He bases his "proof" on the use which Paul makes of the conjunction *kai*, meaning *and, also, even*, etc. By the aid of an electronic computer he was strengthened in his hunch that an author will show a consistent pattern in the use of this conjunction. Hence, granted that the Pauline authorship of Galatians, etc., is beyond dispute but that the *kai*-pattern in *Colossians* differs from that in *Galatians*, etc., this would prove that tradition is wrong in regarding Paul as the author of *Colossians*.

Now if Morton could show that every Greek author, no matter in what sense he employs *kai* (whether in the sense of *and, also, even* or in some adversative sense such as *and yet, nevertheless*), no matter what be the contents or nature of his composition (whether it be narrative, descriptive, didactic, hortatory, or doxological), no matter when, why, or to whom he writes, and no matter whom he employs as his secretary and how much latitude he allows his secretary in the use of *kai*, reveals a consistent pattern in his use of this conjunction, his argument would have some value. As it is, he is basing too much on too little. There is, accordingly, truth in the criticism of the William Toedtman: "So *kais* are the most unreliable *figures* to pour into a computer" (*Time*, March 29, 1963, p. 8).

When all the facts are examined, therefore, it is clear that nothing in the language or style of Colossians can be used as an argument against its authenticity.

(2) *The heresy here combated was that of second century gnosticism. Hence, first century Paul cannot have been its author.*

The use of such words as *fulness* (πλήρωμα, 1:19; 2:9), *mystery*(μυστήριον, 1:26, 27; 2:2; 4:3), *ages* (αἰῶνες, 1:26), *wisdom* (σοφία, 1:9, 28; 2:3, 23; 3:16; 4:5), and *knowledge* (γνῶσις, 2:3), as well as the conception of a whole series of angels (1:16; 2:10; 2:15) points to the heresy of Valentinus.

For detailed explanation of these terms see commentary proper.

Answer: It suffices to affirm that the second century Gnostics did not view Colossians as directed against their beliefs. In fact, they make extensive use

31

of it. Also, the evidence which indicates that *incipient* forms of Gnosticism were already present in the first century is increasing.[19]

(3) *The "high Christology" found in Colossians is un-Pauline. It rather reminds one of the doctrine of the Logos in the Gospel according to John.*

Answer: It is certainly true that nowhere else in those epistles which the Church recognizes as having been written by Paul do we find the doctrine of Christ's pre-eminence and his relation to the Father, the universe, the angels, and the Church in such an expanded form as here in Colossians. But is it not altogether probable that this emphasis upon Christ's uniqueness, his supremacy over all, arose from the implied or expressed denial of the same on the part of the Colossian heretics? Surely, the Christology found here, though more detailed, is not any "higher" than that found in other epistles written by Paul, both earlier (Rom. 9:5, according to the correct reading; I Cor. 8:6; II Cor. 4:4), very shortly afterward (Phil. 2:6), and somewhat later (I Tim. 3:16; Titus 2:13).

Indeed, the arguments against the Pauline authorship of Colossians are rather superficial. Not only does the letter claim to have been written by Paul (1:1; 4:18) but the character of Paul, as revealed in his other letters, is also clearly expressed here:

First, Colossians bears close resemblance to Ephesians. He who wrote Ephesians also wrote Colossians. This argument, however, has little value for those who reject the Pauline authorship of Ephesians even more emphatically than they do that of Colossians. To avoid repetition and for the sake of good order the relation between Colossians and Ephesians is accordingly reserved for a Commentary on Ephesians, D.V.

Secondly, Colossians pictures the same kind of author as the one who addresses us from the pages of such almost universally recognized Pauline epistles as Romans, I and II Corinthians, and Galatians. Philippians, moreover, being like Colossians a Prison epistle, also has the identical hall-mark. Note the items of comparison in the table on pages 33, 34.

Therefore, if the Pauline authorship of *Philippians* be granted, as it certainly should be (see N.T.C. on Philippians, pp. 31-37), the conclusion that Paul also wrote *Colossians* would seem to be logical. Note, therefore, the close resemblance in mode of expression. In addition to the similarity already pointed out (see columns 1 and 3 in the table), I call attention *thirdly* to the following:

Verses 9-11 of *the first chapter* in both epistles (Colossians and Philip-

---

[19] See J. M. Bulman, "Valentinus and his School," in S.H.E.R.K. (20th century Extension), pp. 1146, 1147, and the literature there mentioned; also F. L. Cross (editor), *The Jung Codex: A Newly Discovered Gnostic Papyrus.* For a brief summary of second and third century Gnosticism see A. M. Renwick's article, "Gnosticism," in *Baker's Dictionary of Theology,* pp. 237, 238.

INTRODUCTION

	1	2	3
		Romans, I and II Corinthians, Galatians	
	Colossians	*Galatians*	*Philippians*
1. The author is deeply interested in those whom he addresses	1:3, 9; 2:1	Rom. 1:8, 9; I Cor. 3:1, 2; II Cor. 1:6, 23; Gal. 4:19, 26	1:3-11, 25, 26; 2:25-30
2. He loves to encourage and praise them	1:4-6; 2:5	Rom. 1:8; 15:14; 16:19; I Cor. 1:4-7; II Cor. 8:7; Gal. 4:14, 15; 5:7	4:1, 15-17
3. He traces every virtue of those whom he addresses to God, ascribing all the glory to him alone	1:5, 12, 29	Rom. 8:28-30; I Cor. 1:4; 12:4-11; II Cor. 1:3, 4; 2:14; Gal. 5:22-25	1:6; 3:9; 4:13
4. He writes touchingly about the supremacy of love	3:12-17	Rom. 12:9-21; I Cor. 13; II Cor. 5:14; 6:6; 11:11; 12:15; Gal. 5:6, 13, 14, 22	1:9, 16; 2:1, 2
5. He is filled with gratitude to God who laid hold on him and made him, though unworthy, a minister of the gospel	1:23, 25	I Cor. 15:9; II Cor. 11:16; 12:10; Gal. 1:15-17	3:4-14
6. He lists virtues and vices	3:5-9, 12-14	Rom. 1:29-32; I Cor. 5:9, 10; 6:9, 10; Gal. 5:22, 23	3:2, 19; 4:8

	1	2	3
		Romans, I and II Corinthians,	
	Colossians	*Galatians*	*Philippians*
7. He is never afraid to assert his authority	2:1-4:6	Rom. 12-16; I Cor. 5:13; 16:1; II Cor. 13:1-5	2:12-18; 4:1-9
8. When conditions are at all favorable he thanks God for those addressed and at times assures them of his constant prayer for them	1:3-12	Rom. 1:8-12; I Cor. 1:4-9; II Cor. 1:3-7	1:3-11
9. He warns earnestly against those who are seeking to lead others astray	ch. 2	Rom. 16:17, 18; I Cor. 1:10-17; 5:1; 6:1; ch. 11; II Cor. 13; Gal. 1:6-10, etc.	ch. 3
10. He loves "the gospel"	1:5-7, 23	Rom. 1:16, 17; 2:16 ("*my* gospel"); I Cor. 15:1 Gal. 1:6-9	1:5, 7, 12, 16, 27, etc.

pians) contains a summary of the prayer the apostle uttered for those addressed. Note that although the two prayers are by no means the same, there is a striking resemblance: the author prays that his friends may *grow or abound* in grace, may *bear fruit* abundantly, and may possess ever increasingly the true, experiential *knowledge* of God.

With respect to those who have been reconciled to Christ Col. 1:22 shows that it is God's purpose to present them to himself *without blemish (faultless)*. Phil. 2:15 indicates that this quality of being *without blemish,* not only by and by but even here and now, must be the aim of every believer. An important means to this end is *the word or message of God,* as is clear from Col. 1:25 and Phil. 1:14. *Perfection* is ever the goal (Col. 1:28; cf. Phil. 3:12). *Christ's Spirit* is the Energizer (Col. 1:8; and see verse 29; cf. Phil. 1:19, and see 3:21). As for himself, Paul is *supplying whatever is lacking* in the sufferings of Christ (Col. 1:24), as Epaphroditus *supplied what was lack-*

ing in the service which the Philippians had been rendering to Paul (Phil. 2:30) . Note the *sufferings* or *afflictions* of Christ of which Colossians speaks. Philippians, too, speaks about the desire of the apostle to know *the fellowship of his sufferings* (Phil. 3:10) . Of course, if the Colossians are going to be increasingly fruitful they must cling to the truth *as they learned* it from Epaphras (Col. 1:7) , just as the Philippians must continue in the truth *as they learned it* from Paul (Phil. 4:9) .

Turning now to *the second chapter* of Colossians we note that Paul is having a gigantic *conflict* for the Colossians, etc. (Col. 2:1) . In Philippians he also makes mention of a *conflict* in which they and he were jointly engaged (Phil. 1:30) . Paul's physical *absence* does not prevent his spiritual fellowship with the Colossians (Col. 2:5) and should not prevent the Philippians from remaining steadfast (Phil. 1:27) . There is a reference to a kind of *circumcision* that rises above the merely physical (Col. 2:11) . This reminds us immediately of Phil. 3:3. In the writings that have been traditionally ascribed to Paul it is only in these Prison epistles (Col. 2:18, 23; 3:12; Eph. 4:21; Phil. 2:3) that a word is used ($\tau\alpha\pi\epsilon\iota\nu o\varphi\rho o\sigma\acute{v}\nu\eta$) which, depending upon the context in any particular case, has been translated variously as *self-abasement, humility, lowliness.* Note also the frequent use of the verb *I make full, fill* or *fulfil* ($\pi\lambda\eta\rho\acute{o}\omega$). In the second chapter of Colossians it occurs in verse 10 (see also 1:9, 25; 4:17). This reminds us of Phil. 1:11; 2:2; 4:18, 19. The number of times this verb is used in Colossians, Ephesians, and Philippians contrasts sharply with its far lower frequency in the other epistles (see also on Col. 1:19, including footnote 56) .

The *heavenward* direction in which, according to Col. 3:1, 2, the yearning of the heart should be turned is certainly in line with the *heavenward* call which according to Phil. 3:14 the believer has received. *The things that are upon the earth* (Col. 3:2) which should not absorb our interests are in line with *earthly things* on which the enemies of the cross of Christ set their minds (Phil. 3:19) . The *heart of compassion* demanded of us in Col. 3:12 is similar to the *tender mercy and compassion* mentioned in Phil. 2:1. The beautiful reference to *the peace of God* (Col. 3:15) recalls the similar comforting passage in Philippians (4:7) .

Finally, as to *Col. 4*, peculiar to the epistles of Paul's first Roman imprisonment (except for one occurrence in II Tim. 2:9) is the mention of *bonds* (4:18; cf. Phil. 1:7, 13, 14, 17; Philem. 10, 13) . And the terseness of the command, "And say to Archippus, Attend to the ministry which you have received in the Lord, that you fulfil it" (Col. 4:17) reminds us of the words, similarly crisp, "I entreat Euodia and I entreat Syntyche to be of the same mind in the Lord" (Phil. 4:2) .

The testimony of the early church is in harmony with the conclusion which has been derived from the epistle itself.

Thus Eusebius, having made a thorough investigation of the literature at his command, states: "But clearly evident and plain are the fourteen (letters) of Paul; yet it is not right to ignore that some dispute the (letter) to the Hebrews" (*Ecclesiastical History* III.iii.4,5). Obviously Eusebius, writing at the beginning of the fourth century, knew that the entire orthodox church accepted Colossians as having been written by Paul.

From Eusebius we can go back to Origen (fl. 210-250), who states in his work *Against Celsus,* "And in the writings of Paul . . . the following words may be read in the Epistle to the Colossians, Let no one arbitrarily rob y o u of y o u r prize," etc., quoting Col. 2:18, 19. Note that here *Paul* is specifically mentioned as the author of this letter. Origen, in his several works, quotes from every chapter of Colossians.[20]

From Origen we can go back still farther, to his teacher, Clement of Alexandria (fl. 190-200). In his work *Stromata* or *Miscellanies* he more than once either refers to or quotes from each chapter. To him the author of Colossians is "the apostle." Also in his *Paedagogos* or *Instructor* he quotes from Colossians again and again.

About the same time Tertullian (fl. 193-216) quotes the warning against "philosophy and vain deceit" (Col. 2:8) and ascribes this warning to "the apostle," the very person whom he calls "the same Paul" (*Prescription against Heretics* VII, and cf. VI). Again and again, moreover, he quotes from Colossians such passages as refer to the greatness of Christ. See especially his work *Against Marcion.*

Earlier by a few years, but still for a long time a contemporary of Clement of Alexandria and of Tertullian, was Irenaeus. That he regards Paul as the author of Colossians is clear from his words, "Paul has himself declared. . . . 'Only Luke is with me.' . . . And again he says in the Epistle to the Colossians, 'Luke, the beloved physician greets y o u'" (Col. 4:14, see *Against Heresies* III.xiv.1). Not a single chapter of Colossians remains unquoted or not referred to in the works of Irenaeus. Now when Irenaeus ascribes Colossians to Paul, this testimony should carry considerable weight. He had traveled widely, was intimately acquainted with almost the entire church of his day, and was living in a day and age in which the earliest apostolic traditions were still very much alive.

The Muratorian Fragment (about 180-200), a survey of New Testament books, definitely names Paul as the author of Colossians.

Shortly before this Theophilus of Antioch draws a distinction between the Logos internal and the Logos emitted, and he calls this Logos in his emitted state "the firstborn of all creation" (*To Autolycus* XXII), which strongly reminds one of Col. 1:15. This phrase also occurs in Justin Martyr's *Dialogue with Trypho* LXXXV. Justin Martyr wrote some time between 155

---

[20] For detailed references for Origen and also for earlier writers see the Indices of Texts in *Ante-Nicene Fathers.*

and 161.[21] The Epistle to the Colossians was also included in Marcion's Canon, in the Old Latin, and in the Old Syriac. The witness in favor of Paul's authorship is therefore overwhelming. Testimony, both internal and external, yields but one conclusion, namely, that it was Paul who wrote Colossians.

B. *Philemon*

Since the little letter to Philemon is closely linked with Colossians (Col. 4:10-17; cf. Philem, 2, 23, 24) the Pauline authorship of the latter is a strong argument in favor of identical authorship of the former. Moreover, not only does the writer call himself *Paul,* and this no less than three times (verses 1, 9 and 19), but the request which he presents, and which is the very theme and substance of the letter, is of such a definite and personal character that no good reason can be shown why a forger would have composed it. Moreover, the personality of Paul — combining such traits as deep interest in others, delight in mentioning their good qualities, the conviction that back of every human virtue is God as the Giver, emphasis on the spirit of kindness and pardon — marks this little gem of a letter as strikingly as it does Colossians.

It is not surprising, therefore, that Eusebius gave it a place in his list of acknowledged books (*Ecclesiastical History* III.xxv; cf. III.iii), and that he regarded it as one of the letters of Paul "true, genuine, and recognized." Origen, too, accepts it as a letter of Paul (*Hom. in Jer.* 19). Tertullian was well acquainted with it, and because of his testimony we know that even Marcion accepted it though that heretic rejected I and II Timothy and Titus (Tertullian, *Against Marcion* V.xxi). It is probable that Ignatius borrowed his play on the proper name Onesimus from Paul (cf. Philem. 10, 11, 20 with Ignatius, *To the Ephesians,* chapter 2). The letter is also found in the Muratorian Fragment and in the Old Latin and Old Syriac versions.

The fact that the external evidence for the letter to Philemon is not as extensive as it is for some of Paul's other epistles is easy to understand: the request for the kind reception of the fugitive slave is very brief and contains little material that could be used in doctrinal controversies. From the beginning, however, its acceptance has been almost universal. An attack against it in the fourth and fifth centuries — on the ground that it was unworthy of the mind of Paul and of no value for edification — was answered by Jerome (*Comm. on Philem. pref.*), Chrysostom (*Argum. on Philem.*), and others. A much later attack by F. C. Baur was in line with his rejection of the

---

[21] It is probable that there is an echo of Colossians in such very early writings as *The Epistle of Barnabas* and in Ignatius, *Epistle to the Ephesians,* but why look for merely probable references when so much clear proof has already been furnished?

authenticity of most of the epistles that are traditionally ascribed to Paul (see footnote 16 above), and resulted from the same philosophical bias. He called the little letter "the embryo of a Christian romance," and referred to the fact that whoever wrote it used a few words which the real Paul never uses. His arguments are so easily answered that they hardly deserve comment. One author not unjustly calls this attack on the Pauline authorship of Philemon "one of Baur's worst blunders." Everything in this letter so clearly points to Paul that today those who think otherwise are a very small minority.

Commentary

on

The Epistle to the Colossians

Outline of Colossians

Theme: *Christ, the Pre-eminent One, the Only and All-Sufficient Savior*

I. This Only and All-Sufficient Savior Is the Object of the Believers'
   Faith, chapters 1 and 2
   A. This Truth Expounded Positively, chapter 1
      1. Opening Salutation
      2. Fervent Thanksgiving and Prayer
      3. The Son's Pre-eminence
         a. In Creation
         b. In Redemption
      4. His Reconciling Love toward the Colossians, and Their Result-
         ing Duty to Continue in the Faith
      5. The Apostle's Share in Proclaiming "the Mystery," namely,
         "Christ in y o u the hope of glory"
   B. This Truth Expounded Not only Positively but Now Both Posi-
      tively and Negatively, chapter 2, the Latter over against "the Colos-
      sian Heresy" with Its:
      1. Delusive Philosophy
      2. Judaistic Ceremonialism
      3. Angel-worship
      4. Asceticism
II. This Only and All-Sufficient Savior Is the Source of the Believers' Life,
    and Thus the Real Answer to the Perils by Which They Are Con-
    fronted, chapters 3 and 4
    A. This Truth Applied to All Believers, 3:1-17
       1. Believers should be consistent. They should live in conformity
          with the fact that they were raised with Christ, who is their life
       2. Therefore, they should "put to death" and "lay aside" the old
          vices; and
       3. They should "put on" the new virtues
    B. This Truth Applied to Special Groups, 3:18-4:1
       1. Wives and their husbands
       2. Children and their fathers
       3. Servants and their masters
    C. Closing Admonitions, Greetings, etc., 4:2-18
       1. Prayer urged
       2. Wise conduct and gracious speech stressed

3. A good word for Tychicus and Onesimus, who have been sent
   with tidings and encouragement
4. Greetings
5. Exchange of letters requested
6. Crisp directive for Archippus
7. Closing salutation

Outline of Chapter 1

Theme: *Christ, the Pre-eminent One, the Only and All-Sufficient Savior*

I. This Only and All-Sufficient Savior Is the Object of the Believers' Faith, chapters 1 and 2

A. This Truth Expounded Positively, chapter 1

1:1, 2 1. Opening Salutation

1:3-14 2. Fervent Thanksgiving and Prayer

1:15-20 3. The Son's Pre-eminence

a. In Creation (verses 15-17)

b. In Redemption (verses 18-20)

1:21-23 4. His Reconciling Love toward the Colossians, and Their Resulting Duty to Continue in the Faith

1:24-29 5. The Apostle's Share in Proclaiming "the Mystery," namely, "Christ in y o u the hope of glory"

CHAPTER I

COLOSSIANS

1 1 Paul, an apostle of Christ Jesus through the will of God, and Timothy our brother, 2 to the saints and believing brothers in Christ at Colosse; grace to y o u and peace from God our Father.

1:1, 2

I. *Opening Salutation*

1. Though Paul is in the world and uses the world, he is not of the world. As a letter-writer he makes use of the literary devices of the world but in the process of adopting them he transforms them, raising them to a higher level. In Paul's day a man of the world would often begin a letter by jotting down: a. the name of the writer, b. the name of the person (or persons) addressed, c. the words of greeting. The apostle follows the same method, but he beautifies and sanctifies everything by immediately relating both *sender* and *persons addressed* to Christ ("an apostle *of Christ Jesus*," "brothers *in Christ*"), and by speaking about the work of Christ ("grace and peace") in the very opening salutation.

The apostle writes, **Paul, an apostle of Christ Jesus.** He presents himself as being, in the fullest sense of the term, an official representative of the Anointed Savior, the latter's spokesman. To Christ Jesus he owes his appointment and his authority. Through Paul no one less than Christ Jesus himself is addressing the church. It was from the risen and exalted Lord that Paul had received his difficult but glorious assignment to be *an apostle,* yes, *the* apostle to *the Gentiles,* not *exclusively* but *especially* to them (Acts 9:5, 6, 15, 16; 22:10-21; 26:15-18; Rom. 1:1, 5; Gal. 1:1; 2:9).

Paul continues, **through the will of God.** He had attained his high office neither through *aspiration* (see Acts 9:11), nor through *usurpation* — that was not like Paul! —, nor yet through *nomination* by other men (Gal. 1:1, 16, 17), but by divine *preparation* (Gal. 1:15, 16), having been set apart and qualified by the activity of God's sovereign will (I Cor. 1:1; II Cor. 1:1; Gal. 1:1; Eph. 1:1; II Tim. 1:1; cf. Rom. 15:32; II Cor. 8:5).

Paul adds, **and Timothy our brother** (cf. II Cor. 1:1; Phil. 1:1; I Thess. 1:1; II Thess. 1:1; Philem. 1:1). This is not surprising, since right now Timothy was evidently in Paul's vicinity and wished to extend greetings. Moreover Timothy had spent some time with Paul in Ephesus during the third missionary journey (Acts 19:1, 22), and may thus have become acquainted with some of the people of Colosse who at that time presumably came to hear Paul (Acts 19:10). By calling Timothy "our brother," Paul, though *implying* that his younger associate was not in the full sense of the term an apostle, *was rather emphasizing* the closeness of the relationship between himself and his associate. The apostle loved Timothy deeply and tenderly (Phil. 2:19-23). Paul, Timothy, and the members of the Colossian church all belonged to the same spiritual family. It is, however, Paul, Paul *alone,* who is to be considered the real author of the letter (notice the words "I Paul," in Col. 1:23; cf. 1:24-2:5; 4:3, 7-18), not Paul and Timothy.

Paul continues, **to the saints and believing brothers in Christ at Colosse.** Saints are those who by the Lord have been *set apart* to glorify him. They are *the consecrated ones,* and here the Israel of the new dispensation, whose task it is to proclaim God's excellencies (I Peter 2:9). Saints, then, are persons upon whom the Lord has bestowed a great favor and who have been entrusted with a weighty responsibility. Ideally, saints are *believers.* So also nere: the phrase "to the saints and believing brothers" (note the fact that the definite article *the* is not repeated before the second noun) expresses *one* thought, for saints who are true to their calling are, of course, believing brothers, and that "in Christ," *by virtue of union with him.* The addition of the words "at Colosse" shows that this letter was meant primarily for that congregation, though in a secondary sense it was intended also for the church at nearby Laodicea (4:16), and in fact, for every church throughout the entire dispensation.

The salutation proper is as follows, **grace to y o u and peace from God our Father.** Thus, there is pronounced upon all the saints and believing brothers in Christ at Colosse *grace,* that is, God's spontaneous, unmerited favor in action, his sovereign, freely bestowed lovingkindness in operation, and its result, *peace,* that is, the assurance of reconciliation through the blood of the cross, true spiritual wholeness and prosperity, these two blessings (grace and peace) flowing down from "God our Father." Thus the Greek salutation, "greeting" (*chairein,* cf. Acts 15:23) and the Hebrew, "peace" (*shālōm,* cf. Judg. 19:20) are here combined, deepened and enriched. The *grace* (*cháris*) is that referred to in Eph. 2:8, "For by grace have y o u been saved through faith, and that not of yourselves; it is the gift of God." The *peace* (*eirēnē*) is that great blessing which Christ as a result of his atoning death has bequeathed to us (John 14:27). It surpasses all understanding (Phil. 4:7). Note the brevity of this opening salutation. It is next to the shortest in all of Paul's epistles (I Thess. 1:1 contains the fewest words; Rom. 1:1-7 has the most). Here in Colossians the usual additional reference to the second Person of the Trinity: "and the Lord Jesus Christ" (as in Rom., I and II Cor., Gal., Eph., Phil., II Thess., and Philem.), "and Christ Jesus our Lord" (as in I and II Tim.), "and Christ Jesus our Savior" (as in Titus), is lacking

44

in the best manuscripts. The reason for this is not known. One thing is certain: the apostle is not in any way detracting from the glory and majesty of Christ. He is not trying to exalt the Father at the expense of the Son, for this is the very epistle in which the deity of the second Person of the Trinity, his pre-eminence above all creatures including all the hosts of angels, and his all-sufficiency for salvation, are set forth in the clearest manner and emphasized most strongly. Is it possible that any mention of the Lord Jesus Christ is here purposely omitted in order by way of contrasting effect to single him out for special discussion in the immediately following verses? Note the specific mention of "our Lord Jesus Christ" in verse 3, and further references to him in verses 4, 7, and especially in the paragraph about the Son of God's love in verses 15-20.

For further details about certain aspects of Paul's opening salutations see N.T.C. on I and II Thessalonians, pp. 37-45; on Philippians, pp. 43-49; and on I and II Timothy and Titus, pp. 49-56; 339-344.

---

3 While praying for y o u we are always thanking God, the Father of our Lord Jesus Christ, 4 because we have heard of y o u r faith in Christ Jesus and of the love which y o u cherish for all the saints, 5 by reason of the hope laid up for y o u in the heavens, of which y o u have previously heard in the message of the truth, namely, the gospel, 6 which made its entrance felt among y o u, as indeed in the entire world it is bearing fruit and growing — so also among yourselves from the day y o u heard and came to acknowledge the grace of God in its genuine character, 7 as y o u learned it from Epaphras our beloved fellow-servant who is a faithful minister of Christ on our behalf, 8 and has made known to us y o u r love in the Spirit.

9 And for this reason, from the day we heard it we never stopped praying for y o u, asking that y o u may be filled with clear knowledge of his will (such clear knowledge consisting) in all spiritual wisdom and understanding, 10 so as to live lives worthy of the Lord, to (his) complete delight, in every good work bearing fruit, and growing in the clear knowledge of God; 11 being invigorated with all vigor, in accordance with his glorious might, so as to exercise every kind of endurance and longsuffering; 12 with joy giving thanks to the Father who qualified y o u for a share in the inheritance of the saints in the light 13 and who rescued us out of the domain of darkness and transplanted us into the kingdom of the Son of his love, 14 in whom we have our redemption, the forgiveness of our sins.

1:3-14

II. *Fervent Thanksgiving and Prayer*

1:3-8

A. *Thanksgiving*

3. While praying for y o u we are always thanking God. In letters of that day the opening greeting was frequently followed by thanksgiving. Thus an

ancient letter reads, "I thank the Lord Serapis that when I was in peril on
the sea he saved me immediately." [22] This sequence — salutation followed by
thanksgiving — is also Pauline.[23] However, Paul does not thank any pagan
deity but the only true God. Paul's spontaneous thanksgiving, in which
Timothy joins,[24] and which according to the apostle's explicit testimony, is
always [25] an element in prayer for the Colossians, is offered to God **the Father
of our Lord Jesus Christ** (cf. Rom. 15:6; II Cor. 1:3; 11:31; Eph. 1:3; 3:14).
Our *Lord,* who has a right to that name because he purchased his people
with his blood and is their Sovereign Master, and to whom, as the Anointed
Savior, Paul gladly ascribes this honor, is in his very essence God's only Son.
He is *Son by nature.* We are children *by adoption.* He has the right to call
God *"my* Father" (Matt. 26:39, 42) and to make the majestic claim, "I and
the Father, we are one" (John 10:30; cf. 14:9). Calling God "the Father of
our Lord Jesus Christ" has a very practical purpose, as the apostle shows
plainly in II Cor. 1:3. In his capacity as Father of our Lord Jesus Christ he
is "the Father of mercies and God of all comfort." Via Christ every spiritual
blessing flows down to us from the Father. And if Christ is "the Son of God's
love," as Paul says in this very chapter (Col. 1:13), then God must be the
Father of love, the loving Father. Note also that beautiful word of appropriating faith, namely, *our:* "the Father of *our* Lord Jesus Christ." Hence, in
the sublimest and most comforting sense, he is *our* Father. What a reason
for thanksgiving!

---

[22] A. Deissmann, *Light From the Ancient East* (translated from the German by
L. R. M. Strachan, fourth edition, 1922, pp. 179, 180).

[23] Commentators are agreed that in nearly every one of his letters Paul's thanksgiving and/or doxology follows the salutation. On the details there is some confusion.
According to some otherwise thoroughly conservative commentators, in *all* of Paul's
letters "except Galatians" the opening salutation is followed by thanksgiving. Are
these commentators unaware of the fact that, by implication, they are surrendering
the Pauline authorship of Titus? This should not be done. See N.T.C. on I and
II Timothy and Titus, pp. 4-33, 377-381 (footnote 193). According to others, however, the thanksgiving is omitted not only in Galatians and Titus but also in I Timothy. Now it is true, indeed, that in that letter the opening salutation is not *immediately* followed by thanksgiving or doxology. After an intervening paragraph (I
Tim. 1:3-11) there is, however, also here a thanksgiving, beginning with verse 12.
A correct summary of this matter, accordingly, would point out that in *all* of Paul's
epistles, with the exception of Galatians and Titus, the opening salutation is followed, either immediately or very shortly, by a thanksgiving and/or doxology. For
the doxology see II Cor. 1:3 ff.; for the doxology and thanksgiving, Eph. 1:3 ff.,
and 1:15 ff.

[24] Since both Paul and Timothy are mentioned in the immediately preceding context (verse 1) it is natural to interpret the "we" of verse 3 as a reference to them
rather than as an epistolary plural. See N.T.C. on I and II Thessalonians, p. 82,
footnote 65.

[25] Though it is grammatically possible (with A.V. and A.R.V.) to construe *always*
with *praying,* it is better to join it with *thanking.* This is true in view of the immediately following context (verses 4-8) in which reasons for thanksgiving are given,
and also in view of I Cor. 1:4; Eph. 1:16; Phil. 1:3; I Thess. 1:2; II Thess. 1:3; and
Philem. 3.

4, 5a. Paul says, "While praying for y o u we are always thanking God, the Father of our Lord Jesus Christ" **because we have heard of y o u r faith in Christ Jesus and of the love which y o u cherish for all the saints.** The simplest construction of verses 4-8 is surely that which regards this section in its entirety as setting forth reasons for *thanksgiving.* The actual *petition* starts in verse 9. Both thanksgiving and petition belong to the essence of *prayer* (Phil. 4:6). Now the *early* mention of reasons for thanksgiving to God with respect to certain basic conditions in Colosse is also excellent Christian psychology. There were dangers threatening the church. Certain weaknesses, moreover, are clearly implied (3:5-11; cf. 2:4, 8, etc.). But before Paul even begins to refer to these things he first of all assures those to whom this letter is sent that he is convinced that the work of God's grace is evident in their lives. What a lesson for every parent, counselor, teacher, and pastor, especially in cases where warning or even rebuke would appear to be in order! There is such a thing as Christian tact (see appendix). And *this* tact is in complete harmony with honesty.

Paul mentions the fact that he and Timothy *have heard* (see on verse 8) of *the faith* of the Colossians in Christ Jesus, that is, of their abiding trust in and personal surrender to the Anointed Savior.[26] With *faith* in Christ Jesus he associates *love* for all the saints. These two always go together, for faith is ever operating through love (Gal. 5:6). The same Magnet, Christ Jesus,[27] who attracts sinners to himself and changes them into saints simultaneously draws them into closer fellowship with each other. Thus, ideally speaking, every believer enshrines his fellow-believers — wherever they may dwell and of whatever race they may be — in his heart (John 13:34; Phil. 1:7, 8; I John 4:7-11). Paul continues, **by reason of the hope laid up for y o u in the heavens.** Thus, to faith and love he now adds hope, completing the familiar triad.[28] In the New Testament this triad is not confined to Paul's writings. It also occurs frequently in the sub-apostolic literature. It is entirely possible that Paul did not invent it. It may have belonged to the common stock of earliest Christianity. In fact, these very graces stand out in the teaching and ministry of Jesus. Again and again the Lord while on earth stressed the importance of *faith* (Matt. 6:30; 8:10, 26; 9:2, 22, 29; 14:31; 15:28; 16:8; 17:20; 21:21; 23:23, etc.). His very presence, words of cheer, bright and beautiful promises, and deeds of redemption inspired *hope,* even when he did not use

---

[26] Some are of the opinion that since the preposition ἐν is used, not εἰς, Christ cannot be regarded as the object of faith, but must be viewed as the sphere in which faith is exercised. This interpretation disregards flexibility of use with respect to the verb πιστεύω and its prepositions and cases. See Gram. N.T. Bl.-Debr. sections 187 (6), 206 (2), 233 (2), 235 (2), 397 (2).

[27] The question, "Why *Christ Jesus* instead of *Jesus Christ?*" has been discussed in N.T.C. on I and II Timothy and Titus, p. 51, footnote 19.

[28] See A. M. Hunter, "Faith, Hope, Love — A Primitive Christian Triad," *ET* xlix (1937-1938), p. 428 f.

the very word (Matt. 9:2; 14:27; Mark 5:36; 6:50; 9:23; John 11:11, 23, 40; I Peter 1:3, etc.). He placed great emphasis on *love* and certainly regarded it as the very essence of both law and gospel, the greatest of the triad (Matt. 5:43-46; 19:19; John 13:34, 35; 14:15, 23; 15:12, 13, 17; 17:26; 21:15, 16, 17, etc.). Often, in a most natural manner, he combined these three. A striking instance of this is found in John 11:

1. *Love*

"Now Jesus loved [or: was holding in loving esteem] Martha and her sister, and Lazarus" (verse 5).

"So the Jews were saying, See how he (constantly) loved him" (verse 36).

2. *Hope*

"This illness is not unto death . . ." (verse 4).

"Our friend Lazarus has fallen asleep, but I go in order to wake him up" (verse 11).

"I am the resurrection and the life; he who believes in me, though he die, yet shall he live, and everyone who lives and believes in me shall never, never die" (verses 25, 26a).

Though none of these sayings contain the word *hope*, they are all hope-inspiring.

3. *Faith*

"Do you believe this?" (verse 26b). (Note how closely hope and faith are related.)

"Did I not say to you that if you would believe you would see the glory of God?" (verse 40).

Another striking instance of the combination love, faith, and hope is found in Christ's Upper Room Discourse during the night in which he washed the feet of his disciples, instituted the Lord's Supper and was betrayed. "Having *loved* his own in the world, he loved them to the uttermost" (John 13:1). By washing the feet of his disciples and issuing the new commandment ("that y o u keep on *loving* one another") he underscored the importance of love (13:34). Immediately afterward he exhorted his disciples to have abiding *faith* in God and in himself: "Let not y o u r hearts any longer be troubled. Continue *to trust* in God, also in me continue *to trust*" (14:1). And hard upon this he inspired them with *hope* by assuring them, "In my Father's house there are many dwelling-places. If it were not so, I would have told y o u; for I go to prepare a place for y o u. And when I go and prepare a place for y o u, I come again and will take y o u to be face to face with me, in order that where I am y o u may be also" (14:2, 3).

Hence, it is not surprising to find this triad in the inspired writings of

those who had caught the spirit of Christ's example and teachings. It is
found in several variations of sequence, though the three members of the
triad do not always occur in immediate succession:

a. faith, hope, and love (Rom. 5:1-5; I Cor. 13:13 [the best-known of all
the passages in which the triad occurs]; Heb. 10:22-24; I Peter 1:21, 22).

b. faith, love, and hope (Col. 1:4, 5; I Thess. 1:3; 5:8).

c. hope, faith, and love (I Peter 1:3-8).

d. love, hope, and faith (Eph. 4:2-5; Heb. 6:10-12).

Some have experienced difficulty, however, with the fact that Paul here in
Col. 1:4, 5, in which he follows sequence b., seems to be saying that the *faith*
of the Colossians and their *love* are based on *hope*. Note the words, "by
reason of the hope." How can hope ever be the reason for faith and love?
Many interpreters, apparently despairing of finding any other way out of
this difficulty, resort to the device of reconstructing the sentence or at least
the ideas expressed in it, so as to get rid of the idea that faith and love could
be based on hope.[29] However, such a virtual re-wording of the sentence is
not at all necessary. Christian mental and moral attitudes and activities such
as believing, hoping, and loving, always react upon each other. In general,
the more there is of the one the more there will be of the other. This holds
too with respect to hope. It reacts mightily and beneficially on faith and
love.[30] Christian hope is not mere wishing. It is a fervent yearning, confident
expectation, and patient waiting for the fulfilment of God's promises, a full
Christ-centered (cf. Col. 1:27) assurance that these promises will indeed be
realized. It is a living and sanctifying force (I Peter 1:3; I John 3:3). How

---

[29] Some read verses 3-5 as if these meant: "While praying for y o u we are always
thanking God . . . because we have heard of y o u r *faith* in Christ Jesus and of the
love which y o u cherish for all the saints, and because (we have also heard) of
y o u r *hope*." Others translate: "We give thanks to God . . . (praying always for
y o u, having heard of y o u r faith . . . and of y o u r love . . .) because of the
hope." Thus hope, and it *alone*, is viewed as reason for thanksgiving. Lenski is right
when he states: "But this construction yields a strange resultant thought, namely
that after hearing of *the faith and love* of the Colossians Paul and Timothy are
thanking God, *not* for this faith and love as we should expect but only for *the hope*
laid away for the Colossians. . . . No ordinary reader would refer the διά- phrase
back so far in order to get such a thought and then pass on." In one form or another
this construction which connects *hope* with the apostle's thanksgiving, and avoids the
difficulty of making it the reason for faith and love, is advocated by G. G. Findlay ("A Biblical Note," *Exp*, first series, 10 [1879], pp. 74-80), Athanasius, Calovius,
Conybeare, Eadie, Hofmann, Michaelis, Storr, etc. Opposed to them are Bruce,
Calvin, De Wette, Ellicott, Erasmus, Lenski, Lightfoot, C. F. D. Moule, Ridderbos,
Robertson, etc. Commentators of this latter group believe that it makes good sense
to say that faith and love are based on hope. With this judgment I am in agreement,
and this also for the grammatical reason that the words "by reason of the hope" are
in the original joined more closely with "faith . . . and love" than with "always
thanking God."

[30] The interaction of the elements in Christian experience has been discussed in
N.T.C. on John 7:17, 18.

then should not the hope of glory, a glory of which we have already received the first instalment (II Cor. 1:22; 5:5; Eph. 1:14), strengthen our *faith* in the One who merited all these blessings for us, namely, the Lord Jesus Christ? And how should it not enhance our *love* for those with whom we are going to share this bliss everlastingly? How should it not intensify our sense of oneness with the saints of all the ages? And if this be true even with respect to hope as an attitude and activity of heart and mind, it is surely not less true with respect to hope as an objective reality, namely, *the thing hoped for*, which is the sense in which the word is used here in Col. 1:5a, as also in Gal. 5:5 and Titus 2:13 (to which some interpreters would add Heb. 6:18). As the very context indicates, this hope is "the inheritance of the saints in the light" (Col. 1:12). Therefore we read here that it is "laid up for y o u in the heavens," an expression which immediately reminds one of the heavenly treasure of which Jesus speaks in Matt. 5:20, and of the "inheritance imperishable, undefiled, and unfading reserved in heaven for y o u" of which Peter speaks (I Peter 1:4). It is the glory which shall be revealed to us (Rom. 8:18), the peace and joy that pertains to "our homeland in heaven" (Phil. 3:20; cf. John 14:1-4). This realization of our *hope*, this glory, is so entrancing that as we see it from afar we greet it (Heb. 11:13), with our *faith* in the Giver strengthened, and our *love* for all his children with whom we shall share it enlarged and intensified.

5b-8. Now with respect to this hope Paul continues, **of which y o u have previously heard in the message of the truth, namely, the gospel.** Since the apostle himself explains this statement in verse 7, little comment is needed here. The *main idea* is still thanksgiving for the blessings bestowed upon the Colossians. Note, however, that though this is Paul's chief thought, there is here a certain implication. A warning can easily be read between the lines, to this effect, "O Colossians, I gratefully testify that with respect to this glorious hope y o u have heard a message that was true, uplifting, and fruitbearing (5b, 6). Hence, do not allow yourselves to be led astray by teachers of false doctrine. Cling to the truth that was proclaimed to y o u in the gospel." On the meaning of *gospel* see N.T.C. on Philippians, pp. 81-85. This is the gospel **which made its entrance felt among y o u,[31] as indeed in the entire world it is bearing fruit and growing.** The Colossians are being reminded of the power (cf. Rom. 1:16) and successful course of the gospel, as a reason for gratitude. Here, too, there is the implication, "Don't y o u remember the mighty change that occurred when the message of God's redemptive truth made its first appearance among y o u? That gospel needs no addition or supplement. Its influence is being felt in ever-increasing measure, both extensively, invading region after region, and intensively, pro-

---

[31] Thus rather than simply, "which came to y o u." See Oepke, art. παρουσία, πάρειμι, Th.W.N.T., p. 863 ff.

ducing fruit upon fruit in hearts won for Christ. Do not attempt to exchange God's powerful work for man's beggarly elements" (cf. 2:8).

The rapid progress of the gospel in the early days has ever been the amazement of the historian. Justin Martyr, about the middle of the second century, wrote, "There is no people, Greek or barbarian, or of any other race, by whatever appellation or manners they may be distinguished, however ignorant of arts or agriculture, whether they dwell in tents or wander about in covered wagons, among whom prayers and thanksgivings are not offered in the name of the crucified Jesus to the Father and Creator of all things." Half a century later Tertullian adds, "We are but of yesterday, and yet we already fill y o u r cities, islands, camps, y o u r palace, senate, and forum. We have left y o u only your temples." R. H. Glover (*The Progress of World-Wide Missions*, p. 39) states, "On the basis of all the data available it has been estimated that by the close of the Apostolic Period the total number of Christian disciples had reached half a million."

Now, under God, no human individual was a more effective agent in proclaiming the glorious tidings of salvation than was Paul himself. Rescued by Christ, the very One whom he had formerly bitterly opposed, his heart was filled with love and holy zeal for the truth. He gave his very life for it. He reasoned with Jew and Gentile, pleaded with them (cf. II Cor. 5:20, 21), performed miracles among them, visited them in their homes, wept over them. In short, he loved them. When *present* among them, his example — working with his hands to earn a living, admonishing and encouraging them, dealing with them like a father with his children — made a deep impression. He was always pointing away from self to Christ. When *absent* from them, they were on his mind and he would send them messages, vibrant and throbbing, from the heart to the heart. Circumstances permitting, he would revisit them or would send a delegate to help them solve their problems. In his prayers he carried their burdens to the throne of grace. It causes no surprise that from far and near people came to see and hear him. And those who heard told others, and these still others, etc. The following passages serve to explain how, through the ministry of Paul and of those who gave heed to his preaching, the gospel was bearing fruit and growing:

"All those of (the Roman province of) Asia heard the word of the Lord, both Jews and Greeks" (Acts 19:10).

"The word of the Lord grew and increased mightily" (Acts 19:20).

"From y o u (Thessalonians) the word of the Lord has echoed forth, not only in Macedonia and Achaia, but in every place y o u r faith in God has gone forth, so that it is not necessary for us to say anything, for they themselves are reporting about us what kind of entering in we had among y o u, and how y o u turned to God from those idols of y o u r s, to serve God, the living and real One" (I Thess. 1:8, 9).

"Now I want y o u to know, brothers, that the things that have happened to me have in reality turned out to the advantage of the gospel; so that it has become clear throughout the whole praetorian guard and to all the rest that my bonds are for Christ" (Phil. 1:12, 13).[32]

But though Paul took this leading part in the spread of the gospel, he himself, here in Col. 1:6, is placing all the emphasis upon the fact that by God's power and grace it is *the gospel itself* that is thus bearing fruit and growing. He is saying, as it were, "Do not underestimate the vitality of the seed that is scattered upon the ground (see Mark 4:26-29; cf. Isa. 55:11). That seed is germinating, growing, and bearing fruit." The gospel never *depends* on man, not even on Paul. It is *God's* work in which he is pleased to use man.

What has been said implies also *intensive or inner* growth and fruitbearing, gospel-influence on the lives of the people who heard it and gave heed to it. Think of such fruits as faith, love, and hope (verses 4 and 5), with re-emphasis on love (verse 8). And add to this the several fruits mentioned with such striking beauty in verses 9-12 (cf. Gal. 5:22, 23). Fruits for eternity were in evidence everywhere. And this *everywhere* most definitely also included the Lycus Valley, with re-emphasis now on the church at Colosse. That the gospel was not fruitless there had already been stated in verses 4 and 5 and by implication reaffirmed at the very beginning of verse 6 ("which made its entrance felt among y o u"). To this specific instance of fruitbearing the apostle now returns by continuing, **so also among yourselves from the day y o u heard and came to acknowledge the grace of God in its genuine character.** The *main* note is still thanksgiving. The inference is, "So, Colossians, do not destroy this fruit-bearing tree. Do not listen to those who are trying to deprive y o u of the great blessing that has come to y o u." Not only had they come *to know* the truth, they had come *to acknowledge* it, and this from the very day they had first heard it. Such acknowledgment is more than abstract, intellectual knowledge. It is a joyful acceptance and appropriation of the truth centered in Christ. This truth concerns nothing less than the grace of God, his sovereign love in action, his favor toward the undeserving. They had come to acknowledge this grace of God "in its genuine character," unattenuated by philosophical vagaries or Judaistic admixtures.[33]

With reference to this true gospel of grace which as everywhere so also among the Colossians had been bearing fruit increasingly since the day they had heard and accepted it Paul continues, **as y o u learned it from Epaphras**

---

[32] For a summary of Paul's Mission Strategy see the author's *Bible Survey*, pp. 199-207.
[33] Though something can be said for the rendering, "came to acknowledge truly," it would seem to be best to connect the words ἐν ἀληθείᾳ directly with the immediately preceding τὴν χάριν τοῦ θεοῦ. I favor this construction for two reasons: a. the mention of "the message (or *the word*) of *the truth*" in verse 5; and b. the purpose of the letter, namely, to place *the truth* as to Christ's pre-eminence and all-sufficiency over against the lie that was being propagated by the false teachers.

our beloved fellow-servant, who is a faithful minister of Christ on our [34] behalf. On Epaphras, the "minister" of the church at Colosse, etc., who had come to see Paul in Rome, among other things in order to report to the apostle about conditions in that church and to secure his help in the battle against worldliness and heresy, see *Introduction* III A and IV A. By calling him "our beloved fellow-servant" and "faithful minister of Christ on our behalf" Paul is doing three things: a. he is placing the stamp of his approval on Epaphras and the gospel the latter had taught the Colossians; b. he is by implication condemning any system of thought that is in conflict with this one and only true gospel; and c. he is saying, "Those who reject the gospel according to the teaching of our beloved Epaphras are also rejecting us (Paul and Timothy) and our teaching . . . and remember, we, in turn, represent Christ (see on verse 1) just as also Epaphras is Christ's *faithful minister."* Of course, the *main idea* is *gratitude to God* for the fact that from the mouth of this faithful servant Epaphras the Colossians have heard and have accepted that glorious gospel which is bearing fruit among them. The words of verse 3, "While praying for y o u, we are always thanking God," control everything that follows in verses 4-8. With reference to Epaphras the apostle continues, **and has made known to us y o u r love in the Spirit.** This statement takes up the thought expressed earlier (see verse 4b). That Paul and the other apostles regarded love as the most precious fruit of God's grace is evident not only from I Cor. 13:13 ("and the greatest of these is love") but also from such passages as:

Col. 3:14	I John 4:8
I John 3:14	I Peter 4:8

And was not this the very emphasis of Christ himself? See John 13:1, 34, 35; 15:12; cf. Mark 12:28-31. Probably in order to prevent the impression from taking root that Epaphras had painted too somber a picture of conditions among the Colossian believers the apostle stresses the fact that his worthy fellow-worker had given him an enthusiastic account of their *love.* This is the love "for all the saints," of which Paul had just spoken. It can never be divorced from the love of which God himself is the object. It indicates that intelligent and purposeful delight in the triune God, that spontaneous and grateful outgoing of the entire personality to him who has re-

---

[34] With A.R.V., R.S.V., Bruce, C. F. D. Moule, Ridderbos, Robertson, etc., I accept the reading ἡμῶν instead of ὑμῶν. It is true that either reading would make sense. Yet, the phrase "minister . . . on *our* behalf" would seem to harmonize most exactly with the words *"our* fellow-servant." Epaphras, who probably owed his conversion to Paul, had been the apostle's representative to the churches at Colosse, Laodicea, and Hierapolis (cf. 4:13). Another reason for adopting this reading is the fact that it has stronger textual support, "well-distributed and early witnesses" (thus C. F. D. Moule), which cannot be said in the same degree with reference to the alternative reading.

vealed himself in Jesus Christ, which issues in deep and steadfast yearning for the true prosperity of all his children. With respect to the latter aspect of this love — on which according to the present context the emphasis falls — it makes itself manifest in the three graces of oneness, lowliness, and helpfulness (Phil. 2:2-4); hence, in kindness, true sympathy, and the forgiving spirit (Col. 3:12-14). Note the modifier, "y o u r love *in the Spirit.*" Although there are those who maintain that this simply means "spiritual love" without any reference to the Holy Spirit, this opinion runs counter to the fact that in such passages as Rom. 15:30; Gal. 5:22; and Eph. 3:16, 17 Christian love is decidedly regarded as the fruit of the indwelling Spirit. It is implanted and fostered by him. Also, it is rather characteristic of Paul that, having made mention of God the Father (verses 2 and 3) and of Christ Jesus the Son (verses 3, 4, 7), he should now refer to the third person of the Trinity, namely, the Spirit. Cf. Rom. 8:15-17; II Cor. 13:14; Eph. 1:3-14; 2:18; 3:14-17; 4:4-6; 5:18-21.[35]

1:9-14

B. *Prayer*

9. Paul's 218-word sentence starts here at verse 9 and reaches through verse 20. Beginning at verse 15, however, and continuing through verse 20, Christ's Pre-eminence is set forth. Hence, 1:9-14 can be considered a unit of thought all by itself, a touching description of the prayer of Paul and his associates for the Colossians. In the original this part of the sentence — six verses in all — has 106 words.[36] It begins as follows: **And for this reason, that**

---

[35] The phrase ἐν πνεύματι, though not always referring to the Holy Spirit, frequently does so (Rom. 8:9; cf. 8:16; Eph. 2:22; 5:18; 6:18; cf. Jude 20; I Tim. 3:16; see N.T.C. on I and II Timothy and Titus, p. 140). For the reasons given I cannot agree with Lenski's comments on pp. 31 and 32 of his *Interpretation of Colossians, Thessalonians, Timothy, Titus, Philemon.*

[36] The apostle has been accused of "rambling" or of uttering thoughts that reveal no definite sequence. It is true that ideas crowd his mind in such a manner that logical order is not always *immediately* apparent. Accordingly, interpreters are by no means agreed on the grammatical construction of verses 9-14. Some are of the opinion that the apostle is following a zig-zag course, starting out with thanksgiving in verse 3, changing to earnest petition in verse 9, but turning back to the giving of thanks in verse 12. Now even were this true it would be entirely unobjectionable. How often does not this happen to any believer? I am of the opinion, however, that this view of what the apostle is writing is erroneous. In verse 12 it is not Paul who is giving thanks but the Colossians who will be giving thanks if they "walk worthily of the Lord" (verse 10). Grammatically I view the construction of verses 9-14 as follows:

Verse 9

The conjunction καί does not mean, "Not only other people but also we," nor, "Not only are y o u praying for us but also we for y o u." But rather, "We are not only *thanking* God (as in verses 3-8) but we are *also* praying for y o u."

The participles προσευχόμενοι and αἰτούμενοι (though the former indirectly) have

is, not only because of the love mentioned in the immediately preceding verse but on the basis of *all* the evidences of God's grace in the lives of the Colossians as described in verses 3-8, **from the day we heard it we never stopped praying for y o u.** Paul means that he and those associated with him (Timothy, see verse 1; Epaphras and others mentioned in 4:10-14) started to pray now "as they had never prayed before"; that is, granted that there had been prayer for this church before, the news which had reached the apostle upon the recent arrival of Epaphras had brought about a remarkable upsurge in prayer, in fervent intercession, and this with great regularity ("never stopped praying"). It reminds us of the upsurge in Paul's preaching at Corinth after the arrival of Silas and Timothy (Acts 18:5).[37]

The apostle was a firm believer in "the fellowship of prayer": a. he (and those associated with him) praying for those addressed, and b. the latter in turn being requested to pray for him. For a. see Column 1; for b. Column 2. Note that in each of the following instances *the assurance* that Paul prays for those addressed and *the request* (expressed or implied) that they pray for him occurs *in the same letter.*

---

as their object-clause (non-final) ἵνα πληρωθῆτε κ.τ.λ. What Paul was asking for was that the Colossians might be filled with clear knowledge of God's will.

Verse 10a

The infinitive περιπατῆσαι introduces a "contemplated result" statement: "so as to live lives worthy of the Lord," or more literally, "to walk worthily of the Lord" as A.R.V. has it.

Verses 10b-12a

The four participles καρποφοροῦντες, αὐξανόμενοι, δυναμούμενοι, εὐχαριστοῦντες, describe what happens when people live lives worthy of the Lord, so that the Colossians (and in fact all believers everywhere then and now) may know whether they are living such lives and how they may attain to greater perfection in reaching this goal. These participles may therefore be considered *supplementary* to περιπατῆσαι and in that sense *in apposition* with the meaning of the infinitive.

Verses 12b, 13

Mention of the Father in verse 12a leads to the participial modifier τῷ ἱκανώσαντι κ.τ.λ., and to the relative-clause modifier ὃς ἐρρύσατο κ.τ.λ. of verse 13. These are not merely *descriptive* but also *causal*, supplying reasons for thanksgiving.

Verse 14

Mention of "the Son of his love" in verse 13 gives rise to the relative modifier ἐν ᾧ ἔχομεν κ.τ.λ., setting forth *in summary* the redemptive significance of Christ, a fact on which the apostle is going to expatiate.

Conclusion: there surely is no rambling here. The thoughts follow each other in excellent sequence.

[37] Sometimes more meaning is poured into these simple words than would seem to be warranted. Paul's statement is used in order to strengthen the view that he had never been in Colosse, that he knew nobody there, that the church had just now been founded, etc. See what has been said about this in the *Introduction*, II. The City of Colosse, A. Geography; and see also on 2:1.

1.	2.
Rom. 1:9	15:30
Eph. 1:16	6:18, 19
Phil. 1:4	3:17a; 4:9 (implied)
Col. 1:9	4:3
I Thess. 1:2	5:25
II Thess. 1:11	3:1
Philem. 4	22

On the basis of blessings already received the apostle asks for additional favors. Encouraged by evidences of God's grace already present he requests increasing proofs. That is the meaning of "And for this reason," etc. The Lord does not want his people to ask for too little. In the *spiritual* sphere he does not want them to live frugally, parsimoniously. Let them live richly and royally, in harmony with Psalm 81:1!

Now the prayer which is reported here in verses 9b-14 should be compared with Paul's prayers found in the other epistles of his first Roman imprisonment (Eph. 1:17-23; 3:14-21; Phil. 1:9-11). Combining them we notice that the apostle prays that those addressed may abound in such matters as wisdom, knowledge, power, endurance, long-suffering, joy, gratitude, and love. Also, that Jesus Christ (here "the Son of his love") is regarded as the One through whom these graces are bestowed upon the believer, and that the glory of God (here "the giving of thanks to the Father") is recognized as the ultimate purpose. Truly, one cannot afford to ignore Paul's lessons in prayer-life.

Paul had just used the word *praying*. He now adds **asking**. Praying is the more general and comprehensive term. It indicates any form of reverent address directed to the Deity, whether we "take hold of God" by means of intercession, supplication, adoration, or thanksgiving. *Asking* is more specific. It refers to making definite, humble requests. See also Phil. 4:6; I Tim. 2:1 on various synonyms for prayer. The sentence continues, **that you may be filled with** [38] **clear knowledge of his will (such clear knowledge consisting) in all spiritual wisdom and understanding.** It is vain to try to serve God without *knowing* what he desires of us (Acts 22:10, 14; Rom. 12:2). Now the knowledge here referred to is no abstract, theoretical learning. Such merely theoretical knowledge might be possessed by any nominal Christian, and in fact to a certain extent by a professed unbeliever and even by Satan himself. Neither does Paul have in mind a store of occult information, such

---

[38] "Filled with" is correct, even though the verb πληρόω is here used with the accusative, as in Phil. 1:11 (cf. II Thess. 1:11). Elsewhere the apostle uses it with the dative (Rom. 1:29; II Cor. 7:4) or with the genitive (Rom. 15:13, 14). This simply shows that there is no fixed rule with respect to the case that follows this verb. The tendency, moreover, was toward the accusative.

as acquaintance with passwords. It is not the kind of mysterious *gnosis* which teachers of the *gnostic* type claimed for their "initiates." On the contrary, it is penetrating insight into God's wonderful, redemptive revelation in Jesus Christ, a discernment with fruits for practical life, as the immediately following context (verse 10) also indicates. It results from fellowship with God and leads to deeper fellowship. Hence, this *clear knowledge* (ἐπίγνωσις) is heart-transforming and life-renewing. All the instances of the use of this word in the New Testament point in this definite direction: Rom. 1:28; 10:2; Eph. 1:17; 4:13; Phil. 1:9, 10; Col. 1:9, 10; 2:3; 3:10; I Tim. 2:4; II Tim. 2:25; 3:7; Titus 1:1; Philem. 6; Heb. 10:26; II Peter 1:2, 3, 8; II Peter 2:20; and cf. the cognate verb in I Cor. 13:12. Compare also the Old Testament background: "The fear of Jehovah is the beginning of knowledge" (Prov. 1:7; cf. 9:10; also Ps. 25:12, 14; 111:10). Paul prays that those addressed may *be filled* with such rich, deep experiential knowledge of God's will. No doubt we have here an intentional allusion to the gnostic error with which false teachers were striving to lead the Colossians astray. It is as if Paul were saying: "The *clear knowledge* of God's will which is our basic petition for y o u is incomparably richer and more satisfying than the *knowledge* or *gnosis* that is held out to y o u by the advocates of heresy." The penetrating knowledge which is part of the Christian's spiritual equipment consists in "all spiritual wisdom and understanding." Such *wisdom* is the ability to use the best means in order to reach the highest goal, a life to God's glory. It amounts to *understanding* that is at once spiritual and practical. It is not deceived by the wiles of Satan, the lure of the flesh, or the pretentious claims of false teachers. Such *wisdom and understanding* — for the combination of these two words see Ex. 31:3; 35:31, 35; Isa. 10:13; 11:2; etc. — is the work of the Holy Spirit in human hearts. On the characteristics of true wisdom see also the beautiful passage, James 3:17.

10-12. The practical purpose or contemplated result of this clear knowledge which is the starting-point in Paul's prayer for the Colossians is now stated: **so as to live lives worthy of the Lord** (cf. Eph. 4:1; Phil. 1:27; I Thess. 2:12; III John 6). The apostle and those who are with him pray that the Colossians may "walk" (cf. Gen. 5:22, 24; 6:9, etc.) or conduct themselves in harmony with the responsibilities which their new relationship to God imposes and with the blessings which this new relationship brings. There must be nothing half-hearted about this manner of life. On the contrary, it must be **to (his) complete delight** (see further on 3:22), a conscious striving to please God in everything (cf. I Cor. 10:31; I Thess. 4:1). That this God-glorifying conduct will actually be the result of being filled with *clear knowledge* of his will is easy to see, for the more God's children know him, the more they will also love him; and the more they love him, the more they will also wish to obey him in thought, word, and deed.

By means of four participles the apostle now describes this life of sanctification:

(1) **in every good work bearing fruit.**

Paul attaches high value to good works viewed as the fruit — not the root — of grace. Eph. 2:8-10 is his own commentary.

(2) **and growing in the clear knowledge of God.**[39]

Note that the apostle makes the clear knowledge of God both the starting-point (verse 9) and the resulting characteristic (verse 10) of the God-pleasing life. This is not strange: true, experiential knowledge of God brings about an ever-increasing measure of this very commodity. Thus, though at the very beginning of the story Job already knew God, at a much later time he was able to testify:

> "I had heard of thee by the hearing of the ear;
> But now my eye sees thee;
> Therefore I abhor myself,
> And repent in dust and ashes" (Job 42:5, 6).

Of similar import are such passages as, "They go from strength to strength" (Ps. 84:7). "The path of the righteous is as the dawning light, that shines more and more unto the perfect day" (Prov. 4:18). The very apostle Paul, even when he already knew Christ, is still praying for increased knowledge: "that I may know him" (Phil. 3:10).

(3) **being invigorated with all vigor.**

The maxim, "Knowledge is power" is true in spiritual life more than anywhere else. When a person grows in the clear knowledge of God, his strength and courage increase. The divine indwelling presence enables him to say, "I can do all things in him who infuses strength into me" (Phil. 4:13). Paul adds, **in accordance with his glorious might.** "In accordance with" is stronger than "of" or "by." When the multimillionaire gives "of" his wealth to some

---

[39] What is said of the gospel in verse 6 — bearing fruit and growing — is said of believers here. But this does not rule out the idea that here in verse 10 each participle has its own modifier. Since, in view of Gal. 5:19, 22; Phil. 1:22, it is not unnatural that "bearing fruit" should take as its modifier "in every good work," and since, in view of II Peter 3:18, it is not illogical that "growing" or "increasing" be associated with "in the clear knowledge of God," and finally, since here in Col. 1:10 these two modifiers (ἐν παντὶ ἔργῳ ἀγαθῷ and τῇ ἐπιγνώσει τοῦ θεοῦ) are rather widely separated, there is no compelling reason to depart from those English renderings (A.V., A.R.V., R.S.V., N.E.B.) which associate the first modifier with καρποφοροῦντες, the second with αὐξανόμενοι. The only slight change I suggest (see my rendering) is to retain the chiastic word-order that is found in the original; hence,

modifier   participle

participle   modifier

good cause he may be giving very little; but when he donates "in accordance with" his riches, the amount will be substantial. The Holy Spirit gives not only "of" but "in accordance with." Eph. 1:19-23 shows why God's might is indeed "glorious." What this *strength in action* (κράτος) enables believers to do is stated in the words **so as to exercise every kind of endurance and longsuffering.** Endurance is the grace to bear up under, the bravery of perseverance in the performance of one's God-given task in spite of every hardship and trial, the refusal to succumb to despair or cowardice. It is a human attribute and is shown in connection with *things,* that is, *circumstances* in which a person is involved: affliction, suffering, persecution, etc. *Longsuffering* characterizes the person who, in relation to those who oppose or molest him, exercises patience, refusing to yield to passion or to outbursts of anger. In the writings of Paul it is associated with such virtues as kindness, mercy, love, goodness, compassion, meekness, lowliness, forbearance, and the forgiving spirit (Rom. 2:4; Gal. 5:22; Eph. 4:2; Col. 3:12, 13). In distinction from *endurance* this *longsuffering* is not only a human but also a divine attribute. It is ascribed to God (Rom. 2:4; 9:22), to Christ (I Tim. 1:16), as well as to man (II Cor. 6:6; Gal. 5:22; Eph. 4:2; Col. 3:12, 13; II Tim. 4:2). Another distinction is that longsuffering is shown in one's attitude *not* to things but to persons. Considered as human virtues both endurance and longsuffering are divine gifts (Rom. 15:5; Gal. 5:22), and both are inspired by hope, by trust in the fulfilment of God's promises (Rom. 8:25; I Thess. 1:3; II Tim. 4:2, 8; Heb. 6:12).

(4) **with joy** [40] **giving thanks to the Father.**

Due to strength imparted by God, believers are able, even in the midst of tribulation, to give thanks with joy and to rejoice with thanksgiving (cf. Matt. 5:10-12; Luke 6:22, 23; Acts 5:41; II Cor. 4:7-17; Phil. 1:12-21). It is to the Father that this thanks is given, for it is he who through "the Son of his love" (verse 13) freely gives us all things (Rom. 8:32). Paul stresses the necessity of thanksgiving again and again (II Cor. 1:11; Eph. 5:20; Phil. 4:6;

---

[40] I follow N.N.'s punctuation here. The thought expressed in verse 11 probably does not need one more modifier dragging on behind. Besides, by separating the phrase "with joy" from the participle "giving thanks," the latter would be the only participle (of the four) having no modifier.

Lightfoot's argument to the effect that "with joy" when added to "giving thanks" would be meaningless because thanksgiving "is in itself an act of rejoicing" is hardly convincing. Authors, both sacred and secular, frequently add such modifiers in order to stress a certain aspect of the word modified. If "with joy" added to "giving thanks" is pleonastic, why should not the same be true in the immediately preceding verse with respect to the modifier "with all vigor" added to "being invigorated"? The New Testament has numerous similar examples. This phenomenon when not overdone serves to make a writer's style interesting and vivid.

It must be admitted, however, that whether one says "so as to exercise every kind of endurance and longsuffering with joy, giving thanks," etc., or "so as to exercise every kind of endurance and longsuffering, with joy giving thanks," etc., makes little difference in resultant meaning.

Col. 3:17; I Thess. 5:18). In the present connection the reasons why the Colossians should thank the Father are given in verses 12b, 13. Here it is pointed out that the Father is the One **who qualified y o u** [41] **for a share in the inheritance of the saints in the light.** Just as in the old dispensation the Lord provided for Israel an earthly inheritance, which was distributed to the various tribes and smaller units of national life *by lot* (Gen. 31:14; Num. 18:20; Josh. 13:16; 14:2; 16:1, etc.), so he had provided for the Colossians *an allotment* or *share* in the better inheritance. These people, drawn mainly from the Gentile world (see *Introduction* III B), had been at one time "separated from Christ, alienated from the commonwealth of Israel, and strangers to the covenants of the promise, having no hope and without God in the world." But "now in Christ Jesus those who were once far off" had been "brought near in the blood of Christ" (Eph. 2:12, 13).

The fact that this share in the inheritance is a matter of *sovereign grace* and has nothing to do with human merit is clear first of all from the very word used, namely, *inheritance:* one *receives* an inheritance as a gift; one does not *earn* it. It is emphasized by the words, "who *qualified* y o u." The best comment on this verse is Paul's statement in II Cor. 3:5: "our sufficiency is from God." It is God who *makes worthy* [42] those who in themselves are not worthy, and who thus *enables* them to have a share in the inheritance.

The inheritance *of the saints* means the inheritance of redeemed believers, that is, of those human individuals who, having been drawn out of darkness and having been brought into the light, are consecrated to God. Though some commentators are of the opinion that here in Col. 1:12 *saints* refers to *angels*, there is no basis for this view. Paul loves the word *saints*, using it again and again in his epistles. Not once does he employ it to indicate the angels, always the redeemed (see Rom. 1:7; 8:27; 12:13; 15:25, 26, 31; 16:2, 15; I Cor. 1:2; 6:1, 2; 14:33; etc.). Even I Thess. 3:13 is no exception; see N.T.C. on that passage.

This inheritance "of the saints" is at the same time the inheritance "in the light." This is "the light of the *knowledge* of the glory of God in the face of Jesus Christ" (II Cor. 4:16). It is "the *love* of God poured out in our hearts through the Holy Spirit" (Rom. 5:5); "the *peace* of God that surpasses all understanding" (Phil. 4:7); "the *joy* inexpressible and full of glory" (I Peter 1:8).

The fact that in Scripture the word *light* is actually used metaphorically to symbolize all of these ideas and more besides is clear from the following passages, in every one of which the word *light* is used in an interpretive context:

---

[41] The textual support for ἡμᾶς is weaker. It is probably due to assimilation: see ἡμᾶς in verse 13.
[42] In the Dutch language the basic idea of the verb can be brought out by the verb *verwaardigen*.

The word *light* used in close connection with:

(1) *holiness, being sanctified* (Acts 20:32; 26:18, 23). These passages are especially important since they occur in Paul's own speeches.

(2) *the divine revelation: truth,* and *insight into that revelation: knowledge* (Ps. 36:9; II Cor. 4:4, 6)

(3) *love* (I John 2:9, 10)

(4) *glory* (Isa. 60:1-3)

(5) *peace, prosperity, liberty, joy* (Ps. 97:11; Isa. 9:1-7).

Since God himself is in his very being holiness, omniscience, love, glory, etc., and since to his people he is the Source of all the graces and blessings mentioned above under (1)-(5), he is himself *light*. "God is light, and in him is no darkness at all" (I John 1:5). Jesus said, "I am the light of the world" (John 8:12). As such God is in Christ his people's *salvation. Light* and *salvation* are therefore synonyms (Ps. 27:1; Isa. 49:6). So is *light* and the divine *grace* or *favor* (Ps. 44:3).

The opposite of light is *darkness,* which, accordingly, is symbolical of *Satan* and *his angels;* hence, also of sin, disobedience, rebellion, ignorance, blindness, falsehood, hatred, wrath, shame, strife, lack, bondage, and gloom, as is shown by several of the very passages referred to above, under (1)-(5), and by many others.

What the apostle is saying, therefore, here in Col. 1:12, is that the Father of his beloved Son Jesus Christ — hence, also our Father — has in his sovereign grace made the Colossians worthy of, and competent to receive, a share of the inheritance of the saints in the realm of *salvation* full and free. The further question, "Is this realm present or future?" is not difficult to answer. *In principle* the Colossians have already entered it. They have already been "transferred into the kingdom of the Son of his love" (Col. 1:13; cf. Eph. 2:13). The *full possession,* however, pertains to the future. It is "the hope that is laid up for them in the heavens" (Col. 1:15). From the Lord they will receive the reward, namely, the inheritance (Col. 3:24). See also Eph. 1:18; Phil. 3:20, 21; and cf. Heb. 3:7–4:11.[43] Paul *prays* — for it must be borne in mind that this is still part of the prayer — that for all this the Colossians may be constantly and joyfully thanking God.

13, 14. Verses 13 and 14 *summarize* the divine work of redemption. The details follow in verses 15-23. This reminds us of Romans, where 1:16, 17 summarizes what is described in greater detail in Rom. 1:18–8:39.

Paul's heart was in his writing. He never wrote in the abstract when he discussed the great blessings which believers have in Christ. He was ever deeply conscious of the fact that upon *him,* too, though completely unworthy, the Father had bestowed these favors. Hence, it is not surprising that, deeply

---

[43] The futuristic reference of Col. 1:12 does not receive its due in Lenski's interpretation of the passage.

moved by what he is writing, he changes the wording, from "y o u" to "us": verse 13, "who qualified *y o u* . . ."; verse 14, "and who rescued *us.* . . ." Besides, note how all the main ideas of verses 12-14 — *darkness, light, inheritance, remission of sins* [44] — occur also in Acts 26:18, 23, passages that record *Paul's own* experience and predict the experience of the Gentiles to whom he was now sent. The apostle, accordingly, in describing the kindnesses which had been conferred upon the Colossians and upon himself and his associates, yes, even upon all rescued sinners, echoes the very words which the Savior had used in addressing him, even "Saul," the great and dreadful persecutor:

"I am Jesus whom you are persecuting. But rise and stand upon your feet since for this purpose I have appeared to you . . . delivering you from the people and from the Gentiles, to whom I am sending you, to open their eyes that they may turn from *darkness* to *light* and from the power [or: jurisdiction] of Satan to God, that they may receive *remission* of sins and an *inheritance* among those who are sanctified by faith in me" (Acts 26:15b-18, quoted in part).

So Paul writes: **and who rescued** [45] **us.** He drew us to himself, delivering us from our condition of wretchedness. The verb *rescued* in the present context implies both the utterly hopeless darkness and misery in which, apart from God's mercy, "we" (the Colossians, Paul, etc.) had been groping about, and the glorious but arduous redemptive work that was necessary to emancipate us from our wretched state. The Father rescued us by sending his Son into the flesh (Col. 1:22; 2:9; cf. Gal. 1:15, 16; 4:4, 5) in order:

a. to die for our sins on the cross (Col. 1:22; 2:14; cf. Gal. 2:20; 6:14), and

b. to rise and ascend to heaven, whence he poured the Spirit into our hearts (Col. 3:1; cf. II Thess. 2:13; John 16:7), so that we, having been called (Col. 1:6, 7; cf. Gal. 1:15, 16; Phil. 3:14), were "made alive" (Col. 2:13; cf. Eph. 2:1-5; John 3:3; Acts 16:14), and by an act of genuine conversion accepted Christ Jesus as Lord and were baptized (Col. 2:6, 12; cf. Acts 9:1-19).

This entire process is covered by the words, "He rescued us," [46] and this,

---

[44] Notice even ἐξουσίας in Acts 26:18 and here in Col. 1:13.

[45] In the original "who qualified y o u," etc. (verse 12) is a participial modifier, but "who rescued us," etc. (verse 13) is a relative clause. The latter gives to the thought expressed a degree of independence, so that it is not so closely joined with that which precedes. The *prayer* begins to merge with a *description* of the generosity of the Father (verse 13) and with a summarizing statement regarding the redemptive work accomplished by means of the Son (verses 13b, 14).

[46] It is sometimes argued that since ἐρρύσατο is aorist, the reference must be to one definite act. On this assumption some commentators are of the opinion that the expression "He rescued us" refers solely to Christ's death on the cross; others, solely to conversion and baptism. But the aorist tense does not necessarily refer to just *one act.* On the contrary, the aorist *summarizes,* viewing all that happened as *one fact.* See also N.T.C. on John 2:20.

out of the domain of darkness, the sphere in which Satan exercises his usurped jurisdiction (Matt. 4:8-11; Luke 22:52, 53; cf. Acts 26:18) over human hearts, lives, activities, and over all "the powers of the air," "the spiritual hosts of wickedness in the heavenly places" (Eph. 2:2; 6:12). (For the meaning of *light* and *darkness* see above on verse 12.) Helpless, hopeless slaves were we, chained by our sins in Satan's prison . . . until the Conqueror came to our rescue (cf. II Cor. 2:14). It was God in Christ who rescued us **and transplanted us into the kingdom of the Son of his love.** He brought us out of the dark and dismal realm of false ideas and chimerical ideals into the sun-bathed land of clear knowledge and realistic expectation; out of the bewildering sphere of perverted cravings and selfish hankerings into the blissful realm of holy yearnings and glorious self-denials; out of the miserable dungeon of intolerable bonds and heart-rending cries into the magnificent palace of glorious liberty and joyful songs.

"Out of my bondage, sorrow and night,
Jesus, I come, Jesus, I come;
Into Thy freedom, gladness and light,
Jesus, I come to Thee;
Out of my sickness into Thy health,
Out of my want and into Thy wealth,
Out of my sin and into Thyself,
Jesus, I come to Thee.

"Out of the fear and dread of the tomb,
Jesus, I come, Jesus, I come;
Into the joy and light of Thy home,
Jesus, I come to Thee;
Out of the depths of ruin untold,
Into the peace of Thy sheltering fold,
Ever Thy glorious face to behold,
Jesus, I come to Thee."

(W. T. Sleeper)

It is probable that the underlying figure is one which those addressed — both Gentile and Jew — readily understood. These people knew that earthly rulers would at times transplant a conquered people from one country to another (II Kings 15:29; 17:3-6; 18:13; 24:14-16; 25:11; II Chron. 36:20; Jer. 52:30; Dan. 1:1-4; Ezek. 1:1; see also above: *Introduction, II. The City of Colosse,* C). So also "we" have been transplanted, and this *not* from liberty into slavery but from slavery into liberty. Let us then stand in that liberty. Let us not think that our deliverance is only of a partial character, or that by means of mystic rites, painful ceremonies, worship of angels, or any other means (then or now) we must slowly work our way up from sin

63

to holiness. *Once for all* we have been delivered. We have been transplanted not out of darkness into semi-darkness, but out of dismal darkness into "marvelous light" (I Peter 2:9). We have *even now* arrived in "the kingdom of the Son of his (the Father's) love." [47] Here is what may truly be called "realized eschatology." *In principle* we already in this present life partake of the promised glory. God has already begun a good work in us, and as to the future each one of us is able to testify:

> "The work thou hast in me begun
> Shall by thy grace be fully done" (cf. Ps. 138:8; Phil. 1:6).

"We" have received the Holy Spirit. And his indwelling presence is the "earnest" (first instalment and pledge) of our inheritance (Eph. 1:4; cf. II Cor. 1:22; 5:5). It is the guarantee of still greater glory to come. This follows also from the fact that the Christ who merited this glory for us is "the Son of the Father's love." He is both the Object of this love (Isa. 42:1; Ps. 2:7; Prov. 8:30; Matt. 3:17; 17:5; Luke 3:22) and its personal manifestation (John 1:18; 14:9; 17:26). How then shall not the Father "together with him" freely give us all things? (Rom. 8:32). We have been transplanted into the Kingdom of the Son of God's love, **in whom we have our redemption,** that is, our *deliverance as the result of the payment of a ransom.* Just as according to Israel's ancient law the forfeited life could be ransomed (Ex. 21:30), so our life, forfeited through sin, was ransomed by the shedding of Christ's blood (Eph. 1:7).[48] Besides, as A. Deissmann remarks, "When anybody heard the

---

[47] We must be careful at this point not to burden the exegesis with unworkable distinctions; for example, the one according to which "the kingdom of the Son" pertains to the present, but that "of God" to the future. See O. Cullmann, *Königsherrschaft Christi und Kirche im N.T.* Over against that view, which bases too much on I Cor. 15:23 f., Karl L. Schmidt correctly states that it is impossible to speak about the kingdom of Christ without also speaking about the kingdom of God (article βασιλεία in Th.W.N.T., Vol. I, p. 582). A careful examination of such passages as Eph. 5:5, Rev. 12:10, and a comparison of Rom. 14:17 with John 18:36 and with I Cor. 4:20 shows that no sharp distinction, to be applied wherever these two terms or their synonyms are used, is possible. The kingdom of God, to be sure, is everlasting. But so also is the kingdom of the Son (Luke 1:33; Heb. 1:8; II Peter 1:11).

[48] Though, according to the best textual evidence, the *words* "through his blood" (cf. Eph. 1:7) must not be inserted in Col. 1:14, the *idea,* cannot be excluded. Büchsel. to be sure, *denies* that in *any* biblical reference to redemption the idea of a payment of a ransom is present (article ἀπολύτρωσις, Th.W.N.T., Vol. IV, pp. 354-359). But the evidence is clearly on the other side. Matt. 20:28; Mark 10:45 show that Christ came to give his life as a ransom for many. The words "through the redemption that is in Christ Jesus," (Rom. 3:24), in the light of the verse that immediately follows, indicates the payment of a blood-ransom. The same idea is expressed not only in Eph. 1:7, as already mentioned, but also in Heb. 9:15 (cf. verse 12). It is true that by means of a semantic shift a more general connotation — *deliverance, emancipation, release, restoration,* dropping the idea "through the payment of a ransom" — attaches to the word in Luke 21:28; Rom. 8:23; I Cor. 1:30; Eph. 1:14; 4:30; Heb. 11:35. But it is not fair to generalize. Each passage has to be studied in its own specific context. Paul again and again stresses the idea that our

Greek word λύτρον, *ransom* [on which the word ἀπολύτρωσις, *redemption* is based] . . . it was natural for him to think of the purchase-money for manumitting slaves." Hence, "in him," that is, *through spiritual union with him* (Col. 3:1-3), *redemption* full and free is ours. This redemption is, accordingly, emancipation from the curse (Gal. 3:13), particularly from enslavement to sin (John 8:34; Rom. 7:14; I Cor. 7:23), and release to true liberty (John 8:36; Gal. 5:1). Through *Christ's* payment of a ransom and *our* faith in him we have obtained from the Father **the forgiveness** or *remission* (cf. Ps. 103:12) **of our sins.** The chain that held us fast has been broken. Though the apostle uses this *expression* "forgiveness of sins" (which is of such frequent occurrence elsewhere in the New Testament),[49] only here and in Eph. 1:7 (forgiveness of . . . *trespasses*), and though he generally conveys a similar idea by words and phrases that belong to the "justification by faith" family, he was, nevertheless, well acquainted with the *idea* of forgiveness of sins, as is shown by Rom. 4:7; II Cor. 5:19; and in Colossians by 2:13 and 3:13. In fact, in Colossians the idea of forgiveness is even emphasized. See footnote 131.

Justification and remission are inseparable. So are also redemption and remission, though this was at times denied. Thus Irenaeus in his work *Against Heresies* I.xxi.2, written about A. D. 182-188, tells us about certain heretics in his day who taught that here in this life salvation occurs in the following two stages:

a. *Remission of sins* at baptism, instituted by the visible, human Jesus;

b. *Redemption* at a later stage, through the divine Christ who descended on Jesus. In this second stage the person whose sins have already been forgiven attains to *perfection* or *fulness.*

It is *possible,* in view of such passages as Col. 2:9, 10; 4:12, that the errorists at Colosse were already spreading this or a similar notion. In any event, it was through the Holy Spirit, who knows all things even *before* they happen and is therefore able to issue warnings that apply to the future as well as to the present, that the apostle wrote these words. They clearly indicate that when a sinner is transplanted out of the power of darkness into the kingdom of light, he is to be regarded as having been *redeemed,* and that this *redemption* implies *the remission of sins.*

Lord paid an enormous price to obtain redemption for his people. It is in the light of such passages as I Cor. 6:10; 7:23; Gal. 3:13; 4:5; I Tim. 2:6; that Col. 1:14 must be explained. Other relevant passages are Ps. 49:8; Matt. 20:28; Mark 10:45; John 1:29; 3:17; I Peter 1:18, 19; Rev. 5:6, 9, 12; 7:14; 12:11.
[49] See Matt. 26:28; Mark 1:4; Luke 1:77; 3:3; 24:47; Acts 2:38; 5:31; 10:43; 13:38; 26:18. Cf. for a fuller account E. Percy, *Die Probleme der Kolosser und Epheserbriefe,* pp. 85, 86. Also B. B. Warfield, *The Person and Work of Christ,* pp. 429 ff., and E. K. Simpson, *Words Worth Weighing in the Greek New Testament,* p. 8 f.

1:15-20
III. *The Son's Pre-eminence*

Verses 15-20 form a unit. If it was not a literary gem composed by the apostle himself, it was probably a hymn or other fixed testimony of the early church adopted by Paul and reproduced here by him either without change or with alterations suitable to the needs of the Colossian church. It is, in any case, a unit and for that reason is here printed in its entirety. And since it clearly consists of two parts these have been reproduced here in parallel columns.[50] The relation of the theme to its two divisions is as follows. The Son's Pre-eminence is shown:

A. In Creation (verses 15-17)	B. In Redemption (verses 18-20)
15 Who is the image of the invisible God, The firstborn of every creature,	18 And he is the head of the body, the church; Who is the beginning, the first-born from the dead, That in all things he might have the pre-eminence,
16 For in him were created all things In the heavens and on the earth, The visible and the invisible, Whether thrones or dominions or principalities or authorities, All things through him and with a view to him have been created;	19 For in him he [God] was pleased to have all the fulness dwell, 20 And through him to reconcile all things to himself, Having made peace through the blood of his cross, Through him, whether the things on the earth Or the things in the heavens.
17 And he is before all things, And all things hold together in him.	

Very striking and solemn are these lines. Note the following points of correspondence between A. and B.:

	A.	B.
(1) "Who is" in verse	15	18
(2) "The firstborn" in verse	15	18
(3) "For in him" in verse	16	19
(4) "In the heavens and on the earth" in verse	16	cf. 20

[50] In order to emphasize the formal correspondence between A. and B., section B. is often printed as beginning with 18b. Thus both A. and B. would begin with the words "Who is." On the other hand as to *content*, B. should begin as printed, namely, with verse 18a, which clearly pertains to Christ's pre-eminence in the realm of redemption.

Not only do *the same expressions occur* in both columns but they occur *in the same sequence!* There is a definite idea-and-form parallelism. The glory of Christ in Creation is balanced by his majesty in Redemption. There are also other items of resemblance; for example, the expression "all things," occurring four times in verses 15-17 and twice in verses 18-20. And the words "through him" of verse 16 are repeated twice in verse 20.

As to the origin and nature of these impressive, solemn, and carefullv balanced lines, there are *two main* views. See, however, footnote.[51]

---

[51]   A. *Various Views*

(1) Verses 12-20 are to be regarded as a primitive Christian baptismal liturgy, which in verses 15-20 make use of a hymn of Gnostic origin. Ernst Käsemann, "Eine urchristliche Taufliturgie," *Festschrift Rudolf Bultmann zum 65. Geburtstag überreicht* (1949), pp. 133-148.

(2) Col. 1:15-20 is part of a eucharistic liturgy. G. Bornkamm, *Theol. Blätter*, 1942, p. 61.

(3) Col. 1:13-29 shows us a primitive Christian worship-service. There is a definite pattern of arrangement of clauses according to a 3-7, 3-7 numerical scheme. Ernst Lohmeyer, in *Meyer Commentary* (8th ed., 1930).

(4) Col. 1:15-20 constitutes one of the earliest Christian hymns. Paul included this hymn in his letter to the Colossians. O. A. Piper, "The Savior's Eternal Work; An Exegesis of Col. 1:9-29," *Int* 3 (1949), pp. 286-298.

(5) The passage is a Christological confession composed by Paul. This was the opinion to which Martin Dibelius finally arrived. See his commentary, *An die Kolosser, Epheser, an Philemon*, in *Lietzmann's Handbuch zum Neuen Testament*, 3rd ed. revised by H. Greeven, 1953. Ernst Percy also believed that the lines were written by Paul. For proof he pointed to style similarity; cf. Col. 1:16 with I Cor. 3:21; 12:13; and Gal. 3:26-28. See his well-known work *Die Probleme der Kolosser- und Epheserbriefe*, p. 65.

(6) The lines embody traditional forms of predication, Jewish periods, and a Stoic omnipotence-formula. Eduard Norden, *Agnostos Theos*, 1913.

(7) They owe their origin to the Jewish Wisdom literature (Prov. 8:22-31; Ecclus. 1:4; 43:26). H. Windisch, "Die göttliche Weisheit der Juden und die paulinische Christologie," in *Neutest. Studien für Heinrici*, 1914, pp. 220-234. Closely related to this is the suggestion of C. F. Burney that these lines might be a meditation on Prov. 8:22 in connection with Gen. 1:1. See his article, "Christ as the ARXH of Creation," *JTS* xxvii (1925, 1926), pp. 160 ff. Another related view is that the passage, Col. 1:15-20, is "by St. Paul himself, though possibly in words drawn in part from some Hellenistic hymn to the Wisdom or Word of God." C. F. D. Moule, *The Epistle of Paul the Apostle to the Colossians and to Philemon*, p. 61.

(8) They embody an early Christian hymn of praise to Christ, augmented by the words "and he is the head of his body, the Church." The passage is to be regarded as a non-Pauline composition. C. Masson, *Comm. du NT*, Vol. X. By eliminating certain words he arrives at a parallelism that adheres to strict and definite rules.

(9) Whatever be their origin, they show a definite stylistic pattern, a strophic arrangement. But just what was this *strophic* arrangement? Various attempts at reconstruction have been made. In addition to those by Käsemann, Lohmeyer, Norden, and Masson (see above for references to their writings), there are those by P. Benoit, *La Sainte Bible traduite en français sous la direction de l'Ecole Biblique de Jérusalem*; G. Schille, "Liturgisches Gut im Epheserbrief" (doctoral dissertation, Göttingen, 1952); C. Maurer, "Die Begründung der Herrschaft Christi über die Mächte nach Kolosser 1, 15-20," *Wort und Dienst, Jahrbuch der Theologischen Schule Bethel*, n.F.IV (1955), pp. 79-93; and, last but not least, J. M. Robinson, "A

The first of these two acceptable theories is this: Paul himself composed and dictated the lines. Those who favor this view generally add that Col. 1:15-20 is not a hymn.

The second is this: the passage is a pre-Pauline hymn or well-known and oft-repeated early saying or testimony. Paul, having learned this "hymn" or "saying" which had endeared itself to his heart, made it a part of his letter, either with no addition or alteration or else with slight changes to suit his own purpose.

The following arguments have been advanced in favor of *the first* alternative:

(1) Recognizable quantitative meter such as one might expect in a hymn is found here only after considerable conjectural reconstruction.

(2) It was natural for Paul, a highly emotional person who was writing on a lofty theme (Christ's Pre-eminence) to express himself in such a solemn way. And since many Old Testament passages, very familiar to Paul, praised *Jehovah's* majesty in parallelistic phraseology (Ps. 93; 96; 103; 121; 136; 145-150; etc.), the apostle, under the guidance of the Spirit, would almost

Formal Analysis of Colossians 1:15-20," *JBL,* Vol. LXXVI, Part IV (Dec., 1957), pp. 270-288.

(10) Although the formal style and the correspondence between Col. 1:15-18a and 18b-20 do give to these lines a striking and solemn aspect, these characteristics do not prove whether, on the one hand, we are dealing here with a hymn or other liturgical unit or whether, on the other hand, we have here an example of Paul's own preaching concerning the glory of Christ. A hymnal unit is obtained only after considerable reconstruction of the text. H. Ridderbos, *Aan De Kolossenzen,* in *Commentaar op het Nieuwe Testament,* p. 151. He does, however, definitely favor a division of Col. 1:15-20 into *two* — and not into *four* — parts.

B. *Criticism*

Several of these thories are open to serious objection. Thus, in a letter which combats incipient Gnosticism one would hardly look for the incorporation of a Gnostic hymn. Again, though *all things* were created in and through and with a view to Christ and though *all things* cohere in him, there is no need to see any Stoic influence in this idea. As to the possible influence of Wisdom literature, *if* there be any such influence it would pertain to the manner of expression, not directly to the essence. It is at the most marginal, affecting form rather than content. Besides, the poetic personification of Wisdom found in Wisdom literature is not *directly* the Son of God himself whom Paul in Colossians has *immediately* in mind. As to those theories which, *without any textual support,* leave out entirely or re-arrange words, phrases or whole lines, in order to arrive at this or that *precise* strophical scheme, in which everything will be perfectly balanced, I cannot accept them. The very fact that so many of them have been tried out, each claiming to be better than the others, condemns them. As to finding here either a baptismal or a eucharistic liturgy, this, too, is very subjective. It is "found" by those who put it there.

The true reason for Col. 1:15-20 lies ready at hand. That reason is the Christ himself in very person, the One who existed from all eternity, became incarnate, fulfilled his amazingly glorious earthly ministry, suffered and died vicariously, rose from the grave, ascended to heaven, and from the Father's right hand sent forth the Spirit.

naturally express himself in similar language in setting forth the majesty of *Christ.*

(3) There is nothing in this passage that can be considered foreign to Paul's main theme in Colossians.

(4) The Paul of I Corinthians and Galatians writes in similar style. See footnote 51,A.5 above.

Those who disagree might answer as follows:

With respect to (1). Does every hymn have recognizable quantitative meter?

With respect to (2). Would anyone, writing spontaneously in the freely flowing style of a letter, compose a passage consisting of two parts which contain not only the same phrases, but even these same phrases arranged in the same sequence?

With respect to (3). True, but this is not in conflict with either theory.

With respect to (4). At best the passages to which Percy refers furnish only partial proof. They do not contain a true and full stylistic parallel to what is found in Col. 1:15-20.

Now though the first theory may, after all, be correct, there would seem to be a stronger argument in support of *the second.* Note the following:

(1) The primitive Church had not only its Old Testament Psalms but also other hymns. Cf. I Cor. 14:26. Paul loved "psalms and hymns and spiritual songs."

Is not this clearly stated in Col. 3:16?

Very vividly illustrated in I Tim. 3:16?

And also clearly motivated by John 3:16?

The early church also had its famous "reliable sayings" (I Tim. 1:15; 3:1; 4:8, 9; II Tim. 2:11-13; Titus 3:4-8). All such sayings, testimonies, confessions, and songs were passed from mouth to mouth and from heart to heart, until they had embedded themselves in the very soul of the community, where all the fears, hopes, struggles, and joys of believers played around them. It would not be strange, therefore, if Paul here in Col. 1:15-20 were actually quoting, either exactly or with some additional word of application, a saying or hymn which had already secured for itself a place of prominence in the life of the Church.

Note, moreover, that Col. 1:15-20 bears testimony to the greatness of Christ, which is the very theme of I Tim. 3:16. That passage, as already indicated, in all probability was another hymn. In this connection it may be of some significance that a generation after Paul's death Pliny the Younger, describing the Christians of his day to the emperor Trajan, states, "They affirmed, moreover, that the sum-total of their guilt or error was this, that they were in the habit of meeting on a certain fixed day before it was light, when they sang in alternate verses a hymn to Christ as to a God . . ." (*Letters* X.xcvi).

(2) The relative pronoun "who" in "who is" (verses 15, 18, especially the latter) "is not obviously natural" (C. F. D. Moule, *op. cit.*, p. 62). It has all the appearance of having been borrowed from a hymn in which it may have been preceded by such words as, "We thank our glorious Lord Jesus." This is comparable to the antecedant presupposed by the hymn quoted in I Tim. 3:16. See N.T.C. on I and II Timothy and Titus, pp. 137, 138.

(3) The carefully constructed nature of the passage, Col. 1:15-20, the parallelistic correspondences pertaining to its two parts, the recurrence of words and phrases *in the same sequence* in these two sections, is more natural in a hymn than in the free-flowing style of a letter.

Before attempting a study of the separate parts, the passage should be seen in its entirety. The following points should be noted:

(1) The passage indicates *at least* the following, namely, that only about thirty years after Jesus had suffered a shameful death on the cross divine honor was ascribed to him. His pre-eminence both in Creation and Redemption, his exaltation above every creature, was being clearly proclaimed by the apostle Paul. However, if the passage is a quotation from an earlier source, as is distinctly possible, it would mean that the recognition of Jesus as God even antedated Paul! See John 20:28; cf. 1:1-18.

(2) By insisting so strongly on the greatness of Christ, this passage implies that he is able to grant to the Colossians the things which Paul, in his beautiful prayer (verses 9-14), had requested for them. That is the connection between the prayer and the "hymn" or testimony. Such assurance was necessary, for the apostle had asked nothing less than *clear* knowledge of God's will, *all* spiritual wisdom and understanding, bearing fruit in *every* good work, and *all* vigor so as to exercise *every* kind of endurance and long-suffering.

(3) Col. 1:15-20 pictures a Christ who holds in his almighty hand and embraces with his loving heart both the realm of creation and that of redemption. He who is "the firstborn of all creation" is also "the firstborn from the dead." He who died on the cross knows by name the most distant star. He not only knows it but guides it. Still better: he controls it in such a manner that it will serve the interests of his people (Rom. 8:28). The so-called "laws of nature" have no *independent* existence. They are the expression of *his* will. And because he delights in *order* and not in confusion it is possible to speak of *laws*. He who in answer to prayer grants assurance of salvation is also able in answer to prayer to grant rain!

The present-day application of this truth is immediately evident. Since the Christ of Calvary rules the heavens and the earth in the interest of his kingdom and to the glory of his Name, always over-ruling evil for good, neither automation nor bomb nor communistic menace nor depression nor economic unbalance nor fatal accident nor gradual decline in mental vigor nor hallucination due to nervous disorder nor any invader from outer space (about which some people have nightmares!) will ever succeed in separating us from his love (Rom. 8:35, 38). He who tells us how to go to heaven and actually brings us there, also knows how the heavens go; for he, all things having been created and "holding together" in him, through him, and unto him, causes them to perform their mission and to go to the place predestined by him.

(4) Over against the heretics who threatened the Colossian church and proclaimed Christ's *in*sufficiency, this passage sets forth his *all*-sufficiency for salvation. This salvation implies not only being saved from the wrath of God, from the sentence of condemnation, and from eternal punishment, but also being spiritually regenerated and strengthened so that one is able to lay aside his old nature with its many vices (Col. 3:5-9) and to put on the new nature with its many virtues (Col. 3:1-3, 12-17). It is the *all*-sufficient Christ, he and he alone, who brings his people to glory. Thus the apostle, even in this grand passage, Col. 1:15-20, is really dealing with the practical implications of faith in Christ. In contrast with this faith the notions of the errorists fade away into worthlessness.

(5) The passage also clearly teaches that Christ's redemptive activity is universe-embracing. In Christ God was pleased to reconcile *all things* to himself. See on 1:20.

Turning now to the first of the two parts into which the section, verses 15-20, is divided we note the Son's Pre-eminence

A. *In Creation*

15. Paul writes, **Who is the image of the invisible God.** This reminds us of Gen. 1:27 which reports that man was created as God's image. As such man was given dominion over the rest of creation. It is significant that Psalm 8, in which this dominion is described in some detail, is by the author of the epistle to the Hebrews interpreted Messianically (Heb. 2:5-9). But though this reference to man's creation as God's image and consequent dominion may well have been in the background, it does not do full justice to the idea conveyed here in Colossians with respect to the Son. *Man, though God's image, is not God.* But, as the image of the invisible *God, the Son is,* first of all, *himself God.* "In him all the fulness of the godhead dwells bodily" (Col. 2:9; cf. Rom. 9:5). "In him all the treasures of wisdom and knowledge are hidden" (2:3). Secondly, as the *image* of the invisible God, *the Son is God Revealed.* In Paul's writings this identification of the Son with God himself, the Son being *God's image* or *God made manifest,* is not new. Also in a letter to the Corinthians, written earlier by several years, the apostle had called Christ "the image of God" (II Cor. 4:4). With this should be compared the apostle's description of his Lord in Philippians (a letter written probably shortly after Colossians), namely, "existing in the *form* of God" (see N.T.C. on Phil. 2:6). We have here in Col. 1:15 the same teaching as is found in Heb. 1:3, where the Son is called "the effulgence of God's glory and the very impress of his substance." In different language the apostle John expresses the same thought: "In the beginning was the Word, and the Word was face to face with God, and the Word was God. . . . God himself no one has ever seen. The only begotten God, who lies upon the Father's breast, it is he who made him known" (John 1:1, 18). Cf. also John 10:30, 38; 14:9; Rev. 3:14. It is in the Son that the invisible God has become visible, so that man sees him who is invisible (cf. I Tim. 1:17; 6:16).

Now if the Son is the very image of the invisible God, and if this invisible God is from everlasting to everlasting, it follows that the Son, too, must be *eternally* God's image. With respect to his deity he cannot belong to the category of time and space. He cannot be a mere creature, but must be in a class by himself, that is, raised high above every creature. Accordingly, the apostle continues, **the firstborn of every creature,**[52] that is, *the One to whom belongs the right and dignity of the Firstborn in relation to every creature.* That the phrase "the firstborn of every creature" cannot mean that the Son himself, too, is a creature, the first in a very long line, is clearly established by verse 16. He is prior to, distinct from, and highly exalted above every creature. As the firstborn he is the heir and ruler of all. Note Psalm 89:27:

"I will also make him my firstborn,
　The highest of the kings of the earth." Cf. Ex. 4:22; Jer. 31:9.

The same thought is expressed in Heb. 1:1, 2, "God . . . has spoken to us in his Son, whom he appointed heir of all things, through whom he also made the worlds."

16. The interpretation just given brings verse 15 in harmony with verse 16 which again stresses *Christ's pre-eminence above every creature.* And *that,* let it be re-emphasized, was after all Paul's main theme over against the teachers of error who were disturbing the church at Colosse. We read:

**For in him were created all things
In the heavens and on the earth,
The visible and the invisible.
Whether thrones or dominions or principalities or authorities,
All things through him and with a view to him have been created.**

---

[52] It makes little difference in resultant meaning whether πάσης κτίσεως be rendered "of all creation" (cf. Rom. 8:22) or "of every creature" (cf. Rom. 8:39). In favor of "of every creature" is the absence (here in Col. 1:15) of the article. In connection with πάσης one would expect the article if the sense is "of all creation."

All things — it makes no difference whether they be material or spiritual — were created *in him,* that is, *with reference to* the Son, the firstborn. As two walls and the bricks in these walls are arranged *in relation to* the corner-stone, from which they derive their angle of direction, so it was *in relation to* Christ that all things were originally created. He is their Point of Reference. Moreover, it is *through* him, as the *Agent* in creation, and *with a view to* him or *for* him as creation's *Goal* that they owe their settled state ("have been created"). *All* creatures, without any exception whatever, must contribute glory to him and serve his purpose. But is not God the Father — or else the Triune God — rather than the Son, the One for whom all things were brought into being? And do not passages such as Rom. 11:36, I Cor. 10:31, and Eph. 4:6 point in that general direction? Here it must be borne in mind, however, that the apostle's very emphasis in this letter is that the Son, too, is fully divine. In him all the fulness of the godhead dwells bodily (Col. 2:9). Hence, it is entirely reasonable for him to say that the Son is not only the One to whom all things owe their origin, as the divine Agent in their creation, but is also the Goal of their existence. Of all creatures he is Sovereign Lord. Hence, there is absolutely no justification for trusting in, seeking help from, or worshiping any mere creature, even though that creature be an angel. Angels, too, however exalted they may be, are creatures, and as such are subject to Christ. The *region* to which they or any other created beings belong or which they are thought to occupy, whether that region be heaven or earth or some place in-between, makes no difference. Note the crisscross or chiastic manner in which this thought is expressed:

"For in him were created all things"

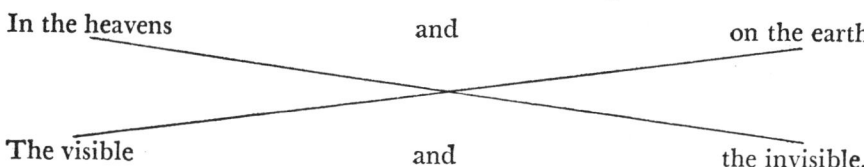

In the heavens   and   on the earth

The visible   and   the invisible.

Here clearly the visible creatures are those viewed as on earth; the invisible as in heaven.

Paul is thinking especially of *thrones or dominions or principalities or authorities.* The teachers of error were constantly referring to these angelic beings. The apostle does not deny their existence (Eph. 1:21, 22). Neither does he reject the idea that they are able to exert influence for good, if still unfallen (on this see N.T.C. on I Tim. 5:21) or for evil, if fallen (Eph. 6:12). The apostle's idea is rather this: angels have no power apart from Christ. In fact, apart from him they cannot even exist. They are *creatures,* nothing more. To the salvation or perfection of the Colossians they, in and by themselves, can contribute naught whatever. They can only *render service* and this always in subjection to Christ and through *his* power. The *good* angels cannot *add* anything to the fulness of riches and resources which believers have in Christ. The *evil* angels cannot separate them from his love (Rom. 8:35-39). In fact, through his death these sinister powers were basically vanquished (Col. 2:15). They are approaching the day when even their ability to do harm in God's universe and in the hearts and lives of earthdwellers will be ended once and for all (I Cor. 15:24, 25).

The enumeration "thrones or dominions or principalities or authorities" is not necessarily an arrangement of angels in four distinct groups, either in an ascending or in a descending scale of eminence, as if there were these four sharply differentiated classes. It is possible, nevertheless, that *thrones* and *dominions* must be viewed as *throne-spirits,* that is, such spirits as are dwelling in the immediate vicinity of God's throne (cf. the cherubim, Rev. 4:6). On this assumption *principalities and authorities,* generally mentioned together (Col. 1:16; 2:10, 15; Eph. 1:21; 3:10; I Cor. 15:24), could be spirits of lesser rank. But, however that may be, what Paul is saying is this: *"These angelic beings* of which false teachers are making so much, *call them by whatever names y o u wish* (Eph. 1:21; Phil. 2:9, 10), *are mere creatures,* and having been created through and for Christ, are subject to him." The inference, of course, is this, also for salvation y o u should expect everything from *him,* from him *alone,* not from him *and the angels!* [53]

17. Now if all things have been created through him and with a view to him (verse 16), it stands to reason that he preceded all created beings in time. In fact, "there never was a time when he was not." He was "begotten of the Father before all worlds" (Nicene Creed). Accordingly, the "hymn" continues, **And he is before all things.** He is, accordingly, the Forerunner. The doctrine of Christ's pre-existence from eternity is taught or implied in such passages as John 1:1; 8:58; 17:5; II Cor. 8:9; Phil. 2:6; Rev. 22:13. He is indeed the Alpha and the Omega, the first and the last, the beginning and the end. And this temporal priority in turn suggests pre-eminence and majesty in relation to all creatures: **And all things hold together in him.** The central position of Christ is defended here over against those who rejected it. The One with reference to whom, through whom, and with a view to whom all things were created is also the One who maintains them. The unity, order, and adaptation evident in all of nature and history can be traced to the Upholder or Sustainer of all (cf. Heb. 1:1-3).

---

[53] On these thrones, dominions, etc. see also the following: Slav. Enoch 20:1; Test. Levi 3 (*Ante-Nicene Fathers,* Vol. VIII, p. 13); and in Th.W.N.T. the following articles: Schmitz, θρόνος, III, pp. 160-167, especially p. 167; Michel, κυριότης, III, p. 1096; Delling, ἀρχή, I, pp. 477-488, especially pp. 481-483; and Foerster, ἐξουσία, II. pp. 559-571, especially pp. 568-571.

All things *hold together;* that is, they *continue and cohere.*[54]

There is, accordingly, unity and purpose in all of Nature and History. The world is not a chaos but a cosmos. It is an orderly universe, a *system.* This, to be sure, does not always appear on the surface. Nature seems to be "raw in tooth and claw," without harmony and order. Yet, a closer look soon indicates a basic plan. There is adaptation everywhere. For their perpetuation certain plants need certain definite insects. These insects are present, and so wondrously constructed that they can perform their function. The polar bear is able to live where there is ice and snow. It is kept from slipping on the ice by having fur even on the soles of its feet. The yucca plant can live in the hot, dry desert because not only does it have roots reaching down deeply into the soil for water but also leaves so formed that evaporation is very slow. Our lungs are adapted to the air we breathe, and our eyes to the light by which we see. Everywhere there is *coherence.*

This is true also in the daily events of History. Here, too, things are not as they seem. Often Confusion seems to be rampant. A Guiding Hand is nowhere visible. Instead, we hear the cry of battle, the shriek of anguish. The newspapers, moreover, are filled with accounts of burglary, murder, rape, and race-clash. If we compare the wheel of the universe to a machine, we might say that its gear-teeth seem not to mesh. To be sure, one day in the far-flung future, all will be harmony: the wolf shall dwell with the lamb, and the leopard shall lie down with the kid; and the calf and the young lion and the fatling together; and a little child shall lead them. . . . They shall not hurt nor destroy in all my holy mountain; for the earth shall be full of the knowledge of Jehovah, as the waters cover the sea" (Isa. 11:6-9). But that time has not yet arrived. All is chaos now. But is it really? Should we not rather compare our world to a weaving, whose underside forms no intelligible pattern, but whose upperside reveals beauty and design? Or to an international airfield? Though its planes, constantly coming and going, make us dizzy, so that we expect a collision any moment, we need not really hold our breath, for the man in the control-tower directs each take-off and landing. Thus, too, all creatures in all their movements throughout history are being *held together.* And that which holds them together is not Chance or Fate or the laws of Nature or even the "nine orbs, or rather globes" of

---

[54] The verb συνίστημι (alongside of which συνιστάνω and συνιστάω are used) means (transitive): *I cause to stand together, I bring together; I bring someone to someone else;* hence, *I introduce someone to someone else, I recommend* or *commend* a person (Rom. 16:1) or thing. In the sense of *commending* it is sometimes used favorably — as in the well-known passage Rom. 5:8 — ; sometimes with unfavorable overtones (for both unfavorable and favorable sense respectively, see the two occurrences of this verb in II Cor. 10:8). Here in Col. 1:17 it is used intransitively. The form here is 3rd person s. perf. act. indic. Cf. also for intransitive use: Luke 9:32 (*standing with*) and II Peter 3:5 (*continuing and consisting of*). See also on this verb L.N.T. (A. and G.), p. 798.

Scipio's Dream. On the contrary, "all things hold together *in him.*" It is the Son of God's love who holds in his almighty hands the reins of the universe and never even for one moment lets them slip out of his grasp (cf. Rev. chs. 4 and 5). Though the man of flesh regards this as so much pious twaddle, the man of faith proclaims with the inspired author of the Hebrews, "Now we see not yet all things subjected to him. But we behold . . . Jesus . . . crowned with glory and honor" (2:9). The believer knows that while the *rule* of Christ has not been established in every human heart, the *over-rule* is an actual fact even now (Rom. 8:28; cf. N.T.C. on Phil. 1:12). And at the sea of crystal the Church Triumphant will forever praise and glorify God for his mighty works and ways (Rev. 15:1-4).

Summarizing, the hymn has shown that with respect to all creatures, Christ is Firstborn (verse 15), Point of Reference, Agent, Goal (verse 16), Forerunner, and Sustainer — Governor (verse 17).

B. *In Redemption*

18. The section showing the Son's pre-eminence in the sphere of Creation has ended. Here, at verse 18, begins the paragraph describing his equal sovereignty in the realm of Redemption. We read: **And he is the head of the body, the church.** In the writings of Paul this expression is something new, whether we view it as original with him or as *here* taken over by him from a familiar hymn or saying. It is nowhere found in the earlier epistles such as Galatians, I and II Thessalonians, I and II Corinthians, or Romans. Yet, it would be unwise on this account to say that Paul cannot have been either the author or confirmer of the idea that Christ is, indeed, the head of the body, namely, the church. To be sure, in the earlier letters the apostle wrote not about Christ as the head of the church but about the church as the body of Christ (Rom. 12:5; I Cor. 12:12-31, especially verse 27). His purpose was to show that in that *one* body there were many *members* ("foot," "hand," "ear," "eye"); in other words, that in the one organism of the church there were many functions and talents distributed among a large number of believers, and that each "member" should use his gifts to benefit the entire body. He did not then specifically state that the head of this body was Christ. That was not the point at issue in these earlier letters. At Colosse, however, this headship or pre-eminence of Christ was distinctly the truth in need of emphasis, as has already been shown. It is for this reason that this particular aspect of the doctrine is set forth here in Colossians rather than in the earlier epistles.

Nevertheless, it cannot be truthfully maintained that the proposition "Christ is the head of the church" was *absolutely* foreign to Paul's thinking previous to the time when he wrote his Prison Epistles. Is not a *body* supposed to have a *head*? Besides, had not the apostle written, "The head of every man is Christ" (I Cor. 11:3) ? Now if Christ is the head of every man in the church, is he not also the head of the church?

As head Christ causes his church to live and to grow (Col. 2:19; cf. Eph. 4:15, 16). He is its *Organic Head*. As head he also exercises authority over the church; in fact, over all things in the interest of the church (Eph. 1:20-23). He is its *Ruling Head*. It is doubtful whether either of these two ideas is ever completely absent when Christ is called head of the church, though sometimes one connotation and then again the other receives the greater emphasis, as the context indicates. And in such a passage as Eph. 5:23, 24 both ideas (*growth* and *guidance*) are brought to the fore.

Now if the Son of God is the Organic and Ruling Head of the church, then the church is in no sense whatever dependent on any creature, angel or otherwise. This is the clear implication over against the teachers of error. Does not the church receive both its growth and guidance from its living Lord? Is it not energized by his power and governed by his Word and Spirit? Hence, is it not true that in Christ it has all it needs, and also that without him it can accomplish nothing? Cf. John 15:5, 7.

> "Thou, O Christ, art all I want;
> More than all in thee I find." (Charles Wesley, in "Jesus,
> Lover of My Soul")

And what could be a better illustration of the relation of Christ to his church than the underlying idea of the relation of the human head to the body? Advance in scientific knowledge has confirmed the adequacy of the figure used by the early church and by Paul. In a human individual it is to the head that the body, in large measure, owes its *vigorous life* and *growth* (the organic relationship). From the pituitary gland, housed in a small cavity located in the base of the skull, comes the growth hormone (and several other hormones). This hormone is known to be closely related to the health and growth of connective tissue, cartilege, and bone.

Consider also the other functions of the head, those related in large measure to *guidance*. It is in the head that the organs of special sense are mainly located. The brain receives impulses from the outside world (indirectly) and from inside the body. It organizes and interprets these impulses. It thinks. It reacts, and this both voluntarily and involuntarily. Thus it *guides and directs* the actions of the individual. In the *cerebrum* are located, among other things, the areas that control the various parts of the body. The *cerebellum* has been called "the co-ordinator and harmonizer of muscular action." The *medulla* controls such actions as winking, sneezing, coughing, chewing, sucking, swallowing, etc. Here also the cardiac center regulates the rate of heart-beat, while the respiratory center is in charge of the activity of the respiratory organs.

Thus, indeed, when the triune God created the human body with its *organic and ruling head,* he so constructed that head that it could serve as an excellent symbol of the Organic and Ruling Head of the church, the Lord Jesus Christ.

With reference to the latter the "hymn" now continues, **Who is the beginning, the firstborn from the dead.** By his triumphant resurrection, *nevermore to die,* Christ laid the foundation for that sanctified life, that hope and assurance in which his own rejoice (Col. 3:1-17; I Peter 1:3 ff.). This resurrection is also the beginning, principle, or cause of their glorious physical resurrection. Hence, from every aspect the statement is true, "Because I live y o u too will live" (John 14:19). He is the path-breaker, who holds the key of Death and Hades. He has authority over life and death (Rom. 8:29; I Cor. 15:20; Heb. 2:14, 15; Rev. 1:5). It is he who "on the one hand, utterly defeated death, and on the other hand, brought to light life and incorruptibility through the gospel" (II Tim. 1:10). All this is true in order **that in all things he might have the pre-eminence.** It stands to reason that One who is Firstborn, Point of Reference, Agent, Goal, Forerunner, and Sustainer — Governor (verses 15-17) in the sphere of Creation; and Head of the Body, Beginning, and Firstborn from the dead in the realm of Redemption (verse 18), has the right to the title, "the One who has the pre-eminence — the divine sovereignty — *in all things,* that is, among all creatures."

19. Note, however, the words, "that he might have." These words show that this high honor possessed by the Son was a matter of design, the Father's good pleasure. Hence, the text continues, **For in him he [God] was pleased to have all the fulness dwell.**[55]

---

[55] With the majority of translators, ancient and modern, I would make "God" or "the Father" (understood) the subject of the verb *was pleased.* Reasons:

(1) In another poetic line (Luke 2:14) the related noun *good pleasure* means *"God's"* (understood) good pleasure." Cf. also Phil. 2:13, where *"the* good pleasure" similarly means *"his* [God's] good pleasure." Also in Eph. 1:5 the clear reference is to the good pleasure of "the God and Father of our Lord Jesus Christ."

(2) The mental insertion "God" or "the Father" is, after all, not too difficult, for in the preceding context *the Father* has been referred to in relation to the Son (see verses 12, 13, 15). In verse 13 the latter was called "the Son of *his* love," and in verse 15 this Son was described as "the image of the invisible *God.*"

The *alternate rendering,* favored by some (including R.S.V., Abbott, Lenski, C. F. D. Moule, Ridderbos), namely, "for in him all the fulness was pleased to dwell" (or something similar) is certainly possible grammatically. My hesitancy to adopt this rendering is based on the following considerations:

(1) Nowhere else in the New Testament does Paul *thus* personify this fulness. Have we the right to ascribe to Paul — or to the very early church, if the apostle is here quoting a hymn — the style of Clement of Alexandria or of Irenaeus?

(2) It is hardly correct to maintain that in Col. 1:19 (alternate rendering) we have an exactly similar construction as in Col. 2:9, that is, that here in Col. 1:19 just as in Col. 2:9 *fulness* is the subject of a form of the verb *to dwell.* On the contrary, when Col. 1:19 is rendered "for in him all the fulness was pleased to dwell" the

This delight of the Father in the Son was evident even during the old dispensation, yes, even before the world was founded (Ps. 2:7, 8; John 17:5; Eph. 1:9). During the period of Christ's sojourn on earth it manifested itself again and again (Matt. 3:17; 17:5; John 12:28). It was indeed God's good pleasure that in his Son *all* the fulness should dwell. The powers and attributes of Deity were not to be distributed among a multitude of angels. The divine supremacy or sovereignty, either as a whole or in part, was not to be surrendered to them. On the contrary, in accordance with God's good pleasure, from all eternity the plenitude of the Godhead, the fulness of God's essence and glory, which fulness is the source of grace and glory for believers, resides in the Son of his love, in him alone, not in him and the angels. It dwells in him whom we now serve as our exalted Mediator, and it manifests itself both in Creation and Redemption.

Explanatory passages are:

John 1:16, "For out of his fulness we have received grace upon grace."

Col. 2:3, "in whom all the treasures of wisdom and knowledge are stored up."

Col. 2:9, "For in him all the fulness [56] of the godhead dwells bodily."

---

noun *fulness* becomes the subject not directly of a form of the verb *to dwell* but of *was pleased,* and this concept (fulness) is thus invested with a more definitely personal attribute. If any argument can be derived from Col. 2:9 it would rather be in the opposite direction, for in Col. 2:9 *fulness* is, indeed, subject of a form of the verb *to dwell,* just as it is also in Col. 1:19 when the latter is rendered, "For in him he [God] was pleased to have all the fulness dwell." The noun πλήρωμα is then subject to the infinitive κατοικῆσαι.

[56] Much has been written about this term *fulness* (πλήρωμα). The sense of the word must be determined in each separate case by the context. In accordance with this rule the following shades of meaning, each according to its own setting, can be recognized. At least, the following resultant meanings deserve consideration:

Matt. 9:16 and Mark 2:21: the patch that fills up the rent in a garment.
Mark 6:43 and 8:20: basketfuls.
John 1:16: infinite plenitude from which believers receive grace upon grace.
Rom. 11:12: total number of elect Jews (cf. Rom. 11:2, 5).
Rom. 11:25: total number of elect Gentiles.
Rom. 13:10: love as law's fulfilment; that is, love considered as that which fully satisfies the requirements of the law.
Rom. 15:29: the sum-total or abundance of blessings imparted by Christ.
I Cor. 10:26 (in a quotation from Ps. 24:1; LXX 23:1): the sum-total or abundance of that which the earth produces.
Gal. 4:4: the full measure of the time of Christ's first coming as predetermined in God's plan, in accordance with the imperative *need* which this coming satisfied, the Messianic *hope* which it fulfilled, and the golden *opportunity* which it provided.
Eph. 1:10: the fulness of the seasons, the new dispensation.
Eph. 1:23 (very controversial). Among the many interpretations are these three:
  (1) the church as that which Christ completes.
  (2) the church as that which completes Christ, he himself being incomplete without it, as the bridegroom is incomplete without the bride.
  (3) Christ as the fulness of God, the All-Filler.
A more detailed discussion would belong to a Commentary on Ephesians.

20. Now both in Col. 2:9, 10 and here in 1:19, 20 the fulness which dwells in Christ is mentioned with a practical purpose. It is a source of blessing. Thus here in Col. 1:19, 20 we are told that it was the good pleasure or delight of God the Father that in the Son of his love all the fulness should dwell **and through him to reconcile all things to himself,**[57] **having made peace**

Eph. 3:19 and 4:13: the full fruit of the work of Christ imparted to believers by God; the full maturity intended by God; spiritual maturity.

Col. 1:19 and 2:9: fulness of the divine essence and glory considered as the source of unending blessings for believers.

The theory that Paul's *frequent use* of the term (though *not* the term itself) was due, at least in part, to its employment by the false teachers may well be correct. The noun *fulness* is found no less than six times in the ten chapters of Ephesians and Colossians, as often as in the seventy-seven chapters of all of Paul's other epistles. Moreover, the number of times the verb *to make full, fill,* or *fulfil* is used in Colossians, Ephesians, and Philippians (closely related Prison Epistles) contrasts sharply with its far lower frequency in the other epistles (as was stated earlier). Was one of the reasons why the apostle included this line of the "hymn" the fact that it contained the word *fulness* in connection with Christ? And did he, perhaps, intend to convey the meaning, "The fulness of God, and consequently the true source of his people's fulness, about which those who proclaim error are always talking, is found in Christ, in him alone"? The probability that this was one of the reasons why Paul quoted these lines in combating the Colossian heresy must be granted, even though we cannot be sure. Lightfoot is of the opinion that Essene Judaizers derived the word *fulness* and its cognates from a Palestinian source, and that it probably represents the Hebrew root *ml'*, of which it is a translation in the LXX, and the cognate Aramaic root, as the Peshito seems to indicate.

Three additional facts should be mentioned in this connection:

(1) For *the term* πλήρωμα *itself* Paul or the early hymn-writers were by no means dependent upon false teachers. The early Christians were steeped in the terminology of the Old Testament, in which the term *fulness* is used again and again; for example in Ps. 24:1 (LXX 23:1); 50:12 (LXX 49:12); 89:11 (LXX 88:12); 96:11 (LXX 95:11); 98:7 (LXX 97:7). (To that extent I can agree with E. Percy, *op. cit.,* p. 76 ff.)

(2) The theory that the *frequency* of the term in Ephesians and Colossians had something to do with its use by the false teachers by no means indicates that as early as this it already had the sense that was ascribed to it in the elaborate speculations of *second century* Gnosticism.

(3) Since the meaning of a word depends on its use in a given context lengthy arguments with respect to the question whether basically πλήρωμα means *that which is filled* or *that which fills* are not very fruitful.

For further discussion see the following:

J. B. Lightfoot, *op. cit.,* pp. 257-273; J. A. Robinson, "The Church as the Fulfilment of the Christ: a Note on Ephesians 1:23," *Exp,* 5th series, 7 (1898), pp. 241-259; C. F. D. Moule, *op. cit.,* pp. 164-169; and Delling, Th.W.N.T., Vol. VI, pp. 297-304.

[57] εἰς αὐτόν to be written (or with the sense of) εἰς αὐτόν. It was customary for Paul to say that reconciliation is *to God* (Rom. 5:10, twice; II Cor. 5:18, 19, 20). The fact that in these passages (as also in non-theological I Cor. 7:11) the verb καταλλάσσω is used, to which corresponds the noun καταλλαγή (Rom. 5:11; 11:15; II Cor. 5:18, 19), while here in Col. 1:20, 21 and in Eph. 2:16 (nowhere else in the New Testament) the compound verb ἀποκαταλλάσσω occurs, does not detract from the force of this argument. Moreover, *God the Father* is the implied subject in verse 19 (see footnote 55 above).

through the blood of his cross; through him,[58] whether the things on the earth or the things in the heavens. Not only were all things *created* "through him," that is, through the Son of God's love (verse 16), but all things are also (in a sense to be explained) *reconciled* "through him" (verse 20). In both cases *all things* has the same meaning: all creatures without any exception whatever:

> "There rustles a Name O so dear 'long the clouds,
> That Name heaven and earth in grand harmony shrouds."

This is the nearly literal translation of the first lines of a Dutch hymn:

> "Daar ruist langs de wolken een lieflijke naam,
> Die hemel en aarde verenigt te zaam."

Some have objected to the lines for theological reasons.[59] Personally, I see no reason for rejecting the idea expressed in this poem. One might as well reject Col. 1:20! It is all a matter of interpretation. Thus, it is true, indeed, that heaven and earth are not now united, and are not going to be united, in the sense that all rational beings in the entire universe are now *with gladness of heart* submitting themselves, or will at some future date joyfully submit themselves, to the rule of God in Christ. This universalistic interpretation of Col. 1:20 is contrary to Scripture (Ps. 1; Dan. 12:2; Matt. 7:13, 14; 25:46; John 5:28, 29; Phil. 3:18-21; II Thess. 1:3-10; and a host of other passages). It was Origen who was probably the first Christian universalist. In his youthful work *De Principiis* he suggested this thought of universal, final restoration for all. In his later writings he seems to imply it here and there, but obscures it somewhat by the suggestion of a constant succession of fall and restoration. He has, however, had many followers, and among them some have expressed themselves far more bluntly. Some time ago a minister told his audience, "In the end everybody is going to be saved. I have hope even for the devil."

The real meaning of Col. 1:20 is probably as follows: Sin ruined the universe. It destroyed the harmony between one creature and the other, also between all creatures and their God. Through *the blood of the cross* (cf.

---

[58] The phrase "through him," here repeated, though lacking in important manuscripts, is probably genuine. It may be considered a repetition for the sake of emphasis. The very fact that it is a repetition probably accounts for its omission from some texts.

[59] Could that be the reason why the otherwise excellent and very popular rendering by Rev. W. Kuipers, as found in No. 199 of *The New Christian Hymnal*, is as follows:

> "I hear in the air, 'neath the canopy blue,
> Sweet notes of a Name, most resplendent and true"?

This, though probably excellent poetry, is obviously not a true translation of the Dutch lines.

Eph. 2:11-18), however, sin, in principle, has been conquered. The demand of the law has been satisfied, its curse born (Rom. 3:25; Gal. 3:13). Harmony, accordingly, has been restored. Peace was made. *Through Christ and his cross the universe is brought back or restored to its proper relationship to God in the sense that as a just reward for his obedience Christ was exalted to the Father's right hand, from which position of authority and power he rules the entire universe in the interest of the church and to the glory of God.* This interpretation brings the present passage in harmony with the related ones written during this same imprisonment. Note the expression "the things on the earth or the things in the heavens" (or something very similar) not only here in Col. 1:20 but also in Eph. 1:10 and Phil. 2:10.

There is, of course, a difference in the *manner* in which various creatures submit to Christ's rule and are "reconciled to God." Those who are and remain evil, whether men or angels, submit ruefully, unwillingly. In their case *peace,* harmony, is *imposed, not welcomed.* But not only are their evil designs constantly being over-ruled for good, but these evil beings themselves have been, in principle, stripped of their power (Col. 2:15). They are brought into subjection (I Cor. 15:24-28; cf. Eph. 1:21, 22), and "the God of *peace* (!) will bruise Satan under y o u r feet shortly" (Rom. 16:20). The good angels, on the other hand, submit joyfully, eagerly. So do also the redeemed among men. This group includes the members of the Colossian church as far as they are true believers, a thought to which Paul gives expression in the following verses.

---

21 And y o u, who once were estranged and hostile in disposition, as shown by y o u r wicked works, 22 he in his body of flesh through his death has now reconciled, in order to present y o u holy, faultless, and blameless before himself; 23 if, indeed, y o u continue in the faith, founded and firm, and are not moved away from the hope that is derived from the gospel which y o u have heard, which was preached among every creature under heaven, and of which I, Paul, became a minister.

1:21-23

IV. *The Son's Reconciling Love toward the Colossians*
and
Their Resulting Duty to Continue in the Faith

21, 22a. And y o u, who once were estranged and hostile in disposition, as shown by y o u r wicked works, he in his body of flesh through his death has now reconciled.[60]

---

[60] Because of its length this footnote has been placed at the end of the chapter, page 96.

With joy of heart the apostle now testifies that the Colossians, too, had become recipients of this marvelous gift of reconciliation, a reconciliation which for men whose hearts receive Christ has a far more beautiful and intimate meaning than it has for the world in general. Paul reminds the Colossians of the great change that had occurred in their lives, in order that this reminder may cause them to dread the very suggestion of returning to their former manner of life (cf. Col. 3:7). Meaning: "Y o u were separate from Christ, alienated from the commonwealth of Israel, and strangers from the covenants of the promise, having no hope and without God in the world . . . far off . . . darkened in understanding, alienated from the life of God" (Eph. 2:12, 13; 4:18). This state of estrangement, moreover, was not due simply to ignorance or innocence. *There are no innocent heathen!* On the contrary, they were estranged *and hostile in disposition.* It was *their own fault* that they had been and had remained for a long time "far off," for they had actually *hated* God; and when God through conscience and through his revelation in nature and history had made himself known to them to a certain extent, they in their hostility had "suppressed the truth by their wickedness" (Rom. 1:18-23). Such inexcusable human hostility, which is the sinner's condition *by nature,* merits God's wrath (Rom. 1:18; Col. 3:6). By nature sinners are therefore "children of wrath" (Eph. 2:3). Moreover, the inner disposition of aversion to God and antipathy to the voice of conscience which formerly had characterized these Colossians had revealed itself in *wicked deeds,* such as those that are enumerated very specifically in Col. 3:5-9.

But all this was past now, at least basically. Through the blood of the Son of God's love peace had been made. He, meaning this Son of God's love,[61] in his *body of flesh* (that was the *sphere* of the reconciliation), and through his *death* (that was the *instrument*) had brought about a return to the proper relation between the Colossians and their God. A *return,* not as if there had been a time, many, many years ago, when these Colossians had been Christians, but rather in this sense, that the establishment of peace between the Father-heart of God and the soul of the sinner is for the latter a *going back* to *the state* of rectitude in which God originally created man. (The *condition* to which grace brings the rescued sinner is, of course, far better than that before the fall.) By God's sovereign grace the prodigal returns to his home from which he had been *estranged* (see verse 21; also Luke 15:11-24). That is the meaning of *reconciliation.* By Christ's atoning death God is reconciled to the sinner, the sinner to God. "The reconciled God justifies the sinner who accepts the reconciliation, and so operates in his heart by the Holy Spirit that the sinner also lays aside his wicked aliena-

---

[61] The modifiers "in *his* body of flesh through *his* death" make it clear that the subject of the sentence (verses 21-23) is not *God* (as Lightfoot maintains) but Christ. Thus also F. W. Beare, *op. cit.,* p. 175, and Lenski, *op. cit.,* p. 70 very emphatically.

tion from God, and thus enters into the fruits of the perfect atonement of Christ." [62]

Note once more that expression "in his body of flesh," a Hebraism meaning *Christ's human body,* and thus by extension, *his entire physical existence on earth,* in which he satisfied the demands of the law and bore its punishment. (Cf. Luke 22:19; I Cor. 11:27; Heb. 10:10; I Peter 2:24.) It is probable that "body of flesh" [63] is here contrasted with "body, the church" of verse 18. It should be added, however, that the Holy Spirit who inspired Colossians (as well as the rest of Scripture) foresaw the time when the Docetics would be teaching that Jesus Christ appeared to men in a *spiritual* body, and since he had no physical body only *seemed* to suffer and die on the cross. Col. 1:22 gives the lie to that theory.

22b. The purpose of the Son's reconciling work as it affected the Colossians is now stated: **in order to present y o u holy, faultless, and blameless before himself.**[64] Note: *holy,* that is, cleansed from all sin and separated entirely to God and his service; *faultless:* without any blemish whatever (Phil. 2:15), like a perfect sacrifice; and *blameless:* completely above reproach (I Tim. 3:10; Titus 1:6, 7).

The *presentation* here referred to must be viewed as definitely eschatological, that is, as referring to the great consummation when Jesus returns upon clouds of glory. This follows from the conditional clause, "if, indeed, y o u continue in the faith. . . ." It is comforting to know that not only *the apostles* looked forward with joyful anticipation to the time when they would present the fruit of *God's* grace and of *their* labor (they being God's co-workers, I Cor. 3:9) as a pure virgin to Christ the Bridegroom (II Cor. 11:2; Phil. 1:10; 2:16; I Thess. 2:19, 20; I John 2:28), but so does also Christ himself (Eph. 5:27). To him, too, the words of Zeph. 3:17 are applicable, "He will rejoice over you with joy; he will rest in his love; he will joy over you with singing." This glorious *presentation* is here referred to as the purpose of the *reconciliation.*

---

[62] L. Berkhof, *Systematic Theology,* p. 373.
[63] On the meaning of the word *flesh* see N.T.C. on Philippians, p. 77, footnote 55.
[64] Agreement with the subject of the sentence (see footnote 61 above), as well as comparison with the very similar passage Eph. 5:27, inclines me to the conclusion that here in Col. 1:22b "before him" means "before himself" (that is, before the Son of God's love), just as in verse 20 (see footnote 57 above) "to him" means (or may even be written) "to himself" (that is, to God). Note, in this connection, that while it was customary for Paul to say that *reconciliation* was *to God,* he describes *presentation* as being either *to Christ* (Eph. 5:27; II Cor. 11:2) or *to God* (Rom. 14:10); and sometimes does not clearly indicate the One *to whom* believers are to be presented (Col. 1:28; II Cor. 4:14). Of course, in view of such passages as John 14:9 and I John 2:23, it makes very little difference whether Christ is viewed as presenting his children to himself or to God. He cannot do the one without doing the other.

23. Now in connection with this glorious presentation at the Lord's return a condition must be fulfilled. Hence, Paul continues: **if, indeed, y o u continue in the faith, founded and firm. . . .** Divine preservation always presupposes human perseverance. Perseverance proves faith's genuine character, and is therefore indispensable to salvation. To be sure, no one can continue in the faith in his own strength (John 15:5). The enabling grace of God is needed from start to finish (Phil. 2:12, 13). This, however, does not cancel human responsibility and activity. Yes, *activity,* continuous, sustained, strenuous effort (Heb. 12:14). It should be noted, however, that this is distinctly the activity of *faith* (cf. I Tim. 2:15), a faith not in themselves but in God. Thus they will be "founded and firm," that is, firmly established upon the one and only true foundation, the foundation of the apostles (through their testimony). Of this foundation Christ Jesus is the cornerstone (I Cor. 3:11; Eph. 2:20; Rev. 21:14, 19, 20). The conditional clause continues: **and are not moved away from the hope that is derived from the gospel which y o u have heard.** Danger was threatening; and it was of a twofold character, as pointed out earlier (see Introduction, III B; IV A). Hence, the apostle by implication is here warning the Colossians against relapse into their former state with all its soul-destroying vices (Col. 3:5-11) and against the "solution" urged upon them by those who refused to recognize Jesus Christ as the complete and all-sufficient Savior. Let them not allow themselves to be dislodged or shunted away from the *hope* — ardent expectation, complete confidence, watchful waiting — of which the gospel speaks and to which the gospel gives rise, that gospel which the Colossians "have heard," that is, to which they have not only listened but to which they have also given heed. See above on Col. 1:6-8. That gospel, moreover, was not meant for a select few — the Colossian errorists may well have considered themselves an exclusive set! — nor was it confined to any particular region; on the contrary, it was the gospel **which,** in obedience to the Lord's command (Matt. 28:19; especially Mark 16:15), **was preached among every creature under heaven.** It recognized no boundaries whether racial, national, or regional. It is always the "whosoever believeth" gospel. Having reached Rome, from which Paul is writing this epistle, it had actually invaded every large center of the then-known world. More on this under verse 6 above. With deep emotion and humble gratitude the apostle concludes this section and links it with the next paragraph by adding: **and of which I, Paul, became a minister.** The real depth of these words can only be understood in the light of such passages as I Cor. 15:9; Eph. 3:8; and I Tim. 1:15-17. A *minister* [65] of the gospel is one who knows the gospel, has been saved by the Christ of the gospel, and with joy of heart proclaims the gospel to others. Thus he *serves* the cause of the gospel.

---

[65] Obviously the word διάκονος is not here used in the technical sense of *deacon.* For the use of this word see N.T.C. on I Tim. 3:13 and 4:6.

24 I am now rejoicing amid my sufferings for y o u, and what is lacking in the afflictions of Christ I in his stead am supplying in my flesh, for his body, which is the church, 25 of which I became a minister, according to the stewardship of God given to me for y o u r benefit, to give full scope to the word of God, 26 the mystery hidden for ages and generations but now made manifest to his saints; 27 to whom God was pleased to make known what (is) the riches of the glory of this mystery among the Gentiles, which is Christ in y o u, the hope of glory; 28 whom we proclaim, admonishing every man and teaching every man in all wisdom, in order that we may present every man perfect in Christ; 29 for which I am laboring, striving by his energy working powerfully within me.

1:24-29

V. *The Apostle's Share in Proclaiming "the Mystery,"*
namely, "Christ in y o u, the hope of glory"

24a. Expanding the personal reference begun in verse 23 the apostle continues: **I am now rejoicing amid my sufferings for y o u.** The word *now* probably refers to the fact that right at this moment Paul is not making missionary journeys nor *by his presence* ministering to the Colossians, as he hopes to do later (Philem. 22), but is enduring the many details of suffering and hardship — note the plural "my sufferings" — that pertain to his present *imprisonment* (Col. 4:10, 18; Eph. 3:1; 4:1; Philem. 1, 9, 23). But instead of complaining *he rejoices,* for do not these trials confirm his apostleship? Remember Acts 9:16! And is not suffering in behalf of Christ a great privilege also for other reasons? See N.T.C. on Phil. 1:29, 30. And will not his endurance in the midst of many hardships strengthen the Colossians, and in fact believers everywhere, in their faith? Paul has every right to say, "my sufferings *for y o u.*" See also on 2:1.

24b. This positive aspect of enduring sufferings, namely, that such sanctified cross-bearing will be of blessing to the church is brought out meaningfully in the much discussed words which follow, namely, **and what is lacking in the afflictions of Christ I in his stead am supplying in my flesh for his body, which is the church.**
Closeness to Christ causes Paul to write as he does. He is even now reflecting on the afflictions which the Savior endured when he was on earth. Paul knows that he himself in his transitory earthly existence is, in a sense to be explained presently, *filling in* or *supplying* what was lacking in Christ's sufferings. The apostle is undergoing these hardships in the place of Jesus, since Jesus himself is no longer here to endure them. Not as if Paul were doing this all by himself, but he is contributing his share. Other believers contribute theirs. Paul is also convinced of the fact that his afflictions are be-

86

ing borne for the benefit of Christ's glorious body, the church (see above, on verse 18). He knows that by his calm endurance and clear testimony during trial the church will be established in the faith.

In the foregoing paragraph I have made it clear that it is my considered opinion that the apostle is actually saying that he, as one among many, is in a sense supplying what was lacking in *the afflictions which Jesus suffered while on earth*. Percy, *op. cit.*, p. 130, calls this "the only possible interpretation." Ridderbos writes, "Our conclusion can be no other than this, that the expression *the afflictions of Christ* points to the historical suffering of Christ" (*op. cit.*, p. 158).

Of course, this does not mean that there was anything lacking in the atoning value of Christ's sacrifice. It does not mean that good works, the suffering in purgatory, faithful attendance at mass, the purchase of indulgences, or any other so-called merits can be or need be added to the merits of our Lord. Among the many passages that would refute such a theory are Col. 2:14; John 19:30; Heb. 10:11-14; and I John 1:9. But we have no right, in the interest of Protestantism in its struggle with Roman Catholicism, to change the clear grammatical and contextual meaning of a passage. We should bear in mind that although Christ by means of the afflictions which he endured rendered *complete* satisfaction to God, so that Paul is able to glory in nothing but the cross (Gal. 6:14), *the enemies of Christ were not satisfied!* They hated Jesus with insatiable hatred, and wanted to add to his afflictions. But since *he* is no longer physically present on earth, their arrows, which are meant especially for *him*, strike his followers. It is in that sense that all true believers are in his stead supplying what, as the enemies see it, is lacking in the afflictions which Jesus endured. Christ's afflictions overflow toward us. This interpretation is supported by passages such as the following:

"If they called the master of the house Beelzebub, how much more them of his household" (Matt. 10:25).

"Y o u shall be hated of all men for my name's sake" (Mark 13:13).

"If the world hates y o u, know that it has hated me before it hated y o u. . . . But all these things will they do to y o u for my name's sake, because they do not know the One who sent me" (John 15:18-21).

"Saul, Saul, why do you persecute me? . . . I am Jesus, whom you are persecuting" (Acts 9:4, 5).

"The afflictions of Christ overflow toward us" (II Cor. 1:5).

". . . always bearing about in the body the putting to death of Jesus" (II Cor. 1:10).

"I bear on my body the marks of Jesus" (Gal. 6:17).

". . . that I may know him . . . and the fellowship of his sufferings" (Phil. 3:10).

"And when the dragon saw that he had been thrown down to the earth,

he persecuted the woman because she had brought forth the male child"
(Rev. 12:13).[66]

25. Paul has indicated that his sufferings are for the benefit of the church.
He continues, **of which I became a minister, according to the stewardship of
God given to me for y o u r benefit.** Harassed by men who tried to lead them
astray, the Colossians must bear in mind that Paul, who is now addressing
them and to whom indirectly they owe their knowledge of salvation, was
their divinely appointed *steward*. The office of "administrator of spiritual
treasures" had been entrusted to him and to his helpers (I Cor. 4:1, 2; 9:17;
I Tim. 1:4; Titus 1:7). And this, says Paul, is *for y o u r benefit*. In their case
that was true in a special sense, for they had been won over from the Gentiles
(Col. 1:27; 3:5-11), and it was *especially* (not exclusively) to the Gentiles
that Paul had been sent (Acts 13:47; 22:21; Rom. 11:13; 15:16; Gal. 2:8, 9;
Eph. 3:1, 2, 8; I Tim. 2:7; II Tim. 4:17). The stewardship of God had been
given to him, moreover, **to give full scope to the word of God,** that is, to
proclaim the Christ in all his glorious fulness to everyone, regardless of race,
nationality, or social position.

26, 27. That word of God centers in Christ, God's glorious mystery. Hence,
the apostle continues, **the mystery hidden for ages and generations but now
made manifest to his saints.** Paul uses the term "mystery," but *not* as indicating *a secret teaching, rite, or ceremony, having something to do with
religion but hidden from the masses and revealed to an exclusive group,* the
sense in which the term (generally in the plural: *mysteries*) was at that time
being employed outside of the circles of true Christianity. On the contrary,
in the Pauline literature a *mystery* [67] *is a person or a truth that would have
remained unknown had not God revealed him or it.* Such a mystery is said to
have been *revealed in the fullest sense* only then when its significance is translated into historical reality. The mystery of which the apostle is thinking here
in Col. 1:26, 27 had been *hidden;* that is, for ages and generations (lit. "since
the ages and since the generations") it had not been historically realized. It
was present, to be sure, in the *plan* of God and also in *prophecy,* but *not in
actuality. Now,* however, that is, in this present era which began with the
incarnation, and even more specifically with the proclamation of the gospel

---

[66] Because of its length this footnote has been placed at the end of the chapter,
page 97.
[67] The word *mystery* occurs 28 times in the New Testament: 3 times in the Gospels
(Matt. 13:11; Mark 4:11; Luke 8:10); 4 times in the Book of Revelation (Rev.
10:7; 17:5; also 1:20 and 17:7 with a sense differing from that in which it is used by
Paul; probably "symbolical meaning"); and 21 times in Paul's letters (Rom. 11:25;
16:25; I Cor. 2:1, 2:7; 4:1; 13:2; 14:2; 15:51; Eph. 1:9; 3:3; 3:4; 3:9; 5:32; 6:19;
Col. 1:26; 1:27; 2:2; 4:3; I Tim. 3:9; 3:16; II Thess. 2:7). See the entry μυστήριον
in L.N.T. (A. and G.), and the extensive literature there given.

to the Gentiles, it was made manifest to his *saints,* that is, to the entire church of this new dispensation, none excepted. It was there for all to see! To describe more fully what he has in mind Paul continues: **to whom God was pleased to make known what (is) the riches of the glory of this mystery among the Gentiles, which is Christ in y o u, the hope of glory.** The mystery, accordingly, is Christ himself, just as in I Tim. 3:16; cf. Eph. 3:3, 4, 9. It is *Christ in all his glorious riches actually dwelling through his Spirit in the hearts and lives of the Gentiles.* In all the preceding ages this had never been seen, but now every child of God ("saint") could bear witness to it. The Colossians themselves offered proof. To be sure, even during the days of the old dispensation there were *predictions* which, with ever-increasing clarity, foretold that the Gentiles would one day constitute part of God's people (Gen. 22:18; 26:4; 28:14; 49:10; Ps. 72:8; 87; Isa. 54:2, 3; 60:1-3; Micah 4:1, 2; Mal. 1:11, to mention only a few), but in the divine good pleasure the realization of these predictions did not arrive until this present Messianic Age. "Christ in y o u, the hope of glory" had to wait until now. "Christ in y o u" means Christ in y o u *Gentiles,* and that on a basis of perfect equality with Israel, the "middle wall of partition" having been completely removed (Eph. 2:14) !

Christ in y o u, the hope of glory, an Easter theme [68]

1. *Its meaning*

Christ in y o u is here proclaimed as the hope or *solid basis for the expectation of* future, eschatological glory. The content of this glory is set forth in the context: "the inheritance of the saints in the light" (verse 12), "the presentation" of the bride to the Bridegroom (verses 22, 28) ; see also Col. 3:4, 24; Rom. 5:2; 8:18-23; I Cor. 15; Phil. 3:20, 21; I Thess. 2:19; 3:13; 4:13-17; II Thess. 1:10; II Tim. 1:12; 4:8; Titus 2:13. While the apostle included the intermediate state in this concept of glory (II Cor. 5:1-8; Phil. 1:21, 23), his horizon was Christ's second coming and never-ending bliss.

2. *Hopes that deceive*

In all ages men have tried to establish their own basis for belief in immortality and even in a future state of perfection.

a. Some reason from the premise of *unsatisfied desire.* We desire to see a perfect landscape. Yet when, standing on a hill, we think we see one, the descent into the valley with its rotting logs and decaying fruit, disillusions us. Nevertheless, the desire persists. This guarantees future realization.

b. Others derive their proof from *the unheeded voice of conscience.* A voice within me is constantly saying, "Thou shalt do this, that." Yet, no

---

[68] Cf. G. Matheson, "The Pauline Argument for a Future State," *Exp,* first series, 9 (1879), pp. 264-284.

one has ever *fully* obeyed this categorical imperative. Is not this unrelenting demand a prediction of a future state of strict compliance, a state of perfection?

c. There is also the argument from *the enduring character of the self within me.* In a steady line of progress I as a person have already survived successive stages of being. I was an embryo. When that stage ceased my *self* persisted. I was born, became an infant. I survived that stage too. And so after boyhood I became a young man, then a man of middle age, etc. Consequently, as I have survived every one of these stages, will I not also survive the last stage, namely, physical death, and rise to an immortality of bliss and glory?

A moment's reflection is all that is necessary to show the weakness of this type of reasoning in any of its forms. Persistent yearning for the ideal in the realm of beauty, inner compulsion to obey the moral law coupled with the realization that in the here and now one can never obey it fully, and also the self's leapfrogging of biological stages, these facts do not guarantee immortality, much less perfection in a future existence. As to the last argument, even a dog, in proportion to its own life span, passes through and survives various stages, yet does not thereby attain to immortality!

3. Christ . . . the hope of glory

Now over against these fallible reasonings Paul proclaims Christ as the one and only solid basis for the expectation of *immortality* not only, but of future, eschatological *glory.* The evidence, moreover, which Christ gave to the world of a future state of perfection lay not only in his words or deeds but in *himself.* Our persistent yearning for the ideal in the realm of true, spiritual beauty is realized in him. And because his soul is beautiful, words of grace and beauty fell from his lips.

> "Fair are the meadows,
> Fairer still the woodlands,
> Robed in the blooming garb of spring:
> Jesus is fairer, Jesus is purer,
> Who makes the woeful heart to sing."
>
> Crusaders' Hymn

As to the persistent demand of conscience, he was the only one who satisfied it in every respect. He was able to say, "Who of y o u convicts me of sin?" (John 8:46).

> "Weak is the effort of my heart,
> And cold my warmest thought;
> But when I see thee as you art,
> I'll praise thee as I ought."
>
> John Newton

loyalty to Christ which characterized the church as a whole. The prisoner, his heart filled with genuine love for the Colossians, decides to write them a letter. In this letter he takes the positive approach, so characteristic of him, and after a Christ-centered opening saluation, tells the addressees that he is continually thanking God for their *faith* in Christ Jesus and their *love* for all the saints, both of these (faith and love) strengthened by the *hope* laid up for them in the heavens, that is, the inheritance of the saints in the light. That prospect does, indeed, intensify *faith* in the Giver and *love* for all the fellow-recipients.

The hope of obtaining this inheritance is firmly grounded in the world-conquering gospel that has also made its presence felt among the Colossians, through the ministry of ever-faithful Epaphras.

Encouraged by answers to previous prayers, Paul is constantly praying that God may multiply his favors upon the Colossians, so that, while living among those whose doctrines would lead them astray, they may receive an ever clearer insight into the will of God, and may, as a result, live lives that will be spiritually fruitful in every way, and will abound in evidences of sincere and humble gratitude to God. Let them ever bear in mind that it was God who rescued them out of the domain of darkness and transplanted them into the kingdom of the Son of his love.

By means of a ringing testimony — perhaps a hymn which he is quoting — the apostle proclaims Christ as all-sufficient Savior, sovereign in both realms: creation and redemption. Therefore let the Colossians not place their confidence in anything other than Christ, for apart from him no creature has any strength either to help or to hurt. Through Christ the universe is restored to its proper relationship to God, for from his position at the Father's right hand Christ rules the entire universe in the interest of the church and to the glory of God. He who died on the cross to save sinners holds in his hands the most distant star.

If the Colossians will keep clinging to the gospel that proclaims this sovereign and all-sufficient Christ who rescued them from their former wicked life, they will not slip back. On the contrary, this Christ will one day present them holy, faultless, and blameless before himself. Of this glorious gospel Paul had been privileged to become a minister. Because of his loyalty to that gospel he is now a prisoner in Rome, supplying in his flesh what was lacking in the afflictions of Christ. Yes, the afflictions which Christ endured were overflowing to him. But he rejoices in his God-given stewardship, and intends, by God's grace, to give full scope to the word of God, the long-hidden but now revealed mystery, which is "Christ in y o u, the hope of glory." The fact that one day Christ would be living through his Spirit in the hearts and lives of the Gentiles had been long predicted but had now become a reality. This indwelling was itself the guarantee of a glorious future. With reference to the indwelling Christ, Paul concludes the chapter by saying, "whom we proclaim, admonishing every man and teaching every man in all wisdom, in order that we may present every man perfect in Christ; for which I am laboring, striving by his energy working powerfully within me."

---

⁶⁰ In connection with the accusative pronoun ὑμᾶς (y o u), the one at the beginning of verse 21, and the verbal form, if any, with which it is connected either as object or otherwise, the following main possibilities require consideration:

(1) This pronoun is modified, in verse 22, by the nom. pl. aor. pass. participle ἀπαλλαγέντες. Hence, one should read, "And y o u, who once were estranged and hostile . . . but now having been reconciled . . ."

Objections: a. In that case the accusative, rather than the nominative form of the participle would be more natural. b. The textual support for this reading is not very strong (D* G it Ir). c. The question would remain: of what verbal form is this pronoun and its modifying participle the object? This question recurs under (2); hence, may be omitted here.

(2) This pronoun is the object of the aor. inf. παραστῆσαι in verse 22. Therefore, the rendering should be, "to present y o u." The sentence which began in verse 9 continues to the end of verse 23. Verse 22a (νυνὶ . . . θανάτου) is a parenthesis in this sentence. Hence, ". . . for in him he [God] was pleased to have all the fulness dwell, and through him to reconcile all things to himself . . . and y o u, who once were estranged and hostile in disposition, as shown by y o u r wicked works (but now y o u have been reconciled in his body of flesh through his death), to present y o u holy, faultless, and blameless before himself . . ." It is evident that here the first y o u, the one at the beginning of verse 21, is repeated in verse 22, in order to disentangle the construction. It is also clear that the verb which indicates the work of reconciliation and which is included in the parenthesis is ἀποκατηλλάγητε: y o u have been reconciled, 2 per. pl. aor. ind. pass.

Objections: a. It is improbable that the very lengthy sentence (verses 9-20) would be lengthened some more by three additional verses. b. It has been shown that verses 15-20 are a literary unit, probably an ancient hymn, a unit of which verses 21-23 are not a part. c. The main idea of verses 15-20, namely, the pre-eminence of the Son in Creation and Redemption, is not continued in verses 21-23. The attention is shifted rather to the share which the Colossians have in this redemption and to the responsibility this imposes upon them.

(3) This pronoun is the object of the aor. inf. ἀποκαταλλάξαι in verse 20. Therefore, the translation should be, "to reconcile y o u." The sentence ends at the close of verse 21. Hence, ". . . for in him he [God] was pleased to have all the fulness dwell, and through him to reconcile all things to himself . . . whether the things on the earth or the things in the heavens, and (to reconcile) y o u, who once were estranged and hostile in disposition, as shown by y o u r wicked works."

Objections: see b. and c. under (2) above; also a. to a certain extent. Moule, op. cit., p. 72, is correct when he states that this reconstruction makes of verse 21 "a clumsy afterthought to the sentence of verse 20."

(4) The pronoun is not connected with any verbal form. It is left hanging. The apostle wanted to say, "And y o u he has reconciled," but he never actually said ("dictated") it. He used instead the aor. indic. pass., "Y o u have been reconciled" (ἀποκατηλλάγητε), verse 22.

The following arguments have been presented in favor of this theory:

a. For Paul it was not unusual that before an idea had been fully expressed it was already being crowded out by another. He had a fertile mind.

b. This reading ("Y o u have been reconciled") has strong textual support (p⁴⁶ B 33 Ephr).

c. It is much easier to explain the substitution of "He has reconciled" (which would eliminate the anacoluthon) for "Y o u have been reconciled," than vice versa.

These are formidable arguments.

(5) The pronoun is simply the object of the 3 per. sing. aor. ind. act. verb ἀποκατήλλαξεν, he has reconciled.

Grounds:

a. This reading is supported by the majority of the manuscripts and versions. — The question may be raised, however, whether such evidence should not rather be weighed than counted.

b. This reading solves the grammatical problem. There is no longer any break in grammatical sequence. — This argument carries very little weight, for objection (4)c still holds. Hence, No. 5 could be simply a *solution* (?) for the sake of ease, a cutting of the Gordian knot.

c. The somewhat similar acc. pronoun ὑμᾶς in Eph. 2:1 ("and y o u being dead through y o u r trespasses and sins") , which also for a while is left hanging, is "rescued" by the aor. *active* ind. *"he made alive together with* Christ," of verse 5. If Paul used the *active* indic. there, why not also here in Colossians? — This argument probably has some value.

Conclusion

The choice lies between (4) and (5). In either case Paul said or at one time intended to say, "He has reconciled y o u." The more usual rendering, which avoids anacoluthon, may therefore probably be allowed to stand, though it does not solve the difficulties mentioned under (4) b and c. Accordingly, the distinct possibility that the rendering should be based entirely upon (4), retaining the anacoluthon, must be granted.

A.

[66] This interpretation is also supported by the following, more technical considerations:

(1) It does justice to the meaning of the prefix ἀντί. There is no justification for taking this prefix-in-composition, as here used, in any other than the substitutionary sense, as I believe I have proved in my doctoral dissertation, "The Meaning of the Preposition ἀντί in the New Testament," pp. 76, 77, Princeton Seminary, 1948. Photius has stated the case very aptly, "For he does not simply say *I fill up,* but *I fill up instead;* that is, instead of the master and teacher, I, the servant and disciple," etc. (Amphil. 121). See Lightfoot's comment on this, p. 165 of his Commentary.

(2) It is in harmony with the meaning of the expression *to fill up* (or *to supply*) *the deficiencies* (or *what is lacking*) , as used elsewhere in the New Testament: I Cor. 16:17; Phil. 2:30 (see N.T.C. on that passage). In both of these cases the verb ἀναπληρόω is used. The double compound ἀνταναπληρόω occurs only here in Col. 1:24. A different double compound προσαναπληρόω (II Cor. 9:12; 11:9) also lends support to the interpretation given.

(3) It also gives the most natural meaning to the genitive τοῦ Χριστοῦ, interpreting it to mean *endured by Christ.* And according to the context the reference is distinctly to the humiliation experienced by the historical Jesus during his earthly ministry and death. See verses 20 and 22, which speak of *the blood of the cross* and of *the death* of Jesus.

B.

Accordingly, to be rejected are the following theories:

(1) Christ's vicarious atonement must be supplemented by good deeds, etc., as if its merits were otherwise insufficient.

Answer. This has been refuted in the text: Heb. 10:11-14, etc.

(2) The expression *the afflictions of Christ* indicates the sufferings which "the Mystic Christ," "the Messianic Community," or "the Corporate Christ" undergoes and must undergo during this entire dispensation until the end of the world. Along this line, though cautiously, Moule, in his very interesting and helpful Commentary, *op. cit.,* p. 76.

Answer. This violates A (3) above.

(3) *The afflictions of Christ* are those *laid upon* Paul, etc., by Christ.

Answer. This also violates A (3) above.

(4) (This is closely related to, though not identical with, No. (2).) *The afflictions of Christ* are those suffered by the exalted Mediator in heaven. The risen and ascended Christ suffers in his members. Because of the intimate bond of unity between the exalted Christ and his church the latter's sufferings may be called "the afflictions of Christ." Thus John Calvin in his *Commentary;* also Augustine and Luther. A. S. Peake, *op. cit.,* pp. 514, 515, concludes similarly.

Answer. Again a violation of A (3) above.

(5) What has been rendered "what is lacking in the afflictions of Christ" should be interpreted as "the leftover parts of the afflictions of Christ." Thus Lenski, *op. cit.,* p. 73. These "leftover parts" he also simply calls "the leftovers." Though on p. 72 he does not hesitate to use the expression "what is lacking" in his translation, yet on p. 74 he objects to calling these leftovers "deficiencies" or "something that was lacking." I honor him (his memory) for the theological position which in all probability led to his objection, but cannot agree with his reasoning at this point.

Answer. The word ὑστέρημα as used in the New Testament means (sing.) *want, lack, what is lacking, need, absence* (see Luke 21:4; I Cor. 16:17; II Cor. 8:13, 14; 9:12; 11:9; Phil. 2:30; I Thess. 3:10; and so, plur., also here in Col. 1:24). The interpretation *leftover, when it is said that this cannot mean lack or deficiency,* is hard to reconcile with the verb *to supply* (literally *to fill up,* or as we would say *to fill in*). Also if the noun used in the original means *leftover but not lack* we might have expected it (plur.) in such passages as Matt. 14:20; Mark 6:43; 8:8, 19, 20; Luke 9:17; John 6:12, 13. It does not occur in these passages.

See also, in addition to the various Commentaries listed in the Bibliography, Ernst Percy, *op. cit.,* pp. 128-134; Delling, Th.W.N.T., Vol. VI, p. 305; P. J. Gloag, "The Complement of Christ's Afflictions," *Exp,* first series, 7 (1878), pp. 224-236; W. R. G. Moir, "Col. 1:24," *ET,* 42 (1930-1931), pp. 479, 480; Josef Schmid, "Kol.1,24," *BibZ,* 21 (1933), pp. 330-344; and the dissertation of Jacob Kremer, *Was an den Leiden Christi noch mangelt. Eine interpretationsgeschichtliche und exegetische Untersuchung zu Kol.1,24b* (in Bonner, *Biblische Beiträge*), 1956.

Outline of Chapter 2

Theme: *Christ, the Pre-eminent One, the Only and All-Sufficient Savior*
I. This Only and All-Sufficient Savior is the Object of the Believers' Faith, chapters 1 and 2
    B. This Truth Expounded not only Positively but now both Positively and Negatively, chapter 2, the latter over against "the Colossian Heresy" with its:

2:1-10 1. Delusive Philosophy
2:11-17 2. Judaistic Ceremonialism
2:18-19 3. Angel-worship
2:20-23 4. Asceticism

CHAPTER II

COLOSSIANS

2 1 For I want y o u to know how greatly I strive for y o u, and for those at Laodicea, and for all who have not seen my face in the flesh, 2 in order that their hearts may be strengthened, they themselves being welded together in love, and this with a view to all the riches of assured understanding, with a view to the clear knowledge of the mystery of God, namely, Christ; 3 in whom all the treasures of wisdom and knowledge are hidden. 4 I say this in order that no one may mislead y o u by persuasive argument. 5 For, although in the flesh I am absent, yet in the spirit I am with y o u, rejoicing to see y o u r good order and the firmness of y o u r faith in Christ.

6 As therefore y o u accepted Christ Jesus the Lord, (so) in him continue to live, 7 rooted and being built up in him and being established in the faith, just as y o u were taught, overflowing with thanksgiving. 8 Be on y o u r guard lest there be any one who carries y o u off as spoil by means of his philosophy and empty deceit, according to the tradition of men, according to the rudiments of the world, and not according to Christ; 9 for in him all the fulness of the godhead dwells bodily, 10 and in him y o u have attained to fulness, namely, in him who is the head of every principality and authority.

2:1-10

I. *Warning against Delusive Philosophy*

1. It is immediately evident that Col. 2:1 is a clear continuation of the thought expressed in 1:29. Paul was writing *one letter, not four "chapters."* The continuation is: **For I want y o u to know,** the "for" constituting proof for the statement made in the preceding verse. The opening formula, "I want y o u to know," here and in I Cor. 11:3, is substantially the same in meaning as the somewhat differently worded one in Phil. 1:12. Similar is also the expression, "I (or *we*) do not wish y o u to be in ignorance" (Rom.1:13; 11:25; I Cor. 10:1; 12:1; II Cor. 1:8; I Thess. 4:13) . By the use of this formula the apostle stresses the importance of the matter under discussion. He regards the Colossian Heresy, which he is about to refute, as being a very serious danger, and therefore continues: **how greatly I strive for y o u** [71] **and**

---

[71] The rendering of the A.V., "what great conflict I have for you," is more literal, but fails to show the closeness of the connection between Col. 1:29 (A.V. "striving according to his working") and 2:1. In the original for these two verses the apostle uses two words derived from the same stem, which could almost be rendered *agonizing* (1:29) , and *agony* (2:1) . See footnote 70.

for those at Laodicea, and for all who have not seen my face in the flesh. The nature of this *striving* need not be repeated (see on Col. 1:29 above). What Paul means is, "For, in substantiation of what I have just said, I want y o u to know how greatly I strive for y o u, Colossians, and for those at Laodicea, and for all who, *like yourselves,* have never seen me." It is well-nigh certain that the phrase "and for all who" also includes the membership of the church at Hierapolis (see Col. 4:13). As has been shown (see Introduction II A), so close to each other were the three cities that a spiritual danger that affected *one* of them was almost bound to affect the other two also, though not necessarily in the same degree.[72]

Two misconceptions must be avoided at this point:

(1) The view of many that the apostle here implies that he had never been in Colosse.

Answer: Church and *town* must not be confused. It should be borne in mind that when Paul on his third missionary journey was headed for Ephesus there was as yet no church at Colosse for him to visit. On the question, "Was Paul ever in Colosse?" see Introduction II A; III A. The situation, as I see it, may well have been as follows:

On his way to Ephesus, Paul followed the natural route which via Colosse led to Ephesus. He passed through Colosse, and may even have spent a night there. Whether or not he did we simply do not know. His aim, however, was to confirm the churches already established and to reach Ephesus, not to establish new churches on the way to his destination. During his lengthy stay at Ephesus, enquirers from the surrounding region came to hear him (Acts 19:10). Among those who came were also some people from *the three cities,* one of those individuals being Epaphras from Colosse (cf. Col. 4:12). Upon their conversion these men — including Epaphras — carried the great news of salvation back to their respective towns. Thus churches were established. Speaking in general terms, Paul could truly say that these congregations had never seen him.

(2) The idea that the apostle was a total stranger to every member of the three churches.

Answer: Nearly all commentators — even those that cling to No. 1, just refuted — are careful to point out that Paul was, indeed, personally acquainted with *some* of the members of the Colossian church, and perhaps also with some of those that belonged to the other churches in the Lycus Valley. As to the apostle's personal acquaintances and friends in or from Colosse see on Col. 4:12, 17; Philem. 1, 2.

The main idea of Col. 2:1 is, accordingly, that Paul, having received ample information from Epaphras (and perhaps also from others) regarding prevailing conditions in the churches of the Lycus Valley, wants the entire

---

[72] Clearly ὅσοι *here,* as in Acts 4:6; Rev. 18:17, includes those previously mentioned. This ὅσοι is reflected in αὐτῶν of verse 2 and even in ὑμᾶς of verse 4.

membership — also that large majority that has never seen him — to know how much he loves them and how thoroughly he is concerned about them when spiritual danger threatens.

Now both in chapter 1 and in chapter 2 the apostle proclaims Christ as the only and all-sufficient Savior, the Object of the believers' faith. In both chapters, moreover, the predominant tone is *positive:* Christ is set forth in all his majesty and riches as the source of whatever believers may need and especially as the object of their trust and adoration. There is, however, a marked difference between the two chapters. While in chapter 1 the negative element — refutation of error — is merely *implied,* in chapter 2 it is definitely *expressed* (see verses 4, 8, 16, 18, 20-23), and forceful warnings are issued. Even here, however, as stated, it is Christ who is proclaimed (see verses 2, 3, 6, 7, 9-15).

Now though the heresy is *one,* the apostle views it here from a fourfold aspect (cf. Introduction III B). These four divisions, however, are not watertight compartments. There is overlapping, as will be shown as the individual passages are discussed.

2, 3. The purpose of Paul's striving is: **in order that their hearts may be strengthened.** The *heart* of all true pastoral activity is to be an instrument in God's hand to bring the *hearts* of those entrusted to one's care to the *heart* of Christ. The reason is this: once a man's heart has been thoroughly won over and established in grace, the entire person has become the object of God's marvelous transforming power, for the heart is the fulcrum of feeling and faith as well as the mainspring of words and actions (Rom. 10:10; cf. Matt. 12:34; 15:19; 22:37; John 14:1). It is the core and center of man's being, man's inmost self. "Out of it are the issues of life" (Prov. 4:23). "Man looks on the outward appearance, but Jehovah looks on the heart" (I Sam. 16:7). Over against the attack of false teachers these hearts must be *strengthened.*[73] In unity there is strength; hence the continuation is: **they themselves being welded together**[74] **in love.** Not *knowledge,* certainly not *conceit* (see Col. 2:18), but *mutual love* is "the bond of perfection" (Col. 3:14). Such love springs directly from the heart of God in Christ and leads back to him, for God is love (I John 4:8). Now when believers, welded together in love,

---

[73] The basic meaning of the verb παρακαλέω is *I call to my side;* hence, *I summon* (cf. Acts 28:20). But a person may be summoned for various purposes. Hence, the word has a great variety of derived meanings, the exact sense in any given case to be determined by the context. When used, as here in Col. 2:2, with *hearts* it is best translated *strengthen, encourage* (here passive; in Col. 4:8; Eph. 6:22; II Thess. 2:17 active). Cf. also Phil. 2:1: "if therefore (there is) any encouragement in Christ."

[74] Basic meaning of the verb συμβιβάζω is *I cause to come together; I bring, hold, knit,* or *weld together, unite* (Eph. 4:16, literally; here in Col. 2:2 fig.). It is easy to see how this basic meaning developed into other connotations: *I teach* (thus in LXX; e.g., Isa. 40:13, 14: "Who has taught him?" quoted in I Cor. 2:16), *I prove* (cf. Acts 9:22), or *I conclude* (cf. Acts 16:10).

are confronted with the danger of errors and lies, let them unitedly pray about this and discuss it among each other on the basis of God's special revelation (cf. Eph. 3:17-19), **and this with a view to all the riches of assured understanding.**[75] Thorough, rich, gratifying *insight* (see also Col. 1:9; cf. I Cor. 1:19; Eph. 3:4; II Tim. 2:7) into spiritual matters, which implies the ability to distinguish the true from the false, must ever be the goal. Even more definitely this goal is expressed in the words: **with a view to the clear knowledge of the mystery of God, namely, Christ.** The sense in which Christ is, indeed, the mystery of God has been explained in connection with Col. 1:27. See also N.T.C. on I and II Timothy and Titus, pp. 137-141, explanation of I Tim. 3:16. This mystery, progressively revealed to believers who love one another, transcends all human comprehension (Rom. 11:33-36; I Cor. 2:6-16), and is, therefore, also in that sense a divine and very glorious mystery: "the mystery of God, namely, Christ," **in whom all the treasures of wisdom and knowledge are hidden.** The Colossians need not, must not, look for any source of happiness or of holiness outside of Christ. Do false teachers boast about their wisdom and their knowledge? Or about that of the angels? Neither man nor angel nor any other creature has anything at all to offer which cannot be found *in incomparably superior essence and in infinite degree* in Christ. In him *all* the treasures of wisdom and knowledge *are hidden,* like the "hidden treasure" of which Jesus spoke in the parable (Matt. 13:44; cf. Prov. 2:4); *hidden,* indeed, but in order to be unearthed, not in order to remain concealed.[76] That this practical purpose is also in the

---

[75] Literally, "all the riches of the assurance of the understanding." *Assurance* is the meaning that fits every New Testament passage in which πληροφορία is used (besides Col. 2:2 also I Thess. 1:5; Heb. 6:11; 10:22).
[76] The word for *hidden* is pl. of ἀπόκρυφος from which we have derived our words *apocrypha* and *apochryphal*. According to Josephus (*Jewish War* II.viii.7) before being admitted to the full privileges of the order of the Essenes the novice "was made to swear tremendous oaths . . . to conceal nothing from the members of the sect and to report none of their secrets to others, even though he should be tortured to death . . . and likewise carefully to guard the books of their sect and the names of the angels." Irenaeus (*Against Heresies* I.xx.1) reports that the Marcosians "adduce an unspeakable number of *apocryphal* and spurious writings, which they themselves have forged." And Clement of Alexandria (*Stromata* or *Miscellanies* I.15) states, "of *the secret books* of this man, those who follow the heresy of Prodicus boast to be in possession." The false teachers who vexed the Colossians with their dangerous doctrines may similarly have boasted about their *secret, hidden* writings. Lightfoot says, "Thus the word *apocrypha* in the first instance was an honorable appellation applied by the heretics themselves to their esoteric doctrine and their secret books; but owing to the general character of these works the term, as adopted by orthodox writers, got to signify *false, spurious*" (*op. cit.*, p. 174).
It is possible, therefore, although it cannot be proved, that when the apostle here refers to Christ's *hidden* treasures, and implies that they are freely offered to those who would accept them by faith (see Col. 2:9, 10), he is contrasting these real and inexhaustible treasures with the worthless secrets of the false teachers, and this glorious hiding with the concealment practised by the heretics.

apostle's mind here in Colossians is clear from verses 9 and 10. What the apostle means, therefore, is this, "In Christ all these treasures are stored away. Hence, come and discover them and enrich yourselves by means of them."

"Treasures of wisdom *and knowledge,*" says Paul, which is even better than "treasures of wisdom" of which we read elsewhere (Ecclus. 1:25). Jesus, according to his divine nature, knows all things. This knowledge, being divine, is all-comprehensive, direct, simple, unchangeable, and eternal. Peter paid tribute to it when he declared, "Lord, all things thou knowest; thou dost realize that I have affection for thee" (John 21:17). Christ's omniscience is therefore a great comfort for the believer and, via Christ's revelation in Scripture, a bank from which he draws.

But in Christ *knowledge* is never separated from *wisdom,* as it often is among men. Now wisdom is the ability, in concrete situations, to apply knowledge to the best advantage. It uses the most effective means to achieve the highest goal. In the Old Testament the work of creation is ascribed to God's wisdom (Ps. 104:24; Jer. 10:12). Job 28:23 ff. and Prov. 8:22 ff. personify the wisdom by means of which God created all things. The New Testament magnifies the wisdom of God revealed in the foolishness of the cross (I Cor. 1:18-25), in the church (Eph. 3:10), and in the work of God's providence in behalf of Israel and of the Gentiles (Rom. 11:33).

At this point it is necessary to guard against error. The word *wisdom* is used in a threefold sense in Colossians: (a) the wisdom given to Paul and his fellow-workers and to believers in general (Col. 1:9, 28; 3:16; 4:5); (b) the pretended wisdom of the false teachers (Col. 2:23); and (c) the divine wisdom that dwells eternally in Christ (Col. 2:3). These three must not be confused. Sometimes divine wisdom, such as is certainly spoken of here in Col. 2:3, is equated, as to its essence, with human wisdom, as if the former were but an enlarged edition of the latter. So, for example, in connection with *the present passage,* we are told that while *"knowledge* applies to apprehension of truths, *wisdom* superadds the power of reasoning about them and tracing their relation" (Lightfoot, *op. cit.,* p. 174). But although this may be a perfectly valid and useful distinction when we are speaking about *human* wisdom, the wisdom that is ascribed to *Christ* is more than the ability to reason and to trace. Archetypal wisdom differs from ectypal: the divine pattern and the human copy can never be identical, the reason being that God is God, and we are dealing here with Christ as God (see Col. 2:9). Divine wisdom, in a sense far more exalted than human wisdom, devises, plans, guides, directs. It is original, creative. It does what no other wisdom in the entire universe can ever accomplish. *It reconciles seeming irreconcilables.* A few examples will make this clear:

(1) In his wisdom God reconciles the Jew with the Gentile, and both together with himself, performing this great miracle by means of that alto-

gether unlikely object, namely, the cross, which to the Jew was a stumbling-block and to the Gentile foolishness! (I Cor. 1:22-25; Eph. 2:13, 14) .

(2) In his wisdom he satisfies the demands both of his *justice* which asked for the death of the sinner and of his *love* which required the sinner's salvation. The law and the gospel embrace each other on the cross (Rom. 3:19-24; 5:8, 12, 13; 16:27; cf. Ps. 85:10) .

(3) In his wisdom, which Paul extols, the very rejection of carnal Israel results, by various links, in the salvation of "all Israel": "By their fall salvation is come to the Gentiles, to provoke them to jealousy . . . that by the mercy shown to y o u [Gentiles] they [Israel] may now obtain mercy." Paul concludes, "O the depth of the riches and wisdom and knowledge of God," etc.[77]

In Christ, then, for the benefit of believers, all the treasures of this all-comprehensive knowledge and of this sublime, creative wisdom are hidden.

4, 5. With reference at least to what he has just said in verses 1-3 but more probably to all of 1:3–2:3, Paul continues: **I say this in order that no one may mislead y o u by persuasive argument.** Do not exchange *demonstrated facts,* regarding the fulness that is in Christ, for *specious reasoning.* Cf. I Cor. 2:4. The original does not bear out the view of those who think that Paul had one particular person in mind when he issued this warning. There were doubtless many false teachers. Hence, says Paul, as it were, "When someone or other comes with attractive arguments, do not be turned aside by that person and his finespun phrases." He continues, **For, although in the flesh I am absent, yet in the spirit I am with y o u.** Note in connection with this statement:

(1) the fellowship of all believers in Christ. This closeness of loving communion was felt very keenly in the early church (see N.T.C. on Philippians, pp. 51-54; 93-95) .

(2) the vividness of Paul's sense of fellowship with those who for the most part had not seen him and with whom, therefore, he was not personally acquainted. It is reasonable to assume that Epaphras had given the apostle a very graphic account of conditions in the Colossian church (see also 1:7, 8; 4:12, 13) .

(3) the plus-factor in this fellowship. What Paul meant amounted to far more than saying, "In my imagination I can see y o u now, my friends. It just seems as if I am there with y o u." It was that, to be sure, but also more than that, namely, "In heart and spirit I am with y o u, with y o u to help y o u and to rejoice with y o u, as even this letter indicates and as Tychicus and Onesimus will be telling y o u" (Col. 4:7-9) . Proof: note how the apostle, using somewhat similar language asserts himself in the congrega-

---

[77] In my 36 page booklet, *And So All Israel Shall Be Saved,* I have given what I consider to be the correct interpretation of Rom. 11:26a and its context.

tion at Corinth, actually taking part in a matter of discipline, even though he was not bodily present with them (I Cor. 5:3-5) ; and also how warmly he makes his spiritual presence felt in the church at Thessalonica (I Thess. 2:17: "out of sight but not out of heart") .

The report which Epaphras had presented to Paul was, on the whole, favorable. Though he had not in any way minimized the dangers that were threatening the church, yet he had been careful to point out that on the whole the Colossians had not been moved from their foundation. Genuine love was present among them (1:8) , and, as we now learn, also *good order* — there had been no schism and no lack of orderly discipline and behavior — and *sterling, steadfast faith,* for the apostle continues: **rejoicing to see y o u r good order and the firmness of y o u r faith in Christ.**[78]

6, 7. In close connection with the preceding sentence Paul continues: **As therefore y o u accepted Christ Jesus the Lord, (so) in him continue to live.** The chiastic or criss-cross structure of this sentence — with the verbs *accepted* and *continue to live* respectively at beginning and end; and the references to Christ, namely, *Christ Jesus the Lord* and *in him,* in the center (note forward position of "in him") — shows that all the emphasis falls on the necessity of clinging to Christ Jesus the Lord (cf. Eph. 3:11; Phil. 2:11) , as the all-sufficient One, as the Lord whose commandments should be obeyed and whose word should be trusted. The meaning is, "Colossians, do not be misled. Let y o u r life (y o u r "walk" or conduct) continue to be in harmony with the fact that y o u have accepted Christ Jesus the Lord as y o u r tradition. Y o u embraced him with a living faith, just as y o u were taught to do" (see verse 7; cf. Eph. 4:20) . The word *accepted* is here used in its technical sense: *received as transmitted* (cf. I Cor. 11:23; 15:1, 3; Gal. 1:9, 12; Phil. 4:9; I Thess. 2:13; 4:1; II Thess. 3:6) , the line of transmission having been from God to Paul (both directly and indirectly) , to Epaphras, to the Colossians.[79]

By a series of four participles ("rooted," "being built up," "being established," "and overflowing") , the first a *perfect passive* and the other three *present,* Paul now shows what this living *in Christ* (that is, *in vital union with him*) means: **rooted and being built up in him and being established in the faith, just as y o u were taught, overflowing with thanksgiving.** Mean-

---

[78] In agreement with many commentators I cannot see any good reason for accepting Lightfoot's suggestion that Paul is using a military metaphor: "y o u r orderly array and close phalanx." The context does not require this interpretation.
[79] Three kinds of *tradition* are mentioned in the New Testament: (a) the Jewish oral law. Said Josephus, "the Pharisees have handed down to the people a great many observances by succession from their fathers which are not written in the law of Moses" (*Antiq.* XIII.x.6) . Jesus reflects on these man-made additions in Mark 7:8, 9; (b) "the tradition of men" (Col. 2:8; see on that verse) ; and (c) the true God-given gospel, as taught by Christ and his apostles, sometimes called "the apostolic tradition." The reference in Col. 2:6 is to (c) .

ing: "Having then been firmly implanted in Christ (for example, in his love, Eph. 3:17), as the infinite and all-sufficient Source of salvation full and free, and so continuing, constantly avail yourselves of every opportunity of being brought to higher and still higher ground, as a building rises tier by tier,[80] of being established ever more firmly in the activity of faith,[81] as y o u were taught by Epaphras (Col. 1:7; 4:12, 13), and of overflowing with gratitude" (cf. Col. 4:2). Gratitude is that which completes the circle whereby blessings that drop down into our hearts and lives return to the Giver in the form of unending, loving, and spontaneous adoration. Moreover, such giving of thanks increases the sense of obligation (Ps. 116:12-14), so that those who overflow with this grace feel all the less ready to turn away from the abundance which they have in Christ Jesus the Lord, and to follow the advice of false teachers.

Notice that Paul does not pray that the Colossians may *begin* to be thankful, but rather that the ocean of their gratitude may constantly overflow its *perimeter*. Paul is never satisfied with anything short of perfection. Hence he loves to use this word *overflow* or *abound* (Rom. 3:7; 5:15; 15:13; I Cor. 8:8; 14:12; 15:58; ten times in II Cor.; Phil. 1:9, 26; 4:12, 18; I Thess. 3:12; 4:1, 10). See also N.T.C. on I and II Timothy and Titus, p. 75.

8-10. There is a very close connection between verses 6, 7, on the one hand, and verses 8-10, on the other. What has been stated positively in verses 6, 7, namely, "Continue to live in Christ Jesus the Lord," is stated negatively in verses 8-10, the sense of these three verses being, "Do *not* allow yourselves to be carried away by any teaching that is *not according to Christ,* for he will supply all your needs, since in him all the fulness of the godhead dwells bodily and since he is the supreme Ruler of all." We have a restatement, therefore, in somewhat different form, of what the apostle had said in verse 4, "I say this in order that no one may mislead y o u by persuasive argument." It becomes clear, therefore, that in this entire section (verses 1-10) Paul indicates that he was deeply concerned about the false teaching of those whose speculative theories, cleverly presented, might tend to undermine the confidence of the Colossians in Christ as their complete Savior. He calls this subversive system of thought and morals, of rules and regulations "philosophy and empty deceit." He uses words like "man-made tradition" and "worldly rudiments" to describe it.

---

[80] The combination *plant* and *building* is also found in Jer. 24:6 and Eph. 4:15, 16.. Is it correct to speak of a mixed metaphor here? Is it not rather a case of one underlying figure following another in rapid succession? I can see no confusion here.
[81] I take τῇ πίστει to be dative of respect or reference, not (with Lightfoot) instrumental. Also, in contrast with Lenski, I believe that this *faith* is to be taken in the subjective sense, although here, as in Col. 1:23, there is a very close connection between this faith-activity and its object, as the following clause ("just as y o u were taught") indicates.

There is, however, another interpretation of these verses, differing rather sharply from the one set forth in the aforegoing summarizing paragraph. It is to the effect that the apostle here sets Christ over against "the elemental spirits of the universe," the words between quotation marks being the R.S.V. rendering of the Greek phrase which in both A.V. and A.R.V. is translated "the rudiments of the world" (verse 8). For comments about this interpretation which, with due respect for the erudition of those who advocate it, I cannot adopt, see footnote 83 *at the close* of my treatment of the entire passage (verses 8-10).

The apostle, accordingly, continues as follows: **Be on y o u r guard lest there be any one who carries y o u off as spoil by means of his philosophy and empty deceit.** Let not those who were rescued out of the domain of darkness and transplanted into the kingdom of the Son of God's love (see Col. 1:13) be carried off as so much booty and become enslaved once more (cf. Gal. 5:1).

Brought under bondage by someone's "philosophy"! As Josephus has shown, any elaborate system of thought and/or moral discipline was in those days called a *philosophy* (cf. our term "moral philosophy," when the *scientific* aspect is not stressed). Thus he states, "For there are three forms of philosophy among the Jews. The followers of the first school are called Pharisees, of the second Sadducees, and of the third Essenes" (*Jewish War* II.viii.2). When it is borne in mind that in several of its traits the body of error which Paul here opposes resembles Essenism, the relevancy of this quotation from Josephus becomes all the more clear. Philo also, when speaking about Hebrew religion, uses such terms as "philosophy according to Moses" and "Jewish philosophy." Paul is warning against the kind of philosophy that amounts to nothing more than *empty deceit.* It is empty, futile. It is deceptive, for, while it promises big things to those who obey its ordinances, it cannot redeem its promises (see on verse 23). Paul continues: **according to the tradition of men** (see footnote 79 above). This was not *apostolic* tradition, nor was it tradition that belonged to the main stream of *Judaism,* though it did have something in common with Judaism and embraced some of the latter's tenets. It was rather a mixture of Christianity, Judaistic Ceremonialism, Angelolatry, and Asceticism, as verses 11-23 indicate. It was a philosophy **according to the rudiments of the world.** Rudiments are *elements,* either in the physical or in the non-physical realm. The original uses the term *stoicheia,* indicating elements or units in a row or series, like the figures (1, 2, 3, etc.) in a column, or the letters (A, B, C, etc.) in the alphabet; then also the basic elements of which the physical world is held to consist (cf. II Peter 3:10, 12). The ancients sometimes spoke of earth, air, fire, and water as elements. By an easy transition the meaning advances to *rudiments* or *elements of learning;* hence, *elementary teaching* (Heb. 5:12). We speak of "Rudiments of Grammar," "Elements of Arithmetic," etc.

The expression "rudiments of the world" also occurs in Gal. 4:3 (cf. Gal. 4:9). This is admittedly a very difficult passage, proving the correctness of II Peter 3:15, 16. It is true, indeed, that "our beloved brother Paul" sometimes wrote things "hard to understand." One thing should be borne in mind, however, namely, that in Galatians and in Colossians we are dealing with rudiments *of the world,* a modifier that does not occur in Hebrews and in II Peter. Now in Col. 2:8, in harmony with the immediate context which speaks about "the tradition of *men,*" the term *world* (kosmos) must probably be taken in its ethical sense (as often in Paul's epistles), as indicating "mankind alienated from the life of God." These are rudiments of worldly men. They are *worldly* rudiments. In all likelihood that interpretation of the modifier *of the world* also holds for Galatians (cf. Gal. 4:9, "weak and beggarly rudiments"). Worthy of serious consideration, in the light of the contexts (in Gal. 4:3 and 4:9), is therefore the view according to which in Galatians the expression "rudiments of the world" indicates rudimentary teaching regarding rules, regulations, ordinances, by means of which, before Christ's coming into the flesh, people (Jews and Gentiles, each in their own way) tried by their own efforts to achieve salvation. With the coming of Christ and the work of his apostles this sinful, autosoteric tendency and teaching continued, sponsored now by enthusiastic Judaists. In their teaching the latter tried to combine faith in Christ with trust in Mosaic-Pharisaic ordinances. And this same danger of trusting in ordinances to supplement faith in Christ asserted itself also at Colosse (see Col. 2:11-23), though in a somewhat different, more complicated, form. That some of these regulations dealt with angel-worship need not and should not be denied (see verses 15 and 18), just so it be borne in mind that the term *rudiments* itself does not therefore necessarily mean *angels.* It is the erroneous *teaching* that is here condemned.

It thus becomes evident that when the meaning *rudimentary instruction* is ascribed to the word *rudiments,* as used in Col. 2:8 and 2:20, this sense cannot be quickly discarded as if it were definitely out of line with the use of this same word elsewhere in the New Testament.

Now if people will but see the implications of faith in Christ in all his glorious fulness and adequacy, they will die to these rudiments, as verse 20 makes very clear. Cast aside then will be these crude notions regarding regulations and ordinances with respect to such things as circumcision, feasts, food and drink, angel-worship, etc., as means toward the achievement of salvation in all its fulness. It is evident that at least in one respect the rudiments mentioned in Galatians and those against which the apostle warns in Colossians are alike, namely, in being "weak and beggarly" (Gal. 3:9). This philosophy is definitely "of the world," as any system must be that does not give Christ all the honor. It is empty, deceitful, **and not according to Christ.** It has a tendency to take men away from Christ, to weaken their trust in him as all-sufficient Savior. It is not in harmony with the fulness which believers have in him.

Hence, Paul continues: **for in him all the fulness of the godhead dwells bodily.** For the interpretation of all but the adverb ("bodily") see also above on Col. 1:19. When the apostle thus describes Christ he has in mind the latter's *deity*, not just his *divinity*. He is referring to the Son's complete equality of essence with the Father and the Holy Spirit, his *consubstantiality*, not his *similarity*.[82] He is saying that this plenitude of deity has its abiding residence in Christ, and this *bodily*.

Many different interpretations have been given of this adverb; such as, *personally, essentially, universally* (in a manner that embraces or affects the entire universe), *ecclesiastically* (in a manner that affects the entire church), *antitypically, genuinely,* etc. Now all of these can be rejected without much argumentation since they are out of harmony with the immediate context, attach a connotation to the adverb that is out of harmony with the main clause, invest that adverb with too much meaning, and miss the main purpose which the apostle had in mind in writing as he does.

There are, however, two theories that deserve more than passing notice:
A. *The view of Lightfoot (op. cit.,* pp. 182, 183), etc.

According to him *bodily* means "with a bodily manifestation," that is, "as crowned by the incarnation." Expositors of repute have endorsed this attractive view. They appeal to such arguments as the importance which Paul attaches to Christ's incarnation (Gal. 4:4), the possible parallel in John 1:1, 14, the reference in Heb. 10:5 to Christ's body ("a body didst thou prepare for me"), etc.

Objections:

(1) Paul uses the present tense. He does not say that the Word *became* flesh but that the fulness of the godhead *dwells* or *is dwelling* in Christ. And surely that indwelling did not just begin with the incarnation. It is an

---

[82] Note what a difference a single letter makes:

(1) θεότης used here in Col. 2:9 (nowhere else in the New Testament) means *deity;* θειότης used in Rom. 1:20 (and there alone in the New Testament) indicates *divinity.* Cf. German: *Gottheit* und *Göttlichkeit;* Dutch: *godheid* en *goddelijkheid.* The difference has been expressed beautifully by E. K. Simpson in these words: "The *hand* of omnipotence may be traced in the countless orbs that bespangle the heavens, and in the marvelous coadjustments of our comparatively tiny globe; but in the Son we behold the *face* of God unveiled, the express image and transcript of his very being" (*Words Worth Weighing in the Greek New Testament.* See also R. C. Trench, *Synonyms of the New Testament,* par. ii.

(2) ὁμοούσιος, as the Nicene Creed declared, means *of the same substance* or *essence,* the Son being consubstantial with the Father, while the weaker ὁμοιούσιος, preferred by the Arians, means *similar in substance* or *essence.* Though the difference seems to be trivial — only one letter! — it is actually nothing less than that between declaring that Jesus is *God* and saying that he is *man,* a very divine man, to be sure, but man nevertheless. Was not the slogan of these heretics, "There was a time when he was not"?

eternal indwelling. Moule, who is inclined to favor Lightfoot's view, nevertheless correctly observes: "The chief objection to taking σωματικῶς [the adverb] thus, as representing a stress on the fact that the godhead became really embodied, is the present tense κατοικεῖ ["is dwelling"], which is not easy to treat as a reference to a past event in history (like John 1:14, σάρξ ἐγένετο [became flesh]" (op. cit., p. 93) . That is exactly the point!

(2) Lightfoot's argument to the effect that the main clause ("for in him all the fulness of the godhead dwells") refers to the pre-incarnate Christ ("the Eternal Word in whom the pleroma had its abode from all eternity"), but that the adverb ("bodily") which modifies this clause refers to the incarnation, would seem to involve contradiction.

(3) If the adverb "bodily" is interpreted literally, and we should allow this adverb really to modify, in a natural way, the main clause with its verb "dwells" or "is dwelling," would not the objection arise that the Son of God is surely not so dependent upon a physical body (or even upon the human nature) that apart from it the godhead cannot dwell in him?

It is, therefore, not surprising that among the earliest writers few adopted this interpretation, and that even today, with some prominent exceptions, it is widely rejected by scholars.

B. *The view of Percy* (op. cit., p.77), *and, in the main, also of Ridderbos* (op. cit., pp. 176-178) .

They interpret the adverb to mean "in a concentrated, as it were visible and tangible, form." Faith clearly sees that the fulness of the godhead dwells from everlasting to everlasting in Christ, this fact having been thus visibly and tangibly demonstrated by Christ's works both in creation and redemption. It sees that the entire essence and glory of God *is concentrated in Christ as in a body*. It is in that sense that it can be said that this fulness of the godhead *is embodied, given concrete expression, fully realized, in him*. This is but another way of saying that from everlasting to everlasting he is "the image of the invisible God" (see on Col. 1:15).

I believe that this gives the proper sense, a meaning which is also in harmony with the context, both preceding and following. Since, therefore, all the fulness of the indwelling essence of God is thus completely concentrated in Christ, there is no need of or justification for looking elsewhere for help, salvation, or spiritual perfection. Hence, the apostle immediately adds: **and in him y o u have attained to fulness**; that is, in Christ y o u have reached the Source whence flows the stream of blessings that supplies whatever y o u need for this life and for the next. Abide, therefore, in him (John 15:4, 7, 9), and y o u will continue to experience that "out of his fulness we all receive grace upon grace" (John 1:16; cf. Eph. 4:13). To the very utmost limits of human capacity the church that remains in vital union with Christ receives love, joy, peace, longsuffering, kindness, goodness, faithfulness, meekness, self-control (Gal. 5:22), yes, every Christian grace. Christ is the Fountain that never fails. Why, then, O Colossians, commit the folly of hewing out cisterns for yourselves, broken cisterns, that can hold no water (Jer. 2:13)? Why trust in circumcision when y o u have been buried with Christ in baptism (verses 11-14)? How foolish to resort to principalities and authorities when in him y o u have attained to fulness, **namely, in him who is the head of every principality and authority** (cf. verse 15). For the meaning of "principality" and "authority" see on Col. 1:16. He is their head, not in fully the same sense in which he is the head of the church (see on Col. 1:18), which is his body, but in the sense that he is supreme Ruler of all (1:16; cf. Eph. 1:22), so that apart from him the good angels cannot help, and because of him the evil cannot harm believers. It seems that it was especially this last thought which the apostle wished to emphasize (see below on verse 15).[83]

In order to show the connection of verses 11-17 with the verses that immediately precede, verses 9 and 10 which have already been explained will be reprinted here:

---

9 for in him all the fulness of the godhead dwells bodily, 10 and in him y o u have attained to fulness, namely, in him who is the head of every principality and authority, 11 in whom also y o u were circumcised with a circumcision made without hands, by the putting off of the body of the flesh in the circumcision of Christ, 12 having been buried with him in y o u r baptism in which y o u were also raised with him through faith in the operative power of God who raised him from the dead. 13 And y o u, who were dead through y o u r trespasses and the uncircumcision of y o u r flesh, y o u he made alive together with him, having forgiven us all our trespasses, 14 having blotted out the handwritten document that was against us, which by means of its requirements testified against us, and he took it out of the way by nailing it to the cross, 15 and having stripped the principalities and the authorities of their power, he publicly exposed them to disgrace by triumphing over them in him.

16 Therefore allow no one to pass judgment on y o u in questions of food or drink or with respect to a festival or a new moon or a sabbath: 17 things that were only a shadow of those that were coming, but the object casting the shadow is to be found with Christ.

2:11-17

II. *Warning against Judaistic Ceremonialism*

In verses 1-10 the warning against the Colossian Heresy was couched in general terms. With verse 11, however, right in the middle of the sentence, it begins to assume specific form. We now learn that the error that was being propagated at Colosse was basically of a Judaistic character. For a reason not definitely stated but which we can probably infer from the context and

---

[83] Because of its length this footnote has been placed at the end of the chapter, page 135.

from similar warnings in other epistles the teachers of false doctrine were advertising such things as circumcision, rigid adherance to dietary restrictions, and strict observance of festivals and sabbaths. That brief summary makes verses 11-17 a thought-unit. The style, however, changes from the rather easy-flowing didactic evident through verse 15 to the far more crisp, direct, and hortatory that begins at verse 16 and continues with few exceptions (the longest exception being 4:7-14) to the end of the letter. It is *subject-matter*, namely, *warning against Judaism*, that unites 2:11-17. But even this subject-matter is not altogether homogeneous. The heresy which the apostle was combating was a somewhat baffling mixture of Judaistic and Pagan beliefs propagated by men who probably posed as Christians, yes better Christians than the common lot. As has been pointed out earlier (see Introduction II C), it was exactly the type of syncretism that one could expect to find in Jewish-Pagan Colosse. It is not surprising that Paul, who had the entire picture before him all the time, in his discussions and warnings should move with ease from one element of the Colossian Heresy to another and then back again. So also here in verses 11-17 we notice that in the midst of his warnings against Judaism he briefly touches upon two subjects about which he will say more subsequently, namely, Relation to angels (verse 15) and Asceticism (verse 16). Yet, he does this not in a disconnected or rambling manner, but in such a way that verses 11-17 form a unit in which every clause leads to the next one in a very natural and organic manner, as will be indicated.

11, 12. Speaking then about Christ, "the head of every principality and authority," Paul continues: **in whom y o u were circumcized.** Paul's thought at this point can perhaps be paraphrased somewhat as follows: Colossians, do not allow these teachers of error to deceive y o u as if, in order to triumph over the indulgence of the flesh (2:23) and to attain to the full measure of salvation (2:9, 10), y o u need to be literally circumcized (cf. Acts 15:1; Gal. 5:2, 3). *Y o u were already circumcized!* Yes, y o u were circumcized with a circumcision that excels by far the rite that is being recommended so strongly by the teachers of error. Y o u were circumcized **with a circumcision made without hands, by the putting off of the body of the flesh in the circumcision of Christ.**

Note points of difference proving the great superiority of the circumcision which the Colossians had already received:

Y o u r circumcision was:	*The other was:*
(1) the work of the Holy Spirit ("made without hands")	(1) a manual operation (minor surgery!)
(2) inward, of the heart (see Rom. 2: 28, 29; also N.T.C. on Phil. 3:2, 3)	(2) outward

Y o u r circumcision was:	*The other was:*
(3) the putting *off* and casting *away* (note double prefix in ἀπεκδύσει) **of** y o u r *entire* evil nature ("the body of the flesh"), in its sanctifying aspect to be progressively realized	(3) removal of excess foreskin
(4) Christian ("the circumcision of Christ," that is, the circumcision which is y o u r s because of y o u r vital union with Christ)	(4) Abrahamic and Mosaic

As a further description of the circumcision which the Colossians had already received the apostle continues: **having been buried with him in y o u r baptism in which y o u were also raised with him.** Meaning:

(1) Christ suffered, died, was buried in y o u r stead and for your benefit. He bore the guilt and punishment of the law for y o u. He took upon himself the curse that rested upon y o u (Gal. 3:13). When by sovereign grace y o u embraced Christ as y o u r Savior and Lord, y o u received the assurance that y o u r former guilt-laden, damnable selves had been buried with him, and that y o u r state with reference to God's holy law had changed from that of objects of condemnation to that of recipients of justification (Rom. 8:1-4; 5:1). Accordingly, not only were y o u buried with him but y o u were also raised with him.

(2) By means of his entire work of humiliation, including burial, Christ procured for y o u the work of the Holy Spirit (John 16:7). Hence, y o u r s is not only justification but also sanctification, gradual spiritual renewal. The Spirit has implanted in y o u r hearts the seed of the new life (John 3:3, 5). "Y o u died, and y o u r life is hid with Christ in God" (Col. 3:3). Hence, also in this sense, y o u were buried with him and y o u were raised with him.

But why does Paul connect "in y o u r baptism" with this having been buried with Christ and having been raised with him? He does not do this because he attaches any magical efficacy to the rite of baptism. See I Cor. 1:14-17; cf. I Peter 3:21. In the passage now under discussion the apostle definitely excludes the idea that the act of baptizing, in virtue of the action itself, and independent of the condition of the heart of them who here and now professed to believe the gospel, has spiritual value. He carefully adds: **through faith in the operative power** [84] **of God who raised him from the dead.** The man who hears the gospel as it is proclaimed must give his heart to the almighty God whose energizing power raised Christ from the dead. He must also believe that the spiritual power that proceeds from the risen

---

[84] Objective genitive after πίστεως as in Rom. 3:22, 26; Gal. 3:22; Eph. 3:12; Phil. 3:9; and II Thess. 2:13.

Savior (Phil. 3:10) will bestow upon him all he needs for body and soul, for time and eternity.

What then is the meaning of the phrase "in y o u r baptism"? Evidently Paul in this entire paragraph magnifies Christian baptism as much as he, by clear implication, disapproves of the continuation of the rite of circumcision if viewed as having anything to do with salvation.[85] The definite implication, therefore, is that *baptism has taken the place of circumcision.*[86] Hence, what is said with reference to circumcision in Rom. 4:11, as being a sign and a seal, holds also for baptism. In the Colossian context baptism is specifically a sign and seal of having been buried with Christ and of having been raised with him. It is, accordingly, a sign and seal of union with Christ, of entrance into his covenant, of incorporation into Christ's body, the church (I Cor. 12:13). The *sign* of baptism pictures the cleansing power of Christ's blood and Spirit. That vivid portrayal is very valuable (cf. Job 42:5, 6). The *seal* certifies and guarantees the operation of this activity of love and grace in

---

[85] As to discarding circumcision Paul uses language that is definite and strong: Gal. 5:2; Phil. 3:2. In Colossians he opposes this rite *for believers from the Gentiles* in this *new* dispensation. In a religious sense circumcision was, indeed, a blessing in the *old* dispensation. For a person living in that era to receive the sign of entrance into the covenant was certainly not bad in itself. On the contrary, it was a blessing as a *sign* and a *seal* of the righteousness of faith (Rom. 4:11). It was, however, never to be regarded as being in and by itself a vehicle of grace or indispensable to salvation. It stands to reason that with the shedding of Christ's blood on Calvary these *bloody* signs and seals (circumcision and the killing of the Passover lamb) attained their fulfilment, and were rendered moribund. The grievous error of the false teachers was therefore twofold: a. the attempt to force this obsolescent rite upon believers from the Gentiles; b. the view that circumcision was in and by itself a vehicle of grace, imparting to the recipient a blessing which "mere" (?) faith in Christ could never have given him. The error was therefore *a denial of Christ's all-sufficiency!* For more about this see on verses 16, 17.

This entire discussion, however, moves in the realm of moral and spiritual values. It has nothing to do with the physical or health value of circumcision in any age. S. I. McMillen, M.D., in his most interesting book, *None of These Diseases,* published by the Fleming H. Revell Co., has high praise for circumcision as a health measure, especially in the prevention of cervical cancer (pp. 19-21). His remarks and statistics are most interesting and instructive. But that is the physical side. Paul discusses the moral and spiritual question.

[86] I am speaking here about a clear *implication.* The surface contrast is that between *literal* circumcision and *circumcision without hands,* namely, the circumcision of the heart, as explained. But the implication also is clear. Hence, the following statement is correct: "Since, then, baptism has come in the place of circumcision (Col. 2:11-13), the children should be baptized as heirs of the kingdom of God and of his covenant" (*Form for the Baptism of Infants* in *Psalter Hymnal of the Christian Reformed Church,* Grand Rapids, Mich., 1959, p. 86). When God made his covenant with Abraham the children were included (Gen. 17:1-14). This covenant, in its spiritual aspects, was continued in the new dispensation (Acts 2:38, 39; Rom. 4:9-12; Gal. 3:7, 8, 29). Therefore the children are still included and should still receive the sign, which in the present dispensation is, as Paul makes clear in Col. 2:11, 12, is baptism. Surely, God is not less generous now than he was in the old dispensation! Further evidence in support of this position can be found in passages such as the following: Mark 10:14-16; Luke 18:15-17; Acts 16:15, 33; I Cor. 1:16.

the lives of all those who embrace Christ by faith. Baptism, therefore, shows us a God who tenderly condescends to the weaknesses of his people: their doubts and their fears. (Cf. Heb. 6:17; also for the sacrament of communion Luke 22:19.) Surely, Noah did not despise the rainbow (Gen. 9:12-17). Happily married couples do not think lowly of their wedding rings.

The meaning, then, of Col. 2:11, 12 would seem to be as follows (in summary): "Y o u, believers, have no need of external circumcision. Y o u have received a far better circumcision, that of heart and life. That circumcision is y o u r s by virtue of y o u r union with Christ. When he was buried y o u — that is, y o u r former, wicked selves — were buried with him. When he was raised y o u — as new creatures — were raised with him. In the experience of baptism y o u received the sign and seal of this marvelous Spirit-wrought transformation." [87]

13. In the spirit of jubilation and solid Christian optimism Paul continues, **And y o u, who were dead through y o u r trespasses and the uncircumcision of y o u r flesh, y o u he made alive together with him.** In his great mercy God had taken pity on Gentiles as well as on the ancient covenant people. "And y o u" means, "And y o u who were formerly Gentiles, and as such morally and spiritually dead, and this not only because of y o u r individual trespasses against God's holy law but also and basically because of y o u r state before God." That state is here described as "the uncircumcision of y o u r flesh," that is, "y o u r *state* of guilt; hence, y o u r *condition* of sinfulness, impotence, and therefore hopelessness."

Being children of wrath, their physical or literal uncircumcision symbolized their moral and spiritual uncircumcision. The word y o u is repeated for

---

[87] This discussion would hardly be complete if nothing were said with reference to the *mode* of baptism, since it is especially upon passages such as this that immersionists base their claim that baptism by immersion is the only valid baptism. They see in the words "having been buried with him in y o u r baptism" an endorsement of immersion into the water; and in the words, "in which y o u were also raised with him" solid support for emersion out of the water. With all love and respect for our brothers in Christ I venture to say, however, that in connection with baptism Scripture also uses other expressions which, on the basis of this kind of reasoning, would then also have to be regarded as indicating the proper *mode* of baptism. If *being buried with Christ* (Col. 2:11, 12; Rom. 6:4) means that baptism must be by immersion, why should not *being crucified with Christ* (Rom. 6:6) indicate that baptism should be by crucifixion, *being planted with him* (Rom. 6:5 A.V. and original) that it should be by implantation, and *putting on Christ* (Gal. 3:27) that it should be by habilitation? As I see it, John Murray is right when he says, "When all of Paul's expressions are taken into account we see that burial with Christ can be appealed to as providing an index to the mode of baptism no more than can crucifixion with him. And since the latter does not indicate the *mode* of baptism there is no validity to the argument that burial does. The fact is that there are many aspects to our union with Christ. It is arbitrary to select one aspect and find in the language used to set it forth the essence of the mode of baptism" (*Christian Baptism,* p. 31).

the sake of emphasis, as if Paul were saying, "Ponder this! Continue to reflect on it that on y o u, yes even on y o u, so deeply fallen, so hopelessly lost, so utterly corrupt in state and condition, such grace was bestowed." Cf. Eph. 2:1, 5. The predominantly Gentile origin of this church is clear also from such passages as Col. 1:21, 22, 27; 3:5-7 (similar passages in Ephesians are: Eph. 1:13; 2:1-3, 11, 13, 17, 22; 3:1, 2; 4:17, etc.). But the same God, who raised Christ from the dead, also and in that very act made the Colossians alive.

In verses 13, 14, and 15 the apostle in orderly arranged participial modifiers shows us what was implied in this *making alive*. It implied:

(1) granting forgiveness to *us:* "having forgiven us all our trespasses" (verse 13).

(2) blotting out *a writing:* "having blotted out the handwritten document that was against us" (verse 14).

(3) disarming *spirits:* "and having stripped the principalities and the authorities of their power" (verse 15).

In the work of salvation the guilt of our sins must be removed first of all. Hence, when Paul describes how we were made alive together with Christ he begins by saying: **having forgiven us all our trespasses.** Note the striking transition from y o u to us. If it be true that *"all* (both Jew and Gentile) have sinned and fall short of the glory of God" (Rom. 3:23), then all alike need forgiveness. And Paul, who regards himself as "chief of sinners" (I Tim. 1:15) was unable to write about a subject like this without being deeply moved in his own soul, having experienced what God did for him in rescuing him from inevitable damnation.

Forgiveness

1. *Why is it emphasized?*

It is worthy of special attention that the apostle speaks about forgiveness in each of the first three chapters of Colossians. May there not have been a special reason for this? Remember that this letter was going to be read aloud to the assembled congregation of Colosse, yes, to the very church gathered in Philemon's house. And Philemon was the master of Onesimus, the returned runaway whom Philemon must forgive! It is as if I am present when this letter is being read, and as if I hear the lector reading the precious words:

"The Father rescued us out of the domain of darkness, and transplanted us into the kingdom of the Son of his love, in whom we have our redemption, *the forgiveness of our sins.* . . . And y o u who were dead through y o u r trespasses and the uncircumcision of y o u r flesh, y o u he made alive together with him, *having forgiven us all our trespasses.* . . . Put on, therefore, as God's elect, holy and beloved, a heart of compassion, kindness, lowliness, meekness, longsuffering, enduring one another, and if anyone has a complaint against anyone else *forgiving each other.* Just as the Lord *has forgiven* y o u, so do y o u also *(forgive)* " (Col. 1:13, 14; 2:13; 3:12, 13) . And it is as if I can hear the Holy Spirit whisper in the heart of the host of this house-church, "Philemon, if the Lord did all this for *you,* should *you* not, with gladness of heart, forgive Onesimus, and fully *accept* him as a beloved brother?"

But surely not only for Philemon were these words intended but for the entire Colossian congregation, and in fact — as Paul reminds us so beautifully by saying "having forgiven *us* all our trespasses" — for each and every believer both then and now.

2. *What are its characteristics?*

The evidence shows that this forgiveness is:

a. *gracious.* The word used here in the original stresses this fact (see on 3:13, footnote 131) . It is completely unmerited by man (Rom. 3:24; Titus 3:4-7) . It is God's precious *gift* in Christ. May not this be the very reason why the sinner must become as a little child to receive it? Cf. Matt. 18:1-3. The story is told of a man who at a Fair offered $10 gold pieces. Accompanying a pile of these valuable coins there was a sign: "Free, Take one." All day long people passed by. Their smile said, "You can't fool me." The pile remained untouched. Just before closing time a child saw the sign, reached out his hand and took a coin!

b. *bountiful.* When God gives or forgives he does not do so merely *of* his riches but *according to* his riches (Eph. 1:7) . His pardoning love superabounds (Rom. 5:20). Cf. Isa. 1:18; Ps. 103:12.

c. *eager.* God "entreats" men to be reconciled to him, "not counting their trespasses against them" (II Cor. 5:19, 20) . Cf. Ps. 86:5.

d. *certain.* When Paul received his commission he was sent to the Gentiles "to open their eyes, that they may turn from darkness to light and from the power of Satan to God, *that they may receive remission of sins. . . .*" When Festus expressed his doubt about this heavenly vision and the commission given to Paul, the apostle answered, "I am not mad, excellent Festus, but I am telling *the sober truth*" (Acts 26:16-18, 25) . Cf. Ps. 89:30-35.

e. *basic.* When a sinner is rescued out of the domain of darkness and transplanted into the kingdom of the Son of God's love, he receives *forgiveness* first of all. Moral and spiritual cleansing ("holiness") *follows* (Col. 1:13, 14, 22) . Thus also here in Col. 2:13 the very first blessing that is mentioned in connection with making the dead sinner alive is forgiveness. Cf. Rom. 3:24. Note emphasis on *justification* in Rom. 5, *followed by* emphasis on *sanctification,* Rom. 6. "How can a sinner become righteous in the sight of God?" is still basic.

3. *How do we receive it?*

What is the way along which God leads his children toward the full possession and enjoyment of this basic blessing?

a. There must be *genuine sorrow for sin* (God-wrought sorrow, II Cor. 7:10). Cf. Mark 1:4.

b. There must be *a yearning desire to forsake sin.* Those who are eager by the grace of God to put to death their evil nature (Col. 3:5-11) are pronounced forgiven (Col. 3:13). Cf. Prov. 28:13. When the Sunday School teacher asked the class, "What does it mean to repent?" a little boy answered, "To repent means to be sorry enough to quit doing what is wrong."

c. There must be *the disposition of the heart to forgive others* (Col. 3:13; Eph. 4:32). Cf. Matt. 6:14, 15.

14. But, in making us alive (see on verse 13), not only has God in mercy pardoned our transgressions against his holy law, he has even blotted out the law itself viewed in its demanding and curse-pronouncing character, that law which, because of its many rigid requirements and regulations, condemned us all. As a way of salvation and as a curse suspended above our heads God by means of his Son's substitutionary sacrifice abolished it. Says Paul: **having blotted out the handwritten document that was against us, which by means of its requirements** [88] **testified against** [89] **us.** This handwriting or handwritten document is clearly the law (cf. Eph. 2:15). [90] In a

---

[88] The original has given rise to various interpretations, and is difficult. The difficulty concerns two phrases: καθ' ἡμῶν and τοῖς δόγμασιν. If καθ' ἡμῶν is rendered "against us" and τοῖς δόγμασιν is construed with "handwriting" the result may be a translation that is open to the charge of tautology: "the handwriting with its ordinances that was against us, which was contrary to us" (cf. somewhat similar rendering in A.V. and A.R.V., text). J. A. T. Robinson avoids this difficulty by taking καθ' ἡμῶν to mean "in our name" (*The Body*, p. 43 n.). But it is difficult to find substantiation for that meaning. E. Percy (*op. cit.*, pp. 88, 89), followed by Ridderbos (*op. cit.*, pp. 186, 187), construes τοῖς δόμασιν with the *following* clause; hence, "the handwriting that was against us, which by means of its ordinances testified against us." This rendering, in substance, I can adopt. Bruce (*op. cit.*, p. 237) states his objection to it in these words: "It is rather awkward to construe τοῖς δόγμασιν with the following adjective clause, in spite of the parallels which he [Percy] adduces." It cannot be denied, however, that there are these parallels, adduced not only by Percy (*op. cit.*, p. 88, footnote 43) but also by Gram. N.T. Bl.-Debr., par. 475,1. Though placing a modifier in front of the relative clause to which it belongs may be regarded as exceptional, it is not so *very* exceptional, as the evidence which Percy and Bl.-Debr. supply, indicates. Besides, is there not, after all, a good reason for this advanced position of the modifier? Is it not true that, over against the false teachers with their love for ordinances and still more ordinances, the apostle desired to stress the idea that it was exactly because of these ordinances that the law had become our adversary, constantly testifying against us, transgressors? If that be borne in mind, the word-order does not seem so strange.

[89] ὑπεναντίον, where ἀντί has the adversative sense. In Heb. 10:27 τοὺς ὑπεναντίους means *the adversaries*. Also in the LXX this ἀντί-compound is the equivalent of the Hebrew 'ōyēbh (enemy) and çar (adversary, foe). Apart from Christ, the law is the sinner's adversary, bearing testimony *against* him.

[90] It is true that χειρόγραφον, which basically means *handwriting*, and so in its general sense, any *document*, frequently has the technical meaning *bond, certificate of*

sense that law was an adversary, an accuser of transgressors. It confronted men with the stern dictum, "Cursed is every one who does not abide by all things that are written in the book of the law to do them" (Gal. 3:10; cf. Deut. 27:26). Moreover, it contained ever so many rules and regulations of a ceremonial nature, with reference to fasts, feasts, foods, offerings, etc. Since no one was ever able to keep the law either in its moral or ceremonial aspect, it continued for a long time its mission as accuser. With the coming of Christ, born to die, a great change took place. Paul tells the Colossians, harrassed as they were by false teachers who were trying to enforce their Judaistic ceremonies upon them and were even adding rules of their own, "God has completely obliterated [91] the document with its legal demands." How had this been accomplished? Paul answers, **and he took it out of the way by nailing it to the cross.** God annulled the law when his Son satisfied its demand of perfect obedience, bore its curse, and fulfilled its shadows, its types and ceremonies. It was nailed to the cross with Jesus. It died when he died. And because of the substitutionary nature of Christ's sacrifice believers are no longer under the law but under grace (Rom. 7:4, 6; 6:14; Gal. 2:19). This does not mean that the moral law has lost significance for the believer. It cannot imply that he should now forget about loving God above all and the neighbor as himself. On the contrary, the law of love has eternal validity (Rom. 13:8, 9; Gal. 5:14). It is the believer's supreme delight. He obeys it out of gratitude for the salvation that he has already received as a gift of God's sovereign grace. But he has been discharged from the law viewed as a code of rules and regulations, a means of obtaining eternal life, a curse threatening to destroy him.

---

indebtedness. See A. Deissmann, *Light from the Ancient East,* pp. 331, 332. Taken in the latter sense "the Jewish people might be said to have signed the contract when they bound themselves by a curse to observe all the enactments of the law" (Deut. 27:14-26; cf. Ex. 24:3). Thus Lightfoot (*op. cit.,* p. 187). But since the apostle speaks about a handwriting that testified against *us,* and he is obviously writing to Christians from among the *Gentiles,* a way must now be found to make this technical sense of the term fit the Gentiles also. Lightfoot offers as a solution "the moral assent of the conscience which, as it were, signs and seals the obligation." Many commentators, in one way or another, follow this line of interpretation. It is a very attractive theory and lends itself beautifully to sermonizing. It is, however, very difficult to fit into the present context which has in view *a document containing regulations or ordinances.* Moreover, in the clearly parallel passage (Eph. 2:15) what has been abolished through the cross is not "a certificate of indebtedness with our signature on it" but "the law of commandments with its requirements." I agree, therefore, with Beare when he states (*op. cit.,* p. 198), "It represents simply the law as a written code." Cf. also Gal. 3:13, "Christ redeemed us from the curse of the law"; and Rom. 7:6, "But now we are discharged from the law."

[91] The synonymous expression, "he took it out of the way," meaning "he has completely abrogated it" indicates that the literal sense of ἐξαλείφω must not be pressed. Not the literal washing out of a signature or of an acknowledgment of debt is meant here but *the complete destruction of the law, regarded as a code of rules and regulations.*

15. Here follows the last of three important acts whereby God grants to his children the joy of salvation (see on verse 13), the three being: (1) forgiveness of sins, (2) the setting aside of the law (in the sense explained), and now (3) the disarming of the principalities and authorities. Says Paul: **and having stripped the principalities and the authorities of their power, he publicly exposed them to disgrace by triumphing over them in him.**[92] These "principalities and authorities" are angelic beings (see on Col. 1:16), who are here (2:15) pictured as resisting God. It is not exactly clear just why Paul makes mention of them in the present connection. It is possible, nevertheless, that the immediately preceding statement of the abrogation of the law as our *impersonal* accuser may have led to this reference to *personal* accusers, namely, the evil angels.[93] That would certainly be a very natural transition. It also reminds us of the apostle's argumentation in Rom. 8. There, too, having pointed out how the demand of *the law* was satisfied (Rom. 8:1-4), the apostle asks in verse 33, *"Who* shall lay anything to the charge of God's elect?" and in verse 34, *"Who* is he that condemns?" Would anyone say that Paul, well-versed in the Old Testament as he was, did *not* include Satan among those personal accusers? The idea that Satan is the arch-accuser is, indeed, decidedly biblical (Job 1:9-11; Zech. 3:1-5; Rev. 12:10). Of course, the work of Satan and his hosts in their attempt to destroy believers is not confined to that of *accusation.* The baseness of these hordes of evil appears especially in this that first they tempt men to sin, and then, having succeeded in their sinister endeavor, they immediately accuse these same people before God, charging them with those very sins which *they,* these sinister spirits, devised.

Now in the midst of this terrific struggle (cf. Eph. 6:12) the Colossians receive a word of comfort. Says Paul, as it were, Y o u need not be afraid of these hosts of evil, for in principle the battle has already been won. It has been won *for* y o u. God himself has disarmed [94] these principalities and powers. Did he not rescue us out of the domain of darkness? (Col. 1:13).

---

[92] Note the symmetrical structure of verses 14 and 15, in both of which in the original the leading verb occurs between two modifying participles.

[93] Ridderbos rejects this idea as being unsupported by the context (*op. cit.,* p. 189). I would rather leave room for this possibility, for the reasons stated in the text.

[94] Here I agree with Ridderbos as against Lightfoot and others. See Lightfoot's lengthy argumentation to the effect that ἀπεκδυσάμενος must be translated as a true middle, so that the sense would be that Christ *divested himself of* the powers of evil "which had clung like a Nessus robe about his humanity" (*op. cit.,* p. 190). Over against this note:

(1) In the New Testament the middle is occasionally used where the active is expected. See Gram. N.T. Bl.-Debr., par. 316.

(2) In Eph. 6:11, 14; I Thess. 5:8 the verb ἐνδύω is used in the middle voice with the meaning *I put on armor.* Hence, here in Col. 2:15 ἀπεκδυσάμενος middle voice, could well mean *disarming.*

(3) The subject of this sentence is still *God.* It is difficult to think of God as divesting himself of the evil angels as if they were clinging about him like a cloak.

Is not his Son *the head of every principality and authority?* (Col. 2:10). And is it not true that principalities and authorities (as well as thrones and dominions) are but creatures, having been created in him, through him, and with a view to him? (Col. 1:16). Remember, therefore, that, by means of that same Son, God stripped these principalities and authorities of their power. He utterly disarmed them. Did not Christ triumph over them in the desert of temptation? (Matt. 4:1-11). Did he not bind the strong man? (Matt. 12:29), casting out demons again and again to prove it? Did he not see Satan fallen as lightning from heaven? (Luke 10:18). When the devil and his hosts asserted themselves from Gethsemane to Golgotha (Luke 22:3, 53; cf. Ps. 22:12, 16), did not Christ by his vicarious death deprive Satan of even a semblance of legal ground on which to base his accusations? Was not *the accuser of the brothers* cast down, and this not only by means of Christ's vicarious death but also by his triumphant resurrection, ascension, and coronation? (Rev. 12:10; Eph. 1:20-23). Is it not true, then, that by these great redemptive acts God publicly exposed these evil powers to disgrace, leading them captive in triumph, chained, as it were, to his triumphal chariot? [95] Yes, in and through this Son of his love, this triumphant Christ, God has achieved the victory over Satan and all his hosts. And that victory is y o u r life and y o u r joy. Whatever y o u need is in Christ.

16, 17. In line with what he had been saying with respect to the persuasive argumentation (2:3), philosophy, empty deceit, man-made tradition, and worldly rudiments (2:8) that characterized the thinking and propaganda of the false teachers, and the *requirements* of the law (2:14) upon which they superimposed their own *regulations,* Paul now continues, **Therefore allow no one to pass judgment on y o u in questions of eating or of drinking or with respect to a festival or a new moon or a sabbath . . .**

The Jewish aspect of the Colossian Heresy stands out clearly here. Nevertheless, it is also evident that the error went beyond that mixture of Jewish religion and Christianity which is called Judaism, for the Colossian errorists passed judgment not only with respect to *eating* but also with respect to *drinking,* though with respect to the latter subject the Old Testament contains rather few prohibitions (Lev. 10:9; Num. 6:3; Judg. 13:4, 7, 14), though lack of moderation is strongly condemned (Isa. 5:11, 12; Amos 6:6; Prov. 20:1). As to *eating,* the false teachers seem to have superimposed their own regulations upon the Old Testament laws regarding clean and unclean animals (cf. Lev. 11). They also tried to impose restrictions in connection with *festivals* — think of Passover, Pentecost, Feast of Tabernacles, and perhaps others (cf. Lev. 23) —, *new moon* (cf. Num. 10:10; 28:11), and *sabbath* (cf. Ex. 20:8-11; 31:14-16). There was evidence, therefore, of a distinctly ascetic tendency. The main purpose of placing such stress on all such regula-

[95] Cf. Eph. 4:8, and for a favorable application of the metaphor see II Cor. 2:14.

tions was to convince the Colossians that strict observance was absolutely indispensable to salvation, or if not to salvation as such, at least to *fulness,* perfection in salvation (see on verses 9, 10). Paul issues a strong warning against this implied denial of the all-sufficiency of Christ, by continuing, **which things** — even in their legitimate Old Testament context — **are a shadow of those that were coming, but the object casting the shadow is to be found with Christ.**[96]

Why regard as indispensable ordinances as to eating, when the One foreshadowed by Israel's manna is offering himself as the Bread of Life (John 6:35, 48)? How can the observance of the Passover (cf. Ex. 12) be considered a means unto spiritual perfection when "our Passover has been sacrificed, even Christ" (I Cor. 5:7)? What justification could there be for imposing upon converts from the Gentile world the observance of the Jewish sabbath, when the Bringer of eternal rest is urging every one to come unto him (Matt. 11:28, 29; cf. Heb. 4:8, 14)? To be sure, for the time being a shadow that is cast by an approaching person may prove to be of some real value. For example, it is possible that one is eagerly expecting this person but happens to be so situated that, at his approach, for a moment his shadow alone is seen. However, that shadow not only guarantees the imminent arrival of the visitor but even provides a dim outline, describing him. Thus, too, the Old Testament regulations had served a real purpose. But now that Christ and salvation in him had arrived, what further use could such shadows serve? Though it was not wrong for *the Jew,* trained from his infancy in the law, for a period of transition to observe some of these customs as mere *customs,* having nothing whatever to do with salvation, it was certainly wrong to ascribe to them a value which they did not have, and to try to impose them upon the Gentiles. And if this was true with respect to Old Testament regulations, it was certainly even far more true with respect to man-made regulations of an ascetic character that were being superimposed upon, added to,

---

[96] On the basis of the rendering, "But the body is Christ," some are of the opinion that the meaning is, "But it is the body of Christ (the church) that must pass judgment in all such matters." However, the words σκιά (shadow) and σῶμα (*body* or *object*) clearly belong together, and to introduce the church at this point is wholly arbitrary. Also, the reading of the original is: τὸ δὲ σῶμα τοῦ Χριστοῦ, literally, ". . . but the body (or: the object) . . . of Christ," probably meaning, ". . . but the object is to be found with Christ."

The translation, "But *the substance* — or *the reality* — is Christ" is very popular. It may not be missing the truth by much. Nevertheless, it would seem to me that because of the close relation between σκία and σῶμα, which are counterparts, Paul was thinking of *a shadow* and *an object casting the shadow.* The real contrast drawn by the apostle is not precisely between that which was *unreal* and that which is *real* — the Old Testament regulations regarding these matters, and also the matters themselves, were real enough —, but rather between that which was *passing* and should therefore be discarded and that which is *abiding.* The shadow preceded the object casting it: the law with its regulations concerning foods, feasts, etc., foreshadowed salvation in Christ. Why cling to the shadow when the shadow-casting object has itself arrived?

and in some cases perhaps even substituted for the law of God. Thus the all-sufficiency and pre-eminence of Christ was being denied. And that, after all, was the basic error.

---

18 Let no one disqualify y o u by delighting in humility and the worship of the angels, taking his stand on the things he has seen, without cause puffed up by his fleshly mind, 19 and not keeping firm hold on the Head, from whom the entire body, supported and held together by joints and ligaments, grows with a growth (that is) from God.

2:18, 19

III. *Warning against Angel-Worship*

18. Turning now to the subject of angel-worship, which was one of the characteristics of the Colossian Heresy, Paul writes, **Let no one disqualify y o u.**[97] Let no ritualist tell y o u, "Since y o u, Colossians, are not following my rules and regulations, y o u are not in the race or contest at all. Y o u are unfit, unworthy." Particularly, do not begin to feel inferior when such a person, in addition to stressing the importance of all those restrictions as to eating, drinking, etc., tries to put y o u to shame by his attempt to draw a sharp contrast between yourself and himself. Let him not *disqualify* y o u by his **delighting**[98] **in humility** . . . Now sincere humility, is, indeed, a precious virtue (cf. Col. 3:12, and see N.T.C. on Phil. 2:3) , but the humility of which this false teacher boasted was nothing but a thin disguise for insufferable pride, as is clear also from verse 23. This person was as "umble" as Uriah Heep in *David Copperfield*.

Paul continues, **and** (also delighting in) **the worship of the angels.** The question arises, Just what is the relation between *humility* and *the worship of angels?* The answer is not given. Perhaps the suggestion that has been offered by more than one commentator is correct, namely, that the teacher of error was trying to create the impression that he considered himself too insignificant to approach God directly, hence sought to contact Deity through the mediation of angels, and since the angels were willing to perform this service for him — or, in order that they might oblige — worshiped them.

---

[97] The word καταβραβευέτω is related to βραβεύς, judge, umpire, referee. Though the verb is rare, and in the New Testament occurs only here (see, however, Col. 3:15 for the simple βραβεύω), there seems to be no good reason to depart from the etymological meaning: *to make an umpire's decision against* a person, *to judge against* someone, *to declare* (someone) *disqualified.* Thus also R.S.V., N.E.V., and Moule.
[98] For the meaning of θέλων ἐν cf. I Sam. 18:22 (LXX) , "The king *delights* in you." Cf. also I Kings 10:9; Ps. 112:1 (LXX 111:1) .

With respect to the words here translated *the worship of the angels* there is much difference of opinion among commentators. Some prefer the rendering, "angelic piety" or "worship as practised by angels." But the fact that Paul in this epistle constantly emphasizes Christ's pre-eminence above all creatures, including the angels (Col. 1:16, 17, 20; 2:9, 15) and that he says "of *the* angels," seems to indicate that he was combating angel-worship. Not only this, but there is evidence tending to support the theory that angel-worship was practised in the general region in which Colosse was located. Did not the Holy Spirit through John, the disciple whom Jesus loved, strongly condemn angel-worship? See Rev. 19:10; 22:8, 9. And did not John, during a considerable portion of his ministry, have *Ephesus,* only a little over one hundred miles to the west of Colosse, as his headquarters? Moreover, as has been pointed out in footnote 76, the Essenes, whose doctrine in certain respects resembled the one here attacked (though the Colossian errorists may not have been Essenes!), required of those who were about to be admitted to full membership an oath "carefully to guard . . . the names of the angels." The Synod of *Laodicea* — one of the three cities of the Lycus Valley; see Introduction II A — in the year A. D. 363 declared, "It is not right for Christians to abandon the church of God and go away to invoke angels" (Canon XXV). A century afterward Theodoret, commenting on this very Scripture-passage (Col. 2:18), states, "The disease which St. Paul denounces, continued for a long time in Phrygia and Pisidia." Irenaeus, himself from Asia Minor but widely traveled, in his work *Against Heresies* (A. D. 182-188), implies both the widespread presence of angel-worship in the camp of the emissaries of error and the firm stand of the primitive church against this evil practice, when he states, "Nor does she [i.e. the church] perform anything *by means of angelic invocations,* or by incantations, or by any other wicked curious art; but directing her prayers to the Lord who made all things . . . and calling on the name of our Lord Jesus Christ, she has been accustomed to work miracles for the advantage of mankind, and not to lead men into error" (II.xxxii.5). It is known that Michael, a leader of the host of angels, was worshiped widely in Asia Minor, and this worship, too, continued for centuries. So, for example, as late as A. D. 739 the scene of a great victory over the Saracens was dedicated to him. His worship is also implied in inscriptions found in Galatia. And he was given credit for miraculous cures. [99]

From all this it would seem that the rendering "the worship of the angels" is correct. For the theory according to which these angels were "astral spirits," "rulers of the planetary spheres," see footnote 83 above. And for Paul's own teaching respecting angels see not only above, on Col. 1:16, 17; 2:15, but also N.T.C. on I and II Timothy, and Titus, pp. 183-185.

---

[99] Cf. W. M. Ramsay, *The Church in the Roman Empire,* pp. 477-480.

Paul continues, **taking his stand** [100] on the things he has seen.[101]

This man *pretends* (perhaps even *believes*) to have seen something, and he presumes on this experience he has had. He makes the most of it. If any one ventures to contradict him or to question the truth of his theories, he will answer, "But I have seen such and such a vision." In saying this and in relating the vision he will, of course, assume an air of deep insight into divinely revealed mysteries. He prides himself on what he regards as his superior knowledge. He forgets that "Knowledge puffs up but love builds

[100] The words ἃ ἑόρακεν ἐμβατεύων have led to well-nigh endless discussion. Lightfoot fairly gives up the attempt to explain them. He states, "The combination is so harsh and incongruous as to be barely possible; and there was perhaps some corruption in the text prior to existing authorities." By detaching κεν from the word ἑόρακεν, prefixing it to ἐμβατεύων, and making a slight change in the word from which κεν was subtracted, he arrives at the result: ἑώρᾳ (or αἰώρᾳ) κενεμβατεύων, "treading the void while suspended in air," that is, "indulging airily in vain speculations." J. R. Harris, in his article, "St. Paul and Aristophanes," *ET* 34 (1922, 1923), pp. 151-156, saw a parallel between Col. 2:18 and line 225 of *The Clouds* of Aristophanes, where Socrates, suspended in a basket, when asked what he was doing, replies, "I tread on air and contemplate the sun." According to this view Paul, having read *The Clouds*, is here ridiculing the Colossian philosophizers as Aristophanes had satirized Socrates.
The question may well be asked, however, whether such and similar interpretations, all of them based on emendation of the text, are necessary. After all, the basic meaning of ἐμβατεύω seems to be *I step upon, set foot upon* (for illustrations of this use see Liddell and Scott, *Greek-English Lexicon*, Vol. I, p. 539); hence, *I enter into, go deeply into, investigate,* and so *take my stand on.* See G. G. Findlay, "The Reading and Rendering of Colossians 2:18," *Exp*, first series, 11 (1880), pp. 385-398. W. M. Ramsay, on the basis of an inscription from the temple of Apollo of Klaros, dating from the second century A. D., accordingly translates Col. 2:18b, 19a as follows, "taking his stand on what he has seen (in the mysteries), vainly puffed up by his unspiritual mind, and not keeping firm hold on the Head." See *The Teaching of Paul in Terms of the Present Day*, pp. 283 ff. This explanation of the expression is favored by M.M., pp. 205, 206, by Bruce, *op. cit.*, pp. 248-250, and also by R.S.V., A.R.V. (margin), and the *New American Standard Bible*. I believe it also is clearly supported by the context: the man who *takes his stand on* — hence, *brags about* (as the Berkeley Version puts it) — what he has seen, is described as being vainly inflated ("puffed up") by his fleshly mind. Cf. also the entry ἐμβατεύω in L.N.T. (A. and G.), p. 253. Ridderbos (*op. cit.*, p. 194), on the other hand, favors (though with commendable caution) the rendering: "as an initiate entering into that which he claims to have seen." This *entering into* may be compared with the rendering *intruding into* of the A.V. Though by no means denying the possibility that Ridderbos is right, since there is definite evidence in support of this use of the word, I regard the translation *taking his stand on* as probably more nearly in harmony with the context in this instance, as has been indicated.
[101] The insertion *not* (A.V. "which he hath not seen") does not rest on *the best* textual evidence in the original. Perhaps some copyist who did not understand that when Paul said, with reference to this false teacher, "taking his stand on the things he has seen," he meant, "on the things he *pretends* (or even *believes*) to have seen," inserted this *not* in his copy, thinking that otherwise the ritualist would receive too much credit. But the idiom which the apostle uses is very transparent. We may compare Paul's expression "the things he has seen" with Christ's ". . . that those that see may become blind" (John 9:39b), meaning, "that those who *pretend* to see, and are constantly saying, *We see,* may become blind" (cf. John 9:41).

up" (I Cor. 8:1). He is, continues Paul, **without cause puffed up by his fleshly mind.** Note "without cause," that is, though he is filled with an exalted opinion of himself, he has no good reason to feel this way. His mind, moreover, is distinctly the mind *of the flesh,* the attitude or disposition of heart and mind *apart from regenerating grace.*[102] It is important in this connection to observe that for the mind to be "fleshly" or "of the flesh" it is not necessary that it be "fixed on purely physical things." [103] On the contrary, it is "of the flesh" if it bases its hope for salvation on *anything apart from Christ,* as verse 19 clearly indicates. Whether the ground on which it bases this confidence be physical strength, charm, good works, or, as here, transcendental visions, makes no difference. It is "the mind of the flesh" all the same. Note how Paul exposes this individual who pretends to take such pleasure in *humility* or *self-abasement.* He says, as it were, "This man who pretends to be so very *humble* is in reality unbearably *proud.* His mind is *inflated* with the sense of his own importance, as he brags about the things he has seen." Contrast this *tawdry* behavior with respect to *questionable* visions with Paul's own *sensible* reaction in regard to *real* visions (II Cor. 12:1-4).

19. The trouble with this combination philosopher-ritualist-angel worshiper-ascetic-visionary is that he is taking his stand on the things he has seen . . . and **not keeping firm hold on the Head.** He does not cling to Christ. He fails to see that Christ is all-sufficient for salvation, and that all the treasures of wisdom and knowledge are hidden in him (Col. 2:3, 9, 10). Hence, Paul continues, **from whom the entire body, supported and held together by joints and ligaments, grows with a growth (that is) from God.** It should not be necessary to defend the proposition that when the apostle, having just referred to Christ as *the Head,* now speaks about *the entire body,* he is thinking about *the church.* That, *in such a connection,* this is the only possible meaning is clearly implied in such passages as Col. 1:18, 24; 3:15; Eph. 1:22, 23; 4:16. [104]

The underlying figure in this passage is that of the growth of the human body. The aptness of Paul's metaphor has been questioned, and this for two reasons:

Objection No. 1. The apostle implies that in a human body the head is the source of growth. This is faulty, ancient physiology.

Answer. As was indicated in connection with Col. 1:18, the hormone that is

---

[102] See summary of the meanings of σάρξ in Paul's epistles, N.T.C. on Philippians, p. 77, footnote 55. Meaning g. is indicated here.
[103] As L.N.T. (A. and G., p. 547), wrongly interprets this word as used here in Col. 1:18.
[104] It is, indeed, somewhat amazing that Dibelius tries to defend the theory that *the body* is here *the cosmos.* See his interpretation of this passage (and also of Col. 1:18 and 2:10) M. Dibelius-H. Greeven, *An die Kolosser, Epheser, An Philemon,* 1953 (in *Handbuch zum Neuen Testament*).

closely related to the growth of connective tissue, cartilage, and bone structure of the body originates in the pituitary gland which is housed in a small cavity in the base of the skull. And that is only one of several ways in which the head influences the growth of the body.

Objection No. 2. According to Paul "nourishment is ministered" (A.V.) to the body by joints and ligaments. Lightfoot similarly states that one of the two functions of the joints and ligaments is "to supply nutriment" (*op. cit.,* p. 200). But we now know that it is not joints and ligaments but the bloodstream that carries nourishment to the various cells and tissues of the human body. Therefore, Paul was in error.

Answer. The proper rendering is "the entire body *supported and held together* by joints and ligaments." [105] Now the fact that the body is, indeed, thus supported and held together is common knowledge. It is not refuted by the most up to date science. Therefore, instead of hinting that the apostle is basing his argument on "loose physiology" (Moule, *op. cit.,* p. 107), the question may well be asked whether the rendering according to which joints and ligaments "supply nutriment" (or "nourishment") to the body is not "loose translation."

So much for the underlying figure. Now as to the real message which the apostle is here conveying, in the light of the context it is clear that the main idea is that to Christ the entire church owes its growth. *The church need not and must not look for any other source of strength to overcome sin or to increase in knowledge, virtue, and joy.* Just as the human body, when properly supported and held together by joints and ligaments, experiences normal growth, so also the church, when each of its members supports and maintains loving contact with the others, will, under the sustaining care of God, proceed from grace to grace and from glory to glory (cf. I Cor. 12; Eph. 4:16).

---

20 If with Christ y o u died to the rudiments of the world, why, as though y o u were (still) living in the world, do y o u submit to regulations, 21 "Do not handle, Do not taste, Do not touch" — 22 referring to things that are meant for destruction by their consumption — according to the precepts and doctrines of men? 23 Regulations of this kind, though to be sure having a reputation for wisdom because of their self-imposed ritual, humility, and unsparing treatment of the body, are of no value whatever, (serving only) to indulge the flesh.

---

[105] See L.N.T. (A. and G.), p. 305, entry ἐπιχορηγέω, which furnishes the evidence for the use of the word in that sense. And see also N.T.C. on Philippians, p. 74, footnote 50 with reference to the meaning of the simple verb.

2:20-23

IV. *Warning against Asceticism*

20-22. In this paragraph Paul condemns the program of austerity recommended by the proponents of error. The connection between these verses and the immediately preceding warning against the worship of the angels (vss. 18, 19) is obscure. Did the impostors perhaps use their presumed contact with the angelic world as a basis for imposing ascetic restrictions on themselves and on others? Did they say, "It must be true that by following these rules y o u will achieve the victory over fleshly indulgence and obtain fulness of salvation, for an angel showed me this in a vision"? We do not know. One fact is certain. It is this, that the apostle teaches that asceticism, no less than the worship of the angels, does more harm than good. Instead of being a remedy against fleshly indulgence, it fosters and promotes the latter.

The apostle has already warned against the *persuasive arguments* of the deceivers (Col. 2:4). He has described this type of propaganda as *philosophy and vain deceit according to the tradition of men* (2:8). He has shown that if even the law *of God,* as a code of ceremonial ordinances and rules and as a means unto salvation, was blotted out and nailed to the cross, then surely *man-made* instructions regarding eating, drinking, etc., must be discarded (2:14, 16). Such added rules and regulations and the teachings of which they are the outgrowth are nothing but puerile notions, *worldly rudiments.* They amount to no more than high-sounding nonsense that is distinctly worldly in its origin and character. Continuing, therefore, along this line, and directing his attention now to an extreme form of this error, namely, to rigid abstinence, Paul says, **If with Christ y o u died to the rudiments of the world, why, as though y o u were (still) living in the world, do y o u submit to regulations.** "If y o u died with Christ, as, of course, y o u did," for y o u were buried with him (see on verse 12 above) and y o u were raised with him (verse 12 again; also 3:1), then y o u have also in that very act made a complete break with all such rudimentary instruction that bases its hope upon anything apart from Christ and fulness of salvation in him. (For the meaning of the expression "rudiments of the world" see on verse 8; also footnote 83.) What is, perhaps, the most beautiful explanation, in Paul's own words, of the basic meaning of this passage is found in Gal. 2:18-21. There Paul is speaking about *building* (verse 18). He is building by faith, "the faith that is in the Son of God, who loved me, and gave himself up for me." He continues, "I do not nullify the grace of God: for if righteousness [or: justification] were through the law, then Christ died to no purpose." And surely if basing one's hope upon the law was contrary to the principle of salvation *solely* on the basis of the redemptive merits of Christ, then this would be true all the more with respect to trusting in purely human ordinances. By reliance on them the Colossians would be acting as though they were still living in the world, that is, in the sphere of life that is separated from Christ. But to this world Paul and all true believers have been crucified. Says he, "But far be it from me to glory except in the cross of our Lord Jesus Christ, through which the world has been crucified to me, and I to the world" (Gal. 6:14). Away, therefore, with all such weak and beggarly rudiments, such teachings and regulations which draw the heart away from Christ as the only Savior (cf. Gal. 4:9)!

With scornful and stinging ridicule Paul now summarizes these regulations, using for this purpose pithy, sparkling, proverbial language: **Do not handle, Do not taste, Do not touch.** He says, as it were, Why submit to a series of Dont's, as if by adding enough negatives y o u would ever obtain a positive, or as if victory over sin and progress in sanctification would ever be achieved by basing all y o u r confidence in sheer *avoidance*. Says Lightfoot, "Some [of these prohibitions] were doubtless re-enactments of the Mosaic law; while others would be exaggerations or additions of a rigorous asceticism, such as we find among the Essene prototypes of these Colossian heretics; e.g., the avoidance of oil, of wine, or of flesh-meat, the shunning of contact with a stranger or a religious inferior, and the like" (*op. cit.,* p. 203). Of course, in reality we do not know exactly what ascetic rules Paul had in mind when he issued this warning, nor do we know precisely what was their background.[106] That restrictions as to the use of foods and beverages were included is implied in the terse commands. Note especially "Do not taste." It is also clear from the parenthetical statement which follows in verse 22. Whether marriage was also forbidden (cf. I Tim. 4:3) or at least subjected to rigorous restrictions we do not know. It would seem, however, that the prohibitions concerned themselves especially with eating and drinking, for the apostle continues . . . — **referring to things that are meant for destruction by their consumption — according to the precepts and doctrines of men?**[107]

---

[106] What really was the origin and background of this asceticism? For a discussion of this question see the Introduction III B 2. Whether the Colossian errorists had at one time been Essenes we do not know. Resemblance does not necessarily mean identity or even descent.

[107] With most translators and commentators I take the question to be, "If with Christ y o u died to the rudiments of the world, why, as though y o u were (still) living in the world, do y o u submit to regulations, Do not handle, Do not taste, Do not touch, according to the precepts and doctrines of men?" (vss. 20, 21, 22b). The clause — "referring to things that are meant for destruction by their consumption" — (verse 22a) is then construed as a parenthesis within the question. It shows that the regulations — in this case prohibitions — refer mainly to that which is consumed by the body. Therefore, the phrase "according to the precepts and doctrines of men" (verse 22b) is construed as modifying verses 20, 21. Others, however, would connect this phrase with the immediately preceding words, which are then no longer construed as a parenthesis. The result then reads as follows: ". . . refer-

What Paul stresses here is that it is certainly most foolish to base one's hope for victory over sin and for complete salvation on anything pertaining to that which in the process of nature is doomed to destruction. Food and drink regulations (here probably especially the former), having as their purpose the betterment of man's moral and spiritual condition, are based on purely human precepts and doctrines. The parenthetical clause — "referring to things that are meant for destruction by their consumption" (cf. I Cor. 6:13) — corresponds exactly to the teaching of Jesus in Matt. 15:17: "Do y o u not understand that whatever goes into the mouth passes into the stomach, and is discharged into the latrine?" The description of the regulations as being "in accordance with the precepts and doctrines of men" also immediately reminds one of what Jesus said as reported in another verse of that same chapter of Matthew, namely, "teaching (as their) doctrines precepts of men" (Matt. 15:9), which, in turn, is a quotation from Isa. 29:13. The point of all this teaching, both in Isaiah and in the words of Jesus, is not only to show that such man-made ordinances and the doctrines from which they spring are *worthless,* but also and emphatically that they are worse than worthless, that is, actually harmful. Hence, according to the Isaiah passage a woe is pronounced upon those who substitute the commandment of men for the heart-centered fear of Jehovah, and in the context of the Matthew passage Jesus sharply denounces those in his day who nullified the word of God for the sake of their tradition (Matt. 15:6).

23. Entirely in line with this the apostle concludes this section as follows: **Regulations of this kind,**[108] **though, to be sure, having a reputation** [109] **for wisdom because of their self-imposed ritual,**[110] **humility, and unsparing treatment of the body, are of no value whatever, (serving only) to indulge the flesh.**[111]

---

ring to things that are meant for destruction by their consumption, along with (or: as happens also to) the precepts and doctrines of men." Foods and human regulations are both doomed to perish. Cf. H. Ridderbos, *op. cit.,* p. 197, though he adds that the connection is rather loose. The reason I favor the more widely held view is that the words "by their consumption" can hardly be considered to apply not only to foods *but also to the precepts and doctrines of men.*

[108] Literally, *such as,* but the reference is to the regulations and the teaching from which they spring.

[109] The meaning of λόγος depends on the context. Here it seems to have the connotation *reputation,* which is akin to that which it frequently has, namely, *report.*

[110] The compound ἐθελοθρησκία has been called a Christian term. Paul may have coined it himself. No examples of its use before Paul have been found. It reminds one of ἐθελοδουλεία, *voluntary service,* but in the present context the word used by Paul probably means *self-chosen worship, self-imposed cult* or *ritual, self-made religion* (hence, in reality, *would-be religion*).

[111] Meaning: "but serve only to indulge the flesh." Lightfoot, followed by Moule, has serious objections to this and similar adversative renderings. His main objections are: (1) there is no indication that an adversative clause begins with πρὸς πλησμονὴν κ.τ.λ.; and (2) it makes the apostle say what he could not have said.

Here "self-imposed ritual" refers to the worship of the angels of which Paul had spoken in verse 18, and "humility" repeats what he said in that same verse about the sham self-abasement of the teachers of error. The "unsparing treatment of the body" has been explained in verses 20, 21. The home-made piety of these cultists made a deep impression on some people. How serious and godly these propagandists seemed to be, and how humble! Perhaps by copying their example the Colossians, striving against sins of the flesh such as are mentioned in 3:5, 8, 9, would be able to achieve the moral and spiritual victory they were seeking. "Not at all," says Paul. Neglect of the body will never cure the soul. Man's body as well as his soul is dear to the Lord, being a temple of the Holy Spirit (I Cor. 6:19). The soul-body contrast, as if the body were evil and for that reason had to be punished, while the soul was divine, smacks of gnostic dualism or hellenism. The worship of the angels reminds one of polytheism. The humility is definitely faked. In reality these teachers of falsehood are proud. If people are deceived by them and accept their worse than worthless advice, this will flatter the pride of these "philosophers." Any system of religion which is unwilling to accept Jesus Christ as the only and all-sufficient Savior is an indulgence of the flesh, a giving in to man's sinful conceit, as if he, by his own contrivances, were able to perfect Christ's imperfect (?) work. It makes matters worse instead of better.

Again and again Paul condemns sinful pride. In addition to Col. 2:18, 23, see also Rom. 1:21, 22, 30; 12:16; I Cor. 8:1, 2; I Tim. 3:6; 6:4. Cf. James 4:6; I Peter 5:5. It is the haughty spirit that goes before a fall (Prov. 16:18). Not only those who actually swagger before men (Matt. 6:1, 2), nor only those who strut in the presence of the Almighty (Luke 18:10-12), but also those

---

"Such language would defeat its own object by its extravagance." He renders πρός "to check," so that the meaning of the sentence becomes, "All such teaching is powerless to check indulgence of the flesh."

Along with H. Ridderbos (op. cit., p. 198) and many other commentators I believe, however, that the adversative sense is correct, and that we have here a μὲν . . . δέ (implied) sequence. In favor of this rendering and in opposition to Lightfoot's arguments I present the following:

(1) When the contrast is easily supplied from the context, μέν need not always be followed by δέ (expressed). L.N.T. (A. and G., p. 504) cites the following New Testament instances of this omission: besides Col. 2:23 also I Cor. 6:7 and II Cor. 12:12. This answers Lightfoot's first objection.

(2) This translation is in line with what the apostle has already said in verse 18, where he spoke about the fleshly mind, that is, the mind inflated or puffed up with sinful pride. The language of verse 23, when the adversative rendering is adopted, is therefore not much more "extravagant" than is that of verse 18. This in reply to Lightfoot's second argument.

(3) The preposition πρός is far more naturally translated with a view to (the indulgence of the flesh); hence, serving (to indulge the flesh).

(4) As was pointed out in connection with verses 20-22, both in Isaiah 29:13 and in Matt. 15:9 such man-made teaching and the regulations which flow forth from it are described as being definitely harmful. They are not only powerless to check indulgence, but they actually promote the desires of the flesh.

who conceal their revolting conceit behind a mask of humility are an abomination to Jehovah (Prov. 16:5; cf. 3:5; 16:18; 26:12; 29:23; Ps. 101:5b). Is there a danger that the Colossians will slip back into their former *fleshly* life? There is a far better solution than that which is offered by the false teachers. In harmony with all that Paul has so far been saying — see especially 1:9-23, 27, 28; 2:2, 3, 6-10 — that solution is pointed out in Colossians 3.

Summary of Colossians 2

Paul concluded the last paragraph by saying, "I am laboring, *striving* by his energy working powerfully within me." In a new paragraph which begins in what we now call Chapter 2 he once more picks up this idea of *striving*, and writes, "For I want y o u to know how greatly I *strive* for y o u," etc. He is wrestling in prayer, in planning, in dictating this letter, and perhaps in other ways, being deeply concerned over the dangers that are threatening the churches located in the Lycus Valley. These dangers do not touch merely the intellect; no, they touch the heart! Paul writes, "I strive for all who have not seen my face in the flesh . . . that their *hearts* may be strengthened." Heresy is usually a matter of the heart, and so is true soundness. Fully realizing that impostors are placing great stress on such matters as "knowledge," "philosophy," (abstract and worldly!), Paul emphasizes *love*. He fervently hopes and prays that the Colossians and their neighbors may be "welded together in love." Such a unity results in praying together, discussing matters together, worshiping together, the result being that the entire company of believers will obtain a clear knowledge of the mystery of God, even Christ. Having discovered this mystery, no further discoveries need be attempted. *Christ cannot be supplemented*, for in him, "*all* the treasures of wisdom and knowledge are hidden"; hidden, yes, but with a view to being *revealed* to every believer and fully *appropriated*. Continue to cling to Christ Jesus, the Lord, says Paul, just as y o u sometime ago made that wonderful decision to accept him. Continue in what y o u were taught, and let no one carry y o u off as spoil "by means of his philosophy and empty deceit, according to the tradition of men, according to the rudiments of the world, and not according to Christ." Watch out for those "worldly rudiments," those puerile notions advanced by worldly people. Remember that not only *divinity* dwells in Christ but *deity*. Being God in the fullest sense of the term, he is able and eager to supply y o u r *every* need. He is higher than all the angels in the sky, and overrules every sinister device of Satan and his helpers.

In order to gain victory over sin and fulness of salvation it will not be necessary for y o u to be circumcised. In fact, y o u have already received a circumcision that far excels the literal kind. Y o u received the circumcision of the *heart*. It is y o u r s because of y o u r vital union with Christ, having been buried with him and having been raised with him. Y o u received the sign and seal of this in y o u r baptism. Let not the law of Moses with its many ordinances frighten y o u. When Christ died, the law, with all its ceremonial regulations, died with him. It was nailed to his cross! Both the law and Satan have lost all legal claim against y o u. By means of Christ's death on the cross the law lost its hold on y o u (as a means of salvation), and the principalities and powers (angels) that might wish to accuse y o u were openly exposed to disgrace. This holds too with respect to regulations concerning food or drink, festivals, new moon, and sabbath. When once the object that projected its shadow arrives, it is foolish to keep clinging to the shadow. The types are fulfilled in Christ.

Don't be impressed by those people who make a show of their humility, pretending that they are too unworthy to contact God directly and must therefore seek to reach God by the mediation of angels whom they adore and worship. [It is not certain, however, that this was their real reason for worshiping the angels. It is a suggestion that has been offered by many.] Do not allow those pretenders to disqualify y o u, as if y o u r manner of worshiping God (or Christ) is not good enough. Remember, instead of being *really* humble, these impostors are "puffed up by their fleshly mind." They are "not keeping firm hold on the Head, from whom the entire body, supported and held together by joints and ligaments, grows with a growth (that is) from God."

And finally, if with Christ y o u died to the world's puerile notions, why then do y o u submit to ordinances, "Do not handle, Do not taste, Do not touch." Such man-made regulations have merely a show of wisdom. If y o u obey them, thinking that conquest over evil and fulness of salvation lies in that direction, y o u will be worse off than ever before. Such self-imposed ritual serves only *to indulge the flesh.* It feeds man's pride. It will but lead y o u *away from* Christ and fulness of salvation in him.

---

[83] In astrological literature *stoicheia* ("rudiments") is frequently used in the sense of *elemental* (or *astral*) *spirits* or *elemental beings.* It is held by many that this is also the meaning here in Col. 2:8. Bible translators have adopted this rendering: R.S.V., N.E.B., Moffatt, etc. Among the many commentators who favor it are F. W. Beare, *The Epistle to the Colossians* (in *The Interpreter's Bible,* Vol. XI), pp. 191-193: "astral divinities which control the spheres and are thus masters of human fate"; F. F. Bruce, *Commentary on the Epistle to the Colossians* (in *The New International Commentary on the New Testament*), pp. 228-232: "rulers of the planetary spheres"; A. S. Peake, *The Epistle to the Colossians* (in *The Expositor's Bible,* Vol. III), pp. 521-524: "astral spirits"; E. F. Scott, *The Epistles of Paul to the Colossians, to Philemon, and to the Ephesians* (in *The Moffatt Commentary*), pp. 41-43: "personal agencies, angelic beings"; and see also E. Percy, *Die Probleme der Kolosser- und Epheserbriefe,* pp. 156-167: "spiritual beings who stood in relation to the elements of nature."

Arguments that have been used in favor of this rendering, in one form or another, are the following; together with my counter-arguments:

(1) There is a good deal of evidence for the widespread use of the word in this sense.

Answer. "For the sense *elemental beings* the evidence, apart from what may be deduced from the contexts of the word in the New Testament, is later than the

Classical and, in all determinable cases, later than the New Testament, and belongs to the astrological sorts of writings" (C. F. D. Moule, *The Epistles of Paul the Apostle to the Colossians and to Philemon*, in *Cambridge Greek Testament Commentary*, p. 91. Again, "Apparently, therefore, there is no definite evidence, that στοιχεῖον meant 'spirit,' 'angel,' or 'demon,' earlier than Test. Sal., which in its present form is post-Christian, and may not be earlier than the third or fourth century" (E. de Witt Burton, *A critical and exegetical commentary on the Epistle to the Galatians*, pp. 510-518.

Besides, if the word has this meaning in Paul's letters, how is it that in his lists of angels (I Cor. 15:24; Col. 1:16; 2:10, 15; Eph. 1:21; 3:10) he never uses it?

(2) When the apostle says, "according to the *stoicheia* of the world and not according to Christ" he is evidently thinking of Christ as a person. Hence, logic requires that these *stoicheia*, who are here represented as opposing Christ, must also be viewed as personal beings.

Answer. By that same reasoning *tradition* also becomes a person, for it stands in exactly the same relation to Christ as do these *stoicheia*. Note: "according to the tradition of men, according to the rudiments of the world and not according to Christ."

(3) In Galatians 4:3, 9 these *stoicheia* are associated, if not identified, with the angelic powers. Now if that be true in Galatians, why not here in Colossians?

Answer. The appeal to Galatians is not justified. Gal. 4:10, considered as an interpretation of 4:9, rather indicates that Paul was thinking of rudimentary teaching regarding observances. Besides, is it at all reasonable to believe that Paul in Gal. 4:3, 9 (notice how he includes himself in verse 3) would be saying that before his conversion he, the Pharisee, had been in bondage to weak and beggarly angels in control of heavenly bodies and of earth, air, fire, water, etc.? Was Paul an animist before his conversion? A polytheist, perhaps, filled with fear and dread because of these astral spirits who supposedly tyrannized mankind in the period of its minority?

(4) But Paul does indeed say something about the angels in Gal. 3:19: "the law was ordained through angels." Is it not true then that with the coming of Christ these angels became as it were competitors of Christ, and tried to maintain the law, and that Paul now warns against putting oneself in bondage again to these angels? If Paul was not warning against the astral spirits of paganism, may he not have been warning against the law-mediating angels of Judaism?

Answer. The idea that Paul regarded the keeping of the law to be a bondage to angels is devoid of every shred of evidence. Paul never makes the angels responsible in any way for the idea of salvation through law-works. He maintains that the law as such is not an obstruction to the work of Christ but on the contrary is holy and good. And in Gal. 3:19 he clearly represents the angels as adding luster to the law. He does not fight those angels. He favors them.

In addition to the works already cited see also H. N. Ridderbos, *The Epistle of Paul to the Churches of Galatia* (in *The New International Commentary on the New Testament*), pp. 152-154, 161; and H. Fransen, "Enkele Opmerkingen over de exegese van Kol. 2:8 en 9," *GTT* (1952), pp. 65-89.

It is not surprising, therefore, that *many* commentators (although probably still a minority) refuse to adopt this rendering, and interpret *stoicheia* to mean *rudimentary instruction:*

Clement of Alexandria, writing about the year A.D. 200, and clearly basing his interpretation on the context, states that Paul figuratively calls Hellenic philosophy the *stoicheia* of this world (*Stromata* VI.viii).

Tertullian, about the same time, and again in complete harmony with the context, writes that Paul warned the Colossians to beware of subtle words and philosophy, as being vain deceit, such as is according to the *stoicheia* of the world, "not understanding thereby the mundane fabric of sky and earth, but worldly learning, and the tradition of men subtle in speech and in their philosophy" (*Against Marcion* V.xix).

Also, much closer to our own day, C. R. Erdman calls these *stoicheia* "the ritual observances of the Jews" (*The Epistles of Paul to the Colossians and to Philemon,* pp. 67, 68) ; J. B. Lightfoot calls them "rudimentary instruction" (*Saint Paul's Epistles to the Colossians and to Philemon,* pp. 178-181) ; C. F. D. Moule defines them as "elementary teaching — teaching by Judaistic or pagan ritualists . . . contrary to the freedom of the Spirit" (*op. cit.,* p. 92) ; Herman Ridderbos, as "elementary knowledge" and as "the basic principles of the sinful world of mankind" (*Aan De Kolossenzen,* in *Commentaar op het Nieuwe Testament,* p. 171) ; and A. T. Robertson, as "the specious arguments of the Gnostic philosophers with all their aeons and rules of life" (*Word Pictures in the New Testament,* Vol. IV, p. 491).

Among the objections that have been advanced against this interpretation the following two are, perhaps, the most outstanding, my answer being added in each case:

(1) Col. 2:8 implies a sharp contrast between these *stoicheia* and Christ. But when these *stoicheia* are interpreted to mean rudimentary instruction regarding rules, regulations, and observances there is no real contrast. Says Percy, "In addition, there is especially this consideration that the expression τὰ στοιχεῖα τοῦ κόσμου, according to Col. 2:8, 10, as well as according to Gal. 4:3, 9, concerns something that is absolutely opposed to Christ, which does not suit the meaning *religious first principles,* which as such are the 'abiding foundations of all religion,' and will retain their validity when a more advanced stage has been reached" (*op. cit.,* p. 157).

Answer. There is, indeed, a sharp contrast here, for these are the rudiments *of the world,* the world apart from Christ, in which sphere these people had formerly lived. These rudiments are not retained when people turn to Christ. On the contrary, we are distinctly told that believers *have died* to them (Col. 2:20).

(2) The interpretation *rudimentary instruction* regarding rules and regulations is not in harmony with the context. Percy, having pointed out that *stoicheia* has of itself no other meaning than *element, rudiment,* continues, "When in so doing it concerns the rudiments of knowledge, this meaning must arise from the context, which is not true in the present case" (*op. cit.,* p. 157).

Answer. In each case where Colossians uses the word *stoicheia* it is exactly the immediate context which by means of the synonyms *philosophy, empty deceit, the tradition of men* (verse 8), *ordinances, precepts and doctrines of men* (verses 20 and 22), would seem to establish the correctness of this interpretation. Clement of Alexandria and Tertullian gave a basically correct explanation. And it does not speak well for the objectivity of the R.S.V., a Bible-translation which in some respects is excellent, that it did not consider *rudimentary instruction* or a similar rendering *worthy at least of a footnote* (contrast N.E.B.) ! Had R.S.V. retained the rendering of the A.V. ("rudiments") and had it left the elucidation to the Commentaries, instead of foisting its "elemental spirits of the universe" on an unsuspecting Bible-reading public, that procedure would have been even more commendable, and this all the more so because on its title page are printed the words "being the version set forth A. D. 1611," etc.

Outline of Chapter 3:1-17

Theme: *Christ, the Pre-eminent One, the Only and All-Sufficient Savior*

II. This Only and All-Sufficient Savior Is the Source of the Believers' Life, and Thus the Real Answer to the Perils by Which They Are Confronted, chapters 3 and 4

    A. This Truth Applied to All Believers, 3:1-17

3:1-4   1. Believers should be consistent. They should live in conformity with the fact that they were raised with Christ, who is their life

3:5-11   2. Therefore, they should "put to death" and "lay aside" the old vices; and

3:12-17   3. They should "put on" the new virtues

CHAPTER III

COLOSSIANS

3 1 If then y o u were raised with Christ, seek *the things that are above,* where Christ is, seated at the right hand of God. 2 On the things that are above set y o u r minds, not on the things that are upon the earth. 3 For y o u died, and y o u r life is hid with Christ in God. 4 When Christ (who is) our life is manifested, then y o u also will be manifested with him in glory.

3:1-4

I. *Believers Should Be Consistent*

1. Consistency requires that believers *live* in conformity with the fact that they were raised with Christ, who is not only the Object of their faith (chapters 1 and 2) but also the Source of their life (chapters 3 and 4). Of course, the line between these two divisions is not sharp. There is considerable overlapping. There is, however, a difference in emphasis.

Between Colossians 3 and that which precedes there is a close connection. The opening words of Col. 3, **If then y o u were raised with Christ,** resume the thought already expressed in 2:12, 13, "raised with him . . . made alive with him," and are the counterpart of 2:20, "If with Christ y o u died to the rudiments of the world. . . ." The Colossians, it will be recalled, were beset by the danger of relapsing into paganism with its gross sensuality, etc., as is clear from 2:23 and 3:5 ff. The wrong solution of their problem was refuted in chapters 1 and 2, especially the latter. It was indicated that there is no material cure for a spiritual ill, that neglect of the body will never heal the soul's sickness but will aggravate it, that heaven-born individuals cannot gain satisfaction from earth-born remedies. *Christ, he alone,* is the answer, Christ in all the fulness of his love and power, as already implied in both chapters 1 and 2, and set forth with even greater clarity and directness now (chapter 3), in a series of pastoral exhortations. If, then, the Colossians were corporately raised *when* Christ was raised and *with* him, as previously explained (see on 2:12, 13, 20), why should they seek salvation or fulness anywhere apart from him? Why should they resort to broken cisterns when the Fountain is at hand? Christ's resurrection, followed by his ascension and coronation, guarantees their pardon and provides for their purity. To this Savior they had surrendered themselves when they had embraced him by

139

faith. The cleansing power of Christ's blood and Spirit had been signified and sealed to them in baptism. The supply of grace remains plentiful. *Right now* — they need not wait until the day of the Parousia! — they are raised with Christ. They possess within themselves the life of the resurrection. Let the power of Christ's resurrection, therefore, be experienced by them in an ever increasing degree. Let their union with the exalted Christ transform their entire life: mind, heart, and will (Phil. 3:10) . Let them **seek** *the things that are above,* **where Christ is.** The verb *seek* implies persevering effort; hence, the rendering, "Be constantly seeking," is not incorrect. This seeking, moreover, is more than a seeking *to discover.* It is a seeking *to obtain* (cf. Matt. 6:33; 13:45) . The emphasis, though, is not on the seeking but on the object sought. A precise rendering would be, "the things that are above [placed forward for emphasis] be constantly seeking." Seeking to obtain is a common activity, but seeking to obtain *the right treasures* is not nearly so common, and therefore requires emphasis. These things that are above are the spiritual values embedded in the heart of the exalted Mediator in glory, whence, without loss to himself, they are bestowed upon those who humbly ask for them and diligently seek them (Matt. 7:7; I Cor. 12:11; Eph. 1:3; 4:7, 8) . As the context indicates, the apostle has reference to such realities as tenderheartedness, kindness, lowliness, meekness, longsuffering, patience, the forgiving spirit, and above all *love* (3:12 ff.) . Surely, if the hearts of believers are filled with such bounties there will be no room for fleshly indulgence. Here, then, is the true solution.

The Colossians can be assured of the fact that their exalted Christ has both the right and the power to bestow whatever gifts are needed, for he is **seated at the right hand of God** (Ps. 110:1, a phrase applied by Christ to himself in Matt. 22:41-46; 26:64; Mark 12:35-37; 14:61, 62; Luke 20:41-44; 22:66-70) , clothed with majesty and honor.

This comforting truth of the ascension of the Lord and his coronation at the Father's right hand, as a Fountain of blessing for his people, was foreshadowed in the Old Testament (Ps. 8, as interpreted in Heb. 2:1-8; Ps. 68:18, as explained in Eph. 4:7, 8; Ps. 110:1, as has been shown; Isa. 53:12) . It was frequently referred to by the Lord himself (see, in addition to the Gospel-passages in the preceding paragraph, John 14:1-4; 14:13-18; 16:7; 17:5; 20:17) . It was from the very beginning one of the basic themes in the preaching of the church (Luke 24:50-53; Acts 1:6-11; 2:33-36; 3:21; 5:30, 31; 7:56; Rom. 8:32-34; Eph. 1:20-23; 4:7, 8; Phil. 2:9-11; 3:20, 21; I Tim. 3:16; Heb. 1:1-3, 13; 2:1-8; 4:14-16; 8:1, 2; 9:11, 12, 24; 10:12; I Peter 3:21, 22; Rev. 1:12-18; 12:5-12) .

Those that seek to obtain these "things that are above" are not chasing phantoms but are gathering priceless treasures. They are not the kind of people who forget about their duty in the here and now. On the contrary, they are very practical, for the graces that have been enumerated enable them not only to gain victory upon victory in their struggle against fleshly indulgence but also to be truthfully "the salt of the earth" and "the light of the world" (Matt. 5:13, 14).

2. In similar vein Paul continues, **On the things that are above set y o u r minds, not on the things that are upon the earth.**[112] This admonition is very practical. It means that the Colossians are urged to *ponder and yearn for* [113] the things that are above, as previously defined. Now a minister who seeks to help his people in their struggle against immorality should not preach a *series* of sermons on the theme *Immorality,* going into all its sordid details. If he does, his sermons might do more harm than good. Instead of banishing the evil he may be creating a taste for it. Let him, instead, preach *one sermon* on Immorality but *an entire series on The Glory of Service Rendered to Christ and His People.*

This *positive* method of overcoming sin is characteristic of Paul's teaching. Note the following:

"Overcome evil with good" (Rom. 12:21);

"Put on the Lord Jesus Christ and make no provision for the flesh" (Rom. 13:14);

"Walk by the Spirit, and y o u will not gratify the desires of the flesh (Gal. 5:16); and

"For the rest, brothers, whatsoever things are true . . . honorable . . . just . . . pure . . . lovely . . . of good report . . . be thinking about these things . . . and the God of peace will be with y o u" (Phil. 4:8, 9).

The same truth is illustrated in Col. 3:12-17. This is the only effective way to "put to death the members that are upon the earth" (3:5-9a), as is also clear from 3:9a, 10.

3. Accordingly, the apostle continues, **For y o u died, and y o u r life is hid with Christ in God.** In the sense already explained (see on 2:11, 12) the Colossians are dead and buried. It is no longer they that live but Christ that lives in them. They are dead to their old selves and to the world governed by sin. Their life is bound up in the bundle of the living with their Lord and Savior Jesus Christ (cf. I Sam. 25:29). From eternity they were comprehended in him (Col. 3:12; cf. Eph. 1:4). In time they were *from God's side* ingrafted in Christ by the Spirit (John 3:5; Rom. 6:5; II Cor. 3:16; Eph. 2:22), and *as a result* were *from their side* united to Christ by a living faith (Gal. 2:20). Their new life *is hid* with Christ. It is concealed to the world

---

[112] In verse 2 the word-order of the original can be retained without any difficulty. In verse 1, because of the modifier "where Christ is," the emphasis of the original can be best retained by means of italics.

[113] For the verb φρονέω see N.T.C. on Phil. 3:19; cf. Rom. 8:5; 12:16.

141

(I Cor. 2:14; I John 3:2), and is indestructible, everlasting (John 3:16; 10:28; Rom. 8:31-39). And since, as to essence, Christ is in the Father, and the Father is in Christ (John 1:18; 10:30; 17:21; I Cor. 3:23; Col. 1:15), it is evident that Paul is fully justified in saying "Y o u r life is hid with Christ *in God*."

4. Though the world will never be able to see the closeness of the *inner* relationship between believers and their Lord, the *outward* expression of this inner relationship, *the glory,* will one day become clear to all: **When Christ (who is) our** [114] **life is manifested, then y o u also will be manifested with him in glory.** "Christ (who is) our life." This cannot mean identity. To say that our life is "the extension" of Christ's life is ambiguous. Christ and we are not the same in *essence,* as are the Father and the Son. The life of Christ — hence, Christ himself — is, however, the Source and Pattern of our life. Moreover, through the Holy Spirit and Spirit-given faith, Christ is most closely united with us, and we with him. The expression "Christ, our life" must, therefore, be explained in the light of similar ones such as the following:

"Because I live y o u too will live" (John 14:19);

"(We are) always bearing about in the body the dying of Jesus, that the life also of Jesus may be manifested in our body" (II Cor. 4:10);

"It was the good pleasure of God . . . to reveal his Son in me" (Gal. 1:15, 16);

"Christ lives in me" (Gal. 2:20);

"My little children, with whom I am again in labor, until Christ be formed in y o u" (Gal. 4:19);

"But we all . . . are transformed into the same image from glory to glory as from the Lord the Spirit" (II Cor. 3:18); and

"For to me to live (is) Christ, and to die (is) gain" (Phil. 1:21).

When, on the day of his second coming, a day known only to God (Matt. 24:36; I Thess. 5:1, 2), Christ, our life, *is manifested,*[115] his attributes of

---

[114] Though the external evidence for ὑμῶν is at least equally strong as for ἡμῶν, the latter may, nevertheless, be correct. It is not unusual for Paul, a deeply emotional writer, who writes about truths he has himself experienced or himself holds dear, to change from the second to the first person (cf. Col. 1:9 with 1:13; 2:13a with 2:13b; and see on Philem. 6).

[115] In the New Testament the verb φανερόω occurs with great frequency in the writings of John (Gospel, First Epistle, Revelation) and of Paul. For a classification of its meanings in John's Gospel and First Epistle see N.T.C. on the Gospel of John, Vol. II, p. 476, footnote 294. Apart from its occurrences in John and Paul it is found only in the following New Testament passages: Mark 4:22; 16:12, 14; Heb. 9:8, 26; and I Peter 1:20; 5:4. In the letters of Paul the word is used 22 times, as follows:

a. in connection with the display of glory in the words and works of Jesus at his

majesty and power being publicly displayed, then the Colossians too will be manifested *with him* (cf. Rom. 8:32). *Their* public vindication and glory will coincide with *his.* Among the many New Testament passages (in addition to Col. 1:27) which shed further light on the meaning of this glory which God's children will share with their Lord in the day when they will be "like him" and will "bear the image of the heavenly" are especially the following: Matt. 25:31-40; Rom. 8:17, 18; I Cor. 1:7, 8; Phil. 3:20, 21; I Thess. 2:19, 20; 3:13; 4:13-18; II Thess. 1:10; II Tim. 4:7, 8; I Peter 1:13; I John 2:28; 3:2; and Rev. 17:14.

---

5 Put to death therefore y o u r members that (are) upon the earth: immorality, impurity, passion, evil desire, and greed, which is idolatry; 6 on account of which things the wrath of God is coming; 7 in which things y o u also walked at one time, when y o u were living in them. 8 But now y o u, too, lay them all aside: wrath, anger, malice, slander, shameful language from y o u r mouth. 9 No longer lie to one another, seeing that y o u have put off the old man with his practices, 10 and have put on the new man, who is being renewed for full knowledge according to the image of him who created him, 11 where there cannot be Greek and Jew, circumcision and uncircumcision, barbarian, Scythian, slave, freeman, but Christ (is) all and in all.

3:5-11

II. *Therefore, They Should "Put to death" and "Lay Aside" the Old Vices*

5. In close connection with the immediately preceding paragraph Paul continues, **Put to death therefore y o u r** [116] **members that (are) upon the earth.** Note the paradox, "Y o u died" (verse 3) . . . "Put to death therefore y o u r members . . ." (verse 5). A superficial judgment would be that the apostle is here contradicting himself. Some interpreters have, in fact, reached that very conclusion. It is as if on the one hand Paul is saying that the Colossians have already died, yet on the other hand is telling them that they must put themselves to death. How can both be true? The answer is

---

first coming (II Cor. 2:14; I Tim. 3:16; II Tim. 1:10), and the life of Jesus manifested in believers (II Cor. 3:3; 4:10, 11).

b. in connection with the disclosure and realization of *the mystery* of God in the fulness of time (Rom. 16:26; Col. 1:26; and cf. Titus 1:3 "manifested his *word*").

c. in connection with the display of glory of Christ at his *second coming* (Col. 3:4a), in which glorious display believers share (Col. 3:4b), and at which time the works and motives of men will be publicly laid bare (I Cor. 4:5; II Cor. 5:10).

d. in connection with *the divine attributes* made known to men (Rom. 1:19; 3:21).

e. in *a more general sense,* in connection with anything else that is hidden or dark and is brought to light or made visible or plain (II Cor. 5:11; 7:12; 11:6; Eph. 5:13 twice; Col. 4:4).

[116] Though the reading without ὑμῶν deserves the preference, y o u r is clearly *implied.*

that as long as believers are still living on earth their *condition* and their *state* do *not wholly* coincide. As to their *state* they are even now perfect, without any sin, wholly justified! Their old self is dead and buried (Col. 2:11-13). Now it is true that their *condition* is in harmony with this, but only *in principle.* In the words of the Heidelberg Catechism, "Even the holiest men, while in this life, have only a small beginning of this obedience [that is, of obedience to God's commandments]; yet so that with earnest purpose they begin to live, not only according to some but according to all the commandments of God" (Lord's Day XLIV, Answer to Question 114). This *progressive* character of sanctification is also clearly taught by Paul (see below, on verse 10, and cf. II Cor. 3:18; Phil. 1:6; 3:12, 13) and is in harmony with the rest of Scripture (Ps. 84:7; Prov. 4:18; Mark 9:24; also implied in I John 1:8-10). While with respect to *the new life* which was imparted to them by the Holy Spirit believers are so closely united with Christ that they are said to be with him in heaven (Col. 3:3), yet *the old life* is still *of* the earth as well as *on* earth. But there is no reason for despair. The very presence of the new life, the life "in Christ," enables believers progressively to put to death [117] the members that are upon the earth.

When the question is asked what is meant by *the members* that must be put to death the answer is: **immorality, impurity, passion, evil desire, and greed, which is idolatry.** But how can *members* be *vices*? Some expositors regard this to be impossible. They suggest various solutions.[118] Yet it would

---

[117] "Put to death" is the proper translation here, not "Reckon as dead." The command "Put to death" of verse 5 does not have exactly the same meaning as "Consider yourselves to be dead" (Rom. 6:11). And the *passive* νενεκρωμένου in Heb. 11:12 ("as good as dead"; cf. Rom. 4:19) does not change the fact that the *active* νεκρώσατε as used here in Col. 3:5, means *put to death;* for, (a) the active meaning intended here is clearly synonymous with "lay aside" in verse 8, which is not a matter solely of mental reflection or consideration (reckoning) but of voluntary, strenuous effort and exertion; and (b) the real parallel of Col. 3:5 is not so much Rom. 6:11 as Rom. 8:13 (*"put to death* the deeds of the body"), though the verb used there in the original is not the one used here in Col. 3:5 but θανατοῦτε. Hence, I cannot agree here with Bruce (*op. cit.,* p. 267) when he says, " 'Put to death,' or, as we might put it, 'reckon as dead.' "

[118] Thus Lightfoot (*op. cit.,* p. 211) puts a heavy stop after the word *earth.* He then treats the vices ("immorality, impurity," etc.) as "prospective accusatives, which should be governed by some such word as *lay aside.*" Moule (*op. cit.,* p. 116) says "This may well be right." But there is not any need for such a forced reconstruction. Had Paul meant to *imply* the verb *lay aside* he would in all probability have *expressed* it, as he does in Rom. 13:12; Eph. 4:22, 25; Col. 3:8.

Similarly objectionable is Charles Masson's solution (*Commentaire du Nouveau Testament* on this passage). Completely out of line with the context he views "members" as referring to "church-members," and as a vocative, so that the meaning would be, "Y o u, members of Christ's body, must therefore," etc.

Finally, there is Lenski's view (*op. cit.,* p. 157), according to which the words "fornication [= immorality], uncleanness," etc., are "adverbial accusatives of specification," and must be rendered, "as to fornication," etc. So construed the translation becomes needlessly difficult, and the construction lacks clarity. The idea, moreover, that since the imperative νεκρώσατε is an aorist it must refer to one fell blow

seem to me that the difficulty is not nearly as great as some would make it appear to be. John Calvin may be on the right track when he states that these *vices* are called *members* "since they adhere so closely to us." Another very similar way of solving the difficulty, a way which does not imply a rejection of Calvin's view but is clearly in line with it, would be to regard the use of the word *members* (= vices) to be an instance of the figure of speech called *metonymy* ("change of name"), in which, for example, the name of the *cause* or *source* is substituted for the *effect* it produces, the *consequences* that flow forth from it, the *fruit* or *product* it yields. Thus in Num. 3:16 (in the original) the word *mouth* is in the Hebrew substituted for the word *command* that *issued* from the mouth; or just as in American slang the expression, "I'll have none of your *lip*" means, "I will not tolerate any saucy remarks that *issue* from your lips." So here also the command, "Put to death therefore y o u r members that (are) upon the earth: immorality, impurity," etc., means, "Put to death therefore the *effects* produced by, and associated so closely with, the members of y o u r body, such effects, products or works, as immorality, impurity," etc. I am therefore in agreement with Bruce (*op. cit.,* p. 268) when he says, "In Rom. 7:23 Paul speaks of 'the law of sin which is in my members'; here [in Col. 3:5] he goes farther and practically identifies the readers' members with the sins of which they were formerly the instruments. But what he is really thinking of is the practices and attitudes to which his readers' bodily activity and strength had been devoted in the old life." Thus also Ridderbos (*op. cit.,* p. 207) states, "The 'members' are here identified with the sins committed by these members, which in a similar connection in Rom. 8:13 are called 'the deeds of the body.'"

Lists of vices are of frequent occurrence in ancient literature, both pagan (moralistic) and anti-pagan. The recently discovered Dead Sea Scrolls also have such lists.[119] In the letters of Paul they occur in the following passages: Rom. 1:18-32; I Cor. 5:9-11; 6:9, 10; Gal. 5:19-21; Eph. 5:3-6; I Thess. 4:3-7; I Tim. 1:9, 10; II Tim. 3:2-5; Titus 3:3. The difference between the Christian and the non-Christian treatment of these vices is that apart from Christ and the fulness of grace imparted by his Spirit there is no power in all the universe to overcome them. Christ, he alone, supplies that power.

As to arrangement, it is rather obvious that verse 5 lists five vices, and so does verse 8. However, whether there is any significance in this number five as here used is questionable, and if any special meaning attaches to it we must confess that we do not know what it is.[120] It is true, nevertheless, that

---

by which the members are struck dead, cannot be substantiated. The aorist does not always nor necessarily refer to *one* — and only one — deed. In any mood it denotes one *fact* or one *idea,* which in actual historical realization may at times be spread over a lengthy period of time (cf. John 2:20 in the original). *It summarizes!*

[119] See M. Burrows, *The Dead Sea Scrolls,* pp. 375, 386, 387.

[120] Not all agree. Thus Lenski sees in the number five "the half of completeness expressed by ten . . . five is also secular, these are vices" (*op. cit.,* pp. 157, 158).

the first list enumerates vices that describe the sinner as he is in himself, while the second characterizes him in his relation to the neighbor. It is also possible to see in the first list a movement from the surface of life to its center, and in the second the reverse. This will become evident as the various items are studied one by one.

Of the five vices mentioned here in Col. 3:5 the first four are also listed in I Thess. 4:3-7, the last four also in Rom. 1:24-29. The first is *immorality* ("fornication"; see I Thess. 4:3; cf. Matt. 5:32; 15:19; 19:9; John 8:41, etc.). Though referring basically to unlawful sexual intercourse, it probably includes illicit, clandestine relationships of every description. The emphasis, however, is on evil in the sexual realm, particularly evil *deeds.*

These evil *deeds* spring from evil *thoughts,* that is, from *uncleanness,* which is mentioned next (Rom. 1:24; I Thess. 4:7; cf. Matt. 15:19; Mark 7:21, etc.). It is not necessary, however, to limit uncleanness to that which is filthy in *thoughts.* The *intents* of the heart are undoubtedly also included (cf. Heb. 4:12).

That it is the evil *disposition* of the heart and will of man which is *the source* of his wicked thoughts and deeds is clear from the two vices that are mentioned next, namely, *passion* and *evil desire.* It is not easy to distinguish between these, though there may be some merit in Lightfoot's suggestion that the former describes this vice more from its passive, the latter more from its active side. For *passion* see also Rom. 1:26; I Thess. 4:5 ("passion of lust"), etc.; for *evil desire,* Rom. 1:24; I Thess. 4:5, etc. The word *evil* is added because *desire* as such is not necessarily wrong. The word used in the original may also refer to legitimate desire, for example, Christ's desire to eat the Passover with his disciples.[121] But *evil* desire is the inordinate craving for sexual satisfaction, or for other things, such as idol-worship, material possessions, renown, etc. The *emphasis,* in the present context, is, however, on illicit sex relationships, but not to the exclusion of other wicked yearnings. Out of this evil craving arise all kinds of sins. It is therefore *basic,* and is so regarded by Paul himself in Rom. 7:7. In this connection it is also interesting to note that in the Decalogue the sin of *coveting* is mentioned last (Ex. 20:17), as being the source of all the others, and that Jesus, too, considers the lustful heart, that is, the heart filled with evil desire, to be the root whence springs the evil deed, for he says, "Every one who looks on a

---

But even when it is granted that in certain types of literature the number five might have a symbolical significance, it is very doubtful whether such a meaning can be ascribed to it in Colossians. Besides, though it is true that verse 8 (as well as verse 5) lists *five* vices, verse 9 adds another to the list, making *six* in all, or eleven as the sum of both lists. It is therefore better to refrain from dubious numerology.
[121] On the word ἐπιθυμία see N.T.C. on I and II Timothy and Titus, pp. 271, 272, footnote 147.

woman to lust for her has already in his heart committed adultery with her" (Matt. 5:28).

But though by mentioning passion and evil desire the apostle has, as it were, reached the very bottom of every sin, he adds one more vice, one in which all the others are summarized, namely, *self-seeking* or *greed* (cf. Rom. 1:29, etc.). Every sin is basically selfishness, the worship of self instead of the worship of God, the substitution of self for Christ, in one's affections (cf. Col. 3:1-3). It is for this very reason that Paul adds, "which is idolatry" (cf. Eph. 5:5). The young man who gets a girl in trouble may call this "love." He is mistaken. It is self-seeking, greed, at least to a considerable extent. This young man wants "to have more than his due." He is over-reaching, going beyond what is proper (see N.T.C. on I and II Thessalonians, pp. 100, 101). However, the apostle is not thinking particularly about a *young* man but rather about "the *old* man," (see 3:9) that is, the carnal nature of *any* man, regardless of age, the nature of man as it is apart from saving grace.

6, 7. Having listed the vices which formerly characterized the Colossians and by which they are still being tempted, the apostle continues, **on account of which the wrath of God is coming.**[122] By means of what is sometimes called "a prophetic present tense" (cf. John 4:21; 14:3) Paul stresses the fact that the coming of the wrath of God, to be visited upon those who live in such sins, is so certain that it is as if that wrath had already arrived. These sins attract God's displeasure like a magnet attracts iron or like a high steeple on an isolated hill draws lightning. The reference, no doubt, is to the revelation of God's wrath in the coming judgment day (cf. Rom. 2:5-11; Eph. 5:6; II Thess. 1:8-10). Calvin very appropriately observes that the real purpose of this prophecy about the inevitability of God's wrath being visited upon confirmed evildoers is "that we may be deterred from sinning." Accordingly, even such a wrath-statement is filled with mercy!

By God's sovereign grace, however, the Colossians have, in principle, re-nounced this kind of conduct. For them it belongs to the past. Says Paul, **in which things y o u also walked at one time, when y o u were living in them.** Note, "y o u also," that is, "y o u, like other heathen." *Living* and *walking* are almost identical. Nevertheless, in certain contexts, as here, there is a dif-

---

[122] Although the textual support for the additional phrase "upon the sons of dis-obedience" is not weak, the context pleads against its insertion. It is probably an interpolation from Eph. 5:6. Its inclusion here in Col. 3:6 leads to the rendering "among whom" at the beginning of verse 7, and to the strange conclusion that Paul rebukes the Colossians for having walked among the sons of disobedience, an inference which would be contrary to his own teaching (I Cor. 5:10; cf. Titus 2:12) as well as the Lord's (John 17:15; cf. Matt. 5:13, 14).

ference. *Walking* here indicates behavior; *living*, disposition. Thus also Gal. 5:25, "If we live by the Spirit, by the Spirit let us also walk." The Colossians having become "new creatures," are no longer absorbed in these vices of former days. They have become ashamed of their earlier ways. By the power of the Holy Spirit they have been sanctified, cleansed. Their life "is hid with Christ in God" (see above, verse 3). Nevertheless, as pointed out previously, this does not mean that even now the victory has been *fully* won. The flesh is still lusting against the Spirit, and the Spirit against the flesh (Gal. 5:17; cf. Rom. 7:15-24). Hence, the command which follows in verses 8, 9a is very much to the point:

8, 9a. But now y o u, too, lay them all aside: wrath, anger, malice, slander, shameful language out of y o u r mouth. No longer lie to one another. The former vices had not only wrought destruction in the lives of men as individuals, viewed separately (see on verse 5 above), but had also disrupted the relationship between neighbors. This must not continue. Accordingly, *wrath* (Latin: *ira*), that is, settled indignation, when the heart is like a roaring furnace; *anger* or *fury* (Latin: *furor*), the tumultuous outburst, like fire in straw; [123] *malice,* not merely "mischief" but the evil inclination of the mind, the perversity of disposition which bodes ill for man's fellow-man; *slander* or *reviling;* [124] and *shameful language out of y o u r mouth,* that is, abusive speech, all of these *must be laid aside.* Note here the progress in vice, from *wrath* inside the heart, through various stages, to the bitter outward manifestations: slander and abusive language. *Lying,* too, must be discarded (cf. I Tim. 2:7). It must no longer be in evidence in the lives of believers. All manner of hypocrisy and deception has always marked the heathen world. That is true even today. A missionary told us that in answer to his question why a certain enquirer had failed to keep her promise to attend a midweek meeting, the woman answered, "I'm very sorry that I was unable to attend, but, you see, I had to go to the funeral of my mother-in-law in a distant city." Afterward the missionary discovered that the mother-in-law in question had died years ago and that the woman who had invented the excuse had not even been out of the village on the day of the midweek meeting. He added, "They will tell you anything that occurs to their minds just to save face."

Lay aside all these vices, says Paul, just as one *discards* a worn-out garment

---

[123] See C. Trench, *Synonyms of the New Testament,* par. xxxvii. Also N.T.C. on the Gospel according to John, Vol. I, p. 151.

[124] The Greek word used is *blasphemy.* But in Greek this word has a somewhat broader meaning than in English. While in our language it refers to abusive language with respect to God or things religious, that is, to *defiant irreverence,* in the original it refers to insults directed either against God or against men. In the present instance, as the context indicates, the latter is clearly meant: scornful and insolent language directed against a neighbor, slander, defamation, detraction.

or one that no longer fits the person who has been clothed with it. For literal use of the expression "Lay aside" in connection with robes see Acts 7:58. The apostle, well-versed in the Old Testament, knew that the figure of a garment was frequently used in the sacred scriptures to indicate *character*. Sometimes it referred to God-glorifying character, consisting of the fruits of grace, such as righteousness, justice, joy, faithfulness (Job 29:14; Ps. 132:9; Isa. 11:5; 61:10); sometimes to evil character: pride, violence (Ps. 73:6); or to the latters's result: shame and dishonor (Ps. 35:26; 109:29). The garment of righteousness and salvation is ascribed to Jehovah himself (Isa. 59:17). It is therefore understandable that Paul makes use of this figurative manner of speaking (so do other New Testament authors; see Heb. 12:1; James 1:21; I Peter 2:1). It is clearly implied in Rom. 13:12a, 14; Gal. 3:27, "did put on Christ"; Eph. 4:22, 25. With a slight modification of the figure the apostle sometimes speaks of the Christian's duty to *put on* his spiritual *armor* (Rom. 13:12b; II Cor. 6:7; Eph. 6:13-18; and I Thess. 5:8).

9b-11. When Paul urged the Colossians to lay aside the vices that had marked their previous manner of life he was using consistent reasoning. He was, as it were, saying, "Continue to do in practice what y o u have already done in principle." He says, **seeing that y o u have put off** [125] **the old man with his practices, and have put on the new (man).**[126]

As has been shown (see on 2:11, 12), when they were baptized the Colossians had decisively renounced — *put off* and *cast away* — "the old man" (Rom. 6:6; Eph. 4:22), that is, "the body of the flesh," their former manner of existence, their earlier wicked selves, "with its practices," the very practices listed in 3:5, 8, 9a, and had *put on* the new man, Christ (Gal. 3:27), that is, the new nature which believers have as members of Christ. Hence, let them now adorn their baptismal profession of faith with a godly life. Let them "put to death" (verse 5) and "lay aside" (verse 8) all their former vices. Says John Calvin, "The old man is whatever we bring from our mother's womb, and whatever we are by nature. It is called *the old man* because we are first born from Adam, and afterward are born again through

---

[125] Oepke (Th.W.N.T., Vol. II, p. 319) and Lightfoot (*op. cit.*, pp. 214, 215) ascribe an imperative sense to the participles "putting off" and "putting on." However, (1) in this very letter (2:11) the apostle has already mentioned "the putting off of the body of the flesh" as something pertaining to the past, an accomplished fact; and (2) the immediate context (3:2, 3) appears to be a close parallel to 3:8, 9. Both mean, "Do this, *for* y o u have already done that. Do in practice what y o u have already done in principle."

[126] Though it is true that basically the adjective νέον as used here in Col. 3:10 means *new* as to *time* (new versus old), while καινόν as found in Eph. 4:24 indicates *new* as to *quality* (fresh versus worn out), this distinction cannot be pressed here, for the idea of freshness and vigor which might be lacking in the adjective νέον is supplied by the participle ἀνακαινούμενον.

Christ." And Thomas Goodwin, "There are but two men that are seen standing before God, Adam and Jesus Christ; and these two men have all other men hanging at their girdles." Cf. Rom. 5:12-21; I Cor. 15:22, 45-49.

It should be stressed that it is only *in Christ* (by means of vital union with him) that this new man is formed in the believer; also that, because of this very fact, all those who have become new men, whether Jews or Gentiles, can also be called, in their corporate existence, "one new man" in him, as it is expressed in Eph. 2:15, "that he might create in himself of the two one new man." Cf. Gal. 3:28.

Now in each believer this new man is a progressively developing entity, as Paul indicates by continuing, **who is being renewed for full knowledge.** In slightly different language an analogous, though not entirely identical, thought is expressed in II Cor. 4:16, in the words: "Accordingly, we do not lose heart, but (are confident that) though our outer man is decaying, yet our inner man is being renewed day by day." From both of these passages it is evident that the believer's new nature resembles a growing plant. It is being constantly renewed by the Holy Spirit and increases in vigor with a definite goal in mind. The fact that the new man is, as it were, an expanding reality and that salvation means progress is clear not only from these passages and from the references given earlier, in the discussion of verse 5 above (beginning with II Cor. 3:18), but also from the following, to which many others could be added: II Cor. 9:10; 10:15; Eph. 2:21; 4:16; Phil. 2:12, 13; I Thess. 3:12; I Thess. 4:10; II Thess. 1:3; I Tim. 4:15; II Tim. 2:1. When a man is led through the waters of salvation, these are ankle-deep at first, but as he progresses, they become knee-deep, then reach to the loins, and are finally impassable except by swimming (cf. Ezek. 47:3-6). The same thought occurs in Colossians (1:9, 10; 2:19).

The new man is being renewed "for full knowledge" (to which Eph. 4:24 adds "righteousness and holiness"). This knowledge excels by far any so-called knowledge in which the false teachers who disturbed the churches of the Lycus Valley were glorying (see on Col. 2:2, 3, 18). It pertains to both heart and mind, is experiential, and has God's holy will as its object (Rom. 12:2). A true discernment of that will, particularly with reference to its "good pleasure" (Eph. 1:5), is very rewarding. It is a means toward a fuller, richer measure of salvation's joy and peace. A contrast will make this clear. While it is true that here on earth a person's experience with his neighbor will at times cause him to say, "The better I know him and understand his intentions, the less I trust him," in the kingdom of heaven the very opposite truth prevails, namely, "The more we know *him* — that is, the triune God or our Savior Jesus Christ —, and *his* purposes of grace, the more we trust and love him." Paul continues, **according to the image of him who created him.** The standard or yardstick and the aim of the renewal is God's image, the likeness of the very One who created this new man in the hearts and

150

lives of believers, just as he once created the first Adam as his own image (Gen. 1:26, 27). Nevertheless, the new man is not simply the restoration of whatever pertained to the first Adam before the fall. (To mention only one point of difference between the original creation and the new creation: in the state of rectitude Adam had no inkling of knowledge concerning God's redemptive love.) Rather, "Just as we have borne the image of the earthly one, so we shall also bear the image of the heavenly One" (I Cor. 15:49), in whom redemptive love is wholly centralized.

Now this glorious progressive transformation into the image of God recognizes no racial-religious, cultural, or social boundaries. Paul continues, **where there cannot be Greek and Jew, circumcision and uncircumcision, barbarian, Scythian, slave, freeman.**

All racial bigotry, chauvinism, and snobbery is condemned here. Here the truth that before God "all men are equal" receives its best — because infallibly inspired — expression. To be sure, by divine illumination there have always been men who have grasped this truth, at least to a degree. Yet, the vast majority among all races have denied it, if not in theory at least in practice. There was, for example, the Assyrian who considered his gods to be mightier than those of any other nation, stronger even than the God of Israel (II Kings 18:33-35). There was the Jew who knew no fear because, in distinction from the men of other nations, he had "the" temple (Jer. 7:4), and was able to say, "We have Abraham as our father" (but see how Jesus answers him, Luke 3:8). The Edomite considered himself to be superior to other men because he was living in "the cleft of the rock" (Obad. 3). There is also the red man who considers the white man "underbaked," the black man "burnt," but himself "just right," and is sure that the village in which he lives occupies the very center of the earth's surface; the white man who considers himself to be a member of the "superior" race, is sure that a special curse of God rests on those who belong to the opposite race, and that it is his privilege and duty by means of enslavement to perpetuate this curse; and the Negro who says that not the white man but he himself is "superior" and should assert this superiority if need be by force. Of course, not *every* member of any race or class is guilty of this exclusivism and clannishness, but there are many who are. Hindus are by no means the only ones who believe in the caste-system!

In the early days of American history there were men of distinction who regarded the white settlements as representing God's chosen people, destined, because of their extraordinary virtue, to rule the world. There are Germans who put their whole heart into singing, "Deutschland, Deutschland über alles," and Dutchmen who believe that there exists a special covenant between "God, The Netherlands, and the House of Orange." There are fine, evangelical people, "brothers and sisters in Christ," who feel certain that even in the present dispensation national distinctions have value before God (all this in spite of Col. 3:11; cf. Eph. 2:14, 18, 19), and that the Jews will one day rule over the entire world from Jerusalem. And there are males who believe that superiority is somehow linked with sex, and that "Woman is the lesser man."

Now it is not Paul's intention to deny every ethnic, cultural, or social distinction. That there are, indeed, *differences* is freely admitted, and, in fact, sometimes even emphasized. All members of the human body do not have the same function. Thus it is also with Christ's body, the church (Rom. 12:4; I Cor. 12:12-31). Let all work together harmoniously. Similarly, not all have had the same opportunities or advantages (Rom. 3:1, 2). Let the specially privileged recognize their added responsibilities (Rom. 2:9, 12; 3:12; cf. Amos 3:2; Luke 12:47, 48). In certain respects, therefore, it is by no means true that all men are alike. But in two important points they are, indeed, equal! First of all, "all have sinned, and fall short of the glory of God" (Rom. 3:23; cf. 2:11; 3:9-18; 5:12, 18). Secondly, "the same Lord is Lord of all, and is rich to all that call on him" (Rom. 10:11, 12). Those who, by God's sovereign grace, are led to believe in the Lord Jesus Christ are saved regardless of race, culture, or social position (see also Rom. 3:22b, 23, 24; 4:11, 12; 5:18b; 11:32; Gal. 3:13, 14; 3:9, 27-29; Eph. 2:11-22).

Now the present passage (Col. 3:11) is not the only one in which the apostle contrasts certain groups. See also Rom. 1:14, and especially Gal. 3:28. But in each letter the particular contrast which he draws is in keeping with the purpose he has in mind for that letter. Thus, in Galatians, in harmony with its background and intent, the distinctions enumerated are racial-religious ("neither Jew nor Greek"), social ("neither bond nor free"), and sexual ("no male and female"). It reminds one of the prayer of thanksgiving uttered by a *male* Jew who blesses the Lord each morning because he did not make him "a Gentile, a slave, *or a woman!*" Paul says that "in Christ" those distinctions, when they are regarded as marks of preferment by God, are definitely *out*. In our present passage, the contrasts and the reason for stating them thus and not otherwise are as follows:

(1) *racial-religious:* "where there cannot be Greek and Jew, circumcision and uncircumcision." [127] This is stated to counteract the teaching of the ceremonialists (see above, on 2:11-14).

(2) *cultural:* "barbarian, Scythian." Though these two designations both refer to the supposedly uncultured, there is an *implied* contrast here between the cultured and the uncultured. "Knowledge" and "philosophy" are of no help in creating within the heart "the new man." Yet, it was on such human attainments that the false teachers who were troubling the Colossian church placed the emphasis. See on 2:4, 8, 18.

---

[127] Note chiastic arrangement here, very frequent with Paul. The first term, *Greek*, corresponds with the fourth, *uncircumcision;* the second, *Jew*, with the third, *circumcision.* See on Philem. 5.

(3) *social:* "slave, freeman." It is as if Paul were saying, "O Colossians, do not look down on slaves. *Accept Onesimus as y o u r very own, y o u r brother in Christ.* As far as standing before God is concerned there is no distinction between bond and free."

Grace bridges all chasms. Though the Greeks divided mankind into two categories, Greeks and "barbarians"; and though the Romans, after conquering the Greeks politically but having been conquered by them culturally, drew a similar contrast between Greeks-Romans, on the one hand, and "barbarians," on the other; and though the Jews, unconverted to Christ, set Greek over against Jew, grace recognizes no such distinctions, for both Gentile and Jew are reconciled to each other by being reconciled to God through the cross (Eph. 2:13).

Similarly, since the only circumcision that has any value before God is the circumcision of the heart, it stands to reason that before him the question whether or not one has been literally circumcised or has not been literally circumcised has no meaning. See N.T.C. on Phil. 3:2, 3.

And since the world by its "wisdom" did not come to know God (I Cor. 1:21), the cultural distinction also has no value in a person's standing before God. Academic degrees do not make any one a new man. Refinement in customs and manners, in itself not to be despised, is not saving grace. And, on the other hand, being a *barbarian* (Acts 28:4; Rom. 1:14; I Cor. 14:11 twice), a mere "stammerer" to the ears of the more sophisticated, cannot, in and by itself, prevent one from becoming a new man, not even if this barbarian happens to be of the reputedly lowest class, namely, a *Scythian.*

In the seventh century B. C. these Scythians, savage and warlike nomads from the northern steppes, had deluged the countries of the Fertile Crescent, including Palestine, and, having subsequently been repulsed, had left a memory of dread and horror.[128] The account of Herodotus with reference to them is as follows (in part):

---

[128] Lightfoot (*op. cit.,* p. 219) states that "the terror inspired by these invaders has found expression in the prophets." He then refers to Ezek. 28 [38?] and 39, and to Jer. 1:13 ff. and 6:1 ff. Others, too, have identified the Scythians with "Gog and Magog" of Ezek. 38 and 39. Thus Josephus states, "Magog founded those that from him were called Magogites, but who are by the Greeks called Scythians" (*Antiquities of the Jews* I.vi.1). And see J. F. McCurdy's article "Gog and Magog" in *The New Schaff-Herzog Religious Encyclopedia,* Vol. V, pp. 14, 15. Close exegetical study of the Jeremiah and Ezekiel passages has convinced several exegetes, however, that this identification is questionable. In Judg. 1:27 LXX inserts *Scythopolis* as the equivalent of Beth-shean. (Cf. Judith 3:10; II Macc. 12:29.) It is rather commonly supposed, therefore, that a company of Scythians, after their invasion of Palestine, established residence here, and that from this circumstance the place was called "City of the Scythians." For the rest, the only undisputed reference to the Scythians in Scripture is the present passage, Col. 3:11.

"They invaded Asia, after they had driven the Cimmerians out of Europe . . . and made themselves masters of all Asia. From there they marched against Egypt; and when they were in that part of Syria which is called Palestine, Psammetichus, king of Egypt, met them and with gifts and prayer persuaded them to come no farther. . . . They ruled Asia for twenty-eight years; and all the land was wasted by reason of their violence and their arrogance. . . . The greater number of them were entertained and made drunk and were then slain by Cyaxares and the Medes" (I.103-106). "They drank the blood of the first enemy killed in battle, and made napkins of the scalps, and drinking bowls of the skulls of the slain. They had the most filthy habits and never washed with water" (IV.64, 65, 75). Cf. Tertullian, *Against Marcion* I.1, "Marcion was born there, more filthy than any Scythian." Josephus states, "The Scythians delight in murdering people and are little better than wild beasts" (*Against Apion* II.269). In II Macc. 4:47 we read, "Menelaus, the cause of all the evil . . . sentenced to death those unfortunate men who would have been set at liberty uncondemned if they had pleaded even against the Scythians." That "even against the Scythians" speaks volumes! Cf. III Macc. 7:5. And Origen (*Against Celsus* I.1) speaks of "Scythian laws, or more impious even than these, if there be any such."

Nevertheless, even though a man be a Scythian, that as such cannot hinder him from becoming a new man in Christ. That is what Paul is here saying. Or, as Justin Martyr put it so strikingly, "But though a man be a Scythian or a Persian, if he has the knowledge of God and of *his* [God's] Christ, and keeps the everlasting righteous decrees, he is circumcised with the good and beneficial circumcision, and is a friend of God, and God rejoices in his gifts and offerings" (*Dialogue with Trypho,* ch. 28).

And finally, as to "slave, freeman," since "If therefore the Son will make y o u free, y o u will be free indeed" (John 8:36), any bondage that pertains to merely earthly social relationships can have no relevance for salvation. For more extensive discussion of Slavery see on Col. 3:23-4:1; also Commentary on Philemon in this volume, and *Scripture on Slavery,* pp. 233-237.

Paul concludes this paragraph with the words, **but Christ (is) all and in all.** *Christ, as the all-sufficient Lord and Savior, is all* that matters. His Spirit-mediated indwelling *in all* believers, of whatever racial-religious, cultural, or social background they be, guarantees the creation and gradual perfection in each and in all of "the new man, who is being renewed for full knowledge according to the image of him who created him." Thus, most appropriately, the very theme of the entire letter, namely, "Christ, the Pre-eminent One, the Only and All-Sufficient Savior," climaxes this passage.[129]

---

[129] The conjunction "and" in "Christ (is) all *and* in all" shows that "both parts of the phrase must be given recognition" (Moule, *op. cit.,* p. 122). Hence, I Cor.

12 Put on, therefore, as God's elect, holy and beloved, a heart of compassion, kindness, lowliness, meekness, longsuffering, 13 enduring one another, and forgiving each other if anyone have a complaint against anyone. Just as the Lord has forgiven y o u, so do y o u also. 14 And above all these things (put on) love, which is the bond of perfection. 15 And let the peace of Christ, for which y o u were called in one body, rule in y o u r hearts, and be thankful. 16 Let the word of Christ dwell among y o u richly; in all wisdom teaching and admonishing one another, (and) by means of psalms, hymns, and spiritual songs singing to God in a thankful spirit, with all y o u r heart. 17 And whatever y o u do in word or in deed, (do) all in the name of the Lord Jesus, giving thanks to God the Father through him.

3:12-17

III. *They Should "Put On" the New Virtues*

As the calmness of the inland lake, reflecting the beauty of the rising sun, follows the turbulence of warring winds and tempestuous billows, so, in principle, "the peace of Christ" (verse 15) had displaced the restlessness which formerly characterized the Colossians, when they lived apart from Christ, as described in the previous paragraph (see especially verses 5-9). For beauty of style and direct appeal to the heart the present section is unsurpassed. The same can be said about its practical value. If the Colossians will only live the life that is portrayed in such a graphic and yet simple manner in these few lines, their problems will be solved. Of course, only by strength imparted by God and by means of complete reliance on the sustaining power of his sovereign, transforming grace, will they be able to heed the directions given. These directions are introduced as follows:

12, 13. Put on, therefore, as God's elect, holy and beloved. "Put on" is repeated from verse 10. And the word "therefore" means (amplified), "Since y o u have in principle taken Christ into y o u r hearts, *therefore* actually *be* in practice — yes, *be fully* — what y o u have professed to be, and what I, Paul, actually believe y o u have begun to be." Be this "as God's elect." For a twelve-point summary of the doctrine of election in the epistles of Paul see N.T.C. on I and II Thess., pp. 48-50. Note especially the following statements, taken from points 7, 10, and 12: "Election affects life in all its phases, is not abstract. Although it belongs to God's decree from eternity, it becomes a dynamic force in the hearts and lives of God's children. It produces fruits. It is an election not only unto salvation but definitely also (as a link in the chain) unto service. It has as its final aim God's glory, and is the work of his delight" (Eph. 1:4-6).

15:28 and Eph. 1:23 ("all in all" in both cases, omitting "and") are not really parallel.

In apposition with the expression "God's elect" are the ascriptions "holy and beloved." As God's chosen ones, these people, both individually and collectively as far as they are true believers, are *holy*, that is, "set apart" for the Lord and for his work. They have been cleansed by the blood of Christ from the guilt of their sins, and are being delivered, more and more, from sin's pollution, and renewed according to the image of God (see on verse 10 above). They are, moreover, "beloved," and this *especially* by God (I Thess. 1:4; cf. II Thess. 4:13).

Thus, the qualifying designations of honor that were formerly applied to the ancient covenant people of Israel (see I Peter 2:9; then Isa. 5:1; Hos. 2:23; cf. Rom. 9:25) are here used in connection with the members of the church of the new dispensation. The church is the new Israel. Paul continues. (Put on) **a heart of compassion, kindness, lowliness, meekness, long-suffering.** It is immediately evident that these qualities overlap. A person with "a compassionate heart" will also be "kind." One who is lowly or humble

in disposition will also be "meek," etc. Hence, not

but   and so for the others. The expression *heart of compassion* [130] indicates a very deep feeling, "a yearning with the deeply-felt affection of Christ Jesus" (Phil. 1:8). As to the depth of this feeling one thinks of the reaction of Joseph upon seeing Benjamin (Gen. 43:30), or in revealing himself to his brothers (Gen. 45:1-4). Another example would be the tender relationship between David and Jonathan (I Sam. 18:1; 20:4, 17).

The next quality is *kindness*. This is Spirit-imparted *goodness* of heart, the very opposite of the *malice* or *badness* mentioned in verse 8. The early Christians by means of kindness commended themselves to others (II Cor. 6:6). God, too, is kind (Rom. 2:4; cf. 11:22), and we are admonished to become like him in this respect (Luke 6:35). Examples of human kindness would be the same persons already mentioned in connection with "heart of compassion." To avoid repetition, let us add the Good Samaritan of the well-known parable (Luke 10:25-37), Barnabas (Acts 4:36, 37; 15:37), and the apostle Paul himself (I Thess. 2:7-12).

Lowliness or *humility* — a virtue despised by the heathen (as noted earlier) — is also mentioned as a quality which believers should more and more strive to acquire. The person who is kind to others generally does not

---

[130] For a discussion of the word used in the original see N.T.C. on Philippians, p. 58, footnote 39.

have too high an estimate of himself. A happy condition arises when in a church each member counts the other to be better than himself (Phil. 2:3). Of course, there is also such a thing as "feigned humility" (see on 2:18, 23). Good examples of true humility would be the centurion who said, "I am not worthy that thou shouldest come under my roof" (Luke 7:6), and the publican who, in a striking parable, pours out his heart by sighing, "God, be merciful to me, the sinner" (Luke 18:13). According to the entire context, however, it is modest self-appraisal in relation to *the neighbors,* especially to *fellow-believers,* that Paul has in mind. Of course, these two — humility toward God and the same disposition toward men — far from being mutually exclusive, belong together.

Meekness, mentioned next, is definitely not weakness or spinelessness, the characteristic of the person who is ready to bow before every breeze. It is submissiveness under provocation, the willingness rather to *suffer* injury than to *inflict* it. A striking example is Moses (Num. 12:3).

For *longsuffering* see on 1:11. What a longsuffering hero was Jeremiah during his lengthy period of prophetic activity. Think also of Hosea who, instead of rejecting his unfaithful wife, slips away to the haunt of shame, redeems Gomer with fifteen pieces of silver and a homer and a half of barley, and mercifully restores her to her position of honor! [131]

Continued: **enduring one another.** The Colossians are urged to bear with one another in love (cf. Eph. 4:2). Paul was able to say, "Being persecuted we endure" (Cor. 4:12). The example of Job comes to mind (James 5:11). Paul adds, **and forgiving** [132] **each other if anyone have a complaint against anyone. Just as the Lord** [133] **has forgiven y o u, so do y o u also.** For the divine forgiveness see on 2:13. Christ, while on earth, had taught his disciples to pray, "Forgive us our debts, as we also have forgiven our debtors" (Matt. 6:12). It is possible that the expression "Just as the Lord has forgiven y o u, so do y o u also" is a conscious echo of the just quoted petition of the Lord's Prayer, showing that Paul knew that prayer. Anyway, it is identical in spirit and meaning. Jesus had also instructed Peter to forgive "not up to seven times but up to seventy times seven times" (Matt. 18:22), and had added a touching parable ending with the words, "So also my heavenly Father will do to y o u, if each of y o u does not forgive his

---

[131] Of course, this is true only if "the wife of whoredom," namely, Gomer (Hos. 1:2, 3), is to be identified with the "adulteress" mentioned in Hos. 3:1-3.
[132] Here again a form of the verb χαρίζομαι is used, as in 2:13. It stresses the full and gracious character of forgiveness. The noun ἄφεσις, used in Col. 1:14 and Eph. 1:7, (cf. the verb ἀφίημι, *let go, send away*) places greater stress on the thought that the sin is completely *dismissed* (cf. Ps. 103:12).
[133] Textual variants here are "God," "God in Christ" (very likely after Eph. 4:32), and "Christ." The textual support for the reading "the Lord" is, however, clearly the strongest. On the basis of Col. 1:13, 14 and 2:13 (see the explanation of these passages) the reference is to God rather than to Christ, though the difference is minor. When God forgives he does so "in Christ" (Eph. 4:32; cf. Matt. 18:35).

brother from the heart" (Matt. 18:35; cf. Mark 11:25). Moreover, the Lord had underscored these precepts with his own example. While being crucified he had implored, "Father, forgive them, for they know not what they do" (Luke 23:34). When Stephen, while he was being stoned to death, prayed "Lord, lay not this sin to their charge," he was following the example of Christ.

This would seem to be the proper place to point out that Paul here links his admonitions to Christ's person and work, as has been indicated also in connection with Col. 1:28. See the three columns there. The qualities which, according to Paul's teaching here, mark the new man are also ascribed to *Christ*. For his "heart of compassion" and his kindness see Matt. 9:36; 14:14; 15:32; 20:34. His lowliness and meekness are exemplified in Matt. 11:29; 21:5; John 13:1-15; Phil. 2:8; his longsuffering and endurance or forbearance, in Matt. 17:17; John 14:9; I Peter 2:23; and his forgiving spirit, in Matt. 9:2; Luke 7:47; 23:34. Accordingly, when a believer manifests these virtues in his association with his fellow-men he has "put on" Christ (Rom. 13:14). And it is comforting to know that he who has seen Christ has seen the Father (John 14:9; cf. 1:18), and that he who is an imitator of Christ (I Cor. 11:1; I Thess. 1:6) is also an imitator of God (Eph. 5:1).

14. This holds also with respect to *love,* as Eph. 5:2 clearly indicates. The apostle continues, **And above all these things (put on) love, which is the bond of perfection.** This supremacy of love — note "above all these things" — is clear also from I Cor. 13:13. Love heads the list of "the fruits of the Spirit" (Gal. 5:22). In Paul's prayer for the Philippians the petition mentioned first of all is "that y o u r love may abound more and more" (Phil. 1:9). Love dominates the writings of John, where it is mentioned scores of times. With Peter, too, love is supreme (I Peter 4:8). How highly the anonymous author of Hebrews regards it is evident from Heb. 10:24; 13:1. Love is the lubricant that enables the other virtues to function smoothly (Gal. 5:6, 13). It is *intelligent and purposeful self-giving* that Paul has in mind, the fulfilment of both the law and the gospel. In the present context it is especially *mutual* love, love for one another within the Christian community, that is thought of, though it is true that such love overflows its boundaries (I Thess. 3:12). That is of the very essence of love: to overflow. It was this love for one another, as brothers and sisters in the Lord, of which Jesus spoke when he issued his "new commandment" (John 13:34; I Thess. 4:9). See also on Col. 1:8.

Now this love is called "the bond of perfection." This has been interpreted to mean that love is "the grace that binds all these other graces together" (Bruce, *op. cit.,* p. 281). Though this may be correct, and a sensible connotation is thereby ascribed to the expression, it is probably better to interpret it in the light of what Paul himself says in this very epistle, namely, "they themselves being welded together in love" (2:2). *Love, then is "the bond of perfection" in the sense that it is that which unites believers, causing them to move forward toward the goal of perfection.* This interpretation is also in line with the apostle's purpose in writing this letter. It is as if he were saying, "Not *knowledge* or *philosophy* — the kind of knowledge and philosophy of which false teachers boast — or *obedience to human regulations,* but *love* for one another, the spontaneous response to God's love for y o u, is that which will strengthen and unite y o u, and will lead y o u toward the attainment of y o u r spiritual ideal." For the meaning of this ideal see also on 1:28.

15. Paul continues, **And let the peace of Christ, for which y o u were called in one body, rule in y o u r hearts.** This peace is the condition of rest and contentment in the hearts of those who know that their Redeemer lives. It is the conviction that the sins of the past have been forgiven, that the present is being overruled for good, and that the future cannot bring about separation between Christ and his own. Concerning this peace the apostle says in Phil. 4:7, "And the peace of God that surpasses all understanding will keep guard over y o u r hearts and y o u r thoughts in Christ Jesus." It is the peace *of Christ* because it was merited for believers by Christ, is through his Spirit bestowed upon them, and is fostered by this same Lord and Savior (John 14:27; 16:33; 20:19, 21, 26). It is, moreover, patterned after the peace that dwells in the Savior's own heart.

Now this peace also has its social aspect, on which the emphasis falls in the present passage (cf. Eph. 4:3, 4), as is evident from the phrase "for which y o u were called in one body." When men were called out of the darkness into the light they, as seen by God, were not drawn out of their sinful environment as pebbles are picked up from the beach. On the contrary, they were called as a body, for from eternity they had been viewed as a corporate entity "in Christ." In time they were "called" in order that they might promote this spiritual oneness in every way. Now this purpose can be accomplished only when the peace of Christ *rules*[134] in each heart. Let each individual, therefore, constantly ask himself, "Will I have peace within if I do this or do that?" Let him be sure to be at peace with God, for only then can he expect to live in true harmony with his brothers (cf. James 4:1).

Paul adds, **and be thankful.** It is worthy of note how frequently in this brief epistle the apostle refers to the privilege and duty of being thankful (1:3, 12; 2:7; 3:15, 16, 17; 4:2). Gratitude makes for peace and excellent public relations. When a person is overpowered by the feeling of warm and

---

[134] Basically the meaning of βραβευέτω is *let it be umpire.* Since the umpire's decision is very important, it is easy to see how the meaning *let it rule* arose. See also on 2:18, footnote 97.

deep appreciation for benefits received from God he will hardly be able to grudge someone else his wealth or superior talents. Hence, this admonition fits splendidly into the immediate context. Gratitude promotes peace. The exhortation also suits the broader context which mentions some of the blessings believers have received. They are "hid with Christ in God," have received the forgiveness of sins, and are experiencing daily spiritual renewal. Moreover, the apostle is about to mention the further blessings of the indwelling word and of psalms, hymns, and spiritual songs. For all these favors thanksgiving is in order. Though all men *should* give thanks, the Christian *can be expected* to do so. Ingratitude marks paganism (Rom. 1:21). In all probability it also marked the fearfilled alarmists who were vexing the addressees (Col. 2:16-23). Having therefore been rescued from paganism let the Colossians also turn their backs upon these so-called "philosophers." Let them in newness of spirit be joyful and praise the Lord every day. Thus they will be truly and serenely blessed, and in turn will be a blessing to others.

16. Paul has just been saying, "Let the peace of Christ rule in y o u r hearts." At first glance a believer might well ask, however, "If I do this am I not building the edifice of my hope and trust upon a rather insecure, subjective foundation?" After further thought, however, he answers, "Not at all, for I have peace when in my inmost being I, by God's sovereign grace, resolve to live in accordance with the objective word of Christ." Verses 15 and 16 must therefore not be separated. By obedience to the gospel peace is conveyed to the heart. So Paul continues, **Let the word of Christ dwell among** [135] **y o u richly.** The objective, special revelation that proceeds from (and concerns) Christ — "the Christ-word" — should govern every thought, word, and deed, yes even the hidden drives and motivations of every member, and thus should bear sway *among them* all, and this *richly,* "bearing much fruit" (John 15:5). This will happen if believers heed the word (Matt. 13:9), handle it rightly (II Tim. 2:15), hide it in their hearts (Ps. 119:11), and hold it forth to others as being in truth "the word of life" (Phil. 2:16). Though when the apostle wrote this, "the word of Christ" had not yet been entrusted to the written page in the form and to the extent in which we now have it, this does not cancel the fact that for Paul and for all believers in his day as well as, in broader scope, for us today, "All scripture (is) God-breathed and useful for teaching, for reproof, for correction, for training in righteousness, that the man of God may be equipped, for every good work thoroughly equipped" (see N.T.C. on II Tim. 3:16, 17). The logical con-

---

[135] Or "in" with most of the English translations. The immediately succeeding context would seem somewhat to favor the rendering "among," however. Thus also N.E.B., Bruce, Ridderbos. Lightfoot favors "in." The difference is not very important, for only when the word dwells *within* the hearts will it dwell *among* the people.

tinuation is: **in all wisdom** [136] **teaching and admonishing one another.**[137]

For the explanation of these words see on 1:28, where essentially the same thought is expressed in an almost identical statement. The differences are as follows: (1) in 1:28 the apostle relates what he, Timothy, etc., are doing; here (in Col. 3:16) he admonishes the Colossian believers what they should be doing. In both cases the content is the same: admonishing and teaching. Believers, by virtue of their "office" as believers — let them not forget that they are clothed with that *office!* — should do what Paul and his associates are doing by virtue of *their* office, respectively as apostle and apostolic delegates. Each person must do it in accordance with the rights and duties of his particular office. (2) In 1:28 the object is somewhat broader, "every man." Here (Col. 3:16) the emphasis is rather on *mutual* teaching and admonition. And (3) in 1:28 the phrase "in all wisdom" is placed last. In the Colossian passage it is placed first, perhaps to underscore the thought conveyed in the immediately preceding adverb "richly," as if to say, "If the word of Christ is to dwell among y o u *richly,* then *in all wisdom* y o u should admonish and teach each other."

There is something else that should also be done if the word of Christ is to dwell among the Colossians richly. It is stated in these words: **(and) by means of psalms, hymns, and spiritual songs** [138] **singing to God in a thankful spirit,**[139] **with all y o u r heart.**

---

[136] For me the fact that in Col. 1:28, in an almost identical clause, the phrase "in all wisdom" modifies "teaching and admonishing" shows that it should be so construed here also, and not (with Lightfoot) attached to the preceding clause.

[137] Not "themselves." The pronoun ἑαυτούς is not only *reflexive* but can also be *reciprocal.* See L.N.T. (A. and G.), p. 211. In Col. 1:28 the thought is similar: admonishing *every man* and teaching *every man,* not "teaching themselves." Cf. Eph. 5:19. So also in the Colossian context, 3:13 can hardly be rendered "forgiving themselves." This is my answer to Lenski's contrary assertion (*op. cit.*, p. 177), though in 3:13 he, too, renders the pronoun: "each other."

[138] As to the construction there are two main possibilities: (1) Construe "by means of psalms, hymns, and spiritual songs" with the words that precede. Paul would then be saying, "teaching and admonishing one another by means of psalms, hymns, and spiritual songs." This is favored by A.V., A.R.V. (both the old and the new), Moffatt's New Testament Translation, Berkeley Version, and by the commentators Bruce, Lenski, Lightfoot, etc. (2) Link the phrase with the words that follow (see my translation). With minor variations in translation this alternative, which is in agreement with N.N.'s punctuation, is accepted by R.S.V., Amplified New Testament, Dutch Bible (Nieuwe Vertaling), Beare (in *The Interpreter's Bible*), Ridderbos, etc. I agree with the last-mentioned author when in opposing theory (1) he states, "The idea that this mutual teaching and admonishing must be carried out by means of song seems rather unnatural to us" (*op. cit.*, p. 222). I might add that Eph. 5:19, to which the supporters of theory (1) appeal, is, in my estimation, hardly sufficient proof. It is one thing to speak to one another in song. It is something else again to say that *teaching and admonishing* must be done by means of song.

[139] Whether ἐν τῇ χάριτι or ἐν χάριτι is the best reading is not certain. Each has strong textual support. On the basis of I Cor. 10:30, and in line with the immediate context (see verses 15 and 17) the most probable meaning here would seem to be

Paul clearly recognizes the edifying nature of God-glorifying singing. As to the meaning of the terms *psalms, hymns,* and *spiritual songs* (see also Eph. 5:19) a little investigation quickly shows that it may not be easy to distinguish *sharply* between these three. It is possible that there is here some overlapping of meanings. Thus, in connection with *psalms* it is natural to think of the Old Testament Psalter, and, in support of this view, to appeal to Luke 20:42; 24:44; Acts 1:20; 13:33. So far there is no difficulty. However, expositors are by no means agreed that this can also be the meaning of the word *psalm* in I Cor. 14:26 ("When y o u assemble, each one has a psalm").

As to *hymns,* in the New Testament the word *hymn* is found only in our present passage (Col. 3:16) and in Eph. 5:19. Augustine, in more than one place, states that a hymn has three essentials: it must be sung; it must be praise; it must be to God. According to this definition it would be possible for an Old Testament psalm, sung in praise to God, to be also a hymn. Thus when Jesus and his disciples were about to leave the Upper Room in order to go to the Mount of Olives, they "hymned" (Matt. 26:30; Mark 14:26). It is held by many that what they hymned was Psalm 115-118. According to Acts 16:25 in the Philippian prison Paul and Silas were *hymning* to God. Is it not altogether probable that some, if not all, of these *hymns* were *psalms?* Cf. also Heb. 2:12. But if Augustine's definition is correct there are also hymns that do not belong to the Old Testament Psalter; such hymns as the *Magnificat* (Luke 1:46-55) and the *Benedictus* (Luke 1:68-79). Fragments of other New Testament hymns seem to be embedded in the letters of Paul (Eph. 5:14; Col. 1:15-20; I Tim. 3:16, and perhaps others).

The word *song* or *ode* (in the sense of poem intended to be sung) occurs not only in Eph. 5:19 and Col. 3:16 but also in Rev. 5:9; 14:3, where "the new song" is indicated, and in Rev. 15:3, where the reference is to "the song of Moses, the servant of God, and the song of the Lamb." These are not Old Testament Psalms. Moreover, a song or ode is not necessarily a *sacred* song. In the present case the fact that it is, indeed, sacred is shown by the addition of the adjective *spiritual.*

All in all, then, it would seem that when here in Col. 3:16 the apostle uses these three terms, apparently distinguishing them at least to some extent, the term *psalms* has reference, at least mainly, to the Old Testament Psalter; *hymns* mainly to New Testament songs of praise to God or to Christ; and *spiritual songs* mainly to any other sacred songs dwelling on themes other than direct praise to God or to Christ.[140]

The point that must not be ignored is this, that these songs must be sung in a thankful spirit. The songs must be poured forth sincerely, rising from

---

thankfully or *in a thankful spirit,* rather than a. "with grace in y o u r hearts," or b. "charmingly."

[140] See also Trench, *op. cit.,* par. LXXVIII.

within the humbly grateful hearts of believers. It has been said that next to Scripture itself a good Psalter-Hymnal is the richest fountain of edification. Not only are its songs a source of daily nourishment for the church, but they also serve as a very effective vehicle for the outpouring of confession of sin, gratitude, spiritual joy, rapture. Whether sung in the regular worship-service on the Lord's Day, at a midweek meeting, in social gatherings, in connection with family-worship, at a festive occasion, or privately, they are a tonic for the soul and promote the glory of God. They do this because they fix the interest upon the indwelling word of Christ, and carry the attention away from that worldly cacophony by which people with low moral standards are being emotionally overstimulated.

The passage under discussion has often been used in support of this or that theory with respect to what may or may not be sung in the official worship-service. Perhaps it is correct to say that the appeal is justified if one is satisfied with a few broad, general principles; for example, (1) In our services the psalms should not be neglected. (2) As to *hymns*, in the stricter sense of songs of praise, "It is probably true that a larger proportion of the religious poems which are used in public praise should be 'hymns' in the stricter sense. They should be addressed to God. Too many are subjective, not to say sentimental, and express only personal experiences and aspirations which are sometimes lacking in reality" Charles E. Erdman (*op. cit.,* p. 91).

For the rest, it is well to bear in mind that Paul's purpose is not to lay down detailed rules and regulations pertaining to ecclesiastical liturgy. He is interested in showing the Colossians and all those to whom or by whom the letter would be read how they may grow in grace, and may manifest rightly the power of the indwelling word. His admonition, therefore, can be applied to every type of Christian gathering, whether on the Sabbath or during the week, whether in church or at home or anywhere else.[141]

17. A fundamental principle for Christian life and conduct summarizes and climaxes this priceless paragraph, namely, **And whatever y o u do in word or in deed, (do) all** [142] **in the name of the Lord Jesus, giving thanks to God the Father through him.**

For the expression "Whatever y o u do" see also verse 23 and I Cor. 10:31. In connection with "Do all in the name of the Lord Jesus" it should be

---

[141] That Paul's teaching with respect to this subject was given this wide application in the early church is clear from such references as the following: Clement of Alexandria, *The Instructor* II.4; Tertullian, *Apology*, ch. 39; *To His Wife* II.8.

[142] With respect to the wording of the original two points are in order: πᾶν should in all probability be viewed as a nominative absolute, replaced later by the accusative πάντα considered as the object of an implied verb. The implied verb is ποιεῖτε, viewed as a present imperative.

noted that *the name* indicates the Lord Jesus himself as he has revealed himself.[143] "In the name" means, accordingly, "in vital relation with him," that is, in harmony with his revealed will, in subjection to his authority, in dependence on his power. The clause "giving thanks to God the Father through him" (in connection with which see especially Eph. 5:20; then also John 14:6; 15:5b; Rom. 1:8; 7:25; 16:27; I Cor. 1:20) is explained by the fact that it is on the basis of the Son's atonement that sinners are accepted by the Father, and that they ("together with him") receive every blessing. Hence, it is altogether just and fair that *through him* thanksgiving be given to the Father.

The main lessons of this closing paragraph should not escape us. As I see it they are the following:

(1) "Whatever y o u do" is very general. In contrast with the many specific rules and regulations which false teachers were trying to impose upon the Colossians (Col. 2:16-23), Paul simply enunciates a comprehensive principle, and permits believers to work it out for themselves in perfect freedom. After all, the child of God of the new dispensation is not under bondage. Let the Spirit within him rule him.

(2) This Spirit (hence also the Spirit-indwelt believer) operates in connection with the word, that is, the revelation ("name") of the Lord Jesus. Man is "free" only when he abides in Christ. Let him therefore always ask himself, "What shall I do, Lord?" (Acts 22:10). Let him diligently and prayerfully study Scripture. It is in that sense that (1) above is to be understood.

(3) In connection with any and every word and deed the believer should ask himself, "Am I able to thank God the Father for having given me the opportunity to say or do this?" (Cf. Bruce, *op. cit.*, p. 286).

(4) The sovereignty or pre-eminence of the Lord Jesus in relation to the entire universe with all its events and in relation to the believer himself should be joyfully acknowledged. Therefore, too, he should do everything "in the name of the Lord Jesus."

We notice, therefore, that the present paragraph closes as did also the preceding one (see on 3:11), with a reminder of the theme of the entire epistle, Christ, the Pre-eminent One, the Only and All-Sufficient Savior.

Summary of Colossians 3:1-17

By accepting the counsel which Paul here offers, the Colossians will not only win victory upon victory in their battle with "the flesh" (see 2:23; 3:5-9), but will live a life of usefulness for the edification of the church and the benefit of their fellowmen, to the glory of God. Let them, accordingly, be consistent. Having been "raised with Christ" let them seek the things that

---

[143] For proof see N.T.C. on Philippians, p. 117, footnote 98.

are above, not those that are upon the earth, for their *life* (and this section of Colossians concerns the believers' *life*) "is hid with Christ in God." It was heaven that gave them birth, for they were born from above. Their names are inscribed in heaven's register. Their rights are secured in heaven. Their interests are being promoted there. Hence, since they belong to heaven, let their lives be governed according to heavenly standards, and to heaven let their thoughts and prayers ascend, and their hopes aspire. Let them seek to obtain for themselves those heavenly gifts mentioned in verses 12-17. And since Christ "in them" is "the hope of glory" (1:27), it must be true that when Christ (who is) *"our life"* is manifested, then they too "will be manifested with him in glory."

A radical break with former vices is therefore in order. These must in fact be "put to death." Once and for all they must be "laid aside." Since at their baptism the Colossians had publicly repudiated the old man with his evil deeds and had put on the new man, let them therefore now continue to do *in practice* what they had already done *in principle.* The Creator of the new man will enable them to do this. And this applies to *all* true believers. Here every class-distinction disappears completely, for Christ is "all and in all."

In order to bid defiance to the forces of evil let them, however, not concentrate on evil. Let vice be conquered by virtue. Let evil be overcome with good. Let them therefore, having accepted Christ as their Lord and Savior, become imitators of him, so that all his marvelous virtues — a heart of compassion, kindness, lowliness, *above all love* — may also be seen in *them.* Thus, they will be welded into a strong, spiritual unity. Let, therefore, Christ's peace rule in their hearts. Let his word dwell among them, so that in all wisdom they will teach and admonish each other. Let them be so filled with joy and gratitude as to pour forth their very hearts in jubilation, singing not only the psalms of "the sweet singer of Israel" but also hymns of praise and other spiritual songs.

Paul concludes this paragraph by laying down not a set of detailed rules and regulations but a basic principle (which is far better), "And whatever y o u do in word or in deed, (do) all in the name of the Lord Jesus, giving thanks to God the Father through him." Thus once more, as often in this letter, Paul is directing the minds and hearts of the addressees to the only and all-sufficient Savior Jesus Christ, and via that sovereign Mediator, to God the Father.

Outline of Chapter 3:18–4:1

Theme: *Christ, the Pre-eminent One, the Only and All-Sufficient Savior*

II. This Only and All-Sufficient Savior Is the Source of the Believers' Life, and Thus the Real Answer to the Perils by Which They Are Confronted, chapters 3 and 4

B. This Truth Applied to Special Groups, 3:18–4:1

3:18, 19   1. Wives and their husbands

3:20, 21   2. Children and their fathers

3:22–4:1   3. Slaves and their masters

18 Wives, be submissive to y o u r husbands, as is fitting in the Lord.
19 Husbands, love y o u r wives, and do not be harsh toward them.

3:18, 19

I. *Wives and Their Husbands*

A new paragraph begins here. The sublime yet very practical truth that
Christ is the only and all-sufficient Savior and as such the source of the believers' life is now going to be applied to special groups. Paul is thinking of
household groups. What we have here, therefore, is a kind of "table of
household duties," sometimes simply called "house-table." Now it is true
that even in the writings of non-Christian moralists we find codes of domestic behavior.[144] But the notion that the apostle is simply copying their tables,
and coating them with a thin varnish of Christianity — merely (!) adding
"in Christ" — misses the point entirely. Between these pithy directives as
presented here in Colossians — also in Eph. 5:22–6:9; I Tim. 2:8-15; 6:1, 2;
Titus 2:1-10; I Peter 2:12–3:7 — and the maxims of the Stoics and other
moral philosophers, there is, indeed, at times a superficial resemblance, but
there are at least three main differences:

(1) Christianity, as proclaimed by Paul, etc., supplied the *power* to carry
out the commands, that power being the grace of God, mentioned in that
very connection at the close of the list in Titus (Titus 2:1-10, then verse 11;
cf. Phil. 4:13). All other moral philosophies, the very best of them, are trains
lacking engines!

(2) Christianity also presented a new *purpose*. That purpose was *not*
simply "to try to live in agreement with Nature," but "to do everything to
the glory of God" (I Cor. 10:31), that is, "in the name of the Lord Jesus,
giving thanks to God the Father through him," as stated in the Colossian
context (3:17). The only proper way to explain Col. 3:18–4:1 is in the light
of Col. 3:17. And finally,

(3) Christianity, as originating in Christ, supplied the only true *pattern*
for God-glorifying conduct on the part of the very groups here discussed,
namely, wives and their husbands, children and their fathers, servants and
their masters. Christ himself, as the bridegroom, in his matchless love for

---

[144] See Seneca, *Epistles* XV.2; Th.W.N.T., pp. 949-959; 974-978; and Stobaeus, *An-
thologies* IV.

the church, his bride, furnished the standard for the love of *Christian marriage* (Eph. 5:25, 32) .

In his obedience to his parents (Luke 2:51) , in the wonderful manner in which he, in the midst of the tortures of hell, provided for his earthly mother (John 19:25-27) , and in fact in his entire life of obedience to his heavenly Father, culminating in a death in which that obedience was climaxed (Phil. 2:8) , he gave to all an example of patient submission. That example was certainly intended also for *the children*. (He also had a lesson for *the fathers,* Luke 15:20-24.)

Last of all, in his willingness to stoop very low, which he proved by washing the feet of his disciples and by his death on the cross, he gave an object-lesson intended for all, certainly also for *masters and slaves,* as plainly indicated in John 13:13-17.

18. The first admonition is, **Wives, be submissive to y o u r husbands, as is fitting in the Lord.** Suffragists have said that it is positively wicked to use the word "obey" in the marriage contract. They have loudly affirmed that the marriage service in its present "Form" compels the bride to take a vow which she has no intention of keeping. A Prayer Book has eliminated the word "obey" from its Marriage Form. All this, however, does not "eliminate" Col. 3:18! Moreover, a little searching will quickly show that what the passage teaches is the consistent doctrine of Scripture anent this point. See the following passages: Gen. 3:16; Rom. 7:2; I Cor. 14:34, 35; Eph. 5:22-24, 33; I Tim. 2:11-15; Titus 2:5; I Peter 3:1-6. And the reason given here in Col. 3:18 is that such obedience is (and always has been) "fitting in the Lord," being in harmony with his will as revealed in Scripture. A Christian wife will therefore gladly strive to regulate her conduct in harmony with this command. She will not begin to think that her equality in spiritual standing before God and the great liberty which has now become her portion as a believer (Gal. 3:28) entitles her to forget about the fact that in his sovereign wisdom God made the human pair in such a manner that it is natural for the husband to lead, for the wife to follow; for him to be aggressive (in the most favorable sense) , for her to be receptive; for him to invent, for her to use the tools which he invents. The tendency *to follow* was embedded in Eve's very soul as she came forth from the hand of her Creator. Hence any attempt to reverse this order is displeasing to God. Why should a woman be encouraged to do things that are contrary to her nature? Her very body, far from preceding that of Adam in the order of creation, was taken out of Adam's body. Her very name — Ish-sha — was derived from his name — Ish (Gen. 2:23) . It is when the wife recognizes this basic distinction and acts accordingly that she can be a blessing to her husband, can exert a gracious, very powerful, and beneficent influence upon him, and can promote not only his but also her own happiness.

In connection with this command that wives be submissive to their husbands the following should also be noted:

(1) *It does not imply the wives' inferiority to their husbands.* In non-Christian circles wives (in fact, women in general) were regarded as being inferior beings. Among the Greeks, in spite of their high degree of culture, wives, as a rule, were not considered to be the equals or even the companions of their husbands. The Romans, too, regarded women as being intrinsically inferior. Philo, a Jewish philosopher who was greatly influenced by Greek philosophy, regarded *women* as being selfish, jealous, and hypocritical, and *married men* as being no longer free men but slaves.

The status of women in the Qumran community, which has given us the Dead Sea Scrolls, was not enviable. There seem to have been both celibate and non-celibate groups in the Qumran sect (see Miller Burrows, *More Light on the Dead Sea Scrolls*, pp. 358, 383). "One of the most conspicuous differences between the church and the Qumran sect . . . was the entirely different status of women in the two communities" (same author, *The Dead Sea Scrolls*, p. 333; cf. pp. 233, 244, 291; also H. Mulder, *De vondsten bij de Dode Zee*, p. 35).

Christianity changed all this (Gal. 3:28), and is still changing it among those who are being led to accept it.[145] Jesus made some of his most startling revelations to women (John 4:13, 14, 21-26; 11:25, 26; 20:11-18). For the dignity of women in Paul's epistles see N.T.C. on I and II Timothy and Titus, pp. 113, 114.

(2) *It is not absolute.* If a husband should ever ask his wife to do something which in her conscience (illumined by Scripture) she knows to be wrong, she has the right and the duty to disobey her husband (Acts 5:29).

(3) *It is issued in a context of love,* of which wives must be the objects, for Paul continues:

19. Husbands, love [146] y o u r wives, and do not be harsh toward them. The best commentary is Paul's own, in Eph. 5:25-33. A discussion of the

---

[145] For the status of woman for many centuries under Islam see S. M. Zwemer, *Across the World of Islam,* chapters V and VI, especially p. 135. For her status outside Christendom in general see J. S. Dennis, *Christian Missions and Social Progress* (3 volumes), especially Vol. I, pp. 104-125. Credit for more recent progress in her status must be given, at least in part, to the influence of Christianity.

[146] The verb used is a form of ἀγαπάω. Paul uses φιλέω only twice (I Cor. 16:22; Titus 3:15). The verb ἀγαπάω is pushing out the verb φιλέω, taking over its functions and (at least in the present case) retaining its own as well. Full, Christian love is what is here meant, a love which sublimates all other. On the relation between the two verbs see N.T.C. on the Gospel according to John, Vol. II, pp. 494-501, footnote 306.

contents of that magnificent passage does not belong here but in a Commentary on Ephesians. The love of a husband for his wife is *sexual,* to be sure, but also rises above the sexual. It is *natural affection,* but it is also far more than that. It is the love for one's wife as "a sister in the Lord." This love acts as a moderating influence upon the husband's exercise of authority. It is true that the primary responsibility for the final decision with respect to a matter rests with the husband, but the method of reaching that decision leaves ample room for mutual deliberation and gentle persuasion, in the course of which, perhaps, at times the *husband's* tentative conclusion may finally prevail, at other times the *wife's,* her partner having come to see that she was right. Thus, the husband, having fully committed himself to the principle that his love for his wife must be a true reflection of the deep, sacrificial love of Christ for the church (Eph. 5:25, 32), acts toward her as a man of understanding, is never "harsh" or "cross," but is considerate toward her,[147] and honors her in every way (I Peter 3:7). In such a marriage each seeks to please and benefit the other (Prov. 31:12; I Cor. 7:33, 34), and to promote the other's welfare, and this not only physically and culturally but also, and in fact mainly, spiritually. The husband views his wife as his equal in the sense that she is "a joint-heir of the grace of life" (I Peter 3:7). See also Gen. 24:67 (Isaac's love for Rebekah) and 29:20 (Jacob's love for Rachel).

---

20 Children, obey y o u r parents in all things, for this is well-pleasing in the Lord. 21 Fathers, do not exasperate y o u r children, in order that they may not lose heart.

3:20, 21

II. *Children and Their Fathers*

20. Children, obey y o u r parents in all things, for this is well-pleasing in the Lord.[148] This admonition is completely in line with such passages as Ex. 20:12; 21:15-17; Lev. 20:9; Deut. 5:16; 21:18; Prov. 1:8; 6:20; 30:17; Mal. 1:6; Matt. 15:4-6; 19:19; Mark 7:10-13; 10:19; 18:20; Eph. 6:1-3. Disobedience to parents is one of the vices of paganism (Rom. 1:30). It marks the ever-increasing wickedness of "the last days" (II Tim. 3:2). The soul-destructive falsehood that would abolish all parental authority — the very word "authority" being anathema in certain educational circles! —, so that children no longer need to pay any attention to their father's instruction or

---

[147] Lenski is right when he states, "This negative [do not be harsh toward them] is on the order of a litotes: ever be considerate toward them . . ." (*op. cit.,* p. 182).
[148] The reading *"to the Lord"* has slight support.

to their mother's teaching, is directly contrary to the clear teaching of Scripture, both Old and New Testament. Godly parents do not inflict upon their children the cruelty of telling them that they should do "just as they please." According to both Scripture and experience children are not only immature but also sinful by nature, wholly incapable *by nature* to choose the good (Ps. 51:5). And because of this the admonition in the form in which it is found here is very comprehensive: the children are exhorted to obey their parents "in all things," always subject to the limitation of Acts 5:29.

Such obedience is *well-pleasing*. This word is generally (though *not* expressly here in Col. 3:20) modified by "to God" or "to the Lord" (Rom. 12:1; 14:18; II Cor. 5:9; Eph. 5:10; Phil. 4:18; cf. Heb. 13:21). This modifier may certainly also be viewed as *implied* in our present passage. That God is pleased with this obedience is clear from the fact that he himself in the Decalogue pronounced a special blessing upon it (Ex. 20:12; Deut. 5:16), to which the apostle refers in the parallel Ephesian passage (Eph. 6:2, 3). For that matter, obedience to God's commandments is always well-pleasing to him! That it is carried out "in the Lord," that is, in fellowship with and dependence upon him, is understood by every child, whether older or younger, who from the heart is able to sing:

"When we walk with the Lord
In the light of his Word,
What a glory he sheds on our way!
While we do his good will
He abides with us still,
And with all who will trust and obey.
Trust and obey, for there's no other way
To be happy in Jesus,
But to trust and obey." (J. H. Sammis)

21. One of the most striking characteristics of these brief admonitions is their *reciprocal* character. In enjoining God-glorifying domestic relationships they do not stress the duty of wives at the expense of that of husbands, of children at the expense of that of fathers, or of slaves at the expense of that of masters. Outside of special revelation there is very little of this balance. Often the duty of the first member in each group is stressed, and little or nothing is said about the second. In ancient times when things went wrong *all* the blame was heaped on wives, children,[149] and slaves. But Paul, having admonished husbands as well as wives, and having just now reminded the children of their obligation to their parents, in all fairness proceeds to

---

[149] *Today* in civilized (?) countries, on *parents!* Or on *society, the environment.* Do these deserve *all* the blame?

issue a directive to the fathers also: **Fathers,**[150] **do not exasperate** [151] **y o u r children, in order that they may not lose heart.**

Fathers should create an atmosphere which will make obedience an easy and natural matter, namely, the atmosphere of love and confidence. They should bring up their children in the discipline and instruction of the Lord (Eph. 6:4) .[152] When fathers are unjust or overly severe, a spirit of sullen resignation is created in the hearts of their offspring. The children "lose heart," thinking, "No matter what I do, it's always wrong." There should be no nagging, no *constant* "Don't do this" and "Don't do that." Though the negative admonition ("Don't") cannot and must not be avoided and is at times definitely in place (note the repeated "Thou shalt not" of the Decalogue, in the teaching of Jesus, and in Paul's epistles, including this very passage!) , the *emphasis* must be on the positive (Rom. 12:21) . A good father spends time with his children, teaches, entertains, and encourages them, and by his example as well as by outright, verbal instruction, points them to Christ. Though the rod of correction may at times be necessary, it must be used with discretion, since wise reproof is generally better than a hundred stripes (Prov. 13:24; 23:13, 14; then 17:10) . Paul's admonition not to embitter the children — hence, to be kind to them — is quite different from the advice given to fathers by Ben Sira: "He who loves his son will whip him often. . . . Bow down his neck in his youth, and beat his sides while he is young" (Ecclus. 30:1, 12) . How friendly and fatherly!

---

22 Slaves, obey in all things those who according to the flesh are y o u r masters, not with eye-service as men-pleasers but with singleness of heart, fearing the Lord. 23 Whatever y o u do, put y o u r soul into the work, as for the Lord and not for men, 24 knowing that from the Lord y o u will receive the recompense, namely, the inheritance. (It is) the Lord Christ (whom) y o u are serving. 25 For, the wrong-doer will receive (the consequences of) what he has wrongly done. And there is no partiality.

1 Masters, render to y o u r slaves that which is fair and square, knowing that y o u also have a Master in heaven.

---

[150] The possibility that the word "fathers" has here the meaning "parents" must be granted (see also Heb. 11:23) . However, the fact that in the preceding verse the more usual word for *parents* is used would rather seem to indicate that in the present passage "fathers" means just that. Though the responsibility for the education of the children rests on both parents, and father will consult mother, the probability is that the father is here regarded as the head of the family.

[151] The verb is ἐρεθίζετε, meaning *stir up*. One can stir up for good (II Cor. 9:2) for evil (as here in Col. 3:21) . In the latter case the resultant meaning is *exasperate, embitter*. In the present passage there is also considerable textual support for the synonym παροργίζετε, *provoke to anger*. There is very little difference in meaning. Perhaps the latter verb was inserted here from Eph. 6:4.

[152] For a 15-point discussion of *Principles and Methods of Education in Israel* see N.T.C. on I and II Timothy and Titus, pp. 296-301.

3:22–4:1

III. *Slaves and Their Masters*
See also *Scripture on Slavery, pp. 233-237*

22. **Slaves, obey in all things those who according to the flesh are y o u r
masters** . . . Nowhere in Scripture is it stated that slavery *as such* is a divine
ordinance, such as marriage (Gen. 1:18, 24), the family (Gen. 1:27, 28),
the sabbath (Gen. 2:3), and human government (Gen. 9:6; Rom. 13:1).
In and by itself it is not pleasing to God that one man should *own* another
man. The fact, moreover, that Paul addresses slaves and their masters on a
basis of equality is significant, and implies their spiritual equality before
God.

The Roman world was full of slaves. It has been estimated that in Rome
itself at one time about a third of the inhabitants belonged to this social
class. They had become slaves as prisoners of war, or as convicts, or through
debt, kidnaping, purchase, or birth from slave-parents.

Now Paul did not recommend outright revolt by the slaves against their
masters. On the contrary, he took the social structure as he found it and
endeavored by peaceful means to change it into its very opposite. His rule,
in summary, amounted to this, "Let the slave wholeheartedly obey his master, and let the master be kind to his slave." Thus the ill-will, dishonesty,
and laziness of the slave would be replaced by willing service, integrity, and
industry; the cruelty and brutality of the master, by considerateness and
love. And a new and gloriously transformed society would replace the old.

The Pauline material dealing with this subject is found mainly in the
following passages: Eph. 6:5-9; Col. 3:22–4:1; I Tim. 6:1, 2; and Titus 2:9,
10. With this should be compared what Peter says in I Peter 2:18-25. Of
these five little paragraphs only the first two mention the reciprocal duties
of slaves *and their masters.* One of the reasons why more attention is paid to
the slaves than to the masters could well be that among those addressed
there were many more of the former than of the latter (see I Cor. 1:26).
The probable reason why *in Colossians* the apostle devotes far more attention to a. slaves and their masters than to b. wives and their husbands, and
children and their fathers (combined) has been pointed out in the Introduction IV A 4 (Onesimus and his master Philemon).

Now when Paul instructs the slaves to obey their masters "in all things,"
he probably means, "not only in matters pleasant and agreeable but also
in matters unpleasant and disagreeable." He cannot have meant, "in *absolutely* all things" (see Acts 5:29). As Paul says elsewhere, by means of this
obedience they would "adorn the doctrine of God our Savior" (Titus
2:10). The expression "those who according to the flesh — that is, those

who as concerns earthly relationships [153] — are y o u r masters" implies, "Y o u r *real* Master is in heaven," a thought on which Paul will expand presently.

Now this obedience must be not with eye-service as **men-pleasers** but with **singleness of heart, fearing the Lord.** They must not obey simply "to catch the eye" of their master for selfish purposes. Instead of striving to please men, with the ulterior motive of seeking profit for themselves, they should "with singleness of heart," that is, with an *undivided* mind, hence, with sincerity and uprightness (cf. I Chron. 29:17), render service to their earthly masters, and in so doing show reverence for their Lord.

23, 24. Whatever y o u do (cf. with verse 17), **put y o u r soul into the work** (literally, "work from the soul"), **as for the Lord and not for men . . .** In spirit people cease to be slaves as soon as they begin to work for the Lord, and no longer in the first place for men. This was, accordingly, the most helpful advice anyone could ever have given a slave. Moreover, by means of his *wholehearted* cooperation with his master, rendering obedience to him in every way, and doing this while his master was fully aware of the fact that the service was being rendered by a Christian, the slave was promoting the cause and honor of his Lord. The master would begin to think, "If the Christian religion does this for slaves, it must be wonderful." Paul continues, **knowing that from the Lord y o u will receive the recompense, namely, the inheritance.** Even though from his earthly master the slave may receive far less than he should, yet from his heavenly Lord he will receive *the full amount* which *by God's grace* has been allotted to him.[154]

Though salvation is entirely "by grace" and definitely not "of works" (Eph. 2:8, 9; Titus 3:5), yet this gracious *recompense of eternal life* will be given "according to works" (II Cor. 5:10; Rev. 20:12, 13; then also Eccl. 12:14; I Cor. 3:10-15; 4:5; Gal. 6:7). The recompense is, moreover, "the inheritance," probably implying the following ideas: a. it is *a gift* (a person does not *earn* an inheritance), b. it is *inalienable* (I Kings 21:3; Heb. 9:15), c. it *was willed* to the person who receives it, and in that sense, is therefore his *by right* (cf. Isa. 1:27); and it implies *the death of the testator* (Heb. 9:16).

---

[153] On the various meanings of the word *flesh* see N.T.C. on Philippians, p. 77, footnote 55. Meaning c. is indicated here.
[154] The word rendered *recompense* is acc. of ἀνταπόδοσις, in the New Testament occurring only in this one passage. Here ἀντί expresses the idea of *full, complete return.* The noun ἀνταπόδομα means *requital,* used in a favorable sense in Luke 14:12; unfavorably in Rom. 11:9. The cognate verb ἀνταποδίδωμι, used in favorable sense (Luke 14:14; Rom. 11:35; I Thess. 3:9), in unfavorable sense (Rom. 12:19; II Thess. 1:6; Heb. 10:30), has the root-meaning *I render a full return for something received.* See my doctoral dissertation "The Meaning of the Preposition ἀντί in the New Testament," in the library of Princeton Seminary, Princeton, N.J., pp. 83, 84.

Now slaves, as a rule, are not heirs (Gen. 15:3; Rom. 8:15-17; Gal. 4:7). But the slaves to whom Paul is here referring *do* inherit, for their Master is Christ: **(It is) the Lord Christ (whom) y o u are serving.**[155] Let them therefore always live "as under the eye" of their Lord! For the expression "the Lord Christ" see also Rom. 16:18. These are the only two occurrences in the New Testament. The anointed Lord is the slave's employer. What a privilege and honor!

25. Paul continues, **For,** implying, perhaps, "Y o u should obey these instructions, for" **the wrong-doer will receive (the consequences of) what he has wrongly done. And there is no partiality.** According to Ridderbos this has reference solely to *the master* of the slave. It means that even though the slave may at times have to suffer an injustice from the hand of his master, that master will not be left unpunished (*op. cit.*, p. 230). Lenski, on the other hand, refers it solely to *the slave*, "The wrong done remains on the slave's back, and he will carry it to judgment." He points out that "masters are not mentioned until later" (*op. cit.*, p. 185). Lightfoot's opinion differs from both. Says he, "It seems best to suppose that both are included" (*op. cit.*, p. 229). I believe that this last position is the right one. My reason is that an almost exactly parallel idea is expressed in Eph. 6:8, only now with respect to the *right*-doer (instead of *wrong*-doer, as here in Col. 3:25), in a context in which it is definitely mentioned that the statement concerns *both bond and free.* The sentence in Ephesians is as follows, ". . . knowing that whatever good anyone does, he will receive the same again from the Lord, whether he be a slave or free." Says Lightfoot, commenting on Col. 3:25, "The warning is suggested by the case of the slave, but it is extended [in the next verse, Col. 4:1] to the case of the master."

If the slave fails to heed the admonitions that have been issued, he will reap what he has sown. No one in the church of Colosse must begin to think that since the apostle has dealt so kindly with Onesimus he also approves of what the latter did to his master. The rule (Gal. 6:7) is universal. It applies to every slave, no matter who he is. And it applies even to every master. With God there is no *partiality* (Lev. 19:15; Mal. 2:9; Acts 10:34;

---

[155] Some prefer to render this as an imperative, "Serve the Lord Christ," giving as a reason that otherwise the word "for" which introduces verse 25 has no meaning. However, whether one renders the verb as an imperative or as an indicative, in either case something has to be supplied in order to obtain a reasonable thought-connection. This is a case of "abbreviated expression." See N.T.C. on John 5:31. Besides, the difference is rather insignificant, as, in either case, the point is that Paul wants these slaves ever to bear in mind that they are really serving not first of all and most of all an earthly but a heavenly Master, and that this should be their attitude. The preceding "knowing that" would seem to point to the indicative here. Thus also A.V., A.R.V. (old and new), R.S.V., Berkeley.

Eph. 6:9; James 2:1) ; literally "no acceptance of face" (hence, "respect of persons") .[156]

4:1. By an easy transition the final admonition belonging to this table of domestic duties follows: **Masters,**[157] **render to y o u r slaves that which is fair and square, knowing that y o u also have a Master in heaven.** More literally translated, the first part would read, "Masters, that which is just and that which is fair,[158] to the slaves grant." The masters must remember that they, too, have a Master. The commended centurion understood this (Matt. 8:5-13, see especially verse 9). The unmerciful servant of the parable related in Matt. 18:23-35 did not. Let the masters then realize that just as their slaves are accountable to them, so they, in turn, will have to answer to the Master in heaven. If they understand this, they will not treat their slaves harshly. They will "forbear threatening" (Eph. 6:9), and will, instead, show the same consideration to their servants as they themselves expect to receive from the One who exercises authority over them. What we have here, therefore, is an application of the Golden Rule (Matt. 7:12) to the master-slave relationship.

The summary of admonitions addressed to separate groups ends, accordingly, with the mention of the all-sufficient, pre-eminent Master, even "the Lord Christ" (cf. 4:1 and 3:24), for it is he who is the source of the believers' life, the One who is ever ready to enable every believer, to whatever group he belongs, to live to the glory of God.

Summary of Colossians 3:18–4:1

The all-sufficient Christ is also the source of life for household groups. They, too, must draw their inspiration from him, for it is from him that they derive *power* to do what is right and proper, the *purpose* to do all in the name of the Lord Jesus, and the *pattern* of obedience.

In the present paragraph wives are told to be submissive to their husbands; husbands to love their wives; next, children, to obey their parents; fathers, to be kind to their children; and finally, slaves to obey their masters, "not with eye-service as men-pleasers but with singleness of heart, fearing the Lord"; and masters, to render to their slaves what is fair and square, remembering that they (these masters) , too, have a Master in heaven.

---

[156] Moule has an interesting paragraph on the Greek word rendered *partiality* (*op. cit.,* p. 132).

[157] In the original the vocatives *wives, husbands, children, fathers, slaves, masters* (3: 18–4:1) are all preceded by the generic article, a not uncommon usage (Gram. N.T., p. 757).

[158] It is not true that ἰσότης must always be rendered *that which is equal* or *equality.* There are instances of the use of this word in the sense of *fairness* also in other authors (see M.M., p. 307). Used in connection with the word *justice* (or "that which is just") it is natural to treat the two concepts as synonyms and to use the English idiom "fair and square" (or something similar) in the translation.

COLOSSIANS

Because of their *reciprocal character* — admonitions being addressed not only to wives but also to their husbands, not only to children but also to their fathers, not only to slaves but also to their masters — these exhortations are eminently fair. That the counsel given in each case is fair also appears from its *content*. Wives are told to do that which accords with the manner in which they were created. Children, too, are not told to do whatever they please — which would be cruel advice — but to obey those who love them most and who are best qualified to judge what is best for them. Slaves are shown the only road to true, spiritual freedom, namely, to remember, in the midst of all their toil that they are really working "for the Lord." The same holds with respect to the other classes mentioned: husbands, fathers, and masters.

These admonitions were evidently addressed to household groups of *believers*. What happens when either the wife or the husband or the master is not a believer? What is the rule in such a case for, respectively, the husband or the wife or the slave? Scripture has not left us in the dark on this question. See the following passages: Acts 5:29; I Cor. 7:12-16; I Tim. 6:1 (contrast verse 2); Titus 2:9, 10; I Peter 2:18-21; 3:1, 2.

Outline of Chapter 4:2-18

Theme: *Christ, the Pre-eminent One, the Only and All-Sufficient Savior*
II. This Only and All-Sufficient Savior Is the Source of the Believers' Life, and Thus the Real Answer to the Perils by Which They Are Confronted, chapters 3 and 4

      C. Closing Admonitions, Greetings, etc., 4:2-18

4:2-4	1. Prayer urged
4:5, 6	2. Wise conduct and gracious speech stressed
4:7-9	3. A good word for Tychicus and for Onesimus, who have been sent with tidings and encouragement
4:10-15	4. Greetings
4:16	5. Exchange of letters requested
4:17	6. Crisp directive for Archippus
4:18	7. Closing salutation

CHAPTER IV

COLOSSIANS 4:2

4 2 Persevere in prayer, keeping alert in it with thanksgiving; 3 at the same time praying also for us, that God may open to us a door for the message, to speak forth the mystery concerning Christ, on account of which I am in prison, 4 (praying) that I may make it clear, (and may speak) as I ought to speak.

4:2-4

I. *Prayer Urged*

2. As Paul is now approaching the close of the letter he issues certain admonitions of a general nature, as in 3:1-17; with emphasis on the positive, cf. 3:12-17. It is not surprising that, having spoken about *the word* (3:16), the apostle now stresses the importance of *prayer*, for word and prayer belong together: in the former God speaks to us, in the latter we to him. Says Paul: **Persevere in prayer.** Prayer is the most important expression of the new life. As such it is the means of obtaining for ourselves and for others the satisfaction of needs, both physical and spiritual. It is also a divinely appointed weapon against the sinister attack of the devil and his angels, the vehicle for confession of sin, and the instrument whereby the grateful soul pours out its spontaneous adoration before the throne of God on high. Accordingly, perseverance in prayer is urged. See also Acts 1:14; Rom. 12:12; Eph. 6:18. This is in keeping with the teaching of Jesus in which he admonished his disciples to persevere in prayer, and not to lose heart when a petition is not immediately answered (Acts 18:1-8). Paul adds, **keeping alert in it.** This admonition *to remain fully awake* in prayer reminds one of Matt. 26:41; Mark 14:38; Luke 22:40, 46. Yet, in these Gospel passages the wakefulness referred to is to be taken more literally, as the respective contexts indicate. What the apostle has in mind is that, while continuing in prayer, the worshiper shall be alive to such matters as: a. his own needs and those of the family, church, country, world, b. the dangers that threaten the Christian community, c. the blessings received and promised, and (last but not least) d. the will of God. Cf. Acts 20:31; II Cor. 16:13; I Thess. 5:6; I Peter 5:8; Rev. 3:2, 3. From the Greek verb which expresses this necessity of being vigilant — a form of *grēgoreō* (I am awake, I remain alert) — the early Christians coined a favorite proper name: *Gregory.*

179

Now when one is deeply and humbly conscious of blessings received and promised he will express his gratitude to God. Hence, Paul continues: **with thanksgiving.** Cf. Eph. 5:20; 6:18; Phil. 4:6; I Thess. 5:18; and see also above, on Col. 3:15, 17. It is worthy of note that the apostle wedges his admonitions to particular groups (3:18–4:1) in between two reminders to give thanks to God (2:17 and 4:2), as if to say, "Wives, husbands, children, fathers, slaves, masters, obey these instructions *spontaneously,* prompted by gratitude for the many blessings received."

It should be borne in mind that the man who issues this directive is a prisoner. However, *this* prisoner is able to thank God even for his chains (Phil. 1:12-14). Surely, on the basis of the thought expressed so beautifully in Rom. 8:28 the believer can be thankful for whatever happens to him.

3, 4. In these prayers the needs of Paul and his companions must be included. Accordingly, the apostle continues, **at the same time praying also for us.**[159] Like Daniel before him (Dan. 2:18), and probably also Esther (Esth. 4:6), Paul felt the need of being remembered in prayer. Moreover, Timothy (Col. 1:1) and Epaphras (4:12) must be remembered similarly, and doubtless also those mentioned in 4:10, 11, 14. This is by no means the only time that the apostle asked to be thus remembered. See above, on 1:9, the parallel columns. See especially *Eph. 6:18-20.* This passage from Ephesians, in fact, should be constantly borne in mind in the interpretation of Col. 4:2-4 in its entirety. "Brothers, do pray for us" (I Thess. 5:25) was Paul's constant appeal. Now when he urged this upon his fellow-workers and fellow-believers he had something very definite in mind. Hence, stating the contemplated result of the prayer, and using an idiom that may have belonged to the common speech of that day,[160] as it is also a metaphor among us, he continues, **that God may open to us a door for the message.** A *door,* then as now, is an opportunity to enter, a means of approach or access. In the present context it is an opening for *the word* or *message.* Cf. I Cor. 16:9; II Cor. 2:12; Rev. 3:8. Now the apostle did not intend to say: Pray that *by my release from imprisonment* I may again be able to proclaim the message of salvation. No, he wanted that door right here and now! That this was not an absurd request, as if it would be impossible for a prisoner to have an open door, is shown by such a passage as Acts 28:30, 31. And if the objection be raised that such freedom as there presupposed did not necessarily continue, and that before his release the apostle was transferred from his "rented house" to the soldiers' barracks, or that in some other way he was placed under stricter custody, the answer is that even this added severity would not completely remove the open door, as is clearly shown in Phil. 1:12-18. As there

---

[159] It is not necessary to assume a literary or epistolary plural here, nor in I Thess. 2:18; 3:1. See N.T.C. on these passages.
[160] A. Deissmann, *op. cit.,* p. 300, footnote 2.

indicated, from a certain point of view the seeming disadvantage was in reality an advantage, as Paul's chain made it very clear that his was not a fair-weather religion, but something far more precious and real. Nevertheless, humanly speaking, circumstances could easily change. When Paul made this prayer-request was he thinking, perhaps, of a summons before the Roman tribunal for a hearing, probably not the first one? And is he now saying, in effect, "O Colossians, do pray that, when we are called to give an account before the authorities, we may speak forth very freely and that our message may also gain entrance into the hearts of those who hear"? Besides, testifying openly and clearly before every type of audience and under all circumstances is not easy. Hence, this man of God who in a sense already had an open door is not at all inconsistent when he now asks that prayer may be offered so that he may (at all times and under all circumstances) have an open door. This explanation is also in line with the parallel passage, Eph. 6:19, and with what follows immediately here in Colossians, namely, **to speak forth the mystery concerning Christ,**[161] its content being Christ himself as the source of salvation, full and free, for both Gentile and Jew, a secret no longer *concealed* but now, O glorious paradox!, a *secret* fully *revealed*, and not revealed only but *realized* in the hearts and lives of people of every class, station, and nationality. See further on 1:26, 27 and on 2:2 above. Paul continues, **on account of which I am in prison,** hence all the more in need of, and entitled to, being remembered in y o u r prayers (cf. 1:24). That it was indeed as a result of the proclamation of this mystery — especially its disclosure *to the Gentiles!* — that Paul was fettered and in custody follows from the many references in which it is clearly indicated that the Jews, filled with fury because Paul preached the gospel to Jew *and Gentile* without distinction, had accused him before the civil authorities (Acts 18:12, 13; 21:28; 22:21-30; 23:26-30; 24:1-9; 25:1, 2, 6, 7; 26:19-21, 32).

Now Paul wishes to be remembered in prayer for two reasons: a. so that he may continue to proclaim the blessed contents of the mystery, as has been indicated, and b. that he may do this in the proper manner. As to b., therefore, he continues: **(praying) that I may make it clear, (and may speak) as I ought to speak.** When a *good* message is proclaimed in a *bad* way it can do more harm than good. How often have not those who, though innocent, were imprisoned or otherwise molested, made matters worse both for themselves and for the cause which they were defending, by failing to observe this truth. When the apostle now asks to be remembered in prayer so that he may not fall into this error but may speak *as he should,* he probably had in mind some or all of the following particulars: a. Pray that I may speak *clearly* ("that I may make it clear"), b. *boldly,* that is, without fear or restraint ("telling all," see Eph. 6:19, ἐν παρρησίᾳ), c. yet also *graciously* (see

---

[161] or simply, "the mystery, namely, Christ." See N.T.C. on I Tim. 3:16. Christ is in any event the heart and essence of the mystery.

the context, Col. 4:6a) , and d. *wisely,* so that I may know exactly what approach to use when questioned by groups or individuals of various backgrounds: visitors who come to see me in prison, soldiers who guard me, and the Roman authorities before whom I may be summoned.

---

5 Conduct yourselves wisely toward outsiders, making the most of the opportunity. 6 Let y o u r speech always be gracious, seasoned with salt, so that y o u may know how to answer each individual.

4:5, 6

II. *Wise Conduct and Gracious Speech Stressed*

5. In the spirit of the principles to which Paul has bound himself and in connection with which he has just now asked the Colossians to remember him and his companions in prayer (see verses 3 and 4 above) he now urges them to adhere to a similar way of life. Says he, **Conduct yourselves wisely toward outsiders.** To the Jew every non-Jew was an "outsider." And to the Christian every non-Christian is, in a sense, an outsider. See I Cor. 5:12, 13; I Thess. 4:12; I Tim. 3:7. In the days of the early church believers were often slandered by these outsiders. For example, they were called *atheists* because they served no visible gods, *unpatriotic* because they did not burn incense before the image of the emperor, and *immoral* because, of necessity, they would often meet behind locked doors. The apostle knew that the best way to defeat this slander was for Christians daily to conduct themselves not only *virtuously* instead of *wickedly* but also *wisely* instead of *foolishly.* See Appendix, *Scripture on Tactfulness.* It was then as it is now: in the long run the reputation of the gospel depends on the conduct of its devotees. It is as if the apostle were saying, "Behave wisely toward outsiders, always bearing in mind that though few men read the sacred scrolls, all men read y o u."

But not only does such wise conduct, so that believers use the best means to reach the highest goal, serve as a weapon against vilification and character-assassination, it also has a positive purpose, namely, to win outsiders for Christ. Paul was fully aware of the fact that the most effective way for Christians to spread the gospel so that it would be accepted was to conduct themselves in such a manner that the heathen would say, "Behold how they love each other, and, in spite of all we have said about them, even love us and treat us with kindness, returning good for evil." That Paul had this positive purpose in mind is also evident from the fact that he adds: **making the most of the opportunity.** If the participle used in the original has fully retained its etymological significance, the apostle literally said, ". . . *buying* *up* the opportunity." The sense then would be "Do not just sit there and wait for opportunity to fall into y o u r lap, but go after it. Yes, buy it." "Buy up the entire stock of opportunity" (Moule, *op. cit.*, p. 134) . "Count not the cost. Winning even one soul for Christ is worth it (cf. Prov. 11:30; Rom. 11:14) , and so is salvation itself" (Matt. 13:44, 45) . But in any event the minimal meaning is, "Avail yourselves of every opportunity to be a blessing to others."

One thought which, though not here expressed, may very well have been in the background is this: the days are evil and are speeding toward the great consummation of all things. "The night is far gone; the day is at hand." Therefore, make the most of the opportunity while y o u have it. Cf. Rom. 13:11, 12; I Cor. 7:29; Gal. 6:9, 10; and especially Eph. 5:16.

6. See also on Col. 3:8, 9, 16. Paul has asked the Colossians to pray that *his* manner of speaking might always be the very best (see above, on verse 4) . So, having as it were set the example, he now admonishes the addressees to be similarly careful in the use of *their* tongue: Let y o u r speech always be gracious . . . Note *always,* that is, both in addressing a group or in talking to the neighbor, both when conversing with an equal or when replying to someone in authority, to rich and poor alike, not only in proclaiming the message of salvation but also in discussing the weather. When gracious speech becomes their habit they will not use improper language when suddenly confronted with a difficult situation; for example, when summoned to appear before a worldly judge or when persecuted for the faith.

Just what is "gracious speech"? By non-Christians of Paul's day the same expression was used. However, what they meant by it was *sparkling conversation,* speech dotted with witty or clever remarks. When Paul uses the term he has reference to the type of language that results from the operation of God's grace in the heart. *Negatively,* such speech will not be abusive (Rom. 1:29-32; II Cor. 12:20; Gal. 5:19-21, 26; Eph. 4:31; Titus 3:2) . Neither will it be vindictive. It will be patterned after the example of Christ who "when he was reviled did not revile in return" (I Peter 2:23) . Positively, it will be truthful and loving. Perhaps the best *description* of gracious speech is found in the words of Paul himself: "speaking truth in love" (Eph. 4:15) , and the best *example* in the words of Jesus, "Father, forgive them, for they know not what they do" (Luke 23:34) .

A further description of this kind of gracious speech is: seasoned with salt. Those whom the Lord calls "the salt of the earth" (Matt. 5:13; Mark 9:49, 50; Luke 14:34, 35) must not be insipid in their language. Salt prevents corruption. It is hard to believe that this idea was absent from the mind of Paul, for in the parallel passage he says, "Let *no corrupt* speech proceed from y o u r mouth, but only such (speech) as is good for edification, as fits the need, that it may impart grace to those who hear" (Eph. 4:29) . But not only does salt have preservative power. It also has pungency and flavor. Speech flavored with salt is, accordingly, not empty or insipid, but thought-provoking and worth-while. It is not a waste of time. Also, such speech does not repel. It attracts, has spiritual charm. Accordingly, it is distinctive: a Christian is known by his speech as well as by his conduct.

Now in their conversations believers must be mindful not only of the particular occasion that evokes their remarks but also of the person addressed. Hence, the apostle continues: **so that y o u may know how to answer each individual.** In other words, they should speak the right word at the right time to the right person. This reminds us of I Peter 3:15, "But in y o u r hearts reverence Christ as Lord, always being ready to make a defense to anyone who asks y o u to give an account for the hope that is in y o u, yet with gentleness and reverence." The Holy Spirit himself will help them to do this. Hence, they need not be frightened (Matt. 10:19, 20; Mark 13:11). Christ will give them a mouth and wisdom (Luke 21:14, 15).

---

7 All my affairs will Tychicus make known to y o u, the beloved brother and faithful minister and fellow-servant in the Lord, 8 whom I am sending to y o u for this very purpose, that y o u may know our circumstances and that he may strengthen y o u r hearts. 9 (He is) accompanied by Onesimus, the faithful and beloved brother, who is one of y o u. They will acquaint y o u with everything (that has taken place) here.

4:7-9

III. *A Good Word for Tychicus and for Onesimus, Who Have Been Sent with Tidings from Rome and with Encouragement*

7, 8. All my affairs will Tychicus make known to y o u. Tychicus [162] was one of Paul's intimate friends and highly valued envoys. He hailed from the province of Asia, and had accompanied the apostle when at the close of the third missionary journey the latter was returning from Greece through Macedonia and then across into Asia Minor and so to Jerusalem on a charitable mission (Acts 20:4); that is, on that trip Tychicus had traveled in advance of Paul from Macedonia to Troas, and had been waiting for the apostle in that city. And now, some four years later, having spent some time with Paul in Rome during the latter's first Roman imprisonment, Tychicus had been commissioned by the apostle to carry to their destination not only the epistle to the Colossians, as implied here in Col. 4:7, 8, and the one to Phi-

---

[162] For the meaning of the name see N.T.C. on Philippians, pp. 138, 139, footnote 116, where the explanation of many other personal names is also given. For more on Tychicus, e.g., his relation to Paul after the latter's first Roman imprisonment, see N.T.C. on Titus 3:12 and on II Tim. 4:12.

lemon, as a comparison of 4:9 and Philem. I, 8-22, would appear to indicate, but also the letter that has been transmitted to us as the Epistle to the Ephesians (see Eph. 6:21, 22, which is almost identical with Col. 4:7, 8). The description of Tychicus as **the beloved brother and faithful minister and fellow-servant in the Lord** is nearly like that of Epaphras (though not in word-order). There is *essential* identity. Hence, see on Col. 1:7. And the reasons for recommending Tychicus so highly are also similar to those given in the case of Epaphras. It stands to reason that Tychicus, having just now spent some time with Paul and being a man of sound judgment, would be the right person to supply all the necessary information about Paul and his companions and fellow-Christians in Rome. Besides, paper was not as plentiful and cheap as it is today, the circumstances under which Paul, the "aged" prisoner (see on Philem. 9) had to dictate his letters were not altogether favorable, certain things are better *said* than *written;* hence, for such and similar reasons Paul continues: **whom I am sending** [163] **to y o u for this very purpose, that y o u may know our circumstances.**[164] Not only this, however, but also, **and that he may strengthen y o u r hearts,** probably by stilling y o u r fears (cf. Phil. 1:12-14), by delivering to y o u this very letter, and in general by orally supplying the "atmosphere" of consolation and spiritual strengthening based upon the promises of God.

9. The apostle continues: **(He is) accompanied by Onesimus, the faithful and beloved brother, who is one of y o u. They will acquaint y o u with everything (that has taken place) here.**

It is not necessary to repeat what is said about Onesimus in Introduction IV B and in N.T.C. on Philemon (see especially on verses 8-22) in this volume. The emphatic recommendation of Onesimus to the entire church of Colosse was, and no doubt was meant to be, a powerful support for the plea in behalf of him which Paul addressed to Philemon, the slave's master, one of the members of that church. What has been affirmed by many a commentator, namely, that the very preservation of the Epistle to Philemon proves that this plea was successful is probably correct. By calling Onesimus "the faithful and beloved brother" the apostle underscores before the entire church verse 16 of his personal letter to Philemon. By permitting Onesimus to stand at the side of Tychicus as an informant regarding everything pertaining to Paul and the church in Rome the apostle is telling the Colossians, including Philemon, that he regards the man who by God's transforming grace is now living up the meaning of his name — Onesimus: *profitable, helpful* — to be also *wholly reliable.*

---

[163] ἔπεμψα, epistolary aorist.
[164] Though the reading "that he may know y o u r circumstances" has the support of p[46] and other manuscripts, it must be considered inferior because of the context (see verse 9b).

10 Aristarchus, my fellow-prisoner, greets y o u; so does Mark, the cousin of Barnabas — concerning whom y o u received instructions; if he comes to y o u receive him — ; 11 and Jesus who is called Justus. Of those who are of the circumcision these are the only co-workers for the kingdom of God who have been a comfort to me. 12 Epaphras, who is one of y o u, a servant of Christ Jesus, greets y o u, always wrestling for y o u in his prayers that y o u may stand firm, mature and fully assured in all the will of God. 13 For I can testify concerning him that he has put himself to much trouble for y o u and for those in Laodicea and those in Hierapolis. 14 Luke, the beloved physician, greets y o u, and so does Demas. 15 Extend greetings to the brothers in Laodicea, and to Nympha and the church in her house.

23 Epaphras, my fellow-prisoner in Christ Jesus, greets y o u, 24 (and so do) Mark, Aristarchus, Demas, and Luke, my fellow-workers.

Col. 4:10-15   Philem. 23, 24

IV. *Greetings*

This section in Colossians may be divided into two parts: a. vss. 10-14, in which three of Paul's companions of Jewish birth — Aristarchus, Mark, and Jesus Justus — , and also three of Gentile birth — Epaphras, Luke, and Demas — send greetings to the Colossians; and b. verse 15, in which the apostle requests the Colossians to forward his greetings to "the brothers in Laodicea and to Nympha and the church in her house."

A look at the parallel columns reveals the following:

(1) Due largely to the fact that in the Colossian passage Paul enlarges on Mark, on "those of the circumcision," and on Epaphras, this passage is lengthier by far than the corresponding list of greetings in Philemon.

(2) In Colossians six men send greetings, in Philemon only five. Jesus Justus is not mentioned in the smaller letter. We do not know for what reason his name is omitted. The order of the names also is different. The Colossian list mentions Aristarchus, Mark, Jesus Justus, Epaphras, Luke, and Demas in that sequence. In Philemon the order is: Epaphras, Mark, Aristarchus, Demas, and Luke.

Taking the names one by one, in the order in which they are mentioned in Colossians, we begin with

Aristarchus

10a. Aristarchus, my fellow-prisoner, greets y o u. The native town of
this man, or at least the place with which he was mainly associated, was
Thessalonica. At Ephesus, during Paul's lengthy ministry there (third missionary journey, outward bound) he was with the apostle, and, recognized
by the Ephesian rioters as one of Paul's traveling companions, he, along
with another man from Macedonia, Gaius, was on the spur of the moment
seized by the mob (Acts 19:29). Later we again find him in Paul's company
on the return from this same journey. In fact, Tychicus, from "Asia," (see
above, on verse 7) and Aristarchus and Secundus from Thessalonica, are
mentioned as Paul's travel-companions in the same verse (Acts 20:4). This
was the trip on which delegates from various churches of predominantly
Gentile origin were carrying aid to the needy in Jerusalem. We meet Aristarchus once more in the very beginning of the account of Paul's Voyage
Dangerous (Acts 27:2). He started out with Paul and probably accompanied the apostle all the way to Rome. (For the idea of Lightfoot, that Aristarchus disembarked at Myra, there is no evidence whatever.) From Rome
he is now sending greetings both to the Colossians and to Philemon.

Now a glance at the parallel columns above indicates a rather striking
peculiarity that requires some attention. In Colossians Aristarchus is called
"my fellow-prisoner," but in Philemon no such qualifying designation is
added. Along with others he is designated "my fellow-worker" (see on
Philem. 1). Conversely, in Philemon it is Epaphras who is described as "my
fellow-prisoner in Christ Jesus," but in Colossians, though much is said
about Epaphras, that specific designation is not used with respect to him.
From this circumstance and from the fact that Aristarchus was not "under
arrest" when Paul as a *prisoner* among other *prisoners* started on his journey to Rome, and that Epaphras, too, somewhat later, was delegated to
Rome *as a free man,* the probably warranted inference has been drawn that
when Aristarchus, here in Col. 4:10, and Epaphras, in Philem. 23, are
called *fellow-prisoners,* this must not be taken in a *strictly* literal sense.
These men may well have volunteered to share Paul's imprisonment, assisting him in every possible way. They must have been glad to do this
since they, as well as Paul, were captives in Christ's train (II Cor. 2:14; cf.
10:5).[165]

---

[165] The root meaning of αἰχμάλωτος is *one caught with the spear;* hence, a *war-
captive,* and so simply *a captive* or *prisoner.* See N.T.C. on II Tim. 3:6. It is not
wrong, therefore, to render συναιχμάλωτος *fellow-prisoner.* Since the apostle was
himself a prisoner in the literal sense of that term it is hard to believe that in
speaking of "fellow-prisoners" he was using this term in an *exclusively* spiritual
sense, though it must be admitted that not only in II Cor. 2:14 but also elsewhere
the apostle uses military terminology with respect to the service rendered to the
cause of Christ (Phil. 2:25; Philem. 2; and II Tim. 2:3). Paul's use of the word
captive or *prisoner,* even when used in a literal sense, often has a spiritual over-

Mark

10b. So does Mark, the cousin of Barnabas.

Mark, the one whom we recognize as the writer of the second Gospel, was also associated with Paul in Rome at this time, and as such is sending greetings both to the Colossians and to Philemon. We now learn that he was a cousin of Barnabas. This could be the reason why, some twelve years earlier, the latter had treated him with such extraordinary kindness. This happened just after Mark, on Paul's first missionary journey, had deserted his senior partners and had gone home. Because of this act of disloyalty and cowardice Paul had refused to accept the suggestion of Barnabas that Mark be given another chance and be taken along on the second missionary journey (Acts 15:36-41). There had been "a sharp contention" about this matter between Paul and Barnabas. But by now, Mark seems to have redeemed himself. The apostle no longer regards him as a liability, but recommends him warmly, and even includes him among those who have been a comfort to him (see on verse 11). Moreover, this favorable attitude continued, for even in his very last letter that has come down to us Paul says, "Mark . . . is very useful to me for (the) ministry" (II Tim. 4:11).

What factors or agencies did the Holy Spirit use in bringing about this favorable change in the life of John Mark? In all probability one or more of the following:

a. "The kindly tutelage of Barnabas, that true 'son of encouragement.'" Not *entirely* was it due to this but "no doubt in great measure" (F. F. Bruce, *op. cit.,* p. 305).

b. The stern discipline of Paul, shown in refusing to take Mark with him on the second journey. Perhaps Mark needed exactly that seeming harshness.

c. The influence of Peter who calls Mark "my son" (I Peter 5:13). A consistent early tradition links these two men. Peter knew *by experience* that there was hope for those who had fallen into the sins of disloyalty and cowardice.

The Holy Spirit may well have used all three factors and others also to perform his marvelous work in the mind and conscience of "the man who came back."

Paul continues, **concerning whom y o u received instructions; if he comes to y o u receive him.**

What these instructions were and who had issued them we do not know. Either it was Paul himself, in which case he here underscores what he had previously ordered regarding Mark; or else it was Barnabas, Peter, or some other person deemed to be invested with a degree of authority, in which

tone. Thus, when he refers to himself as "a prisoner," he adds "of Christ Jesus." We may well assume, therefore, that here, too, the word "fellow-captive" or "fellow-prisoner" has that spiritual overtone.

case the apostle here endorses these earlier directives. The first alternative would seem the more probable. In any event it is clear that Mark, being now somewhere in Paul's vicinity, was about to make a trip to Asia Minor, and that his itinerary would include Colosse. The apostle bespeaks a whole-hearted "acceptance" for him.

There is no reason to doubt that Mark made this tour, even though there is no further specific record of it. There are, however, two lines of evidence which link Mark with the churches of the general region of Asia Minor during apostolic times:

a. We know that Peter was closely associated with the churches of this region, for he addressed his first epistle to them (I Peter 1:1, 2). Also his second? Cf. II Peter 3:1. And in Peter's letter *Mark's* greetings are conveyed to these churches (I Peter 5:13).

b. We also know that during Paul's second Roman imprisonment Mark was at a place where he could easily be picked up by Timothy, who at that time was in all probability continuing his work in *Ephesus*, province of "Asia." See N.T.C., on I and II Timothy and Titus, p. 43, 321.

Jesus Justus

11. . . . and Jesus who is called Justus. Of those who are of the circumcision these are the only fellow-workers for the kingdom of God who have been a comfort to me.[166]

The name of this Jew who had become a Christian is a combination of the Greek equivalent (Jesus) of Joshua or Jeshua, and a Latin surname (Justus), which, meaning "the just" or "the righteous," may well have been regarded by those of Jewish origin as representing the Hebrew *Zadok* (I Kings 1:32) ; cf. also *Zedekiah* (Jer. 1:3, "Jehovah is righteousness" or "righteousness is of Jehovah"). The same cognomen is found also in Acts 1:23, "Joseph called Barsabbas, who was surnamed Justus," a Jewish Christian, and in Acts 18:7, "Titus Justus," a Roman or Latin who had been attracted to the synagogue. The name Justus was rather common among both Jews and non-Jews, and could be used both by itself or as a surname.

About this man (not mentioned in Philemon) we have no other authentic item of information than that which is given here in Col. 4:11. However, the little that is said about him, as he joins others in sending greetings to the believers in the church of Colosse, is very favorable. We are told that of

---

[166] Though not all are in agreement with respect to the proper punctuation and grammatical construction of verse 11b, it is clear that the word *circumcision* does not end a clause. The sense is not: "Aristarchus, Mark, and Jesus Justus, who are of the circumcision; these are the only fellow-workers for the kingdom of God," etc. Paul certainly would not have denied that such men as Epaphras, Luke, and others were also fellow-workers and had also been a source of consolation to him. The idea is that *from among those of Jewish origin* these three men were the only fellow-workers who had been a comfort to him.

Jewish Christians the three persons just mentioned — namely, Aristarchus, Mark, and Jesus Justus — [167] were the only fellow-workers who had been of *comfort* — that shade of meaning of the word παρηγορία predominates here — to Paul. For the term "fellow-workers" see on Philem. 1. Note the striking modifier after the word *fellow-workers:* "fellow-workers *for the kingdom of God*." Did the apostle thus qualify the term in order to convey the idea, "Especially among the Jews with their great emphasis upon *the kingdom* I should have received more co-operation"? Besides, had he not preached "the kingdom of God" among these very people almost from the moment of his arrival in Rome? See Acts 28:31. In that passage and also here in Col. 4:11 the term "kingdom of God" obviously has reference to the divine realm as a *present* reality. It indicates the dispensation of salvation which in its present phase began with the coming of Christ. God is using Paul and others as his agents in the establishment of this reign of God in the hearts of men. See also on Col. 1:13.

It must not escape our attention that the apostle's statement with reference to these three men as the *only* Jewish-Christian fellow-workers who had been a comfort to him implies deep disappointment with other people of his own race. Paul was painfully aware of his estrangement from his own people (Rom. 9:1-5). And he was not insensitive to the fact that the Judaists (Jews who confessed Jesus but over-emphasized the law) regarded him with suspicion (Acts 15:1, 2, 24; 21:20, 21; Gal. 2:12; Phil. 3:23). It cannot be wrong to regard Phil. 1:14-17; 2:20, 21; II Tim. 4:16 as shedding further light on the apostle's feelings anent this matter. All the more, therefore, does he appreciate the co-operation he is receiving from Aristarchus, Mark, and Jesus Justus!

Epaphras

12-13. To the greetings from three Jewish Christians Paul now adds those from three of Gentile origin, namely, Epaphras, Luke, and Demas. Verses 12 and 13 concern Epaphras, the evangelist of Colosse, Laodicea, and Hierapolis. To some extent the interpretation of these verses has already been given. With respect to this brother and the apostle's high regard for him see Introduction III A 1; see also on Col. 1:7. In his quality as "fellow-prisoner"

---

[167] The combination "Aristarchus . . . and Mark . . . and Jesus who is called Justus" (verses 10, 11) would seem to make it well-nigh certain that all three were *Jewish* Christians. Though a few modifiers are added, these three names are, nevertheless, mentioned in one breath, being linked by ". . . and . . . and . . ." I cannot agree, therefore, with A. S. Peake who, in commenting on this passage in the *Expositor's Greek Testament* (Vol. III, p. 546), states, "Aristarchus is probably not included, for he went as one of the deputation sent by the Gentile Christians with the collection for the church at Jerusalem," nor with Lenski who defends this same idea even more vigorously: "He was a Thessalonian, and thus not a Jew." Acts 17:1-4 implies that among the converts at Thessalonica there were also some Jews.

(Philem. 23) Epaphras has been discussed in connection with Aristarchus (see above on verse 10a). On the three cities to which reference is made in verse 13 see Introduction II and III. Paul writes: **Epaphras, who is one of y o u, a servant of Christ Jesus, greets y o u.** In the spiritual sense Paul uses the word *doulos* (servant) specifically only with respect to himself (Rom. 1:1; Gal. 1:10; Phil. 1:1; Titus 1:1), Timothy (Phil. 1:1) and Epaphras (here in Col. 4:12). A servant of Christ Jesus is one who has been bought with a price and is therefore owned by his Master, on whom he is completely dependent, to whom he owes undivided allegiance and to whom he ministers with gladness of heart, in newness of spirit, and in the enjoyment of perfect freedom (Rom. 6:18, 22; 7:6), receiving from him a glorious reward (Col. 3:24). Every true Christian is in a sense such a servant. See N.T.C. on Phil. 1:1 for more on this concept. It is to the church in Colosse and to Philemon that Epaphras is sending his "best regards."

Paul continues: **always wrestling for y o u in his prayers.** For "wrestling" or "striving" in prayer see also Rom. 15:30, and cf. what the apostle says about himself in Col. 2:1. Epaphras was deeply in earnest as he again and again invoked God's favor upon the Colossians and besought the Lord to help them so that they might not be led astray but might stand firm in the true faith. Further, **that y o u may stand firm, mature.** For the meaning of the word "mature" see above on 1:28; also N.T.C. on Phil. 3:15 (especially p. 176, footnote 156 there).

When Paul further defines the object or contemplated result of Epaphras' prayer by adding, **fully assured in all the will of God,** he must be using the perfect participle "fully assured" in the sense of the cognate noun in Col. 2:2 (see on that passage). Thorough, rich, gratifying insight into all spiritual matters is meant; understanding which not only penetrates the mind but also fills the heart with satisfying conviction. Epaphras does not want these churches that are dear to his heart to be deluded by error. They must remain true to their confession of faith in the all-sufficient Savior Jesus Christ. It is for that reason that he wrestles for them in prayer.

And it is exactly that wrestling in prayer which is probably the best explanation of the words, **For I can testify concerning him that he has put himself to much trouble for y o u and for those in Laodicea and those in Hierapolis.** The Colossian Heresy had undoubtedly affected all three churches founded by Epaphras. Hence, it is in connection with the danger that threatened them all that he betakes himself to the throne of grace in earnest and repeated intercession.[168]

---

[168] This explanation is in harmony with the context. Another interpretation, the one suggested, for example, by E. F. Scott, *The Epistles of Paul to the Colossians, to Philemon and to the Ephesians,* p. 90, would connect the "trouble," to which Epaphras put himself, with the earthquake which about the year A. D. 60 shook the Lycus Valley. See above, Introduction, II B. Paul, according to this theory, is conveying the idea that Epaphras had been laboring to provide financial help for the

Luke

14a. Luke, the beloved physician, greets y o u.

From a comparison with verse 11 we learn that Luke was a Christian from the Gentiles. The present passage shows that he was at Rome just now and was a doctor and a person of amiable personality, beloved by his Lord, by believers generally, and by Paul specifically. He was to become the author of the third Gospel. Note that he and Mark, who wrote the second Gospel, were together in Rome. It is not at all surprising but gratifying that in spite of lengthy arguments to the contrary, thoroughly conservative scholarship is more and more arriving at the conclusion that in composing his own Gospel Luke made use of Mark's as one of his sources.[169]

Luke was a remarkable person, always loyal to Paul, to the gospel, and to his Lord. Frequently he had been Paul's companion in travel, as is indicated by the "we" sections in Acts (16:10-17; 20:6-16; 21; 27; 28). He had been with Paul on the second missionary journey, namely, at Troas and at Philippi. He had evidently been left behind at the latter place (Acts 16:17-19). Toward the close of the third tour he seems again to have joined Paul at Philippi (Acts 20:6), and he accompanied him to Jerusalem. For a while we do not see him. But suddenly he re-appears, for he is in Paul's company on the long and dangerous sea-journey to Rome (Acts 27). And it is from Rome during this, Paul's first, Roman imprisonment, that he is sending his greetings to the Colossians and also to Philemon. Later, the apostle, experiencing his second and final Roman imprisonment, would write these touching words, "Luke is the only one with me" (II Tim. 4:11a). This would be followed by, "Pick up Mark and bring him with you. . . ."

Luke and Paul had much in common. Both were educated men, men of culture. Both were big-hearted, broad-minded, sympathetic. Both were believers and missionaries.

Demas

14b. . . . and so does Demas.

Yes, Demas, too, is a fellow-worker (Philem. 24), one of Paul's assistants in the ministry who wishes to be remembered to the church in Colosse and to Philemon. Paul does not yet know that one day this man will be a deep disappointment to him, and that with reference to this assistant in the gospel-ministry he will, during his second Roman imprisonment, write these

---

stricken inhabitants. However, there is no precise and consistent testimony with reference either to the exact date or extent of this earthquake. Besides, had the apostle meant this, we might have expected a clearer reference to it.

[169] Cf. Zahn, *Einleitung*, II, pp. 404 ff. (Eng. trans., III, pp. 101 ff.) ; H. J. Cadbury, *The Style and Literacy Method of Luke*, pp. 73 ff.; and N. B. Stonehouse, *Origins of the Synoptic Gospels*, p. 49.

plaintive words, "Demas has deserted me, because he fell in love with the present world, and has gone to Thessalonica" (II Tim. 4:10). And with that tragic statement Demas will disappear from sacred history.

15. Having finished the section in which six men—three of Jewish and three of Gentile birth—send their greetings to the Colossians, the apostle now asks that certain greetings be forwarded to believing neighbors. His request is: **Extend greetings to the brothers in Laodicea, and to Nympha and the church in her house.**[170]

Note that Hierapolis (see on verse 13 above) is no longer mentioned. We simply do not know what may have been the reason for this. The apostle wants the addressees to convey his greetings to the brothers in nearby Laodicea. On the *geography* of the three cities — Colosse, Laodicea, Hierapolis — in their relation to each other and to Ephesus, and on their *history*, see Introduction II A (including maps 1, 2, 3), and II B. In Laodicea Paul singles out for separate greetings Nympha and the church in her house.[171] Did he know Nympha personally? Perhaps a group of Laodiceans living close together, but separated at some inconvenient distance from the others, met at her house for worship. So special greetings are extended to them and their hostess. For the house-church idea see Philem. 2.

---

16 And when this letter has been read among y o u, see to it that it is read also in the church of the Laodiceans, and that y o u also read the one from Laodicea.

---

[170] Or, "and to Nymphas and the church in his house." Not only do the manuscripts vary between Nympha (feminine) and Nymphas (masculine), but correspondingly also between "in *her* house" and "in *his* house." Some even have "in *their* house." In the latter case it is probable that a scribe erroneously included a reference to "the brothers" and so arrived at the phrase "in *their* house." As between *her* and *his*, the textual attestation for the former is qualitatively the strongest. Besides, it is not difficult to understand that a scribe, not deeming it proper to speak of the church in *her* house, would change this to *his*. All in all, therefore, it would seem that the reading "Nympha and the church in her house" deserves the preference. For the names Nympha, Nymphas, see N.T.C. on Philippians, p. 139, footnote 116.

[171] F. W. Beare, in his comment on this passage (in *The Interpreter's Bible*, Vol. 11, p. 239) opines that it was the church of Hierapolis which met at the home of Nympha. But, after the analogy of Rom. 16:23, written from Corinth (see Rom. 16:1, 23; cf. I Cor. 1:14), and I Cor. 16:19, written from Ephesus (I Cor. 16:8), it would seem more natural that when a house-church and the owner of the house are mentioned in close connection with a city (clearly implied or even mentioned by name), this church belongs to that particular community and not to some other place on the map.

4:16

V. *Exchange of Letters Requested*

16. **And when this letter has been read among y o u.** The letter, after it
has been delivered to the proper ecclesiastical authorities at Colosse by
Tychicus, will be read by the lector to the congregation assembled for worship. Now when this has taken place, says Paul, **see to it that it is read also
in the church of the Laodiceans.** The believers of nearby Laodicea will not
only be *interested* in this letter coming from the beloved apostle Paul, they
will also be spiritually *benefited* by it. So it must also be read in their midst.
So far there are no difficulties. But now Paul continues: **and that y o u also
read the one from Laodicea.** Altogether too large a literature has been built
up around these few words. Countless conjectures have been made regarding this "letter from Laodicea." [172]

The main ones are as follows. Paul had reference to:

(1) *A letter written by the Laodiceans.*

According to most of the advocates of this view it was addressed to the
apostle himself.

This theory was strongly advocated, among others, by Theodore of Mopsuestia (A. D. 350-428), classical representative of the school of Antioch.
John Calvin's defense of this view was no less vigorous. Said he, "Afflicted
with double mental aberration are those who think that it was written by
Paul to the Laodiceans. I have no doubt that it was an epistle sent to Paul,
the perusal of which might be profitable to the Colossians, as neighboring
towns usually have many things in common. However, . . . some worthless
person, I know not who, had the audacity to forge an epistle that is so insipid that it is impossible to conceive of anything more foreign to the spirit
of Paul." [173]

No doubt Calvin was influenced by eagerness to reject the spurious *Epistle
to the Laodiceans;* perhaps also by hesitancy to accept a "lost" Pauline
epistle.

Among the many objections to theory (1) are the following:

a. If Paul had this letter in his possession, why should he ask the Colossians to get it from the Laodiceans?

b. How did he know that the Laodiceans had made a copy of their letter,
before sending it to Paul? But if they had made such a copy, how did the

---

[172] See J. B. Lightfoot's summary of theories, *op. cit.,* p. 274 and his lengthy discussion that follows the summary.
[173] The original statement is found in *Commentarius In Epistolam Pauli Ad Colossenses (Corpus Reformatorum,* vol. LXXX), Brunsvigae, 1895. — The marginal explanation of Col. 4:16 in the Dutch *Staten Bijbel* (I own a copy printed in 1643!)
defends the same view.

apostle know that they would be willing to give it to the Colossians and to let them read it to the church assembled for worship?

c. Why should he place these two on a par: a letter written by himself to the Colossians, under inspiration of the Holy Spirit, and an uninspired communication supposedly sent to him by the Laodiceans?

(2) *A letter written by Paul from Laodicea; perhaps Galatians or I Timothy or I Thessalonians or II Thessalonians.*

Objections:

a. Although Paul may very well have passed through Laodicea (see Introduction III A), namely, on his way to Ephesus (third missionary journey), the design of that trip was to confirm already established churches along the route of travel, and to reach Ephesus in order to spend some time there, as he had promised. On the trip there must have been little or no time for letter writing.

b. In all probability none of the letters to which reference was made was written from Laodicea. Galatians and I and II Thessalonians seem to have been written from Corinth (N.T.C. on I and II Thessalonians, pp. 15, 16). I Timothy probably originated in Macedonia (Philippi? see N.T.C. on I and II Timothy and Titus, pp. 39-41).

(3) *A letter written by Paul to Philemon.*

Since, according to this theory Philemon lived in Laodicea, this letter when it reached Colosse via Laodicea could be called "the letter from Laodicea."

Objection:

This theory has been discussed in some detail. See Introduction IV B; and see on Philem. 1, 2. Philemon, in all probability, did not live in Laodicea but in Colosse. Accordingly, there is no solid support for this view.

(4) *The letter to the Laodiceans which today is known as "the Apocryphal Epistle to the Laodiceans."* [174]

---

[174] It is a short apocryphal writing that occurs in many manuscripts of the Vulgate. It usually follows Colossians. But it antedates the Vulgate and can be found in old-Latin manuscripts before Jerome. And even in the Greek-speaking portion of the church between the fourth and eighth centuries reference is often made to "Paul's Epistle to the Laodiceans." The conclusion is warranted that it existed in Greek as well as in Latin; and if in Greek, it must have originated not later than the first half of the third century A. D. Its genuineness was defended by Gregory the Great (sixth century), Aelfric of Cerne (tenth century), John of Salisbury (twelfth century), and many others. It is found in several older editions of the English, German, Dutch and other Bibles. "For more than nine centuries this forged epistle hovered about the doors of the sacred Canon, without ever finding admission or being peremptorily excluded. At length the revival of learning dealt its death-blow to this as to so many other spurious pretensions" (Lightfoot, *op. cit.*, p. 299). For the Latin text of this forgery see Lightfoot, *op. cit.*, pp. 287-289; for Lightfoot's reconstruction of the Greek text, *op. cit.*, pp. 293, 294; and for two forms of the letter in its old English dress, *op. cit.*, pp. 298, 299.

195

Objections:

a. This letter is nothing but "a cento of Pauline phrases strung together without any definite connection or any clear object" (Lightfoot).

b. Jerome already stated that "it is rejected by all." The Council of Nicea (A. D. 787) warned against it.

c. It was obviously fabricated to satisfy curiosity with respect to Col. 4:16b.

d. Since such a disproportionately large part of this small letter was lifted from Paul's Epistle to the Philippians, it is evident that it does not even fit the Lycus Valley situation.

(5) *The canonical Epistle of Paul to the Ephesians.*

This theory has gained many adherents. It is generally linked with the "circular letter" view of Ephesians, though the latter theory is not really dependent upon it. According to this interpretation of Col. 4:16b, as soon as "Ephesians" in its circuit of the churches has been read to the church of Laodicea it must, in accordance with Paul's wishes, be sent on to Colosse in exchange for "Colossians."

Evaluation:

Conclusive proof for the correctness of this theory is lacking. It is supplied neither here in Colossians nor in Eph. 1:1. (The discussion of the latter passage would be appropriate in a Commentary on Ephesians.) On the other hand, though it is merely a theory, it is not exposed to the objections that count against the preceding four. It proceeds on the valid assumptions that both letters to which reference is made in Col. 4:16 were written *by the apostle Paul* and *to churches.* According to this theory, then, "Ephesians," reaching the Colossians from Laodicea, will thus truthfully become the letter "from the Laodiceans."

(6) *A genuine letter of Paul addressed to the Laodiceans, but now lost.*

As before (see above, under (5)), when this letter reaches the Colossians it will be the letter "from the Laodiceans."

Evaluation:

Here, too, proof is lacking, and here, too, the theory is free from the objections mentioned as valid against the first four.

The fact that this theory proceeds from the assumption that a letter written by Paul can have been "lost," in the sense that it was not handed down to posterity, should not count as a valid objection. Not all of Paul's letters have been preserved (see I Cor. 5:9). Those favoring this theory are of the opinion that the reason why, in God's providence, Paul's letter to the Laodiceans was not preserved may well have been that the distinctive portion of the epistle — that wherein it differed from Colossians —, though certainly of real value for the membership in the Lycus Valley (at least for that of Laodicea and Colosse), was lacking in *abiding* and *universal* significance.

It must be borne in mind that Tychicus had to pass through Laodicea in order to reach Colosse. In all probability he traveled the road which Paul himself had used, but now Tychicus traveled it in reverse (from W. to E.). See Introduction II A, map 4. Would it not have been strange if, having delivered "Ephesians" to the elders at Ephesus, and being on his way to deliver "Colossians" to the authorities at Colosse, he would have had no missive from Paul to the church of Laodicea through which town he was passing? Both theories supply this need. According to (5) Tychicus could have told the Laodiceans, "Paul's letter which I left at Ephesus will be sent to y o u presently. Having read it, send it on to the Colossians, who will send y o u, in exchange, the letter which we are going to deliver to them." According to (6) Tychicus, welcomed by the Laodiceans, would deliver to them Paul's letter addressed specifically to them. That letter itself probably contained a request that it (or a copy of it) be sent to the Colossians in exchange for the one addressed to them.

Against (6) it is sometimes urged that Paul would hardly have asked the Colossians to convey his greetings to the brothers in Laodicea, and to Nympha and the church in her house (Col. 4:15), if at the same time he had been writing a letter addressed specifically to the Laodiceans. Others, however, answer that for a heart so filled with love and friendliness such a thing can be considered neither impossible nor unnatural. Besides, objections have also been advanced against (5), particularly against the circular letter theory.

There are times, in the course of exegesis, when a precise answer is impossible, and the choice must be left between two alternatives, in this case theory (5) and theory (6).

---

17 And say to Archippus, Attend to the ministry which you have received in the Lord, that you fulfil it.

4:17

VI. *Crisp Directive for Archippus*

17. And say to Archippus. Archippus was a member of the family of Philemon who lived in Colosse, and at whose home the church was accustomed to gather for worship. In Philem. 2 the apostle bestows on him the signal honor of calling him "our fellow-soldier." See in this volume, on Philem. 1, 2. As he was probably *the son* of Philemon and Apphia he cannot have been very old. We may, perhaps, compare him to Timothy to whom Paul, after his release from the present Roman imprisonment, was going to write, "Let no one despise your youth" (I Tim. 4:12). Those words were addressed to Timothy when he was perhaps somewhere between 34 and 39 years of age. See N.T.C. on I and II Timothy and Titus, p. 157.

Now for this companion-in-arms, Archippus, the apostle has a special message. He expresses it in language which, because of its terse, commanding character, must have sounded all the more direct and unequivocal. Paul tells the church of Colosse to say to Archippus, **Attend to the ministry which you have received in the Lord, that you fulfil it.** Nothing further is said about the nature of this "ministry." Nor are we told why Archippus had to be thus admonished. Some have thought that the reason was that he lacked diligence or energy, that he was somewhat on the lazy side, always postponing to the indefinite future ("mañana") the tasks that needed immediate attention. The objection to this theory is that in that case Paul would hardly have called him "our fellow-*soldier*." Perhaps a safer method of reaching a probable answer to the double question: a. "What was this ministry?" and b. "Why did Paul choose this method of reminding Archippus of his responsibility?" is to study the exact meaning of the expression used. Archippus must attend to the *ministry*. The word in italics is the equivalent of the Greek *diakonia*. In Paul's writings it has several meanings.[175] Prominent among these meanings is, however, the spiritual one, according to which the word has reference to the office of *the ministry*, and the service implied in that office. In the present instance we can, perhaps, proceed even farther in arriving at a reasonable conclusion with respect to the sense of the term in Col. 4:17. The latter passage has a very close parallel in II Tim. 4:5, as follows:

Col. 4:17b	II Tim. 4:5b
"Attend to the ministry which you have received in the Lord, that you fulfil it."	"Do the work of an evangelist, your ministry discharge to the full."

Now in Timothy's case that "ministry" was "the work of an evangelist" or gospel-preacher (Acts 21:8; Eph. 4:11). Timothy, who, when Paul will

---

175 Paul uses it 22 times. Not in every instance are commentators and translators in complete agreement as to its exact, contextual significance. Thus, in I Cor. 12:5 it is rendered variously: *service, ministration, dispensation, ministry;* and similar variety obtains with respect to the meanings assigned to it in II Cor. 3:7, 8, 9 (twice). Fairly certain, however, is the meaning *relief, care* (for the poor), *contribution* (to relieve the needy), in Rom. 15:31; II Cor. 8:4; 9:1, 12, 13. *Service,* of some kind or of any kind whatever, seems to be the meaning in I Cor. 16:15 and in II Cor. 11:8. In many passages *spiritual office* (for example, that of apostle or of evangelist) and/or its *administration* ("ministry" or "the ministry") is clearly shown to be the meaning in the light of the specific context in which the word is used. It is then defined in such terms as the *diakonia* "of reconciliation," the *diakonia* "for the building up of the body of Christ" or is used as a synonym of an expression like "the work of an evangelist." Clear examples of this usage — though in a few cases even this is disputed — are the following: Rom. 11:13; 12:7; II Cor. 4:1; 5:18; 6:3; Eph. 4:12; I Tim. 1:12; II Tim. 4:5, 11. It would seem that Col. 4:17 also belongs here. As to the meaning of *the cognate verb* see N.T.C. on I and II Timothy and Titus, p. 135, especially footnote 67; and for *the cognate noun* see the same volume, p. 130, especially footnote 65.

be writing these words, will be in Ephesus as Paul's envoy, must "herald the word, being on hand in season, out of season." He must "reprove, rebuke, admonish, with all longsuffering and teaching" (II Tim. 4:2).

In Colosse, too, someone must have been in charge of the flock. When Colossians was being written and brought to its destination it could not have been Epaphras, the minister of the churches in the Lycus Valley, for just now he was with Paul in Rome, from which he is sending greetings (4:12). Who was it? In view of the striking similarity between Col. 4:17 and II Tim. 4:5b, the conclusion does not seem unreasonable that this interim-shepherd was none other than Archippus. Further, since he, too, just like Timothy, was probably rather young and somewhat diffident, wondering perhaps whether the church would give him — a man so inexperienced — its full co-operation in this important work, the apostle, very tactfully, or-ders *the congregation* itself to encourage him by saying to him, as it were, "Go right ahead, we are with you and we promise to help you in every way. The task you are trying to perform was given to you by the Lord, and you are discharging it with strength imparted by him." Hence, "Attend to the ministry which you have received in the Lord, that you fulfil it." All this is, of course, no more than a reasonable conjecture.

---

18 The greetings by my own, Paul's, hand. Remember my bonds. Grace (be) with y o u.

4:18

VII. *Personal Greeting, Reminder, Benediction*

18a. The greeting by my own, Paul's, hand. It was customary for Paul to write a few words of greetings with his own hand (see II Thess. 3:17; cf. I Cor. 16:21). He had a twofold purpose in doing this:

a. to mark the autographed letter as a genuine one, an authentic product of the mind and heart of Paul (II Thess. 3:17); and

b. to discourage the spread of spurious letters (see II Thess. 2:1, 2).

It is also clear from this that Paul was in the habit of dictating his letters (see, in addition to the references given above, Rom. 16:22; Gal. 6:11; and see on Philem. 19).

18b. Remember my bonds. It is a sign of Paul's true greatness that he did not deem himself to be too exalted to solicit continued sympathy and inter-cession in behalf of himself, a prisoner! See on 1:9; cf. 4:3.

18c. Grace (be) with y o u. In this shortest possible form the benediction is also found in I Tim. 6:21 (cf. II Tim. 4:22b). But though brief it is rich in meaning, for grace is the greatest and most basic blessing of all. It is God's favor in Christ to the undeserving, transforming their hearts and lives and leading them on to glory. The apostle, who in his opening salutation had spoken of *grace* (followed by *peace*), now closes this letter by again authoritatively pronouncing *this* grace (note the article; hence really "the grace") upon the believers in Colosse.[176]

Seed Thoughts of Colossians 4:2-18

(1) "Persevere in prayer." Sometimes the answer does not come at once because we are not as yet ready to receive the blessing; sometimes, because the blessing is not yet ready for us. Besides, if whenever we prayed God *immediately* granted the petition, would we appreciate his blessings? (verse 2a).

(2) ". . . keeping alert in it *with thanksgiving.*" Paul was *a prisoner* when he wrote this. How true are the lines:

> "Stone walls do not a prison make,
> Nor iron bars a cage." (Lovelace)

From his first Roman imprisonment the apostle wrote four letters that have come down to us: Colossians, Philemon, Ephesians, and Philippians. Colossians overflows with "thanksgiving" (1:3, 12; 2:7; 3:15, 16, 17; 4:2); Ephesians, with "grace" (1:2, 6, 7; 2:5, 7, 8; 3:2, 7, 8; 4:7, 29; 6:24) and "glory" (1:6, 12, 14, 17, 18; 3:13, 16, 21); Philippians, with "joy" (1:4, 18, 25; 2:2, 17, 18, 28, 29; 3:1; 4:1, 4, 10); and all four with "love" (see especially Philem. 1, 5, 7, 9, 16, and cf. 12), (verse 2b).

(3) ". . . praying also for us, that God may open to us a door for the message." The prisoner prays not for a door of *exit* from prison, but for a door for the *entrance* of the message (verse 3).

(4) ". . . (praying) that I may make it clear, (and may speak) as I ought to speak." Not only *what* we say but also *how* we say it is important (cf. Eph. 4:15), (verse 4).

(5) ". . . making the most of the opportunity" or ". . . buying up the opportunity." For some "Time is *money*." For Paul it is "opportunity" to conduct oneself wisely toward outsiders (verse 5).

(6) ". . . so that y o u may know how to answer each individual." Not only *what* we say and *how* we say it is important (see No. 4 above) but also *to whom* we say it (verse 6).

(7) "All my affairs will Tychicus make known to you . . ." Some things are better *said* than *written* (verses 7 and 8).

(8) ". . . Onesimus, the faithful and beloved brother"; "Mark, the

---

[176] Some manuscripts add "Amen," but this addition may stem from liturgical usage or may have been added by a scribe who happened to remember that this was the concluding word in Galatians and, according to the best reading, also in Romans.

cousin of Barnabas . . . if he comes to y o u receive him." Brother *A* is very generous in his willingness to overlook the sin which brother *B* committed against brother *C*, but not nearly as eager to forgive *D*'s trespass against himself *(A)*. Paul, however, does both. He forgives Onesimus for having wronged Philemon, but he also forgives Mark for having wronged himself, i.e., Paul (see Acts 13:13; 15:38; II Tim. 4:11), (verses 9 and 10).

(9) "Of those of the circumcision these are the only co-workers for the kingdom of God who have been a comfort to me." The most privileged individuals are not always the most profitable (verse 11).

(10) "Epaphras, who is one of y o u, a servant of Christ Jesus, greets y o u, always wrestling for y o u in his prayers that y o u may stand firm, mature and fully assured in all the will of God." The mark of a great leader is that he is eager to speak well of a person and to bolster confidence in him. Paul did this again and again (verses 12 and 13).

(11) "Luke, the beloved physician, greets y o u, and so does Demas." Here these two are mentioned favorably, in one breath. Later the contrast would become apparent, and Paul would write, "Demas has deserted me, because he fell in love with the present world . . . Luke is the only one with me." Two kingdom workers may be working side by side, doing the same kind of work, as far as men can see. God sees the heart (verse 14; cf. II Tim. 4:10, 11).

(12) ". . . and the church in her house." In a sense every home should be a house-church (verse 15).

(13) ". . . see to it that it is read also in the church of the Laodiceans, and that y o u also read the one from Laodicea." This not only because these two *letters* were important to the two churches, but also because the two *congregations* should be important to each other (verse 16).

(14) ". . . that you fulfil it." Every God-given task must be fulfilled (verse 17).

(15) "Remember my bonds." A truly great man is not too proud to ask that he be remembered in prayer (verse 18).

Paul's Epistle to the Colossians

Chapter 1

1 Paul, an apostle of Christ Jesus through the will of God, and Timothy our brother, 2 to the saints and believing brothers in Christ at Colosse; grace to y o u and peace from God our Father.

3 While praying for y o u we are always thanking God, the Father of our Lord Jesus Christ, 4 because we have heard of y o u r faith in Christ Jesus and of the love which y o u cherish for all the saints, 5 by reason of the hope laid up for y o u in the heavens, of which y o u have previously heard in the message of the truth, namely, the gospel, 6 which made its entrance felt among y o u, as indeed in the entire world it is bearing fruit and growing — so also among yourselves from the day y o u heard and came to acknowledge the grace of God in its genuine character, 7 as y o u learned it from Epaphras our beloved fellow-servant, who is a faithful minister of Christ on our behalf, 8 and has made known to us y o u r love in the Spirit.

9 And for this reason, from the day we heard it we never stopped praying for y o u, asking that y o u may be filled with clear knowledge of his will (such clear knowledge consisting) in all spiritual wisdom and understanding, 10 so as to live lives worthy of the Lord, to (his) complete delight, in every good work bearing fruit, and growing in the clear knowledge of God; 11 being invigorated with all vigor, in accordance with his glorious might, so as to exercise every kind of endurance and longsuffering; 12 with joy giving thanks to the Father who qualified y o u for a share in the inheritance of the saints in the light 13 and who rescued us out of the domain of darkness and transplanted us into the kingdom of the Son of his love, 14 in whom we have our redemption, the forgiveness of our sins.

15 Who is the image of the invisible God, the firstborn of every creature, 16 for in him were created all things in the heavens and on the earth, the visible and the invisible, whether thrones or dominions or principalities or authorities, all things through him and with a view to him have been created; 17 and he is before all things, and all things hold together in him. 18 And he is the head of the body, the church; who is the beginning, the firstborn from the dead, that in all things he might have the pre-eminence, 19 for in him he [God] was pleased to have all the fulness dwell, 20 and through him to reconcile all things to himself, having made peace through the blood of his cross, through him, whether the things on the earth or the things in the heavens.

21 And y o u, who once were estranged and hostile in disposition, as shown by y o u r wicked works, 22 he in his body of flesh through his death has now reconciled, in order to present y o u holy, faultless, and blameless before himself; 23 if, indeed, y o u continue in the faith, founded and firm, and are not moved away from the hope that is derived from the gospel which y o u have heard, which was preached among every creature under heaven, and of which I, Paul, became a minister.

24 I am now rejoicing amid my sufferings for y o u, and what is lacking in the afflictions of Christ I in his stead am supplying in my flesh, for his body, which is the church, 25 of which I became a minister, according to the stewardship of God given to me for y o u r benefit, to give full scope to the word of God, 26 the mystery hidden for ages and generations but now made manifest to his saints; 27 to whom God was pleased to make known what (is) the riches of the glory of this

mystery among the Gentiles, which is Christ in y o u, the hope of glory; 28 whom we proclaim, admonishing every man and teaching every man in all wisdom, in order that we may present every man perfect in Christ; 29 for which I am laboring, striving by his energy working powerfully within me.

Chapter 2

1 For I want y o u to know how greatly I strive for y o u, and for those at Laodicea, and for all who have not seen my face in the flesh, 2 in order that their hearts may be strengthened, they themselves being welded together in love, and this with a view to all the riches of assured understanding, with a view to the clear knowledge of the mystery of God, namely, Christ; 3 in whom all the treasures of wisdom and knowledge are hidden. 4 I say this in order that no one may mislead y o u by persuasive argument. 5 For, although in the flesh I am absent, yet in the spirit I am with y o u, rejoicing to see y o u r good order and the firmness of y o u r faith in Christ.

6 As therefore y o u accepted Christ Jesus the Lord, (so) in him continue to live, 7 rooted and being built up in him and being established in the faith, just as y o u were taught, overflowing with thanksgiving. 8 Be on y o u r guard lest there be any one who carries y o u off as spoil by means of his philosophy and empty deceit, according to the tradition of men, according to the rudiments of the world, and not according to Christ; 9 for in him all the fulness of the godhead dwells bodily, 10 and in him y o u have attained to fulness, namely, in him who is the head of every principality and authority, 11 in whom also y o u were circumcised with a circumcision made without hands, by the putting off of the body of the flesh in the circumcision of Christ, 12 having been buried with him in y o u r baptism in which y o u were also raised with him through faith in the operative power of God who raised him from the dead. 13 And y o u, who were dead through y o u r trespasses and the uncircumcision of y o u r flesh, y o u he made alive together with him, having forgiven us all our trespasses, 14 having blotted out the hand-written document that was against us, which by means of its requirements testified against us, and he took it out of the way by nailing it to the cross, 15 and having stripped the principalities and the authorities of their power, he publicly exposed them to disgrace by triumphing over them in him.

16 Therefore allow no one to pass judgment on y o u in questions of food or drink or with respect to a festival or a new moon or a sabbath: 17 things that were only a shadow of those that were coming, while the object casting the shadow is to be found with Christ.

18 Let no one disqualify y o u by delighting in humility and the worship of the angels, taking his stand on the things he has seen, without cause puffed up by his fleshly mind, 19 and not keeping firm hold on the Head, from whom the entire body, supported and held together by joints and ligaments, grows with a growth (that is) from God.

20 If with Christ y o u died to the rudiments of the world, why, as though y o u were (still) living in the world, do y o u submit to regulations, 21 "Do not handle, Do not taste, Do not touch" — 22 referring to things that are meant for destruction by their consumption — according to the precepts and doctrines of men? 23 Regulations of this kind, though to be sure having a reputation for wisdom because of their self-imposed ritual, humility, and unsparing treatment of the body, are of no value whatever, (serving only) to indulge the flesh.

COLOSSIANS

Chapter 3

1 If then y o u were raised with Christ, seek *the things that are above,* where Christ is, seated at the right hand of God. 2 On the things that are above set y o u r minds, not on the things that are upon the earth. 3 For y o u died, and y o u r life is hid with Christ in God. 4 When Christ (who is) our life is manifested, then y o u also will be manifested with him in glory.

5 Put to death therefore y o u r members that (are) upon the earth: immorality, impurity, passion, evil desire, and greed, which is idolatry; 6 on account of which things the wrath of God is coming; 7 in which things y o u also walked at one time, when y o u were living in them. 8 But now y o u, too, lay them all aside: wrath, anger, malice, slander, shameful language from y o u r mouth. 9 No longer lie to one another, seeing that y o u have put off the old man with his practices, 10 and have put on the new man, who is being renewed for full knowledge according to the image of him who created him, 11 where there cannot be Greek and Jew, circumcision and uncircumcision, barbarian, Scythian, slave, freeman, but Christ (is) all and in all.

12 Put on, therefore, as God's elect, holy and beloved, a heart of compassion, kindness, lowliness, meekness, longsuffering, 13 enduring one another, and forgiving each other if anyone have a complaint against anyone. Just as the Lord has forgiven y o u, so do y o u also. 14 And above all these things (put on) love, which is the bond of perfection. 15 And let the peace of Christ, for which y o u were called in one body, rule in y o u r hearts, and be thankful. 16 Let the word of Christ dwell among y o u richly; in all wisdom teaching and admonishing one another, (and) by means of psalms, hymns, and spiritual songs singing to God in a thankful spirit, with all y o u r heart. 17 And whatever y o u do in word or in deed, (do) all in the name of the Lord Jesus, giving thanks to God the Father through him.

18 Wives, be submissive to y o u r husbands, as is fitting in the Lord. 19 Husbands, love y o u r wives, and do not be harsh toward them. 20 Children, obey y o u r parents in all things, for this is well-pleasing in the Lord. 21 Fathers, do not exasperate y o u r children, in order that they may not lose heart. 22 Slaves, obey in all things those who according to the flesh are y o u r masters, not with eye-service as men-pleasers but with singleness of heart, fearing the Lord. 23 Whatever y o u do, put y o u r soul into the work, as for the Lord and not for men, 24 knowing that from the Lord y o u will receive the recompense, namely, the inheritance. (It is) the Lord Christ (whom) y o u are serving. 25 For, the wrong-doer will receive (the conquences of) what he has wrongly done. And there is no partiality.

Chapter 4

1 Masters, render to y o u r slaves that which is fair and square, knowing that y o u also have a Master in heaven.

2 Persevere in prayer, keeping alert in it with thanksgiving; 3 at the same time praying also for us, that God may open to us a door for the message, to speak forth the mystery concerning Christ, on account of which I am in prison, 4 (praying) that I may make it clear, (and may speak) as I ought to speak.

5 Conduct yourselves wisely toward outsiders, making the most of the opportunity. 6 Let y o u r speech always be gracious, seasoned with salt, so that y o u may know how to answer each individual.

7 All my affairs will Tychicus make known to y o u, the beloved brother and faithful minister and fellow-servant in the Lord, 8 whom I am sending to

y o u for this very purpose, that y o u may know our circumstances and that he may strengthen y o u r hearts. 9 (He is) accompanied by Onesimus, the faithful and beloved brother, who is one of y o u. They will acquaint y o u with everything (that has taken place) here.

10 Aristarchus, my fellow-prisoner, greets y o u; so does Mark, the cousin of Barnabas — concerning whom y o u received instructions; if he comes to y o u receive him — ; 11 and Jesus who is called Justus. Of those who are of the circumcision these are the only co-workers for the kingdom of God who have been a comfort to me. 12 Epaphras, who is one of y o u, a servant of Christ Jesus, greets y o u, always wrestling for y o u in his prayers that y o u may stand firm, mature and fully assured in all the will of God. 13 For I can testify concerning him that he has put himself to much trouble for y o u and for those in Laodicea and those in Hierapolis. 14 Luke, the beloved physician, greets y o u, and so does Demas. 15 Extend greetings to the brothers in Laodicea, and to Nympha and the church in her house.

16 And when this letter has been read among y o u, see to it that it is read also in the church of the Laodiceans, and that y o u also read the one from Laodicea.

17 And say to Archippus, Attend to the ministry which you have received in the Lord, that you fulfil it.

18 The greetings by my own, Paul's, hand. Remember my bonds. Grace (be) with y o u.

Commentary

on

The Epistle to Philemon

Outline of Philemon

Theme: *Paul's Request for the Kind Reception of the Fugitive Slave Onesimus*

   I. Opening Salutation, verses 1-3

  II. Thanksgiving and Prayer, verses 4-7

 III. Plea in Behalf of Onesimus, Including Request for Lodging, verses 8-22

 IV. Greetings and Closing Salutation, verses 23-25

EPISTLE TO PHILEMON

PHILEMON

1 Paul, a prisoner of Christ Jesus, and Timothy our brother, to Philemon our beloved (brother) and fellow-worker 2 and to Apphia our sister and to Archippus our fellow-soldier and to the church in your house; 3 grace to y o u and peace from God our Father and the Lord Jesus Christ.

1-3

I. *Opening Salutation*

For the form or structure of Paul's letters see on Col. 1:1, 2. For a discussion of the persons addressed here in Philem. 1, 2, and for all other matters of an introductory nature see the opening section of this book, the Introduction to Colossians and Philemon.

1, 2. The Salutation opens with the words **Paul, a prisoner.** Cf. verse 9; also Eph. 3:1; 4:1; II Tim. 1:8. He adds **of Christ Jesus.** In every reference to himself as a prisoner Paul always stresses the fact that as such he belongs to his Lord, for it was while engaged in *his* service and thus for *his* sake that he was imprisoned. Moreover, all the details of the imprisonment as well as its outcome, whether it be the death-sentence or acquittal, are in the hands that were pierced for this prisoner, those very hands that now control the entire universe in the interest of the church (Eph. 1:22). Paul's imprisonment is therefore a very honorable one. The mention of himself as a prisoner of Christ Jesus is also very tactful, probably implying, "In comparison with the *sacrifice* that I am making is not the *favor* which I am asking you to grant a rather easy matter?" See Summary at the close of this chapter for a discussion of the apostle's tactfulness as shown in this letter. See also in the Appendix, "Scripture on Tactfulness." Paul continues, **and Timothy our brother.** For this addition see on Col. 1:1. For "brother" see also Philem. 7 and 20, where this designation of intimate spiritual relationship and tender love is applied to Philemon (giving us the right to insert it parenthetically after the words "our beloved" in verse 1), and verse 16, where it is used with reference to Onesimus.

The letter is addressed **to Philemon our beloved (brother) and fellow-worker.** In Christ and for his sake, Philemon, a resident of Colosse, is loved by Paul, by Timothy, and by every believer who has heard of him. He is loved by Christ and has the characteristics of a brother. In the companion-letter, Colossians, Paul speaks of Epaphras as "beloved *fellow-servant*" (1:7), of Tychicus and Onesimus as "beloved *brothers*" (14:7, 9), and of Luke as "the beloved *physician*" (4:14). Philemon is also called "fellow-worker." It is not impossible that he had been assisting Paul in spiritual work during the latter's prolonged ministry in Ephesus and had continued his evangelical labors after the apostle's departure from Asia Minor. But, aside from this, would not what is recorded concerning him in Philem. 7 entitle him to be called fellow-worker? Paul had many fellow-workers. Among them were such *men* as Urbanus (Rom. 16:9), Timothy (Rom. 16:21), Apollos (I Cor. 3:9), Titus (II Cor. 8:23), Epaphroditus (Phil. 2:25), Syzygus and Clement (Phil. 4:3), Jesus Justus (Col. 4:11), Mark, Aristarchus, Demas, and Luke (Philem. 23); *the married couple* Aquila and Priscilla or Prisca (Rom. 16:3); and such *women* as Euodia and Syntyche (Phil. 4:2) and those mentioned in Rom. 16. What should be stressed in this connection is the fact that the apostle considers them fellow-workers not only in the sense that they were *his* but also in the sense that they were *God's* co-laborers. And in the latter sense Paul himself was also a fellow-worker (I Cor. 3:9).

Very closely associated with Philemon and mentioned in one breath with him as those to whom the opening salutation and in a more general sense the entire letter is addressed are two other persons. Hence, the sentence continues, **and to Apphia our sister and to Archippus our fellow-soldier.** After mentioning them and "the church in *your* (Philemon's) house," and pronouncing upon them all (y o u) the salutation proper (verse 3), the writer again more specifically addresses Philemon himself (using the pronouns *you* and *your,* not y o u and y o u r) throughout the entire body of the letter (verse 6b is probably no exception), returning to the plural (y o u r), as was to be expected, in the reference to the prayers of the congregation (verse 22) and in the closing salutation (verse 25). The inference would seem to be warranted that Philemon, who with the aforementioned exceptions, is addressed in the singular throughout, is the head of the family, and that Apphia and Archippus are members of this family. Apphia may well have been Philemon's wife, and Archippus their son. Although this view of the matter cannot be demonstrated beyond possibility of contradition, deviating theories have failed to convince many apart from those who propose them. It is not difficult to understand this use of the second person singular throughout the body of the letter. The missive is a request for the kind reception of the fugitive slave Onesimus who is being returned to his master. It is, accordingly, in the final analysis up to Philemon himself — not up to Apphia, Archippus, or even the church — whether this request will be granted. But although Philemon himself must make the decision, the others, too, must hear the letter. Let them therefore assist Philemon to do his duty. Let them also hear how Paul, by the inspiration of the Holy Spirit, would solve the important problem of the fugitive slave. Their minds, too, will thus be illumined and their sympathies broadened.

Apphia is called "our sister." This is true not *literally* or *physically,* as Mary and Martha were sisters of Lazarus (John 11:1), nor *metaphorically,* referring to a church (II John 13), but *spiritually:* Apphia is "our sister" in the sense in which Timothy is "our brother," namely, as belonging to the family of faith. She is our sister *in the Lord.* Archippus is called "our fellow-soldier," a title which in the New Testament is given to only one other person, namely, Epaphroditus (Phil. 2:25). With respect to this same Archippus the apostle has issued a crisp command (Col. 4:17). Lest anyone in hearing this command should begin to hold this young brother in low esteem, Paul, with wonderful *tact* bestows upon him this title of honor, meaning "our companion in arms." Cf. N.T.C. on Philippians 2:25.

Paul adds, **and to the church in your house.** Since in the first and second centuries church-buildings in the sense in which we think of them today were as yet not available, families would hold services in their own homes. Such services would be attended by the members of the household: father, mother, children, servants. If the house was large enough to accommodate others, they, too, were invited. The early church numbered many hospitable members, ready and eager to offer the facilities of their homes for religious purposes. Thus, in Jerusalem "many were gathered together and were praying" in the house of Mary, the mother of John Mark (Acts 12:12). Lydia graciously invited Paul, Silas, Timothy, and Luke to use her home as their headquarters (Acts 16:15, 40). Wherever Aquila and Priscilla went they would if at all possible welcome the worshipers to their home. Hence, both at Ephesus (I Cor. 16:19) and at Rome (Rom. 16:3-5) there was "a church in their house." Laodicea, too, had its house-church (see on Col. 4:15). So did Corinth, at the home of Gaius (Rom. 16:23). If the number of believers in any town was small, one house-church might be sufficient; if large or widely separated, more than one would be necessary. So it is not surprising that Philemon, too, had shown similar hospitality. Since the membership of the Colossian church was probably small numerically (see Introduction II B 4) it is entirely possible that the entire congregation gathered for worship in his home.[177]

---

[177] The transition from private house, whose owner had offered its facilities for public worship, to spacious church-edifice, built expressly for congregational services, was probably gradual. Cf. the transition from buggy to automobile. Thus the oldest known church discovered by archaeologists was in reality a modified once-private dwelling. The house had been built A. D. 232-233 at Dura Europos in eastern Syria on the Euphrates. Three of its rooms had been changed into a chapel with room for 100 people. For full description see C. Hopkins and P. V. C. Baur, *Christian Church at Dura-Europos;* cf. G. E. Wright, *Biblical Archaeology,* pp. 245-247. Even earlier is

3. The opening salutation proper follows in the familiar words, **grace to y o u and peace from God our Father and the Lord Jesus Christ.** Thus there is pronounced upon Philemon, Apphia, Archippus and the entire congregation that gathers at Philemon's house *grace,* that is, God's spontaneous, unmerited favor in action, his sovereign, freely bestowed loving-kindness in operation, and its result, *peace,* that is, the conviction of reconciliation through the blood of the cross, true spiritual wholeness and prosperity, these two blessings (grace and peace) coming from God our Father and the Lord Jesus Christ. For further details of explanation and for a discussion of the question whether this salutation is an exclamation, a declaration, or perhaps merely an expression of a pious wish, see N.T.C. on I and II Thessalonians, pp. 40-45, 153, 154.

---

4 I thank my God always, making mention of you in my prayers, 5 because I hear of your love and of the faith which you have, (the latter) toward the Lord Jesus, and (the former) for all the saints, 6 (praying) that the sharing to which your faith gives rise may be energetically stimulated for Christ by the clear recognition of all the good that is ours. 7 For I have derived much joy and comfort from your love, because the hearts of the saints have been refreshed through you, brother.

4-7

II. *Thanksgiving and Prayer*

4, 5. As usual the salutation is followed by the thansgiving and the prayer. The apostle can honestly write: **I thank my God always,**[178] **making mention of you in my prayers.** He continues, **because I hear of your love and of the faith which you have, (the latter) toward the Lord Jesus, and (the former) for all the saints.** Epaphras, the spiritual leader of the Colossian church, a Colossian himself (Col. 4:12, 13), and now with Paul (Philem. 23), must have given the apostle much valuable information about conditions in that congregation. In that connection he had also made mention of Philemon's work for the Lord and of his generosity and hospitality. The fugitive slave Onesimus in all probability supplied further details. After his conversion his attitude toward his master must have changed sufficiently to say some good things about him. And there may have been other informers. Thus the apostle had heard about Philemon's love. Had he not

---

the implied distinction in I Cor. 11:18, 22, between strictly private homes and what must have been a rather spacious gathering-place for the church. With the conversion of Constantine (A. D. 323-337) church architecture received the boost it needed.

[178] See on Col. 1:3, footnote 25, for the reason why the word *always* should be construed with "I thank my God," rather than with "making mention."

opened his house for religious services? See verses 1, 2. Had he not "re-freshed the saints" in other ways also? See verse 7. This love for God's conse-crated children had its root, as always, in faith directed toward the Lord Jesus.[179]

6. Verse 6 follows naturally. It is connected not only with verse 4, because it gives the content of Paul's prayer for Philemon, but also with verse 5. In the latter passage mention was made of the addressee's "love for all the saints." This love was demonstrated in a willingness on the part of Philemon to share his bounties with others. Undoubtedly he had made many valuable contributions, both material and spiritual, to the welfare of the little com-munity. Let him then demonstrate this same attitude of liberality, and at the same time the genuine character of his faith, in still another respect, namely, by showing mercy to Onesimus. This thought, which pervades the entire letter and is about to be expressed in verses 8-21, underlies the statement in verse 6. This is true no matter which of the following two renderings of this admittedly difficult passage be adopted. Whether the sense be:
a. (praying) that your participation in the faith may become clearly known by y o u r good deed, etc., or

---

[179] Some believe that both the love and the faith have the Lord Jesus and all the saints as objects. They interpret *faith* to mean *fidelity*. As a result, these interpreters also deny the chiastic structure of the passage. But the fact that the love is for *the saints,* and the faith is directed toward *the Lord,* is clear from the parallel pas-sages: Eph. 1:15; Col. 1:14.
Note, accordingly, the chiastic structure of the sentence:

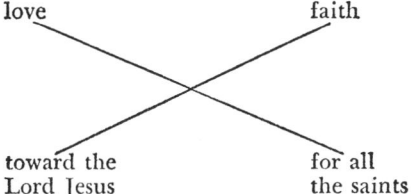

This criss-cross structure occurs frequently in Paul. See N.T.C. on Phil. 2:3, 8, 12; on Col. 1:10; 1:16; 3:11; and on I Tim. 3:16. In the present instance the reason for this arrangement is probably the following: the apostle wants Philemon, who has already manifested his love to others, to show kindness to Onesimus also. Hence, this being uppermost in Paul's mind, he mentions *love* first of all and traces it to its source, namely, genuine faith in the Lord Jesus. This enables him to refer now to the objects of this love: all the saints (verse 5b), which connects immediately with the next verse (verse 6) in which he prays that this *sharing* which he has just now commended in Philemon may become very effective. *Implied* is clearly the thought: "Now take one more step, beloved brother; extend this same kindness and love to Onesimus." And so, in verse 7, the apostle once more praises Philemon for the man-ner in which he has refreshed the hearts of the saints, adding that he (Paul) him-self has been gladdened and comforted by this. It will be evident that the chiastic structure in this instance lends itself best to Paul's purpose. *Love toward the saints* naturally occupies the two places of greatest importance in this causal modifier (verse 5), the first and the last place.

213

b. (praying) that the sharing to which your faith gives rise may be energetically stimulated for Christ by the clear recognition of all the good that is ours, in either case the basic *implication* is the same. It is a prayer that Philemon, who has already shown his unselfishness in so many ways, may take the next step also.[180]

---

[180] The differences in translation arise mainly from the fact that the passage contains several important words and phrases with different possible meanings or constructions; especially the following:
(1) Does κοινωνία as here used mean *participation* (in) or does it mean *sharing* (one's bounties with others?)
(2) Hence also: Does τῆς πίστεως mean *in the faith* or does it mean *of your faith,* that is, *springing from your faith?*
(3) What does εἰς Χριστόν mean and what does it modify?
(4) Does ἐν ἐπιγνώσει here signify *by the clear recognition* or rather *in the clear (or full) knowledge?*
(5) Does ἀγαθοῦ have reference to *the blessings* or *privileges that we enjoy* and which should stimulate us to show kindness to others, or does it have reference to *the good that we do?*
(6) And, as if this were not enough, there is the question as to which *reading* is correct: ἐν ἡμῖν or ἐν ὑμῖν. Is it *the good that is ours* or *the good that is y o u r s?*
Without going into great detail my answers are as follows: As to (1) Either meaning can be given to this word which frequently has the sense *fellowship.* For extensive discussion see N.T.C. on Philippians, pp. 51-54 and 93-95. However, if the meaning *participation* (in) is adopted, the reading ὑμῖν instead of ἡμῖν also receives the preference ("that your participation in the faith may become clearly known by your good deed"). But why the change from *your* to *y o u r?* Besides, there is another objection to the adoption of the reading ὑμῖν, as will be indicated under (6) below.
As to (2) The answer to the preceding determines this also. Hence, I prefer the rendering *springing from your faith* or *to which your faith gives rise.*
As to (3) The phrase εἰς Χριστόν is more naturally rendered *for Christ* than *in Christ.* As to what it modifies, it does not make much difference in the resultant meaning of the entire clause whether one translates "may be energetically stimulated (or "may become effective") for Christ by the clear recognition of all the good that is ours," or "may be energetically stimulated by the clear recognition of all the good that is ours for Christ (i.e., to his glory) ."
As to (4) The rendering *in the clear knowledge* makes it difficult to arrive at an intelligible meaning for the entire sentence. On the contrary, the translation *by the clear recognition* ("by the acknowledging," R.V.) leads to a sensible result which is in harmony with Pauline thought, as indicated in the explanation.
As to (5) Though the word used in the original may indicate either *that which is morally good* (Rom. 2:10) or *blessing, privilege* (Rom. 14:16), the latter yields the better meaning in the present context, as shown in the explanation.
As to (6) It has already been shown that, with the exception of the salutations at the beginning and close (vss. 1-3, 25) and the reference to "y o u r prayers " in verse 22, the letter is specifically addressed throughout to one person, namely, Philemon (see on verses 1, 2). Even the greetings are addressed to him alone (vss. 23, 24). Therefore, the sudden appearance, here in the body of the letter (verse 6), of the second person plural (ὑμῖν) would be very strange indeed. On the other hand, that Paul, reflecting on the goodness of God in Christ toward Philemon, would immediately include himself and in fact all believers as objects of this divine love and care, and would therefore write "the good that is *ours,*" is easy to understand.
An entirely different meaning is given to the passage by E. J. Goodspeed. He renders verses 5 and 6 as follows: "I hear of the love and faith you have in the

The fact that the entrancing contemplation of the blessings of redemption — "all the good" — that are ours in Christ should evoke in our hearts the response of love and that not only God but also fellow-believers should be included in the object of this love, is not foreign to Pauline thought. The companion-epistle begins with this very idea: ". . . the love which y o u cherish for all the saints by reason of the hope laid up for y o u in the heavens" (Col. 1:4, 5). And the best commentary on Philem. 6 is probably the one found in Col. 3:13, "Just as Christ has forgiven y o u, so do y o u also forgive." Cf. Eph. 4:32; 5:2. The more thoroughly Philemon recognizes how greatly he himself has been benefited, the more inclined will he be to extend mercy and pardon to others, specifically to Onesimus. And the very fact that Philemon has manifested such a fine spirit in the past convinces the apostle that he is not writing in vain.

7. Hence, he continues, **For I have derived much joy and comfort from your love, because the hearts** [181] **of the saints have been refreshed through you, brother.** As has been indicated, this verse is closely connected with the preceding. Also, of course, with verse 4 ("I thank my God"), for verse 7, as well as verse 5, shows why Paul was so thankful. In times of hardship or need Philemon had on more than one occasion given *rest* to the weary, after the example and promise of Christ. See Matt. 11:28.[182] That such rest or refreshment had been given specifically to slaves, as some maintain, is not stated here. What Paul by means of these words *implies* but does not yet expressly *state,* is rather this, that since in the past Philemon has shown such pity and generosity to believers, let him do it again. This time let him lavish his love and sympathy on Onesimus. Paul himself will derive joy and comfort from this, as had been the case so often in the past when he had heard about the acts of kindness performed by Philemon. When the apostle writes, ". . . because the hearts of the saints have been refreshed through you, brother," this word *brother* is a fitting climax, showing how deeply the apostle loves the man whom he here addresses, how highly he esteems him, and how completely he trusts him.

Lord Jesus and all his people, and I pray that through coming to know every good thing about us as Christians they may effectually share your faith." Objections: (1) What does he mean by "the love and the faith in . . . all his people"? (2) Why should the apostle pray that "all his people" [the saints] may effectually share Philemon's faith? They already have that faith! — Other renderings or reconstructions are even less probable and require no discussion.

[181] On σπλάγχνα see footnote 39, p. 58 of N.T.C. on Philippians.

[182] In that passage, as the *Greek* has it, the Lord *twice* used a form of the word which here in Philem. has been rendered *refreshed.* It indicates *rested,* and thus *revived,* having obtained fresh courage and vigor. And in the *Syriac* translation of the Matthew passage the word, in one form or another, occurs no less than *three* times. This is an even more striking play upon words, and may reflect the actual idiom of Galilee, hence also of Jesus: "Come to me . . . and I will *rest* y o u . . . for I am *restful* [here *the Greek* has *meek*] . . . and y o u will find *rest* for yourselves."

8 Accordingly, although in Christ I am quite free to order you (to do) your duty, 9 yet for love's sake I rather appeal to you — since I am such a person as Paul, an old man, and now also a prisoner of Christ Jesus — 10 I appeal to you in the interest of my child, whom I have begotten in my bonds, Onesimus, 11 who formerly to you was useless, but now both to you and to me is useful, 12 whom I am sending back to you; (yes, even) him, that is, my very heart, 13 whom I could have wished to keep with me, in order that in your behalf he might render service to me in the bonds of the gospel; 14 but without your consent I did not wish to do anything, that your goodness might not be compulsory but voluntary.

15 Moreover, perhaps the reason why he was parted (from you) for a short period was this, that you might have him back forever, 16 no longer as a slave but something better than a slave, a brother beloved, especially to me but how much more to you, both in the flesh and in the Lord. 17 If then you consider me a partner, accept him as (you accept) me. 18 But if he has caused you any loss or owes you anything, charge that to my account. 19 I, Paul, do myself write this with my own hand, I will repay it — not to mention to you that you owe me your very self besides. 20 Yes, brother, let me have some benefit from you in the Lord. Refresh my heart in Christ.

21 Confident of your obedience I am writing to you, knowing that you will do even better than I say. 22 At the same time, prepare a guest room for me, for I am hoping that through y o u r prayers I shall be granted to y o u.

8-22

III. *Plea in Behalf of Onesimus, Including Request for Lodging*

It may seem as if this *plea* and this *request* have nothing in common, and should be treated under separate headings. The conviction that there may, nevertheless, be a subtle relation, as will be pointed out (see on verse 22), has led me to treat them under one theme.

8, 9. Accordingly, since you are the kind of person who delights in refreshing the hearts of God's people, a firm believer in loving and sharing (vss. 4-7), hence, **although in Christ I am quite free to order you (to do) your duty, yet for love's sake I rather appeal to you.** Paul is conscious of his authority as an apostle of Christ. There were times when he even laid stress on this right to rule the church in matters of faith and conduct, a commission given to him by his Lord (Rom. 1:1; I Cor. 5:3, 4; 9:1; II Cor. 10:13, 14; 12:12; Gal. 1:1; II Tim. 1:1, 11; 4:1; Titus 1:1). Yet, as he now unburdens his heart in the interest of Onesimus he prefers not to emphasize his apostolic prerogative. He would rather base his appeal on intelligent and purposeful Christian love, that very love which Philemon has been showing to all the saints (verse 5). One cannot really say that even here Paul *completely* excludes any appeal to his authority as Christ's official ambassador. If that were true, he would, of course, not even have mentioned it at all. In this respect verses 8, 9 may be compared to verse 19, where the apostle says, "not to mention to you that you owe me your very self," *but mentions it, nevertheless!* So also here in verses 8, 9, the reference to authority is made to flash before Philemon's mind for just a moment, only to recede entirely to the background when the spotlight is turned on the most dynamic motivating power in the entire universe, namely, love. In a tone of deep affection and gentle persuasion the plea continues: **since I am such a person as Paul, an old man,**[183] **and now also a prisoner of Christ Jesus.** Just how old Paul was when this was written we do not know. At Stephen's death he was "a young man" (Acts 7:58). Based on this fact and on various other data in the book of Acts and in the epistles, many are of the opinion that by now the apostle was in the neighborhood of sixty years of age. If that may not seem old to us, it must be borne in mind not only that man's average span of life was shorter in those days than it is now, but also that, as a result of all his labors and afflictions (see the stirring account in II Cor. 11:23-33, to which other hardships were added subsequently) this valiant servant of Christ had "grown old" in the service of his Lord and Master. Did he not bear in his body "the marks of the Lord Jesus"? (Gal. 6:17). Was he not the man with "a thorn in the flesh"? (II Cor. 12:7). And was he not even now also a prisoner of Christ Jesus? (see on verse 1). Surely, Philemon cannot refuse a reasonable request coming from a man who had shown his willingness at all times to surrender his all in the service of the King of Kings!

10, 11. Continues Paul: **I appeal to you in the interest of my child, whom I have begotten in my bonds, Onesimus.** That is the order of the sentence in the original. It should be preserved in the translation (cf. A.R.V.). This is not the case in A.V. and in R.S.V. The reason why this point must be stressed is that the apostle obviously has planned this statement with great care. Hence, before he ever mentions the name of the person in whose interest he is writing, he first of all seeks to create in the mind of Philemon a favorable impression of him and also sympathy for the one who is writing. Read the sentence again as Paul wrote (or dictated) it, and contrast it with what he might have written: "I am writing to you about Onesimus, that reputedly good-for-nothing slave or yours who, probably after robbing you, ran away from you." Note with what affection the apostle calls Onesimus "my child"; even more touchingly, "whom I have begotten in my bonds"; hence, "the child of my imprisonment"; *"my* child, who by God's grace was

---

[183] I cannot agree here with Lightfoot, C. F. D. Moule, and others who, with an appeal to Eph. 6:20, defend the theory that πρεσβύτης here means πρεσβευτής (ambassador). Is not this a clear violation of the context? Having just now (vss. 8, 9a) declared in unmistakable language that he does *not* wish to base his request on the authority with which his office as an apostle has invested him, he would turn right around and, almost in the same breath, appeal after all to his high prerogative as Christ's ambassador. That makes little sense.

by my personal ministry here in prison led to a saving knowledge of Christ."
We picture it thus: While still at the home of Philemon the slave had heard
about Paul, and about his gospel, zeal, loving heart, etc. Arrived in Rome as
a fugitive and in dire straits, he had taken refuge with the apostle. The
latter was used by God to change the slave into a brother beloved, the thief
into a fellow-servant. Paul continues: **who formerly to you was useless, but
now both to you and to me is useful.** Note with what tact the apostle balances the modifiers, so that the first ends with the word *useless,* the second
with *useful.* The latter, however, is the more emphatic because while Onesimus is said to have been useless with reference to only *one* person, namely,
Philemon, he is described as useful to *two* individuals, "to you and to me."
There is a play on the word *Onesimus,* meaning *profitable, helpful,* or more
precisely, on its synonym *useful* (euchrēstos) as contrasted with *useless*
(achrēstos).[184] Onesimus who formerly to you was *useless,* not minding his
duties, a pilferer and a runaway; hence, totally untrue to the meaning of his
name, has now become *useful,* for as a Christian he will work for you with a
new attitude, striving to please you for Christ's sake, and thus pleasing me
also. Undoubtedly, there is also a reference here to the services which Onesimus, had he remained with Paul, could have rendered to him to lighten
the burden of his imprisonment, for the apostle refers to this in verse 13.

    Paul has already appealed to Philemon's outgoing personality (vss. 4-7,
9a), to his (Paul's) own age and imprisonment for Christ (9b), and to the
fact that Onesimus has become a believer (verse 10). He now reminds
Philemon of the fact that it will be in his own interest to extend a welcome
to the returning fugitive. Will not the latter serve his master far better than
ever before?

12-14. To all this another, perhaps even more stirring, argument is added
in the words: **whom I am sending back** [185] **to you; (yes, even) him,**[186] **that
is, my very heart.**[187] Onesimus is being sent back, but by no means alone.
Big-hearted Paul sees to it that, instead of forcing this slave to beg for mercy

---

[184] Lenski's denial of this play on words is surprising. The pun is too obvious. One
is reminded of II Thess. 3:11, "not busy workers but busybodies."
[185] ἀνέπεμψα epistolary aorist. That this word should here be taken in a legal sense,
as if an accused were being "sent up" to someone in higher authority, has not been
established. The simple sense is probably the best in the present connection.
[186] "whom . . . him." This resumption of a relative by means of a pronoun occurs
frequently in Hebrew. Whether or not the present resumption must be regarded as
a Semitism is, perhaps, not as important as is the fact that obviously this repetition
is for the sake of emphasis: this very slave, who had made himself so obnoxious, has
now become the object of Paul's most tender affection.
[187] On σπλάγχνα in the sense of *heart,* both here and in verses 7 and 20, see footnote 39, p. 58 of N.T.C. on Philippians. The additional words of the A.V., "thou
therefore receive him," are based upon a reading for which the textual evidence is
definitely weak. For the idea itself see, however, verse 17, which is probably the
source of the words inserted here in verse 12.

all by himself, he returns supported by: a. Tychicus (see explanation of Col. 4:7-9), b. a letter from Paul addressed to the entire congregation of Colosse, in which love and the spirit of forgiveness is emphasized, and c. a letter dealing specifically with the case of Onesimus. Surely, never did a runaway return to his master in better company! Onesimus is "my very heart," writes Paul. So deeply does he feel himself attached to this newly won convert to the Christian faith. See also Col. 4:9. How could Philemon reject Paul's very heart?

In similar vein the apostle continues, **whom I could have wished to keep with me, in order that in your behalf he might render service to me in the bonds of the gospel.** "For an instant," says Paul, as it were, "it occurred to me that I should keep Onesimus with me to render personal service to me in my imprisonment.[188] But immediately my better judgment said, No, that cannot be. Not I but Philemon must make the final decision regarding Onesimus." Paul is speaking about help that might have been rendered to himself by Onesimus, serving in behalf of Philemon. Note "in your behalf he." Here the apostle, with marvelous generosity, is assuming that Philemon had been wishing that he himself could render such service to Paul; and also that, prevented by distance from doing so, Philemon, had he but known all the circumstances, would have been only too happy to substitute the services of Onesimus for his own. However, Paul is also convinced that it would have been wrong for him *to act* on this assumption and to have kept Onesimus with him in Rome. Why would it have been improper? Says Paul: **but without your consent I did not wish to do anything, that your goodness might not be compulsory but voluntary.** There is not even a hint here that *even now* Paul wants Philemon to send Onesimus back to Rome to be of assistance to the apostle. Such an idea is simply read into the text. On the contrary, Paul, the prisoner is rather expecting that he will be released and is already asking that at Colosse lodging be prepared for him (verse 22). Paul's actual purpose in verses 10-14 is to show Philemon what a very valuable man Onesimus has become. He is profitable, Paul's very heart, one whom Paul would have been glad to retain. "Hence, Philemon, you better forgive and forget." Cf. verse 17.

"Had I kept him with me," says Paul, as it were, "this would hardly have been fair to you. It would have placed you before an accomplished fact. In that case, your subsequent acquiescence or approval would have been a matter of coercion, not of spontaneous volition." Here Paul is imitating God as a beloved child (cf. Eph. 5:1). Was not this the reason why God had issued the probationary command in the Garden of Eden, namely, in order to give man an opportunity to serve God *of his own accord?* And had not Paul, in II Cor. 8:1-6, praised the churches of Macedonia because they had made

---

[188] For similar service see what is said about Epaphroditus in Phil. 2:25b.

their generous contributions "of their own accord"? Cf. also Ex. 35:29; 36:5. Philemon would have been deprived of the privilege of making such a spontaneous contribution — in this case consisting of the service of Onesimus — had Paul presumed on his goodness.

15, 16. Still another reason why Philemon should grant Paul's request in the interest of Onesimus is now presented: **Perhaps the reason why he was parted (from you) for a short period was this, that you might have him back forever.** Note that with a love that covers all things (I Peter 4:8; cf. I Cor. 13:7) the pleader here places the most charitable construction possible upon the case of Onesimus. He does not say, "Perhaps the reason why he ran away from you after committing larceny," etc., but "Perhaps the reason why *he was parted* (from you) ," etc. In other words, Paul, though by no means clearing Onesimus of guilt, wants Philemon to see and consider God's glorious, overruling providence. "Behold *the hand of God,* in this happening," says he, as it were. God used the evil deed of Onesimus to bring about good, and this both for the runaway himself and for Philemon. The latter had been parted for a short period from *a slave;* he is joined forever to *a brother!* The bond between master and slave had been severed for the brief span intervening between the flight and the return. The bond between the two as brothers in Christ would never be severed, neither here nor in the hereafter. That was God's grand design, his marvelous plan.

Here again there is no hint of any intention on Paul's part that Onesimus be returned to him, to be of assistance to him in Rome. If anything, the very opposite: "that *you* might have him back," writes Paul.[189]

Having said, "that you might have him back forever," the apostle continues, **no longer as a slave but something better than a slave, a brother beloved.** This passage makes it clear that Paul does not consider immediate, forced emancipation the true solution of the slavery problem. He does not say, "that you might set him free," but "that you might have him back, no longer as a slave but something better than a slave, a brother beloved." When a slave becomes a "brother beloved," he ceases to be a slave, though he is still, as in this case, a servant. Paul adds, **especially to me but how much more to you.** At first glance these words seem somewhat illogical, for if it be true that by saying "especially to me" Paul is already singling out the most prominent example among all those to whom Onesimus would now be a brother beloved, how can he add, *"how much more* to you"? I have found the following solutions:

(1) The word translated *especially,* as here used, really means *exceed-*

---

[189] I am therefore in full agreement with C. F. D. Moule who states (*op. cit.,* pp. 146, 147) , "But the τάχα γάρ, following what is said in v. 14, makes it difficult to interpret the present verse otherwise than as a reference to the possibility of its *not* being his master's intention (γνώμη) to part with Onesimus."

ingly or *immensely* [what about *intensely?*]. This will allow for the expression "how much more," without violating logic.[190]

(2) This is in reality an illogicality springing from enthusiasm: "most of all to me — more than most of all to you."

If either of these two solutions must be accepted I, for one, prefer the first, as the second is really no solution at all. Is there not a third possibility? It could be the following:

(3) When Paul begins to write this modifier, he is comparing his own relation to Onesimus with the relation in which believers in general would now stand to this converted man. And since to him, Paul, and to no one else, had been granted the privilege of becoming the spiritual father of Onesimus (verse 10), he is fully justified in calling him "a brother beloved *especially to me.*" However, as the apostle continues to describe the person in whose interest he is writing this stirring appeal, he now compares his own relation to him with the relation which specifically Philemon would bear to him. From a certain aspect the latter relationship would excel the former, and this for the reason which Paul immediately adds, namely, **both in the flesh and in the Lord.** The "flesh" relationship which existed between the master and the servant did not obtain between the "father" and the "child." Between Paul and Onesimus there was only a spiritual relationship, though it was, indeed, a very beautiful one. Between Philemon and Onesimus there was, in addition, also this "flesh" relationship. In both of these relationships Onesimus, it is here assumed, would now be very dear to Philemon. Inquiry into the question just what is meant by the words, "both in the flesh and in the Lord," has resulted in such answers as the following:

(1) both as a fellow-Colossian and as a brother in the Lord;

(2) both in the affairs of this world and in the affairs of the higher life.

The latter, it would seem to me, deserves the preference here, in harmony with the use of the word "flesh" ($\sigma\acute{\alpha}\rho\xi$) in such passages as Gal. 2:20; Phil. 1:22, 24.[191] Both at work and in church the new and sanctified relationship between master and servant, brother and brother, will assert itself.

17. On the basis, then, of all these grounds which Paul has presented in support of his plea, let Philemon take favorable action: **If then you consider me a partner, accept him as (you accept) me.** The original means "Take Onesimus *to yourself* just as you do me." This is more than just extending a hearty welcome to a person upon arrival. Moreover, when Paul writes, "If then you consider me a partner," he means more than, "If you look upon me as a friend." The *partner* here is the *koinōnos,* the *sharer* in

---

[190] In other words, $\mu\acute{\alpha}\lambda\iota\sigma\tau\alpha$ is here used in an elative sense.

[191] For a classification of the various shades of meaning which this word has in the epistles of Paul see N.T.C. on Philippians, p. 77, footnote 55. Meaning c. would seem to be indicated here.

the *koinōnia* (spiritual fellowship). This fellowship always implies *sharing* (see on verse 6), and at times must be so rendered.[192] Let, therefore, all the rights and privileges pertaining to any one who is included in this blessed fellowship be given to the one who is now returning as a humble penitent, a sincere child of God!

18-20. All the while, as Paul was writing or dictating, there was present in his mind one final matter which might, after all, prove to be a real obstacle in the path leading to complete reconciliation. The apostle knew very well that any one traveling all the way from Colosse to Rome would need money. He also was not ignorant of the fact that lack of trustworthiness in matters relating to material things was characteristic of slaves. After his release from the present (first Roman) imprisonment he was going to write to Titus: "Urge slaves to be submissive in every respect to their own masters . . . *not pilfering, but evincing the utmost trustworthiness*" (Titus 2:9, 10). It is possible that Onesimus had told Paul that he had committed theft. More probable, it would seem to me, is the supposition that Paul was entertaining justified suspicions that such a wrong had been committed. This would account for the use of the significant two-letter word *If* in verse 18. Paul was not sure, but suspected it! [193] This possible hindrance to the establishment of the proper, Christian relationship between master and returning servant must be removed. Therefore, gracious, big-hearted Paul continues: **But if he has caused you any loss or owes you anything, charge that to my account.** Had Paul come into an inheritance in recent years, that he was able to make this generous offer? On the basis of the fact that according to Acts 24:26 Felix detained the apostle, hoping that the latter would purchase his freedom; of Acts 28:30, which contains a reference to Paul's "own rented quarters"; and of the passage now under discussion, some have arrived at this conclusion. In any event Paul either had some money or knew where he could get it. He was entirely sincere in offering compensation for the loss which Philemon might have suffered. So, using commercial phraseology, he says, "Charge that to my account." He continues, **I, Paul, do myself write this with my own hand.** In other words, "Here is my promissory note, with my own signature attached to it." This has been interpreted to mean that the entire letter was in Paul's own handwriting. Though this possibility must be granted, it cannot be proved. All the statement actually means is that the promise to reimburse Philemon for the loss suffered was made with Paul's own hand. That the closing salutation was also by Paul's

---

[192] See N.T.C. on Philippians, pp. 51-54 and 93-95, for full discussion.
[193] I prefer this rather common interpretation to the one offered by Lenski (*op. cit.*, pp. 968, 969), according to which the wrong done was simply this, that by fleeing Onesimus had deprived his master of his services. But in that case it is hard to explain Paul's *If*. The fact that the slave had caused his master the loss of his services was undeniable.

own hand is clear from II Thess. 3:17. Possibly the apostle himself, without use of secretary, wrote verses 18-25. But this is merely a conjecture. The offer here made is a very solemn one. It showed how intensely Paul had come to love Onesimus. Was it with somewhat of a sense of benign, fatherly humor that the pleader added: **not to mention** [but he does mention it; hence, probably meaning, not to stress the fact] **to you that you owe me your very self besides?** "Philemon, instead of my owing you this money, you really owe it to me; yes, far more besides, for you owe me your very self, your very life as a believer." [194]

Philemon had been converted either directly, through the instrumentality of Paul, perhaps while the master of Onesimus was on a visit to Ephesus and heard the apostle preach (Acts 19:10), or indirectly, through the labors of Epaphras who, in turn, was indebted to Paul. In either case Paul was able to write, "You owe me your very self." This also shows that the apostle was a firm believer in the principle of reciprocation: the obligation to make a return for favors or blessings received. He believed that this principle applied both to things received from God (see verse 6; also II Cor. 1:34; 8:7, 9; cf. Ps. 116:12) and from men (cf. I Tim. 5:4).

Reflecting then once more on the entire plea, with all the grounds so far mentioned, Paul continues, **Yes, brother, let me have some benefit** [195] **from you in the Lord.** The term of endearment, *brother* (see also verse 7), expressing love and intimate spiritual relationship, fits very well at this point. What is especially striking is the manner in which Paul all but identifies himself with Onesimus. He says, "Let *me* have some benefit from you." In other words, whatever favor Philemon grants to Onesimus is to be viewed as granted to Paul himself. We have a similar instance of the marvelous identifying power of love in the Syrophoenician woman's touching plea in behalf of her daughter. She says to Jesus, "Help *me!*" (Matt. 15:25), and, of course, in the words of Christ himself, "To the extent that y o u have done it to one of these brothers of mine, (even) the least (of them), y o u have done it to *me*" (Matt. 25:40). As a mere human being, acting apart from Christ, it might have been impossible for Philemon to pardon and restore Onesimus. Let him then do it (and thereby impart a benefit to Paul) *in the Lord,* in fellowship with him; reflecting on the blessings which he himself, the master of Onesimus, had received from fellowship with *his* Master, and by means of the grace and power derived from him. Paul adds, **Refresh my heart in Christ.** For the meaning of these words see on verse 7. The apostle is expressing the wish that he, too, may be included in the circle of those to whom Philemon in the past has given rest of heart. And this, in fellowship

---

[194] As I see it, we have here another case of abbreviated expression. See N.T.C. on John 5:31. For a different explanation see Lenski, *op. cit.,* p. 971.

[195] ὀναίμην. This could well be a play on the name Onesimus. It is the only instance of the use of the first person optative in the New Testament.

with Christ. Let him place the entire matter before Christ. If he does this, there can be but one answer. He will surely grant Paul's request. In fact, he will do even more; hence, Paul continues:

21. Confident of your obedience I am writing to you. This obedience to which the apostle refers is *gospel-obedience*. It is a hearkening to the demands of God as expressed in the gospel (cf. Rom. 10:16; Phil. 2:12; II Thess. 3:14). It is, therefore, more than heeding *Paul's* advice and granting his request. It is exactly the gospel as proclaimed by Christ that demands that those who have been greatly benefited shall also show kindness to others. Matt. 18:21-35 proves this point in a striking manner. The apostle states, as it were, that he does not even have to wait until he hears whether or not Philemon has acted according to the stirring plea that was by means of this letter presented to him. He fully trusts Philemon to do what is right and charitable. In fact, he adds, **knowing that you will do even better than I say.** Exactly what Paul may have had in mind when he added these words we do not know. To infer from this rather obscure hint that the apostle *must* have meant, "I know that you will send Onesimus right back to me," or "I know that you will at once emancipate him," is certainly rash. Besides, Paul was not thinking in terms of having Onesimus returned to him, but rather of his own liberation from imprisonment and a journey to Colosse (verse 22). Aside from emancipation, there were other ways in which Philemon was able to do even better than requested. To mention but a few: he might give Onesimus some spare-time to do evangelistic work. He might review his entire relation to his servants on the basis of gospel principles. He might, as a result, urge other masters, too, to treat their servants with greater consideration. He might send a message to Paul, saying, "You asked me to provide a guest room for you. I'll do better than that. You can stay at my own home." And so one could easily continue. But this should suffice to show that those who think that there was *only one* way in which Philemon could do even better than requested are in error.

22. Paul concludes his eloquent plea in words which, on the surface, may seem to have nothing to do with it, and to introduce an entirely new subject, but which actually stand in close connection with it, namely, **At the same time, prepare a guest room for me.** The true interpretation, it would seem to me, is the one given by Lightfoot (*op. cit.*, p. 345), who shows the connection in these words, "There is a gentle compulsion in this mention of a personal visit to Colosse. The apostle would thus be able to see for himself that Philemon had not disappointed his expectations." Paul's tactfulness surely is evident here also, as it is so strikingly throughout the letter. See the Summary which follows the exegesis of this chapter. Paul continues, **for I am hoping that through y o u r prayers I shall be granted to y o u.** Here the second person plural reappears: the prayers to which Paul refers are those not only of Philemon but also af Apphia, Archippus, and in fact of all believers in Colosse. Not only does *he* pray for Philemon (verse 4) and for believers everywhere, but *he also wants believers to pray for him* and for others who are engaged in spiritual warfare. "Brothers, do pray for us," is the language he uses elsewhere (I Thess. 5:25) ; see also on Col. 1:9, the parallel columns. Moreover, he does not say, "Through y o u r prayers I hope to be released from imprisonment," though that, of course, is implied, but phrases it far more beautifully: "I shall be granted to y o u." Here again it becomes evident that Paul, the prisoner, is conscious of that same providential guidance with respect to his own life to which he had already directed the mind of Philemon in verse 15, in order that the latter might also gratefully discern it in whatever had happened to him. Above all, Paul here displays, as he does so often, his firm conviction that God is an answerer of prayer. All the evidence points to the fact that Paul was, indeed, released from his first Roman imprisonment, and made more journeys.[196] No doubt he made use of the guest room prepared for him by Philemon, whether in his own home or elsewhere.

---

23 Epaphras, my fellow-prisoner in Christ Jesus, greets you, 24 (and so do) Mark, Aristarchus, Demas, and Luke, my fellow-workers.
25 The grace of the Lord Jesus Christ (be) with y o u r spirit.

23-25

IV. Greetings and Closing Salutation

A. Greetings

23, 24. Epaphras, my fellow-prisoner in Christ Jesus, greets you, (and so do) Mark, Aristarchus, Demas, and Luke, my fellow-workers.
For these five men and the greetings they send see on Col. 4:10-14.

B. Closing Salutation

25. The grace of the Lord Jesus Christ (be) with y o u r spirit. The best textual evidence supports this reading. One is reminded of Phil. 4:23; cf. also Gal. 6:18; I Cor. 16:23; I Thess. 5:28; II Thess. 3:18; and II Tim. 4:22. Upon Philemon, Apphia, Achippus, and all those who gather for worship in their home, yes, upon all Colossian believers, Paul, as God's official representative, pronounces God's grace, that is, his unmerited favor in the

---

[196] See for this evidence and for a conjecture as to the apostle's itinerary N.T.C. on I and II Timothy and Titus, pp. 23-28, 39, 40.

anointed Lord and Savior, based on his merits, conveyed by his Spirit. If
this pronouncement is accepted with a believing heart, then from this basic
blessing of grace all others flow forth, filling the very *spirit* (pneuma), the
inner personality viewed as contact-point between God and his child, with
the peace of God that passes all understanding!

No one has attached a postscript to this gem of a letter. Information as to
whether Philemon acted in accordance with Paul's stirring, masterly plea
is entirely lacking, though a favorable inference is inescapable. The main
point is this: here is Christianity in action. Here is an actual demonstration
and illustration of *faith working through love!*

Summary of Philemon

of Paul's Masterpiece of Tactful Pleading, in which he asks Philemon that
the runaway slave, Onesimus, who as a penitent and converted man is now
returning to the house from which he fled, be fully accepted.

(1) Listen to me, that is, to Paul, a man who has grown old in the service
of his Lord (verse 9).

(2) I am now a prisoner of Christ Jesus (1, 9). Surely, compared to the
hardships of my imprisonment how small is the favor I am asking of you.

(3) Besides, I am your friend, who loves you, and admires you for the
manner in which you have again and again refreshed the hearts of the saints
(4, 5, 7, 8, 9, 20).

(4) We are in debt to God for all his goodness shown to us (6). Also,
you are in debt to me. In fact, you owe me your very life (19).

(5) Onesimus is my child, my very heart, a brother beloved (10, 12, 16).

(6) It is to your advantage to grant my request that you accept Onesimus,
for the once useless one has become useful. I, for one, surely so regard him
(11, 13, 14).

(7) Favorable action on your part would be in line with God's providential direction, which we should gratefully acknowledge (15, 22b).

(8) The fellowship of all believers in Christ demands this, for not only
you and I are included in this but so is Onesimus (17).

(9) I have confidence in your obedience (21).

(10) I want you to prepare a guest room for me, for I hope, in answer to
the prayers of God's children, to be granted to y o u (22b). Surely, you
would not wish to disappoint my eyes.

These are the ten arguments Paul uses.

Paul's Epistle to Philemon

1 Paul, a prisoner of Christ Jesus, and Timothy our brother, to Philemon our beloved (brother) and fellow-worker 2 and to Apphia our sister and to Archippus our fellow-soldier and to the church in your house; 3 grace to y o u and peace from God our Father and the Lord Jesus Christ.

4 I thank my God always, making mention of you in my prayers, 5 because I hear of your love and of the faith which you have, (the latter) toward the Lord Jesus, and (the former) for all the saints, 6 (praying) that the sharing to which your faith gives rise may be energetically stimulated for Christ by the clear recognition of all the good that is ours. 7 For I have derived much joy and comfort from your love, because the hearts of the saints have been refreshed through you, brother.

8 Accordingly, although in Christ I am quite free to order you (to do) your duty, 9 yet for love's sake I rather appeal to you — since I am such a person as Paul, an old man, and now also a prisoner of Christ Jesus — 10 I appeal to you in the interest of my child, whom I have begotten in my bonds, Onesimus, 11 who formerly to you was useless, but now both to you and to me is useful, 12 whom I am sending back to you; (yes, even) him, that is, my very heart, 13 whom I could have wished to keep with me, in order that in your behalf he might render service to me in the bonds of the gospel; 14 but without your consent I did not wish to do anything, that your goodness might not be compulsory but voluntary.

15 Moreover, perhaps the reason why he was parted (from you) for a short period was this, that you might have him back forever, 16 no longer as a slave but something better than a slave, a brother beloved, especially to me but how much more to you, both in the flesh and in the Lord. 17 If then you consider me a partner, accept him as (you accept) me. 18 But if he has caused you any loss or owes you anything, charge that to my account. 19 I, Paul, do myself write this with my own hand, I will repay it — not to mention to you that you owe me your very self besides. 20 Yes, brother, let me have some benefit from you in the Lord. Refresh my heart in Christ.

21 Confident of your obedience I am writing to you, knowing that you will do even better than I say. 22 At the same time, prepare a guest room for me, for I am hoping that through y o u r prayers I shall be granted to y o u.

23 Epaphras, my fellow-prisoner in Christ Jesus, greets you, 24 (and so do) Mark, Aristarchus, Demas, and Luke, my fellow-workers.

25 The grace of the Lord Jesus Christ (be) with y o u r spirit.

Appendix

Scripture on Tactfulness

In the various textbooks of the biblical sciences this subject is generally neglected. Yet it is by no means of minor importance. Tactfulness is definitely a virtue. Though its presence, sometimes in a remarkable degree, among worldly people cannot be denied (cf. Luke 16:8), yet *in its noblest form* it is a product of special grace. Its parents are Love and Wisdom. It is that skill which, without any sacrifice of honesty or candor, enables a person to speak the right word at the right time, and to do the proper thing in any given situation. It is premeditated prudence, sanctified mother wit, consecrated savoir faire. The tactful person does not shirk his duty even when he is convinced that he must admonish or rebuke. But he has learned the art of doing this without being rude. He is humble, patient, and kind. The apostle Paul draws his picture in I Cor. 13.

God himself is the archetype or model of tactfulness to be imitated by men, as Isa. 28:23-29 teaches so strikingly. In more than one way his divine wisdom coupled with considerateness is shown; for example, in the account of the creation of Eve (Gen. 2:18-24); in his punitive yet also merciful dealing with Adam and Eve immediately after the fall (Gen. 3:9-19); in the manner in which he dealt with Cain (Gen. 4:7, 15), with Abraham (Gen. 12:1-3; cf. chapters 15, 17, 18, 22), and with Jonah (Jonah 4:10, 11). These are but a few instances among ever so many others. In fact, God *always* uses the right approach!

Jesus, during his earthly sojourn, repeatedly demonstrated this quality. The following are but a few examples of his tact in dealing with people: the raising of the daughter of Jairus (see especially Matt. 9:25 and Luke 8:55b); the sending forth of laborers into the spiritual vineyard, selecting those very men who at his suggestion had been praying for such laborers (Matt. 9:37–10:1); his illustrated teaching on the indispensability of humility (Matt. 18:1-3; John 13:1-18); his conversation with the Samaritan woman (John 4:1-42), with Thomas (John 20:24-29), and with grief-stricken Peter (John 21:15-17).

Among purely human biblical examples of tactfulness are the following:
a. in the Old Testament: Abraham's generous proposition made to Lot (Gen. 13:1-13); Joshua's challenge to the elders of Israel, in which he takes the lead in doing for himself and his family what he wants them to do for themselves and their families (Josh. 24:15); Abigail's stirring appeal to David, a supplication presented so tactfully that the latter exclaimed, "Blessed be your discretion" (I Sam. 25:14-33); Nathan's parable of "the little ewe lamb" (II Sam. 12:1-12); Solomon's wise judgment (I Kings

231

3:16-28) ; and Mordecai's earnest entreaty presented to his cousin and foster-child, Queen Esther (Esth. 4:13, 14).

b. in the New Testament: Joseph's contemplated action with respect to Mary (Matt. 1:19) ; John the Baptist's humble recessional (John 3:22-30) ; the considerate action of "the disciple whom Jesus loved" with respect to Mary, the mother of Jesus (John 27:19b) ; Gamaliel's advice (Acts 5:33-42) ; the balanced and forward-looking advice of the Jerusalem Conference (Acts 15:22-29) ; the irrefusable invitation extended to the missionaries by Lydia (Acts 16:15) ; the pacifying words of the town-clerk (Acts 19:35-41) ; Paul's remark to the Sanhedrin, "with respect to the hope of the resurrection of the dead I am on trial," very true and very clever (Acts 23:6-9) ; and his courageous conduct and inspiring words during the Voyage Dangerous in moments when all seemed hopeless (Acts 27:20-26, 33-36).

This trait in the great men of the Old Testament and of the early church must not be minimized. In fact, it is probably not an exaggeration to say that *one* of the reasons for Paul's almost unbelievable success as a missionary was his tact in dealing with men. Thus, for example, he was eager to become "all things to all men" that he might by all means save some (I Cor. 9:22). Hence, he would carefully choose *one* approach to the Jews (Acts 13:16-41), but *another* to the Gentiles (Acts 17:22-31), would not only address large audiences but would also seek out individuals to bring them to Christ (I Thess. 2:11), would work among the people with his hands in order not to burden them (I Thess. 2:9), and in his epistles would be careful, wherever possible, to speak words of praise and encouragement before presenting his reprimanding admonitions. Yet, he never used words of flattery (I Thess. 2:5), and was able, when the occasion demanded this course, to say, "O foolish Galatians! Who has bewitched y o u?" (Gal. 3:1).

Before taking leave of this subject of the use of tact it should be pointed out that this application of *discretion* or *prudence* in practical matters is as it were a theme that runs through the book of Proverbs from beginning to end. See especially Prov. 1:4; 2:1-5; 2:11; 3:1-12; 3:21; 5:2; 8:12; 10:19; 11:22; 15:1, 17, 28; 19:11; 22:24, 25; 25:11.

Scripture on Slavery

In ancient times slavery was widespread. Especially among the Greeks it was common practice to reduce captives and often criminals and debtors to the state of bondage. On the island of Delos sometimes as many as ten thousand slaves were sold in a single day. Among the Romans the lot of the slave seems to have been more cruel than among the Greeks. The slave was not considered to have any rights. The law offered him no protection. To be sure, there are recorded instances of masters who were kind to their slaves, but these are the exceptions. It is not surprising that a civilization which looked upon all foreigners as "barbarians" and upon labor as "unworthy of a free man and vulgar" (cf. N.T.C. on I and II Thessalonians, pp. 66, 67) would welcome slavery.

In the Old Testament we immediately feel the breath of special revelation. We enter a different world. It must be freely admitted that the Old Testament does not regard the possession of slaves to be *always and under all circumstances* a moral evil. Israelites were permitted to impose the punishment of slavery upon those nations whose cup of iniquity was full (Gen. 15:16; Lev. 25:44-46). A burglar who was unable to make restitution according to the law had to be sold into slavery (Ex. 22:1-3). These were divine regulations of a punitive character. But such stipulations were a far cry from divine and indiscriminate permission for any one to go man-stealing for pleasure or profit. The divine approval did not rest on the kidnaper. On this point the law was clear: "Whoever steals a man, whether he sells him or is found in possession of him, shall be put to death" (Ex. 21:16). Accordingly, when in more recent centuries some have tried to defend modern slavery by appealing to Moses they have done so without any shadow of warrant.

The insecure basis of such an appeal becomes even more clearly evident when the cruelty which in every century has been a characteristic of the slave-trade is taken into consideration. Perhaps a single day spent *as a slave* on a "slave schooner" would have changed the mind of many an advocate of slavery. It is just possible that had he himself been shackled to other slaves for sixteen hours a day in a three-feet high 'tween deck, with little — and in case of rough weather with *no* — ventilation, had he seen other slaves die at sea of dysentery, smallpox, or other disease, or, in case of safe arrival, had he — or *she* — stood upon the block exposed to every vulgarity of man's inhumanity to man, and subsequently while at work had he been flogged unmercifully by a so-called "overseer," he would probably never again defend slavery, not even "as an indispensable means of leading heathen to Christ."

It is exactly the *cruelty* of slavery which even the *Old* Testament opposes with every possible emphasis. Note the following:

(1) A man who has purchased a female slave with the intention of making her an inferior wife is not permitted to treat her as a slave (Ex. 21:7-11).

(2) Extreme cruelty to a slave must result in immediate manumission (Ex. 21:26, 27).

(3) Returning a runaway to his master to become enslaved once more is strictly forbidden (Deut. 23:15).

(4) Though there is a difference among commentators with respect to the question whether all of the kindness-to-slaves regulations applied to foreign (non-Hebrew) slaves as well as to Israelites, the preponderance of evidence is certainly in the direction of the divinely imposed mandate of at least showing fairness and mercy to all, including the foreigner. Thus, for example, definite provision was made for the incorporation of foreign slaves into religious fellowship with Israel, and this by means of circumcision (Gen. 17:12, 13, 22, 23, 26, 27) and partaking of the paschal meal (Ex. 22:44).

(5) Among the Israelites an impoverished person could "sell himself" in order thus to pay his debts. But his condition was in reality not that of slavery but rather that of mild indenture or voluntary apprenticeship (Lev. 25:39).

(6) The basic rule in Israel is laid down in Lev. 25:42, 43, namely, "They are my servants whom I brought forth out of the land of Egypt. They shall not be sold as slaves, neither shall you rule over him with harshness. You shall revere God" (Lev. 25:42, 43; cf. Neh. 5:5).

(7) For the Hebrew indentured servant the seventh year was that of emancipation (Ex. 21:1, 2), or if the year of jubilee should arrive before the seventh year then that year of jubilee meant freedom (Lev. 25:39-41).

(8) When a Hebrew had served his term he must not be sent away as a pauper or beggar. On the contrary, "When you let him go away from you into freedom, you must not let him go empty-handed. You shall furnish him liberally with provisions from your flock, from your threshing floor, and from your wine-press. As Jehovah your God has blessed you, you must give to him. You shall remember that you yourself were once a slave in the land of Egypt, and that Jehovah your God redeemed you. That is the reason why I give you this command today" (Deut. 15:13-15).

(9) In fact, the probability existed that at times an indentured servant, given permission to become a free man, would say, "I love my master, my wife, and my children; I will not go out free." Definite provision was made whereby also such a desire could be fulfilled (Ex. 21:5, 6).

APPENDIX

We come to the New Testament. Here in the attitude of the centurion toward his slave one finds the counterpart of (9) above. When conditions were ideal, the servant's "I love my master" (Ex. 21:5), would be answered by the master's, "My servant is precious to me" (Luke 7:2), and vice versa. It fills the heart with pure delight to hear the centurion address Jesus in these words, "Say the word, and *my boy* will be healed" (Luke 7:7). Surely, such "slavery" ceased to be slavery at all! Moreover, the love proclaimed by Jesus, a love extending even to enemies (Matt. 5:43-48), has had its definite effect on the thinking of every consistent believer. Paul proclaimed the truth, "There can be neither Jew nor Greek; there can be neither bond nor free . . . y o u are all one man in Christ Jesus" (Gal. 3:28). God does not favor masters above slaves. With him there is no partiality (Eph. 6:5-9; Col. 3:11, 25). It is not surprising therefore that Paul mentions "kidnapers" or "slave-dealers" in one breath with murderers and sodomites as those against whom the law of God thunders its denunciations (I Tim. 1:9b, 10). The book of Revelation implies that one of the reasons for the fall and desolation of Babylon was the slave-trade (Rev. 18:13).

Thus Old and New Testament combine in showing that though those indeed, are wrong who attach an exclusively "social" value to Christianity, those, too, are in error who assign to it a purpose so abstractly "religious" that it loses all contact with the concrete situations of life. To be sure Christianity is a religion, but a religion that includes definite guide-lines for human action in every sphere. No Christian should ever be afraid to condemn the curse of slavery. He has Scripture, both Old and New Testament, on his side.

All this does not mean that either Jesus or Paul advocated social revolution: immediate emancipation of every slave. Such a sudden upheaval of the entire Roman economy would have resulted in indescribable misery for many a bondman who depended on his master for a living, and would have placed an insurmountable obstacle in the way of the propagation of the Christian faith.

Enforced emancipation has by no means always been appreciated even by the slaves. The booklet *Strange But True*, pp. 6, 7, relates that when imperial Russia gained control over the Caucasus territory, the viceroy of the Czar advised the local princes to emancipate their house-slaves. When the slaves heard about it, however, they protested bitterly, and insisted that slavery was their hereditary right!

Another somewhat similar scene is touchingly portrayed by Susan Dabney Smedes, one of whose essays is found on pp. 796-800 of *The Heritage of America*. This concerns the aftermath of the Civil War. She writes that even long after Lincoln had issued his Emancipation Proclamation "no apparent change took place among the Burleigh Negroes. Those who worked in the fields went out as usual and cultivated and gathered in the crops.

235

In the house they went about their customary duties. We expected them to go away or to demand wages or at least to give some sign that they knew they were free. But, except that they were very quiet and serious and more obedient and kind than they had ever been known to be for more than a few weeks at a time of sickness or other affliction, we saw no change in them. At Christmas such compensation was made them for their services as seemed just. Afterward fixed wages were offered and accepted. Thomas called them up now and told them that as they no longer belonged to him they must discontinue calling him master. 'Yes, marster,' 'Yes, marster,' was the answer to this." [197]

Now whatever value there may be in the objection that the instances related must have been of an exceptional character, it remains true that especially this second example points in the right direction as to the true solution, and this not only of the slavery question of the past but also of similar problems today. What Paul teaches, not only in his letter to Philemon but also elsewhere, is that *love, coming from both sides* (masters and slaves) *is the only solution.* This love is the response to God's love for his child. Whether that child be black or white, bond or free, makes no difference. It is this love of God which melts cruelty into kindness and in so doing changes despots into kind employers, slaves into willing servants, and all who accept it into "brothers" in Christ. The kingship or rule of God works from within outward, not from without inward. The truth of the gospel contained in passages such as Matt. 5:43-48; 7:12; John 3:16; Acts 10:34, 35; Rom. 3:21-24; 12:9-14; I Cor. 13; Eph. 6:5-9; Col. 3:12-17, 25–4:1, will do far more to solve social questions than any number of bayonets.

Brief Bibliography on Slavery

In addition to articles on slavery in the best encyclopaedias see also the following:

J. O. Buswell, *Slavery, Segregation, and Scripture,* Grand Rapids, 1964. This book contains a good Bibliography, pp. 93-97.

H. S. Commager and A. Nevins (editors), *The Heritage of America,* especially sections 99 ("The Rev. Mr. Walsh Inspects a Slave Ship") and 183 ("Thomas Dabney Does the Family Wash").

J. C. Furnas, *Goodbye to Uncle Tom,* New York, 1956.

A. Grünfeld, *Die Stellung der Sklaven bei den Juden,* Jena, 1886.

E. Hamilton, "The Roman Way," R. Carpenter, "Ancient Rome Brought to Life," and R. Stillwell, "Greece — The Birthplace of Science and Free Speech," three articles in *Everyday Life in Ancient Times,* published by the National Geographic Society, 1951, as reprints of articles that appeared in the issues of Oct., 1941, March, 1944, Nov. 1946, and Jan. 1951.

---

[197] From *The Heritage of America,* edited by Henry Steele Commager and Allan Nevins, Copyright 1939, 1949 by Henry Steele Commager and Allan Nevins. Reprinted by permission of Little, Brown and Company, Publishers.

APPENDIX

M. Mielziner, *Die Verhältnisse der Sklaven bei den alten Hebräer,* Leipsic, 1859, Eng. transl, in *Evang. Review,* 1862, pp. 311-355.

P. Schaff, *Slavery and the Bible,* Mercersburg, 1860.

J. R. Spears, *The American Slave Trade,* New York, 1960.

R. Wallace, "How the Negro Came to Slavery in America," *Life,* Sept. 3, 1956.

For the older literature see the Bibliography at the close of the article "Slavery" in *The New Schaff-Herzog Encyclopaedia of Religious Knowledge,* Vol. X, pp. 449-454.

SELECT BIBLIOGRAPHY

I would especially recommend the following:

Bruce, F. F., *Commentary on the Epistle to the Colossians* (*New International Commentary on the New Testament*), Grand Rapids, Mich., 1957.
Calvin, John, *Commentarius In Epistolam Pauli Ad Colossenses. . . . Ad Philemonem* (*Corpus Reformatorum,* vol. LXXX), Brunsvigae, 1895; English translation (*Calvin's Commentaries*), Grand Rapids, Mich., respectively, 1957, 1948.
Lightfoot, J. B., *Saint Paul's Epistles to the Colossians and to Philemon,* reprint of 1879 edition, Grand Rapids, Mich.
Ridderbos, Herman, *Aan de Kolossenzen* (*Commentaar op het Nieuwe Testament*), Kampen, 1960.

GENERAL BIBLIOGRAPHY

For other titles see List of Abbreviations and Brief Bibliography on Slavery.

Abbott, T. K., *The Epistles to the Ephesians and to the Colossians* (*International Critical Commentary*) , New York, 1916.

Ante-Nicene Fathers, ten volumes, reprint, Grand Rapids, Mich., 1950, for references to Clement of Alexandria, Irenaeus, Justin Martyr, Origen, Tertullian, etc.

Barclay, W., *The Letters to the Philippians, Colossians, and Thessalonians* (*The Daily Study Bible Series*) , second edition, Philadelphia, 1959.

Barnes, A., *Notes on the New Testament, Ephesians, Philippians and Colossians,* reprint, Grand Rapids, Mich., 1949; also *Thess.-Philemon.*

Barnett, A. E., *The New Testament: Its Making and Meaning,* Nashville, 1946.

Beare, F. W., *The Epistle to the Colossians* (*Interpreter's Bible,* Vol. XI) , New York and Nashville, 1955.

Benoit, P., *La Sainte Bible traduite en francais sous la direction de l'École Biblique de Jerusalem,* 1949.

Berkhof, L., *New Testament Introduction,* Grand Rapids, Mich., 1916.

Berkhof, L., *Systematic Theology,* Grand Rapids, Mich., 1949.

Bible, Holy, In addition to references to Bible-versions other than English, there are references to the following English translations: A.V., A.R.V., R.S.V., Berkeley, N.E.B., New American Standard, Moffatt, Goodspeed. These are references. The *translation* which is found in N.T.C. and followed in the exegesis is the author's own.

Bieder, W., *Brief an die Kolosser,* Zurich, 1943.

Bruce, F. F., *Commentary on the Epistle to the Colossians* (*New International Commentary on the New Testament*) , Grand Rapids, Mich., 1957.

Buckler, W. H., and Calder, W. M., *Monumenta Asiae Minoris Antiqua,* Vol. VI. *Monuments and Documents from Phrygia and Caria,* 1939.

Burney, C. F., "Christ as the ARXH of Creation," *JTS* xxvii (1925, 1926) , pp. 160 ff.

Burrows, M., *The Dead Sea Scrolls,* New York, 1956.

Burrows, M., *More Light on the Dead Sea Scrolls,* New York, 1958.

Calvin, John, *Commentarius In Epistolam Pauli Ad Colossenses. . . . Ad Philemonem* (*Corpus Reformatorum,* vol. LXXX) , Brunsvigae, 1895; English translation (*Calvin's Commentaries*) , Grand Rapids, Mich., respectively, 1957, 1948.

Charlesworth, M. P., *Trade Routes and Commerce of the Roman Empire,* 1924.

Conybeare, W. J., and Howson, J. S., *The Life and Epistles of St. Paul,* reprint, Grand Rapids, Mich., 1949.

Cullmann, O., *Königsherrschaft Christi und Kirche im N.T.,* 1950.

Deissmann, A., *Light From the Ancient East* (translated by L. R. M. Strachan) , New York, 1927.

Dennis, J. S., *Christian Missions and Social Progress* (3 volumes) , New York, Chicago, Toronto, 1899.

Dibelius, M., *An die Kolosser, Epheser, an Philemon* (Lietzmann's *Handbuch zum Neuen Testament*) , 3rd edition, revised by H. Greeven, Tübingen, 1953.

GENERAL BIBLIOGRAPHY

Dodd, C. H., *Colossians and Philemon* (*Abingdon Commentary*), 1929.

Erdman, C. R., *The Epistles of Paul to the Colossians and Philemon*, Philadelphia, 1933.

Findlay, G. G., "The Reading and Rendering of Colossians 2:18," *Exp,* first series, 11 (1880), pp. 385-398.

Findlay, G. G., "On Colossians 2:22, 23," *Exp,* first series, 12 (1880), pp. 289-303.

Forschungen in Ephesos veröffentlicht vom Österreichschen archäologischen Institute, 1906-1953.

Fransen, H., "Enkele Opmerkingen over de exegese van Kol. 2:8 en 9," *GTT* (1952), pp. 65-89.

Glover, R. H., *The Progress of World-Wide Missions,* New York, N.Y., 1925.

Goodenough, "Paul and Onesimus," *HTR,* 22 (1929), pp. 181-183.

Goodspeed, E. J., *New Solutions to New Testament Problems,* Chicago, 1927.

Goodspeed, E. J., *The Meaning of Ephesians,* Chicago, 1933.

Goodspeed, E. J., *The Key to Ephesians,* Chicago, 1956.

Greeven, H., "Prüfung der Thesen von J. Knox zum Philemon brief," *TZ,* 79 (1954), pp. 373-378.

Greijdanus, S., *Bizondere Canoniek,* Kampen, 1949, two volumes.

Grollenberg, L. H., *Atlas of the Bible,* tr. of *Atlas van de Bijbel*), London and Edinburgh, 1956.

Grosheide, F. W., "Kol. 3:1-4; I Petr. 1:3-5; I Joh. 3:1, 2," *GTT* 54 (1954), pp. 139-147.

Hamilton, W. J., *Researches in Asia Minor, Pontus, and Armenia,* 1842.

Harris, J. R., "St. Paul and Aristopanes," *ET* 34 (1922, 1923), pp. 151-156.

Harrison, P. N., "Onesimus and Philemon," *ATR,* XXXII (1950), pp. 286-294.

Hendriksen, W., *Bible Survey,* Grand Rapids, Mich., sixth printing, 1961.

Hendriksen, W., *More Than Conquerors, An Interpretation of the Book of Revelation,* Grand Rapids, Mich., thirteenth edition, 1963.

Hendriksen, W., *The Bible on the Life Hereafter,* Grand Rapids, Mich., second printing, 1963.

Holtzmann, H. J., *Kritik der Epheser- und Kolosserbriefe,* 1872.

Hopkins, C., and Baur, P. V. C., *Christian Church at Dura-Europos,* New Haven, 1934.

Hurlbut, J. L., *A Bible Atlas,* New York, Chicago, San Francisco, 1940.

Johnson, Sherman E., "Laodicea and its Neighbors," *BA,* Vol. XIII (Feb. 1950), pp. 1-18.

Johnson, Sherman E., "Early Christianity in Asia Minor," *JBL,* 77 (March 1958), pp. 1-17.

Käsemann, E., "Eine urchristliche Taufliturgie," *Festschrift Rudolf Bultmann zum 65. Geburtstag überreicht,* 1949.

Keller, W., *The Bible as History,* New York, N.Y., 1956.

Knox, J., *The Epistle to Philemon* (Interpreter's Bible, Vol. XI), New York, 1955.

Knox, J., *Philemon among the Letters of Paul,* Chicago, 1959.

Kraeling, E., *Rand McNally Bible Atlas,* New York, Chicago, San Francisco, 1956.

Kremer, J., *Was an den Leiden Christi noch mangelt. Eine interpretationsgechichliche und exegetische Untersuchung zu Kol. 1, 24b* (Bonner, *Biblische Beiträge*), 1956.

Kuiper, H. J. (editor), *The New Christian Hymnal,* Grand Rapids, Mich., 1929.

Lenski, R. C. H., *Interpretation of Colossians, Thessalonians, Timothy, Titus, Philemon,* Columbus, Ohio, 1946.

Lightfoot, J. B., *Saint Paul's Epistle to the Colossians and to Philemon,* reprint of 1879 edition, Grand Rapids, Mich.

GENERAL BIBLIOGRAPHY

Loeb Classical Library, New York (various dates), for The Apostolic Fathers, Eusebius, Horodotus, Josephus, Philo, Pliny, Plutarch, Strabo, Xenophon, etc.

Lohmeyer, E., *Die Briefe an die Kolosser und an Philemon (Meyers Kommentar)*, Göttingen, 1930.

Lukyn, W. A., *The Epistles of Paul to the Colossians and to Philemon (Cambridge Greek Testament for Schools and Colleges)*, Cambridge, 1907.

Marsh, F. B., *A History of the Roman World from 146-30 B. C.*, second edition, London, 1953.

Masson, C., *L'Épître de Saint Paul aux Colossiens (Commentaire du Nouveau Testament, X)*, 1950.

Matheson, G., "The Pauline Argument for a Future State," *Exp,* first series, 9 (1879), pp. 264-284.

Maurer, C., "Die Begründung der Herrschaft Christi über die Mächte nach Kolosser 1:15-20," *Wort und Dienst, Jahrbuch der Theologischen Schule Bethel,* n.F.IV (1955), pp. 79-93.

Mayerhoff, E. Th., *Der Brief an die Colosser mit vornehmlichter Berücksichtigung der drei Pastoralbriefe kritisch geprüft,* Berlin, 1838.

Mitton, C. L., *The Formation of the Pauline Corpus of Letters,* London, 1955.

Moule, C. F. D., *The Epistles of Paul the Apostle to the Colossians and to Philemon* ("Cambridge Greek Testament Commentary"), Cambridge, 1957.

Mulder, H., *De vondsten bij de Dode Zee,* 's-Gravenhage, 1957.

Müller, J. J., *The Epistles of Paul to the Philippians and to Philemon (The New International Commentary on the New Testament)*, Grand Rapids, Mich., 1955.

Murray, J., *Christian Baptism,* Philadelphia, 1952.

National Geographic Magazine, "Lands of the Bible Today" (Dec. 1956); in the same issue, "Jerusalem to Rome in the Path of St. Paul." Also published by National Geographic: *Everyday Life in Ancient Times,* 1953.

Norden, E., *Agnostos Theos,* 1913.

Paulus, H. E. G., *Philologisch-kritischer Kommentar über das Neue Testament,* Lübeck, 1800.

Peake, A. S., *Critical Introduction to the New Testament,* 1909.

Peake, A. S., *The Epistle to the Colossians (The Expositor's Bible,* Vol. III), Grand Rapids, Mich., 1943.

Percy, E., *Die Problem der Kolosser- und Epheserbriefe,* Lund, 1946.

Piper, O. A., "The Savior's Eternal Work; An Exegesis of Col. 1:9-29," *Int,* 3 (1949), pp. 286-298.

Pope, R. M., "Studies in Pauline Vocabulary; Redeeming the Time," *ET* 22 (1910, 1911), pp. 552-554.

Radford, L. B., *The Epistle to the Colossians and the Epistle to Philemon (The Westminster Commentary)*, London, 1931.

Ramsay, W. M., *Historical Geography of Asia Minor,* London, 1890.

Ramsay, W. M., *The Church in the Roman Empire,* London, 1893.

Ramsay, W. M., *Cities and Bishoprics of Phrygia* (two vols.), London, 1895-1897.

Ramsay, W. M., *The Letters to the Seven Churches of Asia,* London, 1904.

Ramsay, W. M., *The Teaching of Paul in Terms of the Present Day,* London, 1913.

Rendtorff, H., *Das Neue Testament Deutsch, 8. Die Kleineren Briefe des Apostels Paulus,* Göttingen, 1949.

Ridderbos, Herman, *Aan de Kolossenzen (Commentaar op het Nieuwe Testament)*, Kampen, 1960.

Robertson, A. T., *Word Pictures in the New Testament,* New York and London, 1931, Vol. IV, on Philemon and Colossians, pp. 464-513.

GENERAL BIBLIOGRAPHY

Robinson, J. A., "The Church as the Fulfilment of the Christ: a Note on Ephesians 1:23," *Exp*, 5th series, 7 (1898), pp. 241-259.

Robinson, J. A. T., *The Body*, 1952.

Robinson, J. M., "A Formal Analysis of Colossians 1:15-20," *JBL*, Vol. LXXVI, Part IV (Dec. 1957), pp. 270-288.

Rutherford, John, "St. Paul's Epistle to the Laodiceans," *ET*, 19 (1907, 1908), pp. 311-314.

Schille, "Liturgisches Gut im Epheserbrief," doctoral dissertation, Göttingen, 1952.

Schultze, V., *Altchristliche Staedte und Landschaften*, II, Kleinasien, 1922.

Scott, E. F., *The Epistles of Paul to the Colossians, to Philemon, and to the Ephesians (Moffatt Commentary)*, New York, 1930.

Simpson, E. K., *Words Worth Weighing in the Greek New Testament*, London, 1946.

Stonehouse, N. B., *Origins of the Synoptic Gospels*, Grand Rapids, Mich., 1963.

Thiessen, H. C., *Introduction to the New Testament*, Grand Rapids, Mich., 1943.

Trench, R. C., *Synonyms of the New Testament*, edition, Grand Rapids, Mich., 1948.

Van Leeuwen, J. A. C., *Paulus' Zendbrieven aan Efeze, Colosse, Filemon, en Thessalonika (Kommentaar op het Nieuwe Testament)*, Amsterdam, 1926.

Vincent, M. R., *The Epistles to the Philippians and to Philemon (International Critical Commentary)*, New York, 1906.

Wiggers, F., "Das Verhältniss des Apostels Paulus zu der christlichen Gemeinde in Kolossä," *TSK* (1838), pp. 165-188.

Windisch, H., "Die götliche Weisheit der Juden und die paulinische Christologie," *Neutest. Studien für Heinrici*, 1914.

Wood, J. F., *Discoveries at Ephesus*, 1877.

Wright, G. E., *Biblical Archaeology*, London and Philadelphia, 1957.

Young, E. J., "The Teacher of Righteousness and Jesus Christ, Some Reflections Upon the Dead Sea Scrolls," *WTJ*, Vol. XVIII, No. 2 (May, 1956), p. 145.

Zahn, Th., *Einleitung in das Neue Testament*, 1897-1900.

Zwemer, S. M., *Across the World of Islam*, London and Edinburgh, 1929.

roma
dennis hopper
brad pitt chr
BRAD
PITT
DIANE
KRUGER
KILL
BILL 2
INGL RIOUS
BASTERDS
THE NEW FILM BY
ROLLING
QUENTIN TARANTINO/PRODUCED BY LAWRENCE BENDER
KILL
KILL BIL
THE FOURTH FILM BY QUENTIN TAR
KILL BILL
OUT NOW

TOM SHONE

TARANTINO
A RETROSPECTIVE

With over 250 illustrations

Thames & Hudson

For Gavin
TS

First published in the United Kingdom in 2017
by Thames & Hudson Ltd, 181A High Holborn,
London WC1V 7QX

Reprinted in 2018

Design and layout © 2017 Palazzo Editions Ltd
Text © 2017 by Tom Shone

Created and produced by
Palazzo Editions Ltd
15 Church Road
London SW13 9HE
www.palazzoeditions.com

Design by Amazing15

Sources for images on the cover: Front © Nicolas Guerin/Contour by Getty Images. Back cover,
clockwise from top: *Reservoir Dogs* (Entertainment/REX/Shutterstock), On the set of *Reservoir
Dogs* (Collection Christophel/Alamy), *The Hateful Eight* (Everett Collection Inc/Alamy), *Pulp Fiction*
(Vista/REX/Shutterstock), *Kill Bill* (AF Archive/Alamy Stock Photo).
Please see picture credits on page 255 for further image copyright information

British Library Cataloguing-in-Publication Data
A catalogue record for this book is available from the British Library

ISBN 978-0-500-51948-6

Printed and bound in China

To find out about all our publications, please visit **www.thamesandhudson.com**.
There you can subscribe to our e-newsletter, browse or download our current catalogue,
and buy any titles that are in print.

PAGES 2–3: Portrait by Levon Biss, 2012.

CONTENTS

INTRODUCTION

WHEN Quentin Tarantino writes a movie, the first thing he does is go to the stationery store and buy a 250-page notebook, along with some black and red felt pens. He used to write in public— restaurants, bars, coffeehouses, in the backs of station wagons, anywhere but home—but he recently wrote *Django Unchained* on the balcony of his bedroom in his large rambling mansion in the Hollywood Hills. The balcony overlooks a swimming pool, an orange tree, and, in the distance, green-ridged canyons. He keeps some small speakers on the balcony so that he can listen to his mixtapes.

Tarantino gets up at around 10 a.m. or 11 a.m., unplugs his landline, moseys out onto the balcony, and puts in a full work day—six to eight hours if it's going well. He finds dialogue the easiest to write. To hear him tell it, he's not writing his characters' speech so much as transcribing it. Sometimes the best moments come when he thinks he's finished a scene. He had no idea that the gang in *Reservoir Dogs* would start arguing by themselves about the color of their names, for example. Nor did he know Mr. Blonde was going to pull a straight razor from his boot.

OPPOSITE: Framed by a projected clip from *Pulp Fiction*. RIGHT: At home in the Hollywood Hills, 2013.

"My head is a sponge," he said of his writing process. "I listen to what everyone says; I watch for little idiosyncratic behaviors. People tell me a joke, and I remember it. People tell me an interesting story in their life and I remember it . . . When I go and write my new characters, my pen is like an antenna—it receives that information, and, all of a sudden, these characters come out more or less fully formed. I don't write their dialogue; I get them talking to each other."

Frequently while writing, Tarantino will ring up friends and say "Listen to this," and then read them what he's written—not so much to get their approval but rather to hear it through their ears. After befriending film critic Elvis Mitchell at the 2004 Sitges Film Festival, Tarantino read the script for *Death Proof* to him on a hotel patio in Los Angeles.

"Even the car had a life of its own—and not just in the KITT 2000 sense either," noted Mitchell. "Tarantino's admiration for the characters came with awe because his reading demonstrated how each of the creations took on a self-involved, argumentative life of their own . . . The fascinating thing about hearing him read the pages aloud is how each of the characters has something very specific at stake—in most cases, a hunger to be understood on their own terms."

RIGHT: Surrounded by his craft, Tarantino is photographed by Patrick Fraser at his home in California, 2013.

Once Tarantino has finished a script, he types it out using one finger on a Smith Corona typewriter/word processor that he inherited from an old girlfriend and has used since *Reservoir Dogs*. Despite an IQ of 160, the dyslexic Tarantino dropped out of junior high school in Harbor City, Los Angeles, in ninth grade. Since he can neither spell nor punctuate very well—"My stuff is unreadable," he claimed—he frequently gives the script to a friend or a typist to transcribe for him. Then he makes thirty to thirty-five copies and throws a party at his house.

"I send it out to Harvey Weinstein and other people, and then my friends just show up all day long and get their copies of it and drink champagne, and we celebrate. All day long, people come by and they pick up their copy— I don't watermark them or anything—and we hang out and we talk and we have food and drinks."

Inside the house, the walls are covered with movie posters. There are bronze sculptures of Mia Wallace from *Pulp Fiction*; Louis, Melanie, and Max Cherry from *Jackie Brown*; and Mr. Blonde from *Reservoir Dogs*, all of which Tarantino commissioned from an artist in Texas. A movie theater built into one wing of the house was designed to resemble an old-fashioned

> ## "If I were writing a Quentin character, he would be loud, lovely, soft, and so sweet you might not believe it— and, above all, he would be a mad motherf***er."
> ## —Paul Thomas Anderson

cinema, with wall-to-wall diamond-patterned carpeting, velvet ropes supported by short brass poles, and about fifty red seats in graduated rows for guests. At the front is a red sofa on which Tarantino sits when he's alone. When he comes home at night after a late double feature, it is not unheard of for him to head into his movie theater and watch a third or fourth movie, with his head tipped back, eyes wide, mouth slightly open.

Nobody knows the clichés of the Quentin Tarantino interview better than the man himself—a "motormouth" and "manic," he is always "lumbering" into a room, "gesticulating wildly," etc.—but his voice can be surprisingly soft and his hand gestures almost feminine, and he often touches the dimple in his chin when making a point. His ego gives off a strong hum, but so boundless are his enthusiasms, whether for his own work or other people's, that it almost comes across as an act of generosity.

"If I were writing a Quentin character, he would be loud, lovely, soft, and so sweet you might not believe it—and, above all, he would be a mad motherfucker," his friend, director Paul Thomas Anderson, told *Vanity Fair* in 2003. "I would cast someone with large balls, a lumbering walk, and a gentle, gentle touch."

TOP: Striking his signature pose for a portrait by Martyn Goodacre, 1994.
BOTTOM: With long-time producer Harvey Weinstein, at the Hollywood premiere of *Inglourious Basterds*, August, 2009.

That gentleness comes out the most with his actors. An actor himself, he delights in the Oprah-esque wish-fulfillment aspect of casting, often bypassing formal channels to tell an actor he has written a part specifically for them.

"I was doing a play in London, and one night, after the curtain, Quentin showed up in my dressing room," said Daryl Hannah of how Tarantino came to cast her in *Kill Bill*. "He said he'd flown to London to see me in the play because he wanted to tell me he'd written a part for me in this movie. I'd never met him before. He said he saw me in some cable movie I did, which I never even saw and don't remember the name of. I went, 'Uh-huh. Where's *Candid Camera*?' You don't know whether to believe it or not, and then a few months later he sends me the script. It was just awesome."

Before making a final decision, Tarantino likes to hang out with an actor he is considering for a lead in one of his films, a routine he established after spending an evening getting drunk with Tim Roth on the Sunset Strip while casting *Reservoir Dogs*. Before casting John Travolta in *Pulp Fiction*, he invited the actor around to his apartment; they ended up singing "You're the One That I Want" into the early hours of the morning.

He likes to shoot scenes long, sometimes as long as ten minutes, with few cuts, a style he first established in *Reservoir Dogs*. On set, he bounds everywhere, talking to everyone, his jackhammer laugh sounding every ninety seconds or so, but when giving directions to his actors, he goes into a huddle. "Quentin whispers his directions to you, which is cool; it makes one feel like an accomplice," noted David Carradine during the making of *Kill Bill*. "He is very excited, extremely focused on the impact of the moments he is attempting to capture . . . [He] walks a razor's edge between obsessed visionary and doting mother hen."

Tarantino is one of the few directors working today who doesn't use a video monitor. He checks the framing of each shot before it begins but stays focused on what is happening in front of the camera. During the dance scene at Jack Rabbit Slim's in *Pulp Fiction*, he danced alongside John Travolta and Uma Thurman, just out of frame, and applauded when they were finished. "For thirteen hours you have completely captivated us," he told his stars.

During production, Tarantino screens a lot of movies. "Quentin has the greatest knowledge of cinema of anyone you'll run into, and that's infused into the day's work," said Brad Pitt of the shoot for *Inglourious Basterds,* where every Thursday was movie night, with the director screening everything from *The Good, the Bad and the Ugly* to German propaganda films to obscure gems such as *Dark of the Sun*.

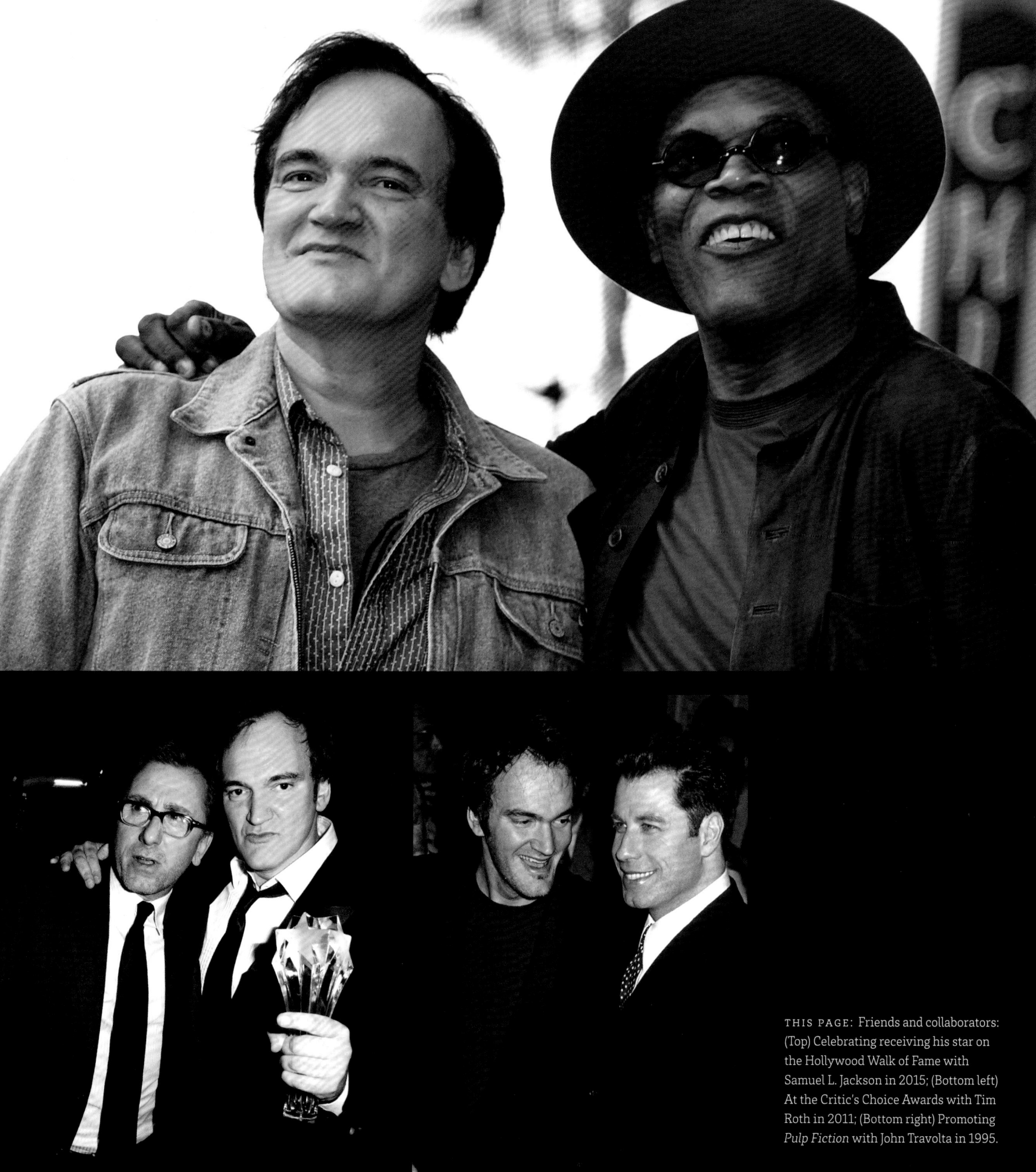

THIS PAGE: Friends and collaborators: (Top) Celebrating receiving his star on the Hollywood Walk of Fame with Samuel L. Jackson in 2015; (Bottom left) At the Critic's Choice Awards with Tim Roth in 2011; (Bottom right) Promoting *Pulp Fiction* with John Travolta in 1995.

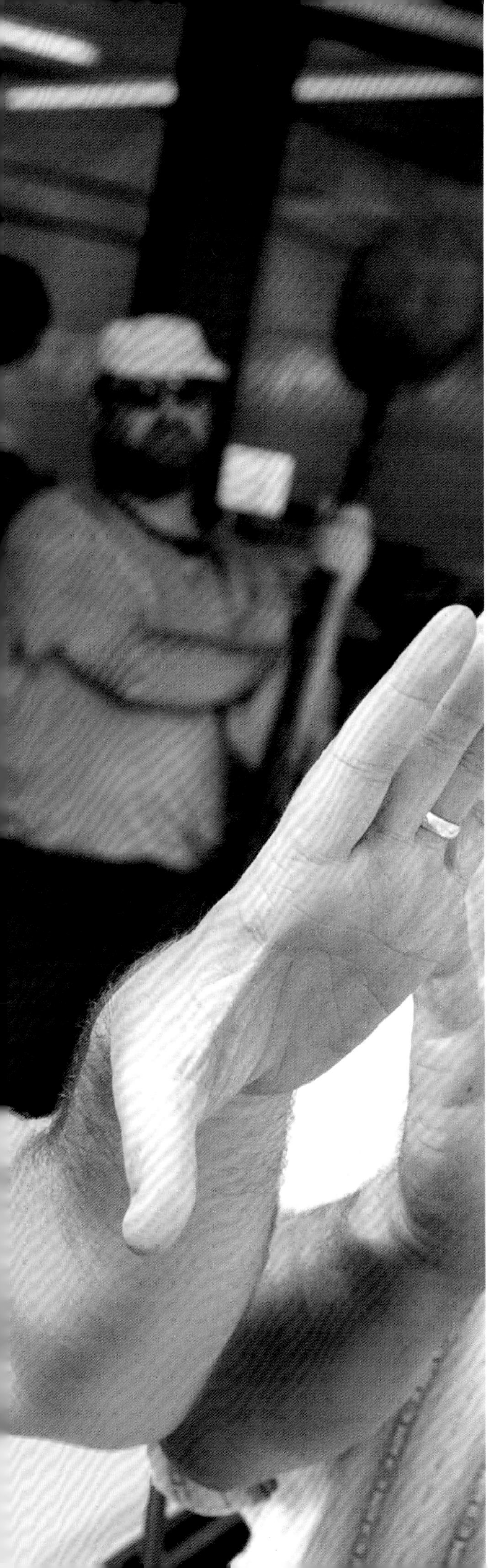

Once the week's shooting is done, Tarantino likes to party, often staying up late on Saturday and sleeping it off on Sunday before being ready for work again on Monday. "Quentin is very determined about having fun," said Carradine. "He pursues it with a resoluteness, a rigor, that is irresistible and cannot fail." On *Kill Bill*, Tarantino and his crew hit the bars in Beijing, which stayed open all night, and took ecstasy on the Great Wall of China. On *Django Unchained*, they visited the bars of New Orleans. "We would be out till six or seven in the morning and then just sleep all day and recuperate Sunday, maybe show a movie, and be back at it Monday," Tarantino said. "The weekend comes and all I want to do is smoke out to veg. It's just shutting down."

Until her sudden death by heatstroke in 2010 while walking her dog in Bronson Canyon, Sally Menke edited every one of Tarantino's films, from *Reservoir Dogs* to *Inglourious Basterds*, working out of a specially converted private house rather than on the studio lot. By the time they made *Kill Bill*, their rhythm had become so instinctive that they didn't speak until five months into the shoot, Menke editing the rough cut of both movies while Tarantino continued to film.

"We're kinda like a movie husband and wife," said Menke of their collaboration. "The thing with Tarantino is the mix-and-match. We do study other films and other scenes but only to get the vibe we need for our scene—like for *Kill Bill*

LEFT: Framing a shot on the set of *Death Proof*, 2006. ABOVE: The "movie husband and wife." Quentin with friend and editor Sally Menke at the American Cinema Editors Awards, Beverly Hills, 2007.

when Uma's facing off the Crazy 88, we looked at some Sergio Leone close-ups to see how we wanted to cut that scene. Our style is to mimic, not homage, but it's all about recontextualizing the film language to make it fresh within the new genre. It's incredibly detailed."

Tarantino is an avid audience watcher. He saw *Jackie Brown* thirteen times at the Magic Johnson Theaters upon its release and drove to eight different theaters around Los Angeles in his yellow-and-black Mustang to gauge audience reaction to *Death Proof*. He attended an 11 a.m. showing of *The Hateful Eight* on Christmas Day at the Del Amo Mall in Torrance, where he grew up and where a large section of *Jackie Brown* was shot.

Tarantino's views on the cinematic experience are paradoxical. On the one hand, he sees it as a radically subjective experience: "If a million people see my movie, I want them to make a million different movies in their head," he said, hence his reluctance to settle such debates as what the title of *Reservoir Dogs* means or what the suitcase in *Pulp Fiction* contains. At the same time, he added, "I like fucking with your emotions, and I like it when it's done to me. That's my thing. The audience and the director, it's an S-and-M relationship, and the audience is the M. It's exciting! When you go out and have pie afterward, you've got some shit to talk about. You went to the movies that night!"

It is the tension generated by these two positions—the director as genial sadist, yanking the audience's chain; and the director as tender lover, feeding their subjectivity—that makes Tarantino the filmmaker he is. He directs from the front row.

"I am first and foremost a film fanatic," he told interviewers when he first exploded onto the scene with *Reservoir Dogs* in 1992. And "I am first and foremost a film geek." While most directors would say that with a note of fond self-deprecation for their younger apprentice selves, Tarantino said it as if pinning the highest badge of honor to his chest. In some ways, he sees himself as a film fan before he sees himself as a film director. It forms the core of his identity.

While working at Video Archives in Manhattan Beach, Tarantino would collect clippings about new Brian De Palma pictures—*Scarface* in 1983, say, or *Body Double* in 1984—and arrange them in a scrapbook in the months leading up to the release. On the day the film came out, he would go to the first show, at noon, by himself. Then, having gotten the plot out of the way, he would see a midnight showing that night with a friend.

"From seventeen to twenty-two, I used to make lists of every movie I saw in a given year in the theaters, including revival theaters," Tarantino said. "If it was a new release, I circled the number. And I would pick my favorite movies and give out my little awards. It was always the same amount back then; it was 197 or 202. And

"I don't consider myself just as a director, but as a movie man who has the whole treasure of the movies to choose from and take whatever gems I like, bring things together that have never been matched up before."

"I have loved movies as the number one thing in my life so long that I can't ever remember a time when I didn't."

BELOW: Often taking a minor role in his movies, Tarantino played the getaway driver, Mr. Brown, in his first major film, *Reservoir Dogs* (1992).

that's when I was broke and I was paying for those movies myself. Back at my most voracious moviegoing, 200 was the average."

Shooting *Breathless* (1960) on lightweight Arriflex cameras from the back of shopping trolleys, Jean-Luc Godard exploded the syntax of American gangster movies and refashioned it into his own distinct form of cinematic jazz. And, in the process, he gave the world a template for the independent movie. Tarantino would do something similar with *Reservoir Dogs* and *Pulp Fiction*, films that mixed explosive violence, long takes, and hilariously profane riffs on everything from burgers to Madonna—and in the process ushered independent moviemaking into its second, $100-million phase. "Miramax is the house Quentin Tarantino built," Miramax founder Harvey Weinstein said. "Because of his stature, he has carte blanche." Tarantino stands, in the words of the writer Clancy Sigal, "at the Hollywood crossroads where guilty laughter and sadistic brutality merge."

Like Godard's, too, Tarantino's films glint with borrowings, references, and homages to other films—pinning a line here, a scene there, a character in this script, a situation in that one, before executing an abrupt left turn that leaves the cliché hanging.

"Call it plagiarism, call it intertextuality, but Tarantino has the ability to make anything sound

his own," said James Mottram in his book *The Sundance Kids*. In 1993, Graham Fuller called Tarantino "not so much a postmodern auteur as a *post*-postmodern one, for he is feverishly interested in pop-cultural artifacts and ideas that themselves spring from earlier incarnations or have already been mediated or predigested." He does this to not just show off how clever he is for making the connection or congratulate the audience for being in on the joke, but so that everyone can engage in the game of juggled expectations that results. He wants, above all, to *play*.

"In the first ten minutes of nine out of ten movies—and this applies to a whole lot of independent films that are released, not the ones that can't find a release—the movie tells you what kind of movie it's gonna be," Tarantino said. "It tells you everything that you basically need to know. And, after that, when the movie's getting ready to make a left turn, the audience starts leaning to the left; when it's getting ready to make a right turn, the audience moves to the right; when it's supposed to suck 'em in, they move up close. You know just what's gonna happen. You don't know you know, but you know. Admittedly, there's a lot of fun in playing against that, fucking up the breadcrumb trail that we don't even know we're following and using an audience's own subconscious preconceptions against them so they're actually having a viewing experience

and are actually involved in the movie. Yeah, I'm interested in doing that just as a storyteller. But the heartbeat of the movie has to be a human heartbeat."

When he first arrived on the scene, the critical rap on Tarantino was immediate, unanimous, and almost wholly wrong: Here, they said, was a callow master of blood-spattered spectacle, the pied piper of movie mayhem, making ultraviolent movies with no connection to the real world. Review after review repeated the same mantra: violence, violence, violence. And: no connection whatsoever to reality. Film critic David Thomson wrote, "Tarantino does not seem to know, much less possess, the life alluded to in [Howard Hawks's] films. His characters are all taken from actors and acting classes. It is a safe bet that Tarantino has known few if any gangsters. He has certainly never seen a head blown off. But he treasures every hood from the history of American film." The charge was repeated so much that even his colleagues began to repeat it. "The one problem people have with Quentin's work is that it speaks of other movies instead of life," said his cowriter on *Pulp Fiction*, Roger Avary. "The big trick is to live a life, and then make movies about that life."

To be fair, Tarantino has aided and abetted this myth himself, baiting interviewers with

such statements as, "To me, violence is a totally aesthetic subject. Saying you don't like violence in movies is like saying you don't like dance sequences in movies," and "I don't even know what gratuitous *means*."

But a life spent watching movies is still a life—Tarantino's films are much more grooved by the particulars of his experience than people think, which is not quite the same thing as saying that they are autobiographical. He distinguishes sharply between the films he makes like *Kill Bill*,

ABOVE: Photographed in 2007 at his recently purchased New Beverly Cinema in West Los Angeles, where he continues to do the vast majority of monthly programming and exclusively screens film prints.

VINCENT

In Paris, you can buy beer at McDonald's. Also, you know what they call a Quarter Pounder with Cheese in Paris?

JULES

They don't call it a Quarter Pounder with Cheese?

VINCENT

No, they got the metric system there, they wouldn't know what the fuck a Quarter Pounder is.

JULES

What'd they call it?

VINCENT

Royale with Cheese.

JULES

(repeating)
Royale with Cheese. What'd they call a Big Mac?

VINCENT

Big Mac's a Big Mac, but they call it Le Big Mac.

JULES

What do they call a Whopper?

VINCENT

I dunno, I didn't go into a Burger King.

ABOVE: Tarantino is renowned for his memorable dialogue in which characters like Jules and Vincent in *Pulp Fiction* riff on pop culture before pulling off their next crime.

which are set in the "movie-movie universe, where movie conventions are embraced, almost fetish-ized," and those of the "other universe, where *Pulp Fiction* and *Reservoir Dogs* take place, in which reality and movie conventions collide." His best work resounds with the shock of that collision. Plots veer off suddenly at perpendicular angles and movie-ish happenings are dropped into the laps of unmovieish characters who freak out, squabble, lose the plot, or miss out on everything because they are on the toilet. Guns misfire, people get shot over pop tarts, thieves fall out over what color-coded names they are going to pick. And the audience laughs in recognition, not because they have ever committed a diamond heist or shot someone over pop tarts, but because when his characters open their mouths, they sound like *this*:

The truly great thing about this exchange is the dud note at the end. Vincent's non sequitur often gets as big of a laugh from audiences as the lines that precede it. A lesser writer than Tarantino would have given him a wittier payoff, but Tarantino's ear seeks out something that stays true to the strange little hiccups and misfires that trip up everyday conversation. "Maybe his greatest gift as a screenwriter is that complete immersion in loving to hear people talk," wrote film critic Elvis Mitchell, "particularly people who have enormous confidence in expressing themselves verbally, part Robert Towne, part Chester Himes and part Patricia Highsmith."

There is, in other words, plenty of reality in Tarantinoland—albeit not in the bright pop-art production design of his movies, nor their winking assemblage of genre tropes—but rather every time one of his characters opens their mouth. His films are black comedies about the gulf between movies and reality, where the reality is supplied by the way people speak. Like all revolutionary ideas, Tarantino's insight seems obvious now, but it rests on a simple observation: "Most of us don't talk about the plot in our lives," he once noted. "We talk all around things. We talk about bullshit. And we talk about stuff that interests us. Gangsters don't just talk about gangster-plot-related stuff, polish their bullets, talk about this murder, that murder. They talk about something on the radio; they talk about the chicken dinner they had last night; they talk about this girl they met."

It's true. Gangsters in *The Godfather* (1972) certainly didn't sit around talking about the lyrics of their favorite songs. Martin Scorsese's *Goodfellas* (1990) didn't get into disputes about their favorite TV shows, although the pool-hall argument about the meaning of the word "mook" in *Mean Streets* (1973) is an obvious precursor to Tarantino's gutter talk. Until he came along, people in movies generally didn't admit to going to the movies to anything like the extent that Tarantino and his friends did. By the late 1980s, however, with the video and home theater revolutions, pop culture had reached such a level of penetration into people's lives that it was beginning to show up on its own radar. By 1990, *Seinfeld*'s Jerry and George could be heard debating whether Superman had a sense of humor or not ("I never

heard him say anything really funny"). In 1988's *Die Hard*, Alan Rickman's Hans Gruber taunts John McClane (Bruce Willis): "Another orphan of a bankrupt culture who thinks he's John Wayne? Rambo?" To which McClane replies, "I was always kinda partial to Roy Rogers actually . . . *yippee ki-yay, motherfucker*!"—the best line of Tarantino dialogue not actually written by Quentin Tarantino.

"He seems to think the way the audience thinks, and to have grasped how sick we are of seeing through every limp scenario in two minutes," wrote Sarah Kerr in her review of *Pulp Fiction* for the *New York Review of Books*.

Tarantino hot-wired the zeitgeist of the mid-nineties in a way that no filmmaker has done since, retuning the ears of cinemagoers with his crazily entertaining and ferociously profane dialogue in much the same way David Mamet did for 1980s theatergoers. He introduced the idea that violence could be funny into the mainstream and (over)impressed an entire generation of filmmakers. In the years following *Pulp Fiction*, it was impossible to miss the mushroom patch of films featuring characters pulling off crimes while riffing on pop culture, from *Bad Boys* to *Love and a .45* to *Lucky Number Slevin* to *The Usual Suspects* to *Too Many Ways to Be No. 1*. "You'd be hard-pressed to find a coffee shop, public library, or backseat of a station wagon in Southern California where screenwriters-marque aren't aping his low-tech DIY scribbling," noted Mitchell, "hunched over legal pads and English composition notebooks in ways that will produce kinks and muscle strains some westside chiropractor will eventually have to beat and adjust out of them as they're trying to reproduce Tarantino™ sweat and caffeine stains on their own work—the film version of predistressed Martin Margiela shoes."

The spate of copycats has receded now. Twenty-five years on from *Reservoir Dogs*,

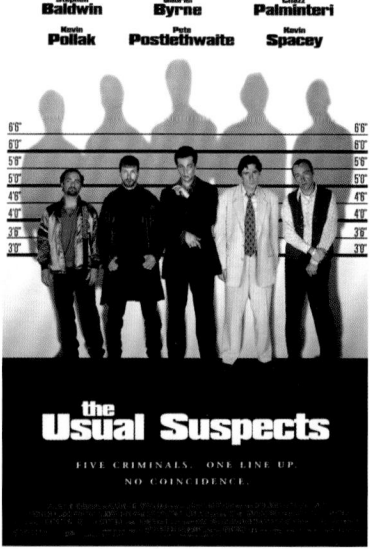

the controversy over its violence seems almost quaint. Critics thought *that* film was just a "flashy, stylistically daring exercise in cinematic mayhem." They should try *Kill Bill*. Tarantino is a different filmmaker these days, having exchanged the streetwise deconstructive comedy of his early work for the rambunctious burlesque of period genre pieces like *Inglourious Basterds* and *Django Unchained*—luridly sadistic spins in the B-movie-mobile that find their reality not in the mouths of the characters but in the cruelties of history, as remixed and redressed by Quentin Tarantino. The former *enfant terrible* is now fifty-four and a double Oscar winner. He's part of the canon from which he once quoted.

"I'm not a Hollywood outsider anymore," he said during a screening of *Django Unchained* at the Directors Guild, a Hollywood institution Tarantino famously resisted for the first two decades of his career. "I know a lot of people. I like them. They like me. I think I'm a pretty good member of this community, both as a person and as far as my job and contributions are concerned. Back in 1994, I think they were all pretty impressed with me, and that was cool, but I felt like an outsider, a maverick punk, and I was hoping I wouldn't fuck it up. I still do things my own way, but I didn't go away, either. I still kind of feel like I'm always trying to prove I belong here."

Here are the films that prove he does.

LEFT: The director with the fame of a movie star. Quentin poses for the cameras at the 2008 Cannes Film Festival.

EARLY YEARS

"I WANTED a name that would fill up the entire screen," said Connie McHugh, Tarantino's mother, a trainee nurse from Cleveland, Ohio, who had done everything she could to put some distance between her and her working-class redneck family. Her father owned a garage and was violent; her mother was an alcoholic. At the first opportunity, she bolted to California to live with an aunt and was just fourteen when she met Tarantino's father, Tony, a wastrel who fancied himself an actor and boasted of having attended classes at the Pasadena Playhouse while horseback riding in Burbank. Barely into boys, she married him just to get out of the house, but the relationship lasted only four months. She never told him she was fourteen. He had left by the time she realized she was pregnant.

> **"I come from a mixed family, where my mother is art house cinema and my father is B-movie genre cinema. They're estranged, and I've been trying to bring them together for all of my career to one degree or another."**

"His father did not even know that Quentin was born," said Connie, who named the child after her two favorite fictional characters, the one Burt Reynolds played in *Gunsmoke*, Quint Asper, and Miss Quentin in William Faulkner's *The Sound and the Fury*. The Nobel laureate and the star of *Smokey and the Bandit*. From the beginning, he was remixing the canon.

It sounds like a Tarantino movie—from that shotgun marriage of Faulkner and Reynolds to the figure of the teen bride left at the altar, her child raised in secret. It sounds like *Kill Bill: Volume 1* to be precise, in which Uma Thurman's Bride, left for dead at her own wedding and believing her own unborn child also dead, embarks on a course of bloody revenge that finally leads her to the door of her ex-lover and pretend "father of the bride," Bill.

But that is Tarantino's method: embedding the personal within the generic like a series of Russian dolls. "My movies are painfully personal, but I'm never trying to let you know how personal they are," he said. "It's my job to make it be personal, and also to disguise that so only I or the people who know me know how personal it is. *Kill Bill* is a *very* personal movie. It's not anyone's business. It's my job to invest in

PAGE 24: Aged twenty-eight, on the set of his first feature film, *Reservoir Dogs*, in 1991. LEFT: Quentin's estranged father Tony Tarantino, pictured in 2015. OPPOSITE: What a pair! Quentin's mother named her son after Quint Asper in *Gunsmoke* (top) and the character Miss Quentin in William Faulkner's *The Sound and the Fury* (bottom).

it and hide it inside of genre. Maybe there are metaphors for things that are going on in my life, or maybe it's just straight up how it is. But it's buried in genre, so it's not a 'how I grew up to write the novel' kind of piece. Whatever's going on with me at the time of writing is going to find its way into the piece. If that doesn't happen, then what the hell am I doing?"

A few weeks before he started shooting *Reservoir Dogs*, Tarantino was accepted into the Director's Lab workshop at the Sundance Film Festival and went there with Steve Buscemi to work on a couple of scenes from the film before an audience of professionals that included Terry Gilliam, Stanley Donen, and Volker Schlöndorff. "Have you done your subtext work?" one of the filmmakers asked him.

"No, what's that?" replied the twenty-eight-year-old.

"Ah, you see. You think because you wrote it, you know everything. But you don't know everything. You've done the writer work. You haven't done the director work. You need to do your subtext work."

He sat down and wrote, "What does Mr. White want from this scene more than anything else in the world? And what do I as a filmmaker

want the audience to take away from this scene more than anything else in the world?"

All of a sudden, Tarantino realized, "the more I wrote, the more I realized that the movie was a father–son story. And that Mr. White was functioning as Mr. Orange's father at that moment. And Mr. Orange was functioning as a son. But he was a son who betrayed his father. But his father doesn't know about the betrayal. And he's trying to hide it from them as long as he can because the guilt is really starting to hit him. Yet Mr. White has faith in Joe Cabot, who is his metaphorical father in this situation. And what does he keep saying? 'Just don't worry about it. Wait for Joe to get here. When Joe gets here, it's all gonna be fine. It's all going to be fine.' And what happens when Joe gets there? He kills Mr. Orange. And then actually Mr. White has to choose between his father—his metaphorical father—and his metaphorical son. And naturally he chooses his metaphorical son, and he's wrong. But he's wrong for all the right reasons. That was pretty heavy.

Many of his films would revisit the revenge motif and the theme of fathers, and even those that didn't would bristle with the cockiness of a teenager who has been let off the leash, with no father around to show him the ropes and teach him the rules. He would find it instead in the movies. His own films would be fascinated with a particular, hyperviolent almost cartoonish form of masculinity filled with wild boasts, rococo threats, and self-styled codes—codes he would then delight in striping bare, subject to pitiless deconstruction and humiliation.

"In a weird way, since I grew up basically without a father, you kind of go looking for it in other places," Tarantino said. "You get torn in all these different directions. When I was a kid, I totally didn't accept any of the prescribed things of right or wrong. I wanted to find a right or wrong inside my own heart. And since I didn't

have somebody showing me the way, I went looking for it, and, in a way, I guess I kind of found it with Howard Hawks's movies. I saw the ethic that he was proposing in his films, about men and their relationships with each other and with women . . . A girl I was talking to about this said I picked the right guy. He did a better job for me than half the fathers out there. I don't mean to drill this into my movies, but I guess they end up coming to the surface."

For a few years, Connie parked the kid with her mother to look after while she attended nursing school. At nineteen, she got a job in a doctor's office in Hacienda Heights and met her second husband, a twenty-five-year-old musician called Curt Zastoupil, after a gig he played at a piano bar in Monrovia Court. He was a scruffy vest and T-shirt kind of guy with a goatee who drove a cool Volkswagen Karmann Ghia. They married, moved to Manhattan Beach—a middle-class suburb just south of the airport—and sent for Quentin to join them. A bright, hyperactive, precocious child who preferred the company of adults to children, he tried to read every billboard and advertisement during the three-day drive from Knoxville to Los Angeles. He adored his new stepfather, insisted on taking his name, was obsessed with having his photograph taken with him in photo booths, and wore his rugged hiking boots to school.

"We were actually a bunch of kids living together," said Connie, who later invited Curt's younger brother, Cliff, and her younger brother, Roger, to live with them for a while. Together, they made up a motley male crew who babysat Quentin after Connie got a job at medical insurance company Cigna. "My brother said it was like being raised in Disneyland. When I was home with Quentin, our life revolved around him. We had hunting falcons; we fenced. We got kicked out of one apartment for our outrageous hobbies—fencing on a balcony. My husband

ABOVE: An early influence on Quentin was *Rio Bravo* director Howard Hawks. OPPOSITE: Films that first inspired a love of the movies included John Boorman's *Deliverance* and Mike Nichols's *Carnal Knowledge*.

was very eclectic. We had eclectic friends. We never left Quentin with a babysitter; if we went to an archery range, he'd come in the back of the car. We took him to every movie, regardless of whether it was appropriate, from the time he was three." Aged six, he saw a double-bill of Sam Peckinpah's ultra-violent western *The Wild Bunch* (1969) and John Boorman's hillbilly horror-story, *Deliverance* (1972).

"That scared the living shit out of me," Tarantino said. "Did I understand Ned Beatty being sodomized? No. But I knew he wasn't having any fun." Taken to see Mike Nichols's scalding sex-war bulletin *Carnal Knowledge* (1971) when he was eight, Tarantino saw the scene in which Art Garfunkel begs Candice Bergen to have sex with him—"Come on, let's do it, let's do it"—and piped up from the back row: "What's he want to do, Mom?" It brought the house down.

"My mom and her friends would take me to cool bars and stuff where they'd be playing cool, live rhythm-and-blues music and I'd be drinking Shirley Temples—I think I called them James Bonds because I didn't like the name Shirley Temple—and eat Mexican food while Jimmy Soul and a cool band would be, you know, playing in some lava lounge-y kind of seventies cocktail lounge," said Tarantino. "It was really cool. It made me grow up in a real big way. When I would hang around with kids I'd think they were really childish. I used to hang around with really groovy adults."

A free-for-all can seem like fun until it gets too unstable. Then you want to know what the rules are. When Tarantino was nine, his mother and Curt divorced; Tarantino came home from school to find the home empty, just like that. Curt was gone. Connie didn't want to talk about it. Quentin buried himself in comic books. It was almost as if he had broken up with Curt. When a drama teacher told him what a cool surname

it was, he quietly reverted to Tarantino. He was writing scripts by then, had been since the sixth grade, when he scribbled out a Burt Reynolds pastiche modeled on *Smokey and the Bandit* called "Captain Peachfuzz and the Anchovy Bandit," plus another script inspired by his massive crush on Tatum O'Neal, the precocious teen star whose picture was plastered all over his locker at school.

"He used to write Mother's Day stories for me, little dramas," said Connie. "Every year, I'd get a Mother's Day story. But he would always kill me in the story. And then he'd tell me how badly he felt about me dying and how much he loved me."

The relationship between mother and son was deteriorating. They moved to the South Bay area of Los Angeles, a depressing sprawl of ticky-tacky tract houses near the Los Angeles International Airport that was caught between the expensive beaches and the dangerous gang quarter to the east. She enrolled him in yet another new school, where he started skipping classes, hiding in the bathroom until his mother went to work, and then spending the rest of the

day at home, reading comic books and watching television. Connie would come home to hear him enacting loud, foul-mouthed battles from the kung-fu movies he had seen at Carson Twin Cinema with his G.I. Joe models. "It's not me, Mom; it's G.I. Joe!" he would yell down the stairs when she complained about his language. "He was sleeping all day, watching TV all night, and scribbling on paper," she recalled. "Pardon me if I didn't recognize that was genius. I thought it was avoidance of responsibility and living in a dream world. Nothing was important except movies, Hollywood . . . It drove me crazy."

He'd stopped liking school some time after kindergarten, unable to focus and bored by everything except history, which reminded him of the movies. In the ninth grade, he dropped out. "They called my mom, and when she asked me, I said, 'Yeah, I quit school,'" he recalled. "A couple days later, she said, 'I'm gonna let you quit, but you have to get a job.'"

Age fifteen and at a loss for what to do, he'd get into trouble, staying out late and drinking, and even shoplifting an Elmore Leonard novel from Kmart. After he was caught by the police,

"My movies are painfully personal, but I'm never trying to let you know how personal they are. It's my job to make it be personal, and also to disguise that so only I or the people who know me know how personal it is."

"My parents said, 'Oh, he's going to be a director someday,' and I didn't know what that was. I wanted to be an actor because when you're a little kid you want to be involved in movies."

RIGHT: Acting teacher Jack Lucarelli, pictured at the Beverly Hills Film Festival in April 2010, taught Tarantino about life in the film industry and later turned up as a rifleman in Tarantino's Oscar-winning *Django Unchained*.

Connie grounded him for the whole summer. He spent it reading in his room and, in the end, asked to enroll at the James Best acting school in Toluca Lake, which was named after *The Dukes of Hazzard* alumnus who had played Sheriff Rosco P. Coltrane. Dressed like a gang member, with a leather jacket, bandana, and single earring, Tarantino would engage in long arguments with his teacher, Jack Lucarelli, trying to convince him of the virtues of Sylvester Stallone. A fellow student, Rich Turner, would then give him a ride back to his house, always dropping him off at an exit off the busy Interstate 405 rather than his actual house. "He'd just disappear down the side of the freeway," recalled Turner. "I never once got to see his house."

Lying about his age, Tarantino got a job as an usher at one of Southern California's Pussycat porno theaters. "To me, it was the most ironic situation," he recalled. "I finally got a job at a movie theater, and it's a place where I don't want to watch the movies." He also conducted market research at a shopping mall near his home in Torrance and got work as a headhunter for a company with clients in the aerospace industry, before finding his way to Video Archives in Manhattan Beach.

Located in a six-building mini shopping mall close to a busy intersection on Sepulveda Boulevard, Video Archives was a tiny store whose customers barely had enough room to squeeze down the aisles. Movies played on the monitors all day long. The staff watched what they wanted: If they felt like watching Pier Paolo Pasolini, Pasolini it was. "I thought it was the coolest place I had ever seen in my life," said Tarantino. "The case could be made that it was really *too* terrific. I lost all my ambition for the first three years."

When one of the other clerks left in 1985, Roger Avary persuaded the store owner to take on the twenty-one-year-old Tarantino. It wasn't long before he was organizing mini–film festivals for the customers, using two shelves as a revolving showcase for some of his favorite

ABOVE: The one place where he didn't want to watch the movies. Quentin's first job was at a Pussycat porno theater in Southern California.

"When I make a film, I am hoping to reinvent the genre a little bit. I just do it my way. I make my own little Quentin versions of them. I consider myself a student of cinema. It's almost like I am going for my professorship in cinema and the day I die is the day I graduate. It is a lifelong study."

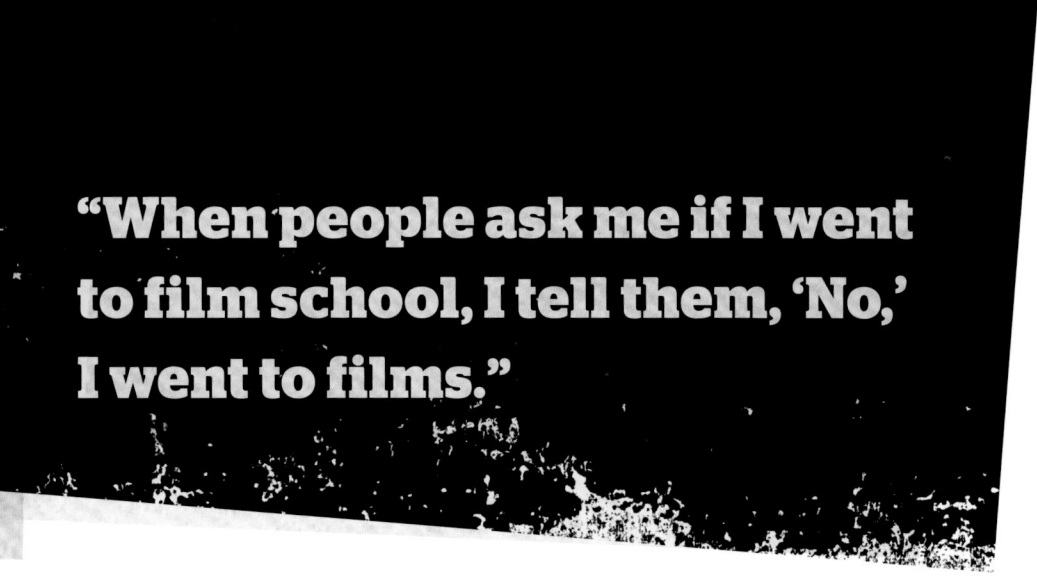

"When people ask me if I went to film school, I tell them, 'No,' I went to films."

subgenres: "Two Guys and a Girl" movies (*Jules and Jim*, *Bande à part*, and Howard Hawks's *A Girl in Every Port*); "A Bunch of Guys on a Mission" movies (*Where Eagles Dare* and *The Guns of Navarone*); "The Teacher I'll Never Forget" genre (*To Sir, with Love* and *Dead Poets Society*); "Mother Nature Goes Apeshit" movies (*Frogs*, *Willard*, and *Night of the Lepus*).

"Every week I would change it—David Carradine week or Nicholas Ray week or swashbuckler movies," Tarantino said. "For the most part, I tried to gear it for the customer. A housewife comes and, say, she wants something. I am twenty-four and she's fifty-four, so I'm not going to try to give her *Eraserhead* or *Forbidden Zone* or some kung-fu movie. If she likes Tom Hanks? I am not going to steer her toward *Bachelor Party*, but I could very well steer her toward *Nothing in Common*. 'Have you seen *Nothing in Common* with Tom Hanks and Jackie Gleason?'"

PAGES 34–35: Always obsessed with the movies, Tarantino is pictured at a video store in Glasgow, Scotland, in the early nineties. BELOW: Just a few of the many films Tarantino studied and showcased while working at movie store Video Archives.

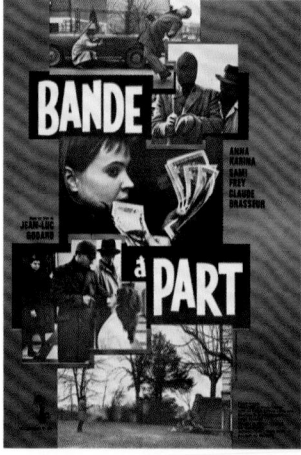

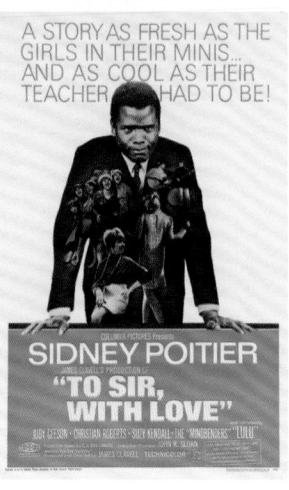

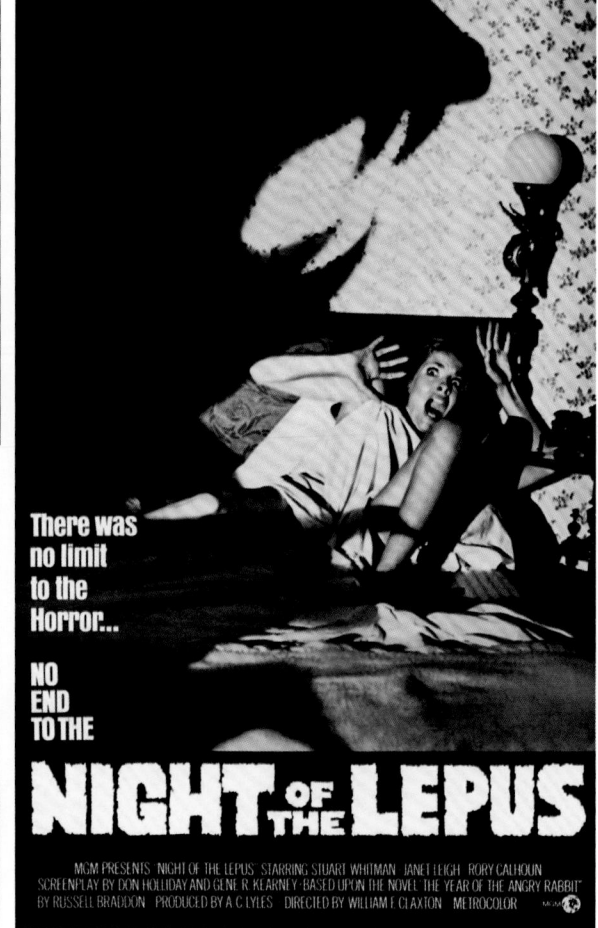

Video Archives was more than just a day job. "The store was my *Village Voice*, and I was the Andrew Sarris," said Tarantino, meaning it was the place where he sharpened his tastes and codified his personal canon. But it was even more that that. He would one day be famous for the accuracy of his ear for everyday speech, and, in particular, for the sound of people engaged in mock-pedantic arguments over the finer points of pop culture. Video Archives was where he did the majority of his arguing, where this devotee of the hang-out movie did the majority of his hanging out, developing his ear and fine-tuning his rhetorical strategies. "It was 'Who knows more?'" said Avary. "And he won. Quentin is a database. I decided a long time ago to give up the fight."

After three years of this, though, even Tarantino was beginning to spin his wheels, wondering if he'd spend his entire life talking about movies rather than making them. His ambition resurfacing, at one point he brought all of the staff together to talk with them about an employee takeover. "'Go to your parents and borrow the $6,000, you and you and you and you. This is all legit.' Nobody was interested. I loved the place. I was really, really invested in it. The truth of the matter is, if we had done that, I may not have made *Reservoir Dogs*. I would have been working at, and owning, Video Archives."

As Avary said, "For Quentin, it was either grand success or video store clerk. There was nothing in between." Time for this rambler to get rambling.

ABOVE: From video store clerks to Oscar winners. Quentin Tarantino and Roger Avary collect the Best Screenplay Academy Award for *Pulp Fiction* in 1995.

THE SCRIPTS

ONE night, Tarantino was at the home of his acting school buddy Craig Hamann in the San Fernando Valley, drinking Black Russians while watching back-to-back reruns of *Miami Vice*, when on came episode sixteen of the third season, "Theresa," featuring a twenty-year-old Helena Bonham Carter as Crockett's heroin-addicted girlfriend.

"Wow," said Hamann. "How did they get her in the show?"

"Geez, look at that wide shot," said Tarantino.

"But they go and ruin it with a cheesy cutaway."

"Hey, Craig, we gotta make our own movie, man."

"That's cool, Quint. But how we gonna pay for it?"

They got too blitzed to figure it out that night but the next morning Tarantino returned to the idea during a phone conversation.

"We gotta do this movie, Craig. Got any ideas?"

"Well, there is one."

"What is it? Shoot."

"Well . . ."

"Come on, pitch it."

"It's about a guy who hires a hooker for his best pal's birthday. But it all goes wrong."

"My first concern is to tell a story that will be dramatically captivating. What counts is that the story works and that viewers will be caught up in my film."

Tarantino liked it and told his friend to write it. A few months later, he was handed a 30-to-40-page script at a coffee shop on Ventura Boulevard. "Mind if I take it home and add a few scenes and things?" he asked. He expanded the script into an 80-page feature, *My Best Friend's Birthday*, which they shot on and off over the next three years for just $5,000. They used an old 16mm Bolex camera containing only a hundred feet of film, which meant the can had to be changed every two and a half minutes. Only thirty-six minutes of the film remain after a lab fire destroyed much of it, enough to ascertain that it may be the only known instance in which a Quentin Tarantino performance saves a Quentin Tarantino film.

As the motor-mouthed DJ Clarence who works for a local station called K–BILLY radio, he is the only bright spot in a series of murkily lit, jerkily staged black-and-white scenes. When we first meet him, he is spinning a riff about how *The Partridge Family* stopped him from committing suicide at age three ("I thought: I'll watch *The Partridge Family*, then I'll kill myself") and insulting callers ("No, I don't do requests . . . I don't care what Unruly Julie plays on her show"). Over the course of the film, he accidentally snorts itching powder he believes to be cocaine, tracks down a hooker for his "best friend," and debates the relative merits of Brando and Elvis ("I'm no fag, but I always said, if ever I had to fuck a guy—I mean had to because my life depended on it—I'd fuck Elvis") to an accompaniment of Sweet's "Ballroom Blitz." Tarantino's voice is unmistakable, even if the film is a mess. The speech would end up in *True Romance*, as would the heroine: a call girl who leaves her pimp.

MISTY
See, for the past three years, I worked at Kmart in Cleveland.

CLARENCE
Really? What department?

MISTY

Records and tapes.

CLARENCE

You lucky dog. I worked at Kmart, too.

MISTY

Really?

CLARENCE

Yeah, out here. I always tried to get into records and tapes, but they stuck me in women's shoes.

MISTY

No kidding? I always felt sorry for those guys in women's shoes. Some of those old ladies would come in and make you try on fifty pairs of shoes before they made up their mind.

CLARENCE

Yeah, but I had a foot fetish, so it evened itself out.

After several years of not being able to afford processing fees, Tarantino finally retired his footage to see what he'd got.

"I started putting it together, and I was heartbroken," he said. "This was not what I thought it was going to be. It was useless. To finish it would've meant another year and a half of 'Okay, now we go into post-production.' So I said, 'Well, that's my film school.' I learned how *not* to make a movie. So I started writing scripts in order to get money to do a real movie."

Hamann had been working as an assistant for an agent, Cathryn Jaymes, and introduced her to Tarantino. She decided to take a chance on the young filmmaker and started championing his early work around Hollywood. But Tarantino's

PAGE 38: The cast of *True Romance* in a promotional shot for the film, 1993. PAGE 39: Christian Slater in *True Romance* as movie-loving fugitive Clarence Worley—a character Tarantino based partly on himself. ABOVE AND OPPOSITE: The lovebirds hit the road. Alabama (Patricia Arquette) and Clarence make off with a stolen stash of cocaine in *True Romance*.

muse was proving an oddly ginger creature at this time. He seemed most comfortable only when taking over other people's scripts—putting his own stamp on them so indelibly that they became his. His next two projects both started life as something called *The Open Road*, an eighty-page *After Hours*–ish yuppie-in-peril movie about a businessman who picks up a crazy hitchhiker and winds up in a hellish midwestern town, written by Tarantino's buddy at Video Archives, Roger Avary. In Tarantino's rewrite, the businessman became a Detroit comic-book clerk, also called Clarence, who hits the road not with a hitchhiker but a hooker called Alabama, all the while scribbling away at a script he is working on about two violent runaways called Mickey and Mallory. Handwritten and held together by a rubber band in a folder, the script eventually reached a sprawling five hundred pages.

"I saw no way to end it," said Tarantino, who eventually split the script in two, forming *True Romance* and *Natural Born Killers*. The former would eventually be filmed by Tony Scott after Tarantino did a rewrite on Rutger Hauer's *Past Midnight* for CineTel and found himself on the set of Tony Scott's *The Last Boy Scout*, made for the same company. Scott invited Tarantino to a party and asked to read his scripts. Tarantino gave him both *True Romance* and *Reservoir Dogs*, telling him, "Read the first three pages. If you don't like it, throw it away."

It was Tarantino's way of weeding out the faint of heart. The original *True Romance* script started with a long discussion about cunnilingus. Tarantino had been unable to get it past the studios' lowest-level readers. Again and again, he heard: too violent, too vile, too vulgar. "Ugh! Hated characters," wrote one reader for Miramax. "Who cares about these people, their story? They're both shit, to quote the characters." Another reader, disgusted with the f-bombs in the script, wrote to Tarantino's manager:

Dear Cathryn,

How dare you send me this fucking piece of shit. You must be out of your fucking mind. You want to know how I feel about it? Here's your fucking piece of shit back. Fuck you.

Reading both scripts on a flight to Europe, Scott was delighted. "By the time I landed, I wanted to make both of them into movies. When I told Quentin, he said, 'You can only do one.'" Scott picked *True Romance*. "For me, it was one of the fullest, most accomplished scripts that I'd ever read. The movie is such a strange mixture. It's a black comedy to me."

Scott's biggest changes were to chronology; the story was originally told out of sequence, like *Reservoir Dogs*, and ended with Clarence dying in a Mexican stand-off, leaving Alabama to make off with the cash.

INT. RED MUSTANG—MOVING—DAY

Alabama's driving fast down the freeway. The deejay on the radio is trying to be funny. Then the song "Little Arrows" by Leapy Lee starts playing. Alabama breaks down and starts crying. She pulls the car over to the side of the road.

INT. RED MUSTANG—ROADSIDE—DAY

The SONG continues. She wipes her eyes with the napkin she pulls out of her pocket and tosses it on the dashboard. She picks up the .45 and puts it in her mouth.

She pulls back the hammer and looks up to see her reflection in the rear view mirror. She turns it away and looks straight ahead.

Her finger tightens on the trigger.

Her eyes catch the napkin on the dashboard, partly opened and she can see the words.

ALABAMA
(reading from the napkin)
You're so cool.

She tosses the gun aside.

Alabama gets out of the car, opens the trunk and takes out the briefcase. She looks around for, and finally finds, the Sergeant Fury comic book Clarence bought her.

And, with the comic book in one hand and the briefcase in the other, Alabama walks away from the Mustang forever.

FADE OUT.

BELOW: Christian Slater receives direction from *True Romance* director Tony Scott on location in Los Angeles.

ABOVE LEFT: Alabama reclines on the hood of her pink Cadillac. ABOVE RIGHT AND OPPOSITE: Christopher Walken (Vincenzo Coccotti) makes up for passing up a role in *Reservoir Dogs* with his turn in *True Romance* playing the mob hit man who tortures Clifford (Dennis Hopper).

"Clarence was me; I could blow my own head off, a punk rock move," said Tarantino. "*True Romance* is probably my most personal script because the character of Clarence was me at the time when I wrote it. He works in a comic-book shop; I was working in a video store. When my friends from that time see *True Romance*, they get melancholy; it brings back a certain time for us. It was weird when I first saw the movie because I was looking at a big-budget version of my home movies, or memories."

The sunniest film to be made from a Tarantino script, Scott's *True Romance* tempers his hard-edged nihilism with the honeyed glow of Scott's advertising-industry background. It's a vibrant, pop-art fairytale with pink Cadillacs shot against heavily filtered skies and Christian Slater and Patricia Arquette as the *Badlands*-style lovebirds hitting the road with a stash of stolen cocaine. The plot is a succession of bad guys, each strutting the stage for a few minutes before making way for the next, including Gary Oldman as a dreadlocked drug dealer with a milky eye, Brad Pitt as a guy so stoned he barely registers armed thugs on his porch ("Don't condescend me"), and Bronson Pinchot as a Hollywood producer's errand boy.

But the movie belongs to Dennis Hopper as Clarence's security cop dad, Clifford, and Christopher Walken as the mob hit man sent to interrogate him. Both actors passed on the opportunity to appear in *Reservoir Dogs* and make up for it with a beautiful piece of cool-dude sparring, with Hopper sucking on a Chesterfield and launching on a wildly insulting rococo riff about Sicilians having "black blood pumpin' through their hearts," and Walken so amused by the balls on the guy that for a few brief seconds you almost think he's going to spare him. Unable to contain their laughter during many takes, they ebulliently improvised the lines "You're part eggplant," and "You're a cantaloupe."

The speech about the Sicilians originated from a friend who had once crashed at Tarantino's apartment. "The one thing I knew Cliff had to do was insult the guy enough that he'd kill him, because if he got tortured he'd end up telling him where Clarence was, and he didn't want to do that," said Tarantino. "I knew how the scene had to end, but I don't write dialogue in a strategic way. I didn't really go about crafting the scene; I just put them in the room together. I knew Cliff was going to end up doing the Sicilian thing, but I didn't know what Coccotti was going

to say. They just started talking, and I jotted it down. I almost feel like a fraud for taking credit for writing dialogue, because it's the characters that are doing it. To me, it's very connected to actors' improv with me playing all the characters. One of the reasons I like to write with pen and paper is it helps that process—for me, anyway."

That he should have reached so deep for a speech signaling the sacrifice of a father for his son is telling. Tarantino's work would abound in father-son relationships of varying mixtures of devotion and destructiveness. There is the relationship in *Reservoir Dogs* between Mr. Orange and Mr. White, played by Harvey Keitel ("the father I never had"), which turns from fierce loyalty to murder, via betrayal. There is Butch Coolidge in *Pulp Fiction*, raised without a father but treasuring the watch he left him. And most comprehensively of all there is Bill in *Kill Bill*, Tarantino's most wholehearted exorcism of all his ambivalence toward fathers and father figures, which he has called "the subtext that actually borders on text." But the most straightforwardly touching is the scene that plays out between Clarence and Cliff in *True Romance*, reconciling after an estrangement of three years in a scene Tarantino called "the most autobiographical I have ever written."

"People come up to me and say, 'You write great dialogue,' and I feel like a fraud taking credit for it. It's the characters who write the dialogue."

CLARENCE

Look, Goddamnit, I never asked you for a
Goddamn thing! I've tried to make your
parental obligation as easy as possible.
After Mom divorced you did I ever ask you
for anything? When I wouldn't see ya for
six months to a year at a time, did I ever
get in your shit about it? No! It was always:
'Okay,' 'No problem,' 'You're a busy guy,
I understand.' The whole time you were a
drunk, did I ever point my finger at you and
talk shit? No! Everybody else did. I never
did. You see, I know that you're just a bad
parent. You're not really very good at it.
But I know you love me. I'm basically a
pretty resourceful guy. If I didn't really need
it I wouldn't ask. And if you say no, don't
worry about it. I'm gone. No problem.

Natural Born Killers was not so lucky. After
Tarantino tried and failed to direct it himself for
$500,000, he spent a year and a half struggling
to raise cash. He finally sold it to two ambitious
film school graduates, Jane Hamsher and Don
Murphy, in 1991 for $10,000, just as *Reservoir
Dogs* went into production. When *Dogs* became
an unexpected hit, he attempted to buy the

ABOVE: Woody Harrelson and Juliette
Lewis pose for a promotional shot for
Natural Born Killers, 1994. OPPOSITE:
Father and son Clifford and Clarence
have a volatile relationship in
True Romamce, a characterization
that Tarantino calls his most
autobiographical.

screenplay back, but it was too late: It was sold to Warner Bros. as a vehicle for director Oliver Stone, who tried to poach half the cast of *Dogs*, including Tim Roth, Steve Buscemi, and Michael Madsen. "Oliver Stone called me and said, 'If I make this picture with you, I get $2.5 million, and the budget of the movie is $20 million," recalled Madsen. "But if I do it with Woody [Harrelson], I get $30 million and my fee is $5 million. So that's what I'm going to do. Meanwhile, Quentin was calling me, saying, 'Don't do *Natural Born Killers* with Oliver; he's gonna fuck it up!'"

Stone rewrote the script, retaining some of Tarantino's distinctive dialogue, including Mallory's "Eenie, meenie, minie, moe" spiel in the opening scene, and Wayne and Mickey's discussion of serial killer ratings ("Manson beat you." "Yeah, it's pretty hard to beat the king."). But in Tarantino's version, Mickey and Mallory are just supporting players. His main focus instead is on the Geraldo-like TV journalist played by Robert Downey Jr. in Stone's film, Wayne Gale, and his production team: a cameraman, a soundman, and an assistant, named Scott, Roger, and Julie after Tarantino's coworkers at Video Archives.

INT. NEWS VAN—MOVING—DAY

Roger's picking through a box of donuts. Scott PANS over to him, then slowly ZOOMS in on him.

ROGER
Where the fuck's the chocolate cream filled? Did anyone get my chocolate cream filled? If you did, it's mine.

CU of Roger, looking into CAMERA.

ROGER
I pointed at a chocolate cream filled. You saw me do it, didn't you?

Wayne starts talking. We PAN from Roger to a CU of Wayne.

WAYNE
You were there. Did you see him put it in a box?

We PAN back to a CU of Roger.

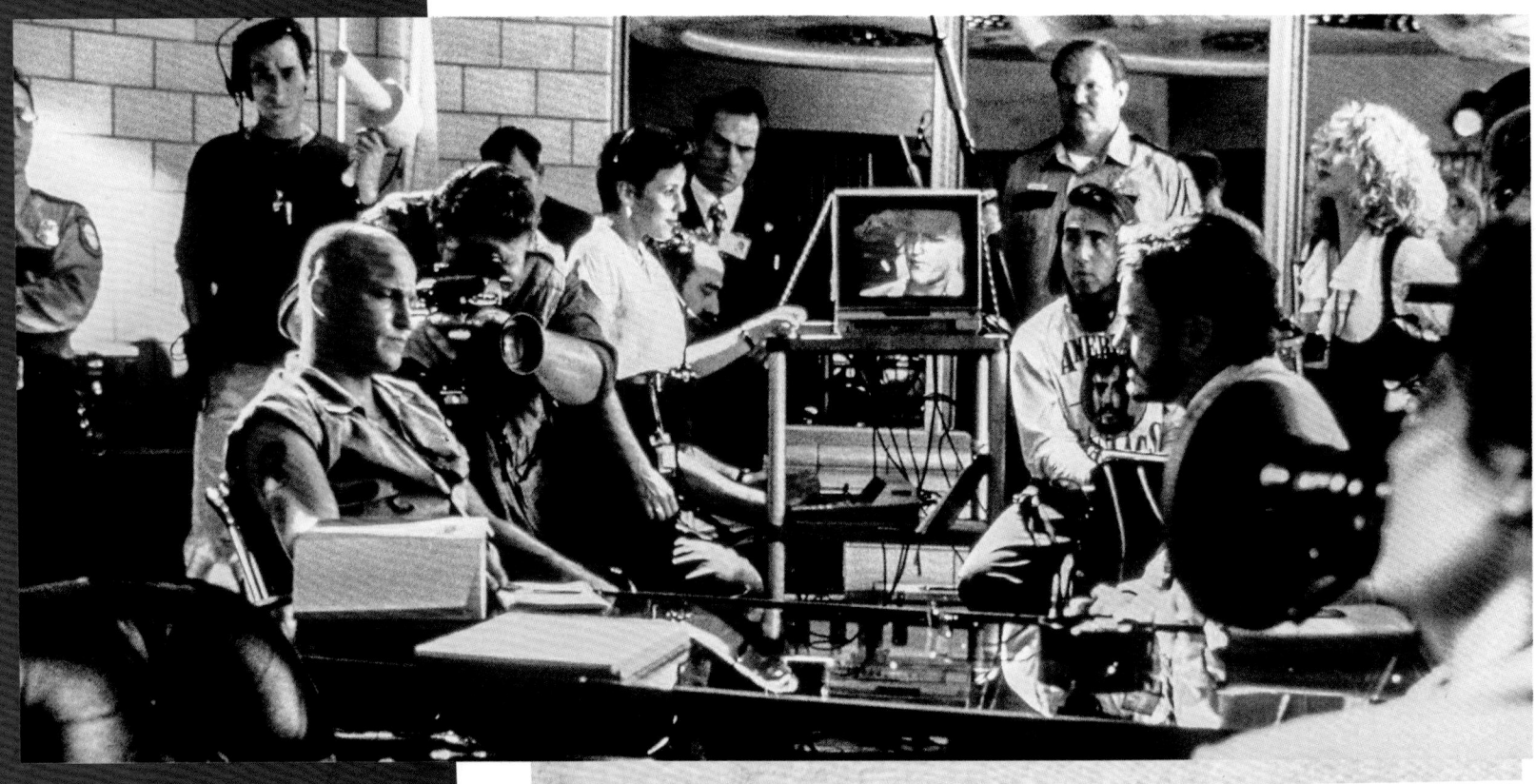

ROGER

At the time, I was too busy explaining to Scott the finer points of film.

We ZOOM back to a WIDE SHOT.

SCOTT (O.S.)

Yeah, right. You know what he said? He said, *Indiana Jones and the Temple Of Doom* is Spielberg's best film.

Wayne starts laughing. We hear Scott laugh too.

WAYNE

(to Roger)
You can't be serious?

ROGER

(preoccupied)
I'm as serious about that as I am about going back to the donut store, and dipping that stupid Mexican's head into the batter for forgetting my chocolate cream filled. Gimme that other box.

It's hard to see such a scene, with its glancing yet relaxed humor, surviving the full-on, double-barreled, twelve-film-stock assault of an Oliver Stone movie. If nothing else, the dense, layered collage of Robert Richardson's cinematography on *Natural Born Killers* anticipates the similar weave of styles he would bring to his later work for Tarantino—on *Kill Bill*, *Inglourious Basterds*, and *Django Unchained*—but "as a satirist, he's an elephant ballerina," wrote Janet Maslin in the *New York Times*. "Scratch the frenzied, hyperkinetic surface of *Natural Born Killers* and you find remarkably banal notions about Mickey, Mallory, and the demon media." Others concurred. "Satire requires a certain cool detachment, and Stone's sensibility is white-hot and personal," wrote Hal Hinson in the *Washington Post*. "Our culture may be drifting toward the sort of calamity that Stone describes in *Natural Born Killers*, but the hysteria he depicts seems to come from within him."

By far the best commentary on the film, though, was provided by Tarantino himself: "I wish [Stone] had just fucking ripped it off," he said, after requesting to have his screenplay credit downgraded to "story by." "His biggest problem is that his obviousness cancels out his energy and his energy pumps up his obviousness. He's Stanley Kramer with style" —an analysis worthy of Pauline Kael herself.

OPPOSITE: Glorified crime. The media hangs on every word during an interview with convict Mickey in *Natural Born Killers*. ABOVE: Director Oliver Stone shot much of *Natural Born Killers* with the camera tilted at a 45 degree angle and with colored filters to express the tension and madness felt by the characters.

"If you like my stuff, you might not like this movie. But if you like [Oliver's] stuff, you're probably going to love it."

All this, including the cherry-red Malibu that Tarantino bought himself from his *Natural Born Killers* money and that John Travolta would drive in *Pulp Fiction*, was to come. By his mid-twenties, Tarantino was not a happy man. Living in a one-bedroom apartment under the flight paths of LAX, driving a clapped-out Honda Civic, attending acting classes and collecting rejection slips, he was, as the 1980s drew to a close, just another twenty-five-year-old genius-in-bud on the fringes of the movie business. The joke amongst his friends was, if you wanted to get a letter to Quentin, just address it to "Quentin Tarantino, the Outskirts of the Film Industry." It would get to him. "I definitely had an angry-young-man thing going through most of my twenties because I wanted people to take me and my shit seriously, all right, and I was very full of piss and vinegar about it," he said. "It was then out of frustration that I wrote *Reservoir Dogs*."

Attending a barbecue at his acting buddy Scott Spiegel's home on July 4, 1989, Tarantino was introduced to producer Lawrence Bender. A lanky, good-looking Jewish kid from the Bronx who had tried his hand at ballet before injuries led him into acting and then producing, Bender had just pulled together the budget for Spiegel's 1989 stalker-slasher movie *Intruder*, only to see it go straight to video, and was toying with the idea of quitting the business. He was, in other words, nursing the exact same hangover of ambition and disillusionment that Tarantino was.

"We were both struggling," said Bender. "We were both outsiders. We both were trying to fight our way into the system."

Introduced to the twenty-five-year-old, he paused. "Tarantino," he said. "That name seems so familiar . . . I read a script, but I think it was another Tarantino, *True Romance* or something like that . . ."

"*That's my script!*" yelled Tarantino.

"Oh really? That was a really cool script. That was really cool."

Bender asked him what he was working on at the moment. Tarantino showed him his script for *Natural Born Killers* and told him about another idea he had for a movie about a failed heist, told from the point of view of the rendezvous and playing out in real time. Gradually, everyone turns up and "someone's been shot, someone's been wounded, someone's been killed, someone's an undercover cop, but you never see the heist."

"As he was telling me the story, I just knew we were off and running to something really great," said Bender, who told him to go and write it. Covered for the moment by residual checks from an appearance on *The Golden Girls*, Tarantino went off to the stationery store and purchased a notebook and a set of felt-tip pens—two red, two black. He wrote the script for *Reservoir Dogs* in just three and a half weeks, although the idea had been bubbling away ever since his days at Video Archives, when he organized a shelf of heist movies like *Rififi*, *Topkapi*, and *The Thomas Crown Affair*.

OPPOSITE: Woody Harrelson and Juliette Lewis as husband and wife murderers Mickey and Mallory Knox in *Natural Born Killers*. ABOVE: The young Hollywood hotshot in 1993.

"I hated it—I *hated* it—where they'd do the robbery and, just by some little quirk, fate steps in and fucks 'em over," said Tarantino. Instead, in a style he would later characterize as "answers first, questions later," the derailment of the gang's plan would be his starting point. Each character would then get their own "chapter," each providing a partial answer to the mystery. "I've always considered *Reservoir Dogs* as the pulp novel I'll never write," he said. "I didn't know if the dramatic structure would work. It was a theory I had, that if you were to take a novelistic structure and put it into film, it would be very cinematic. Edit it like that. Tell a story like that."

One night a few weeks later, Bender received a call from Tarantino at his apartment in West Hollywood. "He didn't have a car, and I couldn't afford photocopying, so I drove over to his place," said the producer, who found Tarantino crouched over his girlfriend's old Smith Corona, laboriously typing out the pages one by one. All the friends

he used to type up his scripts had dried up. What Bender read was full of bad spelling, completely unformatted, sometimes illegible, and quite clearly brilliant.

"Wow, this is extraordinary," he said. "Can you give me some time to raise some money?"

"No, I've heard that all before," said Tarantino, who had been burned one too many times. "Forget it. I don't trust that."

He wanted to self-finance *Reservoir Dogs* as a super-low-budget, black-and-white, 16mm film for $10,000, casting friends and playing Mr. Pink himself, with Bender as Nice Guy Eddie. "No one was going to give me money and I'm not going to spend another Goddamn year talking about making movies," he recalled. "I'd spent a six-year string to get deals on films. No one was going to take a chance and go, 'Here's a million dollars.'"

Bender asked for six months.

"No way. I'll give you two months with an option for one more month."

They signed an agreement on a paper napkin. Tarantino moved back in with his mother to save on rent while Bender did the rounds with his script. One financier offered them $1.6 million if they gave it an ending like *The Sting* with everyone who was dead jumping to life. Another was willing to give them $500,000 as long as his girlfriend could play the role of Mr. Blonde. One potential buyer was reportedly ready to mortgage his house—but only if he could direct the movie. "I had a feeling inside I didn't let out that we were about to do something really great," recalled Bender. "It's not like I could know it from experience. But I felt it deep in my gut."

Within seven months, they would be shooting. "I was going to go really guerrilla-style with it, like the way Nick Gomez did with *Laws of Gravity*," said Tarantino. "I'd lost faith in anyone giving me money . . . and that's when I got the money."

ABOVE: Having finally caught their big break, Tarantino relaxes with producer Lawrence Bender on the set of *Pulp Fiction* in 1994. PAGES 54–55: Portrait by Levon Biss, 2012.

THE DIRECTOR

RESERVOIR DOGS

1992

"THIS MOVIE is dedicated to these Following Sources of Inspiration: Timothy Carey, Roger Corman, André de Toth, Chow Yun-Fat, Jean-Luc Godard, Jean-Pierre Melville, Lawrence Tierney, Lionel White..."

SO DECLARES the opening page of the script for *Reservoir Dogs*, making no bones about its borrowings, including Lionel White, the writer of Stanley Kubrick's *The Killing*, and Timothy Carey, who starred in it; Chow Yun-Fat whose 1987 film *City on Fire* features an undercover cop infiltrating a band of thieves as they prepare to rob a jewelry store for a balding patriarchal boss; veteran character actor and star of 1945's *Dillinger*, Lawrence Tierney, whom Tarantino would cast as his mob boss, Joe Cabot; French director Jean-Pierre Melville ("the Godard I haven't grown out of") whose smartly trench-coated gangsters were the epitome of *nouvelle vague* chic; and, of course, Godard himself, whose *Breathless* (1960) and *Bande à part* (1964), formed so much of Tarantino's remix-and-match aesthetic.

"Great artists steal, they don't do homages," he declared. "If my work has anything it's that I'm taking this from that and that from that and mixing them together and if people don't like it then tough titty, don't go and see it, all right?"

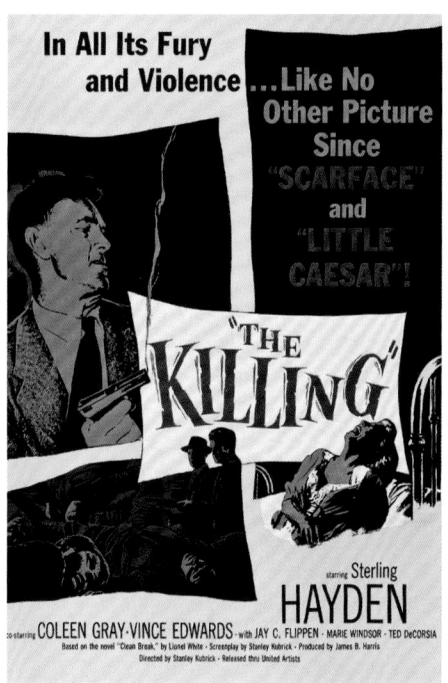

ABOVE: Tarantino working on scenes for *Reservoir Dogs* with Steve Buscemi (center) and Tom Sizemore (right) at the Sundance Film Festival's Director's Lab workshop. LEFT: Tarantino's debut clearly borrows plot structures and themes from gangster films including Stanley Kubrick's *The Killing* (1956) and Max Nosseck's *Dillinger* (1945).

"This movie was never meant to be everything for everybody. And I don't mean that as a slam. I'm just saying I made it for myself and everybody else is invited."

ABOVE: Deep in thought on the set of his first feature film. Tarantino has often spoken of how *Reservoir Dogs* was "the complete, utter payoff of perseverance." OPPOSITE: The Dogs. The scenes at Uncle Bob's Pancakes marks Tarantino's first shoot as a fully-fledged director.

The method that had produced Tarantino's early scripts had now developed into a creative method that was to be his mainstay for the next three decades. Drawing inspiration and sometimes whole plot ideas from the plot-bank to a degree that might make some writers sweat, Tarantino would then proceed to render his version of it, so wholly other as to burn off accusations of plagiarism in the heat of the adjective "Tarantinoesque." Remixers, rappers, Andy Warhol, and Jean-Luc Godard would understand. From *The Taking of Pelham One Two Three* (1974), for example, he took the idea of a gang of thieves, all named after colors, but it took Tarantino to set them all against one another, arguing over who should be what color. In fact, not even *he* did that, by his account. "The characters started squabbling like schoolkids over which colors they got," he said. They just kept talking to each other so I wrote it down and I was like 'Wow.'" Tarantino let his characters pinball freely within his tightly controlled narrative structure: "If a character does something real that doesn't fit with the plan, well, that's what he does. I don't play God and mess with it. That's how I work: letting

the characters improvise, and I'm like a court reporter writing it down."

Or someone planning a heist. So many directors have made their debuts with heist movies—not just Tarantino himself with *Reservoir Dogs* but Woody Allen with *Take the Money and Run*, Michael Mann with *Thief*, Wes Anderson with *Bottle Rocket*, Bryan Singer with *The Usual Suspects*—that a lurking similarity between the act of grand larceny and the hit-and-run aesthetic of first-time filmmakers begins to emerge. Both involve a gang of strangers coming together to execute a long-gestating plan, which depends on its execution to go undetected. Both involve the collision of the plan with the unexpected contingencies and accidents that happen on the day, requiring feats of improvisation from the gang members who must quickly adapt to events as they unfold. Both, if successful, involve making off with a large bundle of cash, though both are also predicated on Murphy's law: If something can go wrong, it will go wrong.

If the first member of Tarantino's gang was Lawrence Bender, the second was Monte Hellman, the cult director of two of Tarantino's

favorite westerns, *The Shooting* and *Ride in the Whirlwind*. Through a connection of Bender's, Tarantino met with Hellman in an ice cream parlor on Hollywood Boulevard called C. C. Browns, where Hellman at first thought he was being offered the film to direct. Emboldened by the recent sale of his *True Romance* script, Tarantino stuck to his guns: This one was for him. Hellman instead came on as executive producer, and went to one-time porno video distributor Live Entertainment, where an executive named Richard Gladstein took up the project, giving them a list of ten actors' names: If they could get one of the actors from the list, he would give them $1.3 million, if two: $2 million. On the list of names were Christopher Walken, Dennis Hopper, and Harvey Keitel.

It turned out that the wife of Bender's acting coach, Lily Parker, knew Keitel from the Actors Studio and managed to get a copy of the script to him. "She simply said, 'I have a screenplay I think you're going to like,'" said Keitel. "When I read it, I was just very stirred. Quentin had a new way of seeing those ancient themes of camaraderie, trust, betrayal, redemption."

Having read it late one Saturday night, Keitel called Bender on Sunday morning and left a message on his answering machine in his unmistakable Brooklyn brogue. "Hello, I'm calling for Lawrence Bender. This is Harvey Keitel speaking. I read the script for *Reservoir Dogs* and I'd like to talk to you about it . . ."

When Tarantino first went to meet Keitel prior to casting him, the actor "opened the door, and it was this tall, gawky-looking guy staring at me, and he said, 'Harvey Kee-tel?' And I said, 'It's Kye-tel.' And it began from there. I offered him something to eat, and he ate a lot. I said, 'How'd you come to write this script? Did you live in a tough-guy neighborhood growing up?' He said no. I said, 'Was anybody in your family connected with tough guys?' He said no. I said, 'Well, how the hell did you come to write this?' And he said, 'I watch movies.'"

They had their Mr. White. Not only that but with Keitel onboard, Tarantino and Bender were able to raise $1.5 million, keep Tarantino in place as director, and start casting the rest of the gang. Knowing both Christopher Walken and Dennis Hopper, Keitel tried to entice them onboard. They both passed, but the script was now circulating among agents and actors, acquiring a reputation as a hot script. Out of his own pocket, Keitel flew them all to New York—himself in first class, Tarantino and Bender in coach—to oversee casting sessions in a small office space on Fifty-Seventh Street. More than sixty actors turned up and took turns abusing a tied-up Bender, who played the captured cop.

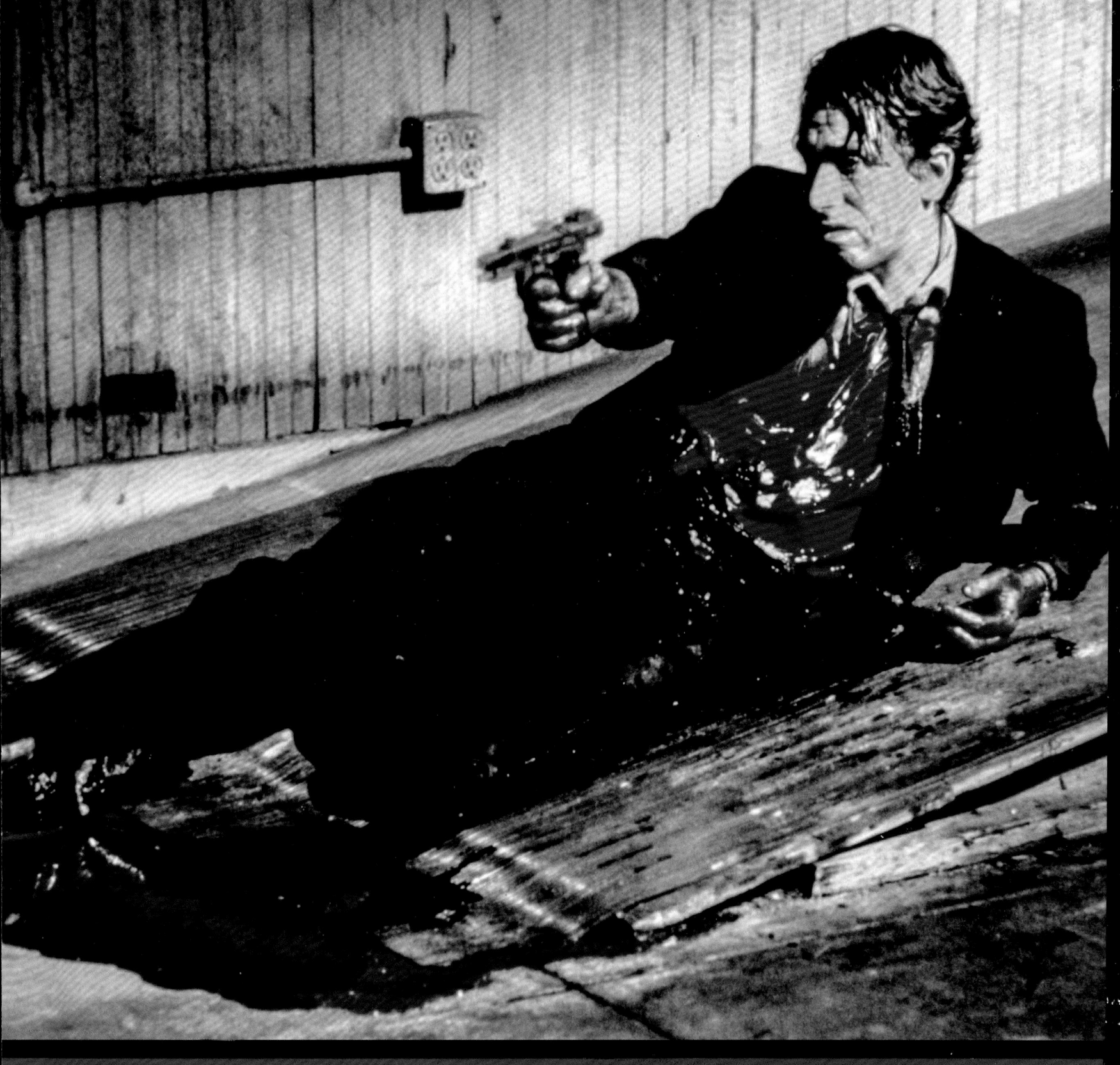

"I like the idea that the audience is laughing and that, BOOM, the next moment there is blood on the walls."

ABOVE: Like a director dishing out the roles, mob boss Joe Cabot, played by Lawrence Tierney (right), gives the gang their aliases. OPPOSITE: Mr. Blonde (Michael Madsen) takes a shot.

Candidates included George Clooney, Samuel L. Jackson, Robert Forster, and Vincent Gallo. James Woods was offered a role, widely assumed to be Mr. Orange, and was later furious with his agent for not accepting the cash offers. "We knocked ourselves out just getting the right collection of guys," said Tarantino.

Michael Madsen originally read for the part of Mr. Pink, which Tarantino had written for himself. He had never met the director before. "He was standing there with his arms folded, Harvey sitting on the couch in bare feet," recalled Madsen. "I made my case for playing Mr. Pink, and Quentin said, 'Okay, show me what you got.' For one of the only times in my life I'd rehearsed the dialogue, so I did a couple of Mr. Pink scenes. When I was done, Quentin looked at me and went: 'Is that it? Okay, good. You're not Mr. Pink. You're Mr. Blonde—and if you're not Mr. Blonde, then you're not in the movie.'"

Steve Buscemi originally looked at Nice Guy Eddie and Mr. Orange but after reading the script wanted Mr. Pink. On the last day of auditions, Tarantino went out to the waiting room to see Steve Buscemi, telling him, "'I wrote the part of Mr. Pink for myself, so you've got to go in there and you've got to *take* it. Or else you're not gonna get it. Now I'm not going to fuck you up, but I ain't giving you jack shit. You've gotta *take* it.

From. Me. Now go in there and do it.' And he did it, actually." Tarantino told him he had the part when he ran into him in the men's room later that day. "Quentin comes in and he's taking a leak in the next stall and he says, 'Oh, by the way, I cast you as Mr. Pink,'" said the actor.

Back in Los Angeles, British actor Tim Roth liked the part of Mr. Orange but refused to read for it. Taking him to a deli, Keitel tried to persuade him, but still he refused. Finally, Tarantino took him to one of the actor's favorite bars, the Coach and Horses pub on Sunset Boulevard, and the two got roaring drunk together. "I'll read anything for you!" declared Roth at around 2 a.m., so Tarantino started scribbling down the dialogue on beer mats, then went and bought more beers from a 7-Eleven and decamped to the actor's apartment, where they read the script all the way through five times. "We were so gone," recalled Roth later. "That's the only time I've read for years." He got the part.

The last member of the gang was editor Sally Menke, whose biggest credit to that point had been editing *Teenage Mutant Ninja Turtles.* "I got in touch, and Tarantino sent me this script for a thing called *Reservoir Dogs,* and I just thought it was amazing," she said. "It floored me. Scorsese was a hero of mine, especially as he used a female editor in Thelma Schoonmaker, and this script just had that tone. Later, when I found out Harvey Keitel was attached, I was more determined to get this job than ever. I was hiking up in Canada on a remote mountain in Banff when I saw a phone box and I stopped to call LA and they confirmed I'd got the gig. I let out a yell that echoed around the mountain."

Assembling his team together at Harvey Keitel's house in Malibu, some of the actors—Eddie Bunker (Mr. Blue), Lawrence Tierney—started swapping stories about the jail time they'd done. "Richard Gladstein and I looked at one another and go: 'This is it, this is the movie, we're in it,' said Bender. The ensemble knitted together so well Keitel compared them to the twelve apostles on *The Last Temptation of Christ*. Afterwards, Tarantino drove back to his apartment in Glendale, slightly drunk, the happiest he could ever remember being. *If I keep this movie in focus I've got a terrific movie*, he recalled thinking to himself. *I could put these fuckers in white shirts against white walls and I'd have a movie.*

Starting on July 29, 1991, *Reservoir Dogs* was shot in just five weeks—thirty days—on location in the San Fernando Valley. The first week they shot the opening scene in Uncle Bob's Pancakes and the office; the second week, they did the outdoor sequences, including the chase, shootout, and Mr. Pink's carjacking; weeks three and four were devoted to the scenes in the warehouse, which was actually an old funeral home on the corner of North Figueroa and Fifty-Ninth Streets in Highland Park. Cinematographer Andrzej Sekula shot with the slowest film stock Kodak makes—50 ASA—because it would make the colors pop like Tarantino wanted. They had to flood the warehouse lights, raising the temperature as high as 110 degrees Fahrenheit. It was so hot that the blood pooling around actor Tim Roth—which was actually syrup, regulated by an onset medic ("Okay, one more pint and he's dead.")—dried and stuck him to the floor. It took them fifteen minutes to get Roth loose.

"I wanted the reds to be eye-popping red, the blues to be blue, the black to be black, no gray," said Tarantino. "Every shot in the movie was miserable to get. I mean that warehouse was an oven. It roasted you, but it was worth it because it gave you those deep, deep colors."

Tarantino directed most of the movie expecting to get a tap on the shoulder any minute and be ejected from the set. He and Bender joked that they were the most inexperienced people there. Shooting Mr. Pink's gunfight and escape, they didn't have enough money to shut down the entire street and had only two cops to direct traffic. Tarantino told an astounded Buscemi, "Okay, what's going to happen is you're going to take the gun, you're going to empty it on the cops, and, if the light is green, you're going to drive away."

"If the light is *green*?" replied Buscemi. "You mean you're *not* stopping traffic?"

"Well, kind of, we're stopping it from this side and this side. And the cops said, 'If you're going with the light, you can go.'"

In the end, Buscemi had to run a stop sign. Crouched down in the back seat of the car, Tarantino heard the walkie-talkie crackle: "That was totally illegal! You ran a stop sign; the cops are pissed!"

They staged the robbery in rehearsal so that they all knew what happened, but they didn't shoot it. For the torture scene, Tarantino asked the actor who was playing the cop, Kirk Baltz, to improvise the speech in which he pleads with Michael Madsen not to set him on fire. The dialogue hadn't been written into the script. "I knew this guy had just had a child," said Baltz, "and at one point in the rehearsal I came up with the line and I said, 'I got a kid now . . .' and as soon as I said that Michael stopped in his tracks. He just stopped. He turned to me, he turned to Quentin and he said, 'I don't want him to say it,' and Quentin said, 'I like that; we're going to keep it.'"

The only cast member to give the director trouble was Tierney, to whom Tarantino had in part dedicated the script (in which he utters the line "dead as Dillinger"). Tierney had done jail time for drunk driving and assault. Before shooting began, Tarantino met Norman Mailer, who had cast Tierney in an adaptation of his own novel, *Tough Guys Don't Dance*, at a party at the Actors Studio in New York. Tarantino recalled: "I said, 'Hey, you worked with Lawrence Tierney, I'm thinking about hiring him.' He said he was a problem. He said, 'Look, Lawrence will slow you down about 20 percent. If you allow for it you'll be

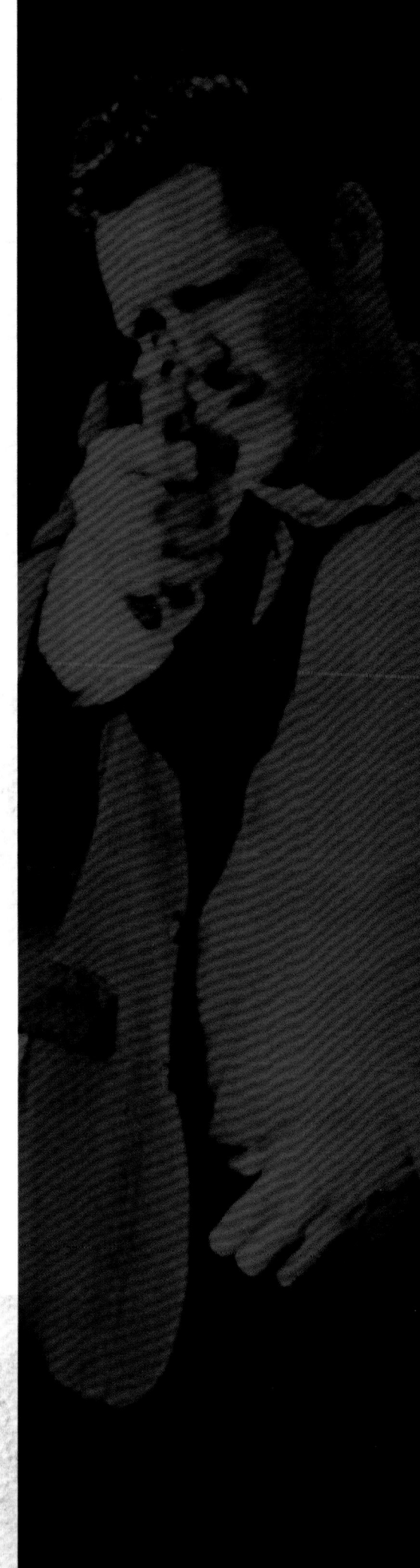

fine.' Fuck you, Norman Mailer! He slows you down 80 percent! What's this 20 percent bullshit? My friend said, 'Is he personally challenging you?' No, Lawrence likes me. He's a nice guy. It's not that he's personally challenging me; he personally challenges the entire concept of filmmaking."

A few days into shooting, Tierney started blaming Michael Madsen for making him forget his lines.

"This is the deal," said Tarantino. "I want you to go practice with Michael and then we can get this just right."

"I don't need your advice, cocksucker," growled the seventy-two-year-old.

"Fuck you, Larry," shot back Tarantino.

Another time, after they'd wrapped for the day, Tierney went home, got drunk and unloaded a .357 Magnum in his apartment, the bullets penetrating into the apartment next door where a family was sleeping. He was thrown in jail and then taken from his bail arraignment to the set. "He's got like five years hanging over his head right now," railed Tarantino. "He's got a record that goes back forty years. He's a felon; he shouldn't be having a gun in the first place." By the end of the shoot, he was at his wit's end. "I can't take this guy," he confided to Chris Penn, who played Nice Guy Eddie.

They finished editing just three days before the Sundance Film Festisval of 1992, delivering prints that were still wet. The program described the film as "Jim Thompson meets Samuel Beckett." Gladstein watched as the ear-slicing scene provoked a firestorm of protest. "Going in, I didn't realize—stupidly, foolishly,

ignorantly—that Sundance didn't show films in this genre," Gladstein told writer Peter Biskind. "Watching the movie with that audience was shocking. You heard these gasps."

Tarantino refused to back down. At the last screening of *Dogs* at the Egyptian Theater, he was asked, "So how do you justify all the violence in this movie?"

He replied, "I don't know about you, but I love violent movies. What I find offensive is that Merchant Ivory shit."

The film got no prizes, but became easily "the most-talked about movie of the festival," as the *Los Angeles Times* wrote. "It was completely wild," said Roth. "They were selling tickets on the buses for a hundred dollars a piece."

It still lacked a distributor, as Miramax's Harvey Weinstein circled, nervous about the ear-slicing scene. "Without this scene you have a mainstream movie," Harvey told Tarantino. "With this scene, you put it in a box. Without this scene, I could open this movie in three hundred theaters, as opposed to one. Thirty seconds could change the movie in the American marketplace."

Weinstein used his wife, Eve, and her sister Maude as guinea pigs. "When the ear scene came on, they were out of their seats like jumping jacks," he said. "Forget it; there go the women."

On her way out, Eve turned to her husband and said, "I don't care how good the movie is, this is disgusting!"

Weinstein recalled: "They were circling outside the screening room, pissed off at me,

"That scene would not be as disturbing without the song because you hear the guitar strain, you get into it, you're tapping your toe and you're enjoying Michael Madson doing his dance, and then—voom!— it's too late, you're a coconspirator."

"I want to make
hard-dick movies
and I want them
all to come from
the same place as
Reservoir Dogs;
from the same
artist, from the
same man."

pissed off at Quentin, pissed off at the movie. Angry." Embarrassed, Weinstein apologized to the director. "I didn't make it for your wife," snapped Tarantino.

Eve and Maude stood outside the theater for fifteen minutes, and then they returned and watched the rest of the film. "I thought you hated the movie; how come you came back?" he asked. "We wanted to find out what happened," replied Eve.

The scene stayed in.

Reservoir Dogs was released on October 23, 1992. That much we know. All other attempts to date the film come with an asterisk. Yes, Tarantino's gangsters sit around in coffee shops, talking about the meaning of Madonna's "Like a Virgin," but otherwise their pop culture intake—Stealers Wheel, Pam Grier movies, the TV shows *Get Christie Love* and *Honey West*—harkens back to Tarantino's childhood in the 1970s, while their natty black suits and skinny ties hail from the decade before that. They look like gangsters from the sixties, groove on music from the seventies, and hold court like nineties coffee-shop philosophers. We already seem to have entered the magpie-ish pop-cultural bric-a-brac sale of Tarantino's imagination, as later

represented by Jack Rabbit Slim's in *Pulp Fiction*, where Marilyn Monroe brushes shoulders with Buddy Holly, only because it's Jayne Mansfield's night off—"a wax museum with a pulse" as Travolta's Vincent Vega puts it, providing the neatest self-encapsulation of the films of Quentin Tarantino the director would ever give us.

Reservoir Dogs may not have dated easily, but the original reviews, on the other hand—oh boy. The reviews make 1992 sound like 1892. It was a dusty and distant period when Bob Dole scolded Hollywood for being a "nightmare of depravity," academics published learned articles about the "new brutality" in film, and Michael Medved fretted nightly over the parade of violent films denigrating Christian values, promoting extra-marital sex and swearing, while honest God-fearing Americans pulled the bed-sheets up around their armpits for protection. Into this atmosphere came Tarantino's film.

"The only thing Mr. Tarantino spells out is the violence," said Julia Salmon in the *Wall Street Journal*.

"This movie isn't really about anything. It's just a flashy, stylistically daring exercise in cinematic mayhem," said the *New York Daily News* in a review headlined "*Reservoir Dogs* overflows with violence."

"I didn't have an idea of how to shoot a single scene . . . but I was the happiest I'd ever been in my life. I was living my dream and my dream was going to be great."

> "To me, violence is just one of the many things you can do in movies. Saying you don't like violence in movies is like saying you don't like slapstick, like saying you don't like dance sequences."

Even the movie's fans subscribed to the cavalcade-of-unending-violence narrative. "It's so well made, the violence is so gratuitous, and the general reception has been so delighted, that attention must be paid," said Stanley Kauffmann in the *New Republic*.

Twenty-five years later, enough time may have elapsed for us to break the news to the movie's critics gently: *Reservoir Dogs* is not that violent.

There are a couple of shoot-outs, and we see a cop being badly beaten, but contrary to legend, we do not see the ear slicing: As Mr. Blonde settles into the cop's lap, the camera averts its gaze to take in a patch of wall.

Famously, we do not see anything of the heist itself, nor Mr. Blonde going crazy in the bank. It's all prelude and aftermath.

"A heist caper without a heist, an action movie that's helplessly in love with talk, a poem to the sexiness of storytelling, and a slice of precocious wisdom about life," said *L.A. Weekly*, calling Tarantino "a maestro of the mood swing" who delights in jamming the audience's radar, gleefully outfoxing us with zig-zags from hilarity to horror and back, leaving the audience giddy with delight: You laugh because someone just made light of murder. Then you laugh that you could even laugh about such a thing. And then you're laughing just because you're laughing, because the movie is so damn *good*.

There's not an inch of fat on it: At ninety-nine minutes, it moves like a bullet. No wonder people complained about violence: not the violence meted out by the characters, or the violence of their talk, but the violence done unto film form. Exposition? Gone. Chronology? Scrambled, although none of the flashbacks *feel* like flashbacks—you're never straining to get back to the warehouse—and when we find out the identity of the undercover cop it doesn't dent the suspense. It raises the stakes still further. These guys cannot possibly trust one another, and yet can't afford *not* to if they are to get to the bottom of who set them up.

MR. PINK

For all we know, he's the rat.

MR. WHITE

That kid in there is dying from a fuckin' bullet I saw him take so don't you be calling him a rat!

The script is constructed as a series of dialogues, in which speaker A attempts to convince speaker B that the opposite of what he thinks is actually the case: Mr. Brown attempts to persuade everyone "Like a Virgin" is about dick; Mr. Pink attempts to persuade everyone tipping is a ludicrous societal norm; Mr. White

attempts to persuade Mr. Orange he is not about to die; Mr. Pink attempts to persuade Mr. White they've all been set up; the cop tries to convince Mr. Blonde not to torture him; and so on.

In *Ars Rhetorica* Aristotle identified three types of rhetoric—*ethos*, which invokes the trustworthiness or credibility of a speaker on a particular subject; *pathos*, an appeal to the audience's emotions; and *logos*, an appeal to pure logic. Mr. White uses pathos to argue for Mr. Orange's innocence: *the kid suffered, don't you be calling him a rat*. Joe Cabot's name is cleared with an appeal to ethos—his credibility and character.

MR. WHITE

Me and Joe go back a long time. I can tell you straight up. Joe definitely didn't have anything to do with this bullshit.

To which Mr. Pink responds by opening a can of pure logos on Mr. White's ass.

MR. PINK

'Oh you and Joe go back a long time.' I known Joe since I was a kid. But me saying Joe definitely couldn't have done it is ridiculous. I can say I definitely didn't do it, cause I know what I did or didn't do. But I can't definitely say that about anybody else, cause I don't definitely know. For all I know, you're the rat.

MR. WHITE

For all I know *you're* the rat.

MR. PINK

Now you're using your head.

Here is the patented Tarantino tone—hard, assaultive, ferociously intelligent, skeptical. The voice of someone who has been burned one too many times. If heists are indeed an allegory for moviemaking, then each of the characters here are storytellers, laying out

OPPOSITE AND ABOVE: Mr. White (Keitel) steps up to comfort and defend injured Mr. Orange (Tim Roth).

and insisting on *their* version of events over the other.

When the cop tries to convince Mr. Blonde not to torture him, Mr. Blonde responds with the most frightening speech of all.

MR. BLONDE

Now, I ain't gonna bullshit you. I don't really care about what you know or don't know. I'm gonna torture you regardless. Not to get information, but because torturing a cop amuses me. There's nothing you can say, I've heard it all before. There's nothing you can do. Except pray for a quick death, which you ain't gonna get.

Tarantino's framing of Madsen is terrific: The slow dolly reveals him to be in the room with them, stood there sucking on his soda. Tarantino knows that what is kept out of the shot is just as important as what he keeps in. The most disturbing thing about the torture scene is not the ear severing itself, which we never see, but the long Steadicam shot following Mr. Blonde as he walks out of the warehouse to get the gasoline from the boot of his car. The music recedes and is replaced on the soundtrack by birds, and the sound of children playing. It's almost like a crack in the cinema itself has opened up, letting in the daylight world beyond, the breaking of the spell the moment at which you most realize its potency.

"That is actually my favorite thing in the film, one of my favorite things I'll ever do in a film," Tarantino would later say. "In the same shot he picks up the can and goes back in—*voom*—the song is playing again, he goes right back into the dance . . . That to me is pure cinema."

Another instance: the cut taking us from the credits to the second scene, showing us Mr. Orange squirming in agony in the back of the car. Tarantino does it with a fade out—one of his most powerful tools, as *Pulp Fiction* would prove—so we hear Orange's whimpers before we see him, and the effect is merciless, edged with mockery: One minute they're exiting the diner in glorious slo-mo, their banter still ringing in our ears, George Baker belting out "Little Green Bag" on the soundtrack; the next they're bleeding out in the backs of cars, crying and cradling one another, their plans in tatters, their machismo stripped bare. In one cut, God—or the next best thing, the director—unzips the plan.

"Like Huston and Kubrick, who used their intricate (but botched) heist plots to demonstrate the existential absurdity of a perfect crime, Tarantino, in *Reservoir Dogs*, has made a nihilist comedy about how human nature will always undercut the best-laid plans," wrote Owen Gleiberman in *Entertainment Weekly*.

Meanwhile out trundle poor doomed Mr. Blue (Eddie Bunker) and Mr. Brown (Tarantino), oblivious to the fate that awaits them. "In that opening scene these guys don't know they're

peripheral characters," said Tarantino. "As far as they're concerned, they're the stars of the movie, you know?"

Here, in embryonic form, is the mock-heroic pop-cosmos of *Pulp Fiction*, in which the lead of one story is the supporting player in the next, all subscribing to the comforting belief, sometimes delusion, that in the movie of their lives they are the star. Tarantino had been mulling over the idea for an anthology movie since his Video Archives days, when he first came up with the idea of a series of interlinking films, not unlike Fernando Di Leo's "Milieu trilogy"—*Caliber* (1972), *La mala ordina* (*Manhunt*, 1972), and *Il Boss* (*The Boss*, 1973)—which featured a mob flunkie who double crosses his own boss, as well as an inter-racial duo of hit men, one black, one white, whose personalities clash. It was while editing *Dogs* that Tarantino got his breakthrough. What if he did it not as an anthology movie at all, but rather something more akin to Salinger's Glass family, whose members would move from one book to the next, the star of one story becoming a small character in the second and a supporting character in the third? "I love the idea that each of these characters could be the star of their own movie," Tarantino said, "and, as far as they're concerned, when they come in, they are."

Upon its release in the United States *Reservoir Dogs* took only $3 million, but internationally it was a smash, taking $20 million. "He was signing autographs for a year," said his manager, Cathryn Jaymes. This, too, would feed into the new movie, as Tarantino went on a global victory lap, accompanying the film to festivals. The girlfriend of one character became French, another Irish. He almost made his two hit men English as a vehicle for Tim Roth and Gary Oldman, but settled for giving one of them a recent trip to Amsterdam and supplying them with observations culled from his trip to Paris to see a John Cassavetes retrospective. "In the Paris McDonalds they serve beer," he noted, incredulously. "And they don't call it a Quarter Pounder, because they have the metric system here: Le Royale with Cheese! They don't know what a fucking Quarter Pounder *is* . . ."

PULP FICTION

1994

"With *Pulp Fiction*, people were like, 'Wow, I have never seen a movie like that before. A movie can do that?'"

TARANTINO had been working at Video Archives, trying to come up with a way of shooting a movie for peanuts when he hit upon the idea of an anthology movie. "The stories would be the oldest chestnuts in the world," he said. "You've seen 'em a zillion times, all right—the guy who's supposed to take out the boss's lady, 'but don't touch her'; the boxer who's supposed to throw the fight but doesn't."

The third story is what Tarantino claimed was "kind of like the opening five minutes of every Joel Silver movie": Two hit men go and kill somebody. "They look really sinister and mean, like really bad guys, like the ones in *Dogs*," he explained. "Then I spend the rest of the film deconstructing these characters. When you follow them through the rest of the morning, you see their clothes are dirty, bloody, and wrinkled . . . They literally decompose right in front of your eyes."

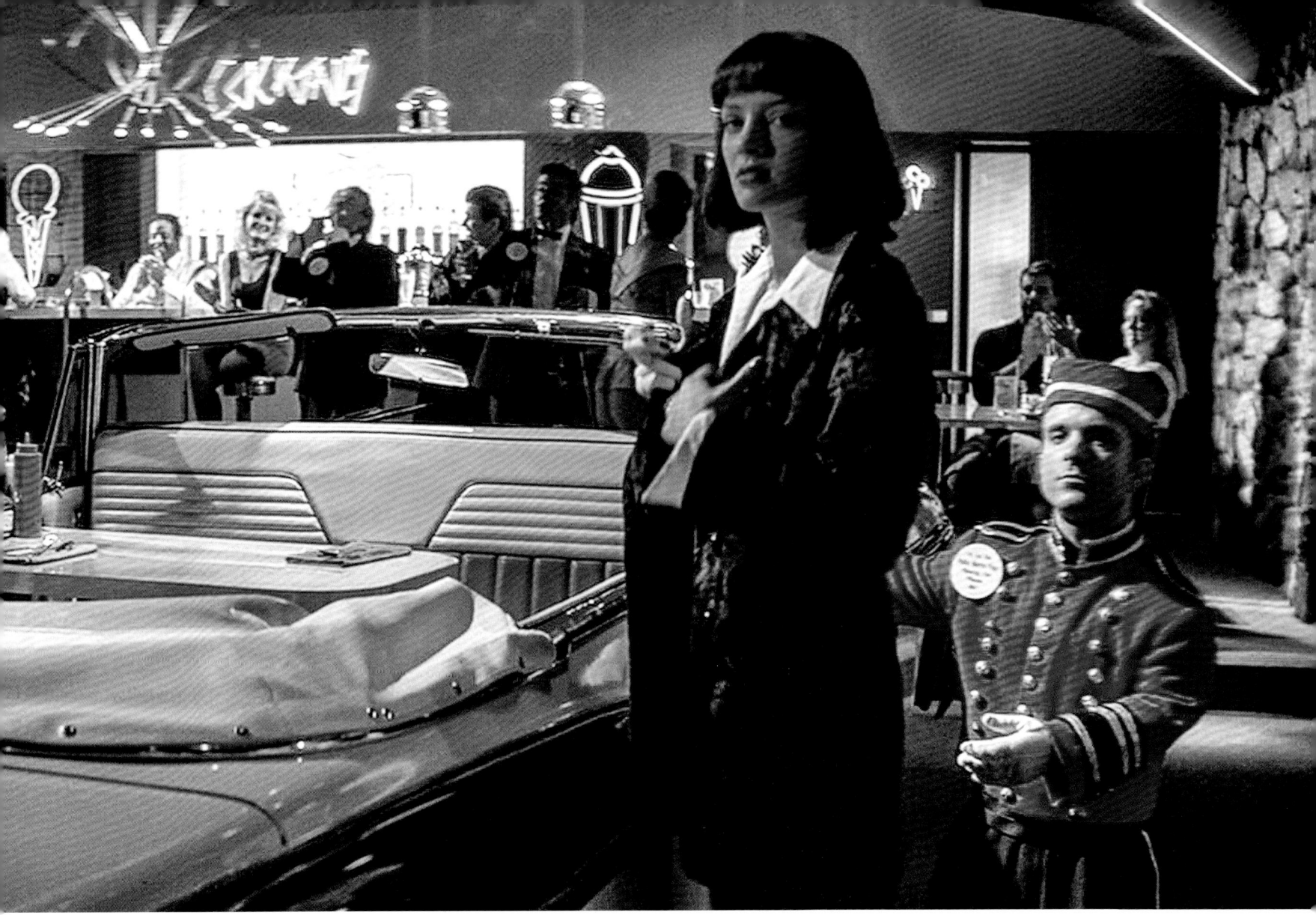

To interviewers, Tarantino always pitched the film as a three-way riff on the original stories written in the 1920s and 1930s by the likes of Raymond Chandler and Dashiell Hammett for the pulp magazines. But as that reference to his own *Reservoir Dogs* makes clear, he was deconstructing his *own* mythos as "the gun guy," as well as raising a middle finger to those who dinged him about the all-male line up of *Dogs*.

"The most interesting character I ever wrote was Mia because I have no idea where she came from," he said. "I knew nothing more about Mia than Vincent did. All I knew were the rumors. I didn't know who she was at all, until they got to Jack Rabbit Slim's and she opened her mouth. Then all of a sudden this character emerged with her own rhythm of speech. I don't know where she came from and that's why I love her."

With the $50,000 he'd made on *Reservoir Dogs* and the promise of $900,000 from TriStar Pictures for *Pulp Fiction*, Tarantino packed a suitcase full of crime novels and flew off to Amsterdam. He settled in a one-room apartment next to the canal with no phone or fax. He would get up, walk around Amsterdam, drink twelve cups of coffee, and spend his morning writing in dozens of notebooks. In between writing bouts, he would watch obscure French gangster films, read voraciously—Leigh Brackett's *No Good from a Corpse*, Anaïs Nin's diaries—and continued to accompany *Reservoir Dogs* on its global tour.

Upon reading Tarantino's final draft—159 pages, completed in May 1993, with the words "LAST DRAFT" on its cover to forestall studio interference—TriStar's Mike Medavoy passed.

OPPOSITE: As well as making a name for the director, *Pulp Fiction* gave Samuel L. Jackson (Jules Winnfield) his big Hollywood break and propelled John Travolta (Vincent Vega) back into the spotlight. ABOVE: Mia (Uma Thurman) makes the best of an awkward situation as she and Vincent are shown to their table in Jack Rabbit Slim's.

THIS PAGE: Pumpkin (Tim Roth) and Honey Bunny (Amanda Plummer) plan and execute their impromptu restaurant robbery. OPPOSITE: Tarantino's "cool cast": Samuel L. Jackson, Uma Thurman, John Travolta, and Bruce Willis (Butch Coolidge).

"They were scared of it. And they didn't think it was going to be funny," said Tarantino, who had also submitted a cast list. "It read like, for, say, the role of Pumpkin, 'This role will be offered to Tim Roth'—who ultimately played it. 'If Tim Roth turns it down, this role will be offered to the next person on the list and so on.' There were no maybes about it. It was how it is. And Medavoy read the list, and we had a big meeting about it, and he goes: 'Tim Roth is a very fine actor, but Johnny Depp is also on your list. I would rather offer the part to Johnny Depp. And if he turns it down, we should go to Christian Slater. That would be my order.'"

Tarantino asked him, "Do you actually think that Johnny Depp, in the role of Pumpkin—who's only in the last scene and the first scene—do you actually think that would mean a dollar's worth of difference at the box office?"

"It won't mean a dime, but it will make me feel better," replied Medavoy.

"There's nothing else to be said after that," said Tarantino. "That says it all. I don't want to make movies that way."

All the other major studios had passed before Bender took it to Harvey Weinstein at Miramax, who read it en route to a vacation in Martha's Vineyard. "What is this, the fucking telephone book?" he asked, eyeing the 159 pages. Three hours later, he called Richard Gladstein, who was now working as head of production for Miramax and later detailed their conversation to author Peter Biskind:

"Oh my God, this is brilliant. The opening of this is unbelievable. Does it stay this good?"

"It stays this good."

"Okay, don't leave the office; I'm gonna keep reading."

Forty-five minutes later, Weinstein called back.

"The main character just died."

"Right."

"What happens at the end?"

"Harvey, just keep reading."

"Richard, is it a happy ending?"

"Yes."

"Oh my God! He comes back! Doesn't he? I'll call you back."

Half an hour later, he called back.

"Fuck it, we have to make this movie. It's unbelievable . . . *Start negotiating!*"

A little while later, he called back again.

"Are you closed yet?"

"*I'm into it.*"

"Hurry up! We're making this movie."

"Back then, I got much more excited by cool casting. I liked the idea of taking an actor I've always liked but wasn't being used much anymore and putting him in the movie and showing people what he could do."

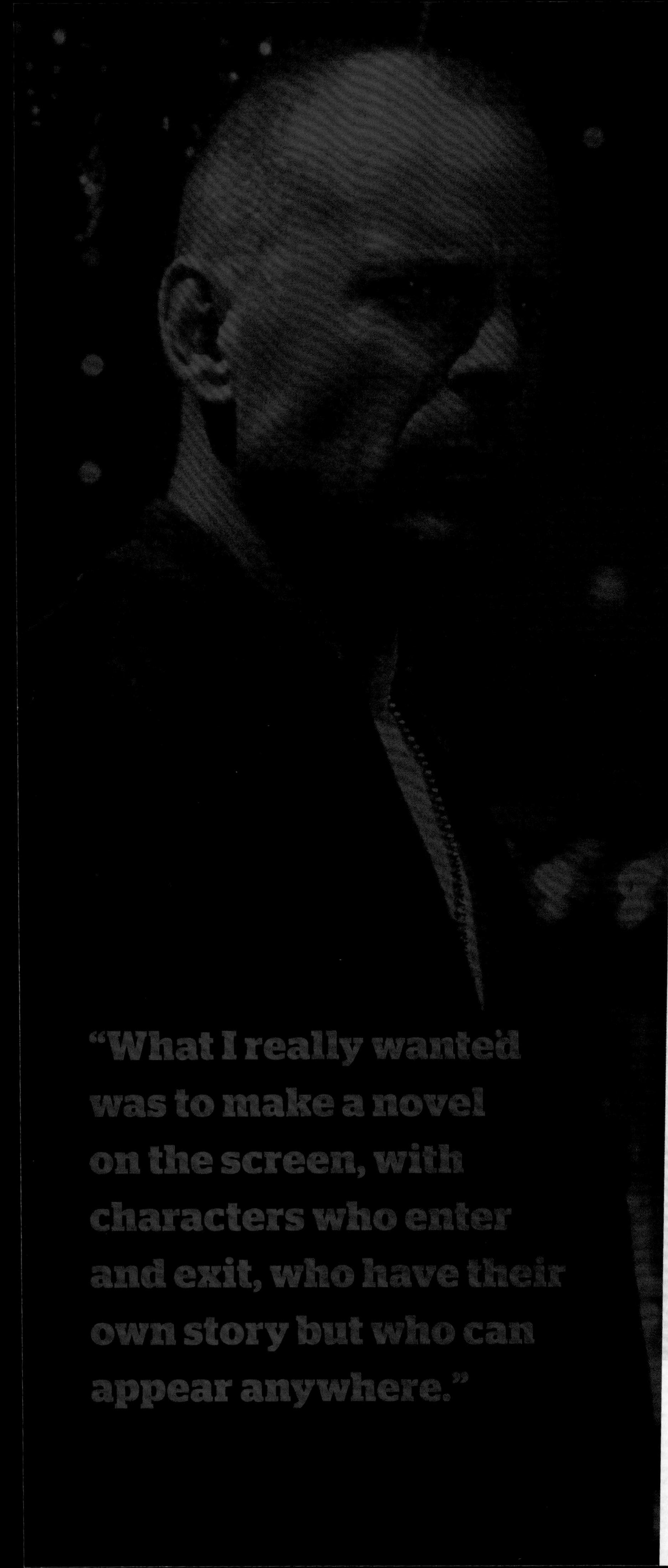

"What I really wanted was to make a novel on the screen, with characters who enter and exit, who have their own story but who can appear anywhere."

Initially, Tarantino didn't have Travolta in mind for the part of hit man Vincent Vega; he'd written it for Michael Madsen. He first approached Travolta for the part of Seth Gecko in his vampire script, *From Dusk Till Dawn,* which he'd written years earlier but had now resurfaced in the wake of *Dogs*'s success. Since his experience with Tim Roth, Tarantino had developed a habit of spending at least a day hanging out with any actor he was considering casting in a lead part in one of his movies. So he invited Travolta to his apartment on Crescent Heights in West Hollywood. Tarantino recalled, "I open the door, and [Travolta] says, 'Okay, let me describe your apartment to you. Your bathroom has this kind of tile, and da-da-da-da. The reason I know this is, this is the apartment that I lived in when I first moved to Hollywood. This is the apartment I got *Welcome Back, Kotter* in.'"

They talked until sunrise, playing Tarantino's collection of board games based on *Grease* and *Saturday Night Fever.* "Playing with John was cool," he said. "It's my dream to do a *Reservoir Dogs* game." Finally, he leveled with Travolta about the state of his career. He hadn't even been able to see *Look Who's Talking Too.* "Don't you remember what Pauline Kael said about you?" he asked. "What Truffaut said about you? What Bertolucci said about you? Don't you know what you mean to American cinema, John?"

Both hurt and touched by his infatuation with his career ("How can you not respond to that?"),

Travolta nonetheless wasn't drawn by *From Dusk Till Dawn*. "I'm not a vampire person," he told him.

"After meeting John, I kept thinking of him whenever I was writing," said Tarantino. When he found out that Madsen had accepted a part in *Wyatt Earp,* a copy of the *Pulp Fiction* script arrived at Travolta's door with a handwritten note attached that simply said, "Look at Vincent." After reading it, Travolta told Tarantino, "This is one of the best scripts I've ever read—one of the best roles I could ever have—but good luck, because I don't think you'll get me in it."

Tarantino had to fight. Harvey Weinstein wanted Sean Penn or Daniel Day-Lewis. James Gandolfini was also in consideration. During a late night telephone call with Weinstein, Tarantino's agent, Mike Simpson, hammered out a term sheet of his demands—final cut, a two-and-a-half hour running time, final choice of actors—telling him, "You're going to agree to it right now, or there's no deal. We've got two other buyers waiting outside to get this. You've got fifteen seconds to agree to it. If I hang up, it's over . . ." Simpson recalled, "Harvey kept talking, arguing, and I said, 'Okay, fifteen, fourteen.' When I got to eight, Bob Weinstein goes, 'Harvey, we have to say yes.' Harvey says, 'Okay, fuck it.'"

Harvey Weinstein breathed easier once they cast Bruce Willis, a huge fan of *Reservoir Dogs* who wanted to work with the young director, even if it meant taking a pay cut: His fee on *Die Hard 2*

was as much as the entire budget of *Pulp Fiction*. Willis was initially suspicious of the role of Butch: "Bruce is all, 'What? I'm not going to play the lead? I'm going to be bound up by some hillbilly in a pawnshop so that *John Travolta* can be the lead?'" recalled Simpson. But Willis came around after meeting the director at a barbecue at Harvey Keitel's house, during which the two of them went for a walk on the beach together.

"One of reasons I cast Bruce Willis in *Pulp Fiction* is, to me, Bruce Willis was the only star out and around at the time that looked like he could be a star of the fifties," said Tarantino, who had heard he was difficult to work with. "You couldn't have heard more bad things about somebody than Bruce, about how he'd tell you what lens to put in the camera." In the end, the actor would ask to change only one word of his script: "I'm sorry, baby. I had to crash that Honda," instead of "car." Tarantino conceded that it was funnier that way. "After working with Bruce, I will never listen to rumors about how difficult this star or that star is," he said. "I'd work with him again in a second."

"The most interesting character I ever wrote was Mia because I have no idea where she came from. I didn't know who she was at all, until they got to Jack Rabbit Slim's and she opened her mouth."

With Willis on board, Miramax was able to sell foreign rights for $11 million, recouping the Weinstein's original $8.5 million investment at a stroke.

Despite having been told by Tarantino at Sundance that the part of Jules had been written for him, Samuel L. Jackson almost lost out to Puerto Rican actor Paul Calderon after his audition had the director applauding. Weinstein urged Jackson to fly immediately to Los Angeles to "blow [Tarantino's] balls off." Arriving at the audition hall angry, tired, and hungry, with a takeout burger in his hand, he was told by someone in the casting office, "I love your work, Mr. Fishburne." Jackson was furious. "In comes Sam with a burger in his hand and a drink in the other hand and stinking like fast food," Gladstein told *Vanity Fair*. "Me and Quentin and Lawrence were sitting on the couch, and he walked in and just started sipping that shake and biting

that burger and looking at all of us. I was scared shitless. I thought that this guy was going to shoot a gun right through my head. His eyes were popping out of his head. And he just stole the part."

Just about every actress in Hollywood auditioned for the role of Mia—Michelle Pfeiffer, Meg Ryan, Holly Hunter, Rosanna Arquette—but Tarantino knew almost from the get-go that he wanted Uma Thurman. "When we were flying back to LA I could see in his eyes that it was Uma," said Bender. She turned down the role initially, put off by the scene showing the anal rape of her crime-boss husband Marsellus Wallace (Ving Rhames). But after a three-hour dinner at The Ivy in Los Angeles, followed by a marathon discussion at Thurman's New York apartment about rape, she signed on.

"It was like a relationship," said Bender. "One was afraid to commit to the other first in

OPPOSITE AND ABOVE: Uma Thurman swiftly became Tarantino's muse on set. BELOW: Samuel L. Jackson blew the director and producers away with his audition for the role of Jules Winnfield, marking the first of six collaborations with Tarantino.

case they said no. It was like this slow dance, the two of them."

She wasn't the only one perturbed by the scene. It turned out to be the dealbreaker for almost all the black actors Tarantino talked to for the part of Marsellus. "It's very hard to talk a black man into doing anything where he's being raped," he told *Playboy*. "I was thinking, please, let him not have as much of a problem as everyone else, because he's just so good. Ving sensed this and said, 'Let me ask you, how explicit is this shit gonna get?' I said, 'It's not going to be that bad, but you're going to know what's going on. Do you have a problem with that?' He says, 'Not only do I not have a problem, you have to understand that because of the way I am, I don't get offered many vulnerable characters. This man might end up

being the most vulnerable motherfucker I will ever play.'"

When it came to filming the rape scene, Rhames was as good as his word, although at one point Rhames turned to the director and asked, "Okay, so we're going to see his butt, right? Well, what's going to be down there to protect that?"

He pointed to Whitaker's groin.

"You won't see anything," Tarantino reassured him.

"I'm not talking about what you're going to show. I don't care if it's on camera, in focus or not. I don't want dick touching anus. What are you going to put down *there*?"

Finally, a prop guy was dispatched and came back with a turquoise velvet jewelry pouch. They all burst out laughing. Ving said "Duane, you just put your dick in this little bag and I'll be okay."

Principal photography began on September 20, 1993, at the Hawthorne Grill in suburban Los Angeles. It was the first of the film's seventy locations and sets, where the couple played by Tim Roth and Amanda Plummer go from breakfast to robbery. Dressed in baggy corduroys, a stained Speed Racer T-shirt, and a scruffy suede baseball jacket, Tarantino skipped around the set like a kid in an amusement park. He embodied a much more relaxed and confident figure than the anxious debutante who shot *Dogs*. He had employed much of the same crew, including cinematographer Andrzej Sekula, editor Sally Menke, costume designer Betsy Heimann, and production designer David Wasco.

Wasco built the movie's main set, a $150,000 re-creation of an Atomic-age Googie-style diner called Jack Rabbit Slim's that was chock-full of cinematic kitsch—Roger Corman posters, cars as booths, and a huge speedometer on the dance-floor—in a warehouse in Culver City. Tarantino was on a "creative and imaginative high . . . just living my dream."

Also on set was his old friend Craig Hamann, an ex-heroin addict who advised the cast on how to lovingly caress a "rig" (needle and spoon) and how to indicate the way a heroin high comes in waves, not all at once. To replicate a heroin high, he told Travolta, "Drink as much tequila as you can and lay in a warm pool or tub of water." Travolta did so happily with his wife in their hotel suite. For the scene in which the overdosed Mia is reanimated with a shot of adrenaline to the heart, they shot the stab backward, for accuracy.

"We had different ideas on how she would react to the adrenaline shot," said Thurman. "But the one I did was inspired by something I didn't witness but had heard about from the crew and cast on *The Adventures of Baron Munchausen*. There was a tiger in Spain that they had oversedated to film safely, and they had to give it some adrenaline to revive it. That was my inspiration."

OPPOSITE: Ving Rhames as crime boss Marsellus Wallace. TOP: Shooting Mia's overdose. Tarantino's own cherry-red Malibu can be seen on the right. BOTTOM: On the Jack Rabbit Slim's set designed by David Wasco.

"Most editing is painstaking but this was an exciting scene to edit because it had momentum of its own and an obvious magic—it's Travolta, dancing in front of me."

—Sally Menke

The scene she most dreaded, though, was her dance scene with Travolta. Tarantino brought in a video of Godard's *Bande à part* to show her Anna Karina's dancing in that film—unchoreographed, like a teenager dancing in her room, not a dancer dancing on a stage. It didn't matter if the dancing was good, bad, or indifferent, he said. He wanted Thurman and Travolta to enjoy themselves.

"Quentin recommended the Twist," said Travolta. "And I said, 'Well, little Johnny Travolta won the Twist contest when he was eight years old, so I know every version. But you may add other novelty dances that were very special in the day.' He said, 'What do you mean?' I said, 'There was the Batman, the Hitchhiker, the Swim, as well as the Twist.' And I showed them to him, and he loved them. I said, 'I'll teach Uma the steps, and when you want to see a different step, call it out.'"

Tarantino filmed the scene with a handheld camera, calling out, "*Watusi! Hitchhiker! Batman!*" when he wanted them to switch, dancing in his sweatshirt and baggy pants alongside them. At the end of a long day, he applauded his stars.

"That scene with Uma Thurman and John Travolta dancing in Jack Rabbit Slim's diner in *Pulp Fiction* was unusual in that it was filmed to playback, to the actual Chuck Berry song," said editor Sally Menke. "It was easy to cut in that respect, and oh my God, it was glorious. We chatted about using the long shot, the medium close-ups, and when to focus on the hands. Most editing is painstaking, but this was an exciting scene to edit because it had momentum of its own and an obvious magic—it's Travolta, dancing in front of me."

After filming wrapped on November 30, 1993, Tarantino's first rough cut came in at more than three-and-a-half hours in length. The first time they screened it, the projectionist asked Menke, "Did I get the reels mixed up?" Among the biggest challenges was cutting down the Jack Rabbit Slim's sequence, originally punctuated by lots of long silences of the sort Mia Wallace praises in the script ("Why do we feel it's necessary to yak about bullshit in order to be comfortable?"). Vince and Mia also had a much longer initial meeting at her house, with Mia training a video camera on him while they play a pop quiz.

MIA

Now I'm gonna ask you a bunch of quick questions I've come up with that more or less tell me what kind of person I'm having dinner with. My theory is that when it comes to important subjects, there's only two ways a person can answer. For instance, there's two kinds of people in the world, Elvis people and Beatles people. Now Beatles people can like Elvis. And Elvis people can like the Beatles. But nobody likes them both equally. Somewhere you have to make a choice. And that choice tells me who you are.

VINCENT

I can dig it.

MIA

I knew you could. First question, *Brady Bunch* or *The Partridge Family*?

VINCENT

The Partridge Family all the way, no comparison.

MIA

On *Rich Man, Poor Man*, who did you like, Peter Strauss or Nick Nolte?

VINCENT

Nick Nolte, of course.

MIA

Are you a *Bewitched* man, or a *Jeannie* man?

VINCENT

Bewitched, all the way, though I always dug how Jeannie always called Larry Hagman, "Master!"

PAGES 90–91: Tarantino filmed Mia and Vincent's dance scene with a handheld camera, applauding his actors from the sidelines. THIS PAGE AND OPPOSITE: "An obvious magic." While editing the scenes in Jack Rabbit Slim's, Menke and Tarantino focused on alternating between long shots and intense close-ups to find the right balance of tension and intimacy.

As they neared release, Tarantino did his best to lower expectations, pointing to the Damon Wayans movie *Mo' Money,* which made $34 million on an $8 million budget. But Weinstein had other plans. In May, Miramax flew some of the cast and crew to the Cannes Film Festival, where Weinstein implemented what he called an "Iron Curtain" strategy for the film, giving only one press screening on the morning of the evening premiere for full impact.

After Janet Maslin's rave review in the *New York Times* ("a work of such depth, wit and blazing originality that it places him in the front ranks of American filmmakers"), Weinstein made copies and slipped them under the doors of the jury members. Tarantino told Weinstein that he would skip the event if *Pulp Fiction* was going to be shut out, as *Reservoir Dogs* had been at Sundance, but on the night of the awards the festival's president, Gilles Jacob, urged Weinstein to make sure that he and the cast attend the ceremony.

"We figured we'd get screenplay or director, some prize like that," said Weinstein. "So they go through all the prizes, and I look at Quentin and say, 'I think we're going to get the big one,' and I'm bouncing up and down on my seat, and Quentin just looks at me like, nah, and then bang! Clint Eastwood gets up on stage and gives the Palme d'Or to *Pulp Fiction.* Thank God Bruce Willis was there to cool me down."

When a woman protested the award, shouting "*Pulp Fiction* is shit!" Tarantino gave her the middle finger. "I don't make movies that bring people together," he announced upon collecting the award, "I make movies that split people apart."

After the ceremony, Willis threw a party at the Hotel du Cap and put it on his tab—about $100,000. By the end he was more in the hole than Travolta, who figured that, what with flying his own jet and wanting to stay in a different hotel with his wife and kids, he wound up paying $30,000 for the privilege of appearing in Tarantino's film. "I think it *cost* me money to do this movie," he said. "But it was well worth it. Quentin's script is like Shakespeare."

BELOW: Picking up the Palme d'Or at the 47th Cannes Film Festival, 1995. OPPOSITE: With the iconic poster art.

2.A boo[k]
ing lurid s[ub]
matter, an[d]
being charac[-]
teristically
printed on
rough,
unfinished
paper.

STRAIGHTING
MORTARLESS BLDG. SUPPLY
RICK'S
RICK'S
FRAME
FOREIGN

PANAVISION
PANAFLEX
A
PANAVISION

"I was on a creative and imaginative high. I was just living my dream."

Tarantino was wrong. He doesn't just make movies that split people apart. He makes movies that bring people together *and* split them apart, have them run into one another by accident, mow each other down, and then go for a pancake-and-bacon breakfast at the Hawthorne Grill.

"Everybody knows the old E. M. Forster distinction between story and plot: 'The king died and then the queen died' is a story. 'The king died and then the queen died of grief' is a plot," Anthony Lane reminded readers of the *New Yorker* in his review of *Pulp Fiction* when it was released in cinemas later that year. "Fair enough, but what Forster failed to foresee was the emergence of a third category, the Quentin Tarantino plot, which goes something like this: 'The king died while having sex on the hood of a lime-green Corvette, and the queen died of contaminated crack borrowed from the court jester, with whom she was enjoying a conversation about the relative merits of Tab and Diet Pepsi as they sat and surveyed the bleeding remains of the lords and ladies whom she had just blown away with a stolen .45 in a fit of grief.'"

Even today, after a dozen viewings, after every exchange of dialogue has been burned into memory and a thousand and one copycats featuring thuggish disquisitions on Coca-Cola or mac 'n' cheese have come and gone, it's possible to watch Tarantino's foxy masterpiece and be startled. A hold-up in a diner ("People never rob restaurants, why not?") interrupted by an urgent need to pee. A hit man assassinated while sitting on the john. An overdose victim dropped into the middle of a marital dispute straight out of *I Dream of Jeannie*. A boxer who double crosses his impassive crime boss—a man rumored to have had someone thrown out of a fourth-story window after a dispute over foot massages—only to run into the kingpin as he plods across a suburban intersection, bearing a cardboard tray of fast food and cola. The boxer runs his Honda into him, crashes, wakes up, and the two men duke it out, before staggering into a pawn shop, where they are taken captive by hillbillies, the two men's titanic battle suddenly dwarfed and forgotten by this freak incursion of a third plot element.

OPPOSITE: Serious on set filming the Butch and Marsellus crash scene.
THIS PAGE: Tarantino and producer Lawrence Bender (right) take a break during filming with Bruce Willis and Maria de Medeiros, who played Butch's girlfriend, Fabienne.

TOP: Offering direction to Maria de Medeiros. BOTTOM: "I don't need you to tell me how fucking good my coffee is." Tarantino took on the role of Jimmie, an accomplice who helps Jules and Vincent dispose of Marvin's body.

"The structure allows him to show his characters as helplessly interconnected and helplessly isolated at the same time, and so he gets across a sense of the mystery of the world, and the smallness of the people in it," wrote Sarah Kerr in the *New York Review of Books*, declaring simply, "the couch potatoes have produced their first genius."

Tarantino's method here is to take the staples of genre, familiar even to the most glancing of aficionados, and subject them to the scuff-marks and the wear and tear of a universe surprisingly like our own, where guns misfire, people need to pee, and shit happens. This juxtaposition was there in *Reservoir Dogs*, too, but it played out in a tightly controlled form between what the gang said (talk about Madonna) and what they did (rob banks).

If *Reservoir Dogs* was the film in which Tarantino proved himself, *Pulp Fiction* was going to be the film in which he enjoyed himself. From its very first scene—Amanda Plummer and Tim Roth's impromptu hold-up, shot in deep-roasted colors by Sekula, and ending in an exhilarating freeze-frame that triggers the reverbed twang of Dick Dale's Stratocaster kicking off "Misirlou"— Tarantino allows the delirium to propel his action and loosen his grip on form, pushing it upwards and out to make a beautiful Möbius strip, the supporting player of each tale the star of the next.

"Even the plots feel like subplots," noted Anthony Lane. "Somewhere, you tell yourself, up above this gutter life the main event is going on. It's a bizarre trick; imagine erasing the hero from *King Lear*, leaving nothing but squabbling brothers and sisters and an old guy strapped to a chair."

Bizarre but not without precedent, the movie scoops up a gleeful grab bag of ingredients and influences—surf-guitar music, film noir, Godard— but its chief precedent is surely the theater of the absurd. That includes Luigi Pirandello's

Six Characters in Search of an Author, Samuel Beckett's *Waiting for Godot*, and most of all, Tom Stoppard's *Rosencrantz and Guildenstern Are Dead*, in which the two messengers bring a letter to the English king requesting that Hamlet be executed, only to be intercepted and executed themselves. The two characters get only a handful of lines between them but are given an entire play to ponder the *Hamlet*-like niceties of their fate as life's bit-players, unwittingly swept up in someone else's drama. "We do on stage things that are supposed to happen off," Guildenstern says. "Which is a kind of integrity, if you look on every exit as being an entrance somewhere else."

That's very close to the pop theology of Jules Winnfield, who, escaping a hail of bullets, concludes that a "miracle" has occurred. "We should be fuckin' dead now, my friend! We just witnessed a miracle, and I want you to fucking acknowledge it!" The line works on two levels,

for of course the audience has just witnessed a resurrection of sorts: Vincent's own, since after being shot up in the bathroom by Butch, he is now walking the earth again thanks to the miracle of Tarantino's looping chronology. Butch, too, escapes on a motorcycle named "Grace."

If there is a God here, one that resembles the vengeful deity of Ezekiel 25:17 ("You will know I am the Lord when I lay My vengeance upon you"), it is Tarantino, who descends from on high to appear among his creations, cackling gleefully as The Wolf (Harvey Keitel) hoses down Jules and Vincent in his backyard. Keitel here plays a role very close to his role as the behind-the-scenes fixer and facilitator in *Reservoir Dogs*—a nod of affection to the star, and also a signal of how much Tarantino was operating outside the rule book that governed his debut. The film was trailed into cinemas by his reputation for violence, but again, we see almost nothing.

And what we do see has the spastic rhythm not of movie violence but real life: After Butch passes out at the wheel of his Honda, the car doesn't crash but rather trundles gently to a stop on the sidewalk next to a "no renting" sign. Then: fade-out.

There are half a dozen fade-outs in the film, most of them after something momentous: Vincent and Mia's dance, Mia's overdose, Butch crashing his Honda, Marsellus passing out after their fight—in order to jump forward a small period of time: *now what*. In each case, the effect is suspenseful, eerie, and catlike. It confirms our sense of Tarantino not so much as an action director but as a *reaction* director.

Tarantino's direction had grown exponentially in strength since *Reservoir Dogs*, allowing scenes to run long when other directors would cut them short and cutting them short where they would go long. His long takes were now supplemented with a series of Godardian extreme close-ups: Mia Wallace's feet, padding to the record player; the back of Marsellus's head, with that single, intriguing bandage—a marvelous little dab of mystery, better even than that famously glowing suitcase.

All of Tarantino's tenderness toward his characters seems to flow through these close-ups. The movie is at its most Godardian around Uma Thurman, glittery-eyed with mischief, black bob modeled on Anna Karina in *Vivre sa vie*, her panther-like gait as entrancing to Tarantino as Karina's was when she walked the length of that record store while Godard dollied his camera alongside her, as if that was what God invented tracking shots *for*.

Like Godard's, Tarantino's casting aims for a curated lack of depth, which is most apparent in Travolta's dance at Jack Rabbit Slim's. The star of *Saturday Night Fever* doing the Twist in worn socks like an uncle at Christmas—it's like watching Picasso draw a stick man. There's also a wonderful moment when Travolta and Butch first catch sight of each other in Marsellus's bar, taking an instant

dislike to one another, like dogs in the street. "You looking at something my friend?" asks Butch. "You ain't my friend," snarls Vincent. There's no reason for their antagonism, besides a chill wind blowing from a future in which one of them will kill the other. It's a clash of the icons—the seventies meets the eighties—the universe as unable to stand such concentration of iconicity as it can atoms colliding, or Ghostbusters crossing their streams. The cosmos goes on the fritz.

For all that he did for the film's box office, it's unclear whether Willis's mucho macho minimalism is quite right for the hyperverbal Tarantino, who can write well for all kinds of men and women— except the strong, silent type. Nothing looks more out of place in the movie than Willis's inscrutable little moue when Marsellus gives his "fuck pride" speech. That's what the whole Butch segment is about—the unmanning of Butch—but Willis shows little inclination toward masculine deconstruction. When, having escaped sodomization by Zed and Maynard, he returns bloodied and limping to Fabienne (Maria de Medeiros), only to have to abruptly switch gears into sweet talk—"Did you get the pancakes, the blueberry pancakes?"—Willis makes sure it is women, and not Butch, who are the butt of the joke. He may be too guarded and self-protective

ABOVE: John Travolta and Bruce Willis share a joke on set. OPPOSITE: "I solve problems." Winston Wolfe, played by Harvey Keitel, offers his assistance to the crime duo.

a performer to risk humiliation. That makes him a lonely man in the world of Quentin Tarantino.

Samuel L. Jackson, on the other hand, is another matter. Voice scaling octaves, eyes popping, Jackson is the face and voice of Tarantino's long years in the wilderness given furious form. Each one of his line readings lets off firecrackers of indignation and wounded scorn: "The motherfucker that said that shit never had to pick up itty-bitty pieces of skull on account of your dumb ass." Only Richard Pryor could have given the line as much splenetic spin.

Jackson and Travolta are great mirrors. If Jackson revs the movie up, Travolta slows it down and soothes it with that sleepy, half-smiling delivery of his, like a boy with a secret. During the dinner date with Mia, he can barely look her in the eye, his own baby-blues averted, and whether it's out of modesty or embarrassment is hard to say. By the end, the pair seems like an expression of the war going on within Tarantino's own nature, between the slacker and the adrenaline junkie, the couch potato and the pulp aficionado, torn between hanging out and cracking the whip. In *Pulp Fiction*, they find an immaculate, hummingbird balance. The movie feels wired

yet leisurely, laid-back yet alert. It comes full circle at the end of a tight, deliberate two-and-three-quarter hours, as *Reservoir Dogs* did, with a Mexican standoff, only, this time, instead of mutual annihilation, we get an act of unilateral disarmament that allows everyone to tuck their guns in their shorts and walk away happy.

"When, toward the end of *Pulp Fiction*, the curve of the story bends back to meet itself, there is something deeply, musically satisfying—a formal magic that is also very moving," David Thomson wrote. Who would have guessed it? Three acts, a romance, redemptive character arcs, quotes from the Bible, and a happy ending.

Made for $8.5 million, *Pulp Fiction* earned $214 million worldwide and was the first independent film to break $200 million. It established Miramax as a mini-studio, jumpstarted John Travolta's ailing career, and changed the course of independent filmmaking. It was "the first independent movie that broke all the rules," said Weinstein. "It set a new dial on the movie clock."

Nominated for seven Academy Awards, including best picture and best director, it won best original screenplay for Tarantino and his collaborator Roger Avary. "*Pulp Fiction* broke the mold of what I was expecting to happen with my career," Tarantino said later. "Normally, if you made a film like *Reservoir Dogs* for the studios, they'd say, 'That guy's pretty good. Maybe, if we match him with more commercial subject matter, that will take it to the next step.' So I do my little art thing, *Pulp Fiction*, in my little auteur way, and maybe it makes $30 million to $35 million. 'Okay, now we're ready to bring him into the studio system for real. Let's give him *Dick Tracy* or *The Man From U.N.C.L.E.* movie,' something like that. Well, that didn't happen. I didn't have to wrap my voice in some commercial project to get it across. My voice, me being me, became huge, so I never had to do that. I rise or fall by my ability."

"I'm not the kind of guy who wants to put *Pulp Fiction* into perspective twenty years later. One of the things I'm proudest about is that I went out to make an omnibus movie. Three separate stories. Then I wanted to make it so it would actually work together to tell one story. And I did that."

INTERMISSION

FOUR ROOMS

1995

FROM DUSK
TILL DAWN

1996

"**I** DON'T have the fame of a movie director in America; I have the fame of a movie star," said Tarantino of his life post-*Pulp Fiction*. Walking into a bar in Los Angeles, in no time, he'd have a couple of girls on his arm. A steady stream of fans would always approach his table. People would honk at him when they saw him in his car, and follow him down the streets with posters and photos to sign. He was happy to talk movies with them, but as time went on, getting accosted in his local record store when all he wanted to do was browse and do his "regular-guy shit" got to be too much.

When Chasen's restaurant closed its doors in April 1995, Tarantino was accompanied there by his friend and fellow filmmaker Robert Rodriguez.

"As soon as he opened the door, people were already there with *Pulp Fiction* posters, mobbing him," said Rodriguez. "He said, 'Man, that guy, I signed his poster, and he looked at me like I was a dick 'cause I didn't sign all ten.'"

When another director friend, Alexandre Rockwell, asked him to contribute to an anthology film that would consist of four different stories all taking place on the same night and in the same hotel, Tarantino decided to hold a mirror up to his newfound fame. His story would be about an obnoxious celebrity called Chester Rush: a motor-mouthed comedy star who takes over a suite at the hotel, guzzling Cristal champagne ("It's fuckin' Cristal, everything else is piss"), peeling off hundred-dollar bills to pay someone to cut off a person's little finger with a meat cleaver for a bet.

"The character started off being comical, because I thought I could play a character like that really well, and then he ended up shouldering some of my own baggage as—for want of a better word—a celebrity," Tarantino said. "I play more or less myself in the worst light I could."

The idea for the anthology came after Tarantino's stint as a houseguest at the Manhattan apartment of Rockwell and his girlfriend, Jennifer Beals. "I had the feeling that there was a new wave of us," said the director, who had first met Tarantino, along with Allison Anders, Richard Linklater, and Robert Rodriguez, at Sundance in 1992. "I thought it would be cool to do something together."

Minus Linklater, who was shooting *Before Sunrise* in Vienna, the group booked a room at the Chateau Marmont to eat junk food, drink, and hash out the continuity between the segments. "It was like a pajama party or something," said Rockwell. "It was Quentin's

fantasy night, you know. We all met in a room with videos and popcorn, whatever. We all sat and talked 'bout the film and we all kinda told each other about the basic outlines . . . And it was amazing when we got the scripts together, because it was remarkable how not one of the stories didn't fit."

All the stories had to take place on the same night and feature the character of the bellhop, Ted. Ted was to have been played by Steve Buscemi, until the actor pointed out that he had already played a bellhop in the Coen Brothers' *Barton Fink*—"With that hesitation and with four directors, he sort of freaked out a bit," said Rockwell—so they approached Tim Roth instead.

OPPOSITE: Poster for *Four Rooms*, starring Tim Roth as the bellhop, Ted. ABOVE: *Four Rooms* directors (from left to right) Alexandre Rockwell, Allison Anders, Tarantino, and Robert Rodriguez.

ABOVE: Taking on the role of comedian Chester Rush in his own directed segment, "The Man from Hollywood," Tarantino starred alongside Bruce Willis, Paul Calderon, and Jennifer Beals. RIGHT: Robert Rodriguez (left) and Tarantino a again on vampire crime thriller *From Dusk Till Dawn*. Sarah Kelly (center) documented the trials and tribulations on the set in her 1997 film *Full Tilt Boogie*.

In Anders's story, "The Missing Ingredient," a coven of witches (including Madonna, Ione Skye, and Lili Taylor) try to resurrect a fifties stripper; in Rockwell's "The Wrong Man," Ted the bellhop is embroiled in a nasty domestic dispute between a husband (David Proval) and his wife (Jennifer Beals); in Rodriguez's "The Misbehavers," a hotel room is trashed by two kids while their parents go out on the town. Finally, in Tarantino's "The Man From Hollywood," a brattish comedy star, Chester Rush (Tarantino), takes over the hotel's suite with his entourage and, borrowing the premise from an episode of *Alfred Hitchcock Presents*, bets his friend that he can't light a Zippo ten times in a row: if he can, he gets Chester's red Chevy Malibu. If he can't, he loses a pinkie. He fails—and loses his finger—on his first try.

"It was like, you know, that's such a old, time-worn device," said Tarantino. "The way to make it fresh is to let real life get into it. It could just as easily not happen on the first one as the last one. It's like the whole idea, the whole story is the build-up to an event and you think you're getting on the ride and then there is no ride—*boom*, it's over."

It was a pretty slender idea—a single left turn that leaves the audience empty-handed and then asks them to find that emptiness funny. If the film had offered Tarantino a refuge from the expectations hanging over him after *Pulp Fiction* and a return to the pre-fame camaraderie he had enjoyed during his Video Archives days, production showed that for the daydream it now was. Anders couldn't help but notice that Tarantino's set on the movie was several times larger than all the others. "All of our rooms would have fit inside his," she said. "It was a metaphor for what was going on."

Arguing with her over who should direct one final piece at the end of the credits, Tarantino told Anders, "You know, you're always saying we're like a band, like the Beatles, where everyone bickers—no, I want to sing lead, no,

I want to sing lead—and just makes one record and then splits up."

Anders replied, "Well there are other kinds of bands that make one hit and disappear, like the Buckinghams, where everybody kisses each others' ass."

"Well I would like a little more of the ass-kissing model right now," Tarantino responded.

"Yeah, as long as it's your ass being kissed," Anders said.

Four Rooms wrapped right before Christmas 1994 and was edited through March 9. Bob and Harvey Weinstein stood guard to make sure they got it down from a rough cut lasting over two-and-a-half hours to a trim ninety minutes. "You really couldn't cut Robert's; it's like a comic strip," said Rockwell. "Quentin shot his in long takes so it's hard to cut his. So the pressure was building on me and Allison."

Rockwell later described the controversy. "I said to Bob and Harvey, 'Well, okay, everybody is going to do some cutting right?' And Harvey and Bob crack up and say, 'Who's going to tell Quentin he has to cut?' Harvey says, 'Well I'll tell him Alex is cutting, but then he's going to think he can add minutes to *his* room.'" In the end, Rockwell ended up with the shortest segment, followed by Anders, Tarantino, and then Rodriguez. Miramax proved gun-shy with the finished film, deliberately bypassing all the festivals except Toronto, before finally releasing it on December 25, 1995—a review-proof date.

"That amounts to an act of mercy, since the less said about this career-denting fiasco, the better," said Janet Maslin in the *New York Times*.

"On the useful scale of the Michelin guide, one is worth a trip ('The Misbehavers'), another is worth a detour ('The Man From Hollywood')," said Roger Ebert. "This story line is appropriately Tarantinonian, but the timing is off (except for one key shot), and the dialogue is all over the map."

"**I used to like to walk and be in my own head, and I can't really do that now. If I was trying to pick up a girl every night, it would be the greatest thing in the world, but I'm not.**"

ABOVE: "I guess I must have become a big shot." Tarantino writes for and highly respects his audience but often has to outrun fans and paparazzi.

The film played for a few weeks, then quickly disappeared, its flimsy contrivance completely unable to withstand the weight of expectation resting on the filmmaker post–*Pulp Fiction*, in addition to the countervailing forces of backlash now in session against him. *Tarantinonian*. They weren't reviewing him so much as his reputation.

"I became an adjective sooner than I thought I was going to," noted the director, who began telling interviewers, "I used to like to walk and be in my own head, and I can't really do that now. If I was trying to pick up a girl every night, it would be the greatest thing in the world, but I'm not." He would read phrases such as "the dangerously overexposed Quentin Tarantino," and think, *You're the motherfuckers who overexposed me.*

Apart from an episode of *ER* ("Motherhood"), Tarantino would direct nothing for a year, seeking refuge from the pressures of following up *Pulp Fiction* by hosting *Saturday Night Live* and appearing on talk shows, and in an episode of *The Simpsons*. He was offered *Speed* and *Men in Black* but turned both down. He did a script

polish for Tony Scott on *Crimson Tide* ("You can tell which is my stuff; it was the shit about the comic books and the *Star Trek* bathroom humor") and an uncredited rewrite on Julia Sweeney's *It's Pat,* although only one of his jokes made it.

His greatest contribution to the cause of world cinema was arguably his championing of Wong Kar-wai's love letter to Hong Kong, *Chungking Express,* released through Rolling Thunder Pictures, the distribution arm of Miramax that Harvey Weinstein had given him to play with. "I just started crying," he said of watching the film, not because the movie was sad, but because he was "just so happy to love a movie this much."

Increasingly, it was acting that preoccupied him. While scouting locations for *Pulp Fiction,* he had squeezed in a cameo in Rory Kelly's 1994 romantic comedy *Sleep with Me,* in which he recycled an old Tarantino-and-Avary riff from his Video Archives days about *Top Gun* being a gay allegory ("They're saying no, go the gay way, be the gay way, go for the gay way, all right").

TOP: "You ever watch *Star Trek*? . . . Now, I'm Captain Kirk, you're Scotty, I need more power." Tarantino's pop-culture imbued dialogue in Tony Scott's *Crimson Tide* (1995) is some of the film's best known. BOTTOM: Brigitte Lin in a scene from Wong Kar-wai's *Chungking Express* (1994), produced by Tarantino for Miramax's Rolling Thunder Pictures.

In 1995, he started dating Mira Sorvino, who had won an Oscar the same year he had. When he was hanging out with the actress and her actor father, Paul, the family's table talk reawakened "old dreams and desires from when I was a little boy." The couple took roles together in *Destiny Turns on the Radio,* where Tarantino played Johnny Destiny, a suave, finger-snapping pseudo-deity who pops up periodically to remind the characters that they live in a town of "limitless possibilities." As with most of his performances, he was playing not so much a character as a master of ceremonies: Quentin Tarantino, Patron Saint of Indiehood, a hip hood ornament by which filmmakers could declare their aesthetic *bona fides.* One of his new friends from this period was Steven Spielberg, who told him, "You're like a cinema raconteur."

Cameos followed in Rockwell's *Somebody to Love,* in which he played a bartender; Virginie Thévenet's *Hands Up,* a bootlegger who falls in love with a woman involved in the S-and-M scene; and in Rodriguez's *Desperado,* a drug mule who delivers a lengthy monologue about

pissing into a glass before being shot dead. But his performance suffered from the same knowing sense of *deus-ex-machina* dislocation, as if he were floating above the action rather that submitting to it. He broke the fourth wall. He was thrown by the reviews, disputing them for years to come, "because every review—I think I'm really funny in that movie, I think I kick ass in that scene—is not about me being bad, but 'We're sick of this guy. We just don't want to see his face anymore.'" They weren't faulting his performance, because he wasn't giving one.

That is not true of *From Dusk Till Dawn,* the vampire shoot-'em-up that Rodriguez directed from the script Tarantino had originally written for $1,500. The script had been created in order for special effects expert Robert Kurtzman to showcase the talents of his company, KNB. (In return, it agreed to provide the special effects for the ear-severing scene in Tarantino's *Reservoir Dogs,* free of charge.) "This is a full-on drive-in picture," said Tarantino, happy to leave his script in the hands of Rodriguez while he played one of two brother bank robbers on the lam—"a couple

of real mean motor scooters"—alongside George Clooney. The pair bonded, swapping fan letters in their trailers.

Tarantino recalled of Clooney: "He was always encouraging me, 'Fuck those assholes about *Destiny Turns on the Radio*! Fuck them! You were the best thing in the movie, man! You got my respect and you got the respect of other people, and you're going to be great in this movie!'"

It certainly showed canniness on Clooney's part: It was a version of the bonding they were required to show on screen. As the younger brother, Richard Gecko, a pale geek on a short fuse that keeps threatening to blow up their plans, "Tarantino isn't bad, and generates a few laughs with his straight-faced portrait of dementia and lasciviousness," according to *Variety*.

"Tarantino in a sly, mercifully restrained mood," judged the *New York Times*.

"The reviews basically said, 'Even Quentin was pretty good!'" said Tarantino. "I really worked hard, and I was proud of what I had done."

TOP: Kate Fuller (Juliette Lewis), Jacob Fuller (Harvey Keitel), and Seth Gecko (George Clooney) make their assult on the undead in *From Dusk Till Dawn*. BOTTOM: Writer Tarantino (bottom right) and director Robert Rodriguez (top right) fool around with cast and crew on the set of *From Dusk Till Dawn*.

"I just had such a good time with those characters. It's two movies put together, and you kind of flip a switch. And we don't indicate it to the audience."

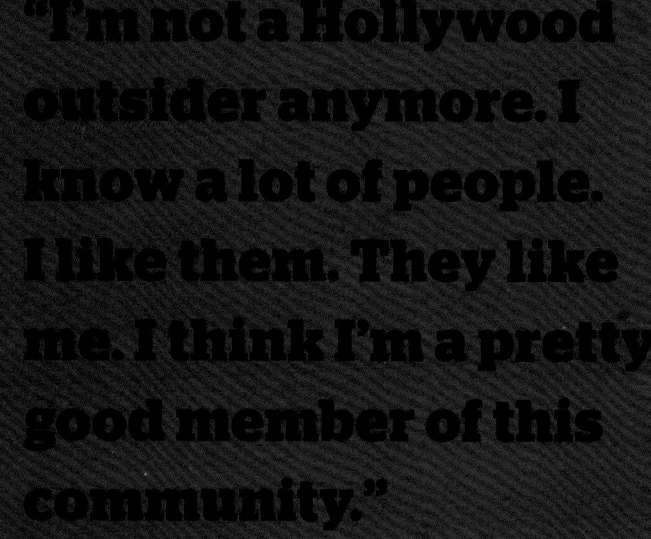

"I'm not a Hollywood outsider anymore. I know a lot of people. I like them. They like me. I think I'm a pretty good member of this community."

The film did well, taking $10 million on course to an eventual $26 million against such solid opposition as Terry Gilliam's *12 Monkeys* and Oliver Stone's *Nixon*. This was despite the film's double-jointed plot in which the Gecko brothers take a preacher's family hostage only to have their differences obliterated by a seemingly unending shoot-out with vampires on the border of Mexico. It is a weak echo of the middle section of *Pulp Fiction*, where Protagonist A duels Antagonist B only to find themselves united against Even Bigger Badass C. "It's Harvey Keitel who anchors *From Dusk Till Dawn*," wrote *Entertainment Weekly*'s Owen Gleiberman. "Acting from beneath a grizzled beard and Southern-comfort drawl, he gives Jacob a quiet moral authority. When he argues with young Scott about what they should do as they approach the Mexican border (the father has more experience; the son has seen more TV crime shows), it's the kind of urgent saturated-with-pop moment that Tarantino can bring alive like no one else."

In the end, it was the Weinsteins who got Tarantino back to the director's chair, with an adaptation from one of his favorite novelists, Elmore Leonard. Tarantino had read Leonard's novel, *Rum Punch*, before it was published just before he finished *Pulp Fiction*: "I read it and I saw it. I just kind of saw the movie."

Lawrence Bender had approached Leonard's publishers about adapting it but they let it go, not wishing to be tied in. After *Pulp Fiction*'s success, however, three more Elmore Leonard novels became available—not just *Rum Punch*, but also *Killshot*, *Bandits*, and *Freaky Deaky*. The Weinsteins bought the rights for all of them for Tarantino to produce.

"I just read to familiarize myself with it," Tarantino said. "Lo and behold, I saw the same movie I saw the first time, when I read it. It just came back again. I thought, I want to do this."

JACKIE BROWN

1997

"I had wanted for a long time to adapt Elmore Leonard. He was the first novelist I read as a kid that really spoke to me."

"**J**ACKIE BROWN wasn't my follow-up to *Pulp*. I wasn't trying to top *Pulp*," Tarantino said. "I was trying to go *underneath* it." He had spent the three years since his Cannes-conquering 1994 hit attending film festivals, acting in his friends' movies, and trying his best to shut out the inquiries from press and fans alike as to when he was going to make another film. Even after news broke that he was adapting Elmore Leonard's *Rum Punch*, the drumbeat in the press was constant: Why was he taking so long?

"I didn't want to do what most movie adaptations do, all right?" he said once the film was finished. "I wanted this to be a thing unto itself, I wanted it to have the integrity of his novel. And that takes time. To not just reduce the plot, but to actually keep his mood, his flavor, keep his thing and add a little bit of mine. All this time there was all these articles, what's Quentin doing, what's Quentin doing, when's Quentin gonna do something else? Well, Quentin was writing, okay? Quentin was doing what Quentin does, all right?"

Actually, Quentin was doing something that was, for him, unusual: his first adapted screenplay. It was Leonard's 1978 novel *The Switch*, the prequel to *Rum Punch* that first introduced the characters Ordell, Louis, and Melanie, and which Tarantino had been busted trying to shoplift from the local Kmart the year he decided to go to drama school, and it was Leonard's writing, he said, that first "opened my eyes to the dramatic possibilities of everyday speech. As I started reading more and more of his novels, it kind of gave me permission to go

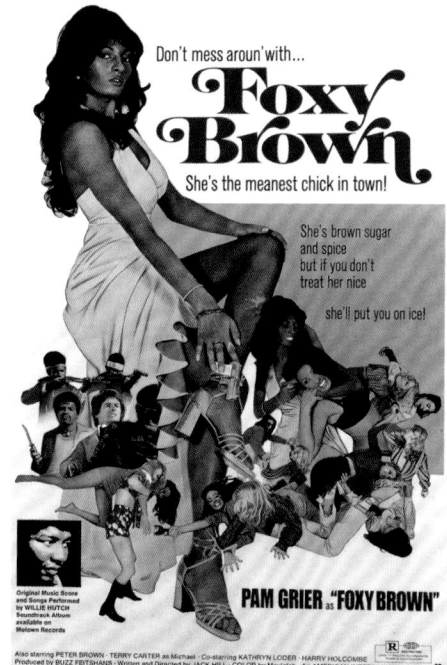

my way with characters talking around things as opposed to talking about them. He showed me that characters can go off on tangents and those tangents are just as valid as anything else. Like the way real people talk. I think his biggest influence on any of my things was *True Romance*. Actually, in *True Romance* I was trying to do my version of an Elmore Leonard novel in script form." With *Jackie Brown*, the aim was simple. "Let me do a more mature film, let me do a more character-based film," he told Rodriguez. "Let me do a movie that people would expect from me when I was forty-five."

Tarantino's biggest entry point into *Rum Punch* was the character of Ordell, the dandyish arms dealer who would be played by Samuel L. Jackson. The year he spent writing, Tarantino went far into character. "The entire year I was Ordell," he said. "He's who I identified the most with in the piece. I was Ordell when I was writing the script. I walked around like him. I talked like him. I spent a whole year basically being Ordell. I couldn't shut him off and I didn't want to. And in a weird way, Ordell is the rhythm of the movie. Like his character, the way he talks, the way he dresses—everything about him is how this movie should play. He is the old school of soul music. He's the personification of that, and I completely identify with that. If I wasn't an artist, I would probably be exactly like fuckin' Ordell."

It's the film that bears the closest kinship with Tarantino's teenage years. In the course of condensing the book's 350-page plot to a two-hour-and-forty-minute movie, he changed the location from Miami to the South Bay of Los Angeles, where he grew up, so that he could

match Leonard's embeddedness rather than mimic it, adding the character of Beaumont (Chris Tucker), Ordell's hapless underling.

He also shifted the dramatic focus onto the forty-four-year-old flight attendant, a white woman named Jackie Burke, who is struggling to keep her job while the feds use her as a pawn to bring down Ordell. It would be his first movie with a female lead. When he tried to come up with actresses who might play Jackie, Tarantino came up with only a handful of names. She had to be forty-four but look like she was thirty-four; she had to look great but also like she could handle anything.

"Then Pam popped in my head," he said. "Then it became very easy. Casting a black woman in her forties as this character gave it a depth. Pam brings a weight to that. She's lived life, and Pam also is gorgeous. She looks like she's thirty-five and has a quality where she looks like she can handle anything. She can keep her cool when the situation gets hot. All right? Well, Pam has that in spades. That is Pam Grier."

Tarantino had first seen Grier's *Coffy* when he was thirteen. He had grown up watching the queen of blaxploitation in *Women in Cages*, *Fort Apache*, *The Bronx*, and *Foxy Brown*, and "like every other boy my age, I had a big old thing for her," he said. She had actually auditioned for the part that went to Rosanna Arquette in *Pulp Fiction*, but by one of those wild coincidences that happen only in real life or Quentin Tarantino films, the director was on a street corner of Highland Avenue one day when he saw Grier in a car, sitting in traffic. Running over, he called through her open window, "*Pam Grier!*"

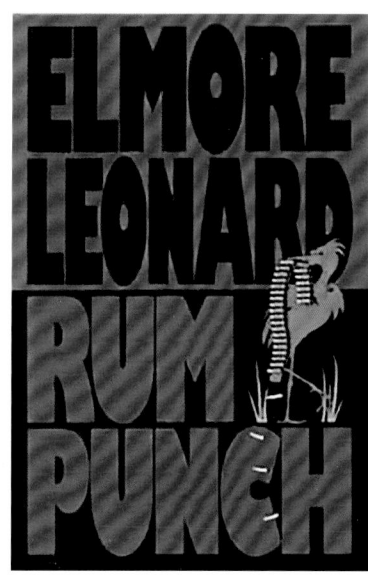

OPPOSITE: Pam Grier as Jackie. TOP: His new muse. Tarantino had grown up watching Pam Grier, the "queen of blaxploitation," in films such as *Foxy Brown*, and wrote the role of Jackie for her. BOTTOM: Tarantino's first adapted screenplay was based on one of his favorite novels, Elmore Leonard's *Rum Punch*.

"I did not want people to take what I had to offer for granted. I saw that could very easily be the case. Doing an adaptation gives you a once removed quality."

"Mr. Tarantino, what a pleasure."

"I'm writing a movie for you," he told her excitedly. "It's based on *Rum Punch*, the Elmore Leonard book!"

"That sounds amazing."

"It's my version of *Foxy Brown*."

But the traffic started moving again, and Tarantino, waving his goodbyes, was forced back to the sidewalk.

"Can you believe that?" asked her boyfriend.

"No, I can't," replied Grier. "Don't believe everything a Hollywood director tells you."

She assumed it was just talk until, sometime later, she got several notices from her local post office that a package had arrived for her without the correct postage. "I kept getting these notices from the post office saying that I had an envelope from Los Angeles with 44 cents due," she recalled. "And I'm thinking it must be a mattress advertisement or something. After the third notice, I said, 'Okay, I'll pay the 44 cents,' and they brought me this envelope that had 'QT' written in the upper-left-hand corner. It's funny because the envelope had a lot of stamps on it—he really licked all these little stamps and put them on the envelope himself."

Reading the script, Grier assumed Tarantino wanted her for the part of Ordell's stoner girlfriend, Melanie, the more "typical" black part: the arms dealer's girl. She called him up at his office.

"Jesus, Pam, I sent the script to you weeks ago," said Tarantino. "I thought you were passing on it."

"I just got it today. They were holding it 'cause you didn't pay enough postage."

"Oh. Well, anyway . . . How'd you like it?"

"It was great. I'd really like to audition for the role of Melanie. I think I could do a great job."

Tarantino laughed. "Bridget Fonda is playing Melanie," he told her. "You're Jackie Brown, Pam. I told you I was writing a script for you. I loved *Foxy Brown*, and I wrote this in your honor."

Meeting the director at his office, she found it festooned with posters from her films: *Coffy, The Big Bird Cage, Foxy Brown, Sheba, Baby*. "Did you put up all these posters because you knew I was coming in?" she asked.

"No—I almost took them *down* because I knew you were coming in," he replied.

Harder was coming clean to Leonard about the changes Tarantino had made to his novel. "Nothing, not studios, nothing, has ever made me more scared than I was when I changed his heroine in *Rum Punch* from a white woman to a black woman," he said. "I was actually scared to talk to him. The phone just weighed five hundred pounds. And it gained a hundred pounds every time I glanced at it. And then I started thinking, you know what, I can't be that way, I've got to go my way. But that didn't really make it any easier to talk to him about it." Just before he started to shoot, he finally plucked up the courage to call the writer.

"I've been afraid to call you for the last year," he told Leonard.

"Why? Because you changed the title of my book? And you're casting a black woman in the lead?" asked Leonard.

"Yeah," said Tarantino.

"You're a filmmaker," replied Leonard. "You can do whatever you want. I think Pam Grier is a terrific idea. Go ahead."

OPPOSITE: On set at the Del Amo Mall. In interviews, Pam Grier had nothing but positive words to say about her experience working with the director: "When you work with Quentin, it's liberation. He's a maestro, and the crew are his orchestra."

"I wasn't trying to top *Pulp Fiction* with *Jackie Brown*. I wanted to go underneath it and make a more modest character study movie."

PAGES 126–127: Tarantino wanted to give Jackie a sense of calm and order in the opening scenes as she prepares for work before chaos ensues. ABOVE: Talking through a scene with Oscar-nominated Robert Forster (Max Cherry).

For the part of Max Cherry, the bail bondsman who aids, abets, and falls in love with Jackie Brown, Tarantino hopped back and forth between four actors: Paul Newman, Gene Hackman, John Saxon, and Robert Forster. Forster was best known as the TV cameraman in Haskell Wexler's *Medium Cool* (1969) and had auditioned for the Joe Cabot role in *Reservoir Dogs*, only to lose it to Lawrence Tierney. Tarantino was still halfway through adapting *Rum Punch* when he came across the actor in his local coffee shop, told the actor to read the book, and then disappeared. He returned six months later to surprise him at the same table.

"I walked out to the patio and here he was sitting in my seat," said Forster. "And as I approached the table, he lifted up a script and handed it to me and said 'Read this; see if you like it.' So, you know, in one fell swoop, and without the usual chasing and auditioning and hoping and begging and whatever it takes to get a job, this guy handed me the best job

in my career. It's hard to explain other than 'miracles do happen.'"

When Tarantino was still prepping the film, he visited Forster's house and discovered that his father had been an elephant trainer for the Ringling Brothers' Circus. He collected a few family photographs and elephant-training tools from Forster and placed them in a glass cabinet in Max Cherry's office; he thought of them thenceforth as the photographs and tools of Max Cherry's father. "Robert Forster's face is backstory," he said. "That was so with both him and Pam Grier. If you've been an actor in this business for as long as they have, you've seen and fucking done it all, all right? They've had heartbreaks and success and failure and money and no money, and it's right there. They don't have to do anything."

Working for the first time with Guillermo Navarro, the cinematographer who had shot *Desperado* and *From Dusk Till Dawn*, Tarantino screened, as prep, Robert Culp's *Hickey and*

"I kind of grew up surrounded by black culture. I went to an all black school. It is the culture that I identify with. I can identify with other cultures too; we all have a lot of people inside of us, and one of the ones inside of me is black. Don't let the pigmentation fool you; it is a state of mind. It has affected me a lot in my work."

Boggs and Peter Bogdanovich's *They All Laughed.* "A masterpiece, I think," said Tarantino of the latter. "It captures a fairy-tale New York. It makes New York look like Paris in the twenties. It makes you want to live there. And we kind of used it. And then we watched *Straight Time*, one of the best LA crime movies ever. But I wanted *Jackie Brown* to look more like a movie than that. *Straight Time* is too gritty."

Increasingly disgruntled with the press, Tarantino also insisted on a closed set for the first time, excluding TV cameras and journalists. The media chatter box who had accompanied *Reservoir Dogs* on its global tour was shutting up. The privacy made for some unusual on-set bonding.

"One day he declared that we would have 'skirt day,'" wrote Grier in her autobiography, *Foxy*. "In the morning all the men in this crew (the usual suspects with whom he always worked) showed up wearing kilts and skirts and we laughed all day long."

They started shooting on May 25, making such good progress that at one point, ahead of schedule, Tarantino asked Grier and Jackson to shoot an extra scene. Jackson refused, saying he wasn't ready and didn't want to shoot it cold. "As if we were his teenage kids, Quentin proceeded to pit us against each other," recalled Grier in her autobiography *Foxy*. "A master manipulator, he told Sam, 'I just talked to Pam. She's ready. Why aren't you?'

"'I don't want to do it,' he said simply.

"'Pam is waiting for you,' he urged Sam, poking subtly at his ego. 'She's all ready,' he repeated. His method worked perfectly, as Sam took the bait. 'I guess I can do it, then,' he said. Quentin came running over to me and said with a sparkle in his eye, 'He's gonna do it—once he knew you would.'

"'Is he going to take it out on me?' I asked. 'What did you say to him? Are you getting me in trouble here?'"

"It's not like that," he reassured her.

ABOVE: Pam Grier and Samuel L. Jackson had dynamic chemistry as Jackie and Ordell.

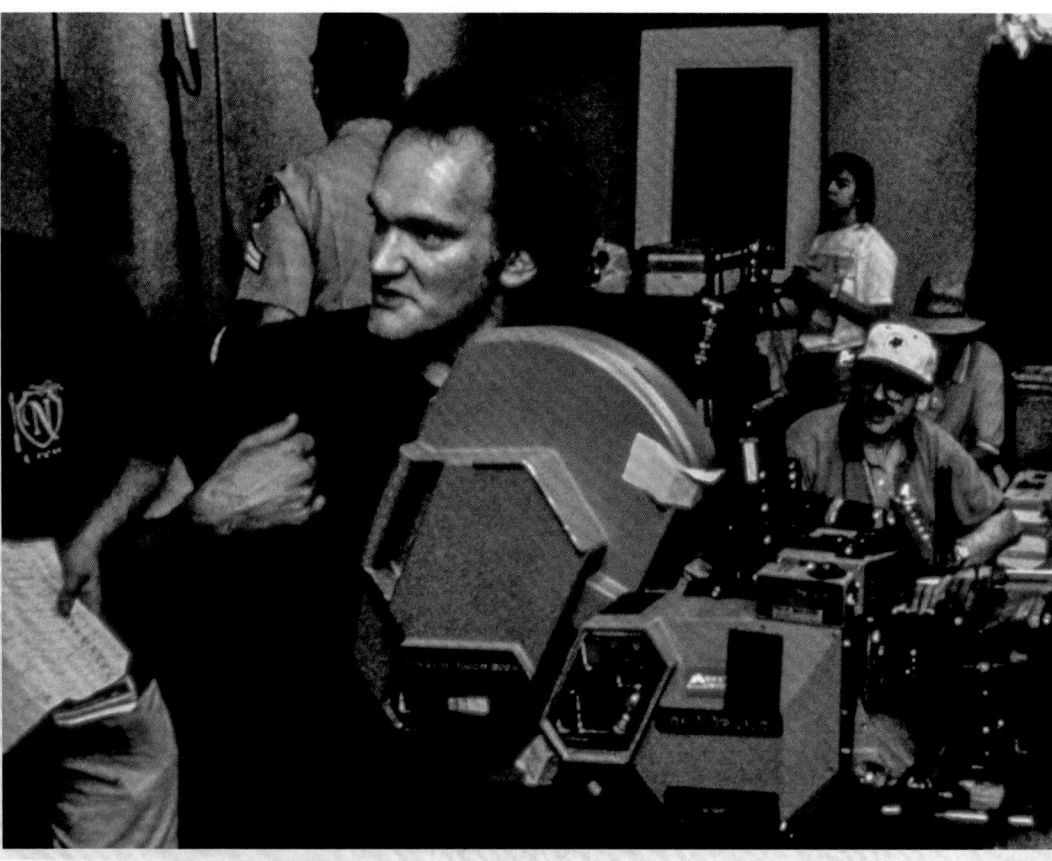

ABOVE: A "mature cinematic effort." From behind the camera, Tarantino prepares his crew for a scene. OPPOSITE: Promotional shot for the film with the core cast members Michael Keaton, Bridget Fonda, Robert De Niro, Samuel L. Jackson, and Pam Grier.

Another time, shooting the scene in Jackie Brown's kitchen with Max Cherry where Brown is frustrated and afraid but trying to hide it, Grier started to cry spontaneously. She knew she had nailed the take when the crew applauded.

"That was it," she said. "That was the performance, right?"

"You got another one in you?" asked Tarantino.

"Yeah," said Grier, stunned. "I can do it again. But why?"

"I'd like you to try it one more time without the tears," he said. "I need you to look stronger."

When the film wrapped, Tarantino gave only one interview, to the *New York Times*'s Lynn Hirschberg at his new home in the Hollywood Hills. He told her, "It's a quiet film, but my idea of quiet may not be anyone else's," and complained about the roughing up he'd gotten in the press.

"The main thing people took shots at was that I didn't make another movie right away. I'm never going to be the director that makes a movie a year. I don't see how directors do that and live a life. I did the talk shows and magazine articles and profiles and all, and people started writing that 'Quentin Tarantino is a master of self-promotion.' I just did the publicity rounds. You could take 30 percent of my fame away and I'd be just fine."

He spent the first few weeks of release watching it in theaters, seeing it thirteen times at the Magic Johnson to see how it was going down. "The whole first four weeks it was there, I just lived there," he said. "It's a hangout movie. *Jackie Brown* is better the second time. And I think it's even better the third. And the fourth time . . . Maybe even the first time we see it we go, 'Why are we doing all this hanging out? Why can't we get to more of the plot?' But now the second time you see it, and the third time you see it, you're not thinking about the plot anymore. You're waiting for the hangout scenes."

Elmore Leonard and Quentin Tarantino have a lot in common—a feel for scuzzy low life, great

130

dialogue, and an absurdist take on the human theater. Here, for example, are Ordell and Louis in Leonard's original *The Switch*.

"You notice in the drive?" Ordell said to Louis. "He's got an AMC Hornet, man, pure black, no shit on the outside at all, your plain unmarked car. But inside—tell him, Richard."

Richard said, "Well, I got a rollbar. I got heavy-duty Gabriel Striders. I got a shotgun mount in front."

"He's got one of those flashers," Ordell said. "Kojak reaches out, puts up on his roof?"

"Super Fireball with a magnetic bottom. Let's see," Richard said, "I got a Federal PA one-seventy electronic siren, you can work it wail, yelp, or hi-lo. Well, in the trunk I keep a Schermuly gas grenade gun, some other equipment. Night-chuk riot baton. An M-17 gas mask." He thought a moment. "I got a Legster leg holster. You ever see one?"

And here are Ordell and Louis in Tarantino's *Jackie Brown*.

LOUIS

Who's your partner?

ORDELL

Mr. Walker. He runs a fishing boat in Mexico. I deliver the merchandise to him, gets it to my customers. On all my bulk sales, anyway. Nigga didn't have a pot to piss in or a window to throw it out 'fore I set 'em up. Now, motherfucker's rollin' in cash. He got himself a yacht, with all kinds of high tech navigational shit on it.
(*back to video*)
AK-47, the very best there is.

GLORIA, a tall, Amazonian, bikini-clad, black woman faces camera and describes the AK-47.

ORDELL (CONT'D)

When you absolutely, positively, gotta kill every motherfucker in the room, accept no substitute. That there is the Chinese one. I pay eight-fifty and double my money.

Both writers clearly like their gear and watch a lot of TV. Tarantino's Ordell uses the word "motherfucker" more. The chief difference, though, is the moral value they place on their characters' talk. In Leonard's novels, the big talkers are invariably fools, show-offs who can't keep their mouths shut, sunk by their own loose talk, his greatest admiration reserved instead for the laconic types who play their cards only when necessary. Tarantino is the exact opposite, a hyper-articulate motor-mouth whose scripts buzz with thrilling rodomontade, for whom the talk *is* walking the walk, which is why Samuel L. Jackson all but walks off with *Jackie Brown*.

A loquacious gangster dandy in white beach-wear, with a long ponytail and wispy Chinese-sage beard, Ordell is a far meaner critter than Jules Winnfield in *Pulp Fiction*, but he inspires some of the funniest dialogue Tarantino has written, particularly in his early exchanges with Beaumont, as he talks him into getting into the back of his trunk so he can put a bullet in him.

BEAUMONT

I'm still scared as a motherfucker, O.D.
They talking like they serious as hell
giving me time for that machine gun shit.

ORDELL

Aw, come on, man, they just trying to put
a fright in your ass.

BEAUMONT

Well, if that's what they doin', they done
did it.

ORDELL

How old is that machine gun shit?

BEAUMONT

About three years . . .

ORDELL

Three years? That's a old crime, man! They
ain't got enough room for all the niggas
running around killing people today, now
how are they gonna find room for you?

Samuel L. Jackson knows how to fire off Tarantino's
dialogue like no other, but he makes Ordell's
silences menacing, too, sitting in the dark, waiting
for Jackie like a rattlesnake. Tarantino goes
all De Palma for the action, telling the money
exchange three ways and splitting the screen in
two to explain how Jackie lays her hands on a
gun. Although, oddly, Grier seems most over-
directed in the scenes where she reverts to her
blaxploitation sass—the crux of it for Tarantino,
whose directions you can almost hear hanging

in the air after the cameras roll—and much more
natural in the earlier scenes, where she conveys
the weary ache in Jackie's forty-four-year-old
bones. Sitting down with Max Cherry, the first
thing they discuss is how to quit smoking without
gaining weight. The next time they meet he
talks about his hair plugs. Eschewing the shock
and audacity of *Pulp Fiction* while running
nearly as long, *Jackie Brown* worked a mellow,
soulful groove that was new to Tarantino's work,
possessed of a ruefulness about age and the
passage of time that is written in the faces of its
lead actors.

OPPOSITE: With gun in hand, Samuel
L. Jackson partakes in a trademark
Tarantino promo shot. TOP: "It's a
hangout movie. It's about hanging out
with the characters." Melanie, Ordell,
and Louis spend much of the early part
of the film chilling out and watching
television. BOTTOM: Ordell and
Beaumont (Chris Tucker) talk it out.

TOP: Guns, girls, and money are Ordell's main obsessions. BOTTOM: Cast and crew including Tarantino, Jackson, and Lawrence Bender prepare for the scenes in which Ordell coaxes Beaumont into his car trunk and murders him. OPPOSITE: "If I wasn't an artist, I would probably be exactly like fuckin' Ordell."

"Perhaps the most remarkable thing about *Jackie Brown* is how unfoolish and—a very un-Tarantino word—how *wise* this film looks and sounds while espousing a then-thirty-four-year-old, non-black, male filmmaker's vision of Jackie's predicament," wrote film critic Nick Davis. "Though the colors and songs are all Tarantino-brite, the framings are contemplative and often very simple, even amidst key episodes in the criss-crossy plot."

Many critics faulted its leisurely pace and low energy level. "In virtually every scene of Quentin Tarantino's *Jackie Brown*, you know you're watching a movie by the creator of *Pulp Fiction* and *Reservoir Dogs*, but the fizz—the exhilaration—is gone," wrote Owen Gleiberman in *Entertainment Weekly*. "In Tarantino's earlier pictures, the material, refracted through a prism of pop sources, fused chemically in the filmmaker's brain. Whatever he put on screen, be it John Travolta dancing or Michael Madsen slicing off someone's ear, he was so entranced by the mad-scientist power of his own imagination that we shared in his wide-eyed gaze. In *Jackie Brown*, Tarantino is still entranced, only in a more detached, self-conscious way."

However, just as many enjoyed its soulful groove. "The film is best (and most patiently) enjoyed as a set of laid-back sketches that don't always head anywhere, even if a filmmaker of Mr. Tarantino's talents can make schmoozing such an end in itself," said A. O. Scott in the *New York Times*. "There's hardly a scene in *Jackie Brown* that doesn't, somewhere within the banal chatter, hide a tough little grace note."

It's the quietest Quentin Tarantino movie by far, some of those grace notes either shorn of dialogue or entirely silent. Picture Ordell sitting in his van, the camera tight on his knitted brow as he thinks, thinks, thinks, then looks up and says

"The hardest thing to give up in *Jackie Brown* was Ordell ... I was Ordell. It was so easy to write Ordell. I was Ordell for the year I was writing the script. I had to really work hard in letting go of Ordell and letting Sam play him and not being a jerk about stuff."

simply, "It's Jackie Brown." Or his and Jackie's argument on his balcony, muffled by the French windows, while Louis (Robert De Niro) looks on. In one of the picture's better running gags, Tarantino makes Louis, the companion of this motor-mouth, almost monosyllabic; De Niro nods and grimaces his way through whole conversations in thuggish pantomime. And that's *before* he gets stoned with Melanie (Bridget Fonda), the stoned surfer chick draped over Ordell's couch like a Balthus teen, bewitching Louis with every rub of her long, perfectly tanned legs.

That's all we see of her at first—that and a pair of hands refilling Ordell's drink. It's a great way of introducing a character, with little dabs of mystery, but also offers caustic commentary: That's all she is to these men. Fonda's mutinous backchat about the idiocy she sees unfolding in that house ("He's just repeating shit he heard on TV") and in the parking lot during the money exchange is one of the best things in the movie.

"When the camera is on Melanie then Melanie is the most important person on screen," noted Anthony Lane, spotting the same egalitarianism that underpinned *Reservoir Dogs* and *Pulp*

Fiction, calling it the "most democratic and least volatile Tarantino movie to date—he seems to be tempering his taste for junk melodrama."

Jackie Brown is also Tarantino's first, if not last, attempt at a love story, albeit unrequited. Max is fifty-six, Jackie is forty-four. "When was the last time you went to the movies—let alone a Tarantino movie—and saw a fond, unironic kiss between a couple who are a hundred years old?" asked Lane.

Like the best onscreen romances, Max and Jackie's is all the more bewitching for going unspoken, their parting no less sweet for that. "I never lied to you, Max," Jackie admits during their final moments together, and with his crinkled smile, we know Max genuinely believes her. Here, inside this San Fernando Valley bail bonds office, a forlorn gentleman shares a common thought with Tarantino's slowly dissolving camera: *Farewell, my lovely.*

But it's Forster's performance that is the keeper. "He's like a wall, this Max, smart but quiet and self-contained, and when Forster acts with Grier—the scenes are mostly long conversations—we realize what Tarantino is getting at," wrote David Denby in the *New Yorker.* "These two actors, sitting across a table in some dim bar, don't open anything up; they're

not particularly expressive. But they're not cheap or flashy either; their strength lies in a kind of impervious power, and it's possible that their very lack of range and flexibility seems a form of integrity for Tarantino."

Some critics consider *Jackie Brown* Tarantino's best film, although the opinion tends to reveal either disgruntlement over the perceived hype for *Pulp Fiction,* in the same way that a liking for the *White Album* often signals a distain for the Beatles' chart-toppers, or overveneration of *Vertigo* masks a strong wish that Alfred Hitchcock had been French. It's the Tarantino movie that people who don't like Tarantino say they like in order to subtly communicate the fact that they don't like Tarantino, praise for it a back-handed compliment to the rest of the work. "For all the much-copied riffs and routines, sometimes Tarantino's characters are eloquent and human in their talk especially in *Jackie Brown,*" says David Thomson in his *Biographical Dictionary of Film.* "I see it as the best evidence yet that Tarantino could become a maker of great comedies."

Jackie Brown seems to offer a tantalizing glimpse of the filmmaker Tarantino chose *not* to become. Imagine critics had provided a warmer welcome for this more "mature" Tarantino. Imagine Pam Grier had gotten an

PAGES 136–137: Louis begins to lose his patience with Melanie, resulting in unplanned, disastrous consequences. OPPOSITE: Juxtaposition. Jackie and Ordell have a heated argument on the balcony at Ordell's apartment as quiet, monosyllabic Louis looks on. ABOVE: Tarantino's first attempt at a love story plays out between Max and Jackie. LEFT: Bridget Fonda as Ordell's surfer chick floozy, Melanie.

"I am a method writer. I become the characters as I am writing them. That is how I am able to get them to talk to each other. I am everybody. I am Louis. I am Melanie."

Oscar nomination alongside Robert Forster for her performance in the film, as Tarantino hoped she would ("Who was better than her that year?"). Imagine fans had embraced the film in the same way they had *Pulp Fiction* and pushed its box-office take closer to $100 million. What then? The film did well, grossing $40 million domestically on a budget of $12 million, a hit by anyone's standards, but not a *Pulp Fiction*-size hit, and so it was perceived by many as a disappointment, which Tarantino seemed to internalize.

"I was not given that much credit for the long, three-dimensional aspects at the time," he said. "When the movie came out, it was like, 'Get fucking to it. Get on with it.' Now everyone seems to feel differently about it." When it was all over, "the fact that it was just a little bit once removed made me a little bit disconnected from it. That's why I haven't done another adaptation

since then. I want to *naturally* fall into the next thing that's going to turn me on."

About a year and a half after the film opened, a big international producer said to Tarantino, "Quentin, now that it's all said and done, do you wish you had cast bigger stars in *Jackie Brown*?"

"No, I thought they were fantastic," replied the director.

"Yeah, but it could have done better."

"What do you mean? $15 million on a movie starring Pam Grier and Robert Forster, that's pretty good."

"Yeah, but that's all you."

"Great, lucky me. If I'm enough of a name that people will go see my movie, then I don't have to cast an actor who can open the film."

All this would be righted with his next movie, about revenge no less. There would be absolutely no question who wrote it, who directed it, and whose name was the opener.

OPPOSITE: Robert De Niro as Louis.
ABOVE: "Who was better than her?" Tarantino was desperate for Pam Grier to receive an Oscar nomination alongside Robert Forster.

KILL BILL

2003/2004

"Pressure is the name of the game for a director. Pressure is the job. Having said that, there is nothing better than having people anticipating your next movie and that they want you to blow them away. It inspires you."

TOP: The old gang. The remaining members of the Deadly Viper Assassination Squad look over the Bride's "dead" body. RIGHT: "We were in the throes of a very artistic love affair. She's my actress." Tarantino and his muse, Uma Thurman, originally developed the idea for *Kill Bill* while on the set of *Pulp Fiction* in 1994.

"**W**HEN I was first starting out I looked at the great action directors, and to me those were the *real* directors," Tarantino told *Vanity Fair* while editing *Kill Bill* with Sally Menke in a small bungalow just south of the Paramount lot. "That was cinema. With *Kill Bill,* I wanted to test myself, see how good I am. I wanted to risk hitting my head on the ceiling of my own talent. The only reason for me to do it was to raise the bar. I used to say, '*Kill Bill* has to be to fight scenes what the "Ride of the Valkyries" scene in *Apocalypse Now* is to battle scenes, or else I will have failed.' Completely. If this doesn't just fucking rock, then I'm just not as good as I think I am."

He first had the idea for the film while "batting ideas around" with Uma Thurman on the set of *Pulp Fiction.* They started talking about vengeance movies. Tarantino mentioned how much he liked 1970s kung-fu movies. In a matter of minutes they had hashed out what would become the opening scene—a beaten bride, mown down and left for dead at her own wedding party. The bride is an assassin, trying to go straight, who has been viciously attacked by her old gang, a band of female killers called the Deadly Viper Assassination Squad, not unlike the all-female gang in *Fox Force Five*, Mia Wallace's TV pilot—one blonde, one Japanese, one black, one French, one who specializes in knives, and so on.

Tarantino was so excited that he went home and wrote thirty pages of the script in a multicolored felt-tip frenzy, discussing the project with Thurman every opportunity he could in between takes. Filming his cameo in Robert Rodriguez's *Desperado*, right after *Pulp Fiction* wrapped, Tarantino excitedly pitched his work-in-progress. Videotape footage shot by Rodriguez reveals the idea for the opening scene to be pretty far advanced.

"*Fade up. A wall covered in red blood and brains. The camera pans off the wall to a young man dressed in a tuxedo lying dead on the floor, blown apart by a shotgun blast. A woman's voice. 'That's Tim. Arthur's best friend.' Move to a plump dead young woman in a frilly pink dress, wedding bouquet in her dead hand. 'That's my best friend from work, Erica …'*"

"Oooh," interjects Rodriguez, behind the camera.

"*We move past a bloody, dead little boy. 'I don't know who that is. Some little kid, I guess, I don't remember him being there . . .'*"

"Oh shit."

"*We move over and see a pretty young woman wearing a white wedding gown, two bullet holes in her body, one in her head. We slowly zoom in to her dead-looking face. 'I laid in a coma for five years. When I woke, every emotion in me was dead. Every emotion that is, except one, desire. The desire for revenge.' We dissolve to a matching close-up of a young woman. To your car, moving, sunset. The young woman is behind the wheel of a big car, white wedding gown on, outrageous orange and red sunset process shot playing in the background. She's talking into the camera. She put her dress back on . . .*"

"Wow! She put her dress back on…"

"Yeah."

"*One man did all this to me. I've killed eighteen men in the last week, didn't feel a thing. Those eighteen dead bodies were just eighteen*

steps. Steps I've climbed to get to him, and to him is where I'm driving, because there's no one left worth killing except him. The him I'm talking about's name is Bill. When I get to where I'm going, I'm going to kill Bill."

"Oooh."

"*Then the music and the title song begins …*"

Then Thurman heard nothing. The thirty handwritten pages went back into the drawer while Tarantino disappeared into his World War II script, *Inglourious Basterds*. "Are we ever going to do *Kill Bill*?" she would ask whenever they saw one another. "Someday. Someday," the filmmaker would reply. The pair drifted apart, and then ran into one another again at a Miramax Oscar party in 2000.

"I had really sort of lost touch with him," said Thurman. "I asked him, 'What happened to those pages? Did you lose them?'" Tarantino said he still had them in a drawer. Returning home that night, he took out the thirty pages, read them again, and said to himself, "'That's what I'm going to do.' It just so happened that her birthday was the following Sunday, so I went to her party and told her, 'This is your present: I'm gonna finish writing *Kill Bill*. In two weeks.'"

A year and a half later, he had his script—all 220 pages of it. When Uma's husband, Ethan Hawke, first read it, he said, "Quentin, if this is the epic you're doing before you do your epic, I'm afraid to see your epic." Drawing for inspiration on Toshiya Fujita's *Lady Snowblood* revenge films, Tarantino seemed to take genre conventions personally. "When I was doing *Kill Bill*, I was the Bride," he said. "People noticed that when I was writing, I was getting much more feminine in my outlook. All of a sudden, I was buying things for my apartment or house. I'd buy flowers for the house and start arranging them. I don't normally wear jewelry, and suddenly I'm wearing jewelry. My friends said, 'You're getting in touch with your feminine side. You're nesting, adorning yourself.'"

The person he had in mind was clearly his mother: the only other pregnant bride he knew, if not left at the altar then certainly abandoned by his father before his birth, so that he, like Beatrix's daughter, was raised for a period without one parent knowing of his existence. This would be the film where his ambivalence about fathers and father figures came home to roost. "The subtext that actually borders on text," he would call it.

"Like most men who never knew their father, Bill collected father figures," says Esteban Vihaio (Michael Parks). To play him, Tarantino wanted an actor who had done something similar in his own life and career, Warren Beatty, but it was to prove an uphill climb. The script "was so wholly other to him," said Tarantino. "He goes, 'Okay, Quentin, let me just ask you a question here. Don't be offended by it—I'm just curious: What would your answer be if somebody were to ask, 'What stops this from just being one fight after another where each one tops the last one?' I went, 'Well, Warren, that's a pretty Goddamn good description of a martial arts movie. A kung-fu film with a lot of great fights, and each

one is better than the last? That's what I'm goin' for, and if I do it, I will be very happy.'"

Beatty signed on in 2001, but then Thurman and Hawke conceived a child. Tarantino, faced with the decision of whether to wait for her or find someone else, decided to delay the movie a year. "I definitely thought about it for two to three weeks," he said. "She was having her baby, and this was mine. She was going to let me decide. And I decided. It needed to be her. If you're Sergio Leone and you've got Eastwood in *A Fistful of Dollars* and he gets sick, you wait for him."

The year-long hiatus provided more than enough time for the love affair between Tarantino and the terminally indecisive Beatty to sour. The disintegration of the relationship was detailed by David Carradine in *The Kill Bill Diary*. During a meeting at which the star's commitment seemed to waver, Beatty suddenly blurted out, "Look, I don't give a shit about Chinese kung-fu movies, and I hate spaghetti westerns, though I like Clint personally, and I wouldn't go to a Japanese samurai movie if you paid me!" Tarantino realized he was "saying that for effect, and, well, you know, it had an effect, all right? It

just wasn't romantic. The relationship between a director and his star has to have a little romance to it. And Warren was saying 'Hey, how long is this really going to take? How much time do I really have to put in? Do I really need to do all that training?' So I'm thinking 'I was really writing this character for you, about you, all this time, and I'm thinking, *Shit!*' And we had another meeting, to try and put it back together—I mean, Warren had been a part of the film for a year—and I was saying how I wanted him to act, to be sort of like David Carradine in this movie, and Warren said suddenly, 'Why don't you offer it to David?'"

Three days after Lawrence Bender held a dinner to introduce Beatty to Michael Madsen, who would be playing his brother Budd, Madsen got a phone call from the director. "He goes, 'Well, I just fired Warren,'" recalled Madsen. "And I said, 'Oh my God. You did?' And he said, 'Yeah, yeah. He doesn't understand what the movie's about, he doesn't want to do it, and I don't want him to do it.' I said, 'Well, who in the name of God is going to play Bill?' And he goes, 'Are you ready?' And I said, 'Yeah, I'm ready, Goddamnit. Who is it?' And he said, 'David Carradine.' And I remember that I was completely and totally stunned. I mean, it so took me off guard. I wouldn't have thought of David in a million years."

Taking his first meeting with the director at a Thai restaurant, Carradine, who had skidded along the bottom of the horror and straight-to-video action-movie market for two decades since making the seminal *Kung Fu* TV series in the seventies, was so astounded to be offered the part that he could barely find his Maserati afterwards.

"I'd never done action films before, and I'd definitely never done a Hong Kong action film. I was stepping into the unknown, and the unknown was scary."

In early April of 2002, the principal actors, including Tarantino, who planned on playing sadistic kung-fu master Pai Mei himself, met for a six-week training program with Yuen Woo-Ping, the martial arts choreographer of the *Matrix* trilogy and *Crouching Tiger, Hidden Dragon*. Just three months after giving birth, Thurman had to master three styles of kung-fu, two styles of sword fighting, knife throwing, knife fighting, hand-to-hand combat, and Japanese. "It was literally absurd," said the actress, after hitting herself in the head with a 10 pound samurai sword the first time she swung it. "I get shot in the head, raped, kicked, beaten, and sliced by samurai swords. The movie should have been called 'Kill Uma.'"

To the actress's horror, Tarantino threw out most of the choreography they had learned the day they started shooting in Beijing. "I've never done action films before," said the director, whose communication with the Chinese crew, few of whom spoke English, provided a constant level of frustration. "We screwed up every way you could screw up when it came to scheduling

this movie. Because we just didn't know what the fuck we were doing. Other people do storyboards and shit, but we didn't do any of that crap. It was impossible to figure out how you're going to shoot it all in your head."

For the shoot's first sequence—known as "Crazy 88," for the number of yakuza thugs the Bride reputedly kills at the House of Blue Leaves nightclub—Tarantino devised a complicated traveling shot to kick off the carnage. Starting behind the bandstand, the Steadicam walked screen right, swung out from beneath the stairway, and followed the Bride as she strode across the room and down a side hallway. It then rose and continued to follow her from an overhead angle, and descended again as she entered the bathroom, swinging to find the House of Blue Leaves's owner and her manager, following them up a staircase. The cameraman at this point stepped onto a crane that swept across the dance floor, past the band, to the opposite staircase, where it craned in and boomed down to reveal Sofie Fatale (Julie Dreyfus). The camera then followed her into the bathroom before continuing past her to the wall of a stall, inside of which is the Bride, waiting. Richardson and his crew spent just six hours rehearsing the shot and took a full day to complete it. In his diary of the shoot Richardson noted:

June 18: The difficulty of filming the martial arts sequences is beyond what most of us imagined. Quentin wants to shoot shot by shot (editorial order), regardless of the number of lighting shifts necessary. Difficult, needless to say, but if the procedure leaves Quentin more comfortable, we should do it. Critics surround. Let them psychoanalyze themselves.

THIS PAGE: In order to perfect Tarantino's exacting vision for the film, Uma Thurman and the cast meticulously trained in the art of kung-fu under the direction of renowned martial arts choreographer Yuen Woo-Ping. OPPOSITE: Putting skills to the test as Beatrix fights the Crazy 88.

Tarantino and Thurman argued almost daily, with Thurman lobbying for everything from wardrobe changes to dialogue rewrites. "It's a movie about a woman who challenges five people to duels. That's pretty much it," she complained. "He is brilliant, but my job was to take this character out of his wildly creative, seemingly improvisational world and make her human. If the movie was going to be more than a cartoon, it was up to me." During the eight weeks of shooting that were required for *Kill Bill*'s twenty-minute finale, she came to the realization that "in some ways I was in a silent film. The physicality of the movie is what it's about for him."

As Tarantino grappled with the logistics of his newly improvised fight sequences, the production began to fall behind schedule. David Carradine arrived on set after an extended stay in Los Angeles, amid a swirl of rumors about the production. "Everyone out there is betting on whether *Kill Bill* is in trouble—behind schedule, over budget, all that," he noted in his diary. "Does Harvey Weinstein still love Quentin? Can Quentin still deliver? Will the picture get back on track?" Finally, worried Miramax executives called Tarantino and demanded, "What's going on? Do we have a runaway train here?" The director lost it. "Don't be talking to me about this shit!" he yelled. "If I'd wanted more days, I could've just asked for them! If I wanted that much more money, I could've just asked for it, and I would've gotten it! The money I was spending, that was my money! I didn't give a fuck what any of those motherfuckers say except for Harvey and Bob! They all work for me!"

Arriving on set in the last month of shooting in Beijing, Weinstein was shown some footage by editor Sally Menke from the rough cut she had assembled and came up with the idea of splitting the movie into two parts. He called Tarantino immediately to reassure him: "Quentin, it's amazing," he said. "You just make your movie.

You just keep making it as good as this, and however long it takes is how long it takes. You don't fucking worry about nothing." Menke was not surprised. "Very early on, we started talking about it being split into two, so it wasn't a surprise, given the quantity of scenes," she said. "I have to say that it *was* a relief. It meant we could get everything in that we loved so dearly, rather than going, 'Ohhh. We have to see that go.'"

When Tarantino finally wrapped in China and returned to Los Angeles in September, with further shoots still set for Mexico and Los Angeles, a shoot that had been scheduled to last for twenty-one days had instead taken seventy-six. "Quentin told me once that when he was conceiving this movie, he thought he didn't want to just make a movie, he wanted to live it," noted Carradine. "To make it his life, his whole universe, for however long it took. To lose himself in it. Well, we've all done that with him. *Kill Bill* and Super Cool ManChu have become our lives."

When the film finally wrapped in March of 2003, Tarantino had shot 840,300 feet of film—109 hours—and the budget, $39 million going in, had climbed to $55 million. It was a nervous Weinstein who started devising marketing campaigns for two movies that now needed to do blockbuster business if they were to turn a profit, as Tarantino edited furiously to get the first film finished for release in October 2003 and the second for April 2004. Weinstein was worried that women would be turned off by the violence. "Don't worry," Tarantino reassured him. "I think thirteen-year-old girls will love *Kill Bill*. I want young girls to be able to see it. They're going to love Uma's character, the Bride. They have my permission to buy a ticket for another movie and sneak into *Kill Bill*. That's money I'm okay not making."

Thurman's reaction was simpler. "I am really so happy with it," she said. "And so happy that it's over."

OPPOSITE: Behind the camera on set in Beijing. PAGES 152–153: Tarantino and Thurman discuss the action-filled scenes in the House of Blue Leaves nightclub. ABOVE: Posters for the two installments.

"Sure, *Kill Bill* is a violent movie. But it's a Tarantino movie. You don't go to see Metallica and ask the f***ers to turn the music down."

Once the credits are over, *Kill Bill* opens on a quiet shot of a house in suburban Pasadena, its lawn strewn with children's toys. Distantly, a barking dog and an ice cream truck can be heard. Drawing up in a yellow station wagon, a young woman (Uma Thurman) walks up the path and rings the bell. The door is opened by a young black woman (Vivica A. Fox), who is immediately punched in the nose. Vicious hand-to-hand combat commences and quickly turns her living room to rubble. Shattering pictures and glass tables, the pair go at each other with feet, fists, knives, and fire fenders, the melee only interrupted by her daughter's return from school.

"Nikki, in your room, now," says her mother.

"I have no wish to kill you before the eyes of your daughter," says Thurman to Fox, before doing just that, with a knife in the kitchen, crunching brightly colored cereal underfoot. Thus the twin themes of *Kill Bill* are simultaneously introduced: bloody revenge

and the difficulty of combining a career as a highly paid international assassin with good housekeeping.

Beatrix Kiddo (Thurman) seeks revenge on the Deadly Viper Assassination Squad, led by Bill (David Carradine), for killing her fiancé and (she thinks) unborn child. But why did he do that? Why did Bill act in the first place? For no reason other than that Beatrix abandoned her career as an international assassin in order to become a mom. The very idea of such normalcy offends him. She's in denial of her nature, he tells her.

BILL

Superman didn't become Superman. Superman was born Superman. When Superman wakes up in the morning, he's Superman. His alter ego is Clark Kent. His outfit with the big red "S", that's the blanket he was wrapped in as a baby when the Kents found him. Those are his clothes. What Kent wears—the glasses, the business

ABOVE: Beatrix first seeks revenge on fellow mother Vernita Green (Vivica A. Fox) at her surburban Pasadena home.

suit—that's the costume. That's the costume Superman wears to blend in with us. Clark Kent is how Superman views us. And what are the characteristics of Clark Kent? He's weak . . . he's unsure of himself . . . he's a coward. Clark Kent is Superman's critique on the whole human race.

BEATRIX

Are you calling me a superhero?

BILL

I'm calling you a killer. A natural born killer. Moving to El Paso, working in a used record store, goin' to the movies with Tommy, clipping coupons. That's you, trying to disguise yourself as a worker bee. That's you tryin' to blend in with the hive. But you're not a worker bee. You're a renegade killer bee. And no matter how much beer you drank or barbecue you ate or how fat your ass got, nothing in the world would ever change that.

The self-quotation should tip us off here, for the story Tarantino tells in *Kill Bill* is also Tarantino's story. He, like Kiddo, tried to quit the assassination business: He tried to put his reputation as the "gun guy" behind him. First, he deconstructed it in *Pulp Fiction*, and then he settled down to make the quiet caper movie that got praised by critics for its "maturity": *Jackie Brown*, a film filled with characters raging quietly against the dying of the light and fretting about their fat asses, as Kiddo wants to. But the film was received poorly, or at least not with the raise-the-rafters chorus Tarantino had expected.

TOP: Vernita Green, Budd, O-Ren Ishii, and Elle Driver ominously approach the church to assassinate their former accomplice. BOTTOM: "You're a renegade killer bee." Bill can't fathom Beatrix's desire to lead a "normal" life.

"It's really cool, because the Chinese way of doing action is there's not really a schedule. There's no shot list. I had certain shots in my mind that I knew I wanted to do from like a year and a half of writing about them but me and the master, Yuen, came up with new things as we were doing it."

BELOW: The skill of kung-fu shown in all its glory by Robert Richardson's expert cinematography. OPPOSITE: Beatrix shows off her skills but she is no match for her trainer, Pai Mei, played by renowned martial arts master Gordon Liu.

Tarantino stewed in his own juices for a few years and came back with a raucous, ultraviolent mixtape of spaghetti western, blaxploitation flick, Japanese anime, and Asian action movie, all whipped up to slake a seemingly unfathomable thirst for bloodlust. It's his renegade killer bee movie.

"What truly distances the movie from its models is the fan boy giddiness that Tarantino brings to the party," said *Slate*'s David Edelstein of the long climactic fight sequence in which the Bride takes on eighty-eight yakuza fighters, the lights dropping so they are suddenly blue silhouettes gyrating against a great grid, as insouciant and elegant as a dance number. "It's like *An American in Paris* with arterial spray."

Elvis Mitchell wrote in the *New York Times* that "the movie, which quivers with a geek-adrenaline rush in some ways feels as if its time may have passed. It seems like a film Mr. Tarantino might have made *before Pulp Fiction*."

This is close to the mark. Actually, the movie of Tarantino's that *Kill Bill: Volume 1* most forcefully resembles is the one he never made—the "flashy, stylistically daring exercise in cinematic mayhem" critics thought they had found in *Reservoir Dogs* and *Pulp Fiction* and did find in *Natural Born Killers*. He even employed

Stone's cinematographer, Robert Richardson, to shoot the film in flashing, five-blade swiss-army-knife style.

"This is the movie-movie universe, where movie conventions are embraced, almost fetishized," he said, "as opposed to the other universe where *Pulp Fiction* and *Reservoir Dogs* take place, in which reality and movie conventions collide."

That is a game-changing statement, marking as big a break as can be found in a director's career in the modern era. *Kill Bill* didn't just do things differently. It did a different thing. As Jules Winnfield says in a different context in *Pulp Fiction*, it "ain't the same fuckin' ballpark; it ain't the same league; it ain't even the same fuckin' *sport*." Jettisoning the contrast-driven streetwise comedy of his early films, he instead dove into the genre looking-glass, where blood the color of raspberries spurts comically from the stumps of severed arms and torsos, characters drive against obvious black-and-white back-projected roads, and B-movie storm clouds hurl B-movie rain.

Everything is recognizably Tarantino, and yet everything is changed utterly. That knife fight amid the cereal boxes clearly came from the same part of the director's brain that cued up

Vincent Vega's assassination to the ejection of pop tarts from Butch's toaster in *Pulp Fiction*, but where the violence in that film was spasmodic, off-screen, and arrived as the punchline to a joke about the gap between movies and reality, in *Kill Bill* it obeys the tightly choreographed chop-socky convention. Vernita's little girl looks on as if taking in a boxing match on TV. And when they pause and open their mouths, we get the biggest change of all:

> **VERNITA**
> Be that as it may, I know I do not deserve mercy or forgiveness. However, I beseech you for both on behalf of my daughter.

Beseech? *Be that as it may*? Tarantino's writing always had its higher register, of course, but it was always punctuated by his extraordinary ear for the filthy, profane rhythms of black street vernacular.

> **VINCENT**
> Jules, did you ever hear the philosophy that once a man admits that he's wrong that he is immediately forgiven for all wrongdoings? Have you ever heard that?

> **JULES**
> Get the fuck out my face with that shit! The motherfucker that said that shit never had to pick up itty-bitty pieces of skull on account of your dumb ass.

In *Kill Bill*, the characters all speak in a new, ornate idiom of Tarantino's own devising. They speak of taking their "satisfaction" with one another like eighteenth-century fops, and use the pronouns "whom" and "one" ("When one manages the difficult task of becoming queen of the Tokyo underworld, one doesn't keep it a secret, does one?") as if they had all swallowed dictionaries. The first order of business for some critics, when *Kill Bill: Volume 1* was released, was a small period of mourning for the loss of the colloquial in Tarantino's writing.

"The filmmaker who, in *Pulp Fiction,* appeared to have discovered a new way of writing dialogue for the movies—pop-surreal, nasty, and blazingly funny—has settled into a pseudo-suave idiom that lies across the screen like a lead-filled vest," wrote the *New Yorker*'s David Denby, who had cheered up for the second film but not by much: "The pop encyclopedist and video-store genius has become a megalomaniac, and the exhilarating filmmaker he might have been is disappearing fast."

Certainly, the film, which was conceived as one film and shot as one film, was not served by its original broken-backed release. Denied the bulk of the Bill material and the meat of Thurman's performance, *Volume 1*'s parade of non-stop bloodshed, interrupted only by an interminable sequence with Sonny Chiba (Hattori Hanzo) reciting Shaolin mumbo-jumbo and arguing at ear-splitting volumes about sake, seemed a Far Eastern copy of the filmmaker who had once supplied John Travolta and Samuel L. Jackson with their patter about foot massages.

In retrospect, seeing *Volume 1* without seeing *Volume 2* was like quitting *Apocalypse Now* just at the point where we reach Kurtz's compound, for *Volume 2* had all the dark poetry and thematic punch its predecessor lacked. There were Beatrix's battles with Michael Madsen's ex-assassin, Budd, a fatalistic drunk living in a trailer home. There was also Daryl Hannah's one-eyed hellion, against vast, voluptuous Texan landscapes straight out of Sergio Leone. Facing West, not East, the film spoke Tarantino's native language, not his second—and best of all, finally, we got Bill. Soft-spoken, preternaturally cool, his weathered face held aloft by superb bone structure, Carradine made Bill a creature of magnificent perversity, sweet-talking Thurman as if bidding her goodbye and menacingly pretending to be the father of the bride. He would marry her, or murder her, or both.

Finally given a human pulse to track, Thurman comes alive in their scenes together. "Thurman, whose speaking voice has a lyric, teasing quality—if Dusty Springfield had been an actress, she would have been Ms. Thurman—is just the performer to convey Mr. Tarantino's mordant slyness," wrote Elvis Mitchell in the *New York Times*. "[Tarantino's] movies are about loss and betrayal, and *Kill Bill: Volume 2* is a double-burger helping of those motifs. It is rich, substantial and sustained, yet also greasy kids' stuff, a wrapper filled with an extra large order of chili fries, stained with ketchup, salt, and cheese."

Finally editing the two volumes together in 2011, Tarantino introduced *Kill Bill: The Whole*

OPPOSITE: Having brutally murdered Budd, Elle (Daryl Hannah) prepares to defend herself against a formidable Beatrix. TOP: One-eyed. Tarantino and Hannah joke around on set. BOTTOM: Michael Madsen, in his second film with Tarantino, plays drunk ex-assassin Budd.

Bloody Affair to American audiences at the New Beverly Cinema on March 27, his birthday—a date of obvious significance given the film's autobiographical resonance. He incorporated a longer thirty-minute anime sequence and showed the fight with the Crazy 88 in full color. But by far the most important change he made was to remove the spoiler from the end of *Volume 1* tipping off the audience to the survival of Beatrix's daughter, thus synchronizing the audience's shock with hers in the final reel. It's the biggest shock of the movie: Thurman's face crumples, falls, then feigns pain as she play-acts a gunfight with her daughter, all the movie's frenzy now revealed as so much child's play, before mother and child curl up in bed to watch *Shogun Assassin*—a hushed recreation of Tarantino's own childhood.

Her final confrontation with Bill has the eerie stillness of opium dens, cobras, Freudian primal scenes, and Oedipal wrongs righted. Beatrix kills Bill using the Five Point Palm Exploding Heart Technique—by literally breaking his heart. He drops to the ground unceremoniously, like a puppet with its strings cut, the very flatness of the tableau, after the dexterity of all that has preceded it, conveying the significance of what we are witnessing. The final shot of the film shows Beatrix, curled up on the floor of her bathroom in Pasadena, sobbing, while her daughter watches cartoons next door, overcome to have been granted the normalcy she has craved for so long.

Would Tarantino? Both films were giant hits, the first volume taking $180 million worldwide and the second $152 million. *Jackie Brown* was left in the dust. Bill's soliloquy about Superman would hang over the later half of Tarantino's career, somewhere between a threat and a promise. He had experienced, with *Jackie Brown*, what it was to be Clark Kent: vulnerable, bruised, human, mortal, but also praised for his maturity, growth. He had also, with *Kill Bill*, tasted superpower, invulnerability, a rebound at the box office, but involving a rejection of the normalcy—the naturalistic texture of daily life—so coveted by Beatrix. Which, going forward, would he chose?

"I wrote a movie I wanted to see. I make my movies for my fans but I consider myself the biggest fan. So I make it for me and everyone else is invited."

DEATH PROOF

2007

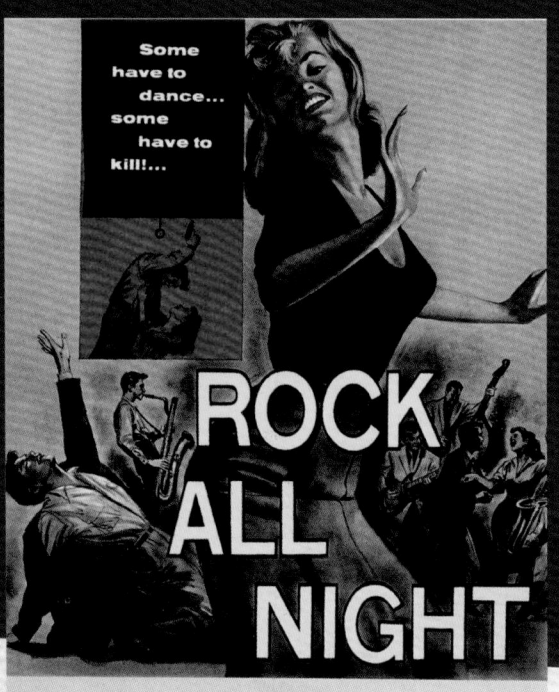

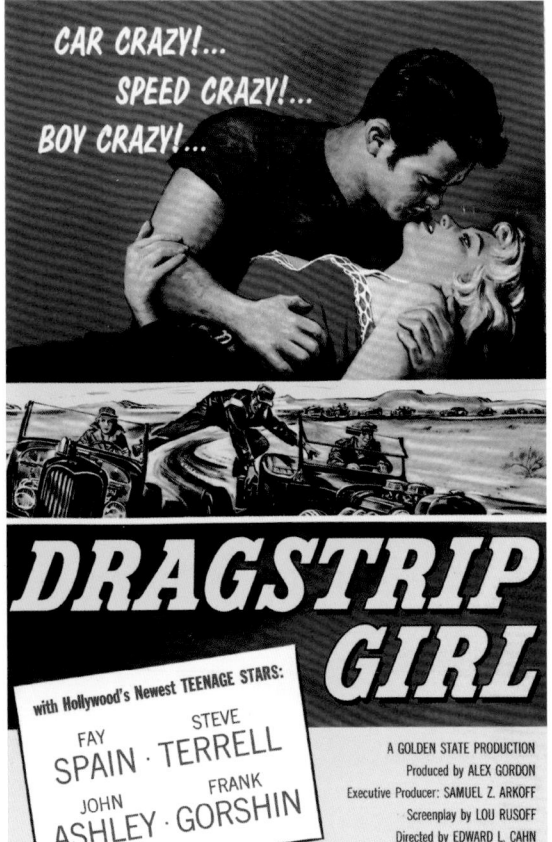

LEFT: The 1957 slasher film double bill of *Rock All Night* and *Dragstrip Girl* provided the inspiration for *Grindhouse.* OPPOSITE: The distinctive poster art for Tarantino and Rodriguez's double feature.

"ONE of the things I always loved about exploitation movies is that, even in the midst of all that's going on, you all of a sudden start caring about the characters," Tarantino told *Wired* when *Death Proof* was released as part of a double bill called *Grindhouse,* alongside Robert Rodriguez's *Planet Terror.* "Especially when you're watching it with modern audiences. When I show these films to my friends, I say, 'Look, there's some funny stuff in these movies but, please, laugh because it's funny, not to show that you're superior to it and show how cool you are—don't laugh at it, laugh with it. And if you resist the temptation to just ridicule this shit and take it at face value, you'll be surprised. All of a sudden, you get into the movie."

The idea for *Death Proof* came to Tarantino after ploughing through a bout of slasher films from the late 1970s to mid-1980s with director Robert Rodriguez. The pair were in the habit of watching movies together at Tarantino's house. One day, admiring a poster for a 1957 double bill of *Dragstrip Girl* and *Rock All Night,* Rodriguez said, "We should do a double feature. I'll do one, and you do one."

"We came up with most of the movie right there," Rodriguez said later.

TOP LEFT AND OPPOSITE: Part slasher film and part chick flick, Tarantino's focus in the film was the scenes with his eight female stars. BOTTOM LEFT: More fantastical, Rodriguez's half of the double bill featured an exotic dancer whose leg is eaten by flesh-craving zombies and fitted with a machine-gun prosthetic. TOP RIGHT: Fear and temptation. Stuntman Mike lures in his first unsuspecting victim.

For his half of the double bill, Rodriguez wanted to make a movie about an exotic dancer whose career is cut short when her right leg is eaten by flesh-craving zombies, and she's fitted with a machine-gun prosthetic.

Tarantino, meanwhile, had long had a fascination for the way stuntmen would "death-proof" their cars so as to be able to survive horrific, high-speed crashes. He'd had a conversation with a friend about how he wanted a Volvo because he "didn't want to die in some auto accident like the one in *Pulp Fiction*," to which his friend had replied, "Well, you could take any car and give it to a stunt team, and for ten or fifteen thousand dollars, they can death-proof it for you."

The phrase stuck in Tarantino's head. His film was about a deranged stuntman who stalks and murders sexy young women with his car. The whole thing would be a kind of slasher movie, except turned on its head, its first half a kind of chick-flick hang-out movie. "I realized that if I did my own slasher film, it'd just be too self-reflective. So I decided that I should do it the way I did *Reservoir Dogs*, which was my weird version of a heist film. So this is my weird version of a slasher film."

It would be Tarantino's first script featuring an almost-all-female cast, drawing on his many years hanging out with female friends. Hearing the director read the script aloud to him, film critic Elvis Mitchell noted, "I could hear the excitement as he served up dialogue that showed how much time he'd spent sitting around listening to women and soaking up their attitudes and cadences, too." As such, it would mark a return to the universe of *Reservoir Dogs* and *Pulp Fiction*, wherein movie conventions brush up against real life and get their fenders dented.

"To me, the whole thing about *Kill Bill* was that I created my own kind of reality. In that world, cartoons can come in and show you stuff, and airplanes have holders for samurai swords. But there's nothing about *Death Proof* that plays fantastical. It all takes place in the real world . . . You could get a car to do this. You could meet a guy like Stuntman Mike. And if you do, you're fucked. When he's coming at you at a hundred miles per hour, there's not a damn thing you can do about it."

The part of Jungle Julia went to Sidney Poitier's daughter, Sydney Tamiia Poitier, who

"I realized that if I did my own slasher film, it'd just be too self-reflective. So I decided that I should do it the way I did *Reservoir Dogs*, which was my weird version of a heist film. So this is my weird version of a slasher film."

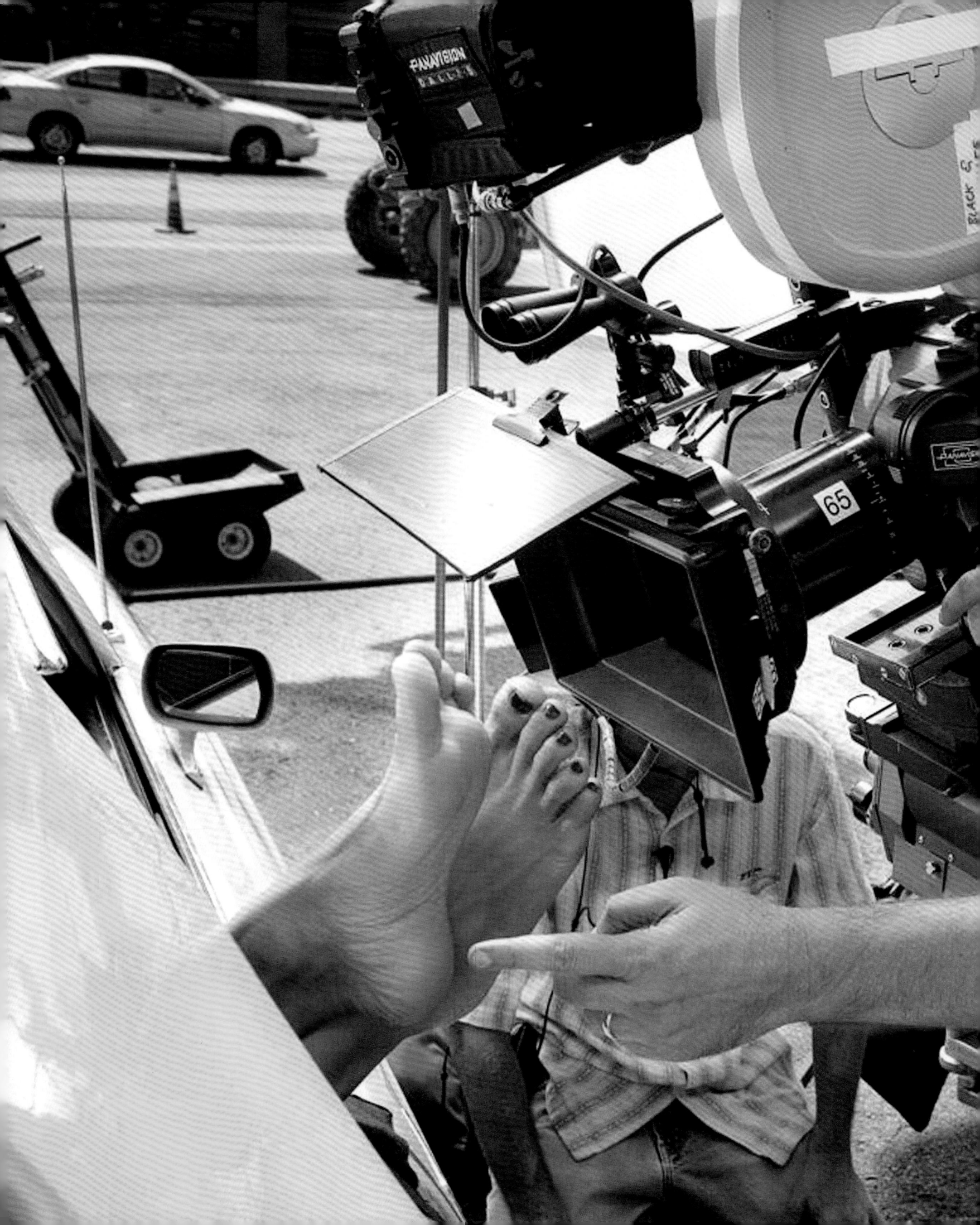

had auditioned for a role in *Kill Bill*. Opening the script, the first thing she read was, "Arlene's feet tapping on the dashboard, and then cut to Jungle Julia's feet walking down the hallway," so when she went in for the audition, one of the first things she did was sit down on the chair, kick off her shoes and put her feet up on the table.

Vanessa Ferlito (Arlene) was already a friend of the director's. "He's an empath," she said. "He listens to every word and everything you say. He wrote the role for me because this was something I was rambling about with a guy. He just listens and then two years later he's like, 'Remember that story . . .' I'm like, 'Who? Which one?' He just pays attention. When you think he's not, he knows and listens. He doesn't miss anything."

The role of Stuntman Mike was intended for Mickey Rourke, but after initial talks, the actor dropped out for reasons unclear. Tarantino considered replacing him with Willem Dafoe, John Malkovich, and Sylvester Stallone, but Stallone told him, "There's no way. I have two daughters, and this fellow, his hobby is putting teenagers in his car and smashing them into a wall. That's not going to work."

Instead he went to Kurt Russell. "My whole thing is not to go to the next guy—y'know, the one that's almost like the guy—because it gives me an opportunity to rethink my whole movie," he said. "There's a wonderful aspect that Kurt has that's fantastic, and it mirrors Stuntman Mike

a lot. He's a working professional and he's been in this business for a long time. He's done all this episodic television—he did all those TV series, *The High Chaparral*s and the *Harry O*s. And he's worked with fucking everybody. Literally. So he knows the life that Stuntman Mike's had."

Early on in the shoot, Russell asked Tarantino, "Does this guy turn into a coward?"

Tarantino replied, "Well, yeah, kinda, sorta." After the first take of the scene at the end, in which the girls pull Mike out of the car while he screams, Tarantino pulled Russell aside. "Kurt, do you think you could take it down just a little bit?" he asked.

Russell replied, "I never thought I'd hear you say 'take it down a bit.'"

The change worked, and they used the next take in the final movie. "It was kind of fascinating seeing this character just totally fall apart in front of you," said Rosario Dawson (Abernathy). "Playing him as such a cowardly lion is such a brave and interesting choice . . . You can see that a bit easier with someone like Kurt, who's playing him like some washed up stunt man who is kinda corny, and kinda cute, and you're like, 'Eh, he's harmless . . .' I have to say it if it was Mickey I'd be, 'You're a dumbass and you deserve to die if you get in a car with that guy.' Because he seems really scary. There's no way you could think otherwise."

Tarantino embraced mistakes in filming. If the shot was out of focus for half a second, "we'd just

PAGES 174–175: "I appreciate the female foot, but I've never said that I have a foot fetish." Tarantino focuses the camera on his favourite body part during a take. OPPOSITE: Kurt Russell played a cowardly version of Stuntman Mike, adding extra dimensions to the character. ABOVE LEFT: DJ Jungle Julia (Sydney Tamiia Poitier) chills at the Texas Chili Parlor with Arlene (Vanessa Ferlito). ABOVE RIGHT: Tarantino and Kurt Russell discuss the set up of a scene.

"CGI has fully ruined car crashes. When you watched them in the 1970s, it was real cars, real metal, real blasts. They're really doing it and risking their lives."

ABOVE: Not a fan of CGI creations, Tarantino wanted the crash scene to be as realistic as possible.

say to each other, 'Hey, it's grindhouse!'" But for his car chases, Tarantino had six weeks to film and wanted the crash to be as realistic as possible "about what happens to people in a crash—you kind of get ripped apart," he said.

He also wanted the audience complicit. "If, at the last second, the girls had braked and missed it, they would be pissed off," he said. "They'd be totally mad. That's the thing: to get them complicit, get them wanting it and waiting for it. Then—BANG!—it happens, it's so much more horrible than you ever could have imagined. But— too late! You wanted it to happen. You willed it into being. You are complicit in it. Now take your medicine! And you should feel a little ashamed, feel a little bad, but feel like you came. Now light the cigarettes! We didn't pull any punches at all."

To make the experience authentically B-grade, Tarantino and Rodriguez edited out "missing reels" and scratched the prints with pens and needles. Tarantino's assistant would take out the film and thrash it against the bushes in the driveway. "We kept asking the lab to make this section dirtier," he said. "We never even got it—we were too careful. We should have gotten it dirtier in some places. The lab had a lot of fun, though, not being careful. Want to smoke a cigarette over that? No problem."

Forced to chop out thirty minutes in order to fit inside the three-hour double-feature running time, Tarantino concentrated on retaining the scenes with his actresses, all eight of them, as they hang out in bars, texting their no-good, no-show boyfriends. "I was like a brutish

American exploitation distributor who cut the movie down almost to the point of incoherence. I cut it down to the bone and took all the fat off it to see if it could still exist, and it worked."

Despite largely positive reviews in the United States, *Grindhouse*, given a disastrous Easter weekend release, took $25 million at the American box office and just $384,191 overseas. The double-bill format seemed to confuse audiences, as did the fake trailers for non-existent films and the missing reels and scratchy celluloid. "Did anyone besides Tarantino and Rodriguez ever really care about the grindhouse movie genre that much to begin with?" asked *Variety*.

"Oh, it was disappointing," says Tarantino. "I'm really well versed on a lot of directors' careers, you know, and when you look at those last five films when they were past it, when they were too old, and they're really out of touch with the times, whether it be William Wyler and *The Liberation of L.B. Jones* or Billy Wilder with *Fedora* and then *Buddy Buddy* or whatever the hell. To me, it's all about my filmography, and I want to go out with a terrific filmography. *Death Proof* has got to be the worst movie I ever make. And for a left-handed movie, that wasn't so bad, all right?—so if that's the worst I ever get, I'm good. But I do think one of those out-of-touch, old, limp, flaccid-dick movies costs you three good movies as far as your rating is concerned."

Tarantino here commits the sin of inverted pride, as if trying to outdo even his critics with his powers of self-damnation. Once released from the task of hauling the dead weight of Rodriguez's *Planet Terror* around cinemas and expanded to

TOP: With Robert Rodriguez at the Los Angeles premiere of *Grindhouse*, 2007. BOTTOM: Tarantino and Rodriguez with their almost all-female cast at the Los Angeles premiere.

ABOVE: Preparing for a
close-up, the camera focuses
in on Stuntman Mike.

113 minutes for the DVD release, *Death Proof,* still
coming in as his shortest film since *Reservoir Dogs*,
is a down-and-dirty ode to burnt rubber and bent
fender that is graced with tender, wonderfully frank
portraiture of the all-female gangs at its centre, like
J. G. Ballard's *Crash* as rewritten by Toni Morrison.

"At times it's like a grindhouse version of *The
View*," wrote *Slate*'s Dana Stevens, applauding
that "the women emerge as separate, vibrant
personalities: not the slut, the nice girl, and the
quiet best friend, but three rowdy, unapologetically
sexual party girls who care more about each other
than the dudes trying to get into their pants." Can
you be exploitative and sing a hymn to female
empowerment at the same time? Apparently so,
if you are Quentin Tarantino.

Not least among its pleasures was a return,
after his visits through the genre looking-glass in
Kill Bill, to a recognizable patch of planet Earth
you'd be tempted to call "reality"—or, if that
seems too much of a stretch, then, certainly a
place where you can buy a decent taco.

"His films don't take place in a vacuum,"
noted Elvis Mitchell in his introduction to
the screenplay. "The sense of community is
undeniable, and controls the conception of the
characters because the characters actually live
in a real place . . . In *Death Proof* it is Austin,
Texas, which is an amalgam of college town,
music magnet and laid-back dreamscape
. . . Austin's floating sense of anything-can-
happen, and the inviting hypervoluble Texan
friendliness that can take a wrong turn if too
many tequilas have been downed, are part of
the ambiance of *Death Proof*."

Three party girls—an Austin DJ known as
Jungle Julia (Sydney Tamiia Poitier) and her
friends Shanna (Jordan Ladd) and Arlene or
"Butterfly" (Vanessa Ferlito)—are planning a
night of margaritas and Mexican food at the
Texas Chili Parlor to celebrate Julia's birthday.
Tarantino shot the movie himself and appeared
as a bartender at the Texas Chili Parlor, which
was furnished with his own jukebox. The place
seems to bring out the Godard in him. The
scene alternates between long shots and slinky
close-ups of needle hitting groove, a rack of
tequila shots, and of Ferlito's behind as she
sidles up to the jukebox to put on Joe Tex's
1966 hit "The Love You Save (May Be Your
Own)." On film, Tarantino's attitude to these
women is somewhere between a wolf whistle

> **"I was like a brutish American exploitation distributor who cut the movie down almost to the point of incoherence. I cut it down to the bone and took all the fat off it to see if it could still exist, and it worked."**

and a high five: A lustful big brother, he ogles their bodies shamelessly, but he also celebrates their victories like an honorary soul sister granted inner-sanctum access to their rowdy, randy chatter.

ARLENE
We didn't do "the thing."

SHANNA
Excuse me for livin' but what's "the thing?"

ARLENE
You know, everything but.

SHANNA
They call that "the thing?"

ARLENE
I call it "the thing."

SHANNA
Do guys like "the thing?"

ARLENE
Well, they like it better than no-thing.

The Spice Girls by way of Harold Pinter.

Also at the bar, chowing down on a nachos grande platter, filmed in oblique, backlit three-quarter profile, like Elvis on a snack break, is Stuntman Mike, a weathered, scarred hunk who claims to have performed stunt work on several television series.

"There are few things as fetching as a bruised soul on a beautiful angel," he tells Arlene before showing her his car, a steel-reinforced Dodge Charger painted in dusty black primer with a skull stenciled on its hood. It's "death proof," he claims.

Tarantino allows the scene to play on and on, and as his camera arcs around the room, the dread becomes increasingly hard to dispel. Mike charms the girls and scores a lap dance from Arlene. Then, after they have left the bar, he pursues them in his car and kills them with a head-on collision on an empty, winding country road. The scene is set to the lost gem "Hold Tight" by Dave Dee, Dozy, Beaky, Mick & Tich. Tarantino shows the crash three times, the women's bodies pulled apart over and over, their deaths quite unlike any other movie deaths, sickening and hateful and heartbreaking, like

ABOVE: Tarantino makes a cameo in the film as the bartender at the Texas Chili Parlor.

crazy things. Just for fun, Bell straps herself to the hood of a roaring 1970 Dodge Challenger with nothing more than two belts tied to the window posts. When Stuntman Mike shows up, a classic battle unfolds across backcountry Texas terrain that hasn't seen anything like it since Steven Spielberg's 1971 film *Duel*. It's the most singularly effective piece of action Tarantino has ever shot. At a certain point, Tarantino goes "back to the basics of character, action, and story," wrote A. O. Scott in the *New York Times*. "*Death Proof* is a decidedly modest picture, fittingly enough given its second billing in this double feature. But its scaled-down ambition is part of its appeal."

Death Proof would be Tarantino's swansong to the contemporary era, a kinetic action poem that is also an elegy for old-school stunt work— what Stuntman Mike calls the days of "real cars crashing into real cars, with real, dumb people driving 'em."

Tarantino was disconcerted by the film's reception. "It's like in a breakup, when she's the one that does the leaving, and you're shaken," he said, taking consolation from his friends Tony Scott and Steven Spielberg. "One of the things Spielberg said that was cool was, he goes, 'Well, Quentin, you've been pretty lucky. You've had a success, to one degree or another, every time out. It's almost like playing the game and not paying for it. All right? Today you paid for it. And it can make you a more well-rounded person, having done that. But the other thing, though, is the next time you have a success it's going to be even sweeter because you learned what it's like to have the cards fall the other way.' My confidence was rocked, but in this way: Instead of taking a job, or writing something new, I went back to *Inglourious Basterds*, old material that I knew was good. I said, let me solve it now, quit fucking around and just solve it."

seeing an artist deface his own work: these same bodies and souls that Tarantino so tenderly delineated now fed into the grinder.

"It's as if he couldn't decide whether to be a humanist or a nihilist," said David Denby in the *New Yorker*, although the correct answer is, of course: both.

"He's a predatory humanist," wrote David Edelstein in *Slate*, much closer to the mark, "a movie freak who loves women onscreen almost as much as he loves to punish women onscreen, and who (this is what makes him an artist) gets off most on his own ambivalence."

The film mirrors that ambivalence exactly: it's divided into two halves, like panels of a diptych. On one side is a vision of macho Mike, triumphant and rendered in period style with scratches on the negative and "missing" reels. The opposing panel, by contrast, is blemish-free, with deeply saturated colors, and a fearless new breed of woman at its center: Abernathy (Rosario Dawson), Kim (Tracie Thoms), Lee (Mary Elizabeth Winstead), and Zoë Bell (as herself) on a day off from a Hollywood movie shooting in the area. The women riff about vintage speedsters and movies like *Vanishing Point* and *Dirty Mary Crazy Larry*.

The only thing capable of beating a stuntman, it turns out, is two stuntwomen: in *Death Proof*, Tarantino does everything the old-fashioned way, with fast cars and real human beings doing

ABOVE: Fear in their eyes. Julia, Shanna (Jordan Ladd), and Lanna (Monica Staggs) prepare to meet their fate. OPPOSITE: Evil reigns as Stuntman Mike drives his "death-proofed" car towards the unsuspecting girls.

"My confidence was rocked a little. It's like in a breakup, when she's the one that does the leaving, and you're shaken."

INGLOURIOUS BASTERDS

2009

"If I couldn't make *Inglourious Basterds* as good as I thought it should be then I would have just not done it. But I knew I had to write it."

"THIS ain't your daddy's World War II movie," said Tarantino of *Inglourious Basterds,* his giddily brutal, camply entertaining Second World War remix about a group of Jewish-American GIs taking revenge on the Nazis. Tarantino first started the script in 1998, right after making *Jackie Brown.* "I guess I was a little precious about it because it was my first original script since *Pulp Fiction,*" he told the *Guardian.* "It just got bigger and bigger in my head. It became about the words on the page rather than the film. I couldn't turn my brain off. I couldn't stop coming up with new avenues, new ideas. Suddenly it was like, what the fuck? Am I too big for movies now? Are movies too small for me? I mean, what's *that* about?"

Shelving the script to make *Kill Bill* and *Death Proof,* he returned to it and wondered if the story wouldn't be better served as a twelve-part TV miniseries. Having dinner with French film director Luc Besson and his producing partner Pierre-Ange Le Pogam, he told them about the idea and got a friendly telling-off from Besson. "I'm sorry, you're one of the few directors who actually makes me want to go to the movies," the director told him, "and the idea that I might have to wait five years to go into a theater and see one of your movies is depressing to me."

Deciding to cut the script back down to what it had been originally—a *Dirty Dozen*–style movie about a bunch of guys on a mission—Tarantino took six months to reduce his magnum opus to a 160-page script, starting in January 2008 and writing through July. He did a rewrite on the older material in the first two chapters after finding the original character of Shosanna— "a real badass, a Joan of Arc of the Jews"—too similar to the Bride in *Kill Bill.* Instead, he made her more of a survivor and wrote everything after Chapter Two in one big go.

He had one roadblock: history. In particular, he had to decide what to do with the character of Hitler, who, everyone knows, did not meet a grisly end at the hands of American scalp-hunters. One day, after a long writing stint, he realised that the characters he was writing didn't know they were part of history.

"I was listening to music, pacing around, and finally I just grabbed a pen, went over to a piece of paper and wrote, 'Just fucking kill him!'" Tarantino said. "I put it near my bedside table so I would see it when I woke up the next morning and could decide after a night's sleep if it was still a good idea. I saw it, paced around awhile, and said, 'Yeah, that's a good idea.' I went out on the balcony and started writing. And I just fucking killed him.

"I can honestly say that when I conceived of that ending, it was one of the most exciting moments of inspiration I've ever had as a writer. I was like: 'Use the nitrate prints to blow up the theater!' Because it could do that. And when I came up with that idea, it was one of the eureka moments of my artistic life. It really was. 'Oh my God, how come nobody ever thought of that before?'"

OPPOSITE: Eli Roth as one of the Basterds, Sergeant Donny Donowitz. TOP: Martin Wuttke plays a fictionalized Adolf Hitler. BOTTOM: Shosanna (Mélanie Laurent) prepares the nitrate prints to blow up the theater.

ABOVE: Tarantino took inspiration from World War II propaganda films such as *Confessions of a Nazi Spy*, *Man Hunt*, and *This Land is Mine*.
OPPOSITE: "Brad was a blast in this role." Tarantino was full of praise for Brad Pitt's portrayal of the Basterd First Lieutenant Aldo Raine.

Even Lawrence Bender was surprised when Tarantino called in July to announce that he had finalized the long-gestating *Basterds* script. "He's read me all kinds of stuff over the years, but I always assumed it was something he was going to have and never do," said Bender, who, in the years since Tarantino began the project, had seen World War II become something of a cottage industry in Hollywood. *Saving Private Ryan* and *The Thin Red Line had* both arrived in 1998, followed by *Band of Brothers* on HBO in 2001. Tarantino wanted to roll back the clock to such films as Anatole Litvak's *Confessions of a Nazi Spy* (1939), Fritz Lang's *Man Hunt* (1941), and Jean Renoir's *This Land Is Mine* (1943), all propaganda films in which you rooted for the heroes and cheered the death of the Nazis.

Tarantino said, "What struck me about those movies was that they were made during the war, when the Nazis were still a threat, and these filmmakers probably had had personal experiences with the Nazis or were worried to death about their families in Europe. Yet these movies are entertaining, they're funny, there's humor in them. They're not solemn, like *Defiance*. They're allowed to be thrilling adventures."

Tarantino had long wanted to work with Brad Pitt, whose agent was shared with Uma Thurman. "As I was writing the script, it went from, 'Oh, Brad could be good in this,' to, 'Brad would be damn good in this,' to, 'Brad would be fuckin' awesome in this,' to, 'Okay, now, I need to fuckin' get Brad, because if I *don't*, what am I going to *do*?'"

Visiting the actor at his home in the South of France toward the end of the summer, the pair did a tour of the property in a dune buggy with Pitt's kids to see the huge vineyard and the on-site recording studio where Pink Floyd recorded *The Wall*. Then they returned to Pitt's home to talk about the movie over several bottles of wine and some hash. Finally peeling off in the early hours of the next morning, Tarantino returned to his hotel room with a sliver of hash Pitt had cut from his brick, along with a Coke can to use as a pipe.

"All I know is we talked about the backstory," said Pitt. "We talked about movies till the wee hours of the night, and I got up the next morning, and I saw five empty bottles of wine lying on the floor—five! And something that resembled a smoking apparatus, I don't know what that was. Apparently I had agreed to do the movie, and six weeks later I was in a uniform."

To meet the accelerated production schedule that would allow them to make the 2009 Cannes Film Festival, the rest of the cast was quickly assembled. Initially, Tarantino had Leonardo DiCaprio in mind for the pivotal role of Hans Landa. A fan of Tarantino's writing, DiCaprio was among the first to receive a copy whenever the director finished a script. DiCaprio was "curious about playing the role," but Tarantino wanted to use a native German speaker.

Insistent that everyone speak their character's mother tongue, Tarantino wanted, above all, to avoid the contrivance of Germans speaking perfect English. He auditioned numerous actors for the role, but none quite worked. As the clock ticked down, he considered that he might have written an unplayable part. "I was getting worried. Unless I found the perfect Landa, I was going to pull the movie. I gave myself one more week and then I was going to pull the plug. Then Christoph Waltz came in and it was obvious that he was the guy; he could do everything. He was amazing. He gave us our movie back."

Born in Vienna to a theatrical family, Waltz was a journeyman character actor who had worked mostly in the theater and on German television, playing villains. He had once played Friedrich Nietzsche in a French-German coproduction about the life of Richard Wagner, but had come across nothing like Tarantino's script before.

"I was completely thrown by it," Waltz said of the five-chapter behemoth filled with lengthy, sinuous conversations, complete with misspellings—"Basterds" for "Bastards," "Bostin" for "Boston," "there knee's" for "their knees,"—and beneath his hand-scrawled title, the words "Last Draft." Waltz read through the entire script during his first audition in Berlin, and afterwards told the casting agent, "Look, if that's it, it will have been more than just worthwhile. Thank you!"

Waltz said, "When Quentin called me back for a second audition, I said, 'I feel exactly the same, only now it's 200 percent better.' And a few days later I got the call."

With his Landa in place, Tarantino started shooting right away at Studio Babelsberg in Potsdam, Germany. He then moved the shoot to Paris, where he commandeered a 1904 bistro with peeling paint, Art Deco stained glass, and a wall of windows overlooking an intersection of identifiably Parisian streets in the Eighteenth Arrondissement for the scene in which Landa and Shosanna (Mélanie Laurent)—hunter and hunted—first cross paths.

Tarantino worked closely with Waltz, keeping him from rehearsing too much with the other actors so that they didn't get too comfortable around him. "He wanted this insecurity on their part," said Waltz, who went through the script, page by page, with the director, building the character from the ground up.

"It was just for a big movie, we had a nice pace. And well, it made it harder. Maybe it made it a tad less fun, because it was a lot of pressure. But I was hoping all that energy would go into the film."

"What do you think, Christoph?" Tarantino asked him over dinner one night in Germany. "In the script it says that the calabash is your pipe, but what if it's not? Maybe you don't smoke a pipe. Maybe this is simply a prop for your interrogation of Perrier LaPadite (Denis Ménochet). You've learned he smokes a pipe, so you're going to buy this pipe just before you show up. It's going to be this Sherlock Holmes pipe and at the right moment in the interrogation you bring it out to say, 'I'm on to your motherfucking ass.'"

Waltz replied, "Oh, no, it's definitely a prop! I don't smoke a pipe!"

Every Thursday was movie night. Eli Roth remembered them screening an obscure 1968 actioner called *Dark of the Sun*, in which a bar burns down amid machine gunfire. Four months later, while shooting the climactic inferno sequence, "[Tarantino] had a camera move, and his only direction to me was: '*Dark of the Sun*.' And I knew exactly what he meant. He didn't rip off the shot, but it was a mood, a feeling, and we realized that that was what we were looking for."

Said Brad Pitt, "Quentin has the greatest knowledge of cinema of anyone you'll run into,

TOP: Chillingly polite Landa intimidates Charlotte LaPadite (Léa Seydoux) and her sisters in the film's opening scenes. LEFT: Til Schweiger as the quietly stern Basterd Sergeant Hugo Stiglitz. OPPOSITE, TOP: Tarantino screened Kenneth More's *Dark of the Sun* for his cast, using it as inspiration for the final inferno scene. OPPOSITE, BOTTOM: Cinematographer Robert Richardson begins the shoot at the basement bar La Louisiane.

and that's infused into the day's work. But the set is church. He is God, his script is Bible, and no heretics allowed."

When Mélanie Laurent questioned a line in the script, she encountered this reception. "I had this expression to say that really seemed improbable to say in French," she said. "I told him, but there was no negotiating. He said, 'We can invent. Who's to say we can't invent new expressions?' He likes certain sounds. He likes certain words in French and he wants to hear them."

Scrambling to meet their May deadline in time for Cannes, Tarantino and editor Sally Menke had to forgo their usual test screening. Some pretty well-known sequences were cut from the film, including the scene where Michael Fassbender's character (Lieutenant Archie Hicox) meets with the Basterds, and the characters played by Maggie Cheung and Cloris Leachman were eliminated altogether.

"It was down and dirty," said Menke. "We physically ran out of time, especially with a couple of moments with Shosanna, where we knew it wasn't quite right." When the first wave of mostly negative reviews hit, "we knew ahead of time that we were going to put some things back in and address certain scenes, so it wasn't a surprise. It was like, 'Okay, let's get back from France! Let's go do this work, because we're opening soon!'" Working around the clock to get the film ready for its September release, even Tarantino sounded exhausted.

"I don't know if I really want to work *this* fast ever again, on this big a film," he said. "We've always worked best under some sort of a deadline. You can fuck around with a movie too much. We like rushing the judgment. It's like, 'We're going this way, and that's it.' *Bam!*"

Inglourious Basterds begins with the best game of cat-and-mouse in Tarantino's work since

A strike force of crack mercenaries fight the hottest battles in all the blazing fury of today's strife-torn Congo!

ROD TAYLOR · YVETTE MIMIEUX · JIM BROWN

DARK OF THE SUN

KENNETH MORE

Dennis Hopper discussed Italian genealogy with Christopher Walken in *True Romance*. Taking place inside the confines of a single room in a farmhouse, the scene is a marvel of carefully choreographed camera movement and tightly coordinated performances.

An SS patrol, led by Colonel Hans Landa (Christoph Waltz), questions a French farmer about a family of Jews who may be hiding on his property. Landa is polite, even flirtatious, and Tarantino increases the tension gradually, the camera circling Landa and the farmer like an ever-tightening noose, before slipping through the floor to show the terrified family members prostrate, their hands over their mouths and their eyes wide in fear. The interrogation continues, the bonhomie of Landa's chatter only heightening the lethal tension of the scene, which Tarantino then punctuates with a sight gag: After asking the farmer if he can smoke, Landa pulls out a pipe so comically large it wouldn't be out of place in a *Naked Gun* movie. Or a Magritte painting. Or both.

Welcome to the weird, topsy-turvy world of late-period Tarantino: a self-contained universe of broad burlesque humor, immense cruelty, and counterfactual revenge fantasy. With its multilingual chatter, *Inglourious Basterds* marks the farthest distance, both geographically and historically, from Tarantino's own patch of turf, and it shows—not so much in the solecisms detected by Laurent as in the thick fur of movie references.

Tarantino's initial impulse—to write a *Dirty Dozen*–style men-on-a-mission movie—quickly unspools into five different chapters, all of them paying lip service to cinema. In the first, we get the Basterds, led by Lieutenant Aldo Raine (Brad Pitt), a blunt, jaw-jutting, Kentucky-fried simpleton whose eight-soldier team—a kind of Jewish Dirty Dozen—has parachuted behind enemy lines to kill and collect Nazi scalps.

"Quite frankly," Raine tells one victim, "watching Donny beat Nazis to death is the closest we ever get to going to the movies."

In another strand, a German movie star, Bridget von Hammersmark (Diane Kruger) plots against Hitler with a British commando and film critic (Michael Fassbender) who is attempting to pass himself off as an SS officer. In a stroke of

"I was trying to do a spaghetti western but using World War II iconography."

casting that borders on the camp, Mike Myers plays the stereotypically British General assigning him the mission.

In the third chapter, called "German Night in Paris" and generally considered the most compelling, a French Jew named Shosanna (Mélanie Laurent), who escaped Landa's death squad, reinvents herself as the proprietress of a Paris movie house. But she runs right into Landa again when he orders a strudel in the restaurant where she works as a waitress. Hypnotizing his prey with a twinkling eye, giant grin, and unctuous charm ("Don't forget the cream"), Waltz tortures his lines with exquisite relish, drawing out every syllable until it plops into the audience's lap.

The performance is Brechtian: Hans Landa isn't so much a character as he is the movie's leering master of revels and sadist-in-chief. He's almost a kind of director, lording it over all the other characters, not just the best thing in the movie, but very nearly the *only* thing in the movie. "The delight we take in Landa creates an odd imbalance in the film," wrote Ryan Gilbey in the *New Statesman*. Manohla Dargis in the *New York Times* agreed, writing that "The film's most egregious failure—its giddy, at times gleeful embrace and narrative elevation of the seductive Nazi villain—can largely be explained as a problem of form. Landa simply has no equal in

the film, no counterpart who can match him in verbal dexterity and charisma, who can be the Jules Winnfield and Mia Wallace to his Vincent Vega as Mr. Jackson and Uma Thurman are to John Travolta in *Pulp Fiction*."

Tarantino's work had always featured these figures—genially sadistic tyrants, filibustering the movies in which they appear—but, in the latter half of Tarantino's career, they would come to dominate, pushing everyone else to the side: Landa in *Inglourious Basterds*, Calvin Candie in *Django Unchained*, Marquis Warren in *The Hateful Eight*, a movie composed of nothing *but* director figures, all staging their own version of events.

Here, Brad Pitt sinks comfortably into character-acting second gear, content merely to roll his Southern-flavored vowels around like chewing tobacco. He's no match for the polyglot Landa, who finishes whole speeches in the time it takes

PAGES 198–199: Raine and Donowitz prepare to scalp their Nazi victims. OPPOSITE, TOP: Landa attempts to strike a deal with the Basterds. OPPOSITE, BOTTOM LEFT: The stellar cast included Mike Myers as British General Ed Fenech. OPPOSITE, BOTTOM RIGHT: A little light entertainment as undercover agents Lieutenant Hicox (Michael Fassbender) and Bridget von Hammersmark (Diane Kruger) keep watch over their SS counterparts. RIGHT: Shosanna surveys the scene as she welcomes Hitler and his Nazi comrades to her cinema.

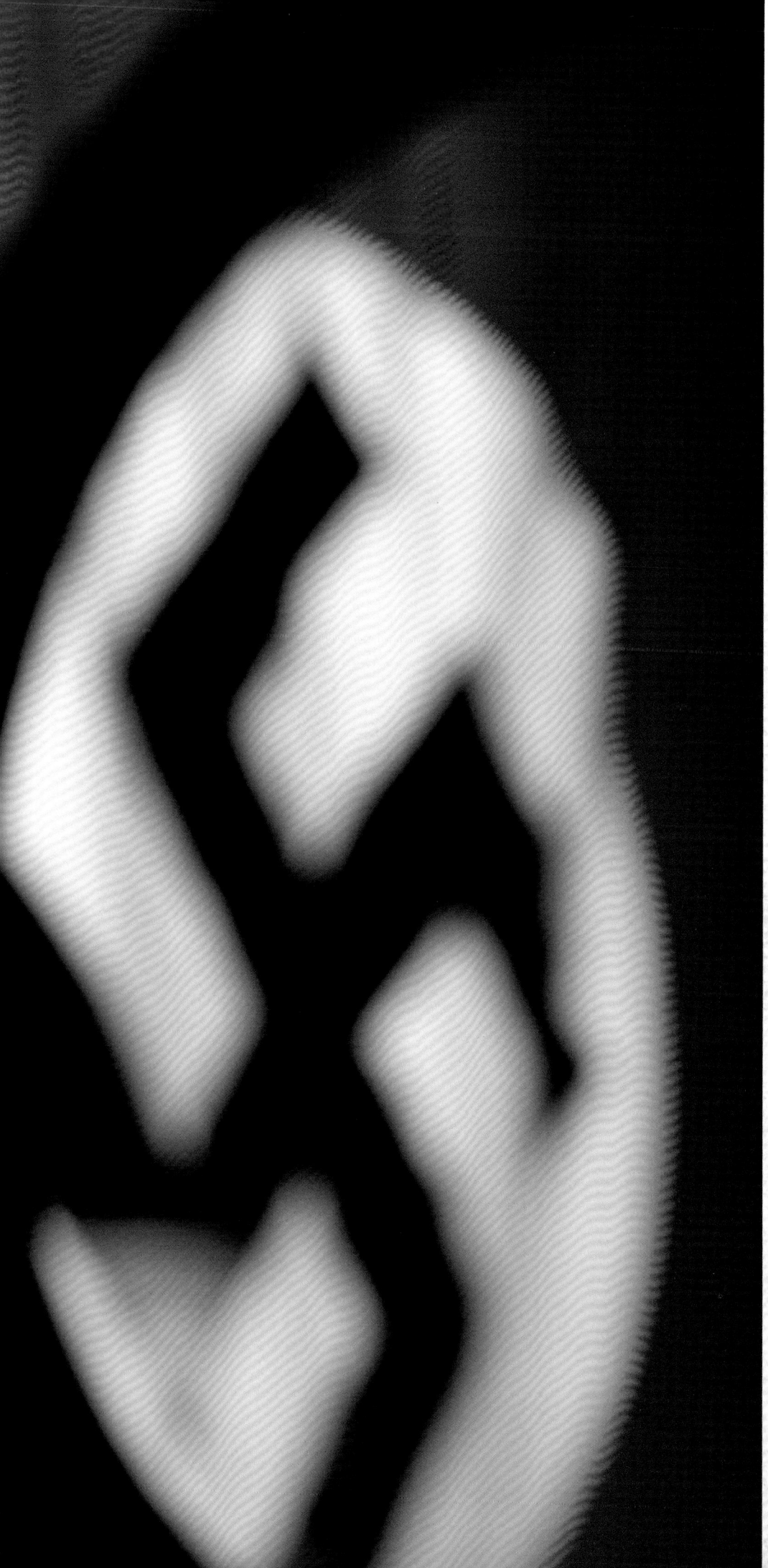

Raine to summon a monosyllable. The movie grows wispier as it goes, Shosanna's plan and the Basterds' mission coming together in the final chapter, "The Revenge of the Giant Face," in which the Basterds spray the Nazi command with machine gun fire in Shosanna's Art Deco movie house to David Bowie's "Cat People," before the whole place goes up in a nitrate inferno. When the smoke clears, little is left. It's a curiously weightless climax, and among the movie's more haunting images: a close-up of Laurent's face is projected onto a blanket of smoke in a hellish echo of Giuseppe Tornatore's *Cinema Paradiso*.

With its movie critic and projectionist heroes, its visual nods to *The Searchers* (1956), its name checks for B-movie stars (Raine, a play on Aldo Ray, and Hugo Stiglitz among them), references to G. W. Pabst and Leni Riefenstahl, as well as a riff on *King Kong* as representative of "the story of the negro in America," *Inglourious Basterds* is easily Tarantino's most self-consciously movieish movie—a sonnet to cinephilia.

"In a sense, *Inglourious Basterds* is a form of science fiction," wrote J. Hoberman in the *Village Voice*. "Everything unfolds in and maps an alternate universe: The Movies." It could be argued that all of Tarantino's films map that universe. Although when the characters in *Reservoir Dogs* sat around arguing about their names, you didn't need to have seen *The Taking of Pelham One Two Three* to get the joke.

LEFT: Putting on her war paint, Shosanna prepares to avenge her enemies and meet her fate.

"When I conceived of that ending, it was one of the most exciting moments of inspiration I've ever had as a writer."

When he wrote *Pulp Fiction*, Tarantino was careful to draw on all the "old chestnuts" a mainstream cinema audience might be familiar with, raiding the B-movie bank for crossover appeal. As his career progressed, Tarantino would look over his shoulder less, embarking on a series of vertiginous descents down the rabbit hole.

"This time, he has pulled the film-archive door shut behind him," said the *New Yorker*'s David Denby of *Inglourious Basterds*. "There's hardly a flash of light indicating that the world exists outside the cinema except as the basis of a nutbrain fable."

Critics were as confused as the film. Some critics took the bait and mistook it for a film about World War II, rather than a film about World War II movies. Jonathan Rosenbaum wrote that the film "seems morally akin to Holocaust denial" and that Tarantino had "become the cinematic equivalent of Sarah Palin, death-panel fantasies and all."

In his one-star *Guardian* review, Peter Bradshaw wrote the movie off as "a colossal,

complacent, long-winded dud, a gigantic two-and-a-half-hour anti-climax."

The New York Times thought it "unwieldy," "interminable," "repellent," and "vulgar."

Salon's Stephanie Zacharek more accurately concluded, "Tarantino has taken a huge leap and made a movie that doesn't fully work, which presents those of us who love his work, hate his work, or love-hate his work—which should cover just about everybody—with a confounding question: Do we praise the leap, or shake our fists at the result?"

By far the most interesting critical reaction, though, came from Germany, where reception to the film bordered on a kind of pop-cultural catharsis. In the Frankfurter Allgemeine Zeitung, Claudius Seidl expressed his joy at having seen a film "that presents the downfall [of the Third Reich] not as a tragedy but as a farce . . ."

He noted that "when Inglourious Basterds had its German premiere in Berlin, after one particularly nasty scene in which Christoph Waltz plays the SS man Hans Landa, an old-school murderer, sadist, and middle-brow intellectual, spontaneous applause broke out."

In its review, the Berlin daily newspaper Tagesspiegel wrote that Inglourious Basterds "isn't camp, it isn't pulp—you miss the point using such categories with Tarantino—but rather a vision never before seen in the nearly exhausted world of cinematic images." It also wrote that the movie offered "catharsis! Oxygen! Wonderful retro-futuristic insanity of the imagination!"

Writing about the final scene, in which Hitler, Goebbels, and company are incinerated in a Paris cinema, Die Zeit's reviewer said simply, "Hurray! They're torched!"

OPPOSITE: Mélanie Laurent as resourceful refugee-turned movie-theater proprietress Shosanna Dreyfus. ABOVE: "A basterd's work is never done." Donowitz and Private First Class Omar Ulmer (Omar Doom) pose as Italian filmmakers who enter the cinema to kill Hitler and Goebbels in the film's final scenes.

DJANGO UNCHAINED

2012

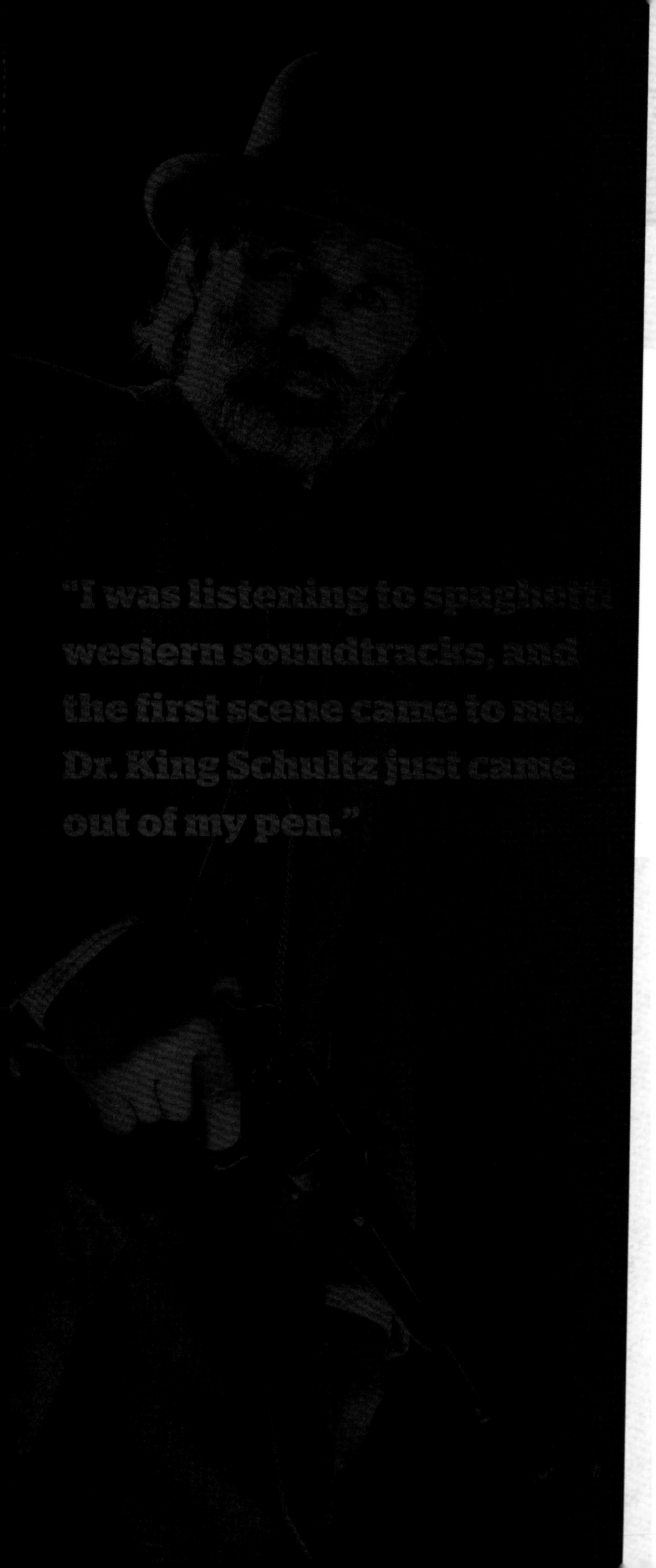

FAR LEFT: Following their successful collaboration on *Inglourious Basterds*, Tarantino cast Christoph Waltz as the enigmatic bounty hunter Dr. King Schultz. LEFT AND OPPOSITE: Jamie Foxx, in the titular role, strikes a pose reminiscent of Sergio Corbucci's *Django* (1966), an inspiration for Tarantino.

"I was listening to spaghetti western soundtracks, and the first scene came to me. Dr. King Schultz just came out of my pen."

ENJOYING a day off near the end of the promotional tour for *Inglourious Basterds*, Tarantino went to a record store in Japan and found a "treasure trove" of spaghetti western soundtracks. The country had been enjoying a huge resurgence of interest in the genre at the time. Tarantino had been doing a lot of thinking himself about Sergio Corbucci, a film critic who directed a number of spaghetti westerns in the 1960s, most notably the ultraviolent *Django* (1966), starring Franco Nero as a drifter seeking to avenge the death of his wife.

"I was actually writing a piece on Corbucci and describing his kind of western," said Tarantino, who had loaded up on soundtracks and returned to his room, where the first scene of *Django Unchained* came to him more or less complete. "The Corbucci piece put all those images in my head. I was listening to spaghetti western soundtracks, and the first scene came to me. Dr. King Schultz just came out of my pen."

Tarantino saw two white slave traders dragging a chain gang through the Texas woods. Then, a German bounty hunter appears out of the darkness and declares that he intends to acquire Django, one of the slaves. Envisioned as an "ubermasculine black male figure of folklore"—a black Paul Bunyan or Pecos Bill—Django is freed, rescues his wife from bondage, and evolves into an angel of black vengeance, killing white people and getting paid for it. In essence, the film was a kind of superhero origin story.

"I got the chance to take a slave character and give him a heroic journey, make him heroic, make him give his payback. To show this epic journey and give it the folkloric tale that it deserves."

"There haven't been that many slave narratives in the last forty years of cinema, and usually when there are, they're done on television, and for the most part they're historical movies, like history with a capital H," noted Tarantino. "It ends up becoming soul-deadening, because you're just watching victimization all the time. And now you get a chance to put a spin on it and actually take a slave character and give him a heroic journey, make him heroic, make him give his payback, and actually show this epic journey and give it the kind of folkloric tale that it deserves—the kind of grand-opera stage it deserves."

Tarantino's initial impulse was to get Django's transformation out of the way at the beginning of the film, and then cut to years later "like, way after the Civil War"—but he wanted to take a break from the time-jumping storytelling style he was associated with and liked Django's origin story too much. He liked the idea of following one character from beginning to end. Armed with that first scene and his trove of spaghetti western soundtracks, Tarantino returned to Los Angeles and set to work on the balcony off the bedroom of his house in the Hollywood Hills, typing with one finger on his Smith Corona typewriter/word processor.

Upon finishing the initial script in late April 2011, Tarantino invited a group of friends, including Samuel L. Jackson, to his home to look at what he called his 166-page "novel." Tarantino had Jackson in mind for Django, but the actor was, at 62, a little too old for the part and so Tarantino gave him instead the role of the loyal Stephen, who the actor called "the most despicable negro in cinematic history." Jackson relished the challenge after playing one of the most beloved, Dr. Martin Luther King Jr., on Broadway.

Tarantino met with Will Smith while the actor was shooting *Men in Black 3* in New York. They went over the script but Smith wasn't sure of it and didn't know if there would be time to address his reservations. "Let me just see how I feel, and if you don't find anybody, let's talk again," Smith told the director.

Tarantino met six more actors—Idris Elba, Chris Tucker, Terrence Howard, Michael K. Williams, the singer Tyrese—before meeting with Jamie Foxx. Tarantino quickly realized he wouldn't have to fret about putting Foxx through the paces.

"Jamie understood the material," said Tarantino. "But mostly he was the cowboy. Forget the fact that he has his own horse—and that is actually his horse in the movie. He's from Texas; he understands. We sat there talking, and I realized, wow, if this were the 1960s and I was casting a Django western TV show and they had black guys as stars of those in the 1960s, I could see Jamie on one of those. And that's what I was looking for, a Clint Eastwood."

OPPOSITE: "The cowboy." Tarantino found his Clint Eastwood in Jamie Foxx. ABOVE: Setting the tone for the rest of the film, the brutal opening scenes turn the status quo on its head as freed slaves take revenge on their owner.

Nervous, Jamie Foxx asked his representatives to contact Jackson for his thoughts on the Django role. "At the end of the day all I could tell them was it's Quentin Tarantino, first of all," said Jackson, "and second of all, if it was ten to fifteen years ago we wouldn't be having this conversation because I'd be doing that role, and if you need to know anything more then you're calling the wrong person."

After missing out on the role of Hans Landa in *Inglourious Basterds*, Leonardo DiCaprio called Tarantino to let the director know how much he liked the role of plantation owner Calvin Candie.

"I actually wrote him to be a much older man," Tarantino said, "so we sat down together and talked about it and I went home and asked myself, *Can this work as a younger person? What do I lose and gain by changing that?*" It was not a typical calculation: Normally it's the actor's job to change and fit into the character."

But Tarantino's interest was piqued. "All of a sudden I thought about a bored, petulant boy emperor," he said. "Caligula, Louis XIV, where his daddy's daddy's daddy was the cotton man. He's the idle, decadent rich."

Sitting down at the table to read through the script, DiCaprio expressed some trepidation. Tarantino describes the initial read: "He's like, 'Do I have to say this this many times? And do I have to say "nigger" like—'and I said, 'Yeah, you do.' And he'd say, 'Well, is there a way'— 'No, you can't.' Because this is how it is. This is the reality of how it goes. So once he realized you're either all in or all out, he went home, and the next day he was all in."

OPPOSITE AND ABOVE: Having missed out on a role in *Inglourious Basterds*, Leonardo DiCaprio was keen to take on a Tarantino character, settling on evil plantation owner Calvin Candie.

WANTED
DEAD OR ALIVE
SHIRLEY BACALL

Tarantino was more improvisational in devising shots on *Django* than he was on his previous collaborations with cinematographer Robert Richardson, which involved handwritten shot lists provided each morning. "When we're outside, it's Sergio Leone and Sergio Corbucci," Tarantino told Richardson. "Inside, especially in Candie's mansion, it's Max Ophüls."

Shooting began the last week of November 2011 in Lone Pine, California, before moving to Jackson Hole, Wyoming, and Louisiana, finally wrapping on July 24, 2012—a long shoot. "We shot that film forever," said Jackson.

Hours in a coffin-sized metal sauna full of centipedes and worms left Kerry Washington with nightmares. In DiCaprio's climactic monologue —a rant inspired by a racist phrenology book in the actor's collection—he lost his voice a couple of times, and on the sixth take, slammed his hand on the table and hit a glass, blood pouring all over the table. Foxx hurt his back. In training, bees startled Christoph Waltz's horse, who threw him, breaking the actor's pelvis, and putting him out of action for two-and-a half months. Northern California had a snowless December for the first time in a hundred years during the shoot, forcing Tarantino to ship sets to Wyoming to shoot, losing several actors in the process: Joseph Gordon-Levitt, Anthony LaPaglia, Kevin Costner, and his replacement, Kurt Russell, who was replaced by Walton Goggins in late March.

"Making this movie was really hard," said Tarantino. "When you make an epic and you go through months and months with an army of people in extreme cold and heat, the hardest thing is remembering why you wanted to do it in the first place. It's easy to get lost."

The Weinsteins, *Django*'s producers, were aiming for a Christmas release in order to be eligible for the 2012 Academy Awards. "At some point in the process, we had to make that decision," said Tarantino. "Do we have an Oscar movie, or do we not? And we all thought we did."

Post-production was squashed down to four months.

It was complicated by the fact that, for the first time, Tarantino was finishing a movie without editor Sally Menke, who had been found dead of heatstroke after going on a hike in Griffith Park shortly after the release of *Inglourious Basterds*. He worked instead with Fred Raskin, who began cutting while Tarantino was still shooting. The rough cut came in at just under four and a half hours.

"Quentin's method of working is to shoot the entire script and boil it down to its essentials in editing," said Raskin, who wrestled to reduce three major scenes: the Mandingo fight, the dog scene, and the almost-castration scene in the barn. But the original cut didn't quite hit the mark. "Even though the film played really well in test screenings, you could tell they were traumatized. People applauded at the end, but it wasn't the whole theater bursting into applause."

Tarantino had to negotiate with the Weinsteins for the three extra weeks he needed to shoot a new final sequence. In exchange, Tarantino agreed to forgo a chunk of his profit participation. The final budget was an estimated $83 million, making it the priciest movie Tarantino had made yet.

The shootout was one of the pricier additions. Originally, Schultz kills Candie, Butch Pooch kills Schultz, Django puts his hands in the air and is captured, and then it goes to the scene in the barn. "But the movie felt done at that point," said Raskin, "so Quentin took it down to the bare essentials: Django comes in and takes them out."

PAGES 218–219: Samuel L. Jackson's Stephen, "the most despised Negro in cinematic history," susses out Broomhilda's connection to the Candyland guests. OPPOSITE: The unlikely camaraderie between Schultz and Django is trademark Tarantino. TOP: "If all I had to do was cut a hole in a bag, I could've cut it better myself." Known for inserting wit where it doesn't quite belong, Tarantino's KKK scene is a beautifully shot stampede accompanied by comic dialogue. BOTTOM: Freed from his shackles, Django swaps his rags for a more splendid outfit.

A companion piece of sorts to *Inglourious Basterds*, *Django Unchained* marked another spin in the period-B-movie mobile, continuing the revenge theme that, since *Kill Bill*, had come to dominate Tarantino's filmmaking to the point of monomania. A genre arabesque kept aloft by prodigious feats of verbiage, *Django* is effectively two movies in one. The first is a kind of western set in the American South in 1858, where a German immigrant bounty hunter, King Schultz (Christoph Waltz), silver-tongued, trim of beard, and florid of rhetoric, buys a slave, Django (Jamie Foxx), who can help him find three brothers for whom he has a warrant. First glimpsed in shackles and rags on a cold Texas night, Django is soon kitted out like Gainsborough's Blue Boy, posing as Schultz's valet, while dispensing rough justice to white slavers. "Killin' white folks for money—what's not to like?" he says of the job.

Or, from the audience's perspective: a cross-racial Tarantino buddy movie—what's not to like? It had been a long time since Tarantino availed himself of the companionable pleasures of a double act. His ego-powered writing had

granted characters less inclination toward playing well with others as time went on. Most of the killers in *Kill Bill* were solo operatives, and in *Inglourious Basterds,* Hans Landa stood alone. But the chat that flows between Django and Dr. Schultz, eyes twinkling, mustache twitching, resuscitated something of the similarly cross-racial camaraderie between Jules and Vincent in *Pulp Fiction*, even if Tarantino seems far more interested in Django's verbose companion than in Django himself.

His infatuation with Waltz seems to know no bounds. An explanation of Dr. Schultz's German origins—which might have merited just a line—spills over into the film's plot, the pair searching for Django's German-speaking wife, Broomhilda von Shaft. This search-and-rescue mission, modeled on the legend of Siegfried as recounted by Schultz, unfolds in a spirit of burlesque merriment that is closer to Mel Brooks than Sergio Leone. Some of the scenes, most notably a KKK rally led by Don Johnson's Big Daddy, in which the night riders complain petulantly that they can't "see fucking shit" through the holes in their hoods, are among

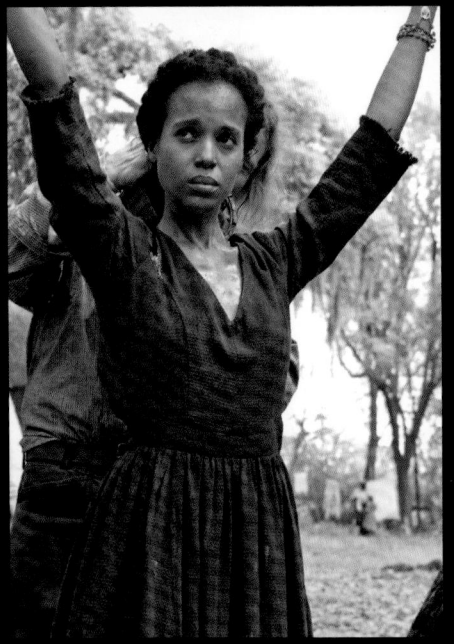

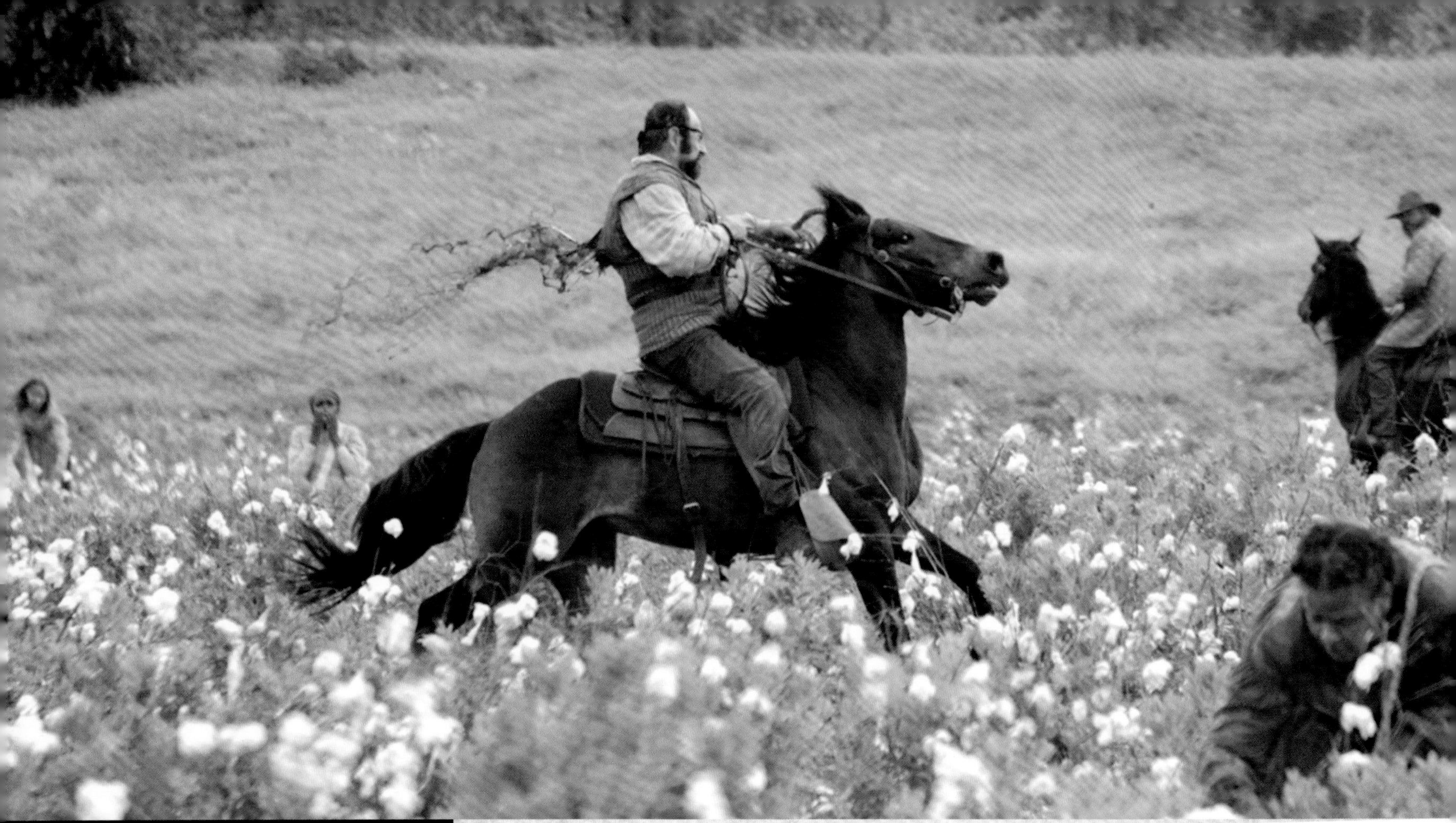

TOP: Beauty in the violence. Robert Richardson's superb cinematography won him an eighth Academy Award nomination. BOTTOM: Django's wife, Broomhilda—the damsel in distress—is enslaved at Candyland. OPPOSITE, TOP: Leonardo DiCaprio in a promotional shot for the film. OPPOSITE, BOTTOM: Django and Schultz arrive at the Candyland mansion.

the funniest Tarantino has written. ("I think—*we* all think the bags woz a nice idea, and I'm not pointing any fingers, but they could have been done better" concludes one, that self-correction from "I to "we" just perfect.)

At the same time, cinematographer Robert Richardson delivers some of the most beautiful images in any Tarantino film, from the spray of blood on white flowers, to a horse galloping riderless. "He has such a fine eye, and his traveling shots of horses and riders are a hint of what tremendous cowboy flicks he might have made, in a straighter age," wrote Anthony Lane in the *New Yorker*. But something happens to the pace and the poise of *Django Unchained* as the hunters head South and the screen fills with the word "Mississippi."

The second half of the film finds Tarantino quitting those beautiful Leone-inspired vistas and hunkering down in the heat, stillness, and stagnation of Candyland, the plantation where Django's wife, Broomhilda (Kerry Washington), is enslaved by her master, Calvin Candie (Leonardo DiCaprio), a brocaded foppish epicurean who lords over brutal "Mandingo" wrestling matches between his slaves, in which arms are broken and eyeballs are popped from their sockets. Tarantino's theater of cruelty here finds its most detestable, debonair ringmaster, played with almost indecent flair by DiCaprio, delivering long, hateful speeches on phrenology while he raps his fingers on the skull of a former manservant. There's only one problem: The picture already has its big talker, Schultz, who now has to choose between long passages of near silence and competing feats of loquacity. He turns the film into a Mexican standoff of dueling mouths.

CALVIN CANDIE
White cake?

DR. KING SCHULTZ
I don't go in for sweets, thank you.

CALVIN CANDIE
Are you brooding 'bout me getting the best of ya, huh?

DR. KING SCHULTZ

Actually, I was thinking of that poor devil you fed to the dogs today, D'Artagnan. And I was wondering what Dumas would make of all this.

CALVIN CANDIE

Come again?

DR. KING SCHULTZ

Alexandre Dumas. He wrote *The Three Musketeers*. I figured you must be an admirer. You named your slave after his novel's lead character. If Alexandre Dumas had been there today, I wonder what he would have made of it?

CALVIN CANDIE

You doubt he'd approve?

DR. KING SCHULTZ

Yes. His approval would be a dubious proposition at best.

Who knew that the writer who penned *Reservoir Dogs* and *Pulp Fiction*—masterpieces of hard American demotic—would write such fragrant, frilly-laced exchanges? Tarantino has always had a soft spot for rhetorical archaism: In *Pulp Fiction*, Samuel L. Jackson says "Well, allow me to retort," to his captive audience of terrified preppies, but you could see the fear on their faces, and the scene lasted just five minutes; it had you pinned to your seat before you even knew what was happening. DiCaprio's phrenology lecture, by contrast, is delivered during a dinner table scene lasting twenty-

five minutes, more than enough time for the suspicions to gather that Calvin Candie is, like Bill before him, a world-class bore.

The film ends with Django taking his revenge, redecorating the walls of Candie's Southern mansion with blood that "has its own ballet movements," as David Thomson wrote in the *New Republic.* "It's Jackson Pollock on speed; and it spouts from bodies the way oil arrives in *Giant* or jism comes in a porno movie. It can't wait to get out of the bodies."

The viewer is pondering how many of Tarantino's movies make the same plot transition, from movement to confinement to explosion, like an antsy teenager trapped in his room. By the time Tarantino shows up as an Australian redneck, the film has "mislaid its melancholy, and its bitter wit, and become a raucous romp," wrote Anthony Lane. "It is a tribute to the spaghetti western, cooked *al dente,* then cooked a while more, and finally sauced to death."

The film won Oscars for Christoph Waltz for Best Supporting Actor and Tarantino for Best Original Screenplay, the film's taboo-busting take on slavery lending it a weight that played well with the Academy, for all the film's snickering wit. "In placing his story of righteous payback in the Old South rather than the Wild West, and in making its agent a black former slave, Tarantino exposes and defies an ancient taboo," wrote A. O. Scott in the *New York Times.* "When you wipe away the blood and the anarchic humor, what you see in *Django Unchained* is moral disgust with slavery, instinctive sympathy for the underdog and an affirmation (in the relationship between Django and Schultz) of what used to be called brotherhood."

TOP: Like many Tarantino characters, sadistic Calvin Candie delights in violently asserting his authority. BOTTOM: Tarantino makes a brief cameo as an Australian redneck. OPPOSITE: Shooting the bloody massacre at Candie's mansion.

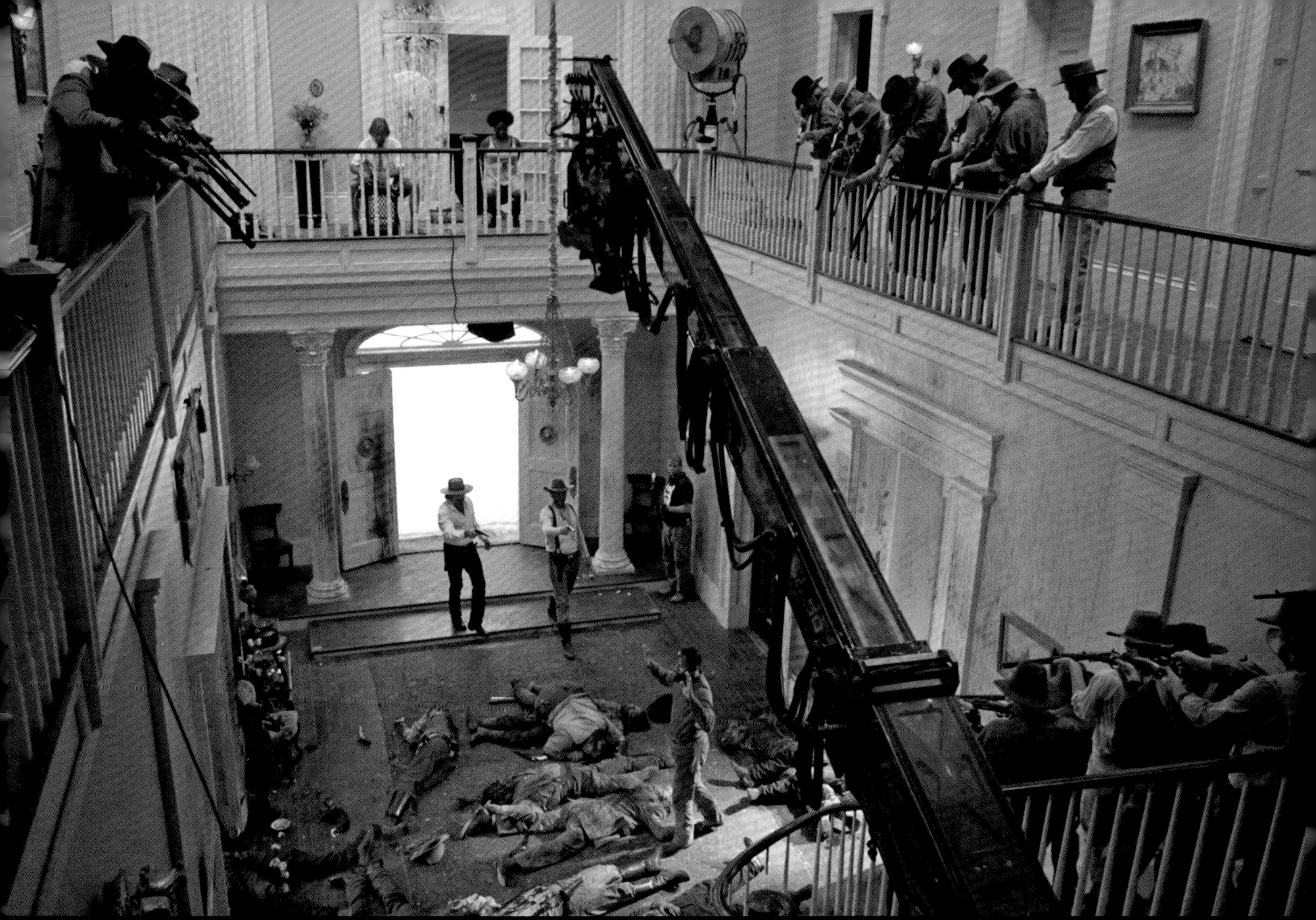

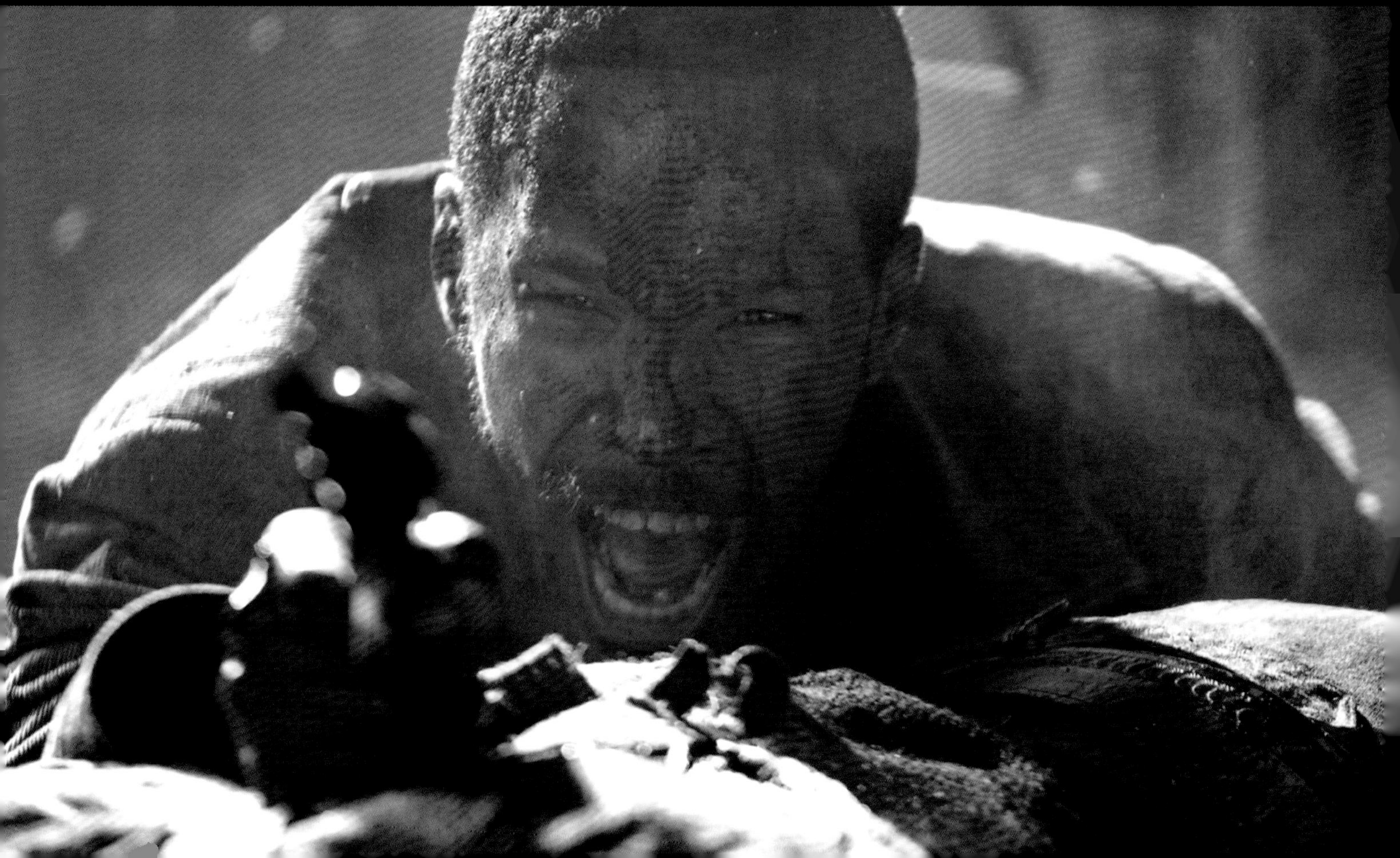

THE HATEFUL EIGHT

2015

ABOVE: The blizzard forces John Ruth (Kurt Russell) to offer transport to his fellow bounty hunter Major Marquis Warren (Samuel L. Jackson). OPPOSITE: After the "very depressing" leak of the script, the energy of the cast and positive audience reaction at the live reading in Los Angeles prompted Tarantino to finally make the movie.

WHILE perusing his collection of shows like *Bonanza*, *The Big Valley*, and *The Virginian* after shooting *Django Unchained*, Tarantino came up with the kernel of the idea that became *The Hateful Eight.* "Twice per season, those shows would have an episode where a bunch of outlaws would take the lead characters hostage . . . I thought, 'What if I did a movie starring nothing but those characters? No heroes. Just a bunch of nefarious guys in a room, all telling backstories that may or may not be true. Trap those guys together in a room with a blizzard outside, give them guns, and see what happens.'"

In Tarantino's version, a bounty hunter, John Ruth (Kurt Russell), is trying to deliver a fugitive named Daisy Domergue (Jennifer Jason Leigh) to Red Rock, where she'll be hanged and he'll collect a $10,000 reward. Along the way, the pair gets caught in a blizzard and ends up trapped with six other strangers in Minnie's Haberdashery, a ramshackle roadside inn.

Owing as much to the parlor-room whodunit as the wide-screen western, the script prompted its own round of sleuthing when, in January 2014, gossip website Gawker published a link to a leaked draft of the script. Tarantino was "devastated," suing Gawker and announcing that he was no longer planning to make the movie.

"Y'know, all my movies are surrounded by some sort of stupid controversy that is really only of the moment. Then cut to eight years later, you're watching it on TNT. All right, so how f***ing controversial is it?"

"It was very much a work in progress," said producer Stacey Sher. "Then . . . Boom! The next thing we knew, people were saying they'd read the script, and suddenly it was on the Internet. I absolutely thought it was not going to happen. I thought he was just going to publish it and not make the movie."

So few people had seen the script at that point that suspicion quickly narrowed down to just six suspects: Michael Madsen, Tim Roth, Bruce Dern, *Django Unchained* producer Reginald Hudlin, and two unnamed agents who had been given the script by Hudlin or one of the actors. "It was one of six," insisted Tarantino, finally calming down after a trip to the Cannes Film Festival for a twentieth-anniversary screening of *Pulp Fiction*. If Tarantino knows who the culprit is, he has never said.

Deciding to roll with what had happened, Tarantino gave a live script reading at the Theater at Ace Hotel, Los Angeles, four months after the script was leaked, with Samuel L. Jackson, Kurt Russell, Dern, Walton Goggins, and Madsen. "The energy in that theater was so big," said Madsen. "It was just big. And afterwards Quentin said, 'Wow, that really went well. I didn't think it would go that well.' And we were like, 'Yeah, it did, man.' It seems to me like that's when he made the decision to make the movie."

In early June, Tarantino called producer Stacey Sher, and the project was back on. He rewrote the script, making changes to its ending. "The ending wasn't meant to be the end. It was an end," he said. "The Lincoln letter was brought up once, and that was it. I knew I wanted to do more with the letter." Most of the actors who participated in the reading ended up with parts in the film, except for Amber Tamblyn, who had read the part of Daisy but was replaced by Jennifer Jason Leigh.

Wanting to shoot in the Rocky Mountains in the middle of winter using old-fashioned Ultra Panavision 70, Tarantino had to refurbish and test the lenses he wanted to use—the same ones

used to film 1959's *Ben-Hur*—to make sure they could withstand the extreme cold. "They had an incredibly wet summer, so we should have an incredibly snowy winter," he enthused. "Should be deep snow, the Rockies right behind us, and part of the idea for shooting it out there is that cold makes for misery."

Beginning in January 2015, the team shot on location in Telluride, where the temperature sometimes dipped to minus ten or minus twenty degrees Fahrenheit. Despite having rehearsed the material, they never knew more than three days in advance what the weather was going to be, which wreaked havoc with their running order and threw the whole shoot off. They ended up having to follow the weather. If it was snowing, they would head outside for the falling snow scenes. It if was overcast or foggy, they were in the stagecoach. If it was sunny, they headed into a full-size version of Minnie's Haberdashery built outdoors. "So the idea of starting a scene and emotionally taking it till its very end, that was all gone," said Tarantino.

Shooting inside the one-room cabin that had been built on a soundstage, Tarantino maintained a chilly thirty-five-degree room temperature inside the set so that the actors' breath would be visible.

"It was bitter cold," said Leigh. "Do I get out of the stagecoach and walk to the tent where there's a heater that's a football field away? Or do I just sit in the snow?"

Almost all of Tarantino's movies to this point had been without original scores—although parts of *Kill Bill* were scored by Robert Rodriguez, intercut with portions of Ennio Morricone's old scores—but for *The Hateful Eight*, Tarantino went to Morricone himself.

"There was something about this movie, more than the others—and maybe I was a little precious about it—but I thought it deserved its own theme, something that hadn't been in anything else," Tarantino said.

While he was in Rome to collect unclaimed prizes for *Pulp Fiction* and *Django Unchained* at the David di Donatello Awards, Tarantino dropped around to the composer's house. When Morricone asked when he planned to start shooting, Tarantino told him the film had already wrapped.

"Oh, that's not going to work," said Morricone, who was about to start work on a Giuseppe Tornatore film in a few weeks.

But he remembered that he had some music left over from John Carpenter's 1982 version of *The Thing*, and realized he could repurpose it. He recorded a string version, a brass version,

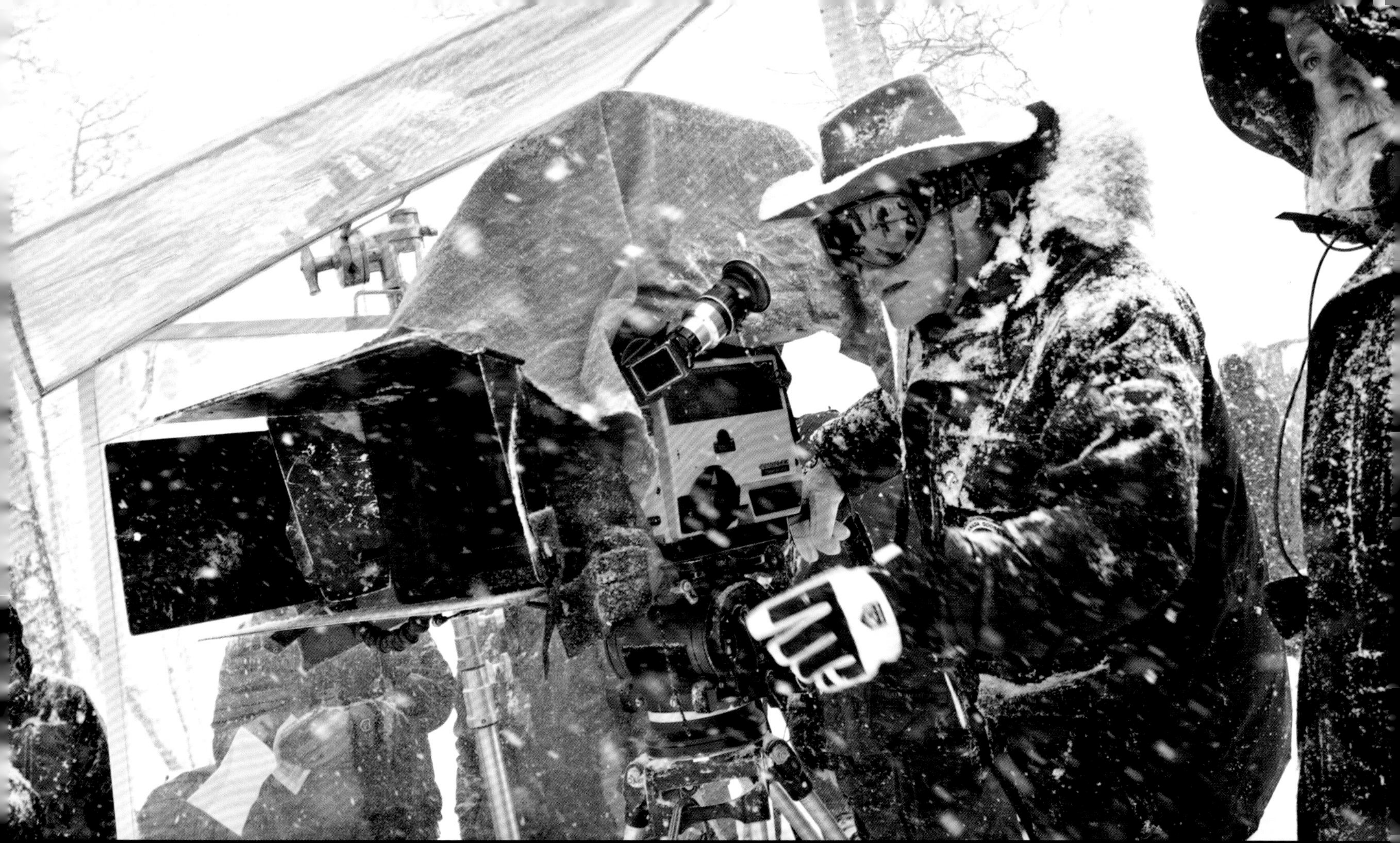

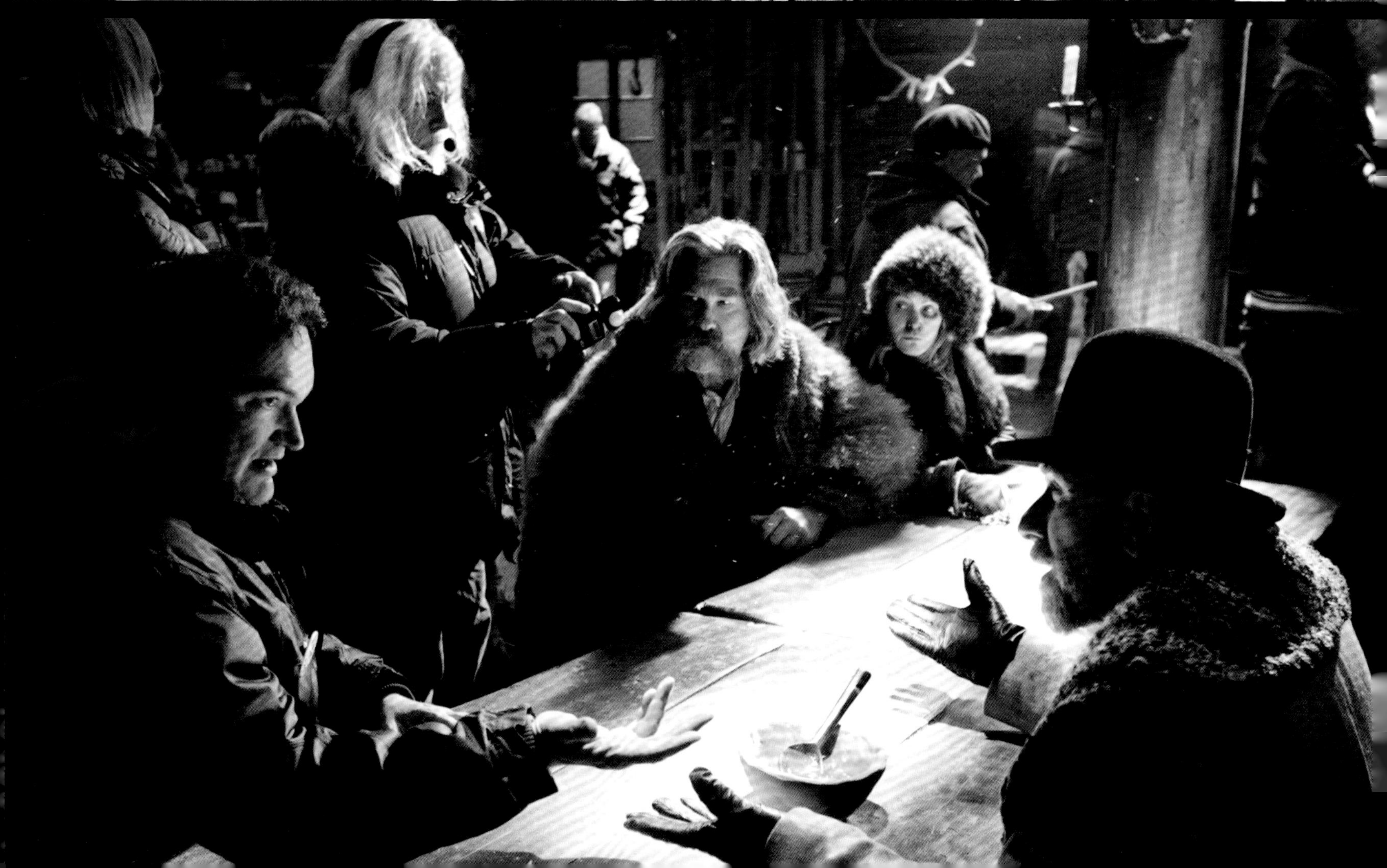

and a full orchestral version for Tarantino to use as he saw fit. *The Thing*'s air of wintery claustrophobia and paranoia made a perfect fit in the composer's mind.

"Quentin Tarantino considers this film a western," Morricone said. "For me, this is not a western."

Listening to the intense, propulsive, brooding score—written without Morricone having seen the film, and closer in some ways to the motifs of the Italian horror or giallo movie—Tarantino was at first non-plussed. "I needed to listen to it for two or three days even before I talked about it with my editor," he said. "Then I go, 'What do you think about it?' And he said, 'It's weird. I like it. But it's weird. It's not what I was expecting.' And I said, 'Me too!'"

By the end, mostly thanks to the weather, the $44 million production had gone $16 million over budget. It would also cost the Weinstein Company another $10 million to find and refurbish enough 70mm projectors to show the film in Tarantino's preferred format, most theaters having converted to digital projection. The fact that *Django Unchained* and *Inglourious Basterds* had kept the company afloat with a combined gross of $746 million helped. Releasing the film in 2,500 digital-projection theaters, the Weinsteins bankrolled a one-hundred–theater, limited-run 70mm road show, complete with an old-school twelve-minute intermission and souvenir program. The director was "on edge" in the last few weeks before release. On Christmas Day, Tarantino dropped into the end of an 11.00 a.m. screening of the film at the Del Amo Mall in Torrance, where he had done much of his teenage movie-watching.

"I watched the last chapter play," he said. "It was real dark when I got there and I couldn't see anything and then there was a close-up of Sam Jackson and his white sleeve, and it lit up the theater and I went, holy shit, it's sold out. On Christmas Day. I went outside and hung by

KRISTOPHER TAPLEY
VARIETY

"The industry march toward digital standardization is inevitable. But **Quentin Tarantino's** new film **"The Hateful Eight"** is a reminder that, underlying the romance of those who rage against the dying of the flickering projector light, is an unyielding passion.

Filmed in the **Ultra Panavision 70** format, capturing big, bold frames that allow for unique and creative visual storytelling flourishes, this dynamic genre piece is a testament to the benefits of embracing the hard work that forged the industry. New frontiers will surely, and necessarily, spark new creative revolutions, but the ghosts of cinema have something to teach us yet."

THE 8TH FILM BY
QUENTIN TARANTINO

THE HATEFUL EIGHT

SEE IT EXCLUSIVELY AT THIS LOCATION IN
GLORIOUS 70MM

OPPOSITE: Samuel L. Jackson as Major Marquis Warren. *The Hateful Eight* marked his eighth collaboration with Tarantino. ABOVE: Poster advertising the release of *The Hateful Eight*'s limited run in one hundred specially refurbished 70mm projector cinemas.

PAGES 234–235: The tension is too much to bear for John, Daisy, and General Sandy Smithers (Bruce Dern) as the Hateful Eight start to turn on each other. ABOVE: Down but not out. Daisy Domergue is bruised and battered by her captor, John Ruth. OPPOSITE: Major Warren stands guard over his cadavers.

the Johnny Rockets and watched the people come out. They were hanging onto their programs and I could see they really liked the film. I was surprised how touched I was, to see people heading out to their cars and clutching their *Hateful Eight* programs."

Set in the wide, open plainland of Wyoming and filmed in sumptuous, wide-screen 70mm Ultra Panavision, *The Hateful Eight* nevertheless amounts to Tarantino's most cramped movie. Much of the first half is spent in a stagecoach, and the rest of the movie—barring brief trips to a stable and an outhouse—is spent in a lonely saloon where a collection of characters seeking shelter from a blizzard serve each other coffee and stew.

En route to Red Rock with Daisy Domergue, John Ruth unhappily takes on two additional passengers—Major Marquis Warren (Samuel L. Jackson), a bounty hunter, former Union officer, and an old acquaintance of Ruth's, who is transporting the cadavers of three men wanted dead or alive; and Chris Mannix (Walton Goggins), a garrulous Southerner who will soon be assuming the post of Red Rock's sheriff. Already ensconced by the fireplace at Minnie's is an aged Confederate general (Bruce Dern); a dandyish and punctiliously eloquent British hangman (Tim Roth); a gruff and taciturn diarist (Michael Madsen); and a Mexican wanderer who is temporarily managing the place (Demián Bichir).

Everyone is said to be strangers but—cued up by the sinister swells of Ennio Morricone's score—doubts form. As suspicions rise in this hothouse of unwanted intimacy, sparks fly

"*Django* was definitely the beginning of my political side, and I think *Hateful Eight* is the logical extension and conclusion of that. In a weird way, *Django* was the question and *Hateful Eight* is the answer."

and violence finally erupts, igniting a Grand Guignol finale of crime and punishment. "There is some real heat—some real hate—in the confrontation between Mr. Jackson and Mr. Dern, whose acting rises above the mannered self-consciousness that Mr. Tarantino's writing often calls forth," wrote A. O. Scott in the *New York Times*.

However, the bigger contest by far is between Quentin Tarantino: writer and Quentin Tarantino: director. At the very start of his career, the writer-director told an audience at the 1992 Toronto Film Festival, "I never see myself as a writer, I see myself as a director who writes stuff for me to do." But, as he later told Robert Rodriguez, writing later became "more and more important to me. That first real flash of excitement is always when I'm writing something that should go this way and all of a sudden inspiration happens and it goes somewhere else and I'm party to it."

In *The Hateful Eight*, the writer in Tarantino has the director in him pinned to the ground, defeated. It's a *Bonanza*-style Agatha Christie mystery, with Marquis in the Hercule Poirot role, except Tarantino hasn't bothered to concoct the mystery himself. There's no body and no crime to solve, and in the absence of a clear set-up, the characters are forced to concoct controversy themselves. They are,

like characters in an Ionesco play debating the contrivance by which they have been made to meet, miniature dramatists who turn the saloon into a stage, perform, take their bows, and are blown away: Reservoir Dogs reduced to their barest dramatic DNA.

"A beastly brew: a blend of Agatha Christie and Sergio Leone, spiked with postmodernist poison," concluded Anthony Lane in the *New Yorker*, singling out Jennifer Jason Leigh's performance as Daisy Domergue as the highlight. "One slow look that she gives, raising her face, with a black eye and a crinkled grin, to fill the screen, may be the most convincing portrait of wickedness—and of its demonic appeal—in all of Tarantino. With that smile alone, Leigh possesses the film."

"Consider his last on-set bloodbath, *Reservoir Dogs*, nowhere near as accomplished a piece of moviemaking but full of psychological cross-currents and emotional quandaries," wrote David Edelstein in *New York* magazine. "Tarantino has left emotional quandaries behind. He's in the grindhouse revenge ether now, high on his own silly, can-you-top-this gross-out carnage. You wonder what he has up his sleeve in *The Hateful Eight*, but gorgeous as that sleeve might be, what's up it is crap. The movie is a lot of gore over a lot of nothing. I hope that won't be Tarantino's epitaph."

OPPOSITE: The appearance of Daisy's brother, Jody, played by Channing Tatum, is one of the film's biggest surprises. TOP: Michael Madsen, in his third Tarantino film, plays the "cow puncher" Joe Gage. BOTTOM: No one to trust. Paranoia sets in as new Red Rock sheriff Chris Mannix (Walton Goggins) keeps watch. PAGES 240–241: Armed and dangerous. The climactic western-inspired gun fight ensues.

"I was in a real kind of funky area when I wrote the script. I kind of had a lot of anger in me, and so it all came out in the script. And that was good. That was a good place to put it."

EPILOGUE

TARANTINO has spoken often of his desire to quit directing once he reaches ten movies. "I think it's pretty safe to say that directing is a young man's game," he told the *Hollywood Reporter* in 2013. "Directors really don't get better as they get older. When I was making *Pulp Fiction*, I would have died for the movie, and if I don't feel that way, I don't want to put my name on it. I almost feel that I owe it to people who like my stuff. I don't want to burn out, all right? If a guy like me likes my stuff, maybe he saw *Reservoir Dogs* when he was twenty, or maybe he saw *Reservoir Dogs* when he was my age, or maybe this guy I'm talking about isn't even born yet, all right? Maybe he's born today and he's going to catch up with my shit when he gets older. I don't want him to have to make excuses for the last twenty years of my career, because I've championed directors before, and you're always making excuses. That's my big thing: I'm not going to burn out."

to movies is the day I want to quit. It's not a part-time thing. It's my life."

PAGE 242: Portrait by William Callan, 2016. ABOVE: The next project? Tarantino has spoken of his desire to adapt another Elmore Leonard novel, *Forty Lashes Less One*, as a TV miniseries.

Over the years, there have been enough almost-Tarantino movies to form a bizarro-world B-career. After *Reservoir Dogs* in 1992, he considered adapting the Marvel comic book *Luke Cage: Hero for Hire*, one of Marvel's first African-American heroes, and discussed the role with Laurence Fishburne. After the success of *Pulp Fiction* in 1994, his name was linked with an adaptation of *Modesty Blaise*, the comic strip/adventure novel Vincent Vega was seen reading on the toilet, as well as a version of *The Man from U.N.C.L.E.* He also spent decades talking up a possible project, known as either *Double V Vega* or *The Vega Brothers*, teaming up *Reservoir Dogs*'s Vic Vega (Michael Madsen) and *Pulp Fiction*'s Vincent Vega (John Travolta). As the years ticked by, he even factored in the actors' advancing ages. "I actually came up with a way I could have done it, even being older and dead, where they all had older brothers and both of their brothers got together because the two guys died," he said. "And they wanted revenge or something like that."

In the late 1990s, there was talk of him taking on a "small-scale, plot-driven" version of *Casino Royale*—the one Ian Fleming novel that, at that point, hadn't been given serious treatment—but after Pierce Brosnan departed the franchise in 2005, Tarantino lost interest. "That wouldn't have been just throwing my hat in the franchise ring; that would have been subversion on a massive level, if I could have subverted Bond," he said.

There was also talk of an adaptation of Len Deighton's Cold War spy thriller, *Berlin Game*; a remake of *The Psychic*, Lucio Fulci's 1977 horror film about a clairvoyant, with possibly Bridget Fonda in the lead; and a project the director fancifully described as "a cool sex movie" set in Stockholm, with a couple of Americans visiting a couple of Swedish friends. Tarantino described the latter as "kind of like the girls in *Death Proof*, just going out drinking, having a good time, hooking up."

He hasn't spoken of any of these projects in years. More likely to see the light of day is the TV miniseries he has talked of adapting from Elmore

Leonard's 1972 novel, *Forty Lashes Less One,* about two death-row prisoners, an Apache and a black former soldier who are given a chance to be set free if they can hunt down and kill the five worst outlaws in the West. Tarantino owns the rights and has completed twenty pages of a script, and he recently reiterated his desire to make a stablemate for *Django Unchained* and *The Hateful Eight.* "If you're going to call yourself a western director today, you need to do at least three," he said. "And I would really like to do it as a miniseries, like an hour an episode, four or five hours—I'd write and direct it all. And it's right along the lines of *Django* and *Hateful Eight,* as it deals with race, and it all takes place in a territorial prison. It's a really good book, and I've always wanted to tell that story, so we'll see."

He has also mentioned his desire to make a children's film, a Howard Hawks–style screwball romantic comedy, a biopic about abolitionist John Brown, and a "reimagining of a 1930s gangster movie, set in Australia. "It would be a *Bonnie and Clyde*–ish story with a couple of outlaws in Australia." Then there is his possible prequel to *Inglourious Basterds,* adapted from the material that didn't make it into the final shooting script, involving Aldo and Danny and "following a platoon of black troops that were court-martialed and they escape. They are in France, they are going to be hung in London, and their whole thing is to get to Switzerland. And they end up getting into an adventure, and they meet the Basterds," he said. "So I could still do that."

The most eagerly awaited of his projects is probably *Kill Bill: Volume 3.* Having put Beatrix Kiddo through so much in the first two films, he's in no hurry to shatter her hard-won domestic peace but recently said, "I wouldn't be surprised if the Bride made one more appearance before the whole thing is said and done. I've been talking to Uma about it just a little bit. I'm thinking, 'Okay, now, thirteen years later, what would be going on with Sofie Fatale; what would be going on with Elle Driver?'" He already has a plot in place: "Sofie Fatale will get all of Bill's

ABOVE: Leaving his mark on Hollywood. Tarantino's hand and footprints on the historic Walk of Fame outside Grauman's Chinese Theatre, California.

money. She'll raise Nikki [the daughter of Vivica A. Fox's character], who'll take on the Bride. Nikki deserves her revenge every bit as much as the Bride deserved hers."

After three period pieces in a row, he also longs to get back to the present. "It would be really great to do another movie where a TV's on in the background or somebody turns on a radio, and then I can score my scene that way, and then turn it off when I want the music to stop. Or they get into a car and drive for a while, and I can actually do a little montage of them driving to some cool song. That would be really great. I haven't done that in a long time, and I'm really looking forward to it."

Beyond that, the pages are blank. Tarantino has spoken often of turning his attention to writing novels and film criticism, although he won't rule out television or theater work. In 2007, he bought a revival theater, the New Beverly Cinema, and became the programming director there, frequently screening prints from his private collection.

"I've started to realize that I'm a frustrated theater owner," Tarantino said. "I'll move out of Los Angeles—somewhere where I can live to a hundred, maybe Montana or something, someplace with good air—and buy some little movie theater. I'll have all my prints, and I'll just show them, and that'll be my thing. I'll be the crazy old guy in town that has that little movie theater. That seems like a really cool old-guy life!"

RIGHT: Planning for retirement. Tarantino is pictured outside his New Beverly Cinema in Los Angeles.

FILMOGRAPHY

Release/broadcast dates are for the United States (general release) unless stated.

Love Birds in Bondage
Unfinished short, 1983
(Novacaine Films)
Directors & Screenplay: Quentin Tarantino, Scott Magill
Cinematography: Scott Magill
Editor: Scott Magill
Cast: Quentin Tarantino (boyfriend)

My Best Friend's Birthday
Unfinished short, 1987, 69 minutes
Director: Quentin Tarantino
Screenplay: Quentin Tarantino, Craig Hamann
Cinematography: Roger Avary, Scott Magill, Roberto A. Quezada, Rand Vossler
Producers: Quentin Tarantino, Craig Hamann, Rand Vossler
Editor: Quentin Tarantino
Cast: Quentin Tarantino (Clarence Pool), Craig Hamann (Mickey Burnett), Crystal Shaw Martell (Misty), Allen Garfield (Entertainment Magnate), Al Harrell (Clifford), Rich Turner (Oliver Brandon)

Vegetables
Short video film, 1989, 90 minutes
Director: Laura Lovelace
Cast: Quentin Tarantino

Past Midnight
(Cinetel Films)
First shown October 1991 (Vancouver International Film Festival), 100 minutes
Director: Jan Eliasberg
Screenplay: Frank Norwood
Cinematography: Robert D. Yeoman
Producer: Lisa M. Hansen
Editor: Christopher Rouse
Associate Producer: Quentin Tarantino
Cast: Rutger Hauer (Ben Jordan), Natasha Richardson (Laura Mathews), Clancy Brown (Steve Lundy)

Reservoir Dogs
(Live Entertainment/Dog Eat Dog Productions)
First shown January 21, 1992 (Sundance Film Festival),
Opened October 23, 1992 (limited general release),
99 minutes
Director: Quentin Tarantino
Screenplay: Quentin Tarantino, Roger Avary
Cinematography: Andrzej Sekula
Producer: Lawrence Bender
Editor: Sally Menke
Cast: Quentin Tarantino (Mr. Brown), Harvey Keitel (Mr. White), Tim Roth (Mr. Orange), Michael Madsen (Mr. Blonde), Edward Bunker (Mr. Blue), Steve Buscemi (Mr. Pink), Chris Penn (Nice Guy Eddie Cabot), Lawrence Tierney (Joe Cabot)

Eddie Presley
First shown March 1992 (South by Southwest Film Festival), 106 minutes
Director: Jeff Burr
Screenplay: Duane Whitaker
Cinematography: Thomas L. Callaway
Producers: William Burr, Chuck Williams
Editor: Jay Woelfel
Cast: Quentin Tarantino (cameo as asylum attendant), Duane Whitaker (Eddie Presley), Lawrence Tierney (Joe West)

True Romance
(Morgan Creek Productions/Davis-Films/August Entertainment/Sterling MacFadden)
Opened September 10, 1993, 120 minutes
Director: Tony Scott
Screenplay: Quentin Tarantino
Cinematography: Jeffrey L. Kimball
Producers: Gary Barber, Samuel Hadida, Steve Perry, Bill Unger
Editors: Michael Tronick, Christian Wagner
Cast: Christian Slater (Clarence Worley), Patricia Arquette (Alabama Whitman), Dennis Hopper (Clifford Worley), Val Kilmer (Mentor), Gary Oldman (Drexl Spivey), Brad Pitt (Floyd), Christopher Walken (Vincenzo Coccotti), Samuel L. Jackson (Big Don), Michael Rapaport (Dick Ritchie)

Killing Zoe
(Davis-Films/Live Entertainment/PFG Entertainment)
First shown October 1993 (Raindance Film Festival),
Opened September 1994, 96 minutes
Director & Screenplay: Roger Avary
Cinematography: Tom Richmond
Producer: Samuel Hadida
Editor: Kathryn Himoff
Executive producers: Quentin Tarantino, Lawrence Bender, Rebecca Boss
Cast: Eric Stoltz (Zed), Julie Delpy (Zoe), Jean-Hugues Anglade (Eric), Gary Kemp (Oliver), Bruce Ramsay (Ricardo)

The Coriolis Effect
(Secondary Modern Motion Pictures/Vanguard International Cinema)
First shown March 26, 1994 (New York New Directors and New Films Festival), 33 minutes
Director & Screenplay: Louis Venosta
Cinematography: Paul Holahan
Producer: Kathryn Arnold
Editor: Luis Colina
Cast: Quentin Tarantino (voice of Panhandle Slim), Dana Ashbrook (Ray), Corrine Bohrer (Suzy), David Patch (Terry), Jennifer Rubin (Ruby), James Wilder (Stanley)

Pulp Fiction
(Miramax/A Band Apart/Jersey Films)
First shown May 21, 1994 (Cannes Film Festival),
Opened October 14, 1994, 154 minutes
Director: Quentin Tarantino
Screenplay: Quentin Tarantino, Roger Avary
Cinematographer: Andrzej Sekula
Producer: Lawrence Bender

Editor: Sally Menke
Cast: Quentin Tarantino (Jimmie), John Travolta (Vincent Vega), Uma Thurman (Mia Wallace), Samuel L. Jackson (Jules Winnfield), Bruce Willis (Butch Coolidge), Ving Rhames (Marsellus Wallace), Amanda Plummer (Honey Bunny), Tim Roth (Pumpkin), Harvey Keitel (The Wolf), Christopher Walken (Captain Koons), Eric Stoltz (Lance)

Natural Born Killers

(Warner Bros./Regency Enterprises/Alcor Films/Ixtlan/New Regency Pictures/J D Productions)
Opened August 26, 1994, 118 minutes
Director: Oliver Stone
Story & Screenplay: Quentin Tarantino, David Veloz, Richard Rutowski, Oliver Stone
Cinematography: Robert Richardson
Producers: Jane Hamsher, Don Murphy, Clayton Townsend
Editors: Brian Berdan, Hank Corwin
Cast: Woody Harrelson (Mickey Knox), Juliette Lewis (Mallory Knox), Tom Sizemore (Det. Jack Scagnetti), Robert Downey, Jr. (Wayne Gale), Tommy Lee Jones (Warden Dwight McClusky)

Sleep with Me

(August Entertainment/Castleberg Productions/Paribas Film Corporation)
First shown September 10, 1994 (Toronto International Film Festival), 86 minutes
Director: Rory Kelly
Screenplay: Duane Dell'Amico, Roger Hedden, Neal Jimenez, Joe Keenan, Rory Kelly, Michael Steinberg
Cinematography: Andrzej Sekula
Producers: Roger Hedden, Michael Steinberg, Eric Stoltz
Editor: David Moritz
Cast: Quentin Tarantino (Sid), Meg Tilly (Sarah), Eric Stoltz (Joseph), Craig Sheffer (Frank), Lewis Arquette (Minister), Todd Field (Duane)

Somebody to Love

(Cabin Fever Entertainment/Initial Productions/Lumière Pictures)
First shown September, 1994 (Venice Film Festival), Opened September 27, 1996, 102 minutes
Director: Alexandre Rockwell
Screenplay: Sergei Bodrov, Alexandre Rockwell
Cinematography: Robert D. Yeoman
Producer: Lila Cazès
Editor: Elena Maganini
Cast: Quentin Tarantino (Bartender), Rosie Perez (Mercedes), Harvey Keitel (Harry Harrelson), Anthony Quinn (Emillio), Michael DeLorenzo (Ernesto), Steve Buscemi (Mickey)

Destiny Turns on the Radio

(Rysher Entertainment/Savoy Pictures)
Opened April 28, 1995, 102 minutes
Director: Jack Baran
Screenplay: Robert Ramsey, Matthew Stone
Cinematography: James L. Carter
Producer: Gloria Zimmerman
Editor: Raúl Dávalos
Cast: Quentin Tarantino (Johnny Destiny), Dylan McDermott (Julian Goddard), Nancy Travis (Lucille), James Le Gros (Thoreau), Jim Belushi (Tuerto)

Crimson Tide

(Hollywood Pictures/Don Simpson-Jerry Bruckheimer)
Opened May 12, 1995, 116 minutes
Director: Tony Scott
Screenplay: Michael Schiffer, Richard P. Henrick, Quentin Tarantino (uncredited)
Cinematography: Dariusz Wolski
Producers: Jerry Bruckheimer, Don Simpson
Editor: Chris Lebenzon
Cast: Denzel Washington (Hunter), Gene Hackman (Ramsey), Matt Craven (Zimmer), George Dzundza (Cob), Viggo Mortensen (Weps), James Gandolfini (Lt. Bobby Dougherty)

Desperado

(Columbia Pictures Corporation/Los Hooligans Productions)
First shown May 1995 (Cannes Film Festival), Opened August 25, 1995, 104 minutes
Director & Screenplay: Robert Rodriguez
Cinematography: Guillermo Navarro
Producers: Bill Borden, Robert Rodriguez
Editor: Robert Rodriguez
Cast: Quentin Tarantino (Pick-up Guy), Antonio Banderas (El Mariachi), Salma Hayek (Carolina), Joaquim de Almeida (Bucho), Steve Buscemi (Buscemi)

Four Rooms

Anthology film with Allison Anders, Alexandre Rockwell, and Robert Rodriguez
Tarantino segment "The Man from Hollywood" (Miramax/A Band Apart)
First shown September 16, 1995 (Toronto International Film Festival), Opened December 25, 1995, 98 minutes
Director & Screenplay: Quentin Tarantino
Cinematographer: Andrzej Sekula
Producer: Lawrence Bender
Editor: Sally Menke
Cast: Quentin Tarantino (Chester), Jennifer Beals (Angela), Paul Calderon (Norman), Bruce Willis (Leo–uncredited)

Hands Up

First shown 1995
Director & Screenplay: Virginie Thévenet
Producer: Kaz Kuzui, Fran Rubel Kuzui
Cast: Quentin Tarantino, Charlotte Gainsbourg

From Dusk Till Dawn

(Dimension Films/A Band Apart/Los Hooligans Productions/Miramax)
Opened January 19, 1996, 108 minutes
Director: Robert Rodriguez
Screenplay: Quentin Tarantino, Robert Kurtzman

Cinematography: Guillermo Navarro
Producers: Gianni Nunnari, Meir Teper
Editor: Robert Rodriguez
Cast: Quentin Tarantino (Richard Gecko), George Clooney (Seth Gecko), Harvey Keitel (Jacob Fuller), Juliette Lewis (Kate Fuller), Ernest Liu (Scott Fuller), Salma Hayek (Santanico Pandemonium)

Girl 6
(Fox Searchlight Pictures/40 Acres & A Mule Filmworks)
Opened March 22, 1996, 108 minutes
Director: Spike Lee
Screenplay: Suzan-Lori Parks
Cinematography: Malik Hassan Sayeed
Producer: Spike Lee
Editor: Samuel D. Pollard
Cast: Quentin Tarantino (Director #1), Theresa Randle (Girl 6), John Turturro (Murray)

Curdled
(A Band Apart/Tinderbox Films)
First shown September 6, 1996 (Toronto International Film Festival), Opened September 27, 1996, 88 minutes
Director: Reb Braddock
Screenplay: Quentin Tarantino (segment "Gecko Brothers News Report"), Reb Braddock, John Maass
Cinematography: Steven Bernstein
Producers: John Maass, Raul Puig
Executive Producer: Quentin Tarantino
Editor: Mallory Gottlieb
Cast: Quentin Tarantino (Richard Gecko), William Baldwin (Paul Guell), Angela Jones (Gabriela), Bruce Ramsay (Eduardo), Lois Chiles (Katrina Brandt)

Jackie Brown
(Miramax/A Band Apart/Lawrence Bender Productions/Mighty Mighty Afrodite Productions)
Opened December 25, 1997, 154 minutes
Director & Screenplay: Quentin Tarantino
Cinematography: Guillermo Navarro
Producer: Lawrence Bender
Editor: Sally Menke
Cast: Pam Grier (Jackie Brown), Samuel L. Jackson (Ordell Robbie), Robert Forster (Max Cherry), Bridget Fonda (Melanie Ralston), Michael Keaton (Ray Nicolette), Robert De Niro (Louis Gara), Chris Tucker (Beaumont Livingston)

God Said, 'Ha!'
(Oh, Brother Productions)
First shown March 14, 1998 (South by Southwest Film Festival), 85 minutes
Director & Screenplay: Julia Sweeney
Cinematography: John Hora
Editor: Fabienne Rawley
Producer: Rana Joy Glickman
Executive producer: Quentin Tarantino
Cast: Quentin Tarantino (himself), Julia Sweeney (herself)

From Dusk Till Dawn 2: Texas Blood Money
(A Band Apart/Dimension Films/Los Hooligans Productions)
Released on video March 16, 1999, 88 minutes
Director: Scott Spiegel
Screenplay: Scott Spiegel, Duane Whitaker
Cinematography: Philip Lee
Producers: Michael S. Murphey, Gianni Nunnari, Meir Teper
Executive producers: Quentin Tarantino, Lawrence Bender, Robert Rodriguez
Editor: Bob Murawski
Cast: Robert Patrick (Buck), Bo Hopkins (Sheriff Otis Lawson), Duane Whitaker (Luther), Muse Watson (C. W. Niles), Brett Harrelson (Ray Bob)

From Dusk Till Dawn 3: The Hangman's Daughter
(A Band Apart/Dimension Films/Los Hooligans Productions)
Released on video January 18, 2000, 94 minutes
Director: P. J. Pesce
Screenplay: Álvaro Rodríguez
Cinematography: Michael Bonvillain
Producers: Michael S. Murphey, Gianni Nunnari, Meir Teper, H. Daniel Gross
Executive producers: Quentin Tarantino, Lawrence Bender, Robert Rodriguez
Editor: Lawrence Maddox
Cast: Marco Leonardi (Johnny Madrid), Michael Parks (Ambrose Bierce), Temuera Morrison (The Hangman), Rebecca Gayheart (Mary Newlie), Ara Celi (Esmeralda)

Little Nicky
(Avery Pix/Happy Madison Productions/New Line Cinema/RSC Media/Robert Simonds Productions)
Opened November 10, 2000, 90 minutes
Director: Steven Brill
Screenplay: Tim Herlihy, Adam Sandler, Steven Brill
Cinematography: Theo van de Sande
Producers: Jack Giarraputo, Robert Simonds
Editor: Jeff Gourson
Cast: Quentin Tarantino (Deacon), Adam Sandler (Nicky), Patricia Arquette (Valerie Veran), Harvey Keitel (Dad), Rhys Ifans (Adrian), Tommy 'Tiny' Lister (Cassius)

Iron Monkey
Re-released version of the 1993 film *Siu nin Wong Fei Hung chi: Tit ma lau*
(Film Workshop/Golden Harvest Company/Long Shong Pictures/Paragon Films)
Opened October 12, 2001, 90 minutes
Director: Woo-Ping Yuen
Screenplay: Tan Cheung, Tai-Mok Lau (as Tai-Muk Lau), Elsa Tang (as Pik-yin Tang), Hark Tsui, Richard Epcar
Cinematography: Chi-Wai Tam, Arthur Wong
Producers: Quentin Tarantino, Hark Tsui
Editors: Chi Wai Chan, Stephanie Johnson, Angie Lam, Marco Mak, John Zeitler
Cast: Rongguang Yu (Dr. Yang/Iron Monkey), Donnie Yen (Wong Kei-Ying), Jean Wang (Miss Orchid), Sze-Man Tsang (Wong Fei-Hong)

Kill Bill: Volume 1
(Miramax/A Band Apart/Super Cool ManChu)
Opened October 10, 2003, 111 minutes
Director & Screenplay: Quentin Tarantino
Cinematography: Robert Richardson
Producer: Lawrence Bender
Editor: Sally Menke
Cast: Uma Thurman (The Bride), David Carradine (Bill), Lucy Liu (O-Ren Ishii), Vivica A. Fox (Vernita Green), Daryl Hannah (Elle Driver), Michael Madsen (Budd), Julie Dreyfus (Sofie Fatale)

Kill Bill: Volume 2
(Miramax/A Band Apart/Super Cool ManChu)
Opened April 16, 2004, 137 minutes
Director & Screenplay: Quentin Tarantino
Cinematography: Robert Richardson
Producer: Lawrence Bender
Editor: Sally Menke
Cast: Uma Thurman (The Bride), David Carradine (Bill), Lucy Liu (O-Ren Ishii), Vivica A. Fox (Vernita Green), Daryl Hannah (Elle Driver), Michael Madsen (Budd)

My Name Is Modesty: A Modesty Blaise Adventure
(Miramax)
Released on DVD September 28, 2004, 78 minutes
Director: Scott Spiegel
Screenplay: Lee Batchler, Janet Scott Batchler
Cinematography: Vivi Dragan Vasile
Producers: Marcelo Anciano, Michael Berrow, Ted Nicolaou, Sook Yhun (uncredited)
Executive producers: Quentin Tarantino (uncredited), Paul Berrow, Michelle Sy
Editor: Michelle Harrison
Cast: Alexandra Staden (Modesty Blaise), Nikolaj Coster-Waldau (Miklos), Raymond Cruz (Raphael Garcia), Fred Pearson (Professor Lob)

Hostel
(Hostel/International Production Company/Next Entertainment/Raw Nerve)
First shown September 17, 2005 (Toronto International Film Festival, Opened January 6, 2006, 94 minutes
Director & Screenplay: Eli Roth
Cinematography: Milan Chadima
Producers: Chris Briggs, Mike Fleiss, Eli Roth
Executive producers: Quentin Tarantino, Scott Spiegel, Boaz Yakin
Editor: George Folsey Jr.
Cast: Jay Hernandez (Paxton), Derek Richardson (Josh), Eythor Gudjonsson (Oli), Barbara Nedeljakova (Natalya)

Daltry Calhoun
(L. Driver Productions/Map Point Pictures/Miramax)
Opened September 25, 2005, 100 minutes
Director & Screenplay: Katrina Holden Bronson
Cinematography: Matthew Irving
Producer: Danielle Renfrew
Executive producers: Quentin Tarantino, Erica Steinberg
Editor: Daniel R. Padgett
Cast: Elizabeth Banks (May), Johnny Knoxville (Daltry

Calhoun), Beth Grant (Dee), Laura Cayouette (Wanda Banks)

Freedom's Fury
Documentary film
(WOLO Entertainment/Cinergi Pictures Entertainment/Moving Picture Institute)
Opened September 7, 2006 (Hungary), April 8, 2008 (Wisconsin Film Festival), 90 minutes
Directors: Colin K. Gray, Megan Raney
Screenplay: Colin K. Gray
Cinematography: Megan Raney
Producer: Kristine Lacey
Executive producers: Quentin Tarantino, Lucy Liu, Amy Sommer, Andrew G. Vajna
Editor: Michael Rogers

Death Proof
Originally released as part of the double feature *Grindhouse* in April 2007 alongside *Planet Terror* (next column)
(The Weinstein Company/Dimension Films/Troublemaker Studios/Rodriguez International Pictures)
First shown May 22, 2007 (Cannes Film Festival), Opened July 21, 2007, 113 minutes
Director & Screenplay: Quentin Tarantino
Cinematography: Quentin Tarantino
Producers: Quentin Tarantino, Elizabeth Avellán, Robert Rodriguez, Erica Steinberg
Editor: Sally Menke
Cast: Quentin Tarantino (Warren), Kurt Russell (Stuntman Mike), Zoë Bell (as herself), Rosario Dawson (Abernathy), Vanessa Ferlito (Butterfly), Sydney Tamiia Poitier (Jungle Julia), Tracie Thoms (Kim), Rose McGowan (Pam), Jordan Ladd (Shanna)

Hostel: Part II
(Lionsgate/Screen Gems/Next Entertainment/Raw Nerve/International Production Company)
Opened June 8, 2007, 94 minutes
Director & Screenplay: Eli Roth
Cinematography: Milan Chadima
Producers: Chris Briggs, Mike Fleiss, Eli Roth
Executive producers: Quentin Tarantino, Leifur B. Dagfinnsson, Scott Spiegel, Boaz Yakin
Editor: George Folsey Jr.
Cast: Lauren German (Beth), Roger Bart (Stuart), Heather Matarazzo (Lorna), Bijou Phillips (Whitney), Richard Burgi (Todd)

Diary of the Dead
(Artfire Films/Romero-Grunwald Productions)
First shown September 8, 2007 (Toronto International Film Festival), Opened February 22, 2008, 95 minutes
Director & Screenplay: George A. Romero
Cinematography: Adam Swica
Producers: Sam Englebardt, Peter Grunwald, Ara Katz, Art Spigel
Editor: Michael Doherty
Cast: Quentin Tarantino (cameo as Newsreader), Michelle Morgan (Debra Moynihan), Joshua Close

(Jason Creed), Shawn Roberts (Tony Ravello), Amy Lalonde (Tracy Thurman)

Sukiyaki Western Django
(A-Team/Dentsu/Geneon Entertainment/Nagoya Broadcasting Network/Sedic International/Shogakukan/Sony Pictures Entertainment/Sukiyaki Western Django Film Partners/TV Asahi/Toei Company/Tokyu Recreation)
Opened September 15, 2007 (Japan), 121 minutes
Director: Takashi Miike
Screenplay: Takashi Miike, Masa Nakamura
Cinematography: Toyomichi Kurita
Producers: Nobuyuki Tohya, Masao Ôwaki
Editor: Yasushi Shimamura
Cast: Quentin Tarantino (Piringo), Kôichi Satô (Taira no Kiyomori), Yûsuke Iseya (Minamoto no Yoshitsune), Masanobu Andô (Yoichi), Kaori Momoi (Ruriko)

Planet Terror
Originally released as part of the double feature *Grindhouse* in April 2007 alongside *Death Proof* (previous column)
(The Weinstein Company/Dimension Films/Troublemaker Studios/Rodriguez International Pictures)
First shown October 15, 2007 (Screamfest Horror Film Festival), 105 minutes
Director & Screenplay: Robert Rodriguez
Cinematography: Robert Rodriguez
Producers: Quentin Tarantino, Robert Rodriguez, Elizabeth Avellán, Erica Steinberg
Editors: Ethan Maniquis, Robert Rodriguez
Cast: Quentin Tarantino (Rapist 1/Zombie eating road kill), Rose McGowan (Cherry Darling), Freddy Rodriguez (Wray), Josh Brolin (Dr. William Block), Marley Shelton (Dr. Dakota Block)

Hell Ride
(Dimension Films)
First shown January 21, 2008 (Sundance Film Festival), Opened August 8, 2008, 84 minutes
Director & Screenplay: Larry Bishop
Cinematography: Scott Kevan
Producers: Larry Bishop, Shana Stein, Michael Steinberg
Executive producers: Quentin Tarantino, Bob Weinstein, Harvey Weinstein
Editors: Blake West, William Yeh
Cast: Larry Bishop (Pistolero), Michael Madsen (The Gent), Eric Balfour (Comanche), Julia Jones (Cherokee Kisum), David Carradine (The Deuce), Vinnie Jones (Billy Wings), Leonor Varela (Nada), Dennis Hopper (Eddie)

Inglourious Basterds
(The Weinstein Company/Universal Pictures/A Band Apart/Studio Babelsberg/Visiona Romantica)
Opened August 21, 2009, 153 minutes
Director & Screenplay: Quentin Tarantino
Cinematography: Robert Richardson
Producer: Lawrence Bender
Editor: Sally Menke
Cast: Quentin Tarantino (cameo as First Scalped Nazi/

American Soldier), Brad Pitt (Lt. Aldo Raine), Mélanie Laurent (Shosanna), Christoph Waltz (Col. Hans Landa), Eli Roth (Sgt. Donny Donowitz), Michael Fassbender (Lt. Archie Hicox), Diane Kruger (Bridget von Hammersmark)

Kill Bill: The Whole Bloody Affair
Re-edited amalgamation of *Kill Bill: Volume 1* and *Kill Bill: Volume 2*; see individual listings for production details.
(A Band Apart)
Opened March 27, 2011, 247 minutes

Django Unchained
(The Weinstein Company/Columbia Pictures)
Opened December 25, 2012, 165 minutes
Director & Screenplay: Quentin Tarantino
Cinematography: Robert Richardson
Producers: Reginald Hudlin, Pilar Savone, Stacey Sher
Editor: Fred Raskin
Cast: Quentin Tarantino (cameo as LeQuint Dickey Mining Co. Employee/Robert), Jamie Foxx (Django), Christoph Waltz (Dr. King Schultz), Leonardo DiCaprio (Calvin Candie), Kerry Washington (Broomhilda von Shaft), Samuel L. Jackson (Stephen), Walton Goggins (Billy Crash)

She's Funny That Way
(Lagniappe Films/Lailaps Pictures/Venture Forth)
First shown August 29, 2014 (Venice Film Festival), Opened August 21, 2015, 93 minutes
Director: Peter Bogdanovich
Screenplay: Peter Bogdanovich, Louise Stratten
Cinematography: Yaron Orbach
Producers: George Drakoulias, Logan Levy, Louise Stratten, Holly Wiersma
Editors: Nick Moore, Pax Wasserman
Cast: Quentin Tarantino (as himself), Imogen Poots (Isabella Patterson), Owen Wilson (Arnold Albertson), Jennifer Aniston (Jane Claremont), Kathryn Hahn (Delta Simmons), Will Forte (Joshua Fleet), Rhys Ifans (Seth Gilbert)

The Hateful Eight
(Double Feature Films/FilmColony)
Opened December 25, 2015 (limited 70mm version), Opened December 30, 2015 (general release), 187 minutes
Director & Screenplay: Quentin Tarantino
Cinematography: Robert Richardson
Producers: Richard N. Gladstein, Shannon McIntosh, Stacey Sher
Editor: Fred Raskin
Cast: Samuel L. Jackson (Major Marquis Warren), Kurt Russell (John Ruth), Jennifer Jason Leigh (Daisy Domergue), Walton Goggins (Sheriff Chris Mannix), Tim Roth (Oswaldo Mobray), Michael Madsen (Joe Gage), Bruce Dern (General Sandy Smithers), James Parks (O.B.), Channing Tatum (Jody)

Television/Internet

The Golden Girls
Television series, one episode ("Sophia's Wedding: Part 1")
(Witt-Thomas-Harris Productions/Touchstone Television)
First broadcast November 19, 1988, 30 minutes
Director: Terry Hughes
Screenplay: Susan Harris, Barry Fanaro, Mort Nathan
Producers: Paul Junger Witt, Tony Thomas
Cast: Bea Arthur (Dorothy Zbornak), Betty White (Rose Nylund), Rue McClanahan (Blanche Devereaux), Estelle Getty (Sophia Petrillo), Jack Clifford (Max Weinstock), Quentin Tarantino (Elvis impersonator)

All-American Girl
Television series, one episode ("Pulp Sitcom")
(Sandollar Television/Heartfelt Productions/Touchstone Television)
First broadcast February 22, 1995, 30 minutes
Director: Terry Hughes
Screenplay: Tim Maile, Douglas Tuber
Cinematography: Daniel Flannery
Producer: Bruce Johnson
Editor: Jimmy B. Frazier
Cast: Margaret Cho (Margaret Kim), Jodi Long (Katherine Kim), Clyde Kusatsu (Benny Kim), Amy Hill (Yung-hee Kim), Quentin Tarantino (Desmond)

ER
Television series, one episode ("Motherhood")
(Constant c Productions/Amblin Television/Warner Bros. Television)
First broadcast May 11, 1995, 48 minutes
Director: Quentin Tarantino
Screenplay: Lydia Woodward
Cinematography: Richard Thorpe
Producer: Christopher Chulack, Paul Manning
Editor: Jim Gross
Cast: Anthony Edwards (Mark Greene), George Clooney (Doug Ross), Sherry Stringfield (Susan Lewis), Noah Wyle (John Carter), Julianna Margulies (Carol Hathaway), Eriq La Salle (Peter Benton)

Dance Me to the End of Love
Internet short
(A-Acme Film Works)
First shown online October 27, 1995, 6 minutes
Director: Aaron A. Goffman
Screenplay: Quentin Tarantino, Aaron A. Goffman
Cinematography: Rand Vossler
Producer: Aaron A. Goffman
Cast: Quentin Tarantino (Groom), Sylvia Binsfeld (Bride), Nick Rafter (Groom in Chains), Laura Bradley (Girl), Marc Anthony-Reynolds (Boy)

Saturday Night Live
Television series, one episode ("Quentin Tarantino/Smashing Pumpkins")
(Broadway Video/NBC Productions)
First broadcast November 11, 1995, 90 minutes
Director: Beth McCarthy-Miller
Writers: Ross Abrash, Cindy Caponera, James Downey, Hugh Fink, Tom Gianas, Tim Herlihy, Steve Higgins, Norm Hiscock, Steve Koren, Erin Maroney, Adam McKay, Dennis McNicholas, Lorne Michaels, Lori Nasso, Paula Pell, Colin Quinn, Frank Sebastiano, Andrew Steele, Fred Wolf
Art direction: Peter Baran
Producer: Lorne Michaels
Editor: Ian Mackenzie
Cast: Quentin Tarantino (guest host), Jim Breuer, Will Ferrell, Darrell Hammond, David Koechner, Norm MacDonald, Mark McKinney

Alias
Television series, four episodes ("The Box: Part 1", "The Box: Part 2", "Full Disclosure", "After Six")
Broadcast between January 20, 2002 and February 15, 2004, each episode 45 minutes
(Touchstone Television/Bad Robot)
Directors: Jack Bender, Maryann Brandon, Lawrence Trilling
Screenplays: J. J. Abrams, Jesse Alexander, John Eisendrath, Alison Schapker, Monica Breen
Cinematography: Michael Bonvillain, Donald E. Thorin Jr.
Producers: Jesse Alexander, Sarah Caplan, Jeff Pinkner, Chad Savage, Lawrence Trilling
Editors: Virginia Katz, Mandy Sherman, Fred Toye, Mary Jo Markey
Cast: Quentin Tarantino (McKenas Cole), Jennifer Garner (Sydney Bristow), Ron Rifkin (Arvin Sloane), Michael Vartan (Michael Vaughn), Carl Lumbly (Marcus Dixon)

CSI: Crime Scene Investigation
Television series, two episodes ("Grave Danger: Part 1" and "Grave Danger: Part 2")
(Jerry Bruckheimer Television/CBS Productions/Alliance Atlantis Productions)
First broadcast May 19, 2005, each episode 120 minutes
Director & Story: Quentin Tarantino
Screenplay: Naren Shankar, Anthony E. Zuiker, Carol Mendelsohn
Cinematography: Michael Slovis
Producers: Kenneth Fink, Richard J. Lewis, Louis Milito
Editor: Alec Smight
Cast: William Petersen (Gil Grissom), Marg Helgenberger (Catherine Willows), Gary Dourdan (Warrick Brown), George Eads (Nick Stokes), Jorja Fox (Sara Sidle)

Duck Dodgers
Television series, one episode with two segments ("Master & Disaster" and "All in the Crime Family")
(Warner Bros. Animation), 30 minutes
First broadcast October 21, 2005
Directors: Spike Brandt, Tony Cervone
Screenplay: Kevin Seccia, Mark Banker
Art direction: Mark Whiting
Producer: Bobbie Page
Cast: Quentin Tarantino (voice of Master Moloch), Joe Alaskey (Duck Dodgers/Martian Commander X-2/Rocky), Bob Bergen (The Eager Young Space Cadet/Mummy)

The Muppets' Wizard of Oz
Television movie
(Jim Henson Company/Fox Television Studios/Touchstone Television/Muppets Holding Company/Muppet Movie Productions)
First broadcast May 20, 2005, 120 minutes
Director: Kirk R. Thatcher
Screenplay: Debra Frank, Steve L. Hayes, Tom Martin, Adam F. Goldberg
Cinematography: Tony Westman
Producers: Martin G. Baker, Warren Carr
Editor: Gregg Featherman
Cast: Quentin Tarantino (Kermit's Director), Ashanti (Dorothy Gale), Jeffrey Tambor (Wizard), David Alan Grier (Uncle Henry), Queen Latifah (Aunt Em), Steve Whitmire (voice of Kermit the Frog), Dave Goelz (voice of The Great Gonzo), Eric Jacobson (voice of Miss Piggy)

#15SecondStare
Television series, fourteen episodes
(Crypt TV)
First broadcast January 17, 2016, each episode 1 minute
Only cast and crew involved in more than one episode are listed here.
Directors: Wesley Alley, Steven Shea
Screenplay: Wesley Alley
Producers: Jack Davis, Eli Roth, Wesley Alley
Executive producers: Quentin Tarantino, Jason Blum, Vanessa Hudgens, Katie Krentz, Gaspar Noé, Jordan Peele, Joel Zimmerman
Cast: Brian C. Chenworth, Breeanna Judy, Ellen Smith

"When I'm doing a movie, I'm not doing anything else. It's all about the movie. I don't have a wife. I don't have a kid. Nothing can get in my way . . . I've made a choice, so far, to go on this road alone. Because this is my time. This is my time to make movies."

Select Bibliography

Books

Bailey, Jason. *Pulp Fiction: The Complete Story of Quentin Tarantino's Masterpiece*. Minneapolis: Voyageur Press, 2013.

Bernard, Jami. *Quentin Tarantino: The Man and His Movies*. New York: HarperPerennial, 1996.

Biskind, Peter. *Down and Dirty Pictures: Miramax, Sundance and the Rise of Independent Film*. London: Bloomsbury, 2016.

Carradine, David. *The Kill Bill Diary: The Making of a Tarantino Classic as Seen Through the Eyes of a Screen Legend*. New York: Bloomsbury Methuen Drama, 2007.

Clarkson, Wensley. *Quentin Tarantino: The Man, the Myths and his Movies*. London: John Blake, 2007.

Dawson, Jeff. *Quentin Tarantino: The Cinema of Cool*. New York: Applause, 1995.

Grier, Pam and Andrea Cagan. *Foxy: My Life in Three Acts*. New York: Grand Central Publishing, 2010.

Mottram, James. *The Sundance Kids: How the Mavericks Took Back Hollywood*. London: Faber & Faber, 2011.

Peary, Gerald, ed. *Quentin Tarantino: Interviews*. Jackson: University Press of Mississippi, 2013.

Roston, Tom. *I Lost it at the Video Store: A Filmmakers' Oral History of a Vanished Era*. Jenkintown: The Critical Press, 2015.

Sherman, Dale. *Quentin Tarantino FAQ: Everything Left to Know about the Original Reservoir Dog*. Milwaukee, Hal Leonard, 2015.

Waxman, Sharon. *Rebels on the Backlot: Six Maverick Directors and How They Conquered the Hollywood Studio System*. New York: HarperCollins, 2005.

Death Proof: A Screenplay. New York: Weinstein Books, 2007.

Features and interviews

Amis, Martin. "The Writing Life: A Conversation Between Martin Amis and Elmore Leonard." *Los Angeles Times*, February 1, 1998.

Appelo, Tim. "*Django* to the Extreme: How Panic Attacks and DiCaprio's Real Blood Made a Slavery Epic Better." *Hollywood Reporter*, January 10, 2013.

Bailey, Jason. "Imagining the Quentin Tarantino-Directed *Natural Born Killers* That Could Have Been." *Flavorwire*, August 25, 2014.

Bailey, Jason. "Quentin Tarantino is a DJ." *The Atlantic*, October 14, 2014.

Baron, Zach. "Quentin Tarantino Explains the Link Between His *Hateful Eight* and #BlackLivesMatter." *GQ*, December 8, 2015.

Bauer, Erik. "Method Writing: Interview with Quentin Tarantino." *Creative Screenwriting*, January/February 1998.

Beaumont-Thomas, Ben. "Quentin Tarantino Says Next Film Will be Another Western." *Guardian*, November 27, 2013.

Becker, Josh. "Quentin Tarantino Interview: On the Set of *Reservoir Dogs*." www.beckerfilms.com, 1992.

Biskind, Peter. "Four x Four." *Premiere*, November 1995.

Biskind, Peter. "The Return of Quentin Tarantino." *Vanity Fair*, October 14, 2003.

Brody, Richard. "*Inglourious* in Europe." *New Yorker*, August 20, 2009.

Brown, Lane. "In Conversation: Quentin Tarantino." *Vulture*, August 23, 2015.

Buckmaster, Luke. "Quentin Tarantino: Australian Films had a Big Influence on my Career." *Guardian*, January 15, 2016.

Carroll, Kathleen. "*Reservoir Dogs* Overflows with Violence: 1992 Review." *New York Daily News*, October 23, 1992.

Carroll, Larry. "*Inglourious Basterds* Exclusive: Brad Pitt Says Movie 'Was a Gift.'" www.mtv.com, August 19, 2009.

Ciment, Michel and Hubert Niogret. "Interview with Quentin Tarantino." Translated by T. Jefferson Kline. *Positif*, November 1994.

Dargis, Manohla. "Tarantino Avengers in Nazi Movieland." *New York Times*, August 20, 2009.

Debby, David. "Americans in Paris." *New Yorker*, August 24, 2009.

Ebert, Roger. "Reviews: *Chungking Express*." rogerebert.com, March 15, 1996.

Fleming, Michael. "Playboy Interview: Quentin Tarantino." *Playboy*, November 2003.

Fleming, Michael. "Playboy Interview: Quentin Tarantino." *Playboy*, December 3, 2012.

Fleming Jr, Mike. "Quentin Tarantino on Retirement, Grand 70mm Intl Plans for *The Hateful Eight*." www.deadline.com, November 10, 2014.

Galloway, Stephen. "Director Roundtable: 6 Auteurs on Tantrums, Crazy Actors and Quitting While They're Ahead." *Hollywood Reporter*, November 28, 2012.

Garrat, Sheryl. "Quentin Tarantino: No U-turns." *Telegraph*, September 15, 2007.

Gerston, Jill. "Film; Finally, Bruce Willis Gets Invited to the Ball." *New York Times*, October 2, 1994.

Gettell, Oliver. "Quentin Tarantino and Robert Rodriguez Look Back on *From Dusk Till Dawn*." *Entertainment Weekly*, November 3, 2016.

Gilbey, Ryan. "*Inglourious Basterds*." *New Statesman*, August 20, 2009.

Gordon, Devin. "Q&A: Quentin Tarantino." *Newsweek*, April 4, 2007.

Grow, Kory. "Ennio Morricone Goes Inside *Hateful Eight* Soundtrack." *Rolling Stone*, January 11, 2016.

Guerrasio, Jason. "Samuel L. Jackson on Finding the Right Skin Tone for *Django Unchained* and Making Leonardo DiCaprio Become Comfortable with the N-word." *Vanity Fair*, December 20, 2012.

Haselbeck, Sebastian. "An Interview with Kurt Russell." The Quentin Tarantino Archives [www.wiki.tarantino.info].

Hirschberg, Lynn. "Quentin Tarantino, pre-*Pulp Fiction*." *Vanity Fair*, July 5, 1994.

Hirschberg, Lynn. "The Two Hollywoods; The Man Who Changed Everything." *New York Times*, November 16, 1997.

Hiscock, John. "Quentin Tarantino: I'm Proud of my Flop." *Telegraph*, April 27, 2007.

Hoberman, J. "Quentin Tarantino's *Inglourious Basterds* Makes Holocaust Revisionism Fun." *Village Voice*, August 18, 2009.

Horn, John. "Quentin Tarantino Looks Back: *Reservoir Dogs* a Father-Son Story." *Los Angeles Times*, February 12, 2013.

Jagernauth, Kevin. "Quentin Tarantino Says he Didn't Fall Out with Will Smith Over *Django Unchained* Plus New Pic from the Film." *IndieWire*, November 15, 2012.

Jakes, Susan. "Blood Sport." *Time*, September 30, 2002.

Kerr, Sarah. "Rain Man: *Pulp Fiction*—A Film by Quentin Tarantino." *New York Review of Books*, April 6, 1995.

Labrecque, Jeff. "Quentin Tarantino Discusses his Plan to Retire and the Idea of Having Children." *Entertainment Weekly*, December 22, 2015.

La Franco, Robert. "Robert Rodriguez." *Wired*, April 1, 2007.

Lane, Anthony. "Love Hurts." *New Yorker*, January 7, 2013.

Lewis, Andy. "Making of *Hateful Eight*: How Tarantino Braved Sub-Zero Weather and a Stolen Screener." *Hollywood Reporter*, January 7, 2016.

Lim, Dennis. "*Inglourious* Actor Tastes the Glory." *New York Times*, August 12, 2009

Longworth, Karina. "Quentin Tarantino Emerges with his Most Daring Film Yet." *Village Voice*, December 19, 2012.

MacFarquhar, Larissa. "The Movie Lover." *New Yorker*, October 20, 2003.

McGrath, Charles. "Quentin's World." *New York Times*, December 19, 2012.

Morgan, Kim. "Basterds, Sam Fuller and Snoopy: Talking to Tarantino." *Huffington Post*, September 19, 2009.

Nashawaty, Chris. "*Jackie Brown* Blu-ray: Pam Grier talks Quentin Tarantino's Film." *Entertainment Weekly*, October 4, 2011.

Pappademas, Alex. "Triumph of His Will." *GQ*, June 30, 2009.

Pavlus, John. "A Bride Vows Revenge." *American Cinematographer*, October 2003.

Perez, Rodrigo. "What's Left? Quentin Tarantino Talks the Remaining Movies he Could Make Before Retirement." *IndieWire*, December 15, 2015.

Pride, Ray. "Interview Flashback: Quentin Tarantino Talks *Jackie Brown* and Quentin Tarantino." www.newcityfilm.com, December 29, 1997.

Rose, Charlie. "Quentin Tarantino on his Popular Film, *Pulp Fiction*." www.charlierose.com, October 14, 1994.

Rosenbaum, Jonathan. "Recommended Reading: Daniel Mendelsohn on the New Tarantino." www.jonathanrosenbaum.net, August 17, 2009.

Salisbury, Brian. "The Badass Interview: Robert Forster on *Jackie Brown*'s Latest Home Video Release." www.birthmoviesdeath.com, October 3, 2011.

Sancton, Julian. "Tarantino is One Basterd Who Knows How to Please Himself." *Vanity Fair*, August 20, 2009.

Scott, A. O. "The Black, the White and the Angry." *New York Times*, December 24, 2012.

Scott, A. O. "Review: Quentin Tarantino's *The Hateful Eight* Blends Verbiage and Violence." *New York Times*, December 24, 2015.

Scherstuhl, Alan. "Quentin Tarantino's *The Hateful Eight* Refuses to Play Nice." *LA Weekly*, December 15, 2015.

Sciretta, Peter. "Quentin Tarantino Talks Vega Brothers, the *Pulp Fiction* and *Reservoir Dogs* Sequel/Prequel." www.slashfilm.com, April 7, 2007.

Seal, Mark. "Cinema Tarantino: The Making of *Pulp Fiction*." *Vanity Fair*, February 13, 2013.

Secher, Benjamin. "Quentin Tarantino Interview: 'All my Movies are Achingly Personal.'" *Telegraph*, February 8, 2010.

Singer, Matt. "In Praise of *Death Proof*, One of Quentin Tarantino's Best Movies." *IndieWire*, December 28, 2012.

Soghomonian, Talia. "Tarantino Says Will Smith was First Choice for *Django Unchained* Lead." *NME*, January 28, 2013.

Solomons, Jason. "Interview with Sally Menke: 'Quentin Tarantino and I Clicked.'" *Guardian*, December 6, 2009.

Sordeau, Henri. "Quentin Tarantino Talks *Inglourious Basterds*." www.rottentomatoes.com, August 11, 2009.

Spitz, Marc. "*True Romance*: 15 Years Later." *Maxim*, April 25, 2008.

Stasukevich, Iain. "Once Upon a Time in the South." *American Cinematographer*, January 2013.

Tapley, Kristopher. "*The Hateful Eight*: How Ennio Morricone Wrote His First Western Score in 40 Years." *Variety*, December 11, 2015.

Taylor, Ella. "Quentin Tarantino: The *Inglourious Basterds* Interview." *Village Voice*, August 18, 2009.

Thomson, David. "*Django Unchained* is All Talk with Nothing to Say." *New Republic*, January 5, 2013.

Tyrangiel, Josh. "The Tao of Uma." *Time*, September 22, 2003.

Verini, Bob. "Tarantino: Man with Sure Hand on his Brand." *Variety*, November 7, 2012.

Walker, Tim. "Michael Madsen Interview: How *The Hateful Eight* Star Ducked and Dived his Way Through Hollywood." *Independent*, January 2, 2016.

Wise, Damon. "'Resist the Temptation to Ridicule This': Quentin Tarantino Talks *Grindhouse*." *Guardian*, May 4, 2007.

Wise, Damon. "*The Hateful Eight*: A Rocky Ride from Script to Screen." *Financial Times*, December 18, 2015.

Whitney, Erin. "Quentin Tarantino Wanted to Massively 'Subvert' James Bond with *Casino Royale*." *Huffington Post*, August 24, 2015.

Wooton, Adrian. "Quentin Tarantino Interview (I) with Pam Grier, Robert Forster and Lawrence Bender." *Guardian*, January 5, 1998.

Wright, Benjamin. "A Cut Above: An Interview with *Django Unchained* Editor Fred Raskin." *Slant*, January 15, 2013.

Yuan, Jada. "Tarantino's Leading Man." *Vulture*, August 25, 2015.

"*Death Proof*: Quentin Tarantino Interview." http://www.indielondon.co.uk/Film-Review/death-proof-quentin-tarantino-interview.

Interview on *The Rachel Maddow Show*. NBC, February 11, 2010 [http://www.nbcnews.com/id/35367550/ns/msnbc-rachel_maddow_show/print/1/displaymode/1098/].

"The Lost, Unmade and Possible Future Films of Quentin Tarantino." www.indiewire.com, March 27, 2013.

"Quentin Tarantino: 'It's a corrupted cinema.'" *The Talks*, October 28, 2013.

"Quentin Tarantino, 'Unchained' and Unruly." *NPR*, January 2, 2013 [http://www.npr.org/2013/01/02/168200139/quentin-tarantino-unchained-and-unruly].

Reservoir Dogs: Ten Years, directed by Quentin Tarantino. Artizan, 2002 [DVD].

"ZDF Quentin Tarantino Interview (*Kill Bill*)." https://www.youtube.com/watch?v=bIGhtVN2lrY.

Picture Credits

T: Top; B: Bottom; C: Centre; L: Left; R: Right

PAGE 256: Portrait by Nicolas Guerin, 2008.

"Two more. That's it. And then drop the mic.
Boom. Tell everybody match that sh*t!"